THE BOOK OF SAINTS

THE
BOOK OF SAINTS

A DICTIONARY OF PERSONS CANONIZED
OR BEATIFIED BY THE CATHOLIC CHURCH

COMPILED BY

THE BENEDICTINE MONKS OF
ST AUGUSTINE'S ABBEY, RAMSGATE

FIFTH EDITION
ENTIRELY REVISED
AND RE-SET

THOMAS Y. CROWELL COMPANY

NEW YORK   ESTABLISHED 1834

FIRST EDITION 1921
SECOND EDITION 1931
THIRD EDITION 1934
FOURTH EDITION 1939
FIFTH EDITION, RE-SET, 1966

© 1966 A. AND C. BLACK LTD

LIBRARY OF CONGRESS CATALOG CARD NO. 66–22140

1   2   3   4   5   6   7   8   9   10

PRINTED IN THE UNITED STATES OF AMERICA

NOTE TO THE FIFTH EDITION

The Book of Saints meets a steady demand for information in a compact form over the whole range of beatified or canonized servants of God. For this reason another edition has been called for and has been prepared. The fourth edition was so much enlarged and extended in scope as to be almost a new work by comparison with its predecessors. This, the fifth edition, is substantially the same as the last, but many inaccuracies inevitable in a work of such enormous scope have been corrected, and legendary information replaced more often by the bald facts of research. Moreover a large number of additions have been made, including those beatified or canonized in the last twenty-five years.

The compilers wish to acknowledge particularly a debt to Dr. Emil Kisban for the use of his researches into the saints of the Hungarian Pauline Order, and to the Benedictine fathers of the Abbaye Sainte-Marie at Paris for their work on the lives of the early saints and martyrs.

March 1966

FOREWORD TO THE FOURTH EDITION

The Book of Saints first appeared in 1921. It was a pioneer work and it certainly filled a gap in English hagiological literature. The fact that it was several times reprinted proves that it achieved success, and the demand for this new edition shows that a considerable public still finds it useful.

Since 1921, however, several similar dictionaries, some of which are evidently indebted to *The Book of Saints*, even to the extent of embodying verbatim transcriptions therefrom, have been put on the market. These later works have inevitably rendered our *Book of Saints* more or less out of date. For this reason and also in view of a number of valuable suggestions and corrections made by reviewers of former editions, we put it to the publishers, when they asked us to prepare this fourth edition, that, in fairness to our readers and to ourselves, a re-casting of the whole work was imperative. This we now offer to the public. A few observations on this new *Book of Saints* are, however, necessary for a proper appreciation of its scope, and we therefore beg the reader not to skim the following pages.

The original *Book of Saints* was conceived, planned, directed and in part written by a very great scholar, namely, the Right Rev. Dom Thomas Bergh (d. 1924), monk of Ramsgate and Abbot Visitor of the English Province of the Benedictine Subiaco Congregation. Abbot Bergh was helped in the compilation of the book by monks of the community, two especially. His policy was to leave intact the entries contributed by the others, correcting only here and there when he deemed it necessary. For this reason the work is somewhat uneven. Another point that needs mentioning is Abbot Bergh's bent of mind. Although he was a scholar of high standing in matters biblical, theological and hagiological, his outlook was definitely conservative. This explains his unwillingness to discard ancient legends especially if sanctioned by liturgical use. He would certainly never have approved of the ruthlessly iconoclastic methods of some modern writers. This explains some of the well-founded criticism levelled at his work.

The Book of Saints which we now offer to the public has been compiled on a different method and from a different angle. One of the Fathers of this community of Ramsgate has re-written the whole book, entry by entry. It has then been revised and checked by two other Fathers. All three have kept before their minds the most recent findings of hagiological research. They do not always agree with these findings, but in most cases they let the reader know when the data given in the book are uncertain or debatable.

The book remains anonymous. We are only too happy to follow the example set us by its original compiler. Moreover, by doing so, we are acting, even in a small work like this, according to the best Benedictine traditions.

Some further observations as to the aim and use of the book as now revised seem to be called for. As regards its aim, we must first of all repeat here the words written by Abbot Bergh in the original preface: "The present compilation aims at no more than the stretching of the historical framework of a saint's life." The saints, however, included in this new edition are considerably more numerous than those included by Abbot Bergh. The additions comprise not only those saints who have been canonized or beatified or whose cult has been officially recognized by the Holy See since 1921, but also a great number of others omitted in the first edition. The expansion of this latter category is due to our adoption of a more liberal criterion in judging claims to recognized sainthood, and also to our desire to include, within reasonable limits, every holy person whose memory is venerated, or whose feast is celebrated, as that of a saint in a particular country or diocese or religious order.

It is of course beyond human power to achieve absolute completeness. This is especially the case where there are a number of saints of the same name, belonging to the same country, and presenting similar—usually very jejune—biographical data: this phenomenon is common among Irish saints, e.g., Bracan, Brendan, Conall, Conan, etc. The most plausible hypothesis in such cases is that one individual saint, by being venerated in different localities, has achieved a kind of multiple personality, whence it has now become impossible to say to which particular place he originally belonged. Possibly, in other instances, two or three saints of the same or similar name have been blended into one by popular piety.

We may also note here that the present volume, although aiming at accuracy, is not, except in the case of most of the Benedictine saints, a work of original research. The compilers have for the most part adopted what they consider to be the sanest conclusions of modern critical hagiography.

To facilitate the use of this book we will now outline briefly the method followed in its compilation. The entries are drawn up on the following plan. We give

(i) The name of each saint in alphabetical order. If there are several saints of the same name, we follow the order of their respective feast days in the calendar. The spelling of proper names, whether of saints or of places, has created some difficulty. In the case of a great number of saints' names the spellings are so various that it would require too much space to enter each form under a separate heading.[1] For certain names in common use at the present time (e.g., James, John, Paul, Peter) we have in each

[1] We would recommend *Baptismal Names* by Joseph L. Weidenham, S. T. L., Washington, 1919, as a very useful reference book, particularly for variant forms of saints' names.

case inserted a special entry giving its different forms in modern European languages. For the spelling of place names the *Encyclopaedia Britannica* usually, but not invariably, has been followed.

(ii) The saint's surname or his distinctive appellation, if any; for instance: James *Kisai*, James *of Tarantaise*, James *the Almsgiver*.

(iii) The saint's hagiological rank, viz., *Saint* (St) or *Blessed* (Bl).

(iv) The liturgical group to which the saint belongs, e.g. *Martyr* (M), *Confessor* (C), etc.‖*Confessor* (C), however, has often been omitted as understood, as also *Monk*, *Nun*, when that is obvious from the entry itself.

(v) The religious order, if any, to which the saint belonged.

(vi) The present state of the saint's cult, that is, whether the name of the saint is included in the Roman Martyrology (RM), whether the cult has been approved—*Approved Cult* (AC), or whether it is an unofficial *Popular Cult* (PC). By *Approved Cult* (AC) we mean that there is positive historical evidence of a saint having been venerated as such, even if, as in many instances among the Cornish and Welsh saints, that evidence rests solely on ancient church dedications and there is no other official recognition by the Church, such as an approved liturgical office. *Popular Cult* (PC) is affixed to the names of those saints who are invariably styled so, or are given the title of *Blessed*, or are usually referred to as *Saint* or *Blessed* in ancient writers, but whose veneration has never been accompanied by any recognized external sign of cult.

(vii) The date of the saint's feast. Note that feast days of saints, especially of those not included in the Roman Martyrology, often vary from diocese to diocese or from one religious order to another. In these cases we sometimes give more than one date, but we usually confine ourselves to the date of death, which is the normal day for celebrating a saint's feast.

(viii) The year of the saint's death, whether definite, e.g., *d. 890* or approximate: *d.c.* (*circiter*: about) *890*. Failing this, we give the century, or if even this is unverifiable, we put an interrogation mark (?). When possible, as in the case of the more recent saints, two figures are given, that of their birth and that of their death, e.g. 1810-1890.

(ix) The text of each entry, which gives only the chief features of the saint's career. Legendary matter is not altogether excluded, but, when admitted, some warning is usually given. To write of St Catherine of Alexandria without mention of the wheel, or of St Laurence of Rome ignoring the gridiron, would probably be more confusing than useful, even though scholars question the historicity of the episodes in which these instruments figure.

In the case of some early martyrs whose names are listed in the martyrologies in the genitive, it is hardly possible, in the absence of other evidence, to determine the sex of the saint. Thus, for example, *Passio S. Zenaidis* might refer to a holy man named Zenaides or to a woman named Zenais.

ABBREVIATIONS

(i) Chronological

a.	ante, i.e., before.
c.	circiter (or circa), i.e., about.
d.	died.
p.	post, i.e., after.
cent.	century.

(ii) Canonical

AC.	Approved Cult.
Bl, BB.	Blessed.
PC.	Popular Cult.
RM.	Roman Martyrology.
St, SS	Saint, saints.

(iii) Liturgical

Ab.	Abbot.
Abs.	Abbess.
Bp., Bps.	Bishop, -s.
C., Cc.	Confessor, -s.
Card.	Cardinal.
Comp.	Companions.
Dr	Doctor of the Church.
H., HH.	Hermit, -s.
Mk.	Monk.
M., MM.	Martyr, -s.
N.	Nun.
V., VV.	Virgin, -s.
W.	Widow.

(iv) Religious Orders

Barn.	Barnabites.
Bridg.	Bridgettines.
CM.	Congregationis Missionis (Vincentians, Paulists).
CP.	Congregationis Passionis (Passionist Fathers).
C.SS.R.	Congregationis Sanctissimi Redemptoris. (Redemptorists)
Orat.	Oratorians.
O. Carm.	Carmelites.
OCD.	Discalced Carmelites.
O. Cart.	Carthusians.
OFM.	Ordinis Fratrum Minorum. (Franciscans)
OFM. Cap.	Capuchins.
O. Merc.	Mercedarians.
O. Minim.	Minims.
OP.	Ordinis Praedicatorum. (Dominicans)
O. Praem.	Praemonstratensians.
OSA.	Augustinians.
OSA. Erem.	Augustinian Hermits.
OS. Bas	Basilians.
OSB.	Benedictines.
OSB. Cam.	(Benedictine) Camaldolese.
OSB. Cel.	(Benedictine) Celestines.
OSB. Cist.	(Benedictine) Cistercians.
OSB. Hum.	(Benedictine) Humiliati.
OSB. Oliv.	(Benedictine) Olivetans.
OSB. Silv.	(Benedictine) Silvestrines.
OSB. Vall.	(Benedictine) Vallumbrosans.
OSB. Virgil.	(Benedictine) Montevirginians.
OS. Trin.	Trinitarians.
OSU.	Ursulines.
SJ.	Jesuits.
Tert.	Tertiary.

A

AARON (St) Ab.   AC. June 22
d. *p*.552. A Briton who crossed into Armorica (Brittany) and lived as a hermit in the island of Cesambre, now St Malo. Eventually he was joined by a group of disciples and became their abbot. Among the disciples was St Malo, who arrived from Wales about the middle of the 6th cent.

AARON (St) 1st High Priest
RM. July 1
15th cent. B.C. Great grandson of Levi, son of Jacob, and the first of the Jewish High Priests, to which office he was appointed by God Himself. He was the elder brother of Moses, the Hebrew Law-giver, with whom he shared the leadership of the people of Israel. Like Moses he never entered the Land of Promise, but died on Mt Hor, on the borders of Edom. In art he is represented with a rod in flower, a censer and a Jewish mitre.

AARON (St) M.   RM. July 1
See Julius and Aaron (Aakon).

AARON (Bl) Abp. OSB.   PC. Oct 9
d. 15 May 1059. He was the first abbot (1040) of the Benedictine monastery of Tyniec in Poland. In 1046 he became the first archbishop of Cracow. According to the Polish legend he had been a monk of Cluny under St Odilo.

ABACHUM (St) M.   RM. Jan 19
See Marius, Martha, etc.

ABB (St) V. Abs.   AC. Aug 25
Otherwise Ebba, q.v.

ABBAN (St) Ab.   AC. March 16
5th cent. An Irish saint, contemporary with St Patrick and nephew of St Ibar. Founder of Kill-Abban Abbey in Leinster.

ABBAN (St) Ab.   AC. Oct 27
6th cent. Nephew of St Kevin; founder of many monasteries, mostly in S. Ireland. His name is especially connected with that of Magh-Armuidhe, now Adamstown, in Wexford. The lives of this saint, of the foregoing St Abban, and of sundry others of the same name are hopelessly confused.

ABBO (St) Bp.   AC. Sept 19
Otherwise Goeric, q.v.

ABBO (St) Ab. M. OSB. AC. Nov 13
c.945–1004. Born near Orleans, he took the habit at Fleury (St Benoît-sur-Loire) and was reputed one of the greatest scholars of his age. He was invited by St Oswald of Worcester to take charge of the abbey school of Ramsey in Huntingdonshire, where he stayed for two years. He was then appointed abbot of Fleury (988), where he introduced the Cluniac observance. He was often called in as mediator between the king of France and the Holy See. He was martyred at La Réole in Gascony by monks whom he had set out to reform.

ABBO (St) Bp. OSB.   PC. Dec 3
d. *c*.860. Monk and abbot of the monastery of St Germain at Auxerre. In 857 he was chosen bishop of the same city, but resigned in 859 and died shortly after.

I

ABBRICI (Bl)
See Magdalen Abbrici.

ABDAS (St) M.   **RM. May 16**
Otherwise Audas, q.v.

ABDECHALAS (St) M. RM. Apr 21
See Simeon and Comp.

ABDIAS (ABDIS, OBADIAH) (St)
Prophet.   **RM. Nov 19**
9th cent. B.C. The name means Servant of the Lord. He is the fourth of the twelve minor prophets. Some identify him with Ahab's steward (3 Kings XVIII, 3). His prophecy is contained in a single chapter of twenty-five verses. He foretells the destruction of Edom. The RM. locates his memory at "Samaria in Palestine".

ABDIESUS (HEBEDJESUS) (St) M.
    RM. Apr 22
4th cent. He was one of the vast multitude of Persians, named and unnamed, martyred under King Shapur (Sapor) II. This persecution lasted from A.D. 341 to A.D. 380. Abdiesus is styled a deacon in the RM., and is probably not to be identified with another martyr of the same name who was bishop of Cashcar.

ABDON and SENNEN (SS) MM.
    RM. July 30
3rd or 4th cent. Persian nobles, brought to Rome as captives, who devoted themselves to the service of the imprisoned Christians and to burying the bodies of the martyrs. Some authorities place their martyrdom in the reign of Decius, others in that of Diocletian. They are still annually commemorated by the Roman Church on July 30.

ABEL (St) Patriarch.   **AC. Jan 2**
The second son of Adam, killed by his brother Cain. He is invoked in the litany for the dying, and there is a reference to his sacrifice in the Canon of the Mass.

ABEL, THOMAS (Bl)   **AC. July 30**
See Thomas Abel.

ABEL (St) Abp. OSB.   **PC. Aug 5**
d. c.751. English, or Irish, in origin, he accompanied St Boniface to the Continent. He was chosen archbishop of Reims, his election being ratified by the council of Soissons (744) and by Pope St Zachary, but he could not take possession of his see, which was occupied by the intruder Milo. He retired to Lobbes, where he became abbot and died.

ABELLON (Bl) OP.   **AC. May 15**
See Andrew Abellon.

ABERCIUS (St) Bp.   **RM. Oct 22**
d. c.167. Bishop of Hierapolis in Phrygia, in which see he is stated to have succeeded the famous Papias. Imprisoned for his zeal against paganism, he was set free and died in peace at Hierapolis. His epitaph, composed by himself and discovered in 1882, is now in the Lateran Museum. It sheds vivid light on several points of Christian doctrine, e.g., baptism, the eucharist, the Roman primacy. Its authenticity is beyond doubt.

ABIBAS (ABIBO) (St) C. RM. Aug 3
1st cent. Second son of Gamaliel (Acts V 34, XXII 3), at whose feet St Paul had sat. Like his father he became a Christian. He lived till his eightieth year. In 415 his remains were found at Capergamela, near Jerusalem, together with those of SS Stephen, Gamaliel and Nicodemus.

ABIBUS (St) M.   **RM. Nov 15**
d. 322. A deacon of Edessa in Syria,

martyred by burning under the emperor Licinius, and buried with his friends SS Gurias and Samonas.

ABIBUS (St) M.   AC. Dec 9
See Samosata, Martyrs of.

ABILIUS (St) Bp.   RM. Feb 22
d. c.98. According to Eusebius, he was third bishop, in succession to SS Mark and Anianus, of Alexandria in Egypt, to which see he was appointed c.84.

ABLEBERT (St) Bp.   AC. Jan 15
Otherwise Emebert, q.v.

ABRA (St) V.   AC. Dec 12
c.342–360. Daughter of St Hilary of Poitiers, born to him before he was raised to the episcopate. Following his advice she consecrated herself to God as a nun, but died in her eighteenth year. Her feast is kept at Poitiers.

ABRAHAM (ABRAAMIOS) (St) Bp. M.   AC. Feb 5
d. c.344–348. Bishop of Arbela in Assyria. He was put to death in the village of Telman under Shapur II of Persia.

ABRAHAM (ABRAAMES) (St) Bp.
                            AC. Feb 14
d. c.422. A hermit in Syria, who succeeded in converting a village in the Lebanon by borrowing money to pay its taxes. Eventually he became bishop of Harran (Charres) in Mesopotamia. He had a great influence on Theodosius the Younger and his court. He died at Constantinople while on a visit to the emperor.

ABRAHAM (St) C.   RM. March 16
d. c.366. Surnamed Kidunaia, from the name of his parish at Beth-Kiduna. Flying from a wealthy home and a promising marriage, he lived as a hermit in a desert near Edessa. At the entreaty of his bishop he was ordained and appointed to the town of Beth-Kiduna, which he completely converted to Christianity. His life was written by St Ephrem, who was his personal friend and admirer. The episodes connected with his niece Mary are now considered spurious.

ABRAHAM (St) Ab.   RM. June 15
d. c.480. Born on the banks of the Euphrates, he journeyed to Egypt, where he fell among thieves, who held him captive five years. He succeeded in escaping and boarded a ship bound for Gaul. He settled near Clermont in Auvergne as a solitary. Eventually he was given charge as abbot of the monastery of St Cyriacus (St Cyrgues) and was ordained priest. His protection is invoked against fever.

ABRAHAM (St) Patriarch
                            RM. Oct 9
20th cent. B.C. The Father of all believers and progenitor of the Hebrew nation. Born at Ur in Chaldea, Abram, whom God renamed Abraham—the father of many, migrated at God's command to Canaan, the land which God had promised him. Here he lived a pastoral and nomad life. In his Seed—Christ, the Messiah—all nations have been blessed, in accordance with the covenant which God made with him. He died at the age of one hundred and seventy-five.

ABRAHAM (St) H.   AC. Oct 27
d. 367. Surnamed "the Poor" or "the Child". Born at Menuf in Egypt, he became a disciple of St Pachomius. After twenty-three years he retired to a cave, where he spent seventeen years. His cult is widespread among the Copts.

ABRAHAM (St) Abp.   AC. Oct 28
6th cent. Built the monastery of the

Abrahamites by the Golden Gate at Constantinople and the monastery of the Byzantines near Jerusalem. Eventually he became archbishop of Ephesus. He was a writer on ecclesiastical subjects.

ABRAHAM (St) Bp.   AC. Dec 6
474–c.558. Born at Emesa in Syria, while still very young he was chosen abbot of a monastery at Kratia in Bithynia. Later he was made bishop of the same place. Twice he secretly fled in search of quiet: the second time he found a refuge in a Palestinian monastery, where he died.

ABRAHAMITE MONKS (SS) MM.
RM. July 8
Between 830 and 840. This group of monks belonged to the monastery founded by St Abraham of Ephesus (q.v., Oct 28) at Constantinople. They were put to death under the emperor Theophilus for their brave defence of the cult of images.

ABRAN (St)   AC. May 8
See Gibrian.

ABROSIMUS (St) M.   AC. Apr 22
d. 341. His name is also spelt Abrosima. A Persian priest stoned to death with many of his flock under King Shapur II. The Greeks keep his feast on Nov. 10.

ABSALE (ABSALON) (St) M.
RM. March 2
See Lucius, Absalon and Lorgius.

ABUDIMUS (ABUDEMIUS) (St) M.
RM. July 15
4th cent. A native of the island of Tenedos in the Aegean, who was martyred under Diocletian.

ABUNDANTIUS (St) M.
RM. March 1
See Leo, Donatus, etc.

ABUNDANTIUS (St) M.
RM. Sept 16
See Abundius, Abundantius, etc.

ABUNDIUS (St) M.   RM. Feb 27
See Alexander, Abundius, etc.

ABUNDIUS (St) Bp.   RM. Apr 2
d. 469. A Greek priest who became bishop of Como in N. Italy. He was an able theologian and was entrusted by St Leo the Great with a mission to the emperor Theodosius the Younger, which resulted in the calling of the Council of Chalcedon (451). St Abundius is represented in art either with a hart or raising a dead child to life.

ABUNDIUS (St) C.   RM. Apr 14
d. c.564. Sacristan of St Peter's, Rome. St Gregory the Great makes mention of his humble but divinely favoured life. His feast is kept as a double major at St Peter's.

ABUNDIUS (St) M.   RM. July 11
d. 854. Parish priest of Ananelos, a village in the mountains near Cordova in Spain. He entertained no thought of martyrdom, but suddenly found himself drawn into the conflict. He valiantly confessed Christ before the tribunal of the Moorish Caliph of Cordova, was beheaded and his body thrown to the dogs.

ABUNDIUS (St) M.   RM. Aug 26
See Irenaeus and Abundius.

ABUNDIUS, ABUNDANTIUS, MARCIAN and JOHN (SS) MM.
RM. Sept 16
d. c.303. Their laus in the RM. reads as follows: "At Rome on the Flaminian Way, the memory of the holy martyrs Abundius, priest, and Abundantius, his deacon, whom the emperor Diocletian ordered to be beheaded ten miles from

the city, together with Marcian, a senator, and John, his son, whom Abundius had raised from the dead." Their *Acta*, however, are by no means trustworthy.

ABUNDIUS (St) M.   RM. Dec 10
See Carpophorus and Abundius.

ABUNDIUS (St) M.   RM. Dec 14
See Justus and Abundius.

ACACIUS
Note. The following variant spellings of this and all the following entries under the same name should be noted:— ACHATIUS, ACHACIUS, ACATHIUS, ACHATHIUS, ACHATES, and even, more rarely, AGATIUS, AGATHIUS.

ACACIUS (St) Bp.   AC. March 31
d. *c.*251. Surnamed by the Greeks Agathangelos (the Good Angel) and the Wonder-worker. He was a bishop in Hither Asia, and, under the Decian persecution, he is said so to have impressed his judges by his defence of Christianity that he was set free. His *Acta* seem to be genuine. He is held in great veneration in the East.

ACACIUS (St) Bp.   RM. Apr 9
d. *p.*421. Bishop of Amida (Diarbekir) in Mesopotamia, and distinguished for his charity to the Persian prisoners, for whose ransom he melted down and sold the sacred vessels of his church. This won for him the friendship of King Bahram V of Persia, who is said to have forthwith ceased to persecute his Christian subjects.

ACACIUS (St) M.   RM. Apr 28
See Patrick, Acacius, etc.

ACACIUS (St) M.   RM. May 8
d. *c.*303. A Cappadocian centurion in

the Roman army stationed in Thrace, who was tortured and beheaded at Byzantium under Diocletian. Constantine the Great built a church in his honour. He is the S. Agario venerated at Squillace in Calabria and the San Acato of Avila and Cuenca in Spain.

ACACIUS (St) M.   June 22
The story of a martyrdom of St Acacius and ten thousand Roman soldiers under his command on Mt Ararat, which had great vogue in the later Middle Ages, is now discarded as pure romance.

ACACIUS (St) M.   RM. July 28
d. *c.*310. A martyr at Miletus under the emperor Licinius.

ACACIUS (St) M.   RM. Nov 27
See Hirenarchus, Acacius, etc.

ACCA (St) Bp. OSB.   AC. Oct 20
*c.*660–742. A Northumbrian disciple of St Bosa of York and of St Wilfrid, and a constant companion of the latter in his journeys in England, Italy and Frisia. St Wilfrid appointed him abbot of St Andrew's at Hexham. In 709 Acca succeeded Wilfrid as bishop of the same place. For a time he was exiled from his see. St Bede was his great friend and dedicated several works to him. Acca is described by Bede as "great in the sight of God and man", and he was certainly one of the most learned Anglo-Saxon prelates of his day.

ACCURSIUS (St) M. OFM.
RM. Jan 16
See Berardus, Peter, etc.

ACEPSIMAS (St) and Comp. MM.
RM. Apr 22
d. 10 Oct. 376. An octogenarian bishop of Hnaita in W. Persia, who was racked and flogged to death under Shapur II. The Acts of his martyrdom are quite

genuine. With him suffered two priests Aithala and Joseph. The Roman Martyrology commemorates many others who suffered about this time in the same persecution. See Persia, Martyrs of.

ACEPSIMAS (St) H.   AC. Nov 3
5th cent. A hermit who lived for sixty years in a cave near Cyrrhus in Syria in the time of Theodosius I. He died shortly after his ordination to the priesthood.

ACESTES (St) M.   AC. July 2
1st cent. According to the legend he was one of the three soldiers who led St Paul to execution: having been converted by him, they were beheaded after him.

ACHACIUS, or ACHATIUS (*several*)
See under Acacius.

ACHARD (St) Ab. OSB.
RM. Sept 15
Otherwise Aichardus, q.v.

ACHARIUS (St) Bp.   AC. Nov 27
d. 640. Monk of Luxeuil under St Eustace. In 621 he was chosen bishop of Noyon-Tournai, and as such fostered the missionary efforts of St Amandus of Maestricht and obtained from King Dagobert I the erection of the see of Térouanne, in which he placed his friend St Omer.

ACHE and ACHEUL (SS) MM.
AC. May 1
Otherwise Acius and Aceolus, q.v.

ACHERIC and WILLIAM (SS) Mks. OSB.   PC. Nov 3
d. after 860. Hermits, and afterwards monks in a monastery founded by Bidulph, archdeacon of Metz, in the Vosges mountains in the diocese of Strasburg.

ACHILLAS and AMOES (SS) HH.
AC. Jan 17
4th cent. Achillas, in Latin Achilleus, is mentioned by Rufinus. He is venerated by the Greeks at the beginning of Lent, together with Amoes. They both lived as solitaries in Egypt and are called in the Greek liturgy "the flowers of the desert".

ACHILLAS (St) Bp.   RM. Nov 7
d. 313. Successor to St Peter the martyr in the see of Alexandria. He raised to the priesthood the man who afterwards became world-famous as the heresiarch Arius. St Athanasius extols the virtues of St Achillas, who was maligned by the party of Meletius on account of the purity of his doctrine.

ACHILLES (St) Bp.   AC. May 15
d. c.330. In Latin Achillius. Metropolitan of Larissa in Thessaly. He is supposed to have assisted at the 1st Council of Nicaea. Since 978 his relics have been venerated at Presba (Achilli) in Bulgaria.

ACHILLEUS (St) M.   RM. Apr 23
See Felix, Fortunatus and Achilleus.

ACHILLEUS (St) M.   RM. May 12
See Nereus, Achilleus, etc.

ACHILLEUS KEWANUKA(SI) (St) M.   AC. June 3
d. 1886. Before entering the service of King Mwanga of Uganda, he was a clerk. See Uganda, Martyrs of.

ACINDYNUS (St) M.   RM. Apr 20
See Victor, Zoticus, etc.

ACINDYNUS, PEGASIUS, APHTHONIUS, ELPIDEPHORUS and ANEMPODISTUS (SS) MM.
RM. Nov 2
d. 345. Persian Christians, priests and

clerics, who suffered for the Faith under Shapur II.

ACISCLUS and VICTORIA (SS) MM.   RM. Nov 17
d. 304. Brother and sister, natives of Cordova in Spain, who suffered martyrdom probably under Diocletian. Their home was turned into a church. They are the principal patron saints of Cordova and are greatly venerated throughout Spain and S. France.

ACIUS (ACHE) and ACEOLUS (ACHEUL) MM.   AC. May 1
d. *c*.303. The former a deacon, the latter a subdeacon, martyred near Amiens under Diocletian. Their cult is widespread in the diocese of Amiens. Their *Acta*, however, are not trustworthy.

ACTINEA and GRAECINA (SS) VV. MM.   AC. June 16
4th cent. The former was beheaded at Volterra in Etruria in the persecution of Diocletian. In 1140 her remains, together with those of Graecina, were found in the Camaldolese church of SS Justus and Clement.

ACUTIUS (St) M.   RM. Sept 19
See Januarius and Comp.

ACYLLINUS (St) M.   RM. July 17
See Scillitan Martyrs.

ADAL-, AETHEL-, AL-, ADRE-, AU-, EDIL-, ETHEL-
Note. All these prefixes to names of Teutonic origin are more or less interchangeable. Thus, Etheldreda, Ediltrudis, Audrey, are one and the same personage. That which appears the more usual manner of spelling a saint's name in English has, as a rule, been followed here.

ADA (St) Abs.   AC. Dec 4
End of 7th cent. Niece of St Engebert, bishop of Mans. She was a nun at Soissons and was appointed abbess of Saint-Julien-des-Prés at Mans. Her name has the variants: Adenette, Adna, Adnette, Adrechildis.

ADALAR (ADALHER) (St) M. OSB.   RM. June 5
d. 755. Monk-priest and companion of St Boniface, with whom he was martyred at Dokkum in Frisia.

ADALARD (St) Ab. OSB.   AC. Jan 2
c.751–827. His name is also written Adalhard, Adelhard, Adalardus, Adelardus, Alard. Grandson of Charles Martel, and one of Charlemagne's chief advisers. The ups and downs of his political career belong to general history. He entered the monastery of Corbie in Picardy, of which he became abbot. Driven into exile, he secured the foundation of New Corbie (Corvey) in Saxony. Throughout his career he remained a great abbot.

ADALARD (Bl) Mk. OSB.   PC. July 15
d. *c*.824. Surnamed the younger. Monk of Corbie under the abbot St Adalard. Died in his twentieth year.

ADALBALD (St) M.   AC. Feb 2
d. 652. Surnamed "D'Ostrevant". Born in Flanders, a son or grandson of St Gertrude of Hamage. He served at the court of Dagobert I and married a Gascon lady named Rictrude, who is also venerated as a saint, as also were their four children, Maurontius, Clotsindis, Eusebia and Adalsindis. Adalbald was slain by some relatives of his wife who disapproved of the match, and was thereafter venerated as a martyr.

ADALBERO (Bl) Bp.   PC. Jan 1
d. 1128. A brother of Godfrey Le
Barbu, count of Louvain. Successively
canon of Metz and bishop of Liége,
where he founded the abbey of Saint-
Gilles.

ADALBERO (Bl) Bp. OSB.
PC. Apr 28
d. 909. He belonged to the family of the
counts of Dillingen, and was uncle to
St Ulric. Monk (850) and afterwards
abbot of Ellwangen, abbot-restorer of
Lorsch and bishop of Augsburg (after
887). Chief adviser of Arnulf of Bavaria,
tutor to his son Louis and regent of the
Empire during the latter's childhood.
He was well versed in science and the
arts, chiefly as a musician.

ADALBERO (St or Bl) Bp.
AC. Oct 6
1045–1090. Son of Count Arnold of
Lambach. A student at Paris with St
Altmann of Passau. Eventually he
became bishop of Würzburg and sided
with Gregory VII against Henry IV.
On this account he was driven from his
see (1085) and retired to the Benedictine abbey of Lambach in Austria, to
the foundation of which he had largely
contributed. It was there that he died.
Cult approved in 1883.

ADALBERO (Bl) Bp.   PC. Dec 15
d. 1005. Of the family of the dukes of
Lorraine. Educated at the Benedictine
abbey of Gorze, he became bishop of
Verdun, but was transferred in the
same year (984) to Metz. He was
zealous in spreading the Cluniac observance by founding monasteries and
churches.

ADALBERT (St) Abp. M. OSB.
RM. Apr 23
956–997. In Czech Voitech. Born in
Bohemia and educated by St Adalbert

of Magdeburg. He was consecrated
bishop of Prague (983), but disheartened
at the result of his labours, he went to
Rome and became a Benedictine at the
abbey of SS Boniface and Alexius on
the Aventine. Twice he returned to his
former mission, and twice he had to
abandon it. However, on each occasion
he preached instead in Poland, Prussia,
Hungary and even Russia, with signal
success; hence he is styled the Apostle of
the Slavs. He was martyred by the
Prussians near Danzig.

ADALBERT (St) Abp. OSB.
AC. June 20
d. 981. Monk of St Maximin of Trèves,
he was chosen by the emperor Otto III
to evangelize Russia. On their arrival
there in 961, all his companions were
killed, and he himself escaped with
difficulty. He was then appointed abbot
of Weissenburg, and in 968 first archbishop of Magdeburg with jurisdiction
over the Wends. He did much to encourage learning, especially as abbot of
Weissenburg.

ADALBERT (St) Mk.   RM. June 25
d. c.740. A Northumbrian by birth who
became a monk of Rathmelgisi and
accompanied St Willibrord as one of his
deacons to Friesland. He laboured
especially round Egmont, of which
abbey he became the patron saint.

ADALBERT (Bl) Mk. OSB.
PC. Nov 23
d. p.1045. Monk of Cassoria—Cas-
sauria, Pescara—in the Abruzzi, under
his abbot, St Guy. He retired to Mt
Caramanico near Chieti, where he
founded the abbey of St Nicholas.

ADALGIS (ADELGIS, ALGIS) (St)
Priest H.   AC. June 2
d. c.686. An Irish monk, disciple of St
Fursey. He evangelized the country

around Arras and Laon. In the forest of Thiérarche in Picardy he founded a small monastery, around which afterwards grew up the village of Saint-Algis.

ADALGIS (St) Bp.   AC. Oct 7
c.850. Bishop of Novara *c*.830–*c*.850. An important churchman under the emperor Lothair. Venerated at Novara, where he is buried in the church of San Gaudenzio.

ADALGOTT (St) Bp. OSB.Cist.
AC. Oct 3
d. 1165. Professed as a monk under St Bernard at Clairvaux. In 1150 he became abbot of the Black Benedictines at Dissentis and bishop of Chur, where he founded a hospital for the poor and proved himself an excellent pastor.

ADALGOTT (Bl) Ab. OSB.
AC. Oct 26
d. 1031. Monk of Einsiedeln and from 1012 abbot of Dissentis, both of which abbeys are in Switzerland.

ADALSINDIS (St) Abs. AC. May 3
c.680. Sister of St Waldalenus, abbot-founder of Bèze. She became abbess of a convent near Bèze under the supervision of her brother.

ADALSINDIS (St) N. OSB.
PC. Dec 25
c.715. One of the daughters of SS Adalbald and Rictrudis, who took the veil at Hamay-les-Marchiennes, in the diocese of Arras, under her own sister St Eusebia.

ADAM (St) Ab. OSB.   AC. May 16
d. *p*.1212. Born at Fermo. First hermit, and then monk and abbot, of San Sabino on Mt Vissiano, near Fermo. His relics are enshrined in the cathedral of Fermo, where his feast is kept.

ADAM (Bl) Mk. OSB.Cist.
PC. Dec 22
d. *c*.1210. Priest and sacristan in the Cistercian abbey of Loccum in Saxony. Remarkable, like most Cistercian saints, for his devotion to our Lady.

ADAM and EVE (SS)   AC. Dec 24
First parents of the human race. Adam died aged nine hundred and thirty years. Their feast is given different dates in the martyrologies: Jan 18–23, March 24, April 24, Dec 19, Dec 24. The last date is the most common.

ADAMNAN (St) Mk. OSB.
AC. Jan 31
d. *c*.680. An Irish pilgrim who became a monk at Coldingham, near Berwick, under the abbess St Ebba. Cult confirmed by Leo XIII in 1898.

ADAMNAN (St) Ab.   AC. Sept 23
c.630–704. Surnamed McRonan. Called also Adam, Aunan, Eunan. An Irish saint who became abbot of Iona (679) and zealously advocated the Roman observance of Easter, which however his own abbey did not adopt. He is best remembered for his life of St Columba, a most important hagiographical document.

ADAUCTUS (St) M.   RM. Aug 30
See Felix and Adauctus.

ADAUCTUS and CALLISTHENE (SS) M. V.   AC. Oct 4
c.312 and *p*. These two saints were Ephesians, father and daughter. The former suffered under Maximinus Daza *c*.312. Callisthene escaped martyrdom and devoted herself to works of charity till her death at Ephesus.

ADAUCUS (ADAUCTUS) (St) M.
RM. Feb 7
d. 304. An Italian who held the office of

finance minister at the imperial court of Diocletian in Phrygia. The emperor sacrificed him on discovering his religion. A large number of Christians were martyred with him, their town, Antandro, being burnt over their heads.

ADDAI and MARI (SS) Bps.
AC. Aug 5
2nd cent. They are styled "Our Holy Apostles" alike by Syrians and Persians. Addai was probably a missionary bishop at Edessa in the second century. Of Mari nothing trustworthy is known.

ADEGRIN (ADALGRIN, ALDE-GRIN) (St) Mk. OSB.   PC. June 4
d. 939. A knight who joined St Odo, the future abbot of Cluny, at Baume, and shortly after embraced the eremitical life near the same abbey.

ADELA (St) W.   PC. Feb 24
c.1062–1137. Youngest daughter of William the Conqueror. In 1080 she married Stephen of Blois, played a great part in political affairs, and generously endowed abbeys and churches.

ADELA (St) W. OSB.   PC. Sept 8
d. 1071. Wife of Count Baldwin IV of Flanders, who, in her widowhood, received the habit from Pope Alexander II (1067) and retired to the Benedictine convent of Messines, near Ypres, where she died.

ADELA (St) W. Abs. OSB.
PC. Dec 24
d. c.730. Daughter of Dagobert II, king of the Franks. In her widowhood she founded and became first abbess of Pfalzel (*Palatiolum*) near Trèves.

ADELAIDE (St) Abs. OSB.
AC. Feb 5
d. c.1015. Abbess of Bellich (Willich)

near Bonn, and of Our Lady of the Capitol at Cologne. Both were Benedictine convents founded by her father.

ADELAIDE (ALEYDIS) (St) V. OSB. Cist.   AC. June 15
d. 1250. A young nun of the Cistercian convent of La Cambre who was visited with many physical afflictions. She became blind, contracted leprosy, and was struck with paralysis. She had to be segregated from her community. She offered up her sufferings for the souls in purgatory and had visions of their being set free through her intercession. Her life was written by a contemporary. Cult confirmed in 1907.

ADELAIDE (St) W. Empress.
AC. Dec 16
c.930–999. Daughter of the king of Burgundy, she was married (947) to Lothair II of Italy, on whose death she was treated with great brutality by Berengarius of Ivrea. She was rescued by the emperor Otto the Great, who married her. Again left a widow (973), she was ill-treated by her son and daughter-in-law. In her old age she became the regent of the Empire. Throughout her life she received strong support from the abbots of Cluny, with whom she was on terms of close friendship. Before her death she retired to a convent.

ADELBERT (*several*)
Otherwise Adalbert, q.v.

ADELELMUS (Fr. ALLEAUME, Sp. LESMES, ELESMES) (St) Ab. OSB.
AC. Jan 30
d. c.1100. Born at Laudun, Poitou. He became a soldier. On his return from a pilgrimage to Rome he met at Issoire St Robert, founder of Chaise-Dieu, and joined his community. He seems to have been abbot there for a time. In

1079 he was called to Burgos, Old Castile, by Queen Constance of Burgundy, wife of Alphonsus VI of Castile. Adelelmus received from the king a church and a hospital by the gates of Burgos, where the great abbey of St John (now the church of St Lesmes) was founded with the saint as first abbot.

ADELELMUS (ADELHELM) (Bl) Ab. OSB.   **PC. Feb 25**
d. 1131. A monk of St Blasien in the Black Forest, he was sent to found the monastery of Engelberg in Switzerland, of which he became prior and subsequently abbot.

ADELELMUS (St) H.   PC. Apr 27
d. 1152. Born in Flanders, he became a disciple of St Bernard of Thiron, and afterwards founder of the monastery of Etival-en-Charnie.

ADELGOTT
Otherwise Adalgott, q.v.

ADELHEIDIS (Bl) V. OSB.Cist.
PC. Dec 27
d. 1273. Of the family of Thöningen. She sanctified herself as a recluse under the obedience of the Cistercian abbey of Tennenbach.

ADELIN, ADELINUS
Otherwise Hadelin, q.v.

ADELINA (Bl) V. OSB.Cist.
PC. Aug 28
c.1170. Daughter of Bl Guy, brother of St Bernard of Clairvaux. She was educated at Juilly and became a nun, and afterwards abbess, of the Cistercian convent of Poulangy, diocese of Langres.

ADELINA (St) V. OSB. AC. Oct 20
d. 1125. Granddaughter of William the Conqueror and sister of St Vitalis of Savigny. She became abbess of La Blanche at Moriton (les Dames Blanches de Mortain) in Normandy, founded by her brother.

ADELINDIS (Bl) W. OSB.
PC. Aug 28
d. c.930. In her widowhood she founded and eventually became a nun—and perhaps abbess—of Buchau, on the Federsee in Wurtemburg.

ADELOGA (HADELOGA) (St) V. OSB.   AC. Feb 2
d. c.745. A Frankish princess who was the foundress and first abbess of the great Benedictine nunnery of Kitzingen in Franconia.

ADELPHUS (St) Bp.   RM. Aug 29
5th cent. The RM. has: "At Metz in France the memory of St Adelphus, bishop and confessor." Nothing more is known about him. His cult at Metz from early times is indisputable.

ADELPHUS (St) Ab. OSB.
AC. Sept 11
d. c.670. Grandson of St Romaricus, and his successor (653) as abbot of Remiremont. He died at Luxeuil.

ADELTRUDIS (St) Abs. OSB.
AC. Feb 25
Otherwise Aldetrudis, q.v.

ADEODATUS
Saints of this name are better known as Deusdedit or Dieudonné, q.v.

ADERALD (St) C.   AC. Oct 20
d. 1004. Archdeacon of Troyes. He led a pilgrimage to Palestine, and on his return "with much booty in the shape of holy relics" he built for their reception the Benedictine abbey of St Sepulchre at Samblières.

ADHERITUS (ABDERITUS, ADERY) (St) Bp.   RM. Sept 27
d. 2nd cent. A Greek by birth, successor of St Apollinaris in the see of Ravenna. Since the early Middle Ages his body has been enshrined in the Benedictine basilica of Classe near Ravenna.

ADILIA
Otherwise Adela, or Otillia, q.v.

ADJUTOR (AYUTRE) (St) H. OSB.
AC. Apr 30
d. 1131. A Norman knight, lord of Vernon-sur-Seine, who fought in the Crusades and on his return became a monk at Tiron. He afterwards led the life of a recluse at Vernon-sur-Seine, where he died.

ADJUTOR (St) C.   RM. Sept 1
See Priscus, Castrensis, etc.

ADJUTOR (St) M.   RM. Dec 18
See Victurus, Victor, etc.

ADJUTUS (St) M. OFM.
RM. Jan 16
See Berardus, Peter, etc.

ADJUTUS (St) Ab.   RM. Dec 19
Otherwise Avitus (or Avy), q.v.

ADO (St) Bp. OSB.   RM. Dec 16
799–875. Born in Burgundy and educated under Lupus Servatus at Ferrières, he was professed as a Benedictine at Ferrières, but the abbot of Prüm, near Trèves, succeeded in enlisting his services as headmaster of the monastic school at Prüm. After some years the jealousy of certain monks drove him from Prüm, and he travelled to Rome. On his return to France he stayed for a while at Lyons and in 859 was made bishop of Vienne. He proved an altogether admirable prelate. He is best remembered, however, as the compiler of the martyrology which bears his name and of other minor writings which unfortunately "were responsible for the perpetuation of a number of baseless and misleading statements". (Att.)

ADOLPH (St) Ab. (or Bp.) OSB.
AC. June 17
See Botulph and Adulph.

ADOLPHUS (St) Bp. OSB.Cist.
AC. Feb 11
c.1185–1224. Born in Westphalia, of the family of the counts of Tecklenburg, he became a canon of Cologne, but resigned to become a Cistercian at Camp on the Rhine. In 1216 he was nominated bishop of Osnabrück, where he became known as "the almoner of the poor". He died on June 30.

ADOLPHUS LUDIGO-MKASA (St) M.   AC. June 3
From a tribe of herdsmen. See Uganda (Martyrs of).

ADOLPHUS and JOHN (SS) MM.
RM. Sept 27
d. c.850. Two brothers, born at Seville of a Moorish father and a Christian mother, who were martyred at Cordova under Abderrahman II.

ADRIA (St) M.   RM. Dec 2
See Eusebius, Marcellus, etc.

ADRIAN
Note. This name is in certain cases also spelt with an initial H.

ADRIAN (St) Ab. OSB.   AC. Jan 9
d. 710. An African by birth, he became abbot of Nerida, not far from Naples. Pope Vitalian chose him to be archbishop of Canterbury, but he declined

the office and recommended instead St Theodore of Tarsus, with whom he came to England as assistant and adviser. He became abbot of SS Peter and Paul, afterwards St Augustine's, Canterbury, where he supervised a flourishing school. He was eminent for his learning as well as his sanctity. His cultus revived in 1091, when his body was discovered.

ADRIAN (St) M.   RM. March 1
See Hermes and Adrian.

ADRIAN and Comp. (SS) MM.
AC. March 4
d. c.875. Adrian was a missionary bishop on the isle of May in the Firth of Forth, who was martyred by the Danes together with some fellow missionaries who were monks. The saint's connexion with Hungary seems to be a myth.

ADRIAN and EUBULUS (SS) MM.
RM. March 5 and 7
d. 308. Both were martyred at Caesarea in Palestine when they came to visit the Christians there—Adrian on March 5 and Eubulus two days later.

ADRIAN (St) M.   AC. March 19
d. c.668. A disciple of St Landoald. He was murdered by robbers while begging alms for his community near Maestricht, and afterwards locally venerated as a martyr.

ADRIAN III (St) Pope   RM. July 8
d. 885. He became pope in 884, and almost at once set out to take part in the diet of Worms, intending to ask for help against the Saracens. He died on his way, near Modena, and was buried at Nonantola. Cult confirmed in 1892.

ADRIAN BEANUS (St) M.
O.Praem.   RM. July 9
See Gorkum (Martyrs of).

ADRIAN FORTESCUE (Bl) M.
AC. July 9
1476–1539. Born at Punsbourne in Hertfordshire, he was first cousin to Anne Boleyn. In 1499 he married Anne Stonor. He was a knight of St John and most faithful in the discharge of his duties. He refused the oath of supremacy, and was for this reason beheaded on Tower Hill by order of Henry VIII. Beatified by Leo XIII in 1895.

ADRIAN (St) M.
RM. March 4. Aug 26. Sept 8
d. c.304. Adrian, a pagan officer at the imperial court at Nicomedia, befriended the Christian prisoners and was himself cast into prison, where he and his fellow prisoners were tended by his wife St Natalia, q.v. All the prisoners were martyred on March 4. Natalia survived to transfer her husband's relics to Argyropolis. In later times the relics were translated to Rome. St Adrian is the patron of soldiers and butchers.

ADRIAN (Bl) M. OP.   AC. Dec 21
13th cent. Adrian, a Friar Preacher, and twenty-seven companions were put to death by the Mohammedans in Dalmatia.

ADRIO, VICTOR and BASILLA (SS) MM.   RM. May 17
? Martyrs of Alexandria, whether at the hands of pagans or Arians is not known.

ADULPHUS
Otherwise Adolphus or Adolph, q.v.

ADVENTOR (St) M.   RM. Nov 20
See Octavius, Solutor and Adventor.

AE
Note. Names of saints beginning with this diphthong are frequently spelt with A or E only as the initial letter. Thus for

Aelphege we have also Alphege (Alphage) and Elphege.

AEDAN
Among many variants of the name the following are the commonest: Aidan, Aedhan, Edan. The Celtic variants are: Maidhoc, Maodhog, Mogue, and, in Brittany, Dé. See Aidan.

AEDESIUS (St) M.   RM. Apr 8
d. c.306. His *laus* in the RM. is as follows: "At Alexandria, the memory of St Aedesius, martyr, a brother of blessed Apphian, who, under Maximian Galerius the emperor, openly withstood an impious judge because he handed over to pimps virgins consecrated to God. He was laid hold of by the soldiery, afflicted with most cruel punishments, and drowned in the sea for the Lord Christ."

AEDH MacBRICC (St) Bp.
AC. Nov 10
6th cent. The name is also spelt Aod and Aedsind, and it is latinized as Aidus. He was a disciple of St Illadan at Rathlihen in Offaly, and is said to have founded churches at Rathugh and other places in his native Meath, where he held the office of bishop.

AEDH, AEDHAN
Note. Holweck lists eighteen more Irish saints of the name of Aedh, and twenty under Aedhan, but the historical data are hopelessly confused.

AEGIDIUS
One of the most popular saint's names in the Middle Ages. In Italian: Egidio; in French: Gilles; in Spanish and Portuguese: Gil; in English: Giles, q.v.

AELGIFU (St) W. OSB.
AC. May 18
Otherwise Elgiva, q.v.

AELPHLEAH, AELPHEGE (St) Bp.
Otherwise Elphege, q.v.

AELRED (St) Ab. OSB.Cist.
AC. Jan 12
1109–1167. Born in the north of England, Aelred became master of the household of King David of Scotland. In 1133 he joined the Cistercian community of Rievaulx in Yorkshire. Soon he was made abbot, first of Revesby, then of Rievaulx itself. Austere with himself, he was, we are told, remarkably gentle with his monks, of whom he dismissed not one in seventeen years. His ascetical treatises, especially that *On Spiritual Friendship*, are full of charm.

AEMILIAN—AEMILIANA—AEMILIO—AEMILIUS
Otherwise Emilian—Emiliana—Emilio—Emilius, q.v.

AENGUS (OENGUS, OENGOBA) (St) Bp.   AC. March 11
d. c.830. Known as "the Culdee". He is said to have been first a monk of Clonenagh and then of Tallacht Hill. He is best remembered as the composer of a celebrated metrical hymn to the saints, called Felire (Festilogium, metrical martyrology). Though he was famous in his day, no early account of him is extant and he is not commemorated liturgically in any Irish diocese. From Tallacht Hill he returned to Clonenagh, where he became abbot and bishop.

AESCHILUS (St) Bp. M.
AC. June 12
Otherwise Eskill, q.v.

AETHELGIFU
Otherwise Ethelgiva or Elgiva, q.v.

AETHELHARD (St) Bp. AC. May 12
Otherwise Ethelhard, q.v.

AETHERIUS (*several*)
Otherwise Etherius, q.v.

AETIUS (St) M.   RM. March 10
See Forty Armenian Martyrs.

AFAN (St) Bp.   AC. Nov 16
6th cent. A Welsh saint of the Cunedda
family, by some supposed to have been
a bishop. He has given its title to the
church of Llanafan (Brecknock).

AFFROSA (St) VM.   RM. Jan 4
Otherwise Dafrosa (or Daphrosa), q.v.

AFRA (St) VM.   RM. May 24
? A martyr of Brescia, connected by
legend with SS Faustinus and Jovita.
The rest of the legend is untrustworthy.

AFRA (St) M.   RM. Aug 5
d. *c*.304. A martyr who suffered at
Augsburg, probably under Diocletian.
She was venerated there from early
times, and the great Benedictine abbey
of that city was dedicated to her. The
story of her being a converted harlot
from Cyprus is worthless.

AFRICA (Martyrs of) (SS)
By Africa here is meant only North
Western Africa, or *Africa Latina*.
North Eastern Africa goes under the
heading Egypt or Ethiopia. The following anonymous groups of martyrs are
mentioned in the Roman Martyrology:

RM. Jan 6
d. *c*.210. A number of Christians of
either sex burnt at the stake under
Septimius Severus.

RM. Feb 11
d. *c*.303. Martyrs known as the "Guard-
ians of the Holy Scriptures". They
chose to die rather than to deliver the
sacred books to be burnt. They suffered
under Diocletian. St Augustine mentions especially those of Numidia.

RM. Apr 5
d. 459. A large group martyred on
Easter Sunday while assisting at Mass,
under Genseric, the Arian king of the
Vandals. The lector, who was at the
moment intoning the Alleluja, had his
throat pierced by an arrow.

RM. Apr 9
? A group of Christians martyred at
Masyla (*Martyres Massylitani*).   St
Augustine and Prudentius sang their
praises.

RM. Oct 16
? Two hundred and twenty Christians
were put to death on this day, where,
when and how is not known.

RM. Oct 30
? A group of Christians, numbering between one (and) two hundred, massacred in one of the early persecutions.
No other details are available.

RM. Dec 16
d. 482. A great number of women
butchered under Hunneric, Arian king
of the Vandals.

AFRICANUS (St) M.   RM. Apr 10
See Terence, Africanus, etc.

AFRICUS (St) C.   AC. Nov 16
7th cent. A saint of Comminges in S.
France, celebrated for his zeal for orthodoxy. His shrine was destroyed by the
Calvinists, but his cultus still endures.
Tradition makes him bishop of that
city, but his name is not mentioned in
the French Episcopologia.

AGABIUS (St) Bp.   RM. Aug 4
c.250. An early bishop of Verona. His
existence is uncertain.

AGABUS (St) C.   RM. Feb 13
1st cent. A prophet twice mentioned in
the Acts of the Apostles. (XI 28; XXI
10–12.) A Carmelite legend has led to
his being usually represented in art

robed in the Carmelite habit and holding the model of a church.

AGAMUND (St) M. OSB.
AC. Apr 9
See Theodore and Comp.

AGANUS (St) Ab. OSB. PC. Feb 16
c.1050–1100. An abbot of St Gabriel's
at Airola in Campania, diocese of St
Agatha dei Goti.

AGAPE (St) M.   RM. Jan 25
See Donatus, Sabinus, and Agape.
Note. The genitive case Agapis in the
RM. may designate a saint of either sex.

AGAPE (St) VM.   RM. Feb 15
c.273. A maiden martyred at Terni, who
belonged to a group of virgins formed
by St Valentine into a community.
From the 6th to the 12th century there
was a church at Terni dedicated to her.

AGAPE, CHIONIA and IRENE (SS)
VV. MM.   RM. Apr 3
d. 304. Three sisters who were burnt
alive with several companions under
Diocletian at Salonika. All suffered on
April 3 except Irene, who was exposed
in a brothel and put to death two days
later.

AGAPE (St) VM.   RM. Aug 1
Otherwise Charity. See Faith, Hope,
and Charity.

AGAPE (St) VM.   RM. Dec 28
See Indes, Domna, etc.

AGAPITUS (St) Bp. RM. March 16
4th cent. Bishop of Ravenna.

AGAPITUS (St) Bp. RM. March 24
3rd cent. Bishop of Synnada in Phrygia.

AGAPITUS (St) M.   RM. Aug 6
See Sixtus II and Comp.

AGAPITUS (St) M.   RM. Aug 18
d. c.274. A boy of fifteen who bravely
confessed Christ and was martyred at
Palestrina, near Rome. He is the
patron saint of Palestrina, where as
early as the 5th century a church was
dedicated to him by Pope Felix III
(483–492).

AGAPITUS (St) M.   RM. Sept 20
See Eustace, Theopistus, etc.

AGAPITUS I (St) Pope.
RM. Sept 20 (and Apr 22)
d. 536. A Roman by birth and archdeacon of the Roman Church, he was
elected pope in May 535 and died at
Constantinople on April 22, 536. As
pope he showed great strength of
character in deposing the Monophysite
patriarch of Constantinople. His body
was taken back to Rome on Sept 20,
on which date he is commemorated a
second time in the RM. In common
with many other Italian saints of the
same period he owes his cult to the
devotion of St Gregory the Great.

AGAPITUS (St) M.   RM. Nov 20
See Bassus, Dionysius, etc.

AGAPIUS (St) M.   RM. March 24
See Timolaus, Dionysius, etc.

AGAPIUS (St) M.   RM. Apr 28
See Aphrodisius, Caralippus, etc.

AGAPIUS and Comp. (SS) MM.
RM. Apr 29
c.259. The Spanish saints Agapius and
Secundinus, bishops or priests, were
banished to Cirta, Numidia, in the
persecution under Valerian. There they
suffered martyrdom together with
Tertulla and Antonia, virgins, and a
certain woman with her twin children.
The martyr Emilian mentioned by the
RM. is not mentioned in the *Acta*.

AGAPIUS (St) M.   RM. Aug 19
See Timothy, Thecla and Agapius.
St Agapius is also commemorated
separately on Nov 20, q.v.

AGAPIUS (St) M.   RM. Aug 21
See Bassa, Theogonius, etc.

AGAPIUS (or AGAPITUS) (St) Bp.
                         RM. Sept 10
d. 447. Bishop of Novara in Piedmont
from 417–447. Successor to St Gaudentius, "whose footsteps he followed".

AGAPIUS (St) M.   RM. Nov 2
See Carterius, Styriacus, etc.

AGAPIUS (St) M.   RM. Nov 20
d. c.306. Martyred at Caesarea in
Palestine under Diocletian. He was
thrice imprisoned for the Faith. Again
arrested, he was chained to a murderer
and taken to the amphitheatre to be
thrown to the wild beasts. His companion was pardoned, and liberty was also
offered to Agapius if he would renounce
Christ. He refused, and a bear was let
loose upon him which almost mauled
him to death. He was taken back to
prison and on the following day
weighted with heavy stones and cast
into the sea. He is also commemorated
on Aug 19.

AGATHA (St) VM.   RM. Feb 5
d. c.250. Born either at Catania or
Palermo in Sicily, she suffered martyrdom at Catania. According to the
legenda, she was handed over to a pros-
titute and her breasts were cut off. St
Peter cured her of this mutilation while
she was in prison, where she subsequently died. Her cult spread throughout the Church. Her name is in the
litany of the saints, in the canon of the
Mass, and in all the martyrologies,
Greek and Latin. In art she is represented holding a pair of pincers or bearing

her breasts on a platter: later these
were mistaken for loaves, whence arose
the custom of blessing bread on a dish
on St Agatha's day. The miracles by
which she has preserved Catania from
successive eruptions of Mt Etna are
well accredited. She is the patroness of
wet-nurses, bell-founders and jewellers.

AGATHA (St) W.   PC. Feb 5
d. 1024. Wife of Paul, count of Carinthia. A model of devotion to her domestic duties and of patience under the
brutal ill-treatment of her jealous husband, whom she converted. She is
highly venerated in Carinthia.

AGATHA LIN (Bl) VM. AC. Feb 18
1817–1858. A Chinese school-teacher,
born at Ma-Tchang and beheaded for
the Faith at Mao-ken on Jan. 28. She
was beatified on May 2, 1909.

AGATHA (St) V. OSB.   AC. Dec 12
d. c.790. Nun of Wimborne, disciple of
St Lioba, with whom she crossed over
to Germany to help St Boniface in his
missionary labours.

AGATHANGELUS (St) M.
                         RM. Jan 23
d. c.309. Agathangelus was converted
and baptized by St Clement, bishop of
Ancyra, while the latter was a prisoner
in Rome. He followed the bishop to the
East, and both were martyred at Ancyra.
Their Acta are most romantic, but unfortunately spurious.

AGATHANGELUS and CASSIAN
(BB) MM. OFM. Cap.   AC. AUG 7
d. 1638. Agathangelus of Vendôme—his
baptismal name was Francis Noury—
became a Capuchin friar at Vendôme
and eventually was sent to Egypt (1633)
to work for the reconciliation of the
dissident Coptic Christians. There he
joined his fellow-Capuchin, Fr Cassian

of Nantes. Their mission failed and they passed on into Abyssinia. They were at once reported to King Fasilidas by a German Protestant and stoned to death on entering the country. They were beatified in 1905.

AGATHIUS (St) M.   RM. May 8
Otherwise Acacius, q.v.

AGATHO (St) Pope.   RM. Jan 10
d. 681. Pope from June 27, 678, to Jan 10, 681. He was a Sicilian of Palermo and probably a monk, whether Benedictine or Basilian is not certain. As pope he convened the 6th oecumenical council held at Constantinople in 680 against the Monothelites. He restored St Wilfrid to the see of York.

AGATHO (St) M.   RM. Feb 14
See Cyrion, Bassian, etc.

**AGATHO and TRIPHINA (SS) MM.
     RM. July 5**
d. ? 306. Sicilian martyrs about whom nothing further is known. There is doubt even as to the sex of the latter saint.

AGATHO (St) Ab.   AC. Oct 21
4th cent. Hermit and abbot in Egypt. Often quoted in the *Lives of the Fathers of the Desert.*

AGATHO (St) M.   RM. Dec 7
d. 250. This Agatho has been identified with St Besas, whom the RM. mentions on Feb 27 together with SS Julian and Eunus, q.v.

AGATHOCLIA (or AGATHOLICA) (St) VM.   RM. Sept 17
? The *laus* of the RM. is as follows: "On the same day the birthday of St Agathoclia, the handmaid of a certain infidel woman, who for a long time afflicted her with stripes and other tor-

ments to make her deny Christ. She was at last taken before the judge and treated with even greater cruelty, and as she persisted in the confession of the Faith, her tongue was cut out and she was cast into the fire." It is probable that she was a Greek, but at a later period she was said to have been a Spaniard, perhaps because she was the patron saint of Mequinenza in Aragon.

**AGATHODORUS (St) Bp. M.
     RM. March 4**
See Basil, Eugene, etc.

**AGATHODORUS (St) M.
     RM. Apr 13**
See Carpus, Papylus, etc.

**AGATHONICA (St) VM.
     RM. Apr 13**
See Carpus, Papylus, etc.

**AGATHONICA (St) VM.
     RM Aug 10**
See Bassa, Paula and Agathonica.

AGATHONICUS, ZOTICUS and Comp. (SS) MM.   RM. Aug 22
? 3rd cent. Agathonicus, a patrician, was put to death in the neighbourhood of Constantinople under Maximian Herculius. Zoticus, a philosopher of Bithynia, and several of his disciples were martyred about the same time. A magnificent basilica was built in their honour at Byzantium.

**AGATHOPODES (AGATHOPUS) and THEODULUS (SS) MM.
     RM. Apr 4**
d. 303. Agathopodes, a deacon, and Theodulus, a young reader, of the church of Thessalonica were martyred by drowning under Maximian Herculius for refusing to give up the sacred books.

AGATHOPODES (AGATHOPUS)
(St) C.   RM. Apr 25
See Philo and Agathopodes.

AGATHOPUS (St) M.   RM. Dec 23
See Theodulus, Saturninus, etc.

AGERANUS (AYRAN, AYRMAN)
(St) M. OSB.   PC. May 21
d. 888. Ageranus was a monk of Bèze in
the Côte d'Or. When the Normans invaded Burgundy (886–889) most of the
monks escaped, but Ageranus remained
with four other monks—Genesius, Ber-
ard, Sifiard and Rodron—the boy
Adalaric and the priest Ansuinus. All
were massacred by the invaders.

AGERICUS (AGUY, AIRY) (St) Ab.
OSB.   PC. Apr 11
d. c.680. A disciple of St Eligius (Eloi)
who became abbot of St Martin's at
Tours.

AGERICUS (AGUY, AIRY) (St) Bp.
                          RM. Dec 1
c.521–591. Successor of St Desiderius
in the see of Verdun (554). He was
greatly admired by his contemporaries
SS Gregory of Tours and Venantius
Fortunatus. He was buried in his own
home, which was turned into a church.
Around it was built in 1037 the Benedictine abbey of Saint-Airy.

AGGAEUS (St) M.   RM. Jan 4
See Hermes, Aggaeus and Caius.

AGGAEUS (AGGEUS, HAGGAI)
(St) Prophet   RM. July 4
d. c.516 B.C. The tenth of the Minor
Prophets. He belongs to the period after
the exile, and the purpose of his divine
message was to forward the rebuilding
of the Temple of Jerusalem.

AGIA (AIA, AUSTREGILDIS, AYE)
(St) N. OSB.   AC. Apr 18

d. c.714. Wife of St Hidulphus of
Hainault. Both desiring to become religious, she entered the nunnery of Mons
(Castrilocus), while he joined the monks
of Lobbes. She is especially venerated
by the Beguines of Belgium.

AGIA (AIA, AYE) (St) W. AC. Sept 1
6th cent. Mother of St Lupus of
Sens.

AGILBERT (AGLIBERT) (St) Bp.
OSB.   PC. Oct 11
d. c.685. A Frankish monk of Jouarre
under the abbot Ado. He studied scripture in France and then crossed over to
England and preached in Wessex. He
was invited to remain as bishop of the
West Saxons, and as such he came in
contact with St Wilfrid. The two saints
were leaders of the "Roman party" in
the synod of Whitby. When King
Coinwalch grew impatient of the presence in his realm of a foreign bishop,
Agilbert returned to France and was
made bishop of Paris in 668. He was
buried at Jouarre.

AGILBERTA (AGUILBERTA, GIL-
BERTA) (St) Abs. OSB. AC. Aug 10
d. c.680. Second abbess of Jouarre,
elected about the year 660. She was a
relative of St Ebrigisil, of St Ado,
founder of Jouarre, and of St Agilbert,
bishop of Paris.

AGILEUS (St) M.   RM. Oct 15
d. c.300. An African Christian who
suffered martyrdom at Carthage. His
relics were afterwards translated to
Rome. He was held in great veneration
in the Latin Church, especially in Africa.
We have a sermon of St Augustine's in
the martyr's honour.

AGILO (Bl) Ab. OSB.   PC. Aug 27
d. 957. Monk of St Aper at Toul. He
was invited by St Gerard of Brogne to

restore monastic discipline at Sithin (Saint-Bertin).

AGILULPH (St) M. Abp. OSB.
                                      AC. July 9
d. *p.*720. Monk and abbot of Stavelot-Malmédy and archbishop of Cologne. His martyrdom was the result of the zealous discharge of his ministry, and, it seems, of the connivance of Charles Martel.

AGILUS (St) Ab.   AC. Aug 30
*c.*580–650. A young Frankish nobleman who became a monk under St Columbanus at Luxeuil. He remained at Luxeuil under the founder's successor, St Eustace, but went with him in 612 to evangelize Bavaria. On his return to France he became abbot of Rebais, near Paris. He is known also as Aile, Ail, Aisle, Ayeul, Ely.

AGLIBERT (St) M.   RM. June 24
See Agoard, Aglibert, and others.

AGNELLUS of PISA (Bl) C. OFM.
                                      AC. March 13
1194–1236. Born at Pisa, Agnellus was received by St Francis himself among the Friars Minor and sent by him to open a house at Paris. He was later appointed by Francis the first Provincial of the Order in England. Agnellus arrived at Dover in 1224 and founded houses at Canterbury and Oxford. He worked also for some time in London. At Oxford he established a school which became famous, and at Oxford he died. Cult confirmed in 1892.

AGNELLUS (St) Ab. OSB.
                                      RM. Dec 14
d. *c.*596. Hermit and afterwards abbot of San Gaudioso near Naples. He is one of the patron saints of the city and, the RM. adds, "was often seen to free the

besieged city from its foes by the banner of the cross".

AGNES (St) VM.   RM. Jan 21
d. *c.*304. A Roman maiden, aged twelve or thirteen years, who was martyred under Diocletian and buried beside the Via Nomentana, where a basilica in her honour has stood since the time of Constantine the Great. St Ambrose, St Damasus and Prudentius sang her praises. Her name occurs in the canon of the Mass, and as a special patroness of chastity she is one of the most popular of saints. Unfortunately the details of her *Acta* are not trustworthy. In art she is usually represented with a lamb.

AGNES OF BENIGAMIN (Bl)
V. OSA. Disc.   AC. Jan 22
Otherwise Inés de Benigamin, q.v.

AGNES DE (Bl) M.   AC. Feb 18
d. July 12, 1841. Born of Christian parents at Bai-den in W. Tonkin, she died in prison for the Faith at Namdinh. Beatified in 1909.

AGNES of BOHEMIA (Bl) V. Poor Clare   AC. March 2
1200–1282. Born at Prague, daughter of the king of Bohemia, she was educated by the Cistercian nuns of Trebnitz and twice betrothed. She refused to marry, and, with the help of Pope Gregory IX, became a Poor Clare in a foundation of her own at Prague, to which St Clare sent five nuns from Assisi. Agnes remained here till her death, forty-six years later.

AGNES of MONTEPULCIANO (St)
V. OP.   RM. Apr 20
1268–1317. Born near Montepulciano in Tuscany, she entered the convent *del Sacco* at the age of nine. At fourteen she was given charge of the temporalities, and at fifteen she was made first abbess of the convent at Procena. After some

seventeen years she was asked to return to Montepulciano to take charge of a new house of Dominican nuns. Here she spent the remainder of her life. Canonized by Benedict XIII in 1726.

AGNES of POITIERS (St) Abs.
AC. May 13
d. 588. Chosen by St Radegund to be abbess of the nunnery of Holy Cross at Poitiers, Agnes adopted the Rule of St Caesarius, handed to her by the holy bishop himself. She is best known as the friend of the poet St Venantius Fortunatus.

AGNES of VENOSA (Bl) V. OSB.
Mont.   PC. Sept 1
d. c.1144. Said to have been one of the dancing girls sent to tempt St William of Vercelli. She repented and joined the Monteverginian nuns at Venosa, where she became abbess.

AGNES of BAGNO (Bl) V. OSB.
Cam.   AC. Sept 4
d. c.1105. A Camaldolese nun at Santa Lucia, near Bagno di Romagna in Tuscany. Her cult was confirmed in 1823. Her relics are enshrined in the village church of Pereto.

AGNES TAQUEA (Bl) M.
AC. Sept 10
d. 1626. Wife of Bl Cosmas Taquea. A native Japanese woman beheaded at Nagasaki. She and her husband belong to the group of fifty-one Christians who were martyred on the same day with Bl Charles Spinola, SJ., q.v. Beatified in 1867.

AGNES of BAVARIA (Bl) V.
PC. Nov 11
d. 1532. Daughter of Louis IV, duke of Bavaria, she was educated by the Poor Clares of St James at Munich, where she died aged seven.

AGNES of ASSISI (St) V. Abs. Poor Clare   AC. Nov 16
1198–1253. Younger sister of St Clare, whom she followed, aged sixteen, to the Benedictine convent of Panso, near Assisi, and then to San Damiano. She became the first abbess of Monticelli at Florence, opened houses at Padua, Venice and Mantua, and returned to San Damiano, where she died three months after her sister. Cult confirmed by Benedict XIV.

AGNES TSAO-KOUY (Bl) WM.
AC. Nov 24
1826–1856. A young Chinese widow who served the missionaries as catechist. She was killed by "cage torture" at Sy-Lin-Hien. Beatified in 1900.

AGOARD, AGLIBERT and others (SS) MM.   RM. June 24
5th to 7th cent. The RM. has the legend: "In the neighbourhood of Paris, in the village of Creteil, the passion of the holy martyrs Agoard and Aglibert, and numberless others of both sexes." The Bollandists fix the date of their martyrdom between the 1st and the 3rd centuries, but in all probability it took place between the 5th and the 7th.

AGOBARD (St) Bp.   AC. June 6
c.769–840. A native of Spain, he escaped in his youth from the invading Saracens and joined the clergy of Lyons in France. He became archbishop of that city in 813. He played a prominent part in both the ecclesiastical and the political affairs of his time. But his greatest work was done as a theologian, chiefly in the field of liturgy, and he has left many important writings.

AGOFREDUS (St) Mk. OSB.
AC. June 21
d. 738. Brother of St Leutfrid (Leffroi)

and monk of Holy Cross (La-Croix-Saint-Leuffroi), a Benedictine abbey in the diocese of Evreux, Normandy.

AGRECIUS (AGRITIUS) (St) Bp.
RM. Jan 13
d. c.333. Bishop of Trèves and predecessor in that see of St Maximinus. He took part in the council of Arles (314). According to his life composed in the 11th century, he was aided by St Helen, wife of Constantine, who procured for him the garment of our Lord, known as the Holy Coat of Trèves.

AGRICOLA (St) Bp.   AC. Feb 5
d. 420. He is listed as the eleventh bishop of Tongres in a catalogue of the 10th century transcribed from the ancient diptychs.

AGRICOLA (St) Bp.   AC. Feb 26
d. c.594. Said to have been bishop of Nevers between 570 and 594.

AGRICOLA (St) Bp.   RM. March 17
d. 580. In French Arègle or Agrèle. Bishop of Châlon-sur-Saône. His contemporary St Gregory of Tours enlarges upon the austerity of his life.

AGRICOLA (or AGRICOLUS) (St) Bp.   AC. Sept 2
c.630–700. Son of St Magnus, bishop of Avignon. At the age of sixteen he was professed a monk at Lérins, where he remained sixteen years. His father called him to Avignon and made him his co-adjutor, and in 660 he became bishop of the city. He built a church in Avignon to be served by the monks of Lérins and also a convent for Benedictine nuns. By his blessing he put an end to an invasion of storks. All the above particulars are based on documents dating only from the 15th century, and only since 1647 has Agricola been the patron saint of Avignon.

AGRICOLA (St) M.   RM. Nov 4
See Vitalis and Agricola.

AGRICOLA (St) M.   RM. Dec 3
? A martyr in Pannonia, details of whose life have not come down to us, but whose name appears in all the ancient registers.

AGRICOLA (St) M.   RM. Dec 16
See Valentine, Concordius, etc.

AGRIPPINA (St) VM.   RM. June 23
d. c.262. A Roman maiden who was martyred, it is surmised, under Valerian. She is especially venerated by the Sicilians and by the Greeks, both claiming to have her relics, the former at Mineo, the latter at Constantinople.

AGRIPPINUS (St) Bp.   AC. Jan 30
d. c.180. The ninth bishop of Alexandria after St Mark.

AGRIPPINUS (St) Bp.   PC. June 17
d. 615. Bishop of Como in N. Italy. There are well-founded doubts about his claim to the title of saint.

AGRIPPINUS (St) Bp.   AC. July 9
d. 538. Bishop of Autun, who ordained St Germanus of Paris to the deaconate and the priesthood.

AGRIPPINUS (ARPINUS) (St) Bp.
RM. Nov 9
2nd or 3rd cent. Bishop of Naples, where he has been greatly venerated from time immemorial. His relics are enshrined under the high altar of the cathedral of Naples with the bodies of SS Eutychius and Acutius, companions of St Januarius.

AGRITIUS (St) Bp.   RM. Jan 13
Otherwise Agrecius, q.v.

AGUY
An abbreviated popular form of the names Agericus and Agritius, q.v.

AIA (St) W.   **AC. Sept 1**
Otherwise Agia, q.v.

AIBERT (AYBERT) (St) H. OSB.
            AC. Apr 7
c.1060–1140. Born at Espain, near Tournai, he became a monk at the abbey of St Crespin, where for twenty-three years he was provost and cellarer; then he retired to live as a recluse. His devotion to the Holy Sacrifice took the form of saying two masses daily, one for the living and one for the dead.

AICHARDUS (AICARD, ACHARD) (St) Ab. OSB.   **RM. Sept 15**
d. c.687. Born at Poitiers, the son of an officer at the court of Clotaire II. He was educated at the abbey of St Hilaire at Poitiers and early in life was professed as a monk of Ansion in Poitou. Here he spent thirty-nine years; afterwards he became abbot of St Benedict's at Quinçay, near Poitiers. Finally he succeeded St Philibert at Jumièges, where he ruled close on a thousand monks.

AICHARDUS (Bl) Mk. OSB. Cist.
            PC. Sept 15
d. c.1170. Entered Clairvaux (c.1124) and made his profession in the hands of St Bernard, who sent him to several foundations. Having returned to Clairvaux he was made novice-master by St Bernard himself.

AID (St) Ab.   **AC. Apr 11**
? An abbot of Achard-Finglas in Co. Carlow, possibly one and the same with St Aed or Maedhogh of Clonmore.

AIDAN (or MAEDOC) (St) Bp.
            AC. Jan 31
d. 626. The first bishop of Ferns in Co. Wexford, Eire, where he founded and ruled a monastery as well. In his youth he had become a monk under St David in Wales and he returned later in life to live some time with him. His life contains much legendary matter.

AIDAN (AEDAN) (St) Bp.
            RM. Aug 31
d. 651. An Irish monk of Iona who, at the request of St Oswald king of Northumbria, was sent to evangelize N. England. He fixed his see at Lindisfarne (Holy Island) where he ruled as abbot and bishop, his diocese reaching from the Forth to the Humber. His apostolate, furthered by numberless miracles, was most fruitful, as is witnessed by the writings of St Bede. He died at Bamborough. In art he is represented sometimes with a stag near him, suggested by a legend that by his prayer he once rendered invisible a deer pursued by huntsmen.

AIDAN (St) Bp.   **AC. Oct 20**
d. 768. An Irish bishop in Mayo.

AIGNAN (AGNAN) (St) Bp.
            RM. Nov 17
Otherwise Anianus, q.v.

AIGULPHUS (AYOUL, AIEUL, AOUT, HOU) (St) Bp.   **AC. May 22**
d. p.835. After an excellent education he chose to live as a recluse. However, about the year 812 he was against his will placed in the see of Bourges, which he governed till his death.

AIGULPHUS (AYOU, AYOUL) (St) Ab. M. OSB.   **RM. Sept 3**
c.630–676. Born at Blois, at the age of twenty he entered Fleury, then in its first fervour of Benedictine observance. He was sent first to Montecassino to rescue the relics of St Benedict, and then (c.670) as abbot to Lérins to introduce the Benedictine Rule. Some malcontents—laymen, it appears—opposed him and caused him to be taken, with

four of his monks, to an island near Corsica where they were done to death.

AILBE (ALBEUS, AILBHE) (St) Bp.
AC. Sept 12
We transcribe Donald Attwater's excellent summary: "A commemoration of the feast of St Ailbe (*Albeus*) is made throughout Ireland, but his recorded life is a confusion of valueless legends and contradictory traditions. He is venerated as the first bishop at Emly, in the early 6th century, and is reputed as author of a monastic rule."

AILRED (St) Ab. OSB. Cist.
AC. Jan 12
Otherwise Aelred, q.v.

AIMARD (Bl) Ab. OSB. AC. Oct 5
Otherwise Aymard, q.v.

AIMÉ (AMÉ) (St) Ab. OSB.
RM. Sept 13
Otherwise Amatus, q.v.

AIMO (AIMONIUS) (St) Mk.
PC. Feb 13
d. *c.*790. Founder of the nunnery of St Victor at Meda in the archdiocese of Milan.

AIMO (AYMO, HAIMO) (St) Mk.
OSB.   AC. Apr 30
d. 1173. Born in the diocese of Rennes, Aimo joined the community of Savigny in Normandy. Falsely suspected of leprosy, in order not to be sent away, he offered to serve two religious who were actually lepers. Afterwards he was admitted to profession, and ordained priest and appointed to various offices. He had many severe trials and was favoured with mystical experiences.

AIMO TAPARELLI (Bl) C. OP.
AC. Aug 18
1395-1495. A native of Savigliano in Piedmont and a member of the family of the counts of Lagnasco. He became a Dominican, and was appointed chaplain to Bl Duke Amadeus of Savoy and inquisitor general for Lombardy and Liguria. He died a centenarian. Cult confirmed in 1856.

AIRALDUS (AYRALDUS) Bp.
O. Cart.   AC. Jan 2
d. 1156? Carthusian prior of Portes, in the diocese of Belley, and, from 1132 to 1156, bishop of St John of Maurienne in Savoy.

AIRY (St) Bp.   RM. Dec 1
Otherwise Agericus, q.v.

AISLE (AILEU) (St) Ab. AC. Aug 30
Otherwise Agilus, q.v.

AITHALAS (St) M.   RM. Apr 22
d. 377. One of the band of Persian martyrs whose leader was St Acepsimas, q.v.

AIZAN and SAZAN (SS) MM.
AC. Oct 1
d. *c.*400. Two brothers, petty chieftains in Abyssinia, very zealous in spreading the gospel in their own country. They were great friends of St Athanasius.

AJOU (AJON) (St) Ab. M. OSB.
RM. Sept 3
Otherwise Aigulphus, q.v.

AJUTRE (St) H. OSB. AC. Apr 30
Otherwise Adjutor, q.v.

ALACOQUE, MARGARET MARY
(St) V.   RM. Oct 17
See Margaret Mary Alacoque.

ALACRINUS (Bl) Bp. OSB. Cist.
PC. Jan 5
d. 1216. Cistercian prior of Casamari, diocese of Veroli, he was sent as papal

legate to Germany under Popes Innocent III and Honorius III.

ALADIUS (St) Bp. AC. Oct 1
Otherwise Albaud, q.v.

ALANUS (St) Ab. OSB. Cist.
PC. June 28
Otherwise Almus, q.v.

ALANUS (Bl) H. OSB. AC. July 18
d. 1311. An Austrian monk who in the jubilee year of 1300 journeyed to Rome and afterwards joined the Italian community of Sassovivo. In 1311 he became a recluse.

ALANUS de RUPE (ALAIN de la ROCHE) (Bl) C. OP. PC. Sept 8
c.1428–1475. A native of Brittany, he became a Dominican at Dinan, diocese of St Malo and was stationed at the Dominican houses of Paris, Lille, Ghent, and Zwoll, where he died. He is famous for his zeal in spreading the devotion of the Holy Rosary. Cult not yet officially confirmed.

ALANUS and ALORUS (SS) Bps.
AC. Oct 26
5th cent. Two bishops of Quimper in Brittany, concerning whom no reliable particulars have come down to us, except the fact of the popular and liturgical cult given to them from early ages.

ALANUS (St) Ab. OSB. AC. Nov 25
7th cent. Abbot-founder of Lavaur in Gascony.

ALARICUS (ADALRICUS, ADAL-RAI) (Bl) H. OSB. AC. Sept 29
d. 975. Son of Duke Burkhard II of Swabia. Educated, and then a monk, at Einsiedeln in Switzerland. Eventually he became a recluse on the small island of Uffnau, on the lake of Zurich.

ALBAN BARTHOLOMEW ROE (Bl) M. OSB. AC. Jan 21
d. 1642. A Suffolk man of Protestant parentage, who was educated at Cambridge and became a Catholic at Douai and a Benedictine under the name of Alban at Dieuleward (now Ampleforth) in 1612. He laboured in the English mission from 1615 to 1642 and was martyred for his priesthood at Tyburn.

ALBAN (St) M. RM. June 21
d. c.400. A Greek priest of Naxos who, sent into exile by the Arians, preached the gospel in parts of Germany about Mainz. Here he was again attacked by the Arians and put to death. The Benedictine abbey at Mainz, dedicated in his honour, has preserved his memory.

ALBAN (St) M. RM. June 22
3rd or 4th cent. Venerated as the protomartyr of Britain. He was a citizen of Verulam converted by a persecuted priest whom he sheltered in his house. He was executed on Holmhurst Hill. On that spot King Offa erected the Benedictine abbey of St Alban's by which name Verulam has since been known.

ALBAUD (ALADIUS) (St) Bp.
AC. Oct 1
d. c.520. Bishop of Toul. He built the church of St Aper (Epvre), his predecessor in the see, which was at a later period the abbey church of the Benedictine monastery of Saint-Aper.

ALBERIC (St) Ab. OSB. Cist.
AC. Jan 26
d. 1109. One of the three founders of the Cistercians. He was first a hermit at Collan, near Châtillon-sur-Seine; then he followed St Robert to Molesmes (1075) and was prior there and afterwards accompanied him to Cîteaux (1093) where he was again prior and

succeeded St Robert as abbot in 1100. The old Cistercian martyrology adds: "He had a filial devotion to our Lady, from whom he received the white cowl."

ALBERIC CRESCITELLI (Bl) M.
AC. July 9

1863–1900. Born at Altavilla, Beneventa, he entered the Pontifical Seminary for Foreign Missions at Rome. Ordained in 1887, he went next year to work in the Shensi Province of China. After labouring there twelve years, he was moved to Ningkiang. Captured in the Boxer Rising, he was tortured and beheaded. Beatified 1951.

ALBERIC (St) H. OSB. Cam.
AC. Aug 29

d. c.1050. A Camaldolese monk who lived as a recluse at Bagno de Romagna in the diocese of Sarsina. His relics are enshrined in the Camaldolese church of S. Anastasio, diocese of Montefeltro.

ALBERIC (St) Ab. OSB. PC. Oct 28
d. 779. Abbot of Stavelot-Malmédy. His feast is kept together with that of four other abbots of the same monastery.

ALBERIC (St) Bp. OSB. AC. Nov 14
d. 784 (Aug 21). Nephew of St Gregory of Utrecht, he became cathedral prior, and on his uncle's death in 775, bishop of St Martin's at Utrecht. He was a highly educated man, a great friend of Alcuin. His apostolate among the pagan Teutons was exceedingly fruitful.

ALBERIC (Bl) Mk. OSB. AC. Dec 24
10th cent. Monk of Gladbach. Others call him Albert, and give him the title of saint.

ALBERT of CASHEL (St) Bp.
AC. Jan 8

7th cent. Patron saint of Cashel in Ireland. According to the—rather un-

reliable—account of his life, he was an Englishman who laboured in Ireland and afterwards evangelized Bavaria, went to Jerusalem and on his return died and was interred at Ratisbon.

ALBERT (St) King   AC. Feb 24
Otherwise Ethelbert, q.v.

ALBERT of TRENT (St) Bp. M.
AC. March 27

d. 1181. A holy Bishop of Trent who fell a victim in the wars between the Emperor Frederick Barbarossa and his vassals.

ALBERT of MONTECORVINO (St) Bp.   AC. Apr 5
d. 1127. Of Norman origin, Albert settled with his parents at Montecorvino and became bishop there. In his old age, he lost his sight and was given a coadjutor who treated him with contempt and cruelty. The saint went through this trial with heroic patience.

ALBERT THAR-ISPAN (Bl)
AC. May 9

d. 1492. Count of the Cumanian tribes in Hungary, he entered the Pauline Order, in which he lived and died renowned for his austerities.

ALBERT of BERGAMO (Bl) Tert. OP.   AC. May 11
d. 1279. Also called "Albert the Farmer". He was a peasant farmer who helped the poor and destitute. For his generosity he was persecuted by his shrewish wife and jealous relatives. He was a native of Ogna near Bergamo, but later lived at Cremona and died there. He was a Dominican tertiary. Cult approved in 1748.

ALBERT of BOLOGNA (Bl) Ab. OSB. Vall.   AC. May 20
d. 1245. Born at Bologna, a member of

the Parisi family. He became a monk at, and eventually abbot of a Vallumbrosan abbey near Bologna, which afterwards was called S. Alberto.

ALBERT of CSANAD (St) Mk.
AC. May 28
d. c.1492. Hungarian Pauline monk. He was a Latin poet and orator. He died in the monastery at Bajcs. His body was reputed to remain incorrupt.

ALBERT (ARIBERT) of COMO (St) Bp. OSB.   AC. June 3
d. c.1092. A hermit at Rho, and afterwards monk and abbot of San Carpofero. He died bishop of Como.

ALBERT QUADRELLI (St) Bp.
AC. July 4
d. 1179. Born at Rivolta d'Adda in the diocese of Cremona, he was parish priest of his native town for twenty-five years and in 1168 was chosen bishop of Lodi.

ALBERT of GENOA (St) C. OSB. Cist.   AC. July 8
d. 1239. Albert, or Lambert, was born at Genoa and was professed as a laybrother of the Cistercian abbey of Sestri da Ponente, near that city. Eventually he lived as a hermit near the abbey. His cult is very popular.

ALBERT of VALLUMBROSA (Bl) Mk. OSB. Vall.   AC. Aug 1
d. 1094. A disciple of St John Gualbert, he was cellarer for forty years, and also claustral prior. His cult was approved with that of St Rudolph (q.v.) in 1602.

ALBERT of TRAPANI (St) C. OC.
RM. Aug 7
d. 1306. A native of Trapani in Sicily, he entered very young the Carmelite monastery of his native town situated on Mt. Trapani. After his ordination, he was stationed at the Carmelite house

of Messina, where he devoted himself with marvellous success to the conversion of the Jews. Cult confirmed in 1454.

ALBERT (St) Ab. OSB. AC. Sept 5
d. 1073. Abbot-founder of Butrio, in the diocese of Tortona.

ALBERT of PONTIDA (Bl) Ab. OSB.   AC. Sept 5
d. 1095 (May 1). A soldier of Bergamo, who was severely wounded and vowed, if he were cured, to become a religious. He first went as a pilgrim to Compostella and afterwards founded the Benedictine abbey of Pontida, near Bergamo, dedicated to St James, and placed it under the obedience of St Hugh of Cluny. His relics were enshrined at Santa Maria Maggiore of Bergamo, and in 1928 were brought back to Pontida.

ALBERT of JERUSALEM (St) Bp.
AC. Sept 25
c.1149–1214. An Italian canon regular who became successively prior general of his Institute, bishop of Bobbio, bishop of Vercelli, and in 1205, under Pope Innocent III, patriarch of Jerusalem. He is best known as co-founder of the Carmelite Friars, for whom, at the request of St Brocard, he wrote a rule. He was assassinated by an evil-liver whom he had rebuked.

ALBERT of SASSOFERRATO (Bl) C. OSB.   AC. Oct 25
d. 1330 (Aug 7). A monk of Santa Croce di Tripozzo before the Camaldolese had taken possession of that house. Cult confirmed in 1837.

ALBERT the GREAT (St) Bp. Dr OP.   RM. Nov 15
1206–1280. A Swabian by descent, Albert was sent to the university of Padua where he joined the Dominicans. Appointed lector of theology, he taught

at Cologne and Paris. Here St Thomas Aquinas was his disciple, and Albert was the first to recognize Thomas's genius and to foretell the future work of his pupil. Albert became provincial of his Order in Germany and, in 1260, accepted under obedience the see of Ratisbon. He resigned two years later and retired to Cologne, where he spent the rest of his life teaching and writing. Albert was the chief pioneer in the application of the Aristotelian system to theology. His printed works fill thirty-eight quarto volumes and deal with all branches of learning. For this reason he is called "the Great" and "*Doctor Universalis*". He was beatified in 1622 and was equivalently canonized by being declared a Doctor of the Church in 1931.

ALBERT of LOUVAIN (St) Bp. M.
RM. Nov 21
c.1166–1192. Born at Mont César in Louvain and chosen bishop of Liége in 1191. His election was opposed by the emperor Henry VI who favoured another candidate. St Albert appealed to Pope Celestine III, who decided in his favour, and Albert was consecrated at Reims on Sept 29, 1192, but he was murdered by three German knights only two months afterwards (Nov 24). Cult confirmed in 1613.

ALBERT of HAIGERLOCH (Bl)
Mk. OSB.   AC. Nov 26
d. 1311. Of the family of the counts of Haigerloch in Hohenzollern. He was a monk of Oberaltaich in Bavaria from 1261 to 1311, where he sanctified himself in the offices of prior and parish priest.

ALBERT of SASSOVIVO (Bl) Ab.
OSB.   PC. Dec 10
d. *p.*1102. A son of Count Walter (Gualterio), the benefactor who gave to St Mainardus the site to found the abbey of the Holy Cross at Sassovivo. Bl Albert became a monk there, and eventually third abbot of the monastery.

ALBERT (St) Bp.   RM. Dec 13
Otherwise Autbert, q.v.

ALBERT of GAMBRON (St) Ab.
OSB.   AC. Dec 29
7th cent. A courtier who became a hermit and afterwards the abbot-founder of the small abbey of Gambron-sur-l'Authion, where the Rules of St Benedict and St Columbanus were observed simultaneously.

ALBERTA (St) VM.   AC. March 11
d. *c*.286. One of the first victims of the persecution under Diocletian. She suffered at Agen in company with St Faith and others of the same city.

ALBERTINUS (St) C. OSB.
AC. Aug 31
d. 1294. A monk of the monastery of the Holy Cross of Fonteavellana—head house of a Benedictine congregation which in 1570 was united with the Camaldolese. He was elected prior general of his congregation and succeeded in making peace between the bishop and the people of Gubbio. Cult confirmed by Pius VI.

ALBEUS (St) Bp.   AC. Sept 12
Otherwise Ailbe, q.v.

ALBINA (St) VM.   RM. Dec 16
d. 250. A young Christian maiden who suffered at Caesarea under Decius. The RM. mentions Formiae, now Mola di Gaeta in the Campagna, as the place of her death, and her relics have certainly from time immemorial been enshrined at Gaeta near Naples. The Greeks maintain that her body was miraculously translated after martyrdom.

ALBINUS of BRIXEN (St) Bp.
AC. Feb 5
See St Genuinus.

ALBINUS (AUBIN) (St) Bp.
RM. March 1
d. c.554. A native of Vannes. Monk and abbot of Tincillac, between Angers and Saumur, and then bishop of Angers (c.529–554). He took a prominent part in the third council of Orleans (538). The abbey of Saint-Aubin at Angers was erected in his memory. Saint-Aubin de Moeslain (Haute Marne) is to this day a popular place of pilgrimage.

ALBINUS (St) Bp. OSB. AC. Sept 5
Otherwise Alvitus, q.v.

ALBINUS (AUBIN, ALPIN) (St) Bp.
RM. Sept 15
d. c.390. The successor of St Justus in the see of Lyons between 381 and 390. He is said to have built the church of St Stephen and to have chosen it for his cathedral.

ALBINUS (ALBUINUS) (St) Bp.
OSB.   AC. Oct 26
d. p.760. An Anglo-Saxon monk, whose native name was Witta, but who latinized it as Albinus when setting out as a fellow-worker with St Boniface in the conversion of Germany. In 741 he was consecrated bishop of Buraburg in Hesse.

ALBURGA (St) WN. OSB.
AC. Dec 25
d. c.800. Sister to King Egbert of Wessex and wife of Wulstan of Wiltshire. She founded Wilton abbey, near Salisbury, whither she retired and took the veil in her widowhood.

ALCMUND (ALCHMUND) (St) M.
AC. March 19
d. c.800. Prince of the royal house of

Northumbria, who after many years of exile among the Picts of Scotland met his death in Shropshire in circumstances which led to his being venerated as a martyr, first at Lilleshall and then at Derby.

ALCMUND (St) Bp. OSB.
AC. Sept 7
d. 781. The seventh bishop of Hexham.

ALCOBER (JOHN) (Bl) OP.
AC. Dec 30
See John Alcober.

ALCUIN (FLACCUS ALBINUS) (Bl) Ab. OSB.   PC. May 19
d. 804. A native of York, who was educated at the monastic cathedral of that city and became a monk there. Eventually he was ordained deacon and appointed headmaster of his old school. He travelled to Italy to obtain the *pallium* for his bishop and at Parma met Charlemagne who forthwith enlisted his services in the cause of education. The monk became, in fact, the "minister of education" of the Frankish Empire and founded and directed the school (*schola palatina*) where Charlemagne himself became a pupil. In his old age Alcuin was given, among others, the abbey of St Martin of Tours, where he presided as abbot and restored the monastic observance with the help of St Benedict of Aniane. He was a very prolific writer, chiefly on theology and liturgy. Many martyrologies list his name as a *beatus*.

ALDA (ALDOBRANDESCA) (Bl) W. OSB. Hum.   AC. Apr 26
1249–1309. A Sienese maiden who married a very pious husband and lived with him in conjugal continency. Upon the death of her husband Alda joined the third order of the Humiliati and

devoted her life to almsdeeds and mortification. She is greatly honoured at Siena. Variants of her name are Aude, Blanca and Bruna.

ALDATE (ELDATE) (St) C.
AC. Feb 4

5th cent. A Briton who lived in W. England and became celebrated for his patriotism in stirring up his fellow-countrymen to resist the heathen invaders of the land. In some legends he is given as bishop of Gloucester. Many churches bear his name as their titular saint, but trustworthy data of his life are lacking.

ALDEBRANDUS (HILDEBRAND) (St) Bp.
AC. May 1

1119–1219. Born at Sorrivoli, diocese of Cesena, he became provost of Rimini, where he was known for his brave, outspoken stand against all licentiousness: once indeed he had to flee for his life on account of his frank preaching. In 1170 he became bishop of Fossombrone of which town he is now the principal patron saint.

ALDEGUND (St) V. Abs. OSB.
RM. Jan 30

630–684. Sister of St Waldetrudis, abbess of Mons. She became the foundress and first abbess of Maubeuge. She died from cancer of the breast, and, we are told, "in an ecstasy of serene joy".

ALDEMAR (St) Ab. OSB.
AC. March 24

d. c.1080. Surnamed "the Wise". Born at Capua, he became a monk at Montecassino. He was sent as a director to St Laurence's nunnery at Capua; but he was so much talked about on account of his miracles that he was recalled to Montecassino. He founded the Abbey of Bocchignano in the Abruzzi and several other houses which he ruled

with much success. He was a great lover of animals.

ALDERICUS (ALDRIC, AUDRY) (St) Bp.
AC. Jan 7

d. 856. Chaplain to the emperor Louis the Pious, and bishop of Le Mans (832). He excelled alike as a saintly prelate and as an able administrator of public affairs. Some of his works are still extant.

ALDERICUS (ALDRIC, AUDRI) (St) Bp. OSB.
AC. Oct 10

790–841. Born in the Gatinais, he became a Benedictine at Ferrières. The archbishop of Sens attached him to the clergy of the archdiocese. Then he was summoned to the palace as "master and chancellor" (*magister et cancellarius*). Lastly he was raised to the archbishopric of Sens (828). He was a zealous fosterer of ecclesiastical studies.

ALDETRUDIS (ADELTRUDIS) (St) V. Abs. OSB.
AC. Feb 25

d. c.696. Daughter of SS Vincent Madelgarus and Waldetrudis, and a niece of St Aldegund of Maubeuge, she was confided to her aunt's care at this nunnery, of which she became second abbess.

ALDHELM (ADHELM, ALDELMUS) (St) Bp. OSB.
RM. May 25

639–709. A native of Wessex who became a monk at Malmesbury. He was educated partly at Malmesbury and partly under St Adrian at Canterbury. He was given charge of the school at Malmesbury and in 675 was made abbot. Lastly in 705 he was named first bishop of Sherborne. Aldhelm was the first Anglo-Saxon to attain distinction as a scholar and a Latin poet. His love of books is one of the most attractive traits of his character. He has been described as the first English librarian.

ALDO (Bl) OSB.   AC. March 31
d. late 8th cent. Count of Ostrevant, he became a monk at Hasnon abbey in Belgium, which had been founded by his brother John. Aldo was chosen second abbot.

ALEMAN   AC. Sept 16
See Louis Allemand.

ALENA (St) VM.   AC. June 18
d. c.640. Born of pagan parents near Brussels, Alena was baptized without their knowledge. She was put to death while secretly journeying to hear Mass.

ALETH (Bl) W.   PC. Apr 4
d. 1105. Wife of Tecolin and mother of several saintly children, the most famous of whom is St Bernard of Clairvaux. In 1250 her relics were transferred to Clairvaux.

ALEXANDER (St) Bp. M.
RM. Jan 11
? A native of Fermo, near Ancona, who became bishop of his native city, and was martyred under Decius. His relics are enshrined in the cathedral.

ALEXANDER AKIMETES (St) Ab.
AC. Jan 15
d. 430. A Greek who became a monk in Syria and eventually founded a *laura* by the Euphrates, where he soon had some four hundred monks under his rule. He was a somewhat restless archimandrite, fond of new places and faces. He is best known as the founder of the "sleepless" (*akoimetoi*) monks who sang the divine office in relays without intermission day and night. One of these houses he established at Constantinople.

ALEXANDER (St) M.   RM. Jan 30
3rd cent. The RM. describes him as a martyr under Decius "glorious for his venerable age". Some writers have identified him with St Alexander of Jerusalem (see March 18).

ALEXANDER (St) M.   RM. Feb 9
? A martyr of Rome who was accompanied in his confession and death by thirty-eight others. On this same day the RM. mentions another St Alexander, martyred at Soli in Cyprus together with St Ammonius. See Ammonius and Alexander.

ALEXANDER of LUGO (Bl) M. OP.
AC. Feb 10
d. 1645. A Spanish Dominican martyred by the Turks.

ALEXANDER (St) M.   RM. Feb 18
See Maximus, Claudius, etc.

ALEXANDER of ADRUMETUM (St) M.   (RM.) Feb 21
d. c.434. A martyr of the group Verulus, Secundinus, etc., q.v.

ALEXANDER of ALEXANDRIA (St) Bp.   RM. Feb 26
c.250–326. Patriarch of Alexandria, who, as such, convicted of heresy and condemned Arius, one of his own clergy, and on the other hand realized the great gifts of Athanasius, whom he made his deacon and favoured with his confidence. Both the patriarch and his deacon assisted at the council of Nicea (325) where Arius was again condemned. Alexander died shortly after his return to Alexandria.

ALEXANDER, ABUNDIUS, ANTIGONUS, and FORTUNATUS (SS) MM.   RM. Feb 27
? A group of martyrs who suffered either in Rome (the RM.) or in Thessaly (according to the Ven. Bede), when and how is not known.

31

ALEXANDER (St) M.
RM. March 10

See Caius and Alexander.

ALEXANDER and THEODORE (SS) MM.
RM. March 17

? Their names are mentioned both in the Hieronymian and in the Roman Martyrologies. It has been conjectured that they should be identified with SS Alexander and Theodulus, commemorated in the RM. on May 3.

ALEXANDER of JERUSALEM (St) Bp. M.
RM. March 18

d. 251. A fellow-student with Origen at Alexandria, he became bishop of his native city in Cappadocia and was imprisoned for the Faith under Severus. On his release he journeyed to Jerusalem where he was made coadjutor to Narcissus the bishop of the holy city—the first recorded example of an episcopal translation and coadjutorship. Here he received Origen, now an exile, and founded for him a library and a school. Alexander died in chains at Caesarea in Palestine under Decius.

ALEXANDER (SS) MM.
RM. March 24

Two martyrs of the same name included in the group Timolaus and Comp., q.v.

ALEXANDER (St) M.
RM. March 27

3rd cent. A soldier, described in the RM. as having suffered as a Christian in Pannonia under Maximian Herculeus. It seems that he should be identified with the anonymous martyr of Thrace of May 13.

ALEXANDER (St) M.
RM. March 28

See Priscus, Malchus, and Alexander.

ALEXANDER RAWLINS (Bl) Priest M.
AC. Apr 7

d. 1595. A secular priest born in Gloucestershire (?) educated at Reims and ordained in 1590. He was captured while labouring in the York mission and martyred for his priesthood. Beatified in 1929.

ALEXANDER and Comp. (SS) MM.
RM. Apr 24

d. 178. A Greek by birth and the friend and companion of St Epipodius of Lyons. He was arrested. Thirty-four others suffered at the same time.

ALEXANDER, EVENTIUS and THEODULUS (SS) MM.
RM. May 3

d. c.113. Three Roman martyrs buried on the Via Nomentana. The RM. erroneously identifies the Alexander of this group with Pope St Alexander I.

ALEXANDER I (St) Pope
RM. May 3

Pope from c.107 to c.113. See the preceding notice. See S. Quirinus (March 30).

ALEXANDER and ANTONINA (ANTONIA) V. (SS) MM.
RM. May 3

d. 313. The *laus* of the RM. is as follows: "At Constantinople the birthday of the martyrs SS Alexander, the soldier, and Antonina, a virgin. In the persecution of Maximian she was condemned to the stews by Festus the Governor. But she was secretly delivered by Alexander, who changed garments with her and remained there in her place. She was afterwards commanded to be tortured with him; and both were together cast into the flames, with their hands cut off, and were crowned after ending a mighty contest."

ALEXANDER (Bl) Mk. OSB. Cist.
PC. May 3
c.1180–1229. Born in Scotland a descendant of Scottish kings, he entered as a lay-brother the Cistercian abbey of Foigny (*Fusciniacum*), diocese of Laon.

ALEXANDER VINCIOLI (Bl) Bp.
OFM.   AC. May 3
d. 1363. Born at Perugia, he joined the Franciscans. Pope John XXII chose him as his penitentiary and named him bishop of Nocera in Umbria. Bl Alexander died at Sassoferrato.

ALEXANDER (St) M.   RM. May 20
See Thalelaeus, Asterius, etc.

ALEXANDER (St) M.   RM. May 29
See Sisinius, Martyrius and Alexander.

ALEXANDER (St) M.   RM. June 2
See Photinus (Pothinus), Sanctius, etc.

ALEXANDER (St) Bp. RM. June 4
8th cent. A bishop of Verona, of whom nothing further is known.

ALEXANDER (St) Bp. M. RM. June 6
d. 590. Bishop of Fiesole in Tuscany, a brave defender of the Church against the kings of Lombardy. His opponents waylaid him and drowned him in the R. Reno, near Bologna.

ALEXANDER of NOYON (St) M.
RM. June 6
See Amantius, Alexander, etc.

ALEXANDER (St) M.   RM. July 9
See Patermuthius, Copres and Alexander.

ALEXANDER (St) M.   RM. July 10
One of the Seven Brothers, q.v.

ALEXANDER (St) M.   RM. July 21
See Victor, Alexander, etc.

ALEXANDER (St) M.   RM. Aug 1
See Leontius, Attius, etc.

ALEXANDER (St) Bp. M.
RM. Aug 11
d. 270. Surnamed Carbonarius (charcoal-burner) from the trade he was following when appointed bishop of Comana in Pontus on the recommendation of St Gregory Thaumaturgus. He was a philosopher who adopted this trade through humility. He was burnt at the stake.

ALEXANDER (St) M. RM. Aug 26
? Patron of Bergamo, where a church has been dedicated to him from the 4th century. A later manuscript makes him a centurion of the Theban legion who escaped from prison but was retaken.

ALEXANDER (St) Bp. RM. Aug 28
d. ? 336. Patriarch ? or Bishop of Constantinople from 313 to 336, i.e. during the period of the struggle of the church against Arianism. He assisted at the first council of Nicea (325) and took a firm stand against Arius. Indeed, the RM. adds "by the power of his (Alexander's) prayers Arius, condemned by the judgment of God, brake in the midst and his bowels poured out".

ALEXANDER (St) M.   RM. Sept 9
See Hyacinth, Alexander and Tiburtius.

ALEXANDER (St) Bp. M.
RM. Sept 21
2nd cent. A bishop in the neighbourhood of Rome. His miracles attracted the attention of the people and he was arrested and martyred on the Claudian Way, some twenty miles from Rome. St Damasus translated his relics and enshrined them in one of the Roman churches.

ALEXANDER (St) M. RM. Sept 28
See Mark, Alphius, etc.

ALEXANDER (St) M. (RM.) Oct 5
3rd cent. One of the "innumerable multitude" put to death at Trèves by the
prefect Rictiovarus during the persecution of Diocletian.

ALEXANDER SAULI (St) Bp. Barn.
                              RM. Oct 11
1534–1593. A native of Milan who
joined the Barnabites in 1550. Ordained
priest, he became a zealous preacher and
confessor and was for many years
director of St Charles Borromeo. He
was elected general of his Congregation,
and, in 1569, bishop of the Corsican
diocese of Aleria which he completely
reformed during his 20 years' rule. In
1592 Pope Gregory XIV commanded
him to accept the transfer to Pavia,
where he died the following year in the
course of his first pastoral visitation.
Beatified in 1741–1742 and canonized
in 1904.

ALEXANDER (St) M. RM. Oct 17
See Victor, Alexander and Marianus.

ALEXANDER, HERACLIUS and
Comp. (SS) MM.   RM. Oct 22
? Alexander, a bishop, made by his
preaching such an impression on the
multitude that many, both Jews and
pagans, became Christians. He was
arrested and tortured, and such was his
constancy that Heraclius, one of the
soldiers of the guard, was at once converted. Others followed his example.
All were put to death together with St
Alexander. Neither place nor year is
recorded.

ALEXANDER (St) M.   RM. Nov 9
4th cent. A martyr of Salonica under
Maximian Herculeus.

ALEXANDER (St) M. RM. Nov 24
d. 361. A martyr at Corinth under
Julian the Apostate.

ALEXANDER BRIANT (Bl) Priest
M. SJ.   AC. Dec 1
d. 1581. A secular priest, who was admitted into the Society of Jesus in
prison, cruelly tortured to make him
disclose the whereabouts of Father
Parsons SJ. and martyred at Tyburn
together with BB. Ralph Sherwin and
Edmund Campion SJ. for complicity
in a fictitious plot. He was only twenty-
five years of age. Beatified in 1886.

ALEXANDER (St) M. RM. Dec 12
See Epimachus.

ALEXANDRA, CLAUDIA, EUPH-
RASIA, MATRONA, JULIANA,
EUPHEMIA, THEODOSIA, DER-
PHUTA and a Sister of DER-
PHUTA (SS) MM.
                          RM. March 20
d. c.300. Christian women, natives of
Amisus in Paphlagonia, burnt to death
under Diocletian.

ALEXANDRA (St) VM.
                            RM. May 18
See Theodotus, Thecusa, etc.

ALEXANDRIA (Martyrs of)
The RM. makes mention of the following anonymous groups of martyrs put to
death for Christ at Alexandria in Egypt:

                            RM. Jan 28
d. 356. A great number of Catholics
were ordered to be put to death by an
Arian officer while they were in church
assisting at the Holy Sacrifice offered by
St Athanasius. St Athanasius himself
was able to escape.
                            RM. Feb 28
d. 260. The *laus* of the RM. concerning
this group of martyrs reads as follows:
"At Alexandria . . . the commemoration of the holy priests, deacons, and
many others who, in the time of the
emperor Valerian, when a most deadly

pestilence was raging, freely met their death whilst ministering to the sick; whom the religious faith of pious persons is wont to honour as martyrs."

RM. March 17

d. 390. During the reign of the emperor Theodosius, a heathen mob of worshippers of Serapis massacred a multitude of Christians who refused to join in the sacrifices to the pagan idol. Theodosius had the temple of Serapis destroyed and a Christian church built on its site.

RM. March 21

d. 342. The RM. reads: "At Alexandria, the commemoration of the holy martyrs who were slain on Good Friday under the emperor Constantius and Philagrius the Prefect, when the Arians and heathens rushed into the churches." St Athanasius who escaped from the tumult has left a description in his Second Apology.

RM. May 13

d. 372. A great number of Catholics of both sexes were put to death or exiled from Alexandria when, for the fifth time, St Athanasius had been driven from his flock under the Arian emperor Valens. The RM. makes special mention of those massacred in the church of Theonas.

RM. Aug 10

c.257. The RM. has this *laus*: "At Alexandria the commemoration of the holy martyrs who in the persecution of Valerian, under Emilian the Governor, were long tormented with various and sharp tortures, and obtained the crown of martyrdom by divers kinds of deaths". St Dionysius of Alexandria has left a graphic account of them all.

ALEXANDRINA di LETTO (Bl)
Abs Poor Clare   PC. Apr. 3
1385–1458. Born at Sulmona, she joined the Poor Clares when fifteen years of age and after some twenty-three years founded a convent of her order at Foligno of which she became first abbess. Here she initiated a new Franciscan reform, which was blessed and encouraged by Pope Martin V.

ALEXIUS FALCONIERI (St) C.
RM. Feb 12 and 17
One of the Seven Holy Founders of the Servite Order, q.v.

ALEXIUS (Bl) M. OP.   AC. June 1
d. 1622. A Japanese catechist and novice of the Dominican missionaries in Japan. He was burnt alive on the day of the great martyrdom, Sept 10, at Nagasaki. Beatified in 1867.

ALEXIUS DELGADO (Bl) M. SJ.
AC. July 15
1556–1570. A native of Elvas in Portugal, he became a Jesuit novice, and was only fourteen years old when he was killed by Calvinist French pirates near Palma on his way to the W. Indies with a group of Jesuits under the leadership of Bl. Ignatius de Azevedo, q.v. Beatified in 1854.

ALEXIUS (ALEXIS) (St) C.
RM. July 17
d. early 5th cent. A saint originally distinguished with the anonymous title of "the man of God", at a later period he was named Alexis or in Latin Alexius. The legend of his life came from the East and spread throughout the West in the 10th century, when the Greek monks were given the Benedictine abbey of St Boniface on the Aventine, which they renamed SS Boniface and Alexius. The *laus* of the RM. sums up the legend somewhat as follows: Alexius the son of a Roman senator, in order to serve God in humility, on his wedding day fled from his parental home disguised as a beggar. He set sail for

Edessa where after seventeen years an image of our Lady proclaimed him "the man of God". Alexius fled again and eventually returned to Rome and for years lived unrecognized as a beggar in his own home. After his death a mysterious voice again proclaimed him "the man of God". This attractive legend made St Alexius one of the most popular of "popular saints". However, only this seems certain: that the saint lived, and died and was buried at Edessa.

ALEXIUS NACAMURA (Bl) M.
AC. Nov 27

1619. A Japanese layman, born in Figen, of the royal family of Firando. Beheaded with ten companions at Nagasaki. Beatified in 1867.

ALEYDIS (St) V.   AC. June 15
Otherwise Adelaide, q.v.

ALFANUS (ALPHANUS) (St) Bp. OSB.   PC. Oct 9

d. 1085. A monk of Montecassino, who was consecrated at Rome archbishop of Salerno in 1058. It was he who assisted Pope St Gregory VII on his deathbed.

ALFERIUS, (ALPHERIUS, ADAL-FERICUS) (St) Ab. OSB.
AC. Apr 12

930–1050. A Norman by origin, he was born at Salerno and belonged to the family of Pappacarbone. Sent as an ambassador to France, he fell ill at the abbey of Chiusa, and on his recovery betook himself to Cluny and was professed under St Odilo. The duke of Salerno asked for his return, and Alferius settled at Mt. Fenestra, near Salerno, and there founded the abbey of La Cava, under the Cluniac observance. Soon the abbey counted its affiliated houses by hundreds and became a potent civilizing influence in S. Italy. Cult confirmed in 1893.

ALFONSO
Note. This is the modern spelling of Alphonsus in Spanish, Portuguese and Italian; the French spell it Alphonse. The old Spanish spelling is Alonso, and the Portuguese Alonzo. All are derivatives of the original Spanish name Ildephonsus or Aldephonsus. See Alphonsus.

ALFRED (St) Bp. OSB. PC. Aug 15
Otherwise Altfrid, q.v.

ALFREDA (ELFREDA, ETHEL-FREDA) (St) V. OSB.   AC. Aug 2
Otherwise Etheldritha, q.v.

ALFRICK (St) Bp. OSB. A.C. Nov 16

d. 1005. Monk and abbot of Abingdon, and afterwards, successively, bishop of Wilton (990) and archbishop of Canterbury (995). He governed the church very ably in the critical times of the Danish invasion of Kent.

ALFWOLD (St) Bp. OSB.
AC. March 26

d. 1058. A monk of Winchester who was chosen bishop of Sherborne in 1045. He was known for his great devotion to SS Cuthbert and Swithun, whose cult he propagated.

ALGERIC (St) Bp.   RM. Dec 1
Otherwise Agericus, q.v.

ALICE (St) V.   AC. Feb 5
Otherwise Adelaide (or Adelhid). q.v.

ALICE RICH (Bl) V. OSB. PC. Aug 24

c.1270. Sister of St Edmund, archbishop of Canterbury. She joined the Benedictine nuns of Catesby, and became their prioress.

ALIPIUS (ALYPIUS) (St) Bp.
RM. Aug 15

d. c.430. Disciple and lifelong friend of

St Augustine. They were baptized together at Milan on Easter Eve, 387. Upon their return to Africa they spent some time in solitude as religious. St Alipius then visited Palestine. About the year 393 he became bishop of Tagaste and was St Augustine's chief assistant in all his public work.

ALIPRANDUS (or LEUPRANDUS) (St) Ab. OSB.   AC. July 24
8th cent. An abbot of the monastery of St. Augustine in Ciel d'Oro (*in coelo aureo*) at Pavia. He was related to the royal family of the Lombards.

**ALIX LE CLERC (Bl) V. Foundress
                              AC. Jan 9**
1576–1622. Born of noble parents in Lorraine, at first she led a frivolous life, but soon gave herself to God, under the guidance of St Peter Fourier. She founded under his direction the Congregation of Canonesses of St Augustine devoted to the teaching of poor children. A great mystic as well as an active foundress, she was described by one of her spiritual daughters as "the child of silence". Beatified in 1947.

**ALKELD (or ATHILDA) (St) V.
                        PC. March 27**
? 10th cent. Two Yorkshire churches are dedicated to this saint, of whom nothing else is known, except that an ancient painting represents her being strangled by Danish pirates.

ALKMUND (St) M.   AC. March 19
Otherwise Alcmund, q.v.

**ALLAN (ALLEN) (St) C.
                           AC. Jan 12**
Otherwise Elian, q.v.

**ALLEAUME (ALEAUME) (St) Ab.
                           AC. Jan 30**
The French form of Adelelmus, q.v.

ALLOYNE (St) C.   RM. Oct 1
Otherwise Bavo, q.v.

ALLUCIO (St) C.   AC. Oct 23
d. 1134. Born in the diocese of Pescia in Tuscany, Allucio started life as a herdsman. Eventually his fellow citizens entrusted him with the direction of an almshouse at Val di Nievole, near Pescia, and he became in fact the second founder of that charity. He had some followers who were named the Brethren of St Allucio. Cult confirmed by Pius IX.

ALLYRE (St) Bp.   RM. July 7
Otherwise Illidius, q.v.

ALMACHIUS (or TELEMACHUS), St. HM.   RM. Jan 1
d. *c*.400. A hermit who came to Rome from the East, and publicly protested against the gladiatorial combats in the Roman amphitheatre. He was seized and cut to pieces by order of the prefect Alipius. As a consequence, the emperor Honorius is said to have abolished such spectacles.

ALMEDHA (ELED, ELEVETHA) (St) VM.   AC. Aug 1
6th cent. A descendant of King Brychan of Brecknock. The tradition is that she suffered martyrdom on a hill near Brecknock.

ALMIRUS (ALMER, ALMIRE) (St) Ab.   PC. Sept 11
d. *c*.560. A native of Auvergne, he was educated at Menat, where he met SS Avitus and Carilefus. With them he went to Maine. After a short stay at Micy, St Almirus lived as a hermit at Grécz-sur-Roc, where he died.

ALMUS (ALME, or ALANUS) (St) Ab. OSB. Cist.   PC. June 28
d. 1270. Cistercian monk of Melrose

37

who became the first abbot of the Scottish monastery of Balmerino, founded in 1229 by Ermengardis, widow of William I of Scotland.

ALNOTH (St) M.   AC. Nov 25
d. *c*.700. A cowherd attached to St Werburg's monastery at Weedon (Northants). Later he lived as a hermit at Stowe, near Bugbrooke. He was put to death by robbers and venerated as a martyr.

ALODIA (St) VM.   RM. Oct 22
See Nunilo and Alodia.

ALONSO or ALONZO
Otherwise Alphonsus, q.v.

ALORUS (St) Bp.   AC. Oct 26
See Alanus and Alorus.

ALOYSIUS, or LUDOVICUS
Note. These are two Latin forms of the French Louis, radically identical with Chlodovicus and Clovis. The modern languages have usually derived variants from both forms: thus in Italian: Luigi, Lodovico; in Spanish: Luis, Ludovico; in Portuguese: Luiz, Ludovico; in Catalan: Lluis, Ludovic; in German: Aloys, Ludwig; in English: Lewis (Aloysius), Ludovic.

ALOYSIUS RABATA (Bl) C. OC.
**   AC. May 11**
c.1430–1490. A Sicilian friar of the Carmelite monastery of Randazzo. He died from the effects of a blow on the head from an assailant whom he refused to bring to justice. Cult confirmed by Gregory XVI.

ALOYSIUS GONZAGA (St) C. SJ.
**   RM. June 21**
1568–1591. Born in the castle of Castiglione in Lombardy, he served as a page at the courts of Tuscany, Mantua and Spain, and in his eighteenth year entered the Society of Jesus, after having overcome the opposition of his family. Within six years he fell sick while nursing the plague-stricken and died. He was beatified in 1605 and canonized in 1726. Benedict XIII declared him special protector of young students and Pius XI proclaimed him patron of Christian Youth. Oversentimental biographies and cheap art have rather obscured his attractive personality.

ALPAIS (Bl) V.   AC. Nov 3
d. 1211. Born in the small village of Cudot, diocese of Sens, of a peasant family, she helped her parents in the fields until still very young she became bed-ridden with leprosy. For a long time her only food was the Eucharist. Her patience and gentleness made a great impression on her contemporaries. Cult confirmed by Pius IX in 1874.

ALPHAEUS (St) C.   AC. May 26
1st cent. Mentioned in Matt. X 3 as the father of St James the Less. The Greek liturgy commemorates him on this day. The apocryphal books have embellished his life, but they deserve no credence.

ALPHAEUS and ZACHAEUS (SS)
MM.   RM. Nov 17
d. 303. Alphaeus was a reader and exorcist at Caesarea in Palestine, and Zachaeus, his cousin, a deacon at Gadara beyond the Jordan. They were beheaded at Caesarea under Diocletian.

ALPHAGE or ALPHEGE (St) Bp.
M. OSB.   RM. Apr 19
Otherwise Elphege, q.v.

ALPHANUS (St) Bp. OSB.
**   PC. Oct 9**
Otherwise Alfanus, q.v.

ALPHERIUS (St) Ab. OSB.
AC Apr 12
Otherwise Alferius, q.v.

ALPHIUS, PHILADELPHUS and CYRINUS (SS) MM.   RM. May 10
d. 251. Sicilian saints, said to have been brothers. They appear to have suffered under Decius. They are held in great veneration in Sicily (chiefly at Lentini, of which town they are patron saints) and also among the Greeks.

ALPHIUS (St) M.   RM. Sept 28
See Mark, Alphius, etc.

ALPHONSUS LEZINIANA (Bl) M. OP.   AC. Jan 22
d. 1745. A Spanish Dominican who was one of the companions of Bl Francis Gil in Tonkin, and was martyred with him.

ALPHONSUS of ASTORGA (St) Bp. OSB.   AC. Jan 26
9th cent. A bishop of Astorga who retired and became a monk at the abbey of St Stephen de Ribas de Sil, in Spanish Galicia.

ALPHONSUS de ROJAS (Bl) C. OFM.   AC. March 21
d. 1617. Successively professor at Salamanca, tutor to a young duke, canon of Coria and a Franciscan friar. His feast at Coria is kept on March 26.

ALPHONSUS NAVARRETE (Bl) M. OP.   AC. June 1
d. 1617. Born at Valladolid, he entered the Dominican Order and worked first as a missionary in the Philippine Islands, whence, in 1611, he was sent to Japan where he was appointed provincial vicar. He converted, we are told, many thousands to Christianity. He was beheaded on the isle of Tacaxima. Beatified in 1867.

ALPHONSUS de MENA (Bl) M. OP.
AC. June 1
d. 1622 (Sept 10). Born at Logroño, in Spain, he became a Friar Preacher at Salamanca. He was a nephew of Bl Peter Navarrete, whom he accompanied to Japan. Here he was burnt alive at Nagasaki with the group led by Bl Charles Spinola, SJ. Beatified in 1867.

ALPHONSUS de VAENA (Bl) M. SJ.
AC. July 15
d. 1570. Born at Toledo, he entered the Society of Jesus as a coadjutor. He belonged to the band of Jesuit martyrs led by Bl Ignatius de Azevedo. Beatified in 1854.

ALPHONSUS PACHECO (Bl) M. SJ.   AC. July 25
1550-1583. Born at Minayá in Catalonia, he joined the Jesuits in 1566 and was sent to Goa, where he was ordained priest. After a very laborious apostolate among the Goanese he was killed with Bl Rudolph Acquaviva at Salsette, near Goa. Beatified in 1893.

ALPHONSUS MARY LIGUORI (St) Bp. Dr. Founder CSSR.
RM. Aug 2
1696-1787. Born near Naples of a distinguished family, he became a barrister, but soon abandoned this promising career and became a priest in 1726. He joined a society of priests engaged in catechizing the peasants of the country districts, and this led him to the foundation of the congregation of the Most Holy Redeemer, which was approved in 1749. In 1762 an order of the pope forced the saint to accept the bishopric of Sant' Agata de' Goti, which he held until 1775, when he was compelled to resign through ill-health. He returned to live with the members of his own congregation. Throughout all these years he produced a steady output of

ascetical, theological and historical works. Canonized in 1839, and declared Doctor in 1871.

ALPHONSUS de OROZCO (Bl) C. OSA Erem. AC. Sept 19
1500–1591. Born at Oropesa in Castile, he studied at the university of Salamanca, where as an undergraduate he was drawn to the Augustinian Hermits by the sermons of St Thomas of Villanueva. After his profession Bl Alphonsus became preacher at the court of Philip II of Spain. He was a prolific writer and his works are reckoned among the classics of Spanish literature. Beatified in 1882.

ALPHONSUS RODRIGUEZ (St) C. SJ. RM. Oct 31
1531–1617. Born at Segovia in Spain, he became a merchant and married, but lost his wife and children, and at the age of 44 was received into the Society of Jesus as coadjutor and sent to Palma in Majorca. From 1580 to 1604 he was doorkeeper of the college of Montesión. In this office he edified the whole island. Beatified in 1825 and canonized in 1888.

ALPINIAN (St) C. RM. June 30
See Martial, Alpinian and Austriclinian.

ARALDUS (Bl) Mk, OSB. Cist.
PC. Nov 11
d. c.1250. A lay-brother of the Cistercian abbey of Isenhagen.

ALRICK (St) C. AC. June 30
12th cent. An English hermit associated with St Godric, who assisted him at his death.

ALTFRID (St) Bp. OSB.
PC. Aug 15
d. 874. Monk and headmaster of the school at the abbey of Corvey in Saxony.

In 851 he became bishop of Hildesheim. He was known throughout the Frankish empire as a fosterer of peace and goodwill, a champion of his Benedictine brethren, an upholder of the ecclesiastical canons, and a devout client of our Lady.

ALTHEUS (St) C. AC. Dec 26
Otherwise Tathai, q.v.

ALTHRYDA (ALFRIDA, ETHELDRYTHA) (St) V. OSB. AC. Aug 2
Otherwise Etheldritha, q.v.

ALTIGIANUS and HILARINUS (SS) MM. OSB. PC. Aug 23
d. 731. Two monks killed by the Saracens at Saint-Seine, diocese of Langres, Côte d'Or.

ALTINUS (ATTINUS) (St) Bp. M.
AC. Oct 19
1st of 4th cent. An alleged disciple of our Lord, founder of the churches of Orleans and Chartres. Others state that he was a martyr of the 4th cent.

ALTMAN (St or Bl) Bp. AC. Aug 8
c.1020–1091. Born in Westphalia, he studied at Paris, became a canon regular, chaplain to the emperor Henry III and finally bishop of Passau in 1065. He upheld the authority of St Gregory VII against Henry IV and was driven from his see, but he continued to exercise great influence throughout the Germanies. He was buried at the Benedictine abbey of Göttweig in Austria, which he had founded. Cult confirmed by Leo XIII.

ALTO (St) Ab. OSB. AC. Feb 9
d. c.760. A monk, probably Irish, who crossed over into Germany (c.743) and settled as a hermit in a wood near Augsburg. King Pepin made him a grant of

that place, and there the saint founded an abbey, since called Altomünster (Alto's monastery). St Boniface dedicated its church in 750.

ALUINUS (St) Bp. OSB. AC. Sept 5
Otherwise Alvitus, q.v.

ALVAREZ, BARTHOLOMEW (Bl) M. SJ.   AC. Jan 12
See Bartholomew Alvarez.

ALVAREZ, EMMANUEL (Bl) M. SJ.   AC. July 15

ALVAREZ, FRANCIS (Bl) M. SJ.

ALVAREZ, GASPAR (Bl) M. SJ.
Three Jesuit martyrs belonging to the group of Bl Ignatius de Azevedo, q.v.

ALVARO (ALVAREZ) of CORDOVA (Bl) C. OP.   AC. Feb 9
d. c.1430. He became a Dominican at Cordova in 1368 and worked with great success in Andalusia, France and Italy. He was chosen by the queen-mother of Spain, Catherine, daughter of John of Gaunt, as her adviser and as tutor of her son John II. Bl Alvaro opposed the Avignon pope Peter de Luna. His priory near Cordova became a centre of learning and piety. Cult confirmed in 1741.

ALVARO GARCIA (Bl) M.
PC. June 11
See Peter Rodriguez and Comp.

ALVITUS (AVITUS, ALUINUS, ALBINUS) (St) Bp. OSB. AC. Sept 5
d. c.1063. He was born in Spanish Galicia and belonged to the family of Rudesind, the great abbot-bishop of

Mondoñedo. St Alvitus became a Benedictine at Sahagún (Cluniac observance) and in 1057 was appointed bishop of León by King Ferdinand I. He transferred the relics of St Isidore from Seville to León.

AMABILIS (St) V.   PC. July 11
d. c.634. According to tradition she was a daughter of an Anglo-Saxon king. She became a nun of Saint-Amand at Rouen.

AMABILIS (St) C.   AC. Nov 1
d. 475. It seems that he was precentor of the cathedral at Clermont and afterwards parish priest of Tiom in Auvergne. He is invoked as a protector against fire and snakes.

AMADEUS of CLERMONT (Bl) C. OSB. Cist.   AC. Jan 14
d. c.1150. Lord of Hauterives (Drôme), he left the world with 16 of his vassals (c.1119) and entered the Cistercian abbey of Bonnevaux. Later he spent some time at Cluny to attend to the education of his son Bl Amadeus of Lausanne. He founded four monasteries: Léoncel, Mazan, Montperoux and Tamis. Returned to Bonnevaux where he died.

AMADEUS (Bl) Bp. OSB. Cist.
AC. Jan 28
c.1110–1159. Son of (Bl) Amadeus of Clermont, he was educated at Cluny and afterwards served in the court of the emperor Henry V. In 1125 he became a monk at Clairvaux under St Bernard, by whom he was sent in 1139 to govern as abbot the abbey of Hautecombe in Savoy. In 1144 the pope put him under obedience to accept the bishopric of Lausanne. During the last years of his life he was also co-regent of Savoy and chancellor of Burgundy. Cult approved by St Pius X.

AMADEUS IX of SAVOY (Bl) C.
AC. March 30

1435–1472. Born at Thonon, son of the Duke of Savoy, he began to rule in 1455. He suffered from epilepsy, but nevertheless governed in such a way as to endear himself to all his subjects, until compelled to resign in favour of his wife. He was proclaimed a saint immediately after his death, but was beatified only in 1677. He was an ancestor of the royal house of Savoy, which chose him for its patron.

AMADEUS of PORTUGAL (Bl) C.
OFM.   PC. Aug 10

See Amedeus of Portugal

AMADOR, AMADOUR (several)

Otherwise Amator, q.v.

AMAETHLU (MAETHLU) (St) C.
AC. Dec 26

6th cent. A Welsh saint who has left his name to Llanfaethlu, a church founded by him in Anglesey.

AMANDUS of ELNON (St) Bp.
RM. Feb 6

c.676. Born near Nantes, he lived for fifteen years as a solitary at Bourges. At the age of 33 he journeyed to Rome and received from the pope his commission as a missionary bishop. As such he preached in Flanders, to the Slavs in Carinthia and the Basques in Navarre. He founded many monasteries in all these places, of which the best known is Elnon, near Tournai, where he retired in his old age and died a nonagenarian. In art he is represented carrying a church in his hand.

AMANDUS (St) Bp.   RM. June 18

d. c.431. Successor of St Delphinus as bishop of Bordeaux (c.404). He is chiefly known from the works of St Paulinus of Nola, whom St Amandus converted and prepared for baptism.

AMANDUS and ANSELM (SS)
Abbots OSB.   AC. Nov 18

Amandus d. 708: Anselm later in the 8th cent. St Amandus succeeded St Aigulphus as abbot of Lérins, in 676 and ruled the monastery with a firm hand. St Anselm, another abbot of Lérins, lived later in the 8th century.

AMANDUS or AMANTIUS (AMATIUS)

Note. There are a number of other saints of this name, belonging to the 4th, 5th, 6th and 7th centuries, of whom only the bare fact of their existence is known. Among these, the following are likely identifications: (1) Amandus, abbot-founder of Moissac, d. 644, feast Feb 6. (2) Abbot-founder of Nantes, 7th cent., feast id. (3) Count of Grisalba, near Bergamo, d. April 6th, 515, feast Apr. 6th. (4) Abbot-founder of Saint-Amand-de-Boixe, feast May 22. (5) A Scottish hermit at Beaumont, diocese of Reims, 6th cent., feast June 16. (6) Abbot-founder of Saint-Amand de Coly (Dordogne), diocese of Limoges, 6th cent., feast June 25. (7) A hermit in a solitude at the meeting of the rivers Glanne and Vienne, diocese of Limoges, 5th cent., feast Oct 16. (8) The first bishop of Strasburg, d. 346, feast Oct 26. (9) A bishop of Worms, 4th cent., feast id. (10) A bishop of Rodez (otherwise Amantius) 4th cent. He is mentioned in the RM. on Nov 4. (11) A bishop of Avignon, id. (12) A bishop of Rennes, 4th cent., feast Nov 13.

AMANTIUS (St) M.   RM. Feb 10

See Zoticus, Irenaeus, etc.

AMANTIUS (St) C. RM. March 19

See Landoald and Amantius.

AMANTIUS (St) Bp.   RM. Apr 8

d. 440. Successor of St Provinus in the

see of Como. He is still held in great veneration in his diocese.

AMANTIUS, ALEXANDER, and Comp. (SS) MM.   RM. June 6
? Said to have been four brothers, priests. Amantius is given as bishop of Noyon, who evangelized Cannes, diocese of Carcassonne, where he was martyred with the other three.

AMANTIUS (St) M.   RM. June 10
See Getulius, Cerealis, etc.

AMANTIUS (St) C.   RM. Sept 26
d. c.600. A priest of Città di Castello (*Tiphernum*) near Perugia, who was personally known to St Gregory the Great and held in great veneration by the holy pontiff. He is the patron saint of Città di Castello.

AMARAND (St) Bp. OSB. AC. Nov 7
d. p.700. Abbot of Moissac, who became bishop of Albi some time between 689 and 722.

AMARANTHUS (St) M. RM. Nov 7
3rd cent. A martyr venerated at Albi in S. France. The fact of his martyrdom is attested by St Gregory of Tours. Other data are lacking.

AMARINUS (St) M. Ab. OSB.
RM. Jan 25
d. 676. Abbot of a monastery in the Vosges. Companion in martyrdom of St Praejectus (St Priest), bishop of Clermont. The valley of Saint-Amarian in Alsace is named after him.

AMASIUS (St) Bp.   AC. Jan 23
d. 356. A Greek, driven from the East by the Arians, who became second bishop of Teano in 346. His cult is still

flourishing in several dioceses of central Italy.

AMASWINTHUS (St) Ab.
AC. Dec 22
d. 982. Monk and abbot for forty-two years of a monastery at Silva de Málaga in Andalusia.

AMATA (St) V. Poor Clare
PC. Feb 20
d. c.1250. A niece of St Clare of Assisi, healed by her aunt of a disease and thereby converted to the life of the cloister. Her name is in the Franciscan martyrologies.

AMATA (Bl) V. OP.   AC. June 10
d. 1270. A Dominican nun of San Sisto in Rome. A co-foundress of the convent of St Agnes at Valle di Pietro, Bologna.

AMATOR (AMADOR) (St) C.
AC. March 27
? A Portuguese hermit, of the diocese of Guarda, to whom several churches are dedicated in his country. He has often been confused with St Amator of Rocamadour (see below, Aug 20).

AMATOR, PETER and LOUIS (SS)
MM.   RM. Apr 30
d. 855. Amator was born at Martos, near Cordova, in which latter city he studied and was ordained priest. He, together with a monk, Peter by name, and a lay-man called Louis was put to death by the Saracens for having publicly confessed Christ.

AMATOR (AMATRE, AMADOUR)
(St) Bp.   RM. May 1
d. 418. Bishop of Auxerre. He had been married to a holy woman venerated locally as St Martha. St Amator ordained as a priest his successor St Germanus,

who has left us the biography of his predecessor.

AMATOR (AMADOUR) (St) C.
AC. Aug 20

? An incorrupt body was found buried beneath the church of Our Lady at Rocamadour in 1166, and thus originated "St Amadour". Various identifications, including one with the publican Zacchaeus, have been made, but beyond a general agreement since the 17th cent. that he was a hermit of an unknown date, no information can be given.

AMATOR (St) Bp.   RM. Nov 26
3rd cent. Bishop of Autun. There is nothing further known for certain about him.

AMATUS RONCONI (Bl) Mk. OSB.
AC. May 8

d. 1292. Born near Rimini, after having four times made the pilgrimage to Compostella he became a lay-brother at the abbey of San Giuliano near his native town.

AMATUS (St) Bp.   RM. Aug 31
d. 1093. He was Bishop of Nusco near Naples. He has been claimed as a monk of Montevergine, but the date of his death renders this impossible.

AMATUS (AMAT, AMÉ, AIMÉ, AMADO) (St) Ab. OSB.
RM. Sept 13

c.567–630. Born at Grenoble, he entered as a boy the abbey of St Maurice of Agaune in Switzerland where he lived as a monk hermit for over thirty years. St Eustace induced him to migrate to Luxeuil. Here he turned the heart of St Romaricus to God, and when this nobleman founded the abbey of Habendum (*Remiremont: Romarici mons*) in 620, under the Benedictine Rule, St

Amatus was made its first abbot. Here he lived until his death.

AMATUS (St) Bp. OSB.
RM. Sept 13

d. 690. Abbot of Agaune, he became the tenth bishop of Sion in Valais—*Sedunensis*, not *Senonensis* (Sens). As a result of a false accusation, he was banished to the abbey of Péronne, and then to that of Breuil, diocese of Arras, where he lived as one of the monks, and where he died.

AMBICUS, VICTOR and JULIUS (SS) MM.   RM. Dec 3
4th cent. Christians martyred at Nicomedia under Diocletian, whose imperial residence was in that city.

AMBROSE FERNANDEZ (Bl) M. SJ.   AC. March 14
1551–1620. Born at Sisto in Portugal, he went to Japan to seek his fortune, which he found in 1577 by entering the Society of Jesus as a lay-brother. He died in the horrible prison of Suzota (Omura) of apoplexy, aged 69. Beatified in 1867.

AMBROSE (St) C.   AC. March 17
d. c.250. A rich nobleman of Alexandria, who befriended and helped Origen financially. He suffered imprisonment for the Faith under Maximinus, but was released and died a confessor.

AMBROSE SANSEDONI (Bl) C. OP.   RM. March 20
1220–1287. Born at Siena, he joined the Dominicans in 1237 and was a fellow student of St Thomas Aquinas under St Albert the Great. He excelled as a preacher, and in the performance of this office he travelled through Germany, France and Italy. He was also Master of the Sacred Palace. His death was hastened by the vehemence of his preaching. In art he is represented as

holding in his hand a model of his native city. Cult confirmed in 1622.

AMBROSE KIBUKA (St) M.
RM. June 3

d. 1886. Page to King Mwanga of Uganda; he was baptized on Nov 17, 1885, and burnt alive the following year. See Uganda (Martyrs of).

AMBROSE AUTPERTUS (St) Ab. OSB.
AC. July 19

d. c.778. Born in Gaul, he was Charlemagne's tutor at the court of Pepin the Short. He went to Italy as the king's envoy and visited the Benedictine abbey of St Vincent by the river Volturno, in the duchy of Benevento, and forthwith entered there as a monk. Eventually he became abbot. He was an able exegete and his works were considered as authoritative as those written by the greatest of the Latin Fathers. In fact, though not in title, he is one of the Doctors of the Church.

AMBROSE (St) M.
RM. Aug 16

d. c.303. A centurion put to death under Diocletian at Ferentino in central Italy. His *Acta* are preserved only in a MS. of the 14th century.

AMBROSE PICCOLOMINI and PATRICK de' PATRIZI (BB) Mks OSB. Oliv.
PC. Aug 21

d. ? 1347. With Bl Bernard Tolomei they were co-founders of Montoliveto Maggiore, near Siena. They are always called *Beati* by the Olivetans.

AMBROSE (St) Bp.
AC. Aug 28

d. p.450. A bishop of Saintes, whose episcopate lasted for about fourteen years. He is mentioned in the life of his successor St Vivian and is honoured together with him in the diocese of La Rochelle.

AMBROSE (St) Bp.
AC. Sept 3

d. c.455. Bishop of Sens, of whom nothing else is known.

AMBROSE EDWARD BARLOW (Bl.) M. OSB.
AC. Sept 10

d. 1641. Baptized a Catholic, he was educated a Protestant, but was reconverted to the Faith and studied for the priesthood at Douai and Valladolid. In 1615 he was professed a monk at St Gregory's, Douai, now Downside; but he asked to be affiliated to the Spanish abbey of Celanova; and the community granted his petition. He was sent to the English mission in his native Lancashire, where he laboured for twenty-four years. Four times he was imprisoned and released, the fifth time he was executed at Lancaster for his priesthood. Beatified in 1929.

AMBROSE (St) Bp.
RM. Oct 16

d. c.752. The thirteenth bishop of Cahors. Eventually he resigned and lived as a recluse. After a pilgrimage to Rome he died at Ernotrum (now Saint-Ambroise-sur-Arnon), in Berry.

AMBROSE (St) Ab.
RM. Nov 2

523 and 582. There were two abbots of this name of the abbey of Agaune, St Moritz, Switzerland. The former, who had formerly been abbot of Ste Barbe, near Lyons, is the one commemorated by the RM.; the latter died in 582.

AMBROSE TRAVERSARI (Bl.) Ab. OSB. Cam.
PC. Nov 20

1376–1439. Born at Portico, near Florence, he studied under the Greek humanist Chrysoloras at Venice, and became a typical "all round" Renaissance scholar. In 1400 he joined the Camaldolese at Santa Maria degli Angeli, at Florence; here he continued his studies, wrote much, chiefly in Greek, and collected a large library. He was the soul of the Council of Florence for the reunion of the Greeks. In 1431 he became abbot-general. He was both a great churchman and a great scholar.

AMBROSE (St) Bp. Dr. RM. Dec 7
c.340–397. Born in Gaul, where his father, who belonged to the Roman nobility, was praetorian prefect. Still very young, Ambrose became a barrister at Rome and before his thirty-fifth year was appointed governor of Liguria and Aemilia with his headquarters at Milan. The whole province was rent by the Arian controversy. When in 374 the bishop of Milan died, Ambrose, as governor, went to the cathedral to ensure peace and order in the new election, with the result that he himself, though a catechumen, was elected by acclamation, after a child had been suddenly heard to cry out "Ambrose for bishop". Ambrose's objections were overruled and he was consecrated on Dec 7, 374 (the day on which his feast is now kept). He proved to be one of the greatest and most beloved bishops of all time. He excelled as an administrator, as a writer, as a protector of the poor, as the "hammer of Arianism". He was prompt and outspoken in withstanding the tyranny of the emperors. His courage in reproving Theodosius the Great was a noble example of Christian heroism. He died on Good Friday, April 4, 397, He is one of the four great Latin Fathers and Doctors.

AMÉ, AIMÉ (St)
Otherwise Amatus, q.v.

AMEDEO (St) C.
               RM. Feb 12 and Apr 18
One of the Seven Holy Founders of the Servite Order, q.v.

AMEDEUS IX (Bl.) C.
               AC. March 30
d. 1472. The third Duke of Savoy. His cult was authorized by Innocent XI.

AMEDEUS of PORTUGAL (St) C.
               PC. Aug 9
1420–1482. Of a noble Portuguese family, he became a Hieronymite, but later decided to become a Franciscan. After much opposition, he was allowed to enter as a lay brother at Assisi. His life was quasi-eremetical, but later he was made a priest, and founded several houses "of the regular observance". Sixtus IV treated him with great honour. In 1568, his houses were united to those of the Franciscan Observants.

AMELBERGA
Note. Variant forms of this name are: Amalberga, Amalburga, Amalia, Amelia.

AMELBERGA (St) V. OSB.
               RM. July 10
d. c.772. She was a nun of Münsterbilsen in Flanders, receiving the veil from St Willibrord. Her relics were transferred to the abbey church of St Peter at Ghent in 1073.

AMELBERGA (St) W. OSB.
               AC. July 10
d. 690. Born in Brabant, she was a niece, or sister, of Bl. Pepin of Landen. She was married to Count Witger and mother of SS Gudula, Emebert, and Reineldis. When Witger became a Benedictine monk at Lobbes, she joined the nunnery of Maubeuge under the same rule. Often confused with the preceding.

AMELBERGA (St) Abs. OSB.
               AC. Nov 21
d. p.900. Abbess of Susteren. She educated in her convent two daughters of the king of Lorraine.

AMICUS and AMELIUS (SS) MM. AC. Oct 12

d. 773. French knights who took part in Charlemagne's campaign against the Lombards in Upper Italy, where they were killed, or fell in battle, and have been venerated as martyrs ever since at Mortara in Lombardy.

AMICUS (St) Mk. OSB. AC. Nov 2

d. c.1045. Born near Camerino, he became a secular priest, then a hermit and finally a monk of St Peter's at Fonteavellana, founded by St Dominic of Sora in 1025 (not that governed by St Peter Damian). St Peter's was at that time a daughter-house of Montecassino, and for this reason St Amicus is often called a monk of Montecassino, and was held in special veneration at that abbey.

AMICUS (St) Ab. OSB. AC. Nov 2

Early 11th cent. Abbot of Rambara.

AMIDAEUS (AMIDEI, AMADIO) (St) C. OSM. RM. Feb 12 (Apr 18)

One of the Seven Holy Founders of the Servite Order, q.v.

AMMIA (St) Matron RM. Aug 31

See Theodotus, Rufina and Ammia.

AMMIANUS (St) M. RM. Sept 4

See Theodore, Oceanus, etc.

AMMON, EMILIAN, LASSA and Comp. (SS) MM. AC. Feb 9

? A band of forty-four Christians martyred at Membressa in Africa.

AMMON and Comp. (SS) MM. RM. Sept 1

d. c.322. Ammon, a deacon, was put to death under Licinius at Heraclea in Thrace, together with forty young women, his converts. The executioner killed St Ammon by placing a red-hot helmet on his head. Both the Greeks and the Latins commemorate their passion.

AMMON, THEOPHILUS, NEOTERIUS and Comp. (SS) MM. RM. Sept 8

? These three, together with twenty-two more Christians, suffered at Alexandria. The Bollandists give the names of all, but no other data are known.

AMMON the GREAT (St) Ab. AC. Oct 4

d. c.350. Of a wealthy Egyptian family, Ammon married, and for eighteen years he and his wife lived as brother and sister. Then by mutual agreement they embraced the religious life. Ammon retired to the Nitrian desert and eventually had under his charge from four to five thousand monks or hermits. In his later years Ammon ate only once every three or four days. He is one of the earliest and greatest hermit-monks.

AMMON, ZENO, PTOLEMY, INGEN, and THEOPHILUS (SS) MM. RM. Dec 20

d. 249. The first four were soldiers. They, together with Theophilus, were present when a Christian on trial at Alexandria showed signs of wavering. They forthwith encouraged him and were beheaded on that account.

AMMONARIA, MERCURIA, DIONYSIA, and a second AMMONARIA (SS) MM. RM. Dec 12

c.250. A band of holy women of Alexandria martyred under Decius. Mercuria is described as an aged woman, Dionysia as the mother of many children and the two Ammonarias as young girls.

AMMONIUS (St) M. RM. Jan 18

See Moseus and Ammonius.

AMMONIUS and ALEXANDER (SS) MM. RM. Feb 9
? Two Christians martyred at Soli in Cyprus.

AMMONIUS (St) M. RM. Feb 12
See Modestus and Ammonius.

AMMONIUS (St) M. RM. Feb 14
See Dionysius and Ammonius.

AMMONIUS (St) M. RM. March 26
See Theodore, Irenaeus, etc.

AMMONIUS (St) M. RM. Nov 26
See Faustus, Didius, etc.

AMNICHAD (AMNUCHAD) (Bl.) H. OSB. AC. Jan 30
d. 1043. Born either in Ireland or in Scotland, he travelled to Germany and became first a monk, and then a recluse, at Fulda.

AMO (AMON) (St) Bp. AC. Oct 23
4th cent. Second known bishop of Toul, the successor of St Mansuetus in that see.

AMOES (St) H. AC. Jan 17
See Achillas and Amoes.

AMOR (AMOUR) (St) M. AC. Aug 9
? Venerated in the Franche-Comté together with St Viator. Their relics are enshrined at Saint-Amour, in Burgundy.

AMOR (AMATOR, AMOUR) (St) Ab. OSB. AC. Aug 17
8th cent. Companion of St Pirmin in the evangelization of Germany. Abbot-founder of Amorbach in Franconia.

AMOR (AMOUR) of AQUITAINE (St) H. AC. Oct 8
9th cent. Born in Aquitaine, he lived as a recluse at Maestricht. Eventually he founded Münsterbilsen nunnery, in the diocese of Liége. He has been wrongly identified with St Amor, founder of Amorbach.

AMOS (St) Prophet RM March 31
8th cent. B.C. One of the minor prophets, a shepherd of Tekoah (Koa) near Bethlehem, who aptly describes himself as "a herdsman plucking wild figs" (VII 13). He was—the RM. says—"transfixed with an iron bar through the temples". He was buried in his native place.

AMPELIUS (St) M. RM. Feb 11
See Saturninus, Dativus, etc.

AMPELIUS (St) Bp. AC. July 7
d. c.672. Bishop of Milan during the Lombard period. He wielded a great influence for good among the invading Lombards.

AMPELUS and CAIUS (SS) MM. RM. Nov 20
d. c.302. They are presumed to have been Sicilians, martyred at Messina under Diocletian. Actually nothing is known about them.

AMPHIANUS (APPIAN, APIAN) (St) M. RM. Apr 2
d. c.305. A young Christian of Lycia, Asia Minor, who entered the governor's house when the latter was on the point of offering sacrifices to idols and boldly reproached him for his crime of idolatry. He was forthwith arrested and most cruelly tortured to death.

AMPHIBALUS (St) M. AC. June 24
d. c.304. The supposed fellow-martyr of St Alban of Verulam. In the original *Acta* it is only said that St Alban put on the priest's cloak (*amphibalus*) and was arrested *instead* of the priest who had taken refuge in his house—not *with* the

priest. Geoffrey of Monmouth took the word *amphibalus* to be the name of the priest.

AMPHILOCHIUS (St) M.
RM. March 27
See Philetus, Lydia, etc.

AMPHILOCHIUS (St) Bp.
RM. Nov 23
d. *c*.400. Fellow-student of St Basil under Libanius, a successful lawyer at Constantinople, a hermit, and finally one of the group of Cappadocian bishops, friends of St Basil, appointed by the latter to counteract Arianism in Cappadocia. Amphilochius was appointed to the see of Iconium. He opposed the Macedonian heretics, against whom he wrote a work on the Holy Ghost highly commended by St Jerome. He presided at the synod of Sidon which condemned the Messalians, who asserted that prayer is the only means of salvation.

AMPHION (St) Bp.   RM. June 12
d. *p*.325. The RM. describes him as "an excellent confessor in the time of Galerius Maximian". He was then bishop of Epiphania in Cilicia. During the Arian troubles he was elected by the Catholic party to Nicomedia. Amphion was one of the "illustrious confessors" who attended the council of Nicea. St Athanasius approved of his writings.

AMPLIATUS, URBAN and NARCISSUS (SS) MM.   RM. Oct 31
1st cent. St Paul mentions these three saints in Romans XVI. 8 sqq: "Salute Ampliatus, most beloved by me in the Lord. Salute Urban our helper in Jesus Christ. Salute them that are of Narcissus's household who are in the Lord". Later, chiefly Greek, traditions have made Ampliatus a bishop, and all three disciples of our Lord, and preachers of the gospel with St Andrew in the Balkan

countries. The RM. adds "they were slain by Jews and Gentiles".

AMULWINUS (AMOLVINUS) (St) Ab. Bp. OSB.   AC. Feb 7
d. *c*.750. He was an abbot-bishop (*chorepiscopus*) of Lobbes, successor of St Erminus (d. 737).

AMUNIA (St) W. OSB. AC. March 11
d. *c*.1069. The mother of St Aurea (Oria), whom she joined in her widowhood as a recluse under the obedience of the abbot of San Millán de la Cogolla, in La Rioja, Spain.

ANACHARIUS (AUNACHARIUS, AUNACHAIRE, AUNAIRE) (St) Bp.
RM. Sept 25
d. 604. Born near Orleans and educated at the court of King Guntram of Burgundy, he became bishop of Auxerre in 561. He ordered the Litany of the Saints to be sung daily in the chief centres of population by rotation and enforced the recitation of the Divine Office in all churches of the diocese.

ANACLETUS (ANENCLETUS) (St) Pope, M.   RM. July 13
1st cent. One of the earliest popes, he is now regarded as identical with St Cletus, q.v.

ANANIAS (St) M.   RM. Jan 25
1st cent. The disciple at Damascus who baptized St Paul (Acts IX), and who, according to tradition, evangelized Damascus, Eleutheropolis and other places, and was ultimately martyred.

ANANIAS and Comp. (SS) MM.
AC. Feb 25
d. *c*.298. A martyr-priest of Phoenicia under Diocletian. Thrown into prison, he converted his gaoler, Peter, and seven soldiers of the guard. All were put to death together.

ANANIAS (St) M.   RM. Apr 21
See Simeon, Abdechalas, etc.

ANANIAS (St) M.   RM. Dec 1
? A layman, martyred at Arbela, either
the Persian or the Assyrian (Erbel)
town of that name.

**ANANIAS, AZARIAS and MISAEL
(SS)   RM. Dec 16**
7th cent. B.C. Named otherwise Sidrach,
Misach and Abdenago (AV. Shadrach,
Meshach, Abed-nego.) The three children cast into the fiery furnace by order
of the king Nebuchadnezzar (Dan. III).
The RM. adds: "whose bodies are
buried near Babylon in a certain cave".

**ANASTASIA the PATRICIAN (St)
VH.   AC. March 10**
6th cent. Her life is counted by many as
a pious legend, the first of many similar
historiettes. She belonged to the nobility of Byzantium, and found favour in
the eyes of the emperor Justinian, thus
exciting the empress's jealousy. Anastasia escaped first to a nunnery near
Alexandria, and after the empress's
death, when the emperor instituted a
search for her, she disguised herself in
male attire and lived in Scythia as a
monk-hermit for twenty-eight years.
The Greeks keep her feast on March 10.

ANASTASIA (St) M.   RM. Apr 15
See Basilissa and Anastasia.

**ANASTASIA and CYRIL (SS) MM.
                            RM. Oct 28**
d. ? 253. All that we know concerning
these two saints is given in the RM.:
"At Rome, the passion of SS Anastasia
the Elder, the Virgin, and Cyril, Martyrs. The former was bound with chains
in Valerian's persecution under the
Prefect Probus, tortured . . . her breasts
cut off, her nails torn out, her teeth
broken, her hands and feet cut off, and

being beheaded . . . she passed to her
Spouse; Cyril, who offered her water
when she begged thereof, received martyrdom for his reward". Unfortunately
the whole *passio* is a fictitious composition and it is doubtful that the saints
ever existed.

ANASTASIA (St) M.   RM. Dec 25
d. *c.*?304. She is one of the best known
martyrs on account of her being commemorated in the second Mass of
Christmas and mentioned in the Canon
of the Mass and in the Litany of the
Saints. She suffered at Sirmium in
Dalmatia, her relics were translated to
Constantinople and her cult spread to
Rome under the influence of Byzantine
officials who dwelt in the aristocratic
quarters by the Forum where there is
a basilica dedicated in her honour, the
ancient *titulus Anastasiae*. The *Acta* of
her martyrdom are worthless.

ANASTASIUS (St) M.   AC. Jan 6
4th cent. A martyr at Syrmium, Pannonia.

**ANASTASIUS, JUCUNDUS,
FLORUS, FLORIANUS, PETER,
RATITES, TATIA, and TILIS (SS)
MM.   AC. Jan 6**
4th cent. Martyres at Syrmium, Pan-
nonhalma.

ANASTASIUS (St) Bp.   AC. Jan 7
d. 977. Archbishop of Sens from 968 to
977, he began the building of the cathedral, and greatly favoured the monks
of Saint-Pierre-le-Vif, in whose church
he was buried.

ANASTASIUS (St) M.   RM. Jan 9
See Julian, Basilissa, etc.

**ANASTASIUS (St) Ab. OSB.
                            RM. Jan 11**
d. *c.*570. A notary of the Roman church,

who became monk and abbot of Suppentonia (Castel Sant' Elia), diocese of Nepi, near Mt Soracte. St Gregory the Great narrates that, at the summons of an angel, St Anastasius and his monks died in quick succession.

ANASTASIUS the PERSIAN (St) M.
RM. Jan 22

d. 628. Magundat had been a soldier in the army of Chosroes, the Persian king. Baptised as Anastasius, he became a monk at Jerusalem. He was arrested at Caesarea in Palestine, tortured and taken to the Persian king in Assyria, who ordered his execution. His head was brought to Rome and enshrined in a church dedicated to him and St Vincent, the Spanish martyr. Hence, his wide-spread cult in the West.

ANASTASIUS (St) M. AC. March 20

d. c.797. The archimandrite (superior) of the *laura* of St Sabas, at Jerusalem. The *laura* (a cluster of hermitages) was attacked by robbers and all its monks massacred with the archimandrite at their head. The Greeks keep their feast on the anniversary of their death.

ANASTASIUS the SINAITE (St) C.
? RM. Apr 21

d. c.678. A Palestinian hermit, who eventually fixed his abode on Mt Sinai, hence his surname "the Sinaite". He took part in all the Christological controversies of his time, in Syria, in Egypt, and elsewhere. He has left ascetical and theological writings of considerable value.

ANASTASIUS I (St) Patriarch
? RM. Apr 21

d. 599. Often confused with his namesake "the Sinaite". He was patriarch of Antioch and a resolute opponent of the imperial politico-theological rule. For this reason he was threatened with

deposition by Justinian, and actually banished from his see after twenty-three years by Justin II. He was restored to Antioch by St Gregory the Great and the emperor Maurice.

ANASTASIUS and Comp. (SS)
MM.   RM. May 11

d. 251. Anastasius, a tribune in the army of the emperor Decius, was converted to Christianity on witnessing the courage of the martyrs whom in his capacity of tribune he was torturing to death. A few days after his conversion he was arrested and beheaded with all his family and servants. Their relics are venerated at Camerino in central Italy.

ANASTASIUS (St) C.   AC. May 11

? The patron saint of the city of Lérida in Spanish Catalonia. He is probably to be identified with one of the many *Anastasii* martyrs listed here, although the people of Lérida assert that their Anastasius was a native of that city.

ANASTASIUS (St) Bp. RM. May 20

d. 610. Bishop of Brescia in Lombardy. He greatly contributed to the conversion of the Lombards from Arianism. St Charles Borromeo solemnly translated his relics in 1581.

ANASTASIUS (St) Bp. RM. May 30

d. 680. A convert from Arianism, who became bishop of Pavia in Lombardy 668–680. He is commonly called Anastasius II, to distinguish him from one of his predecessors in the see.

ANASTASIUS, FELIX and DIGNA
(SS) MM. OSB.   RM. June 14

d. 853. Anastasius was a deacon of the church of St Acisclus at Cordova, who became a monk of the double abbey of Tábanos, near the same city. Felix was born at Alcalá (*Complutum*) of a Berber family, was professed a monk in Asturias but joined the community of Tábanos, being desirous of martyrdom. Digna belonged to the nunnery of the double abbey. The three were among the first to confess Christ at Cordova, and were beheaded by order of the Caliph.

ANASTASIUS (St) M.   RM. June 29
See Marcellus and Anastasius.

ANASTASIUS (SS) Cc. RM. Aug 13
See Maximus, Homologetes and Comp.

ANASTASIUS (St) Bp.   AC. Aug 14
11th cent. Benedictine Abbot (996–1006) of Pannonhalma in Hungary, and then second Archbishop of Eszterzom and Primate of Hungary.

ANASTASIUS (St) Bp. RM. Aug 17
d. ? 553. Bishop of Terni at the time of the invasion of Totila. Said to have come from Syria and to have been a hermit near Perugia. The Bollandists state that there has been a confusion between a hermit martyr and a bishop of Terni. St Anastasius the bishop did not find a place in the RM. until 1518.

ANASTASIUS CORNICULARIUS (St) M.   RM. Aug 21
d. 274. A military tribune (*cornicularius*, sub-officer) converted to Christ on beholding the courage of the young St Agapitus. This happened at Salone, twelve miles from Palestrina, near Rome. The RM., however, gives Salona in Dalmatia, as the place of martyrdom. The story itself is a duplication of that of St Anastasius of Camerino (May 11) and, as regards its location in Dalmatia, of that of St Anastasius the Fuller (see below, Sept 7). All is very confused.

**ANASTASIUS the Fuller (St) M.
                           RM. Sept 7**
d. 304. A fuller of Aquileia, not far from Venice. He crossed into Dalmatia and continued to ply his trade at Salona and to profess his religion openly, painting a conspicuous cross on his door. He was seized and drowned. He is now commonly identified with the Anastasius of August 21.

**ANASTASIUS, PLACID, GENESIUS and Comp. (SS) MM.
                             RM. Oct 11**
? The RM. has this entry: "The passion of SS Anastasius, a priest, Placid, Genesius, and their companions". And this is all we know about them.

ANASTASIUS of CLUNY (St) Mk. OSB.   AC. Oct 16
c.1020–1085. A native of Venice and a man of considerable substance and learning, he became a monk of Mont-Saint-Michel in Normandy, but left the abbey, being dissatisfied with the abbot, who was accused of simony. In 1066 St Hugh of Cluny made his acquaintance and invited him to join Cluny. After about seven years Gregory VII ordered him to go to Spain to preach to the Moors. He did so, but after another seven years returned to Cluny; then he lived for a time as a recluse near Toulouse. Recalled again to Cluny, he died on the way.

ASTERICUS (ASTRICUS, ASCRICK) (St) Bp. OSB.   AC. Nov 12
d. c.1035. A native of Bohemia, he became a monk and accompanied St Adalbert to the Bohemian mission. He became the first abbot of Brevnov, but had to flee to Hungary where he was appointed the first abbot of Pannonhalma, recently founded by King Stephen and the Archbishop of Kalocsa. Anastasius was the king's ambassador, sent to negotiate the recognition of the new Hungarian kingdom by Pope Sylvester II. He brought the Holy Crown of Hungary to St Stephen.

ANASTASIUS II (St) Pope
? PC. Nov 19
d. 498. He was pope for only two years: 496–498. On account of his conciliatory attitude towards the Acacian schism of Constantinople he was maligned by the intransigents. As a result his memory remained under a cloud for centuries, and this led Dante to give the saintly pontiff a place in hell (Inferno, XI, 4). The pope's name is found with the title of Saint in many calendars on Sept 8.

ANASTASIUS (St) M. RM. Dec 5
? The *laus* of the RM. is as follows: "The passion of St Anastasius the martyr, who in his ardent desire for martyrdom gave himself up, of his own accord, to the persecutors". Nothing else is known about him.

ANASTASIUS (St) M. RM. Dec 19
See Cyriacus, Paulillus, etc.

ANASTASIUS I (St) Pope
RM. Dec 19
d. 401. The RM. has this *laus:* "At Rome, the death of Pope St Anastasius I, a man of extreme poverty and apostolic solicitude. St Jerome in his writings saith that Rome did not deserve to possess him for long . . ." The saintly pope is given similar praises by SS Augustine and Paulinus of Nola. He stopped the spread of the errors attributed to Origen.

ANASTASIUS II the YOUNGER (St) Patriarch, M.   RM. Dec 21
d. 609. In 599 he succeeded St Anastasius I in the see of Antioch. During his episcopate there took place at Antioch a rising of the Syrian Jews against the tyranny of the emperor Phocas, and Anastasius was murdered by the mob and was looked on as a martyr.

ANATHALON (St) Bp. RM. Sept 24
1st cent. The oldest catalogues give him as the first bishop of Milan, sent there by St Barnabas whose disciple he was. As first bishop of Milan he evangelized the surrounding district, including Brescia, where he died.

ANATOLE KIRIGGWAJJO (St) M.
RM. June 3
d. 1886. He came from a tribe of herdsmen and was one of the young pages of King Mwanga of Uganda. Martyred together with several others. See Uganda (Martyrs of).

ANATOLIA and AUDAX (SS) MM.
RM. July 9
d. *c*.250. There are two *legenda* connected with these martyrs, who suffered under Decius. The martyrology of St Jerome makes Anatolio a Roman maiden, denounced with her sister Victoria, by their rejected lovers. They were confined to a prison near Rieti, here their miracles converted Audax, one of the guards. The RM., however, does not mention Victoria, and places the scene of the martyrdom at Thora, in the diocese of Rieti, not far from the small village now called Sant' Anatolia. Otherwise the two stories agree.

ANATOLIUS (St) Bp.   AC. Feb 3
9th cent. A Scottish bishop who went as a pilgrim to Rome and settled as a hermit at Salins in the Jura, where at a later date a church was built in his honour. Another completely different legend makes him a 4th cent. Bishop of Galicia.

ANATOLIUS (St) Bp.   AC. Feb 7
? A supposed bishop of Cahors whose relics were venerated at the abbey of Saint-Mihiel, diocese of Verdun. The whole account of his life bristles with inaccuracies.

ANATOLIUS (St) M. RM. March 20
See Photina, Joseph, etc.

ANATOLIUS (St) Bp.   RM. July 3
d. c.283. Head of the Aristotelian school
at Alexandria, his native city. He excelled as a philosopher and a mathema-
tician. About the year 269 he was chosen
bishop of Laodicea. St Jerome com-
mends his works.

ANATOLIUS (St) Bp.   AC. July 3
d. 458. Patriarch of Constantinople from
449 to 458. The Bollandists have vindicated his claims to sanctity. His feast is
kept by the Byzantine Catholics.

ANATOLIUS (St) M.   RM. Nov 20
See Eustace, Thespesius and Anatolius.

ANCINA, JUVENAL (Bl.)
                          AC. Aug 31
See Juvenal Ancina.

ANDÉOL (St) Bp.   RM. Oct 15
Otherwise Antiochus, q.v.

ANDEOLUS (St) M.   RM. May 1
d. 208. A subdeacon of Smyrna sent to
France by St Polycarp. He is said to
have been martyred near Viviers on the
Rhône.

ANDOCHIUS, THYRSUS ar.d
FELIX (SS) MM.   RM. Sept 24
2nd cent. Andochius, a priest, and
Thyrsus, a deacon of Smyrna, sent to
Gaul by St Polycarp. They established
themselves at Autun where they converted their host, a rich merchant, by
name Felix. All three were martyred
together. Their cult was wide-spread
throughout Gaul.

ANDREW (St) ? Bp. ? M. ? Jan 13
d. ? 235. The supposed twelfth bishop
of Trèves, whom some chroniclers make
also a martyr.

ANDREW of PESCHIERA (Bl.)
C. OP.   AC. Jan 19
d. 1485. Called "the Apostle of the
Valtellina". He was born at Peschiera
on the southern shore of Lake Garda,
diocese of Verona. At the age of fifteen
he became a Friar Preacher at Brescia,
studied at San Marco in Florence, and
afterwards for forty-five years carried
out a most successful apostolate in the
Valtellina district on the borders of
Switzerland and Italy.

ANDREW of SEGNI (Bl.) C.
                           AC. Feb 1
d. 1302. Born at Anagni of the noble
family of Conti, he became a Franciscan
and then a recluse in the Apennines.
Troubled in life by the demons, he
became celebrated for his assistance to
those who invoked his aid against them.
Cult confirmed in 1724.

ANDREW CORSINI (St) Bp. OC.
                            RM. Feb 4
1302–1373. Born in Florence of the
illustrious Corsini family. After wasting
his early years in dissipation, he joined
the Carmelites in 1318, and embarked
on a life of the most austere penance.
He studied in Paris and at Avignon, and
was made prior at Florence. Bishop of
Fiesole from 1360, he continued his
extraordinary life of penance, was a
father of the poor, and mediator between
the quarrelsome Italian states of that
time. He died on Jan 6.

ANDREW of ELNON (Bl) Ab.
OSB.   AC. Feb 6
d. c.690. Monk and disciple of St
Amandus at Elnon, whom he succeeded
as abbot. His relics were "raised" together with those of St Amandus in 694.

ANDREW and APONIUS (SS) MM.
                         AC. Feb 10
1st cent. Martyred at Bethlehem, it is

said, during the persecution mentioned in Acts XII, in which St James the Great was put to death.

ANDREW CONTI (Bl) C. OFM.
AC. Feb 15
d. 1302 (Feb 1). Andrew of the counts of Segni, or Andrew of Anagni, as he is called from his birthplace, was a nephew of Pope Alexander IV. He became a Franciscan lay-brother and remained in that position although offered a cardinal's hat by Pope Boniface VIII. He was equipollently beatified in 1724.

ANDREW NAM-THUNG (Bl) M.
AC. Feb 18
c.1790–1855. A native catechist of Cochin-China and mayor of his village. He died on the way to exile at Mi-Tho, E. Cochin-China. Beatified in 1909.

ANDREW of FLORENCE (St) Bp.
RM. Feb 26
d. c.407. The successor—according to Gams, the predecessor—of St Zenobius in the see of Florence. Gams lists a second Andrew as a successor—with an interrogation mark.

ANDREW of STRUMI (Bl) Ab.
OSB. Vall.
AC. March 10
d. 1097. Born at Parma, he was the disciple and chief supporter of the deacon St Arialdo in the campaign against simony at Milan. After his master's martyrdom, Andrew became a Vallumbrosan monk, and was made abbot of San Fedele at Strumi on the Arno. He excelled as a peacemaker between Florence and Arezzo.

ANDREW de' GALLERANI (Bl) C.
AC. March 19
d. 1251. He was a distinguished Sienese soldier, who accidentally killed a man whom he had heard blaspheming. Exiled

from Siena, he led a life of extraordinary penance and charity until he was allowed to return to his native city, where he founded the Brothers of Mercy, which lasted until 1308.

ANDREW of MONTEREALE (Bl)
C. OSA. Erem.
AC. Apr 12
1397–1480. Born at Mascioni, diocese of Rieti, at the age of fourteen he became an Augustinian hermit at Montereale. Ordained priest, he preached and laboured for fifty years throughout Italy and France, disciplining himself by severe fasts. He was for a time provincial of his order in Umbria. Cult confirmed in 1764.

ANDREW HIBERNON (Bl) C.
OFM.
AC. Apr 18
1534–1602. Born at Alcantarilla, near Murcia, in Spain, of noble but poor parents, he worked in order to help his sister financially, but was robbed of his savings and, disillusioned, joined the Conventual Franciscans as a lay-brother. In 1563 he passed over, at Elche, to the Alcantarine Reform. He converted many Moors by his frank simplicity. He died while helping to introduce the reform at Gandia. Beatified in 1791.

ANDREW FOURNET (St) C.
RM. May 13
1752–1834. Born at Maillé, near Poitiers. After several false starts, he was ordained and appointed parish priest of his native town, which he served unremittingly, even at the risk of his life, during the French Revolution. In 1807 he, with Elizabeth des Anges, founded the Congregation of the Daughters of the Cross for nursing and teaching. Beatified in 1926 and canonized in 1933.

ANDREW (St) M.   RM. May 15
See Peter, Andrew, etc.

ANDREW ABELLON (Bl) COP.
AC. May 15
1375–1450. A Dominican friar, prior of the royal monastery of St Mary Magdalen at Saint-Maximin, in France. Cult confirmed in 1902.

ANDREW BOBOLA (St) M. SJ.
RM. May 16
1592–1657 (May 16). Called by the schismatics *Duszochwat* (robber of souls). He was a Pole, who joined the Society of Jesus at Vilna in 1611 and spent his whole life reconciling dissident Orthodox with the Holy See. For this reason he was cruelly tormented and partially flayed alive and finally put to death by a gang of Cossacks at Janov, near Pinsk. Beatified in 1853, canonized in 1938.

ANDREW FRANCHI (Bl) Bp. OP.
AC. May 30
1335–1401. Of the family dei Franchi Boccagni. He was born at Pistoia, where he took the Dominican habit and eventually (1378) was chosen bishop. One year before his death he resigned and retired to his old friary. Cult confirmed in 1921.

ANDREW TOCUAN (Bl) M.
AC. June 1
d. 1619 (Nov 18). A Japanese layman, born at Nagasaki, he was a member of the confraternity of the Holy Rosary, and was burnt alive together with Bl Leonard Kimura because he had sheltered the missionaries. Beatified in 1867.

ANDREW TSHOCHINDA (Bl) M.
AC. June 1
d. 1617 (Oct 1). A Japanese layman and member of the confraternity of the Holy Rosary. Martyred at Nagasaki for having given shelter to the Dominican missionaries. Beatified in 1867.

ANDREW CACCIOLI (Bl) C. OFM.
AC. June 3
d. 1254 (or 1264). Born at Spello, near Assisi, he was ordained priest and was possessed of considerable wealth. He gave it all to charity and became one of the first seventy-two followers of St Francis. He favoured a strict interpretation of the Franciscan Rule, against the innovations of Brother Elias, and was for this reason persecuted and imprisoned. He died at Spello, where he had founded a friary. Cult confirmed by Clement XII.

ANDREW KAGWA (St) M.
RM. June 3
d. 1886. A native of Uganda and royal bandmaster of King Mwanga. Baptized in 1881, he was condemned to death for the Faith, and after his right arm had been severed from his body he was beheaded in 1886. See Uganda (Martyrs of).

ANDREW of CRETE (St) Bp.
AC. July 4
c.660–740. Surnamed also "of Jerusalem". He was born at Damascus, became a monk of Mar Saba and then of the Holy Sepulchre at Jerusalem, a deacon of St Sophia at Constantinople, and finally archbishop of Gortyna in Crete. He excelled as a writer of homilies and panegyrics of saints; he also considered to be the initiator of the *Kanon* of the Byzantine Liturgy.

ANDREW WOUTERS (St) M.
RM. July 9
d. 1572. One of the martyrs of Gorkum (see under Gorkum). He was a secular priest at Heinot near Dortrecht in Holland. He led a scandalous life, but when the Calvinists tried to compel him to renounce the Catholic faith, he expiated his past by a brave confession, was imprisoned at Briel with the other

martyrs and hanged with them. Beatified in 1675, canonized in 1867.

ANDREW of RINN (Bl) M.
AC. July 12

1459–1462. A boy, aged three, alleged
to have been put to death by Jews out
of hatred of Christ at Rinn, near Inns-
bruck. The facts are doubtful. Benedict
XIV allowed the continuation of the
local *cultus* but refused to proceed to
Andrew's canonization.

ANDREW ZORARD (St) M.
AC. July 17

d. *c*.1010. A hermit of Polish origin, he
lived on Mount Zobar, in Hungary,
near a Benedictine monastery, under
whose influence he trained St Benedict
of Szkalka (q.v.). His life was written
by Bl. Maur OSB. Canonized 1083.

ANDREW the TRIBUNE and
Comp. (SS) MM.   RM. Aug 19

d. *c*.303. An officer in the army of Maximian Galerius, who took part in an
expedition against the Persians. Accused
with a number of his comrades of being
a Christian, he and they were expelled
from the army and took refuge in the
Taurus mountains in Cilicia, but were
tracked and put to death.

ANDREW of TUSCANY (St) Ab.
OSB.   AC. Aug 22

d. *c*.880. An Irish or Scottish pilgrim to
Rome, who settled at Fiesole and became
the abbot-restorer of San Martino in
Mensula. These seem to be the only
trustworthy facts in his life, which has
come down to us largely embellished
with fiction.

ANDREW (St) M.   RM. Aug 29
See Hypatius and Andrew.

ANDREW DOTTI (Bl) C. OSM.
AC. Sept 3

1256–1315 (Aug 31). Born at Borgo San

Sepolcro, Italy, from being a military
captain he followed St Philip Benizi into
the Servite Order and accompanied him
on his preaching expeditions. He retired
to the solitude of Montevecchio, where
he died. Cult confirmed in 1806.

ANDREW KIM (Bl) M.
AC. Sept 22

d. 1846. Of one of the noblest families
of Korea, he was ordained at Macao,
S. China, and returned to Korea as the
first native priest, and was arrested
almost immediately and put to death.
Beatified with many others in 1925.

ANDREW, JOHN, PETER, and
ANTONY (SS) MM.   RM. Sept 23

d. *c*.900. According to the Greek Menology these saints were deported from
Syracuse to Africa by the Saracens, at
that time masters of Sicily. They were
there subjected to savage tortures and
put to death.

ANDREW CHAKICHI (Bl) M.
AC. Oct 2

d. 1622. A Japanese boy, aged eight,
son of BB. Louis and Lucy Chakichi
and brother of Francis. He was beheaded
with his mother and his brother Francis; their father was burnt at the stake.
The four were beatified together in
1867.

ANDREW the CALABYTE (St) M.
RM. Oct 20

d. 766. A native of Crete, and a monk
there, who went to Constantinople and
openly denounced the emperor Constantine Copronymus for heresy on account of the latter's edict against the
veneration of images. The emperor
ordered the brave monk to be put to the
torture and finally abandoned him to
the mob, who led him through the
streets in derision and stabbed him to
death.

ANDREW of BAUDIMENT (Bl) Ab. OSB. Cist. PC. Nov 10 (Apr 29) d. 1142. A Cistercian monk of Pontigny, he became the abbot-founder of Chablis (*Caroli-loci*).

ANDREW AVELLINO (St) C. Theatine RM. Nov 10 1521–1608. Born near Naples and christened Lancelot. Ordained priest, he was at first an ecclesiastical lawyer and as such was entrusted with the reform of a certain nunnery, being nearly killed in the enterprise. He then joined the Theatine Clerks Regular and took the name of Andrew. He worked with great success, chiefly in Lombardy where he became a personal friend and advisor of St Charles Borromeo. He died at Naples, in his eightieth year, at the foot of the altar when beginning Mass. Beatified in 1624 and canonized in 1712.

ANDREW TRONG (Bl) M. AC. Nov 18 1817–1835. A native soldier of Cochin-China attached to the Society of Foreign Missions of Paris. He was arrested with other Christians in 1834. His mother assisted at his execution at Hué and received his falling head into her lap. Beatified in 1900.

ANDREW (St) M. RM. Nov 28 See Stephen, Basil, etc.

ANDREW the APOSTLE (St) M. RM. Nov 30 1st cent. A native of Bethsaida in Galilee, elder brother of St Peter and like him a fisherman. He was a disciple of St John the Baptist and the first to be called to Christ's apostleship. He is said to have evangelized Asia Minor and Greece and to have been crucified at Patras in Achaia. The *Acta* of his martyrdom seem to date from the 4th century. His alleged relics, stolen from Constantinople in 1210, rest now at Amalfi in S. Italy. St Andrew is the patron saint of Scotland, Russia and Greece; his name occurs in the Canon of the Mass and in the embolism of the Lord's prayer. His emblem in art is the traditional cross of his martyrdom—shaped like an X.

ANDREW of ANTIOCH (Bl) C. OSA. AC. Nov 30 1268–1348. A descendant of Robert Guiscard, he was born at Antioch of Norman parents. He joined the Canons Regular of the Holy Sepulchre at Jerusalem and was sent into Europe to collect funds for the Eastern houses of his order. In this quest he died at Annecy (March 27).

ANDREW DUNG (or LAC) (Bl) M. AC. Dec 26 1785–1839. A native priest of Tonkin. Arrested with Bl. Peter Thi, both were beheaded on Dec 21. Beatified in 1900.

ANDRONICUS and JUNIAS (SS) MM. AC. May 17 1st cent. Disciples of St Paul, who makes mention of them in Romans XVI, 7: 'Salute Andronicus and Junias, my kinsmen and fellow-prisoners, who are of note among the Apostles, who also were in Christ before me". This is all we know about them. The Greeks celebrate their feast on May 17; their names have been dropped from the RM.

ANDRONICUS and ATHANASIA (SS) HH. RM. Oct 9 5th cent. Husband and wife, citizens of Antioch in Syria, where the former was a silversmith or banker. On the death of their two children they agreed to separate and live as hermits in Egypt. Years later they met and occupied adjoining cells, Andronicus not recognizing his wife until after her death. They are particularly venerated in Egypt and Ethiopia.

ANDRONICUS (St) M. RM. Oct 11
See Tharacus, Probus and Andronicus.

ANECTUS (St) M.   RM. March 10
See Codratus, Dionysius, etc.

ANECTUS (ANICETUS) (St) M.
                              RM. June 27
d. 303. Nothing really is known about him. Baronius, who wrote the *laus* for the RM., places him at Caesarea in Palestine under Diocletian, but remarks that the Greek *Acta* are very vague.

ANEMPODISTUS (St) M.
                                RM. Nov 2
See Acindynus, Pegasius, etc.

ANESIUS (St) M.   RM. March 31
See Theodulus, Anesius, etc.

ANEURIN (or GILDAS) and GWINOC (SS) CC.   AC. Oct 26
6th cent. Welsh monks, father and son. The latter has left some Celtic poems of a certain literary value.

ANGADRESIMA (ANGADRISMA, ANGADREME) (St) Abs. OSB.
                                AC. Oct 14
d. *c*.695. Cousin to St Lambert of Lyons, monk of Fontenelle. She herself received the veil at the hands of St Ouen. Eventually she became abbess of the Benedictine nunnery of Oroër-des-Vierges, near Beauvais.

ANGELA of FOLIGNO (Bl) W. Tert. OFM.   AC. Jan 4
1248–1309. Born at Foligno of good family, she led a worldly self-indulgent life in the married state, until her conversion, when she became a Franciscan tertiary. After the death of her husband

and children she gave herself up completely to God and to penance and became the leader of a large group of tertiaries, men and women. At the request of her confessor, Friar Arnold, she dictated to him an account of her visions and ecstasies in which she reveals herself as one of the greatest of mystics. Cult confirmed in 1693.

ANGELA de' MERICI (St) V. Foundress   RM. May 31
1474–1540 (Jan 24). Born at Desenzano on Lake Garda, diocese of Verona, she devoted herself to the education of girls, and the care of sick women. She was joined by several companions, and this led to the foundation of the Institute of St Ursula in 1535, the first specifically teaching order of women established in the Church. Canonized in 1807.

ANGELELMUS (St or Bl) Bp. OSB?   PC. July 7
d. 828. He is said to have been abbot of SS Gervase and Protase at Auxerre. He was bishop there from *c*.813 to 828.

ANGELICO (Bl) C. OP.
                              PC. March 18
1387–1455. His baptismal name was John. Born in the province of Mugello near Florence, he became a Dominican in 1407 at Fiesole. He resided for a time at San Marco in Florence, which he decorated with his wonderful paintings, and died at the Dominican friary of La Minerva at Rome. He is one of the best known and admired religious painters of all times. He is usually called *il Beato Angelico*, although he has never been officially beatified.

ANGELINA of MARSCIANO (Bl) W. Tert. OFM.   AC. July 15
1377–1435. Born at Montegiove in Umbria, she married in her fifteenth year and was left a widow at seventeen. She

was inspired to found a convent of regular tertiaries of St Francis at Foligno. It was finished in 1397, and before her death there were a hundred and thirty-five such houses under her direction as superior general. Cult confirmed in 1825.

ANGELUS
Note. This is the Latin form of a name which is very common in Latin countries: Angelo in Italian; Ange in French; Angel in Spanish; Anjo in Portuguese.

ANGELUS of FURCI (Bl) C. OSA.
AC. Feb 6
1246–1327. Born at Furci in the Abruzzi, diocese of Chieti, he joined the Augustinians at an early age, studied in Paris where he became lector of theology, and on his return to Italy spent the rest of his life as professor of theology at Naples. Without giving up his teaching he became for a time provincial of his order and refused several bishoprics. Cult confirmed in 1888.

ANGELUS of GUALDO (Bl) C. OSB. Cam.
AC. Feb 14
c.1265–1325 (Jan 25). A native of Gualdo, diocese of Nocera, on the borders of Umbria. In his youth he travelled barefoot from Italy to Compostella. He was professed a Camaldolese lay-brother and for forty years lived as a hermit walled up in his cell. All his life he was distinguished for his extreme simplicity, innocence and gentleness. Cult confirmed in 1825.

ANGELUS of BORGO SAN SEPOLCRO (Bl) C. OSA. Erem.
AC. Feb 15
d. c.1306. A native of Borgo San Sepolcro in Umbria, and a scion of the family of Scarpetti. He entered the order of Augustinian Friars and became a fellow-student of St Nicholas of Tolentino. It is said that Bl. Angelus worked in England and founded several friaries there. He was famed as a wonder-worker: once, it was narrated, he asked pardon for a man condemned to death and was refused this request, but after the man's execution he raised him to life again. Cult approved in 1921.

ANGELUS PORTASOLE (Bl) Bp. OP.
PC. Feb 22
c.1296–1334. A native of Perugia, he was elected bishop of Iglesias, in Sardinia, in 1330. He died at Ischia.

ANGELUS CARLETTI, of CHIVASSO (Bl) C. OFM.
AC. Apr 12
d. 1495. Born at Chivasso, diocese of Ivrea, near Turin, he studied law at Bologna and practised at Monferrato. Elected a senator, he left all to become a Friar Minor at Genoa. In the order he filled important offices; preached among the Saracens and the Waldensians and against usurious money-lenders; wrote a book of "Moral Cases" (the *Summa Angelica*), and effected many conversions. Cult approved by Benedict XIV.

ANGELUS of JERUSALEM (St) M. OC.
RM. May 5
1145–1220. Born in Jerusalem of convert Jewish parents. He was one of the early friar-hermits of Mt Carmel (1203). Commissioned to obtain the approval of Honorius III for the Rule written by St Albert for the use of the new friars, he journeyed to Rome and shortly after went to preach in Sicily, where he was killed by a man whose crimes he had denounced.

ANGELUS of MASSACCIO (Bl) M. OSB. Cam.
AC. May 8
d. 1458. A Camaldolese monk of Santa Maria di Serra in the Marches of Ancona. He was put to death by the

heretics, called Fraticelli or Bertolani, on account of his vehement preaching in defence of the Catholic faith.

ANGELUS AGOSTINI MAZZIN-GHI (Bl) C. OC.   AC. Aug 16
1377–1438. Born at Florence, a member of the Agostini family, he was professed a Carmelite in his native city. After his ordination he was professor of theology, prior at Frascati and Florence, and provincial. He died in retirement, revered by all as a model religious. Cult approved in 1761.

ANGELUS of ACQUAPAGANA (Bl) C. OSB. Cam.   AC. Aug 19
1271–1313. He became a Camaldolese at Val di Castro and then lived as a hermit near Acquapagana, diocese of Camerino, under the authority of the Silvestrines. Cult confirmed in 1845.

ANGELUS of FOLIGNO (Bl) C. OSA. Erem.   AC Aug 27
1226–1312. Born at Foligno, at the age of twenty he became an Augustinian Friar, and like Bl. Angelus of Borgo San Sepolcro, he was linked in friendship with St Nicholas of Tolentino. He founded three houses of the order in Umbria. Cult confirmed in 1891.

ANGELUS ORSUCCI (Bl) M. OP.   AC. Sept 10
1573–1622. A native of Lucca, in Italy, he became a Dominican there and passed over to Valencia in Spain to finish his studies. Eventually he went to the missions of the order in the Philippine Islands and Japan. Here he was arrested and for four years languished in the horrible prison of Omura until he was burnt alive at Nagasaki. Beatified in 1867.

ANGELUS (St) M.   RM. Oct 10
See Daniel, Samuel, etc.

ANGELUS of ACRI (Bl) C. OFM. Cap.   AC. Oct 30
1669–1739. Born at Acri, diocese of Bisignano, in Calabria. Twice he attempted unsuccessfully to become a religious, the third time, after a tempestuous novitiate, he was professed as a Capuchin. His public life as a preacher was again quite unsuccessful in the beginning and "tempestuously successful" afterwards. Beatified in 1825.

ANGELUS SINESIUS (Bl) Ab. OSB.   PC. Nov 27
d. c.1386. Born at Catania, he joined the Benedictines at the abbey of San Nicolo del' Arena and eventually was chosen abbot of San Martino della Scala at Palermo, whence he influenced all the Sicilian Benedictine abbeys in restoring monastic observance.

ANGILBERT (St) Ab. OSB.   AC. Feb 18
c.740–814. Nicknamed "Homer" at the court of Charlemagne, because he was a fluent verse-writer. His early life was worldly, if not dissipated. He excelled, however, as a minister and filled several important offices. As a reward Charlemagne gave him the abbey of St Riquier (*Centula*) and Angilbert became a model abbot. He introduced the continuous chanting of the office, using his three hundred monks and one hundred boys in relays, enriched the library and completed the buildings. He has always been venerated with a public cult.

ANGLINUS (St) Ab. OSB.   AC. Oct 28
d. c.768. The tenth abbot of Stavelot-Malmédy, in the province of Liége, Belgium.

ANGUS of KELD (St) AC. March 11
Otherwise Aengus, q.v.

ANIANUS (St) Bp.   RM. Apr 25
1st cent. According to the Acts of St
Mark and Eusebius, he was a disciple
and immediate successor of St Mark in
the see of Alexandria. He is said to have
been a shoemaker.

ANIANUS (St) M.   RM. Nov 10
See Demetrius, Anianus, etc.

ANIANUS (AIGNAN) (St) Bp.
                              RM. Nov 17
d. 453. Fifth bishop of Orleans. He is
best known in history as the prelate who
organized the defence of his episcopal
city at the time of the invasion of the
Huns under Attila and interviewed the
latter on his approach to Orleans, thus
saving the city.

ANIANUS (AGNAN) (St) Bp.
                              AC. Dec 7
5th cent. Fifth bishop of Chartres. We
know nothing else about him.

ANICETUS (St) Pope M. RM. Apr 17
d. 160. A Syrian by descent, he was
pope from about 152 till 160. During his
pontificate St Polycarp of Smyrna
visited Rome to settle with the pope the
question of the date of Easter. Anicetus
took a firm stand against the Gnostics.
It does not seem that he died a martyr,
although he is venerated as such.

**ANICETUS, PHOTINUS (PHOTI-
US) and Comp. (SS) MM.**
                              RM. Aug 12
c.305. Martyrs of Nicomedia under Diocletian. Anicetus and Photinus were
closely related by blood. They are only
known through Acts of no historical
value.

ANINUS (St) H.   PC. March 16
? A Syrian hermit famous for his austerities and his miracles; his date is
uncertain.

ANNA the PROPHETESS (St) W.
                              RM. Sept 1
1st cent. "Daughter of Phanuel, of the
tribe of Asher; she was far advanced in
years, and lived with her husband seven
years from her virginity. And she was a
widow until four score and four years;
who departed not from the temple by
fastings and prayers serving night and
day. Now she at the same hour (of our
Lord's being brought to the temple)
coming in, confessed to the Lord; and
spoke of Him to all that looked for
the redemption of Israel". (Luke II,
36–38). The Greeks keep her feast on
Feb 3.

ANNAM (Martyrs of) BB.
                    AC. July 11 and Nov 19
1798–1853 and 1736–1861. The two
major beatifications of 1900 and 1909
comprise martyrs who suffered between
these dates in Indo-China, most of
them between 1833 and 1840 or between 1859 and 1861. There are 64 in
the first group and 28 in the second.
Each receives a special notice in this
book. See also Dominican Martyrs,
beatified in 1906, and 1951.

ANNE LINE (Bl) M.   AC. Feb 27
d. 1601. A gentlewoman, née Higham,
born at Dunmow in Essex. A convert,
she was hanged at Tyburn for harbouring priests. Beatified in 1929.

**ANNE of St BARTHOLOMEW (Bl)
V. OCD.   AC. June 7**
1549–1626. Anne García was born at
Almendral, diocese of Avila, Spain, the
daughter of poor shepherds. A shepherdess herself in her early years, she
was the first to join St Teresa's reform
at Avila as a lay-sister. Eventually she
became St Teresa's secretary and companion in her foundations throughout
Spain. In 1606 she was sent to establish
the reform in France, was promoted to

the choir, and appointed prioress at Pontoise and Tours. She was the foundress of the convent at Antwerp, primarily intended for English refugees. She has left some delightful religious verse. Beatified in 1917.

ANNE MARY TAIGI (Bl) Matron
AC. June 9

1769–1837. Born at Siena, daughter of a druggist named Giannetti, whose business failed, she was brought to Rome and worked for a time as a domestic servant. In 1790 she married Dominic Taigi, a butler of the Chigi family in Rome, and lived the normal life of a married woman of the working class. In the discharge of these humble duties and in the bringing up of her seven children she attained a high degree of holiness. Endowed with the gift of prophecy, she read thoughts and described distant events. Her home became the rendezvous of cardinals and other dignitaries who sought her counsel. Beatified in 1920.

ANNE MARY JAVOUHEY (Bl) V.
Foundress   AC. July 15

1779–1851. Her childhood took place during the years of the French Revolution and she was accustomed to hide persecuted priests, to care for them and to keep watch while they said Mass. After the persecution she founded at Cabillon the Institute of St Joseph of Cluny, and seven years later, in 1812, moved it to Cluny. Fired with apostolic zeal she sent her nuns to work in far distant regions, and herself laboured for several years in French Guiana, with heroic courage. Beatified in 1950.

ANNE PELRAS and ANNE MARY THOURET (BB.) VV. MM. OC.
AC. July 17

See Carmelite Nuns of Compiègne.

ANNE (St) VH.   AC. July 23

c.840–918. Called also Susanna. A maiden of Constantinople who, while in her first youth, was left an orphan with a large fortune and was importuned to marry by unsuitable suitors. She refused, spent her money in the service of the poor, and finally lived half a century as a solitary on the Leucadian promontory of Epirus.

ANNE (St) Mother of Our Lady.
RM. July 26

1st cent. The gospels do not mention the names of our Lady's parents. Tradition gives them as Joachim and Anne (Hannah—"Grace"). St Anne's *cultus* already appears in the 6th century in some of the Eastern liturgies and in the 8th in the West, but it did not become general till the 14th century was well advanced. St Anne is usually represented as teaching her little daughter to read the Bible.

ANNE MARY ERRAUX and ANNE JOSEPH LEROUX (BB.) VV. MM. OS. Ursulae.   AC. Oct 23

See Ursuline Nuns.

ANNE or EUPHEMIANUS (St) W. H.   AC. Oct 29

d. 820. Born at Constantinople, a maiden of good family, she was married against her will but, after the death of her husband, under the name of Euphemianus and in male attire, became a monk at an abbey on Mt. Olympus. Here she made rapid progress in virtue, and was asked to take charge of an abbey built by the patriarch of Constantinople. She declined, and died instead in a small out-of-the-way monastery. The Greeks keep her feast.

ANNEMUNDUS (St) Bp. M.
AC. Sept 28

d. 657. Called in French either Annemond or Chamond, and by St Bede, in error, Dalphinus. He was archbishop of Lyons and friend and patron of the young St Wilfrid of York, to whom he gave shelter for three years in his diocese. St Wilfrid was present when Annemundus was murdered at Châlon-sur-Saône by order of Ebroin.

ANNO (HANNO, ANNON) (St) Bp.
AC. May 13

d. 780. A native of Verona, who became bishop there and is remembered chiefly in connection with the translation of the relics of SS Firmus and Rusticus.

ANNO (Bl.) Mk. OSB. AC. Sept 29
See Catholdus, Anno, etc.

ANNON (St) Bp.   RM. Dec 4
c.1010–1075. Son of a poor knight, he eventually became archbishop-elector of Cologne (1056) in spite of the hostility of his flock who thought him insufficiently well-born for their see. After a crowded career, full of political events, in which he took a great, and often leading, albeit not uniformly edifying part, he retired to the Benedictine abbey of Siegburg, which he had founded, and spent there the last twelve months of his life in rigorous penance.

ANNOBERT (ALNOBERT) (St) Bp. OSB.   AC. May 16
d. p.689. Monk of Almenèches, who was raised to the see of Séez about the year 685.

ANONYMOUS
Note. By counting up the number of saints listed anonymously in the RM. under such headings as companions, many, a great number, twenty, seventy, one hundred, etc., we reach the approximate figure of 36,000.

ANSANUS (St) M.   RM. Dec 1
c.304. A scion of the Anician family of Rome, he became a Christian when twelve years old. His own father accused him to the authorities, but the boy contrived to escape, and converted so many pagans, first at Bagnorea and then at Siena, that he was called "the Baptizer". He was at last arrested and beheaded.

ANSBALD (St) Ab. OSB. AC. July 12
d. 886. Born in Luxemburg of the counts of Querry, he became a monk of Prüm, and afterwards abbot of Saint-Hubert in the Ardennes, and finally of Prüm in 860. In 882 his abbey was burnt down by the Normans, and he succeeded in restoring it with the help of Charles the Fat.

ANSBERT (St) Bp. OSB. RM. Feb 9
d. c.700. From being chancellor at the court of Clotaire III he became a monk at Fontenelle under St Wandrille. He was chosen the third abbot and in 683 was promoted to the see of Rouen. Pepin of Heristal banished him to the monastery of Hautmont on the Sambre, where he died.

ANSCHAR (ANSGAR, SCHARIES) (St) Bp. OSB.   RM. Feb 3
801–865. Born near Amiens, he was received as a boy by the Benedictines of Old Corbie in Picardy, and educated there under St Adelard as abbot and St Paschasius Radbert as headmaster. After his monastic profession he was transferred to New Corbie in Saxony, whence he was taken by King Harold of Denmark to evangelize the heathen Danes. For thirteen years he worked there as first archbishop of Hamburg and legate of the Holy See; his mission extended to Sweden, Norway and N. Germany. The success achieved by his personal efforts was unfortunately not lasting and most of those northern churches relapsed into paganism.

ANSEGISUS (St) Ab. OSB.
AC. July 20

c.770–833. Monk of Fontenelle at eighteen, he was soon chosen by Charlemagne to be the restorer of several abbeys, and he ruled successively those of St Sixtus at Reims, St Meuge near Châlons, St Germer at Flaix, Luxeuil and Fontenelle. He excelled as a canonist, and wrote a collection of capitularies, which became the official law-book of the Empire. "His life," writes Father Thurston, "is a characteristic example of Benedictine work for Christianity and civilization such as went on throughout the Dark Ages of Europe," typical of that "all-roundness which characterized most of them".

ANSELM (St) Ab. OSB. AC. March 3
d. 803. Brother-in-law of the Lombard King Aistulph, and duke of Friuli, Anselm became a monk and founded the abbey of Fanano, near Modena, and a second at Nonantola. To both he attached sundry hospitals and hostels. Aistulph's successor, King Desiderius, banished him to Montecassino, but after seven years he was restored to Nonantola by Charlemagne.

ANSELM of LUCCA (St) Bp. OSB.
RM. March 18

1036–1086. Born at Mantua. His uncle Pope Alexander II nominated him bishop of Lucca; but Anselm refused to accept investiture from the emperor Henry IV. Later counselled by Gregory VII he accepted investiture, took possession of his see and then had scruples and withdrew to the Cluniac abbey of Polizone where he was professed as a Benedictine. Gregory VII recalled him to Lucca and the saint obeyed. He tried to reform the canons, who raised a revolt, and Anselm again withdrew. A man of great learning, he excelled as a canonist. He was Gregory VII's staunch supporter. Before his death at Mantua he became apostolic legate in Lombardy.

ANSELM (St) Abp. Dr. OSB.
RM. Apr 21

c.1033–1109. Born at Aosta in Piedmont, he became a Benedictine at Bec in Normandy under Bl Herluin. He became abbot at Bec and succeeded Lanfranc in the see of Canterbury in 1093. For his resistance to King William Rufus's encroachments on ecclesiastical rights he was exiled to the Continent. In 1098 he assisted at the council of Bari, and, at the pope's request, resolved the theological doubts of the Italo-Greek bishops. On Rufus's death Anselm returned to Canterbury, at the invitation of the new king Henry I, whom, however, he had also to oppose on the question of investitures. Hence a second exile, terminating in a triumphal return (1106). In spite of his somewhat stormy career, Anselm was one of the gentlest of saints. He stands out also in Church History as the link between St Augustine of Hippo and St Thomas Aquinas, and is known as the Father of Scholasticism. He was officially declared a Doctor of the Church in 1720. His life was written by his own secretary, the monk Eadmer of Christ Church, Canterbury.

ANSELM (St) Ab. OSB. PC. Nov 18
c.750. Abbot of Lérins. Mentioned in most menologies together with St Amandus of Lérins.

ANSFRIDUS (St) Bp. OSB.
AC. May 3

d. 1010. Count of Brabant and a knight in the service of the emperors Otto III and Henry II. In 992 he built the convent of Thorn for his daughter and wife, being himself desirous of becoming a monk. He was appointed instead archbishop of Utrecht. As such, he founded the Benedictine abbey of Hohorst (Heiligenberg) and, when stricken with blindness, he retired there and realized his ambition of taking monastic vows. There too he ended his days.

ANSGAR (St) Bp. OSB. RM. Feb 3
Otherwise Anschar q.v.

ANSILIO (St) Mk. OSB. AC. Oct 11
d. late 7th cent. A monk whose relics were enshrined at the Benedictine abbey of Lagny, diocese of Meaux.

ANSOVINUS (St) Bp.
RM. March 13
d. 840. A native of Camerino in Italy, who from being a hermit at Castel Raimondo, near Torcello, was raised to the episcopal see of his native town. He accepted the office on condition that his see should be exempt from the service of recruiting soldiers, then imposed upon most bishops in their capacity of feudal lords.

ANSTRUDIS (AUSTRUDE, AUS-TRU) (St) V. OSB.   AC. Oct 17
d. 688. Daughter of SS Blandinus and Salaberga, the founders of the nunnery of St John the Baptist at Laon. Mother and daughter were successively the first two abbesses. She had to suffer much at the hands of Ebroin, the mayor of the palace and oppressor of all the saints of that period.

ANSUERUS and Comp. (SS) MM. OSB.   AC. July 17
d. p.1066. He belonged to the nobility of Schleswig and was a monk and abbot of the Benedictine monastery of St Georgenberg, near Ratzeburg in Denmark, whence he and his monks evangelized that country. Ansuerus and twenty-eight of his community were stoned to death in the antichristian reaction which took place among the Wends after the emperor Henry III's death.

ANSURIUS (ADURI, ASURIUS, ISAURI) (St) Bp. OSB.   AC. Jan 26
d. 925. He was bishop of Orense in Spanish Galicia and helped in the foundation of the Benedictine abbey of Ribas de Sil. He was elected to the see in 915, and in 922 he resigned and became a monk at the above-mentioned monastery. After his death he was venerated there, together with seven other bishops who had followed his example.

ANTHELMUS (St) Bp. O. Cart.
RM. June 26
1105-1178. A Savoyard nobleman who, ordained priest early in life, went on a chance visit to the Charterhouse of Portes and stayed there as a monk. In 1169 he was chosen prior of the Grande Chartreuse, and it is owing to his efforts that the Carthusians, from being more or less a branch of Benedictine Monachism, became definitely a new religious order. In 1163 he accepted the bishopric of Belley under obedience to the pope, and so much did he endear himself to the people that, after his death, the city was called for a time Anthelmopolis. He was sent to England to try to bring about a reconciliation between King Henry II and St Thomas Becket. To the end of his life his heart was in his beloved Charterhouse which he revisited on every possible occasion.

ANTHEROS (St) Pope.   RM. Jan 3
d. 236. A Greek who was pope only a few weeks. It is not quite certain whether he died a martyr, as his name is not mentioned in the *Depositio Martyrum*. He was buried in the catacomb of St Callistus.

ANTHES (St) M.   RM. Aug 28
See Fortunatus, Caius, and Anthes.

ANTHIA (St) M.   RM. Apr 18
See Eleutherius and Anthia.

ANTHIMUS (St) Bp. M.
                        RM. Apr 27
d. 303. Bishop of Nicomedia where he
was beheaded for the Faith under Diocletian. His death was followed by a
wholesale slaughter of the Christian
communities of the district.

ANTHIMUS (St) M.   RM. May 11
d. 303. A priest at Rome, who is said to
have converted the pagan husband, a
prefect, of the Christian matron Lucina,
well known for her charity to her imprisoned fellow-Christians. The martyr,
thrown into the Tiber but miraculously
rescued by an angel, was afterwards recaptured and beheaded.

ANTHIMUS (St) M.   RM. Sept 27
d. *c*.303. Mentioned in the legendary
Acta as a companion martyr of SS
Cosmas and Damian, q.v.

**ANTHOLIAN   (ANATOLIANUS)
(St) M.   RM. Feb 6**
c.265. Mentioned by St Gregory of
Tours as one of the martyrs of Auvergne
under Valerian and Gallienus. Fellow-
sufferers were SS Cassius, Maximus,
Liminius and Victorinus.

ANTHOLIN (St) Ab.   RM. Jan 17
Otherwise Antony, q.v.

ANTHONIUS (St) M. RM. May 11
Otherwise Anthimus, q.v.

ANTHONY
Note. From the Greek Anthonios and
the Latin Anthonius or Antonius. The
usual modern forms are: in Italian and
Portuguese: Antonio; in Spanish: Antonio or Anton; in Catalan: Antoni; in
French: Antoine; in German: Anton;
in English: Antony, q.v.

ANTHUSA (St) V.   RM. July 27
8th cent. First a recluse, and then abbess
of a nunnery near Constantinople.
Known for her open veneration of the
images of saints. For this reason she had
to appear before the emperor Constantine Copronymus, by whose orders she
was put to the torture. The empress,
however, befriended Anthusa, who
lived to an advanced age.

ANTHUSA the ELDER (St) M.
                        RM. Aug 22
See Athanasius, Anthusa, etc.

ANTHUSA (St) VM.   RM. Aug 27
? Called St Anthusa the Younger, to
distinguish her from St Anthusa of
Seleucia (Aug 22). She was probably a
Persian and suffered in that country.
She is said to have been sewn up in a
sack and drowned in a well.

**ANTIDIUS (ANTEL, ANTIBLE,
TUDE) (St) Bp. M.   RM. June 17**
d. *c*.265. Disciple and successor of St
Froninus in the see of Besançon. He was
put to death by a horde of Vandals at a
place called Ruffey.

ANTIGONUS (St) M.   RM. Feb 27
See Alexander, Abundius, etc.

ANTIMUS (St) Ab. OSB.
                        AC. Jan 28
8th cent. He was, it seems, one of the
first abbots of Brantôme, an abbey
founded by Charlemagne in 769 and
destroyed by the Normans in 817.

ANTINOGENES (St) M.
                        RM. July 24
See Victor, Stercatius and Antinogenes.

**ANTIOCH in SYRIA (Martyrs of)
(SS)**
The following anonymous groups of

martyrs put to death at Antioch in Syria are given in the RM.:

RM. March 11

*c.*300. "Many holy martyrs . . . under Maximian set upon red hot gridirons and condemned not to death but continued torture," while others were afflicted with other cruel torments.

RM. Nov 6

d. 637. "Ten holy martyrs, who are said to have suffered at the hands of the Saracens," i.e., after their seizure of Antioch. Some records put their number at forty or more.

RM. Dec 24

d. 250. Forty Christian maidens put to death under Decius.

ANTIOCHUS (St) M.   RM. May 21
See Nicostratus, Antiochus and Comp.

ANTIOCHUS and CYRIACUS (SS) MM.   RM. July 15
3rd cent. The RM. has this *laus*: "At Sebaste the passion of St Antiochus the physician who was beheaded under the governor Hadrian; and when milk flowed forth from the severed head in place of blood, Cyriacus, the executioner, was converted to Christ, and himself also suffered martyrdom."

**ANTIOCHUS (ANDEOL) (St) Bp.
                         RM. Oct 15**
5th cent. When St Justus, bishop of Lyons, joined the solitaries in Egypt, the priest Antiochus was sent to seek him out and induce him to return to his see. The priest's efforts were in vain, and on his own return to Lyons he was himself chosen bishop.

ANTIOCHUS (St) M.   RM. Dec 13
d. *c.*110. A martyr of Solta (*Sulci*), a small island near Sardinia, under the emperor Hadrian. The island is now also known as the *Isola di Sant' Antioco.*

ANTIPAS (St) M.   RM. Apr 11
d. *c.*90. The martyr referred to in Apoc. II: 13 as a "faithful witness" put to death at Pergamum. Details of his martyrdom are not reliable, and it is unlikely that he was bishop of Pergamum.

ANTOINETTE
French diminutive form of the names Antonia, Antonina, q.v.

ANTOINETTE ROUSSEL (Bl.) V. OCD.   AC. July 17
See Carmelite Nuns of Compiègne.

ANTONIA of FLORENCE (Bl.) W. OFM.   AC. Feb 28
1400–1472. Born in Florence, she was left a widow in early life and joined the Franciscan tertiaries. Chosen superioress at Aquila, she adopted the original rule of the Poor Clares. She contracted a painful disease, which afflicted her for fifteen years, but this and other trials she bore bravely under the guidance of St John Capistran. Cult confirmed in 1847.

ANTONIA (St) VM.   RM. Apr 29
See Agapius and Comp.

ANTONIA (or ANTONINA) VM.
    RM. June 12 (March 1 and May 4)
d. ? 304. There are no verifiable data about this martyr. She seems to be triplicated in the RM., March 1 and May 4, and is claimed by three different places called Cea. Very likely she suffered at Nicomedia.

**ANTONIA of BRESCIA (Bl) V. OP.
                         PC. Oct 27**
1407–1507. Having entered as a young girl at the Dominican convent of Brescia, she was, at the age of sixty-six, chosen prioress of St Catherine's Convent at Ferrara, which she ruled justly

but rigorously. She was deposed and underwent other trials, always with much patience and humility.

ANTONINA (St) VM.   RM. May 3
See Alexander and Antonina.

ANTONINUS of SORRENTO (St)
Ab. OSB.   RM. Feb 14
d. 830. A Benedictine monk in one of the daughter houses of Montecassino. Forced to leave his monastery by the wars raging in the country, he became a hermit, until he was invited by the people of Sorrento to live among them. He did so as abbot of St Agrippinus. He is now venerated as the patron saint of the town.

ANTONINUS (St) M.   RM. Apr 20
See Victor, Zoticus, etc.

ANTONINUS (St) Bp. OP.
                            RM. May 10
1389–1459 (May 2). A Florentine of the Pierozzi family, he joined the Friars Preachers at Fiesole, and while still very young was made prior of the Minerva at Rome. In 1436 he founded San Marco at Florence, and in 1446 he was against his will appointed archbishop of that city. He was the "people's prelate" and "the protector of the poor". He also distinguished himself as a writer on moral theology and international law. Canonized in 1523.

ANTONINUS (St) M.   RM. July 6
See Lucy, Antoninus, etc.

ANTONINUS (St) M.   RM. July 29
See Lucilla, Flora, etc.

ANTONINUS (St) M.   RM. Aug 22
d. 186. A converted executioner at Rome under Commodus. However, see Eusebius, Pontian etc. (Aug 25).

ANTONINUS (St) M.   RM. Sept 2
? It is not certain whether the Pamia mentioned in the RM. is a town named Apamea in Syria or Pamiers in France. In both places there are traditions connected with a martyr named Antoninus.

ANTONINUS (St) M.   RM. Sept 3
See Aristaeus and Antoninus.

ANTONINUS (St) M.   RM. Sept 30
3rd cent. A soldier of the Theban Legion, martyred on the banks of the Trebbia, near Piacenza, in Italy. His blood, kept in a phial, is said to have the same miraculous properties as that of St Januarius.

ANTONINUS (St) M.   RM. Oct 25
See Marcellinus, Claudius, etc.

ANTONINUS (St) Bp.   RM. Oct 31
d. 660, Surnamed Fontana. He was archbishop of Milan for one year. In 1581 St Charles Borromeo enshrined his relics beneath a magnificent altar in the church of St Simplician.

ANTONINUS, ZEBINAS, GERMANUS and ENNATHA (SS) MM.
                            RM. Nov 13
d. 297. Martyrs under Galerius at Caesarea in Palestine. St Ennatha, a virgin, was burnt alive; her male fellow-sufferers were beheaded.

ANTONY (St) M.   RM. Jan 9
See Julian, Basilissa, etc.

ANTONY MARY PUCCI (St) C.
OSM.   AC. Jan 12
1819–1892. A native of Poggiole, Tuscany, he made his profession as a Servite in 1843. Appointed pastor of Viareggio, he devoted himself to teaching the catechism, administration of the sacraments and solicitude for the poor, the sick and the plague-stricken. Canonized in 1962.

ANTONY
ANTONY

ANTONY (St) Ab.   RM. Jan 17
251–356. The patriarch of all monks.
Born at Coma in Upper Egypt, at the
age of twenty he gave away his property,
which was considerable, to the poor and
lived as a hermit near his native place.
About the year 305 he established a
community at Fayum and another
shortly after at Pispir. Thus he was the
first to establish the religious life as we
know it today, by gathering together
large groups of hermits into loose communities. Soon he became famous
throughout Egypt and beyond, and was
in great demand as an advisor by people
of every rank. He was a personal friend
of St Athanasius and his staunch supporter against the Arians, whom he
arraigned as heretics in a public sermon
preached at Alexandria at the invitation
of Athanasius, when he was ninety years
old. Athanasius himself became St
Antony's biographer. St Antony died in
his hermitage on Mt. Kolzim, near the
Red Sea. In art he is frequently shown
with a T-shaped cross and a pig. The
latter, perhaps originally the symbol of
evil, became associated with a privilege
of the Hospital Brothers of St Antony
founded in the 17th century. St Antony's
fire was apparently an epidemic form of
erysipelas against which the saint's
intercession was invoked.

ANTONY, MERULUS and JOHN
(SS) Mks. OSB.   RM. Jan 17
6th cent. Three monks of St Andrew's
on the Coelina Hill, Rome. St Gregory
the Great, who was their abbot, has left
us an account of their virtues and
miraculous power.

ANTONY FATATI (Bl) Bp.
    AC. Jan 19
c.1410–1484 (Jan 9). Born at Ancona,
he held successively the office of Archpriest of Ancona, vicar-general of Siena,
canon of the Vatican at Rome, bishop of

Teramo and bishop of Ancona. His
feast is celebrated in all these places.
Cult approved by Pius VI.

ANTONY of AMANDOLA (Bl) C.
OSA. Erem.   AC. Jan 28
c.1355–1450. A native of Amandola in
the Marches of Ancona, he joined the
Augustinian Hermits and followed in
the footsteps of St Nicholas of Tolentino, with whom he was on terms of
friendship. His cult was confirmed in
1759, and he is honoured chiefly at
Ancona.

ANTONY MANZONI (or MANZI)
(Bl) C.   PC. Feb 1
c.1237–1267. Surnamed "the Pilgrim".
Born at Padua of a wealthy family, he
gave all his patrimony to the poor and
spent the rest of his life living on alms
and tramping his way to Loreto, Rome,
Compostella and Palestine. On account
of his wandering habits, his relatives,
especially his two sisters who were
nuns, looked on him with marked disfavour.

ANTONY DEYNAN (St) M.
    RM. Feb 5
d. 1597. Born at Nagasaki of Japanese
parents, he was an altar boy (thirteen
years old) and a tertiary of St Francis,
when he was crucified for the Faith at
his native town. Beatified in 1627, canonized in 1862. See Japan (Martyrs of).

ANTONY of STRONCONE (Bl) C.
OFM.   AC. Feb 7
1391–1461. Antony dei Vici became a
Franciscan lay-brother in his twelfth
year. Notwithstanding his humble
status, he was chosen to assist Bl
Thomas of Florence in an important
mission on behalf of the Holy See. After
more than ten years combating the
heresy of the Fraticelli, he was recalled
to the friary of the Carceri, in Umbria,

where he lived and practised rigorous penance for the rest of his life. Cult confirmed in 1687.

ANTONY CAULEAS (St) Bp.
RM. Feb 12

829–901. Born near Constantinople, he became monk and then abbot of a monastery of that city. Eventually he became patriarch, the second after Photius, the effects of whose schism he laboured to remove.

ANTONY of SAXONY, GREGORY of TRAGURIO, NICHOLAS of HUNGARY, THOMAS of FOLIGNO, and LADISLAS of HUNGARY (BB) MM. OFM.
PC. Feb 12

d. 1369. Franciscan friars put to death for the Faith by King Bazarath at the village of Widdin (in modern Yugoslavia) and in the presence of the heretic monk by whom they had been arrested.

ANTONY (St) M.
RM. Feb 14

See Bassus, Antony and Protolicus.

ANTONY (St) Mk. OSB.
AC. March 9

10th cent. A monk of Luxeuil, who became a recluse at Froidemont, in Franche-Comté.

ANTONY OF MILAN (Bl) OFM.
PC. March 15

See Monaldus of Ancona, etc.

ANTONY FUSTER (Bl) C. OP.
PC. Apr 5

14th cent. A disciple of St Vincent Ferrer, he was called "the Angel of Peace". He is highly honoured at Vich in Catalonia.

ANTONY PAVONI (Bl) M. OP.
AC. Apr 9

1326–1374. Born at Savigliano, he joined the Dominicans and became their prior in his native town, and finally inquisitor-general for Liguria and Piedmont. On Low Sunday, 1374, he preached a vigorous sermon against heresy at Brichera, and on leaving the church was killed by heretics. Cult confirmed in 1856.

ANTONY NEYROT (Bl) M. OP.
AC. Apr 10

d. 1460. A native of Rivoli, diocese of Turin, in Piedmont, he was professed a Friar Preacher. He was captured by Moorish pirates and carried off to Tunis, where he apostatized to Islam and married. After a few months he repented, put on the Dominican habit, publicly confessed Christ, and was stoned to death. Cult approved by Clement XIII.

ANTONY, JOHN and EUSTACE (SS) MM.
AC. Apr 14

d. 1342. Officials of the court of the grand duke of Lithuania, at Vilna. Antony and John, who were brothers, were crucified for having refused to eat meat on an abstinence day. Eustace became a Christian on witnessing their heroic fortitude, and was himself martyred for the Faith. They are the patron saints of Vilna.

ANTONY de' PATRIZZI (Bl) C. OSA. Erem
AC. Apr 27

d. 1311. Born at Siena, Antony became a Hermit Friar of St Augustine at the friary of Monticiano, of which he eventually became superior. Cult confirmed in 1804.

ANTONY (St) Ab. OSB. AC. May 4

6th cent. A supposed disciple of St Benedict and companion of St Maurus on his mission to France. He was the abbot-founder of Saint-Julian at Tours. He is surnamed "du Rocher" because he ended his days as a recluse on a spot called le Rocher. The story of St Maurus's mission to France is now discarded by all historians, with the exception of a few of French nationality.

ANTONY MIDDLETON (Bl) M.
AC. May 6
d. 1590. Born at Middleton Tyas, Yorks, he was educated at Reims for the secular clergy. He was hanged, drawn and quartered at Clerkenwell, London, for his priesthood. Beatified in 1929.

ANTONY of FOLIGNO (Bl) C.
AC. May 13
d. c.1398. A pilgrim from Hungary, and Franciscan tertiary, he was noted for his works of mercy. His relics are preserved in the Cathedral of Foligno.

ANTONY MARY GIANELLI (St) Bp.
AC. June 7
1789–1846. Born at Cerreto near Genoa, he was ordained priest in 1812 and, after twelve years spent as a devoted parish priest, was consecrated bishop of Bobbio in 1838. As a parish priest he organized a congregation of missioners and another of teaching sisters. Canonized in 1951.

ANTONY of PADUA (St) C. Dr OFM.
RM. June 13
1195–1231. A native of Lisbon and christened Ferdinand, he joined the Canons Regular at an early age, but a few years later (1212) passed over to the recently founded Friars Minor at Coimbra. Bent on martyrdom he sailed for Africa, but illness and storm brought him to Italy, where under the guidance of St Francis, he began his career as a preacher—"the hammer of heretics"—and as a wonder-worker. He died at Padua and was canonized by Gregory IX in the following year. "He is one of the most 'popular' saints of the Church, with a great reputation for retrieving lost belongings of careless people". (Att.) In art he is usually represented bearing the Child Jesus in his arms and holding a lily.

ANTONY MARY ZACCARIA (St) C. Founder
RM. July 5
1502–1539. Born at Cremona he studied medicine, but changed his mind and became a secular priest. His zeal, moulded on that of St Paul, knew no bounds. In 1530 he founded the congregation of clerks regular under the patronage of St Paul, called Barnabites from their headquarters at the church of St Barnabas at Milan. It was approved in 1533. He died as a result of his unceasing apostolic toil. Canonized in 1897.

ANTONY VAN HORNAER and ANTONY VAN WERDEN (SS) MM.
RM. July 9
See Gorkum (Martyrs of).

ANTONY FRANCISCO (Bl) M. SJ.
AC. July 15
d. 1583. Born at Coimbra in Portugal. After his profession as a Jesuit in 1570, he was sent to India, and after his ordination he took charge of the mission of Arlin on the peninsula of Salsette, near Goa. He was martyred with Bl Rudolph Acquaviva, q.v.

ANTONY CORREA, ANTONY FERNANDEZ and ANTONY SUAREZ (BB) MM. SJ.
AC July 15
d. 1570. Three Jesuits—companions of Bl Ignatius de Azevedo, q.v.

ANTONY TURRIANI (or TURRIANO, of TORRE) (Bl) C. OSA. Erem.
AC. July 24
d. 1694. Born at Milan, he studied medicine at Padua and practised at Milan. Then he became an Augustinian Friar Hermit. After several apostolic journeys, including three years at

Compostella in Spain, he died at Aquila in the kingdom of Naples. Cult confirmed in 1759.

ANTONY della CHIESA (Bl) C. OP. AC. July 28
1394–1459 (Jan 22). Born at San Germano, near Vercelli, in Piedmont, he belonged to the family of the Marquis della Chiesa. He became a Dominican and ruled, as prior, the friaries of Como, Savona, Florence and Bologna, sharing in the apostolic labours of St Bernadine of Siena. Cult confirmed in 1819. Bl Antony was a collateral ancestor of Pope Benedict XV.

ANTONY DICH (Bl) M. AC. Aug 12
d. 1838. A wealthy native farmer of Tonkin, attached to the Foreign Missions of Paris. He was beheaded for sheltering Bl James Nam, a priest. Beatified in 1900.

ANTONY PRIMALDI and Comp. (BB) MM. AC. Aug 14
d. 1480. An aged artisan, eminent for his piety, of the city of Otranto in Italy. When the Turks raided that city in 1480, they gave the inhabitants the choice between death and apostasy. Antony became the leader and spokesman of eight hundred citizens, all men who chose death for Christ, and were accordingly hacked to pieces. Cult approved in 1771.

ANTONY of ST FRANCIS (Bl) M.
AC. Aug 17
d. 1627. A Japanese Catechist, who was burnt at Nagasaki. A co-worker with Bl Francis of Saint Mary, q.v.

ANTONY DSHMANANDA (Bl) M.
AC. Aug 19
d. 1622. A Japanese sailor on board the ship of Bl Joachim Firaiama. He was beheaded at Nagasaki. Beatified in 1867.

ANTONY IXIDA and Comp. (BB) MM. AC. Sept 3
d. 1632. A Japanese Jesuit, famed for his learning and eloquence, who with five Franciscan and Augustinian friars was tortured for thirty-three days, by the application of scalding water, in a vain effort to make them apostatize. Finally they were burnt alive at Nagasaki. Beatified in 1867.

ANTONY of ST BONAVENTURE (Bl) M. OFM AC. Sept 8
1588–1628. A native of Tuy in Galicia, Spain, he studied at Salamanca, became a Franciscan, and was appointed to the mission of Manila in the Philippines. Here he was ordained priest and crossed over to Japan, where it is on record that he reconciled over 2,700 apostates. He was burnt alive at Nagasaki. Beatified in 1867.

ANTONY of ST DOMINIC (Bl) M.
Sept 8
d. 1628. A Japanese youth of twenty years, tertiary of St Dominic, companion of Bl. Dominic Castellet. He was beheaded at Nagasaki. Beatified in 1867.

ANTONY KIUN (Bl) M. SJ.
AC. Sept 10
1572–1622. A native of the province of Mikata in Japan, he was received into the Society of Jesus at Omura, and burnt alive at Nagasaki. Beatified in 1867.

ANTONY of COREA (Bl) M.
AC. Sept 10
d. 1622. Born in Corea, catechist under the Jesuit Fathers in Japan, he was beheaded at Nagasaki. Beatified in 1867.

ANTONY SANGA (Bl) M.
AC. Sept 10
d. 1622. A Japanese catechist beheaded with Bl Charles Spinola, q.v.

ANTONY VOM (Bl) M. AC. Sept 10
d. 1622. Son of Bl Clement Vom. Beheaded at Nagasaki with his father.
Beatified in 1867.

ANTONY (St) M.   RM. Sept 23
See Andrew, John, etc.

ANTONY MARY CLARET (St) Bp.
Founder   AC. Oct 24
1807–1870. Born at Sallent in Catalonia, he started life as a weaver, but
soon became a student for the secular
priesthood. He was ordained in 1835
and devoted himself to missionary work
among the people, helped by a group of
priests, whom he formed into the
Institute of "Missionary Sons of the
Immaculate Heart of Mary"—Clare-
tians. Bl Antony was raised to the see of
Santiago de Cuba, and in 1856 was made
confessor to Queen Isabella II and was
exiled with her in 1868. Both in Cuba
and in Spain he encountered the hostility of the Spanish liberal (i.e., anti-
clerical) politicians. He had the gifts of
prophecy and miracles. Canonized in
1950.

ANTONY (St) M.   RM. Nov 7
See Melasippus, Antony and Carina.

ANTONY BALDINUCCI (Bl) C.
SJ.   AC. Nov 7
1665–1717. Born at Florence, he became
a Jesuit in 1681. He worked as a missionary chiefly in the Colli Albani near
Rome, adopting very unconventional
methods of preaching and calling people
to penance. Beatified in 1893.

ANTONY QUINH-NAM (Bl) M.
**   AC. Nov 24**
1768–1840. A native catechist and
physician of Cochin-China, who became
attached to the Foreign Missions of
Paris. He was imprisoned for the Faith

in 1838, and strangled two years later.
Beatified in 1900.

ANTONY KIMURA (Bl) M.
**   AC. Nov 27**
1595–1619. A Japanese of the royal
family of Firando, aged twenty-three,
a relative of Bl Leonard Kimura. He
was beheaded with ten companions at
Nagasaki. Beatified in 1867.

ANTONY BONFADINI (Bl) C.
OFM.   AC. Dec 1
1400–1482. Born at Ferrara, he joined
the Franciscan Friars of the Observance
and was sent to the mission of the Holy
Land. He died at Cotignola, diocese of
Faenza. Cult confirmed in 1901.

ANTONY GRASSI (Bl) C. Orat.
**   AC. Dec 13**
d. c.1672. Priest of the Oratory at Fermo in the Italian Marches, and its
superior from 1635 until his death. In
1621 he was struck by lightning, but
this only seemed to increase his marked
serenity of manner. He had the gift of
reading consciences and excelled as a
director of souls. Beatified in 1900.

ANTONY (St) M.   RM. Dec 15
See Irenaeus, Antony, etc.

ANTONY of LÉRINS (St) H.
**   RM. Dec 28**
d. c.520. Born in Lower Pannonia, he
served God as a recluse in several places
north of the Alps until he found rest for
the last two years of his life as a monk at
Lérins.

ANYSIA (St) M.   RM. Dec 30
d. 304. A maiden of Salonika, put to
death by a soldier when she resisted an
attempt to drag her to a pagan sacrifice.

ANYSIUS (St) Bp.   RM. Dec 30
d. c.407. The successor of St Ascolus in

the see of Salonika. He was a friend of St Ambrose, Vicar Apostolic of Pope Damasus in Illyria, and loyal defender of St John Chrysostom.

AOUT (St) C.   **RM. Oct 7**
Otherwise Augustus, q.v.

APELLES (APELLIUS), LUCIUS (LUKE) and CLEMENT (SS) MM.
      RM. Apr 22 and Sept 10
1st cent. Apelles and Lucius are described by the RM. as "from among the first disciples of Christ". They are usually identified with the "Apelles, approved in Christ" and "Lucius, my kinsman" mentioned by St Paul (Rom. XVI, 10, 21). These names are duplicated in the RM., in the second entry (Sept 10) a third name Clement being added. Tradition adds that St Apelles was bishop of Smyrna, and Lucius bishop of Laodicea.

APER (St) Bp.
Otherwise Aprus, q.v.

APHRAATES (St) H.   **RM. Apr 7**
4th cent. A Persian hermit who settled at Edessa in Mesopotamia, and later on removed to Antioch in Syria, where he valiantly opposed Arianism during the reign of Valens. Some authors have endeavoured to identify him with the famous "Aphraates the Syrian", the ecclesiastical writer.

APHRODISIUS (St) M.
      RM. March 14
See Peter and Aphrodisius.

APHRODISIUS, CARALIPPUS, AGAPIUS, and EUSEBIUS (SS) MM.   **RM. Apr 28**
1st cent. A French legend, now universally rejected, makes this Aphrodisius an Egyptian who sheltered the Holy Family during their flight into Egypt.

He is alleged to have been martyred with the other three in Languedoc. Their story is told by Gregory of Tours.

APHRODISIUS and Comp. (SS) MM.   **RM. Apr 30**
? An Egyptian priest put to death at Alexandria with a group of some thirty of his flock.

APHTHONIUS (St) S.   **RM. Nov 2**
See Acindynus, Pegasius, etc.

APIAN
Otherwise Amphianus, Apphianus, Appianus, Appian, Apphian. Here we adopt the spelling Appian, q.v.

APODEMIUS (St) M.   **RM. Apr 16**
See Saragossa (Martyrs of).

APOLLINARIS SYNCLETICA (St) V.   **RM. Jan 5**
$c.450$. The heroine of a religious romance who disguised herself in boy's clothes and lived undiscovered in an Egyptian hermitage as a disciple of one of the Saints Macarius.

APOLLINARIS the APOLOGIST (St) Bp.   **RM. Jan 8**
d. $c.180$. Claudius Apollinaris, a bishop of Hierapolis in Phrygia, is now only known from the *Apologia* for the Christian Faith which he dedicated to Marcus Aurelius towards the middle of the 2nd cent.

APOLLINARIS (St) Bp. M.
      RM. June 21
See Cyriacus and Apollinaris.

APOLLINARIS (St) Bp. M.
      RM. July 23
? 1st cent. He is usually described as a disciple of St Peter. He certainly was the first bishop of Ravenna and was repeatedly put to the torture for the Faith

and died of its effects. The exact date is not known. His shrine at the Benedictine abbey of Classe at Ravenna became famous throughout Christendom.

APOLLINARIS and TIMOTHY (SS) MM.   RM. Aug 23
3rd cent. Apollinaris was the executioner in the gaol at Reims, who became a Christian on witnessing the fortitude of St Timothy under repeated torture. Both were beheaded for Christ and their tomb became famous in that district.

APOLLINARIS SIDONIUS (St) Bp.
                                    AC. Aug 23
See Sidonius Apollinaris.

APOLLINARIS FRANCO and Comp. (BB) MM. OFM.
                                    AC. Sept 10
d. 1622. Born at Aquilar del Campo in Old Castile, he studied law at Salamanca, and entered the Franciscan Order of the Observance, and eventually was sent to Japan (1614) as commissary general of the missions of his order there. He was arrested in 1617 and detained in the horrible prison of Omura until he was burnt alive on Sept 10. The "Companions" include Japanese martyrs of various dates, beatified in 1867. See Japan (Martyrs of).

APOLLINARIS (AIPLONAY) (St) Bp.   RM. Oct 5
d. c.520. Elder brother of St Avitus of Vienne, he became bishop of Valence, where he died after a glorious and indefatigable apostolate. He is the patron saint of the diocese.

APOLLINARIS (Bl or St) Ab. OSB.
                                    PC. Nov 27
d. 828. The fourteenth abbot of Montecassino, he governed the archabbey for eleven years. He has always been greatly venerated at Montecassino.

APOLLINE (St) VM.   RM. Feb 9
Otherwise Apollonia, q.v.

APOLLO (St) Ab.   AC. Jan 25
c.316–395. An Egyptian hermit who, after forty years of solitude in the Thebaid, became the abbot of over five hundred monks near Hermopolis. He left the desert, in order to withstand Julian the Apostate.

APOLLO, ISACIUS and CROTATES (CODRATUS) (SS) MM.
                                    RM. Apr 21
d. c.302. Three servants at the palace of Alexandra, wife of Diocletian, described as martyrs at Nicomedia. Alexandra however never existed, and the story is part of the legend of St George.

APOLLONIA (APOLLINE) (St) VM.
                                    RM. Feb 9
d. 249. An aged deaconess of Alexandria, martyred under Decius. Her teeth were broken with pincers, and for this reason she is invoked against toothache and is represented in art holding a tooth in pincers. Finally she was led to a kindled pyre to be burnt alive unless she renounced Christ, and "of her own accord leaped into the pyre, being kindled within by the greater fire of the Holy Ghost". (RM.).

APOLLONIUS (St) M. RM. Feb 14
See Proculus, Ephebus and Apollonius.

APOLLONIUS (St) M.
                                    RM. March 8
See Philemon and Apollonius.

APOLLONIUS and LEONTIUS (or LEONTINUS) Bps. MM.
                                    RM. March 19
? Neither the see nor the date of martyrdom of these two bishops is known. Their names, however, already occur in

the martyrology of St Jerome. The Portuguese have claimed them for their see of Braga.

APOLLONIUS and Comp (SS) MM.
RM. Apr 10
? A priest and five companions martyred at Alexandria under Decius.

APOLLONIUS the APOLOGIST (St) M.
RM. Apr 18
d. *c*.190. A Roman senator, denounced as a Christian by one of his own slaves and condemned to be beheaded. His eloquent defence of the Faith (*apologia*) delivered before the Senate at his trial is one of the most priceless documents of Christian antiquity. It was discovered in an Armenian text in 1874.

APOLLONIUS (St) M. RM. June 5
See Marcian, Nicanor, etc.

APOLLONIUS (St) Bp. RM. July 7
? A bishop of Brescia in Lombardy. He is mentioned in the acts of SS Faustinus and Jovita which, however, cannot be relied upon. His relics are enshrined in the cathedral of Brescia.

APOLLONIUS (St) Bp. AC. July 8
d. *p*.326. Bishop of Benevento. He went into hiding during the last persecution under Diocletian.

APOLLONIUS (St) M. RM. July 10
d. early 4th cent. A native of Sardis in Lydia, Asia Minor, he was scourged and crucified at Iconium.

APOLLONIUS and EUGENE (SS) MM.
RM. July 23
? Roman martyrs, the former was pierced with arrows at the stake, the latter was beheaded.

APONIUS (St) M. AC. Feb 10
See Andrew and Aponius.

APPHIA (St) M. RM. Nov 22
See Philemon and Apphia.

APPIAN (St) Mk. OSB. AC. March 4
d. *c*.800. Born in Liguria, he became a Benedictine at the abbey of St Peter of Ciel d'Oro at Pavia. Eventually he became a recluse at Commacchio on the shores of the Adriatic, and evangelized that country.

APPIAN (St) M. RM. Apr 2
d. 306. A martyr at Caesarea in Palestine in the persecution of Galerius and Maximian.

APPIAN and Comp. (SS) MM.
RM. Dec. 30
See Mansuetus, Severus, etc.

APRONIA (EVRONIE) (St) V.
AC. July 15
5th and 6th cent. Born near Trèves. Sister of St Aprus (Evre), bishop of Toul, at whose hands she received the veil. She died at Troyes.

APRONIAN (St) M. RM. Feb 2
d. *c*.304. A Roman executioner who was converted to Christianity when taking the martyr St Sisinnius before the tribunal, and was himself thereupon put to death.

APRUS (APER, APRE, EPVRE, EVRE) (St) Bp. RM. Sept 15
d. 507. Born near Trèves, he became a very able and just lawyer. He gave up this profession to be ordained priest, and in time was chosen bishop of Toul, which see he governed for seven years. Some authorities reject the tradition of his having been a lawyer.

APULEIUS (St) M. RM. Oct 7
See Marcellus and Apuleius.

AQUILA (St) M. RM. Jan 23
See Severian and Aquila.

AQUILA (St) M.   RM. March 23
See Domitius, Pelagia, etc.

AQUILA (St) M.   RM. May 20
d. 311. An Egyptian, torn to pieces with
iron combs under Maximinus Daza.
The prefect Arianus, who had ordered
this torture, subsequently became a
Christian and a martyr in the same persecution.

AQUILA and PRISCILLA (SS)
RM. July 8
1st cent. Husband and wife, belonging
to the Jewish diaspora, who worked as
tentmakers at Rome, whence they were
banished with all other Jews under
Claudius. They settled at Corinth,
where they received St Paul into their
house (Acts XVIII, 3). Under Nero
they returned to Rome and St Paul
sends greetings to them as follows:
"Salute Prisca and Aquila my helpers
in Christ, who have for my life laid down
their own necks" (Rom. XVI, 3-4).
There is a tradition in Rome that they
were martyred there.

AQUILA (St) M.   RM. Aug 1
See Cyril, Aquila, etc.

AQUILINA (St) VM.   RM. June 13
d. 293. A young girl—said to have been
no more than twelve years old—who
was tortured and beheaded at Byblus in
Syria. The account of her passion is not
trustworthy.

AQUILINA (St) M.   RM. July 24
See Niceta and Aquilina.

**AQUILINUS, GEMINUS, EUGENE,
MARCIAN, QUINTUS, THEO-
DOTUS and TRYPHON (SS) MM.**
RM. Jan 4
c.484. A band of martyrs put to death in
Africa under the Arian Hunneric, king
of the Vandals. Their acts are now lost,

but it seems that Ven. Bede had access
to them in the eighth century.

AQUILINUS (St) M.   RM. Jan 29
d. 650. A Bavarian by birth, who flying
from the prospect of high ecclesiastical
preferment at Cologne, went to Paris
and then to Milan, preaching against
Arianism. On this account he was assassinated by the Arians. His relics are
venerated at Milan.

**AQUILINUS, GEMINUS, GELA-
SIUS, MAGNUS and DONATUS
(SS) MM.   RM. Feb 4**
? 3rd cent. Martyrs at Forum Sem-
pronii, which has been interpreted very
doubtfully as Fossombrone in central
Italy. No details survive.

**AQUILINUS and VICTORIAN
(SS) MM.   RM. May 16**
? Martyrs in the Province of Isauria, in
Asia Minor and, as such, registered by
Ven. Bede in his martyrology. Nothing
else is known about them.

AQUILINUS (St) M.   RM. May 17
See Heradius, Paul, etc.

AQUILINUS (St) Bp.   RM. Oct 19
c.620-695. A native of Bayeux, he spent
forty years in the service of Clovis II.
On his return from the war against the
Visigoths, he and his wife agreed to give
themselves up to works of charity. They
retired to Evreux, and Aquilinus was
soon made bishop of that city. He
managed, however, to live more as a
hermit than a prelate.

ARABIA (Martyrs of)   RM. Feb 22
By the term Arabia is here understood,
conformably to the usage of the period,
the countries, mainly desert, east of the
Jordan, and, again, the mountainous
districts south of the Dead Sea. The
RM. has this entry: "In Arabia, the

memory of many holy martyrs, who were cruelly slain under the emperor Galerius Maximian".

ARABIA (St) M.   RM. March 13
See Theusetas, Horres, etc.

ARATOR, FORTUNATUS, FELIX, SILVIUS and VITALIS (SS) MM.
                         RM. Apr 21
? St Arator is said by the RM. to have been a priest of Alexandria in Egypt, put to death with the other Christians named above, in one of the earlier persecutions. No particulars are now extant.

ARATOR (St) Bp.   AC. Sept 6
d. *c*.460. The fourth bishop of Verdun.

ARBOGAST (St) Bp.   RM. July 21
d. *c*.678. Born in Aquitaine, not as has been maintained in Ireland or Scotland. He was living as a recluse in Alsace when King Dagobert II forced on him the see of Strasburg, which he ruled with great humility and wisdom. At his own request he was interred in the place set apart for the burial of criminals. A church was soon built over his tomb. In art he is represented as walking dry-shod over a river.

ARCADIUS (St) M.   RM. Jan 12
d. *c*.302? A prominent citizen of Caesarea in Mauretania (near Algiers) who under Maximianus Herculeus was slowly and barbarously mutilated until he died under the torture.

ARCADIUS (St) Bp. M.
                         RM. March 4
See Basil, Eugene, etc.

ARCADIUS (St) Bp.   AC. Aug 1
d. *a*.549. Bishop of Bourges, he took part in the Council of Orleans in 538. Buried at Saint Ursin.

ARCADIUS, PASCHASIUS, PROBUS, EUTYCHIAN and PAULILLUS (SS) MM. RM. Nov 13
d. 437. All of these were Spaniards, exiled to Africa by the Vandal Arian King Genseris, where they became the protomartyrs of the Vandal persecution. Paulillus was only a boy, the little brother of SS Paschasius and Eutychian. "As he could not be turned from the Catholic Faith he was long beaten with rods, and condemned to the basest servitude" (RM.).

ARCANUS (St) Ab. OSB. PC. Sept 1
See Giles and Arcanus.

ARCHANGELA GIRLANI (Bl) V. OC.   AC. Feb 13
1461–1494. A native of Trino, in the Monferrato, Italy, she became a Carmelite at Parma and, at the request of the Gonzagas, was sent to found a new Carmel at Mantua. She was its first prioress, a living pattern of perfection. Cult confirmed in 1864.

ARCHANGELUS CANETULI (Bl) C. OSA.   AC. Apr 16
d. 1513. Born at Bologna, he became an Augustinian canon regular, conspicuous for his gifts, natural and supernatural. He died as archbishop-elect of Florence.

ARCHANGELUS of CALAFATIMI (Bl) C. OFM.   AC. July 30
d. 1460. Born at Calafatimi in Sicily, he was a hermit at the time when Pope Martin V suppressed the Sicilian hermitages. He then joined the Franciscans of the Observance and was a great promoter of this new branch throughout Sicily. Cult confirmed in 1836.

ARCHELAIS, THECLA and SUSANNA (SS) VV. MM. AC. Jan 18
d. 293. Three Christian maidens of the Romagna who retired to Nola in the

Campagna in order to escape death; but there too they were accused of being Christians, tortured, taken to Salerno and beheaded.

ARCHELAUS, CYRIL and PHOTIUS (SS) MM. RM. March 4
Nothing is known about these martyrs.

ARCHELAUS (St) M. RM. Aug 23
See Quiriacus, Maximus, etc.

ARCHELAUS (St) Bp. RM. Dec 26
d. *c.*278. Bishop of Kashkar in Mesopotamia. He seems to have been a formidable opponent of Manicheism during his life, but the writings against these heretics attributed to him are not his work.

ARCHIPPUS (St) RM. March 20
1st cent. St Paul calls him "my fellow-soldier" (Philem. 2) and mentions him also in his epistle to the Colossians (IV, 17). Tradition, basing itself on St Paul's words, has made Archippus the first bishop of Colossae.

ARCONTIUS (St) Bp. M. AC. Jan 19
8th (or 9th) cent. Bishop of Viviers, killed by a mob for having upheld the rights of his church.

ARCONTIUS (St) M. RM. Sept 5
See Quintius, Arcontius and Donatus.

ARDALION (St) M. RM. Apr 14
d. *c.*300. An actor who suddenly proclaimed himself a Christian while engaged in ridiculing Christianity on the stage. He was roasted alive in the public square.

ARDANUS (ARDAING, ARDAGNE, ARDAGNUS, ARDAN) (St) Ab. OSB. AC. Feb 11
d. 1058. The thirteenth abbot of the Benedictine monastery of Tournus, now in the diocese of Autun. He restored the monastic buildings and was a father to the people during the famine of 1030–1033.

ARDO (St) Ab. OSB. AC. March 7
d. 843. A native of Languedoc, he changed his baptismal name of Smaragdus on entering the abbey of Aniane under its first abbot St Benedict. He became director of the schools attached to the abbey, St Benedict's travelling companion and secretary—and eventually also his biographer—and his successor at Aniane when St Benedict went to reside at Aix-la-Chapelle. His cult was well established at Aniane at an early date.

ARDUINUS (ARDWYNE, ARDOIN) (St) AC. July 28
? 7th cent. He is patron saint of Trepino in S. Italy. An improbable legend makes him one of four English pilgrims who died in this region in the 7th century.

ARDUINUS (St) AC. Aug 15
d. 1009. A priest of Rimini who lived first as a hermit and ended his days in the monastery of San Gudenzio, but did not however take vows there.

AREDIUS (ARIGE, AREGIUS, etc.) (St) Abp. PC. Aug 10
d. *p.*614. An outstanding archbishop of Lyons; his political activities have come down to us in an unfavourable light. He has a local cult only.

AREDIUS (YRIEIX, YRIEZ) (St) Ab. AC. Aug 25
d. 591. Born at Limoges, after a period of service at the court of the Frankish kings he became the abbot-founder of the abbey of Atane in the Limousin, which later on was called after him, as was also the village of Saint-Yrieux which grew up around the abbey. He

was famous for his evangelical travels throughout Gaul. Other variants are: Yriel, Ysary, Ysère, Yséry.

AREGLOE, AREGLE, Bp.
RM. March 17

Otherwise Agricola, q.v.

ARESIUS, ROGATIUS and Comp. MM.   RM. June 10
? A band of seventeen African martyrs, particulars concerning whom have been lost. Some martyrologies class them with the Roman martyrs, Basilides and others, commemorated on the same day.

ARETAS and Comp. (SS) MM.
RM. Oct 1

? According to the RM. St Aretas suffered at Rome with five hundred and four others. The first to mention this number was Usuardus. Some try to identify this group with that mentioned on Oct 24. See Nagran (Martyrs of).

ARETAS (St) M.   RM. Oct 24
See Nagran (Martyrs of).

ARETIUS (ARECIUS, AREGIUS) and DACIAN (SS) MM. RM. June 4
? Roman martyrs who were buried in the catacombs on the Appian Way.

ARGARIARGA (St) V.   AC. Sept 9
Otherwise Osmanna, q.v.

ARGEUS, NARCISSUS and MAR-CELLINUS (SS) MM.   RM. Jan 2
d. 320. Three brothers enrolled as soldiers in the army of the emperor Licinius who suffered martyrdom at Tomi in Pontus, on the Black Sea. Marcellinus was only "a boy enrolled as a recruit, who, on refusing to perform military service, was first flogged most cruelly, then kept long in prison, and lastly thrown into the sea." His brothers were beheaded.

ARGYMIRUS (St) M. Mk.
RM. June 28

d. 858. A native of Cabra, near Cordova, who held high official position among the Mohammedans of that city. He was deprived of his office on account of his Christian faith and became a monk. Shortly after he openly denounced Mohammed and confessed Christ and was beheaded.

ARIADNE (St) M.   RM. Sept 17
d. c.130. A Christian woman slave of a Phrygian prince, who was flogged for refusing to join in the heathen rites celebrated on the anniversary of her master's birthday; it is said that she took refuge in a chasm in the rock which miraculously opened before her and closed on her entering, thus affording her a tomb and the crown of martyrdom.

ARIALDUS (St) M.   AC. June 27
d. 1066. A deacon of Milan, who distinguished himself for his zeal against the rampant simony of his time, chiefly at Milan. For this reason he was first excommunicated and, after much persecution, killed by the party of the simoniac archbishop of Milan. Cult approved in 1904.

ARIAN, THEOTICUS and Comp. (SS) MM.   RM. March 8
c.311. Arian, governor of Thebes, in Egypt, with Theoticus and three others was converted to Christianity on witnessing at Alexandria the martyrdom of SS Apollonius and Philemon. The judge ordered them to be drowned in the sea.

ARIGIUS (St) Bp.   AC. May 1
535–604. Bishop of Gap for twenty years, he was one of the great pastors of the time. Cult confirmed by St Pius X.

ARILDA (St) VM.   AC. Oct 30
? A maiden of Gloucestershire who met her death in defence of her chastity. The church at Oldbury-on-the-Hill is dedicated to her.

ARISTAEUS and ANTONINUS (SS) MM.   RM. Sept 3
? Aristaeus is said to have been bishop of Capua, but modern research inclines rather to identify him with the Egyptian martyr Aristaeus, venerated by the Greeks on Sept 3. Similarly the child-martyr, Antoninus, seems to be a duplicate of St Antoninus of Apamea, commemorated in the RM. on Sept 2. At Capua there is no record of either saint.

ARISTARCHUS (St) Bp. M.
**   RM. Aug 4**
1st cent. A native of Salonika and a companion of St Paul in his travels (Acts XX, 4; XXVII, 2). He was arrested with the apostle at Ephesus, and shared his imprisonment. He is described as "his fellow-worker" (Philem. 24). Tradition makes him the first bishop of Salonika and adds that he was beheaded in Rome with St Paul.

ARISTIDES (St)   RM. Aug 31
2nd cent. An Athenian philosopher, famous for his *Apologia* for Christianity, which he presented to the emperor Hadrian in 125. The text, long lost, has now been recovered in Syriac, Armenian and Greek. See Barlaam and Josaphat.

ARISTION (St) M.   RM. Feb 22
1st cent. One of the seventy-two disciples of our Lord. He preached in Cyprus and died there a martyr, at Salamis. Others assert that he was martyred at Alexandria.

ARISTOBULUS (St) M.
**   RM. March 15**
1st cent. One of the seventy-two dis-ciples of our Lord. Perhaps he is the Aristobulus mentioned by St Paul (Rom. XVI, 11). He has been identified with Zebedee, the father of SS James and John, and Britain has been allotted to him as the place of his labours and martyrdom—all without the slightest foundation.

ARISTON, CRESCENTIAN, EUTYCHIAN, URBAN, VITALIS, JUSTUS, FELICISSIMUS, FELIX, MARCIA, and SYMPHOROSA (SS) MM.   RM. July 2
d. *c*.285. A band of martyrs put to death in the Campagna, S. Italy, under Diocletian. Nothing more is known about them.

ARISTONICUS (St) M. RM. Apr 19
See Hermogenes, Caius, etc.

ARMAGILLUS (ARMEL) (St) C.
**   AC. Aug 16**
d. *c*.570. Born in S. Wales, a cousin of St Samson. A Cornish church was dedicated to him—St Erme. He crossed over to Brittany and founded Saint-Armel-des-Boscheaux and Plou-Ermel (Ploermel). Like all the Celtic names of that period, Armel has taken countless variants. Here are a few: Ermel, Erme, Ermin, Arthmael, Armail, Arzel, Armahel, Hermel, Thiarmail. In Latin it is translated as Armagillus.

ARMAND (St) C.   AC. Jan 23
Otherwise Ormond, q.v.

ARMEL (St) C.   AC. Aug 16
Otherwise Armagillus q.v.

ARMENTARIUS (St) Bp.
**   AC. Jan 30**
d. *p*.451. First bishop of Antibes in Provence. An old church is dedicated in his name at Draguignan.

ARMENTARIUS (St) Bp.
RM. Jan 30

d. *c*.711. Bishop of Pavia. During his episcopate the see of Pavia was withdrawn from the jurisdiction of the metropolitan see of Milan and directly attached to the Roman Church.

ARMOGASTES and Comp. (SS) MM.   RM. March 29

d. *p*.460. Armogastes and Saturus, high officers at the palace, suffered in Africa during the Arian persecution under the Vandal king, Genseric. First they were tortured, then sent to labour in the mines, then condemned to slavery as cowherds near Carthage. They were not put to death "lest the Romans should venerate them as martyrs." The other names given in the RM., Archimimus and Masculas, thought to be martyrs of this group, apparently refer to Armogastes, with the meaning "President of the Theatre, a native of Mascula" or possibly we should understand "Archimimus, the Masculan".

ARMON (St) Bp.   RM. July 31
Otherwise Germanus of Auxerre, q.v.

ARNOLD (ARNALD, ARNAUD) (Bl) Ab. M. OSB.   AC. March 14
d. 1254. Born at Padua of the noble family de'Cattanei, he became a Benedictine at St Justina, Padua, and eventually its abbot. The tyrant Ezzelino da Romano, after persecuting him for a long time, imprisoned him at Asolo and loaded him with chains. He bore it all patiently for eight years and died in prison at the age of seventy.

ARNOLD (St) C.   AC. July 8
d. *p*.800. A Greek by birth, attached to the court of Charlemagne. He was famed for his charity to the poor. He has left his name to the village, Arnold-Villiers (Arnoldsweiler) near Jülich.

ARNOLD (Bl) Ab. OSB.
AC. Nov 30

d. 1155. A Benedictine of the abbey of St Nicasius at Reims, who became abbot of Gemblours.

ARNULF (ARNULPHUS, ARNULPH, ARNOUL) (Bl) Mk. OSB. Cist.   AC. June 30
d. 1228. Surnamed "Cornibout" or "of Villers". He was born at Brussels, and after a pleasure-loving youth, he became a lay-brother at the Cistercian abbey of Villers in Brabant, where he atoned for his past by long years of prayer and penance. He attained to a high degree of mystical prayer.

ARNULF (St) Bp. M.   AC. July 1
d. 1160. Archbishop of Mainz from 1153. He was murdered by his own diocesans and is venerated as a martyr.

ARNULF (St) Bp.   RM. July 18
d. 640. A courtier of high standing in the palace of the Austrasian kings, he determined to become a monk at Lérins. His wife took the veil and Arnulf was just on the point of retiring to Lérins when he was made bishop of Metz (*c*.610). A few years before his death he resigned and retired to a hermitage near the abbey of Remiremont.

ARNULF (St) Bp. OSB. RM. Aug 15
c.1040–1087. Born in Flanders, after some years in the armies of Robert and Henry I, kings of France, he became a Benedictine at the abbey of St Medard at Soissons. After his profession he lived as a recluse under the abbot's obedience. In 1082 he was obliged to accept the bishopric of Soissons. Some time after he resigned and founded the abbey of Oudenbourg in Flanders, where he died.

ARNULF (St) H.   AC. Aug 22
9th cent. The relics of this saint were

venerated at Arnulphsbury, or Eynes-
bury, in Huntingdonshire. He has been
described as an English hermit of that
district, but he is probably a duplicate
of St Arnulf of Metz.

ARNULF (St) Bp. OSB. AC. Sept 19
d. 1070. Born at Vendôme, he became
a Benedictine at the abbey of Holy
Trinity in his native city. In 1063 Pope
Alexander II consecrated him bishop of
Gap. As such he restored the cathedral
of his episcopal city. He is the principal
patron saint of Gap.

ARNULF (St) M. OSB.
                                AC. Oct 31
d. c.840. A monk of Novalese, in Piedmont, who was put to death by the Saracens.

ARNULF (St) Bp.   AC. Nov 15
d. 871. Bishop of Toul from 847 to 871.
He was a firm and outspoken opponent
of the divorce of King Lothair.

ARONTIUS (ORONTIUS) (St) M.
            RM. Aug 27 and Sept 1
See Honoratus, Fortunatus, etc.

ARPINUS (St) Bp.   RM. Nov 9
Otherwise Agrippinus, q.v.

ARSACIUS (URSACIUS) (St) C.
                               RM. Aug 16
d. 358. A Persian soldier in the Roman
army, who on his conversion retired to
live as a recluse in a high tower overlooking Nicomedia. He forewarned its
inhabitants of the impending destruction of their city by the great earthquake of 358. Some survivors found
refuge in the tower, where Arsacius had
already died in the attitude of prayer.

ARSENIUS (St) Bp.   AC. Jan 19
d. 959. A native of Constantinople of
Jewish descent, he became the first

bishop of Corfu, of which he is now
venerated as the principal patron.

ARSENIUS the GREAT (St) H.
                               RM. July 19
d. c.449. Surnamed also "the Roman"
and "the deacon", being actually a
Roman deacon. He was summoned by
Theodosius the Great to Constantinople
to become the tutor of Arcadius and
Honorius, the emperor's sons (c. 383).
After ten years in that thankless office
(c.393) he abandoned the court and
retired to the desert of Skete as a hermit. A hermit he remained for the rest
of his life, living in various places in
Egypt and ever "weeping over the
feebleness of Arcadius and the foolish-
ness of Honorius." He breathed his last
at the rock of Troë, near Memphis.

ARSENIUS (St) M. OSB.
                               AC. Aug 30
See Pelagius, Arsenius and Sylvanus.

ARSENIUS (St) M.   RM. Dec 14
See Heron, Arsenius, etc.

**ARTALDUS (ARTHAUD,
ARTAUD) (Bl) Bp. O. Cart.**
                               AC. Oct 7
1101–1206. Served at the court of
Amadeus III of Savoy, and then became a Carthusian at Portes (1120). In
1140 he founded the charterhouse of
Arvières-en-Valromey in Savoy. He
was an octogenarian when he was appointed bishop of Belley (1188) but
resigned after two years (1190) and
returned to Valromey where he died.
Cult approved in 1834.

**ARTAXUS, ACUTUS, EUGENDA,
MAXIMIANUS, TIMOTHY,
TOBIAS and VITUS (SS) MM.**
                               AC. Jan 2
3–4th cent. Martyrs at Syrmium, Pannonia.

ARTEMAS (St) M. AC. Jan 25
? Said to have been a boy of Pozzuoli (Puteoli) who was stabbed to death with iron pens by his pagan school-fellows. It seems, however, that the whole story is a pious romance.

ARTEMAS (St) Bp. AC. Oct 30
1st cent. One of St Paul's disciples, he is mentioned by the apostle in his letter to Titus (III, 12). A later tradition has made of him a bishop of Lystra. He is venerated by the Greeks.

ARTEMIUS (ARTHEMIUS) (St) Bp. AC. Jan 24
d. 396. An imperial legate who, on his way to Spain, fell sick in Gaul and settled at Clermont, in Auvergne, where eventually he became bishop.

ARTEMIUS (St) Bp. AC. Apr 28
d. 609. A native of Sens where he became bishop. He admitted to public penance a Spaniard, named Baldus (in modern French Bond), whom he trained to be a great saint.

ARTEMIUS, CANDIDA and PAULINA (SS) MM. RM. June 6
d. 302. Artemius, gaoler of one of the Roman prisons, with his wife Candida and daughter Paulina, was converted to Christ by St Peter the exorcist and baptized by St Marcellinus. Artemius was beheaded, and his wife and daughter buried alive under a pile of stones.

ARTEMIUS (St) M. RM. Oct 20
d. 363. An officer of high rank under Constantine the Great. A pronounced Arian, he was made by Constantius prefect of Egypt and, as such, persecuted St Athanasius and harassed the Catholics, nor is there any record of his having renounced Arianism. He was beheaded as a Christian under Julian the Apostate.

He is called by the Greeks the Megalo-martyr.

ARTEMON (St) M. RM. Oct 8
d. c.305. A priest of Laodicea (in Phrygia) burnt to death under Diocletian.

ARTHELAIS (St) V. AC. March 3
6th cent. One of the patron saints of Benevento, whither she is said to have fled from Constantinople to escape the attentions of the emperor Justinian.

ARTHEN (St)
? This saint seems untraceable. He appears to be one and the same with the St Arvan or Aroan who has left his name at St Arvans and Cwmcarvan in Monmouthshire. Stanton's Menology, following Challoner, identifies St Arvan with Maruanus, a companion of SS Banca (or Breaca) and Sennen (6th century).

ARWALD (SS) MM. AC. Apr 22
d. 686. Two brothers, sons of Arwald, a prince in the Isle of Wight, whose proper names are lost. They were put to death by soldiers of King Ceadwalla, then a pagan, on the day after their baptism.

ASAPH (St) Bp. RM. May 1
d. c.600. One of St Kentigern's monks in N. Wales. He succeeded St Kentigern as abbot and bishop, leaving his own name to the see. Moreover, he founded Llanasa in N.E. Flintshire. Many of his kinsfolk—Deiniol, Tysilo, etc.—are also venerated as saints.

ASCELINA (St) V. OSB. AC. Aug 23
1121-1195. A relative of St Bernard and early Cistercian mystic. She entered the convent of Boulancourt (Haute-Marne).

ASCLAS (St) M.   RM. Jan 23
d. *c*.287. Martyred under Diocletian by being thrown into the Nile at Antinoe.

ASCLEPIADES (St) Bp. M.
                              RM. Oct 18
d. 217. St Serapion's successor in the see of Antioch, from 211 to 217. He is usually given the title of martyr, probably on account of all that he underwent during the persecution of Severus.

ASCLEPIODOTUS (ASCLEPIA-DORUS) (St) M.   RM. Sept 15
See Maximus, Theodore and Asclepiodotus.

ASELLA (St) V.   RM. Dec 6
d. *c*.406. St Jerome, who became her panegyrist, calls her "a flower of the Lord," and tells us that this Roman maiden took the veil at the age of ten, and retired to a small cubicle at twelve, where she lived for long years until she became "the mother of many virgins". Pallasius visited her in Rome, where she had her community.

ASICUS (ASCICUS, or TASSACH) (St) Bp.   AC. Apr 27
d. *c*.490. One of the earliest disciples of St Patrick, by whom he was placed at the head of the monastery and diocese of Elphin, of which he is now venerated as the patron saint. He excelled as a coppersmith, and some remarkable specimens of his handiwork yet remain.

ASPASIUS (St) Bp.   AC. Jan 2
d. *c*.560. A bishop of Eauze—now Auch —who took part in the councils of Orleans, 533, 541 and 549, besides holding a provincial council at Aauze in 551. He is honoured in the diocese of Meaux, and especially at Melun.

ASPREN (ASPRONAS) (St) Bp.
                              RM. Aug 3
1st cent. The tradition, dating from time immemorial, concerning this saint is recorded by the RM. as follows: "At Naples in Campania, the birthday of St Aspren the bishop, who was cured of infirmity by St Peter the Apostle, and afterwards baptized and ordained bishop of that city". It seems however that he should not be dated before the end of the 2nd or beginning of the 3rd century.

ASTERIA (HESTERIA) (St) VM.
                              RM. Aug 10
d. *c*.307. A martyr venerated according to a Passio of doubtful validity, at Bergamo in Lombardy. She was a sister of St Grata, and both were associated in the burial of the martyr, St Alexander (Aug 26).

ASTERICUS (ASTRICUS) (St) Bp. OSB.   AC. Nov 12
Otherwise Anastasius, q.v.

ASTERIUS (St) M.   RM. March 3
See Marinus and Asterius.

ASTERIUS (St) M.   RM. May 20
See Thalelaeus, Asterius, etc.

ASTERIUS (St) Bp.   RM. June 10
d. *p*.362. Formerly an Arian who, after his conversion, became bishop of Petra in Arabia, and earned the hatred of the heretics by publishing the story of their intrigues at the council of Sardica (347). Banished to Libya by Constantius, but recalled by Julian the Apostate, he was present at the council of Alexandria in 362, and was chosen to be the bearer of the letter from the council to the Church of Antioch. He died shortly after.

ASTERIUS (St) M.   RM. Aug 23
See Claudius, Asterius, etc.

ASTERIUS (St) M.   RM. Oct 21
d. *c*.223. A Roman priest under Pope St Callistus, whose body he secretly

buried. For this reason he himself was cast into the Tiber at Ostia by order of the emperor Alexander. The Christians recovered his body and buried it at Ostia, where it is now enshrined in the cathedral.

ASTERIUS (St) Bp. AC. Oct 30
d. *c*.400. Bishop of Amasea in Pontus, Asia Minor. He was renowned as a preacher: twenty-one of his sermons are still extant.

ASTIUS (St) Bp. M. RM. July 7
See Peregrinus, Lucian, etc.

ASYNCRITUS (St) Bp. RM. Apr 8
See Herodion, Asyncritus and Phlegon.

ATHAN (St)
Place-name near Pontypridd. No record.

ATHANASIA (St) W. RM. Aug 14
d. 860. Born in the island of Aegina of an ancient Greek family. Her first husband died fighting against the Saracens; her second husband, with her consent, left her to become a monk. She turned her house into a convent, and numerous disciples gathered around her whom she ruled as an abbess.

ATHANASIA (St) H. RM. Oct 9
See Andronicus and Athanasia.

ATHANASIUS (St) RM. Jan 3
See Zozimus and Athanasius.

ATHANASIUS (St) Bp. AC. Jan 26
? He is honoured at Sorrento in S. Italy. Nothing is known about him. Perhaps he is to be identified with St Athanasius of Naples (July 15).

ATHANASIUS (St) Bp. AC. Jan 31
d. *c*.885. A native of Catania in Sicily. During the invasion of the Saracens he fled to Patras in Peloponnesus, became a Basilian monk, and eventually also bishop of Modon.

ATHANASIUS (St) Ab. AC. Feb 22
d. *c*.818. Born at Constantinople, he became abbot of the Paulo-Petrian monastery, near Nicomedia. He had to suffer much at the hands of the Iconoclast emperor, Leo the Armenian.

ATHANASIUS (St) Bp. Dr.
RM. May 2
c.297–373. History has given him the titles, amply deserved, of "Father of Orthodoxy", "Pillar of the Church", and "Champion of Christ's Divinity". A native of Alexandria, he began his public career when, still a deacon, he denounced Arius as a heretic. He accompanied his bishop to the council of Nicea, and on his return to Alexandria (328) was made patriarch of that city, which he governed for over forty years. His life-work was the defeat of Arianism and the vindication of the divinity of Christ. For this cause he was five times exiled from his see: 335–338 to Trèves; 341–346 to Rome; 356–362 to the desert; 362–363 and a second time during four months of 363 again to the desert. Through it all he managed to guide his flock, and to write for them most illuminating treatises on Catholic dogma. One of his most attractive characteristics was his unfailing humour, which often proved a deadly weapon against his adversaries. He is revered in the universal Church as one of the four great Greek Doctors, and in the East as one of the three Holy Hierarchs. He is the pioneer of scientific theology.

ATHANASIUS BADZEKUKETTA (St) M. RM. June 3
d. 1886 (May 17). A page to King Mwanga of Uganda and a Keeper of the Royal Treasury. He was baptized in 1885 and martyred by the king's

soldiers in the following year. See Uganda (Martyrs of).

ATHANASIUS (St) M. RM. July 5
d. 452. A deacon of Jerusalem. He denounced the heretic Theodosius, who had supplanted the Catholic St Juvenal in the see of Jerusalem. For this act he was seized by the soldiery and beheaded.

ATHANASIUS the ATHONITE (St) Ab.   AC. July 5
c.920–1003. Born at Trebizond, he embraced the monastic life in Bithynia, whence he migrated to Mt Athos. Here he founded a laura (961), which became the first nucleus of what has ever since been a wholly monastic republic. When he died he ruled as abbot-general over some sixty communities of hermits and monks living on Mt Athos. Shortly after the founder's death the monks became schismatics.

ATHANASIUS (St) Bp. RM. July 15
d. 872. Son of the duke of Naples, he was made bishop of that city at the age of eighteen. After he had ruled it for twenty years he began to suffer from the exactions of relatives, in whose hands rested the civil authority of Naples. Imprisoned, and then exiled, he died at Veroli and was buried at Montecassino, whence his body was transferred to Naples.

ATHANASIUS, ANTHUSA and Comp. (SS) MM.   RM Aug 22
d. c.257. Athanasius was bishop of Tarsus in Cilicia. Anthusa, a noble lady of Seleucia, was baptized by him together with two of her slaves, Charisius and Neophytus. The three men were martyred under Valerian; Anthusa survived twenty-three years. The Acts of St Anthusa which relate this story closely resemble those of St Pelagia of Tarsus.

ATHELM (St) Bp. OSB. PC. Jan 8
d. 923. Paternal uncle of St Dunstan. A monk, and then abbot, of Glastonbury, he was appointed first bishop of Wells in Somerset, and in 914 transferred to the see of Canterbury.

**ATHENODORUS (St) Bp. M.
RM. Oct 18**
d. c.269. A Native of Neo-Caesarea in Cappadocia and a brother of St Gregory the Wonder-Worker (Thaumaturgus). After their conversion the two brothers studied under Origen at Caesarea and then became bishops, Athenodorus of an unnamed see in Pontus. He suffered martyrdom under Aurelian.

**ATHENODORUS (St) M.
RM. Nov 11**
d. c.304. A martyr of Mesopotamia under Diocletian, who, according to the RM. "was tormented with fire and tried with other punishments . . . at length he was condemned to capital punishment, but when the executioner fell to the ground, and none other dared smite him with the sword, he fell asleep in the Lord in prayer".

**ATHENOGENES (St) Bp. M.
RM. Jan 18, July 16**
? On Jan 18 the RM. has: "In Pontus, the birthday of St Athenogenes, an aged theologian, who, when about to consummate his martyrdom by fire, sang a hymn of joy, which he left in writing to his disciples". The martyr is to be identified, it seems, with the bishop who suffered at Sebaste in Armenia with ten disciples, under Diocletian (RM. July 16). The hymn referred to above, is, according to St Basil, the beautiful *Phos hilaron*, feature of the vespers service in the Byzantine liturgy.

ATHEUS (St) C.   AC. Dec 26
Otherwise Tathai, q.v.

ATHILDA (St) VM.   AC. March 27
Otherwise Alkeld, q.v.

ATTALA (ATTALUS) (St) Ab. OSB.
AC. Apr 3
d. *c*.800. A Benedictine monk and abbot of a monastery at Taormina in Sicily.

ATTALAS (St) Ab.   RM. March 10
d. 627. Born in Burgundy, he was professed a monk at Lérins, whence he passed over to Luxeuil under St Columbanus, whom he followed to Bobbio in N. Italy, helping him in the foundation of the abbey and succeeding him as abbot (615). It was during his abbacy that most of the monks stood out against the severity of the Columbanian Rule.

ATTALIA (ATTALA) (St) Abs.
OSB.   AC. Dec 3
c.697–741. A niece of St Ottilia. She became a Benedictine nun and abbess of St Stephen's nunnery at Strasburg.

ATTALUS (St) M   RM. June 2
See Photinus, Sanctius, etc.

ATTALUS (St) M.   RM. Dec 31
See Stephen, Pontian, etc.

ATTICUS (St) Bp.   AC. Jan 8
d 425 (Oct. 10). A convert from heresy, he opposed St John Chrysostom and was intruded as bishop of Constantinople during the latter's second banishment. However, he repented of his opposition and submitted to Pope Innocent's ruling. Afterwards he lived as an eminently virtuous prelate.

ATTICUS (St) M.   RM. Nov 6
? The RM. has: "In Phrygia St Atticus, Martyr". Nothing else is known about him.

ATTILANUS (St) Bp. OSB.
RM. Oct 5
c.939–1009. A native of Tarazona, near Saragossa, he became a Benedictine at Moreruela under St Froilan, who chose him as prior of the abbey. The two sees of León and Zamora becoming vacant, Froilan was appointed to the former and Attilanus to the latter, and they were consecrated together on Whit-Sunday, 990. St Attilanus was canonized in 1089.

ATTIUS (St) M.   RM. Aug 1
See Leontius, Attius, etc.

ATTO (ATTHO) (St) Bp. OSB. Vall.
RM. May 22
d. 1153. Born at Badajoz in Spain—some Italian writers claim him for Florence in Italy. He became a Benedictine at Vallumbrosa, and eventually abbot-general of the congregation and bishop of Pistoia. He wrote the lives of St John Gualbert and of St Bernard of Parma and a work on Compostella in Spain.

ATTO (St) Bp. OSB.   AC. June 1
d. *c*.1044. Benedictine monk at Oña, in Old Castile, under St Enneco. Afterwards bishop of Oca-Valpuesta.

ATTO (St) Ab. OSB.   AC. Nov 19
d. p. 1010. First abbot of Tordino, near Teramo, a house founded by Montecassino in 1004.

ATTRACTA (ATHRACHT) (St) V.
AC. Aug 11
? 5th cent. She seems to have been a contemporary of St Patrick. She certainly was a recluse, first at Killaraght, on Lough Gara, and then at Drum, near Boyle. Both places eventually grew into nunneries under her direction. She is venerated throughout Ireland.

AUBERT (*several*)
Otherwise Autbert, q.v.

AUBIERGE (St) V.   RM. July 7
Otherwise Ethelburga, q.v.

AUBIN (AUBYN) (St) Bp.
RM. March 1
Otherwise Albinus, q.v.

AUCEJAS and LUCEIA (SS) MM.
RM. June 25
See Lucy and Companions.

AUCTUS, TAURION and THESSALONICA (SS) MM.
RM. Nov 7
? Martyrs at Amphipolis in Macedonia. Nothing else is known of them.

AUDACTUS (ADAUCTUS) (St) M.
RM. Oct 24
See Felix, Audactus, etc.

AUDAS (or ABDAS) (St) Bp. M.
RM. May 16
d. 420. A Persian bishop, martyred together with seven priests, nine deacons and seven virgins. Their death marked the beginning of a widespread persecution of Christians throughout the kingdom.

AUDAX (St) M.   RM. July 9
See Anatolia and Audax.

AUDIFAX (St) M.   RM. Jan 19
See Marius, Martha, etc.

AUDÖENUS (St) Bp.   RM. Aug 24
Otherwise Ouen, q.v.

AUDOMARUS (St) Bp. RM. Sept 9
Otherwise Omer, q.v.

AUDREY (AWDREY) (St) V.
RM. June 23
Otherwise Etheldreda, q.v.

AUGULUS (AUGURIUS, AULE) (St) Bp. M.   RM. Feb 7
d. c.303. His name appears in the martyrology of St Jerome as a bishop. Others describe him as a martyr put to death in London under Diocletian. French writers usually identify him with St Aule of Normandy.

AUGURUS (St) M.   RM. Jan 21
See Fructuosus, Augurius and Eulogius.

AUGUSTA (St) VM. AC. March 27
5th cent. Daughter of the Teuton duke of Friuli. Her conversion to Christianity so enraged her father that he killed her with his own hand. She has been venerated from time immemorial at Serravalle, near Treviso, in N. Italy.

AUGUSTALIS (AUTAL) (St) Bp.
RM. Sept 7
? c.450. A bishop in Gaul, probably at Arles.

AUGUSTINE SCHÖFFLER (Bl) M.   AC. May 1
1822–1851. Born at Mittelbronn in Lorraine, he joined the Paris Society of Foreign Missions and was sent to Annam where he was beheaded for the Faith. Beatified in 1900.

AUGUSTINE WEBSTER (Bl) MO Cart.   AC. May 4
d. 1535. Prior of the Charterhouse of Axholme, England; he was arrested at the London Charterhouse and executed at Tyburn.

AUGUSTINE of NICOMEDIA (St) M.   RM. May 7
See Flavius, Augustus and Augustine.

AUGUSTINE NOVELLO (Bl) C. OSA. Erem.   AC. May 19
d. 1309. Born at Taormina, in Sicily. After taking his doctorate in law at Bologna, he was appointed chancellor to King Manfred of Sicily. Left for dead on the battlefield at Benevento, after his recovery he joined the Augustinian friars as a lay-brother with the name

Augustine. His gifts were soon discovered and he was commanded to receive priest's orders. Eventually he became prior-general of the Order, confessor to the pope, and legate. Cult confirmed in 1759.

AUGUSTINE OF CANTERBURY (St) Bp. OSB.   RM. May 26 (28)

d. 604. He shares with St Gregory the Great the title of Apostle of the English. He was prior of St Andrew's on the Caelian Hill when he was sent by Pope Gregory the Great with a band of forty companions to evangelize England. The missionaries landed at Ebbsfleet near Ramsgate, Thanet, in 597. Soon Augustine had converted the king of Kent with thousands of his subjects to the Faith. He was consecrated bishop at Arles (597) and established his see at Canterbury. He was not so successful in his relations with the Celtic missionaries. He died shortly after St Gregory the Great. Whether he followed the Benedictine Rule has been questioned.

AUGUSTINE HUY (Bl) M.
AC. June 13

d. 1839. A native soldier of Tonkin sawn asunder with Bl Nicholas The.

AUGUSTINE TCHAO (Bl) M.
AC. July 9

d. 1815. He was among the soldiers who escorted Bl John Gabriel Dufresse to Pekin, and was converted by his behaviour. Ordained priest, he laboured in the Province of Su-Tchuen. He was arrested while on his ministry, and being already sick, died of ill-usage, in prison. Beatified 1900.

AUGUSTINE FANGI (Bl) C. OP.
AC. July 22

d. 1493. He was born at Biella, where he joined the Dominicans. After a crowded apostolic life and great bodily sufferings he died at Venice. Cult approved in 1872.

AUGUSTINE GAZOTICH (Bl) Bp. OP.   AC. Aug 3

1262–1323. A native of Trau in Dalmatia, he became a Friar Preacher at the age of twenty. Eventually he was sent to preach among the Siavs and Hungarians and in 1303 was chosen bishop of Zagreb in Croatia. Later he was translated to Lucera (Nocera) in Italy. His characteristic was gentleness, and he had the gift of healing. Beatified by Clement XI.

AUGUSTINE OF LUCERA (Bl) Bp. OP.   AC. Aug 3

d. 1323. A Dalmatian by birth, he entered the Dominican Order and studied at Paris. He was made Bishop of Zagreb, and later of Lucera. Cult approved in 1722.

AUGUSTINE CANNINI (Bl) M. OSM.   AC. Aug 11

See Laurence Nerucci, etc.

AUGUSTINE of HIPPO (St) Bp. Dr. Founder   RM. Aug 28 (see also Feb 28, Apr 2, May 4)

Nov 13, 354—Aug 28, 430. A native of Tagaste in N. Africa. In spite of his early training by his mother St Monica, he spent his youth in vice, and all but became a Manichaean. A professor of rhetoric by profession, he taught successively at Tagaste, Carthage, Rome (383) and Milan (384–386). Under the influence of St Ambrose, of St Paul's epistles and of some neoplatonist writings, he was converted and was baptized at thirty-two by St Ambrose at Easter 387. The same year he left for Africa, his mother dying at Ostia. From 388 to 391, he lived a sort of monastic life with a few friends near Tagaste. In 391 he was ordained priest at Hippo and three years later coadjutor-bishop of the same city. From this time on he devoted all his energy and extraordinary intellectual gifts to the defence of

Christian faith and morals and to the refutation of heresy and schism, thus opposing Manichaeans, Priscillianists, Donatists, Pelagians and Semipelagians, and Arian Vandals. His leading ideas and principles on religious life are still followed by numerous canons, friars, hermits and nuns. He is one of the most prolific, and certainly the most influential, of all the doctors. His two works, the *Confessions* and the *City of God*, are reckoned among the world's classics. In his life he is a miracle of divine grace, since even the child of his sin, Adeodatus, is now venerated as a saint. His relics are enshrined in the basilica of St Peter.

AUGUSTINE AMBROSE CHEVREUX (Bl) M. OSB. AC. Sept 2
d. 1792. The last superior-general of the French Benedictine congregation of St Maur—the Maurists. He was imprisoned with a numerous band of ecclesiastics at the Carmelite monastery of Paris (*Les Carmes*) and put to death in the general massacre of Sept 2. Beatified in 1931.

AUGUSTINE, SANCTIAN and BEATA (SS) MM. AC. Sept 6
d. 273. Three Spanish Christians, who fled to Gaul in time of persecution and were martyred near Sens, where they are still venerated.

AUGUSTINE OTA (Bl) M. SJ. AC. Sept 25
1622 (Aug 10). A native of Firando, Japan, who helped the missionaries as a catechist, was imprisoned at Iki, received into the Society of Jesus in prison, and beheaded at Iki. Beatified in 1867.

AUGUSTINE and PAULINUS (SS) Mks. OSB. AC. Nov 5
6th cent. According to the Cassinese tradition, they were monks sent by St Benedict to the foundation of Terracina.

AUGUSTINE MOI (Bl) M. AC. Dec 18
d. 1839. A poor day-labourer in Tonkin, a Dominican tertiary, he was strangled because he refused to trample on the crucifix. Beatified in 1900.

AUGUSTUS CHAPDELAINE (Bl) M. AC. Feb 27
1814–1856. Born in France, the ninth child of a peasant. After his ordination to the priesthood in the Paris Society of Foreign Missions, he served as a curate, and then went to China to work as a missionary priest in the apostolic vicariate of Kwang-si. He was put to death with every refinement of cruelty. Beatified in 1900.

AUGUSTUS (St) M. RM. May 7
See Flavius, Augustus, and Augustine.

AUGUSTUS (St) C. RM. Sept 1
See Priscus, Castrensis, etc.

AUGUSTUS (St) C. RM. Oct 7
6th cent. An abbot of Bourges in France, friend of St Germanus of Paris. He is chiefly notable for having discovered the body of St Ursinus, apostle of that district.

AULAIRE (St) VM. RM. Feb 12
Otherwise Eulalia of Barcelona, q.v.

AULD (St) Bp. Feb 4
Otherwise Aldate, q.v.

AUNAIRE (St) Bp. RM. Sept 25
Otherwise Anacharius, q.v.

AUREA (ORIA) (St) V. OSB. AC. March 11
d. *c.* 1069. An anchoress, attached to the Benedictine abbey of San Millán de la Cogolla in the old kingdom of Navarre,

Upper Ebro, Spain. She lived under obedience of the abbot and was directed by St. Dominic of Silos. She died at the age of twenty-seven.

AUREA (AURA) (St) WM.
RM. July 19

d. 856. Born at Cordova, daughter of infidel parents, in her widowhood she became a Christian and a nun at Cuteclara, where she remained for more than twenty years. She was then denounced as a Christian by her own family and beheaded.

AUREA (St) VM.   RM. Aug 24

d. c.270. The Acts of St Aurea's martyrdom are described as a "hagiographical romance". But her existence is vouched for by the early cultus at her shrine at Ostia.

AUREA (St) Abs.   RM. Oct 4

d. 666. A Syrian lady, placed by St Eligius at the head of the nunnery of St Martial at Paris (633). She governed the community thirty-three years and died of the plague, together with one hundred and sixty of her nuns.

AUREA (St) Abs.   AC. Oct 6

8th cent. A young girl of Amiens who retired to Boves and eventually became the abbess of a numerous community.

AURELIA and NEOMISIA (SS) VV.
RM. Sept 25

? Born in Asia, they visited Palestine and Rome. At Capua they were maltreated by the Saracens (?) but escaped under cover of a thunderstorm. They took shelter at Macerata, near Anagni, where they died.

AURELIA (St) V. OSB. RM. Oct 15

d. 1027. A French princess who spent fifty-five years as a recluse at Strasburg under the obedience of a Benedictine abbey. Her name has been associated with that of St Wolfgang.

AURELIA (St) M.   RM. Dec 2
See Eusebius, Marcellus, etc.

AURELIAN (St) Bp.   AC. May 10

(1st or) 3rd cent. Disciple of St Martial of Limoges, and eventually bishop of that city.

AURELIAN (St) Bp.   RM. June 16

d. c.550. Raised to the see of Arles in 546, he was appointed papal legate in Gaul by Pope Vigilius. He founded two monasteries, one for monks and one for nuns, and drew up for each a monastic rule, based on that of St Caesarius.

AURELIAN (St) Bp. OSB. AC. July 4

d. 895. Monk and abbot of Ainay and afterwards archbishop of Lyons.

AURELIUS (St) Bp.   AC. July 20

d. 429. Bishop of Carthage, metropolitan, friend and fellow-worker of St Augustine of Hippo. He was among the first to detect and oppose Pelagianism. He was forced by the violence of his adversaries to invoke the civil power against them, much against his own will.

AURELIUS of CORDOVA (St) M.
RM. July 27

See George, Aurelius, and the translation of their relics to Paris, in the RM. Oct 20.

AURELIUS and PUBLIUS (SS)
Bps. MM.   RM. Nov 12

2nd cent. Two bishops who wrote against the Montanists or Cata-Phrygians. They were martyred, probably in Asia, according to others in N. Africa.

AUREUS, JUSTINA and Comp.
(SS) MM.   RM. June 16

? During an invasion of the Huns, St

Aureus, bishop of Mainz, was driven from his see and was followed by his sister, Justina, and others. On their return, while the bishop was celebrating Mass, he and the others were murdered in the church.

AUSONIUS (St) Bp. M.
AC. May 22
1st (or 3rd) cent. Supposed to have been a disciple of St Martial of Limoges, and first bishop of Angoulême.

AUSPICIUS (St) Bp.   RM. July 8
d. c.130. Said to have been the fourth bishop of Trèves and successor of St Maternus (c.130). It seems, however, that he should be identified with a first-century bishop of Toul of the same name.

AUSPICIUS (St) Bp.   AC. July 8
d. c.475. According to Sidonius Apollinaris, he was bishop of Toul. He was buried at Saint-Mansuy.

AUSPICIUS (St) Bp.   AC. Aug 2
Before 4th cent. Said to have been the first bishop of Apt.

AUSTELL (St) C.   AC. June 28
6th cent. A disciple of St Mewan or Mevan of Cornwall. He lived probably in the district where a place-name preserves his memory. Some modern writers conjecture that Austell (Hawystill) is a woman saint, one of the daughters of the famous Brychan of Wales, who has perhaps left her name to Aust of Awst in Gloucestershire.

AUSTIN (ST)
Otherwise Augustine (especially St Augustine of Canterbury).

AUSTINDUS (St) Bp. OSB.
AC. Sept 25
d. 1068. A native of Bordeaux, he became a monk and then abbot of Saint-Orens, at Auch, where he introduced the Cluniac observance. In 1041 he was elected archbishop of Auch and proved a brave upholder of the rights of his church against simoniacal customs.

AUSTREBERTA (EUSTREBERTA) (St) V. Abs. OSB.   RM. Feb 10
630–704. Born near Thérouanne, in Artois, daughter of St Framechildis and the count palatine Badefrid. She received the veil at the hands of St Omer in the nunnery of Abbeville (Port-sur-Somme) of which she became abbess. As abbess she governed Pavilly in Normandy and proved a most successful ruler.

AUSTREGILDIS (St) W.
AC. Apr 18
Otherwise Agia, q.v.

AUSTREGISILUS (AOUSTRILLE, OUTRILLE) (St) Bp.   RM. May 20
551–624. Born at Bourges, he was educated as a courtier, but preferred the life of a monk and entered the abbey of Saint-Nizier at Lyons, where he became abbot. In 612 he was elected bishop of Bourges. He has always been honoured as a saint.

AUSTREMONIUS (STREMOINE) (St) Bp.   RM. Nov 1
(1st or) 3rd cent. One of the seven missionaries sent from Rome to evangelize Gaul. He preached in Auvergne and was the first bishop of Clermont-Ferrand.

AUSTRICLINIAN (St) C.
RM. June 30
See Martial, Alpinian and Austriclinian.

AUSTRUDE (St) V.   AC. Oct 17
Otherwise Anstrudis, q.v.

AUTBERT (St) Mk. OSB. AC. Feb 1
d. 1129. A Benedictine monk of Landevenec in Brittany, who became chaplain to the nuns of St Sulpice, near Reims. He is honoured liturgically at Reims.

AUTBERT (St) Bp.   AC. Sept 10
d. p. 709. A bishop of Avranches, famous because he founded the abbey-church and monastery of Mont-St-Michel *in periculo maris* on the Normandy coast.

AUTBERT (St) Bp.   RM. Dec 13
d. *c*.669. Bishop of Cambrai-Arras. As such he was a great fosterer of monastic life and the founder of monasteries, among others, of the great abbey of St Vedast (Saint Vaast) at Arras. He does not seem, however, to have been a monk himself. Under him Hainault and Flanders became a vast monastic colony.

AUTBODUS (St) C.   AC. Nov 20
d. 690. An Irish missionary who preached in Artois, Hainault, and Picardy, and died as a hermit near Laon.

AUTEL (St) Bp.   RM. Sept 7
Otherwise Augustalis, q.v.

AUTHAIRE (OYE) (St) C.
AC. Apr 24
7th cent. A courtier at the palace of King Dagobert I of France, and father of St Ouen of Rouen. He is the patron saint of the village La-Ferté-sous-Jouarre, where he usually resided.

AUTHBERTUS (AUDBERT, AUBERT, ALBERT) (*several*)
Otherwise Autbert, q.v.

AUTONOMUS (St) Bp. M.
RM. Sept 12
d. *c*.300. Said by the Greeks to have been an Italian bishop, who, to escape the fury of the persecution under Dio-

cletian, fled into Bithynia in Asia Minor, where he made many converts and afterwards was martyred.

AUTOR (ADINCTOR, AUTEUR) (St) Bp.   AC. Aug 9
5th cent. The thirteenth bishop of Metz. In 830 his relics were translated to the abbey of Marmoutier.

AUXANUS (St) Bp.   RM. Sept 3
d. 568. Known in Milan as Sant' Ansano. He was bishop of that city, where he has always been held in great veneration.

AUXENTIUS (St) H.   RM. Feb 14
d. *c*.470. Born in Syria, of Persian parents, he served as a soldier in the guards of the emperor Theodosius the Younger. Later he retired to live as a hermit in Bithynia. He was accused of heresy at the council of Chalcedon, but most successfully vindicated his orthodoxy.

AUXENTIUS (St) M.   RM. Dec 13
See Eustratius, Auxentius, etc.

AUXENTIUS (St) Bp.   RM. Dec 18
d. p. 321. A soldier in the army of the emperor Licinius, he had to suffer for refusing to take part in idolatrous practices. However, he survived the persecution and became a priest and lastly bishop of Mopsuestia in Cilicia.

AUXIBIUS (St) Bp.   RM. Feb 19
1st cent. Said to have been baptized by St Mark and consecrated by St Paul as first bishop of Soli in Cyprus.

AUXILIUS (St) B.   AC. March 19
d. *c*.460. A companion of St Patrick, he was made bishop and resided at Killossey.

AUXILIUS (St) M.   RM. Nov 27
See Basileus, Auxilius and Saturninus.

AUXILIUS, ISSERNINUS and SECUNDINUS (SS) Bps. AC. Dec 6
5th cent. Fellow-workers under St Patrick in the evangelization of Ireland. The decree signed by the four, reminding the Irish clergy that appeals from the judgment of Armagh may be made to Rome, is still extant.

AVA (or AVIA) (St) Abs. OSB.
AC. Apr 29
d. p. 845. A niece of King Pepin, in her childhood and youth she was blind, but was cured miraculously by St Rainfredis. She entered a nunnery at Denain in Hainault, where she became abbess.

AVENTINUS of CHARTRES (St) Bp.   AC. Feb 4
d. c.520. Bishop of Chartres, in which office he succeeded his brother St Solemnis.

AVENTINUS of TROYES (St) H.
RM. Feb 4
c.538. Born in central France, he acted as almoner to St Lupus, bishop of Troyes, until he retired to live as a hermit. The spot where he thus lived is now called Saint-Aventin.

AVENTINUS (St) M.   AC. June 7
d. 732. Born at Bagnères in the Pyrenees, he became a recluse in the valley of Larboush, where the Saracens discovered him, and put him to death.

AVERTANUS (St) C. OC.
AC. Feb 25
d. 1380. A native of Limoges, where he was professed as a Carmelite laybrother. He died outside Lucca while on a pilgrimage to Palestine.

AVITUS (St) M.   RM. Jan 27
? The RM. mentions a martyr of this name in Africa, who is probably to be identified with the St Avitus, venerated in the Canary Islands as their apostle and first bishop.

AVITUS of VIENNE (St) Bp.
RM. Feb 5
d. c.520. Born in Auvergne and brother to St Apollinaris, bishop of Valence. Their father St Isychius, a Roman senator, had been bishop of Vienne. Avitus succeeded him. As a bishop he commanded the respect of his flock, as also of the pagan Franks and Arian Burgundians. He converted the Burgundian king Sigismund. St Avitus was also an elegant writer.

AVITUS II of CLERMONT (St) Bp.
AC. Feb 21
d. 689. Bishop of Clermont in Auvergne from 676 to 689. He was one of the great bishops who defended and developed the church training of the epoch.

AVITUS (AVY) (St) Ab.
RM. June 17
d. c.530. First a monk of Menat in Auvergne, then abbot of Micy, near Orleans, finally a hermit in the French province of Perche, where he was forced by numerous followers to build, and govern, a new monastery.

AVITUS I of CLERMONT (St) Bp
AC. Aug 21
d. c.600. Eighteenth bishop of Clermont, contemporary of St Gregory of Tours, whom he ordained deacon.

AVITUS (or ADJUTUS) (St) Ab.
RM. Dec 19
? The RM. calls him Adjutus. It seems that he was an abbot of Micy, near Orleans. If so, there must have been two of the same name, and almost contemporaries, in the same abbey (see Avitus, June 17).

AYBERT (St) H. OSB.   Apr 7
Otherwise Aibert, q.v.

AYE (St)   AC. Apr 18 or Sept 1
Otherwise Agia, q.v.

AYMARD (Bl) Ab. OSB.
                                    AC. Oct 5
d. 965. He succeeded St Odo in the
abbacy of Cluny (942); but, after about
ten years he became blind and resigned
his office to St Majolus, giving to all
during the rest of his life an example of
wonderful resignation. Many writers
call him saint.

AZADANES and AZADES (SS) MM.
                                    RM. Apr 22
d. 341–342. The former a deacon, the
latter an officer of high standing at the
court of the Persian king, Shapur II.
They were martyred together with
Abdesus and others.

AZARIAS (AZARIAH) (St)
                                    RM. Dec 16
6th cent. B.C. One of the three youths
cast into the fiery furnace at Babylon by
order of Nebuchadnezzar. The Baby-
lonian officials gave him the name of
Abednego.

AZAS and Comp. (SS) MM.
                                    RM. Nov 19
d. c.304. About one hundred and fifty
Christian soldiers martyred in Isauria,
Asia Minor, under Diocletian.

B

BABILAS (BABYLAS), URBAN, PRILIDIAN and EPOLONIUS (SS) MM. RM. Jan 24
d. *c.*250. Babilas was bishop of Antioch, the most celebrated occupant of that see after St Ignatius. The other three were his pupils. Babilas died in chains awaiting execution under Decius; the three youths were put to death.

BABILLA (St) VM. RM. May 20
Otherwise Basilla, q.v.

BABOLENUS (St) Ab. AC. June 26
d. *c.*677. Monk of Luxeuil under St Columbanus, and afterwards first abbot of St Peter, later St Maur-des-Fossés, near Paris. He was helped by St Fursey in the erection of many churches and hospitals in the diocese of Paris.

BABOLENUS (St) Ab. OSB.
AC. Aug 31
d. *c.*640. Fourth abbot of Bobbio in Italy, where he introduced the Benedictine Rule in place of that of St Columbanus.

BACCHUS (St) M. RM. Oct 7
See Sergius and Bacchus.

BADARN (PADARN) (*several*)
Otherwise Paternus, q.v.

BADEMUS (St) M. AC. Apr 10
*c.*380. A native of Persia, founder and abbot of a monastery near Beth-Lapat in his own country. He suffered martyrdom under Shapur II.

BADILO (St) Ab. OSB. AC. Oct 8
d. *c.*870. A Benedictine monk of Vezelay

(Yonne), who became abbot of Leuze (*Lutsa*) in Hainault.

BADULFUS (BADOUR, BADOLF) (St) Ab. OSB. AC. Aug 19
d. *c.*850. Monk and abbot of Ainay, Lyons. The new *Proprium* of Lyons has a commemoration on Aug 19.

BAGLAN (SS)
? There are two Welsh saints of this name, both attributed to the fifth century, but beyond the fact of there being existing churches dedicated to their honour, and a mention in an ancient litany, nothing is known of them.

BAIN (BAINUS, BAGNUS) (St) Bp. OSB. AC. June 20
d. *c.*710. Monk of Fontenelle under St Wandrille. In 685 he was raised to the see of Thérouanne, which then included Calais. After twelve years he resigned and went back to Fontenelle, and three years later became its abbot. Towards the end of his life he had to govern, in addition, the abbey of Fleury which Pepin had just restored. He is the principal patron saint of Calais.

BAISIL (St)
? Patron of a church in the Llandaff diocese. There is no record of such a saint in Welsh hagiology. It may be that *Baisil* is only a misspelling of some other appellative.

BAITHIN (St) Ab. AC. June 9
d. *c.*598. Also called Comin or Cominus, and described as first cousin to St Columba, whom he succeeded as abbot

of Iona. He is said to have died on the anniversary of the death of St Columba.

BAJULUS (St) M.   RM. Dec 20
See Liberatus and Bajulus.

BALBINA (St) VM.   RM. March 31
d. *c.*130. The RM. has this *laus:* "At Rome, the birthday of St. Balbina the Virgin, daughter of blessed Quirinus the martyr; she was baptized by Pope Alexander, and chose Christ as her Spouse in her virginity; after completing the course of this world she was buried on the Appian Way near her father". Later on, her relics were enshrined in the church dedicated in her name on the Aventine. Modern writers query the truth of all the above statements, admitting merely that there was a Roman virgin of this name.

BALDA (St) Abs. OSB.   PC. Dec 9
d. late 7th cent. Third abbess of Jouarre in the diocese of Meaux. Her relics were enshrined in the abbey church of Nesle-la-Reposte, diocese of Troyes.

BALDEGUNDIS (St) Abs.
                              PC. Feb 10
*c.*580. Abbess of Saint-Croix, Poitiers, one of the most ancient of French nunneries.

BALDERIC (BAUDRY) (St) Ab.
                              AC. Oct 16
7th cent. He and his sister, St Bova, were children of Sigebert I, king of Austrasia. Eventually he became the abbot-founder of Montfaucon in Champagne as well as the founder and protector of a a nunnery at Reims where his sister took the veil.

BALDOMERUS (or GALMIER) (St) Mk.   RM. Feb 27
d. *c.*650. By trade a locksmith at Lyons, later in life he retired to the monastery of St Justus under Abbot Viventius, and

was ordained sub-deacon. He is the patron saint of locksmiths, and is represented in art carrying pincers and blacksmith's tools.

BALDRED (St) Bp.   AC. March 6
d. 756. A Scottish bishop alleged to have been the successor of St Kentigern or Mungo at Glasgow, and to have ended his life as a hermit on the coast of the Firth of Forth. Some identify him with St Balther, the hermit of Tinningham.

BALDUS (St) H.   AC. Oct 29
Otherwise Baud, Baudin, or Bond. See Bond.

BALDWIN (St) Ab. OSB. Cist.
                              AC. July 15
d. 1140. An Italian, who became a monk of Clairvaux under St Bernard and one of the most beloved disciples of the holy founder. He was sent back to Italy as abbot of San Pastore in the diocese of Rieti. He is the principal patron saint of Rieti.

BALDWIN (BALDUINUS, BAUDOIN) (St) M.   AC. Oct 16
d. *c.*680. Son of St Salaberga and brother of St Anstrude, abbess at Laon. He was archdeacon at Laon, and was murdered in circumstances which have led to his being honoured as a martyr.

BALIN (BALANUS, BALLOIN) (St)
                              AC. Sept 3
7th cent. Said to have been the brother of St Gerald (March 13) and one of the four sons of an Anglo-Saxon king. He and his brothers, after accompanying St Colman of Lindisfarne to Iona, retired into Connaught in Ireland and settled at Tecksaxon, "the house of the Saxons," in the diocese of Tuam.

BALSAMUS (Bl) Ab. OSB.
                              AC. Nov 24
d. 1232. Tenth abbot of Cava, which he

governed from 1208 to 1232. He is described by John of Capua, as "the gem of the priesthood and the crown of prelates". Cult approved in 1928.

BALTHASAR (St)   AC. Jan 6
One of the Magi, q.v.

BALTHASAR de TORRES (Bl) M. SJ.   AC. June 20
1563–1626. Born at Granada, he became a Jesuit (1579), was sent to India (1586), taught theology at Goa and Macao, and passed over to Japan (1606) where he remained during the terrible persecution which broke out soon after. He was burnt alive at Nagasaki. Beatified in 1867.

BALTHASAR of CHIAVARI (Bl) C. OFM.   AC. Oct 17
d. 1492. A Friar Minor and fellow preacher with Bl Bernadinus of Feltre. He is venerated in the diocese of Pavia. Cult confirmed in 1930.

BALTHER (BALDRED, BAL-REDUS) (St) Mk. OSB.
                            AC. March 6
d. 756. A monk-priest of Lindisfarne, who became an anchorite at Tinningham on the Scottish border, where he lived on Bass Rock, near North Berwick, surrounded by the sea. His relics were enshrined at Durham, with those of St Bilfrid, the anchorite.

BANDARIDUS (BANDERIK, BANDERY) (St) Bp.   AC. Aug 9
d. 566. Bishop of Soissons from 540 to 566 and founder of Crépin abbey. He was banished by Clotaire I and worked for seven years, without making himself known, as a gardener in an English abbey. At length Clotaire discovered his place of refuge and recalled him to his see. He was buried in the abbey he had founded.

BANKA (St) V.   AC. June 4
Otherwise Breaca, q.v.

BAPTIST or BAPTISTA (*several*)
See under John Baptist.

BARACHISIUS (St) M.
                            RM. March 29
See Jonas, Barachisius, and Comp.

BARADATES (St) H.   AC. Feb 22
d. *c*.460. Theodoret in his *Philotheus* gives a glowing account of this Syrian solitary, whom he calls "the admirable Baradates". The emperor Leo I of Constantinople wrote to consult Baradates regarding the council of Chaldedon.

BARAT, MAGDALEN (St)
                            RM. May 25
See Mary-Magdalen Sophie Barat.

BARBARA (St) VM.   RM. Dec 4
? One of the most popular saints of the Calendar. According to the extant legend, first told by Metaphrastes in the 10th century, she was shut up in a tower by her father, who himself killed her for being a Christian, whereupon he was struck dead by lightning. According to the RM. this happened at Nicomedia under Maximinus Thrax. But the whole legend is obviously spurious, and some doubt whether she ever existed. She is the patron saint of firework makers, artillerymen, architects, founders, stonemasons, grave-diggers, fortifications, magazines, and a protectress against lightning, fire, sudden death and impenitence. In art she is usually represented holding a tower and with the palm of martyrdom.

BARBASYMAS (BARBASCEMIN) and Comp. (SS) MM.   AC. Jan 14
d. 346. Bishop of Seleucia-Ctesiphon in

Persia. Under Shapur II he was incarcerated for eleven months with sixteen companions in an infected prison. After being tortured, they were all put to death.

BARBATIAN (St) C.   RM. Dec 31
5th cent. A priest of Antioch who came to Rome and there attracted the attention of the empress Placidia Augusta. She induced him to fix his residence at Ravenna, near the imperial court, where she built for him a monastery. By his prudent advice he rendered signal services to the state.

BARBATUS (BARBAS) (St) Bp.
RM. Feb 19
*c.*612–682. A native of Benevento where, as a priest and later as a bishop (663), he rendered signal services to his native town, especially when it was besieged by the emperor Constans II of Byzantium. He assisted at the sixth general council, held at Constantinople, at which the Monothelites were condemned.

BARBE (St) VM.   RM. Dec 4
The French for Barbara, q.v.

BARBEA (St) M.   RM. Jan 29
See Sarbelius and Barbea.

BARDO (St) Bp. OSB.
AC. June 10
982–1053. Born at Oppershofen and educated at Fulda, where he received the Benedictine habit and became a dean. In 1029 he was chosen abbot of Werden on the Ruhr, in 1031 abbot of Hersfeld, and in the same year archbishop of Mainz. He was for a time the Chancellor and Grand Almoner of the Empire. He was noted for his love of the poor, the destitute, and of animals. He was also noted for his austerities, which Pope St Leo IX considered too severe and advised him to relax.

BARDOMIAN, EUCARPUS and
Comp. (SS) MM.   RM. Sept 25
? Twenty-eight martyrs of Asia Minor in one of the early persecutions.

BARHADBESCIABAS (St) M.
AC. July 20
d. 355. A deacon of Arbela in Persia beheaded under Shapur II.

BARLAAM (St) M.   RM. Nov 19
d. *c.*304. A martyr of Caesarea in Cappadocia under Diocletian. His memory has been preserved in one of St Basil's homilies, preached in his honour.

BARLAAM and JOSAPHAT (SS)
RM. Nov 27
? These two supposed saints are the protagonists of a Christian version of a Buddhist romance. The present Greek text dates from the 7th century and was popularized by St John Damascene. By a piece of great good fortune the entire text of the apology for Christianity of Aristides, the Athenian, was embodied in the romance and has thus come down to us.

BARNABAS (St) Apostle M.
RM. June 11
1st cent. A native of Cyprus and one of the seventy-two disciples. He is one of the most attractive characters of the New Testament, and the early chapters of the Acts of the Apostles are full of his name and deeds. It was he who "introduced" St Paul to the Apostles and thus to the Church. He was not one of the twelve, but has always been honoured as an apostle. An old tradition has it that he died a martyr in Cyprus. His name is in the Canon of the Mass.

BARNABAS of POLAND (St) H.
OSB. Cam.   AC. July 9
See Justus of Poland.

BARNARD (St) Bp. OSB.
AC. Jan 23

777–841. Born in the Lyonnais, he was educated at the court of Charlemagne. He restored the abbey of Ambournay and became a monk therein and finally abbot. In 810 he was raised to the see of Vienne, and became one of the most influential prelates of his age. As archbishop he founded the abbey of Romans (c.837) where he was buried. Cult as a saint approved in 1907.

BARNOCH (St) C.   AC. Sept 27
Otherwise Barrog, q.v.

BARONTIUS and DESIDERIUS (SS) Mks. OSB.   RM. March 25
c.725. Barontius was a gentleman of Berry who became a monk at Lonrey, diocese of Bourges. As a result of a vision he asked permission to become a hermit, set out for Italy, and established himself in the district of Pistoia. There he lived a most austere life with another monk, Desiderius, by name, who is also honoured as a saint.

BARR (FINBAR, BARROCUS) (St) Bp.   AC. Sept 25
6th cent. A native of Connaught, who founded, and presided over, a monastic school at Lough Eire, thus originating the city of Cork, of which he became first bishop. He died at Cloyne.

BARRFOIN (BAIRRFHIONN BARRINDUS) (St)   AC. May 21
6th cent. Said to have had charge of the church founded by St Columba at Drum Cullen Offaly, and afterwards to have lived at Killbarron, near Ballyshannon, in Donegal. It is added that he reached America on one of his missions by sea, and informed St Brendan the Navigator of his discovery. By some he is said to have been a bishop. The details of his life are very vague.

BARROG (BARRWG, BARNOCH) (St) H.   AC. Sept 27
7th cent. A disciple of the great Welsh St Cadoc, he has left his name (often spelled Barruc or Barnoch) to Barry Island, off the coast of Glamorgan, where he lived as a hermit.

BARSABAS and Comp. (SS) MM.
AC. Oct 20

d. c. 342. A Persian abbot and his eleven monks put to death under Shapur II near the ruins of Persepolis.

BARSABAS (St) M.   RM. Dec 11
d. c.342. A Persian abbot, who, with several of his monks, suffered under Shapur II. Some identify him with St Barsabas of Oct 20, others with St Simeon Barasbae, commemorated on Apr 21.

BARSANUPHIUS (St) H.
RM. Apr 11

d. c.540. An anchorite near Gaza, in Palestine, greatly venerated among the Greeks, who keep his feast on Feb 6. He became by letter the counsellor of the entire region.

BARSENORIUS (St) Ab. OSB.
AC. Sept 13

7th cent. Successor of St Leutfrid (Leufroy) as abbot of La-Croix-Saint-Leuffroi, in the diocese of Evreux. His relics are at Fécamp.

BARSES (BARSO, BARSAS) (St) Bp.   RM. Jan 30
d. c.379. A bishop of Edessa in Syria, banished to W. Egypt on the frontiers of Libya by the Arian emperor Valens. He died in exile.

BARSIMAEUS (BARSAMJA) (St) Bp. M.   RM. Jan 30
? According to the RM., a bishop of Edessa, who, after converting many to the Faith, suffered under Trajan. The

story, however, of his martyrdom is now rejected.

BARTHOLOMAEA BAGNESI (Bl) V. OP.   AC. May 27

1511–1577. Born at Florence, she became a Dominican nun in 1544, and until her death was afflicted with many and varied sufferings, including diabolical obsessions. Cult approved by Pius VII.

BARTHOLOMAEA CAPITANIO (St) V. Foundress   AC. July 27

1807–1836. Together with St Vincenza Gerosa (q.v.) she founded the Italian Sisters of Charity of Lovere. In spite of her extreme youth, she was the real driving force in her Institute throughout her short life. The Institute was approved in 1840, and has 500–600 communities today.

BARTHOLOMEW ALVAREZ (Bl) M. SJ.   AC. Jan 12

d. 1737. A Portuguese, born near Braganza, who joined the Jesuits at Coimbra in 1723. He was sent to Tonkin, where he was arrested in March, 1736, and beheaded the following year.

BARTHOLOMEW ALBAN ROE (Bl) M. OSB.   AC. Jan 21

See Alban Bartholomew Roe.

BARTHOLOMEW AIUTAMI-CRISTO (Bl) H. OSB. Cam.

AC. Jan 28

d. 1224. He received the surname Aiutamicristo ("Christ help me") because this ejaculation was always on his lips. he was born at Pisa, and became a Camaldolese lay-brother at the monastery of San Frediano in his native city. Cult approved in 1857.

BARTHOLOMEW (Hugh) AMIDEI (St)   RM. Feb 12

See Seven Holy Founders.

BARTHOLOMEW of CERVERE (Bl) M. OP.   AC. Apr 21

1420–1466. Born at Savigliano in Piedmont. He taught theology at Turin and afterwards was appointed inquisitor in Piedmont. For his zeal in exercising his office he was killed by heretics at Cervere, diocese of Fossano. Cult approved by Pius IX.

BARTHOLOMEW PUCCI-FRANCESCHI (Bl) C. OFM.

AC. May 23

d. 1330 (May 6). A wealthy married layman of Montepulciano, who, with his wife's consent, became a Franciscan friar, and is usually described as having become "a fool for Christ's sake". Cult confirmed in 1880.

BARTHOLOMEW of DURHAM (St) H. OSB.   AC. June 24

d. c.1193. A native of Whitby who, after being ordained a priest in Norway, became a Benedictine at Durham, and was subsequently given leave by the abbot to lead an eremitical life on Farne Island, in the cell consecrated of old by St Cuthbert. There he spent forty-two years and there he died.

BARTHOLOMEW de VIR (Bl) Bp. OSB. Cist.   PC. June 26

d. 1157. As bishop of Laon (1113–1151) he helped St Norbert in the foundation of Prémontré. In 1121 he built the Cistercian abbey of Foigny, where he became a monk in 1151.

BARTHOLOMEW SONATI (Bl) M. OSM.   AC. Aug 11

See Laurence Nerucci, etc.

BARTHOLOMEW LAUREL (Bl) M. OFM.   AC. Aug 17

d. 1627. Born at Mexico City, he became a Franciscan lay-brother and in 1609 was sent to Manila, where he studied medicine. In 1622 he crossed over to Japan and a few years later was burnt alive at Nagasaki.

BARTHOLOMEW MONFIORE (Bl) M.   AC. Aug 19
d. 1622. A Japanese sailor in the ship of Bl Joachim Firaiama. He was beheaded at Nagasaki. Beatified in 1867.

BARTHOLOMEW (St) Apostle M. RM. Aug 24
1st cent. One of the Twelve, he is usually identified with Nathanael (John I). He is said to have preached in Asia Minor, N.W. India and Greater Armenia, and to have been flayed alive. His relics are enshrined in Rome on the island in the Tiber called after him, Isola di San Bartolomeo.

BARTHOLOMEW GUTIERREZ (Bl) M. OSA.   AC. Sept 3
1538–1632. A native of Mexico, he joined the Augustinian Friars (1596), was ordained at Puebla and sent to Manila in 1606. In 1612 he went to Japan as prior of Ukusi. He worked most zealously, though his life was in continual danger. At last, in 1629 he was betrayed, imprisoned for three years at Omura, and burnt alive at Nagasaki. Beatified in 1867.

BARTHOLOMEW XIKIEMON (Bl) M.   AC. Sept 10
d. 1622. A Japanese layman, beheaded at Nagasaki. He belongs to the group of Bl Charles Spinola, q.v.

BARTHOLOMEW of BRAGANZA (Bl) Bp. OP.   AC. Oct 23
c.1200–1271. Born at Vicenza, he received the Dominican habit at the hands of St Dominic himself at Padua. In 1233 he founded a sort of military order—the *Fratres Gaudentes*—for the preservation of public order. In 1252 he was sent to Cyprus as bishop of Nimesia, whence he was translated to Vicenza (1256). Cult approved in 1793.

BARTHOLOMEW of MARMOU-TIER (Bl) Bp. OSB.   AC. Nov 11
d. 1067. Abbot of Marmoutier, and archbishop of Tours from 1052 to 1067. He was a tireless worker in the face of many difficulties. He strove unavailingly to bring back Berengarius to the Catholic Faith.

BARTHOLOMEW of ROSSANO (St) Ab.   RM. Nov 11
d. 1065. Of Greek extraction, he was born at Rossano, in Calabria. He followed St Nilus to the foundation of Grotta-ferrata, at Frascati, near Rome, under St Basil's Rule and in the Greek rite. St Bartholomew is rightly considered its second founder. He excelled as a composer of Greek hymns. It was he who persuaded Pope Benedict IX to reform his life and do penance at Grotto-ferrata.

BARTHOLOMEW XEKI (Bl) M. AC. Nov 27
d. 1619. A Japanese layman of the royal family of Firando, beheaded at Nagasaki. Beatified 1867.

BARTHOLOMEW FANTI (Bl) C. OC.   AC. Dec 5
1443–1495. Born at Mantua, where he joined the Carmelites. He was the instructor of St John Baptist Spagnuolo, and was famous as a preacher and director of souls as well as for his gift of healing. Cult confirmed in 1909.

BARTHOLOMEW (BARTOLO) BUONPEDONI (Bl) C. AC. Dec 14
d. 1300. Born near San Geminiano, in Italy. he was first a lay-servant at the Benedictine abbey of San Vito, at Pisa. Later he became a Franciscan tertiary. When he was thirty years of age the

bishop of Volterra ordained him priest, and he served the village of Peccioli, near Volterra. The last twenty years of his life he spent as a leper ministering to his fellow-sufferers with infinite patience. Cult confirmed in 1910.

BARULAS (St) M.   RM. Nov 18
See Romanus and Barula.

BARYPSABAS (St) M. AC. Sept 10
1st cent. A hermit from the East who suffered martyrdom in Dalmatia. A Greek legend has it that Barypsabas had carried to Rome a vessel containing some of the Precious Blood which flowed from the side of our Lord on the Cross.

BASIL (St) Bp.   AC. Jan 1
*c.*475. A priest of Arles who became second bishop of Aix, in Provence.

**BASIL and PROCOPIUS (SS) CC.
                              RM. Feb 27**
d. *c.*750. Two courageous defenders of the veneration of images against the emperor Leo the Isaurian.

**BASIL, EUGENE, AGATHO-
DORUS, ELPIDIUS, AETHERIUS,
GAPITO, EPHREM, NESTOR and
ARCADIUS (SS) Bps. MM.
                              RM. March 4**
4th cent. Missionary bishops: the first seven preached in the Crimea and S. Russia; the last two in Cyprus. All are honoured by the Greeks, on March 7, as martyrs.

BASIL (St) Bp.   RM. March 6
d. 335. Consecrated bishop of Bologna by Pope St Sylvester, he ruled his diocese for twenty years, 315–335.

**BASIL of ANCYRA (St) M.
                              RM. March 22**
d. 362. A priest of Ancyra in Galatia, who distinguished himself as a staunch

upholder of orthodoxy against Arianism. Under Julian the Apostate he was cruelly martyred. His Acts appear to be genuine.

**BASIL the YOUNGER (St) H.
                              AC. March 26**
d. 952. An anchorite near Constantinople who was seized as a spy and put to the torture by the imperial officers. Miracles proved his sanctity, and he continued to live and exercise his gift of prophecy. His life was written by his disciple Gregory who shared his solitude.

**BASIL and EMMELIA (SS)
                              RM. May 30**
d. *c.*370. Parents of SS Basil the Great, Gregory of Nyssa, Peter of Sebaste and Macrina the Younger. They were exiled under Galerius Maximinus, but returned after the peace of the Church to their native city of Caesarea in Cappadocia. St Basil was educated by his mother St Macrina the Elder.

**BASIL the GREAT (St) Bp. Dr.
                      RM. June 14 (and Jan 1)**
329–379 (Jan 1). Born at Caesarea in Cappadocia. His parents, his paternal grandparents, his two brothers and one sister, are all honoured as saints. After his studies at Constantinople and Athens, Basil visited the monastic colonies of Egypt, Palestine and Syria, and founded one himself on the river Iris, in Pontus, for which he wrote his Rules, still the standard works of their kind in the East. In 370 he was made metropolitan of Caesarea, and at once entered upon his brave fight for orthodoxy against Arians and Macedonians, who had the support of the imperial authorities at Byzantium. Nothing daunted, Basil saved the whole of Cappadocia for the Catholic faith. For this purpose he spent himself in preaching and writing doctrinal works, in both of which activities he excelled as much as in the

administration of his diocese. His work on the Holy Ghost is still unsurpassed in Catholic theology. He edited also the Eucharistic Liturgy which bears his name. In the East Basil is the first of the three Holy Hierarchs, in the West one of the four Greek Doctors.

BASIL (St) M.   RM. Nov 28
See Stephen, Basil, etc.

BASILEUS (St) M.   RM. March 2
See Jovinus and Basileus.

BASILEUS (St) Bp. M. RM. Apr 26
d. 319. Bishop of Amasea in Pontus, martyred by drowning in the sea under Licinius. The RM. adds that one of his disciples, by name Elpidiphorus, instructed by an angel, recovered the body and gave it Christian burial.

BASILEUS (St) M.   RM. May 23
See Epitacius and Basileus.

BASILEUS, AUXILIUS and SATURNINUS (SS) MM.
                            RM. Nov 27
? Basileus, a bishop of an unknown see, was put to death at Antioch in Syria together with Auxilius and Saturninus. Nothing further is known about them.

BASILIAN (St) M.   RM. Dec 18
See Theotimus and Basilian.

BASILIDES, TRIPOS, MANDAL and Comp. (SS) MM. RM. June 10
270–275. A group of twenty-three Christians martyred at Rome on the Aurelian Way, under Aurelian. Probably to be identified with the next group (June 12).

BASILIDES, CYRINUS, NABOR and NAZARIUS (SS) MM.
                            RM. June 12
? The RM. has this *laus:* "At Rome on

the Aurelian Way, the birthday of the holy martyrs Basilides, Cyrinus, Nabor, and Nazarius, soldiers who were cast into prison in the persecution of Diocletian and Maximian, under the prefect Aurelius for the confession of the Christian name, scourged with scorpions and beheaded." It seems, however, more likely that this group is the result of confusion of names in the martyrologies: Basilides is probably the Roman martyr of June 10: Cyrinus (or Quirinus) the martyr of June 4; Nabor and Nazarius, two Milanese martyrs, of whom nothing can be ascertained.

BASILIDES (St) M.   RM. June 30
d. 205. A soldier of the guard of the prefect of Egypt, told off to execute St Potamiana, whom he defended from the insults of the mob. He was rewarded with the gift of faith, for which he was martyred shortly after under Septimius Severus.

BASILIDES and Comp. (SS) MM.
                            RM. Dec 23
See Theodulus, Saturninus, etc.

BASILISCUS (BASILICUS) (St) M.
                            RM. March 3
See Cleonicus, Eutropius and Basiliscus.

BASILISCUS (St) M.   RM. May 22
d. 312. Bishop of Comana in Pontus, Asia Minor. He was beheaded under Maximin the Thracian and his body thrown into a river near Nicomedia. It was recovered and translated to Comana. This was the martyr who appeared to St John Chrysostom on the eve of the holy doctor's death.

BASILISSA (St) VM.   RM. Jan 9
See Julian, Basilissa, etc.

BASILISSA (St) M.   RM. March 22
See Callinica and Basilissa.

BASILISSA and ANASTASIA (SS) MM.   RM. Apr 15

d. *c*.68. Noble Roman ladies, disciples of the Apostles Peter and Paul, whose bodies they buried. They were martyred themselves under Nero. Some modern writers have cast doubts on their existence.

BASILISSA (St) VM.   RM. Sept 3

d. *c*.303. The RM. has her full story: "At Nicomedia, the passion of St Basilissa virgin and martyr; though she was only nine years of age, yet by the power of God, she overcame scourges, fire and the beasts under the governor Alexander, in the persecution of the emperor Diocletian; by this she converted the governor to the faith of Christ, and at length she gave up her spirit to God, while she was at prayer outside the city."

BASILISSA (St) Abs. OSB.
PC. Dec 5

d. *c*.780. A Benedictine abbess at the nunnery of Oehren (*Horreum*) in the diocese of Trèves.

BASILLA (St) M.   RM. May 17

See Adrio, Victor and Basilla.

BASILLA (St) VM.   RM. May 20

d. 304. A Roman maiden, betrothed to a pagan patrician, whom she refused to marry on becoming a Christian. Forced to choose between her bridegroom and death, she at once chose the latter and was accordingly martyred for Christ. This summary of her *Acta* shows that they conform to a type common in hagiological literature.

BASILLA (St) V.   RM. Aug 29

? A holy woman, who, according to the RM., died at Smyrna. Other martyrologies, instead of Smyrna, have Sirmium in Pannonia (now Mitrovica).

BASINUS (St) Bp. OSB.
AC. March 4

d. *c*.705. Monk and abbot of the Benedictine monastery of St Maximin at Trèves, he succeeded St Numerian as bishop of the city. In this capacity he greatly helped the English missionaries, notably St Willibrord. He died at St Maximin, whither he had again retired in his old age.

BASOLUS (BASLE) (St) H.
RM. Nov 26

c.555–620. A native of Limoges, he became a monk at Verzy, near Reims, and then a hermit, living for forty years in a cell on the top of a hill overlooking the city. He was celebrated as a wonder-worker.

BASSA (St) M.   RM. March 6

See Victor, Victorinus, etc.

BASSA, PAULA and AGATHONICA (SS) VV. MM.
RM. Aug 10

? Three Christian maidens registered in the accepted lists as having been martyred at Carthage.

BASSA, THEOGONIUS, AGAPIUS and FIDELIS (SS) MM. RM. Aug 21

d. 304. Bassa, wife of a pagan priest, was martyred with her three sons at Edessa (Larissa) in Greece under Diocletian. Like the mother of the Maccabees, she chose to suffer last in order to encourage her children in their agony. Their cult is ancient, though the *Acta* are untrustworthy.

BASSIAN (St) Bp.   RM. Jan 19

d. 413. A Sicilian by birth, he became bishop of Lodi in Lombardy. He was held in high esteem by his friend St Ambrose of Milan, with whom he attended the council of Aquileia (381) and whom he assisted at his death (390).

BASSIAN (St) M.   RM. Feb 14
See Cyrion, Bassian, etc.

BASSIAN (St) M.   RM. Dec 9
See Peter, Successus, etc.

**BASSUS, ANTONY and PROTO-
LICUS (SS) MM.   RM. Feb 14**
? A group of martyrs who were cast
into the sea at Alexandria in Egypt.
Some ancient accounts add nine fellow-
sufferers to this group.

BASSUS (St) M.   RM. May 11
See Maximus, Bassus and Fabius.

**BASSUS, DIONYSIUS, AGAPI-
TUS and Comp. (SS) MM.**
                         RM. Nov 20
? A band of forty-three Christians put
to death at Heraclea in Thrace.

BASSUS (St) Bp. M.   RM. Dec 5
d. c.250. Bishop of Nice in Gaul. He
was martyred under Decius by having
his body transfixed with two huge
nails.

BATHILDIS (St) Queen, OSB.
                         RM. Jan 30
d. 680. An English girl sold as a slave to
the mayor of the palace of the kingdom
of Neustria. King Clovis II married her
in 649, and she became the mother of
three future kings. After her husband's
death she was for eight years regent of
France (656–664). When Clotaire III
came of age, she entered the nunnery of
Chelles, which she had founded, and
lived there as a simple nun. Her biography was written by a contemporary.

**BATHUS, WEREKA and Comps.
(SS) MM.   AC. March 26**
d. 370. They were Goths who embraced
Christianity to the great irritation of
their King, Jungerich or Athanaric.
They were all burnt to death in a church.

BAUDACARIUS (St) Mk. OSB.
                         AC. Dec 21
d. 650. Monk of Bobbio, in N. Italy. His
relics were solemnly translated in 1483.

BAUDELIUS (St) M.   RM. May 20
2nd (or 3rd) cent. A native of Orleans,
a married man, who worked zealously
in the cause of Christianity. He was
martyred at Nîmes. His cult spread
throughout France and N. Spain: there
are some four hundred churches dedicated in his honour.

BAUDRY (St) C.   AC. Oct 16
Otherwise Balderic, q.v.

BAVO (St) H. OSB.   RM. Oct 1
c.589–654. Born in Brabant, in the district of Liège, in his early years he led a
very irregular life. Left a widower, he
was converted by a sermon of St
Amandus and entered upon a course of
canonical penance. Next he founded the
abbey of St Peter on his estate at Ghent
(later called St Bavo's), and became a
monk under St Amandus. Finally he
lived as a recluse in the forest of Mal-
médun, and in a cell by St Peter's.

BAYA and MAURA (SS) VV.
                         AC. Nov 2
10th cent.? Recluses in Scotland, St
Baya being the instructress of St Maura,
and the latter in her turn the abbess of
a community which attached itself to
her. Some authors identify St Baya
with St Begha or Bee. Possibly they
should be identified with SS Maura and
Britta, q.v.

BEAN (St) Bp.   AC. Oct 26
d. p.1012. Bishop of Mortlach in Banff,
from which see he was later transferred
to Aberdeen.

BEAN (St) Bp.   RM. Dec 16
? Bishop of Leinster in Ireland.

BRANDAN (BREANDAN) (St) Ab.
AC. Jan 11
5th cent. An Irishman who crossed into
Britain and had to suffer much there at
the hands of the Pelagians. He took
refuge in a monastery of Gaul, of which
he eventually became abbot.

BEATA (St) M.   RM. March 8
See Cyril, Rogatus, etc.

BEATA (St) M.   AC. Sept 6
See Augustine, Sanctian.

BEATRIX II of ESTE (Bl) N. OSB.
AC. Jan 18
d. 1262. A niece of Bl Beatrix I of
Este (see May 10). Being bereft of her
husband (or fiancé) at an early age, she
founded, in the teeth of much opposition, the Benedictine convent of St
Antony at Ferrara and became a nun
there. Cult confirmed in 1774.

BEATRIX of LENS (Bl) N. OSB.
Cist.   AC. Jan 19
d. p.1216. Born at Lens, in the diocese
of Arras. She founded the Cistercian
monastery of Epinlleu near Mons, and
became a nun there.

BEATRIX d'ORNACIEUX (Bl)
NO. Cart.   AC. Feb 13
d. 1309 (Nov 25). A Carthusian nun
of Parménie, and one of the foundresses
of the Esmue nunnery of the same order.
For many years she had remarkable
mystical experiences as well as diabolical
persecutions. Cult confirmed in 1869.

BEATRIX I of ESTE (Bl) VN.
OSB.   AC. May 10
1206–1226. Daughter of the Marchese
Azzo d'Este, she was left an orphan at
the age of six. When she was fourteen
she secretly left her home, and, against
the wishes of her relatives, became a
Benedictine nun at Solarola, near

Padua. Shortly afterwards she was transferred to Gemmola, where she died a
victim of loving self-immolation. Cult
confirmed in 1763.

BEATRIX (St) M.   RM. July 29
See Simplicius, Faustinus and Beatrix.

BEATRIX (Bl) N. OSB. Cist.
PC. July 29
d. 1268. Cistercian nun of Valfleury, who
became prioress of Our Lady of Nazareth, near Lier, in Brabant. Cult not
yet officially approved.

BEATRIX (BRITES) da SILVA (Bl)
Abs. OSB. Cist.   AC. Aug 16
1424–1490. Born in Portugal, a daughter
of the count of Viana. At the age of
twenty she accompanied Princess Isabel
of Portugal to the Spanish court. Soon
after she entered the Cistercian nunnery
of St Dominic of Silos at Toledo. Later
she founded the Congregation of the
Immaculate Conception (Conception-
ists) under the Benedictine Rule. After
Bl Beatrix's death Cardinal Cisneroo
gave them the rule of St Clare. Cult
confirmed in 1926.

BEATUS (St) Mk.   AC. Feb 19
d. 789. A native of Asturias, in Spain,
monk and priest of Liébana, famous for
his firm stand against Helipandus,
Archbishop of Toledo and other
Adoptionists. When the Adoptionists
were condemned, the saint retired to
the monastery of Valcavado, where he
wrote his commentary on the Apocalypse.

BEATUS (St) Bp.   AC. March 8
Otherwise Beoadh, q.v.

BEATUS (St) H.   RM. May 9
? An early hermit, venerated as the
apostle of Switzerland. His hermitage
was at the place now called Beatenberg,
above the lake of Thun.

BECAN (BEGAN) (St) Ab.
AC. Apr 5
6th cent. One of the "twelve Apostles of Ireland". He was connected by blood with St Columba. He founded a monastery at Kill-Beggan, Westmeath, which centuries later became a Cistercian abbey. He also gave its name to the church and parish of Imleach-Becain, Meath.

BECAN (St) H.   AC. May 26
6th cent. An Irish hermit in the time of St Columba. He lived in the neighbourhood of Cork.

BECHE, JOHN (Bl) M.   AC. Dec 1
See John Beche.

BEDE the YOUNGER (St) Mk. OSB.   AC. Apr 10
d. 883. One of the chief officials at the court of Charles the Bald of France, who became a Benedictine at the abbey of Gavello, near Rovigo, in N. Italy. He refused several bishoprics. His relics were translated to Subiaco in the 19th cent.

BEDE the VENERABLE (St) Dr. OSB.   RM. May 27
673–735. Born at Wearmouth, he was offered as a child to the double abbey of SS Peter and Paul at Wearmouth-Jarrow, was professed there under the founder St Benedict Biscop, and there he spent his whole life, "always writing, always praying, always reading, always teaching". He was ordained priest by St John of Beverley, and it was owing to this dignity, then rather rare among monks, that he was styled Venerable, the title by which priests were usually addressed at that time, much as nowadays they are called reverend. The Bible was his principal study, and then history. His *Ecclesiastical History of the English People* has earned for him the title of Father of English History. He is the type of the Benedictine scholar of all periods, and has been declared Doctor of the Church. He died on Ascension Eve, and his dying words were *Gloria Patri et Filio et Spiritui Sancto*.

BEE (St) V.   AC. Oct 31
Otherwise Bega, q.v.

BEGA (BEGH, BEE) (St) V.
AC. Oct 31
d. 681. An Irish maiden who founded a nunnery on the promontory of St Bee's Head, in Cumberland, which still perpetuates her memory, as does also the name of the village, Kilbees, in Scotland. Two other saints of the same name are mentioned by hagiographers, a nun in Yorkshire and an abbess at Kilbees.

BEGGA (St) W. Abs. OSB.
RM. Dec 17
d. 698. Daughter of Bl Pepin of Landen and of St Ida, and sister of two other saints. She married Angisilus (Ansegis), son of St Arnulf of Metz, and of their union was born Pepin of Heristal, the founder of the Carolingian dynasty. After her husband's death St Begga founded a nunnery at Andenne on the Meuse, which she governed as abbess.

BELINA (St) VM.   AC. Feb 19
d. 1135. A peasant girl of the district of Troyes (France), who died in defence of her chastity, threatened by the feudal lord of the territory. Canonized in 1203.

BELLATANUS and SAVINUS (BB) HH. OSB. Cam.   AC. May 19
? Camaldolese hermits of Montacuto in the neighbourhood of Perugia.

BELLINUS (St) Bp. M.   RM. Nov 26
d. 1151. A bishop of Padua who suffered death in the faithful discharge of

pastoral duties, and was canonized three centuries later by Pope Eugene IV.

BENEDICT
Note. In Latin Benedictus; in Italian: Benedetto; in French: Benoît; in Spanish: Benito; in Portuguese: Bento; in Catalan: Benet (accent on the second syllable); in German: Benedikt; in English: Benet and Benedict.

BENEDICT BISCOP (St) Ab. OSB.
RM. Jan 12

628–690. A Northumbrian by birth, Biscop Baducing made two pilgrimages to Rome early in life, and after the second became a monk at Lérins. After a third journey to Rome he returned to England and founded the abbey of Wearmouth and Jarrow (674–682). Twice more he visited Rome, whence he brought the precentor of the Vatican to train the English monks in the Roman ways. He was the spiritual father of the Venerable Bede.

BENEDICT RICASOLI (Bl) H.
OSB. Vall.   AC. Jan 20

d. 1107. Born at Coltiboni, in the diocese of Fiesole. He entered the monastery founded by his parents for the monks of Vallumbrosa on a mountain near Coltiboni. Later he became a hermit in a cell near by. Cult confirmed in 1907.

BENEDICT of ANIANE (St) Ab.
OSB.   AC. Feb 11

751–821. A Visigoth, by name Witiza, born in Languedoc, he served as a cup-bearer at the court of Pepin and Charlemagne. In 774 he became a monk at Saint-Seine, near Dijon, and was appointed cellarer. In 782 he founded an abbey on his native estate, in Languedoc, by the brook Aniane. The emperor ordered him to undertake the oversight of all the abbeys of Languedoc, Provence and Gascony, and eventually also

the reform of all the French and German houses. As a kind of model abbey St Benedict, with the help of Louis the Pious, founded the abbey of Corneli-münster, near Aix-la-Chapelle. It was at Aix-la-Chapelle that he presided over a meeting of all the abbots of the empire (817)—a turning point in Benedictine history.

BENEDICT REVELLI (St) Bp.
OSB.   AC. Feb 12

c.900. He is said to have been a Benedictine monk of Santa Maria dei Fonti, and then a hermit on the island of Gallinaria, in the Gulf of Genoa. In 870 he was chosen Bishop of Albenga towards the western end of the Ligurian riviera. Cult confirmed by Pope Gregory XVI.

BENEDICT (MANETTUS) DELL' ANTELLA (St)   RM. Feb 12
See Manettus.

BENEDICT of CAGLIARI (St) Bp.
OSB.   AC. Feb 17

d. p.1112. Monk of the monastery attached to the basilica of St Saturninus, at Cagliari, in Sardinia. He was bishop of Dolia, also in Sardinia, from 1107 to 1112. In his old age he resigned and returned to his abbey, where he died shortly after.

BENEDICT CRISPUS of MILAN
(St) Bp.   RM. March 11

d. 725. Archbishop of Milan, he governed his see for forty-five years. He composed the epitaph for the tomb of Ceadwaller, king of Wessex, buried in St Peter's Rome.

BENEDICT (St) Ab. Founder
RM. March 21

c.480–550. Born in the district of Norcia, in Umbria, central Italy, he was sent to Rome for his studies; but fled from the moral dangers which beset him and joined (*c*.500) a sort of community of ecclesiastical students at Affile. Shortly after he retired to a cave near Subiaco—now the Sacro Speco—to live as a hermit. Here his sanctity was soon discovered and many disciples flocked to him; for these he built a *laura*, composed of twelve small monasteries, himself retaining the command over all. About the year 530 he left Subiaco for Montecassino, where on the road to Naples he founded the great arch-abbey and where he lived till his death, famous as a wonder-worker. Here, too, he promulgated his Rule, which is justly considered one of the most potent factors in building up the civilization of Christian Europe. Eventually it became the norm for all western monks, and was simply called "The Holy Rule". The little we know of St Benedict's own personality shows him to us as a strong but lovable character. He died standing erect in prayer before the altar. It is generally considered that he was a deacon, but not a priest. His life was written by St Gregory the Great, Dialogues Bk II. The French tradition maintains that the remains of St Benedict were translated to Fleury in 703. This is contested by the monks of Montecassino. It seems that a translation of at least some of St Benedict's relics to Fleury in the 8th century must be admitted. Proclaimed Patron of Europe by Paul VI in 1964.

BENEDICT of CAMPANIA (St) H.
RM. March 23
d. *c*.550. A contemporary of St Benedict of Montecassino, and a hermit in the Campagna, who was delivered by a miracle from death by burning at the hands of Totila the Goth.

BENEDICT the MOOR (St) C.
OFM.   RM. Apr 4
1526–1589. Called in Italian "il Moro"
—"the Black". He was in fact born of Negro parents, serfs near Messina in Sicily. He first became a hermit and then joined the Friars Minor of the Observance at Palermo as a lay-brother. Nevertheless, he was appointed guardian and novice-master of the friary and he excelled in both offices. His heart, however, was in the kitchen, whither he returned in his old age. Beatified in 1743 and canonized in 1807.

BENEDICT (BÉNÉZET) the
BRIDGE-BUILDER (St) C.
AC. Apr 14
d. 1184. A shepherd boy of Avignon who, as the result of a vision, asked the blessing and help of the bishop of the city to build a bridge at a dangerous ford over the Rhône. A series of miracles accompanied the carrying out of the work.

BENEDICT JOSEPH LABRE (St) C.
RM. Apr 16
1748–1783. A native of Amettes, then in the diocese of Boulogne-sur-Mer. He came of a family of small shopkeepers and was educated by an uncle, a priest. He tried without success to join the Trappists. Then he found his vocation as a pilgrim-beggar, tramping from shrine to shrine throughout Europe, living on alms, and spending long hours before the Blessed Sacrament. He died in Rome during Holy Week. He was beatified in 1860 and canonized in 1883.

BENEDICT of URBINO (Bl) C.
OFM. Cap.   AC. Apr 30
1560–1625. Born at Urbino, of the family de' Passionei, he was a lawyer at Urbino before he joined the Capuchin friars at Fano (1584). He was the companion of St Laurence of Brindisi, whom he followed to Austria and Bohemia. He died at the monastery of Fossombrone. Beatified in 1867.

BENEDICT of SZKALKA (St) M.
AC. May 1
d. 1012. A hermit on Mount Zobor in Hungary near the Benedictine monastery. He was trained by St Andrew Zorard (q.v.). Renowned like his master for his austerity and gifts of contemplation, he was killed by marauders in 1012. Canonized in 1083.

BENEDICT II (St) Pope RM. May 8
d. 685. A Roman by birth, he was chosen pope in 683, but his enthronement was delayed a year awaiting the arrival of the confirmation from Constantinople. He governed the Church eleven months.

BENEDICT XI (Bl) Pope, OP.
RM. July 7
1240–1304. A native of Treviso, Nicholas Boccasini, as he was called in baptism, joined the Dominicans and became their ninth master-general. Eventually he was created cardinal-bishop of Ostia and papal legate. He was elected pope in 1303. He continued to the end his religious observances and penances. Beatified in 1736.

BENEDICT d'ALIGNAN (Bl) Bp.
OFM.   PC. July 8
d. 1268. A Benedictine abbot who was chosen bishop of Marseilles. He made a pilgrimage to the Holy Land, and on his return resigned the bishopric and joined the Friars Minor.

BENEDICT (St) Bp.   AC. July 15
d. c.820. Bishop of Angers in the reign of Louis the Pious.

BENEDICT de CASTRO (Bl) M.
SJ.   AC. July 15
d. 1570. A native of Chacim, diocese of Miranda in Portugal. He belonged to the group of Jesuit martyrs under the leadership of Bl Ignatius Azevedo, q.v., killed by Calvinistic pirates.

BENEDICT of AREZZO (Bl) C.
OFM.   AC. Aug 31
d. 1281. One of the first companions of St Francis of Assisi, and subsequently one of the first Franciscan provincials. He was sent to Greece, Rumania, the Holy Land and Constantinople, where he gave the Franciscan habit to the Emperor.

BENEDICT of MACERAC (St) Ab.
AC. Oct 22
d. 845. A Greek abbot who fled from Petras and settled at Macerac, in the diocese of Nantes. His relics were later transferred to the abbey of Redon.

BENEDICT of SEBASTE (St) Bp.
RM. Oct 23
d. c.654. An alleged bishop of Sebaste in Samaria, who had to escape to Gaul during the persecution of Julian the Apostate. He built a hermitage near Poitiers which later became the abbey of St Benedict of Quincay. Not all the above details, however, are above suspicion.

BENEDICT, JOHN, MATTHEW, ISAAC and CHRISTINUS (CHRISTIAN) (SS) MM. OSB.
RM. Nov 12
d. 1005. Italian Benedictines who followed St Adalbert of Prague to the mission among the Slavs, and were massacred by robbers at their monastery near Gnesen (May 11). They were canonized by Julius II.

BENEDICT de PONTE (Bl) C. OP.
PC. Nov 22
13th cent. Dominican missionary among the Tartars. He died immediately after preaching a sermon.

BENEDICTA (St) VM. RM. Jan 4
See Priscus, Priscillian and Benedicta.

BENEDICTA (St) V.   RM. May 6
6th cent. A nun of the convent founded in Rome by St Galla, of whom St Gregory the Great narrates that her death was foretold to her by St Peter in a vision.

BENEDICTA (St) VM. ?
                                RM. June 29
? The RM. styles her simply "a virgin in the territory of Sens". Later legends add that she was a sister of SS Augustine and Sanctian, all three natives of Spain, and that they passed into France and were martyred under Aurelian.

BENEDICTA and CAECILIA
(SS) Abs. OSB.   PC. Aug 17
10th cent. These two daughters of the king of Lorraine became nuns and successive abbesses of Susteren in the Rhineland.

BENEDICTA (St) VM. RM. Oct 8
? The RM. has only this *laus*: "In the country of Laon (the birthday) of St Benedicta, Virgin and Martyr." Further details, added by later writers, are conflicting.

BENEDICTINE MARTYRS (BB)
                                AC. Dec 1
See Richard Whiting, Hugh Faringdon and John Beche.

BÉNÉZET (St) C.   AC. Apr 14
See Benedict the Bridge-Builder.

BENIGNUS (St) M.   RM. Feb 13
d. *c*.303. A priest of Todi in Umbria, put to death under Diocletian.

BENIGNUS (St) Ab. OSB.
                                AC. March 20
d. 725. Monk and abbot of Fontenelle, he was exiled from the abbey and retired to Flay where the monks asked him to be their abbot. After the victory of Charles Martel, he returned to Fontenelle, retaining the government of Flay, and died shortly after.

BENIGNUS (St) M.   RM. Apr 3
See Evagrius and Benignus.

BENIGNUS (St) Mk. OSB. Cist.
                                PC. June 20
13th cent. Cistercian monk at Breslau, in Silesia, martyred by the Tartars with many other members of his abbey. The Cistercian menologies commemorate him on June 20.

BENIGNUS (St) Bp. M. RM. June 28
6th cent. This bishop is mentioned in a decretal of Pope Pelagius II as desirous of resigning his see. He appears to have retired to Utrecht; at any rate the RM. places him there, and his relics were there rediscovered in 996.

BENIGNUS VISDOMINI (Bl) Ab.
OSB. Vall.   AC. July 17
d. 1236. A Florentine priest, who fell into sin, repented and entered the abbey of Vallombrosa. He became abbot-general but, always conscious of his past guilt, resigned and died as a hermit.

BENIGNUS (St) Mk. OSB.
                                AC. July 21
See John and Benignus.

BENIGNUS (St) M.   RM. Nov 1
3rd cent. A martyr venerated at Dijon from early times, over whose tomb there was erected the magnificent abbey church—now cathedral—of St Benignus. His alleged connexion with St Polycarp of Smyrna is rejected by most modern writers.

BENIGNUS (BENEN) (St) Bp.
                                AC. Nov 9
d. *c*.466. "Benen, son of Sessenen, St Patrick's Psalmsinger." A favourite disciple of St Patrick, whom he succeeded as chief bishop of the Irish church. He preached, it is said, chiefly in Clare and Kerry and founded a monastery at Drumlease. His connexion with Glastonbury has no historical foundation.

BENIGNUS (St) Bp.   RM. Nov 20
d. *c*.477. Archbishop of Milan, during whose pontificate the Heruli, under Odoacer, occupied the city.

BENILDIS (St) M.   RM. June 15
d. 853. A woman of Cordova, who was so moved by the fortitude displayed by St Athanasius, a Spanish priest, during his martyrdom at the hands of the Moors, that she braved death at the stake on the following day. Her ashes were thrown into the Guadalquivir.

BENILDUS (Bl) C.   Aug 13
1805–1862. Peter Romancon of Thuret, diocese of Clermont, France, joined the Brotherhood of Christian Schools, and combined the work of education with a life of prayer and devotion to his religious rule. Beatified April 4 1948.

BENINCASA (Bl) Ab. OSB.
**   AC. Jan 10**
d. 1194. Eighth abbot of La Cava, near Salerno, from 1171 to 1194. It was during his abbacy that a hundred monks were sent from Cava to staff the new monastery of Monreale founded by the king of Sicily in that island. Cult confirmed in 1928.

BENINCASA (Bl) C. OSM.
**   AC. May 11**
1376–1426. A native of Florence, who joined the Servites at Montepulciano. He spent his whole life as a hermit, first at Montagnata, near Siena, and then in the almost inaccessible cave of Montechiello. Cult confirmed in 1829.

BENJAMIN (St) M.   RM. March 31
c.421. A Persian deacon who, having been imprisoned for the Faith, and refusing as a condition of his release to cease preaching Christianity, was tortured to death under Isdegerdes.

BENNO (St) Bp.   RM. June 16
1010–1106. Born at Hildesheim and educated at the abbey of St Michael in his native city. He became canon of Gozlar, chaplain to the emperor Henry III and finally bishop of Meissen. He is one of the protagonists in the quarrel between Pope Gregory VII and Henry IV. He upheld the former but not at all times with equal zeal. In later years he preached to the Wends. His canonization in 1525 roused Luther to fury.

BENNO (Bl) Bp. OSB.   AC. July 12
d. 1088. A Swabian, he was educated and professed as a Benedictine at Reichenau, where he was taught by Bl Herman the Cripple. He himself became the headmaster at Gozlar in Hanover, and finally of the cathedral school of Hildesheim. He was also the official architect to Henry III. He was archbishop of Osnabrück (1067) and as such always upheld the pope's cause. He founded Iburg abbey where he retired to die.

BENNO (Bl) Bp. OSB.   AC. Aug 3
d. 940. A Swabian, canon of Strasburg, he became a hermit on Mt Etzel, in Switzerland, St Meinrad's former hermitage. He lived there with a few disciples, thus becoming the founder of the abbey of Einsiedeln, which still exists. In 927 he was called to the see of Metz. Striving to remedy abuses, he was attacked and blinded by those whom he had rebuked. He resigned and returned to Einsiedeln, which had already grown into a numerous community.

BENTIVOGLIO de BONIS (Bl) C.
OFM.   AC. Jan 2
d. 1232 (Dec 25). Born at San Severino, in the Italian Marches, he was one of St Francis's earliest disciples, and as such he is mentioned in the *Fioretti*. Cult confirmed by Pius IX.

BENVENUTA BOJANI (Bl) V. Tert. OP.   AC. Oct 30

d. 1292. The seventh of seven daughters, christened by her parents Benvenuta, although they had asked for a son. Having become a Dominican tertiary at an early age, she spent her whole life at her home in Cividale, N. Italy, busy with her domestic duties, praying, and working miracles. Cult approved in 1763.

BENVENUTUS SCOTIVOLI (St) Bp. OFM.   RM. March 22

d. 1282. Born at Ancona, he studied law at Bologna, where he was a fellow-student of St Sylvester. Soon he was appointed archdeacon of Ancona, and finally bishop of Osimo. Before his consecration he professed the Franciscan Rule and donned the Franciscan habit. Canonized by Martin IV.

BENVENUTUS of RECANATI (Bl) C. OFM.   AC. May 21

d. 1289. Born at Recanati, near Loreto, of the Mareni family. He joined the Friars Minor as a lay-brother and was mostly employed in the kitchen, where he was constantly favoured with ecstasies and visions. Cult confirmed by Pius VII.

BENVENUTUS of GUBBIO (Bl) C. OFM.   AC. June 27

d. 1232. An uncouth soldier, he was received into the Franciscan order by St Francis himself. At his own request the new friar was allowed to tend lepers, a task which he carried out with the utmost charity. Cult authorized by Gregory IX.

BEOADH (BEATUS) (St) Bp. AC. March 8

d. between 518 and 525. Aeodh (Aidus), an Irish saint, acquired the prefix *Bo* on account of the greatness of his virtues, and was appointed bishop of Ardcarne

(Roscommon). The "Bell of St Beoadh", a beautiful work of art, was long in veneration as a relic of the saint.

BEOC (BEANUS, DABEOC, MOBEOC) (St) Ab. AC. Jan 1

5th (or 6th) cent. By race he was a Cambro-Briton. He crossed over from Wales to Ireland and founded a monastery on an island in Lough Derg, Donegal.

BEOCCA, ETHOR and Comp. (SS) MM. OSB.   AC. Apr 10

d. *c.*870. The Danes, in their continuous raids on England, singled out the Anglo-Saxon abbeys as the special object of their ferocity. Thus at Chertsey Abbey in Surrey, they put to death SS Beocca, abbot, Ethor, monk-priest, and some ninety monks; at Peterborough, they killed St Hedda, abbot, and others of his community; at Thorney Abbey, St Torthred and others. All were justly venerated as martyrs.

BERACH (BARACHIAS, BERACHIUS) (St) Ab. AC. Feb 15

6th cent. From his birth he was placed under the care of his uncle, St Freoch. He afterwards became St Kevin's disciple, and founded an abbey at Clusin-Coirpte, in Connaught. He is the patron saint of Kilbarry, County Dublin.

BERACHIEL   AC. Apr 20

See Seven Angels who stand before the throne of God.

BERARDUS, PETER, OTTO, ACCURSIUS and ADJUTUS (SS) MM. OFM.   RM. Jan 16

d. 1220. Sent by St Francis to evangelize the Mohammedans of the West, these friars travelled from Italy to Aragon, then to Coimbra in Portugal, to Seville and finally to Morocco, where they were beheaded. Berardus, Peter and Otto were priests, Adjutus and Accursius lay-brothers. Canonized in 1481.

BERARIUS (St) Bp.   AC. Oct 17
d. *c.*680. Bishop of Le Mans. During his episcopate St Scholastica's relics were translated from Montecassino to Le Mans.

BERCHAM (St) Bp.   AC. Apr 6
Otherwise Berthanc, q.v.

**BERCHARIUS (St) Ab. M. OSB.
                RM. Oct 16**
d. 696. Monk of Luxeuil and first abbot of Hautvilliers, which had been founded by St Nivard, bishop of Reims. St Bercharius himself founded two new houses, Moutier-en-Der for monks, and Puelle-moutier for nuns. He went on pilgrimage to Rome and Palestine and on his return settled at Moutier-en-Der. A young monk, whom he had corrected, fatally stabbed him by night. Bercharius died, forgiving his murderer, and is venerated as a martyr.

**BERCHTOLD of RATISBON (Bl)
OFM.   AC. Dec 14**
13th cent. A Franciscan missionary who worked in Germany, Austria and Hungary, and converted thousands by his ardent sermons.

**BERCTHUN (BERTIN) (St) Ab.
OSB.   AC. Sept 24**
d. 733. A disciple of St John of Beverley and by him appointed first abbot of Beverley, where he died.

**BERCTUALD (St) Ab. OSB.
                         AC. Jan 9**
Otherwise Brithwald, q.v.

BERE, RICHARD (Bl) M. AC. May 4
d. 1537. Born at Glastonbury and educated at Oxford and the Inns of Court,

he was starved to death with another Carthusian monk of the London Charterhouse in Newgate prison, Aug-Sept 1537.

BEREGISUS (St) C.   AC. Oct 2
d. *p.*725. A priest, confessor of Pepin of Heristal, with whose help he founded the abbey of Saint-Hubert, in the Ardennes. It is not certain if he was himself a monk, although some writers call him abbot.

**BERENCARDUS (BERENGER)
(St) C. OSB.   AC. May 26**
d. 1293. Born near Toulouse, he became a Benedictine at the abbey of St Papoul in Languedoc. After his ordination he filled the offices of novice-master, almoner and master of works (*operarius*) of the abbey. He was noted for his kind charity and patience.

**BERENGARIUS (Bl) Ab. OSB.
                        AC. Oct 29**
d. 1108. First abbot of the Benedictine abbey of Formbach in Bavaria (1094–1108).

BERENICE (St) M.   AC. Oct 4
See Domnina, Berenice and Prosdoce.

**BERLINDA (BERLINDIS, BEL-
LAUDE) (St) V. OSB.   AC. Feb 3**
d. 702. A niece of St Amandus, she became a Benedictine nun of St Mary's convent, at Moorsel, near Alost, in Belgium, and afterwards a recluse at Meerbeke.

**BERNARDETTE (BERNAR-
DETTA) BERNADA (St) V.
                         RM. Apr 16**
1844–1879. Born at Lourdes, Bernadette Soubirous was the daughter of a miller in very poor circumstances. When she was fourteen years of age, she was favoured with a series of apparitions of our Lady, who chose the uneducated

peasant girl to reveal to the world the healing shrine at Lourdes. In 1866 she joined the Institute of the Sisters of Notre Dame at Nevers, where her one desire was to remain hidden and forgotten by the world. Canonized in 1933.

BERNARD of CORLEONE (Bl) C. OFM. Cap.   AC. Jan 19

1605–1667. Born at Corleone in Sicily, Philip Latini, a shoemaker by trade, was reckoned "the best swordsman of Sicily". After mortally wounding another man, he fled from the police and took sanctuary in the church of the Capuchin friars at Palermo. He joined them as a lay-brother (1632) and henceforth became "a prodigy of austerity" till his death. Beatified in 1768.

BERNARD of LIPPE (Bl) Bp. OSB. Cist.   PC. Jan 23

d. 1217. Count of Lippe in Westphalia. He professed the Cistercian Rule and was made abbot of Dünemunde, and later bishop of Semgallen in Kurland.

BERNARD SCAMMACCA (Bl) C. OP.   AC. Feb 16

d. 1486. A native of Catania, he belonged to a wealthy family, and in his youth gave himself up to riotous living until having been gravely wounded in a duel, he came to reflect on his folly, he changed his ways and joined the Friars Preachers. As a friar he atoned by a life of continuous penance for his former evil courses. Cult approved in 1825.

BERNARD of CARINOLA (St) Bp. RM. March 12

d. 1109. A native of Capua, he was appointed bishop of Forum Claudii in 1087 by Pope Victor III. He transferred the see (1100) to Carinola in Campania. St Bernard died in extreme old age. He is now the principal patron saint of Carinola.

BERNARD of THIRON (or of ABBEVILLE) (St) Ab. OSB. AC. Apr 14

1046–1117. Born near Abbeville, Bernard professed the Benedictine Rule at St Cyprian's, Poitiers, and later was appointed prior of St Sabinus. After some twenty years in this office he retired as a recluse to Craon. He was next made abbot of St Cyprian's, but soon retired again to the forest of Thiron in Picardy, where he founded the Congregation of that name, of which the main feature was hard manual labour. The Congregation spread rapidly throughout France, England and Scotland. Cult as a saint confirmed in 1861.

BERNARD the PENITENT (Bl) Mk. OSB.   AC. Apr 19

d. 1182. A native of Provence who, owing to some horrible crime which he had committed, was sentenced by the bishop of Maguelone to seven years public penance. He performed this penance loaded with seven heavy iron bands, which he dragged from shrine to shrine—Compostella, Rome, Palestine—until he came to the abbey of St Bertin (Sithin), where he first lived as a hermit and then ventured to ask the monks to receive him in their community.

BERNARD of MENTHON (St) C. OSA.   RM. May 28

d. c.1081. For forty years he served the bishop of Aosta as vicar-general of the diocese, visiting every mountain and valley in the Alps, and taking particular care of travellers. For this purpose he established two hospices on the great and little passes which bear his name, placing them under Augustinian canons regular. Pius XI named him patron saint of mountaineers.

BERNARD, MARY and GRACIA (GRACE) (SS) MM. OSB. Cist.
AC. June 1

d. *c.*1180. Children of Almanzor, the Mohammedan caliph of Lérida in Catalonia. Their Moorish names were respectively Achmed, Zoraida and Zaida. Achmed was converted to Christianity and became a Cistercian monk at Poblet (Populetum) near Tarragona, under the name of Bernard. He in his turn converted his two sisters, who were in some way affiliated to the Cistercian Order. As a result of their endeavour to convert their brother Almanzor, they were handed over by him to the executioners and martyred *in odium fidei*. They are the patron saints of Alcira, in Valencia, Spain.

BERNARD of BADEN (Bl) C.
AC. July 15

1428-1458. Margrave of Baden, he renounced the rights of his title in favour of his brother and offered himself to several European courts to organize a crusade against the Turks. He died without having attained his object. Cult confirmed in 1481 and again in 1769.

BERNARD of RODEZ (de RUTHENIS) (Bl) Card. OSB.
AC. July 19

d. 1079. Abbot of St Victor at Marseilles (1064). A fast friend of SS Gregory VII, Hugh of Cluny and William of Hirschau, he zealously fostered the Cluniac observance. He was made cardinal and sent as papal legate to Germany (1077) and Spain (1078).

BERNARD DUE (Bl) M.
AC. Aug 1

1755-1838. A native priest of Tonkin, after labouring for many years on the mission, he was living in retirement but spontaneously offered himself to the pagan soldiers as a Christian priest, and was beheaded at the age of eighty-three. Beatified 1900.

BERNARD of CLAIRVAUX (St)
Ab. Dr. OSB. Cist.   RM. Aug 20

1090-1153. Born near Dijon, at the age of twenty-two he joined (1112) the recently founded struggling abbey of Cîteaux, after having persuaded thirty other young noblemen to follow him thither. Scarcely had he finished his novitiate when he was sent as abbot-founder to Clairvaux (1115) and as such became the real founder of the Cistercians. During his lifetime he established sixty-eight Cistercian houses, was the adviser of popes, kings and councils, the preacher of the second crusade (which, however, was a failure), the arbiter of Europe, who, as has been said, "carried the 12th century on his shoulders". In the theological field, he confuted Abelard, wrote profusely on the love of God, commented for his monks on the *Song of Songs*, sent a noble treatise, *De consideratione*, to his former monk, Pope Eugene III, and produced many other works. His *Treatise on the Love of God* is considered the best. Canonized in 1174 and declared a doctor in 1830.

BERNARD of VALDEIGLESIAS (St) Mk. OSB. Cist.
AC. Aug 20

d. *p.*1155. A monk of Valdeiglesias in Spanish Galicia. He is the patron saint of Candelada. Possibly but not certainly a Cistercian.

BERNARD TOLOMEI (Bl)
Founder, OSB. Oliv.   RM. Aug 21

1272-1348. Born at Siena, he was educated by his uncle, a Dominican friar. He studied law, and filled several municipal offices, including that of *podestà* (mayor). In 1313 he withdrew to a place ten miles from the city and there he became the founder of the abbey and Congregation of Montoliveto. He was summoned to Avignon to give an account of this new foundation, and received papal approval (1324). After years spent in wonderful deeds of charity, he died of the pestilence whilst nursing the sick, together with a large number of his monks. Cult officially approved in 1644. Among the Olivetans he is usually given the title of Saint.

BERNARD of OFFIDA (Bl) C.
OFM. Cap.   **AC. Aug 22**
1604–1694. An Italian peasant, born at Appignano, diocese of Ascoli-Piceno. He took his vows as a Capuchin lay-brother at Offida and here, and at the friary of Fermo, he became famous for his wisdom and miracles.

BERNARD of ARCE (St) C.
RM. Oct 14
9th cent. Either an Englishman or a Frenchman, who undertook a pilgrimage to the Holy Land and Rome and then lived as a recluse at Arpino in the Campagna. His relics are enshrined at Rocca d'Arce.

BERNARD of BAGNOREA (or of Castro) (St) Bp.   AC. Oct 20
d. *p.*800. A native of Bagnorea, he was chosen bishop of Vulcia in Tuscany, whence he transferred the see to Ischia di Castro.

BERNARD CALVO (St) Bp. OSB.
Cist.   **AC. Oct 24**
d. 1243. A native of Manso Calvo, in Catalonia, he became a Cistercian and eventually the first abbot of Santas Creus, near Tarragona. In 1233 he was chosen bishop of Vich.

BERNARD de la TOUR (Bl) C.
O. Cart.   **PC. Oct 30**
d. 1258. A Carthusian monk of Portes, diocese of Belley, who became the thirteenth superior general of the Order.

BERNARD of HILDESHEIM (St)
Bp.   **RM. Nov 20**
Otherwise Bernward, q.v.

BERNARD OF TOULOUSE (Bl)
M. OP.   **PC. Dec 3**
d. 1320. A Dominican friar, who in his campaign against the Albigenses was seized by them, put to torture and sawn in two.

BERNARD degli UBERTI (St) Bp.
OSB. Vall.   **RM. Dec 4**
d. 1133. A native of Florence, he was professed a monk at Vallombrosa. He was appointed successively abbot of San Salvi, general of Vallombrosa, cardinal (1097), papal legate and finally bishop of Parma (1106), at that time the storm-centre of the anti-pope's supporters. Twice he was exiled, but he proved a most successful prelate.

BERNARD (or BERARD) PALEARA (St) Bp. OSB.   AC. Dec 19
d. 1122. A monk of Montecassino, chosen bishop of Teramo in 1115. He is venerated as the principal patron saint of Teramo.

BERNARDINUS of SIENA (St) C.
OFM.   **RM. May 20**
1380–1444. Born on Sept 8 at Massa Maritima near Siena, of the family degl'Albizzeschi. He took the Franciscan habit (Sept 8, 1402), and was ordained priest (Sept 8, 1404) and, having preached his first sermon (Sept 8, 1417), his career as a preacher ended only with his life. He was accounted the foremost Italian missioner of the 15th century. He was particularly eloquent when preaching on the Holy Name of Jesus, devotion to which he spread far and wide. He was also responsible for the revival of discipline among the Franciscans, and from 1438 to 1442 he was vicar-general of the order. Canonized

in 1450. In art he is represented holding to his breast the monogram of the Sacred Name—IHS.

BERNARDINUS REALINO (St) SJ.
RM. July 2

1530–1616. A native of Modena, he became a lawyer, but when aged thirty-four joined the Society of Jesus. He worked for ten years at Naples and was then appointed rector of the college at Lecce, where he died. Canonized in 1947.

BERNARDINUS of FELTRE (Bl) C. OFM.   AC. Sept 28

c.1439-1494. A native of Feltre, his baptismal name was Martin Tomitani. He took his vows as a Franciscan and was first employed as a teacher in various houses of the order, but developed before long into a tempestuous preacher, the terror of all evil-doers, but especially of usurers. To protect the people against these he suggested the establishment of *monti di pietà*, of which he organized over thirty in various Italian cities. Beatified in 1728.

BERNARDINUS of FOSSA (Bl) C. OFM.   AC. Nov 27

d. 1503. Bernardino Amici was born at Fossa, diocese of Aquila in central Italy. In 1445, he received the Franciscan habit, and after filling successfully several offices in the order, he embarked on a career of mission-preaching throughout Italy, Dalmatia and Bosnia, being still engaged in this apostolate when he died at Aquila.

BERNO (St) Ab. OSB. AC. Jan 13

d. 927. A native of Burgundy and a monk of St Martin, Autun. He was abbot restorer of Baume-les-Messieurs, where he gave the habit to St Odo in 909, and the abbot-founder of Gigny, Bourg-Dieu, Massay and finally of Cluny (910), which he governed till 926.

In that year he resigned and was succeeded by St Odo. History, whether sacred or profane, has done less than justice to St Berno for his great work for the Church and for civilization.

BERNOLD (Bl) Mk. OSB.
AC. Nov 25

d. c.1050. A monk-priest of Ottobeuren in Bavaria, renowned as a wonder-worker, especially after his death.

BERNWARD (BERWARD) (St) Bp. OSB.   RM. Nov 20

d. 1022. Bernward is one of the most attractive figures of medieval Germany —a German St Dunstan. He excelled as an architect, painter, sculptor, decorator and metal-smith. He was also the tutor of the emperor Otto III. In 993 he was made bishop of Hildesheim. He died "after having assumed the habit of St Benedict". (See Butler-Thurston.) Canonized in 1193.

BERONIGUS, PELAGIA and Comp. (SS) MM.   RM. Oct 19

? A group of fifty-one Christians put to death at Antioch in Syria in one of the early persecutions.

BERTELLIN (St) C.   AC. Sept 9

Otherwise Bettelin, q.v.

BERTHA (Bl) Abs. OSB. Vall.
AC. March 24

d. 1163. Born in Florence, a member of the Alberti family (she is often wrongly called de'Bardi). She became a nun at the Vallombrosan convent of St Felicitas at Florence, whence Bl Qualdo Galli, the general of the Vallombrosans, sent her to Cavriglia in the Valdardo, as abbess. She died ten years later on Easter Sunday.

BERTHA (St) M.   AC. May 1

d. p.680. Abbess-foundress of Avenay,

diocese of Châlons-sur-Marne. She was perfidiously put to death and is venerated as a martyr.

BERTHA (St)   AC. May 15
See Rupert and Bertha.

BERTHA (St) W. OSB. AC. July 4
d. *c*.725. A lady of high station, who after her husband's death entered the nunnery of Blangy, in Artois, which she had founded, and became its abbess.

BERTHA of MARBAIS (Bl) W.
OSB. Cist.   PC. July 18
d. 1247. A near relative of the count of Flanders, she married the chatelain of Molembais. Left a widow, she became a Cistercian at Ayvrières. Her family founded the nunnery of Marquette, whither she was sent as abbess. She has a liturgical cult in the diocese of Namur.

BERTHALDUS (BERTAUD) (St) H.
AC. June 16
d. *c*.540. A hermit in the Ardennes who was ordained priest by St Remigius.

BERTHANC (BERCHAN) (St) Bp.
AC. Apr 6
d. *c*.840. A Scottish saint, who is said to have been a monk of Iona and later bishop of Kirkwall in the Orkneys. He seems to have died in Ireland, and his tomb was shown at Inishmore in Galway Bay. Hence perhaps his surname of Fer-da-Leithe (the man of two parts or countries).

BERTHARIUS (St) Bp.
See Betharius.

BERTHARIUS (St) Ab. M. OSB.
AC. Oct 22
d. *c*.884. A scion of the royal house of France, he was professed at Montecassino and chosen as its abbot in 856. While kneeling in prayer he was mar-

tyred, with several of his monks, by a band of invading Saracens. He is the author of homilies, poems, etc. One of the altars of Montecassino is consecrated in his name.

BERTHOALD (St) Bp. AC. Oct 13
7th cent. Fifth bishop of Cambrai Arras.

BERTHOLD (St) C. OC.
AC. March 29
d. *c*.1195. A Frenchman and a brilliant student at the university of Paris, he set out for Palestine as a crusader. There he joined the group of hermits who dwelt on Mt Carmel and eventually was appointed by his brother Aymeric, Latin patriarch of Antioch, their first superior general. For all practical purposes he may be considered the founder of the Carmelite order.

BERTHOLD of SCHEDA (Bl) C.
O. Praem.   PC. July 13
d. *c*.1214. Founder of the Premonstratensian abbey of Frodenburg (Vrundeberg). He was a brother of Bl Menrich of Lübeck.

BERTHOLD of GARSTEN (Bl) Ab.
OSB.   AC. July 27
1090–1142. Born on the shores of the lake of Constance, Berthold belonged to the family of the counts of Bogen. After a short period of married life he was left a widower at the age of thirty and at once joined the Benedictines of Blasien in the Black Forest. He became their prior, and then prior of Göttweig in Austria and abbot of Garsten in Styria, where he founded a hospice for the poor. He enjoyed a great reputation as a confessor.

BERTHOLD (BERTOLDO) (St) C.
OSB.   AC. Oct 21
d. 1111. An Anglo-Saxon by descent, his parents having fled from England at

the Norman Conquest, Berthold was born at Parma. He spent his whole life as a lay-brother in the service of the nuns of St Alexander in that city.

BERTHOLD (Bl) Ab. OSB.
PC. Nov 3
d. 1197. A monk of Engelberg in Switzerland, who excelled as a transcriber of books. He became the third abbot of the monastery (1178). His memory is liturgically celebrated at Einsiedeln and Engelberg.

BERTILIA (St) V. AC. Jan 3
d. c. 687. A noble maiden who together with her husband took a vow of perpetual continence, and on the death of the latter lived as a recluse near a church she had founded at Maroeuil (Marolles) in Flanders.

BERTILLA (MARY) BOSCARDIN (St) V. AC. Oct 20
1888–1922. St Mary Bertilla, more widely known as St Bertilla among her people, was a member of the congregation entitled Teachers of St Dorothy, Daughters of the Sacred Hearts. Born at Brendola (Vincenza) in Northern Italy. She earnestly devoted her life of obedience to the service of the sick and of children. Canonized in 1961.

BERTILLA (St) V. OSB. AC. Nov 5
d. c.705. A nun at Jouarre, near Meaux, where she held the offices of infirmarian, headmistress of the convent school and prioress. When St Bathildis restored the nunnery of Chelles, St Bertilla was made its first abbess and she governed it for half a century. Great numbers flocked to her convent, including many Anglo-Saxon girls.

BERTILO (Bl) M. OSB.
AC. March 26
d. c.878–888. Abbot of St Benignus, at Dijon. The Normans sacked his abbey and massacred him and several of his community at the foot of the altar.

BERTINUS the YOUNGER (Bl) C. OSB. AC. May 2
d. c.699. Monk of Sithin under its founder, St Bertinus the Great.

BERTINUS (St) Ab. OSB.
RM. Sept 5
d. c.709. Born near Constance, he became a monk at Luxeuil under St Waldebert, who had introduced there the Benedictine Rule. He was sent to help St Omer, bishop of Thérouanne, by whom he was made abbot of Sithin (afterwards called St Bertin). Under his government the community increased in a remarkable manner, and he was obliged to establish several new houses. He is one of the greatest of Benedictine abbots.

BERTOARA (St) Abs. AC. Dec 4
d. p.614. Abbess of Notre-Dame-de-Sales, in Bourges (612–614) under the Columbanian Rule.

BERTRAM (St) C. AC. Sept 9
Otherwise Bettelin, q.v.

BERTRAND (BERTRAM, BERTRAN, EBERTRAM) (St) Ab. OSB.
AC. Jan 24
7th cent. One of St Bertinus's disciples, and one of St Omer's helpers in the evangelization of N. France and Flanders. At a later date he was made abbot of Saint-Quentin.

BERTRAND (St) Bp. M. AC. June 6
1260–1350. Born near Cahors, he became dean of the cathedral chapter of Angoulême, from which position he was raised to the patriarchate of Aquileia. He met his death in defence of the rights of his church. Cult approved by Benedict XIV.

BERTRAND (BERTICHRAMNUS) (St) Bp.   AC. June 30

d. 623. A native of Autun, he was educated by St Germanus at Paris, and appointed archdeacon of that city and some time later bishop of Le Mans. He took a great interest in agriculture and wine-growing. He was especially noted for his benefactions to the poor.

BERTRAND of GARRIGUE (Bl) C. OP.   AC. Sept 6

d. 1230. A native of Garrigue, diocese of Nîmes. He was already a secular priest when he became a disciple of St Dominic and helped him in his first foundation at Paris. He was the constant companion of the holy founder until his appointment as provincial of the Dominicans in Provence. Cult confirmed by Leo XIII.

BERTRAND of COMMINGES (St) Bp.   AC. Oct 16

d. 1123. The most celebrated of the bishops of Comminges (now included in the diocese of Toulouse), he may be considered as the second founder of his episcopal city. He was its pastor for fifty years—energetic, fearless, enterprising, zealous. Canonized by Alexander III.

BERTRAND of GRANDSELVE (Bl) Ab. OSB. Cist.   AC. Oct 23

d. 1149 (July 11). Cistercian abbot of Grandselve for twenty years. He was often favoured with heavenly visions.

BERTUIN (St) Bp. OSB. AC. Nov 11

d. c.698. An Anglo-Saxon monk of the small abbey of Othelle. He was consecrated a missionary bishop, left for Rome where he spent two years, and finally became the abbot-founder of the abbey of Malonne, in the territory of Namur, henceforward the centre of his missionary labours.

BERTULFUS (BERTHULPH) (St) Ab. OSB.   AC. Feb 5

d. 705. Born in Pannonia, a pagan, he migrated to Flanders, where he became a Christian and a priest. Count Wambert entrusted to him the administration of his estate, and gave him the land of Renty. Here the saint founded an abbey whither he retired after his benefactor's death.

BERTULFUS (St) Ab.   AC. Aug 19

d. 640. Of Frankish origin, he entered the abbey of Luxeuil and was professed there under St Eustace. Then he migrated to Bobbio, where he was chosen abbot on St Attalas's death (627). As abbot of Bobbio he is best remembered for having obtained from Pope Honorius I the exemption of his abbey from episcopal jurisdiction, the first case recorded in history.

BESAS (St) M.   RM. Feb 27

See Julian, Cronion and Besas.

BESSARION (St) H.   RM. June 17

d. c.400. One of the fathers of the Egyptian desert, greatly venerated among the Greeks, who keep his feast on June 6.

BETHARIUS (St) Bp.   AC. Aug 2

d. c.623. He was Bishop of Chartres from 595 to 623 and was present at the Council of Sens. His life is of doubtful authenticity.

BETTELIN (BETHLIN, BETHELM) (St) H. OSB. AC. Sept 9

8th cent. Disciple of St Guthlac of Croyland. After the death of his master, Bettelin and his companions lived on at Croyland under Kenulphus, first abbot of the monastery founded there by King Ethelbald of Mercia. A saint of the name of Bettelin was patron of the town of Stafford.

BETTO (St) Bp. OSB.   PC. Feb 24
d. 918. A Benedictine monk of the abbey of Sainte-Colombe, at Sens, who became bishop of Auxerre in 889.

BEUNO (St) Ab.   AC. Apr 21
d. c.630. A Welshman by birth, he was the founder of monasteries at Llanveynoe in Herefordshire and Llanymyech; but his name is chiefly connected with that of Clynnog in Carnarvonshire. Legend makes him the uncle of St Winefride and claims that he restored her to life.

BEUVE (St) V. OSB.   AC. Apr 24
Otherwise Bova, q.v.

BIANOR and SYLVANUS (SS) MM.   RM. July 10
4th cent. Martyrs beheaded in Pisidia, in Asia Minor. Their extant Greek Acts are untrustworthy.

BIBIANA (VIBIANA, VIVIAN) (St) VM.   RM. Dec 2
? A virgin martyred at Rome. This is all that is certain about her. Her *Acta* are a medieval romance, much read and admired throughout Europe, and especially in Germany and Spain, as witness the great number of churches dedicated in her honour. They have given rise to a number of spurious entries in the RM.; see St Dafrosa, and SS Priscus, Priscillian and Benedict.

BIBLIG (PEBLIG) (St)   AC. July 3
Otherwise Byblig, q.v.

**BIBLIS (or BIBLIDES) (St) M.
                          RM. June 2**
One of the martyrs of Lyons. See Photinus, Sanctius, etc.

BICOR (St) M.   RM. Apr 22
A bishop martyr under Shapur II.

BIEUZY (St) M.   AC. Nov 24
7th cent. A native of Britain who followed St Gildas to Brittany. We have no particulars of his life or of the martyrdom which closed it.

BILFRID (BILLFRITH) (St) H. OSB.   AC. March 6
d. c.758. A monk-hermit of Lindisfarne and an expert goldsmith, who bound in gold the Lindisfarne copy of the Gospels, written and illuminated by bishop Eaddfrid. In life and in death he was the centre of great popular veneration.

BILHILD (St) W. OSB. AC. Nov 27
c.630–c.710. Born near Würzburg, Bilhild married the duke of Thuringia. After the death of her husband, she became the abbess-foundress of the nunnery of Altenmünster in Mainz.

BIRGITTA (St) W.   RM. Oct 8
Otherwise Brigid of Sweden, q.v.

BIRILLUS (St) Bp.   RM. March 21
d. c.90. Said to have been consecrated first bishop of Catania in Sicily by St Peter the Apostle, with whom he had travelled from Antioch. He died in extreme old age.

BIRINUS (St) Bp.   RM. Dec 3
d. c.650. A Roman missionary priest commonly said to have been a monk, who offered himself for the foreign missions and was sent by Pope St Honorius to Britain. He was consecrated bishop at Genoa and on his arrival in England converted Cynegils, king of the West Saxons, and was given Dorchester in Oxfordshire for his see. He is known as the "Apostle of Wessex".

BIRNSTAN (BIRRSTAN, BRYNSTAN) (St) Bp. OSB.   AC. Nov 4
d. c.934. Successor of St Frithestan in

the see of Winchester and a disciple of St Grimbald. He was noted for his devotion to the holy souls in Purgatory.

BITEUS (St) C.   AC. July 22
Otherwise Movean, q.v.

BITHEUS and GENOCUS (SS) CC.
                      AC. Apr 18
6th cent. Two British monks who accompanied St Finian of Clonard to Ireland, and there attained a great reputation for sanctity.

BLAAN (St) Bp.   AC. Aug 10
Otherwise Blane, q.v.

BLADUS (St) Bp.   AC. July 3
? According to tradition, one of the early bishops of the Isle of Man.

BLAESILLA (St) W.   AC. Jan 22
d. 383. Daughter of St Paula and a disciple of St Jerome. In her widowhood she consecrated herself to God. She died in Rome aged twenty.

**BLAISE (BLASIUS, BLASE) (St)
Bp. M.**   RM. Feb 3
d. c.316. According to his legendary acts, which became widely known in W. Europe at the time of the crusades, Blaise was a physician who became bishop of Sebaste in Armenia, where he was martyred. One of his miracles was the saving of the life of a boy who had half swallowed a fish-bone which could not be extricated; hence the rite of the *Blessing of St Blaise*, incorporated in the Roman Ritual, against affections of the throat. His feast is observed with much solemnity throughout the East, as was also the case, in ancient times, in the West.

**BLAISE of AUVERGNE (Bl) C.
OP.**   AC. Apr 5
14th cent. A disciple of St Vincent

Ferrer, and like him an impassioned Dominican preacher.

**BLAISE and DEMETRIUS (SS)
MM.**   RM. Nov 29
? Martyrs of Veroli in central Italy. Their connexion with St Mary Salome is discarded by most writers.

**BLAITHMAIC (BLATHMAC,
BLAITHMALE) (St) M.**   AC. Jan 15
d. c.823. An Irish abbot, who, desirous of martyrdom, crossed over to England, then a prey to heathen Danes. He was murdered by the Danes on the altar steps of the abbey church at Iona. Walafrid Strabo narrates his life in verse.

BLANCA (Bl) W.   AC. Apr 26
Otherwise Alda, q.v.

BLANCHE (*several*)
Otherwise Gwen, q.v.

BLANDA (St) M.   RM. May 10
See Calepodius, Palmutius, etc.

BLANDINA (St) M.   RM. June 2
See Photinus (Pothinus), Sanctius, etc.

BLANDINUS (St) H.   AC. May 1
See Salaberga.

BLANE (BLAAN, BLAIN) (St) Bp.
                      AC. Aug 10
6th cent. A Scottish bishop, disciple of SS Comgall and Canice in Ireland, who flourished in the 6th century, and was buried at the place now called Dunblane. There has been much controversy over the actual dates of his life; but the above summary is now commonly agreed upon by scholars.

BLATH (FLORA) (St) V. AC. Jan 29
d. 523. In the Irish martyrologies several saints are registered under the name

Blath (latinized Flora). The one best remembered was a lay-sister, the cook in St Brigid's nunnery at Kildare, where she earned a great reputation for sanctity.

BLEDRWS (St)
? There is a church in Cardiganshire named after St Bledrws, but it has not been found possible to identify the saint.

BLEIDDAN (BLEWDIAN) (St) Bp. RM. July 29
Otherwise Lupus of Troyes, q.v.

BLENWYDD (St)
? The dedication of a chapel to this saint in the Isle of Anglesey is all that perpetuates his memory.

BLIDULF (BLADULPH) (St) Mk. AC. Jan 2
d. c.630. A monk of Bobbio, who courageously denounced the heresy of the Lombard king Ariovald.

BLINLIVET (BLEVILEGUETUS) (St) Bp.   AC. Nov 7
9th cent. The twenty-fifth bishop of Vannes in Brittany. Before his death he resigned and became a monk at Quimperlé.

BLITHARIUS (BLIER) (St) C. AC. June 11
7th cent. A native of Scotland, who passed over into France with St Fursey, and settled at Seganne in Champagne, where he is still held in great veneration.

BLITMUND (St) Ab.   AC. Jan 3
d. 660 ?. Monk of Bobbio under St Attalas. He followed St Walaricus (St Valéry) to France, where they founded the abbey of Leucone (later on called Saint-Valéry; now the village of the same name). St Blitmund survived his master and ruled the abbey as its second abbot.

BOADIN (St) H. OSB.   AC. Jan 11
? An Irishman who passed over to France and became a Benedictine monk there.

BOBINUS (St) Bp. OSB. AC. Jan 31
d. c.766. A native of Aquitaine, monk of Moutier-la-Celle, which was enriched by his benefactions when he became bishop of Troyes (760).

BOBO (BEUVON) (St) H.   AC. May 22
d. c.985. A knight of Provence, who fought bravely against the invading Saracens and then retired as a hermit to lead a life of penance. He died at Pavia in Lombardy while on a pilgrimage to Rome.

BODAGISIL (St) Ab.   AC. Dec 18
d. 588. A Frankish courtier, who later became the founder and first abbot of an abbey on the banks of the Meuse. St Venantius Fortunatus and St Gregory of Tours are loud in his praises.

BODFAN (BOBOUAN) (St)   AC. June 2
7th cent. The patron saint of Abern in Carnarvon. The only extant tradition about him is that the great inundation that formed Beaumaris Bay impelled him, with his father and other relations, to embrace the religious life.

BODO (St) Bp. OSB.   AC. Sept 11
d. p.670. A native of Toul, brother to St Salaberga. He married, but by mutual consent both he and his wife became religious. He entered an abbey at Laon, which, however, he was forced to leave in order to become bishop of Toul. He founded Etival, Bon-Moutier, and Affonville abbeys.

BOETHARIUS (St) Bp.   AC. Aug 2
7th cent. Chaplain of King Clotaire II, and afterwards bishop of Chartres (c.595).

BOETHIAN (St) M. OSB.
                                    AC. May 22
7th cent. A disciple of St Fursey and an Irishman by birth. He built the monastery of Pierrepont, near Laon, in France, and was eventually murdered by those whom he had felt bound to rebuke. His shrine is still a place of pilgrimage.

BOËTHIUS (Bl) C.   AC. Oct 23
See Severinus Boëthius.

BOGUMILUS (i.e. THEOPHILUS) (St) Bp. OSB. Cam.   AC. June 10
d. 1182. A native of Dobrow, a little Polish town on the Wartha. After his studies at the university of Paris he was appointed parish priest of Dobrow, and then archbishop of Gnesen. As such he founded the Cistercian abbey of Coronowa. In spite of his wisdom and zeal his clergy paid little heed to his admonitions. He resigned in 1172 and became a Camaldolese monk at Uniejow. Cult approved in 1925.

BOISIL (St) Ab.   AC. Feb 23
Otherwise Boswell, q.v.

BOLCAN (OLCAN) (St) Bp.
                                    AC. Feb 20
d. c.480. Baptized by St Parick and sent by him to study in Gaul, Bolcan was subsequently by the same saint consecrated bishop of Derkan in N. Ireland. His school there was one of the best equipped in the island. Another St Bolcan is venerated in the diocese of Elphin. He is known as St Olcan of Kilmoyle.

BOLONIA (St) VM.   AC. Oct 16
d. 362. A maiden of fifteen who was martyred under Julian the Apostate, and who has left her name to the village of Saint Boulogne in the Haute Marne.

BONA (St) V.   AC. Apr 24
Otherwise Bova, q.v.

BONAJUNCTA (St) C.
                                    RM. Aug 31 and Feb 12
i.e. Buonagiunta, one of the Seven Holy Founders of the Servite Order, q.v.

BONANNUS (Bl) C. OSB. Cel.
                                    AC. Jan 1
d. c.1320. A Benedictine of the Celestine Congregation, monk of the monastery of St Laurence in the Abruzzi.

BONAVENTURE of MEACO (Bl) M. Tert. OFM.   AC. Feb 5
d. 1597. A native of Meaco in Japan, this saint became a Franciscan tertiary and helped the Franciscan missionaries as a catechist. He was crucified at Nagasaki. Beatified in 1862.

BONAVENTURE TORNIELLI (Bl.) C. OSM.   AC. March 31
1411–1491. Born at Forli, he became a Servite in 1448. At the order of the pope Sixtus IV he preached continually throughout the papal states and S. Italy. He was for some years vicar-general of the Servites. Cult confirmed in 1911.

BONAVENTURE BADUARIO of PERAGA (Bl) C. OSA. Erem.
                                    PC. June 10
1332–1386. A native of Peraga, near Padua, where he was professed as an Augustinian hermit. After having been general of the Order he was created cardinal-priest of St Caecilia—the first of the Order to attain that honour. He was killed in Rome by an arrow, probably in retaliation for his defence of the rights of the Church.

BONAVENTURE (St) Bp. Dr.
OFM.　　　　　RM. July 14

1221–1274. Born at Bagnorea, near Viterbo. His baptismal name was John. The name Bonaventure (good fortune) was given to him by St Francis of Assisi, who cured him miraculously when he was a small child, and exclaimed: *O buona ventura!* At the age of twenty he became a Franciscan, and at thirty-six minister-general of the Order. He was nominated archbishop of York, but refused the honour. Finally in 1273 he was created cardinal bishop of Albano. He died during the general council of Lyons. A disciple of Alexander of Hales and a friend and admirer of St Thomas Aquinas, Bonaventure is known as the "Seraphic Doctor", and was officially given the title of Doctor of the Church by Sixtus V. Besides theological and philosophical works, St Bonaventure has left us sundry ascetical treatises, and a touchingly beautiful life of St Francis of Assisi written with the aim of promoting unity among the Friars Minor. Canonized in 1482.

BONAVENTURE GRAU (Bl) C.
OFM.　　　　　AC. Sept 11

1620–1684. Born at Riudoms, near Barcelona, left a widower after a short period of married life, he joined the Friars Minor at Escornalbou. To escape notoriety for his mystical gifts he went to Rome where he was made doorkeeper at St Isidore. He founded several retreat-convents in the Roman province of his order. His advice was sought by popes and cardinals. Cult approved in 1906.

BONAVENTURE of POTENZA
(Bl) C. OFM.　　　AC. Oct 26

1651–1711. A native of Potenza in Lucania. He entered the Franciscan order at Nocera and spent his life as a missioner in S. Italy, chiefly at Amalfi, and as a novice master. He died in an ecstasy singing psalms.

BONAVENTURE BUONACCORSI
(Bl) C. OSM.　　　AC. Dec 14

d. 1313. A native of Pistoia in Tuscany and the leader of the Ghibellines there, he was converted in 1276 by St Philip Benizi, who was acting as a peace-maker between the parties. He followed St Philip into the Servite Order and as a Servite friar went about preaching peace. The people called him "il Beato" even during his lifetime. Cult approved in 1822.

BONAVENTURE TOLOMEI (Bl)
C. OP.　　　　　PC. Dec 27

d. 1348. Born at Siena in Tuscany. As a child he was favoured with divine charismata, but in early manhood he abandoned himself for four years to a life of impurity and sacrilege. He repented, visited on foot all the celebrated shrines and subsequently entered the Dominican order. He died while tending the plague-stricken in Siena.

BONAVITA (Bl) C. Tert. OFM.
　　　　　　　　　PC. March 1

d. 1375. A blacksmith of Lugo, near Ravenna. He was a Franciscan tertiary, wholly devoted to prayer and good works.

BOND (BALDUS) (St) H. AC. Oct 29

7th cent. A penitent hermit venerated at Sens in France. See Arthemius (Apr 28).

BONET (BONT) (St) Bp.
　　　　　　　　　RM. Jan 15

Otherwise Bonitus, q.v.

BONFILIUS MONALDI (St)
　　　RM. Jan 1 and Feb 12

One of the Seven Holy Founders of the Servite Order, q.v.

BONFILIUS (St) Bp. OSB.
AC. Sept 27

1040–1125. A native of Osimo in Piceno, he became a monk, and then abbot, of the monastery of Our Lady, at Storace. In 1078 he was made bishop of Foligno: but in 1096, after a pilgrimage to the Holy Land, he resigned and retired to the abbey of Santa Maria della Fara, diocese of Cingoli, where he died.

BONIFACE of LAUSANNE (St) Bp.
AC. Feb 19

d. 1265. Born in Brussels and educated by nuns of La Cambre (*Camera S. Mariae*), near his native city. He then studied at Paris, where he taught dogma, afterwards transferring his chair to the university of Cologne. About the year 1230 he was made bishop of Lausanne, but resigned (1239) and henceforth lived at the Cistercian convent, La Cambre, as chaplain to the nuns. The Cistercians claim him for their order.

BONIFACE of SAVOY (Bl) Bp.
O. Cart.   AC. March 13

d. 1270. A member of the ducal house of Savoy, who became a Carthusian monk (and prior) and then bishop of Valence, and finally archbishop of Canterbury (1241). Besides his fame as a saint, the fact that he was uncle to Henry III's wife explains the appointment, which, however, proved very unpopular in England. He died in Savoy and was buried at Hautecombe. Cult confirmed in 1830.

BONIFACE CURITAN (St) Bp.
AC. March 14

d. c.660. A bishop of Ross, very likely a Roman by birth, who evangelized the Picts and Scots, one of the chief features of his mission being the introducing of the Roman discipline and observance, as opposed to the Celtic usages. He is said to have founded a very great number of churches.

BONIFACE of VALPERGA (Bl) Bp.
PC. Apr 25

d. 1243. Monk of the Benedictine abbey of Fruttuaria, who was chosen prior of the Augustinian canons regular of St Ursus at Aosta (1212) and finally bishop of Aosta (1219–1243).

BONIFACE IV (St) Pope
RM. May 8

d. 615. Born at Valeria in the Abruzzi, he became, according to a tradition which cannot, however, be substantiated, a Benedictine monk of St Sebastian, in Rome. He was pope from 608 to 615 and is best remembered for his dedication of the Pantheon to our Lady and all the saints. St Columbanus addressed to him a famous—or notorious —letter.

BONIFACE of TARSUS (St) M.
RM. May 14

d. c.307. A martyr beheaded at Tarsus in Cilicia, whither, his fictitious acts add, he had gone from Rome to recover the bodies of certain martyrs. His own relics are enshrined in the church of SS Alexius and Boniface on the Aventine.

BONIFACE (St) Bp.   RM. May 14
6th cent. Bishop of Ferentino in Tuscany at the time of the emperor Justin. He is commemorated by St Gregory the Great.

BONIFACE (Bl) Mk. OSB. Cist.
PC. June 4

d. c.1280. Monk and prior of the great Cistercian abbey of Villers in Brabant.

BONIFACE (St) Bp. M. OSB.
RM. June 5

680–755. An Anglo-Saxon, whose baptismal name was Winfrid, born at

Crediton in Devon. At the age of five he entered a monastery at Exeter, there to become a Benedictine monk. He was transferred to Nutshulling, diocese of Winchester, where he became head of the abbey school and was ordained priest in 710. In 716 he set out for Germany on his first missionary expedition, which proved a failure. In 718 he left England again, this time for Rome, to get the pope's blessing on his enterprise, and forthwith evangelized Bavaria, Hesse, Friesland, Thuringia and Franconia. In 723 Gregory II consecrated him regionary bishop with full jurisdiction over the Germanies. In 731 he was made by the pope metropolitan beyond the Rhine, in 738 papal legate, and in 747 archbishop of Mainz. A few years before his death he founded the abbey of Fulda (where his body now rests) as the focus of German missionary activities. Before this he had already established a great number of abbeys and nunneries, with attached schools, and to staff them he had invited bands of monks and nuns from England. He was martyred in his old age, with fifty-two companions at Dokkum. He was responsible for the organization of the Frankish church. Always on the best of terms with the Carolingians, he became their mentor and support. He is rightly styled the Apostle of Germany. Among the apostles of all time he stands on a par with St Paul and St Francis Xavier.

BONIFACE (St) M. OSB.
RM. June 19
Otherwise Bruno of Querfurt. See Bruno-Boniface.

BONIFACE (St) M.   RM. Aug 17
See Liberatus, Boniface, etc.

BONIFACE and THECLA (SS) MM.
RM. Aug 30
d. c.250. Their *Passio* makes them the parents of the "twelve brothers" commemorated on Sept 1. They are supposed to have been martyred under Maximiab (though their *Passio* does not say this) at Hadrumetum, i.e. Soussa in Tunisia.

BONIFACE I (St) Pope RM. Sept 4
d. 423. A Roman priest who was elected pope in 418. He was opposed by the anti-pope Eulalius and later on was troubled by the ever-recurring claims of the Patriarch of Constantinople. Gently but firmly he defended the rights of the Roman see. St Augustine dedicated to him several treatises against Pelagianism.

BONIFACE (St) M.   RM. Oct 5
Said to be the name of one of the martyrs who suffered with St Palmatius and Comp., q.v.

BONIFACE (St) M.   RM. Dec 6
See Dionysia, Dativa, etc.

BONIFACE (St) M.   RM. Dec 29
See Callistus, Felix and Boniface.

BONITUS (BONT) (St) Bp. OSB.
RM. Jan 15
623–c.710. A native of Auvergne who became successively chancellor to King Sigebert III, governor of Provence, and bishop of Clermont in Auvergne. After ten years as bishop, he resigned, owing to a scruple of conscience, and retired to the Benedictine abbey of Manlieu, where he became a monk and died in extreme old age.

BONITUS (St) Ab. OSB. AC. July 7
d. c.582. Fourth successor of St Benedict as abbot of Montecassino. During his abbacy the Lombards under Zoto of Benevento plundered and destroyed the arch-abbey (c.581). The monks saved themselves by flight and were

housed in the Lateran in Rome. Bonitus died shortly after.

BONIZELLA (Bl) W.   PC. May 6
d. 1300. The wife of Naddo Piccolomini of Siena. In her widowhood she devoted herself and all her wealth to the service of the poor in the district of Belvederio.

BONONIUS (St) Ab. OSB. Cam.
RM. Aug 30
d. 1026. A native of Bologna and a Benedictine monk of St Stephen's in the same city. He became a disciple of St Romuald, by whom he was sent to preach the gospel in Egypt and Syria. On his return he was made abbot of Lucedio in Piedmont.

BONOSA (St) M.   RM. July 15
See Eutropius, Zosima and Bonosa.

BONOSUS and MAXIMIAN (SS)
MM.   RM. Aug 21
d. 362. Two officers of the Herculean Cohort at Antioch, under Julian the Apostate. They were tortured and beheaded for refusing to change Constantine's Christian banner—the *labarum*—for a new idolatrous standard.

BONUS, FAUSTUS, MAURUS and
Comp. (SS) MM.   RM. Aug 1
d. ? Bonus, a priest, with Faustus, Maurus and nine companions, was martyred at Rome under Valerian.

BORIS and GLEB (SS) MM.
AC. July 24
See Romanus and David.

BOSA (St) Bp. OSB.   AC. March 9
d. 686. Monk of Whitby under St Hilda, he was consecrated bishop of York by St Theodore (678) when the titular of that see, St Wilfrid, was in exile. St Bede praises St Bosa in the following

words: "a man beloved by God . . . of most unusual merit and sanctity."

BOSWELL (BOISIL) (St) Ab.
AC. Feb 23
d. c.664. Abbot of Melrose. He counted SS Cuthbert and Egbert among his monks. Both had a great admiration for him, as had also St Bede. His favourite reading was the Gospel of St John.

BOTULPH and ADULPH (SS) CC.
OSB.   AC. June 17
d. c.680. Brothers, sons of noble Saxon parents. They were educated, and received the Benedictine habit, in Belgian Gaul. Adulph is said to have been raised to the episcopate. Botulph returned to England and became one of the foremost missionaries of the 7th century. He founded an abbey at Ikanhoe, formerly thought to be near Boston in Lincolnshire, but now generally supposed to be Iken in Suffolk. More than seventy English churches were dedicated to St Botulph, including four at the gates of the city of London.

BOTWID (St) M.   AC. July 28
d. 1100. A Swede, converted to the Faith in England, who became an aspostle in his own country. He was murdered by a Finnish slave whom he thought he had converted and whom he had set free.

BOVA and DODA (SS) VV. OSB.
RM. Apr 24
7th cent. St Bova was a sister, and St Doda a niece, of St Balderic (Baudry), the founder of Montfaucon and of the nunnery of St Peter at Reims. He appointed Bova first abbess of this convent and she was succeeded by Doda.

BRADAN and ORORA (CRORA)
(SS)   AC. Oct 20
? Two saints venerated in the Isle of

Man. In the church of St Bradan, Kirk-Braddan, near Douglas, Mark, the bishop of Sodor, held a synod in 1291. In a map of the 16th century, reference is made to the churches of SS Patrick and Crora.

BRANNOCK (St) Ab.   AC. Jan 7
6th cent. A saint who appears to have migrated from S. Wales into Devon, and to have founded a monastery at Braunton, near Barnstaple. The traditions concerning him are very untrustworthy. See also Brynach.

BRANWALLADER (St) Bp.
AC. Jan 19
? 6th cent. Said to have been a bishop in Jersey. King Athelstan, who founded Milton Abbey in Dorset, had this saint's relics translated there in 935.

BRAULIO (St) Bp.   RM. March 26
d. 646. A monk of St Engratia's monastery, Saragossa, he was sent to Seville to study under St Isidore. He was ordained priest by his own brother, John, whom he succeeded as archbishop of Saragossa. He was a ready writer and excelled chiefly as a hagiographer.

BREACA (St) V.   AC. June 4
5th–6th cent. A disciple of St Brigid who is said to have gone from Ireland to Cornwall (c.460) with several companions and to have landed on the eastern bank of the river Hayle. Variants of her name are: Breague, Branca, Banka, etc.

BREGWIN (St) Bp. OSB. AC. Aug 26
d. 765. The twelfth archbishop of Canterbury (761–765). His life was written by Eadmer. Letters of his to St Lullus of Mainz are still extant.

BRENACH (St) H.   AC. Apr 7
Otherwise Brynach, q.v.

BRENDAN the VOYAGER (St) Ab.
RM. May 16
c.489–583. One of the three most famous saints of Ireland. He was born on Fenit peninsula, Kerry, and educated for five years under St Ita, becoming afterwards a disciple of St Finian at Clonard and of St Gildas at Llancarfan in Wales. He was a great founder of monasteries, the chief of which was Clonfert. To his monks he gave a Rule of remarkable austerity. He is best known in history for his voyages, in which, it is said, he reached the American continent. Though they can scarcely be admitted as historical facts, they have nevertheless had some influence on history, since legends of St Brendan's journey to discover the Isles of the Blessed were popular throughout Europe. St Brendan is most fittingly venerated as the patron saint of sailors.

BRENDAN of BIRR (St) Ab.
AC. Nov 29
d. c.562. A contemporary of St Brendan the Voyager, and his fellow-disciple under St Finian at Clonard. His abbey of Birr was somewhere near Parsonstown in Offaly. He was the great friend and adviser of St Columba, who in a vision saw the soul of St Brendan carried by angels to heaven at the moment of his death.

BRETANNION (St) Bp. RM. Jan 25
d. c.380. Bishop of Tomi in Scythia on the Black Sea, near the mouth of the Danube. The Arian emperor, Valens, exiled him for his brave defence of Christ's divinity, but was compelled by popular discontent to recall him.

BRIACH (St) Ab.   AC. Dec 17
d. c.627. An Irishman who became a monk in Wales under St Tudwal, whom he accompanied to Brittany. He built a monastery at Guingamp. He died at Bourbiac.

BRIANT, ALEXANDER (Bl) M.
AC. Dec 1
See Alexander Briant.

BRIAVEL (BREVILE) (St) H.
AC. June 17
? The name of this saint (possibly a variant of Ebrulfus) is perpetuated as that of the patron saint of the parish of St Briavels in the Forest of Dean in Gloucestershire; but no record of his life is extant.

BRICE (BRITIUS, BRIXIUS) (St) Bp.
RM. Nov 13
d. 444. A disciple of St Martin of Tours, but, unlike his master, a proud, ambitious and even licentious cleric. Nevertheless, he was chosen to be St Martin's successor at Tours, and during twenty years he continued to be a very unsatisfactory ecclesiastic, being for this reason eventually driven from his see. He went to Rome, repented, and was reinstated at Tours, and such was his change of manners that his flock proclaimed him a saint immediately after his death. His cult spread throughout N. Europe.

BRICTIUS (St) Bp.
RM. July 9
d. c.312. Bishop of Martola near Spoleto in Umbria, imprisoned for the Faith under Diocletian. He escaped death, and died a confessor under Constantine.

BRIDGET (several)
Otherwise Brigid, q.v.

BRIEUC (BRIOCUS, BRIOC) (St) Bp.
AC. May 1
c.420–510. Born in Cardiganshire, he was educated in France by St Germanus of Auxerre. He laboured very successfully first in his native land, and then in Brittany, where he founded two abbeys, one near Tréguier, and the other where the town of St Brieuc now stands. He is greatly venerated in Cornwall.

BRIGID (BRIGA) (St) V. AC. Jan 21
6th cent. Known as St Brigid of Kilbride and venerated in the diocese of Lismore. It is recorded that her famous namesake of Kildare visited her more than once at Kilbride.

BRIGID (BRIDGET, BRIDE, FFRAID) (St) V. Foundress
RM. Feb 1
c.450–525. Born at Faughart, near Dundalk, she took the veil in her youth and founded the nunnery of Kildare, the first to be erected on Irish soil. Around her name there have been formed hundreds of legends, the key-note of them all being mercy and pity for the poor. In art St Brigid is represented holding a cross, with a flame over her head, and sometimes with a cow near her, since she is reputed to be the protectress of those engaged in dairy work. A greatly venerated Saint, she is the patron of Ireland after St Patrick.

BRIGID (St) V.
AC. Feb 1
9th cent. Alleged sister of St Andrew, abbot of St Donatus at Fiesole in Tuscany. It is said that she was carried by angels to her brother's deathbed. She died as a recluse in the Apennines. Most modern writers discard all this as pure fiction.

BRIGID AND MAURA (SS)
AC. Jan 28
? Venerated as daughters of a Scottish chieftain, said to have been martyred in Picardy while on a pilgrimage to Rome. They are most probably to be identified with SS Maura and Britta (q.v.).

BRIGID of SWEDEN (BRIDGET, BIRGITTA) (St) W. Foundress
RM. Oct 8
1304–1373. Born of a noble Swedish family, Brigid married, before she was fifteen, a Swedish prince, with whom she

lived happily for twenty-eight years, and to whom she bore eight children. She proved to be the ideal busy, home-loving wife. In her widowhood she founded the monastery of Wadstena (1344), thus instituting the Order of the Most Holy Saviour, known as "the Bridgettines". She is also famous for the visions and revelations with which she was favoured by God, and which she recorded in writing. She died in Rome on her return from Jerusalem (July 23) and was canonized eighteen years later (1391). In art she is represented clothed in the religious habit of her Order, bearing a pilgrim's staff, holding a heart marked with a cross and with our Saviour near her.

BRINSTAN (St) Bp.   AC. Nov 4
Otherwise Birnstan, q.v.

BRIOC, (BRIOCUS) (St) Bp.
AC. May 1
Otherwise Brieuc, q.v.

BRITHWALD (BRIHTWALD,
BERTHWALD, BERCTUALD) (St)
Bp. OSB.   AC. Jan 9
d. 731. An Anglo-Saxon, educated probably at Canterbury; afterwards monk and abbot of Reculver in Kent. He was elected archbishop of Canterbury in 692 and governed that see for thirty-seven years.

BRITHWOLD (St) Bp. OSB.
AC. Jan 22
d. 1045. A monk of Glastonbury. He was chosen bishop of Ramsbury (1005), whence he removed the see to Old Sarum. He was a great benefactor of Malmesbury and Glastonbury, where he was buried.

BRITO (BRITONIUS) (St) Bp.
AC. May 5
d. 386. Bishop of Trèves. A stout op-

ponent of the Priscillian heretics, whom he nevertheless always refused to hand over for punishment by the state.

BRITWIN (BRITHWIN, BRITHUN)
(St) Ab. OSB.   AC. May 15
d. c.733. Abbot of Beverley. He received his great friend and patron, St John of Beverley, into his monastery, after the latter had resigned the bishopric of York.

BRIXIUS (St) Bp.   RM. Nov 13
Otherwise Brice, q.v.

BROCARD (St) C. OC.   AC. Sept 2
d. 1231. St Berthold's successor as prior of the Frankish hermits of Mt Carmel. At his request St Albert, patriarch of Jerusalem, drew up for them the rule under which they developed in the West into the Order of Mt Carmel. He was highly respected by the Mohammedans.

BRON (St) Bp.   AC. June 8
d. c.511. A disciple of St Patrick, consecrated bishop of Cassel-Irra, near the town of Sligo.

BRONACH (BROMANA) (St) V.
AC. Apr 2
? Called the Virgin of Glen-Seichis and registered in the martyrologies of Tallaght and Donegal. Glen-Seichis is the old name of Kilbrony or Kilbronach, in Co. Down, which takes its present appellation from her.

BRONISLAVA (Bl) V. O. Praem.
AC. Aug 30
d. 1259. A cousin of St Hyacinth of Poland. She was a professed Premonstratensian nun in Poland, but died a recluse. Cult confirmed in 1839.

BROTHEN and GWENDOLEN
(SS)   AC. Oct 18
? 6th cent. Welsh saints, of whom

nothing is known but the names and the fact that they were given a public cult in Wales. St Brothen is still the patron saint of Llanbrothen in Merionethshire. Dolwyddelen and Llanwyddelan in Montgomeryshire suggest a St Gwendolen; this and similar names are diminutives of Gwen (white) and are equivalent to our Blanche and its allied forms.

BRUNO and Comp. (SS) MM.
AC. Feb 2
See Ebsdorf (Martyrs of).

BRUNO (St) Bp.   RM. May 27
d. 1045. Appointed bishop of Würzburg in 1033 and best remembered as the fosterer of church-building throughout the diocese, on which work he spent all his private fortune. While he was dining with the emperor Henry III at Bosenburg on the Danube, a gallery gave way, killing the saintly bishop on the spot.

BRUNO SERONKUMA (St) M.
RM. June 3
d. 1885. A soldier of King Mwanga of Uganda. He was baptized on Nov 18, 1885, and burnt alive a few weeks later, having refused a drink on the road to martyrdom. See Uganda (Martyrs of).

BRUNO-BONIFACE (St) M. OSB.
Cam.   RM. June 19 and Oct 15
d. 1009. Born at Querfurt, and educated at the cathedral-school of Magdeburg. He accompanied Otto III to Italy (996) and there he received the Camaldolese habit from St Romuald. He was made Archbishop of Mersburg, and sent to evangelize Prussia and Russia. He was martyred with eighteen companions (Feb. 14). Note that St Boniface of the RM. on June 19 and St Bruno on Oct 15 are one and the same person. Bruno was the baptismal, and Boniface the monastic, name of the saint.

BRUNO of SEGNI (St) Bp. OSB.
RM. July 18
1049–1123. Born at Solero (Asti) in Piedmont, he studied in the monastery of St Perpetuus at Asti, and at Bologna. He first became known as the opponent of Berengarius. In 1079 Gregory VII made him bishop of Segni; but he left the see and became a monk, and then abbot, of Montecassino. The pope, however, although allowing him to become a monk, had not definitely accepted his resignation of the see, and eventually Bruno had to return to it. Among other offices held by the saint were those of librarian of the Holy Roman See and cardinal legate. He was a profound theologian, and his work on the Holy Eucharist is still very useful. Canonized in 1183.

BRUNO (St) Founder   RM. Oct 6
1030–1101. Born at Cologne, he studied at Reims and Paris, and became chancellor of the diocese of Reims. In 1084 he retired with six companions to La Grande Chartreuse, near Grenoble, and there he founded his order, or rather a monastery of monk-hermits, under the Benedictine rule, which at a later period grew into the Carthusian Order. Bl Urban II, who had been St Bruno's student at Reims, called the saint to Rome, to be a papal counsellor. Even here, though never fully released from the pope's service, St Bruno managed to establish another Charterhouse at La Torre in Calabria, whither he was allowed to retire. He refused the see of Reggio. St Bruno excelled as a biblical exegete, writing on the psalms and on St Paul's epistles.

BRUNO (St) Bp.   AC. Oct 11
c.925–965. Called "the Great", a title which nowadays would seem rather to belong to the founder of the Carthusians. This Bruno was the youngest son

of the emperor, Henry the Fowler, and St Matilda. From childhood, we are told, he was devoted to learning; Prudentius was his bedside book. In 953 he was made bishop of Cologne, being already commendatory abbot of Lorsch and Corvey. As archbishop his political influence was a factor in the consolidation of the German States.

BRUNO (Bl) C. OSB.   AC. Dec 24
d. *c.*1050. A Benedictine lay-brother of the abbey of Ottobeuren in Bavaria.

BRYNACH (BERNACH, BERNACUS) (St) C.   AC. Apr 7
? 5th cent. An Irishman who settled in Wales, where he built a cell and a church at a place called Carn-Englyi (Mountain of Angels), overhanging Nevern (Pembrokeshire). Some authors identify him with St Brannock of Braunton.

BRYNOTH (St) Bp.   AC. May 9
d. 1317 (Feb 6). A Swede, bishop of Scara in W. Gothland. Canonized in 1498.

BUDOC (BUDEAUX) (St) Bp.
                          AC. Dec 9
? 7th cent. A Breton, educated in Ireland, where he became abbot of Youghal. Returning afterwards to Brittany, he succeeded SS Samson and Maglorius in the see of Dol. He has given his name to several places in Devon and Cornwall.

BUITHE (BUITE, BOETHIUS) (St) C.   AC. Dec 7
d. 521. A Scot, who spent some years in Italy and elsewhere on the continent and, returning to Scotland, evangelized the Picts. From him it seems that Carbuddo (Castrum Butthi) takes its name.

BULGARIA (Martyrs of) (SS)
                          RM. July 23
9th cent. During the war between the Greek emperor, Nicephorus, and the Bulgars, not as yet Christians, many Catholics, besides those slain in battle, were put to death on account of their Faith. There is much uncertainty as to the exact circumstances, but they have always been reckoned as martyrs.

BURCHARD (Bl) Ab. OSB. Cist.
                          PC. Apr 19
d. 1164. A favourite monk and disciple of St Bernard at Clairvaux. He was appointed successively abbot of Balerne (1136) and of Bellevaux (*c.*1157).

BURCHARD (Bl) Ab. OSB.
                          AC. June 25
d. 1122. Monk of the Benedictine abbey of St Michael at Bamberg, and first abbot of Mallersdorf in Bavaria.

BURCHARD (Bl) Bp. OSB.
                          AC. Aug 20
d. 1026. A native of Hesse who, after studying at Coblentz, became a monk at Lobbes. In 1006 he was compelled by the emperor Otto to accept the bishopric of Worms. He is famous as a compiler of canons and decretals.

BURCHARD (St) Bp. OSB.
                          RM. Oct 14
d. *c.*754. An English priest and monk who joined the German mission under St Boniface (*c.*732). He was consecrated first bishop of Würzburg (Herbipolis), and founded there several Benedictine abbeys, of which the most important was St Andrew's, afterwards called after him. About the year 753 he resigned his bishopric to a monk of Fritzlar and spent the remaining months of his life in monastic retirement.

BURGINUS and GUILMINUS (BB) Mks. OSB.   PC. Nov 18
d. *p*.1065. Two Benedictine monks who were among the pioneers of the priory of Thouacé in Anjou, founded by St Florentius.

BURGUNDOFARA (or FARA) (St) Abs. OSB.   RM. Apr 3 and Dec 7
d. 657. Blessed by St Columbanus in her infancy, Burgundofara early developed a religious vocation in spite of the fierce opposition of her father, a noble Frankish courtier. In the end he had to give way and founded for her the nunnery of Brige (Brie) or *Evoriacum*—later called Faremoutiers, i.e. Fara's Monastery—over which she ruled for thirty-seven years. Many English nun-saints were trained under her.

BURIANA (St) V.   AC. June 4
6th cent. An Irishwoman who lived as a recluse in Cornwall. The place-name St Buryan, opposite the Scilly Islands, perpetuates her memory.

BUZAD BANFY (Bl) M., OP.   AC. Dec 8
d. 1241. A Hungarian Count who became a famous friar preacher. Killed in front of the altar by the Tartars when they invaded Pesth.

BYBLIG (BIBLIG, PEBLIG, PIBLIG, PUBLICIUS)   AC. July 3
? 5th cent. A holy man connected with Carnarvon and honoured with a cult in parts of Wales, of whom, however, nothing certain is known.

C

CADELL (St) ?
7th cent. A Welsh saint, giving its name to Llangadell in Glamorgan.

CADFAN (St) Ab. AC. Nov 1
d. early 6th cent. A native of Brittany, who came over to Wales and founded several monasteries. His name is chiefly associated with those of Towyn in Merionethshire and Bardsey Island (Ynys Enlli).

CADFARCH (St) AC. Oct 24
6th cent. A Welsh saint, disciple of St Illtyd, and member of a family of saints. He is said to have founded churches at Penegoes and Abererch.

CADOC (DOCUS, CATHMAEL, CADVAEL) (St) Bp. M. AC. Jan 24
d. c.580. A Welsh monk, founder of the great monastery of Llancarfan not far from Cardiff, which became a veritable house of saints. Accompanied by St Gildas, St Cadoc later continued his religious life on an island off the coast of Vannes in Brittany. He returned to Britain and is said to have taken spiritual charge of the Britons, his compatriots, in the Eastern counties, during their last struggle with the conquering Saxons, by whom he was martyred near Weedon (Benevenna).

CADOG (GADOGA) (St) ?
5th cent. The titular saint of Llangadock in Carmarthen, not to be confused with the later St Cadoc or Docus.

CADROE (CADROEL) (St) Ab. OSB. AC. March 6
d. 976. The son of a Scottish prince, he was sent to Ireland to be educated at Armagh. He came to England and is said to have saved London from destruction by fire. Then he passed over to France and took the Benedictine habit at Fleury. Shortly after he was made abbot of the new foundation of Waulsort on the Meuse and finally called to Metz to restore St Clement's.

CADWALLADOR (St) King AC. Nov 12 (Oct 9)
d. c.682. A chieftain in Wales of the ancient British race, not to be confused with the Anglo-Saxon St Ceadwalla.

CAECILIA, CAECILIANUS, CAELESTINE
Otherwise often written Cecilia, Cecilanus, Celestine, and sometimes Coelestine.

CAECILIA (Bl) V. OP. AC. June 9
See Diana, Caecilia and Amata—the first Dominican nuns.

CAECILIA (St) Abs. OSB. PC. Aug 17
See Benedicta and Caecilia.

CAECILIA (St) VM. RM. Nov 22
2nd–3rd cent. One of the most famous of martyred Roman maidens. Having suffered for Christ, she was buried in the cemetery of St Callistus. Her name is in the Canon of the Mass. At about the same time there suffered at Rome SS Valerian and Tiburtius who were buried in the cemetery of Praetextatus. What connexion they had with St Caecilia, it is difficult now to ascertain. The relics of

all three rest at present beneath the high altar of the basilica of St Caecilia in Trastevere. All this is certain, and certain too it is that as early as the 4th century St Caecilia was already celebrated as one of the greatest Roman martyrs. The acts, however, which we now possess cannot be admitted as history. St Caecilia is the patron saint of musicians. In art she is represented playing the organ or the harp.

CAECILIA of FERRARA (Bl) V. OP.   **PC. Dec 19**
d. 1511. Married to a very virtuous husband, they separated by mutual consent to become religious, and she joined the Dominican nuns at Ferrara.

CAECILIAN (St) M.   **RM. Apr 16**
See Saragossa (Martyrs of).

CAECILIAN (St) C.   **RM. June 3**
Otherwise Caecilius, q.v.

CAECILIUS (St) Bp.   **RM. May 15**
See Torquatus, Ctesiphon, etc.

CAECILIUS (CAECILIAN) (St) C.   **RM. June 3**
3rd cent. A priest of Carthage, who, according to the RM., brought St Cyprian to the faith of Christ. St Cyprian never ceased to revere Caecilius's name, adding it to his own, and on Caecilius's death taking charge of his wife and children.

CAEDMON (St) Mk. OSB.   **AC. Feb 11**
d. c.680. A Northumbrian, attached first as a farm-servant and then as a lay-brother to the community of Whitby under St Hilda. He was the first of the Anglo-Saxons to write in verse.

CAELIAN (St) M.   **RM. Dec 15**
See Faustinus, Lucius, etc.

CAELLAINN (CAOILFIONN) (St) V.   **AC. Feb 3**
? 6th cent. An Irish saint listed in the Martyrology of Donegal. A church in Roscommon perpetuates her memory.

CAEREALIS, PUPULUS, CAIUS and SERAPION (SS) MM.   **RM. Feb 28**
? Martyrs at Alexandria in Egypt. Some ancient MSS read Cerulus or Celerius for Caerealis. Caius was added to the group by Baronius.

CAEREALIS (St) M.   **RM. June 10**
See Getulius, Caerealis, etc.

CAEREALIS and SALLUSTIA (SS) MM.   **RM. Sept 14**
d. 251. Caerealis, a soldier, and his wife Sallustia were instructed in the Faith by Pope St Cornelius, and martyred at Rome under Decius.

CAESAREA (St) V.   **AC. May 15**
? An Italian maiden, who in defence of her virtue took refuge in a cave, near Otranto, S. Italy, and lived therein as a recluse. This cave is now a place of popular pilgrimage.

CAESAREUS (St) M.   **RM. Apr 20**
See Victor, Zoticus, etc.

CAESARIA (St) V.   **AC. Jan 12**
d. c.530. Sister of St Caesarius of Arles, and abbess of the great nunnery founded by her brother in that city. According to the testimony of her contemporaries, Gregory of Tours and Venantius Fortunatus, she was a person of outstanding gifts.

CAESARIUS (St) C.   **AC. Jan 29**
1st cent. Deacon of Angoulême under its first bishop St Ausonius.

CAESARIUS of NAZIANZUS (St) C. RM. Feb 25

d. 369. Brother of St Gregory Nazianzen and physician at the imperial court of Byzantium, even under Julian the Apostate, who endeavoured unsuccessfully to drag Caesarius back to paganism. The saint, however, remained a catechumen nearly all his life, and was baptized only after a narrow escape from death in an earthquake at Nicea in Bithynia. We owe all these details to the funeral oration delivered by his brother Gregory.

CAESARIUS of ARLES (St) Bp. RM. Aug 27

470–543. A native of Châlon-sur-Saône, at the age of twenty he became a monk at Lérins, and at the age of thirty (500) was chosen bishop of Arles. A great churchman, he presided over several councils, notably over that of Orange (529) which condemned Semi-pelagianism. He founded the great nunnery afterwards called by his name at Arles, for which he drew up a monastic rule and of which his sister St Caesaria became abbess. He was zealous for decorum in liturgical worship. He excelled as a preacher, and his homilies may still be read with much profit. His people looked upon him as their leader even in social and political affairs, and he always proved worthy of their trust. During the distress caused by the siege of Arles in 508 he sold the treasures of his church to relieve the poor. He is said to have been the first archbishop in Western Europe to receive the *pallium* from the pope.

CAESARIUS and JULIAN (SS) MM. RM. Nov 1

? The former was an African deacon, the latter a priest. Both were martyred at Terracina, and their names appear in the earliest martyrologies. The church of St Caesarius on the Appian Way in Rome, now a title of one of the cardinal deacons, is dedicated to St Caesarius the African.

CAESARIUS, DACIUS and Comp. (SS) MM. RM. Nov 1

? A group of seven martyrs who suffered at Damascus.

CAESARIUS (St) Bp. AC. Nov 1

d. *p*.627. The nineteenth or the twenty-second bishop of Clermont.

CAESARIUS (St) M. RM. Nov 3

See Germanus, Theophilus, etc.

CAESARIUS (St) M. RM. Dec 28

d. 309. Father of a notorious Arian, Eudoxius by name, his own past life had not been above reproach; but he atoned for it all by his heroic death at the stake at Arabissus in Armenia, under Galerius Maximian.

CAESIDIUS and Comp. (SS) MM. RM. Aug 31

3rd cent. Known only from the unreliable *Acta* of St Rufinus (Aug 11), in which he is said to have been the son of that saint, and to have been martyred, with a group of Christians, on the shores of Lake Fucino, sixty miles east of Rome.

CAGNOALD (St) Bp. AC. Sept 6

d. *c*.635. Brother of St Faro and St Burgundofara. He became a monk at Luxeuil under St Columbanus, and afterwards the sixth bishop of Laon.

CAIAN (St) AC. Sept 25

5th cent. A son or grandson of King Brychan of Brecknock. His church at Tregaian in Anglesey perpetuates his memory.

CAIDOC and FRICOR (ADRIAN) (SS) HH. AC. Apr 1
7th cent. Two Irishmen who evangelized the country of the Morini in N. France. St Ricarius, the future founder of Centula (Saint-Riquier), was one of their converts. Their relics are still venerated at the parish church of Saint-Riquier, diocese of Amiens.

CAILLIN (St) Bp. AC. Nov 13
7th cent. Associated with St Aedan (Maidhoc) of Ferns. It is narrated of him that he turned certain unbelieving Druids into stone.

CAIMIN (CAMMIN) of INNISKEL-TRA (St) Ab. AC. March 24 or 25
d. 653. An Irish recluse who had led a life of great austerity on an island in Lough Derg, to which his reputation for sanctity attracted many disciples. Later in life he founded a monastery and church on the island of the Seven Churches. He was a fellow-worker with St Senan. A fragment of the Psalter of St Caimin, copied with his own hand, still exists.

CAIRLON (CAORLAN) (St) Bp. AC. March 24
6th cent. An Irish abbot, said to have died and to have been restored to life by St Dageus. Afterwards, when St Cairlon had been made archbishop of Cashel, St Dageus placed himself and his monks under his rule.

CAIRNECH (St) AC. May 16
Otherwise Carantac, q.v.

CAIUS (St) M. RM. Jan 4
See Hermes, Aggaeus and Caius.

CAIUS FRANCIS (St) M. Tert. OFM. RM. Feb 5
d. 1597. A Japanese soldier, recently baptized and received as a Franciscan tertiary, who insisted on being arrested with the friars. He was crucified with twenty-five companions at Nagasaki. Beatified 1627, canonized in 1862.

CAIUS (St) M. RM. Feb 28
See Caerealis, Pupulus, etc.

CAIUS and Comp. (SS) MM. RM. March 4
d. 254-259. Caius, an officer of the imperial palace, was with twenty-seven (some MSS have thirty-seven) other Christians thrown into the sea at Nicomedia.

CAIUS and ALEXANDER (SS) MM. RM. March 10
d. c.172. Two Christians martyred at Apamea in Phrygia under Marcus Aurelius. They had previously distinguished themselves as firm opponents of the Montanists.

CAIUS and CREMENTIUS (SS) MM. RM. Apr 16
d. 304. Martyrs or (according to Fortunatus) Confessors of the faith at Saragossa, they belong to the group "Martyrs of Saragossa". See Saragossa.

CAIUS of MELITENE (St) M. RM. Apr 19
See Hermogenes, Caius, etc.

CAIUS (St) Pope RM. Apr 22
d. c.296. Nothing reliable is known about the life or death of this pope. He is said to have been a Dalmatian, and the pope who recognized officially the six orders preceding the priesthood. He suffered ill-treatment under Diocletian, but was not a martyr.

CAIUS XEYMON (Bl) M. Tert. OP. AC. June 1
d. 1627. A Japanese born of Christian parents on the isle of Amakusa. He be-

came a Dominican tertiary and helped the friars in their missionary work. He was burnt alive at Nagasaki (Aug 17). Beatified in 1867.

CAIUS and LEO (SS) MM.
RM. June 30
? Martyrs either in Africa or in Rome. Caius was a priest and Leo a subdeacon.

CAIUS of SALERNO (St) M.
RM. Aug 28
See Fortunatus, Caius and Anthes.

CAIUS of MILAN (St) Bp.
RM. Sept 27
1st cent. He is said to have been the successor of St Barnabas the Apostle in the see of Milan, which he governed for twenty-four years. He is also said to have baptized the martyr St Vitalis and his sons SS Gervase and Protase. St Charles Borromeo enshrined his relics in the church of St Francis at Milan (1571).

CAIUS (St) M.   RM. Oct 3
See Dionysius, Faustus, etc.

CAIUS of CORINTH   RM. Oct 4
See Crispus and Caius.

CAIUS, FAUSTUS, EUSEBIUS, CHAEREMON, LUCIUS and
Comp. (SS) MM.   RM. Oct 4
3rd cent. Victims at Alexandria of the persecution under Valerian (257). Caius and Faustus are probably the saints of those names commemorated with St Dionysius of Alexandria, their bishop, on Oct 3. Eusebius, a deacon, survived to become bishop of Laodicea, and died in 269. Chaeremon, who had already suffered under Decius, was sent into exile. Of Lucius nothing certain is known.

CAIUS (St) M.   RM. Oct 21
See Dasius, Zoticus, etc.

CAIUS of COREA (Bl) M.
AC. Nov 15
d. 1627. A former Corean bonze who fled from his country to Nagasaki, where he harboured Dominican friars. A tertiary OP.

CAIUS (St) M.   RM. Nov 20
See Ampelus and Caius.

CAJETAN (GAETANO) (St)
Founder   RM. Aug 7
1480-1547. Born at Vicenza, in Lombardy, a scion of the family of the counts of Thienna (Tiene). He renounced the dignities offered him in Rome in order to devote his life to the service of the sick and the poor at Vicenza. Later, with Peter Caraffa (afterwards Pope Paul IV), he founded the congregation of clerks regularly called *Theatines*, from Theate (Chieti), in the Abruzzi, where Caraffa was bishop. The institute, characterized by absolute trust in divine providence, played a part in the counter-Reformation. St Cajetan died at Naples; he was canonized in 1671.

CALAIS (St) Ab.   AC. July 1
Otherwise Carilefus, q.v.

CALANICUS (St) M.   RM. Dec 17
See Florian, Calanicus, etc.

CALEPODIUS, PALMATIUS, SIMPLICIUS, FELIX, BLANDA
and Comp. (SS) MM.   RM. May 10
d. 222-232. A number of Roman martyrs who suffered under Alexander Severus, during the pontificate of Callistus I. Calepodius, a priest, was the first to suffer; he has given its name to a Roman catacomb. St Palmatius, of consular rank, died with his wife and children and forty-two of his household. St Simplicius, a senator, was martyred with sixty-five of his family and

dependents. SS Felix and Blanda were husband and wife. All were victims of an outburst of fury on the part of the heathen mob.

CALETRICUS (St) Bp. AC. Sept 4
529–c.580. Born at Chartres he became bishop of that city after the death of St Lubinus (c.557).

CALIMERIUS (St) Bp. M.
                        RM. July 31
d. c.190. A Greek, educated in Rome by Pope St Telesphorus, he became bishop of Milan. He was the apostle of the valley of the Po. Under the emperor Commodus he was martyred by being cast headlong into a deep well. He is buried under the high altar of his church at Milan.

CALIMERIUS of MONTECHIERO (Bl) C. OP. PC. Nov 28
d. 1521. A Friar Preacher who spent his life preaching throughout Italy. When a nonagenarian and unable to climb into the pulpit he persuaded others to lift him into it in order that he might preach.

CALIXTUS (*several*)
Otherwise Callistus, q.v.

CALLINICA and BASILISSA (SS) MM. RM. March 22
d. 250. Rich ladies of Galatia in Asia Minor, who spent their fortune in succouring the Christians imprisoned for their faith. Both were martyred on that account.

CALLINICUS (St) M. RM. Jan 28
See Thyrsus, Leucius and Callinicus.

CALLINICUS (St) M. RM. July 29
? 3rd cent. A native of Gangra, the chief town of Paphlagonia in Asia Minor. He was burnt to death. Metaphrastes gives full details of his martyrdom, and he is held in high esteem in the Eastern Churches.

CALLIOPE (St) M. RM. June 8
d. ? 250. An Eastern martyr, beheaded for Christ. Neither the place nor the exact date of her martyrdom is known. Her acts are untrustworthy.

CALLIOPUS (St) M. RM. Apr 7
d. c.303. A martyr, who, under Diocletian, was crucified head downwards at Pompeiopolis in Cilicia.

CALLISTA (St) M. RM. Sept 2
See Evodius, Hermogenes and Callistus.

CALLISTHENE (St) V. AC. Oct 4
See Adauctus and Callisthene.

CALLISTRATUS and Comp. (SS) MM. RM. Sept 26
d. c.300. A body of fifty African soldiers put to death at Constantinople under Diocletian. They were sewn up in sacks and cast into the sea.

CALLISTUS, CHARISIUS and Comp. (SS) MM. RM. Apr 16
3rd cent. Nine Christians of Corinth, martyred by being thrown into the sea.

CALLISTUS I (St) Pope M.
              RM. Oct 14 (and Aug 14)
d. c.222. A Christian slave of Rome, of outstanding natural gifts, who was made deacon by Pope St Zephyrinus, whom he succeeded as pope (217). For his lenient attitude towards repentant sinners he incurred the wrath of the rigorists—notably St Hippolytus, Tertullian and Novatian. He condemned Sabellianism and other heresies. As deacon he had superintended the Christian cemetery on the Appian Way, which is still known by his name. He was probably martyred. He is honoured

as a martyr at Todi on Aug 14 and is mentioned in the RM. on this date.

CALLISTUS (St) M.   AC. Oct 15
d. 1003. A native of Huesca, in Aragon, who, together with St Mercurialis, passed over to France and died there fighting against the Saracens. They are still venerated in the diocese of Tarbes.

CALLISTUS, FELIX and BONI-FACE (SS) MM.   RM. Dec 29
? Roman martyrs, whose names are listed in all the Western martyrologies, but about whom nothing is known.

CALLIXTUS, CALIXTUS (several)
Otherwise Callistus, q.v.

CALMINIUS (CALMILIUS) (St) H.   AC. Aug 19
d. c.690. A hermit in Gaul who founded the abbeys of Villars (*Calminiacum, Saint Chaffe*), and Mauzac, near Riom.

CALOCERUS (St) Bp. RM. Feb 11
d. c.130. A disciple of St Apollinaris, whom he succeeded in the see of Ravenna.

CALOCERUS (St) M.   RM. Apr 18
? Nothing reliable is known about this martyr. His acts, which belong to a much later period, connect him with SS Faustinus and Jovita, and make him an officer of the emperor Hadrian at Brescia in Lombardy.

CALOCERUS and PARTHENIUS (SS) MM.   RM. May 19
d. 250. Two brothers, eunuchs in the palace of Tryphonia, wife of the emperor Decius. They were martyred at Rome in the Decian persecution.

CALOGERUS the ANCHORET (St) M.   RM. June 18
d. c.486. A Greek who received the monastic habit at the hands of the pope

at Rome, and lived for thirty-five years as a recluse near Girgenti in Sicily, after having evangelized the isles of Lipari.

CALOGERUS (St) Ab. AC. June 18
See Gregory, Demetrius and Calogerus.

CALUPAN (St) H.   AC. March 3
d. 575. Monk of Meallet in Auvergne, and afterwards a recluse in a neighbouring cave.

CAMELIAN (St) Bp.   AC. July 28
d. c.525. Successor of St Lupus in the see of Troyes (478–c.525).

CAMERINUS (St) M.   RM. Aug 21
See Luxorius, Cisellus and Camerinus.

CAMILLA (St) V.   AC. March 3
d. c.437. A native of Civitavecchia who became a disciple of St Germanus of Auxerre at Ravenna and accompanied his corpse to Auxerre. She settled near that place as a recluse and died there.

**CAMILLA GENTILI (Bl) V.
                         AC. May 18**
d. 1486. A maiden of holy life who is venerated in the church of the Dominican friars at San Severino. Cult approved in 1841.

CAMILLA VARANI (Bl) Abs. Poor Clare.   AC. May 31
d. 1527. Abbess of a convent founded by her father at Camerino, in Italy. Cult confirmed in 1843.

CAMILLUS de LELLIS (St) Founder.   RM. July 18
1550–1614. A native of the Abruzzi in central Italy, who after some years of soldiering, tried to join the Capuchins, but had to leave them on account of a disease of the feet, which proved incurable. Ultimately he found his vocation in the service of the sick, for whom

he founded the nursing congregation of the Ministers of the Sick, approved in 1591. Before this, St Camillus had been ordained priest by Thomas Goldwell of St Asaph, the last English bishop of the old hierarchy. Canonized in 1746, and declared by Leo XIII patron saint of the sick and of their nurses.

CAMILLUS CONSTANZI (Bl) M. SJ.   AC. Oct 12

1572–1622. An Italian Jesuit and a missionary in Japan, who was banished from that country as a Christian, but returned and was burnt to death over a slow fire at Firando (Sept 15). Beatified in 1867.

CAMIN or INNISKELTRA (St) Ab.   AC. March 24 or 25

Otherwise Caimin, q.v.

CAMPANIA (Martyrs of) (SS)   RM. March 2

6th cent. Christians put to death by the Lombards. They numbered several hundreds (the RM. mentions eighty). As to their claim to the title of martyrs, we have the testimony of St Gregory the Great, their contemporary.

CAMPION, EDMUND (Bl) M. SJ.   AC. Dec 1

See Edmund Campion, SJ.

CANDIDA (St) W.   AC. Jan 27

d. c.798. Mother of St Emerius, the founder of the abbey of St Stephen of Bañoles. She died as a recluse near the monastery, in the diocese of Gerona, Spain.

CANDIDA (St) M.   RM. June 6

See Artemius, Candida and Paulina.

CANDIDA (St) VM.   RM. Aug 29

? One of a group of martyrs who suffered on the Ostian Way, outside the gates of Rome. In the 9th century Pope St Paschal I enshrined her relics in the church of St Praxedes.

CANDIDA the ELDER (St) VM.   RM. Sept 4

d. c.78. An aged woman who is said to have welcomed St Peter when passing through Naples on his way to Rome and to have been miraculously cured by him of a malady. In her turn she converted St Aspren, who became the first bishop of Naples.

CANDIDA the YOUNGER (St)   RM. Sept 10

d. ? 586. A married woman of Naples, who sanctified herself by fulfilling perfectly her duties as a wife and as a mother. The RM. described her as "famous for her miracles".

CANDIDA (St) VM.   RM. Sept 20

d. c.300. A martyred maiden of Carthage under Maximian Herculeus. The date of her martyrdom is contested; see the Bollandists on this controversy.

CANDIDA (St) M.   RM. Dec 1

See Lucius, Rogatus, etc.

CANDIDUS of ROME (St) M.   RM. Feb 2

See Fortunatus, Felician, etc.

CANDIDUS (St) M.   RM. March 10

One of the Forty Armenian Martyrs, q.v.

CANDIDUS, PIPERION and Comp. (SS) MM.   RM. March 11

d. c.254–259. Twenty-two African martyrs who suffered either at Carthage or at Alexandria, most probably under Valerian and Gallienus. Particulars are lost.

CANDIDUS (St) M.   RM. Sept 22

See Theban Legion.

CANDIDUS (St) M.   RM. Oct 3
? A Roman martyr, buried on the Esquiline Hill, in the place called "*ad Ursum Pileatum*".

CANDIDUS (St) M.   RM. Dec 15
See Faustinus, Lucius, etc.

CANDRES (St) Bp.   AC. Dec 1
5th cent. A regionary bishop who evangelized the territory of Maestricht. He is still liturgically commemorated in the diocese of Rouen.

**CANICE (CANICUS, CAINNECH, KENNY, KENNETH) (St) Ab.
      RM. Oct 11**
*c.*515–599. Born in N. Ireland, he was trained to the monastic life under St Finian of Clonard, and St Cadoc in Wales. Then he went to Glasnevin. He founded the monastery of Agahanoe and perhaps of Kilkenny, and later preached in Scotland under St Columba and was the first to build a church in the place now known as St Andrews. He has always been very popular in Ireland; the city of Kilkenny is named after him.

CANION (St) C.   RM. Sept 1
See Briscus, Castrensis, etc.

CANNATUS (St) Bp.   AC. Oct 15
5th cent. Bishop of Marseilles after St Honoratus.

CANNERA (CAINDER, KINNERA) (St) V.   AC. Jan 28
d. *c.*530. An Irish maiden who lived as a recluse near Bantry. She died after visiting St Senan and receiving Holy Communion at his hands. She was buried on St Senan's island of Enniscorthy.

CANOG (CYNOG) M.   AC. Oct 7
d. *c.*492. Eldest son of King Brychan of Brecknock. He met his death as a result of an inroad of barbarians at Merthyr-Cynog. Several churches in Wales were dedicated to him. In Brittany he is known as St Cenneur.

CANTIAN and CANTIANILLA (SS) MM.   RM. May 31
See Cantius, Cantian, etc.

CANTIDIUS, CANTIDIAN and SOBEL (SS) MM.   RM. Aug 5
? Egyptian martyrs of whom nothing is known except the fact of their martyrdom.

**CANTIUS, CANTIAN, CANTIANILLA and PROTUS (SS) MM.
      RM. May 31**
d. *c.*304. Two brothers and their sister, said to have belonged to the Roman family of the Anicii. They were martyred at Aquileia, whither they had retired, together with their tutor, Protus by name, under Diocletian. We have still a panegyric preached in their honour by St Maximus of Turin.

CANUTE (KNUD) LAVARD (St) M.   RM. Jan 7
d. 1133. A nephew of St Canute, king of Denmark, with whom he is sometimes confused. He was duke of Schleswig, and his life was spent mostly in war against the viking pirates. He was slain as a result of a conspiracy of the Danes, headed by a kinsman of his, pretender to the throne. Canonized in 1171 and venerated as a martyr.

**CANUTE (KNUD) (St) King, M.
      RM. Jan 19**
d. 1086. Natural son of Sweyn III, king of Denmark, and great-nephew of Canute, king of England, he succeeded to the Danish throne as Canute IV. He displayed a warlike zeal for the spreading of the gospel in Denmark itself,

Courland, Livonia and elsewhere. He was prevented by treachery from helping the Anglo-Saxons against their Norman conquerors. Though well liked by his people, he was killed in a church by a party of malcontents, headed by his brother Olaf (July 10). As this crime was prompted by opposition to the laws he had enacted to enforce the payment of tithes, he was considered a martyr and as such was canonized by the Holy See, at the request of Eric III, king of Denmark, in 1101.

CAPITO (St) Bp. M.   RM. March 4
See Basil, Eugene, etc.

CAPITO (St) M.   RM. July 24
See Meneus and Capito.

CAPITOLINA and EROTHEIS (SS) MM.   RM. Oct 27
d. 304. A Cappadocian lady and her hand-maid, martyred under Diocletian.

**CAPPADOCIA (Martyrs of) (SS)
                          RM. May 23**
d. 303. A group of martyrs, put to death in Cappadocia, under Galerius, after having suffered exquisite tortures.

CAPRASIUS (St) Ab.   RM. June 1
d. c.430. A native of Gaul, he retired to the island of Lérins to live as a hermit. Thither he was followed by SS Honoratus and Venantius, and together they went to the East to visit the monastic colonies there. Venantius died in Greece; the other two returned to Lérins, where St Honoratus founded the famous abbey, and on his being appointed bishop of Arles, he was succeeded by Caprasius as abbot.

CAPRASIUS (St) M.   RM. Oct 20
d. 303. A native of Agen in S. France, who, owing to fear, concealed himself during the persecution of Diocletian;

but on hearing of the courage of St Faith at the stake, he came forth and boldly confessed his religion. He was forthwith beheaded.

CARADOC (St) Ab.   AC. Apr 13
d. 1124. A Welshman, harpist at the court of King Rhys of S. Wales, who became a monk at Llandaff, and then lived as a hermit in different places—on Barry Island, at St Issels, etc.—in S. Wales. He had much to suffer during the English invasion under Henry I. He was buried with great honour in the cathedral of St David's.

CARALIPPUS (St) M.   RM. Apr 28
See Aphrodisius, Caralippus, etc.

CARANTAC (CARANTOG, CAIRNACH, CARNATH) (St) AC. May 16
5th cent. A Welsh prince who laboured under St Patrick in the evangelization of Ireland.

CARANTOCK (St) Ab. AC. May 16
6th cent. A Welsh abbot, founder of the church of Llangranog. He is associated with Crantock in Cornwall and Carhampton in Somerset. He is also highly venerated in Brittany. Some writers identify him with St Carantac.

CARANUS (St) Bp.   AC. Dec 24
7th cent. A saint commemorated in the Aberdeen breviary. He belonged to E. Scotland.

CARAUNUS (CERAUNUS, CHERON) (St) M.   RM. May 28
5th cent. A Christian of Roman descent, he preached the gospel in Gaul, and was killed by robbers near Chartres. A church and monastery were built over his tomb.

CARDEÑA, Martyrs of
See Stephen of Cardeña.

148

CARILEFUS (CARILEPHUS, CARILEFF, CALAIS) (St) Ab.
AC. July 1

d. c.536. A French monk, friend and companion of St Avitus. He was the abbot-founder of the abbey of Anisole in Maine. His cult is found chiefly at Blois.

CARINA (St) M.   RM. Nov 7
See Melasippus, Antony and Carina.

CARISSIMA (St) V.   AC. Sept 7
5th cent. A native of Albi, in France. She retired to a forest near the city, then to the nunnery of Viants (Vious). She is liturgically commemorated at Albi.

CARITAS (St) VM.   RM. Aug 1
Otherwise Charity. See Faith, Hope and Charity.

CARLOMAN (Bl) Mk. OSB.
AC. Aug 17

707–755. Eldest son of Charles Martel, and brother of Pepin the Short. On his father's death he became king of Austrasia. As such, he promoted the foundation of the abbeys of Fulda, Lobbes, Stavelot, etc., helped St Boniface in the evangelization of the Germanies, and endeavoured to remedy the injustice done by Charles Martel with regard to ecclesiastical property. On St Boniface's advice he left the kingdom to his brother, received the Benedictine habit at the hands of Pope St Zachary and was a monk first on Mt. Soracte and then at Montecassino, where he was employed in the kitchen and as the shepherd of the abbey. Having been sent to maintain peace between Pepin and the Lombards, he died in a monastery at Vienne. He has an altar dedicated to him at Montecassino.

CARMELITE NUNS of COMPIÈGNE (BB) MM   AC. July 17
d. 1794. Sixteen nuns of the Carmel of Compiègne, guillotined in Paris during the French Revolution. They went to the scaffold singing the *Salve Regina*. Beatified in 1906. Each is given a separate notice in this book.

CARMES (Martyrs des) (BB)
AC. Sept 2

See September (Martyrs of).

CARNATH or CARNECH (St) Ab.
AC. May 16

Otherwise Carantac, q.v.

CARON (St) ? Bp.   AC. March 5
? The title saint of Tregaron in Cardiganshire. Nothing is known about him.

CARPONIUS, EVARISTUS and PRISCIAN (SS) MM.   RM. Oct 14
d. c.303. Three brothers who, with their sister St Fortunata, were among the Christians martyred under Diocletian at Caesarea in Palestine. Their relics were translated to Naples.

CARPOPHORUS, EXANTHUS, CASSIUS, SEVERINUS, SECUNDUS and LICINIUS (SS) MM.
RM. Aug 7

d. c.295. Christian soldiers who were put to death at Como in N. Italy, under Maximian Herculius.

CARPOPHORUS (St) M
RM. Aug 27

See Ruphus and Carpophorus.

CARPOPHORUS (St) M.
RM. Nov 8

See Four Crowned Martyrs.

CARPOPHORUS and ABUNDIUS (SS) MM.   RM. Dec 10
d. 290–300. A priest and his deacon who suffered under Diocletian. Rome, Spoleto and Seville have been given as the place of their martyrdom.

CARPUS, PAPYLUS, AGATHONICA, AGATHODORUS and Comp. (SS) MM.   RM. Apr 13

d. 150 (or 250). Carpus was the bishop of Thyatira, Papylus, his deacon, Agathonica, the latter's sister, and Agathodorus, their servant. They were martyred with many others at Pergamos in the time of Marcus Aurelius or of Decius.

CARPUS (St)   RM. Oct 13

1st cent. The Carpus of Troas on the Hellespont with whom St Paul (II Tim. IV, 13) says "he had left his cloak". Nothing more is known about him. Some Greek writers make him a bishop.

CARTERIUS (St) M.   AC. Jan 8

d. 304. A priest of Caesarea in Cappadocia, who suffered under Diocletian. He is venerated by the Greeks.

CARTERIUS, STYRIACUS, TOBIAS, EUDOXIUS, AGAPIUS and Comp. (SS) MM.   RM. Nov 2

d. c.315. Ten Christian soldiers in the army of the emperor Licinius, burnt at the stake at Sebaste in Armenia.

CARTHAGE the ELDER (St) Bp.   AC. March 5

d. c.540. The successor of St Kieran in the see of Ossory. He is said to have been the son or grandson of King Aengus.

CARTHAGE (CARTHACH MOCHUDA) the YOUNGER (St) Bp.   AC. May 14

d. c.637. Born in Kerry, he founded (c.590) an abbey at Rathin in Westmeath, of which he was abbot-bishop, and for which he wrote a monastic rule in verse. Shortly before his death (c.635) he and his community were expelled. He led his monks to the banks of the Blackwater and there established the monastery-school of Lismore. Cult confirmed in 1903.

CARTHUSIAN MARTYRS (BB)   AC. May 4

1535–1540. Eighteen monks of the Carthusian Order in England, put to death for their allegiance to the Holy See under Henry VIII. Beatified in 1886. Each is given a separate notice in this book.

CASDOE (St) M.   RM. Sept 29

See Dadas, Casdoe and Gabdelas.

CASILDA (St) V.   AC. Apr 9

d. c.1050. A native of Toledo and said to have been of Moorish parentage. She became a Christian and led the life of an anchoress near Briviesca in the province of Burgos. She is greatly venerated throughout Spain, chiefly in the provinces of Burgos and Toledo.

CASIMIR of POLAND (St) C.   RM. March 4

1460–1483. The second son of King Casimir IV of Poland. His father wished him to seize the crown of Hungary which was offered to him by a powerful party among the Hungarians: but the prince refused to employ force and was imprisoned by his father for three months. The remainder of his life he devoted to prayer and study. He died of consumption in 1483. He is the patron saint of Poland and Lithuania.

CASPAR (GASPAR) (St)   AC. Jan 8

One of the Magi, q.v.

CASPAR CRATZ (Bl.) M. SJ.   AC. Jan 12

See John Caspar Cratz.

CASPAR SADAMAZU (Bl) M. SJ.   AC. June 20

d. 1626. A native of Omura in Japan, he was received into the society of Jesus at

Bungo 1582. He acted as secretary to several provincials, the last being Bl Francis Pacheco, with whom he was buried alive at Nagasaki. Beatified in 1867.

CASPAR de BONO (Bl) C. Minim.
AC. July 14
1530–1604. A native of Valencia in Spain, he became a silk merchant, then a trooper and finally a Minim friar. After his ordination in 1561 he was twice appointed corrector provincial of the Spanish province of Minims. Beatified in 1786.

CASPAR ALVAREZ (Bl) M. SJ.
AC. July 15
d. 1570. Born at Oporto in Portugal, he became a Jesuit lay-brother, and was one of a band of martyrs who suffered with Bl Ignatius de Azevedo. Beatified in 1854.

CASPAR and MARY VAZ (BB)
MM.   AC. Aug 17
d. 1627. Husband and wife, natives of Japan and tertiaries of St Francis, martyred at Nagasaki. Caspar was burnt alive and his wife beheaded. Beatified in 1867.

CASPAR COTENDA (Bl) M.
AC. Sept 11
d. 1622. A Japanese belonging to the royal family of Firando. He was martyred at Nagasaki. Beatified in 1867.

CASPAR FISOGIRO (Bl) M.
AC. Oct 1
d. 1617. A Japanese Christian, member of the Confraternity of the Holy Rosary. He was beheaded at Nagasaki for having befriended Bl Alphonsus Navarrete, OP. Beatified in 1867.

CASPAR del BUFALO (St)
Founder   AC. Dec 28
1786–1836. A native of Rome, who studied for the priesthood at the Roman College, and was ordained in 1808. He was exiled to Corsica for refusing to swear allegiance to Napoleon. On his return in 1814 he founded at Giano, diocese of Spoleto, the first house of the Missioners of the Most Precious Blood for mission work at home. After much opposition it received the approval of the Holy See, but by that time Caspar was already dead. Canonized in 1955.

CASSIA (St) M.   RM. July 20
See Sabinus, Julian, etc.

CASSIAN (St) M.   RM. March 26
See Peter, Marcian, etc.

CASSIAN (St) Ab.   AC. July 23
Otherwise John Cassian, q.v.

CASSIAN of AUTUN (St) Bp.
RM. Aug 5
d. c.350. Bishop of Autun 314–350, he succeeded St Reticius, and was famous for miracles. A life composed in the 9th century makes him an Egyptian by origin.

CASSIAN VAZ LÓPEZ-NETO (Bl)
OFM. Cap.   AC. Aug 7
1607–1638. Born at Nantes in France but of Spanish descent, he took the Capuchin habit at Angers, and was sent to Egypt to preach to the Copts, together with Bl Agathangelus, q.v. He was stoned to death on entering Abyssinia. Beatified in 1904.

CASSIAN of BENEVENTO (St) Bp.
AC. Aug 12
d. c.340. Bishop of Benevento in S. Italy. His relics are enshrined in the church of St Mary in the same city.

CASSIAN of IMOLA (St) M.
RM. Aug 13
250? The *laus* of the RM. reads as

follows: "The birthday of holy Cassian the martyr. When he refused to worship idols, the persecutor summoned certain boys who hated Cassian as their schoolmaster, and afforded them the opportunity of killing him. As their efforts were puny, so was his suffering bitter above the ordinary and his death protracted". The story is from Prudentius.

CASSIAN of TODI (St) Bp. M.
RM. Aug 13

4th cent. A convert of St Pontian, bishop of Todi, in Central Italy, and his successor in that see. He was martyred under Maximian Herculeus. It is possible that St Cassian of Imola was celebrated at Todi, and this gave rise to the notion of a second saint.

CASSIAN (St) M.   RM. Dec 1
See Lucius, Rogatus, etc.

CASSIAN (St) M.   RM. Dec 3

d. 298. During the trial of St Marcellus (Oct 30) at Tangier under Diocletian, Cassian, as the *exceptor* (official shorthand-writer or recorder) of the court, was taking down the *acta* of the proceedings. Indignant at the injustice done to the martyr, he threw down his pen and declared himself a Christian. He was arrested and a few weeks later he too suffered martyrdom. His acts are quite authentic; he is also mentioned in one of the hymns of Prudentius.

CASSIUS, VICTORINUS, MAXIMUS and Comp. (SS) MM.
RM. May 15

d. *c*.264. A group of martyrs of Clermont in Auvergne, who suffered at the hands of Chrocas, chief of the invading Teutonic barbarians.

CASSIUS of NARNI (St) Bp.
RM. June 29

d. 558. Bishop of Narni from 537 to 558.

St Gregory the Great has left on record the virtues of this holy prelate.

CASSIUS (St) M.   RM. Aug 7
See Carpophorus, Exanthus, etc.

CASSIUS, FLORENTIUS and Comp. (SS) MM.   RM. Oct 10

d. 303. Christians put to death by the emperor Maximian Herculeus at Bonn in Germany.

CASTOR and DOROTHEUS (SS) MM.   RM. March 28

? Two martyrs who suffered at Tarsus in Cilicia in one of the early persecutions.

CASTOR and STEPHEN (SS) MM.
RM. Apr 27

? Two martyrs who suffered at Tarsus in Cilicia in one of the early persecutions. Some writers identify them with the preceding pair.

CASTOR (St) Bp.   AC. Sept 2

d. *c*.420. A native of Nîmes, who married a wife and settled at Marseilles. After a short time they separated by mutual consent and both became religious. Castor founded the monastery of Manauque, and shortly after was chosen bishop of Apt. St John Cassian wrote the *De Institutis Coenobiorum* at Castor's request.

CASTOR, VICTOR, and ROGATIAN (SS) MM.   RM. Dec 28

? African martyrs of whom the names only are known.

CASTORA GABRIELLI (Bl) W.
PC. June 14

d. 1391. A Franciscan tertiary, wife and widow of Santuccio Sanfonerio, a lawyer at Sant' Angelo in Vado in Umbria. She sanctified herself by the daily practice of the domestic virtues.

CASTORIUS (St) M.
                    RM. July 7 and Nov 8
See Claudius, Nicostratus, etc., and
Four Crowned Martyrs.

CASTRENSIS (St) Bp.
                    RM. Sept 1 and Feb 11
See Priscus, Castrensis, etc.

CASTRITIAN (St) Bp.   RM. Dec 1
d. 137. The predecessor of St Calimerius in the see of Milan. He governed
that see for forty-two years.

CASTULUS (St) M.   RM. Jan 12
See Zoticus, Rogatus, etc.

CASTULUS (St) M.   RM. Feb 15
See Saturninus, Castulus, etc.

CASTULUS (St) M. RM. March 26
d. 288. An officer of the palace in Rome
of the emperor Diocletian. For having
sheltered some of his fellow Christians
he was put to the torture and buried
alive. A cemetery was named after his
burial place on the Via Labicana.

**CASTULUS and EUPREPIS (SS)
MM.   RM. Nov 30**
? Roman martyrs of whom nothing is
known.

CASTUS and EMILIUS (SS) MM.
                              RM. May 22
d. c.250. Two African martyrs, who
suffered under Decius. They at first
gave way under torture, but repented,
and on being seized a second time, were
burned to death. Their contemporary,
St Cyprian, and also St Augustine are
loud in their praise of these two martyrs.

**CASTUS and SECUNDINUS (SS)
Bps.   RM. July 1**
c.305. Two saints much venerated in S.
Italy. The martyrologies register them as
of Sinuessa (Mondragone) near Caserta.

CASTUS (St) M.   RM. Sept 4
See Magnus, Castus and Maximus.

CASTUS (St) M.   RM. Oct 6
See Marcellus, Castus, etc.

CATALDUS (St) Bp.   RM. May 10
7th cent. Born in Munster, Ireland, he
was first a pupil, and then the headmaster, of the monastic school of Lismore. On his return from a pilgrimage
to the Holy Land, he was chosen bishop
of their city by the people of Taranto,
in S. Italy. He is the titular of the
cathedral of Taranto and the principal
patron saint of the diocese.

CATELLUS (St) Bp   AC. Jan 19
9th cent. Bishop of Castellamare, south
of Naples. He was an intimate friend of
St Antoninus, OSB. He is venerated as
the principal saint of the city and diocese of Castellamare.

CATHALDUS (CATHAL) (St) Bp.
                              RM. May 10
Otherwise Cataldus, q.v.

**CATHAN (CATAN, CADAN) (St)
Bp.   AC. May 17**
6th or 7th cent. He seems to have been
bishop in the Isle of Bute, often called
after him Kil-Cathan. His tomb is
shown at Tamlacht near Londonderry,
but the Scots contend that he rests in
the Isle of Bute. Possibly there were two
saints of the same name.

CATHERINE dei RICCI (St) V. OP.
                              RM. Feb 2
1522–1590. Born at Florence, she became in 1535 a regular tertiary of St
Dominic, and filled the offices of novice-
mistress and prioress. She was famous
for her ecstasies in which she beheld and
enacted the scenes of our Lord's passion. It is narrated that she met in vision

St Philip Neri, still alive in Rome. Three future popes were among the thousands who flocked to her convent to ask her prayers. Canonized in 1746.

CATHERINE of BOLOGNA (St) V. Poor Clare.   RM. March 9

1413–1463. Born at Bologna, she was a maid of honour to Margaret d'Este. At the age of thirteen, she joined an Augustinian community at Ferrara. Later they became Poor Clares. Catherine was appointed novice-mistress and then abbess of a daughter convent of Poor Clares at Bologna. Here she spent her life praying for sinners, favoured by God with amazing visions, and committing to writing her mystical experiences. Canonized in 1712.

CATHERINE of SWEDEN (St) Bridg.   RM. March 24

1331–1381. Born in Sweden, the fourth child of St Brigid, she married Eggard Lydersson, a life-long invalid, with whom she lived in continency, and whom she tended with great devotion. With the consent of her husband she joined her mother St Bridget in Rome, and accompanied her to Jerusalem. After the death of her husband and mother she returned to Sweden and became abbess of Vadstena. In 1375–1380 she was again in Rome, obtaining the approval of the Salvatorian Order (the Bridgettines) and promoting the canonization of her own mother. Cult confirmed in 1484.

CATHERINE TOMAS (St) V. OSA. RM. Apr 5

1533–1574. Born on the island of Majorca. She joined the canonesses regular of St Augustine at Palma and there she spent her whole life, subject to a great number of strange phenomena and mystical experiences; during the last years of her life she was continually in ecstasy. Canonized in 1930.

CATHERINE of PALLANZA (Bl) V. OSA.   AC. Apr 6

c.1437–1478. A native of Pallanza, diocese of Novara. At fourteen years of age she began to live the life of a recluse in the mountain district above Varese, near Milan. Disciples gathered round her and she gathered them into a community under the rule of St Augustine. Cult confirmed in 1769.

CATHERINE of SIENA (St) V. Tert. OP.   RM. Apr 30

1347–1380. Born at Siena in Tuscany, the twenty-fifth child of a wool-dyer, Catherine Benincasa received the habit of the third order of St Dominic at the age of sixteen, continuing, however, to live at home. Soon her sanctity attracted a number of persons, clerical and lay, round her—the *Caterinati*—of whom she was a sort of leader. She worked among the poor of Siena and was most active and successful in the conversion of hardened sinners. She had especially at heart the unity and welfare of the Church and was instrumental in persuading Pope Gregory XI to abandon Avignon and return to Rome. She tried to heal the great schism of the West, rallying all Italy around Pope Urban VI. In 1378 she was summoned by the pope to Rome and there died, fighting still in the cause of the true pope. She has left over four hundred letters and a *Dialogue* which is one of the most remarkable mystical works of all time. Canonized in 1461 and declared patron saint of Italy in 1939.

CATHERINE of PARC-AUX-DAMES (Bl) V. OSB. Cist. PC. May 4

13th cent. A daughter of Jewish parents of Louvain, her name was Rachel. The Chaplain of the duke of Brabant was a frequent visitor to her home, and the little Rachel was an eager listener when he would defend the Catholic religion against the attacks of her Jewish father. When she was twelve years old, she secretly left her home, received baptism and joined the Cistercian nuns at Parc-aux-Dames, near Louvain, where she lived till her death.

CATHERINE of CARDONA (Bl) V.
PC. May 21

1519–1577. Born at Naples of a noble Spanish family, she lived for a time at the court of Philip II of Spain; then she retired to live as a recluse near Roda in S. Spain. She remained there for twenty years until she was received into a Carmelite convent, where, however, she continued to live as an anchoress. St Teresa speaks very highly of her.

CATHERINE TANACA (Bl) M.
AC. July 12

d. 1626. Wife of Bl John Tanaca. Both were beheaded at Nagasaki, Japan. Beatified in 1867.

CATHERINE SOIRON (Bl) V. M.
AC. July 17

d. 1794. She, and her sister Teresa, were the door-keepers (*tourières*) for the Carmelite nuns at Compiègne and were guillotined with them at Paris. They were not in vows. Beatified in 1904.

CATHERINE MATTEI (Bl) V.
Tert. OP.   AC. Sept 4

d. 1547. Born at Racconigi in the diocese of Cuneo, daughter of a poor working man. She took the Dominican habit of the third order and tried faithfully to imitate her namesake of Siena. She too is said to have been favoured with signal mystical experiences. Cult confirmed in 1810.

CATHERINE (Bl) M.   AC. Sept 10

d. 1622. A Japanese widow. She was beheaded at Nagasaki together with Bl

Charles Spinola and his fifty-one companions. Beatified in 1867.

CATHERINE of GENOA (St) W.
RM. Sept 15

1477–1510. Born in Genoa, of the noble Fieschi family, she married Julian Adorno when she was sixteen. She led a life of active charity, devoting herself to the service of others both at home and in the hospitals and poor quarters of the city. At first her work was made exceedingly difficult by the attitude of her profligate husband, whom she succeeded in converting to better ways. She wrote a treatise on Purgatory and a Dialogue between the soul and the body—two outstanding documents of Christian mysticism. Canonized in 1737.

CATHERINE of ALEXANDRIA (St)
VM.   RM. Nov 25

d. c.310. According to a legend she was a maiden martyred at Alexandria under Maximus Daza, but there is no early evidence for this. Her alleged relics have been enshrined for the last thousand years in the Orthodox monastery of Mt. Sinai. In art she is represented with the spiked wheel of her martyrdom, or arguing with the pagan philosophers.

CATHERINE LABOURÉ (St) V.
RM. Dec 31

1806–1875. Born in the Côte d'Or, daughter of a yeoman farmer, she became a Sister of Charity of St Vincent de Paul in 1830, and spent her whole life much as the ordinary Sister of Charity spends it, except for a series of visions with which she was favoured by God. The first "miraculous medal" was struck as the result of one of these visions. She died in the convent of Enghien-Reuilly and was canonized in 1947.

CATHOLDUS, ANNO and DIE-THARDUS (BB) Mks. OSB.
AC. Sept 29
d. late 8th cent. Three Benedictine monks who preached the gospel in the diocese of Eichstätt. Catholdus was a monk of Herrieden (built in 790).

CATULINUS (CARTHOLINUS), JANUARIUS, FLORENTIUS, JULIA and JUSTA (SS) MM.
RM. July 15
? Carthaginian martyrs. Their bodies were enshrined in the basilica of Fausta at Carthage. Of St Catulinus, a deacon, we have a panegyric preached by St Augustine. Nothing else is known about them.

CATUS (St) M.   RM. Jan 19
See Paul, Gerontius, etc.

CAWRDAF (St)   AC. Dec 5
6th cent. The son and successor of Caradog, chieftain of Brecknock and Hereford. He ended life as a monk under St Illtyd.

CE
Note. In many names this syllable is often written Cae, or Che, or Ke, or Kae, etc.

CEADDA (St) Bp.   RM. March 2
Otherwise Chad, q.v.

CEADWALLA (CADWALLA) (St) King.   AC. Apr 20
d. 689. King of Wessex, who, while yet a pagan, showed himself not less cruel and crafty than other conquerors of his race and time. He was converted by St Wilfrid and journeyed to Rome, where he was baptized by Pope St Sergius and died while yet wearing the white robe of the neophytes. There is no evidence of an ancient cult.

CEALLACH (KELLACH) (St) Bp.
AC. May 1
6th cent. A disciple of St Kieran of Clonmacnoise, who became bishop of Killala but ended his life as a hermit, by some accounts as a martyr. There are several other saints of the same name.

CEARAN (CIARAN) (St) Ab.
AC. June 14
d. 870. An Irish abbot of Bellach-Duin, now Castle-Kerrant, Co. Meath, surnamed The Devout.

CECILIA, CECILY
Otherwise Caecilia, q.v.

CEDD (St) Bp. OSB.   AC. Jan 7
d. 664 (Oct 26). Brother of St Chad of Lichfield. He was a monk of Lindisfarne who evangelized the midlands of England and afterwards was made bishop of the East Saxons. He founded the abbeys of Tilbury and of Lastingham. At the synod of Whitby he abandoned the Celtic for the Roman observances. In his old age he retired to his own foundation at Lastingham in Yorkshire to die under monastic obedience.

CEITHO (St)   AC. Nov 1
6th cent. One of five brothers, saints of the great Welsh family of Cunedda. A church at Pumpsant was dedicated to the five brothers. That at Llangeith, in Cardiganshire, was founded by St Ceitho.

CELE-CHRIST (St) Bp.
AC. March 3
d. *c.*728. St Cele-Christ, otherwise *Christicola* (worshipper of Christ), for many years led an eremitical life but ultimately was forced to accept a bishopric in Leinster.

CELERINA (St) M.   RM. Feb 3
See Laurentinus, Ignatius and Celerina.

CELERINUS (St) M.   RM. Feb 3
d. *p.250*. An African who, without
shedding his blood, earned the title of
martyr on account of the sufferings he
endured under Decius during a visit to
Rome. Set at liberty, he returned to
Carthage where he was ordained deacon
by St Cyprian. A church was dedicated
in his name at Carthage.

CELESTINE (St) M.   RM. May 2
See Saturninus, Neopolus, etc.

CELESTINE V (St) Pope
                           RM. May 19
Otherwise Peter Celestine, q.v.

CELESTINE I (St) Pope.
                           RM. July 27
d. 432 (Aug 1). Born in Campania, he
joined the Roman clergy and succeeded
St Boniface I as pope (422). Three great
events stand out in his pontificate: he
supported the campaign of St Germanus
of Auxerre against Pelagius; he sent
St Palladius to preach in Ireland shortly
before St Patrick's mission there; and
he condemned Nestorianism, presiding,
through his legates, over the council of
Ephesus (431).

CELLACH (CEILACH, KEILACH
—latinized as CELSUS).
Note. Colgan enumerates no less than
thirty-three Celtic saints named Cellach.
Most of them, however, are evidently
the same person.

CELLACH (CEILACH, KEILACH)
(St) Bp.   AC. Apr 1
9th cent. Archbishop of Armagh, possibly before his consecration abbot of
Iona and founder of the abbey of Kells.

CELLACH (in the RM.: CELSUS)
(St) Bp.   RM. Apr 1
d. 1129. Cellach McAedh, a native of
Ireland, seems to have been a Benedic-

tine of Glastonbury. He certainly was
for a time at Oxford, and in 1106 was
consecrated archbishop of Armagh. He
proved to be a great prelate, restorer of
ecclesiastical discipline throughout the
island. When dying he sent his pastoral
staff to St Malachy, then bishop of
Connor, who in fact became his successor.

CELLOCH (St) Ab.   AC. March 26
Otherwise Mochelloc, q.v.

CELSUS (*several*)
Otherwise Cellach, q.v.

CELSUS of ANTIOCH (St) M.
                               RM. Jan 9
See Julian, Basilissa, etc.

CELSUS (St) M.
              RM. July 28 and May 10
See Nazarius and Celsus.

CELSUS and CLEMENT (SS) MM.
                              RM. Nov 21
? Roman martyrs of whom the names
only have come down to us.

CENSURIUS (St) Bp.   RM. June 10
d. 486. The successor of St Germanus
in the see of Auxerre. He governed that
see from 448 to 486. He was buried in
the church of St Germanus, which he
himself had built.

CENTOLLA and HELEN (SS) MM.
                               RM. Aug 13
d. ? *c*304. Two Spanish maidens who
suffered martyrdom near Burgos.

CEOLFRID (GEOFFREY) (St) Ab.
OSB.   AC. Sept 25
642–716. A Northumbrian who became
a monk at Gilling in Yorkshire, whence
he migrated to Ripon, where St Benedict's Rule was observed. After a visit
to Canterbury, he became novice-master

157

at Ripon, but later migrated to Wear-mouth, at St Benet Biscop's invitation (672). Eventually he became abbot of Wearmouth-Jarrow, which he governed for twenty-six years. He was a great abbot and deserves a special recognition for the help he gave to St Bede, who was one of his monks. In 716 he re-signed and died at Langres in Cham-pagne on his way to Rome.

CEOLLACH (St) Bp.   AC. Oct 6
? 7th cent. An Irish prelate who for a short time governed as bishop the diocese of the Mercians or Mid-Angles. Thence he retired to Iona but returned to die in his native country.

CEOLWULPH (St) King, Mk. OSB.
AC. Jan 15
d. 764. King of Northumbria, fosterer of learning and of the monastic life. To him St Bede dedicated his Ecclesiastical History. He ended his days as a monk at Lindisfarne.

CERA (CIAR, CYRA, CIOR,
CEARA) (St) V.   AC. Jan 5
7th cent. An Irish abbess, a native of Tipperary, who governed two nun-neries, one at Kilkeary and the other at Tech Telle, now Tehelly.

CERATIUS (CÉRASE) (St) Bp.
AC. June 6
d. c.455. Bishop of Grenoble in France. Cult confirmed in 1903.

CERAUNUS (CERAN) (St) Bp.
AC. Sept 27
c. p.614. Bishop of Paris. His relics were formerly enshrined in the church of St Geneviève.

CERBONIUS (St) Bp.   RM. Oct 10
d. c.580. One of the African bishops driven from their sees by the Arian Van-dals. He settled at Piombino (*Popu-lonium*) in Tuscany and is said to have become a bishop there.

CERBONIUS (St) Bp.   RM. Oct 10
d. ? c.400. Bishop of Verona in Italy, of whom nothing is known.

CERNEUF (St) M.   AC. Feb 23
Otherwise Sirenus, q.v.

CESLAS (Bl) C. OP.   AC. July 17
d. 1242. A native of Poland, who re-ceived the habit of the Friars Preachers together with St Hyacinth, from the hands of St Dominic himself. He acted as spiritual director to the duchess St Hedwig of Poland. The successful resistance of the people of Breslau in Silesia to the Mongols in their great invasion of 1240, is attributed to the prayers of the saint.

CETTIN (CETHAGH) (St) Bp.
AC. June 16
5th cent. A disciple of St Patrick, con-secrated bishop to assist him in his apostolic work. Some authorities dis-tinguish Cethagh from Cettin.

CEWYDD (St)   AC. July 1
6th cent. A Welsh saint who flourished in Anglesey.

CH
Note. Saint's names beginning with Ch, should also be looked for under Ca, Co, or K, the spelling being frequently very uncertain and variable.

CHAD (CEADDA) (St) Bp.
RM. March 2
d. 673. Brother of St Cedd. Educated at Lindisfarne under St Aidan, and in Ireland. On returning to England, he was made abbot of Lastingham, where at that time, i.e., before the synod of Whitby, St Columba's Rule was strictly observed. During one of St Wilfrid's

absences in France, St Chad was made archbishop of York, but was removed by St Theodore of Canterbury. St Chad readily withdrew, and St Theodore arranged for him to exercise his episcopate in Mercia. The saint fixed his residence at Lichfield and there he died shortly after.

CHAEREMON (St) M.   RM. Oct 4
See Caius, Faustus, etc.

**CHAEREMON and Comp. (SS)
MM.   RM. Dec 22**
d. *p*.250. Bishop of Nilopolis in Egypt. He was already a very old man when the Decian persecution broke out. He was forced to flee to the mountainous district of the Arabian desert with several companions, and they were never seen again.

CHAFFRE (St) Ab. OSB. AC. Oct 19
Otherwise Theofrid, q.v.

CHAINOALDUS (CHAGNOALD, CAGNOU) (St) Bp.   AC. Sept 6
d. 633. Brother of St Faro and of St Fara. A disciple of St Columbanus, whom he accompanied to Bobbio and helped in the foundation of the abbey there. Afterwards he became bishop of Laon.

**CHALCEDON (Martyrs of) (SS)
                          RM. Sept 24**
d. 304. A band of forty-nine martyrs who suffered at Chalcedon under Diocletian. They seem to have been the choir of singers of the church of Chalcedon.

**CHAMOND (ANNEMOND) (St)
Bp. M.   AC. Sept 28**
d. 657. A courtier in the palace of King Clovis II who became archbishop of Lyons. The arch-tyrant Ebroin, mayor of the palace, caused the saint to be assassinated. St Wilfrid of York took

part in the ceremony of the enshrining of the relics of the martyr.

**CHARALAMPIAS and Comp. (SS)
MM.   AC. Feb 18**
d. 203. Martyrs of Magnesia in Asia Minor in the persecution under Septimius Severus. St Charalampias was a priest. With him suffered two soldiers and three women.

CHARBEL (St) M.   AC. Sept 5
d. 107. A martyr of the Antiochene Church under Trajan. Feast kept by the Maronites on the above date.

CHARISIUS (St) M.   RM. Apr 16
See Callistus, Charisius, etc.

CHARISIUS (St) M.   RM. Aug 22
See Athanasius, Anthusa and Comp.

CHARITINA (St) VM.   RM. Oct 5
d. *c*.304. A Christian maiden who breathed forth her soul in the torture chamber. She suffered under Diocletian and probably at Amisus on the Black Sea.

CHARITON (St) M.   RM. Sept 3
See Zeno and Chariton.

CHARITY (St) VM.   RM. Aug 1
Otherwise Caritas or Agape. See Faith, Hope, and Charity.

**CHARLEMAGNE (Bl) Emperor.
                          AC. Jan 28**
742–814. Son of Pepin the Short. King of the Franks in 768, on Christmas Day of the year 800, he was crowned first Holy Roman Emperor by Pope St Leo III. Popular devotion to Bl Charlemagne took root chiefly at the time of the great quarrel between the pope and Frederick Barbarossa; in France it was made compulsory by the state in 1475. Benedict XIV confirmed, or allowed, the

title of Blessed given to the emperor. His feast is observed still in several German dioceses.

CHARLES of SEZZE C. OFM.
AC. Jan 6

1613–1670. A native of Sezze in the Roman Campagna. He professed the Franciscan rule as a lay-brother at Rome. His was a life of great mystical experiences, and it is narrated that his heart was pierced by a ray of light proceeding from the Sacred Host, which left a visible wound. Canonized in 1959.

CHARLES of SAYN (Bl) Ab. OSB. Cist.
AC. Jan 29

d. 1212. A soldier who became a Cistercian at Hemmerode (1185). In 1189 he was chosen prior of Heisterbach and in 1197 abbot of Villers in Brabant. In 1209 he resigned and returned to Hemmerode to prepare for death. He has always been venerated as a *beatus*, at any rate by the Cistercians.

CHARLES the GOOD (Bl) M.
AC. March 2

d. 1127. Son of St Canute of Denmark. He fought in the second Crusade and on his return succeeded Robert II as count of Flanders. His rule was a continuous defence of the poor against the profiteers of his time, both clerical and lay. He was called "the Good" by popular acclamation and was done to death in the church of St Donatian at Bruges as a result of a conspiracy of the rich people whom he had offended. Cult confirmed in 1883.

CHARLES LUANGA (St) M.
RM. June 3

d. 1886. A servant of King Mwanga of Uganda. See Uganda (Martyrs of). He was baptized in Nov 1885, and burnt alive the following June at Namuyongo.

CHARLES de la CALMETTE
AC. Sept 2-3

See September Martyrs.

CHARLES SPINOLA (Bl) M. SJ.
AC. Sept 11

d. 1622. Though born at Prague he belonged to the Italian noble house of Spinola. He became a Jesuit in 1584 and in 1594 was sent to the missions of Japan. He worked there until 1618 when he was arrested and kept in prison for four years. He was then burnt to death with twenty-four companions. Each of them is given separate notice in this book. Beatified in 1867.

CHARLES of BLOIS (Bl) C.
AC. Sept 29

1316–1364. Nephew of Philip VI of France. He married Joan of Brittany in 1341 and claimed her dukedom against John de Montfort. This led to the war in which he was engaged for the rest of his life, except for nine years spent as a prisoner in the Tower of London. He fell in battle in 1364. Cult confirmed in 1904.

CHARLES BORROMEO (St) C. Bp.
RM. Nov 4

1538–1584. Son of Count Gilbert Borromeo by a Medici mother. His uncle Pope Pius IV appointed him archbishop of Milan and cardinal when he was aged only twenty-two. He did not receive priestly or episcopal orders until the year 1563. He was the most imposing and influential figure of the counter-reformation in Italy. He was a model bishop— zealous, selfless, prodigal even of his life. An attempt was made on his life by evildoers. Canonized in 1610.

CHEF (St) Ab.   AC. Oct 29
Otherwise Theodore, q.v.

CHELEDONIUS (St) M.
RM. March 3
See Hemiterius and Cheledonius.

CHELIDONIA (St) V. OSB.
RM. Oct 13

d. 1152. Born at Ciculum in the Abruzzi, she early fled into the mountains above Tivoli, near Subiaco, where she dwelt as a recluse in a cave, now called Morra Ferogna. From Cuno, cardinal of Frascati, she received the Benedictine habit in the abbey church of St Scholastica at Subiaco, but continued to live as a recluse under the obedience of the abbot. Her body now reposes in the church of St Scholastica. She is one of the patron saints of Subiaco.

CHELY (St) Bp.
RM. Oct 25

Otherwise Hilary of Mende, q.v.

CHERON (St) M.
RM. May 28

Otherwise Caraunus, q.v.

CHERUBINUS TESTA of AVIGLIANA (Bl) C. OSA.
AC. Dec 17

1449–1479. An Augustinian friar-hermit of Avigliana in Piedmont. Cult approved by Pius IX.

CHILIAN (St) Bp. M.
RM. July 8

See Kilian, Colman and Totnan.

CHILLIEN (KILLIAN, CHILIANUS) (St)
AC. Nov 13

7th cent. An Irishman, kinsman of St Fiacre, who became a missionary in Artois. His body was enshrined at Aubigny, near Arras.

CHINA (Martyrs of)

In addition to individual martyrs, there have been various group beatifications: (1) in 1893 a group of 5 Dominicans; (2) 1900 13 martyrs included with the Annamite martyrs 1798–1856; (3) 7 martyrs included in a similar decree of 1909; (4) 29 Franciscan martyrs during the Boxer Rising, beatified in 1946. See also Annam, Korea and individual articles.

CHIONIA (St) VM.
RM. Apr 3

See Agape and Chionia.

CHL

Note. Names so beginning are often spelt Cl or Kl.

CHR

Note. Names so beginning are often Spelt Cr.

CHRISTETA (St) M.
RM. Oct 27

See Vincent, Sabina and Christeta.

CHRISTIAN (Bl) Ab. OSB. Cist.
AC. March 18

d. 1186. His Celtic name was Giolla Croist O'Conarchy. An Irish priest, who professed the Cistercian Rule at Clairvaux under St Bernard and eventually was sent back to Ireland (1142) to introduce the Cistercians there. He was in fact the abbot-founder of Mellifont Abbey. It is said that he became bishop of Lismore and papal legate in Ireland.

CHRISTIAN (Bl) C.
PC. Apr 7

? A priest of Douai, whose relics are in the church of St Albinus.

CHRISTIAN (St) Bp.
AC. June 12

d. 1138. Croistan O'Morgair, brother of St Malachy of Armagh. He was made bishop of Clogher (1126) and obtained several privileges from the Holy See for his diocese.

CHRISTIAN (CHRISTINUS) (St) M. OSB.
RM. Nov 12

See Benedict, John, etc.

CHRISTIAN (Bl) Bp.
AC. Nov 22

d. c.873. Thirty-seventh bishop of Auxerre.

CHRISTIAN (Bl) C. OP. PC. Dec 1
13th cent. One of the first disciples of St Dominic, whom he helped in the foundation of the friary at Perugia.

CHRISTIAN (Bl) Bp. OSB. Cist.
PC. Dec 4
d. 1245. A Cistercian monk, probably belonging to the great abbey of Oliva, near Danzig. He went to Prussia as a missionary (1207), and was nominated bishop in 1215. He was instrumental in introducing the Teutonic Knights there. His efforts to convert Prussia were only partially successful.

CHRISTIANA of the CROSS (Bl) V. AC. Jan 10
Otherwise Oringa, q.v.

CHRISTIANA (St) V. AC. July 24
7th cent. Said to have been the daughter of an Anglo-Saxon king. She crossed over to Flanders where she lived until her death. She is the patron saint of Termonde in Belgium.

CHRISTIANA (St) V. RM. Dec 15
Otherwise Nino, q.v.

CHRISTICOLA (St) Bp.
AC. March 3
Otherwise Cele-Christ, q.v.

CHRISTINA CICCARELLI (Bl) V. OSA. AC. Jan 18
1481–1543. A native of Luco in the Abruzzi and a nun and prioress of the Augustinian hermits, who died at Aquila. Cult confirmed in 1841.

CHRISTINA of SPOLETO (Bl)
Penitent AC. Feb 13
1435–1458. Christina Camozzi (wrongly called Visconti) was born near Lake Lugano, the daughter of a physician. After a few years spent in frivolity she embraced a life of extreme bodily mortifications. She died at Spoleto aged twenty-three. Cult confirmed in 1834.

CHRISTINA (St) VM. RM. March 13
? A Persian maiden who was scourged to death.

CHRISTINA (St) VM. RM. July 24
? A maiden, perhaps a native of Rome, who was put to death near the Lake of Bolsena in Tuscany. Her legendary acts have been confused with those of a St Christina of Tyre, whose very existence, however, is very doubtful.

CHRISTINA the ASTONISHING (*Mirabilis*) (Bl) V. PC. July 24
1150–1224. Born near Liége. In 1182, after a cataleptic fit, she was the subject of a life-long series of most astonishing experiences, recorded by a contemporary Dominican. She died in the convent of St Catherine at Trond. Cult never officially confirmed.

CHRISTINA of STOMMELN (Bl) V. AC. Nov 6
1242–1312. Christina Bruzo, or Bruso, was born at Stommeln, near Cologne. Like her namesake of Belgium, she too could be styled "the Astonishing", since her life is a continuous record of most extraordinary phenomena which indeed tax the faith of the reader. They were recorded by a contemporary Friar Preacher. Cult confirmed in 1908.

CHRISTINA (St) V. OSB.
AC. Dec 26
d. 1160. Nun and recluse of Markgate under the obedience of the abbot of St Alban's. Her spiritual director was Bl Roger of St Alban's.

CHRISTINUS (St) M. OSB.
RM. Nov 12
See Benedict, John, etc.

CHRISTOPHER

Note. The Latin Christophorus means the Christ-Bearer. It was one of the most popular names during the Middle Ages. Its variants are numerous: Cristoforo, Christophe, Cristobal, Tobal, Cristobalón, Kester, Kitt, etc.

CHRISTOPHER of MILAN (Bl) C. OP. AC. March 1

d. 1484. A Friar Preacher who, true to his profession, preached with extraordinary success throughout Liguria and the Milanese. At Taggia, as a result of his preaching, the people built a friary and the saint was made its first prior. He died there. Cult confirmed in 1875.

CHRISTOPHER BALES (Bl) M. AC. March 4

d. 1590. Born at Coniscliffe, Durham. He was educated at Rome and Reims and ordained priest at Douai (1587). In 1588 he crossed over to England and two years later was seized, condemned for his priesthood, and hanged drawn and quartered in Fleet Street, London. Beatified in 1929.

CHRISTOPHER MACASSOLI (Bl) C. OFM. AC. March 11

d. 1485. Born at Milan, he joined the Franciscans and eventually founded a friary at Vigevano, in the province of Milan, where thousands sought his help and advice. Cult confirmed in 1890.

CHRISTOPHER (St) M. RM. July 25

? The RM. makes him a martyr of Lycia under Decius, but beyond the fact of his martyrdom, nothing is known about him. Many legends, however, some of them very beautiful but others unbelievable and absurd, have grown up around his name. The most graceful is that of his carrying an unknown child

across a ford, and being borne down by its weight, despite his own gigantic stature and great strength: the child was Christ, carrying in His hand the weight of the whole world. This episode had led to the usual representation of the saint in art. He is one of the Fourteen Holy Helpers, q.v.

CHRISTOPHER (St) M. RM. Aug 20

See Leovigild and Christopher.

CHRISTOPHER of GUARDIA (St) M. AC. Sept 25

d. *c.*1490. A boy of Guardia, near Toledo, in Spain, who at the age of three years was stolen by Jews at Toledo and crucified at Guardia, under Ferdinand and Isabella. His cult was officially confirmed, with the title of saint, by Pius VII in 1805. He is the principal patron saint of Guardia.

CHRISTOPHER BUXTON (Bl) M. AC. Oct 1

d. 1588. Born at Tideswell in Derbyshire, educated at Reims and Rome, and ordained priest in 1586. Two years later he was hanged, drawn and quartered for his priesthood at Canterbury. Beatified in 1929.

CHRISTOPHER of ROMAGNOLA (Bl) C. OFM. AC. Oct 31

*c.*1172–1272. A parish priest in the diocese of Cesena, who resigned his office, and joined St Francis of Assisi. He was sent to establish the Order in Gascony, where he died at Cahors. Cult approved in 1905.

CHRISTOPHER (Bl) M. PC. Nov 12

d. *c.*1500. A Portuguese knight of the Order of Christ (under the Cistercian Rule), who was beheaded for the Faith by a Mohammedan prince of Ceylon.

CHRODEGANG (St) Bp.
AC. March 6

d. 766. A near relative of Pepin, he became the chief minister to Charles Martel and ultimately bishop of Metz (742). He played an important part in nearly all the important affairs of his time, and took part in several councils. He is known for the rule he wrote for the secular clerks whom he gathered together in chapters of canons with common life. He also introduced the Roman liturgy and chant into his diocese and thus into N. Europe.

CHROMATIUS (St) C.   AC. Aug 11

3rd cent. Said to have been prefect of Rome and father of St Tiburtius the martyr.

CHROMATIUS (St) Bp. RM. Dec 2

d. c.406. Bishop of Aquileia, near Venice, from 387 to 406. St Jerome styles him "a most learned and most holy man", and dedicated to him several of his works. Chromatius was also a friend of St John Chrysostom and of Rufinus. We still possess part of his commentary on St Matthew.

CHRONAN (St) Ab.   AC. Apr 28
Otherwise Cronan, q.v.

CHRYSANTHUS and DARIA (SS) MM.   RM. Oct 25

d. 283. Chrysanthus, an Egyptian, with his wife Daria, a Greek, were distinguished in Rome for their zealous profession and practice of the Christian religion. This led to their martyrdom under Numerian and Carinus.

CHRYSOGONUS (St) M.
RM. Nov 24

d. c.304. A martyr who suffered at Aquileia. His name occurs in the Canon of the Roman Mass. His association with the martyr St Anastasia of Sirmium is now generally rejected.

CHRYSOLIUS (St) Bp. M.
AC. Feb 7

4th cent. An Armenian who evangelized N.E. Gaul, where, it is said, he was consecrated bishop. He had left Armenia during the persecution of Diocletian, but won the crown of martyrdom in Flanders. His relics are venerated at Bruges.

CHRYSOLOGUS (St) Bp. RM. Dec 2
See Peter Chrysologus.

CHRYSOPHORUS (St) M.
RM. Apr 20

See Victor, Zoticus, etc.

CHRYSOSTOM (St) Bp. Dr
RM. Jan 27

See John Chrysostom.

CHRYSOTELUS (St) M. RM. Apr 22
See Parmenius, and Comp.

CHUNIALD and GISLAR (SS) CC.
AC. Sept 24

7th cent. Missionaries, probably of Irish or Scottish origin, who evangelized S. Germany and Austria, under the leadership of St Rupert of Salzburg.

CIAN (St) C.   AC. Dec 11

6th cent. A Welsh saint who ended his life as a hermit in Carnarvonshire. He is sometimes described as a servant of St Peris.

CIANAN (St) Bp.   AC. Nov 24
Otherwise Kenan, q.v.

CIARAN (St) Bp.   AC. March 5
Otherwise Kieran, q.v.

CIARAN (St) Ab.   RM. Sept 9
Otherwise Kieran, q.v.

CICELY (St) VM.   RM. Nov 22
Otherwise Caecilia, q.v.

**CICCO of PESARO (Bl) C. Tert.
OFM.** AC. Aug 4
d. 1350. A native of Pesaro, and a tertiary of St Francis, who led the life of a recluse near Pesaro. Cult confirmed by Pius IX.

CILINIA (St) Matron RM. Oct 21
d. *p.*458. Mother of St Principius, bishop of Soissons, and of St Remigius, bishop of Reims. She died at Laon.

CILLENE (St) Ab. AC. July 3
d. *c.*752. An Irish monk who migrated to Iona and was there elected abbot in 726.

CINDEUS (St) M. RM. July 11
d. *c.*300. A priest of Pamphylia in Asia Minor who was burnt at the stake under Diocletian.

CINNIA (St) V. AC. Feb 1
5th cent. A princess of Ulster converted by St Patrick, who also gave her the veil.

CISELLUS (St) M. RM. Aug 21
See Luxorius, Cisellus and Camerinus.

CISSA (St) H. OSB. AC. Sept 23
Late 7th cent. Monk-recluse in Northumbria. most probably at Lindisfarne.

CIWA (St) V. AC. Feb 8
Otherwise Kigwe, q.v.

CLAIR (St) M. AC. Nov 4
The French spelling of Clarus, q.v.

**CLARE AGOLANTI of RIMINI
(Bl) W. Tert. OFM.** AC. Feb 10
1282–1346. She belonged to the nobility of Rimini and was twice married. During her married life she wasted her time in sinful dissipations. On the execution of her father and brother, as a result of civil disturbances, she completely changed her life. She became a Franciscan tertiary and founded a nunnery,

but never became a nun herself. She practised rigorous penances, some of which were considered extravagant even by her contemporaries. Cult sanctioned in 1784.

**CLARE GAMBACORTA (Bl) W.
OP.** AC. Apr 17
1362–1419. Daughter of the head of the state of Pisa. Being left a widow at fifteen, she wished to become a Poor Clare. Her father strongly opposed this at first, but eventually relented and built for her a nunnery where she introduced the strict Dominican observance. As a superior she was continually beset by financial troubles.

CLARE OF ASSISI (St) V. Foundress
RM. Aug 12
*c.*1194–1253. Born at Assisi. At the age of eighteen she was irresistibly drawn to the ideal of Christian poverty preached by St Francis. She ran away from home and took the veil from St Francis himself, who provided a refuge for her with the Benedictine nuns of San Paolo and finally at San Damiano, where the first convent of Poor Clares was established under her guidance. She governed it for forty years, and popes, cardinals and bishops came to consult her. She was indeed as much instrumental in the rapid spreading of the Franciscan movement as St Francis himself. She was canonized two years after her death. In art she is usually represented with a monstrance in her hand in memory of her having in this attitude miraculously saved her convent from assault.

**CLARE of MONTEFALCO (St) V.
OSA.** RM. Aug 17
*c.*1268–1308. Surnamed Clare of the Cross. She was a native of Montefalco, in the diocese of Spoleto. She joined a convent of Franciscan teriaries. In 1290

she became abbess of Holy Cross Convent with the Rule of St Augustine. There is some doubt as to what rule she followed. Her distinctive devotion was the Passion of Christ: a cross was found depicted on the flesh of her heart after her death. Canonized in 1881.

CLARE XAMADA (Bl) M.
AC. Sept 10
d. 1622. A Japanese matron, wife of Bl Dominic Xamada. Both were beheaded at Nagasaki, in Japan.

CLARITUS (CHIARITO) VOGLIA (Bl) C. PC. May 25
d. 1348. A Florentine, who in 1342 founded a convent of Augustinian nuns at Florence. His wife became a nun there, and he remained in the convent as a manservant till his death.

CLARENTIUS (St) Bp. RM. Apr 26
d. c.620. The successor of St Etherius in the see of Vienne.

CLARUS (St) Ab. OSB. AC. Jan 1
d. c.660. A monk of the abbey of St Ferreol, who was chosen abbot of the monastery of St Marcellus at Vienne in Dauphiny. He was the spiritual director of the convent of St Blandina, where his own mother had taken the veil. Cult confirmed in 1907.

CLARUS (St) H. OSB. AC. Feb 1
d. c.1048. A monk of Seligenstadt, in the diocese of Mainz. He lived for thirty years as a recluse, given to great austerities. His motto was: "Christ and Him crucified".

CLARUS (St) Bp. M. AC. June 1
? A regionary bishop, said to have been sent from Rome to preach the gospel in Aquitaine, where he was martyred. He is not to be confused with St Clarus, bishop of Nantes (Oct 10).

CLARUS (St) Bp. AC. Oct 10
? Bishop of Nantes. Some writers make him a disciple of St Peter and the first apostle of Armorica (Brittany). Others place his apostolate in the third century.

CLARUS (St) M. OSB. RM. Nov 4
d. c.875. He is described as a native of Rochester, who crossed over to France, where he was first a monk and then a hermit in the diocese of Rouen. He was murdered at the instigation of a woman whose advances he had rejected. The village Saint-Clair-sur-Epte is named after him.

CLARUS (St) H. RM. Nov 8
d. 397. Born at Tours in France, he joined the community of Marmoutier under St Martin. He was ordained priest and henceforth lived as a hermit near the same abbey.

CLASSICUS (St) M. RM. Feb 18
See Lucius, Sylvanus, etc.

CLATEUS (St) Bp. RM. June 4
d. c.64. One of the earliest bishops of Brescia, who suffered martyrdom under Nero.

CLAUD or CLAUDE (*several*)
Otherwise Claudius, q.v.

CLAUDIA (St) M. RM. March 20
See Alexandra, Claudia, etc.

CLAUDIA (St) VM. RM. May 18
See Theodotus, Thecusa, etc.

CLAUDIA (St) W. AC. Aug 7
1st cent. A woman mentioned by St Paul in his second letter to Timothy (IV, 21). A much later, and rather improbable, tradition asserts that she was a Briton, the wife of Aulus Pudens, a senator, and the mother of SS Praxedes and Pudentiana.

CLAUDIAN (St) M.   RM. Feb 25
See Victorinus, Victor, etc.

CLAUDIAN (St) M.   RM. Feb 26
See Papias, Diodorus, etc.

CLAUDIAN (St) M.   RM. March 6
See Victor, Victorinus, etc.

CLAUDIUS (CLAUDE) de la COL-
OMBIÈRE (Bl) C. SJ.   AC. Feb 15
1641–1682. Born near Grenoble, he
became a Jesuit in 1659 at Avignon.
While superior of the Jesuits at Paray-
le-Monial he was the spiritual director
of St Margaret Mary Alacoque and was
instrumental in spreading devotion to
the Sacred Heart. Sent to England in
1676 as chaplain to the Duchess of
York, he was arrested and banished for
alleged complicity in the imaginary
"Popish Plot". Beatified in 1929.

CLAUDIUS (St) M.   RM. Feb 18
See Maximus, Claudius, etc.

CLAUDIUS (St) M.   RM. June 3
See Lucillian, Claudius, etc.

CLAUDIUS of BESANÇON (St) Bp.
OSB.   RM. June 6
d. c.699. A native of Franche-Comté, he
was trained to bear arms, but decided to
be a priest and eventually was appointed
canon of Besançon. He next became a
monk, and abbot, of Condat Abbey, in
the Jura mountains, where he introduced, or enforced, the rule of St
Benedict. In 685 he was chosen bishop
of Besançon but retained the direction
of the abbey, to which he retired again
before his death. The abbey was afterwards known as Saint-Claude.

CLAUDIUS, NICOSTRATUS,
CASTORIUS, VICTORINUS and
SYMPHORIAN (SS) MM. RM. July 7
d. c.288. Described in the very untrust-

worthy Acts of St Sebastian as having
suffered martyrdom at the same time as
that saint. They are very likely identical
with the group of saints honoured on
Nov 8 with the Four Crowned Martyrs.
q.v.

CLAUDIUS, JUSTUS, JUCUN-
DINUS and Comp. (SS) MM.
                         RM. July 21
d. 273. A group of eight martyrs who
suffered with St Julia at Troyes in Gaul,
under Aurelian. Their bodies were enshrined in the Benedictine nunnery of
Jouarre, near Meaux.

CLAUDIUS, ASTERIUS, NEON,
DONVINA and THEONILLA (SS)
MM.   RM. Aug 23
d. 303. The first three were brothers
who were accused to the magistrate of
Aegea in Cilicia by their step-mother,
who hoped to inherit their estate. They
were crucified, or according to another
account, decapitated. It is not certain
that the two women were fellow-
sufferers; Donvina is a mistake for
Domina.

CLAUDIUS (St) M.   RM. Oct 25
See Marcellinus, Claudius, etc.

CLAUDIUS, LUPERCUS and
VICTORIUS (SS) MM. RM. Oct 30
d. c.300. Three brothers, sons of the
centurion, St Marcellus. They were
martyred at León in Spain under Diocletian. They are the titular saints of St
Claudius in Galicia, one of the earliest
Benedictine abbeys in Spain.

CLAUDIUS, NICOSTRATUS and
Comp. (SS) MM.   RM. Nov 8
These saints belong to the group of the
Four Crowned Martyrs, q.v. They are
probably the same group as that mentioned in the RM. on July 7, see Claudius, Nicostratus, etc. above (July 7).

CLAUDIUS, HILARIA, JASON, MAURUS (MARIS) and Comp. (SS) MM.   RM. Dec 3

d. ? 283. This group of martyrs, consisting of Claudius, a military tribune, Hilaria his wife, their two sons, and seventy soldiers, belong to the larger group figuring in the legendary acts of SS Chrysanthus and Daria.

CLAUDIUS, CRISPIN, MAGINA, JOHN and STEPHEN (SS) MM.   RM. Dec 3

? African martyrs, of whom nothing is known.

CLEAR (CLEER, CLETHER) (St) Bp.   AC. Oct 10

Otherwise Clarus, q.v.

CLEDOG (CLYDOG, CLEODICUS) (St)   AC. Oct 23

Otherwise Clether, q.v.

CLEDWYN (CLYDWYN) (St) C.   AC. Nov 1

5th cent. Patron saint of Llangledwyn in Carmarthenshire. Alleged to have been the eldest son of King Brychan, and to have succeeded him as ruler of part of his dominions.

CLEMENT (St) Bp. M. RM. Jan 23

d. 309. Bishop of Ancyra in Galatia, martyred under Diocletian.

CLEMENT (St) Ab. OSB.   AC. March 5

c.800. Abbot of Santa Lucia, in Syracuse, the oldest Benedictine monastery in Sicily.

CLEMENT MARY HOFBAUER (St) C. C.SS.R.   RM. March 15

1751–1820. A Slav, born in Moravia, whose real name was John Dvorak. He was the son of a grazier, and he himself started life as a baker and then became a hermit. While on a pilgrimage to Rome he received the habit as a recluse at the hands of the bishop of Tivoli, the future pope Pius VII, who changed John's name into that of Clement Mary. In 1784 he joined the recently founded Redemptorists at Rome and four years later was sent to Warsaw to establish the first house of the congregation beyond the Alps. There the untiring zeal of the Redemptorists met with signal success, though the development of the institute was retarded by the Napoleonic wars. Clement spent the last twelve years of his life at Vienna, firmly planting the Redeptorist institute in German lands, whence it spread to Belgium, Ireland, England and the British Empire. Canonized in 1909.

CLEMENT (Bl) Bp. OP.   AC. March 19

d. 1258. He received the habit from St Dominic himself and preached in Scotland into which country he introduced the Dominicans. He became Bishop of Dumblane.

CLEMENT of ELPIDIO (Bl) C. OSA.   AC. Apr 8

d. 1291. A native of Osimo and a hermit friar of St Augustine. In 1270 he was chosen General of the Order and as such he drew up its constitutions, which were approved in 1287. For this reason he is considered the second founder of the order. Cult approved in 1572.

CLEMENT (St) M.   AC. June 27

d. c.298. A martyr of Cordova, in Spain, under Diocletian. He belongs to the group led by St Zoilus, q.v.

CLEMENT of OKHRIDA (St) C.   AC. July 17

See Seven Apostles of Bulgaria.

CLEMENT (St) M.   RM. Sept 10

See Apelles, Lucius and Clement.

CLEMENT VOM (Bl) M.
AC. Sept 10
d. 1622. A Japanese layman, martyred at Nagasaki. He belongs to the group of Bl Charles Spinola, q.v.

CLEMENT KINGEMON (Bl) M.
AC. Nov 1
d. 1622. A native of Arima in Japan. He was the servant of Bl Paul Navarro, whose life he wrote. He was burnt alive with his master at Ximabarra. Beatified in 1867.

CLEMENT (St) M.   RM. Nov 21
See Celsus and Clement.

CLEMENT I (St) Pope, M.
RM. Nov 23
d. c.100. The third successor of St Peter in the see of Rome, he governed the Church for about ten years. In his capacity as pope, he wrote to the church of Corinth to settle some disputes there; the letter is one of the most important documents of the sub-apostolic age. He is venerated as a martyr, but his martyrdom cannot be proved, much less the legends attached to it. He is mentioned in the Canon of the Mass.

CLEMENT (St) Bp.   AC. Nov 23
? The first bishop of Metz, sent directly from Rome to evangelize that district of Roman Gaul.

CLEMENT of ALEXANDRIA (St) C.   PC. Dec 4
d. c.217. Titus Flavius Clemens succeeded Panthenus as the head of the catechetical school of Alexandria, where he had Origen as one of his pupils. He has left numerous writings. His name was listed in the RM. up to 1751.

CLEMENTIA (Bl) N. OSB.
PC. March 21
d. 1176. Daughter of Adolph, count of Hohenburg. A model wife, she became in her widowhood a nun at Oehren, Trèves.

CLEMENTINUS, THEODOTUS and PHILOMENUS (SS) MM.
RM. Nov 14
? Martyrs of Heraclea in Thrace. Nothing else is known about them.

CLEOMENES (LEOMENES) (St) M.   RM. Dec 23
See Theodulus, Saturninus, etc.

CLEONICUS, EUTROPIUS and BASILISCUS (SS) MM.
RM. March 3
d. c.308. These saints belong to a group of martyrs put to death in the province of Pontus on the Black Sea, under Diocletian. Most of the group—some forty to fifty—seem to have been soldiers in the imperial army; several, however, were crucified, the punishment reserved for slaves. Their martyrdom was closely connected with that of St Theodore (Feb 7).

CLEOPATRA (St) W.   AC. Oct 19
d. 319. A widow of Palestine who succeeded in securing the body of St Varus, martyred under Diocletian, and enshrined it at her home at Derâ'a in Syria. On the day of the dedication of the church her twelve-year-old son died, and he and St Varus appeared in a vision to comfort her.

CLEOPHAS (St) M.   RM. Sept 25
1st cent. One of the two disciples whom Christ met on the way to Emmaus (Luke XXIV). The RM. states that he was murdered by the Jews in the house in which he entertained our Lord on that first Easter day. He is sometimes identified, without any real grounds, with Clopas or Alpheus, the father of St James the Less (Mt 10: 3, Jn 19: 25).

Hegesippus adds that he was a brother of St Joseph.

CLERUS (St) M.   RM. Jan 7
d. *c*.300. A Syrian deacon, martyred at Antioch.

CLETHER (CLEER, CLYDOG, SCLEDOG, Latinized: CLITANUS or CLEODIUS) (St)   AC. Oct 23
d. *c*.520. One of the saints descended from King Brychan of Brecknock, or at least of his clan. He left Carmarthen and went to Cornwall. Several dedications of churches—for instance, St Cleer, near Liskeard—perpetuate his memory. Another Clether, or Cledog, is commemorated on Aug. 19. He is alleged to have died a martyr in Herefordshire.

CLETUS (or ANACLETUS) (St) Pope, M.   RM. Apr 26 (July 13)
d. *c*.91. The second successor of St Peter. He was probably martyred under Domitian. His name is in the Canon of the Mass.

CLICERIUS (St) Bp.   RM. Sept 20
d. *c*.438. Bishop of Milan, of whom no record is extant.

CLINIUS (St) Ab. OSB.
**   RM. March 30**
? A Greek and a Benedictine of Montecassino, who was made superior of the daughter-house of St Peter, near Pontecorvo, where his relics are venerated.

CLODOALDUS (French: CLOUD) (St) Ab.   RM. Sept 7
d. *c*.560. Grandson of King Clovis and of St Clotilde. When his two brothers were murdered he was taken to safety in Provence. Afterwards he became a priest, a recluse, and the abbot-founder of Nogent-sur-Seine, near Versailles, now called after him Saint-Cloud.

CLODULPHUS (French: CLOU) (St) Bp.   RM. June 8
605–696. Son of St Arnulf, bishop of Metz. He too became bishop of Metz, succeeding his father in 656 and ruling over his diocese for forty years.

CLOTILDE (St) Queen RM. June 3
c.474–545. Born at Lyons, daughter of Chilperic, king of Burgundy, she married Clovis, king of the Salian Franks, and was the means of leading her husband to embrace Christianity (496). She had much to suffer on account of the quarrels between her three sons. In old age she retired to Tours, where she died by St Martin's tomb.

CLOTILDE PAILLOT (Bl) M.
**   AC. Oct 23**
1739–1794. Born at Bavay, professed as an Ursuline in 1756, superior of the house of Valenciennes. She was guillotined at Valenciennes. She belongs to the group of the Ursuline martyrs beatified in 1920, q.v.

CLOTSINDIS (CLOTSEND) (St) Abs. OSB.   AC. June 30
c.635–714. Daughter of St Adalbald and of St Rictrudis, later the abbess-foundress of Marchiennes in Flanders. She was educated at Marchiennes by her own mother, the abbess-foundress, whom she succeeded as second abbess (688).

CLOU (St) Bp.   RM. June 8
Otherwise Clodulphus, q.v.

CLOUD (St) Ab.   RM. Sept 7
Otherwise Clodoaldus, q.v.

CLYDOG (St)   AC. Oct 23
Otherwise Clether, q.v.

CLYTANUS (CLITANUS) (St)
**   AC. Oct 23**
Otherwise Clether, q.v.

COCCA (CUCCA, CUACH) (St) V.
AC. June 6
? Patroness of Kilcock on the borders of Cos. Meath and Kildare.

COCHA (COECHA) (St) V.
AC. June 29
6th cent. Said to have cared for St Kieran of Saighir in his infancy. She was afterwards abbess of Ross-Benchuir.

CODRATUS (CHUADRATUS), DIONYSIUS, CYPRIAN, ANECTUS, PAUL and CRESCENS (SS) MM.
RM. March 10
d. *c.*258. Greek martyrs, beheaded at Corinth, under Valerian. Previously to this, Codratus, then a child, appears to have been driven into the woods to escape from the persecution under Decius (250).

CODRATUS (St) M. RM. March 26
Otherwise Quadratus, q.v.

COELESTINE (St) Pope.
RM. May 19
See Peter Celestine.

COEMGEN (St) Ab. AC. June 3
Otherwise Kevin, q.v.

COGITOSUS (St) AC. Apr 18
? 8th cent. He appears to have been a monk of Kildare. If the tradition representing him as the author of the life of St Brigid be trustworthy, we are indebted to him for much interesting information regarding that saint and her times.

COINTHA (QUINTA) (St) M.
RM. Feb 8
d. 249. An Egyptian lady—some say a young maiden—martyred under Decius. She was fastened to the tail of a horse, and dragged by her feet through the streets of Alexandria till she died.

COLAN (St) May 21
The Cornish form of the name of the Welsh Gollen, q.v.

COLETTE (St) V. Poor Clare.
RM. March 6
1381–1447. Nicolette Boilet was born at Corbie, in Picardy, a carpenter's daughter. She tried her religious vocation with the Beguines and the Benedictines, but failed. Next she became a recluse at Corbie, and finally she found her vocation in reviving the Franciscan spirit among the Poor Clares. She was made superioress of the whole order, and her reform spread throughout France, Savoy, Germany and Flanders, many convents being restored and seventeen new ones founded by her. She helped St Vincent Ferrer in the work of healing the papal schism. She died at Ghent, and was canonized in 1807.

COLGAN (St) Ab. AC. Feb 20
d. *c.*796. Surnamed "the Wise" and "the Chief Scribe of the Scots". Abbot of Clonmacnoise, in Offaly. He was a friend of Bl Alcuin.

COLMAN—in Latin: COLMANUS
Note. Probably the most popular baptismal name in the early Irish church. There are ninety-six saints of this name in the martyrology of Donegal, two hundred and nine in the Book of Leinster and many others. Holweck lists seventy-one; several, however, are evidently duplicates.

COLMAN of LISMORE (St) Bp.
AC. Jan 23
d. *c.*702. Abbot-bishop of the monastery of Lismore, in the government of

which he succeeded St Hierlug (Zailug) in 698. Under his rule the fame of Lismore reached its peak.

COLMAN of LINDISFARNE (St) Bp.   AC. Feb 18
d. 676. A native of Connaught and a monk of Iona, he was chosen third abbot-bishop of Lindisfarne. His reluctance to accept the Roman traditions prescribed for England at the synod of Whitby (664) led him to withdraw with his monks to Ireland. Here he founded a monastery on Innisboffin Island, but later was compelled to establish another (Mayo of the Saxons) on the mainland for his English monks as they were not on good terms with their Irish brethren.

COLMAN of ARMAGH (St) C.
AC. March 5
5th cent. A disciple of St Patrick. He died during the lifetime of his master, by whom he was buried at Armagh.

COLMAN Mc O'LAOIGHSE (St) Ab.   AC. May 15
6th cent. Named also Columbanus. He was a disciple of St Columba and of St Fintan of Clonenagh. He founded, and governed, a monastery at Oughaval.

COLMAN of DROMORE (St) Bp.
AC. June 7
6th cent. A native of Argyll who settled in Ireland and became the abbot-founder and bishop of Dromore in Co. Down. He is said to have been the teacher of St Finnian of Clonard. Cult approved in 1903.

COLMAN Mc ROI (St) Ab.
AC. June 16
6th cent. A deacon, disciple of St Columba, and himself abbot-founder of a monastery at Reachrain, now Lambay Island, Dublin.

COLMAN (COLOMANNUS) (St) M.   RM. July 8
See Kilian, Colman and Totnan.

COLMAN ELO (St) Ab. AC. Sept 26
d. c. 610. A nephew of St Columba and the abbot-founder of monasteries at Lynally (Land-Elo, Lin-Alli) and at Muckamore. He is credited with the authorship of the *Alphabet of Devotion*.

COLMAN of STOCKERAU (St) M.
RM. Oct 13
d. 1012. An Irish, or Scottish, pilgrim, who passing through Austria, on his way to the Holy Land, was seized as a spy, racked and hanged with a couple of malefactors, at Stockerau, near Vienna. Miracles were wrought by his dead body, and he was venerated as a saint. He is honoured as one of the patron saints of Austria.

COLMAN of KILROOT (St) Bp.
AC. Oct 17
6th cent. A disciple of St Ailbe of Emly, and abbot-bishop of Kilroot, near Carrickfergus.

COLMAN of SENBOTH-FOLA (St) Ab.   AC. Oct 27
d. c.632. An Irish abbot of Senboth-Fola, in the diocese of Ferns, and associated with St Aidan, bishop of that see.

COLMAN of KILMACDUAGH (St) Bp.   AC. Oct 29
d. 632. A son of the Irish chieftain Duac. He was first a recluse at Arranmore and at Burren in Co. Clare; then he founded the monastery of Kilmacduagh i.e. the church of the son of Duac, and governed it as abbot-bishop. Cult approved in 1903.

COLMAN of CLOYNE (St) Bp.
AC. Nov 24
522–c.600. Born in Cork, a poet and a

royal bard at the court of Cashel. In middle age he was baptized by St Brendan, embraced the monastic life, was ordained priest and preached in Limerick and Cork. Finally he founded the church of Cloyne and was consecrated its first bishop. Cult approved in 1903.

COLMAN of GLENDALOUGH (St) Ab.   AC. Dec 12
d. 659. An abbot of Glendalough, mentioned in the Irish calendars.

COLMOC (MACHOLMOC) (St) Bp.   AC. June 7
Otherwise Colman of Dromore, q.v.

COLOMAN de UNGVAR (Bl) C.
                              AC. June 28
d. c.1510. A Hungarian Pauline monk in Ungvár. He healed the blind, the lame and the lepers.

COLUMBA (COLUM, COLM COLUMBKILL, COLUMCILLE, COLUMBUS, COMBS) (St) Ab.   RM. June 9
c.521–597. The most famous of the saints of Scotland. He was a native of Garton, in Co. Donegal, studied at Moville and Clonard, embraced the monastic life at Glasnevin, was ordained priest, and forthwith embarked upon his life's work of founding monasteries and churches, first in Ireland, and after 563 in Scotland. On Whitsun eve of that year he landed with twelve companions on the island of Iona (Holy Island) where he established the greatest and most celebrated of his monasteries, which became thenceforward the most potent factor in the conversion of Picts, Scots, and the Northern English. The description given of him by his biographer and successor Adamnan, is famous: "He had the face of an angel; he was of an excellent nature, polished in speech, holy in deed, great in counsel . . . loving unto all".

COLUMBA (St) Ab.   AC. Dec 12
d. 548. A native of Leinster and disciple of St Finian. He governed the monastery of Tyrdaglas in Munster.

COLUMBA of RIETI (Bl) V. Tert. OP.   AC. May 20
1467–1501. Angelella Guardagnoli was born at Rieti in Umbria. She became a Dominican of the third order at Perugia and won the confidence of all in that city, so that even the magistrates would ask her advice. She is said to have been ruthlessly persecuted by Lucrezia Borgia. Beatified in 1627.

COLUMBA (St) VM.   RM. Sept 17
d. 853. A native of Cordova and a nun at Tábanos, whence she was driven by the Moorish persecution of 852. She took refuge at Cordova, where at a later date, being called upon to deny Christ, she openly reviled Mohammed and thereupon was beheaded.

COLUMBA (St) VM.   AC. Nov 13
? Said to have been a Christian maiden put to death by a heathen king of Cornwall. She is the patron saint of two parishes in Cornwall.

COLUMBA of SENS (St) VM.
                              RM. Dec 31
d. 273. A Spanish girl who abandoned her country in order to avoid being denounced as a Christian. She went to France with other Spanish Christians and all were put to death near Meaux, under Aurelian. Her shrine was at Sens, and she was formerly venerated throughout France.

COLUMBANUS (St) H.   AC. Feb 2
d. 959. An Irish recluse whose hermitage was near the church of Saint-Bavo at Ghent.

COLUMBANUS (St) Ab.
RM. Nov 21

c.545–615. A native of Leinster and a monk of Bangor. In 580 he left Ireland with a band of monks and worked first in England, then in Brittany and finally in the Vosges district where he founded the great abbey at Luxeuil which he governed for twenty-five years. His outspoken protest against the disorders of the Frankish court led to his exile. He ended his days in N. Italy, in the abbey of Bobbio which he founded shortly before his death. His somewhat intemperate defence of the Celtic, as opposed to some of the Roman observances and the austerity of his rule, make him a rather forbidding personality; but on the other hand, through the numerous abbeys, founded by himself and by his disciples, especially after they had become Benedictine, he exerted a determining and lasting influence on the civilization of Western Europe.

COLUMBANUS JUNIOR (St) M.
AC. Nov 21

d. p.616. A disciple of St Columbanus and a monk at Luxeuil.

COLUMBINUS (St) Ab. OSB.
AC. Sept 13

d. c.680. Successor of St Deicola as abbot of Lure.

COLUMBUS (Bl) C. OP. PC. Nov 8
d. 1229. Dominican prior of Toulouse and Montpellier. He died while preaching at Fréjus. His relics are in the cathedral of Fréjus.

COMBS (St) Ab.
RM. June 9

A corrupt form of the name Columbkill or Columba, q.v.

COMGALL (COMGALLUS) (St) Ab.
AC. May 10

c.516–601. Born in Ulster, he became a monk under St Fintan and eventually the abbot-founder of Bangor (Ben-Chor) where he was teacher of St Columbanus and the band of monks who evangelized Central Europe. He wrote a rather severe rule for his monks. It seems that he lived some time in Wales, Cornwall and Scotland.

COMGAN (St) Ab.
PC. Feb 27

d. c.565. Abbot of Glenthsen or Killeshin. He was assisted in death by St Utha of Munster.

COMGAN (St) Ab.
AC. Oct 13

8th cent. An Irish prince, brother of St Kentigern, who embraced the monastic life in Scotland. His feast is kept in the diocese of Aberdeen.

COMINUS (St)

There are several saints of this name, and they have been confused by hagiographers. The following are the most important:

AC. May 1

A martyr of Catania in Sicily.

AC. June 3

A companion of St Photinus (Pothinus), martyr of Lyons.

AC. June 12

An Irish abbot, patron saint of Ardcavan. See also Baithin (June 9).

COMPANIUS (COMPAGNO, COMPANY) (Bl) Ab. OSB. Cam.
AC. Oct 8

12th cent. First abbot of the Camaldolese abbey of our Lady of Porzia in Italy.

CONALD (St) C.
AC. Sept 24

Otherwise Chuniald, q.v.

CONALL (COEL, CONALD) (St) Ab.
AC. May 22

7th cent. Abbot of the monastery of Inniscoel, Donegal, where there is a holy well called after him.

CONAN (St) Bp.   AC. Jan 26
d. ?c.648. A native of Ireland and a monk of Iona, said to have been a bishop in the Isle of Man.

CONCESSA (St) M.   RM. Apr 8
? A martyr anciently venerated at Carthage.

CONCESSUS (St) M.   RM. Apr 9
See Demetrius, Concessus, etc.

CONCORDIA (St) VM.   RM. Aug 13
See Hippolytus, Concordia and Comp.

CONCORDIUS (St) M.   RM. Jan 1
d. 175. A subdeacon put to death at Spoleto, central Italy, under Marcus Aurelius.

CONCORDIUS (St)   RM. June 23
See John.

CONCORDIUS (St) M.   RM. Sept 2
See Zeno, Condordius and Theodore.

CONCORDIUS (St) M.   RM. Dec 16
See Valentine, Concordius, etc,

CONDEDUS (CONDÉ, CONDÈDE) H. OSB.   AC. Oct 21
d. c.690. An Englishman who became a hermit at Fontaine-de-Saint-Valéry, on the Somme, France. There he heard of the abbey of Fontenelle and asked to be received into the community (c.673). After some years as a monk he obtained leave to preach, while residing as a recluse on an island in the Seine, near Caudebec.

CONGAN (St) Ab.   AC. Oct 13
Otherwise Comgan, q.v.

CONINDRUS (St) Bp.   AC. Dec 28
See Romulus and Conindrus.

CONLETH (St) Bp.   AC. May 3
d. c.519. An Irish recluse at Old Con-

nell on the Liffey. St Brigid came to know him and made him the spiritual director of her nuns at Kildare. Eventually he became the first bishop of this place. He was a metal-worker and very skilled as a copyist and illuminator.

CONNAT (COMNATAN) (St) V.   AC. Jan 1
d. c.590. Abbess of St Brigid's convent in Kildare.

CONOGAN (GWEN—latinized into ALBINUS) (St) Bp.   AC. Oct 16
d. 460. The successor of St Corentin in the see of Quimper, in Brittany. His memory is still held in great veneration.

CONON (St) M.   RM. Feb 26
See Papias, Diodorus, etc.

CONON (St) M.   RM. March 6
d. 250. A Christian from Nazareth in Galilee who worked as a poor gardener at Mandona (Carmel), in Pamphylia, martyred under Decius.

CONON (St) Ab.   AC. March 28
d. 1236. A Basilian monk and abbot of the Greek monastery of Nesi in Sicily.

CONON, Father and Son (SS) MM.   RM. May 29
d. 275. Both were martyred at Iconium in Asia Minor under Aurelian. The boy was only twelve years of age. They were roasted before a slow fire and then racked to death.

CONRAD of MONDSEE (Bl) Ab. M. OSB.   PC. Jan 16
d. 1145. Conrad Bosinlother was born near Trèves and became a Benedictine at Siegburg. In 1127 he was appointed abbot of Mondsee (*Lunaelacensis*) in Upper Austria. His firmness in reclaiming the alienated possessions of the abbey led some nobles to murder him

at Oberwang near Mondsee. From the time of his death he was publicly venerated at his abbey as a martyr.

CONRAD of BAVARIA (Bl) OSB. Cist.   AC. Feb 15

1105–1154. Son of Henry the Black, duke of Bavaria. While a student at Cologne he was drawn to the monastic life by St Bernard, who professed him at Clairvaux. After some years he was granted permission to visit the Holy Land and on his return journey he died near Molfetta in Apulia. Cult approved in 1832.

CONRAD of PIANCENZA (St) C. Tert. OFM.   AC. Feb 19

1290–1354. A nobleman of Piacenza who once when out hunting caused a great conflagration, for which a poor man was unjustly accused and condemned to death. Conrad confessed his guilt and forfeited all his fortune to make restitution. After this he and his wife decided to become religious: she was professed as a Poor Clare, he joined the third order of St Francis as a hermit. He passed the last thirty years of his life as a recluse in Sicily. Cult approved, with the title of Saint, by Paul III.

CONRAD of HILDESHEIM (Bl) C. OFM.   AC. Apr 14

c.1190–? An Italian by birth and one of the first followers of St Francis, by whom he was sent to establish the order in N. Germany. He did so at Hildesheim, where his *cultus* survived till the Reformation.

CONRAD MILIANI of ASCOLI (Bl) C. OFM.   AC. Apr 19

1234–1289. A native of Ascoli Piceno, he joined the Franciscans together with Jerome Masci, afterwards Pope Nicholas IV, whose future elevation he foretold. Conrad was sent to evangelize Libya in N. Africa, whence he was recalled to act as advisor of Jerome Masci, when the latter became a cardinal.

CONRAD of PARZHAM (St) C. OFM. Cap.   RM. Apr 21

1818–1894. Born of poor parents at Parzham near Passau in Bavaria, he joined the Capuchins as a lay-brother at the age of thirty-one and spent more than forty years as doorkeeper at his friary. He was endowed with the gift of prophecy and the power to read hearts. Beatified in 1930 and canonized in 1934.

CONRAD of SELDENBÜREN (Bl) M. OSB.   AC. May 2

d. 1126. A scion of the royal house of Seldenbüren and founder of the Swiss abbey of Engelberg in Unterwalden where he was professed as a Benedictine lay-brother. He was sent to Zurich to defend the rights of his abbey and was murdered there by his opponents. He is venerated as a martyr.

CONRAD (CUNO) of TRÈVES (St) Bp. M.   AC. June 1

d. 1066. Of the noble family of Pfullingen in Swabia. His uncle, St Annon, archbishop of Cologne, appointed him bishop of Trèves, in defiance of the right of election of the Trèves chapter. Conrad was seized on his way to Trèves and cast from the battlements of the castle of Uerzig. He is venerated as a martyr.

CONRAD of HESSEN (Bl) Ab. OSB. Cist.   PC. June 1

d. c.1270. Conrad of Herlesheim in Ober-Hessen entered the Cistercian Order and belonged to the abbey of Haina in which he was cellarer for at least sixteen years.

CONRAD of OTTOBEUREN (Bl) AB. OSB.   PC. July 27

d. 1227. Abbot of Ottobeuren Abbey in

Bavaria from 1193 till his death. He is described as a "lover of the brethren and of the poor".

CONRAD NANTWIN (ANTVIN) (Bl) M.   AC. Aug 1
d. 1286. While making a pilgrimage to Rome, he was unjustly accused and burnt at the stake at Wolfrathshausen, near Munich. His cult was approved by Boniface VIII, and a church is dedicated to him.

CONRAD of ZÄHRINGEN (Bl) Card. Bp. OSB. Cist.   PC. Sept 30
d. 1227. A member of the family of the counts of Seyne. In early life he was made a canon of St Lambert's, Liége; then he passed over to the Cistercians at Villers in Brabant. Subsequently he became successively abbot of Villers (1209), of Clairvaux (1214), of Cîteaux (1217), cardinal-bishop of Porto and Santa Rufina (1219) and papal legate in Languedoc (1224–1226). He died at Bari. The Cistercians have always given him the title of Saint.

CONRAD of FRISACH (Bl) C. OP. PC. Nov 24
d. 1239. A doctor at the university of Bologna whom St Dominic received into the Order and sent to Germany. He died at Magdeburg singing the Psalm, *Cantate Domino canticum novum.*

CONRAD of HEISTERBACH (Bl) C. OSB. Cist.   PC. Nov 25
d. c.1200. A soldier and a minister to the margraves of Thuringia until his fiftieth year, and then a Cistercian at Heisterbach. Cult not yet officially approved.

CONRAD of CONSTANCE (St) Bp. RM. Nov 26
d. 975. Bishop of Constance in Switzerland from 934 till his death. Three times he made the pilgrimage to the Holy Land, and in an age when most prelates were continually involved in secular politics, he succeeded in attending exclusively to ecclesiastical interests. Canonized in 1123.

CONRAD of OFFIDA (Bl) C. OFM. AC. Dec 14
c.1241–1306. A native of Offida, diocese of Ascoli Piceno. When fourteen years of age he joined the Franciscans and throughout his life as a Minorite, he favoured the "spiritual" and eremitical tendencies in the order. He died at Bastia in Umbria while preaching a sermon. Cult confirmed in 1817.

CONRADIN of BRESCIA (Bl) C. OP.   PC. Nov 1
d. 1429. Born at Bornato, in the diocese of Brescia, he was professed a Friar Preacher at Padua (1413) and was chosen prior of Bologna. Here he was twice imprisoned for defending the pope.

CONRAN (St) Bp.   Feb 14
The legend of a holy bishop of the Orkney Islands so named lacks all historical foundation.

CONSORTIA (St) V.   RM. June 22
d. ? 570. Said to have been the foundress of a convent generously endowed by King Clotaire out of gratitude for her having miraculously healed his dying daughter. She was venerated at Cluny, but nothing certain is known about her.

CONSTABILIS (St) Ab. OSB. AC. Feb 17
1060–1124. A native of Lucania, he became a Benedictine under St Leo at the abbey of Cava near Salerno, and in 1122 was chosen its fourth abbot. He built the town of Castelabbate, where he is now venerated as the principal patron saint. Canonized in 1893.

CONSTANTIA (St) M. RM. Sept 19
See Felix and Constantantia.

CONSTANT (St) M.   AC. Nov 18
d. 777. An Irish priest-hermit at Lough Erne who died under circumstances which led to his being venerated as a martyr.

CONSTANTIAN (St) Ab. AC. Dec 1
d. 570. A native of Auvergne, monk at Micy (Orleans) and abbot-founder of Javron abbey.

CONSTANTINE (St) RM. March 11
? The RM. says: "At Carthage, St Constantine, confessor". Nothing is known of him.

CONSTANTINE (St) M.
AC. March 11
d. 576. Said to have been a king of Cornwall, who after a career of vice and greed, led a penitent's life in Wales and Ireland, whence he went as a missionary to Scotland. There he was put to death by pirates. There is little serious historical foundation for this story.

CONSTANTINE (St) King, M.
AC. April 2
d. 874. Constantine II, king of Scotland, was slain in a battle against heathen invaders of his country and was henceforth locally honoured as a martyr. He was buried at Iona.

CONSTANTINE (St) Bp.
RM. Apr 12
d. 529. The first bishop of Gap in France, about whom nothing else is known.

CONSTANTINE (St) Bp.
AC. June 15
d. c.706. Said to have been a monk under St Philibert at Jumièges, and then Bishop of Beauvais.

CONSTANTINE (St) Ab. OSB.
AC. July 21
d. c.560. Disciple and first successor of St Benedict at Montecassino.

CONSTANTINE (St) M.
RM. July 27
One of the Seven Sleepers, q.v.

CONSTANTINOPLE (Martyrs of):
Three anonymous groups of martyrs put to death at Constantinople are commemorated in the RM., viz.—

RM. Feb 8
d. 485. The community of monks of St Dius martyred at the time of the Acacian schism for their fidelity to the Holy See.

RM. March 30
d. 351–359. A great number of people who suffered under the Arian emperor Constantius.

RM. July 8
d. 832. The Abrahamite monks, put to death under the iconoclast emperor Theophilus.

CONSTANTIUS and Comp. (SS)
MM.   RM. Jan 29
d. 170. Constantius, first bishop of Perugia, was put to death with numerous Christians of his flock, under Marcus Aurelius. The Acts of these martyrs are far from trustworthy. See Simplicius, Constantius and Victorian (Aug 26).

CONSTANTIUS of FABRIANO
(Bl) C. OP.   AC. Feb 25
d. 1481. Constantius Bernocchi was born at Fabriano in the Marches of Ancona and at the age of fifteen entered the Dominican Order. He had as masters Bl Conradin and St Antoninus. Appointed prior of the friary of San Marco at Florence, he achieved there a complete reform. He was renowned for his gift of prophecy. Beatified in 1811.

CONSTANTIUS (St) M.
RM. Aug 26
See Simplicius, Constantius and Victorian.

CONSTANTIUS (St) Bp. RM. Sept 1
d. c.520. Bishop of Aquino. He is mentioned with great honour by St Gregory the Great in his Dialogues.

CONSTANTIUS (St) C.
RM. Sept 23
6th cent. Sacristan of the ancient church of St Stephen at Ancona. He is still greatly venerated in that city.

CONSTANTIUS (St) C.
RM. Nov 30
5th cent. A priest of Rome who strongly opposed the Pelagians, at whose hands he had much to endure.

CONSTANTIUS (St) M. RM. Dec 12
See Maxentius, Constantius, etc.

CONTARDO of ESTE (St) C.
AC. Apr 16
d. 1249. Surnamed "the Pilgrim". He belonged to the Este family of Ferrara. He set out on a pilgrimage to Compostella, but died at Broni, diocese of Tortona, in extreme poverty.

CONTARDO FERRINI (Bl.) C.
AC. Oct 17
1859–1902. He was born at Milan and studied at the university of Pavia. After taking degrees in civil and canon law he taught at Messina, Mutina and finally Pavia. A Franciscan tertiary, a member of the Society of Saint Vincent de Paul, and a friend of Mgr Achilles Ratti (later Pope Pius XI), he was the model of a Catholic professor, and remarkable for his "inexhaustible desire for prayer". He died comparatively young at Suna on the shore of Lake Maggiore. Beatified in 1947.

CONTESTUS (St) Bp. AC. Jan 19
d. c.510. Bishop of Bayeux in Normandy from 480 till his death.

CONUS (St) Mk. OSB. AC. June 3
d. c.1200. Benedictine monk of Cardossa in Lucania. His relics were enshrined in the neighbouring village of Diano (1261), the saint's native place.

CONVOYON (St) Ab. OSB. AC. Jan 5
d. 868. A Breton by birth, he became successively archdeacon of Vannes, recluse, monk at Glanfeuil, and lastly abbot-founder of the great Benedictine monastery of St Saviour (831) near Redon, in Brittany. He was driven from his abbey by the Norsemen and died in exile. Cult confirmed, with the title of saint, in 1866.

CONWALL (CONVAL) (St) C.
AC. Sept 28
d. c.630. An Irish priest, disciple of St Kentigern, who preached and died in Scotland.

COPRES (St) M. RM. July 9
See Patermuthius, Copres, etc.

CORBICAN (St) C. AC. June 26
8th cent. An Irish recluse in the Low Countries who spent part of his day helping and instructing the peasants.

CORBINIAN (St) Bp. RM. Sept 8
670–730. A Frank who spent fourteen years as a hermit and then went to Rome, where Pope Gregory II consecrated him bishop and sent him to evangelize Germany. Corbinian fixed his residence at Freising in Bavaria. His last years were made very trying by Duke Grimoald, whose incestuous marriage the saint had denounced.

CORBMAC (St) Ab. AC. June 21
6th cent. A disciple of St Columba,

placed by him over the monastery he had founded at Durrow.

CORDULA (St) VM.   RM. Oct 22
d. *c*.453. An apocryphal saint who belongs to the legendary group of St Ursula and her eleven thousand virgins.

COREA (Martyrs of)   AC. Sept 22
See Laurence Imbert, etc.

COREBUS (St) M.   RM. Apr 18
c.117–138. A prefect of Messina in Sicily converted to Christ by St Eleutherius and martyred under the emperor Hadrian. It seems, however, that the Acts of St Eleutherius and Anthia are entirely fictitious.

CORENTINUS (CURY) (St) Bp.
AC. Dec 12
d. *c*.490. The first bishop of Cornouaille, now Quimper, in Brittany. He had been a recluse at Plomodiern. His cult spread throughout S.W. England, where he was known as St Cury.

CORFU (Martyrs of)   RM. Apr 29
1st cent. Known as "the Seven Holy Thieves". Seven criminals converted to Christ, it is said, by St Jason, a disciple of our Lord (Acts XVII, 5). Their names are given as Saturninus, Inischolus, Faustian, Januarius, Massalius, Euphrasius, and Mannonius. They were martyred in the island of Corfu. The story is from a Greek Menology.

CORMAC (St) Bp.   AC. Sept 14
d. 908. Probably the first bishop of Cashel. He is likewise known as king of Munster and was slain in battle. The "Psalter of Cashel" compiled by him is still extant.

CORMAC (St) Ab.   AC. Dec 12
6th cent. An Irish abbot, friend of St Columba.

CORNELIA (St) M.   RM. March 31
See Theodulus, Anesius, etc.

CORNELIUS (St) Bp.   RM. Feb 2
1st cent. The centurion of the Italic cohort, baptized at Caesarea in Palestine by the apostle St Peter (Acts X). Tradition makes him the first bishop of Caesarea; and as such he is described in the R.M.

CORNELIUS (St) Bp. OSA.
AC. June 4
c.1120-1176. Cornelius Mc Conchailleach, an Irishman by birth, joined the Augustinian canons regular at Armagh in 1140, was chosen abbot there in 1151, and finally became archbishop of that city in 1174. He died at Chambéry in Savoy on his return from a pilgrimage to Rome and is still held in great veneration there.

CORNELIUS (St) M. OFM.
RM. July 9
d. 1572. Born at Dorestat near Utrecht, he took the Franciscan habit at Gorkum, Holland, and was hanged by Calvinists at Briel with eighteen companions. (See Gorkum Martyrs.)

CORNELIUS (St) Pope M.
RM. Sept 16
d. 253. A Roman priest raised to the papal throne after an interregnum of fourteen months. He was opposed by Novatian, the first anti-pope. Cornelius had at once to attend to the condemnation of Novatian's rigoristic principles on the readmission of those Christians who had fallen away during the persecution. Cornelius's pontificate is an excellent illustration of how the papal authority was recognized everywhere by the faithful. He died in the persecution of Gallus. Shortly before his death he had been banished to *Centumcellae* (Civita Vecchia). His name is mentioned in the Canon of the Mass.

CORNELIUS (St) M.   RM. Dec 31
See Stephen, Pontian, etc.

CORONA (Bl) V. OSB. AC. Apr 24
? A Benedictine nun of the convent of
Elche, near Valencia in Spain.

CORONA (St) M.   RM. May 14
See Victor and Corona.

**COSMAS TACHEGIA (ZAQUIRA)
(St) M. Tert. OFM.   RM. Feb 5**
d. 1597. A Japanese Franciscan tertiary,
who served the Franciscan missionaries
as interpreter. He was crucified with St
Peter Baptist and twenty-four companions at Nagasaki. Beatified in 1627:
canonized in 1862.

**COSMAS TAQUEA (Bl) M.
                        AC. June 1**
d. 1619 (Nov 18). A layman, native of
Corea, taken to Japan as a prisoner of
war. There he became a member of the
Confraternity of the Rosary and gave
shelter to Bl John of St Dominic. He
was in consequence burnt alive. Beatified in 1867.

COSMAS (St) Bp. M.   AC. Sept 10
d. 1160. Born at Palermo in Sicily, he
was appointed bishop of Aphrodisia and
consecrated by Eugene III. The Saracens captured his episcopal city and he
died as a consequence of maltreatment
at their hands. Cult approved by Leo
XIII.

**COSMAS and DAMIAN (SS) MM.
                        RM. Sept 27**
d. c.303. Twin Arab brothers, physicians by profession, who were martyred
at Aegea in Cilicia, under Diocletian.
They practised their profession without
taking payment from their patients, and
on this account they are surnamed in
the East *Anargyroi* (the moneyless ones).
Their relics were brought to Rome,
whence their cult spread throughout the

West. They are mentioned in the Canon
of the Roman Mass.

**COSMO di CARBOGNANO (Bl)
                        AC. Nov 5**
Otherwise Gomidas, q.v.

**COTTAM (THOMAS) (Bl) M.
                        AC. May 30**
See Thomas Cottam.

**COTTIDUS, EUGENE and Comp.
(SS) MM.   RM. Sept 6**
? Cappadocian martyrs, whose *Acta*
have not come down to us. St Cottidus
is described as a deacon.

**COTTOLENGO (JOSEPH-BENE-
DICT) (St)   AC. Apr 29**
See Joseph-Benedict Cottolengo.

**CRATON and Comp. (SS) MM.
                        RM. Feb 15**
d. c.273. Craton, a philosopher and professor of rhetoric, was converted to
Christ by St Valentine, bishop of Terni.
He was martyred in Rome together
with his wife, and family.

CREDAN (St) Ab. OSB. AC. Aug 19
d. c.780. Eighth abbot of Evesham in
the Time of King Offa of Mercia.

CREMENTIUS (St) M. RM. Apr 16
See Caius and Crementius.

CRESCENS (St) M. RM. March 10
See Codratus, Dionysius, etc.

CRESCENS (St) M.   RM. Apr 15
? A martyr of Myra in Lycia, Asia
Minor, who perished at the stake.

**CRESCENS, DIOSCORIDES,
PAUL and HELLADIUS (SS) MM.
                        RM. May 28**
d. c.244. Roman Christians who were
burnt to death. Helladius does not seem
to have belonged to this group.

CRESCENS (St) Bp. M.
RM. June 27 and Dec 29
2nd cent. The disciple of St Paul mentioned by him (II Tim. IV, 10) as having gone into Galatia. He is stated to have been appointed bishop of the Galatians. Tradition tells us of his apostolate in France and also that he founded the see of Mainz in Gaul. The RM. adds that he returned to the east and was martyred under Trajan. It is certain that the Crescens who was first bishop of Vienne and the Crescens who worked at Mainz were not the disciples of St Paul, even if they did really exist.

CRESCENS (St) M.   RM. July 18
See Symphorosa and Comp.

CRESCENS (St) M.   RM. Oct 1
See Priscus, Crescens and Evagrius.

CRESCENS (St) Bp.   RM. Nov 28
See Valerian, Urban, etc.

CRESCENTIA HOSS (Bl) V. Tert. OFM.   AC. Apr 5
1682–1744. Born at Kaufbeuren in Bavaria. In 1703, at the request of the Protestant mayor of the town, she was admitted to the convent of the Franciscan regular tertiaries, but the nuns neglected and even persecuted her because she had entered without a dowry. Her Holiness, however, overcame their hostility, and eventually she was made novice-mistress, and superioress. Beatified in 1900.

CRESCENTIA (St) VM. RM. June 15
See Vitus, Modestus and Crescentia.

CRESCENTIAN (St) M. RM. May 31
d. c.130. A martyr who suffered at Sassari, in Sardinia, at the same time as SS Gabinus and Crispulus, in the reign of the emperor Hadrian. He is still held in great veneration there.

CRESCENTIAN (St) M. RM. June 1
d. c.287. A soldier beheaded at Saldo, near Città di Castello (*Tiphernum*) in Italy. His historical existence is doubtful.

CRESCENTIAN (St) M. RM. July 2
See Ariston, Crescentian, etc.

CRESCENTIAN (St) M. RM. Aug 12
See Hilaria, Digna, etc.

CRESCENTIAN, VICTOR, ROSULA, and GENERALIS (SS) MM.
RM. Sept 14
d. c.258. African martyrs, alleged to have suffered at the same time and place as St Cyprian.

CRESCENTIAN (St) M. RM. Nov 24
d. 309. A martyr who suffered at Rome in company with SS Cyriacus, Largus and Smaragdus, expiring on the rack in their presence under Maxentius.

CRESCENTIAN (St) Bp. RM. Nov 28
See Valerian, Urban, etc.

CRESCENTIANA (St) M. RM. May 5
5th cent. Beyond the fact that as early as the time of Pope Symmachus (498–514) a church in Rome was dedicated to her, nothing is known of this martyr.

CRESCENTIO (St) M. RM. Sept 17
See Narcissus and Crescentio.

CRESCENTIUS (St) C. RM. Apr 19
d. c.396. A subdeacon of Florence, a disciple of St Zenobius and of St Ambrose.

CRESCENTIUS (St) M. RM. Sept 14
d. c.300. A boy, only eleven years of age, the son of St Euthymius, q.v., who, in the persecution of Diocletian, was brought from Perugia to Rome, bravely confessed Christ under torture, and was beheaded.

CRESCENTIUS (St) M. RM. Dec 12
See Maxentius, Constantius, etc.

CRESCENTIUS (St) Bp.
Otherwise Crescens (June 27) q.v.

CRESCENTIUS (St) M. RM. Dec 29
See Dominic, Victor, etc.

CRESCONIUS (St) Bp. M.
RM. Nov 28
See Valerian, Urban, etc.

CRETE (Martyrs of) Dec 23
For this group of ten martyrs, who suffered in Crete, see Theodulus, Saturninus, etc.

CREWENNA (St) Feb 1
5th cent. This saint accompanied St Breaca from Ireland to Cornwall. There is no record of him beyond the place-name Crowan near St Erth.

CRISPIN (St) Bp. RM. Jan 7
Two bishops of this name, both saints, governed the see of Pavia in Lombardy: one in the first half of the third century occupied the see for thirty-five years, the second was bishop during the reign of Pope St Leo the Great and in 451 subscribed the acts of the council of Milan. It is apparently the second which the RM. commemorates on Jan 7.

CRISPIN of VITERBO (Bl) C. OFM. Cap. AC. May 23
1668–1750. A native of Viterbo, who joined the Capuchins as a lay-brother and was employed as a cook in the friaries of Viterbo, Tolfa, Rome and Albano. He loved to call himself "the little beast of burden of the Capuchins". Beatified in 1806.

CRISPIN and CRISPINIAN (SS) MM. RM. Oct 25
d. *c.*287. Two brothers, shoemakers by trade, who were beheaded at Soissons in France under Diocletian. They were held in great popular veneration throughout the Middle Ages (see in this connection Shakespeare's Henry V, Act IV, Scene 2) and are still recognized as the patron saints of shoemakers.

CRISPIN (St) Bp. M. RM. Nov 19
4th cent. Bishop of Ecija (*Astiagis*) in Andalusia, beheaded under Maximian Herculeus. He is honoured with a special office in the Mozarabic breviary.

CRISPIN (St) M. RM. Dec 3
See Claudius, Crispin, etc.

CRISPIN (St) M. RM. Dec 5
See Julius, Potamia, etc.

CRISPINA (St) M. RM. Dec 5
d. 304. A wealthy matron of Thebeste in Numidia. She was tortured, forced to undergo the most shameful indignities and ultimately beheaded. We have still a glowing panegyric preached by St Augustine in her honour.

CRISPULUS (St) M. RM. May 30
See Gabinus and Crispulus.

CRISPULUS and RESTITUTUS (SS) MM. RM. June 10
1st cent. Martyrs believed to have suffered under Nero, and probably in Rome. Baronius, however, following Rabanus Maurus, assigns them to Spain. No account of them is extant.

CRISPUS (St) M. RM. Aug 18
See John and Crispus.

CRISPUS and CAIUS (SS) MM. RM. Oct 4
1st cent. Saints of the apostolic age, the only two whom St Paul baptized at Corinth (I Cor. 1, 14). Crispus was ruler of the synagogue in that city (Acts

XVIII, 8). Caius in all likelihood is the same person whom the Apostle styles "my host" (Rom. XVI, 23), and also the "dearly beloved Gaius (Caius)" to whom St John addressed his third epistle. According to traditions, both became bishops: the former of the island of Aegina, the latter of Thessalonica.

CRISTIOLUS (St)   AC. Nov 3
7th cent. A Welsh saint, brother of St Sulian and founder of churches in Pembrokeshire and Anglesey.

CROIDAN, MEDAN and DEGAN (SS)   AC. June 4
6th cent. Three disciples of St Petroc, q.v.

CRONAN BEG (St) Bp.   AC. Jan 7
7th cent. A bishop of ancient Aendrum, Co. Down, mentioned in connection with the paschal controversy in 640.

CRONAN the WISE (St) Bp.
                                    AC. Feb 9
? 8th cent. Surnamed "the wise" on account of his ability in systematizing Irish canon law. He is probably identical with St Roman, bishop of Lismore.

CRONAN of ROSCREA (St) Ab.
                                   AC. Apr 28
d. c.626. Born in Munster, founder of several religious houses in various parts of Ireland, chief among them being that of Roscrea.

CRONAN (St)   AC. June 3
d. 617. Surnamed "the Tanner". A disciple of St Kevin.

CRONIDAS (St) M. RM. March 27
See Philetus, Lydia, etc.

CRONION (St) M.
                   RM. Feb 27 and Oct 30
See Julian, Cronion, etc.

CROTATES (St) M.   RM. Apr 21
See Apollo, Isacius, etc.

CROYLAND (Martyrs of) (SS) OSB.
                                      AC. Apr 9
See Theodore and Comp.

CRUMMINE (St) Bp.   AC. June 28
5th cent. A disciple of St Patrick, placed by him over the church of Leccuine (Lackan) Co. Westmeath.

CTESIPHON (St) Bp.   RM. May 15
See Torquatus, Ctesiphon, etc.

CUAN (St) Ab.   AC. Jan 1
6th cent. An Irish abbot, called Mochua or Moncan, who founded many churches and monasteries, and who lived to close upon his hundredth year.

CUARAN (CURVINUS, CRONAN) (St) Bp.   AC. Feb 9
d. p.700. An Irish bishop, surnamed like several others, "the Wise", who concealed his dignity in order to become a simple monk at Iona, where, however he was recognized by St Columba.

CUBY (CYBY) (St) Bp.   AC. Nov 8
6th cent. A Cornish saint, a cousin of St David of Wales. Consecrated bishop, he settled with ten disciples near Tregony, but later passed some time in Ireland. Ultimately he came to Wales and founded a monastery near Holyhead. He is the patron saint of Llangibbi (Monmouth) and of Llangybi (Carnarvon).

CUCUPHAS (CUCUFATE, CUGAT, GUINEFORT, QOQOFAS) (St) M.   RM. July 25
d. 304. A son of noble parents of Punic descent resident at Scillis in Africa. He crossed over to Spain and was martyred near Barcelona at the place where some centuries later arose the Benedictine

abbey of St Cugat del Valles. He is one of the most celebrated of the Spanish martyrs. Prudentius composed some exquisite stanzas in his honour. Part of his relics were venerated at Paris.

CULMATIUS (St) M. RM. June 19
See Gaudentius and Culmatius.

CUMGAR (CUNGAR, CYNGAR) (St) C. AC. Nov 7
6th (or 8th) cent. A native of Devon, founder of monasteries at Budgworth, Congresbury (Somerset) and at Llangonys (Glamorgan). He is to be identified with St Docuinus, or Doguinus. This seems to be the name which was later corrupted into Oue and Kew. St Cumgar was buried at Congresbury, to which town he has given his name.

**CUMINE the WHITE (St) Ab.
AC. Feb 24 or Oct 6**
d. 669. An abbot of Iona of Irish descent, who wrote a life of St Columba.

CUMMIAN (CUMIAN, CUMMIN) (St) Bp. OSB. AC. June 9
1st half 8th cent. An Irish bishop who in his wanderings through Italy visited Bobbio and remained there as a monk. By this time Bobbio was already a Benedictine abbey; Cummian himself was an ardent advocate of the Roman observances.

**CUMMIAN FADA (St) Ab.
AC. Nov 12**
d. 662. An Irish monk who had charge of the monastic school at Clonfert and became the abbot-founder of the monastery at Kilcummin, where he strenuously defended the Roman computation of Easter against his Celtic brethren.

**CUNCOLIM (Martyrs of)
AC. July 27**
See Rudolph Acquaviva and Comp.

**CUNEGUND (St) V. OSB.
RM. March 3**
d. 1039. Wife of Henry II, Holy Roman Emperor, with whom she lived in conjugal virginity and is, for this reason, venerated as a virgin. She founded the Benedictine nunnery of Kaufungen, which she entered on the first anniversary of her husband's death (1024) and where she earnestly endeavoured to forget her past dignity. Canonized in 1200.

**CUNEGUND (Bl) V. OSB.
AC. May 4**
d. *p*.1052. A Benedictine nun of the convent of Niedermunster in Ratisbon.

CUNEGUND (Bl) V. AC. July 24
Otherwise Kinga, q.v.

CUNERA (St) V. AC. June 12
? A saint venerated more particularly in Germany, but said to have been of British birth. The traditions relating to her are most untrustworthy.

**CUNIALD and GISLAR (SS)
AC. Sept 24**
7th cent. Confessors.

**CUNIBERT (St) Ab. OSB.
AC. Sept 16**
d. *c*.680. Successor of St Humbert as abbot of Maroilles, in the diocese of Cambrai.

CUNIBERT (St) Bp. RM. Nov 12
d. *c*.663. A Frankish courtier who became successively archdeacon of Trèves and archbishop of Cologne. He filled the office of chief minister during the minority of King Sigebert of Austrasia. He was an untiring builder of churches and monasteries.

CURCODOMUS (St) C. RM. May 4
3rd cent. A Roman deacon, sent by the

pope to attend St Peregrinus, first bishop of Auxerre, on his mission into Gaul.

CURÉ d'ARS (St) C.   RM. Aug 9
See John Baptist Vianney.

CURIG (St) Bp.   AC. June 16
6th cent. Stated to have been bishop of Llanbadarn in Wales, in which country several churches are dedicated in his honour. There is, however, great difficulty in distinguishing him from other saints bearing similar names.

CURITAN (St) Bp.   AC. March 14
Otherwise Boniface, q.v.

CURONOTUS (St) Bp. M.
                        RM. Sept 12
d. c.258. A bishop of Iconium in Lycaonia, Asia Minor, martyred under Valerian.

CURY (St) Bp.   AC. Dec 12
Otherwise Corentinus, q.v.

CUTHBERT (St) Bp. OSB.
                        RM. March 20
d. 687. A Briton who in his youth tended his father's sheep until he embraced the monastic life at Melrose. When Ripon abbey was founded he was sent there as guest-master, then he became prior of Melrose. Finally, after the council of Whitby, he was asked to go to Lindisfarne, now under the new Benedictine observance, and was made prior of the abbey. In March, 685, he was consecrated abbot-bishop of Lindisfarne by St Theodore at York. St Cuthbert is one of the most famous of English saints. He was moreover the wonder-worker of England, and his shrine at Durham was one of the most frequented in the Middle Ages: it was already an ancient shrine before St Thomas of Canterbury was born.

CUTHBERT (St) Bp. OSB.
                        PC. Oct 26
d. 758. A monk of Lyminge in Kent who became bishop of Hereford (c.736) and archbishop of Canterbury (c.740). He is best remembered as one of the English correspondents of St Boniface.

CUTHBERT MAYNE (Bl) M.
                        AC. Nov 29
1544–1577. Born near Barnstaple in Devonshire, he was educated as a Protestant, but he was converted to Catholicism while an undergraduate at St John's, Oxford. He was ordained at Douai and sent to the English mission (c.1575). He laboured in Cornwall, but before a year had elapsed was captured and condemned for the crime of saying Mass. He was executed at Launceston. Beatified in 1886, he is the protomartyr of the English seminaries.

CUTHBURGA (St) Abs. OSB.
                        AC. Aug 31
d. c.725. Sister to King Ina of Wessex. She married Aldfrid of Northumbria (688) who allowed her to enter as a nun at Barking under St Hildelid. Some time after 705 she founded, with her sister St Queenburga, Wimborne abbey in Dorset, which she governed as abbess. From this nunnery came forth the band of missionary nuns who helped in the evangelization of Germany.

CUTHMAN (St) H.   AC. Feb 8
9th cent. A south of England saint who lived a holy life as a shepherd near Steyning in Sussex. The old church of that place was dedicated in his honour.

CUTIAS (St) M.   RM. Feb 18
See Maximus, Claudius, etc.

CYBAR (St) Ab.   RM. July 1
Otherwise Eparchius, q.v.

CYBY (St) Bp.   AC. Nov 8
Otherwise Cuby, q.v.

CYNDEYRN (St) Bp.   AC. Jan 14
Otherwise Kentigern, q.v.

CYNFARCH (St)   AC. Sept 8
Otherwise Kingsmark, q.v.

CYNFRAN (St) C.   AC. Nov 11
5th cent. A Welsh saint, one of the sons
of the chieftain Brychan of Brecknock
and founder of a church in Carnarvonshire. There is also a St Cynfran's well.

CYNIBILD (St) C.   AC. March 2
7th cent. A brother of SS Chad and
Cedd who also laboured in the evangelization of the Anglo-Saxons.

CYNIDR (KENEDRUS) (St) Ab.
**   AC. Apr 27**
Otherwise Enoder, q.v.

CYNLLO (St)   AC. July 17
5th cent. A Welsh saint, in whose
honour several churches are dedicated

CYNOG (St) M.   AC. Oct 7
Otherwise Canog, q.v.

CYNWL (St) H.   AC. Apr 30
6th cent. The brother of St Deiniol,
first bishop of Bangor. He lived an
austere life in N. Wales, and after his
death churches were dedicated in his
honour.

CYPRIAN (St) M.   RM. March 10
See Codratus, Dionysius, etc.

CYPRIAN (St) Bp.   AC. Apr 21
d. 582. Bishop of Brescia in Lombardy.
His relics are enshrined in the church of
San Pietro in Oliveto at Brescia.

CYPRIAN (St) M.   RM. July 11
See Sabinus and Cyprian.

CYPRIAN (St) Bp. M. RM. Sept 16
c.210–258. Thascius Caecilius Cypria-
nus was born in Proconsular Africa,
became a lawyer, was converted to
Christianity and was consecrated bishop
of Carthage (c.249). It is as a bishop
that he played a most important part in
the history of the Western Church.
As such he produced numerous treatises
on various theological subjects, one of
the most important being *De Unitate*,
and wrote numerous letters. He is in
fact, like Tertullian, a pioneer of Latin
Christian literature. He is a witness to
the belief of the faithful in the necessary
oneness of the Church founded on the
Rock of Peter. He seconded Pope St
Cornelius's teaching on the reconciliation of fallen Christians. He erred, however, on the doctrine of the validity of
baptism conferred by heretics. Nevertheless, the Roman Church has always
been grateful to his memory and
mentions his name in the Canon of the
Mass. Cyprian went into hiding during
the persecution of Decius, but was
arrested and beheaded under the first
edict of Valerian. The Acts of his
martyrdom are of great charm and
interest.

CYPRIAN and JUSTINA (SS) MM.
**   RM. Sept 26**
The legend is that Cyprian, a pagan
necromancer and astrologer, was converted to Christianity by the virgin
Justina whom he had tried to lead
astray. In the persecution under Diocletian they were both arrested and
beheaded at Nicomedia. There is no
evidence whatever to justify the belief
that these two persons ever existed. The
story is merely a moral fable.

CYPRIAN (St) Bp.   AC. Oct 3
6th cent. Monk of St Victor at Marseilles, and bishop of Toulon (516).
He was a staunch opponent of

Semi-Pelagianism. He has left us the life of his master St Caesarius of Arles.

CYPRIAN (St) M.   RM. Oct 12
See Felix and Cyprian.

CYPRIAN (St) Ab.   RM. Dec 9
d. 586. A monk of Périgueux, France, who ended his life as a hermit on the banks of the Dordogne. St Gregory of Tours has left an account of St Cyprian's life and miracles.

CYR (St) M.   RM. June 16
See Quiricius and Julitta.

CYRA (St)   RM. Aug 3
See Marana and Cyra.

CYRENIA and JULIANA (SS) MM.
RM. Nov 1
d. 306. Two Christian women burnt to death at Tarsus in Asia Minor under Maximin.

CYRIA (St) M.   RM. June 5
See Zenais, Cyria, etc.

CYRIACA, CYRIACUS, etc.
Note. These names, common to many saints, are often found written Quiriacus, Quiriaca, etc. Sometimes they are replaced by their equivalent Latin forms Dominicus, Dominica, etc. Less frequently, the spelling Kyriacus, Kiriacus, etc., is met with.

CYRIACA (St) M.   RM. March 20
See Photina, Joseph, etc.

CYRIACA and Comp. (SS) VV.
MM.   RM. May 19
d. 307. Six Christian maidens who perished at the stake at Nicomedia under Maximinian Galerius.

CYRIACA (DOMINICA) (St) M.
RM. Aug 21
d. 249. A wealthy Roman widow, who sheltered the persecuted Christians and to whose house St Laurence, the deacon and martyr, was accustomed to repair to distribute his alms. The Roman Church of St Mary in *Dominica* perpetuates her name.

CYRIACUS (St) M.   RM. Jan 31
See Tarcisius, Zoticus, etc.

CYRIACUS (St) M.   RM. Feb 8
See Paul, Lucius and Cyriacus.

CYRIACUS and Comp. (SS) MM.
RM. Apr 7
? Eleven Christians, martyred at Nicomedia in Asia Minor.

CYRIACUS (St) M.   RM. May 2
See Exuperius, Zoc, etc.

CYRIACUS (QUIRIACUS) (St) M.
Bp.   RM. May 4
? Most probably a bishop of Ancona in Italy, who while making his pilgrimage to the Holy Land, was martyred under Julian the Apostate. Others assert that he was a bishop of Jerusalem put to death under Hadrian.

CYRIACUS (St) M.   RM. June 5
See Florentius, Julian, etc.

CYRIACUS and JULITTA (SS)
MM.   RM. June 16
Otherwise Quiricus and Julitta, q.v.

CYRIACUS and PAULA (St) MM.
RM. June 18
d. 305. Two Christians, stoned to death at Málaga in Spain under Diocletian. St Paula is registered as a virgin-martyr.

CYRIACUS (St) M.   RM. June 20
See Paul and Cyriacus.

CYRIACUS and APOLLINARIS
(SS) MM.   RM. June 21
? African martyrs, registered in the

Martyrologies, but whose Acts have been lost.

CYRIACUS (St) M.   RM. June 24
See Orentius, Heros, etc.

CYRIACUS (St) M.   RM. July 15
See Antiochus and Cyriacus.

CYRIACUS, LARGUS, SMARAG-DUS and Comp. (SS) MM.
RM. Aug 8 and March 16
d. 304. A group of twenty-four martyrs who suffered in Rome under Diocletian. At their head was St Cyriacus, a deacon, who at a later period gave his name to a church. The Acts are worthless, and the only certain fact is that Cyriacus gave his name to the church.

CYRIACUS (St) H.   AC. Sept 29
d. 556. Hermit and abbot in Palestine. He died in the *laura* of St Sabas. His life was written by St Cyril of Scythopolis.

CYRIACUS (St) Bp.   AC. Oct 27
d. 606. Administrator, and afterwards patriarch, of Constantinople. The Greeks commemorate him on Oct 29.

CYRIACUS, PAULILLUS, SECUNDUS, ANASTASIUS, SINDIMIUS and Comp. (SS) MM.
RM. Dec 19
d. 303. A group of Christians, martyred at Nicomedia under Diocletian. No other particulars are extant.

CYRIL of ALEXANDRIA (St) Bp. Dr.   RM. Feb 9
c.376–444. A native of Alexandria who became patriarch of that city in 412. His name in history is famous as the untiring opponent of Nestorianism, which he denounced to Pope St Celestine I. The pope appointed him to preside at the council of Ephesus in 431, at which Nestorius was definitely condemned. Stressing the truth of Christ's divinity, St Cyril employs a terminology that sometimes seems to favour Monophysitism, and this is the reason why Monophysite Copts, Syrians and Ethiopians venerate him as their chief teacher. He was declared Doctor of the Church by Leo XIII.

CYRIL (St) M.   RM. March 4
See Archelaus, Cyril and Photius.

CYRIL of CONSTANTINOPLE (St) C. OC.   AC. March 6
d. 1235. Born of Greek parents at Constantinople, he was ordained priest and was noted as a teacher of true sanctity. At the age of forty-six he became a Carmelite in Palestine and was prior general for seventeen years.

CYRIL, ROGATUS, FELIX, another ROGATUS, BEATA, HERENIA, FELICITAS, URBAN, SILVANUS, and MAMILLUS (SS) MM.   RM. March 8
? African martyrs—Cyril is described as a bishop—registered in all the ancient lists, but of whom nothing is known.

CYRIL of JERUSALEM (St) Bp. Dr.   RM. March 18
c.315–387. Born near Jerusalem, he became a priest in 345, and patriarch of the city from 350 till his death. Seventeen years of his patriarchate he spent in exile, driven out by the Arians. His name is forever connected with his work as a catechist: his instructions on Christian doctrine, addressed to the catechumens before baptism are gems of theological literature. He was declared Doctor of the Church by Leo XIII. The myth that he ever sided with the Arians is now universally rejected.

CYRIL (St) M.   RM. March 20
See Paul, Cyril, etc.

CYRIL (St) M.   RM. March 29
d. *c*.362. A deacon of Heliopolis in the
Lebanon, who suffered under Julian the
Apostate.

CYRIL (St) Bp.   AC. May 19
5th cent. A bishop of Trèves, whose
relics were enshrined in the abbey
church St Matthias in that city.

CYRIL (St) M.   AC. May 29
d. ? 251. A boy of Caesarea in Cappadocia, who embraced Christianity without his father's knowledge. He was
turned out of his home, arrested and
put to death.

CYRIL and METHODIUS (SS) CC.
                       RM. July 7
d. 869 and 885. Two brothers who are
venerated as the "Apostles of the
Slavs". Cyril, or Constantine, was a
secular priest and Methodius a monk
in a Greek monastery. In 863 they began
to evangelize Moravia. They met with
opposition there and came to Rome to
ask the apostolic blessing on their work.
Cyril now became a monk at SS Boniface and Alexius on the Aventine, and
died shortly after. Methodius was consecrated bishop and returned to preach
in Moravia and Pannonia with permission to celebrate the liturgy in Slavonic.
This concession turned the German
bishops against his work, and they even
put him in prison. His apostolate,
however, met with signal success. He
translated most of the Bible into
Slavonic.

CYRIL (St) Bp. M.   RM. July 9
d. 250. An aged bishop of Gortyna in
Crete, tortured and beheaded under
Decius.

CYRIL (St) Bp.   RM. July 22
d. *c*.300. The successor of Timaeus
(280) in the patriarchate of Antioch. He
had much to endure in the persecution
of Diocletian, but appears to have died
in peace.

CYRIL, AQUILA, PETER, DOMI-
TIAN, RUFUS, and MENANDER
(SS) MM.   RM. Aug 1
This group of martyrs had a local feast
at Philadelphia in Arabia. They were
not martyred there, and Peter is apparently the Apostle, Rugus of Rome,
and Cyril of Times.

CYRIL (St) M.   RM. Oct 2
See Primus, Cyril and Secundarius.

CYRIL (St) M.   RM. Oct 28
See Anastasia and Cyril.

CYRILLA (St) M.   RM. July 5
d. *c*.300. An aged widow of Cyrene,
condemned to death, but who appears
to have expired in the torture chamber.
Several other martyrs suffered at the
same time.

CYRILLA (St) VM.   RM. Oct 28
d. 268–270. The daughter of St Tryphonia and a sharer in the good works
of that saintly Roman widow. She was
put to death under the emperor Claudius II.

CYRINUS, PRIMUS, and THEO-
GENES (SS) MM.   RM. Jan 3
d. 320. Soldiers in the imperial army
who were martyred at Cyzicus on the
Hellespont under the emperor Licinius.

CYRINUS (St) M.   RM. May 10
See Alphius, Philadelphus and Cyrinus.

CYRINUS (St) M.   RM. June 12
See Basilides, Cyrinus, etc.

CYRINUS (St) M.   RM. Oct 25
3rd cent. A Roman martyr under Diocletian of whom mention is made in the
Acts of St Marcellinus, pope and martyr.

**CYRION, BASSIAN, AGATHO
and MOSES (SS) MM.   RM. Feb 14**
? A group of martyrs of Alexandria,
listed together because all perished at
the stake. Cyrion was a priest, Bassian
a lector, Agatho an exorcist, and Moses
a layman.

**CYRION and CANDIDUS (SS)
MM.   RM. March 9**
The two most conspicuous among the
Forty Armenian Martyrs, q.v.

CYRUS and JOHN (SS) MM.
**   RM. Jan 31**
d. c.303. Two physicians of Alexandria
who went to Canopus to assist a woman
and her three daughters who were being
persecuted as Christians. All were martyred together.

CYRUS of CARTHAGE (St) Bp.
**   RM. July 14**
? St Possidius, the biographer of St
Augustine, speaks of a sermon deli-
vered by the latter on the feast of St
Cyrus. Probably he meant St Cyprian.

CYTHINUS (St) M.   RM. July 17
One of the Scillitan Martyrs, q.v.

D

DABEOC (St) Ab.   AC. Jan 1
Otherwise Beoc, q.v.

DABIUS (DAVIUS) (St) C.
       AC. July 22
? An Irish priest who worked in Scotland, where he is the titular of several churches. He may be identical with St Movean or Biteus, disciple of St Patrick.

DACIAN (DATIANUS) (St) M.
       RM. June 4
See Aretius and Dacian.

DACIUS (St) M.   RM. Nov 1
See Caesarius, Dacius, and Comp.

DADAS (St) M.   RM. Apr 13
See Maximus, Quintilian and Dadas.

DADAS (DIDAS), CASDOE, and GABDELAS (SS) MM. RM. Sept 29
*c.*310–368. Dadas, a noble Persian, Casdoe, his wife, and Gabdelas, probably their son, were of the number of the many martyrs who suffered under Shapur (Sapor) II, to whom Dadas was kinsman.

DAFROSA (AFFROSA) (St) M.
       RM. Jan 4
? According to the untrustworthy Acts of St Bibiana, St Dafrosa, her mother, was martyred, under Julian the Apostate.

DAGAN (St) M.   AC. Aug 27
Otherwise Decuman, q.v.

DAGOBERT II (St) King M.
       PC. Dec 23
d. 679. Son of St Sigebert III, and king of Austrasia. He was exiled to a monastery in 656, recalled in 675 and murdered by order of Ebroin, mayor of the palace. His death has been traditionally regarded as a martyrdom.

DAIG MACCAIRILL (DAGAEUS, DAGANUS)
Bp.   AC. Aug 18
d. 586. Son of Cayrill, he was a disciple of St Finian and founded a monastery at Inis Cain Dega (Iniskeen). He was bishop and abbot. The Book of Leinster makes him "one of the Three Master Craftsmen of Ireland".

DALLAN FORGAILL (of CLUAIN DALLAIN) (St) M.   AC. Jan 29
d. 598. A kinsman of St Aidan of Ferns, born in Connaught, and a great scholar. Through his application to study he became blind. He is best remembered for his poem in honour of St Columba, called *Ambra Choluim Kille*. He was murdered at Inis-coel by pirates.

DALMATIUS (St) C.   AC. Aug 3
d. *c.*440. An archimandrite, venerated at Constantinople. He took a lively part in defending the Catholic Bishops against the intrigues of the Nestorians.

DALMATIUS MONER (Bl) C. OP.
       AC. Sept 26
1291–1341. Born near Gerona, in Spain, he joined the Friars Preachers. His life among them was uneventful as regards dignities and offices, which he constantly refused, but was a living pattern of fidelity to the rule. Cult confirmed in 1721.

DALMATIUS (St) Bp. AC. Nov 13
d. 580. Bishop of Rodez, in France, from
524 to 580. He had much to suffer at the
hands of the Arian Visigoth King
Amalric.

DALMATIUS (St) Bp. M.
                                    RM. Dec 5
d. 304. Born at Monza of pagan parents
he preached, after his conversion, in
Gaul and N. Italy until his election to
the see of Pavia. He was martyred under
Maximian Herculeus within a year of
his election.

DAMASCUS (Martyrs of) (BB) MM.
                                    AC. July 10
See Emmanuel Ruiz and Comp.

DAMASUS (St) Pope RM. Dec 11
d. 384. A Spaniard by descent, but probably born in Rome, he served as deacon
the Spanish church of St Laurence
in that city. He was chosen pope in 366
and during his pontificate he greatly
increased the prestige of the Roman See.
He successfully opposed the Arians
and Apollinarians; commissioned his
great friend St Jerome to correct the
Latin Bible; developed the Roman
liturgy; and restored many sacred
buildings and the tombs of the martyrs,
composing inscriptions for them which
have become famous. St Jerome styles
him "an incomparable man".

DAMHNADE (St) V. AC. June 13
? An Irish virgin greatly venerated in
Cavan, Fermanagh, etc. Colgan identi-
fies her with St Dympna, the martyr of
Gheel in Belgium. Nothing certain is
known of her life or date.

DAMIAN (SS) MM. RM. Feb 12
? The Bollandists distinguish two saints
of this name under the date Feb 12: one
a soldier, martyred in Africa, probably
at Alexandria; the other a Roman mar-

tyr whose relics were found in the catacombs of St Callistus and sent to
Salamanca in Spain. Other particulars
are lacking.

DAMIAN, PETER (St) Bp. Dr.
                                    RM. Feb 23
See Peter Damian.

DAMIAN (St) Bp.   RM. Apr 12
d. 710. Bishop of Pavia in Lombardy,
elected to that office in 680. He vigor-
ously opposed the Monothelites, and
acted successfully as peacemaker between the Emperor of Byzantium and
the Lombards.

DAMIAN (St) M.   RM. May 26
Otherwise Dyfan, q.v.

DAMIAN VAZ (Bl) M. AC. June 11
d. 1242. A Portuguese knight of St John,
put to death by the Moors at Tavira,
Algarbes, Portugal (see Peter Rodriguez).

DAMIAN YAMIKI (Bl) M.
                                    AC. Sept 10
d. 1622. A Japanese layman, beheaded
at Nagasaki. He belongs to the group of
Bl Charles Spinola, q.v.

DAMIAN (St) M.   RM. Sept 27
See Cosmas and Damian.

DAMIAN dei FULCHERI (Bl) C.
OP.   AC. Oct 26
d. 1484. A native of Finale (*Finarium*)
near Savona, in Liguria, he took the
Dominican habit at Savona, and
preached in nearly all the cities of Italy.
He died at Reggio d'Emilia. Cult approved in 1848.

DANIEL (St) M.   RM. Jan 3
d. 168. A deacon, said to have been of
Jewish extraction, who aided St Prosdocimus, first bishop of Padua, in his

apostolate in N.E. Italy. He was martyred in 168. His body was discovered many centuries later and solemnly enshrined Jan 3, 1064.

DANIEL (Bl) Ab. OSB. Cist.
						PC. Jan 20
d. 1232. The third abbot of the Cistercian monastery of Cambron, in Hainault.

DANIEL (St) M.			RM. Feb 16
See Elias, Jeremias, etc.

DANIEL and VERDA (SS) MM.
						AC. Feb 21
d. 344. Persian martyrs, greatly honoured in the East, who suffered under King Shapur II. The first was a priest, the second a woman.

DANIEL (St) H. OSB. Cam.
						AC. March 31
d. 1411. A German merchant who through travelling to Venice on business came to know the Camaldolese monks of Murano. He lived a hermit's life under their direction and rule, but in his own house, and was wont to spend long periods with them. He was killed by robbers in his cell.

DANIEL (St) M.			AC. Apr 29
9th cent. A hermit-martyr, the titular of the abbey-church of the Benedictine nuns at Gerona in Spain. According to the legend, which defies all historical verification, he was a native of Asia Minor, and flourished in the times of Charlemagne.

DANIEL (St) M.			RM. July 10
See Leontius, Maurice, etc.

DANIEL (St) Prophet   RM. July 21
5th cent. B.C. One of the four great prophets of the O.T. His life belongs to the Jewish, rather than to the Christian calendar. The RM. mentions Babylon as the place of his death. His

relics are said to have been translated first to Alexandria and then to Venice.

DANIEL (St) Bp.			AC. Sept 11
d. 545. Consecrated first bishop of Bangor by St Dyfrig. The Cathedral of Bangor and other churches are dedicated in his name.

DANIEL, SAMUEL, ANGELUS (ANGELUCCIO), DOMNUS, LEO, NICHOLAS and HUGOLINUS (SS) MM. OFM.			RM. Oct 10
d. 1221. This band of Franciscan missionaries was sent by St Francis himself to preach the gospel to the Moors in Morocco. The leader of the band was Brother Daniel, provincial of Calabria. On their arrival at Ceuta the friars were first treated as madmen, but on their refusal to apostatize to Islam, they were beheaded, having been in the country less than three weeks. Canonized in 1516.

DANIEL the STYLITE (St)
						RM. Dec 11
d. 493. After St Simeon the Elder, the greatest and best known of the pillar-saints. He was a monk near Samosata, on the Upper Euphrates. When travelling with his abbot he came to know of St Simeon Stylites, who lived on the top of a pillar near Antioch. He forthwith determined to follow the same way of life at a spot near Constantinople. Here the emperor Leo I built for him a series of pillars, and here too he was ordained priest by St Gennadius. From the top of his pillar he became the oracle of the whole city. He lived on his pillar for thirty years, during which time he came down only once from it in order to rebuke the usurping emperor Basiliscus for supporting the Monophysites.

DANIEL (Bl) C. OSB. Cist.
						PC. Dec 26
Late 12th cent. Monk and cellarer of the

great Cistercian abbey of Villers in Brabant. He is listed as a *beatus* in the Cistercian catalogues.

DARERCA (St) W.   AC. March 22
? 5th cent. St Patrick's sister. Her name, derived from the Irish *Diar-Sheare*, means constant and firm love. She is reputed to have left fifteen sons, some ten of whom became bishops.

DARIA (St) M.   RM. Oct 25
See Chrysanthus and Daria.

DARIUS, ZOSIMUS, PAUL and SECUNDUS (SS) MM. RM. Dec 19
? A group of martyrs who suffered at Nicaea, of whom nothing else is known.

DARLUGDACH (DARDULACHA, DERLUGDACH) (St) V. AC. Feb 1
d. *c*.524. Successor of St Brigid and second abbess of Kildare.

DASIUS, ZOTICUS, CAIUS and Comp. (SS) MM.   RM. Oct 21
d. *c*.303. A group of fifteen soldiers who suffered martyrdom at Nicomedia under Diocletian.

DASIUS (St) M.   RM. Nov 20
d. *c*.303. A Roman soldier who refused to take part in the heathen orgies of the Saturnalia, and was for this reason martyred at Dorostorum in Mysia, Asia Minor.

DATHUS (DATUS) (St) Bp.
**   RM. July 3**
d. 190. Bishop of Ravenna. His election was due to the miraculous appearance of a dove hovering over his head. He governed his see during the reign of the emperor Commodus.

DATIUS (St) Bp.   RM. Jan 14
d. 552. Bishop of Milan, being elected to that see some time after 530. His

whole diocese was overrun by the Arian Ostrogoths, and he had to flee to Constantinople, where he spent the rest of his life. Here he defended Pope Vigilius in the dispute about the "Three Chapters".

DATIUS, REATRUS (RESTIUS) and Comp., and DATIUS (DATIVUS), JULIAN, VINCENT and 27 Comp. (SS) MM.   RM. Jan 27
? Two groups of African martyrs; the second group suffered under the Arian Vandals. The Arian persecution lasted a century (427–531).

DATIVA (St) M.   RM. Dec 6
See Dionysia, Dativa, etc.

DATIVUS (St) M.   RM. Feb 11
See Saturninus, Dativus, etc.

DATIVUS (St) Bp. M. RM. Sept 10
See Nemesian, Felix, etc.

DAVID (St) Bp.   AC. March 1
5th–6th cent. Born in S. Wales and educated by St Paulinus, the disciple of St Germanus of Auxerre. He founded a monastery at Mynyw (Menevia) in the far west of Pembrokeshire and is honoured as the first bishop in those parts. The place is now called St Davids. The monks followed an exceedingly austere rule and their monastery became a veritable nursery of saints. The foundation of a dozen monasteries and many miracles are attributed to him, but the biography of St David, as handed down to us, is full of anachronisms. He is the principal patron saint of Wales.

DAVID (St) H.   RM. June 26
? 5th cent. Said to have been a native of Mesopotamia who settled in a solitary place outside Thessalonica, where he served God for seventy years. His relics were translated to Pavia in 1054.

DAVID GONSON (Bl) M.
AC. July 12
d. 1541. Son of Vice-Admiral Gonson (or Gunston), and a knight of St John. He was hanged, drawn and quartered at Southwark. Beatified in 1929.

DAVID of SWEDEN (St) Bp. OSB.
AC. July 15
d. c.1080. Tradition makes him an English Benedictine, who had a passionate desire to give his life to Christ by martyrdom. When he heard of the death of St Sigfrid's three nephews he offered himself to the saint and was sent to Sinenga. Eventually he founded a Benedictine abbey, afterwards called Monkentorp, which he governed as abbot. He is said to have been the first bishop of Västeräss.

DAVID (GLEB) (St) C.   AC. July 24
See Romanus and David.

DAVID LEWIS (Bl) M. SJ.
AC. Aug 27
1616–1679. David Lewis (alias Charles Baker) was born in Monmouthshire and educated at Abergavenny. He was converted to the Faith, studied for the priesthood at Rome and became a Jesuit in 1645. He worked in S. Wales for thirty-one years. He was martyred for his priesthood at Usk. Beatified in 1929.

DAVID of HIMMERODE (Bl) Ab. OSB. Cist.   AC. Dec 11
d. 1179. A native of Florence, who took the Cistercian habit at Clairvaux under St Bernard (1131). In 1134 he was sent to Germany as abbot-founder of Himmerode, in the diocese of Trèves. Cult approved by Rome.

DAVID (St) King and Prophet
RM. Dec 29
10th cent. B.C. David "the beloved" and "the man after God's own heart". He is one of the types of Christ in the O.T., and indeed one of the most lovable characters in history. His story is fully told in Kings (Samuel) Bks. I and II and in Paralipomenon (or Chronicles). The Greeks keep his feast, together with those of all the other saints who were ancestors of our Lord, on Dec 19.

DAVINUS (St) C.   ? RM. June 3
d. 1051. A native of Armenia who set out on a pilgrimage to Rome and Compostella. On his way he stopped at Lucca, where he succumbed to a fatal malady and was venerated as a saint.

DAVY (JOHN) (Bl) M.   AC. June 6
See John Davy.

DAY (DYE) (St) Ab.   ? RM. Jan 18
? This saint, otherwise unknown, to whom a Cornish church is dedicated, may possibly be St Deicola, abbot, q.v.

DÉ (St) Bp.   AC. Jan 31
Breton form of the name St Aidan (or Eden) of Ferns.

DECLAN (St) Bp.   AC. July 24
5th cent. A disciple of St Colman who became a bishop in the district of Ardmore.

DECOROSUS (St) Bp. RM. Feb 15
d. 695. For thirty years bishop of Capua, St Decorosus was one of the prelates who assisted at the council of Rome under Pope St Agatho (680).

DECUMAN (DAGAN) (St) M.
AC. Aug 27
d. 706. A Welsh saint who lived as a recluse in Somersetshire, where he was murdered.

DEEL (DEILLE) (St) Ab.
RM. Jan 18
Otherwise Deicola (Dichul), q.v.

DEGADH (St)   AC. Aug 18
Otherwise Dagaeus, q.v.

DEGENHARD (Bl) H. OSB.
                     PC. Sept 3
d. 1374. A native of Bavaria and a monk
of Niederaltaich. After some years in
the abbey he retired to live as a recluse
under BB Otto and Hermann, also
Benedictine monks of Niederaltaich, in
their cell at Frauenau, in the Bavarian
Forest, and afterwards at Breitenau on
the Danube.

DEICOLA (DEICOLUS, DESLE,
DICHUL, DEEL, DELLE, DEILLE,
etc.) (St) Ab.   RM. Jan 18
d. c.625. A monk of Bangor who followed St Columbanus to Burgundy,
where he helped in the foundation of
Luxeuil. When St Columbanus was
compelled to go elsewhere by Queen
Brunehaut, Deicola, too old to travel,
remained behind and founded the abbey
of Lure (Lutra) in the Vosges.

DEIFER (St) Ab.   AC. March 7
6th cent. A Welsh saint, abbot-founder
of Bodfari in Flintshire.

DEINIOL (St)   AC. Sept 11
Welsh form of the name Daniel, q.v.

DELPHINA (Bl) V. Tert. OFM.
                     AC. Dec 9
1283–1358. Born at Château-Puy-
Michel in Languedoc, she became the
wife of St Elzear, and is said to have
been a member of the third order of St
Francis. After her husband's death she
lived in retirement at the court of
Naples. Cult approved by Urban VIII.

DELPHINUS (St) Bp. RM. Dec 24
d. 404. Bishop of Bordeaux. He is best
remembered as having been instrumental in the conversion of St Paulinus
of Nola, and as an untiring opponent
of the Priscillianists.

DEMETRIA (St) VM.   RM. June 21
d. 363. An alleged sister of St Bibiana
and daughter of SS Flavian and Dafrosa,
q.v.

DEMETRIAN (St) Bp.   AC. Nov 6
d. c.912. A native of Cyprus who became
monk and *hegoumenos* of St Antony's
and finally bishop of Khytri, both in his
native island. He is one of the most
venerated of Cypriot saints.

DEMETRIUS of TIFLIS (Bl) M.
                     AC. Apr 9
See Bl Thomas of Tolentino and Comp.

DEMETRIUS, CONCESSUS,
HILARY and Comp. (SS) MM.
                     RM. Apr 9
? A group composed of martyrs from
different localities, but about whom no
particulars are extant.

DEMETRIUS (St) C.   AC. June 18
See Gregory, Demetrius, etc.

DEMETRIUS (St) M.   RM. Aug 14
? A martyr of whose death neither the
place nor circumstances can be verified.
The RM., however, describes him as an
African martyr.

DEMETRIUS (DIMITRI) (St) M.
                     RM. Oct 8
Early 4th cent. Surnamed by the Greeks
"the Megalomartyr", he is, after St
George, the most famous military martyr of the East. His military career, however, is a legend. He was probably a
deacon who suffered at Sirmium in
Dalmatia, under Diocletian, though the
centre of his cult was at Salonika, where
a magnificent basilica was erected in his
name. He is mentioned to this day in
the preparation of the Byzantine liturgy.

DEMETRIUS (St) Bp.   AC. Oct 9
d. 231. The twelfth patriarch of Alexandria, during whose episcopate the

catechetical school of that city attained its highest fame. He was a close friend of Origen, whom later he had to banish from the diocese for being uncanonically ordained.

DEMETRIUS, ANIANUS, EUSTOSIUS and Comp. (SS) MM.
RM. Nov 10
? A band of twenty-three martyrs registered as having suffered at Antioch in Syria. St Demetrius is described as a bishop and St Anianus as his deacon.

DEMETRIUS and HONORIUS (SS) MM.
RM. Nov 21
? Old Roman manuscripts describe these saints as martyrs who suffered at Ostia at the mouth of the Tiber.

DEMETRIUS (St) M.
RM. Nov 29
See Blaise and Demetrius.

DEMETRIUS, HONORATUS and FLORUS (SS) MM.
RM. Dec 22
? These martyrs are stated to have suffered at Ostia at the mouth of the Tiber. They probably are to be identified with SS Demetrius and Honorius of Nov 21.

DEMOCRITUS, SECUNDUS and DIONYSIUS (SS) MM.
RM. July 31
? Martyrs, some say of Phrygia, some of Africa. Nothing really is known about them.

DENIS, DENNIS, DENYS (several)
French forms of the name Dionysius, q.v.

DENISE (several)
French form of the name Dionysia, q.v.

DENTLIN (DENTELIN, DENAIN) (St) C.
AC. March 16
7th cent. The little son of St Vincent

Madelgarus (q.v.) and of St Waldetrudis. He was only seven years old when he died. A church in the duchy of Cleves is dedicated in his honour.

DEOCHAR (THEUTGER or GOTTLIEB) (St) Ab. OSB.
AC. June 7
d. 847. A hermit in the wilds of Franconia, for whom Charlemagne founded the abbey of Herriedon under the Benedictine rule, Deochar becoming its first abbot. In 802 he was appointed *missus regius*. In 819 he took part in the translation of St Boniface's relics to Fulda.

DEODATUS (St) Mk. OSB.
AC. Feb 3
8th cent. A monk of Lagny in the archdiocese of Paris.

DEODATUS (St) Ab.
AC. Apr 24
d. c.525. A hermit, or abbot, in the neighbourhood of Blois. At a later period the town of Saint-Dié grew up round his cell (or monastery).

DEODATUS (DIÉ, DIDIER, DIEUDONNÉ, ADÉODAT) (St) Bp. OSB.
AC. June 19
d. p.680. A bishop who founded (c.660) and was abbot of the monastery of Vallis-Galilaea (Val-de-Galilée—Jointures Abbey).

DEODATUS (St) Bp.
AC. June 19
d. 679. Bishop of Nevers in 655 and then a solitary in the Vosges. Later he was abbot-founder of Ebersheimmünster, near Strasburg. He is often confused with St Deodatus of Vallis-Galilaea.

DEODATUS (St) Bp.
AC. June 27
d. 473. Deacon to St Paulinus, bishop of Nola, and his successor in that see. His relics were brought to Benevento in 839.

DEODATUS (St) M. (or C.)
                                    AC. Sept 27
? A saint of Sora (central Italy) whose relics were enshrined in the cathedral of Sora in 1621.

DEOGRATIAS (St) Bp.
                                    RM. March 22
d. 457. Consecrated bishop of Carthage, in 456, fourteen years after the death of his predecessor, St Quodvultdeus, who had been driven into exile by the Arian Vandals. The Vandal king, Genseric, having brought many Italian captives to Carthage, St Deogratias sold all that he or his church possessed, even the sacred vessels, to ransom them. He was bishop only one year.

DERFEL-GADARN (St)   ?
6th cent. A Welsh saint, a soldier and afterwards a solitary at Llanderfel in Merionethshire. He was greatly venerated by the Catholic Welsh.

DERPHUTA (St) M. RM. March 20
See Alexandra, Claudia, etc.

DERUVIANUS (St) M.
                    AC. May 14 (RM. May 26)
Otherwise Dyfan, q.v.

DERWA (St) M.   AC.?
The patron saint of Menadarva (Merthyr-Dava, i.e. the Martyr Derwa) near Camborne in Cornwall. Nothing is known about this saint. Probably he is no other than St Dyfan (Damian or Deruvianus), one of the missionaries sent to Britain in the 2nd century by Pope St Eleutherius.

DESIDERATUS (DÉSIRÉ) (St) Bp.
                    AC. Feb 10 and 11
6th cent. Successor of St Avitus as bishop of Clermont in Auvergne.

DESIDERATUS (St) H. AC. Apr 30
d. c.569. A French solitary who lived at Gourdon, near Châlon-sur-Saône.

DESIDERATUS (St) Bp. AC. May 8
6th cent. Successor of St Arcadius in the bishopric of Bourges.

DESIDERATUS (St) Mk. OSB.
                                    AC. Dec 18
d. c.700. Son of St Waningus, the founder of Fécamp abbey, he became a monk of Fontenelle. His relics were enshrined at Ghent.

DESIDERIUS (DIDIER) (Bl) Bp.
                                    PC. Jan 20
d. 1194. The thirty-third bishop of Thérouanne and founder of the Cistercian abbey of Blandecques (Blandyke) near Saint-Omer. At the end of his life he resigned and prepared for death in a Cistercian monastery. He is usually styled a saint and is claimed by the Cistercians as one of their own. Cult not yet officially confirmed.

DESIDERIUS (St) Bp. M.
                    RM. Feb 11 and May 23
d. 608. A native of Autun, educated at Vienne, where he became archdeacon and then bishop. An intrepid defender of Christian morality, he was persecuted by Queen Brunhildis, who was also instrumental in securing his murder at the place now called Saint-Didier-sur-Chalaronne. See also May 23, below.

DESIDERIUS (St) M. RM. March 25
See Barontius and Desiderius.

DESIDERIUS (St) Bp. M.
                                    RM. May 23
407? Said to have been a native of Genoa who preached in and became bishop of Langres in France. He was killed at the time of a Vandal invasion while pleading for his people.

DESIDERIUS (St) Pope, OSB.
                                    RM. Sept 16
Otherwise Victor III, q.v.

DESIDERIUS (St) M. RM. Sept 19
See Januarius and Comp.

DESIDERIUS (St) Mk. OSB.
                              AC. Oct 19
d. *c.*705. A monk of Lonrey, and a disciple of St Sigiranus, who became a recluse at La Brenne (*Ruriacus*) in the diocese of Bourges, France.

DESIDERIUS (St) Bp.   AC. Oct 27
d. *c.*625. The successor of St Anacharius (Aunaire) in the bishopric of Auxerre. He has often been confused with St Desiderius of Vienne (Feb 11).

DESIDERIUS (St) Bp.   AC. Nov 15
d. 655. The successor of his own brother St Rusticus as bishop of Cahors (630–655).

DEUSDEDIT (St) Bp. OSB.
                              AC. Jan 14
d. 664. An Anglo-Saxon, Frithona by name. He was the first of his race to occupy the primatial see of Canterbury as the successor of St Honorius. He died a victim to the great pestilence.

DEUSDEDIT (St) C.   RM. Aug 10
6th cent. A poor shoemaker in Rome, contemporary of St Gregory the Great, who relates that he gave away to the poor every Saturday all that he earned at his trade during the week.

DEUSDEDIT (St) Ab. M. OSB.
                              RM. Oct 9
d. 836. Monk of Montecassino, chosen abbot about the year 830. He was especially noted for his generous almsgiving. To extort money from him the tyrant, Sicard of Benevento, ill-treated and imprisoned him. He died in prison of hunger and misery. He is venerated as a martyr.

DEUSDEDIT (ADEODATUS I)
(St) Pope   RM. Nov 8
d. 618. A Roman by birth, he became pope in 615. During his pontificate a pestilence raged in Rome and he worked untiringly for the plague-stricken. In all ancient Benedictine menologies he is called a Benedictine monk, but there is no certain evidence for it.

DEUSDEDIT of BRESCIA (St) Bp.
                              RM. Dec 10
d. *c.*700. A bishop of Brescia who played a leading part in the councils convened against the Monothelite heretics.

DEVEREUX (St) Bp.   AC. Nov 13
Otherwise Dubricius, q.v.

DEVINICUS (DENICK, TEAV-NECK) (St) Bp.   AC. Nov 13
6th cent. A native of N. Scotland who in his old age associated himself with the missionary work of SS Columba and Machar and evangelized Caithness. He is reputed to have been a bishop.

DEVOTA (St) VM.   AC. Jan 27
d. 303. A maiden of Corsica who expired on the rack in the persecution of Diocletian. Her relics are at Monaco on the Riviera di Ponente. She is the patron saint of both Corsica and Monaco.

DEWI (St) Bp.   AC. March 1
Otherwise David of Wales, q.v.

DEYNIOLEN (St)   AC. Nov 22
d. 621. Also known as St Deiniol (Daniel) the Younger. He was abbot of Bangor at the time of the slaughter of his monks and the destruction of their monastery by King Ethelfrid of Northumbria (616). The saint appears to have escaped the massacre.

DIACONUS (St) M.   RM. March 14
6th cent. So described on account of his office of deacon, which he held in the church of the Marsi in central Italy.

St Gregory narrates of him that together with two monks he was put to death by the Lombards.

DIANA, CAECILIA and AMATA (BB) VV. OP.   AC. June 10

13th cent. The three first members of the first house of Dominican nuns at Bologna. Diana, of the ancient family of the Carbonesi, was a native of Bologna. After a very worldly youth she embraced religion against the wish of her family; she died in 1236. The other two later became nuns of the Roman convent of San Sisto. Beatified in 1891.

DIARMIS (DIERMIT, DERMOT) (St) Ab.   AC. Jan 18

6th cent. The spiritual director and teacher of St Kieran of Clonmacnois and later abbot-founder of a monastery on Innis-Clotran Island.

DICHU (St)   AC. Apr 29

5th cent. The first convert made by St Patrick in Ulster. He was originally a swineherd. After his conversion, we are told, he continued to the end faithful to Christ and St Patrick.

DICHUL (St) Ab.   RM. Jan 18

Otherwise Deicola, q.v.

DICTINUS (St) Bp.   AC. July 24

d. 420. An adherent of Priscillianism, he was converted by St Ambrose and recanted his errors at the council of Toledo (400). Soon after he was raised to the bishopric of Astorga in Spain.

DIDACUS (DIEGO) de AZEVEDO (Bl) Bp. OSB. Cist.   PC. Feb 6

d. 1207 (Dec 30). Provost of the cathedral of Osma, in Old Castile, where he obtained a canonry for St Dominic Guzmán. In 1201 he became bishop of Osma. He was sent to Rome by King Alphonsus of Castile and took St

Dominic as a companion on his journey: this was the occasion of the founding of the Dominican Order. Didacus became a Cistercian in order to join the crusade against the Albigenses. He has always been styled a *beatus*, or a saint, by the Cistercians.

DIDACUS CARVALHO (Bl) M. SJ.   AC. Feb 25

1578–1624. Born at Coimbra in Portugal, he joined the Jesuits in 1594. He was sent to India in 1600, where he was ordained priest. In 1609 he migrated to Japan. Here he worked untiringly until 1623, when he was arrested with a number of his flock and carried off to Sendai, suffering many indignities on the way. The story of their martyrdom is a miracle of endurance. Beatified in 1867.

DIDACUS (DIEGO, DIAZ) (Bl) C. OFM. Cap.   AC. March 24

1743–1801. A native of Cádiz, he joined the Capuchins at Seville in 1759, and after his ordination to the priesthood began to preach throughout Spain, but chiefly in Andalusia, of which province he is called "the Apostle". Most of his time which remained over from preaching he spent in the confessional. Beatified in 1894.

DIDACUS PEREZ (Bl) M. SJ.   AC. July 15

d. 1570. A Jesuit novice who formed one of the band of missionaries led by Bl Ignatius de Azevedo, whose martyrdom he shared.

DIDACUS (DIEGO, DIAZ) (St) C. OFM.   RM. Nov 12 (and 13)

c.1400–1463. Born of poor parents in the diocese of Seville, he joined the Franciscans as a lay-brother at Arrizafa. Although remaining a lay-brother, he was appointed, on account of his remarkable ability and goodness, guardian of the principal friary in the Canary Islands, at Fuerteventura (1445). Later he was recalled to Spain, and after a pilgrimage to Rome in 1450, died at the friary of Alcalà, in Castile. His chief devotion was to our Lord in the Bl Sacrament. Canonized in 1588.

DIDIER (St) Bp. M.   RM. May 23
Otherwise Desiderius, q.v.

DIDIUS (St) M.   RM. Nov 26
See Faustus, Didius, etc.

DIDYMUS (St) M.   RM. Apr 28
See Theodora and Didymus.

DIDYMUS (St) M.   RM. Sept 11
See Diodorus, Diomedes, etc.

DIÉ (St) Bp.   AC. June 19
Otherwise Deodatus, q.v.

DIEGO (*several*)
Otherwise Didacus, q.v.
Note. Diego is really a corrupt form of the Spanish name for St James, viz. Santiago (Sant-Iago, San Tiego, San Diego). Only in modern times has Diego been latinized into Didacus.

**DIEMUT (DIEMUDA) (Bl) H. OSB.
                          AC. March 29**
d. *c.*1130. A nun at the Benedictine monastery of Wessobrunn in Bavaria, who was granted leave to live as a solitary under the obedience of the monastery. She spent her time in copying manuscripts, some of which are still extant.

**DIETHARDUS (Bl) Mk. OSB.
                          AC. Sept 29**
See Catholdus, Anno, etc.

DIETRICH (St) Bp. M. AC. Feb 2
See Bruno and Comp.

DIEUDONNÉ (*several*)
The French form for Deusdedit or Adeodatus, q.v.

DIGAIN (St) C.   AC. Nov 21
5th cent. A son of Constantine, king or chieftain of Cornwall. Llangernw, Denbighshire, perpetuates his memory.

DIGNA (St) M.   RM. June 14
See Anastasius, Felix and Digna.

DIGNA (St) V.   RM. Aug 11
4th cent. A maiden of Todi in Umbria, who lived as a solitary in the mountains near her native city during the persecution of Diocletian.

DIGNA (St) M.   RM. Aug 12
See Hilaria, Digna, etc.

**DIGNA and EMERITA (SS) VV.
MM.   RM. Sept 22**
d. *c.*259. Roman maidens martyred under Valerian. They expired standing before their judges and praying. Their relics are enshrined in the church of St Marcellus at Rome.

**DIMAN (DIMAS, DIMA) (St) Bp.
                          AC. Jan 6**
d. 658. Surnamed *Diman Dubh* (Diman the Black). A monk under St Columba, and afterwards abbot and bishop of Connor. He is one of the prelates to whom (640) the Roman church, after the death of Pope Honorius, addressed the epistle on the pascal controversy and on Pelagianism.

DIMITRI (St) M.   RM. Oct 8
Otherwise Demetrius, q.v.

DINGAD (St) C.   AC. Nov 1
5th cent. A son of the chieftain Brychan of Brecknock, who led a monastic or eremitical life at Llandingad in Monmouthshire.

DIOCLES (St) M.   RM. May 24
See Zoëllus, Servilius, etc.

DIOCLETIUS (St) M. RM. May 11
See Sisinius, Diocletius, etc.

DIODORUS (St) M.   RM. Feb 26
See Papias, Diodorus, etc.

**DIODORUS and RHODOPIANUS
(SS) MM.   RM. May 3**
Early 4th cent. Two deacons martyred
under Diocletian in the province of
Caria, Asia Minor.

DIODORUS (St) M.   RM. July 6
See Lucy, Antoninus, etc.

**DIODORUS, DIOMEDES and
DIDYMUS (SS) MM.   RM. Sept 11**
? Martyrs of Laodicea (Kulat-el-Husn
or Ladhikijeh) in Syria.

**DIODORUS, MARIANUS and
Comp. (SS) MM.   RM. Dec 1**
d. 283. Roman martyrs under Numerian.
They are described as being very
numerous. In fact, it appears to have
been a case of a Christian congregation
surprised while assembled at prayer in
the catacombs and disposed of by having
the entrance to their subterranean
oratory blocked up.

DIOGENES (St) M.   RM. Apr 6
See Timothy and Diogenes.

DIOGO (*several*)
The Portuguese form of James or
Didacus, q.v. (Cf. note on Diego.)

DIOMEDES (St) M.   RM. Aug 16
d. 300–311 ? A native of Tarsus in
Cilicia, by profession a physician, and
a zealous propagator of Christianity.
He was arrested at Nicaea in Bithynia
and martyred under Diocletian.

**DIOMEDES, JULIAN, PHILIP,
EUTYCHIAN, HESYCHIUS,
LEONIDES, PHILADELPHUS,
MENALIPPUS and PANTAGAPES
(SS) MM.   RM. Sept 2**
? Some perished at the stake, others

were drowned, or beheaded, or crucified.
Place and other circumstances unknown.

DIOMEDES (St) M.   RM. Sept 11
See Diodorus, Diomedes, etc.

DIOMMA (St)   AC. May 12
5th cent. An Irish saint, said to have
been the teacher of St Declan of Ardmore and other saints. He is now
venerated as the patron saint of Kildimo,
Co Limerick.

DION (St) M.   RM. July 6
See Lucy, Antoninus, etc.

DIONYSIA, DIONYSIUS
Note. These Greco-Latin names became very popular in the Middle Ages
under the corresponding French forms
of Denise, Denis, Denys. Sydney in
English is a corrupt form of St Denys.

DIONYSIA (St) M.   RM. May 15
See Peter, Andrew, etc.

**DIONYSIA, DATIVA, LEONTIA,
TERTIUS, EMILIAN, BONIFACE,
and Comp. (SS) MM.   RM. Dec 6**
d. 484. African martyrs under the Arian
Vandal king, Hunneric. We have a quite
genuine account of their martyrdom
from Victor of Utica. According to him
Dionysia, a widow, perished at the
stake with her little child, Majoricus
(q.v.), and her sister Dativa. Emilian, a
physician, and Tertius, a monk, were
flayed alive. The fanatics seem to have
amused themselves by devising strange
kinds of death for the rest of the heroic
band.

DIONYSIA (St) M.   RM. Dec 12
See Ammonaria, Mercuria, etc.

**DIONYSIUS, EMILIAN and
SEBASTIAN (SS) MM. RM. Feb 8**
? The RM. describes them as Armenian

monks. We know nothing about them, save their bare names. St Emilian is honoured at Trevi on Jan 28.

DIONYSIUS and AMMONIUS (SS) MM.   RM. Feb 14
? Martyrs beheaded, it seems, at Alexandria in Egypt.

DIONYSIUS of AUGSBURG (St) Bp. MM.   AC. Feb 26
d. *c*.303. Venerated as first bishop of Augsburg in Germany. He is said to have been converted to Christ, baptized and later consecrated bishop by St Narcissus. He was martyred under Diocletian. The story, however, is from the Acts of St Afra (Aug 5 q.v.) which date from the 8th century.

DIONYSIUS FUGIXIMA (Bl) M. SJ.   AC. March 5
d. 1622 (Nov 1). A Japanese, born of noble parents at Aitzu, Arima, who became a Jesuit novice and worked under Bl Paul Navarro, with whom he was burnt alive at Ximabara. Beatified in 1867.

DIONYSIUS (St) M. RM. March 10
See Codratus, Dionysius, etc.

DIONYSIUS the CARTHUSIAN (Bl) C. O. Cart.   PC. March 12
d. 1471. Born at Ryckel, near Loos, in Flanders, he gained his doctorate at the university of Cologne in his twenty-second year. In 1423 he entered the Carthusian Order. He excelled as a mystical writer and on this account has been given the title of *Doctor Ecstaticus*. He is commemorated as a *beatus* in several martyrologies.

DIONYSIUS (St) M. RM. March 16
See Hilary, Tatian, etc.

DIONYSIUS (SS) MM.
                              RM. March 24
Two of the same name who suffered together. See Timolaus, and Comp.

DIONYSIUS of CORINTH (St) Bp.
                              RM. Apr 8
d. *c*.180. A bishop of Corinth who was a great leader of the Church in the 2nd century. Several of his letters to various churches are still extant: especially noteworthy is that in which he records the martyrdom of SS Peter and Paul in Rome. The Greeks venerate him as a martyr (Nov 20).

DIONYSIUS (St) M.   RM. Apr 19
See Socrates and Dionysius.

DIONYSIUS (St) Bp.   RM. May 8
d. *p*.193. Said to have been one of the ten missionaries sent with St Peregrinus into Gaul by Pope Sixtus I, early in the 2nd century. He succeeded St Justus in the bishopric of Vienne in Dauphiné. Some have erroneously described him as a martyr.

DIONYSIUS (St) M.   RM. May 12
d. 304. An Asiatic by birth and uncle of the youthful martyr St Pancras, to whom he acted as guardian. They came together to Rome, were converted to Christianity, and martyred under Diocletian, Dionysius dying in prison.

DIONYSIUS of MILAN (St) Bp.
                              RM. May 25
d. *c*.359. The successor of St Protasius in the see of Milan in 351. In 355 he was banished to Cappadocia by the Arian emperor Constantius for having upheld the cause of St Athanasius. He died in exile, but St Ambrose had his remains translated to Milan.

DIONYSIUS (St) M.   RM. June 3
See Lucillian, Claudius, etc.

DIONYSIUS SEBUGGWAO (Bl) M.
AC. June 3

d. 1885. A servant of King Mwanga of Uganda; he was pierced with a lance by the king because he was caught teaching the catechism—the first victim of the persecution. See Uganda (Martyrs of).

DIONYSIUS (St) M.   RM. July 27

One of the Seven Sleepers, q.v.

DIONYSIUS (St) M.   RM. July 31

See Democritus, Secundus and Dionysius.

DIONYSIUS and PRIVATUS (SS) MM.   RM. Sept 20

? Martyrs of Phrygia in Asia Minor.

DIONYSIUS, FAUSTUS, CAIUS, PETER, PAUL and Comp. (SS) MM.   RM. Oct 3

d. 257. A group of Christians from Alexandria in Egypt, banished to Libya under Decius (250) and again brought to trial and martyred at Alexandria under Valerian. There is much confusion as to the identity of each of these martyrs.

DIONYSIUS (St) Bp. M. RM. Oct 9

1st cent. This is Denis the Areopagite who was converted at Athens by St Paul (Acts XVII, 34). Early writers say that he became first bishop of Athens and died a martyr (c.95). Unfortunately, at a much later period he was identified with St Dionysius of Paris, and the works of an ecclesiastical writer of the 5th century—the pseudo-Dionysius—were falsely attributed to him. The confusion is still maintained in the RM., although Pope Benedict XIV intended to remedy it by suppressing the feast altogether.

DIONYSIUS, RUSTICUS and ELEUTHERIUS (SS) MM.
RM. Oct 9

3rd cent. According to St Gregory of Tours, Dionysius, first bishop of Paris, was born in Italy and, with six other bishops, was sent from Rome to Gaul, settled on an island in the Seine and evangelized the surrounding district. He was beheaded at Paris with the priest Rusticus and the deacon Eleutherius under Decius. Their bodies were thrown into the Seine, from which they were rescued and buried by a Christian lady named Catulla. A small chapel was built over their tomb, around which arose the Benedictine abbey of Saint-Denis. About the 7th century this Dionysius began to be identified with St Denis the Areopagite, and this identification gained general acceptance until the 19th century. Now it has been discarded by all writers.

DIONYSIUS of ALEXANDRIA (St) Bp.   RM. Nov 17

d. 265. Called also Dionysius the Great. A native of Alexandria, he studied under Origen, whom he succeeded as a master of the catechetical school. In 248 he became patriarch of Alexandria, but two years later, under Decius, was banished to Libya, whence he continued to govern his diocese. He returned to Alexandria, but was again driven from it under Valerian. He was restored under Gallienus. He was a great theologian; St Athanasius styles him "the teacher of the whole Church".

DIONYSIUS (St) M.   RM. Nov 20

See Bassus, Dionysius, etc.

DIONYSIUS and REDEMPTUS (BB) MM. OC.   AC. Nov 29

d. 1638. Dionysius of the Nativity (Peter Berthelot) was a French shipmaster and trader who became a Carmelite at Goa in 1635 and was ordained in 1638. This same year he was sent on an embassy to Sumatra. A Carmelite lay-brother, Redemptus of the cross (Thomas Rodriguez da Cunha), a Portuguese by birth, was given him as a companion. The embassy proved a failure, and both friars were put to death by the Sumatrans. Beatified in 1900.

DIONYSIUS (St) Pope RM. Dec 26
d. 269. A Roman priest who was chosen pope in 259 and very energetically and successfully restored the Roman church after the persecution of Gallienus. He opposed Sabellius and condemned Paul of Samosata.

DIOSCORIDES (St) M. RM. May 10
? A martyr of Smyrna in Asia Minor.

DIOSCORIDES (St) M. RM. May 28
See Crescens, Dioscorides, etc.

DIOSCORUS (St) M.   RM. Feb 25
See Victorinus, Victor, etc.

DIOSCORUS (St) M. RM. May 18
d. c.305. A reader of the church of Kynopolis in Egypt. He was burnt with hot irons and he died under the torture.

DIOSCORUS (St) M.   RM. Dec 14
See Heron, Arsenius, etc.

DIOSCORUS (St)   RM. Dec 21
See Themistocles and Dioscorus.

DIRUVIANUS (St) M.
              AC. May 14 (RM. May 26)
Otherwise Dyfan, q.v.

DISIBOD (DISIBODE, DISEN) (St) Bp. OSB.   AC. Sept 8
d. c.700. An Irishman—a bishop?—who passed over to the continent with several companions and founded a monastery on a hill in the valley of the Nahe, near Bingen, which became known as Disibodenberg or Disenberg, *Mons Disibodi*. It became famous in a later age on account of the residence there of St Hildegarde.

DISMAS (St)   RM. March 25
The name given by tradition to the Good Thief, q.v.

DIUMA (St) C.   ?
7th cent. A Scottish priest sent with St Cedd to convert Mercia.

DIZIER (St) Bp. M.   RM. May 23
Otherwise Desiderius, q.v.

DOCANUS or DOCCO (St) Ab.
                            AC. Nov 7
Otherwise Cumgar (or Cungar), q.v.

DOCHOW (DOCHAU, DOGWYN) C.   Feb 15
? 473. According to the Vita Samsonis he travelled from Wales to Cornwall and founded a monastery there. In the Ulster Annal he is styled bishop. St Dochtwy appears to be another saint altogether.

DOCUS (St) Bp. M.   AC. Jan 24
Otherwise Cadoc, q.v.

DODA (St) V. OSB.   RM. Apr 24
See Bova (Bona) and Doda.

DODO (Bl) C. H.   PC. March 30
d. 1231. A hermit at Asch in Frisia, who practised astonishing austerities. He is reputed to have received the stigmata.

DODO (St) Ab. OSB.   AC. Oct 1
d. c.750. Born in the territory of Laon. Placed from childhood under St Ursmar, he became a monk at Lobbes and eventually was made abbot of Wallers-en-Faigne.

DODOLINUS (St) Bp.   AC. Apr 1
7th cent. Bishop of Vienne in Dauphiné, France.

DOGFAN (DOEWAN) (St) M.
                          AC. July 13
5th cent. A Welshman, one of the sons of the chieftain Brychan. He is said to

have been put to death by heathen invaders of Pembrokeshire, where a church was built to his memory.

DOGMAEL (St) C.   AC. June 14
5th–6th cent. A Welsh monk of the house of Cunedda. He founded several cells in Pembrokeshire, Brittany and elsewhere.

DOMANGARD (DONARD) (St) C.
AC. March 24
d. *c.*500. The patron of Maghera, Co. Down, who in the time of St Patrick lived as a hermit on the mountain now called after him Slieve-Donard.

DOMETIUS and Comp. (SS) MM.
RM. Aug 7
Otherwise Domitius, q.v.

DOMINATOR (St) Bp. RM. Nov 5
d. ? 495. The fourteenth bishop of Brescia in Lombardy.

DOMINIC
Note. Dominicus, Dominica are latinized forms of Cyriacus (*Kuriakos*) and Cyriaca (*Kuriake*). The Latin Dominicus has the following derivatives in modern languages: in Italian, Domenico; in Spanish and Portuguese, Domingo; in French, Dominique; in English, Dominic.

DOMINIC of SORA (St) Ab. OSB.
RM. Jan 22
d. 1031. Born at Foligno in Etruria, he became a Benedictine and eventually the abbot-founder of several monasteries—at Scandrilia, Sora, Sangro, and elsewhere in the old kingdom of Naples. He died at Sora in Campania when eighty years old.

DOMINIC SAVIO (St) C.
AC. March 9
1842–1857. He was the son of a peasant blacksmith in Piedmont, and became a pupil of St John Bosco, who wrote his life. He died shortly before his fifteenth birthday, having given proof of his high virtue. He is the youngest non-martyr to receive official canonization in the history of the Church. Canonized in 1954.

DOMINIC JORJES (Bl) M.
AC. March 14
d. 1619. A Portuguese soldier, born at Aguilar de Sousa, who settled in Japan, where he gave shelter to Bl Charles Spinola. For this reason he was burnt alive at Nagasaki (Nov 18). Beatified in 1819.

DOMINIC TUOC (Bl) M.
AC. Apr 2
d. 1839. A native of Tonkin, and a priest of the third order of Friars Preachers. He died of his wounds in prison. Beatified in 1900.

DOMINIC VERNAGALLI (Bl) Mk.
OSB. Cam.   AC. Apr 20
d. 1218. A native of Pisa who was professed a Camaldolese at the abbey of St Michael in his native city. He founded a hospital attached to the monastery. Cult confirmed in 1854.

DOMINIC and GREGORY (BB)
CC. OP.   AC. Apr 26
d. 1300. Two Spanish Dominicans who preached in the villages of the Somontano, at the foot of the Pyrenees, near Barbastro, in Aragon. They were killed near Perarúa by the fall of a rock, under which they had sought refuge during a thunderstorm. Their relics are enshrined at Besians, diocese of Barbastro. Cult confirmed by Pius IX.

DOMINIC de la CALZADA (St) H.
RM. May 12
d. *c.*1109. Born at Victoria in Biscay, he

tried unsuccessfully his religious vocation at Valvanera and then became a hermit in Rioja. He devoted his days to making a road—*Calzada* (causeway)—for pilgrims on their way to Compostella. The spot where he lived, now the township of La Calzada, became a great pilgrimage shrine.

DOMINIC of the HOLY ROSARY (Bl) M. OP.   AC. June 1

d. 1622. A Japanese catechist and novice of the Dominican Order. He was beheaded on the day of the great martyrdom—Sept 10, 1622—at Nagasaki. Beatified in 1867.

DOMINIC of FIUNGA (Bl) M.   AC. June 1

d. 1622 (Sept 12). A Japanese catechist, of the third order of Friars Preachers, burnt alive at Omura with Bl Thomas Zumarraga and companions. Beatified in 1867.

DOMINIC CASTELLET (Bl) M. OP.   AC. June 1

1592–1628 (Sept 8). A native of Esparraguera, province of Barcelona. He took the Dominican habit at Barcelona and was sent to the Dominican mission of Japan, of which he was vicar provincial at the time of his martyrdom. He was burnt alive at Nagasaki. Beatified in 1867.

DOMINIC TOMAKI (Bl) M.   AC. June 1

d. 1628 (Sept 8). Son of Bl John Tomaki, beheaded at the age of sixteen with his father and brothers at Nagasaki. Beatified in 1867.

DOMINIC NIFAKI (Bl) M.   AC. June 1

d. 1628 (Sept 8). A child, two years old, beheaded at Nagasaki with his father, Bl Louis Nifaki, and his brother Francis. Beatified in 1867.

DOMINIC XIBIOJE (Bl) M.   AC. June 1

d. 1628 (Sept 26). A Japanese layman, of the third order of Friars Preachers, who sheltered the missionaries. Beheaded at Nagasaki. Beatified in 1867.

DOMINIC of COMACCHIO (Bl) Mk. OSB.   AC. June 21

d. *p*.820. A Benedictine monk of Comacchio, near Venice. According to the legend, it was he who in 820 went as a pilgrim to the Holy Land and brought the relics of St Mark from Alexandria to Venice.

DOMINIC HENARES (Bl) Bp. M. OP.   AC. June 25

d. 1838. A Spaniard by birth and a Dominican friar by profession, he became in 1803 bishop-coadjutor to Bl Ignatius Delgado, vicar apostolic of Tonkin. He was beheaded with his catechist, Bl Francis Chien, during the Annamite persecution. Beatified in 1900.

DOMINIC FERNÁNDEZ (Bl) M. SJ.   AC. July 15

d. 1570. A Jesuit lay-brother. Born at Villa Viciosa in Portugal. A companion of Bl Ignatius de Azevedo, q.v.

DOMINIC NICHOLAS DAT (Bl) M.   AC. July 18

d. 1838. A native soldier in Tonkin, who was strangled during the persecution of the Christians. Beatified in 1900.

DOMINIC DU (alias HANH) OP.   AC. Aug 1

d. 1838. A native of Tonkin, and a priest of the Dominican Order. He was executed in his sixty-seventh year. Beatified in 1900.

DOMINIC de GUZMAN (St) Founder OP.   RM. Aug 4

1170–1221. A native of Calaruega, province of Burgos, in Old Castile, and an Augustinian canon regular at the cathedral of Osma. In 1203 he accompanied his bishop, Bl Diego de Azevedo, to S. France, where the Albigenses were at that time devastating the country. Dominic began his life-long apostolate among the heretics, and in 1206 succeeded in opening a convent at Prouille for nun-converts from Albigensianism. This was the germ of his order of friars known as the Friars Preachers, whom Dominic sent everywhere to preach and teach. The order was approved in 1216 and within a few years it had spread throughout Europe. The Order of Preachers, with that founded by St Francis and known as the Friars Minor, marks the culminating point of that powerful tide of Christian asceticism which had begun with Cluny and been continued by Cîteaux. By his personal charm St Dominic won the enthusiastic affection of his followers. He died at Bologna, and was canonized in 1234.

DOMINIC BARBERI of the MOTHER of GOD (Bl) C. CP.
AC. Aug 27
1792–1849. A native of the Viterbo (Rome) countryside, he entered the Congregation of the Passion and was ordained priest in 1818. Chosen by his superiors as head of the Passionist English Mission, Dominic reached England in 1841 and worked unsparingly until his death at Reading. Cardinal Newman was the most prominent of the distinguished converts Bl Dominic received into the Church. Beatified in 1963.

DOMINIC del VAL (St) M.
AC. Aug 31
d. 1250. In Spain he is usually called San Dominguito—Little Dominic. He was a seven-year-old altar boy at the cathedral of Saragossa, who was kidnapped by Jews and nailed against a wall. His feast is celebrated throughout Aragon.

DOMINIC of NAGASAKI (Bl) M. OFM.
AC. Sept 8
d. 1628. A Japanese catechist. He received the Franciscan habit in the prison at Omura from Bl Antony of St Bonaventure and was burnt alive at Nagasaki. Beatified in 1867.

DOMINIC NACANO (Bl) M.
AC. Sept 10
d. 1622. Son of Bl Matthias Nacano. He was beheaded at Nagasaki. Beatified in 1854.

DOMINIC XAMADA and CLARE, his wife (BB) MM.
AC. Sept 10
d. 1622. Japanese laypersons, beheaded at Nagasaki. Beatified in 1854.

DOMINIC TRACH (Bl) M.
AC. Sept 18
1792–1842. A native priest of Tonkin, and a member of the Dominican third order. He was beheaded for his faith. Beatified in 1900.

DOMINIC SPADAFORA (Bl) C. OP.
AC. Oct 3
d. 1521. A native of Palermo, who, after having finished his studies at Padua, joined the Friars Preachers and spent his life in continuous preaching throughout Italy and Sicily. Cult confirmed in 1921.

DOMINIC LORICATUS (the MAILED) (St) H. OSB.   RM. Oct 14
995–1060. Born in Umbria. By means of a bribe his father had him ordained priest in contravention of canon law, and on learning this, the saint determined to do penance for it during the rest of his life. He first became a hermit and then a Benedictine monk under St

Peter Damian at Fontavellana. He is surnamed "the Mailed" because he wore for years a rough iron coat-of-mail next to his skin.

DOMINIC DOAN (XUYEN) (Bl) M. OP.   AC. Oct 26
1788–1839. A native of Tonkin, and a member of the Dominican order, beheaded with Bl Thomas Du. Beatified in 1900.

DOMINIC UY (Bl) M.   AC. Dec 19
1813–1839. A native catechist of Tonkin, who belonged to the third order of St Dominic. He was strangled at the age of twenty-six. Beatified in 1900.

DOMINIC of BRESCIA (St) Bp.
RM. Dec 20
d. c.612. The successor of St Anastasius in the see of Brescia. St Charles Borromeo translated and enshrined his relics.

DOMINIC of SILOS (St) Ab. OSB.
RM. Dec 20
c.1000–1073. Born at Cañas—then Spanish Navarre, now Rioja—he became a Benedictine at San Millán de la Cogolla. As prior of this great abbey he came into conflict with King García III of Navarre by whom he was exiled from the kingdom. King Ferdinand I of Old Castile received him kindly and sent him as abbot to restore the old monastery of St Sebastian—now St Dominic—of Silos. The saint was most successful in this task and was responsible for a virtual rebuilding of the abbey. He was a lover of the arts, and the scriptorium of his abbey produced under his inspiration the best specimens of Spanish Christian art. The cloisters of the abbey—a gem of Romanesque architecture—stand to this day as the best monument to his enterprise. He was also renowned for rescuing Christian slaves from the Moors. He is one of the best beloved of Spanish saints. At his shrine Bl Aza de Guzmán obtained the child whom she called Dominic, after the abbot of Silos, and who became the founder of the Dominican Friars.

DOMINIC, VICTOR, PRIMIAN, LYBOSUS, SATURNINUS, CRESCENTIUS, SECUNDUS, and HONORATUS (SS) MM.
RM. Dec 29
? African martyrs whose Acts have been lost.

DOMINICA (St) VM.   RM. July 6
? Said to have been a martyr in Campania under Diocletian. Possibly she is to be identified with St Cyriaca—*Dominica*, venerated on this day in the East as a martyr at Nicomedia.

DOMINICA (St) M.   RM. Aug 21
Otherwise Cyriaca, q.v.

DOMINICA ONGATA (Bl) M.
AC. Sept 10
d. 1622. A Japanese woman, beheaded at Nagasaki. See Bl Charles Spinola.

DOMINICAN MARTYRS of TONKIN (BB)   AC. July 27
1856–1862. Between these years the persecution of the Church by the King Tu-Duc raged with particular severity in the Dominican Vicariates of Central Tonkin. Five martyrs were beatified in 1906 (Bl Jerome Hermosilla and Comp.), and in 1917 no less than 2,078 causes were introduced. In 1951 a representative group of 25 of these were selected for immediate beatification. These were: Joseph Diaz Sanjurjo OP., Vic. Ap.; Melchior Garcia Sampedro, OP., Vic. Ap.; Dominic Ninh; Laurence Ngon; Dominic An-Kham; Like Cai-Thin; Joseph Cai-Ta; Dominic Mao; Vincent Truong; Dominic Nguyen; Andrew Tuong; Dominic Nhi;

Peter Da; Joseph Tuan; Peter Dung; Peter Tuan; Vincent Duong; Dominic Mau, priest OP.; Dominic Toai; Dominic Huyen; Joseph Tuan, priest OP.; Dominic Cam, priest and Dominican tertiary; Thomas Hjuong, priest and Dominican tertiary; Paul Doung; Joseph Tuc.

DOMITIAN (St) Bp.   AC. May 7
d. *c*.560. Bishop of Maestricht, and apostle of the Meuse valley. His relics are venerated at Huy.

DOMITIAN and HADELIN (SS) Mks. OSB.   AC. June 15
d. *c*.686. Two disciples of St Landelinus at the abbey of Lobbes. They were connected also, i⸱ seems, with Crépin abbey.

DOMITIAN (St) Ab.   RM. July 1
c.347–440. Born in Rome and left an orphan at an early age, he passed into Gaul and became a monk and a priest at Lérins. Later he founded the monastery of Bebron, now St Rambert de Joux. The sources, however, of St Domitian's life are very unreliable.

DOMITIAN (St) M.   RM. Aug 1
See Cyril, Aquila, etc.

**DOMITIAN of CHÂLONS (St) Bp.
                         RM. Aug 9**
4th cent. ? The third bishop of Châlons-sur-Marne in France, in which see he succeeded his master St Donatian.

DOMITIAN (St) M.   RM. Dec 28
See Eutychius and Domitian.

DOMITILLA (St) VM. RM. May 7
More correctly Flavia Domitilla, q.v.

DOMITIUS, PELAGIA, AQUILA, EPARCHIUS and THEODOSIA (SS) MM.   RM. March 23
d. 361. St Domitius was a Phrygian who died by the sword under Julian the Apostate, probably at Caesarea in Palestine. He is said to have publicly attacked the errors of heathenism in the circus, where the pagans were gathered for the festival games held in honour of the gods. Several others were martyred with him.

DOMITIUS (St) M.   RM. July 5
d. 362. A Persian, or a Phrygian monk, stoned to death under Julian the Apostate, in much the same circumstances as St Domitius of March 23.

DOMITIUS (DOMETIUS) and Comp. (SS) MM.   RM. Aug 7
4th cent. The entry in the RM. is: "At Nisibis in Mesopotamia St Dometius, a Persian monk who with two of his disciples was stoned to death under Julian the Apostate." This Domitius is probably identical with the preceding two of March 23 and July 5.

DOMITIUS (St) C.   RM. Oct 23
8th cent. A priest, or deacon, of the diocese of Amiens, who retired to a solitude and lived as an anchorite.

DOMNA (St) VM.   RM. Dec 28
See Indes, Domna, etc.

DOMNEVA (DOMNA EVA) (St) W. OSB.   AC. Nov 19
Otherwise Ermenburga, q.v.

DOMNINA and Comp. (SS) VV. MM.   RM. Apr 14
269? Maidens who were martyred at Terni, in Umbria, at the same time, it is said, as the bishop St Valentine.

DOMNINA, BERENICE and PROS-DOCE (SS) MM.   AC. Oct 4
d. 303–310. St Domnina and her two daughters were martyred in Syria during the persecution of Diocletian. They are commemorated by several contemporary Greek writers.

DOMNINA (St) M.   RM. Oct 12
d. 303. A Christian woman who, after
cruel torments, died in prison at Anazarbus under the prefect Lysias.

DOMNINUS (St) M. RM. March 21
See Philemon and Domninus.

**DOMNINUS, VICTOR and Comp.
(SS) MM.   RM. March 30**
c.304. St Domninus appears to have
suffered at Thessalonica under Maximian Herculius, together with Philo-
calus, Achaicus and Palotinus. He is to
be identified with St Domninus of Oct
1 (see below), on which day he is
venerated by the Greeks. St Victor and
his companions, some ten in number,
suffered elsewhere, the name of the
place being no longer known.

DOMNINUS (St)   RM. Apr 20
See Marcellinus, Vincent and Domninus.

DOMNINUS (St) M.   RM. Oct 1
The same as Domninus commemorated
on March 30, q.v.

**DOMNINUS (DONNINO) (St) M.
                        RM. Oct 9**
d. 304. A native of Parma, who, while
trying to escape in time of persecution,
was overtaken and beheaded on the Via
Claudia or Aemilia, a few miles out of
Parma at a place now called after him
Borgo San Donnino, where his relics
are held in great veneration.

**DOMNINUS, THEOTIMUS, PHIL-
OTHEUS, SYLVANUS and Comp.
(SS) MM.   RM. Nov 5**
? St Domninus, a young physician, and
St Sylvanus, a Syrian bishop, were to-
gether condemned to work in the mines.
The former was burnt alive somewhere
in Palestine, the latter was martyred
much later. The rest seem to have suf-
fered under Maximian.

DOMNINUS (St) Bp.   AC. Nov 5
4th cent. This St Domninus is given as
the first bishop of Grenoble in France.

**DOMNIO and Comp. (SS) MM.
                        RM. Apr 11**
? According to an old legend, Domnio,
one of the seventy-two disciples of
Christ, was sent from Rome by St
Peter to evangelize Dalmatia, where he
was martyred as first bishop of Salona.
A more probable version states that he
was martyred during the persecution of
Diocletian.

DOMNIO (St) M.   RM. July 16
d. c.295. A martyr of Bergamo in Lombardy under Diocletian.

DOMNIO (St) C.   RM. Dec 28
4th cent. A Roman priest, of whom his
contemporaries SS Jerome and Augustine speak in glowing terms.

DOMNOC (St)   AC. Feb 13
Otherwise Modomnock, q.v.

DOMNOLUS (St) Bp. RM. May 16
d. 581. Abbot of the monastery of St
Laurence, near Paris. In 543 he was
chosen bishop of Le Mans. He was the
founder of many monasteries, hospitals
and churches.

DOMNUS (St) M. OFM. RM. Oct 13
See Daniel, Samuel, etc.

**DOMNUS of VIENNE (St) Bp.
                        RM. Nov 3**
d. 657. Successor of St Desiderius the
martyr in the bishopric of Vienne. He
was most zealous in ransoming the
captives taken in the incessant wars of
that period.

**DONALD (DONIVALD) (St) C.
                        AC. July 15**
8th cent. A holy man of Scotland who

with his nine daughters—the "Nine Maidens", led the life of a religious at Ogilvy in Forfarshire.

DONARD (St)   AC. March 24
Otherwise Domangard, q.v.

DONAS (St) Bp.   RM. Oct 14
Otherwise Donatian, q.v.

DONAT (DUNWYD) (St)
                          AC. Aug 7
The patron saint of St Donat's or Llandunwyd, Glamorgan. This from the English Menology. Nothing more is discoverable.

DONATA (St) M.   RM. July 17
One of the Scillitan Martyrs, q.v.

DONATA, PAULINA, RUSTICA, NOMINANDA, SEROTINA, HILARIA and Comp. (SS) MM.
                          RM. Dec 31
? A band of Roman women martyred in one of the early persecutions and whose relics were enshrined in the catacombs of the Via Salaria.

DONATIAN and ROGATIAN (SS) MM.   RM. May 24
d. 299. Two brothers of Nantes in Brittany put to death by Rictiovarus under Diocletian.

DONATIAN (St) Bp.   RM. Aug 7
? 4th cent. Second bishop of Châlons-sur-Marne.

DONATIAN, PRAESIDIUS, MANSUETUS, GERMANUS, FUSCULUS and LAETUS (SS) MM.
                          RM. Sept 6
5th cent. Some of the more prominent among the Catholics driven from Africa into exile by Hunneric, the Arian king of the Vandals. An account of them is given by Victor of Utica in his history

of that persecution. It is said that the number of exiles reached nearly five thousand in a single year.

DONATIAN (DONAS) (St) Bp.
                          RM. Oct 14
d. 390. A Roman by birth and bishop of Reims from 360 to 390. His relics were translated to Bruges in the 9th century. He has been since venerated as the patron saint of Bruges.

DONATILLA (St) VM. RM. July 30
See Maxima, Donatilla and Secunda.

DONATUS, SABINUS and AGAPE (SS) MM.   RM. Jan 25
? Martyrs whose names are listed in the RM. but of whom no record is extant.

DONATUS (St) M.   RM. Feb 4
See Aquilinus, Geminus, etc.

DONATUS (St) M.   RM. Feb 9
See Primus and Donatus.

DONATUS, SECUNDIAN, ROMULUS and Comp. (SS) MM.
                          RM. Feb 17
d. 304. A group of eighty-nine martyrs who suffered under Diocletian. They were put to death at Porto Gruaro (*Concordia*), not far from Venice.

DONATUS, JUSTUS, HERENA and Comp. (SS) MM. RM. Feb 25
3rd cent. A band of fifty martyrs who suffered in Africa under Decius.

DONATUS (St) M. RM. March 1
See Leo, Donatus, etc.

DONATUS (St) M. RM. Apr 7
See Epiphanius, Donatus, etc.

DONATUS (St) Bp. RM. Apr 30
d. late 4th cent. Bishop of Euraea in

Epirus (Albania). His sanctity is recorded by Sozomen and other Greek writers.

DONATUS (St) M.   RM. May 21
See Polyeuctus, Victorius and Donatus.

DONATUS and HILARINUS (SS) MM.   RM. Aug 7
4th cent. St Donatus was the second bishop of Arezzo. Through confusion with another Donatus he was thought to be a martyr. He had no connexion with St Hilarinus, a martyr of Ostia.

DONATUS (St) Bp. OSB. AC. Aug 7
d. *c.*660. A monk of Luxeuil. Bishop of Besançon in 624. He was a most zealous fosterer of monasticism and founded at Besançon the abbey of St Paul. His *Regula ad Virgines* combines elements of the Rules of St Benedict and of St Columban.

DONATUS (St) Mk. OSB. AC. Aug 17
1179–1198. Born at Ripacandida, in the diocese of Rapallo. He became a monk of the Benedictine congregation of Montevergine at S. Onofrio at Petina (1194). He is now the principal patron saint of Ripacandida.

DONATUS (St) C.   RM. Aug 19
d. *c.*535. A native of Orleans, who lived as a hermit on Mt. Jura near Sisteron in Provence.

**DONATUS of ANTIOCH (St) M.
                          RM. Aug 23**
See Restitutus, Donatus, etc.

**DONATUS and FELIX (SS) MM.
                          RM. Sept 1**
Two of the "Twelve Holy Brothers", so-called, q.v.

**DONATUS of CAPUA (St) M.
                          RM. Sept 5**
See Quintius, Arcontius and Donatus.

DONATUS (St) M.   RM. Oct 5
See Placid, Eutychius, etc.

**DONATUS of FIESOLE (St) Bp.
                          RM. Oct 22**
d. 874. An Irishman who, while passing through Tuscany on his return from a pilgrimage to Rome, was made bishop of Fiesole near Florence. His feast is observed throughout Ireland.

**DONATUS of CORFU (St) C.
                          RM. Oct 29**
? All we know of this saint is that, about the year 600, St Gregory the Great directed that his relics, brought to Corfu by a refugee priest from Asia Minor, should be enshrined in one of the churches of the island.

DONATUS (St) M.   RM. Dec 12
See Hermogenes, Donatus, etc.

DONATUS of ALEXANDRIA (St) M.   RM. Dec 30
See Mansuetus, Severus, etc.

DONNAN (DOUNAN) and Comp. (SS) MM.   AC. Apr 17
d. *c.*616. St Donnan was a monk of Iona under St Columba. He eventually became the abbot-founder of a monastery on Eigg Island in the Inner Hebrides, off the west coast of Scotland. He and his fifty-two monks were massacred by heathen raiders.

DONVINA (St) M.   RM. Aug 23
See Claudius, Asterius, etc.

DORBHENE (St) Ab.   AC. Oct 28
d. 713. Abbot of Iona, descended from a brother of St Columba. A copy of St Adamnan's life of the latter written by St Dorbhene is still in existence.

DORCAS (St) W.   AC. Oct 25
Otherwise Tabitha, q.v.

DORIS (*several*)
Otherwise Dorothy, q.v.

DOROTHEUS (St) M. RM. March 28
See Castor and Dorotheus.

DOROTHEUS of TYRE (St) M.
RM. June 5
d. *c*.362. A priest of Tyre, who was
exiled under Diocletian. On his return
he was chosen bishop of Tyre, and as
such assisted at the council of Nicaea.
Under Julian the Apostate he was
beaten to death at Varna on the Black
Sea. All the above details, however, are
more or less guess-work.

DOROTHEUS the ARCHIMAN-
DRITE (St) Ab.   ? PC. June 5
d. *c*.640. A monk of Gaza, who became
archimandrite of an unknown monastery. His writings were greatly admired
by Abbot de Rancé.

DOROTHEUS the YOUNGER (St)
Ab.   AC. June 5
11th cent. Born at Trebizond, he was
first a monk at Samsun on the Black Sea
and afterwards abbot-founder of a monastery at Khiliokomos nearby.

DOROTHEUS and GORGONIUS
(SS) MM.   RM. Sept 9
d. 303. Favourites of the emperor Diocletian and officials of his body-guard at
Nicomedia. The emperor had them
hanged for their faith. Eusebius of
Caesarea, a contemporary, records their
martyrdom.

DOROTHY (DORA, DOROTHEA)
(St) VM.   RM. Feb 6
d. *c*.300. A virgin-martyr of Caesarea in
Cappadocia who suffered under Diocletian. Her *Acta* are apocryphal.

DOROTHY (St) VM.   RM. Sept 3
See Euphemia, Dorothy, etc.

DOROTHY of MONTAU (St) W.
PC. Oct 30
1336–1394. A peasant girl of Montau in
Prussia, who married a wealthy sword-
smith Albert by name. She bore him
nine children and by her gentle patience
completely changed his surly disposition. After his death Dorothy lived as a
recluse at Marienwerder. Though she
was never canonized her cult is still to
be found in Central Europe.

DORYMEDON (St) M. RM. Sept 19
See Trophimus, Sabbatius and Dorymedon.

DOSITHEUS (St) Mk.   AC. Feb 23
d. *c*.530. A rich young man who became
a Christian at Jerusalem and shortly
after a monk at Gaza. His poor health
prevented him from fasting, and moreover he did not work any miracles: these
facts scandalized his fellow monks. His
abbot, however, considered him a great
saint, since he had completely given up
his own will. This has been the verdict
of history, which has canonized him.

DOTTO (St) Ab.   ? Apr 9
? 6th cent. Said to have been abbot of a
monastery in the Orkney Islands.

DOUAI (Martyrs of) (BB) AC. Oct 29
More than a hundred and sixty "seminary priests" from the English College
at Douai were martyred in England and
Wales during the century following its
foundation in 1568. Over eighty of them
were beatified in 1929. Each receives
here a special notice. A collective feast
is kept in their honour in several English
dioceses.

DRAUSINUS (DRAUSIUS) (St) Bp.
AC. March 7
d. *c*.576. Bishop of Soissons. A great
fosterer of monastic life, he even enlisted the services of the tyrant Ebroin
for the building of a convent near

Soissons. For this reason he is invoked against the machinations of enemies, and St Thomas Becket is said to have visited his shrine before returning to England for the last time.

DREUX (St) H.   RM. Apr 16
Otherwise Drogo, q.v.

DRILLO (St) C.   AC. June 15
Otherwise Trillo, q.v.

DRITHELM (St) H.   AC. Aug 17
d. c.700. A Northumbrian who, terrified by a vision, embraced the monastic life at Melrose, where he lived a life of great austerity in a special cell near the abbey.

DROCTOVEUS (DROCTONIUS— in French DROTTÉ) (St) Ab.
RM. March 10
d. c.580. A disciple of St Germanus of Paris, then abbot of the monastery of St Symphorian at Autun and was afterwards called by his old master to Paris as first abbot of the new monastery of St Vincent and the Holy Cross—afterwards renamed Saint-Germain-des-Prés.

DROGO (Bl) Mk. OSB. AC. Apr 2
10th cent. After a worldly life, Drogo entered the Benedictine abbey of Fleury-sur-Loire, and afterwards migrated to that of Baume-les-Messieurs, where he was engaged in tending the flocks of the abbey.

DROGO (DREUX, DRUON) (St) H.
RM. Apr 16
d. 1186. A Fleming by birth and an orphan, at twenty years of age he disposed of all his property and served as a shepherd in France. Nine times he made the pilgrimage to Rome. Stricken with a most unsightly bodily affliction, he built himself a hut under the shadow of the church of Sebourg in Hainault, where he died aged eighty-four.

DROSTAN (St) Ab.   AC. July 11
d. c.610. An Irishman by birth, monk under St Columba, and first abbot of Deer in Aberdeenshire. He is venerated as one of the apostles of Scotland.

DRUSUS, ZOSIMUS and THEODORE (SS) MM.   RM. Dec 14
? Christians martyred in Syria, probably at Antioch. Some MSS have Drusina for Drusus. St John Chrysostom has left a homily preached on their festival day.

DRUSUS (St) M.   RM. Dec 24
See Lucian, Metrobius, etc.

DRUTHMAR (St) Ab. OSB.
AC. Feb 15
d. 1046. A Benedictine of Lorsch, who in 1014 was appointed by the emperor St Henry II abbot of Corvey in Saxony. Fervour and good observance were marks of his rule.

DUBRICIUS (DUBRIC, DYFRIG, DEVEREUX) (St) Bp. AC. Nov 14
d. c.545. One of the founders of monastic life in Wales. His chief centres of monachism were at Henllan and Moccas, whence he established many other religious houses in what is now Herefordshire and Monmouthshire. He had jurisdiction over Caldey Island and appointed St Samson abbot of the monastery there, and later consecrated him bishop. A later legend makes St Dubricius archbishop of Caerleon. He died on the Isle of Bardsey.

DUBTACH (St) Bp.   AC. Oct 7
d. c.513. Archbishop of Armagh from 497 to c.513.

DULA (St) VM.   RM. March 25
? The slave of a pagan soldier at Nicomedia in Asia Minor. She suffered death at his hands in defence of her chastity.

DULAS (St) M.   RM. June 15
d. 300. A Christian of Zepherinum in Cilicia, martyred after having undergone the most frightful tortures.

DULCARDUS (St) H.   AC. Oct 25
d. 584. Monk of Micy (Saint-Mesmin) in Orleans, and afterwards a hermit near Bourges, where now stands the village of Saint-Doulchard (Cher).

DULCIDIUS (DULCET, DOUCIS) (St) Bp.   AC. Oct 16
d. c.450. Successor of St Phoebadius in the bishopric of Agen in France.

DULCISSIMA (St) VM.
AC. Sept 16
? Nothing is really known about this saint, but from time immemorial she has been venerated at Sutri, formerly in the Papal States, as a virgin-martyr and as the principal patron saint of the town and diocese.

DUMHAID (St) Ab.   AC. May 25
Otherwise Dunchadh, q.v.

DUNCHADH (St) Ab. AC. May 25
d. 717. Abbot of Iona in Scotland from 710 till his death. In his time the Roman customs—tonsure, date of Easter, Benedictine Rule—were finally adopted by the Celtic monks in Scotland.

DUNCHAID O'BRAOIN (St) Ab.
AC. Jan 16
d. 988. Born in Westmeath, he was an anchorite near the monastery of Clonmacnoise until the year 969, when he was chosen abbot of that place. In his old age he retired to Armagh, where he died.

DUNSTAN (St) Bp. OSB.
RM. May 19
c.910–988. One of the great figures in English history—abbot, archbishop, statesman, and saint. An Anglo-Saxon by origin, he was born near Glastonbury, where he was also educated and became a monk. In 943 he was made abbot, and under his rule the monastery became the greatest centre of learning in England. He himself excelled as a goldsmith, an illuminator and a musician. He was summoned to court to be a royal counsellor, but was forced into exile by King Edwy, whom he had rebuked. Dunstan now spent one year at Ghent, then a great centre of monastic restoration. He was recalled to England by King Edgar and became his chief adviser, being promoted to the see of Worcester (957) and to that of Canterbury (961). Moreover, Pope John XII appointed Dunstan his legate in England (961). He now achieved, together with SS Ethelwold of Winchester and Oswald of York, a thorough monastic and ecclesiastical reform throughout England and initiated a vigorous policy of national unification and moral restoration. Active and energetic to the very end, he died peacefully at Canterbury, in his cathedral of Christ Church.

DUTHAC (St) Bp.   AC. March 8
d. 1065. An Irishman by birth, he became bishop of Ross in Scotland, where his memory is preserved in several place-names, e.g., Kilduthie, etc.

DWYNWEN (St) V.   AC. Jan 25
d. c.460. A Welsh saint of the family of Brychan of Brecknock. The maxim "nothing wins hearts like cheerfulness" is attributed to her. Churches dedicated to her are to be found in Wales and Cornwall.

DWYNWEN (St) W.   AC. July 18
Otherwise Theneva, q.v.

DYFAN (DERUVIANUS, DAMIAN) (St) M.   AC. May 14 (RM. May 26)
2nd cent. Said to have been one of the missionaries sent to the Britons by Pope St Eleutherius at the instance of King St Lucius. His church of Merthyr Dyfan shows the popular tradition that he ended his days by martyrdom.

DYFNAN (St) C.   AC. Apr 24
5th cent. A son of the Welsh chieftain Brychan. He founded a church in Anglesey.

DYFNOG (St) C.   AC. Feb 13
7th cent. A Welsh saint of the family of Caradog. He was formerly held in local veneration in Denbighshire.

DYFRIG (St) Bp.   AC. Nov 14
Otherwise Dubricius, q.v.

DYMPNA (DYMPHNA) (St) VM.
RM. May 15
? Popular legend makes her the daughter of an Irish chieftain who escaped to Belgium accompanied by her chaplain St Gerebern. Their relics were discovered at Gheel, near Antwerp, in the 13th century, and since then numberless cases of insanity, epilepsy, etc., have been cured at their shrine. The asylum built at Gheel in the 13th century still stands, equipped with all up-to-date improvements. St Dympna is invoked as the patroness of lunatics.

E

Note. Saints' names beginning with the letter E are often found written with the diphthong AE, or OE, as the initial letter.

EADBERT (St) Bp. OSB. RM. May 6
d. 698. A monk of Lindisfarne who succeeded St Cuthbert as abbot-bishop of the island. He was remarkable for his knowledge of holy scripture.

EADBURGA (*several*)
Otherwise Edburga, q.v.

EADFRID (St) Mk. OSB. AC. Oct 26
d. *c*.675. A Northumbrian monk-priest who preached in Mercia and founded, and was the first superior of, Leominister Priory.

EADGITH (*several*)
Otherwise Edith, q.v.

EADNOT (St) Bp. OSB.   ? Oct 19
d. 1016. Monk of Worcester and abbot of Ramsey. In 1006 he became bishop of Dorchester. As such he helped and seconded St Oswald of York. He died in a battle against the Danes, and is sometimes termed a martyr.

EADSIN (St) Bp.   AC. Oct 28
d. 1050. Archbishop of Canterbury. He crowned St Edward the Confessor on the restoration of the Anglo-Saxon line in England. He resigned his see some years before his death.

EANFLEDA (St) W. OSB.
                          AC. Nov 24
d. *c*.700. Daughter of King St Edwin of Northumbria and of his wife St Ethelburga of Kent, baptized as an infant by St Paulinus. She was a great benefactress of St Wilfrid. In her widowhood she became a nun at Whitby under her own daughter, St Elfleda.

EANSWIDA (EANSWITH) (St) Abs. OSB.   AC. Sept 12
d. *c*.640. Granddaughter of King St Ethelbert of Kent. She was the abbess-foundress (630) of a nunnery on the coast near Folkestone. Her convent was destroyed by the Danes but re-founded for Benedictine monks in 1095. Part of it was swallowed up by the sea, and it was removed to Folkestone. Its successor is now the church of SS Mary and Eanswida.

EASTERWINE (St) Ab. OSB.
                        AC. March 7
Otherwise Esterwine, q.v.

EATA (St) Bp. OSB.   AC. Oct 26
d. *c*.686. An Englishman by origin, he was educated by St Aidan in the Celtic observance at Ripon. When St Wilfrid arrived at this abbey, he left it for Melrose, where he became abbot. After the council of Whitby, however, he adopted fully the Roman observances and was made abbot of Lindisfarne. In 678 he became bishop of the Bernicians, being consecrated by St Theodore, with his see first at Lindisfarne and then at the Benedictine abbey of Hexham.

EBBA THE YOUNGER and Comp. (SS) VV. MM. OSB.   AC. Aug 23
d. *c*.870. Abbess of the great Benedictine

nunnery of Coldingham, on the Scottish border, founded two centuries earlier by St Ebba the Elder. During a Danish incursion St Ebba fearing for her virginity mutilated her face and invited her nuns to do the same. The Danes set fire to the nunnery and all the community perished in the flames.

EBBA the ELDER (St) Abs. OSB.
AC. Aug 25
d. 683. Sister of SS Oswald and Oswy, kings of Northumbria. She took the veil from St Finan at Lindisfarne and founded the double monastery of Coldingham, on the coast of Northumberland, near Berwick, of which she was first abbess. The organization of the abbey resembled that of Whitby in most points. Ebba, we are told, was personally a very holy abbess, but not a great success as an administrator.

EBBO (St) Bp. OSB.   AC. Aug 27
d. 740. A native of Tonnerre and a Benedictine monk of Saint-Pierre-le-Vif, at Sens. About the year 709 he was raised to the see of Sens. In 725 he saved the city when it was besieged by Saracens.

EBERHARD (several)
Note. This Teutonic name, when transliterated into other languages, is often softened into Everhard, Everard, Evard, Erhard, Erard, etc.

EBERHARD (Bl) Mk. OSB. Cist.
PC. March 20
d. c.1150. Count of Mons in Belgium. In expiation of a crime committed as a soldier, he went on pilgrimage to Rome and Compostella and finally asked to be hired as a swineherd at the Cistercian abbey of Morimond. When his identity was discovered, he was induced to continue his life of penance as a monk, and accordingly took the vows. In 1142 he founded Einberg and then Mont-Saint-

George. He is officially venerated by the Cistercians.

EBERHARD of SCHAFFHAUSEN (Bl) Mk. OSB.   PC. Apr 7
1018–1078. Eberhard III, count of Nellenburg, was a relative of Pope St Leo IX and the emperor of St Henry II. In 1050 he founded the Benedictine abbey of Schaffhausen in Switzerland—now a town—and took the habit there.

EBERHARD (Bl) O. Praem.
PC. Apr 17
d. 1178. Premonstratensian monk of Roth, later provost of Marchtal in Swabia when it was handed over to the Premonstratensians in 1166.

EBERHARD of SALZBURG (St) Bp. OSB.   AC. June 22
1085–1164 (June 11). Born at Nuremberg and educated by the monks of Michelberg at Bamberg, he obtained a canonry at Bamberg, which, however, he gave up in order to become a Benedictine at Prüfening (1125). In 1133 he was made abbot of Biburg, and in 1147 archbishop of Salzburg. He was the greatest supporter of the pope in Germany during the investiture controversy.

EBERHARD of EINSIEDELN (Bl) Ab. OSB.   AC. Aug 14
d. 958. Of the ducal family of Swabia. He was already provost of the cathedral chapter at Strasburg when, in 934, he joined his friend Bl Benno at Einsiedeln. After Bl Benno's death he was acknowledged as the first abbot of Einsiedeln. During his rule, the abbey was built and the church dedicated.

EBONTIUS (PONTIUS PONCE, EBON) (St) Bp. OSB.   PC. Oct 3
d. 1104. Born at Comminges, Haute Garonne, France, and a Benedictine of Sainte-Foi of Tomières, he became

abbot of St Victorian (Asán), near Ainsa, in Upper Aragon, and first bishop of Babastro after its recapture from the Moors. It is doubtful, however, whether the fact of his cultus can be proved.

EBREGESILUS (St) Bp. M.
RM. Oct 24
Otherwise Evergislus, q.v.

EBRULFUS (EVROULT) (St) Ab.
AC. July 25
d. *c*.600. Born at Beauvais in France, he became a hermit and afterwards abbot-founder of Saint-Fuscien-aux-Bois.

EBRULFUS (EVROULT) (St) Ab.
RM. Dec 29
517–596. A native of Bayeux in Normandy, he became a courtier at the palace of King Childebert I. He left the court to become a monk at the abbey of Deux Jumeaux, diocese of Bayeux, and later the abbot-founder of Ouche and of other smaller houses.

EBSDORF (Martyrs of) (SS)
AC. Feb 2
d. 880. In the winter of 880 Duke St Bruno led the army of King Louis III against the invading Norsemen. On the marshy heath of Luneberg, at Ebsdorf, in Saxony, the army was caught in ice and snow and defeated by the Norsemen. Bruno, with four bishops, eleven noblemen, and many others were slain and forthwith venerated as martyrs.

ECCLESIUS (St) Bp.   AC. July 27
d. 532. Bishop of Ravenna from 521 till 532. He began the building of San Vitale, at Ravenna, where there is a figure of him in mosaic.

ECHA (ETHA) (St) H. OSB.
AC. May 5
d. 767. An Anglo-Saxon priest and monk-hermit at Crayk, near York.

EDAN (St) Bp.   AC. Jan 31
Otherwise Aidan, q.v.

EDANA (ETAOIN) (St) V.
AC. July 5
? An Irish saint, patron of parishes in W. Ireland. A famous holy well bears her name. She appears to have lived near the confluence of the rivers Boyle and Shannon. Some have thought her to be one and the same with St Modwenna, who is also commemorated on July 5.

EDBERT (St) Bp.   RM. May 6
Otherwise Eadbert, q.v.

EDBERT (St) King, OSB.
AC. Aug 20
d. 768. The successor of St Ceolwulph on the throne of Northumbria. After a prosperous reign of twenty years, he resigned and retired to the abbey of York, where he spent a further ten years in prayer and seclusion.

EDBURGA (*several***)**
Note. The name is spelt in many different ways: Iderberga, Edberga, Eadburga, Ideberga, Idaberga, etc.

EDBURGA of WINCHESTER (St)
Abs. OSB.   AC. June 15
d. 960. Daughter of Edward the Elder, granddaughter of Alfred the Great, she was placed as a child in the nunnery which King Alfred's widow had founded at Winchester, of which she herself later became abbess. Her shrine at Pershore in Worcestershire was famous for its miracles.

EDBURGA of CAISTOR (St) N.
OSB.   AC. June 20
Late 7th cent. The daughter of the pagan Penda, king of Mercia, a nun at Caistor (Domundcaster) Northamptonshire, whence her relics were transferred to Peterborough and later to Flanders.

EDBURGA and EDITH (SS) Ns. OSB. AC. July 18
d. *c*.650. Sisters, Anglo-Saxon princesses, nuns at Aylesbury.

EDBURGA of THANET (St) Abs. OSB. AC. Dec 12
d. 751. Of the royal family of Kent. A disciple of St Mildred, whom she probably succeeded as abbess of Minster-in-Thanet. She was a friend and correspondent of St Boniface, whom she helped with books, altar vestments and other gifts. She had a new church built for her convent at Minster.

EDBURGA (St) N. OSB. AC. Dec 13
7th cent. A nun of Lyminge in Kent.

EDEYRN (St) H. AC. Jan 6
6th cent. The patron saint of a church in Brittany. The legend describes him as a Briton, associating him with King Arthur, and making him end his days as a hermit in Armorica.

EDGAR the PEACEFUL (St) King. PC. July 8
d. 975. The great friend of St Dunstan, whom he took as his adviser. His reign is marked by a strong religious revival in England. Though he enjoyed a local cultus at Glastonbury, he would not nowadays be reckoned a likely candidate for canonization.

EDILBURGA (St) V. RM. July 7
Otherwise Ethelburga, q.v.

EDILTRUDIS (St) V. RM. June 23
Otherwise Etheldreda, q.v.

EDISTIUS (St) M. RM. Oct 12
d. *c*.303. A martyr of Ravenna under Diocletian.

EDITH of POLESWORTH (St) W. OSB. AC. July 15
d. ? 925. There is much confusion as to the identity of this St Edith. She was certainly the widow of a king of Northumbria and died as a nun—probably abbess—of Polesworth in Warwickshire.

EDITH (St) V. OSB. AC. July 18
See Edburga and Edith.

EDITH of WILTON (St) N. OSB. RM. Sept 16
961–984. Daughter of King Edgar and of St Wilfrida. Taken to Wilton abbey shortly after birth, she never left it, so that, in the words of the RM. "she rather knew not this world than forsook it". She was professed before her fifteenth year, her father being present. She declined to accept the government of three abbeys, preferring to remain a simple nun at Wilton. When her father died, she was offered the throne, and refused. She died at the age of twenty-two, St Dunstan assisting her in her last illness.

EDMUND ARROWSMITH (Bl) M. SJ. AC. Aug 28
d. 1628. Born at Haydock, near St Helen's, in Lancashire, of a recusant yeoman family. He was educated at Douai, ordained priest (1612), and sent to the English mission, where he worked from 1613 to 1628, being received into the Society of Jesus in 1623. He was hanged, drawn and quartered at Lancaster, where he exercised his apostolate. Beatified in 1929.

EDMUND RICH (St) Bp. RM. Nov 16
1180–1242. Born at Abingdon, he studied at Oxford and Paris, and became professor of philosophy at Oxford (1219–1226), canon of Salisbury, and archbishop of Canterbury (1233). His uncompromising stand in favour of good discipline, monastic observance, justice in high quarters, brought him

into conflict with King Henry III, with several monasteries and with his own chapter. He was moreover opposed by the papal legate. In 1240 he retired to the Cistercian abbey of Pontigny, where, according to the Cistercian tradition, he lived and died in the Cistercian habit. Canonized in 1246.

EDMUND (St) King M. RM. Nov 20

849–870. King of the East Angles from 855. In the Danish inroad of 870 he was taken prisoner and savagely done to death at Hoxne in Suffolk. He expired with the name of Jesus on his lips. His shrine gave its name to the Benedictine abbey and town of Bury St Edmund's.

EDMUND CAMPION (Bl) M. SJ.
AC. Dec 1

c.1540–1581. "The Pope's Champion". Born in London and educated at Christ's Hospital, he was a brilliant student at Oxford. Reconciled to the Catholic Church, he passed on to Douai and then to Rome, where he joined the Jesuits. Next he worked in Bohemia, and finally, for one year, on the English mission. His extraordinary success caused him to be hunted down relentlessly. He was betrayed, racked and martyred at Tyburn.

EDMUND GENINGS (Bl) M.
AC. Dec 10

d. 1591. Born at Lichfield, and a convert from Protestantism, he studied and was ordained priest at Reims (1590). He passed on to the English mission and was condemned to death for his priesthood the following year. He was hanged, drawn and quartered at Gray's Inn Fields, London. Beatified in 1929.

EDWARD the CONFESSOR (St)
King   RM. (Jan 5 and) Oct 13

1004–1066. Born at Islip, near Oxford, the son of King Ethelred the Unready.

He became king of England in 1042. Considerate, just, gentle and unselfish, his reign was one of peace, prosperity and good government. Some of the nobility opposed him, but the commoners were all for "good King Edward". He was much given to prayer, and hunting. In commutation of a vow to go on pilgrimage to Rome he rebuilt Westminster Abbey, where he was buried. He was canonized in 1161, and his relics solemnly enshrined on Oct 13, 1162, on which day his feast is celebrated throughout Christendom, though the date of his death was Jan 5.

EDWARD WATERSON (Bl) M.
AC. Jan 7

d. 1593. Born in London and a convert. He studied at Reims and was ordained in 1592. The following year he was executed for his priesthood at Newcastle. Beatified in 1929.

EDWARD STRANSHAM (Bl) M.
AC. Jan 21

d. 1586. Born at Oxford, and educated at St John's College there. He studied for the priesthood at Douai and Reims, was ordained in 1580, and sent to the English mission in 1581. He worked in London and in Oxford. He was condemned for his priesthood and executed at Tyburn. Beatified in 1929.

EDWARD the MARTYR (St) King
M.   RM. March 18

d. 979. The son of Edgar the Peaceful, and king of England at the age of thirteen, after his father's death (975). In 979 he was murdered at Wareham in Dorsetshire, at the instigation of his stepmother Elfrida; and he was forthwith popularly acclaimed as a martyr.

EDWARD OLDCORNE (Bl) M. SJ.
AC. Apr 7

d. 1606. A native of York, he was ordained priest at Rome and received into the Society of Jesus in 1587. He worked in the Midlands from 1588 to 1606, and was condemned to death at Worcester for alleged complicity in the Gunpowder Plot. Beatified in 1929.

EDWARD CATHERICK (Bl) M.
AC. Apr 13

d. 1642. Born at Carlton, near Richmond, Yorks. He was educated at Douai and laboured as a missionary priest in England from 1635 till his death. He was executed for his priesthood at York. Beatified in 1929.

EDWARD JONES (Bl) M. AC. May 6

d. 1590. Born in the diocese of St Asaph in Wales and a convert. He studied for the priesthood at Reims, and was ordained in 1588. He was captured and executed for his priesthood in Fleet Street. Beatified in 1929.

EDWARD FULTHROP (Bl) M.
AC. July 4

d. 1597. A gentleman of Yorkshire executed at York for having been reconciled to the Catholic Church. Beatified in 1929.

EDWARD POWELL (Bl) M.
AC. July 30

d. 1540. A Welshman who became a canon of Salisbury and a fellow of Oriel and was well known in Europe as the author of various treatises against Luther. He was chosen by Queen Catherine of Aragon as one of her counsel. After six years in prison he was hanged, drawn and quartered at Smithfield, London, for denying the king's spiritual supremacy. Beatified in 1886.

EDWARD SHELLEY (Bl) M.
AC. Aug 30

d. 1588. A gentleman of Warminghurst,

Sussex, hanged at Tyburn for harbouring priests. Beatified in 1929.

EDWARD BARLOW (Bl) M. OSB.
AC. Sept 10

Otherwise Ambrose Edward Barlow, q.v.

EDWARD JAMES (Bl) M. AC. Oct 1

d. 1588. A native of Breaston, near Derby, and an undergraduate of St John's College, Oxford. After his conversion he studied at Reims and Rome. Ordained priest in 1583, he was condemned and executed at Chichester for his priesthood. Beatified in 1929.

EDWARD CAMPION (Bl) M.
AC. Oct 1

d. 1588. Born at Ludlow in Shropshire, he studied at Jesus College, Oxford. After his conversion he was trained for the Priesthood at Reims and ordained in 1587. He was condemned for his priesthood and executed at Canterbury. Beatified in 1929.

EDWARD COLEMAN (Bl) M.
AC. Dec 3

d. 1678. A gentleman of Suffolk, educated at Peterhouse, Cambridge, and a convert to the Catholic Faith. He was secretary to the duchess of York, and was executed at Tyburn on a false charge of conspiring with a foreign power to restore the Catholic Church in England. He was the first victim of the "Titus Oates Plot". Beatified in 1929.

EDWEN (St) V.　　　　　　AC. Nov 6

7th cent. The alleged patron saint of Llanedwen, Anglesey. She is described as having been a daughter of King Edwin of Northumberland.

EDWIN (St) King M.　　　AC. Oct 12

d. 633. King of Northumbria from 616. He married as his second wife Ethelburga of Kent and was baptized by her chaplain St Paulinus (627). He fell in battle at Hatfield Chase fighting against the pagan Mercians and Welsh. Hence he was venerated as a martyr.

EDWOLD (St) C.   AC. Nov 27
9th cent. Brother of St Edmund the Martyr, king of East Anglia. He lived as a recluse at Carne in Dorsetshire.

EFFLAM (St) C.   AC. Nov 6
d. *c*.700. Son of a British prince who, crossing to France, became abbot of a monastery he had founded in Brittany.

EGBERT (St) Mk. OSB.
AC. March 18
d. *c*.720. Monk, probably of Ripon, where his relics were venerated from about the year 1000.

EGBERT (St) Mk.   RM. Apr 24
d. 729. An English monk of Lindisfarne who migrated to Ireland and lived at Rathelmigisi in Connaught. Here he trained several bands of monks for the German mission. He passed over to Iona to induce the monks to adopt the Roman usages. He succeeded at last: in fact on the day of his death Easter was for the first time celebrated at Iona according to the Roman reckoning.

EGDUNUS and Comp. (SS) MM.
RM. March 12
d. 303. Martyrs at Nicomedia under Diocletian. They were eight in number: they were suspended head downwards over a fire and suffocated by its smoke.

EGELNOTH (St) Bp. OSB.
AC. Oct 30
d. 1038. Surnamed "the Good". Monk of Glastonbury, and archbishop of Canterbury from 1020 till his death.

EGELRED (St) M. OSB. AC. Sept 25
d. *c*.870. A monk-martyr of Croyland

Abbey, put to death with his abbot and many others of the community by the heathen Danes.

EGELWINE (St) C.   AC. Nov 26
7th cent. A prince of the house of Wessex who lived at Athelney in Somersetshire.

EGIDIUS (*several*).
Otherwise Giles, q.v.

EGILHARD (St) M. OSB.
PC. May 25
d. 881. The eighth abbot of Cornelimünster, near Aix-la-Chapelle. He was killed by the Normans at Bercheim.

EGILO (EGILON, EIGIL) (St) Ab.
OSB.   AC. June 28
d. 871. Monk of Prüm, near Trèves, and then abbot there. As abbot he gave the habit to St Humphrey at Prüm. In 860 the emperor Charles the Bald directed him to restore Flavigny, in the diocese of Dijon. Later on he founded the abbey of Corbigny, Yonne

EGINO (EGON) (St) Ab. OSB.
PC. July 15
d. 1122. Born at Augsburg and received as a child-oblate at the abbey of SS Ulric and Afra in the same city. In the conflict between the pope and the emperor he sided with the former, and was for this reason expelled by his abbot, being welcomed at the abbey of St Blasien (Blaise). In 1106 he was recalled to Augsburg and appointed abbot in 1109. He had to suffer much at the hands of the simoniacal bishop Herimann and to flee to Rome in 1120. On his return home he died at Pisa in the monastery of his Camaldolese brethren.

EGWIN (St) Bp. OSB.   AC. Dec 30
d. 717. Consecrated to God in his youth, he eventually became the third bishop

of Worcester (692) and the founder of the abbey of Evesham. Twice he made the pilgrimage to Rome; once, indeed, to appeal to the pope against some of his flock, whose enmity he had incurred for his severity against vice.

EGYPT (Martyrs and Confessors of) (SS)
The RM. lists two groups of anonymous martyrs and confessors of Egypt, as follows:
RM. Jan 5
d. 303. "In Egypt the commemoration of many holy martyrs, who were slain in the Thebaid . . . under Diocletian".
RM. May 21
d. c.357. "At Alexandria, the memory of the holy bishops and priests who were sent into exile by the Arians, and merited to be joined to the holy confessors".

EIGIL (AEIGILUS) (St) Ab. OSB.
AC. Dec 17
d. 822. A monk of Fulda, he became abbot in 817, succeeding Rutgar, who had been deposed by Charlemagne on account of excessive and imprudent severity. Eigil restored peace and union among the large community and had the consolation of paving the way for the abbacy of his great successor St Rhabanus Maurus.

EIGRAD (St) C.   AC. Jan 6
6th cent. A brother of St Samson of York, trained by St Illtyd, and founder of a church in Anglesey.

EILAN (St) C.   AC. Jan 12
Otherwise Elian, q.v.

EINGAN (EINION, ENEON, ANIANUS) (St) H.   AC. Feb 9
6th cent. A British prince who came from Cumberland into Wales and finished his days as a hermit at Llanen-

gan near Bangor. He is said to have been a son of the chieftain Cunedda, whose family claims no less than fifty saints.

EINHILDIS and ROSWINDA (SS) Ns. OSB.   AC. Dec 13
8th cent. Nuns of Hohenburg under St Ottilia. St Roswinda seems to have been St Ottilia's sister. St Einhildis became abbess of Niedermünster near Hohenburg.

EKBERT (EGBERT) (Bl) Ab. OSB.
AC. Nov 25
d. 1075. Monk of Gorze and afterwards abbot of Münsterschwarzach in Bavaria.

EKHARD (Bl) Ab. OSB. AC. June 28
d. 1084. Canon of the cathedral of Magdeburg and first abbot of Huysburg.

ELA (Bl) W.   PC. Feb 1
d. 1261. The widow of William Longsword, she placed herself under the direction of St Edmund Rich. She founded a monastery of Carthusians at Hinton and a convent of Augustinian nuns at Laycock. She became abbess in the latter.

ELAETH the KING (St) AC. Nov 10
6th cent. A Briton from the North driven into Wales by the Picts. He became a monk under St Seiriol in Anglesey. Some poems of his are still extant.

ELAPHIUS (St) Bp.   AC. Aug 19
d. 580. Bishop of Châlons-sur-Marne. According to Gregory of Tours, he was sent as ambassador to Spain and died en route. A later writer of his life states he went to Spain to seek the relics of St Eulalia at Merida.

ELDATE (ELDAD) (St) C.
AC. Feb 4
Otherwise Aldate, q.v.

ELDRAD (St) Ab. OSB.
                          AC. March 13
Otherwise Heldrad, q.v.

ELEAZAR (St) M.   RM. Aug 1
See Machabees.

ELEAZAR (St) M.   RM. Aug 23
See Minervus, Eleazar, etc.

ELEAZAR (St) C.   RM. Sept 27
Otherwise Elzear, q.v.

ELEFREDA (St) V. OSB. AC. Aug 2
Otherwise Etheldritha, q.v.

ELERIUS (St) C.   AC. Nov 3
6th cent. A Welsh saint, mentioned in
the legends concerning St Winefred.
He is supposed to have presided over
a monastery in N. Wales.

ELESBAAN (St) King RM. Oct 27
d. *c*.555. Called by the Abyssinians
Calam-Negus. He was a Christian king
of Ethiopia, who successfully fought
the Jewish usurper Dhu-newas, a persecutor of Christianity. After an eventful
reign, during which he showed more
than once his cruel and revengeful
disposition, he died as an exemplary
monk at Jerusalem. It seems, however,
that he always remained a Monophysite.

ELESMES (St) Ab. OSB.
                          AC. Jan 30
Otherwise Adelelmus, q.v.

ELEUCHADIUS (St) Bp.
                          RM. Feb 14
2nd cent. A Greek by origin, he was
converted by St Apollinaris of Ravenna,
and in his absence he governed the
church there. He succeeded St Adheritus as third bishop of that See.

ELEUSIPPUS (St) M. RM. Jan 17
See Speusippus, Eleusippus, etc.

ELEUTHERIUS (St) Bp. M.
                          RM. Feb 20
d. *c*.310. Said to have been bishop of
Byzantium and a martyr. Most writers,
after the Bollandists, identify him with
St Eleutherius commemorated on Aug
4, q.v.

ELEUTHERIUS of TOURNAI (St)
Bp. M.   RM. Feb 20
d. 532. A native of Tournai, bishop of
that city from 486, who evangelized the
Franks then settled in and near Tournai
and died from wounds inflicted by the
Arian heretics of that district.

ELEUTHERIUS and ANTHIA (SS)
MM.   RM. Apr 18
d. 117–138. Eleutherius, a bishop of
Illyria, his mother Anthia and eleven
others, are said to have been martyred
in Illyria under the emperor Hadrian.
The whole story has been proved to be
merely a pious romance of Greek origin.

ELEUTHERIUS (St) Pope, M.
                          RM. May 26
d. 189. A Greek by origin who became
a deacon of the Roman Church. He
succeeded St Soter as pope in 175. Very
little is known about him. The story of
his sending missionaries to Britain is
abandoned by most modern scholars.

ELEUTHERIUS (St) C.
                          RM. May 29
? An English pilgrim, said to have been
the brother of SS Grimwald and Fulk,
who died at Rocca d'Arce, near Aquino,
in S. Italy. He is venerated there as
principal patron saint.

ELEUTHERIUS (St) M. RM. Aug 4
d. *c*.310. He was a martyr of Tarsus,
and his tomb there became a centre of
pilgrimage. He had a basilica at Constantinople. The *Passio* resumed by the
RM. is unreliable.

ELEUTHERIUS and LEONIDES (SS) MM.   RM. Aug 8
? Martyrs burnt to death at Constantinople.

ELEUTHERIUS (St) Bp.
RM. Aug 16
d. 561. Bishop of Auxerre, 532–561.

ELEUTHERIUS (St) Ab. OSB.
RM. Sept 6
d. *c*.590. Mentioned several times by St Gregory the Great as a well-known wonder-worker. He was abbot of St Mark at Spoleto, whence he migrated to St Gregory's own abbey in Rome, where he lived for many years as a simple monk.

ELEUTHERIUS and Comp. (SS) MM.   RM. Oct 2
d. *c*.303. A soldier-martyr of Nicomedia under Diocletian. The story told in the RM. is wholly untrustworthy.

ELEUTHERIUS (St) M. RM. Oct 9
See Dionysius, Rusticus and Eleutherius.

ELEVETHA (St) VM.   AC. Aug 1
Otherwise Almedha, q.v.

ELFEDA (ETHELFLEDA, EDILFLEDA, ELGIVA) (St) Abs. OSB.
AC. Feb 8
d. 714. Daughter of Oswy, king of Northumbria. She was offered to God as a tiny child at the nunnery of Hartlepool under St Hilda, with whom she migrated to Whitby and whom she succeeded as abbess there. She was one of the most influential personages of her time and was instrumental in reconciling SS Theodore and Wilfrid.

ELFLEDA (St) N. OSB. AC. Oct 23
d. *c*.936. An Anglo-Saxon princess who lived as a recluse at Glastonbury under the obedience of the abbey. She was held in great veneration by St Dunstan.

ELFLEDA (St) Abs. OSB.
AC. Oct 29
d. *c*.1000. Daughter of Earl Ethelwold, founder of Ramsey, where she became a nun and eventually abbess.

ELFRIC (St) Bp. OSB. AC. Nov 16
Otherwise Alfrick, q.v.

ELGAR (St) H.   AC. June 14
d. *c*.1100. Born in Devonshire. After some years of captivity in Ireland, he settled as a hermit in the isle of Bardsey off the coast of Carnarvon.

ELGIVA (St) W. OSB. AC. May 18
d. 971. The mother of Kings Edwy and Edgar, and wife of King Edmund. On the death of her husband she retired to the nunnery at Shaftesbury where she ended her days.

ELIAN (EILAN, ALLAN) (St) H.
AC. Jan 13
6th cent. A Cornish or Breton saint of the family of St Ismael. He has given his name to Llanelian in Anglesey and Llanelian in Denbighshire and was titular of St Allen's church in Cornwall. His name is often confused with that of St Hilary.

ELIAN ap ERBIN (St) C.
AC. Jan 13
? 5th cent. This name appears in some Welsh calendars.

ELIAS, JEREMIAS, ISAIAS, SAMUEL and DANIEL (SS) MM.
RM. Feb 16
d. 309. Five Egyptians who on their return journey from visiting some of their fellow-Christians, condemned to the mines of Cilicia, were themselves arrested at Caesarea in Palestine and

beheaded. The graphic account of their martyrdom is given by Eusebius who at that time was living at Caesarea.

ELIAS (Bl) Ab. OSB.   AC. Apr 16
d. 1042. An Irishman who became monk and abbot (1020) of the Scottish abbey of St Martin the Great at Cologne. The archbishop placed also under his care the abbey of St Pantaleon.

ELIAS, PAUL and ISIDORE (SS) MM.   RM. Apr 17
d. 856. Elias, a priest of Cordova, was put to death by the Moors in his old age together with SS Paul and Isidore, two young men under his spiritual direction. St Eulogius, an eye-witness, has left us an account of their martyrdom.

ELIAS of BOURDEILLES (Bl) Bp. OFM.   PC. July 5
1407–1484. Born in Périgord, of the family of the counts of Bourdeilles, he took the Franciscan habit at the age of ten. He was successively bishop of Périgueux (1437), archbishop of Tours (1468) and cardinal (1483), being also confessor of King Louis XI. He is best known in history for his written defence of St Joan of Arc. The process of his beatification was begun in 1526, but never finished.

ELIAS (ELIJAH) (St) Prophet
RM. July 20
9th cent. B.C. The great prophet of the Old Law, the account of whose eventful life is given in III and IV Kings. His association with Mt Carmel is also to be found there. The Carmelite Order liturgically commemorates this great prophet as its principal patron saint.

ELIAS of JERUSALEM (St) Bp.
RM. July 20
See Flavian and Elias.

ELIAS (St) Bp. OSB.   AC. Aug 26
d. 660. A Benedictine monk of Sicily, who died bishop of Syracuse.

ELIAS (St) Bp. M.   RM. Sept 19
See Peleus, Nilus, etc.

ELIGIUS (ELOI, ELOY) (St) Bp.
RM. Dec 1
588–660. A native of Limoges, he became a very skilful metal-smith, and was appointed master of the mint at Paris under King Clotaire II. In 640 he abandoned this office to become a priest and soon after was consecrated bishop of Noyon. He evangelized the districts round Antwerp, Ghent and Courtrai, founded Solignac Abbey and many other monasteries and convents. He was one of the most lovable of saints and most "popular" throughout the Middle Ages.

ELILANTIUS (Bl or St) OSB.
AC. July 10
See Lantfrid, Waltram, etc.

ELINED (St) VM.   AC. Aug 1
Otherwise Almedha, q.v. The name is also written Ellyw, and the saint is probably the one whose memory is perpetuated in the Welsh place-names of Llanelly and Llanelieu, besides perhaps the Breton Lanhelen.

ELIPHIUS (ELOFF) (St) M.
RM. Oct 16
d. 362. An Irishman—or Scot—by birth, who suffered at Toul in France under Julian the Apostate. His relics were translated in the 10th century to Cologne.

ELISABETH ANNE BAYLEY SETON (Bl) W. Foundress
AC. Jan 4
1774–1821. She was born in New York and grew up as a devout Episcopalian until her thirty-first year when, widowed

by the death of her husband Wm. Magee Seton and with full responsibility for her five children she was reconciled to the Church in 1805 and was confirmed in 1806 by Bishop John Carroll of Baltimore. She is the foundress of the first American Sisterhood, the Sisters of Charity of St Joseph, and is considered by some as the initiator of the American parochial school system. Beatified in 1963.

ELISABETH BARTHOLOMEA PICENARDI (Bl) V. OSM.
AC. Feb 20
1428–1468. Born at Mantua in Italy. After her mother's death she joined the third order of the Servites. Several young girls of the noble families of Mantua banded themselves together to live in community under her direction. Beatified in 1804.

ELISABETH SALVIATI (Bl) Abs. OSB. Cam.
AC. Feb 11
d. 1519. Camaldolese nun and abbess of the convent of San Giovanni Evangelista at Boldrone. Pope Urban VIII allowed pictures of her with the title of *beata* underneath to be printed in Rome.

ELISABETH of HUNGARY, the Younger (St) V. OP.
AC. May 6
d. 1338. Daughter of King Andrew III of Hungary. She refused to marry Wenceslaus, the son of the King of Bohemia, and became a Dominican nun. She died in the Swiss convent at Töss, the last of the Dynasty of St Stephen.

ELISABETH of PORTUGAL (St) Queen, Tert. OFM.
RM. July 8
1271–1336. Born in Aragon, Spain, Isabel was the daughter of King Peter ? II of that kingdom, and was married at twelve years of age to the dissolute and selfish King Denis of Portugal. She distinguished herself as a peace-

maker between the kings of Portugal, Castile and Aragon. After the death of her husband she retired to a Poor Clare convent as a tertiary. She was canonized in 1625.

ELISABETH of SCHÖNAU (St) Abs. OSB.
RM. June 18
1126–1164. At the age of twelve she entered the Black Benedictine—not the Cistercian—convent of Schönau, about sixteen miles N.E. of Bonn. She was professed in 1147, and shortly after she became subject to extraordinary supernatural manifestations. In 1157 she was made abbess of Schönau. Her brother Egbert, who governed the Benedictine monks at the same place, wrote her life.

ELISABETH BICHIER des AGES (Bl) V. Foundress
AC. Aug 26
1773–1832. Of noble rank, she was born in the diocese of Bourges. After the French Revolution she entrusted herself to the guidance of St Andrew Fournet (q.v.), and in spite of grave difficulties at the outset founded the Congregation of the Daughters of the Cross for teaching and service in hospitals. She died at Le Pay, Poitiers. Beatified in 1947.

ELISABETH (St) W.
RM. Nov 5
1st cent. The mother of St John the Baptist. All that we know about her is limited to what we find in the first chapter of St Luke's Gospel.

ELISABETH of HUNGARY (St) Queen, Tert. OFM.
RM. Nov 19
1207–1231. Born at Presburg, the daughter of King Andrew II of Hungary and a niece of St Hedwig. At the age of fourteen she was married to Louis IV, landgrave of Thuringia, and bore him three children. Hers was a very happy married life until 1227 when her husband went to the crusade and died at

Otranto. She now became a Franciscan tertiary and devoted herself to the relief of the destitute, living a life of voluntary poverty until her death at twenty-four. She was canonized three years later (1235).

ELISABETH the GOOD (Bl) V. Tert. OFM.   AC. Nov 25

1386–1420. Born at Waldsee in Würtemberg, she lived her whole life in a small community of Franciscan tertiaries close by. She was subject to mystical experiences including the stigmata, and went for long periods without any natural food. Cult confirmed in 1766.

ELISABETH-ROSE (St) Abs. OSB. AC. Dec 13

d. 1130. A nun of Chelles near Paris, and afterwards abbess-foundress of the nunnery of Sainte-Marie-du-Rozoy, near Courtenay, Loiret.

ELISEUS (ELISHA) (St) Prophet RM. June 14

8th cent. B.C. The holy man on whom fell the mantle of Elias, and who continued the work of that great prophet, as is described in IV Kings. The feast of St Eliseus is liturgically observed in the Carmelite Order, and also generally in the East.

ELLEHER (St) M. OSB. RM. June 5

See Waccar, Gundekar, etc.

ELLIDIUS (ILLOG) (St) C. AC. Aug 8

7th cent. Patron saint, it would appear, of Hirnant (Montgomery), and of a church in the Scilly Isles.

ELLYN (St) VM.   AC. Aug 1

Otherwise Almedha, q.v.

ELMO (Bl) C.   AC. Apr 15

Otherwise Peter Gonzales, q.v. But the name Elmo usually stands for an abbreviation of that of St Erasmus (June 2).

ELOFF (ELOPHIUS) M. RM. Oct 16

Otherwise Eliphius, q.v.

ELOI (St) Bp.   RM. Dec 1

Otherwise Eligius, q.v.

ELOQUIUS (ELOQUE) (St) Ab. OSB.   AC. Dec 3

d. p.665. Disciple and successor of St Fursey as abbot of Lagny (*Latiniacensis*).

ELPHEGE the ELDER (St) Bp. OSB.   AC. March 12

d. 951. Also surnamed "the Bald", probably on account of his monastic tonsure. From being a monk he was raised to the see of Winchester (935). He induced many to become monks, notably his young kinsman St Dunstan, whom he ordained priest. St Ethelwold too received the priesthood from St Elphege.

ELPHEGE the MARTYR (St) Bp. OSB.   RM. Apr 19

954–1012. A Benedictine of Deerhurst abbey in Gloucestershire, then abbot of a monastery near Bath, he was raised to the see of Winchester in 984, and to that of Canterbury in 1006. He was greatly loved by his flock, and during the Danish invasion of 1011 he was urged to escape. He declined, and was taken prisoner and put to death at Greenwich for refusing to ransom himself with the money of the poor.

ELPIDEPHORUS (St) M. RM. Nov 2

See Acindynus, Pegasius, etc.

ELPIDIUS (St) Bp. M. RM. March 4

See Basil, Eugene, etc.

ELPIDIUS (St) M.   RM. Sept 1

See Priscus, Castrensis, etc.

ELPIDIUS (St) Ab.   RM. Sept 2
4th cent. A hermit in Cappadocia who lived for twenty-five years in a cave and gathered round him numerous disciples. His relics were brought to a village in the Marches of Ancona, now called Sant' Elpidio. His emblem in art is a vine in leaf in winter.

ELPIDIUS (St) Bp.   RM. Sept 2
d. 422. The successor of St Antiochus in the see of Lyons. His relics were enshrined in the church of St Justus.

ELPIDIUS, MARCELLUS, EUSTOCHIUS, and Comp. (SS) MM.   RM. Nov 16
d. 362. Elpidius, a dignitary at the court of the emperor Constantius, was degraded by Julian the Apostate and, with several companions, dragged at the tail of wild horses. Finally they were burnt at the stake.

ELPIS (St) VM.   RM. Aug 1
See Faith, Hope (Elpis) and Charity.

ELRIC (St) Bp.   AC. Jan 7
Otherwise Aldericus, q.v.

ELSIAR (St) Mk. OSB.   AC. June 4
d. c.1050. A Benedictine of the abbey of Saint-Savin in Lavedan.

ELSTAN (St) Bp. OSB.   AC. Apr 6
d. 981. Monk of Abingdon under St Ethelwold, celebrated as a model of blind obedience. He succeeded St Ethelwold both as abbot of Abingdon and bishop of Winchester.

ELVAN and MYDWYN (SS)   AC. Jan 1
2nd cent. Said to have been the two Britons sent by King St Lucius to Pope St Eleutherius to beg for missionaries to be sent to Britain (see St Eleutherius, pope).

ELVIS (St) C.   AC. Feb 22
Otherwise Elwyn, or Alleyn, or Allan, or Elian. See below under Elwin.

ELWIN (St) C.   AC. Feb 22
6th cent. Said to have been one of the holy men who accompanied St Breaca from Ireland to Cornwall, and perhaps the title saint of St Allen's church in that country. But the traditions are very perplexing.

ELZEAR (ELEAZARUS) (St) C. Tert. OFM.   RM. Sept 27
1285–1323. A native of Provence, where he inherited the barony of Ansuis as well as the county of Ariano in the kingdom of Naples. Married to St Delphina of Glandèves, he was the perfect type of Christian gentleman. He went to Naples as tutor to Prince Charles and as ambassador, and was for a time regent of the kingdom. According to an old tradition both he and his wife, St Delphine (q.v.), were Franciscan tertiaries.

EMEBERT (ABLEBERT) (St) Bp.   AC. Jan 15
d. c.710. Said to have been a brother of SS Reineldis and Gudula. He was bishop of Cambrai in Flanders.

EMERENTIANA (St) VM.   RM. Jan 23
d. 304? According to legend, Emerentiana, the foster-sister of St Agnes, while as yet only a catechumen, was discovered by the pagan mob praying at the tomb of the recently martyred St Agnes, and was stoned to death. In point of fact St Emerentiana is a Roman martyr of unknown date. Her cult is very ancient.

EMERIC (Bl) Bp.   AC. Aug 1
d. 1318. Bishop of Aosta (1301–1318). Cult approved in 1881.

EMERIC (St) C.   RM. Nov 4
1007–1031. Son of St Stephen, the first
Christian king of Hungary. He was educated by St Gerard Sagredo of Czanad
and gave promise of being a model
king, but died before inheriting the
crown. He was canonized with his father
in 1083.

EMERITA (St) VM.   RM. Sept 22
See Digna and Emerita.

EMERITUS (St) M.   RM. Feb 11
See Saturninus, Dativus, etc.

EMERIUS (St) Ab. OSB.
                          AC. Jan 27
8th cent. A Frenchman by birth, he
founded, and ruled as first abbot, the
Benedictine abbey of St Stephen of
Bañoles, near Gerona, in Spanish Catalonia.

EMETERIUS (St) M. RM. March 3
Otherwise Hemiterius, q.v.

EMIDIUS (St) Bp. M.   RM. Aug 5
Otherwise Emygdius, q.v.

EMILAS and JEREMIAS (SS) MM.
                          RM. Sept 15
d. 852. Two Spanish youths, of whom
the former was a deacon, imprisoned
and beheaded at Cordova under the
caliph Abderrahman.

EMILIAN (AEMILIO) (St) Mk.
OSB.   AC. Jan 7
d. 767. A native of Vannes, and a monk
of Saujon, near Saintes, he died as a
recluse in the forest of Combes,
Bordeaux.

EMILIAN (St) M.   RM. Feb 8
See Dionysius and Emilian.

EMILIAN (St) M.   AC. Feb 9
See Ammon, Emlian, etc.

EMILIAN (or EMINIAN) (St) Ab.
OSB.   AC. March 10
d. 675. An Irishman, who became a
monk, and then abbot, of Lagny in
France.

EMILIAN (St) M.   RM. Apr 29
See Agapius and Comp.

EMILIAN (St) M.   RM. July 18
d. 362. A martyr of Silistria in Bulgaria
under Julian the Apostate.

EMILIAN (St) Bp.   RM. Aug 8
d. c.820. A bishop of Cyzicus, an island
off the southern shore of the sea of
Marmora. He died in exile for his firm
stand against the Iconoclasts.

EMILIAN (St) Bp.   RM. Sept 11
d. 520. A N. Italian hermit, who after
forty years as a recluse, was raised to the
see of Vercelli in Piedmont, where he
died a centenarian.

EMILIAN (St) C.   RM. Oct 11
? According to the RM. he was a hermit
at Rennes in Brittany. No saint of this
name can be found in the Breton
records. Possibly he has been confused
with St Melanius, bishop of Rennes
(d. 567).

EMILIAN (St) Ab.   RM. Nov 12
d. 574. A poor shepherd in La Rioja, in
the old kingdom of Spanish Navarre.
He became a hermit and eventually was
ordained priest by his bishop (of Tarazona) who put him in charge of the
parish of Berceo. The saint, however,
returned to his solitude and there gradually he gathered round him a large
number of disciples of whom he became
the abbot. This gave rise to the great
abbey of La Cogolla, which afterwards
adopted the Benedictine Rule. On this
account the saint is described to this
day in the "Spanish proper" of his

office as the first Spanish Benedictine. He is a minor patron saint of Spain, where he is known as San Millan de la Cogolla—the cowled St Emilian. In art he is usually represented on horseback fighting the Moors.

EMILIAN (St) M.   RM. Dec 6
See Dionysia, Dativa, etc.

EMILIANA (St) V.   RM. Jan 5
6th cent. A Roman lady, and the paternal aunt of St Gregory the Great, from whom we know of her saintly life, visions and death.

EMILIANA (St) M.   RM. June 30
? She is stated to have been a Roman maiden who died a martyr.

EMILIUS (St) M.   RM. May 22
See Castus and Emilius.

EMILIUS, FELIX, PRIAM and LUCIAN (SS) MM.   RM. May 28
? Churches are dedicated to these saints in Sardinia; otherwise nothing is known concerning them.

EMILIUS (St) M.   RM. Oct 6
See Marcellus, Castus, etc.

EMILY BICCHIERI (Bl) V. OP.   AC. Aug 19
1238–1314. A native of Vercelli, who induced her father to build a convent, where she professed the Dominican rule. She was a great success as the first prioress of the convent. Cult confirmed in 1769.

EMILY de VIALAR (St) V. Foundress   AC. Aug 24
1797–1856. Born at Gaillace, in the diocese of Albi, S. France, she was early bereaved of her mother, and while giving herself to prayer and works of charity, managed her father's house until she was thirty-five. Then, on

receiving a large legacy, she decided to devote herself to the foundation of a religious institute, viz., the Sisters of St Joseph of the Apparation (i.e. the apparition of the Angel Gabriel to St Joseph). Great trials befell her, and, losing both her money and her reputation in the diocese of Albi, she established the mother-house at Marseilles. When she died there in 1856, she left behind her houses of the Institute in Europe, Africa and Asia. Canonized in 1951.

EMILY de RODAT (St) Foundress   AC. Sept 19
1787–1852. A native of Château Druelles, near Rodez, in southern central France. In 1816, under the direction of Mgr Marty, later vicar general of Rodez, she started a new teaching institute which has since developed into the present-day Religious Congregation of the Holy Family of Villefranche with houses throughout the world. Canonized in 1950.

EMMA (several)
Otherwise Hemma, q.v.

EMMANUEL (several)
Note. A popular name in the Latin countries: Emmanuele in Italian; Manuel in Spanish, Portuguese and Catalan.

EMMANUEL D'ABREU (Bl) M. SJ.   AC. Jan 12
1708–1737. A Portuguese born at Arouca, he entered the Jesuit Order in 1724 and was sent to China; arrested at Tonkin in 1736, he was martyred in 1737 with three companions.

EMMANUEL (Bl) Bp. AC. Feb 27
d. 1198. Bishop of Cremona (1190–1195). Some writers make him a Cistercian monk of Adwerth, in Frisia, before his episcopate; but Adwerth was only founded in 1192. In 1195 Bl

Emmanuel indeed retired to Adwerth, where he died, possibly in the Cistercian habit.

EMMANUEL (St) M. RM. March 26
See Quadratus, Theodosius, etc.

EMMANUEL RUIZ and Comp. (BB) MM. AC. July 10
d. 1860. During the rising of the Druses against the Christians in the Lebanon, the Franciscan community of Damascus, eight in all, and three Maronite laymen, were offered the alternative of accepting Islam or death; they refused the former and were slain in their own friary. The guardian of the friary was Bl Emmanuel Ruiz, a Spaniard, and most of the other Friars were likewise Spaniards. Beatified in 1926.

EMMANUEL ALVAREZ (Bl) M. SJ. AC. July 15
d. 1570. A Jesuit lay-brother, companion of Bl Ignatius de Azevedo, q.v.

EMMANUEL FERNÁNDEZ (Bl) M. SJ. AC. July 15
d. 1570. A native of Celorico, diocese of Cuarda, Portugal, and a Jesuit cleric, companion of Bl Ignatius de Azevedo, q.v.

EMMANUEL PACHECO (Bl) M. SJ. AC. July 15
d. 1570. A native of Zeita, in Portugal, and a Jesuit novice, companion of Bl Ignatius de Azevedo, q.v.

EMMANUEL RODRÍGUEZ (Bl) M. SJ. AC. July 15
d. 1570. A native of Alconchel, Portugal, and a Jesuit cleric, companion of Bl Ignatius de Azevedo, q.v.

EMMANUEL PHUNG (Bl) M. AC. July 31
c.1796–1859. Born at Dan-nuoc, in Cochin China, he worked as a catechist, and was for this reason garrotted near Chaudoc, in W. Cochin China. Beatified in 1909.

EMMANUEL TRIEU (Bl) M. AC. Sept 17
c.1756–1798. Born in Cochin China of Christian parents, he joined the army, but was afterwards ordained priest at Pong-King and worked under the priests of the Foreign Missions of Paris. While visiting his mother he was arrested and beheaded. Beatified in 1900.

EMMELIA (St) Matron RM. May 30
See Basil and Emmelia.

EMMERAMUS (HAIMHRAMM) (St) Bp. M. OSB. RM. Sept 22
d. c.690. A native of Poitiers, he migrated to Bavaria where he became abbot of a monastery at Ratisbon, and then bishop of that city. While on his way to Rome he was attacked by assassins, and died from the injuries received. His relics were enshrined in the great Benedictine abbey dedicated to his name at Ratisbon, where he is venerated as a martyr.

EMYGDIUS (EMIDIUS) (St) Bp. M. RM. Aug 5
d. c.303. His relics are kept at Ascoli, whither they were transported between 996 and 1052. His legend is historically worthless.

ENCRATIA (ENCRATIS, ENCRATIDE, ENGRACIA) (St) VM. RM. Apr 16
d. ? 304. A Spanish maiden who suffered at Saragossa, where the church now stands dedicated in her name. She is famous for "her ardour in suffering for Christ". Though counted a martyr, she apparently outlived her torments.

ENDA (ENDEUS, ENNA) (St) Ab. AC. March 21
d. c.590. Brother of St Fanchea and

founder of many monasteries, of which the principal was on Arranmore. SS Kieran and Brendan, among others, were his disciples.

ENECO (ENNECO, Spanish: IÑIGO) (St) Ab. OSB.   RM. June 1
d. 1057. Born at Calatayud, and a monk of San Juan de la Peña, in Aragon, where the Cluniac observance had been just then introduced. After much entreaty, King Sancho the Great of Navarre induced him to accept the abbacy of Oña in Old Castile. Under Iñigo's rule the abbey rose to great splendour, and on his death he was much lamented by Christians, Jews and Saracens alike. Canonized in 1259.

ENGELBERT (St) Ab.   AC. Feb 18
Otherwise Angilbert, q.v.

ENGELBERT (St) Bp. M. RM. Nov 7
1186–1225. A typical medieval prince-prelate. Early in his career he gained possession uncanonically of benefices, and thereby incurred excommunication. When this was lifted he became archbishop of Cologne (1216). In this position he was a great success: zealous for the discipline of his clergy, fosterer of monastic life and of learning. He was appointed tutor to the emperor's son, and chief minister of the empire. While defending the rights of a nunnery he was killed by hired assassins, and hence he is venerated as a martyr.

ENGELMER (St) M.   PC. May 14
d. 1096. The son of a poor Bavarian labourer, he became a hermit near Passau, and was murdered by a visitor who hoped to find his treasure.

ENGELMUND (St) Ab. OSB.
                                AC. June 21
d. c.739. An Englishman by birth and education, he received the Benedictine habit at a very early age, and became priest and abbot. He crossed over to Friesland, where he worked most successfully under St Willibrord, at Velsen, six miles north of Haarlem.

ENGHENEDL (St)   AC. Sept 30
7th cent. A Welsh saint to whom a church in Anglesey was dedicated. Nothing is now known about his life.

ENGLAND (Martyrs of) (BB)
                                AC. May 4
1535–1681. British-born Catholics, put to death by Protestants between the two dates given above. They are about six hundred in number. Fifty-four were beatified by Leo XIII in 1886, nine in 1895, and one hundred and thirty-seven by Pius XI in 1929: their common feast is held on May 4. The causes of over a hundred others are now being officially examined in Rome; there are still two hundred and eighty-four whose claim to martyrdom has not yet been considered by the Church. Each of these martyrs who has already been officially acknowledged as Saint or Blessed, receives a separate notice in this book.

ENGLATIUS (ENGLAT, TANG-LEN) (St) Bp.   AC. Nov 3
d. 966. A Scottish saint, said by some to have been a bishop, who lived at Tarves in Aberdeenshire.

ENGRATIA (St) H.   AC. Oct 25
See Fructus, Valentine and Engratia.

ENGUERRAMMUS (ANGILRAM) (Bl) Ab. OSB.   PC. Dec 9
d. 1045. Of a humble family, he was educated at the abbey of Saint-Riquier (*Centula*), where eventually he became a monk and abbot (1022). By his contemporaries he was surnamed "the Wise" or "the learned Abbot". He was a very fluent Latin verse-writer.

ENNATHA (St) VM.   RM. Nov 13
See Antoninus, Zebinas, etc.

ENNODIUS (St) Bp.   RM. July 17
473–521. Magnus Felix Ennodius was a
Gallo-Roman by birth and a professor
of rhetoric, who, after his conversion,
became (c.514) bishop of Pavia in Lombardy. The pope entrusted him with
two missions to Byzantium in connection with the Eutychian controversy.
He is now best remembered as a Christian poet, whose writings, chiefly
hymns, are full of interest.

ENOCH (St) V.   AC. March 25
Otherwise Kennocha, q.v.

**ENODER (CYNIDR or KENEDER)
(St) Ab.   AC. Apr 27**
6th cent. A grandson of the Welsh chieftain Brychan. Llangynidr in Brecknockshire perpetuates his memory, as
also possibly St Enoder or Enodoc in
Cornwall. Very likely he is to be identified with St Enodoch, q.v. In Breton he
is called St Quidic.

**ENODOCH (WENEDOC) (St)
                          AC. March 7**
d. c.520. A Welsh saint of the Brychan
race. Some writers identify him with St
Enoder, q.v., others state that she was a
daughter—instead of a son—of Brychan and call her St Qwendydd. The
traditions are very confused.

ENOGATUS (St) Bp   AC. Jan 13
d. 631. The fifth successor of St Malo
in the see of Aleth in Brittany.

EOBAN (St) M. OSB.   RM. June 5
d. 755. A Benedictine monk-priest said
to have been of Irish descent, who
worked under SS Willibrord and Boniface in the German mission and shared
in the latter's martyrdom.

EOCHOD (St)   AC. Jan 25
d. 597. One of St Columba's twelve
companions, and chosen by him to
evangelize N. Britain. He is called the
apostle of the Picts of Galloway.

EOGAN (St) Bp.   AC. Aug 23
Otherwise Eugene, q.v.

EPAGATHUS (St) M.   RM. June 2
See Photinus (Pothinus), Sanctus, etc.

EPAPHRAS (St) Bp. M. RM. July 19
1st cent. "The most beloved fellow-
servant" of St Paul (Col I, 7). He is
traditionally said to have been bishop of
Colossae and to have suffered martyrdom there. But beyond what we read in
the New Testament (Col I, 7; IV, 12
and Philem 23) we know nothing of his
life.

**EPAPHRODITUS (St) Bp.
                      RM. March 22**
1st cent. St Paul mentions him as an
apostle sent to the Philippians (Phil II,
25). Hence, St Epaphroditus is reputed
first bishop of Philippi in Macedonia.
Two saints of the same name are listed
in ancient catalogues: one as the first
bishop of Andriacia in Lycia, and another as the first bishop of Terracina in
Italy. The three are said to have been
among the seventy-two disciples of
Christ. Very likely they are the same
person, with different local veneration.

EPARCHIUS (St) Bp. RM. March 23
See Domitius, Pelagia, etc.

**EPARCHIUS (French: CYBAR) (St)
AB.   RM. July 1**
504–581. Born duke of Périgord in
France, he renounced his title to become a monk of Sessac. After his ordination to the priesthood he was
"walled-up" at Angoulême (542) where
he lived for the rest of his life, directing

a community who established themselves in the neighbourhood for that purpose.

EPHEBUS (St) M.   RM. Feb 14
See Proculus, Ephebus and Apollonius.

EPHESUS (Martyrs of) (SS)
                                   RM. Jan 12
d. *c*.762. Forty-two monks of a monastery at Ephesus, put to death by the emperor Constantine Copronymus for their firm stand against the Iconoclasts. This entry was made by Baronius, but his source is uncertain. See Stephen, Basil, etc. (Nov 28); in their Acts is mention of thirty-eight martyr monks.

EPHREM (St) Bp. M.   RM. March 4
See Basil, Eugene, etc.

EPHREM the SYRIAN (St) Dr.
                                   RM. June 18
c.300–379. Surnamed also "the Deacon" and "the Harp of the Holy Ghost." He was a native of Nisibis in Mesopotamia and very likely the head of the catechetical school of that city before it was captured by the Persians. Afterwards he became a monk near Edessa and a deacon. Here he spent most of his long life writing copious commentaries on the Bible and composing hymns. He wrote the hymns in his native Syriac so that his people could make use of them and thus retain their Catholic faith and keep free from Arianism. He excelled in his Mariological hymns, which are an important contribution to Catholic dogma. In the terrible famine which raged throughout Mesopotamia a few years before St Ephrem's death the saint was the leader in organizing relief and help for the sick. He died in his monastic cell, revered both in the East and in the West. Benedict XV officially declared him a Doctor of the Church in 1920.

EPHYSIUS (St) M.   RM. Jan 15
d. 303. A martyr said to have been put to death in Sardinia under Diocletian. He is still greatly venerated in the island.

EPICHARIS (St) M.   RM. Sept 27
d. *c*.300. She is said to have been the wife of a Roman senator and to have been martyred at New Rome (Byzantium) under Diocletian.

EPICTETUS, JUCUNDUS, SE-CUNDUS, VITALIS, FELIX and Comp. (SS) MM.   RM. Jan 9
d. ? 250. Twelve African martyrs probably of the Decian persecution. Epictetus was a bishop mentioned by St Cyprian.

EPICTETUS (St) M.   RM. Aug 22
See Martial, Saturninus, etc.

EPIGMENIUS (St) M. RM. March 24
d. *c*.300. A Roman priest martyred under Diocletian. Possibly to be identified with St Pigmenius (q.v.).

EPIMACHUS (St) M.   RM. May 10
d. 250. A native of Alexandria in Egypt, burnt there at the stake under Decius. He is commemorated also on Dec. 12, with his fellow-sufferer St Alexander.

EPIPHANA (St) M.   RM. July 12
? She is mentioned in the Acts of St Alphius, which are wholly unreliable. Nothing really is known about her.

EPIPHANES and ISIDORE (SS) MM.   AC. Aug 4
? Two martyrs, venerated at the Cathedral of Besançon up to the French Revolution. Nothing is known of them.

EPIPHANIA (St) N. OSB. AC. Oct 6
d. *c*.800. A Benedictine nun in the convent of Santa Maria della-Caccia—*Sancta Maria Venationum*—at Pavia in

Lombardy. An old tradition adds that she was a daughter of King Ratchis, who himself became a monk at Monte-cassino.

EPIPHANIUS (St) Bp.   RM. Jan 21
439–497. Born at Pavia, and elected bishop of that city in 467. During his episcopate Odoacer destroyed Pavia, and Epiphanius was largely responsible for the rebuilding of the city. In order to ransom some of his flock who were held captive he travelled to Burgundy and so contracted the fever of which he died.

EPIPHANIUS, DONATUS, RUFI-NUS and Comp. (SS) MM.
RM. Apr 7
The RM. reproduces the names from the martyrology of Usuard, who introduced that of Rufinus. There were thirteen fellow-martyrs, but we have no details, except that Epiphanius was an African bishop.

EPIPHANIUS of SALAMIS (St) Bp-
RM. May 12
c.310–403. A native of Palestine, and a monk from his earliest youth. He became abbot at Eleutheropolis, where he wrote and preached against all heretics, but chiefly against Arianism in imperial circles. He was acclaimed "the oracle of Palestine". In 367 he was raised to the see of Salamis in Cyprus, where he continued his vehement defence of orthodoxy. In his old age he acted occasionally in a very headstrong way. His writings were his most important contribution to the Catholic cause.

EPIPODIUS and ALEXANDER (SS)
MM.   RM. Apr 22
d. 178. Two young friends, citizens of Lyons, put to death under Marcus Aurelius. St Epipodius was decapitated; for Alexander, see Alexander and Comp.

EPISTEMIS (St) M.   RM. Nov 5
See Galation and Epistemis.

EPITACIUS and BASILEUS (SS)
MM.   RM. May 23
1st cent. The former is said to have been first bishop of Tuy in Spanish Galicia, and the latter first bishop of Braga in present-day Portugal—both in the apostolic age.

EPOLONIUS (St) M.   RM. Jan 24
See Babilas, Urban, etc.

EPPO (Bl) Ab. OSB.   AC. June 27
d. 1143. Monk, and second abbot (1122) of Mallersdorf in Bavaria.

EPVRE (EURE) (St) Bp. RM. Sept 15
Otherwise Aprus, q.v.

EQUITIUS (St) Ab.   RM. Aug 11
d. c.540. A contemporary of St Benedict, and the founder of a number of monasteries in the province of Valeria (a district east of Rome). St Gregory the Great gives all we know about him in the first book of his Dialogues.

ERASMA (St) VM.   RM. Sept 3
See Euphemia, Dorothy, etc.

ERASMUS (ELMO, ERARMO,
ERMO) (St) Bp. M.   RM. June 2
d. 303. Stripped of all the later legendary additions our knowledge of this saint is reduced to the fact that he was a bishop of Formiae in Campania, martyred under Diocletian, and that his relics were transferred to Gaeta in 842. The legend of his "Acts" made him patron of sailors and one of the Fourteen Holy Helpers (q.v.), greatly revered throughout Europe in the Middle Ages.

ERASMUS (St) M.   RM. Nov 25
? A Syrian, martyred at Antioch. It is

probable that he is a duplicate of St Erasmus of June 2.

ERASTUS (St) Bp. M. RM. July 26
1st cent. The treasurer of the city of Corinth (Rom XVI, 23) converted by St Paul, and one of his helpers in the apostolate (Acts XIX, 22), especially at Corinth (II Tim IV, 20). The Greek tradition is that he became bishop of Philippi Paneas in Palestine: that of the Latins is that his see was Philippi in Macedonia and that he was a martyr.

ERBIN (ERVAN, ERBYN, ERME or HERMES)　　　　　　　AC. Jan 13
? 5th cent. A Cornish saint who seems to have been related to one of the Cornish or Devonshire chieftains. Churches were dedicated to him in Cornwall.

ERBO (Bl) Ab. OSB.　　AC. Aug 27
d. 1162. A disciple of St Theoger and a monk under him at St George's in the Black Forest. In 1121 he was chosen by St Otto, bishop of Bamberg, to succeed St Erminold in the abbacy of Prüfening, which he governed for forty years, the observance being that of Cluny-Hirschau.

ERCONGOTHA (St) V. OSB.
**　　　　　　　　　　AC. July 7**
d. 660. Daughter of King Ercombert of Kent and of St Sexburga. She was a nun at Farmoutier under her aunt, St Etheburga.

ERCONWALD (ERKENWALD) (St) Bp. OSB.　　RM. Apr 30
d. c.686. An East-Anglian of royal blood. He retired to the kingdom of the East Saxons where he founded two houses—Chertsey abbey, in Surrey, for men; and Barking nunnery, in Essex, for women. He became the abbot of the former and his sister St Ethelburga the abbess of the latter. In 675 he was chosen bishop of London by St Theodore.

EREMBERT (St) Bp. OSB.
**　　　　　　　　　　AC. May 14**
d. c.672. Born at Wocourt near Passy, he became a Benedictine at Fontenelle (c.640) and bishop of Toulouse (c.656) which he ruled for twelve years. In his old age he resigned and went back to die at Fontenelle.

EREMBERT I (Bl) AB. OSB.
**　　　　　　　　　　AC. Jan 24**
d. p.1050. Abbot of Kremsmünster, in Austria, to which office he was elected in 1050.

EREMBERTA (St) Abs. OSB.
**　　　　　　　　　　PC. Oct 16**
Late 7th cent. Niece of St Wulmar, and first abbess of the nunnery of Wierre, which he built for her.

ERENTRUDIS (ERMENTRUDE) (St) Abs. OSB.　　AC. June 30
d. c.718. A sister—or niece—of St Rupert, the apostle of Salzburg. She was the first abbess of Nonnberg in Salzburg, a nunnery founded for her by Rupert.

ERFYL (EURFYL) (St) V. AC. July 5
? A British maiden, foundress of the church of Llanerfyl, Montgomeryshire.

ERGNAD (ERCNACTA) (St) V.
**　　　　　　　　　　AC. Jan 8**
5th cent. A native of Ulster who is said to have received the veil from St Patrick.

ERGOULE (St) V.　　AC. Jan 8
Otherwise Gudula, q.v.

ERHARD (St) Bp.　　RM. Jan 8
d. c.686. He is described as an Irishman, who passed over to the Continent and laboured as a missionary bishop in Bavaria, chiefly in and around Ratisbon. His cult has always been very flourishing at Ratisbon.

ERIC (HENRY) (Bl) C.
AC. March 13
d. 1415. The son of the King of Scandinavia, he inherited the crown on the death of his father, but fled into solitude to lead a life of penance. He went on pilgrimage to Rome and died at Perugia, where he is venerated.

ERIC (HENRY) (St) King, M.
RM. May 18
d. 1160. Eric IX became king of Sweden in 1150 and at once began to exert all his influence to spread the gospel throughout the country. He codified the laws of his kingdom in the same spirit, and is for this reason called "the Lawgiver." He also laboured for the conversion of the heathen Finns. He was murdered as he was leaving a church after hearing Mass.

ERIZZO (Bl) Ab. OSB. Vall.
AC. Feb 9
d. 1094. A native of Florence, and the first disciple of St John Gualbert. At a later period he became the fourth general of the Vallumbrosans. Cult confirmed in 1600.

ERKEMBODEN (St) Bp. OSB.
AC. Apr 12
d. 714. A monk of Sithin at Saint-Omer, who succeeded the founder, St Bertinus, as abbot, and then became bishop of Thérouanne, continuing to rule the abbey. He was bishop for twenty-six years.

ERLAFRID (St) Ab. OSB. AC. Nov 6
d. p.830. Count of Calw in Swabia. Founder of Hirschau Abbey, where he became a monk.

ERLUPH (St) Bp. M.   AC. Feb 10
d. 830. A Scottish missionary in Germany who later became bishop of Werden, and was martyred by pagans.

ERMEL (ARMEL, ERME) (St) Ab.
AC. Aug 16
Otherwise Armagillus, q.v.

ERMELINDA (ERMELINDIS) (St) V.
AC. Oct 29
d. c.595. A Belgian recluse who lived at Meldaert, near Tirlemont.

ERMENBURGA (St) W. OSB.
AC. Nov 19
d. ? c.650. Otherwise known as Domna Ebba (Lady Ebba), abbreviated into Domneva. She was a Kentish princess married to the king of Mercia, and the mother of SS Mildred, Milburga and Mildgytha. In her old age she founded the nunnery of Minster in Thanet, where the place-name Ebbsfleet still perpetuates her memory.

ERMENFRIDUS (St) Ab. OSB.
AC. Sept 25
d. c.670. A courtier then a monk at Luxeuil under its third abbot, St Waldebert. Later he became the abbot-founder of Cusance.

ERMENGARDIS (Bl) W. OSB. Cist.
AC. June 1
c.1067–1147. A native of Angers and wife of the duke of Brittany (1092). Before her death she received the Cistercian habit at the hands of St Bernard (c.1130).

ERMENGOL (St) Bp.   RM. Nov 3
Otherwise Hermengaudius, q.v.

ERMENGYTHA (St) V. OSB.
AC. July 30
d. c.680. A sister of St Ermenburga (Domneva). She lived under the latter's obedience as a nun at Minster in Thanet.

ERMENILDA (ERMENGILD) (St) W. OSB.
AC. Feb 13
d. 703. Daughter of King Erconbert of

Kent and of St Sexburga. She married the king of Mercia and exercised a truly Christian influence over him and the kingdom. On his death, she joined her mother at Minster in Sheppey, eventually succeeding her as abbess. She then migrated to Ely where also she became abbess.

ERMINOLD (St) M. Ab. OSB.
AC. Jan 6
d. 1121. He was offered to God at the abbey of Hirschau as a child and educated and professed there. In 1110 he was chosen abbot of Lorsch; but fearing that this appointment might have been the result of simony he resigned and returned to Hirschau. In 1114 he was chosen the first prior of Prüfening and in 1117 its first abbot. One of the lay-brothers of the community struck him with a piece of timber and caused his death. He has always been venerated as a martyr.

ERMINUS (St) Bp. OSB. RM. Apr 25
d. 737. Born at Laon. After his ordination to the priesthood he professed the Benedictine rule at Lobbes under St Urmar, who appointed him his successor both as abbot and as regionary bishop.

ERNAN (ERNIN) (*several*)
There are various Irish saints of this or a similar name. Perhaps the most notable among them is one described as a nephew of St Columba.

ERNEST (St) Ab. OSB.   PC. Nov 7
d. 1148. Benedictine abbot of Zwiefalten in Germany who joined the crusaders and preached in Persia and Arabia. He was taken prisoner and tortured to death at Mecca.

ERNEY (St)
? The patron saint of a church at Landrake in Cornwall.

EROTHEIS (St) M.   RM. Oct 27
See Capitolina and Erotheis.

EROTIS (EROTEIS) (St) M.
RM. Oct 6
4th cent. A martyr who perished at the stake. The martyrdom seems to have taken place in Greece, though by some Erotis is identified with St Erotheis of Cappadocia, who suffered with St Capitolina.

ERTH (HERYGH, URITH) (St)
AC. Oct 31
6th cent. Brother of St Uny and St Ia (Ives). He crossed from Ireland to Cornwall, where a church is dedicated in his name. He has given his name also to the village of St Erth.

ERVAN (St)   AC. May 29
Otherwise Erbin, q.v.

ERVAN (St) Ab.   AC. Aug 16
Otherwise Armagillus, q.v.

ESDRAS (EZRA) (St) Prophet.
RM. July 13
5th cent. B.C. A Jewish scribe and priest, born in Babylon during the captivity. In 459 he obtained permission to lead a group of exiles back to Jerusalem. He had the walls of the city built, and on the completion of the work concluded a solemn pact between God and the people. Two books of the Vulgate Bible bear his name (Ezra and Nehemiah in the A.V.) although he is not their author. Two others known as the third and fourth books of Esdras, are apocryphal.

ESKILL (St) Bp. M.   AC. June 12
d. c.1080. A fellow-missionary of St Sigfrid in Sweden by whom he was consecrated bishop. Both were English. St Eskill was stoned to death for protesting against a heathen festival at Strengnäss.

ESTERWINE (St) Ab. OSB.
AC. March 7

d. 688. A noble Northumbrian who spent his early years at court, and then entered the monastery of Wearmouth, where he was professed under his kinsman St Benedict Biscop, the founder of the abbey. He succeeded St Benet as abbot and ruled four years, dying before the founder. He was celebrated for his gentleness.

ETERNUS (St) Bp.   AC. July 15
d. *p*.660. The ninth bishop of Evreux in France.

ETHA (St) H. OSB.   AC. May 5
Otherwise Echa, q.v.

ETHBIN (St) Ab.   RM. Oct 19
d. *c*.600. A Briton, educated in France by St Samson. When a deacon he retired to the abbey of Taurac (554), where he remained till the dispersion of the community through a raid by the Franks (556). He then crossed over to Ireland, and there led the life of a hermit near Kildare

ETHELBERT of KENT (St) King.
RM. Feb 24

d. 616. Husband of Bertha, a Christian princess from France, he was reigning in Kent when St Augustine arrived in Thanet. Ethelbert protected the missionaries from the start, and received baptism on Whit-Sunday, 597. Though he never tried to force his subjects into Christianity, hundreds followed his example. He was the founder of the abbeys of Christ Church, and SS Peter and Paul, Canterbury, and of St Andrew's, Rochester

ETHELBERT (St) M.   AC. May 20
d. 793. King of East Anglia. He was treacherously murdered at the instigation of the wife of Offa of Mercia. He has always been venerated as a martyr.

ETHELBERT and ETHELRED (SS) MM.   AC. Oct 17
d. 670. Great-grandsons of St Ethelbert of Kent, cruelly put to death at Eastry near Sandwich. Their shrine was finally set up at Ramsey abbey in Huntingdonshire.

ETHELBURGA (St) W. OSB.
AC. Apr 5

d. *c*.647. Daughter of King St Ethelbert of Kent, she married King St Edwin of Northumbria. She went there accompanied by St Paulinus as her chaplain. After Edwin's death she returned to Kent and founded the nunnery of Lyminge where she became a nun and abbess.

ETHELBURGA (St) Abs. OSB.
RM. July 7

d. *c*.664. The daughter of Anna, king of the East Angles. She became a nun at Faremoutier, in France, where she succeeded, as abbess, the foundress herself, St Fara. She is known in France as St Aubierge.

ETHELBURGA (St) Queen.
PC. Sept 8

See Ina and Ethelburga.

ETHELBURGA (St) Abs. OSB.
AC. Oct 11

d. *c*.678. Sister of St Erconwald of London, who founded for her the nunnery of Barking in Essex. She was made abbess; but as she was quite inexperienced, St Hildelid was fetched from a French nunnery to train her. Eventually she governed alone and proved a great abbess.

ETHELDREDA (ETHELREDA, EDILTRUDIS, AUDREY) (St) Abs. OSB.   RM. June 23
d. 679. At one time the most popular of Anglo-Saxon women saints, a native of

Suffolk, she was a sister to SS Sexburga, Ethelburga and Withburga. She took the veil at Coldingham under St Ebba and then migrated to Ely where she was chosen abbess of the double monastery.

ETHELDRITHA (or ETHEL-FREDA, ALFREDA, ALTHRYDA) (St) V. OSB.   AC. Aug 2
d. 834. Daughter of King Offa of Mercia. She lived as a recluse on Croyland Island, in the desolate marshes of Lincolnshire.

ETHELDWITHA (EALSITHA) (St) W. OSB.   AC. July 20
d. 903. An Anglo-Saxon princess, wife of King Alfred. After his death she retired to a nunnery which she founded at Winchester.

ETHELFLEDA (St) N. OSB.   AC. Oct 23
Otherwise Elfleda, q.v.

ETHELGITHA (St) Abs. OSB.   AC. Aug 22
d. c.720. Abbess of a convent in Northumbria.

ETHELGIVA (St) Abs. OSB.   AC. Dec 9
d. 896. Daughter of King Alfred the Great and abbess of Shaftesbury.

ETHELHARD (St) Bp. AC. May 12
d. 803. A bishop of Winchester, translated to Canterbury in 780.

ETHELNOTH (St) Bp.   AC. Oct 30
Otherwise Egelnoth, q.v.

ETHELRED (St) Ab.   AC. Jan 12
Otherwise Aelred, q.v.

ETHELRED (St) King, Ab. OSB.   AC. May 4
d. 716. A king of Mercia, who resigned the crown to become a monk at Bardney, where he was afterwards elected abbot.

ETHELRED (St) M.   AC. Oct 17
See Ethelbert and Ethelred.

ETHELWALD (OIDILWALD) (St) H. OSB.   AC. March 23
d. 699. A monk of Ripon who succeeded St Cuthbert as a hermit on Farne Island, where he lived for twelve years. He was buried at Lindisfarne.

ETHELWIN (St) Bp.   AC. May 3
8th cent. The second bishop of Lindsey. He was a devoted friend of St Egbert, whom he accompanied to Ireland, where he died.

ETHELWOLD (AEDILAULD) (St) Bp.   AC. Feb 12
d. c.740. One of St Cuthbert's chief helpers. He was prior and then abbot of Old Melrose in Scotland and finally succeeded to the see of Lindisfarne.

ETHELWOLD (St) Bp. OSB.   RM. Aug 1
d. 984. A native of Winchester. When St Dunstan became abbot of Glastonbury in 943 and restored there the Benedictine observance, Ethelwold, already a priest, took the habit and was made one of the deans. In 955 he became abbot of Abingdon and in 963 bishop of Winchester. Together with St Dunstan and St Oswald of York he was a leader in the monastic revival of that century, replacing secular canons by Benedictines, founding or restoring abbeys—Newminster, Milton Abbas, Chertsey, Peterborough, Thorney, Ely, etc. He was indeed worthy of the name given him, "The Father of Monks".

ETHENIA and FIDELMIA (SS) VV.   AC. Jan 11
d. 433. Daughters of King Laoghaire,

and among the first converts made by St Patrick. They received the veil from his hands, and the tradition is that on receiving Holy Communion from him immediately afterwards they died.

ETHERIUS (AETHERIUS) St) Bp. M. RM. March 4
See Basil, Eugene, etc.

ETHERIUS (St) Bp. C. RM. June 14
d. *c.*6th cent. Bishop of Vienne in France.

ETHERIUS (St) M. RM. June 18
d. *c.*303. A martyr who suffered at Nicomedia under Diocletian.

ETHERIUS (St) Bp. C. RM. July 27
d. 573. Bishop of Auxerre, 563–473.

ETHERIUS (ALERMIUS) (St) Bp. C. AC. Aug 27
d. 602. The bishop of Lyons to whom St Gregory the Great recommended St Augustine when the latter was on his way to England.

ETHERNAN (St) Bp. AC. Dec 3
? A native of Scotland who studied in Ireland, and was there consecrated bishop. He then went back to evangelize his country.

ETHERNASCUS (St) Bp.
AC. Aug 18
Otherwise Ernan, q.v.

ETHOR (St) M. AC. Apr 10
See Beocca, Ethor and Comp.

ETTO (HETTO) (St) Bp. OSB.
AC. July 10
d. *c.*670. Said to have been a native of Ireland. He laboured as a missionary abbot-bishop in Belgium, using St Peter's Abbey at Fescau as his headquarters.

EUBULUS (St) M. RM. March 7
See Adrian and Eubulus.

EUCARPIUS (St) M. RM. March 18
See Trophimus and Eucarpius.

EUCARPUS (St) M. RM. Sept 25
See Bardomian, Eucarpus, and Comp.

EUCHARIUS (St) Bp. RM. Dec 8
1st cent. Said to have been the first bishop of Trèves in apostolic times.

EUCHERIUS (St) Bp. OSB.
RM. Feb 20
d. 743. Born at Orleans, he received a good education, especially in theology, and entered the Benedictine abbey of Jumièges on the Seine, in the diocese of Rouen, about the year 714. In 721 he was raised to the see of Orleans. He opposed Charles Martel for the latter's high-handed distribution of ecclesiastical property, and was exiled to Cologne in 737. Here he became very popular, and was sent to Liége. He spent the rest of his life in the abbey of St Trond near Maestricht.

EUCHERIUS (St) Bp. RM. Nov 16
d. 450. A Gallo-Roman by birth and the father, by his wife Galla, of two sons, who became bishops. He himself retired to Lérins in 422, while Galla took the veil. He spent his retirement in praying and writing, several of his ascetical works being still extant. In 434 he was compelled to accept the bishopric of Lyons, where he laboured till his death.

EUDO (EUDON, EUDES ODO) (St) Ab. OSB. AC. Nov 20
d. *c.*760. Abbot-founder of the monastery of Cormèry-en-Velay (Charmillac, afterwards Saint-Chaffre). Before entering upon his duties as abbot he went to Lérins to be instructed in the monastic observance.

EUDOCIA (St) M.   **RM. March 1**
d. 98-117. A native of Heliopolis in Coele-Syria and a Samaritan by blood who led at first a profligate life, but was converted to Christianity and died a penitent. She was beheaded under Trajan.

EUDOXIUS, ZENO, MARCARIUS and Comp. (SS) MM.   **RM. Sept 5**
c.311. A body of Christian soldiers, said to have been more than a thousand in number, martyred at Melitene in Armenia under Constantius I.

EUDOXIUS (St) M.   **RM. Nov 2**
See Carterius, Styriacus, etc.

EUFRIDUS (St) Mk. OSB.
                 AC. Oct 11
7th cent. Monk of the diocese of Asti, venerated in the cathedral of Alba in Piedmont.

EUGENDUS (OYEND) (St) Ab.
                 RM. Jan 1
450–c510. The fourth abbot of Condat, near Geneva, called after him Saint-Oyend, but later Saint-Claude. He entered the abbey at the age of seven and lived there until his death at sixty-one.

EUGENE (several)
Note. The Latin form Eugenius is often used also in English.

EUGENE (St)   **RM. Jan 4**
See Aquilinus, Geminus, etc.

EUGENE (St) M.   **RM. Jan 24**
See Mardonius, Musonius, etc.

EUGENE (St) M.   **RM. March 4**
See Basil, Eugene, etc.

EUGENE (St) M.   **RM. March 20**
See Paul, Cyril, etc.

EUGENE (St) Bp. M.   **RM. May 2**
See Vindemialis, Eugene and Longinus.

EUGENE I (St) Pope.   **RM. June 2**
d. 657. A Roman priest, who acted as vicar for Pope St Martin I during the latter's exile in the Chersonese. After St Martin's death in 655, Eugene was chosen to succeed him. Gentle and affable with the poor, he firmly opposed the Monothelite emperor of Byzantium, who threatened to roast St Eugene alive.

EUGENE III (Bl) Pope OSB. Cist.
                 RM. July 8
d. 1153. A native of Montemagno, between Lucca and Pisa, of the Pignatelli family, he was called Peter in baptism, Bernard in religion, and Eugene on the papal throne. He was an official in the ecclesiastical curia of Pisa, when he entered Clairvaux (1135) and was professed under St Bernard. He was appointed first abbot of Tre Fontane (St Anastasius) near Rome, and in 1145 was chosen pope. His pontificate was a troubled one, the greater part of it being passed at a distance from Rome owing to the hostility of the citizens. St Antoninus fittingly called him "one of the greatest and one of the most afflicted of popes". Cult confirmed in 1872.

EUGENE, SALUTARIS, MURITTA and Comp. (SS) MM.   **RM. July 13**
d. 505. Eugene was raised to the see of Carthage in 481 and was shortly afterwards expelled by the Arian Vandals with many of his flock, some of them young boys who served as lectors in the church. They were banished to the desert of Tripoli, where they had to undergo much hardship. In 488 they were allowed to return to Carthage, but Eugene was banished again some eight years later and died at Albi. They are called martyrs on account of their sufferings.

EUGENE (St) M.   **RM. July 18**
See Symphorosa and Comp.

EUGENE (St) M.   RM. July 23
See Apollonius and Eugene.

EUGENE (St) M.   RM. July 29
See Lucilla, Flora, etc.

**EUGENE (EOGHAN, EUNY,
OWEN) (St) Bp.   AC. Aug 23**
6th cent. An Irishman who laboured as
a missionary in England and on the
Continent, and then returned to his
native country, where he became first
bishop of Ardstraw in Tyrone, a see now
replaced by that of Derry.

EUGENE (St) M.   RM. Sept 6
See Cottidus, Eugene, and Comp.

EUGENE (St) M.   RM. Sept 25
See Paul, Tatta, etc.

**EUGENE II of TOLEDO (St) Bp.
                    RM. Nov 13**
d. 657. A Spanish Goth, born at Toledo,
where he was a cleric under St Helladius. He became a monk of St Engracia
at Saragossa, and the archdeacon of St
Braulio there. Finally, in 646, he was
raised to the primatial see of Toledo.
He was a gifted poet and musician, and
most zealous for all that pertained to
divine worship.

EUGENE (St) Bp. M. RM. Nov 15
? A fellow-labourer of St Dionysius,
archbishop of Paris, martyred, it is said,
somewhere near the city. The RM.
wrongly calls him archbishop of Toledo.
His relics were, it is said, translated to
Toledo many centuries afterwards.

EUGENE (St) C.   RM. Nov 17
d. 422. A deacon of the church of Florence under the bishop St Zenobius. He
had been a disciple of St Ambrose at
Milan.

EUGENE (St) M.   RM. Dec 13
See Eustratius, Auxentius, etc.

**EUGENE and MACARIUS (SS)
MM.   RM. Dec 20**
d. 362. Two priests who were scourged,
banished into the desert of Arabia, and
on their return put to the sword under
Julian the Apostate.

EUGENE (St) Bp.   RM. Dec 30
? A bishop of Milan, of whose life no
record remains.

EUGENIA (St) Abs. OSB. AC. Sept 16
d. 735. Daughter of Adalbert, duke of
Alsace, she succeeded her aunt St
Ottilia, as abbess of Hohenburg.

EUGENIA (Bl) Abs. OSB. PC. Nov 22
d. c.1093. Abbess of the convent of SS
Lucy and Agatha at Matera in S. Italy.

EUGENIA (St) V. M.   RM. Dec 25
d. ? 257. A Roman maiden, martyred
under Valerian and buried in the cemetery of Apronian on the Via Latina. At
a later period she was described quite
groundlessly as a woman who disguised
herself as a monk and who was accused
of a crime she could not commit.

EUGENIAN (St) Bp. M. RM. Jan 8
4th cent. He is stated to have been
bishop of Autun in France, a staunch
defender of the Catholic faith against
Arianism, and a martyr.

EUGRAPHUS (St) M. RM. Dec 10
See Mennas, Hermogenes and Eugraphus.

EUGYPPIUS (St) C.   PC. Jan 15
d. c.511. An African, who was ordained
priest at Rome, he was a companion of
St Severinus of Noricum, whose life he
wrote.

**EULALIA of BARCELONA (St)
VM.   RM. Feb 12**
d. 304. A maiden born at Barcelona,

who suffered martyrdom under Diocletian. In all probability she is identical with St Eulalia of Mérida (see Dec 10) though the Catalonians stoutly deny it. Under the names of Aulaire, Aulazie, Olalla, etc., she is greatly venerated throughout Spanish and French Catalonia.

EULALIA (St) VM.   RM. Dec 10
d. 304. The most celebrated virgin martyr of Spain. Prudentius wrote a long hymn describing her martyrdom, and she is mentioned by St Augustine and others. A native of Mérida, at thirteen years of age, she was burnt at the stake in her native city under Diocletian.

EULAMPIA (St) VM.   RM. Oct 10
See Eulampius, Eulampia and Comp.

EULAMPIUS, EULAMPIA and Comp. (SS) MM.   RM. Oct 10
d. 310. Two young children, brother and sister, martyred at Nicomedia under Gallienus. Their courage, it is added, led to the conversion and martyrdom of two hundred soldiers.

EULOGIUS of TARRAGONA (St) M.   RM. Jan 21
See Fructuosus, Augurius and Eulogius.

EULOGIUS of CORDOVA (St) M.   RM. March 11
d. 859. A prominent priest of Cordova in the middle of the 9th century, when the Moorish persecution was at its height. An outstanding personality for his erudition and courage, he encouraged the Christians of the province in their sufferings, and wrote *The Memorial of the Saints* for their benefit. He himself suffered martyrdom for having protected St Leocritia, a girl converted from Islam.

EULOGIUS of EDESSA (St) Bp.   RM. May 5
d. *p*.381. A priest of Edessa, banished to the Thebaid for his firm stand against Arianism, and chosen bishop of his native town on his return after the death of Valens (375).

EULOGIUS and Comp (SS) MM.   RM. July 3
d. 364–370. A group of Catholics martyred at Constantinople under the Arian emperor Valens.

EULOGIUS of ALEXANDRIA (St) Bp.   RM. Sept 13
d. 607. A Syrian by birth and a monk from early youth, Eulogius was chosen patriarch of Alexandria in 579. He was a great friend of St Gregory the Great, who wrote to tell him about the new mission for the conversion of England.

EUMENES (St) Bp.   RM. Sept 18
3rd cent. Bishop of Gortyna in Crete, who died in exile. He is one of those whom on account of their many miracles, the Greeks surname "the Wonder-Worker".

EUNAN (St) Bp.   AC. Sept 23
7th cent. Identical with St Adamnan of Iona, q.v.

EUNICIAN (St) M.   RM. Dec 23
See Thedulus, Saturninus, etc.

EUNOMIA (St) M.   RM. Aug 12
See Hilarla, Digna, etc.

EUNUS (St) M.   RM. Feb 27 and Oct 30
See Julian, Cronion, etc.

EUPHEBIUS (St) Bp.   RM. May 23
? A bishop of Naples, about whom nothing is known.

EUPHEMIA (St) M. RM. March 20
See Alexandra, Claudia, etc.

EUPHEMIA (Bl) Abs. OSB.
PC. June 17
d. 1180. Daughter of the count of Andechs, she became a nun and abbess of
Altomünster in Bavaria.

**EUPHEMIA, DOROTHY, THECLA
and ERASMA (SS) VV.MM.**
RM. Sept 3
? 1st cent. A group of maidens, martyred at Aquileia. They are venerated at
Venice and at Ravenna.

EUPHEMIA (St) VM. RM. Sept 16
d. 307. A maiden said to have been
burnt at the stake at Chalcedon. She is
one of the most venerated of virgin-
martyrs in the Greek church.

EUPHRASIA (St) V. RM. March 13
d. c.420. Born at Constantinople and
connected by blood with the imperial
family. She was brought up in a convent
in Egypt, and when at a later date she
was asked by the emperor to marry a
senator she refused and remained in the
convent for the rest of her life. An early
life of her is in the *Acta Sanctorum*.

EUPHRASIA (St) M. RM. March 20
See Alexandra, Claudia, etc.

EUPHRASIA PELLETIER (St)
Foundress   RM. Apr 24
1796–1868. A native of Noxmontier, in
W. France, at eighteen she joined the
institute of Our Lady of Charity founded by St John Eudes, and in 1829
founded at Angers the first convent of
the Good Shepherd, a congregation
which today numbers three hundred
and thirty convents throughout the
world and over ten thousand sisters. St
Euphrasia visited London in 1844. She
died at Angers in her seventy-second

year, and was beatified in 1933 and
canonized in 1940.

EUPHRASIA (St) VM. RM. May 18
See Theodotus, Thecusa, etc.

EUPHRASIUS (St) Bp. RM. Jan 14
? Perhaps identical with Eucrathius, a
correspondent of St Cyprian; or else, a
bishop martyred in Africa by the Arian
Vandals.

EUPHRASIUS (St) M. RM. Apr 29
See Corfu (Martyrs of).

EUPHRASIUS (St) Bp. M.
RM. May 15
See Torquatus, Ctesiphon, etc.

EUPHRONIUS (St) Bp. RM. Aug 3
d. p.475. Bishop of Autun in France,
friend of St Lupus of Troyes. A letter
of his written with St Lupus survives
(PL LVIII, col 66–67).

EUPHRONIUS (St) Bp. RM. Aug 4
530–573. Bishop of Tours from 556 till
his death. During his episcopate the
city was burnt, and he worked most
strenuously and successfully to rebuild
it.

EUPHROSYNE (St) VM. RM. Jan 1
? According to the legend, St Euphrosyne was a maiden of Alexandria in
Egypt, who lived as a monk in a monastery, there, her sex not being discovered
till her death many years later. It is only
a replica of similar stories; see SS
Pelagia (Oct 8), Eugenia (Dec 25) etc.
It is doubtful whether St Euphrosyne
ever existed.

EUPHROSYNE (St) VM.
RM. May 7
See Flavia Domitilla, Euphrosyne and
Theodora.

EUPLUS (St) M.   RM. Aug 12
d. 304. A Christian of Catania in Sicily
who was found with a copy of the gospels in his possession, against Diocletian's edict. He was cruelly racked and
martyred on this account. His Acts are
genuine.

EUPORUS (St) M.   RM. Dec 23
See Theodulus, Saturninus, etc.

EUPREPIA (St) M.   RM. Aug 12
See Hilaria, Digna, etc.

EUPREPIS (St) M.   RM. Nov 30
See Castulus and Euprepis.

EUPREPIUS (St) Bp.   RM. Aug 21
1st cent. The first bishop of Verona in
N. Italy. The tradition (now abandoned)
was that he was sent there by St Peter
himself.

EUPREPIUS (St) M.   RM. Sept 27
d. c.303. Mentioned in the legendary
Acta as a companion martyr of SS
Cosmas and Damian, q.v.

EUPSYCHIUS (St) M.   RM. Apr 9
d. 362. A youth of Caesarea in Cappadocia, martyred under Julian the Apostate as leader of a group of Christians
accused of having destroyed the temple
of Fortune in that city.

EUPSYCHIUS (St) M.   RM. Sept 7
d. c.130. A martyr of Caesarea in Cappadocia who suffered under Hadrian.

EURFYL (St) V.   AC. July 5
Otherwise Erfyl, q.v.

EURGAIN (St) V.   AC. June 30
6th cent. A daughter of the chieftain
Caradog in Glamorgan, foundress of
Cor-Eurgain, afterwards Llantwit. Another St Eurgain, wife of a princeling
in N. Wales, founded Llan-Eugain in
Flintshire.

EUROSIA (OROSIA) (St) VM.
                              AC. June 25
d. 714. According to the legend, she was
a native of Bayonne—a more florid
version makes her a native of Bohemia—
who was martyred by the Saracens at
Jaca in the Aragonese Pyrenees, close to
the French frontier. She is to this day
venerated as the patron saint of the diocese of Jaca, and her cult has spread
throughout S. France and N. Italy. Leo
XIII officially confirmed it in 1902.
However, her very existence is doubtful.

EUSEBIA (St) Abs. OSB.
                              AC March 16
d. c.680. Eldest daughter of SS Adalbald and Rictrudis, she was placed by
her mother in the abbey of Hamage
(Hamay) which had been founded by
her grandmother St Gertrude. St Eusebia succeeded as abbess at the age of
twelve, whereupon she was summoned
by her mother to Merchiennes; she went
with all her community, but later was
allowed to return to Hamage and continued to rule her nunnery in peace.

EUSEBIA (St) Abs. M. OSB.
                              AC. Sept 20
d. c.731. Abbess of a nunnery at Marseilles. She, with some forty nuns of her
community, was put to death by the
Saracens at Saint-Cyr.

EUSEBIA (St) VM.   RM. Oct 29
Late 3rd cent. A maiden of Bergamo, in
Lombardy, niece of St Domnio, q.v.,
martyred under Maximian Herculius.

EUSEBIUS (Bl) Founder.
                              AC. Jan 20
d. 1270. At first a Canon of Esztergom,
he became a hermit in the mountains of
Pilis. Gathering disciples there he
founded the Pauline Order of Hermits,
after St Paul, the first Hermit (Jan 15
q.v.). The constitutions were written by

St Thomas Aquinas and received papal approval. He died in Pilis and has always been venerated as Blessed in Hungary.

EUSEBIUS (St) H.   **AC. Jan 23**
d. 4th cent. A Syrian hermit who lived on Mt Coryphe, near Antioch.

EUSEBIUS (St) M. OSB.
                              AC. Jan 31
d. 884. An Irish pilgrim who took the Benedictine habit in the Swiss abbey of St Gall. Eventually he obtained leave to live as a recluse on Mt St Victor in the Vorarlberg. When he was denouncing some godless peasants, one of them struck him with a scythe and killed him. Hence his veneration as a martyr.

EUSEBIUS (Bl) H. OSB. Cam.
                              PC. Feb 10
d. 1501. A member of the Spanish nobility who was sent as ambassador to the republic of Venice. Here, he left all things to don the Camaldolese habit at San Michele, on the isle of Murano.

EUSEBIUS (St) H.   **AC. Feb 15**
5th cent. A hermit of Aschia in Syria, venerated in the East.

EUSEBIUS and Comp. (SS) MM.
                              RM. March 5
? A group of ten martyrs who suffered in Africa.

EUSEBIUS (St) Ab.   **AC. March 5**
d. c.423. A native of Cremona and an intimate friend of St Jerome whom he followed to Rome and to the East. Here he succeeded the holy Doctor as abbot of Bethlehem, and was involved, like his friend, in bitter disputes on Origenism. The tradition that he founded the abbey of Guadalupe in Spain cannot be substantiated.

EUSEBIUS, NEON, LEONTIUS, LONGINUS and Comp. (SS) MM.
                              RM. Apr 24
? According to the Greek menologies, these were eight bystanders, who became Christians on witnessing the martyrdom of St George and were for this reason put to death. The legend should be studied in connection with that of St George.

EUSEBIUS (St) M.   **RM. Apr 28**
See Aphrodisius, Caralippus, etc.

EUSEBIUS of SAMOSATA (St) Bp. M.   **RM. June 21**
d. c.379. Bishop of Samosata in Syria from the year 361, he was a great friend of SS Basil and Gregory of Nazianzos, and a brave defender of orthodoxy against the Arians. He was for this reason banished to France, but recalled four years later. He was killed by an Arian woman who threw a tile at his head.

EUSEBIUS of MILAN (St) Bp.
                              RM. Aug 12
d. 465. Probably a Greek by birth, he succeeded St Lazarus in the see of Milan and governed it for sixteen years. He helped Pope St Leo the Great to repress Eutychianism.

EUSEBIUS (St) C.   **RM. Aug 14**
4th cent. A Roman priest, belonging to the patrician order, who founded the "parish church" called after him the *titulis Eusebii*. The Acts of Eusebius, according to which he publicly preached against Pope Liberius, are entirely spurious.

EUSEBIUS (St) Pope.   **RM. Aug 17**
d. 310. A Greek by birth, he was pope for a few months only, and died in exile in Sicily.

EUSEBIUS, PONTIAN, VINCENT and PEREGRINUS (SS) MM.
RM. Aug 25
d. 192? The only certain fact is that the relics of SS Eusebius and Pontian were sought from Pope Nicholas I and taken to Vienne in 863. The *Passio* which mentions other Christians, including Vincent, Peregrinus, Julius and Antony (or Antoninus) is untrustworthy.

EUSEBIUS, NESTABUS and ZENO (SS) MM.
RM. Sept 8
d. 362. Martyrs massacred by the mob at Gaza in Palestine for having helped in the destruction of a pagan temple there.

EUSEBIUS (St) M.
RM. Sept 21
? A martyr of Phoenicia, who appears to have given himself up voluntarily as a Christian.

EUSEBIUS of BOLOGNA (St) Bp.
RM. Sept 26
d. *c.*400. A bishop of Bologna from about the year 370. He was a great friend of St Ambrose of Milan, and an ardent opponent of Arianism. During his pontificate the relics of the martyrs SS Vitalis and Agricola were discovered.

EUSEBIUS (St) M.
RM. Oct 4
See Caius, Faustus, etc.

EUSEBIUS (St) M.
RM. Oct 22
See Philip, Severus, etc.

EUSEBIUS (St) M.
RM. Nov 5
See Felix and Eusebius.

EUSEBIUS, MARCELLUS, HIPPOLYTUS, MAXIMUS, ADRIA, PAULINA, NEON, MARY MARTANA and AURELIA (SS) MM.
RM. Dec 2
d. 254–259. Roman martyrs under Valerian, Eusebius, a priest, Marcellus, his deacon, Neon and Mary were beheaded; Adria and Hippolytus scourged to death; Paulina died in the torture-chamber; and Maximus was thrown into the Tiber.

EUSEBIUS of VERCELLI (St) Bp. M.
RM. Dec 16
*c.*283–370. A native of Sardinia, he joined the Roman clergy and was in 340 raised to the see of Vercelli in Piedmont. He fought Arianism with all the ardour of his Sardianian temperament, and with Dionysius of Milan and Lucifer of Cagliari was banished to the East. Before returning to Italy under Julian he visited St Athanasius at Alexandria. St Jerome wrote: "on the return of Eusebius, Italy put off her mourning". He was the first bishop who lived with his clergy under a rule, an example which was followed by St Augustine. On account of the sufferings he had to endure in his exile he is venerated as a martyr although he died in peace at Vercelli on Aug 1.

EUSEUS (St) H.
AC. Feb 15
14th cent. A hermit who lived and died near Serravalle in Piedmont. He is regarded as a patron of cobblers, since he plied that trade.

EUSIGNIUS (St) M.
RM. Aug 5
d. 362. An old soldier of the army of Constantius Clorus who, surviving to the age of 110, refused to sacrifice to idols at the bidding of Julian the Apostate and was scourged and beheaded at Antioch in Syria.

EUSTACE (*several*)
Note. The Latin forms of this name, viz., Eustachius and Eustathius, are also used in English.

EUSTACE (EUSTASIUS) (St) Ab.
RM. March 29
d. 625. A favourite disciple and monk of

St Columbanus, whom he succeeded as second abbot of Luxeuil. He ruled over about six hundred monks, and during his abbacy the monastery was a veritable seminary of bishops and saints.

EUSTACE (St) M.   AC. Apr 14
See Antony, John and Eustace.

EUSTACE (St) Bp.   RM. July 16
d. *c*.335. A native of Side in Pamphylia and a confessor during the last persecution, he was made bishop of Beroea in Syria and then transferred against his will to the patriarchal see of Antioch. He was present at the council of Nicaea, and from that time never ceased to oppose Arianism in preaching and writing. The Arians succeeded in deposing and banishing him, and he died in exile.

EUSTACE (EUSTATHIUS) (St) M.
RM. July 28
? A martyr of Galatia who after torture appears to have been cast into a river.

EUSTACE (St) Ab. OSB. Cist.
PC. Sept 7
d. 1211. Born in the Beauvasis, he became a priest of the diocese of Beauvais. He later entered the Cistercian abbey of Flay (Saint-Germer) and was eventually its abbot. Under Pope Innocent III he was apostolic legate in England and on the continent against the Albigenses. He is greatly honoured by the Cistercians.

EUSTACE, THEOPISTES, AGAPI-
TUS and THEOPISTUS (SS) MM.
RM. Sept 20
d. 118. Said to have been a Roman family of distinction—Eustace, an officer, Theopistes, his wife, and Agapitus and Theopistus, their two sons who were martyred under Hadrian. Eustace owed his conversion to the vision of a

stag with a crucifix between its antlers see by him while hunting. Actually, however, nothing certain is known about him, or his supposed family, and their Acts are wholly untrustworthy.

EUSTACE (St) M. (or C.)
RM. Oct 12
? Hagiologists are in complete disagreement as to who this St Eustace was. The RM. describes him as a priest and confessor in Syria; the Bollandists make of him an Egyptian martyr.

EUSTACE, THESPESIUS and
ANATOLIUS (SS) MM.
RM. Nov 20
d. 235. Martyrs of Nicaea in Asia Minor under the emperor Maximinus the Thracian.

EUSTACE (St) M. Bp. RM. Nov 28
See Valerian, Urban, etc.

EUSTACE WHITE (Bl) M.
AC. Dec 10
d. 1591. Born at Louth, in Lincolnshire, he became a convert, and was educated for the priesthood at Reims and Rome. Ordained in 1588, he was condemned to death for his priesthood and executed at Tyburn.

EUSTADIOLA (St) Abs. OSB.
AC. June 8
d. 690. A native of Bourges who married early in life. Having been left a widow she spent all her fortune in building a nunnery in her native town—Moyenmoutier *Medianum monasterium*—whither she retired and became abbess.

EUSTERIUS (St) Bp.   RM. Oct 19
5th cent. The fourth bishop of Salerno, of whom only the name is known.

EUSTOCHIA (St) V.   RM. Sept 28
Otherwise Eustochium, q.v.

EUSTOCHIUM CALAFATO (Bl)
Poor Clare. AC. Feb 1
1437–1468. Daughter of the Countess
Matilda of Calafato, she was born at
Messina in Sicily, where she became a
Poor Clare, and eventually (1446) foun-
ded a convent of stricter observance at
a place called *Monte delle Vergini*
(Maidens' Hill). Cult confirmed in
1782.

EUSTOCHIUM of PADUA (Bl) N.
OSB. AC. Feb 13
1444–1469. The Cinderella of the Cloister. She was the daughter of a nun of
Padua who had been seduced, and her
baptismal name was Lucrezia Bellini.
Gentle and pious, she became a nun in
1461 and for four years was subject to
violent hysteria for which she was
treated as one diabolically possessed:
exorcized, kept in prison, fed on bread
and water, or even deprived of food.
When in her right mind she bore her
treatment with heroic patience and
humility. She died after her profession,
aged twenty-five, and the name of
Jesus was found cauterized on her
breast. She is liturgically honoured at
Padua.

EUSTOCHIUM (St) V. RM. Sept 28
d. 419. The third and best loved daughter of St Paula, the Roman matron who
followed St Jerome to Palestine. She
joined her mother at Bethlehem, where
she collated manuscripts for St Jerome's
translation of the Bible. She succeeded
her mother in the direction of the nunnery at Bethlehem.

EUSTOCHIUM (St) VM.
RM. Nov 2
d. 362. A maiden of Tarsus in Cilicia
condemned to death under Julian the
Apostate. She was barbarously tortured,
and as a consequence died in prison,
while engaged in prayer.

EUSTOCHIUS (St) Bp.
RM. Sept 19
d. 461. The successor (444) of St Brice
in the see of Tours.

EUSTOCHIUS (St) M.
RM. Nov 16
See Elpidius, Marcellus, etc.

EUSTOLIA and SOPATRA (SS)
VV. RM. Nov 9
7th cent. It is uncertain whether both
of these virgins were daughters of the
emperor Maurice of Constantinople
(582–602) or only one of them. They
were from the first revered as saints.

EUSTORGIUS (St) M. RM. Apr 11
d. ? 300. A priest of Nicomedia in Asia
Minor, martyred, probably under Diocletian.

EUSTORGIUS II (St) Bp.
RM. June 6
d. 518. A Roman priest who became
bishop of Milan in 512. He spent large
sums of money in ransoming many of
his flock taken prisoners by the barbarians.

EUSTORGIUS I (St) Bp. M.
RM. Sept 18
d. *p*.331. A Greek by birth, he was
raised in 315 to the see of Milan, where
he exerted all his influence against the
Arians.

EUSTOSIUS (St) M. RM. Nov 10
See Demetrius, Anianus, etc.

EUSTRATIUS, AUXENTIUS,
EUGENE, MARDARIUS and
ORESTES (SS) MM. RM. Dec 14
d. *c*.302. Martyrs under Diocletian at
Sebaste in Armenia. Eustratius was
burnt to death in a furnace; Orestes, a
soldier, roasted on a gridiron; the others
were martyred in various ways.

EUSTREBERTA (St) V. AC. Feb 10
Otherwise Austreberta, q.v.

EUTHALIA (St) VM. RM. Aug 27
? A virgin martyr of Leontini in Sicily.
The Bollandists consider her very existence to be hardly proved.

EUTHYMIUS the GREAT (St) Ab.
RM. Jan 20
378–473. An Armenian, born at Melitene. He was raised to the priesthood and charged with the supervision of all the monasteries of the district. At the age of twenty-nine he became a monk near Jerusalem, retiring afterwards to Jericho and further into the desert, where he established several *lauras*. He opposed Nestorianism and Eutychianism alike, and induced the empress Eudoxia to give up the latter. He is highly revered throughout the East.

EUTHYMIUS of SARDIS (St) Bp.
M. RM. March 11
d. 840? A monk who was made bishop of Sardis in Lydia and bravely opposed the Iconoclasts. He was banished by the emperor Nicephorus, and although he was several times given permission to return on condition of his becoming an Iconoclast, he always refused and remained in exile for twenty-nine years. He was scourged to death.

EUTHYMIUS (St) M. RM. May 5
? A deacon of Alexandria, martyred there.

EUTHYMIUS (St) C. RM. Aug 29
4th cent. A Roman who fled to Perugia with his wife and his child, St Crescentius, during the persecution of Diocletian. He died at Perugia and is venerated there. The *Passio* is untrustworthy.

EUTHYMIUS the THESSA-
LONIAN (St) Ab. AC. Oct 15
d. 886. Surnamed also "the New".

Before his twentieth year became a monk at M. Olympus in Bithynia. Later he migrated to M. Athos and finally restored the monastery of St Andrew, and established a new nunnery, near Salonika. He returned to M. Athos to die.

EUTHYMIUS (St) M. RM. Dec 24
d. 303. A Christian of Nicomedia, foremost in encouraging his fellow-believers during the persecution of Diocletian, and a martyr himself under the same emperor.

EUTROPIA (St) VM. RM. June 15
See Lybe, Levnis and Eutropia.

EUTROPIA (St) W. RM. Sept 15
5th cent. Said to have lived in Auvergne, France. She is first mentioned by Sidonius Apollinaris.

EUTROPIA (St) M. RM. Oct 30
d. ? 253. An African martyr, probably under Valerian.

EUTROPIA (S) VM. RM. Dec 14
See Nicasius, Eutropia, etc.

EUTROPIUS (St) M. RM. Jan 12
See Tigris and Eutropius.

EUTROPIUS (St) M. RM. March 3
See Cleonicus, Eutropius and Basiliscus.

EUTROPIUS (St) Bp. M.
RM. Apr 30
? One of the alleged companions of St Dionysius of Paris. He is honoured as the first bishop of Saintes, and as a martyr.

EUTROPIUS (St) Bp. RM. May 27
d. *p*.475. A native of Marseilles who succeeded St Justin in the see of Orange, in France, at a time when the diocese had been laid waste by the Visigoths.

EUTROPIUS, ZOSIMA and BONOSA (SS) MM. RM. July 15
d. *c.*273. Martyrs of Porto, near Rome, under Aurelian.

EUTYCHES (St) M. RM. Apr 15
See Maro, Eutyches and Victorinus.

EUTYCHIAN (St) M. RM. July 2
See Ariston, Crescentian, etc.

EUTYCHIAN (St) M. RM. Aug 17
See Straton, Philip and Eutychian.

EUTYCHIAN (St) M. RM. Sept 2
See Diomedes, Julian, etc.

EUTYCHIAN (St) M. RM. Nov 13
See Arcadius, Paschasius, etc.

EUTYCHIAN (St) Pope M.
RM. Dec 8
d. 283. A native of Etruria or Tuscany. In 275 he succeeded St Felix I as pope. He is venerated as a martyr; but nothing certain is known about him.

EUTYCHIUS (St) M. RM. Feb 4
4th cent. A Roman martyr under Diocletian. From St Damasus's inscription on the tomb of the martyr we learn that he was left for twelve days in prison without food and then thrown into a well.

EUTYCHIUS and Comp. (SS) MM.
RM. March 14
d. 741. A considerable number of martyrs, put to death at Carrhes by the Mohammedans in Mesopotamia for refusing to deny Christ.

EUTYCHIUS of ALEXANDRIA and Comp. (SS) MM. RM. March 26
d. 356. Eutychius was a subdeacon of the church of Alexandria who, for his stand against Arianism, was condemned to slavery in the mines, but perished from exhaustion on the road thither. His companions were other leading Catholics of Alexandria, four of whom were seized and scourged (but not executed) for showing sympathy for him.

EUTYCHIUS of CONSTANTINOPLE (St) Bp. AC. Apr 6
d. 582. Appointed patriarch of Constantinople in 552, he opposed the emperor Justinian's interference in theological controversies. He was for this reason exiled for twelve years. He is honoured in the East.

EUTYCHIUS (St) M. RM. Apr 15
? A martyr of Ferentino in the Roman Campagna. According to the Dialogues of St Gregory he appeared in a vision to St Redemptus.

EUTYCHIUS (St) M. RM. May 21
See Timothy, Polius and Eutychius.

EUTYCHIUS and FLORENTIUS (SS) CC. RM. May 23
6th cent. Two monks who successively governed a monastery in Valcastoria, near Norcia, Italy. St Gregory the Great has left a glowing account of their virtues and miracles.

EUTYCHIUS (St) RM. Aug 24
1st cent. A Phrygian, disciple of St John the Evangelist (according to the apochryphal *Acta* of St John). He is sometimes identified with the young man raised from the dead by the apostle Paul at Troas (Acts 20).

EUTYCHIUS (St) M. RM. Sept 19
See Januarius and Comp.

EUTYCHIUS, PLAUTUS and HERACLEAS (SS) MM. RM. Sept 29
? Martys in Thrace.

EUTYCHIUS (St) M. RM. Oct 5
See Placid, Eutychius, etc.

EUTYCHIUS (St) M.   RM. Nov 21
See Honorius, Eutychius and Stephen.

EUTYCHIUS (St) M.   RM. Dec 11
4th cent. A Spanish martyr—San Oye
—martyred at Mérida, or at Cádiz.
Nothing certain is known about him.

EUTYCHIUS and DOMITIAN (SS)
MM.   RM. Dec 28
? A priest and his deacon, martyred at
Ancyra, in Galatia.

EUVERT (St) Bp.   RM. Sept 7
Otherwise Evortius, q.v.

EVA of LIÉGE (Bl) V. AC. March 14
d. c.1266. A recluse of Liége who lived
under the Cistercian rule, and who on
the death of Bl Juliana of Cornillon
successfully continued her work in
favour of the institution of the liturgical
feast of *Corpus Christi*. Cult confirmed
in 1902.

EVAGRIUS (St) Bp.   RM. March 6
d. c.380. In 370, after the Arians had
occupied the see of Constantinople for
twenty years, the Catholics chose Evagrius for that see; but a few months later
he was banished by the emperor Valens,
and remained in exile till his death.

EVAGRIUS and BENIGNUS (SS)
MM.   RM. Apr 3
? Martyrs at Tomi on the Black Sea.

EVAGRIUS (St) M.   RM. Oct 1
See Priscus, Crescens and Evagrius.

EVAGRIUS, PRISCIAN and Comp.
(SS) MM.   RM. Oct 12
? A group of martyrs, who suffered either
in Rome or, more probably, in Syria.

EVAL (Uvol, Urfol)   AC. Nov 20
6th cent. A British bishop in Cornwall,
from whom a village in that county is
named.

EVAN (INAN) (St) H.   AC. Aug 18
9th cent. A Scottish hermit in Ayrshire,
where churches are still dedicated to
him.

EVANDUS (St) Bp.   AC.?
d. c.313. First bishop of Urbino.

EVANGELIST and PEREGRINUS
(BB) CC. OSA.   AC. March 20
d. c.1250. These two saints were born
at Verona, became friends at school,
entered together the order of the Augustinian friars, were both endowed with
similar miraculous gifts, and died within
a few hours of each other. Their cult
was approved in 1837.

EVARISTUS (St) M.   RM. Oct 14
See Carponius, Evaristus and Priscian.

EVARISTUS (St) Pope M.
**   RM. Oct 26**
d. c.107. A Hellenic Jew who was raised
to the Roman see about the year 96—
thus becoming the fourth successor of
St Peter. He is honoured as a martyr,
though the fact of his martyrdom is not
established.

EVARISTUS (St) M.   RM. Dec 23
See Theodulus, Saturninus, etc.

EVASIUS (St) Bp. M.   RM. Dec 1
d. ? 362. Said to have been the first
bishop of Asti in Piedmont, whence he
was driven by the Arians, and finally to
have been put to death under Julian the
Apostate at Casale Monferrato. The
accounts given of him are very untrustworthy.

EVASIUS (St) Bp.   RM. Dec 2
? First bishop of Brescia.

EVE (St)   AC. Dec 24
See Adam and Eve.

EVELLIUS (St) M.   RM. May 11
d. *c*.66. Said to have been a counsellor of Nero, converted to Christ on witnessing the patience of the martyrs, and himself martyred at Pisa.

EVENTIUS (St) M.   RM. Apr 16
See Saragossa (Martyrs of).

EVENTIUS (St) M.   RM. May 3
See Alexander, Eventius and Theodulus.

EVERARD (*several*)
Otherwise Eberhard, q.v.

EVERARD HANSE (Bl) M.
                        AC. July 30
d. 1581. A native of Northamptonshire who was educated at Cambridge and became a Protestant minister. After his conversion he was ordained priest at Reims (1581). A few months after he was martyred at Tyburn; when dying he was heard to exclaim: "Oh happy day!" Beatified in 1886.

EVERGISLUS (EBREGESILUS) (St) Bp. M.   RM. Oct 24
? 5th cent. A bishop of Cologne, and a martyr at the hands of heathen robbers. Very probably he died at a much later period and not as a martyr.

EVERILDIS (St) Abs. OSB.
                        AC. July 9
d. late 7th cent. This saint received the veil from St Wilfrid at York at a spot called "the Bishop's Farm", afterwards Everildsham, now Everingham, where she became abbess of a large community. Her two first companions were SS Bega and Wulfreda.

EVERMARUS (St) M.   AC. May 1
d. *c*.700. A pilgrim, murdered by robbers at Rousson, near Tongres, in Belgium.

EVERMOD (St) Bp. O. Praem.
                        AC. Feb 17
d. 1178. A Premonstratensian canon under St Norbert, who preached to the Wends, and eventually was chosen abbot of Gottesgnaden, then abbot of Magdeburg, and finally bishop of Ratzeburg.

EVERMUND (EBREMUNDUS) (St) Ab. OSB.   AC. June 10
d. *c*.720. A native of Bayeux and a courtier. He married and, with his wife's consent, founded several religious houses, the chief of which was Fontenay-Louvet, in the diocese of Séez, where he became monk and abbot. His wife entered one of his foundations as a nun.

EVILASIUS (St) M.   RM. Sept 20
See Fausta and Evilasius.

EVODIUS, HERMOGENES and CALLISTA (SS) MM.   RM. Apr 25
? The RM. mentions this group three times. On Aug 2 they are given as the three sons of Theodota, martyred at Nicea in Bithynia. On the other two dates their martyrdom is placed at Syracuse, and in each of these places, the third name is given as Callista, indicating a sister and not a third brother. There is no *Passio* of the martyrs of Syracuse, and it is possible that they suffered at Nicea. See Theodota.

EVODIUS (St) Bp. M.   RM. May 6
d. *c*.67. The successor of St Peter in the see of Antioch. Tradition makes him a martyr and one of the seventy-two disciples of our Lord.

EVODIUS (St) Bp.   RM. Oct 8
5th cent. A native of Rouen and bishop of that see. His relics were translated to Braine, near Soissons.

EVODIUS (St) Bp.   AC. Nov 12
d. *p*.560. Bishop of Le Puy in France.

EVORTIUS (St) Bp.   RM. Sept 7
d. *c*.340. A Roman cleric who became bishop of Orleans. The abbey of Saint-Euvert (St Evortius) was founded to enshrine his relics.

EVROUL (St) Ab.   RM. Dec 29
Otherwise Ebrulfus, q.v.

EWALD the FAIR and EWALD the DARK (SS) Mks. OSB. RM. Oct 3
d. *c*.695. Two brothers of Northumbrian stock who became monks and priests, and followed St Willibrord to Frisia. After a short apostolate they were martyred together at Aplerbeke, near Dortmund.

EXANTHUS (St) M.   RM. Aug 7
See Carpophorus, Exanthus, etc.

**EXPEDITUS of MELITENE (St) M.
RM. Apr 19**
See Hermogenes, Caius, Expeditus, etc.

EXUPERANTIA (St) V. RM. Apr 26
? A saint whose relics are venerated at Troyes in France. Nothing else is known about her.

**EXUPERANTIUS (St) Bp.
RM. Jan 24**
5th cent. Bishop of Cingoli near Ancona, in Italy. He is believed to have been a native of Africa.

**EXUPERANTIUS (St) Bp.
RM. May 30**
d. 418. Bishop of Ravenna from 398 to 418.

**EXUPERANTIUS (St) M.
RM. Dec 30**
See Sabinus, Exuperantius, etc.

EXUPERIA (St) M.   RM. July 26
See Symphronius, Olympius, etc.

EXUPERIUS (HESPERIUS), CYRIACUS and THEODULUS (SS) MM.   RM. May 2
d. *c*.127. A family of slaves—husband, wife and two sons—owned by a rich pagan of Attalia in Pamphylia. They were martyred for refusing to take part with their master in idolatrous rites.

EXUPERIUS (St) M.   RM. Sept 22
See the Theban Legion.

EXUPERIUS (French: SOUPIRE) (St) Bp.   AC. Aug 1
? 4th cent. A bishop of Bayeux, who appears to have lived in the 4th century, and is honoured at Corbeil under the name of St Spire.

EXUPERIUS (French: SOUPIRE) (St) Bp.   RM. Sept 28
d. 411. Bishop of Toulouse, a benefactor and friend of St Jerome, noted for his generosity in sending large contributions to the poor of Palestine and Egypt.

EXUPERIUS (St) M.   RM. Nov 19
See Severinus, Exuperius and Felician.

**EZECHIEL (St) Prophet
RM. Apr 10**
6th cent. B.C. One of the four greater prophets and the writer of a canonical book of Scripture. The tradition is that he was put to death, while in captivity in Babylon, by one of the Jewish judges who had turned pagan, and that he was buried there in the tomb of Shem. His grave was for the early Christians a place of pilgrimage.

F

FABIAN (St) Pope M.   RM. Jan 20
d. 250. In 236 Fabian succeeded St
Antheros on the papal throne and
reigned fourteen years, until his martyrdom under Decius. St Cyprian, his
contemporary, describes him as an
"incomparable man" and adds that the
glory of his death corresponded with the
purity and goodness of his life. Part of
his relics were taken to the Basilica of
St Sebastian; thereafter the two martyrs were honoured with one feast.

FABIAN (St) M.   RM. Dec 31
See Stephen, Pontian, etc.

FABIOLA (St) W.   AC. Dec 27
d. c.400. A Roman patrician maiden who
was married to a very young man of
equal rank but of dissolute habits, whom
she divorced. She then united herself
with another man, causing great scandal
in Rome. After the latter's death she
performed public penance, and devoted
her great wealth to the care of the sick
in a hospital which she established in
Rome—the first of its kind in the West
—associating herself in this work with
St Pammachius. In 395 she visited her
friend St Jerome in the Holy Land, and
wished to enter the convent at Bethlehem; but was dissuaded by St Jerome.
She returned accordingly to Rome and
founded, and superintended, a hostel
for pilgrims near the city. The veneration in which she was held in Rome was
demonstrated by the great concourse of
people at her funeral.

FABIUS (St) M.   RM. May 11
See Maximus, Bassus and Fabius.

FABIUS (St) M.   RM. July 31
d. 300. A soldier beheaded at Caesarea
in Mauretania, under Diocletian, for
refusing to carry a standard bearing
idolatrous emblems.

**FABRICIAN and PHILIBERT (SS)
MM.   RM. Aug 22**
? Said to have been martyred in Spain.
They are honoured at Toledo.

FACHANAN (St) Bp.   AC. Aug 14
d. late 6th cent. Probably the first
bishop of Ross, in Ireland. He founded
the monastic school at what is now
Rosscarbery, in Co. Cork, and placed
there St Brendan as one of the teachers.
He is venerated as the patron saint of
the diocese of Ross.

**FACIOLUS (St) Mk. OSB.
                    AC. Sept 7**
d. c.950. A Benedictine monk of the
abbey of St Cyprian at Poitiers.

FACUNDINUS (St) Bp. AC. Aug 28
d. c.620. Bishop of Taino in Umbria,
where he is still venerated.

**FACUNDUS and PRIMITIVUS
(SS) MM.   RM. Nov 27**
d. c.300. Born at León in Spain and
beheaded by the River Cea, where the
town of Sahagun now stands. At a later
period the great Benedictine abbey of
Sahagun, round which grew the present
township of that name, was called after
St Facundus (Sant'Facun-Sahagun).

FAGAN (St) AC. Jan 3 (RM. May 26)
Otherwise Fugatius, q.v.

FAGILDUS (St) Ab. OSB.
                              AC. July 25
d. 1086. Benedictine abbot of the monastery of St Martin de Antealtares, at Compostella in Spain. The epitaph on his tomb ends with this line: "A saint, he left the world to live with the saints."

FAILBHE the LITTLE (St) Ab.
                              AC. March 10
d. 754. For seven years abbot of Iona, where he died at the age of eighty.

FAILBHE (St) Ab.   AC. March 22
d. c.680. An abbot of Iona. He was an Irishman and brother of St Finan of Rath. There are some twenty other saints of the same name commemorated in the Irish and Scottish menologies.

FAINA (St) M.   RM. May 18
See Theodotus, Thecusa, etc.

**FAITH, HOPE and CHARITY (SS)
VV. MM.   RM. Aug 1**
d. c.120. The English equivalent of the Greek Pistis, Elpis, Agape, and of the Latin Fides, Spes, Caritas. The legend is that they were three young girls, aged respectively twelve, ten and nine years, daughters of St Wisdom (Sophia, Sapientia) with whom they were martyred in Rome under Hadrian. The story seems to be a myth.

FAITH (FOI) (St) VM.   RM. Oct 6
? A Maiden of Agen in S. France, burnt to death in the same city (under Maximian Herculeus). Her shrine at the abbey of Conques was very famous during the Middle Ages. A portion of her relics was taken to Glastonbury; hence her place in the Sarum calendar and the dedication to her of several English churches.

FAL (FELE) (St) C.   RM. May 16
Otherwise Fidolus, q.v.

FALCO (St) Bp.   AC. Feb 20
d. 512. Bishop of Maestricht from 495 till his death.

FALCO (Bl) Ab. OSB.   AC. June 6
d. 1146. Falco received the Benedictine habit at Cava, at the hands of St Peter, abbot of that monastery. Shortly after he was sent to rule the daughter house of St Mary at Cirzosimo, and in 1141 he succeeded Bl Simon as abbot of Cava. Cult confirmed in 1928.

FALCO (Bl) H.   AC. Aug 9
d. 1440. A native of Calabria, who led a hermit's life in the Abruzzi. His shrine is to be found at Palena. Cult approved in 1893.

**FAMIANUS (QUARDUS) (St) H.
OSB. Cist.   AC. Aug 8**
1090–1150. A native of Cologne, who made the pilgrimage to the Holy Land, to Rome and Compostella, and finally settled near the last named place as a hermit, living for twenty-five years at San Placido on the River Minho. When the Cistercian abbey of Osera was built in the neighbourhood he joined the community and professed the Rule. However, he obtained leave to visit the Holy Land once more and, on his return, died at Gallese in Umbria.

FANCHEA (GARBH) (St) V.
                              AC. Jan 1
d. c.?585. A native of Clogher and sister of St Endeus (Enda). She was the abbess-foundress of a convent at Rossory in Fermanagh, and was buried at Killane.

FANDILAS (St) Mk. M. RM. June 13
d. 853. An Andalusian by birth, he was a priest and abbot of the monastery of Peñamelaria, near Cordova. He was beheaded at Cordova by order of the emir Mohammed.

FANTINUS (St) Ab.   RM. Aug 30
d. *p.*980. A Basilian monk of Calabria,
and abbot of the Greek monastery of St
Mercury. He was already an old man
when his abbey was destroyed by the
Saracens. He then travelled to the East,
where he died.

FARA (St) Abs. RM. Apr 3 and Dec 7
Otherwise Burgundofara, q.v.

FARANNAN (St) Ab.   AC. Feb 15
d. *c.*590. An Irish disciple of St Columba
at Iona. Eventually he returned to Ireland to lead the life of a hermit at All-
Farannan, now Allernan, Sligo, where
he probably died.

FARO (St) Bp.   RM. Oct 28
d. *c.*675. A brother of SS Fara and
Cagnoaldus. He gave up the office of
chancellor which he held at the court of
Dagobert I and became a monk (either
at Luxeuil or at Rebais), a priest, and
finally bishop of Meaux (626). In this
capacity he was a great fosterer of
monasticism.

FASTRED (Bl) Ab. OSB. Cist.
AC. Apr 21
d. 1163. Fastred de Cavamiez was a
native of Hainault who received the
Cistercian habit from St Bernard at
Clairvaux. In 1148 he was dispatched
with a colony of monks to be abbot-
founder of Cambron, in the diocese of
Cambrai. In 1157 he was transferred to
the abbacy of Clairvaux and in 1162 to
that of Cîteaux.

FAUSTA and EVILASIUS (SS) MM.
RM. Sept 20
d. 303. St Fausta, a girl of about thirteen, was being cruelly treated by order
of Evilasius, a heathen magistrate, when,
on seeing her constancy, the latter also
confessed Christ. Both were martyred
together at Cyzicum in Pontus under
Diocletian.

FAUSTA (St) W.   RM. Dec 19
3rd cent. The reputed mother of St
Anastasia of Sirmium.

FAUSTIAN (St) M.   RM. Apr 29
See Corfu (Martyrs of).

FAUSTINA (St) V.   AC. Jan 18
See Liberata (Jan 18).

FAUSTINIAN (St) Bp. RM. Feb 26
4th cent. Said to have been the second
bishop of Bologna. He reorganized the
diocese which had suffered much during
the persecution of Diocletian, and lived
to be a firm defender of the Faith against
Arianism.

FAUSTINUS and JOVITA (SS) MM.
RM. Feb 15
d. *c.*?121. Two brothers, belonging to
the nobility of Brescia, in Lombardy,
and zealous preachers of Christianity,
who were beheaded in their native city,
under the emperor Hadrian. The details
of their Passion are doubtful but their
cult was ancient and widespread. They
are the chief patrons of Brescia.

FAUSTINUS (St) Bp.   RM. Feb 16
d. 381. The successor of St Ursicinus,
about the year 360, in the see of Brescia,
in Lombardy. He is said to have been a
collateral descendant of SS Faustinus
and Jovita and to have compiled their
Acts.

FAUSTINUS and Comp. (SS) MM.
RM. Feb 17
? A group of forty-five martyrs, of
whom nothing whatever is known. The
RM. places them at Rome.

FAUSTINUS, TIMOTHY and
VENUSTUS (SS) MM. RM. May 22
d. *c.*362. Roman martyrs under Julian
the Apostate.

FAUSTINUS (St) M.   RM. June 5
See Florentius, Julian, etc.

FAUSTINUS (St) M.   RM. July 29
See Simplicius, Faustinus and Beatrix.

FAUSTINUS (St) C.   RM. July 29
4th cent. A disciple of St Felix, bishop of Martano, or Spello, near Spoleto, and his attendant at his martyrdom. St Faustinus himself suffered much for Christ before passing away peacefully at Todi in Umbria.

FAUSTINUS, LUCIUS, CANDIDUS, CAELIAN, MARK, JANUARIUS and FORTUNATUS (SS) MM.   RM. Dec 15
? African martyrs, about whom nothing is known.

FAUSTUS (St) Ab.   AC. Feb 15
6th cent. An alleged disciple of St Benedict at Montecassino, and companion and biographer of St Maurus, according to the legendary *Vita Sancti Mauri* of Abbot Odo of Glanfeuil.

FAUSTUS and Comp. (SS) MM.   RM. June 24
? Twenty-four Roman martyrs, whose Acts have been lost. They are very probably to be identified with the group of Roman martyrs commemorated on June 25 (see Lucilla, Flora, etc.).

FAUSTUS (St) M.   RM. July 16
d. 250. A martyr of the Decian persecution, who, crucified and transfixed with arrows, is said to have lingered in his agony for five days.

FAUSTUS (St) M.   RM. Aug 1
See Bonus, Faustus, etc.

FAUSTUS (St) C.   AC. Aug 3
5th cent. Said to have been son of St Dalmatius but the history is of later origin. Faustus became a monk.

FAUSTUS (St) M.   RM. Aug 7
d. c.190. According to tradition, this St Faustus was a soldier martyred at Milan under Commodus.

FAUSTUS, MACARIUS and Comp. (SS) MM.   RM. Sept 6
d. 250. A group of twelve martyrs, beheaded at Alexandria in Egypt under Decius.

FAUSTUS (St) Ab.   AC. Sept 6
d. c.607. Abbot of the monastery of Santa Lucia, at Syracuse, where he taught Zosimus, the future bishop of Syracuse.

FAUSTUS (St) M.   RM. Sept 8
See Timothy and Faustus.

FAUSTUS (St) Bp.   AC. Sept 28
d. c.493. Born in Brittany, Faustus became a monk at Lérins and later the abbot (433) of that monastery. In 452, he was chosen bishop of Riez. He combated with great energy and success both Arianism and Pelagianism; though in his writings he himself is not exempt from semi-Pelagianism. He was one of the most influential bishops of his time.

FAUSTUS (St) M.   RM. Oct 3
See Dionysius, Faustus, etc. This Faustus is identified by the RM. with those of Oct 4 and Nov 19.

FAUSTUS (St) M.   RM. Oct 4
See Caius, Faustus, etc.

FAUSTUS (St) M.   RM. Oct 5
See Placid, Eutychius, etc.

FAUSTUS, JANUARIUS and MARTIAL (SS) MM.   RM. Oct 13
d. 304. Martyrs of Cordova under Diocletian, Prudentius calls them "the Three Crowns of Cordova".

FAUSTUS (St) M.   RM. Nov 19
4th cent. The deacon of St Dionysius of
Alexandria and his companion in exile.
He survived his master and in extreme
old age died a martyr under Diocletian.
See Dionysius, Faustus, etc., and Caius,
Faustus, etc.

FAUSTUS, DIDIUS, AMMONIUS,
PHILEAS, HESYCHIUS, PACHO-
MIUS, THEODORE and Comp.
(SS) MM.   RM. Nov 26
d. c.311. Egyptian martyrs under Maxi-
mian Galerius. It is said that their total
number was six hundred and sixty.
Phileas, Hesychius, Pachomius and
Theodore were bishops, Faustus a priest
of Alexandria.

FAZZIO (FATIUS, FAZIUS,
FACIUS) (St) C.   AC. Jan 18
1190–1272. A native of Verona and a
goldsmith. He founded a charitable
society at Cremona, called the Order of
the Holy Spirit. He made several pilgrimages on foot to Rome and to Compostella.

FEBRONIA (St) VM.   RM. June 25
d. 304. A young nun, barbarously mutilated and finally put to death under
Diocletian at Nisibis in Mesopotamia
(not at Sybapolis in Syria). The legend
adds many ghastly details; but there is
good reason to doubt the very existence
of this saint.

FECHIN (St) Ab.   AC. Jan 20
d. c.665. A native of Connaught, and the
abbot-founder of several Irish monasteries. His name is particularly connected with that of Fobhar (Fore) in
Westmeath. Ecclefechan and St Vigean's, near Arbroath in Scotland, also
perpetuate his memory.

FEDLEMID (St) Bp.   AC. Aug 9
Otherwise Phelim, q.v.

FEIGHIN (St) Ab.   AC. Jan 20
Otherwise Fechin, q.v.

FELAN (St) Ab.   AC. Jan 9
Otherwise Foelan, q.v.

FELE (St) C.   RM. May 16
Otherwise Fidolus, q.v.

FELICIA de MONTMORENCY
(Bl) V. OV.   AC. June 6
1600–1666. Born at Rome of French
parents, Marie Félicie des Ursins became a nun of the Visitation at Autun,
during the life-time of the foundress,
St Jane Frances de Chantal.

FELICIA MEDA (Bl) Poor Clare
                        AC. Oct 5
1378–1444. A native of Milan, who
joined the Poor Clares at the convent of
St Ursula in that city (1400). In 1425
she was made abbess, and after fourteen
years she was sent to Pesaro to establish
a new house which she ruled with equal
success. Cult approved in 1812.

FELICIAN (St) Bp. M.
               RM. Jan 24 and Oct 20
d. 251. A native of Foligno, who was
consecrated bishop of that city by Pope
St Victor I and governed his diocese for
more than fifty years, meanwhile evangelizing the whole of Umbria. He was
arrested under Decius, and died on his
way to martyrdom at Rome.

FELICIAN, PHILAPPIAN and
Comp. (SS) MM.   RM. Jan 30
? A band of one hundred and twenty-six
African martyrs.

FELICIAN (St) M.   RM. Feb 2
See Fortunatus, Felician, etc.

FELICIAN (St) M.   RM. June 9
See Primus and Felician.

FELICIAN (St) M.   RM. July 21
See Victor, Alexander, etc.

FELICIAN (St) M.   RM. Oct 29
See Hyacinth, Quintius, etc.

FELICIAN (St) M.   RM. Nov 11
See Valentine, Felician and Victorinus.

FELICIAN (St) M.   RM. Nov 19
See Severinus, Exuperius and Felician.

FELICINUS (St) Bp.   RM. July 19
Otherwise Felix of Verona, q.v.

FELICISSIMA (St) VM. RM. Aug 12
See Gracilian and Felicissima.

FELICISSIMUS, HERACLIUS and PAULINUS (SS) MM. RM. May 26
d. 303. Martyrs under Diocletian. They suffered in all probability at Todi in Umbria, where their relics are still venerated.

FELICISSIMUS (St) M. RM. July 2
See Ariston, Crescentian, etc.

FELICISSIMUS (St) M. RM. Aug 6
See Sixtus II and Comp.

FELICISSIMUS (St) M. RM. Oct 26
See Rogatian and Felicissimus.

FELICISSIMUS (St) M. RM. Nov 24
d. c.303. A martyr who suffered at Perugia, probably under Diocletian.

FELICITAS (St) M.   RM. March 7
See Perpetua, Felicitas, etc.

FELICITAS (St) M.   RM. March 8
See Cyril, Rogatus, etc.

FELICITAS (St) V.   AC. March 26
9th cent. A nun, in all probability of the Benedictine Order, who professed the Rule in a convent on the Colli Euganei,

or else in that of SS Cosmas and Damian at Padua. Her relics are now at St Justina, Padua.

FELICITAS (St) M.   RM. Nov 23
d. 165. A Roman widow martyred at Rome with her sons under Marcus Antoninus. The RM. identifies her sons with the seven brothers, commemorated July 10 (see Seven Brothers) but modern writers incline to question this identification. This Felicitas may be the saint named in the Canon of the Mass, rather than the companion of St Perpetua, as usually supposed.

FELICULA (St) M.   RM. Feb 14
See Vitalis, Felicula and Zeno.

FELICULA (St) VM.   RM. June 13
d. c.90. A Roman maiden of the apostolic age, thought to have been the foster sister of St Petronilla. After the latter's martyrdom under Domitian she was left for a fortnight in her prison without food or drink, and then was thrown into a ditch to die. Her body was recovered by St Nicomedes.

**FELINUS and GRATIAN (SS) MM.
                                    RM. June 1**
d. 250. Soldiers in the imperial army martyred at Perugia under Decius. Their relics were translated to Arona near Milan in 979.

FELIX (*several*)
Note. This name is one of the most common in Christian Hagiology. In the following notices we list only the best known among them.

**FELIX of BOURGES (St) Bp.
                                    AC. Jan 1**
d. c.580. Bishop of Bourges in France. He took part in the council of Paris A.D. 573. He is still venerated at Bourges.

FELIX and JANUARIUS (SS) MM.
RM. Jan 7
? Said to have suffered martyrdom at Heraclea, a name common to several ancient cities.

FELIX (St) M.   RM. Jan 9
See Epictetus, Jucundus, etc.

FELIX OF NOLA (St) M. RM. Jan 14
d. c.260. The son of a Romano-Syrian soldier who had settled at Nola, near Naples. Felix was ordained a priest and devoted himself to the service of his bishop, St Maximus, especially during the persecution which broke out under Decius. On account of his sufferings during the persecution, he is sometimes referred to as a martyr. St Paulinus, bishop of Nola, has left a glowing account of the popular veneration for St Felix.

FELIX (St) C.   AC. Jan 14
? A Roman priest, venerated also on Jan 14, and often confused with St Felix of Nola.

FELIX O'DULLANY (Bl) Bp.
OSB. Cist.   PC. Jan 24
d. 1202. An Irish Cistercian monk, probably of Jerpoint, Kilkenny. In 1178 he was made bishop of Ossory residing at Aghaoe. He is venerated by the Cistercians as a *beatus*.

FELIX, SYMPHRONIUS (SEM-PRONIUS), HIPPOLYTUS and Comp. (SS) MM.   RM. Feb 3
? A group of martyrs who suffered probably in Proconsular Africa.

FELIX of LYONS (St) Bp. RM. Feb 3
See Lupicinus and Felix.

FELIX of AFRICA (St) M.
RM. Feb 11
See Saturninus, Dativus, etc.

FELIX of ADRUMETUM (St) M.
RM. Feb 21
See Verulus, Secundinus, etc.

FELIX of METZ (St) Bp. RM. Feb 21
2nd cent. Described as the third bishop of Metz, which see he is alleged to have occupied for over forty years in the sub-apostolic age.

FELIX of BRESCIA (St) Bp.
RM. Feb 23
d. c.650. The twentieth bishop of Brescia. He governed the diocese for over forty eventful years during which he was occupied in combating Lombard Arians and other heretics.

FELIX (St) M.   RM. Feb 26
See Fortunatus, Felix and Comp.

FELIX III (or II) (St) Pope
RM. March 1 (Nov 1)
d. 492. A Roman, said to have been an ancestor of St Gregory the Great. He was pope from 483 till his death. The nine years of his pontificate were occupied with controversy against Monophysitism and Eutychianism as also in remedying the evils caused in Africa by numerous apostasies during the Vandal persecution.

FELIX, LUCIOLUS, FORTUNA-TUS, MARCIA, and Comp. (SS)
MM.   RM. March 3
? A group of forty martyrs conjectured to have suffered in N. Africa.

FELIX of RHUYS (St) Ab. OSB.
AC. March 4
d. 1038. A native of the diocese of Quimper in Brittany who became a hermit on Ouessant Island and afterwards a Benedictine at Fleury (Saint-Benoit-sur-Loire). The abbot of Fleury sent him to restore Rhuys abbey, the great Breton monastery founded by St

Gildas, which had been destroyed by the Normans.

FELIX (St) M.   RM. March 8
See Cyril, Rogatus, etc.

FELIX of DUNWICH (St) Bp.
                          RM. March 8
d. 648. A native of Burgundy who brought about the conversion of Sigebert, king of the East Angles, when that prince was in exile, and later was summoned by Sigebert to evangelize East Anglia. St Felix undertook the mission with the approval of St Honorius of Canterbury, and placed his episcopal see at Dunwich, now washed away by the sea. He preached with great success in Norfolk, Suffolk and Cambridgeshire, opening schools on the French model. He is the veritable apostle of the East Angles.

FELIX of AQUILEIA (St) M.
                          RM. March 16
See Hilary, Tatian, etc.

FELIX of GERONA (St) M.
                RM. March 18 and Aug 1
See Narcissus and Felix.

FELIX and Comp. (SS) MM.
                          RM. March 23
5th cent. A group of twenty-one martyrs. Unless their proximity in the RM. to SS Victorian and Comp. implies that they suffered in the same persecution of the Vandals, we can only say that they suffered in Africa.

FELIX of MONTECASSINO (Bl) Mk.   AC. March 23
d. c.1000. A Benedictine of Montecassino, who spent all his life in one of the daughter-houses of the abbey. On account of the many miracles wrought at his tomb the bishop of Chieti raised his relics for veneration.

FELIX of TRÈVES (St) Bp.
                          RM. March 26
d. c.400. Consecrated bishop of Trèves by his friend, St Martin of Tours, in 386. Owing to the fact that this took place under the usurping emperor Maximus, the legality of his election was questioned by the Holy See and St Ambrose, and he consequently resigned. Contemporary writers, particularly St Sulpicius Severus, speak very highly of his virtues.

FELIX (St) M.   RM. March 31
See Theodulus, Anesius, etc.

FELIX of SARAGOSSA (St) M.
                          RM. Apr 16
See Saragossa (Martyrs of).

FELIX of ALEXANDRIA (St) M.
                          RM. Apr 21
See Arator, Fortunatus, etc.

FELIX, FORTUNATUS and ACHILLEUS (SS) MM. RM. Apr 23
d. 212. St Felix, a priest, and his two deacons, Fortunatus and Achilleus, were sent by St Irenaeus of Lyons to evangelize the district of Vienne, in France. After a most successful apostolate they were martyred. The *Acta* are of much later composition.

FELIX of SEVILLE (St) M.
                          RM. May 2
? A deacon, martyred in all probability at Seville where he is held in great veneration.

FELIX of ROME (St) M. RM. May 10
See Calepodius, Palmatius, etc.

FELIX and GENNADIUS (SS) MM.
                          RM. May 16
? Two martyrs venerated from ancient times in the city of Uzalis in Proconsular Africa, where their relics were enshrined.

FELIX of SPOLETO (St) Bp. M.
RM. May 18
d. *c*.304. A bishop, either of Spoleto or of the neighbouring town of Spello (*Hispellum*) in Umbria. He was martyred under Diocletian.

FELIX of CANTALICE (St) OFM. Cap.   RM. May 18
1513–1587. A native of Cantalice, near Rieti, in Apulia, the child of peasant farmers, he started life as a farm labourer, and at the age of thirty joined the Capuchins in Rome as a lay-brother; thereafter for forty years he begged the daily alms for his friary. He was a friend of St Charles Borromeo, and an intimate of St Philip Neri. He was nicknamed *Deo Gratias* on account of his habitual use of this ejaculation. His characteristic virtue was spiritual joy. Canonized in 1724—the first Capuchin friar to attain this honour.

FELIX of ISTRIA (St) M.
RM. May 24
See Zoëllus, Servilius, etc.

FELIX of SARDINIA (St) M.
RM. May 28
See Emilius, Felix, etc.

FELIX (St) H.   AC. May 29
See Votus, Felix and John.

FELIX I (St) Pope M.
RM. May 30 and Dec 30
d. 274. A Roman by birth and pope from 269 to 274. He was the first to condemn the heresy of Paul of Samosata. He is said to have died a martyr under Aurelian; but this appears to be an error, due to confusion with another Felix.

FELIX of NICOSIA (Bl) OFM. Cap.
AC. June 1
1715–1787. A native of Nicosia in Sicily. He began life as an apprentice to a shoemaker; then he sought to become a religious, but failed several times. At last he was professed as a lay-brother, and in the course of his begging expeditions on behalf of his friary at Nicosia, reclaimed numerous sinners and helped the poor and the sick. Beatified in 1888.

FELIX of FRITZLAR (St) M. OSB.
AC. June 5
d. *c*.790. A Benedictine monk of Fritzlar in Germany and a martyr probably at the hands of the heathen Saxons.

FELIX and FORTUNATUS (SS) MM.   RM. June 11
d. 296. Two brothers, born at Vicenza in N. Italy, who suffered under Diocletian at Aquileia.

FELIX of CORDOVA (St) M.
RM. June 14
See Anastasius, Felix and Digna.

FELIX and MAURUS (SS) CC.
AC. June 16
6th cent. Natives of Palestine, father and son, who after a pilgrimage to Rome settled at a place now called San Felice near Narni, in central Italy.

FELIX of APOLLONIA (St) M.
RM. June 17
See Isaurus, Innocent, etc.

FELIX of SUTRI (St) M.
RM. June 23
d. 257. A priest of Sutri in Tuscany, scourged to death under the emperors Valerian and Gallienus.

FELIX of CÎTEAUX (Bl) Mk. OSB. Cist.   PC. June 23
d. 1113. A Cistercian monk, listed in the menologies of the order as a *beatus*.

FELIX (St) M.   RM. July 2
See Ariston, Crescentian, etc.

FELIX of NANTES (St) Bp.
AC. July 7
d. 584. A great bishop who ruled over the see of Nantes for about thirty-three years. He died on Jan 8; July 7 is the anniversary of the translation of his relics.

FELIX (St) M.   RM. July 10
One of the Seven Brothers, MM., q.v.

FELIX (St) M.   RM. July 10
See Januarius, Marinus, etc.

FELIX of MILAN (St) M.
RM. July 12
See Nabor and Felix.

FELIX of COMO (St) Bp.
RM. July 14
d. c.390. Said to have been the first bishop of Como. He was an intimate friend of St Ambrose.

FELIX of PAVIA (St) Bp. M.
RM. July 15
? A martyr, of whom nothing is known. Some identify him with St Felix of Spoleto (May 18).

FELIX (St) M.   RM. July 17
One of the Scillitan Martyrs, q.v.

FELIX (FELICINUS) of VERONA (St) Bp.   RM. July 19
? A bishop of Verona, venerated from ancient times as a saint.

FELIX of MANFREDONIA (St) M.
RM. July 25
See Florentius and Felix.

FELIX of CORDOVA (St) M.
RM. July 27
See George, Aurelius, etc.

FELIX, JULIA and JUCUNDA (SS) MM.   RM. July 27
? The RM. erroneously assigns these

martyrs to Nola. As to St Felix the reference would simply be the date of the consecration of St Felix, bishop of Nola (see Nov 15). SS Jucunda and Julia are in older MSS assigned to Nicomedia in Asia Minor.

FELIX II (St) Pope M. RM. July 29
d. 365. The accounts of the life of this Felix are very conflicting: he does not seem to have been either a pope or a martyr. He certainly was intruded into the see of Rome in the year 355, when Pope Liberius was exiled by the Arian emperor Constantius II. The reasons why he was listed in the RM. are still heatedly debated.

FELIX (FEDLIMID) (St) Bp.
AC. Aug 9
Otherwise Phelim, q.v.

FELIX of PORTO (St) M.
RM. Aug 22
See Martial, Saturninus, etc.

FELIX of PISTOIA (St) H.
RM. Aug 26
9th cent. A hermit of Pistoia in Tuscany, venerated as a saint, about whom, however, almost nothing is known.

FELIX (St) M.
RM. Aug 28 and Sept 1
See Septiminus, Januarius and Felix, a group among the Twelve Holy Brothers.

FELIX and ADAUCTUS (SS) MM.
RM. Aug 30
d. c.304. Martyrs beheaded in Rome under Diocletian. St Felix was a priest; as he was being led to execution, a bystander confessed Christ and was put to death with St Felix. Because this second martyr's name was not known, he was called *Adauctus*, i.e., the one added.

FELIX (St) M.   RM. Sept 1
See Donatus and Felix.

FELIX and AUGEBERT (SS) MM. AC. Sept 6

7th cent. Two English slaves sold in France, and ransomed by St Gregory the Great, who directed that they should be received and educated in a monastery with a view to their becoming missionaries in their native country. Felix was ordained priest, and Augebert deacon; but unfortunately they were killed by pagans in Champagne before they could undertake their mission.

FELIX and another FELIX (SS) Bps. MM. RM. Sept 10

See Nemesian, Felix, etc.

FELIX and REGULA (SS) MM. AC. Sept 11

3rd cent. Brother and sister who at the time of the martyrdom of St Maurice under Maximian Herculeus, took refuge in Switzerland, where they were eventually found and martyred near Zurich.

FELIX and CONSTANTIA (SS) MM. RM. Sept 19

1st cent. Martyrs under Nero, at Nocera, between Naples and Salerno.

FELIX III (IV) (St) Pope RM. Sept 22

d. 530. Less accurately Felix IV. (See above, St Felix II, July 29.) His pontificate lasted from 526 till 530 and his best remembered deed as pope was the building of the church of SS Cosmas and Damian. He was greatly loved in Rome for his simplicity and generosity to the poor.

FELIX of AUTUN (St) M. RM. Sept 24

See Andochius, Thyrsus and Felix.

FELIX and CYPRIAN (SS) MM. Bps. RM. Oct 12

d. c.484. Two African bishops, leaders of a great multitude of Catholics—the number of four thousand nine hundred and sixty-six is usually given by historians—driven out to starvation and death in the Sahara desert by the Arian Vandal king Hunneric. We have the account of their sufferings from Victor of Utica, a contemporary writer.

FELIX (AFRICANUS), AUDACTUS (ADAUCTUS), JANUARIUS, FORTUNATUS and SEPTIMUS (SS) MM. RM. Oct 24

d. 303. Felix was a bishop of Thibiuca in Africa who refused to deliver up the sacred books, and was for this reason put to death. He was one of the first victims of Diocletian's persecution. The accounts we have of the other martyrs mentioned with him are not trustworthy.

FELIX and EUSEBIUS (SS) MM. RM. Nov 5

? 1st cent. Alleged martyrs of Terracina an Italian city between Rome and Naples.

FELIX of THYNISSA (St) M. RM. Nov 6

? An African martyr who suffered at Thynissa, near Hippona (Bona). He was found dead in prison the day before he was to be executed. St Augustine preached a sermon on the martyr's feast day.

FELIX of FONDI (St) Mk. OSB. RM. Nov 6

6th cent. A monk of a Benedictine house at Fondi in S. Italy—a contemporary of St Gregory the Great, by whom he was greatly revered.

FELIX of NOLA (St) Bp. M. RM. Nov 15

d. 287. Said to have been the first bishop of Nola, near Naples, and to have been put to death for Christ with thirty companions.

FELIX of VALOIS (St) C.
RM. Nov 20
1127–1212. We first meet him as a hermit in a forest near Meaux. Eventually—some writers say he was already seventy years old—he, with St John of Matha, organized the Trinitarians in France, a religious order founded for the purpose of ransoming captives from the Moors. He is called "of Valois" because he lived for a time in that province.

FELIX (St) Bp.   RM. Nov 28
See Valerian, Urban, etc.

FELIX of BOLOGNA (St) Bp.
RM. Dec 4
d. 429. A deacon of the church of Milan under St Ambrose, and afterwards the fifth bishop of Bologna.

FELIX (St) M.   RM. Dec 5
See Julius, Potamia, etc.

FELIX of ROME (St) M.
RM. Dec 29
See Callistus, Felix and Boniface.

FEOCK (St) V.   AC. Feb 2
? A saint otherwise unknown, whose name is perpetuated by a church dedication in Cornwall. Possibly she was an immigrant from Ireland. Some have it that Feock is only a variant of the name of St Fiace the friend of St Patrick; others identify St Feock with St Vougas of Brittany.

FERDINAND III (St) King
RM. May 30
1198–1252. King of Castile in 1217, and of León in 1230. For twenty-seven years he was engaged in an almost uninterrupted crusade against the Mohammedans in Spain, from whom he recaptured Cordova (1236), Murcia, Jaen, Cadiz, and finally Seville (1249). He was a wise ruler, and was wont to say

that he "feared more the curse of one old woman than the whole army of the Moors". He was the founder of the university of Salamanca and of the cathedral of Burgos. By his second wife he was the father of Eleanor, wife of Edward I of England. Canonized in 1671.

FERDINAND of ST JOSEPH
AYALA (Bl) M. OSA.   AC. June 1
1575–1617. Born at Ballesteros, diocese of Toledo, Spain, he took the Augustinian habit at Mentilla, and in 1603 was sent to Mexico, and thence to Japan (1605) as vicar provincial. He worked at Ozaka with great success until his capture and execution at Omura. Beatified in 1867.

FERDINAND of PORTUGAL (Bl)
M.   AC. June 5
1402–1443. Surnamed "the Constant" or "the Standard-bearer" (*El Abanderado*), son of King John I of Portugal, he was born at Santarem, and his leanings towards the religious life led him to become the Master General of the military order of Aviz, an order dependent on Cîteaux. In this capacity he led an expedition against the Moors in Africa, but was defeated at Tangier and given up as a hostage. He was imprisoned at Arzilla and remained a prisoner, with never a word of complaint, for five years, finally dying there of neglect. Cult approved in 1470.

FERDINAND of ARAGON (St) Bp.
AC. June 27
13th cent. Related to the royal family of Aragon, then the rulers of the Two Sicilies, he became the fifth bishop of Cajazzo, in that kingdom. His relics are now venerated at Cornello, in Sicily.

FERDINAND SANCHEZ (Bl) M.
SJ.   AC. July 15
d. 1570. Born in Castile, and a Jesuit

novice, he suffered martyrdom under the leadership of Bl Ignatius de Azevedo, q.v.

FEREDARIUS (St) Ab. AC. May 18
d. *p*.863. An Irishman by birth, chosen abbot of Iona in 863. During his abbacy the relics of St Columba were removed to Ireland, for fear of the Danes.

FERGNA (St) Ab.   AC. March 2
d. 637. Surnamed "the White", a kinsman and disciple of St Columba and his successor as abbot of Iona.

FERGUS (FERGUSTUS, FERGUISIUS) (St) Bp.   AC. March 30
6th cent. A bishop of Downpatrick; but the traditions concerning him are vague in the extreme, and he may possibly be identified with St Fergus of Scotland (Nov 18).

FERGUS (St) Bp.   AC. Nov 18
d. *p*.721. An Irish bishop who preached in Perthshire, Caithness, Buchan and Forfarshire. He signed the Acts of the Roman council of A.D. 721, describing himself as a Pict. In the Aberdeen breviary he is called Fergustian.

FERNANDO (*several*)
The Spanish and Portuguese form of Ferdinand, q.v.

FERRAN (*several*)
The old Castilian and Catalan form of Ferdinand, q.v.

FERREOLUS (St) Bp.   AC. Jan 4
d. 581. A native of Narbonne, who became bishop of Uzès. He devoted himself in particular to converting the Jews of his diocese, and is said to have been exiled by King Childebert on that account. He was the founder of a monastery, for which he wrote a monastic rule.

FERREOLUS (FERGÉOL) (Bl) Bp. M.   AC. Jan 16
d. *c*.670. Said to have been bishop of Grenoble in France. Cult confirmed in 1907.

FERREOLUS and FERRUTIO (SS) MM.   RM. June 16
d. *c*.212. Ferreolus, a priest, and Ferrutio, a deacon, are said to have been brothers and natives of Asia Minor. They were sent by St Irenaeus of Lyons to evangelize the country round Besançon, where they worked for thirty years and then were martyred.

FERREOLUS (St) M.   RM. Sept 18
3rd cent. An officer of the imperial army, martyred at Vienne in Gaul, under Diocletian. One tradition makes him superior officer to St Julian of Auvergne (cf. RM. Aug 31).

FERREOLUS (St) Bp. AC. Sept 18
d. *c*.591. Fifth bishop of Limoges in France. He is mentioned with great veneration by St Gregory of Tours.

FERRUTIO (St) M.   RM. June 16
See Ferreolus and Ferrutio.

FERRUTIUS (St) M.   RM. Oct 28
? A Roman soldier stationed at Mainz in Germany, who demanded his discharge from the army rather than take part in idolatrous worship. He was cast into prison, where he died of ill-treatment and hunger.

FESTUS (St) M.   RM. June 24
Otherwise Faustus, q.v.

FESTUS (St) M.   RM. Sept 19
See Januarius and Comp.

FESTUS (St) M.   RM. Dec 21
See John and Festus.

FIACE (FIECH) (St) Bp.
AC. Oct 12

5th cent. An Irish bishop, friend and disciple of St Patrick, in whose honour he wrote a hymn which is still extant.

FIACHAN (FIANCHNE) (St) C.
AC. Apr 29

7th cent. A native of Munster in Ireland, a monk at Lismore, and disciple of St Carthage the Younger.

FIACRE (FIACRIUS, FIAKER, FÈVRE) (St) Ab.
RM. Aug 30

d. c.670. Fiachra, an Irishman, was given land for a hermitage by St Faro of Meaux. Here he lived for the rest of his life, attracting many disciples for whom he built the abbey of Breuil. St Fiacre's shrine is still a place of pilgrimage. As patron of gardeners, he is often represented carrying a shovel.

FIBITIUS (St) Bp.
RM. Nov 5

d. c.500. Abbot of a monastery at Trèves, and the twenty-first bishop of that city.

FIDELIS (St) Bp.
AC. Feb 7

d. c.570. An Eastern by origin, he travelled to Spain with some merchants, and settled at Mérida, where he was trained by St Paul, bishop of the city, whom he succeeded in that office.

FIDELIS (St) M.
RM. March 23

? An African martyr. Some writers place him in the same group of African martyrs as St Felix and his twenty-four companions (March 23).

FIDELIS of SIGMARINGEN (St) M. OFM. Cap.
RM. Apr 24

1577–1622. Mark Rey, born at Sigmaringen, in S. Germany, practised as a lawyer, and came to be known as the "advocate of the poor". In 1612 he joined the Capuchins, receiving the new name of Fidelis, and after his ordination the newly founded Roman Congregation of Propaganda sent him as a missionary to the Swiss Protestants in the Grisons. Incensed at his success, the Calvinists raised the peasants against him by inventing the story that he was a political agent of the Austrian emperor. He was stabbed to death near Grüsch.

FIDELIS of EDESSA (St) M.
RM. Aug 21

See Bassa, Theogonius, etc.

FIDELIS of COMO (St) M.
RM. Oct 28

d. c.304. A soldier martyred in Lombardy under Maximian Herculeus. His body was translated by St Charles Borromeo to Milan, but some of his relics are venerated at Como.

FIDELMIA (St) V.
AC. Jan 11

See Ethenea and Fidelmia.

FIDENTIAN (St) M.
RM. Nov 15

See Secundus, Fidentian and Varicus.

FIDENTIUS and TERENCE (SS) MM.
RM. Sept 27

? The relics of these martyrs were discovered in the 12th century at Todi in central Italy, where they are venerated. Nothing else is known about them. The legend of their martyrdom is quite untrustworthy.

FIDENTIUS (St) Bp.
RM. Nov 16

2nd cent. Some make this saint a confessor, others a martyr, Baronius a bishop. Tradition assigns him to Padua and to the 2nd century. All this is mere surmise and nothing is known about him.

FIDES (St) VM.
RM. Aug 1

Otherwise Faith, q.v.

FIDHARLEUS (St) Ab. AC. Oct 1
d. 762. An Irish saint, the restorer of
Rathin Abbey.

FIDLEMINUS (St) Bp. AC. Aug 9
Otherwise Phelim, q.v.

**FIDOLUS (French: PHAL) (St) Ab.
RM. May 16**
d. c.540. The son of a Roman official in
Auvergne, France. Taken prisoner by
the soldiers of Clovis and sold into
slavery, he was ransomed by Aventinus,
abbot of Aumont, near Troyes. At a
later period Fidolus was himself abbot
of the abbey, which was afterwards
called Saint-Phal.

**FIDWETEN (FIVETEIN, FIDIVI-
TANUS) (St) Mk. OSB. AC. Dec 11**
d. c.888. A Benedictine monk, disciple
of St Convoyon at the abbey of Redon,
in Brittany.

FIECH (St) Bp. AC. Oct 12
Otherwise Fiace, q.v.

FILLAN (St) Ab. AC. Jan 9
Otherwise Foelan, q.v.

FINA (St) V. AC. March 12
Otherwise Seraphina, q.v.

FINAN (St) Bp. AC. Feb 17
d. 661. An Irish monk of Iona, who
succeeded St Aidan in the government
of the Northumbrian church. Attended
by St Cedd and other fellow-missionaries
he evangelized parts of southern England.

**FINAN (FINNIAN) (St) Ab.
AC. Apr 7**
6th cent. A native of Munster and a
disciple of St Brendan, at whose wish
he founded and governed a monastery
at Kinnitty in Offaly of which place he
is patron.

FINBAR (St) Ab. AC. July 4
6th cent. An Irish abbot of Innis-
Doimhle, Wexford.

**FINBARR (FION-BHARR, i.e.
White Head) (St) Bp. AC. Sept 25**
Otherwise Barr, q.v.

**FINDAN (or FINTAN) (St) H. OSB.
AC. Nov 15**
d. 879. A native of Leinster in Ireland
who was carried off as a slave to the
Orkneys by Norse raiders, but managed
to escape to Scotland. He then undertook a pilgrimage to Rome, and became
a Benedictine at the abbey of Farfa in
Sabina. Thence he migrated to the
abbey of Rheinau in Switzerland, where
he was allowed to live as a recluse for
twenty-two years.

FINDBARR (St) Bp. AC. Sept 10
Otherwise Finian, q.v.

**FINGAR (GWINNEAR), PHIALA
and Comp. (SS) MM. AC. Dec 14**
5th cent. Fingar and Phiala, brother
and sister, left their native Ireland and
crossed over to Cornwall, but they were
put to death at Hayle near Penzance by
a pagan chief. Their attendants shared
their crown.

**FINIAN LOBHAR (St) Ab.
AC. March 16**
d. ? c.560. A disciple of St Columba, by
whom he is said to have been made abbot
of Swords near Dublin. He is surnamed
"the Leper", on account of a skin
disease from which he suffered. The
records of his life are most conflicting.

**FINIAN (FINDBARR, WINNIN)
(St) Bp. AC. Sept 10**
d. c.575. Born near Stangford Lough,
he became a monk in Scotland, and was
ordained in Rome. On his return to
Ireland he brought with him biblical

manuscripts which led to the famous incident of the Psalter of St Columba. He was the founder and first abbot-bishop of the monastery of Moville in Co. Down. Wrongly identified with St Frigidian of Lucca.

FINIAN (FINTAN MUNNU) (St) Ab.   **AC. Oct 21**
d. *c*.635. A disciple of St Columba at Iona, and at a later period the abbot-founder of the monastery of Taghmon in Co. Wexford. In Scotland he is called St Mundus.

FINIAN of CLONARD (St) Bp.
                                AC. Dec 12
d. *c*.552. Born at Myshall in Co. Carlow, early in life he became a monk in Wales, and after a long sojourn there returned to Ireland and founded a great number of churches, monasteries and schools. Clonard was the greatest, and it was here that Finian had as pupils the so-called Twelve Apostles of Ireland, among whom was St Columba. Finian indeed became known as the "Teacher of the Irish Saints", Clonard was the greatest school of its period, renowned chiefly for its biblical studies.

FINLUGH (FINLAG) (St) Ab.
                                AC. Jan 3
6th cent. A brother of St Fintan (Jan 3) who crossed to Scotland, where it is thought that he became one of St Columba's disciples. Returning to Ireland he was made abbot of a monastery established by St Columba in Co. Derry.

FINTAN (St) Ab.   **AC. Jan 3**
6th cent. A disciple of St Comgall at Bangor. He is honoured as the patron saint of Doon in Limerick. His holy well is still venerated there.

FINTAN (St) Ab.   **RM. Feb 17**
d. 603. A disciple of St Columba, he led the life of a hermit at Clonenagh in Leix. Soon numerous disciples attached themselves to him, and he became their abbot. Such was the austerity of the life led at Clonenagh that neighbouring monasteries protested.

FINTAN (St) H. OSB.   **AC. Nov 15**
Otherwise Findan, q.v.

FIONNCHU (St) Ab.   **AC. Nov 28**
6th cent. The successor of St Comgall in the abbey of Bangor.

FIRMATUS (St) M.   **RM. Oct 5**
See Placid, Eutychius, etc.

FIRMATUS and FLAVIANA (SS) MM.   **RM. Oct 5**
? Firmatus, a deacon, and Flaviana, a virgin, are venerated on Oct 5 at Auxerre in France. Their names appear already in St Jerome's martyrology, as venerated in France long before the supposed martyrdom of St Placid, Eutychius and Companions (q.v.).

FIRMIAN (FERMANUS, FIR-MINUS) (St) Ab. OSB. AC. March 11
d. *c*.1020. A Benedictine abbot of the monastery of San Sabino Piceno, near Fermo, in the Marches of Ancona.

FIRMINA (St) VM.   **RM. Nov 24**
d. *c*.303. A Roman maiden tortured to death at Amelia (Ameria) in Umbria, under Diocletian.

FIRMINUS (St) Bp.   **AC. Jan 19**
? Third bishop of Gabales (Gévaudan), Mende, in France.

FIRMINUS (St) Ab.   **RM. March 11**
? It seems that Baronius became confused between St Firmian (or Firminus) abbot in the Marches of Ancona (AC. March 11) and Firminus Bishop of Amiens (RM. Sept 1 and 25). No

abbot-saint, of the name of Firminus, has ever been venerated at Amiens.

FIRMINUS (St) Bp.   AC. March 29
6th cent. Bishop of Viviers, in France.

FIRMINUS of ARMENIA (St) M.
RM. June 24
See Orentius, Heros, etc.

FIRMINUS of METZ (St) Bp.
RM. Aug 18
d. 496. Greek, or Italian, by origin, he ruled the see of Metz for eight years.

FIRMINUS of AMIENS (I and II) (SS) Bps.
RM. AC. Sept 1 and Sept 25
2nd–3rd cent. Two bishops of the name Firminus are venerated at Amiens: one on Sept 1, said to have been the third prelate of that city, and another on Sept 25, the supposed first bishop of Amiens. The latter is described as a native of Pampeluna in Spanish Navarre and a convert of St Saturninus, bishop of Toulouse. The former, viz. the third bishop of Amiens, is alleged to have been the son of one of the converts of St Firminus, the first bishop of that city. Some writers consider them to have been one and the same person.

FIRMINUS of UZÈS (St) Bp.
RM. Oct 11
d. 553. A native of Narbonne in S. France, he was educated by his uncle the bishop of Uzès, whom he succeeded as bishop at the age of twenty-two. He died at the age of thirty-seven.

FIRMINUS (St) Bp.   AC. Dec 5
d. 6th cent. The seventh bishop of Verdun.

FIRMUS of ROME (St) M.
RM. Feb 2
See Fortunatus, Felician, etc.

FIRMUS (St) M.   RM. March 11
See Gorgonius and Firmus.

FIRMUS (St) M.   RM. June 1
d. c.290. An Eastern martyr who suffered under Maximian.

FIRMUS (St) M.   RM. June 24
See Orentius, Heros, etc.

FIRMUS of TAGASTE (St) Bp.
RM. July 31
? Of him St Augustine writes that he was *firm* by name but *firmer* yet by faith. Put to the torture, he endured the most frightful sufferings rather than betray the hiding-place of one of his flock. This notice of St Augustine led Baronius to insert St Firmus's name in the RM.

FIRMUS and RUSTICUS (SS) MM.
RM. Aug 9
d. c.290. Two kinsmen, prominent citizens of Bergamo in Lombardy, who suffered at Verona under Maximian. Their *Passio* is not authentic; it seems possible that the relics of two martyrs of these names were translated from Africa to Verona.

FISHER, JOHN (St) Bp. M.
RM. July 9
See John Fisher.

FLANNAN (St) Bp.   AC. Dec. 18
7th cent. An Irish monk consecrated bishop by Pope John IV. He was the first bishop of Killaloe and worked also in the Hebrides and elsewhere, and in spite of all this toil, he managed, we are told, to recite daily the entire Psalter. He is patron of Killaloe diocese.

FLAVIA DOMITILLA, EUPHRO-SYNA and THEODORA (SS) VV. MM.   RM. May 7
2nd cent. Flavia Domitilla was a great-niece of the emperors Domitian and

Titus, and also of St Flavius Clemens. She became a Christian, and on refusing to marry a pagan, was banished from Rome, and eventually martyred with her foster sisters, Euphrosyna and Theodora, at Terracina. The Roman liturgy associates her name with those of SS Nereus and Achilles, who were buried in the cemetery of Domitilla in the Via Ardeatina. Probably there were two Roman ladies named Flavia Domitilla and both martyrs—the one described above and her own niece by marriage.

FLAVIA (St) VM.   RM. Oct 5
See Placid, Eutychius and Comp.

FLAVIAN (St) M.   RM. Jan 28
d. *c*.304. A deputy-prefect of Rome who suffered martyrdom at Civita Vecchia, under Diocletian.

FLAVIAN of CONSTANTINOPLE (St) Bp. M.   RM. Feb 18
d. 449. Appointed patriarch of Constantinople in 447. He refused to give the customary bribe on his accession to the see, and it was not long before he was compelled to denounce the heresy of Eutyches, a favourite of the imperial court. Pope Leo the Great approved his condemnation of Eutychianism by sending him the famous "Dogmatic Letter". At "the Robber Synod" of Ephesus in 449, Flavian appealed to the pope, whereupon he was exiled and maltreated, dying shortly after of his injuries. The Council of Chalcedon (451) proclaimed him a saint and a martyr.

FLAVIAN (St) M.   RM. Feb 24
See Montanus, Lucius, etc.

FLAVIAN and ELIAS (SS) Bps.   RM. July 20
d. (respectively) 512 and 518. St Flavian was patriarch of Antioch, and St Elias patriarch of Jerusalem. Both were exiled by the Monophysite emperor Anastasius (491–518) for strenuously upholding the decrees of the council of Chalcedon. This is the reason for their joint commemoration in the RM.

FLAVIAN (FLAVINIAN, FLAVIUS) of AUTUN (St) Bp.   RM. Aug 23
7th cent. The 21st bishop of Autun in France. The 15th bishop of Autun also called Flavius (d. *c*.544) has also a local cult.

FLAVIAN (St) M.   RM. Dec 22
d. 362. Said to have been an ex-prefect of Rome, branded on the forehead as a slave and exiled to the small village of Acquapendente in Tuscany by order of Julian the Apostate. At Acquapendente he died while in prayer.

FLAVIANA of AUXERRE (St) VM.   RM. Oct 5
See Firmatus and Flaviana.

FLAVIUS, AUGUSTUS and AUGUSTINE (SS) MM. RM. May 7
d. *c*.300. Flavius, bishop of Nicomedia, and his two brothers, were martyred in that city under Diocletian.

FLAVIUS CLEMENS (St) M.   RM. June 22
d. *c*.96. Brother of the emperor Vespasian and uncle of Titus and Domitian, whose niece, Flavia Domitilla, he married. In the year 95 he held the consular office together with Domitian. The following year Domitian had him beheaded as a Christian.

FLAVIUS of AUTUN (St) Bp.   RM. Aug 23
Otherwise Flavian, q.v.

FLOCELLUS (St) M.   RM. Sept 17
2nd cent. A youth martyred at Autun in

France under the emperor Marcus Aurelius (161–180). After having been put to the torture he was flung, half-dead, to the wild beasts in the amphitheatre.

FLORA (St) V.   AC. Jan 29
Otherwise Blath, q.v.

FLORA of BEAULIEU (Bl) V.
      AC. June 11
d. 1347. Born in Auvergne, Flora, at the age of fourteen, entered the order of Hospitallers of St John of Jerusalem at Beaulieu, near Rocamadour. Her spiritual trials and the physico-mystical phenomena which accompanied them make her life of absorbing interest.

FLORA (St) VM.   RM. July 29
See Lucilla, Flora, etc.

FLORA and MARY (SS) VV. MM.
      RM. Nov 24
d. 856. Two Christian maidens of Cordova, in Spain, who gave themselves up to the Moors, and were beheaded by order of Abderrahman II.

FLORENCE (*several*)
Otherwise Florentina, Florentia or Florentius, q.v.

FLORENTIA (FLORENCE) (St) M.
      RM. Nov 10
See Tiberius, Modestus and Florentia.

FLORENTIAN (St) Bp.
      RM. Nov 28
See Valerian, Urban, etc.

FLORENTINA (FLORENCE) (St)
Abs.   RM. June 20
d. c.636. A native of Carthagena in Spain, and the only sister of SS Leander, Fulgentius and Isidore. Losing her parents at an early age, she was placed under the guardianship of St

Leander. She retired to a convent for which St Leander wrote a rule. Eventually she governed it as abbess.

FLORENTINUS and HILARY (SS)
MM.   RM. Sept 27
? Two French solitaries, put to death in Gaul by some invading barbarians. Several places have been suggested as the place of their martyrdom. Pseudun, now Sémont in the diocese of Autun; Sion in the Valais; Suint, in Charollais; and Simond in the diocese of Dijon.

FLORENTINUS of TRÈVES (St)
Bp.   RM. Oct 16
4th cent. The successor of St Severianus in the see of Trèves. There is much controversy about him and about his reputed predecessor St Severinus.

FLORENTIUS of VIENNE (St) Bp.
M.   RM. Jan 3
? The RM. speaks of him as Bishop of Vienne martyred under Gallienus about 275. The local feast also is of a bishop and martyr. But the episcopal catalogues of Vienne place Florentius in the 4th century, and he is said to have assisted at the Council of Valence (374).

FLORENTIUS of SEVILLE (St)
      RM. Feb 23
d. c.485. A saint much venerated in Seville and its neighbourhood.

FLORENTIUS, GEMINIANUS and
SATURUS (SS) MM.   AC. Apr 6
? 4th cent. Martyrs of Sirmium, Pannonia.

FLORENTIUS of OSIMO (St) M.
      RM. May 11
See Sisinius, Diocletius and Florentius.

FLORENTIUS of NURSIA (St) Mk.
      RM. May 23
See Eutychius and Florentius.

FLORENTIUS, JULIAN, CYRIACUS, MARCELLINUS and FAUSTINUS (SS) MM. RM. June 5
d. 250. These martyrs suffered under Decius, being beheaded at Perugia in central Italy.

FLORENTIUS of CARTHAGE (St) M. RM. July 15
See Catulinus, Januarius, etc.

FLORENTIUS and Felix (SS) MM. RM. July 25
d. 235. Two soldiers of the Roman imperial army put to death under Maximinius the Thracian, at Furcona, an ancient town near Aquila in S. Italy. They belong to the group of eighty-three soldiers commemorated on July 24.

FLORENTIUS (St) C. RM. Sept 22
5th cent. A Bavarian by birth and a disciple of St Martin of Tours, by whom he was ordained priest and sent to evangelize Poitou. He eventually retired as a hermit to Mt Glonne in Anjou, where he was followed by numerous disciples. He built for them the monastery afterwards known as Saint-Florentle-Vieux. Here he died in extreme old age.

FLORENTIUS (St) M. RM. Oct 10
See Cassius, Florentius, etc.

FLORENTIUS (St) M. RM. Oct 13
d. 312. A martyr of Thessalonica, who died at the stake, under the emperor Maximinus Daza.

FLORENTIUS of ORANGE (St) Bp. RM. Oct 17
d. c.526. The eighth bishop of Orange in S. France.

FLORENTIUS (St) M. RM. Oct 27
3rd cent. A martyr who suffered at Trois-Châteaux in Burgundy.

FLORENTIUS of STRASBURG (St) Bp. RM. Nov 7
d. c.693. An Irishman by birth, he left his country for Alsace and settled in the wilds of Haselác, where he built a monastery. About the year 678 he was raised to the see of Strasburg, where he founded another monastery— St Thomas's—chiefly for his own countrymen.

FLORENTIUS of CARRACEDO (St) Ab. OSB. AC. Dec 10
d. 1156. Abbot of the Black Benedictine monastery of Carracedo, in the Bierzo Mountains, province of León, Spain. He was greatly revered by King Alphonsus VII of León. After the saint's death the abbey adopted the Cistercian observance. St Florentius is still greatly venerated in his native province.

FLORENTIUS (FLANN) (St) Ab. AC. Dec 15
7th cent. An abbot of Bangor in Ireland.

FLORIAN (St) M. RM. May 4
d. 304. A high Roman officer (*princeps officiorum*) in Noricum, now Upper Austria, who was drowned in the R. Enns (*Anisus*), near Lorch, under Diocletian. He is the patron of Upper Austria and Poland.

FLORIAN, CALANICUS and Comp. (SS) MM. RM. Dec 17
d. c.637. A band of sixty martyrs, slain by the Mohammedan invaders at Eleutheropolis (Beit Jibrin) in Palestine.

FLORIBERT (St) Bp. AC. Apr 27
d. 746. Bishop of Liége, described as "vehement in correcting". He has been confused with St Floribert, abbot of Ghent.

FLORIBERT (FLORBERT) (St) Ab. OSB. AC. Nov 1
d. c.660. Appointed by St Amandus

abbot of the new monasteries of Ghent, Mont-Blandin and Saint-Bavon.

FLORIUS of NICOMEDIA (St) M.
RM. Oct 26
See Lucian, Florius, etc.

FLORUS, LAURUS, PROCULUS and MAXIMUS (SS) MM.
RM. Aug 18
2nd cent. A Greek tradition, which is called in question by some writers, described Florus and Laurus as twin brothers, stone masons by trade, and Proculus and Maximus as their employers. They handed over a temple on which they had been working to Christian worship, and as a punishment were drowned in a well. This is said to have happened in Illyria.

FLORUS (French: FLOUR) of LODÈVE (St) Bp.
AC. Nov 3
d. 389. First bishop of Lodève in Languedoc. He has given his name to the town where his relics are enshrined.

FLORUS (St) M.
RM. Dec 22
See Demetrius, Honoratus and Florus.

FLOS (St) M.
RM. Dec 31
See Stephen, Pontian, etc.

FLOSCULUS (French: FLOU) (St) Bp.
RM. Feb 2
d. *p*.480. Bishop of Orleans, a contemporary of Sidonius Apollinaris.

FLOUR (St) Bp.
AC. Nov 3
Otherwise Florus of Lodève, q.v.

FLOU (St) Bp.
RM. Feb 2
Otherwise Flosculus, q.v.

FOELLAN (FOILAN, FILLAN) (St) C.
AC. Jan 9
8th cent. A native of Ireland, who accompanied his mother, St Kentigerna,

and his kinsman, St Comgan, to Scotland, where he became a missionary monk. The place where he died is now called Strathfillan.

FOILA (FAILE) (St) V. AC. March 3
6th cent. Said to have been the sister of St Colgan. The two were patrons of the parishes of Kil-Faile (Kileely) and Kil-Colgan, in Galway. Kil-Faile has been a noted place of pilgrimage.

FOILLAN (St) Ab. OSB. AC. Oct 31
d. *c*.655. Brother of SS Fursey and Ultan. They left Ireland, their native country, and worked in E. Anglia. St Foillan became the abbot of Burghcastle, near Yarmouth, but when this monastery was destroyed by the Mercians, he crossed over to Belgium. Bl Ita of Nivelles gave him some land at Fosses, where he founded the abbey of that name. He was the religious leader of Nivelles and evangelized Brabant. He was killed by robbers and is venerated as a martyr.

FORANNAN (St) Bp. OSB.
AC. Apr 30
d. 982. An Irish bishop who left his native country and arriving at the abbey of Waulsort on the Meuse joined the community as a monk and in 962 became its abbot. He spent some time at Gorze to study the monastic observance established there by St John (Feb 27) in order to introduce it at Waulsort, which he did most successfully.

FORT (St) Bp. M. AC. May 16
? 1st cent. Venerated as the first bishop of Bordeaux and as a martyr.

FORTCHERN (St) C. AC. Feb 17
? 6th cent. Said to have been converted by St Lornan. He succeeded him for a short time as Bishop of Trim, and then became a recluse.

FORTIS GABRIELLI (Bl) H. OSB.
AC. May 13

d. 1040. A native of Gubbio in Umbria, and a hermit in the mountains near Scheggia, under the guidance of Bl Ludolph, founder of Fontavellana. Later he entered that monastery and was professed there as a monk-hermit. Cult approved in 1756.

FORTUNATA (St) VM. RM. Oct 14

d. 303. A maiden martyred at Caesarea in Palestine under Diocletian. Her relics have been venerated at Naples since the 8th century. The legend adds that her three brothers, SS Carponius, Everistus and Priscian, suffered with her.

FORTUNATUS of SMYRNA (St) M. RM. Jan 9

See Vitalis, Revocatus and Fortunatus.

FORTUNATUS, FELICIAN, FIRMUS and CANDIDUS (SS) MM. R.M Feb 2

? The names have been transferred from the martyrology of Usuard, but nothing is known of them.

FORTUNATUS (St) M. RM. Feb 21

See Verulus, Secundinus, etc.

FORTUNATUS, FELIX and Comp. (SS) MM. RM. Feb 26

? A group of twenty-nine martyrs of whom nothing is known.

FORTUNATUS (St) M. RM. Feb 27

See Alexander, Abundius, etc.

FORTUNATUS (St) M. RM. March 3

See Felix, Luciolus, etc.

FORTUNATUS and MARCIAN (SS) MM. RM. Apr 17

? Martyrs, perhaps of Antioch in Syria, but more probably of some town in Africa.

FORTUNATUS of ALEXANDRIA (St) M. RM. Apr 21

See Arator, Fortunatus, etc.

FORTUNATUS of VALENCE (St) M. RM. Apr 23

See Felix, Fortunatus and Achilleus.

FORTUNATUS (St) C. RM. June 1

d. c.400. A parish priest at a place near Spoleto, in Umbria, conspicuous for his charity to the poor.

FORTUNATUS of AQUILEIA (St) M. RM. June 11

See Felix and Fortunatus.

FORTUNATUS and LUCIAN (SS) MM. RM. June 13

? African martyrs, whose Acts have been lost. Most martyrologies register six or more other names.

FORTUNATUS the PHILOSOPHER (St) AC. June 18

d. c.569. An Italian bishop driven from his see in N Italy by the Lombards. He was much esteemed by St Germanus of Paris. He must not be confused with the better known St Venantius Fortunatus, his contemporary in France.

FORTUNATUS (St) M. RM. July 12

See Hermagoras and Fortunatus.

FORTUNATUS (St) M. RM. Aug 27 and Sept 1

See Honoratus, Fortunatus, etc. (Sept 1), and the Twelve Holy Brothers.

FORTUNATUS, CAIUS and ANTHES (SS) MM. RM. Aug 28

d. 303. Martyred near Salerno under Diocletian. Their relics were enshrined at Salerno in 940, and since then they have been held in great popular veneration. Their Passion has no historical foundation. Fortunatus may be the martyr included in the "Twelve Holy Brothers".

FORTUNATUS of TODI (St) Bp.
RM. Oct 14

d. 537. A bishop of Todi, who saved the city from being sacked by Totila the Goth.

FORTUNATUS (St) M. RM. Oct 15
d. ? 537. A Roman martyr.

FORTUNATUS (St) M. RM. Oct 24
See Felix, Audactus, etc.

FORTUNATUS, VENANTIUS (St) Bp.
AC. Dec 14

See Venantius Fortunatus.

FORTUNATUS (St) M. RM. Dec 15
See Faustinus, Lucius, etc.

FORTY ARMENIAN MARTYRS (SS)
RM. March 10

d. 320. Forty soldiers put to death by the emperor Licinius at Sebaste (Sivas) in Lesser Armenia. They were exposed naked on the ice of a frozen lake, a warm bath being on the bank as a temptation to apostatize. One fell, but his place was taken by one of the guards who was converted by the heroism of the rest. On the morrow all were dead, save the youngest among them. His brave mother carried her child after the corpses of the rest until he too expired in her arms, and then laid his body by their side. Many ecclesiastical writers of that period speak of this group of martyrs—SS Basil, Gregory of Nyssa, Gaudentius of Brescia, Sozomen, etc. They are still greatly venerated in the East.

FOSTER (St) Bp.
RM. Feb 6

The old English form of the name Vedast or Waast. See Vedast.

FOUR CROWNED MARTYRS, The (SS)
RM. Nov 8

There are two groups of martyrs called the Four Holy Crowned Ones—*Sancti Quatuor Coronati*: one group suffered at Albano *c.*305, viz, Severus, Severian, Carpophorus and Victorinus; the other group met their death in Pannonia about the same time: Claudius, Nicostratus, Symphorian and Castorius, to whom a fifth named Simplicius is added. In both cases their names were at first unknown; hence the collective title by which they are generally referred to.

FOURTEEN HOLY HELPERS, The (SS)
AC. Aug 8

A collective feast is celebrated in several places, chiefly in Germany, in honour of fourteen saints, each of whom is believed to grant a special form of help. The usual fourteen are: Acacius (June 22), Barbara, Blaise (Feb 3), Catherine of Alexandria, Christopher (July 25), Cyriacus (Aug 8). Dionysius of Paris (Oct 9), Erasmus (June 2), Eustace (Sept 20), George (April 23), Margaret (July 20), Pantaleon, Vitus—all martyrs—and Giles (Sept 1). See their respective notices.

FRAGAN and GWEN (BLANCHE) (SS)
AC. July 5

5th cent. Refugees from Britain in the troublous times consequent upon the departure of the Romans, and parents of SS Winwaloë, Jacut and Guithern. Churches in Brittany are dedicated to each of them.

FRANCA VISALTA (St) OSB. Cist.
AC. Apr 26

1170–1218. A native of Piacenza in Italy. At the age of seven she was offered to God in the Benedictine convent of St Syrus. She was professed at fourteen and soon, though very young, made abbess. She seems to have been over severe, and she was in fact deposed. After some years she was made abbess of the Cistercian nunnery of Pittoli. Cult confirmed, with the title of Saint, by Gregory X.

FRANCES of ROME (St) W. OSB.
RM. March 9
1384–1440. A native of Rome, she married in 1396 Lorenzo de Ponziani, with whom she lived for forty years, succeeding during all this time in never once annoying him. Her life was a model of fidelity and devotedness to her domestic duties; she patiently bore many severe trials, among them being the death of her children, her husband's banishment and the confiscation of their estates. In 1433 she founded the community of Benedictine Oblates of Tor de' Specci, but it was not until 1436, after the death of her husband, that she could join it. Her biography, with many particulars of visions and revelations, of her devotion to her angel guardian, whom she often saw walking by her side and guiding her, was written by John Matteotti, who had been her confessor during the last ten years of her life. Canonized in 1608.

FRANCES LANEL (Bl) M.
AC. June 26
1745–1794. A native of Eu, diocese of Rouen, she became a Sister of Charity at Rouen, and was later stationed at Cambrai and Arras. She, with three other sisters, was guillotined at Cambrai. Beatified in 1920.

FRANCES de CROISSY and
FRANCES BRIDEAU (BB) MM.
OC.   AC. July 17
d. 1794. Frances de Croissy was born at Paris in 1745 and was professed a Carmelite nun at Compiègne in 1764. She was prioress from 1779 to 1787 and at the time of her death was novice-

mistress. Frances Brideau was born at Belfort in 1752 and professed at Compiègne in 1771. She was the sub-prioress. Both were guillotined at Paris with the rest of the community in 1794. Beatified in 1906.

FRANCES BIZZOCCA (Bl) M.
AC. Aug 17
d. 1627. A Japanese, the wife of Bl Leo, she belonged to the third order of Friars Preachers. She was condemned to death for sheltering missionaries in her house, and was burnt alive at Nagasaki. Beatified in 1867.

FRANCES d'AMBOISE (Bl) OC.
AC. Nov 4
1427–1485. Reared at the court of Brittany, Frances became the wife of Duke Peter of Brittany, and spent her life in endeavouring to please and pacify her jealous husband—no light task—and in charitable works. She was a great benefactress of the Carmelite Bl John Soreth, and herself became a Carmelite in her widowhood (1470) at the convent which she had founded at Nantes. Beatified in 1863.

FRANCES XAVIER CABRINI (St)
Foundress   RM. Dec 22
1850–1917. Born at Sant' Angelo Lodigiano in Lombardy, the thirteenth child of Augustine and Stella Cabrini. In 1874 she was asked by the parish priest to teach in an orphanage at Codogno, diocese of Lodi. In 1877 the orphanage became the mother-house of a new institute, founded by Mother Frances under the title of Missionary Sisters of the Sacred Heart. She made her own profession at the hands of the bishop of Lodi, who in 1880 officially approved the new congregation as a diocesan institute. Mother Cabrini's dream was to send her sisters to China, but on the advice of Pope Leo XIII she dispatched

them instead to the United States. In 1889 she herself accompanied the first batch of missionary sisters to New York, and from that time almost every year she crossed the sea at the head of new bands of missionaries. During her life-time she founded as many as sixty-seven religious houses—schools, orphanages, hospitals, etc.—in N. and S. America, Italy, Spain, England, etc. She died in one of the American foundations, Columbus Hospital, Chicago. She had become an American citizen. Canonized in 1946.

FRANCIS FERDINAND de CAPILLAS (Bl) M. OP.   AC. Jan 15
1606–1648. A native of Vacherim de Campos in Old Castile, Francis joined the Dominicans at Valladolid and was sent to the missions in China. He laboured in Fokien with great success, but political and religious troubles arose in the province, and Francis was executed as a spy. Beatified in 1909, and proclaimed the Protomartyr of China.

FRANCIS GIL de FEDERICH (Bl) M. OP.   AC. Jan 22
1702–1745. A native of Tortosa, Spain, he became a Friar Preacher at Barcelona and was sent to the Philippines. Thence he went to Tonkin in 1732 where after long apostolic labours, he was imprisoned for several years and beheaded at Checo. Beatified in 1906.

FRANCIS of SALES (St) Bp. Dr.
Founder   RM. Jan 29
1567–1622. Born near Annecy, in Savoy, the eldest son of the Seigneur de Nouvelles. He read for the Law at Paris and Padua, but abandoned his legal studies and became a priest in 1593. At once he set out for his apostolate among the Calvinists of the Chablais, where he is said to have made within two years over eight thousand converts. In 1599 he was chosen coadjutor to the bishop of Geneva, whom he succeeded in 1602. Two years later he met St Jane Frances of Chantal, with whom he founded the Order of the Visitation. He was indefatigable in the discharge of his office as a bishop: organized conferences for the clergy, directed them to teach catechism in simple words, insisted on unadorned straightforward preaching, established a seminary at Annecy which he visited regularly. He excelled as an ascetical writer, and his treatise *Introduction to the Devout Life* will always remain a classic. His people loved him and styled him "The Gentle Christ of Geneva". Canonized in 1665; declared a Doctor of the Church in 1877, and patron saint of journalists in 1923.

FRANCIS XAVIER BIANCHI (St)
Barn.   AC. Jan 31
1743–1815. A native of Arpino in Italy who became a Barnabite clerk regular and was ordained priest in 1767—in the teeth of opposition from his family. Owing to overwork and to his austere life, he ruined his health and lost the use of his legs. He was considered and acclaimed as the "Apostle of Naples" for his work for the poor and abandoned and to preserve girls from the danger of an immoral life. Canonized in 1951.

FRANCIS BLANCO (St) M. OFM.
RM. Feb 5
d. 1597. A native of Monterey, in Spanish Galicia. He studied at Salamanca, and was professed as a Franciscan at Villalpando. He first laboured at Churubusco in Mexico, and in 1594 reached Japan from Manila. He was crucified at Nagasaki. Canonized in 1862.

FRANCIS of ST MICHAEL (St) M.
OFM.   RM. Feb 5
d. 1597. Born at Parilla, near Valladolid. He became a Franciscan lay-brother

and in 1593 accompanied St Peter Baptist from Manila to Japan. He was arrested with him at Ozaka (1596) and crucified. Canonized in 1862.

FRANCIS of NAGASAKI (St) M.
RM. Feb 5

d. 1597. A Japanese physician, from Macao, and a member of the third order of St Francis. He served the missionaries as a catechist and was for this reason crucified at Nagasaki. Canonized in 1862.

FRANCIS REGIS CLET (Bl) M. CM.
AC. Feb 17

1748–1820. Born at Grenoble, he joined the Lazarists and was sent to China as a missionary in 1791. Here he laboured for thirty years, in the face of incredible difficulties, and at last, in his seventy-second year, was cruelly tortured and strangled near Hankow. Beatified in 1900.

FRANCIS of FERMO (Bl) M. OFM.
PC. March 15

See Monaldus of Ancona, etc.

FRANCIS of NOSTRA (Bl) Mk.
AC. March 18

d. 1433. A Hungarian Pauline monk of the famous convent of Maria Nostra, he was meek and modest in outward appearance. His body is reputed to have remained incorrupt after death. Venerated by his order as Blessed, though his cult has not been officially confirmed. Called also Francis the Pious.

FRANCIS of PAOLA (St) Founder
RM. Apr 2

1416–1507. Born at Paola in Calabria. At the age of fourteen he settled as a hermit on the sea coast near Paola. Many disciples followed him and eventually their community at Paola grew into the new order of Minim Friars—

Minimi, i.e., the least of all friars. The order was approved by Sixtus IV in 1474. It was this same pope who directed St Francis to travel to France (1482) in order to assist, at Plessis-les-Tours, the dying King Louis XI. At the request of that king's successors Francis remained in France for the rest of his life and died at Plessis. Canonized in 1519.

FRANCIS PAGE (Bl) M. SJ.
AC. Apr 20

d. 1602. Born at Antwerp, he belonged to an English Protestant family of Harrow-on-the-Hill. He was reconciled to the Church, educated at Douai, ordained in 1600, sent to the English mission, captured, received in prison into the Society of Jesus and executed for his priesthood at Tyburn. Beatified in 1929.

FRANCIS VENIMBENE of FABRIANO (Bl) C. OFM.
AC. Apr 22

1251–1322. Born at Fabriano, the son of a physician. He joined the Franciscans in 1267 and was a disciple of St Bonaventure. He founded the first Franciscan library.

FRANCIS COLMENARIO (Bl) C.
AC. Apr 24

d. 1590. A Spanish missionary priest who evangelized the West Indies. He preached also in Guatemala.

FRANCIS DICKENSON (Bl) M.
AC. Apr 30

d. 1590. A native of Yorkshire and a convert, he was educated for the priesthood at Reims, ordained in 1589 and sent to the English mission, where the following year he was hanged, drawn and quartered for his priesthood at Rochester. Beatified in 1929.

FRANCIS JEROME (de GERONIMO) (St) C. SJ.
RM. May 11

1642–1716. Born near Taranto in S.

Italy, and ordained priest in 1666, he entered the Society of Jesus in 1670. From this time on he spent his whole life preaching throughout S. Italy, where his sermons were attended by huge congregations. Canonized in 1839.

FRANCIS PATRIZI (Bl) C. OSM.
AC. May 12

d. 1328. A native of Siena, he was converted by a sermon of the Servite friar, Bl Ambrose Sansedoni, and was himself received into the Servite Order by St Philip Benizi. He was favoured by God with the special grace of reconciling enemies. He died at Siena. Cult approved in 1743.

FRANCIS RONCI (Bl) C. OSB. Cel.
AC. June 4

1223–1294. Born at Abri in S. Italy, he was one of the first disciples of St Peter Celestine and his companions at the hermitages of Orfente and Morrone. In 1285 he became prior of Santo Spirito and Majella and the first General of the Congregation until 1294. It seems probable that he was created Cardinal by St Peter in Sept 1294; he died the following month.

FRANCIS CARACCIOLO (St) C.
Founder   RM. June 4

1563–1608. A scion of the noble Neapolitan family of Caracciolo, he was born in the Abruzzi and during his early years was afflicted with a disease akin to leprosy, of which he was cured on deciding to become a priest. He did so, and in 1588 founded with John Augustine Adorno the order of Minor Clerks Regular, with perpetual adoration of the H. Eucharist as one of its main duties. Francis was the first General of the Order and spent his life in governing it and in preaching. Canonized in 1807.

FRANCIS PACHECO and Comp.
(Bl) MM. SJ.   AC. June 20

1566–1626. A native of Ponte da Lima in Portugal. In 1586 he became a Jesuit and was sent to Macao (1592) where he was ordained priest. He laboured at Macao and in Japan and held the office of rector, provincial, vicar general and administrator of the diocese. He was burnt alive at Nagasaki, together with two other Jesuits from Europe, a Japanese Jesuit, four Japanese laymen and a Korean. All were beatified in 1867.

FRANCIS CHIEN (Bl) M. Tert. OP.
AC. June 25

1796–1838. A Chinese catechist, arrested with Bl Dominic Henares and beheaded at Annam. Beatified in 1900.

FRANCIS ROD (St) M. OFM.
RM. July 9

d. 1572. Born at Brussels, he took the Franciscan habit at Gorkum, Holland. Shortly after his ordination he was hanged by the Calvinists at Briel.

FRANCIS SOLANO (St) C. OFM.
RM. July 14

1549–1610. A native of Andalusia in Spain. He professed the Franciscan Rule among the Observants (1569) and after twenty years of apostolic activities in Spain, he was sent to Peru (1589). Here and elsewhere in S. America he laboured for another twenty years until his death at Lima. Canonized in 1726.

FRANCIS ALVAREZ (Bl) M. SJ.
AC. July 15

d. 1570. A native of Covilhao in Portugal, who became a Jesuit lay-brother. He was martyred with Bl Ignatius de Azevedo, q.v.

FRANCIS ARANHA (Bl) M. SJ.
AC. July 15

d. 1583. A native of Braga in Portugal

who came to Goa with his uncle, and there joined the Society of Jesus (1571) as a coadjutor. He served the mission on the islet of Salsette, where he was martyred with Bl Rudolph Acquaviva, q.v.

FRANCIS MAGALLANES (Bl) M. SJ. AC. July 15
d. 1570. A native of Alcázar do Sal, in Portugal, who became a Jesuit cleric and shared the martyrdom of Bl Ignatius de Azevedo and companions, q.v.

FRANCIS PEREZ GODOY (Bl) M. SJ. AC. July 15
d. 1570. A native of Torrijos, diocese of Toledo, in Spain. He was a Jesuit novice and a companion in martyrdom of Bl Ignatius de Azevedo, q.v.

FRANCIS (CECO) of PESARO (St) Tert. OFM. AC. Aug 13
d. 1350. An early Franciscan tertiary who lived with others in community. Cult confirmed in 1859.

FRANCIS CULOYE (Bl) M. AC. Aug 17
d. 1627. A Japanese tertiary of St Francis, beheaded for having sheltered missionaries. Beatified in 1867.

FRANCIS CUROBIOYE (Bl) M. AC. Aug 17
d. 1627. A native Japanese Christian, and a Dominican tertiary, burnt alive at Nagasaki. Beatified in 1867.

FRANCIS of ST MARY and Comps. (BB) MM. AC. Aug 1
d. 1627. Francis of St Mary was a Spanish friar minor who was burnt alive at Nagasaki on Aug 17, 1627, together with Br Bartholomew Laurel, another Franciscan, of Mexican origin, and a doctor, Gaspar Vaz, a Japanese

tertiary in whose house Fr Francis of St Mary was taken, and Br Antony of St Francis, a native catechist. With them were beheaded the wife of Gaspar Vaz, named Mary, and six Franciscan tertiaries: Louis Soyeman a neighbour, Francis Coufioye baptized in prison, Thomas Wo Jonyemon, formerly a servant of the Jesuits, Luke Kiyemon, a builder of hiding places, Michael Kizayemon another carpenter, and Martin Gomez de Facato who had hidden Franciscan friars. On the same or the preceding day were burnt four Dominican tertiaries: Francis Curobioye, catechist, Gaius Jiyemon, formerly a bonze of Corea, Magdalen Kista, of royal blood, and Frances Bizocca. All were beatified in 1867.

FRANCIS de la ROCHEFOU-CAULD (Bl) Bp. M. AC. Sept 2-3
See September Martyrs.

FRANCIS of JESUS ORTEGA (Bl) M. OSA. AC. Sept 3
d. 1632. A native of Villamediana in Spain. In 1614 he took the habit of the Hermits of St Augustine at Valladolid. In 1622 he was sent to Mexico, and thence with Bl Vincent Carvalho, to Manila, and in 1623 to Japan. He was burnt alive at Nagasaki. Beatified in 1867.

FRANCIS NIFAKI (Bl) M. AC. Sept 8
d. 1628. A native boy of five years of age, beheaded at Nagasaki with his father, Bl Louis Nifaki, and his brother Dominic. Beatified in 1867.

FRANCIS de MORALES (Bl) M. OP. AC. Sept 10
d. 1622. A native of Madrid who became a Dominican and worked for twenty years in the Japanese mission of Satzuma. In 1608 he returned to Fuximi,

and in 1614 to Nagasaki where he was burnt alive with Bl Charles Spinola and companions. Beatified in 1867.

FRANCIS TAQUEA (Bl) M.
AC. Sept 11

d. 1622. A Japanese boy of twelve years of age, a son of Bl Thomas Taquea, beheaded with Bl Caspar Cotenda at Nagasaki. Beatified in 1867.

FRANCIS of ST BONAVENTURE (Bl) M. OFM.   AC. Sept 12

d. 1622. Born in Musaxi, Quanto, Japan. A native catechist who worked under Bl Apollinaris Franco. He was burnt alive at Omura. Beatified in 1867.

FRANCIS of CALDEROLA (Bl) C. OFM.   AC. Sept 13

d. 1407. A native of Calderola, diocese of Camerino. He embraced the Franciscan rule and was a very successful preacher, with the special gift for reconciling enemies. He died at Colfana. Cult approved by Gregory XVI.

FRANCIS of CAMPOROSSO (St) C. OFM. Cap.   AC. Sept 16

1804–1866. An Italian peasant born near Ventimiglia, who became a laybrother in the Capuchin friary of the Immaculate Virgin at Genoa. He spent forty years there and died while nursing cholera victims. Canonized in 1962.

FRANCIS de POSADAS (Bl) C. OP.
AC. Sept 20

1644–1713. Born at Cordova in Spain, he took the Dominican habit at Aracoeli in 1663, and spent the rest of his life giving missions throughout S.W. Spain. He died at Aracoeli. Beatified in 1818.

FRANCIS JACCARD (Bl) M.
AC. Sept 21

1799–1838. Born at Onnion in Savoy. He entered the Seminary for Foreign Missions in Paris and was sent to Cochin-China in 1826. He was strangled in Annam. Beatified in 1900.

FRANCIS CHAKICHI (Bl) M.
AC. Oct 2

d. 1622. A Japanese boy of four years of age, son of BB Louis and Lucy Chakichi. He was beheaded with his mother and his brother Andrew (their father was burnt at the stake) at Nagasaki. Beatified in 1867.

FRANCIS of ASSISI (St) Founder
RM. Oct 4

1181–1226. "The Poor Little Man"—*il Poverello*—one of the best known and loved of saints. A native of Assisi in Umbria, the son of a merchant. In his youth he loved pleasure, until a series of providential happenings led him, in 1209, to found the order of Friars Minor, characterized by a loving, joyous worship of the Sacred Humanity of Christ, and by a profession of poverty which was both individual and collective. The appeal of the new order to that generation may be gauged from the fact that at the General Chapter of 1219 five thousand friars were present. This same year Francis sailed for Palestine and tried to evangelize the Mohammedans, but this mission was a failure. Meanwhile, the new order was passing through a period of painful internal difficulties. Francis returned to Italy, sent friars into all western European countries, with instructions to establish themselves preferably in university centres. His rule was approved by Innocent III, and his life and message received a direct sanction from Christ in 1224, when on September 14 Francis received the stigmata of the Passion on Mt Alvernia. He died still in deacon's orders and was canonized two years after his death.

FRANCIS TITELMANS (Bl) C. OFM. Cap.   AC. Oct 4
d. 1537. A student of Louvain who joined the Capuchins and ended his days tending the sick in the hospital of St James in Rome.

FRANCIS TRUNG (Bl) M. AC. Oct 6
1825–1858. A native of Cochin-China and a corporal in the army there. Born at Phan-xa, beheaded in An-hoa. Beatified in 1909.

FRANCIS BORGIA (St) C. SJ. RM. Oct 10
1510–1572. Born at Gandia, near Valencia, in Spain, of the noble family of de Borja. He was reared at the court of Charles V, married very young, and up to the time of his wife's death (1546) devoted himself to the discharge of his duties at the emperor's court and on his own estates as duke of Gandia. In 1546 he left all and joined the Society of Jesus. As General of the Society, he was one of the greatest instruments of Divine Providence in the counter-reformation. Under him the Society spread throughout Europe and the foreign missions. Austere with himself, Francis was the typical saint of the Spanish nobility — courteous, refined, kind, humble and generous, yet most determined and enterprising. He died at Ferrara, while travelling on an embassy from Pope St Pius V, his great friend, to the kings of France and Spain. Canonized in 1671.

FRANCIS ISIDORE GAGELIN (Bl) M.   AC. Oct 17
1799–1833. A native of Montperreux, diocese of Besançon. He belonged to the Society of Foreign Missions of Paris, and was sent to Cochin-China in 1822, where on his arrival he was ordained priest. He worked zealously until the persecution broke out, when he gave

himself up to the Mandarin of Bongson and was strangled. Beatified in 1900.

FRANCIS DIAZ (Bl) M. OP. AC. Oct 20
d. 1748. A Spanish Dominican missionary in Fo-Kien, China. He was strangled in prison with Bl Francis Serrano at Futsheu. Beatified in 1893.

FRANCIS SERRANO (Bl) M. OP. AC. Oct 20
d. 1748. Born in Spain and sent as a missionary to China, to the province of Fo-Kien. He was arrested with Bl Peter Sanz (1746). Whilst in prison at Futsheu he was elected titular bishop of Tipasa. He was strangled with three other Dominicans. Beatified in 1893.

FRANCIS NÉRON (Bl) M. AC. Nov 3
See Peter-Francis Néron.

FRANCIS XAVIER CAN (Bl) M. AC. Nov 20
1803–1837. Born at Sou-Mieng, in W. Tonkin, he was a catechist attached to the fathers of the Foreign Missions of Paris. He was strangled in prison. Beatified in 1900.

FRANCIS XAVIER (St) C. SJ. RM. Dec 3
1506–1552. Born at the family castle of Javier, in Spanish Navarre, Francis inherited the best characteristics of his race—generosity, love of culture and adventure. He was studying with distinction at the university of Paris when he met St Ignatius Loyola, and in 1534 they took their first religious vows at Montmartre. In obedience to St Ignatius's order, Francis set out on his first journey to the far east in 1540, landing at Goa in 1542. He visited India, Ceylon, Malaya, Japan, and other Far Eastern islands, dreaming all the time of his longed-for apostolate in China.

The difficulties he met with in his missionary labours were well-nigh insurmountable: they proceeded chiefly from the politically-minded European traders. However, he was favoured with such extraordinary graces from heaven, that his mission proved from the start a signal success: it is reckoned that in Japan alone, some forty years afterwards, there were 400,000 Christians. Indeed, Francis Xavier is perhaps the greatest individual missionary the Church has produced since St Paul. Francis died at Sancian, when about to enter China. Canonized in 1602, and proclaimed by Pius X patron of all foreign missions.

FRANCIS GALVEZ (Bl) M. OFM.
AC. Dec 4

1567–1623. A native of Utiel in New Castile. He joined the Friars Minor at Valencia (1591), went to Manila (1609) and thence to Japan (1612). During the persecution he returned to Manila (1614); at Macao he blackened his face in order to be able to enter Japan anew (1618). He preached with great courage, and finally was burnt alive at Yeddo. Beatified in 1867.

FRANCIS FASANI (Bl) C. OFM.
AC. Dec 9

1681–1742. Antony Fasani was born at Luceria and after a devout childhood entered the Franciscan order under the name of Francis. Ordained in 1775 he rose to be provincial and introduced salutary reforms. In prayer he was sometimes raised from the ground. He worked mainly at Luceria and died there in 1742. Beatified in 1951.

FRANCIS XAVIER MAU (Bl) M. Tert. OP.
AC. Dec. 19

d. 1839. A native catechist of Tonkin, strangled with four companions. Beatified in 1900.

FRANCISCAN MARTYRS OF CHINA (BB)
AC. July 9

d. 1900. A group of 29 martyrs, mostly Franciscans or tertiaries, put to death in the Boxer Rising under the Dowager Empress Tze'Hse, and beatified as a representative group of the 100,000 Christians estimated to have been put to death in that persecution. They were nearly all slaughtered in the courtyard of the palace of Yu Sun, viceroy of Tay-yüan-fu of the Scien-fu province. Their names were: (1) Bishop Gregory Grassi, Vicar Apostolic of Northern Scian-si; Bishop Francis Fogolla, his coadjutor; Elias Facchini; Theodore Balat; Andrew Bauer; all friars minor. Sisters Mary Emiliana Grivot; Mary of Peace Guiliani; Mary Clare Nanette; Mary of Sainte Nathalie Kerguin; Mary of St Justus Moreau; Mary Amandina Jeuris; Mary Adolphine Dierk—all Franciscan Missionaries of Mary; John Tciang; John Van; Philip Tciang; Patrick Tun; another John Tcaing—all seminarists; Thomas Sen; Simon Tcing; Peter U-Ngan-Pau; Francis Tciang-Iun; Matthias Fun-Te; James Ien-Kutun; Peter Tchang-Pau-Nien; James Tciao-Tcieum-Sin; Peter Van-al-man—members of the Bishop's household. (2) Bishop Antoninus Fantosanti, Vicar Apostolic of Hunan (now Hengchow) and Joseph Mary Gambaro, both friars minor, tortured to death at Hengchow on July 7. (3) Caesidius Giacomantonio OFM., burned alive at Wanshawan on July 4. Beatified 1946.

FRANCO (FRANCUS) (St) H. OSB.
AC. June 5

d. c.1275. A native of Castel Regni, near Asserigo, in the Abruzzi. He became a Benedictine at the monastery of Colimento, and after twenty years as a cenobite, spent the last fifteen years of his life as a hermit near Asserigo.

FRANCO LIPPI (Bl) C. OC.
AC. Dec 11
d. 1291. A native of Grotto, near Siena. Early in life he fell in with evil companions and became their leader. A fugitive from justice, he joined a band of *condottieri* and excelled them all in crime until about his fiftieth year. Then he became blind, repented, went on a pilgrimage to Compostella, received back his sight, was absolved by Gregory X, and admitted to the Carmelite Order as a lay-brother. He was already over sixty-five, but managed to earn the title of Saint by his fervour in his new life.

FRANCOVEUS (FRANCHY) (St) Mk.   AC. May 16
7th cent. Monk of St Martin de la Bretonnière, he had to suffer much from the jealousy of his fellow-monks. The monastery being destroyed, he lived as a hermit in the Nivernais.

FRATERNUS (St) Bp. M.
RM. Sept 29
d. c.450. Bishop of Auxerre in France. Tradition makes him also a martyr.

FREDEGAND (FREGAUT) (St) Ab. OSB.   AC. July 17
d. c.740. Said to have been an Irish companion of St Foillan. Monk and abbot of Kerkelodor, near Antwerp. It seems probable that he was a fellow-worker with St Willibrord.

FREDERICK of ARRAS (Bl) Mk. OSB.   AC. Jan 6
d. 1020. Son of Geoffrey *le Barbu*, count of Verdun. In 997 he handed over his patrimony to the bishop of Verdun, set out for Palestine, and on his return was admitted to the Benedictine abbey of St Vanne. His friend Bl Richard, abbot of St Vanne, was transferred to the abbey of St Vedast at Arras, and Bl Frederick followed him as prior.

FREDERICK (Bl) Ab. O. Praem.
AC. March 3
d. 1175. Born at Hallum in Frisia he became the abbot-founder of the Premonstratensian abbey of Mariengart in Holland.

FREDERICK (Bl) Ab. OSB.
AC. May 7
d. c.1070. A native of Swabia and a monk of Einsiedeln in Switzerland, he was sent with twelve monks to restore discipline in the abbey of Hirschau (1066). He was calumniated by evil-minded monks and deposed by the Count of Calw, owner of Hirschau, in 1069. He retired to Ebersberg where he died.

FREDERICK (St) Bp. AC. May 27
d. 1121. Chosen bishop of Liège in 1119 in the room of the deposed simoniacal prelate Alexander. He was an excellent bishop, but had to suffer much, and in the end, it is said, was poisoned by Alexander's supporter the count of Louvain.

FREDERICK (FRIDRICH) (St) Bp. M.   RM. July 18
d. 838. Grandson of Radbod, king of the Frisians. In 820 he was appointed bishop of Utrecht and devoted himself especially to combating the evil custom of incestuous marriages, for which reason he was murdered in church at Maestricht.

FREDERICK of RATISBON (Bl) OSA.   AC. Nov 29
d. 1329. Born at Ratisbon of poor parents. He was received as a lay-brother into the order of Augustinian Hermits at Ratisbon and was employed there as carpenter and wood-chopper. Cult approved in 1909.

FREDIANO (FRIGIDANUS, FRIGDIANUS) (St) Bp. RM. March 18
d. 588. An Irishman who went on

pilgrimage to Rome and settled in Italy as a hermit on Monte Pisano. In 566 he was elected bishop of Lucca and formed the clergy of the city into a community of canons regular. He rebuilt the cathedral after it had been burnt by the Lombards. He is greatly venerated at Lucca.

FREMUND (St) M. AC. May 11
9th cent. An Anglo-Saxon hermit, who seems to have been killed by the Danes and to have been honoured as a martyr. His remains were enshrined at Dunstable.

FRIARD (St) H. AC. Aug 1
d. c.577. Hermit on the isle of Vindomitte, near Nantes. With him is mentioned St Secundel.

FRICOR (ADRIAN) (St) H.
AC. Apr 1
See Caidoc and Fricor.

FRIDESWIDE (FREDESWINDA) (St) V. OSB. RM. Oct 19
d. c.735. The daughter of Didan, prince (*subregulus*) of a district bordering the Upper Thames. She was the abbess-foundress of the nunnery of St Mary's under the rule of St Benedict on the site of what is now Oxford. It is said that from her childhood she took for her maxim: "Whatsoever is not God is nothing". She is the patroness of the city and university of Oxford.

FRIGIDAND (St) Ab. OSB.
AC. July 17
Otherwise Fredegand, q.v.

FRIDOLIN (St) Ab. OSB.
AC. March 6
d. c.540. A priest of Irish origin, he is said to have become a monk of Luxeuil. Later he founded the abbey of Säckingen. He is venerated as the apostle of the Upper Rhine.

FRIGIDIAN (FRIDAN, FINNIAN) (St) Bp. RM. March 18
Otherwise Frediano, q.v.

FRITHBERT (FRIDEBERT, FRITHUBEORHT) (St) Bp. OSB.
AC. Dec 23
d. 766. The successor of St Acca in the bishopric of Hexham, which church he ruled for thirty-four years.

FRITHESTAN (St) Bp. OSB.
AC. Sept 10
d. 933. A disciple of St Grimbald consecrated bishop of Winchester by St Plegmund. He ruled the see for twenty-three years.

FRODOBERT (St) Ab. OSB.
AC. Jan 8
d. c.673. A monk of Luxeuil under the third abbot St Waldebert. Abbot-founder of Moutier-la-Celle, near Troyes, where he led a life of continuous prayer and great austerities.

FRODULPHUS (FROU) (St) H. OSB. AC. Apr 21
d. c.750. A disciple of St Medericus (Merry), he became a monk at St Martin's, Autun, whence he was driven by the Saracen invasion and settled at Barjon, Côte d'Or, where he died.

FROILAN (St) Bp. OSB. RM. Oct 3
d. 1006. A native of Lugo in Galicia, at the age of eighteen he undertook, together with his companion Attilanus (q.v.), the reorganization of monastic observance at Moreruela, on the river Esla in Old Castile. After a very successful career as abbot he was consecrated bishop of León. He and St Attilanus were the great restorers of Benedictine monasticism in W. Spain.

FROMUNDUS (St) Bp. OSB. Oct 24
d. p.690. Monk and abbot, and then bishop of Coutances.

FRONTO (St) H.   RM. Apr 14
? 2nd cent. A solitary in the desert of Nitria in Egypt.

FRONTO (St) M.   RM. Apr 16
See Saragossa (Martyrs of).

FRONTO and GEORGE (SS) Bps.
                         RM. Oct 25
? Apostles of Périgueux in France at some early period. Worthless legends have completely obscured their true story.

FROWIN (Bl) Ab. OSB. Cist.
                         PC. Feb 17
d. 1165. A Cistercian of Bellevaux in Savoy and the abbot-founder of Salom in the diocese of Constance. He was a companion of St Bernard when the latter was preaching his crusade.

**FROWIN II of ENGELBERG (Bl)
Ab. OSB.   AC. March 7**
d. 1178. A Benedictine of St Blasien in the Black Forest who was made abbot of Engelberg in Switzerland (1143). He founded the monastic school at Engelberg, a library, etc., and was himself the chronicler of the abbey and an ascetical writer of distinction.

FRUCTULUS (St) M.   RM. Feb 18
See Lucius, Sylvanus, etc.

FRUCTUOSA (St) M.   RM. Aug 23
See Restitutus, Donatus, etc.

FRUCTUOSUS, AUGURIUS and EULOGIUS (SS) MM.   RM. Jan 21
d. 259. Fructuosus, bishop of Tarragoña in Spain, with his two deacons, Augurius and Eulogius, were burnt at the stake under Valerian. When the fire had burnt through their bonds, they stretched out their arms in the form of a cross and thus expired. The account of their official examination is still extant and thoroughly authentic.

FRUCTUOSUS (St) Ab. Bp.
                         RM. Apr 16
d. 665. Born in Spain, the son of a military officer belonging to the royal house of the Visigoths. He became a monk, and then a hermit in the Vierzo Mts, whither he was followed by crowds of disciples. His rule was based on the rule of St Benedict. Fructuosus was eventually forced to accept the bishopric of Dumium and later became archbishop of Braga.

FRUCTUS (FRUTOS), VALENTINE and ENGRATIA (SS) HH.
                         AC. Oct 25
d. c.715. Two brothers and their sister who were living at Sepúlveda in Old Castile at the time of one of the Saracen raids. Valentine and Engratia were killed by the Moors, but Frutos escaped and died a hermit. They are now venerated as the patron saints of Segovia where their relics are enshrined.

FRUGENTIUS (St) M. OSB.
                         AC. Sept 3
d. 675. A Benedictine of Fleury, killed with St Aigulphus, abbot of Lérins, q.v.

FRUMENTIUS and another FRUMENTIUS (SS) MM. RM. March 23
See Victorian, Frumentius, etc.

FRUMENTIUS (St) Bp. RM. Oct 27
d. c.380. A native of Tyre, who in the course of a voyage on the Red Sea, was wrecked on the Ethiopian coast with another young man—perhaps his brother—St Aedesius. Both were taken to the king's palace at Aksum, and attained high offices at court. Eventually Frumentius applied to St Athanasius for the appointment of a bishop for Ethiopia. St Athanasius complied by consecrating Frumentius. Frumentius and Aedesius preached the gospel with

signal success and are for this reason venerated as the apostles of Ethiopia.

FUGATIUS and DAMIAN (SS)
AC. Jan 3 (RM. May 26)
? 2nd cent. The alleged missionaries sent by Pope St Eleutherius to Britain. Their names are also written, Phaganus and Diruvianus, Fagan and Deruvian, Ffager and Dyfan.
See Dyfan.

FULBERT (St) Bp.   AC. Apr 10
d. 1029. The glory of his century. He was an Italian by birth, who became a student at the Benedictine abbey of Reims, under Gerbert (Pope Silvester II). He himself directed as headmaster the cathedral school of Chartres, of which city he was made bishop. A poet and scholar he identified himself whole-heartedly with the Cluniac movement of reform.

FULCRAN (St) Bp.   AC. Feb 13
d. 1006. A bishop of Lodève in Languedoc, famous for his vigorous asceticism and energetic rule. He was consecrated in 949 and ruled his diocese for over half a century.

FULGENTIUS (St) Bp. RM. Jan 1
468–533. An African, belonging to a family of senatorial rank. Early in life he embraced the monastic life and was elected abbot of his monastery; but he had to flee owing to the Vandal persecution. In 508 he was chosen bishop of Ruspe; but was again exiled by the Vandals. He spent his exile in Sardinia where he wrote his numerous works, which are still of the greatest importance for the history of the Arian persecutions. In 523 he returned to Africa and died ten years later.

FULGENTIUS (St) Bp. AC. Jan 16
d. c.633. Brother of SS Isidore and Leander of Seville and of St Florentina.

He was bishop of Ecija, in Andalusia, and one of the leaders of the Spanish church of that time. He is often confused with St Fulgentius of Ruspe (see Jan. 1).

FULGENTIUS (Bl) Ab. OSB.
PC. Dec 10
d. 1122. A Walloon by birth, he was professed a Benedictine at the abbey of St Airy, Verdun. The community of this monastery had to disband, owing to the struggle between Gregory VII and Henry IV. Fulgentius repaired to the abbey of Afflighem in Belgium, where later he was elected abbot.

FULK (FOULQUES, FULCO) (Bl) C.   AC. March 2
d. 1201. Parish priest of Neuilly-sur-Marne in France, commissioned by Innocent III to preach the third crusade, in which Richard Coeur de Lion took part. He died before setting out for the Holy Land.

FULK (St) C.   RM. May 22
d. p.600. A pilgrim to Rome who gave his life in the service of the plague-stricken at Santopadre or Castrofuli, near Arpino, in S. Italy. He is venerated as the patron saint of that district. Cult approved in 1572. The legend is extremely doubtful, but he is certainly the patron saint of Castrofuli.

FULK (St) Ab. OSB.   PC. Oct 10
d. 845. The twenty-first abbot of Fontenelle in Normandy.

FULK (St) Bp.   RM. Oct 26
1164–1229. Born at Piacenza of Scottish parents, he was appointed to a canonry there. Then, after his studies in Paris, he became archpriest and bishop of Piacenza. Six years later he was transferred by Honorius III to the see of Pavia, which he occupied for thirteen years.

FULK (FOLQUET) (Bl) Bp. OSB.
Cist.   PC. Dec 25
c.1155–1231. A Genoese by birth, and a
minstrel by profession, he entered the
Cistercian abbey of Thoronet, of which
he became abbot in 1200. In 1206 he
was raised to the see of Toulouse and
greatly helped St Dominic in the
founding of the Friars Preachers. He
was known as "the Minstrel Bishop".
He is venerated by the Cistercians.

FULRAD (St) Ab. OSB. AC. July 16
d. 784. An Alsatian by origin, he became
a Benedictine at the abbey of St Denis
near Paris, and in 750 was elected its
abbot. From this time his life is identified with that of the Carolingian court,
at which he held offices: viz. councillor,
court chaplain, grand-almoner, ambassador to the pope, etc. His was a
crowded life in the service of the Church
and of the Holy Roman Empire.

FURSEY (St) Ab. OSB. RM. Jan 16
d. c.648. An Irish monk, who established a monastery at Rathmat, whence
he passed over to England and founded
another at Burgh Castle, near Yarmouth,
in East Anglia. He finally crossed over
to France and became the abbot-
founder of Lagny, near Paris. His life is
also famous for his remarkable ecstasies,
of which St Bede and others write.

FUSCA V. and MAURA (SS) MM.
                            RM. Feb 13
d. c.250. Two martyrs of Ravenna under
Decius. Fusca was a young girl and
Maura her nurse.

FUSCIAN (St) M.   RM. Dec 11
See Victoricus, Fuscian and Gentian.

FUSCULUS (St) Bp. M. RM. Sept 6
See Donatian, Praesidius, etc.

FYMBERT (St) Bp.   AC. Sept 25
7th cent. A bishop in the W. of Scotland, said to have been consecrated by
St Gregory the Great.

FYNCANA and FYNDOCA (SS)
VV. MM.   AC. Oct 13
? Two martyrs listed in the Aberdeen
breviary, of whom nothing is known.

G

GABDELAS (St) M. RM. Sept 29
See Dadas, Casdoe and Gabdelas.

GABINUS (St) M. RM. Feb 19
d. 295 (or 296). A Roman Christian and martyr, related to the emperor Diocletian, brother of Pope St Caius and father of the martyr St Susanna. His Acts, however, are quite untrustworthy.

GABINUS and CRISPULUS (SS) MM. RM. May 30
d. c.130. The proto-martyrs of Sardinia. They suffered at Torres, where they had preached the gospel, under Hadrian.

GABRIEL de DUISCO (St) M.
RM. Feb 5
d. 1597. One of the group of twenty martyrs who were crucified at Nagasaki. He was a Japanese Franciscan tertiary.

GABRIEL of OUR LADY of SORROWS (St) CP. RM. Feb 27
1838–1862. Francis Possenti was born at Assisi and educated at Spoleto under the Jesuit Fathers. After two serious illnesses he suddenly developed a religious vocation and joined the Passionist Fathers at Morovalle, near Macerata (1856). Six years later (1862) the young scholastic died of consumption at Isola, in the Abruzzi. He attained perfection by heroic self-denial in small things. Canonized in 1920.

GABRIEL the ARCHANGEL (St)
RM. March 24
St Gabriel is mentioned in the Book of Daniel (VIII, 16; IX, 21) and was the angel sent to Zachary (Luke I, 11–19) and especially to our Lady, to tell her that she was chosen to be the Mother of God (Luke I, 266 sqq). He is for this reason called "The Angel of the Annunciation". His feast was added to the general calendar of the Western Church in 1921. See also Seven Angels.

GABRIEL MARY (Bl) C. OFM.
AC. Aug 27
1463–1532. Gabriel's baptismal name was Gilbert Nicolas, and he was born near Clermont. He was refused admission to several houses of the Franciscan Observants, but finally was received at Notre-Dame-de-la-Fon, near Rochelle. He co-operated with St Jane of Valois, whose confessor he was, in the foundation of the order of the Annonciades (1532). Cult approved in 1647.

GABRIEL of ST MAGDALEN (St) M. OFM. AC. Sept 3
d. 1632. A native of Fonseca in New Castile, and a Franciscan lay-brother. In 1612 he was sent to Manila, where he studied medicine, and in 1622 passed over to Japan and ministered to the sick during the persecutions, at the risk of his own life. He was at last captured and burnt alive at Nagasaki. Beatified in 1867.

GABRIEL PERBOYRE (Bl) M.
AC. Sept 11
1802–1840. Born at Peuch, in the diocese of Montauban, he joined the Vincentians in 1818, and after his ordination (1825) taught theology at Saint-Flaur (1825–1835). Here he received the news of the death of his brother, a

missionary in China, and offered himself to replace him. He arrived in China in 1836 and worked in the mission of Honan. In 1840, after a long incarceration and many tortures, he was strangled at the cross. Beatified in 1889.

GABRIEL JOHN TAURIN DU-FRESSE (Bl) M.   AC. Sept 14
1750–1815. Born at Ville-de-Lezoux, diocese of Clermont, he entered the seminary for foreign missions in 1774, and arrived in China in 1777. In 1800 he was consecrated titular bishop of Tabraca and after fifteen years of continual danger was betrayed by a native Christian and beheaded. Beatified in 1900.

**GABRIEL FERRETTI (Bl) C. OFM.
                              AC. Nov 12**
1385–1456. A native of Ancona, and a scion of the family of the counts Ferretti. He became a Friar Minor at Ancona, and eventually provincial of Piceno (Marches). Cult confirmed in 1753.

**GABRIELLE BOURLA (Bl) M.
                              AC. Oct 17**
1746–1794. Her name in religion was Marie-Ursule, and she belonged to the group of Ursuline Nuns, martyrs of Valenciennes, q.v.

GAIANA (St) VM.   RM. Sept 29
See Rhipsime, Gaiana, etc.

GAIUS (St) (*several*)
Otherwise Caius, q.v.

GAJAN (St) M.   AC. Apr 10
? 4th cent. A deacon martyred in Dacia.

GALATA (St) M.   RM. Apr 19
See Hermogenes, Caius, etc.

GALATION (GALACTEON) and EPISTEMIS (SS) MM.   RM. Nov 5
d. 251. According to the legend, Gala-

tion, already a Christian, converted his wife, upon which each retired to a monastery. They were martyred under Decius at Emessa in Phoenicia. It is now generally agreed that these two martyrs never existed: they are simply the hero and heroine in what may be described as the Christian continuation of the romance of Clitophon and Leucippe.

GALDINUS (St) Bp.   RM. Apr 18
1100–1176. A native of Milan and a member of the Della Scala family. After his ordination he was chancellor and archdeacon of the archdiocese. In 1161 he fled on the approach of the emperor Barbarossa; but, though absent, was elected archbishop of Milan and created cardinal (1165). He returned to Milan and was instrumental in rebuilding the city razed to the ground by Barbarossa. He died immediately after having preached a sermon in his cathedral. The Milanese always invoke him after SS Ambrose and Charles Borromeo.

GALGANUS (St) C.   RM. Dec 5
d. 1181. A native of Siena who at first led a worldly life, but was converted to better ways and became a hermit at Monte Siepe in Tuscany, where he died. He was canonized by Alexander III. In 1196 a church was built on the site of his hermitage which was handed over to the Cistercians in 1201. It is probably for this reason that the Cistercians have always claimed him as one of their own.

**GALL (GALLUS) (St) Bp.
                              RM. July 1**
c. 489–554. A native of Auvergne who became a monk but after being ordained deacon by St Quinctian, bishop of Clermont, was sent to represent him at the court of King Thierry. In 527 he succeeded St Quinctian. He was uncle and teacher of St Gregory of Tours.

GALL (St) Ab. RM. Oct 16
d. *c.*640. An Irishman and a monk of
Bangor who accompanied St Columbanus to England and France, where he
helped in the foundation of Luxeuil. He
was banished, together with St Columbanus, and settled in Switzerland, at a
place on the Steinach, where the great
abbey and town of Saint-Gall sprang up
at a later period, and is venerated as one
of the apostles of Switzerland.

GALLA (St) W. RM. Oct 5
d. *c.*550. A Roman lady, daughter of
Symmachus the younger and sister-in-
law of Boëthius. After her husband's
death she led the life of a recluse in a
small cottage on the Vatican Hill, where
she died of cancer of the breast. Her life
and death are briefly described by St
Gregory the Great.

GALLGO (St) Ab. AC. Nov 27
6th cent. A Welsh saint, founder of
Llanallgo in Anglesey.

GALLICANUS (St) M. RM. June 25
d. *c.*362. Described as a high officer in
the army of Constantine and consul at
Rome, who in the year 330, retired to
Ostia, where he founded a hospital and
ministered to the sick. The RM makes
him a martyr at Alexandria under
Julian the Apostate; but both his
banishment to Alexandria and his
martyrdom are denied by historians.

GALLICANUS (St) Bp. AC. June 25
d. *p.*541. The fifth bishop of Embrun,
in France.

GALLUS (St) RM. July 1
Otherwise Gall, q.v.

GALMIER (St) RM. Feb 27
The French form of Baldomerus, q.v.

GALNUTIUS (St) Ab. AC. March 3
Otherwise Winaloë, q.v.

GAMALIEL (St) RM. Aug 3
1st cent. The Jewish doctor of the Law,
at whose feet St Paul sat (Acts XXII, 3)
and whose counsel saved Peter and
John (ib. V, 34–39). Tradition makes
him a convert to Christianity. The RM.
commemorates the finding of his body,
together with those of SS Stephen,
protomartyr, Nicodemus and Abibo
(415).

GAMELBERT (St) C. AC. Jan 27
720–800. Son of rich Bavarian parents,
he was set by his father to guard his
sheep. Later he went to Rome on pilgrimage, was ordained priest, and
laboured for over fifty years as parish
priest of Michaelsbuch. Cult approved
in 1909.

GAMO (St) Ab. OSB. AC. May 30
8th cent. Monk and then abbot of the
abbey of Brétigny near Noyon.

GANDULPHUS of BINASCO (Bl)
C. OFM. AC. Apr 3
d. 1260. Born at Binasco, near Milan, he
became a Friar Minor during the life-
time of St Francis, and spent all his life
praying and preaching in Sicily.

GANGULPHUS (St) M.
RM. May 11
d. 760. A Burgundian and a courtier,
who retired from public life to lead the
life of a recluse and was killed by his
wife's paramour.

GARBH (St) V. AC. Jan 1
Otherwise Fanchea, q.v.

GARBHAN (St) Ab. AC. March 26
7th cent. The Irish saint who appears to
have left his name to Dungarvan.
Nothing certain is known about him.

GARCIA GONZALEZ (St) M. OFM.
RM. Feb 5
d. 1597. A Spanish Franciscan and

missionary in Japan, crucified at Nagasaki. Beatified in 1627, and canonized
in 1862.

GARCIA (St) Ab. OSB. AC. Sept 29
d. c.1073. A native of Quintanilla, near
Burgos, in Old Castile. He became
monk and abbot (1039) of Artanza, in
Old Castile, and was the counsellor and
companion of King Ferdinand I of
Castile, whom he more than once followed into battle.

GARDINER, GERMAN (Bl) M.
                              AC. March 7
See Jermyn Gardiner.

GAREMBERT (St) Ab. AC. Dec 31
Otherwise Walembert, q.v.

GARIBALDUS (St) Bp. OSB.
                                  AC. Jan 8
d. 762. First bishop of Ratisbon, who
was consecrated by St Boniface c.740.
He had been abbot probably of St
Emmeran at Ratisbon.

GARMIER (GERMIER) St)
                                RM. Feb 27
Otherwise Baldomerus, q.v.

GARMON (St) Bp.   RM. July 31
A French form of the name of St Germanus of Auxerre, q.v.

GARNAT (St)   AC. Nov 8
Otherwise Gervadius, q.v.

GASPAR (several)
Otherwise Caspar, q.v.

GASTON (St) Bp.   RM. Feb 6
A French form of Vedast, q.v.

GATIAN (St) Bp.   RM. Dec. 18
d. ? c.337. Venerated as one of the disciples of St Dionysius of Paris and the
founder and first bishop of the diocese
of Tours, in France.

GAUCHERIUS (GAULTIER,
WALTER) (St) Ab.   AC. Apr 9
d. 1140. The abbot-founder of the
monastery of St John at Aureil in the
Limousin, for Augustinian canons regular. He was also a great benefactor of
St Stephen of Gramont at Muret.

GAUDENTIA and Comp. (SS) VV.
MM.   RM. Aug 30
? St Gaudentia, a Roman maiden, is
said to have suffered with three other
Christians; but the more ancient
martyrologies do not rank her among
the martyrs.

GAUDENTIUS of GNESEN (St)
Bp. OSB.   AC. Jan 5
d. c.1004. Younger brother of St Adalbert of Prague and his fellow-monk at
the Benedictine abbey of Sant' Alessio,
on the Aventine, Rome, and again his
companion on his mission to Prussia.
he escaped the massacre in which his
brother was martyred and in 1000 was
appointed first archbishop of Gnesen
by Otto III.

GAUDENTIUS of NOVARA (St)
Bp.   RM. Jan 22
d. 417. A priest of Ivrea, near Turin,
who was befriended first by St Laurence
of Novara and then by St Eusebius of
Vercelli. He succeeded the former as
bishop of Novara, and governed the
diocese twenty years.

GAUDENTIUS of VERONA (St)
Bp.   RM. Feb 12
d. c.465. Bishop of Verona. His relics
are enshrined at Verona in the ancient
basilica of St Stephen.

GAUDENTIUS of OSSERO (St) Bp.
OSB.   AC. June 1
d. 1044. Bishop of Ossero in Istria. He
was appointed to that see in 1030. Two
years later he journeyed to Rome to
appeal against his persecutors. On his

way back he fell ill at Ancona, and, on his recovery, resigned his see (1042) and became a Benedictine under St Peter Damian.

GAUDENTIUS and CULMATIUS (SS) MM.   RM. June 19
d. 364. Gaudentius, a bishop, and Culmatius, his deacon, are stated in the RM. to have been martyred at Arezzo in Tuscany under Valentinian I. With them suffered Andrew, a layman, with his wife and children and a group of fifty-three companions.

GAUDENTIUS of RIMINI (St) Bp. M.   RM. Oct 14
d. c.360. An Asiatic, who joined the Roman clergy (332) and in 346 became bishop of Rimini. He suffered much at the hands of the Arians, who dominated the council of 357, and was by them done to death.

GAUDENTIUS of BRESCIA (St) Bp.   RM. Oct 25
d. c.410. A pupil of St Philastrius, bishop of Brescia, he became a monk at Caesarea in Cappadocia, but was recalled to Brescia to succeed St Philastrius as bishop and was consecrated by St Ambrose (c.387). In 405 he was sent to the East to defend the cause of St John Chrysostom and was imprisoned near Thrace. He died shortly after.

GAUDIOSUS of BRESCIA (St) Bp.   RM. March 7
d. 445. (?) Bishop of Brescia where his relics are venerated.

GAUDIOSUS of SALERNO (St) Bp.   RM. Oct 26
7th cent. A bishop of Salerno, whose relics are venerated at Naples.

GAUDIOSUS of NAPLES (St) Bp.   RM. Oct 27
d. c.455. Surnamed "the African". He was in fact a bishop of Abitina in N. Africa, exiled by the Arian Vandal king Genseric (440). He took refuge at Naples where he founded a monastery, of which, later, St Agnellus became abbot.

GAUDIOSUS of TARAZONA (St) Bp.   AC. Nov 3
d. c.585. A monk of Asan in the Aragonese Pyrenees, near Benasque, under St Victorian. About the year 565 he was made bishop of Tarazona (not Tarragona) in the province of Saragossa.

GAUFRIDUS (Bl) Ab. OSB.   AC. Sept 9
d. 1139. A disciple of Bl Vitalis, and his successor as abbot of Savigny (1122–1139). Under him the new Benedictine congregation of Savigny spread to Normandy, England, Ireland and numbered some twenty-nine houses.

GAUGERICUS (GAU, GÉRY) (St) Bp.   RM. Aug 11
d. c.625. Gaugericus was born in the diocese of Trèves and was ordained priest by the bishop of that diocese, and later was made bishop of the united dioceses of Cambrai and Arras, which he governed for over thirty-nine years.

GAUSMARUS (Bl) Ab. OSB.   AC. June 3
d. 984. Abbot of St Martin of Savigny (954–984).

GEBETRUDE (GERTRUDE) Abs. OSB.   AC. Nov 7
d. c.675. Third abbess of Remiremont (Habend). Her relics were elevated and her cult approved by Leo IX in 1051.

GEBHARD (St) Bp.   AC. Aug 27
d. 995. Bishop of Constance (979–995). He founded the great Benedictine abbey of Petershausen, near Constance (983), where he was buried.

GEBIZO (St) Mk. OSB. AC. Oct 21
d. *c*.1087. A native of Cologne, he became a monk of Montecassino under Abbot St Desiderius (Pope Victor III) in 1076. He was sent to Croatia by Pope St Gregory VII, to crown King Zwoinimir.

GEBUINUS (St) Bp.   AC. Apr 18
d. 1080. Archbishop of Lyons. He is patron of the cathedral-chapter of Langres.

GEDEON (St) Bp.   AC. Aug 8
d. *c*.796. The thirteenth bishop of Besançon (790–796).

GEDEON (St) Judge   RM. Sept 1
Otherwise Gideon, q.v.

GELASINUS (GELASIUS) (St) M.
AC. Aug 26
d. 297. An actor at Heliopolis in Phoenicia who, having to burlesque the ceremony of baptism, suddenly declared himself a Christian and was stoned to death by the mob. Probably identical with St Genesius (Aug 25).

GELASIUS II (St) Pope OSB.
RM. Jan 29
c.1058–1119. A monk of Montecassino, he became cardinal and counsellor of Pope Pascal II. He was elected Pope in 1118 and carried on the struggle with the Emperor Henry V and his anti-pope. But he died soon after at Cluny. Baronius said that no pontiff, except the martyrs, had suffered so much for the Church.

GELASIUS (St) M.   RM. Feb 4
See Aquilinus, Geminus, etc.

GELASIUS (GIOUA-MAC-LIAG)
(St) Bp.   AC. March 27
d. 1174. Abbot of Derry. He was consecrated archbishop of Armagh in 1138, and is said to have been the first Irish

bishop to whom the pallium was sent. In 1162 he consecrated St Laurence O'Toole archbishop of Dublin.

GELASIUS I (St) Pope RM. Nov 21
d. 496. An African by descent he was raised to the papal see in 492. He showed himself a vigorous pontiff, in fact one of the greatest in that century of great popes. Although he is not the author of the Sacramentary which goes under his name, it probably contains much that is really due to his talent and research.

GELASIUS (St) M.   RM. Dec 23
See Theodulus, Saturninus, etc.

GEMELLUS (St) M.   RM. Dec 10
d. 362. Crucified for the Faith at Ancyra in Galatia (Asia Minor) under Julian the Apostate.

GEMINIAN of MODENA (St) Bp.
RM. Jan 31
d. 348. Deacon to the bishop of Modena and his successor in the see. He gave shelter to St Athanasius as that great bishop passed through Italy on his way to his exile in Gaul. Geminian bravely opposed Jovinianism.

GEMINIAN (St) M.   RM. Sept 16
See Lucy and Geminian.

GEMINUS (St) M.   RM. Jan 4
See Aquilinus, Geminus, etc.

GEMINUS of FOSSOMBRONE (St)
M.   RM. Feb 4
See Aquilinus, Geminus, Gelasius, etc.

GEMINUS (St) Mk.   AC. Oct 9
d. ? 815. A monk of Sanpaterniano de Fano, diocese of Narni, in Umbria. He is claimed both by the Basilians and the Benedictines for their respective orders. He is the patron saint of San Gemini.

GEMMA GALGANI (St) V.
RM. Apr 11
1878–1903. Born at Camigliano, near Lucca, in Tuscany. Her mother died when she was seven years old, and from that time her life was one of domestic trials and intense suffering both spiritual and physical. Through it all, however, she remained at peace and was the subject of various extraordinary supernatural phenomena—visions, ecstasies, revelations, supernatural knowledge, visible intercourse with her guardian angel, prophecy, miracles, and above all the periodically recurring stigmata between 1899 and 1901. She was directed by the Passionist fathers. Her physical infirmities prevented her becoming a Passionist nun, as she ardently desired. She died on Holy Saturday. Beatified in 1933 and canonized in 1940, in the teeth of strong opposition based on the extraordinary nature of her religious experiences.

GEMMA (Bl) V.
AC. May 12
d. 1249. A shepherdess, and afterwards for forty-two years a recluse at Goriano Sicoli, diocese of Sulmona in the Abruzzi. Cult approved in 1890.

GEMMA (HEMMA, EMMA) (St) W. OSB.
AC. June 29
d. 1045. A near relative of the emperor St Henry II. Left a widow, she became the foundress of the double monastery of Gurk in Carinthia, and took the veil among the nuns.

GEMUS (St) Mk. OSB. AC. March 19
? Monk, probably of Moyenmoutier in Alsace. His relics were enshrined at Hürbach.

GENEBALD of LAON (St) Bp.
AC. Sept 5
d. c.555. A bishop of Laon related to St Remigius. For a fault he committed he is said to have performed a seven years' continuous penance.

GENEBRARD (St) M.   AC. May 15
Otherwise Gerebern, q.v.

GENERALIS (St) M.   RM. Sept 14
See Crescentian, Victor, etc.

GENEROSA (St) M.   RM. July 17
One of the Scillitan Martyrs, q.v.

GENEROSUS (St) Ab. OSB.
AC. July 16
d. c.682. An abbot of Saint-Jouin-de-Marnes in Poitou.

GENEROSUS (St) M.   RM. July 17
? Venerated at Tivoli, where his relics are enshrined in the cathedral, under the high altar; but nothing is known about him.

GENESIUS (St) Bp.   AC. June 3
d. 662. Bishop of Clermont in Auvergne. He is described as learned, benevolent, surpassingly good, beloved by old and young, rich and poor.

GENESIUS the COMEDIAN (St) M.
RM. Aug 25
d. c.300. An actor at Rome who, while taking part in a burlesque of Christian baptism in the theatre, was suddenly converted and forthwith martyred. The same story is told of at least three other martyrs. Probably this Genesius is the same as the Saint of Arles, and a popular story has been applied to him. (Cf. Gelasinus above.)

GENESIUS (GENÈS) of ARLES (St) M.
RM. Aug 25
d. c.303. A notary of Arles in S. Gaul, who having refused to put on record an imperial decree against Christians and declaring that he himself believed in Christ, was martyred under Maximian Herculeus.

GENESIUS (St) M.   RM. Oct 11
See Anastasius, Placid, etc.

GENESIUS (St) Bp.   AC. Nov 1
d. c.679. From being prior at Fontenelle he was chosen abbot-chaplain of the palace by Queen Bathildis, and in 658 raised to the see of Lyons. He died at the nunnery of Chelles while on a visit there.

GENISTUS (St) M. OSB. AC. Apr 30
c.1100. A Benedictine monk of Beaulieu in the Limousin, diocese of Limoges. Killed by his nephew at Aynac-en-Quercy. He is venerated as a martyr and as patron saint of Aynac.

GENEVIÈVE (St) V.   RM. Jan 3
c.422–500. Born at Nanterre near Paris. In her seventh year she happened to become known to St Germanus of Auxerre, who befriended her. When fifteen years old she received the veil from the bishop of Paris, and gave herself up to penance and the exercise of charity. When Paris was occupied by the Franks and afterwards threatened by Attila and his Huns, St Geneviève encouraged the people to defend the city. She has always been considered the special protectress and patroness of Paris. There has been in recent times a lively controversy over the authenticity of her life, of which the above is a resumé.

GENGULPHUS (St) M. RM. May 11
Otherwise Gangulphus, q.v.

GENITUS (St)   AC. Jan 17
See Genulfus and Genitus.

GENNADIUS (St) M.   RM. May 16
See Felix and Gennadius.

GENNADIUS (St) Bp. OSB.
                            AC. May 25
d. c.936. A monk at Argeo, near Astorga, in Spain, abbot-restorer of San Pedro de Montes, and a zealous propagator of St Benedict's Rule throughout N.W. Spain. About the year 895 he was raised to the see of Astorga, which he resigned five years before his death, returning to live as a monk-hermit in his beloved San Pedro.

GENNARD (St) Ab. OSB.   Ac. Apr 6
d. 720. Educated at the court of Clotaire III, he became a monk at Fontenelle under St Wandrille, and eventually abbot of Flay (Saint-Germer) in the diocese of Beauvais. Before his death he resigned and returned to die at Fontenelle.

GENNARO (St) M.   RM. Sept 19
The Italian form of Januarius, q.v.

GENNYS (GENEWYS) (St) Bp.
                            RM. July 31
Otherwise Germanus of Auxerre, q.v.

GENOCUS (St) C.   AC. Apr 18
See Ritheus and Genocus.

GENOVEFA (St) V.   RM. Jan 3
Otherwise Geneviève, q.v.

GENTIAN (St) M.   RM. Dec 11
See Victoricus, Fuscian and Gentian.

GENTILIS (Bl)   AC.
d. 1530. The widow of a Venetian tailor, she assisted Bl Marguerite of Ravenna in the foundation of her institute.

GENTILIS (Bl) M. OFM. AC. Sept 5
d. 1340. A native of Matelica in the Marches, Piceno, where he joined the Friars Minor. He spent some time on Mt Alvernia and then went as a missionary among the Mohammedans of Egypt and Persia. He was martyred at Toringa in Persia. Cult approved by Pius VI.

GENUINUS (INGENUINUS) and ALBINUS (SS) Bps.   RM. Feb 5

7th cent. A bishop of the small town of Sabion (which has since disappeared) near Brixen in the Tyrol. With him is commemorated on the same day St Albinus, bishop of Brixen in the 11th century.

GENULFUS (GENOU) and GENITUS (SS)   AC. Jan 17

? 3rd cent. They are said to have been two holy monks so named who lived at Celle-sur-Naton in France. Another St Genulfus is honoured at Cahors as the first bishop of that see.

GEOFFREY (GODFREY) (St) Ab.   AC. June 21

Otherwise Agofredus, q.v.

GEOFFREY (St) Ab.   AC. Sept 25

The Norman form of the Saxon name Ceolfrid, q.v.

GEOFFREY (several)

Otherwise Godfrey, q.v.

GEORGE of LODÈVE (St) Bp. OSB.   AC. Feb 19

d. c.884. Born near Rodez and a Benedictine at Sainte-Foi-de-Conques in Rouergue. After the destruction of the monastery by the Norsemen (862) he became a monk at Vabres, diocese of Rodez. When quite old he was elected to the see of Lodève.

GEORGE of AMASTRIS (St) Bp.   AC. Feb 21

d. c.825. A native of Kromna, near Amastris, on the Black Sea. He was first a hermit on Mt Sirik, then a monk of Bonyssa, and lastly bishop of Amastris. He deserved well of his people during the Saracen attacks, against which he successfully defended his episcopal city.

GEORGE the YOUNGER (St) Bp.   AC. Apr 7

d. c.816. Bishop of Mitylene, the capital of Lesbos. He is called "the Younger" because two of his predecessors in the see and of that century, also named George, are venerated as saints.

GEORGE GERVASE (Bl) M. OSB.   AC. Apr 11

d. 1608. A native of Bosham, Sussex. In his youth he had a very adventurous career under Drake in the W. Indies. He was educated for the priesthood at Douai and ordained priest in 1603. At Douai, too, he was received into the Benedictine Order. Sent to the English mission he was condemned for his priesthood and suffered at Tyburn. Beatified in 1929.

GEORGE of ANTIOCH (St) Bp. M.   RM. Apr 19

d. 814. A monk, who became bishop of Antioch in Pisidia. He was one of the Fathers of the second council of Nicea (787) against the Iconoclasts. Banished by the emperor Leo V. the Armenian, he died in exile.

GEORGE the GREAT (St) M.   RM. Apr 23

d. c.300. It is now almost universally agreed that St George was a martyr who suffered at Diospolis (Lydda, Ludd) in Palestine, probably under Diocletian. All the other legends which have grown up around his name may safely be regarded as fictitious, including the story of the dragon, which seems to have originated in Italy at a comparatively recent period. The Crusaders certainly gave great impetus to devotion to St George in the West, though he was venerated there long before. He is venerated in the East as one of the fourteen Holy Helpers and, universally, as the model of knighthood and avenger of women. He is the acknowledged patron saint of England, Aragon, Portugal and Germany, also of Genoa and Venice, and protector of Ferrara. In the East he is especially honoured as the patron of soldiers. His veneration as protector of England was officially approved by Pope Benedict XIV.

GEORGE SWALLOWELL (Bl) M.
AC. July 26
d. 1594. Born near Durham, he became a Protestant minister and schoolmaster. He was condemned to death for being reconciled to the Church, and executed at Darlington. Beatified in 1929.

GEORGE, AURELIUS and NATALIA, FELIX and LILIOSA (SS) MM.   RM. July 27 (Oct 20)
d. c.852. Martyrs who suffered at Cordova in Spain under the Caliph Abderrahman II. Aurelius and Felix, with their wives, Natalia and Liliosa, were Spaniards; but the deacon George was a monk from Palestine, who, though offered pardon as a foreigner, preferred to throw in his lot with the others.

GEORGE LIMNIOTES (St) M.
RM. Aug 24
d. c.730. A hermit of Mt Olympus in Asia Minor, who had reached the age, it is said, of ninety-five, when he was martyred under Leo the Isaurian for defending the worship of sacred images.

GEORGE and AURELIUS (SS) MM.
RM. Oct 20
See George, Aurelius, etc., July 27. The relics of SS Aurelius and George were translated to the abbey church of St Germain at Paris. The anniversary of this translation is celebrated on Oct 20.

GEORGE of PÉRIGUEUX (St) Bp.
RM. Oct 25
See Fronto and George.

GEORGE of VIENNE (St) Bp.
RM. Nov 2
? A bishop of Vienne in France, who flourished probably at the beginning of the eighth century, though some put Nov 2, 699 as the date of his death. Canonized in 1251.

GEORGE NAPPER (Bl) M.
AC. Nov 9
d. 1610. Born at Holywell Manor, Oxford, and educated at Corpus Christi College, Oxford. He studied for the priesthood at Douai where he was ordained in 1596. Sent to the English mission he laboured in Oxfordshire and was finally condemned for his priesthood and executed at Oxford. Beatified in 1929.

GEORGIA (St) V.   RM. Feb 15
d. c.500. A maiden who became a recluse near Clermont in Auvergne, France.

GERALD (St) Bp. OSB. AC. Feb 6
d. 1077. From being prior at Cluny Gerald was raised by Pope Alexander II to the see of Ostia as successor to St Peter Damian. He was papal legate to France, Spain and Germany, and was arrested and imprisoned by the German emperor, Henry V. He is the principal patron saint of Velletri.

GERALD (St) Ab.   AC. March 13
d. 732. A Northumbrian monk who followed St Colman from Lindisfarne to Ireland and became his successor in the English house built at Mayo for the English monastic colony. He lived to an old age and must have witnessed the introduction of the Roman observances into his abbey.

GERALD of SAUVE-MAJEURE (St) Ab. OSB.   AC. Apr 5
d. 1095. A native of Corbie, he was

educated and became a monk and cellarer at the famous abbey of his native town. He suffered from acute headaches. He was taken by his abbot to Rome and Montecassino, and at Rome Pope Leo IX ordained him priest. On his return to Corbie, he was cured by St Adalard; then he went to Palestine. Next, he was chosen abbot of St Vincent's at Laon and of St Medard at Soissons; but, being expelled by a usurper, he founded Sauve-Majeure, which became the centre of a powerful Benedictine congregation. Canonized in 1197.

GERALD (St) Bp. OSB. AC. May 29

d. 927. A monk of Brou. He became bishop of Mâcon but after some forty years in the episcopate he returned to his old abbey to die.

GERALD of AURILLAC (St) C.
AC. Oct 13

855–909. Gerald, count of Aurillac, led a life of great virtue at a period when it was difficult for one of his rank to do so. He founded a Benedictine abbey on his estate and endowed it in princely fashion. He is the patron saint of Upper Auvergne.

GERALD (Bl) Ab. OSB. Cist.
AC. Oct 16

d. 1177. A native of Lombardy and professed at the Cistercian monastery at Fossanuova in the Roman Campagna, being eventually chosen abbot. He was later promoted to the abbacy of Clairvaux (1170) and was killed by an unruly monk while on a canonical visitation to Igny.

GERALD of BEZIERS (St) Bp.
AC. Nov 5

d. 1123. A canon regular who became bishop of Beziers in S. France. He spent all his revenues in relieving the distress of the poor of the diocese.

GERALD (St) Bp. OSB. PC. Dec 5

d. 1109. Born near Cahors in Gascony, he took the Benedictine habit at Moissac. He accompanied Archbishop Bernard of Toledo to Spain, and was eventually made archbishop of Braga in Portugal (1100).

GERARD (Bl) D. OSB. Cist.
AC. Jan 30

d. 1138. The second and favourite brother of St Bernard of Clairvaux. He was not of the party of thirty who accompanied St Bernard to Cîteaux. He was then soldiering and, on being wounded, made up his mind to become a monk. He entered Cîteaux and followed his brother to Clairvaux where he excelled as a cellarer. St Bernard mourned him deeply when he died.

GERARD (Bl) C. OSB. Cam.
AC. Apr 1

1280–1367. At the age of nine Gerard received the Camaldolese habit at the abbey of the Holy Cross, at Sassoferrato. After his ordination he was entrusted with the care of the parish, which he served with untiring zeal. He died on Nov 18; but his feast is kept by the Camaldolese on Apr 1.

GERARD of ORCHIMONT (Bl) Ab. OSB.   AC. Apr 23

d. 1138. A Benedictine monk and afterwards abbot, of Florennes (1126–c.1136).

GERARD of TOUL (St) Bp.
RM. Apr 23

d. 994. A native of Cologne, who became bishop of Toul in 963. He rebuilt the cathedral and established religious houses in which teaching was given by Greek and Irish monks to the great furtherance of religion and learning in the diocese. He was canonized by Pope Leo IX, his successor in the see.

GERARD (St) C.   AC. Apr 28
639? One of four English pilgrims—the other three were Ardwine, Bernard and Hugh—who died at Galinaro in S. Italy. Many scholars doubt their very existence.

GERARD of BOURGOGNE (Bl)
Ab. OSB. Cist.   PC. Apr 28
d. 1172. The successor of St Fastred as abbot of the Cistercian monastery of Cambron.

GERARD of VILLAMAGNA (Bl) C.
AC. May 13
1174–1242. A native of Tuscany who, as esquire to a knight, took part in the crusades and was taken prisoner. On being ransomed, he returned to Italy, joined the third order of St Francis and lived as a recluse for the rest of his life. Cult approved in 1833.

GERARD de LUNEL (St) C.
AC. May 24
1275–1298. Said to have been a French pilgrim, belonging to the third order of St Francis, who died at Monte Santo, near Ancona, on his return from Palestine. His cult was approved by Benedict XIV and Pius VI, and he is now honoured as the patron saint of Monte Santo.

GERARD TINTORIO (Bl) C.
AC. June 6
d. 1207. A young citizen of Monza in Lombardy, belonging to the upper middle class, who expended his wealth in founding a hospital, where he served the sick, especially lepers. Cult approved in 1582.

GERARD SAGREDO (St) Bp. M.
OSB.   RM. Sept 24
d. 1046. Apostle of Hungary, where he is venerated as St Collert. He was a Venetian by birth and a Benedictine monk and abbot of San Giorgio Maggiore in his native city. On a pilgrimage to Palestine he was stopped when passing through Hungary by King St Stephen and persuaded to work among the Magyars. He became the tutor of Prince St Emeric and, in 1035, first bishop of Csanad. He worked most zealously, but during the pagan reaction after St Stephen's death Gerard was martyred at Buda, and his body cast into the Danube.

GERARD of BROGNE (St) Ab.
OSB.   RM. Oct 3
d. 959. Born in the county of Namur, and trained for the army, as a page of the count of Namur he was sent on a special mission to the French court (918). He stayed in France and joined the Benedictines of St Denis. After some eleven years he was ordained priest, and left for Belgium in order to found a new abbey on his own estate of Brogne. He was its abbot for twenty-two years and during that period was instrumental in introducing St Benedict's Rule into numerous houses in Flanders, Lorraine and Champagne. He was noted for his engaging sweetness of temper.

GERARD MAJELLA (St) C. C.SS.R.
RM. Oct 16
1725–1755. A native of Muro in S. Italy, he was apprenticed to a tailor before asking to be received by the Redemptionists as a lay-brother. He continued his trade in the monastery, where he soon attracted the attention of St Alphonsus de Liguori, who shortened his novitiate. His wonderful and well authenticated life was a series of supernatural phenomena—bilocations, reading of consciences, prophecies, multiplying of food, etc. Canonized in 1904.

GERARD of POTENZA (St) Bp.
RM. Oct 30

d. 1119. A native of Piacenza, who was enrolled among the clergy of Potenza, in S. Italy, and elected bishop there at an advanced age. Canonized by Pope Callistus II.

GERARD de BAZONCHES (St) Mk. OSB.
AC. Nov 4

d. 1123. A Benedictine monk-priest of St Aubin, at Angers.

GERARD (St) Ab. OSB. AC. Dec 6

d. 1109. First prior of the Cluniac house of La-Charité-sur-Loire, in the diocese of Namur. He founded several more Cluniac houses in France and elsewhere and finally governed the abbey of Soigny, but resigned and returned to La-Charité to end his days as a simple religious.

GERARD CAGNOLI (Bl) C. OFM.
AC. Jan 2

1270–1345. He was born of noble parents at Valenzo near Pavia; after the death of his mother he became a hermit on Mt. Etna in Sicily. After some years he entered the Franciscans as a lay brother, and fulfilled the office of cook. He was the recipient of many extraordinary divine favours. Cult confirmed 1908.

GERARDESCA (Bl) W. OSB. Cam.
AC. May 29

d. c.1260. A native of Pisa, who married a citizen of that city. After some years of married life she induced her husband to become a Camaldolese monk at San Salvio, while she lived nearby as a recluse, under the obedience of the abbey. Cult confirmed in 1856.

GERASIMUS (St) Ab. RM. March 5

d. c.475. A monk first in Lycia, Asia Minor, and afterwards in Palestine.

Eventually he himself founded a *laura* on the banks of the Jordan, near Jericho, which grew to be second only to that of St Sabas. "St Jerome's Lion" really belonged to St Gerasimus.

GERBALD, REGINHARD, WINEBALD and WORAD (BB) MM. OSB.
AC. May 25

d. 862. The first two were monks, the two latter deacons of the abbey of St Bertin, all martyred by the Danes.

GERBOLD (St) Bp. OSB. AC. Dec 5

d. c.690. Monk of Ebriciacum under Abbot Alnobert, and afterwards abbot-founder of the abbey of Livray (*Liberiacum*). Eventually he became bishop of Baycux.

GERBRAND (Bl) Ab. OSB. Cist.
PC. Act 13

d. 1218. Second abbot of the Cistercian monastery of Klaarkamp in Frisia, and founder of Bloemkamp (1191). He died at Foigny, in the Laonnais, when returning from a general chapter, and has been venerated there ever since.

GEREBALD (St) Bp. AC. June 12

d. 885. Bishop of Châlons-sur-Seine (864–885).

GEREBERN (GEREBRAND) (St) M.
AC. May 15

7th cent. The aged Irish priest who accompanied St Dympna (q.v.) to Belgium and shared in her martyrdom. He is the patron saint of a village in the Rhineland, where his relics are enshrined.

GEREMARUS (GERMER) (St) Ab. OSB.
RM. Sept 24

d. c.658. A native of Beauvais, attached to the court of Dagobert I. With the consent of his saintly wife he retired to the abbey of Pentale on the Seine, near Brionne, of which he eventually became abbot. He was over-severe, with the result that some of his monks made an attempt on his life, whereupon he resigned and retired to a cave near the abbey to live as a hermit. In 655 he founded Flay abbey, between Beauvais and Rouen, which was afterwards called Saint-Germer.

GEREON and Comp. (SS) MM.
RM. Oct 10
? These martyrs represent a band of Christians—said to have been three hundred and nineteen in number—who suffered at Cologne, where their tomb was shown in the fifth century. They have been wrongly associated with the Theban Legion.

GERINUS (GARINUS, WERINUS) (St) M. **RM. Oct 2**
d. 676. Brother of St Leodegarius (Leger) and, like him, persecuted by Ebroin, mayor of the palace. He was stoned to death near Arras.

GERIUS (St) C. **AC. May 24**
Otherwise Gerard de Lunel, q.v.

GERLAC (St) H. **AC. Jan 5**
d. c.1170. A Dutch soldier of licentious life, who after the death of his wife experienced a moral conversion and led thenceforth a life of most austere penance: he lived in a hollow tree near Valkenberg, his native place. He had a kind of spiritual pact with St Hildegard.

GERLAND (St) Bp. **AC. Feb 25**
d. 1104. Said to have been born at Besançon in France, and to have been related to the Norman conqueror of Sicily, Robert Guiscard. He was certainly consecrated bishop of Girgenti, in Sicily, by Urban II, and laboured for the restoration of Christianity in Sicily after the expulsion of the Saracens.

GERLAND (St) C. **AC. June 18**
13th cent. A knight—either a Templar or a Hospitaller—whose relics are venerated at Caltagirone in Sicily.

GERMAN GARDINER (Bl) M.
AC. March 7
Otherwise Jermyn Gardiner, q.v.

GERMANA (St) M. **RM. Jan 19**
See Paul, Gerontius, etc.

GERMANA (French: GERMAINE) COUSIN (St) V. **RM. June 15**
c.1579–1601. Born at Pibrac, near Toulouse, daughter of a poor farmer. She suffered from scrofula, was neglected by her father and treated with much harshness by her step-mother. She was sent to tend the sheep, and spent her short life in the fields, communing with God in prayer, and practising charity towards others poorer than herself. She died all alone on her straw bed at the age of twenty-two. Canonized in 1867.

GERMANICUS (St) M. RM. Jan 19
d. 156. A youth of Smyrna thrown to the wild beasts in the amphitheatre at the public games. The letter describing his martyrdom—together with that of St Polycarp—is one of the most authentic documents of early ecclesiastical history.

GERMANUS and RANDOALD (SS) MM. OSB. **AC. Feb 21**
d. c.677. Germanus was born at Trèves, and became a monk at Remiremont. Thence he migrated to Luxeuil under its third abbot St Waldebert, who introduced the Benedictine rule into the abbey. At a later date he was made abbot of Granfield in the Val Moutier. He and his prior St Randoald, were put to death by the duke of that district while interceding with him on behalf of the poor.

GERMANUS (St) M.   RM. May 2
See Saturninus, Neopolus, etc.

GERMANUS (St) Bp. M. AC. May 2
d. *c*.460. Of Irish or Scottish origin, he was converted by St Germanus of Auxerre whose name he took. He was martyred in Normandy.

GERMANUS OF CONSTANTI-NOPLE (St) Bp.   RM. May 12
d. 732. A churchman of senatorial rank, who, from being bishop of Cyzieus, was made patriarch of Constantinople (715). He bravely opposed the iconoclast emperor, Leo III, the Isaurian and was forced to resign (732). He died in exile. Several of his writings are still extant.

GERMANUS of PARIS (St) Bp.
RM. May 28
496–576. Born near Autun, he was ordained priest and became abbot of a monastery. In 554 he was promoted to the see of Paris. By him King Childebert I was cured in the body and converted from a licentious life. The king built for him the abbey of St Vincent now known as Saint-Germain-des-Prés. St Germanus is one of those bishops to whom history has given the title of "father of the poor".

GERMANUS (St) Bp.   AC. July 3
d. *c*.474. Said to have been a nephew of St Patrick and a missionary monk in Ireland, Wales and Brittany. Eventually he was sent as a bishop to the Isle of Man, where his memory is still preserved in several place-names under the forms "Gremain" and "Jarman".

GERMANUS (St) M.   RM. July 7
See Peregrinus, Lucian, etc.

GERMANUS of AUXERRE (St) Bp.
RM. July 31
c.378–448. A native of Auxerre, he studied civil law in Rome, and embarked upon a secular career. In 418 he received priest's orders and shortly after became bishop of Auxerre. He had relations with the church in Britain, whither he came twice (in 429, in 447) and where he succeeded in completely stamping out Pelagianism. He led the Britons to their great "Alleluia" victory over the Saxons. He died at Ravenna in Italy on a mission which he undertook on behalf of his people.

GERMANUS (St) Bp. M. RM. Sept 6
See Donatian, Praesidius, etc.

GERMANUS of BESANÇON (St)
Bp. M.   RM. Oct 11
d. *c*.390. Successor of St Desideratus in the see of Besançon. He is said to have been martyred by the Arians.

GERMANUS (St) M.   RM. Oct 23
See Servandus and Germanus.

GERMANUS of CAPUA (St) Bp.
RM. Oct 30
d. *c*.545. Bishop of Capua, and a great friend of St Benedict. He seems to have been sent to Constantinople as papal legate to heal the Acacian schism and to have met with ill-treatment at the hands of the schismatics. St Benedict saw his soul being carried to heaven.

GERMANUS of MONTFORT (St)
Mk. OSB.   AC. Nov 1
c.906–1000. Born at Montfort, he studied at Paris and was ordained priest. Afterwards he entered the abbey of Savigny and was made prior of Talloires. He ended his life as a recluse. His relics were elevated by St Francis of Sales in 1621.

GERMANUS, THEOPHILUS, CAESARIUS and VITALIS (SS)
MM.   RM. Nov 3
d. 250. Martyrs of Caesarea in Cappadocia under Decius.

GERMANUS (St) M.   RM. Nov 13
See Antoninus, Zebinas, etc.

GERMANY (Martyrs of) (SS)
RM. Oct 15
d. 303. This is the same group of martyrs as that listed under St Gereon, twice commemorated in the RM. on Oct 10 (318 martyrs) and on Oct 15 (300 martyrs).

GERMERIUS (St) Bp.   AC. May 16
d. ? 560. Bishop of Toulouse for fifty years. His cult is very ancient.

GERMOC (St) C.   AC. June 24
6th cent. An Irish chieftain, brother of St Breaca, who settled in Cornwall, near Mount's Bay.

GEROLD (St) H.   AC. Apr 19
d. 978. A member of the Rhetian family of the counts of Saxony. He bestowed his lands upon the abbey of Einsiedeln where his two sons, Cuno and Ulric, were monks, and retired to live as a hermit, under the obedience of the abbot of Einsiedeln, in a village near Mitternach.

GEROLD (St) Bp. OSB. AC. June 14
d. 806. One of Charlemagne's courtiers who became a monk of Fontenelle and in 787 was made bishop of Evreux. At a later period he resigned and returned to Fontenelle, where he died.

GEROLD (Bl) M.   AC. Oct 7
13th cent. A pilgrim from Cologne killed by robbers near Cremona and honoured as a martyr at Cremona and at Cologne.

GERONTIUS (St) M.   RM. Jan 19
See Paul, Gerontius, etc.

GERONTIUS (St) Bp. M. RM. May 9
a. 501. A bishop of Cervia, near Ravenna,

who was murdered at Cagli on the Flaminian Way, under circumstances which led to his being honoured as a martyr.

GERONTIUS (GERAINT) (St)
King M.   AC. Aug 10
d. ? 508. Son of Erbin and king of Damnonia (Devon). He fell in battle against the Saxons. He and his wife Enid have been the subject of much romantic legend. Another St Gerontius, king of Cornwall, died in 596. St Gerrans in Cornwall and St Géran in Brittany have one or the other of these for patron saint.

GERTRUDE van OOSTEN (Bl) V.
AC. Jan 6
d. 1358. Gertrude began life as a servant girl at Delft in Holland. Having been jilted by her lover, she entered the *béguinage* in her native town. In her new life she rapidly advanced in the way of perfection and was rewarded with the stigmata. "Van Oosten" is said to be a nickname she earned by her frequent repetition of the hymn *"Het daghet in den Oosten"*. "The day breaks in the East."

GERTRUDE of NIVELLES (St)
Abs. OSB.   RM. March 17
629–659. Younger daughter of Pepin of Landen and of Bl Ida. Ida founded the nunnery of Nivelles for herself and her daughter, but insisted on Gertrude being the first abbess. Though then only twenty years of age, Gertrude performed her duties admirably. At the age of thirty she resigned in favour of her niece Wilfetrudis. She befriended the Irish saints SS Foillan and Ultan.

GERTRUDE of ALTENBERG (Bl)
Abs. O. Praem.   AC. Aug 13
1227–1297. Daughter of Louis IV, landgrave of Thuringia and of St Elisabeth

of Hungary. She was educated and became a nun at the nunnery of Altenberg. She was chosen abbess very young and ruled the house for half a century. Cult authorized by Clement VI.

GERTRUDE of REMIREMONT (St) Abs. OSB.   AC. Nov 7

d. *c*.690. Sister of St Adolphus and granddaughter of St Romaricus, she was educated at the nunnery of Saint-Mont, near Remiremont, where she took the veil, and was abbess after her aunt St Clare (*c*.654). Cult authorized by St Leo IX (1051).

GERTRUDE the GREAT (St) N. OSB.   RM. Nov 16, 17

c.1256–1302. "The Prophetess of devotion to the Sacred Heart". She was born at Eisleben in Germany, and as a child of five years old was offered to God at Helfta in Saxony, a Black Benedictine nunnery which in its early days had for political reasons been fictitiously designated Cistercian. Gertrude had her first mystical experience in 1281, and from that year her life was a continuous familiar communing with Christ, whose Heart she learned to love and worship. Her mystical writings have done much to spread devotion to the Sacred Heart. Her feast was extended to the whole Church in 1677. St Teresa of Avila had a great devotion to her. St Gertrude is patroness of the W. Indies.

GERTRUDE the ELDER (St) W. OSB.   AC. Dec 6

d. 649. A widow, who founded and was the first abbess of the nunnery of Hamaye (Hamay, Hamage) near Douai.

GERULPH (St) M.   AC. Sept 21

d. *c*.746. A Flemish youth, heir to a vast estate, who was treacherously murdered by a relative who hoped to succeed to his inheritance. At the time of his death Gerulph was returning home after having received confirmation. He died with words of pardon on his lips.

GERUNTIUS of MILAN (St) Bp.   RM. May 5

d. *c*.470. Successor of St Eusebius in the see of Milan (*c*.465–470).

GERUNTIUS of ITALICA (St) Bp. M.   RM. Aug 25

d. *c*.100. A missionary in Spain in the apostolic age, said to have been bishop of Talco (Italica, near Seville) and a martyr. A special hymn in the old Mozarabic breviary commemorates him.

GERVADIUS (GERNARD, GARNET) (St) C.   AC. Nov 8

10th cent. An Irish saint, who crossed over to Moray and afterwards became a recluse near Elgin.

GERVASE and PROTASE (SS) MM.   RM. June 19

? 2nd cent. In 386, during the episcopate of St Ambrose, there were discovered at Milan the relics of SS Gervase and Protase, whom the saintly bishop styles the protomartyrs of the city. Even then next to nothing was remembered about them, except their names and the fact of their martyrdom in one of the early persecutions. Their supposed *Acta* have no historical value.

GERVINUS (St) Ab. OSB.   AC. March 3

d. 1075. Born near Reims, and educated at the episcopal school, Gervinus became a canon of that city. Subsequently he entered the Benedictine abbey of St Vannes at Verdun, and became abbot of Saint-Riquier. He enjoyed the friendship of St Edward the Confessor. He is described as great in his devotion to the Divine Office, great in preaching, and great in collecting Greek and Latin MSS. This last was, after the service of God, the great passion of his life.

GERVINUS (Bl) Ab. OSB.
AC. Apr 17

d. 1117. A monk of Saint-Winnoc, and then a hermit at Munster in Aldenburg, he was finally chosen abbot (1095) of Aldenburg (Oudenburg) in Flanders.

GERY (St) Bp.   RM. Aug 11
Otherwise Gaugericus, q.v.

GETULIUS, CAEREALIS, AMANTIUS and PRIMITIVUS (SS) MM.
RM. June 10

d. c.120. Getulius, a Roman, is said to have been the husband of St Symphorosa. He and his brother Amantius, and the two officers sent to capture him, and converted by him, were clubbed to death at Tivoli under Hadrian.

GEZELIN (GHISLAIN, GISLE, JOSCELIN) (St) H.   AC. Aug 6
? A hermit honoured at Slebusrode near Cologne.

GHERARDINO (MANETTUS) SOSTEGNI (St)   RM. Feb 12
See Seven Holy Founders.

GIBARDUS (St) Ab. OSB. M.
AC. Apr 7

d. c.888. Abbot of Luxeuil at the time of the invasion of the Huns. He and his monks fled from the abbey. The barbarians found them and put them to death.

GIBITRUDIS (St) N. OSB.
AC. Oct 26

d. c.655. A nun at Faremoutier under St Fara.

GIBRIAN (St) C.   AC. May 8
d. ? c.515. An Irish hermit, the eldest of five brothers and three sisters, all alleged to have migrated to Brittany and to have become saints there. Their names are given as Tressan, Helan, Germanus, Abran (or Gibrian), Petran, Franca, Promptia, Possenna.

GIDEON (GEDEON) (St)
RM. Sept 1

14th cent. B.C. The Judge of Israel (Judges VI, VII), commemorated with Josua by the Greek and Latin Churches on Sept 1. The Copts keep his feast on Dec 16; and the Armenians on the second Saturday of August.

GILBERT of SEMPRINGHAM (St) C. Founder.   RM. Feb 4
1083–1189. A native of Sempringham in Lincolnshire, who became parish priest of that village in 1123. A group of seven ladies of his parish wishing to live in community, he drew for them a set of rules. This developed into the Gilbertine Order, which came to comprise monks under the Augustinian Rule as well as nuns under that of St Benedict. He was their first master-general until he became blind. The Order counted twenty-two houses in England at the time of the Reformation. Canonized in 1202.

GILBERT (St) Bp.   AC. Apr 1
d. 1245. For twenty years bishop of Caithness, of which diocese he built the cathedral. He was a valued servant of the Scottish kings, and a zealous upholder of Scottish independence against the archbishop of York.

GILBERT (Bl) Ab. O. Praem.
AC. June 6

d. 1152. The abbot-founder of the Premonstratensian monastery of Neuffons (Neufontaines).

GILBERT (Bl) Ab. OSB.
                                  AC. Aug 21
d. 1185. A monk at Saint-Crespin-en-Chaie, Soissons, and then the second abbot of the monastery of St John the Baptist at Valenciennes. He suffered persecution at the hands of the count of Hainault.

GILBERT of HEXHAM (St) Bp.
                                  AC. Sept 7
Otherwise Tilbert, q.v.

GILBERT (Bl) Ab. OSB. Cist.
                                  AC. Oct 17
d. 1167. An Englishman by birth who became a Cistercian, probably at Ourscamp, of which he was made abbot in 1147. In 1163 he was promoted abbot of Cîteaux. The Cistercian writers surname him "the Great", or "the Theologian".

GILDARD (GODARD) (St) Bp.
                                  RM. June 8
d. c.514. Bishop of Rouen for about fifteen years. The RM. unfortunately re-echoes a later fable, according to which Gildard was a brother of St Medard of Soissons "born on the same day, consecrated bishops on the same day, and on the same day withdrawn from this life". In fact Gildard had been dead at least five years when St Medard was consecrated.

GILDAS the WISE (St) Bp.
                                  RM. Jan 29
d. c.570. Often called Badonicus, because born in the year the Britons defeated the Saxons at Bath. He was trained by St Illtyd, and towards the end of his life, crossing over to Brittany, lived as a hermit on the island of Rhuys. St Gildas is famous for a Latin work on the miseries of his fatherland *De excidiis Britanniae*; his authorship of part of it, however, is doubtful.

GILDUIN (St)   AC. Jan 27
1052–1077. A devout canon of Dol, he was elected bishop, but fled to Pope Gregory VII in order to escape the charge. He was released but died on the return journey.

GILES (*several*)
Note. Giles is the English form of the Latin name Aegidius. It was a very common name in the Middle Ages. The other Western European variants are as follows: Italian, Egidio; French, Gilles; Spanish and Portuguese, Gil.

GILES of LORENZANA (Bl) C.
OFM.   AC. Jan 28
c.1443–1518. A native of Lorenzana, in the kingdom of Naples, who began life as a farm-hand. Later he became a Franciscan lay-brother and was allowed to live as a hermit in the garden of the friary. He is famous for his love of animals. Cult approved in 1880.

GILES MARY of ST JOSEPH (Bl)
C. OFM.   AC. Feb 7
d. 1812. Born at Taranto in S. Italy, and a rope-maker by trade. He joined the Alcantarine Franciscans at Naples. He spent the rest of his life as porter of the Neapolitan friary. Beatified in 1888.

GILES of ASSISI (Bl) C. OFM.
                                  AC. Apr 23
d. 1262. The third follower of St Francis of Assisi and one of the most delightful figures of the *Fioretti*. He went to preach to the Mohammedans in Tunis, but his mission was a failure. The rest of his life he spent in Italy, being eagerly consulted by all sorts of people on spiritual matters. He died at Perugia.

GILES of SAUMUR (Bl) Bp.
                                  AC. Apr 23
d. 1266. Chaplain to St Louis, king of

France, with whom he went on crusade. In 1243 he became bishop of Damietta, and in 1245 archbishop of Tyre. He died at Dinant in Belgium.

GILES of SANTAREM (Bl) C. OP.
AC. May 14

1185-1265. A native of Vaozela in Portugal, who became a medical student, and, it is said, practised necromancy. After his conversion, he joined the Dominicans at Palencia, resided a long time at Santarem, and was made provincial for Spain.

GILES (St) Ab. OSB.   RM. Sept 1

d. c.712. If we discard the legends which have been woven round the memory of this saint, the historical residue is as follows: Giles was probably a Provençal by birth, and abbot of a monastery on the Rhône, where the city of Saint-Gilles now stands. He became one of the most "popular" saints of the Middle Ages, and his shrine a much frequented place of pilgrimage. Over one hundred and sixty churches were dedicated in his name in England alone. He is venerated as the patron saint of cripples, beggars, and blacksmiths.

GILES and ARCANUS (SS) OSB.
PC. Sept 1

d. c.1050. Giles was of Spanish birth, and together with the Italian St Arcanus, founded an abbey under the Benedictine rule, to enshrine the relics which they had brought from Palestine. This grew into the present day Borgo San Sepolcro in central Italy.

GILES of CASTAÑEDA (Bl) Ab.
OSB. Cist.   AC. Sept 1

d. c. 1203. Cistercian abbot of the monastery of Castañeda in the Asturias. He is now greatly venerated in the diocese of Astorga, in Spain.

GIRALD (GIRARD, GIRAUD) (St)
Ab. OSB.   AC. Dec 29

d. 1031. A Benedictine monk at Lagny and afterwards abbot of Saint-Arnoul. Richard IV, duke of Normandy, enlisted his services as abbot of Fontenelle, where he was murdered by an unruly monk.

GISELLA (GIZELLA, GISELE) (Bl)
W.   AC. May 7

d. c.1095. First Queen of Hungary, wife of St Stephen, sister of St Henry, Emperor of Germany. After a saintly life of good works she retired to the convent at Passau, where she died and is buried. Canonization not finished.

GISLAR (St) C.   AC. Sept 24

See Chrenrald and Ghislar.

GISLENUS (GHISLAIN, GUIS-
LAIN) (St) Ab. OSB.   RM. Oct 9

d. c.680. A Frankish recluse, living in a forest at Hainault, whither he was followed by numerous disciples. He built for them the abbey of SS Peter and Paul now Saint-Ghislain near Mons, which he governed for thirty years.

GISTILIAN (GISTLIAN) (St) C.
AC. March 2

5th–6th cent. The uncle of St David and a monk of Menevia, or St Davids.

GLADYS (St) W.   AC. March 29

5th cent. A Welsh saint, daughter of Brychan of Brecknock. She became the wife of St Gundleus and mother of St Cadoc.

GLAPHYRA (St) V.   RM. Jan 13

d. c.324. A female slave in the service of Constantia, wife of the emperor Licinius, who, in order to safeguard her chastity, fled to St Basil, bishop of Amasea in Pontus. She was recaptured and condemned to death. She died on the way to martyrdom.

GLASTIAN (St) Bp.   AC. Jan 28
d. 830. The patron saint of Kinglassie in Fife. As mediator between the Picts and Scots, he did much to alleviate the lot of the former when subjugated by their foes.

GLEB (St)   AC. July 24
See Romanus and David.

GLODESIND (St) Abs. OSB.
Otherwise Clotsindis, q.v.

GLODESIND (St) Abs. AC. July 25
d. c.608. Betrothed to a courtier who was arrested on their wedding day and afterwards executed. She took the veil in a nunnery at Metz, of which she became abbess.

GLUNSHALLAICH (St) C.
                        AC. June 3
7th cent. An Irish penitent, converted by St Kevin and buried in the same grave with him at Glendalough.

GLUVIAS (GLYWYS) (St) C.
                        AC. May 2
6th cent. Brother of St Cadoc of Llan-carfan, and possibly sent by him into Cornwall, where he made a monastic foundation. A parish in Cornwall perpetuates his name.

GLYCERIA (St) VM.   RM. May 13
d. c.177. A Roman maiden, living with her father at Trajanopolis in Greece, who was martyred at Heraclea in the Propontis.

GLYCERIUS (St) Bp.   AC. Sept 20
d. c.438. Archbishop of Milan.

GLYCERIUS (St) M.   RM. Dec 21
d. 303. A priest of Nicomedia in Asia Minor, burnt at the stake under Diocletian.

GLYWYS (St) C.   AC. May 2
Otherwise Gluvias, q.v.

GOAR (St) C.   RM. July 6
d. c.575. A secular priest of Aquitaine, who led the life of a hermit near Ober-wesel on the Rhine. His extant life is most untrustworthy. Charlemagne built a stately church over St Goar's hermitage.

GOBAN GOBHNENA (St) C.
                        AC. May 23
6th or 7th cent. Supposed to be the Goban, mentioned in the life of St Laserian as governing the monastery of Old-Leighlin, from which he migrated to Tascaffin, in the present Co Limerick.

GOBAN (GOBAIN) M. OSB.
                        AC. June 20
d. c.670. An Irishman by birth, and a disciple of his countryman St Fursey, under whom he became a monk at Burgh-Castle in Suffolk. He followed his abbot to France and both took to the solitary life in the great forest near the Oise. He was murdered by barbarian marauders at the place now called Saint-Gobain.

GOBERT (Bl) Mk. OSB.
                        AC. Aug 20
d. 1263. Count of Apremont. After fighting as a crusader in Palestine he became a Cistercian at Villers in Brabant.

GOBNATA (GOBNET) (St) V.
                        AC. Feb 11
? 6th cent. St Abban is said to have founded a convent in Ballyvourney, Co Cork, and to have placed St Gobnet over it as abbess. A well still exists there called after her.

GOBRAIN (St) Bp.   AC. Nov 16
d. 725. A Breton monk who became bishop of Vannes, and at the age of eighty-seven resigned his see to retire to a hermit's cell, where he died.

GODARD (St) Bp. OSB. RM. May 4
Otherwise Godehard, q.v.

GODARD (St) Bp.   RM. June 8
Otherwise Gildard, q.v.

GODEBERTHA (St) Abs. AC. Apr 11
d. *c*.700. Born in the diocese of Amiens. In 657 she received the veil from St Eligius, bishop of Noyon, who also composed a rule for her nunnery at Noyon. She was the first abbess.

GODEHARD (GODARD, GOTH-ARD) (St) Bp. OSB.   RM. May 4
d. 1038. A Bavarian, whose father was employed in the service of the canons of Niederaltaich. Godehard joined them and became their provost. He was instrumental in re-introducing the Benedictine Rule at Niederaltaich and was commissioned by the emperor St Henry to revive the Benedictine observance in several German dioceses. Tegernsee, Hersfeld and Kremsmünster received abbots from Niederaltaich. In 1022 the saint was made bishop of Hildesheim and did much to foster religion and culture. Canonized in 1131.

GODELEVA (GODLIVA) (St) M.
AC. July 6
d. 1070. Married very young to Bertulf of Ghistelles, who after ill-treating her for two years had her strangled. She has been venerated as a martyr ever since.

GODFREY (*several*)
Note. This name, in Latin, Godefridus, is variously spelt in English: Godefrid, Geoffrey, Gotfrid, Goffry, etc. In other languages the spelling is: Gottfried, Geoffroy, Gioffredo, Gaufrid, Geofroi, Goffredo, Gofrido, etc.

GODFREY of CAPPENBERG (Bl)
C. O. Praem.   AC. Jan 13
1097–1127. Born at Cappenberg Castle in Westphalia, where, besides being a count, he owned large estates. He made the acquaintance of St Norbert, and in the teeth of violent opposition from his relatives made over his lands to the holy founder, turned his castle into a Premonstratensian abbey and himself joined the order with his brother, while his wife and two sisters took the veil in a nunnery which he founded for them. He died at the age of thirty and not yet a priest.

GODFREY of DUYNEN and GOD-FREY of MERVILLE (SS) MM.
RM. July 9
d. 1572. The former was a secular priest and at one time rector of a school in Paris; the latter was custos of the Franciscan house at Gorkum, Holland, and a painter. Both were hanged with others by the Calvinists at Briel. The group is known as the martyrs of Gorkum, see Gorkum.

GODFREY of LOUDUN (Bl) Bp.
AC. Aug 3
d. 1255. Bishop of Mans from 1234, he was a man of intense activity, and he took a full part in the ecclesiastical affairs of the time. He founded the Charterhouse of Parc d'Orgues, where he was buried. He died at Anagni on a visit to the Pope.

GODFREY (St) Bp. OSB. RM. Nov 8
c.1066–1115. Born in the province of Soissons and placed at the age of five at the abbey of Mont-Saint-Quentin, where in due course he was professed and ordained. In 1096 he was promoted abbot of Nogent-sous-Coucy in Champagne and in 1104 bishop of Amiens. He was rigidly austere, both with himself and with others. In spite of this when he wished to resign and become a Carthusian his people would not allow it. He was a lifelong opponent of simony and incontinency.

GODO (GAON) (St) Ab. OSB.
AC. July 24

d. *c.*690. A native of Verdun, and a nephew of St Wandrille, under whom he was professed at Fontenelle. Afterwards he was the abbot-founder of Oye Abbey, near Sezanne-en-Brie.

GODRIC (St) H. OSB. AC. May 21

d. 1170. A native of Walpole in Norfolk, after years of adventurous seafaring and of many pilgrimages he became a hermit at Finchale in Co Durham, under the obedience of the prior of Durham. There he lived for sixty years, remarkable for his austerities, his supernatural gifts and also for his familiarity with wild animals.

GODWIN (St) Ab. OSB. AC. Oct 28

d. *c.*690. Abbot of the great Belgian monastery of Stavelot-Malmédy.

GOERIC (St) Bp.   AC. Sept 19

d. 647. Also called Abbo. The successor of St Arnulf in the bishopric of Metz.

GOEZNOVEUS (St) Bp. AC. Oct 25

d. 675. A Cornish saint, brother of St Maughan, who crossed into Brittany and became bishop of Léon.

GOFOR (St) C.   AC. May 9

? A Welsh saint, patron of Llanover in Monmouthshire.

GOHARDUS (St) Bp. M. AC. June 25

d. 843. Bishop of Nantes, slain by raiding Normans while celebrating Mass; many monks and priests were killed with him.

GOLLEN (COLLEN, COLAN) (St) C.   AC. May 21

? 7th cent. A saint who has given his name to Llangollen in Denbighshire. His name is connected in legend with Wales, Glastonbury and Rome.

GOLVINUS (GOLWEN) (St) Bp.
AC. July 9

? 7th cent. A Breton saint, but of British origin, whose fame for sanctity led to his promotion to the see of St Pol-de-Léon. He died at Rennes where his relics are still enshrined.

GOMER (St)   RM. Oct 11
Otherwise Gummarus, q.v.

GOMIDAS (Bl) M.   AC. Nov 5

*c.*1656–1707. Gomidas Keumurjian, an Armenian by descent, was born at Constantinople, married at the age of twenty and was ordained a priest of the dissident Armenian Church. In 1696, he and his family made their submission to Rome. This angered the dissidents, who unjustly accused Gomidas to the Turkish authorities as an agent of hostile Western powers. Consequently he was beheaded at Parmark-Kapu, on the outskirts of Constantinople. Beatified in 1929.

GONERI (St) C.   AC. July 18

6th cent. An exile from Britain to Brittany, where he led an eremitical life near Tréguier.

GONSALVO of AMARANTHE (Bl) C.   AC. Jan 16
Otherwise Gundisalvus, q.v.

GONTRAM (St) King
RM. March 28
Otherwise Gunthamnus, q.v.

GONZAGA GONZA (St) M.
RM. June 3

d. 1886. Having spent a long time in prison, he was put to death by King Mwanga of Uganda. See Uganda (Martyrs of).

GOOD THIEF, THE (St)
RM. March 25
1st cent. The repentant thief, to whom the dying Saviour promised paradise.

The name of Dismas has been given him by tradition, and a number of legends have grown up around his name; but except for the episode recorded in the gospel, nothing is known about him.

GORAN (WORANUS) (St) C.
AC. Apr 7

6th cent. Several Cornish churches are dedicated in his honour. He was a friend of St Patrick.

GORAZD (St) C.   AC. July 17
See Seven Apostles of Bulgaria.

GORDIAN and EPIMACHUS (SS) MM.   RM. May 10
d. 250 and 362. Epimachus was martyred at Alexandria under Decius, and his relics were taken to Rome. Gordian suffered at a later date, very probably under Julian the Apostate, and was buried in the same tomb. Their *Acta* are not trustworthy.

GORDIAN (St) M.   RM. Sept 17
See Valerian, Macrinus and Gordian.

GORDIUS (St) M.   RM. Jan 3
d. 304. A soldier of Caesarea in Cappadocia, dismissed from the army on account of his religion. He retired to the desert, but during the persecution under Diocletian gave himself up and was beheaded.

GORGONIA (St)   RM. Dec 9
d. c.375. Daughter of St Gregory Nazianzen senior and of St Nonna, and sister of St Gregory Nazianzen junior, the great Greek theologian. She married and was a model Christian matron.

GORGONIUS and FIRMUS (or FIRMINUS) (SS) MM.
RM. March 11

3rd cent. Martyrs, either of Nicaea in Bithynia, or of Antioch in Syria.

GORGONIUS (St) M.   RM. Sept 9
See Dorotheus and Gorgonius.

GORKUM (Martyrs of (SS)
RM. July 9

d. 1572. A group of nineteen martyrs, ten Franciscans, two Premonstratensians, a Dominican, a canon regular, four secular priests and a layman—put to death with unspeakable cruelty by the Calvinists at Gorkum, near Dordrecht in Holland. Each receives a separate notice in this book. Canonized in 1867.

GORMAN (St) Bp. OSB.
AC. Aug 28

d. 965. A Benedictine of Reichenau, who went to preach the gospel in the North and became bishop of Schleswig in Denmark.

GORMCAL (St) Ab.   AC. Aug 5
d. 1016. An Irish abbot of the monastery of Ardoilen in Galway.

GOSBERT (St) Bp. OSB.
AC. Feb 13

d. c.859. The fourth bishop of Osnabruck and a disciple of St Anschar. His was a particularly laborious episcopate.

GOSCELINUS (GOSLIN, GOZZELINUS) (St) Ab. OSB.
AC. Feb 12

d. 1153. Second abbot of San Solutore, near Turin (1147–1153). The solemn translation of his relics took place in 1472.

GOSWIN (St) Ab. OSB. AC. Oct 9
d. 1165. A native of Douai and a student at Paris, he first taught theology in his native city where he held a canonry; then he professed the Benedictine Rule at Anchin (1113), where he eventually became abbot (c.1130): one of the greatest abbots of that great abbey.

GOSWIN (Bl) OSB. Cist.
AC. Oct 27
d. 1203. A Cistercian monk, first at Clairvaux and then at Chemnion.

GOTHARD (St) Bp.   RM. May 4
Otherwise Godehard, q.v.

GOTTESCHALK (St) M. AC. June 7
d. 1066. A Wendish prince who renounced Christianity because his father had been murdered by Christian Saxons. As the husband of Canute's grandniece he came to England and returned to the Faith, which he henceforth fostered with great zeal. He was murdered at Lenzen by assassins in the service of his brother-in-law. Many doubt whether he has a true claim to the title of either saint or martyr.

GOWAN (GOVAN, GOVEN, COFEN) (St) Matron   AC. Dec 28
5th cent. The wife of King Tewdrig of Glamorgan. The parish of Llangoven in Monmouthshire takes its name from her, and a chapel in Pembrokeshire is likewise dedicated in her honour.

GRACE and PROBUS (SS)
AC. July 5
See Probus and Grace.

GRACIA (St) M. OSB. Cist.
AC. June 1
See Bernard, Mary, etc.

GRACILIAN and FELICISSIMA (SS) MM.   RM. Aug 12
d. c.304. According to the legend, which is untrustworthy, Gracilian, a Christian of Faleria, while in prison awaiting martyrdom, restored the sight of a blind girl and converted her to Christ. They were beheaded on the same day.

GRAECINA (St) VM.   AC. June 16
See Actinea and Graecina.

GRATA (St) W.   RM. May 1
4th (or 8th) cent. A holy woman of Bergamo, zealous in securing Christian burial for the bodies of the martyrs. The evidence regarding her life is very conflicting.

GRATIA of CATTARO (Bl) C. OSA.   AC. Nov 16
1438–1509. A native of Cattaro in Dalmatia. For thirty years he was a fisherman in the Adriatic and then professed the Augustinian Rule as a lay-brother. He was famous for the gift of infused knowledge. Cult approved in 1889.

GRATIAN (St) Bp.   RM. Dec 18
Otherwise Gatian. q.v.

GRATINIAN (GRATIAN) (St) M.
RM. June 1
See Felinus and Gratian.

GRATUS (St) Bp.   AC. Sept 7
d. c.470. Bishop of Aosta. He is now its patron saint.

GRATUS (St) Bp.   AC. Oct 8
d. c.652. A French bishop of Châlons-sur-Saône.

GRATUS (St) Bp.   AC. Oct 11
d. c.506. The first bishop of the ancient see, long suppressed, of Oloron, in S. France.

GRATUS (St) M.   RM. Dec 5
See Julius, Potamia, etc.

GREDIFAEL (St) C.   AC. Nov 13
7th cent. A Breton or Welsh saint who accompanied St Paternus from Brittany to Wales. He is said to have been abbot of Whitland in Pembrokeshire.

GREGORY NAZIANZEN the ELDER (St) Bp. C.   AC. Jan 1
c.276–374. A native of Nazianzos in

Cappadocia, Asia Minor, a state functionary and a pagan, he was converted (325) by his wife, St Nonna. They had three children—all saints: Gregory Nazianzen, junior, the great Father of the Church, Caesarius and Gorgonia. Gregory senior became bishop of his native city (*c*.328) and attached himself to some heretical sect; but was converted to orthodoxy (361) by his more gifted son, Gregory, who, in 372, became his coadjutor. He died when nearly one hundred years of age.

GREGORY of LANGRES (St) Bp.
RM. Jan 4

d. 539. A leading citizen (*comes*) of the district round Autun and the civil governor of the city, firm and severe. Later in life he lost his wife, was ordained priest and became bishop of Langres, and as such gained a reputation for gentleness and understanding. He was the father of St Tetricus (q.v.), and great-uncle of St Gregory of Tours.

GREGORY X (Bl) Pope
RM. Jan 10

d. 1276. Theobald Visconti was a native of Piacenza in Italy, who became archdeacon of Liége, in Belgium. While holding this office he was entrusted with the preaching of the last crusade. He himself accompanied the crusaders to Palestine, and he was still there when elected pope in 1271. He was not yet a priest. The outstanding event of his pontificate was the holding of the council of Lyons, at which the Eastern orthodox became reconciled, unhappily for only a short time, to the Catholic Church. Beatified 1713. His name was inserted in the RM. by Benedict XIV.

GREGORY II (St) Pope RM. Feb 11

d. 731. Roman born and educated at the Lateran, he held the offices of Librarian and Archivist of the Roman Church,

when he was elected pope in 715. He devoted much of his time to the affairs of the Eastern Church, and his pontificate is also famous for the spreading of the gospel among the Teuton races, to whom he sent as missionaries St Boniface and St Corbinian. He fostered Benedictine life everywhere, and restored several Italian abbeys, notably Montecassino. An old tradition makes him in fact a Benedictine monk, and his office figured for centuries in several Benedictine *Propria*. He opposed Iconoclasm and checked the advancing Lombards. He is one of the great popes.

GREGORY of TRAGURIO (Bl)
OFM   PC. Feb 12

See Antony of Saxony.

GREGORY of NYSSA (St) Bp.
RM. March 9

d. *c*.395. A younger brother of St Basil the Great. After his marriage he practised as a professor of rhetoric but abandoned this profession for the priesthood. In 372 his brother Basil nominated him bishop of Nyssa, a small township in Lower Armenia. It was a somewhat unfortunate choice, as Gregory was not a man of affairs, and the Arians were predominant in the diocese. After a period of exclusion from his diocese he regained it in 378 and after his brother's death was the mainstay of orthodoxy throughout Cappadocia. His writings are remarkable for depth of thought and lucidity of expression. Of the three "great Cappadocians"—Basil, Gregory Nazianzen, Gregory of Nyssa—he is the least prolific but the most profound.

GREGORY the GREAT (St) Pope,
Dr.   RM. March 12 and Sept 3

c.540–604. Born in Rome of patrician parents, he became the prefect—*praetor* mayor—of the city. He soon resigned the office, turned his ancestral home on the Caelian Hill into a monastery and became a monk there. Next he was sent to Constantinople as *apocrisarius*—papal nuncio. On his return he was chosen pope (590), and what he achieved in his fourteen years' pontificate makes him one of the most commanding figures in world history. First in importance was his mission to England, whither he sent St Augustine and some forty of his monks from the Caelian Hill; this was important not only on account of the conversion of England itself, but also because of the spreading of the Benedictine Rule among the new races of W. Europe. He promoted likewise the conversion of the Lombards in Italy and of the Goths in Spain; upheld the rights of the Roman see against Constantinople; embellished the Liturgy in its sacramentary and in its chant; defended and befriended monachism; and cared for the poor in Rome, at Ravenna and on his estates in Sicily. He was moreover a prolific writer; his dialogues, compising the only extant life of St Benedict, and his *Regula Pastoralis* are classics in ascetical literature.

GREGORY MAKAR (St) Bp.
AC. March 16

d. *c.*1000. He is described as an Armenian, who became a monk and was elected bishop of Nicopolis in Armenia. He is said to have fled to France and settled as a hermit at Pithiviers in the diocese of Orleans.

GREGORY of ELVIRA (St) Bp.
RM. Apr 24

d. *c.*400. Bishop of Elvira, in S. Spain—a see which has since been translated to Granada. He was one of the champions of the Faith against Arianism, and one of the few bishops who at Rimini (359) consistently refused to compromise with the heretics. In all good faith he sided with the party of Lucifer of Cagliari, but never left the communion of the Roman see.

GREGORY OF BESIANS (Bl) COP.
AC. Apr 26

See Dominic and Gregory.

GREGORY CELLI of VERUCCHIO (Bl) C. OSA.
A C. May 4

d. 1343. A native of Verucchio, in the diocese of Rimini. His mother founded a monastery for the Augustinians in his native town, and Gregory took the habit there. After a time he was dismissed for some unjust reason, but was charitably received by the Franciscans of Monte Carnerio, near Rieti, where he died. Cult confirmed in 1769.

GREGORY NAZIANZEN (St) Bp. Dr.
RM. May 9

*c.*329–390. A native of Arianzos in Cappadocia and eldest son of St Gregory Nazianzen the Elder (q.v.). He read law for ten years at Athens and then joined his friend St Basil in his monastic solitude in Pontus. In 361 he was ordained priest and in 372 consecrated bishop of the small township of Sasima. This see he refused to accept, acting instead as coadjutor to his father at Nazianzos, until, in 380, he was prevailed to accept the see of Constantinople. He was there only one month: after which he resigned and retired to Arianzos where he died in 390. The tragedy of his life was his promotion to the rank of bishop, since his character was not fitted for a life of action. On the other hand, as a writer he stands far above most other Greek Doctors, in fact, he is surnamed by the Greeks "the Divine"—*ὁ Theologos*. He is venerated in East and West as a Doctor of the Church.

GREGORY of OSTIA (St) Bp. OSB.
AC. May 9

d. c.1044. A Benedictine cardinal, bishop of Ostia, who exercised legatine powers in the old kingdoms of Spanish Navarre and Old Castile. He died at Logroño. He is still greatly venerated throughout Navarre and Rioja. His life, however, as handed down to us, is full of conflicting statements.

GREGORY VII (St) Pope, OSB.
RM. May 25

c.1020–1085. A native of Soana, in Tuscany. His baptismal name was Hildebrand. He was sent very young to Rome, where his uncle was superior of the Cluniac abbey of St Mary on the Aventine, and there Hildebrand professed the Benedictine Rule. He accompanied the deposed Pope Gregory VI to Germany, but returned to Rome with St Leo IX, and became abbot of St Paul-outside-the-Walls (1059). From this date begins his close association with the popes, five of whom he served as archdeacon. In 1073 he himself became supreme pontiff and continued his life-long struggle against lay investiture, simony and clerical concubinage. He succeeded in imposing his will on his persistent and childishly cunning enemy the emperor Henry IV of Germany, but nevertheless a few years later he was driven into exile at Salerno where he died. Few men have been so admired by their friends and reviled by their foes. Canonized in 1584.

GREGORY, DEMETRIUS and CALOGERUS (SS) CC. AC. June 18

d. 5th cent. Respectively a bishop, an archdeacon and an abbot, in N. Africa, whence they were driven by Arian Vandals. They settled down at Fragalata, near Messina, in Sicily, and preached the gospel there. They are now honoured as the patron saints of Fragalata.

GREGORY BARBADIGO (St) Bp.
AC. June 18

1625–1697. Venetian-born, he was first bishop of Bergamo and then of Padua, and was created cardinal in 1660. He was equally distinguished as a churchman and as a statesman. His charities were on a princely scale, and his benefactions to Padua numerous and lasting. He was an earnest worker for the reconciliation of the dissident Greeks. Canonized 1960.

GREGORY ESCRIVANO (Bl) M. SJ.
AC. July 15

d. 1570. Born at Logroño, in Old Castile, he was a Jesuit coadjutor, and a companion of Bl Ignatius de Azevedo q.v.

GREGORY LOPEZ (Bl) H.
PC. July 20

1542–1596. A native of Madrid, where he served as page to Philip II. In 1562 he migrated to Mexico and lived as a hermit among the Indians near Zacatecas and later near the capital. His cult spread all over Mexico, but the process of his beatification, begun in 1752, fails to make progress in Rome.

GREGORY of NONANTULA (Bl) Ab. OSB.
AC. Aug 3

d. 933. A Benedictine abbot of the great Italian abbey of Nonantula, near Modena.

GREGORY of UTRECHT (St) Ab. OSB.
RM. Aug 25

c.703–776. A native of Trèves. When a child he met St Boniface, under whom he became a monk. The old apostle loved him as a son and made him abbot of St Martin's at Utrecht. Without relinquishing his office of abbot, St Gregory administered the diocese as well for twenty-two years. During his abbacy St Martin's became a great missionary centre and a nursery of saints.

GREGORY the ILLUMINATOR (St) Bp.   RM. Sept 30

d. c.330. Also surnamed "the apostle of Armenia". Unfortunately his life, as given by tradition, is not well authenticated. The following main facts seem certain: he began to preach to the Armenians and converted their king Tiridates, had himself consecrated bishop and set up his see at Ashtishat, whence his apostolate spread far and wide. Armenian legends, obviously fictitious, about St Gregory run to several volumes.

GREGORY of BURTSCHEID (St) Ab. OSB.   AC. Nov 4

d. 999. A Basilian monk at Cerchiara, in Calabria, who fled from the Saracens and met the emperor Otto III in Rome. The emperor befriended him, invited him to Germany and built for him the abbey of Burtscheid, near Aix-la-Chapelle, under the Benedictine Rule.

GREGORY of EINSIEDELN (St) Ab. OSB.   Ac. Nov 8

d. 996. An Anglo-Saxon by birth, who on a pilgrimage to Rome received the Benedictine cowl on the Caelian Hill at Rome. On his way home he stayed at the Swiss abbey of Einsiedeln, and joined the community (949). He was elected abbot and his rule coincided with the period of the greatest monastic splendour of the abbey.

GREGORY THAUMATURGUS (St) Bp.   RM. Nov 17

c.213–270. A native of Pontus and a disciple of Origen. He was made bishop of Neocaesarea in 240. It is related that on his accession to the see he found just seventeen Christians, and that when he died he left only seventeen pagans. His title of "the Wonder-Worker" explains itself. He is also an ecclesiastical writer.

GREGORY of TOURS (St) Bp.   Nov 17

539–596. This saint was born in Auvergne, and was baptized George Florentius, but took the name Gregory when he was raised to the see of Tours in 573. He was a great bishop much revered by St Gregory the Great. He excelled, however, as a historian, and his writings are now the best historical source of the Merovingian period.

GREGORY DECAPOLITES (St) C.   RM. Nov 20

9th cent. So-called from his birthplace in Asia Minor. He opposed the Iconoclasts zealously and suffered much at their hands.

GREGORY of GIRGENTI (St) Bp.   RM. Nov 23

d. c.638. A Sicilian of the Byzantine rite, who, after a protracted sojourn in the Eastern *lauras*, was nominated by St Gregory the Great bishop of Girgenti (*Agrigentum*) his native town. His interesting commentary on the book of Ecclesiastes is still extant.

GREGORY III (St) Pope   RM. Dec 10

d. 741. A Syrian by birth who reigned as pope from 731 to 741. His was a very stormy pontificate, troubled in the beginning by the foolish excesses of the Iconoclasts and at the end by the incursions of the Lombards. Gregory sought the aid of Charles Martel against the latter, thus establishing a connection with the Franks which was to prove of historic importance.

GREGORY of TERRACINA (St) C. OSB.   AC. Dec 12

d. c.570. A disciple of St Benedict, and, with his brother St Speciosus, monk at Terracina. St Gregory the Great speaks of him in the Dialogues Bk. II.

GREGORY of AUXERRE (St) Bp.
RM. Dec 19

d. *c*.540. The twelfth bishop of Auxerre. He governed the see thirteen years, and died aged eighty-five.

GREGORY of SPOLETO (St) M.
RM. Dec 24

A priest said to have been martyred under Maximinian Herculeus. His *Acta* are not reliable; and doubt has been thrown on his very existence.

GRIGNON de MONTFORT (Bl) C.
AC. Aug 19

See Louis Mary Grignon de Montfort.

GRIMBALD (St) Ab. OSB.
AC. July 8

d. 903. A Benedictine monk, and prior of Saint-Bertin. In 885 King Alfred, then on his way to Rome, invited him to England. Grimbald came, but declined the see of Canterbury offered to him by the king. Eventually he was made abbot of the New Minister at Winchester. He was a restorer of learning in England.

GRIMOALDUS (St) C. RM. Sept 29

d. *p*.1137. Archpriest of Pontecorvo, near Aquino, in S. Italy. Some writers state that he was an Englishman.

GRIMONIA (GERMANA) (St) VM.
AC. Sept 7

4th cent. Said to have been an Irish maiden, martyred in Picardy in defence of her virtue.

GRWST (St) C.   AC. Dec 1

7th cent. The Welsh saint whose memory is perpetuated by the place-name Llanrwst, Denbighshire.

GUALA (Bl) C. OP.   AC. Sept 3

d. 1244. One of the first disciples of St Dominic in Italy and the first Dominican prior of Brescia and Bologna. In 1228 he was made bishop of Brescia, but resigned in 1242 on account of civil strife and retired to the Vallumbrosans of San Sepolcro d'Astino, where he died. Cult approved in 1866.

GUALFARDUS (WOLFHARD)
(St) H. OSB. Cam.   AC. May 11

d. 1127. A native of Augsburg and a saddler, who plied his trade in Verona, till the people began to look upon him as a saint. Then he retired to live as a monk-hermit in the Camaldolese priory of San Salvatore, near Verona.

GUALTERUS (*several*)
Otherwise Walter, q.v.

GUARINUS (GUERIN) (St) Bp.
OSB. Cist.   AC. Jan 6

1065–1150. Originally a monk of Molesmes, he was made abbot of Aulps, near Geneva. At his request his community was affiliated to Clairvaux. Afterwards he was raised to the see of Sion in the Valais.

GUARINUS (St) Bp. OSA.
RM. Feb 6

d. 1159. A native of Bologna, who joined the Augustinian canons regular. After forty years of religious life he was elected bishop of Pavia; but nothing could induce him to accept the post. However, Lucius II created him cardinal bishop of Palestrina. Canonized by Alexander III.

GUASACHT (St) Bp.   AC. Jan 24

4th cent. Son of Maelchu, the master under whom St Patrick worked as a slave in Ireland. Guasacht was converted by Patrick, whom he helped, as bishop of Granard (Longford), in the evangelization of Ireland.

GUDELIA (St) M.   RM. Sept 29

d. *c*.340. A maiden martyred in Persia under Shapur II.

GUDULA (GOULE) (St) V.
AC. Jan 8

d. 712. Daughter of St Amelberga, she was trained by St Gertrude at Nivelles, and afterwards lived at home a life of great holiness. She is the patroness of Brussels. In art she is often shown with a lantern.

GUDWALL (CURVAL) (St) Bp.
AC. June 6

7th cent. A Welsh bishop who founded monasteries in Devon and Cornwall. By many he is supposed to be the Gurval who succeeded St Malo at Aleth in Brittany. His relics are venerated at Ghent.

GUENHAËL (St) Ab.   AC. Nov 3

d. c.550. Guenhael means "white Angel". He was born in Brittany and educated at Landevenec under St Winwaloë, where in due course he became abbot.

GUENNINUS (St) Bp. AC. Aug 19

7th cent. A bishop of Vannes in Brittany, whose relics are enshrined in the cathedral.

GUEREMBALDUS (St) Mk. OSB.
AC. Nov 10

d. 965. A Monk of Hirschau, who, through humility, renounced the bishopric of Spire.

GUERRICUS (Bl) Ab. OSB. Cist.
AC. Aug 19

?1080–?1155. Born at Tournai, he studied there and became canon and headmaster of the cathedral school. He visited Clairvaux to see St Bernard, and stayed there. In 1138 St Bernard sent him as first abbot of Igny, in the diocese of Reims. He was a prolific ascetical writer; some of his writings indeed have been attributed to St Bernard. Cult approved 1889.

GUESNOVEUS (GOUERNOU) (St)
Bp.   AC. Oct 25

d. 675. A bishop of Quimper in Brittany and founder of a monastery near Brest, where he died.

GUETHENOC (GWENTHENOC)
(St)   AC. Feb 6

See Jacut and Guethenoc.

GUEVROCK (GUEROC, KERRIC)
(St) Ab.   AC. Feb 17

6th cent. A Briton who followed St Tadwal to Brittany and succeeded him as abbot of Loc-Kirec. He helped St Paul of León in the rule of the diocese.

GUIBERTUS (St) Mk. OSB.
AC. May 23

d. 962. A noble of Lorraine who served with distinction in several campaigns. He then lived the life of a hermit on his own estate of Gembloux, in Brabant, but eventually he turned it into a monastery and retired himself to the Benedictine abbey of Gorze. Several times, however, he had to leave the peace of Gorze in order to defend the rights of his foundation at Gembloux. He died at Gorze.

GUIDO (*several*)
Otherwise Guy, q.v.

GUIER (St) H.   PC. Apr 4

? Priest and hermit in Cornwall, where a church perpetuates his name.

GUILMINUS (Bl) Mk. OSB.
PC. Nov 18

See Burginus and Guilminus.

GUINGAR (St) M.   AC. Dec 14
Otherwise Fingar, q.v.

GUINGALOC (GUIGNOLE,
GUINVALOEUS)   AC. March 3
Otherwise Winwaloë, q.v.

GUINIZO (St) Mk. OSB.
AC. May 26
d. *c*.1050. A native of Spain who professed the Benedictine Rule at Montecassino, and remained as a hermit on
the holy mountain after one of the
destructions of the abbey.

GUINOC (St) Bp. AC. Apr 13
d. *c*.838. A Bishop in Scotland, commemorated in the Aberdeen breviary.

GUISLAIN (St) Ab. RM. Oct 9
Otherwise Gislenus, q.v.

GUITMARUS (St) Ab. OSB.
AC. Dec 10
d. *c*.765. Fourth abbot of Saint-Riquier
(Centula) in France.

**GULSTAN (GUSTAN, CON-
STANS) (St) Mk. OSB.** AC. Nov 29
d. *c*.1010. A Benedictine of the abbey of
St Gildas of Rhuys, in Brittany, under
St Felix.

**GUMESINDUS and SERVUSDEI
(SS) MM.** RM. Jan 13
d. 852. Two Spanish martyrs, one a
parish-priest, the other a monk, who
suffered at Cordova under Abderrahman II.

GUMMARUS (GOMER) (St) H.
RM. Oct 11
c.717–774. A courtier of King Pepin
who married a wife of extravagant and
tiresome disposition. After long and
patient endurance of her perversity he
was at last obliged to separate from her
and died a recluse. The present Flemish
town of Lierre (Lier) has grown up
and around his hermitage.

**GUNDEBERT (GUMBERT,
GONDELBERT) (St) Bp. OSB.**
AC. Feb 21
d. *c*.676. A Frankish bishop (of Sens)

who resigned and retired into the
Vosges, where he founded the abbey of
Senones (*c*.660).

GUNDEBERT (St) M. AC. Apr 20
8th cent. Tradition describes this saint
as a Frankish courtier, who married St
Bertha (q.v.), and brother of St Nivard.
He separated from his wife, became a
monk and crossed over to Ireland and
was killed there by heathen marauders.

GUNDECHAR (Bl) Bp. AC. Aug 2
1019–1073. Bishop of Eichstätt. The
Pontifical which he drew is still pre-
served and is of great historical interest.
He had been chaplain to the Empress
Agnes.

**GUNDEKAR (KUNDEKAR) (St)
M. OSB.** RM. June 5
See Waccar, Gundekar, etc.

**GUNDELINDIS (GUENDELINDIS)
V. OSB.** AC. March 28
d. *c*.750. A daughter of the duke of
Alsace, and a niece of St Ottilia, whom
she succeeded as abbess in the nunnery
of Niedermünster.

GUNDENIS (St) VM. RM. July 18
d. 203. A maiden martyred at Carthage,
under Septimius Severus.

GUNDISALVUS (Bl) C. OP.
AC. Jan 16
1187–1259. A native of Vizella in the
diocese of Braga, in Portugal. After his
ordination to the priesthood he led the
life of a solitary at Amaranthe, and later
entered the Dominican order. Cult
approved in 1560.

**GUNDISALVUS GARCIA (St) M.
OFM.** AC. Feb 5
1556–1597. Born in the East Indies of
Portuguese parents, he first served the
Jesuits as a catechist, then opened a

flourishing business in Japan, and finally (1591) joined the Franciscans at Manila as a lay-brother. He returned to Japan as an interpreter to St Peter Baptist, with whom he was crucified at Nagasaki. Canonized in 1862.

**GUNDISALVUS (Bl) Ab. OSB. Cist.
AC. June 6**
d. 1466. Cistercian abbot of Azebeyro, in Spanish Galicia.

GUNDISALVUS HENDRIQUEZ (Bl) M. SJ.   AC. July 15
d. 1570. A Portuguese deacon and a Jesuit scholastic, companion of Bl Ignatius de Azevedo, q.v.

**GUNDISALVUS FUSAI (Bl) M. SJ.
AC. Sept 10**
1582–1622. A Japanese who held a high office at court but, after baptism, attached himself to the Jesuit missionaries. He was put in gaol at Omura, and there received into the Society of Jesus by Bl Charles Spinola, with whom he was burnt alive at Nagasaki. Beatified in 1867.

**GUNDISALVUS (St) OSB. Cist.
AC. Oct 10**
d. c.1163. First abbot, or prior, of the Cistercian abbey of Las Junias, in Portugal, founded from Osera in 1135.

GUNDISALVUS of LAGOS (Bl) C. OSA.   AC. Oct 21
d. 1422. A native of Lagos in Portugal. He became an Augustinian, and excelled as a preacher. Cult approved in 1778.

GUNDISALVUS (GONZALO) (Bl) Mk. OSB.   AC. Dec 20
d. c.1073. Monk of the Benedictine abbey of Silos, in Old Castile, under its great abbot St Dominic.

GUNDLEUS (St) H. AC. March 29
d. c.500. Gundleus is the latinized form

of the Welsh Gwynllyw, anglicized as Woollos. He is said to have been the husband of St Gladys and the father of St Cadoc, and to have ended his life as a hermit in Wales. There is a church dedicated to him at Newport.

**GUNDULPHUS (St) Bp.
RM. June 17**
6th cent. A bishop somewhere in Gaul, who is said to have died at Bourges.

GUNIFORT (St) M.   RM. Aug 22
? Said to have been a Northerner— Irish, Scottish or English—martyred at Pavia. His legend resembles that of St Richard the King.

GUNTHER (Bl) Mk. OSB. AC. Oct 9
955–1045. A cousin of St Stephen of Hungary. He began life full of worldly ambition, but was brought to better ways by St Godehard of Hildesheim, and became a monk at Niederaltaich in Bavaria. But his ambitious nature asserted itself once more and he had himself made abbot of Göllingen, but proved a failure. Made wise by experience, he resigned and lived as a hermit for twenty-eight years in the mountains of Bakory, Hungary.

GUNTHIERN (St) H.   AC. July 3
d. c.500. A Welsh prince who adopted the solitary life in Brittany.

**GUNTHILDIS (St) V. OSB.
AC. Dec 8**
d. c.748. An English nun of Wimborne, who, at the request of St Boniface, passed over to Germany, and was abbess of a nunnery in Thuringia, and inspector of all the schools founded by the English nuns in the Germanies.

GUNTHRAMMUS (GONTRAM) (St) King   RM. March 28
d. 592. King of Burgundy. Having

divorced his wife and over-hastily ordered the execution of his physician, he was overcome with remorse and lamented these sins for the rest of his life. On his death he was at once proclaimed a saint.

GURIAS and SAMONAS (SS) MM. RM. Nov 15

d. 305. Martyrs beheaded at Edessa in Syria under Diocletian.

GURLOËS (St) Ab. OSB. AC. Aug 25

d. 1057. A Benedictine monk, prior of Redon Abbey, who in 1029 became abbot of Sainte-Croix of Quimperlé in Brittany.

GURVAL (St) Bp.   AC. June 6

Otherwise Godwall, q.v.

GUTHAGON (St) C.   AC. July 3

8th cent. An Irishman who crossed over into Belgium, where he became a recluse.

GUTHLAC (St) H. OSB. AC. Apr 12

667–714. From being a warrior in the army of Ethelred, king of Mercia, Guthlac entered the Benedictine abbey of Repton, a double house under the abbess Elfrida where he was duly professed. Afterwards he asked to leave to become a recluse in the heart of the Lincolnshire fens: here he spent the last fifteen years of his life. At a later period the abbey of Croyland was erected on the site of his cell.

GUY

Note. This is the English form of the Latin Vitus and also of Guido. Variants in other languages are: Gui, Gwin, Guidone, Viton, Wido, Witen, Wit, Wye, Wyden.

GUY (GUIDO) (St) Ab. OSB. AC. March 31

d. 1046. Born near Ravenna, Guy became a Benedictine at the abbey of St Severus in that city, of which he was chosen abbot. Afterwards he was promoted to the abbey of Pomposa, near Ferrara. He loved sacred learning, and at his request, St Peter Damian delivered lectures on the scriptures to his monks for two years. Towards the end of his life he was fiercely, though unjustly, persecuted by the bishop of Ravenna.

GUY of VICOGNE (Bl) O. Praem. AC. March 31

d. 1147. Founder of the Premonstratensian abbey of Vicogne, in the diocese of Arras, whither he retired and was superior of the community.

GUY de GHERARDESCA (Bl) H. AC. May 20

d. 1099. A native of Pisa, who led the life of a solitary at Campo in the diocese of Massa Maritima, in Italy.

GUY of ACQUI (Bl) Bp. AC. June 2

d. 1070. Bishop of Acqui in Monferrato, Piedmont, from 1034 till 1070. Cult confirmed in 1853.

GUY VIGNOTELLI (Bl) C. Tert. OFM.   AC. June 16

c.1185–1245. A rich citizen of Cortona who gave up his wealth on hearing a sermon by St Francis of Assisi. He was received into the third order of St Francis by the holy Founder himself. Ordained a priest, he lived the rest of his life as a recluse near Cortona.

GUY (St) Ab. OSB.   AC. June 18

d. *p.*940. The successor of Bl Berno in the abbey of Baume. About the year 940 he resigned and retired to a hermitage near Fay-en-Bresse.

GUY MARAMALDI (Bl) C. OP. AC. June 25

d. 1391. A native of Naples who became a Dominican, taught philosophy and theology, established a friary at Ragusa, and died as the General Inquisitor for the kingdom of Naples. Cult confirmed in 1612.

GUY (St) C.   RM. Sept 12
d. *c*.1012. Surnamed "the Poor Man of Anderlecht". He was a native of Brabant and the sacristan of Our Lady of Laken, and afterwards for seven years a pilgrim in the Holy Land. On his return he was admitted to the public hospital at Anderlecht, near Brussels, where he died.

GUY of DURNES (Bl) Ab. OSB. Cist.   AC. Sept 23
d. *c*.1157. A monk of Clairvaux, and one of St Bernard's most beloved disciples. He was sent to be abbot-founder of Our Lady of Cherlieu, in the diocese of Besançon. At the request of St Bernard he revised the Cistercian liturgical chant, which was approved in the general chapter of 1150.

GUY of CASAURIA (Bl) Ab. OSB.
                                AC. Nov 23
d. 1045. A Benedictine of Farfa, who was promoted abbot of Casauria, near Chieti.

GWEN (BLANCA, BLANCHE) (St)
                                AC. July 5
See Fragan and Gwen.

GWEN (St) W.   AC. Oct 18
5th cent. Said to have been the sister of St Nonna and therefore aunt to St David of Wales. She is alleged to have been the mother of SS Cuby and Cadfan.

GWEN (CANDIDA, BLANCHE) (St) WM.   AC. Oct 18
d. *c*.492. Reputed to have been a daughter of Brychan of Brecknock, murdered by the heathen Saxons at Talgarth.

GWENDOLINE (St) V. OSB.
                                AC. March 28
Otherwise Gundelindis, q.v.

GWENDOLINE (GWENDOLEN) (St) V.   AC. Oct 18
See Brothen and Gwendolen.

GWENHAEL (St) Ab.   AC. Nov 3
Otherwise Guenhael, q.v.

GWERIR (St) H.   AC. Apr 4
? A hermit near Liskeard in Cornwall, at whose grave King Alfred is said to have been cured of a serious malady. St Gwerir's cell was after his death occupied by St Neot.

GWINOC (St) C.   AC. Oct 26
See Aneurin and Gwinoc.

GYAVIRE (St) M.   RM. June 13
d. 1886. Known as the "good runner of messages". He was put to death by order of King Mwanga of Uganda. See Uganda (Martyrs of).

H

Note. Names beginning with a vowel to which by some an aspirate is prefixed, by others not, will be found either under the letter H or under the initial vowel, according as the one or the other form may appear the more usual or the more authentic.

HABACUC (HABAKKUK) (St)
Prophet   **RM. Jan 15**
6th cent. B.C. One of the twelve lesser prophets. He prophesied in Judaea during the time of captivity. The reason why his name has been inserted in the RM. is the alleged finding of his relics by bishop Zebenus of Eleutheropolis under Theodosius the Great (379–395). Churches have been dedicated to him in the Holy Land.

HABAKUK (St) M.   **RM. Jan 19**
Otherwise Abachum. See Marius, Martha, etc.

HABENTIUS (St) M.   RM. June 7
See Peter, Wallabonsus, etc.

HABERILLA (HABRILIA) (Bl) V.
OSB.   **AC. Jan 30**
d. *c.*1100. A virgin who became a recluse under the obedience of the abbot of Mehrerau, in Switzerland. Mehrerau at that time was a Black Benedictine monastery.

HABET-DEUS (St) Bp. M.
                          AC. Feb 17
d. *c.*500. Bishop of Luna in Tuscany, an ancient city now in ruins. He was martyred by the Arian Vandals (?), and is now venerated at Sarzana.

HADELIN (St) Ab. OSB. AC. Feb 3
d. *c.*690. A native of Gascony who followed St Remaclus first to Solignac and then to Maestricht and Stavelot. He became the founder of Celles, in the diocese of Liége. He lived as a hermit near Dinant on the Meuse.

HADELIN (St) Ab. OSB.
                          AC. June 15
See Domitian and Hadelin.

HADELIN (ADELHEIM) (St) Bp.
OSB.   **AC. Nov 10**
d. *c.*910. Monk and abbot of Saint-Calais, and then bishop of Séez from *c.*884 till 910.

HADELOGA (St) V. OSB.
                          AC. Feb 2
Otherwise Adeloga, q.v.

HADRIAN (*several***)**
See Adrian.

HADUIN (HARDUIN) (St) Bp.
                          AC. Aug 20
d. *c.*662. A bishop of Le Mans, founder of several monasteries including Notre-Dame-d'Evron.

HADULPH (St) Bp. OSB.
                          AC. May 19
d. *c.*728. A prelate who simultaneously held the offices of abbot of Saint-Vaast and bishop of Arras–Cambrai.

HADULPH (St) M. OSB.
                          RM. June 5
Otherwise Hathawulf. See Waccar, Gundekar, etc.

HALWARD (HALLVARD) (St) M.
AC. May 14
d. c.1043. A scion of the royal family of Norway. He is said to have met his death while defending from ill-usage a woman who had appealed to him for help. He is the patron saint of Oslo.

HARDOIN (St) Bp.   AC. Nov 29
7th cent. Bishop of St Pol-de-Léon in Brittany. The name is variously written: Ouardon, Wardon, Hoarzon, Huardo, etc.

HARDUIN (Bl) Mk. OSB. AC. Apr 20
d. 811. Born in the diocese of Rouen he became a Benedictine at Fontenelle (749). After a time he asked leave to live as a recluse near the abbey, and spent his leisure time copying the writings of the Fathers.

HARDULPH (St)   AC. Aug 21
? The church at Breedon-on-the-Hill in Leicestershire was dedicated to this saint, of whom nothing is known. He may be identical with the hermit of Bredon or Breedon mentioned in the life of St Modwenna, q.v.

HARMON (St) Bp.   RM. July 31
Otherwise Germanus of Auxerre, q.v.

HAROLD (St) M.   AC. March 25
d. 1168. A child said to have been put to death by Jews in Gloucester.

HARTMANN (Bl) Bp.   AC. Dec 23
d. 1164. A native of Polling in Austria, who was educated by the Augustinians of Passau, and became dean of the cathedral at Salzburg (1122) and eventually bishop of Brixen. He was highly respected by emperors and popes as well as by the poor people of his diocese. He did much for the canons regular, but was also a great benefactor of other religious, notably of the Benedictines. Cult confirmed in 1784.

HARTWIG (Bl) Bp.   AC. June 14
d. 1023. Twenty-first archbishop of Salzburg (991-1023).

HARUCH (St) Bp. OSB. AC. July 15
d. c.830. Abbot and regionary bishop in the territory of Werden.

HATEBRAND (St) Ab. OSB.
AC. July 30
d. 1198. A native of Frisia, who professed the Benedictine Rule of St Paul's, in Utrecht. In 1183 he became abbot of Olden-Klooster in his native land, and as such he revived the Benedictine life throughout Frisia.

HATHAWULF (St) M. OSB.
RM. June 5
See Waccar, Gundekar, etc.

HATTO (Bl) Mk. OSB.   AC. July 4
d. 985. Born of a noble Swabian family, he left all his property to the Benedictine abbey of Ottobeuren, and became a monk therein. Afterwards he lived as a recluse; but the abbot thought that he was showing too much attachment to his old property, and recalled him back to community life—a call which he at once obeyed.

HEBED JESUS (St) M. RM. Apr 22
Otherwise Abdiesus, q.v.

HEDDA and Comp. MM. OSB.
AC. Apr 9
d. c.870. Hedda was the abbot of Peterborough (Medehampstead). He and eighty-four monks of his community were slain by the Danes, and thenceforward venerated as martyrs.

HEDDA (St) Bp. OSB. RM. July 7
d. 705. An Anglo-Saxon monk and abbot, probably of Whitby, who in 676 was made bishop of the divided diocese

of Wessex. He resided first at Dorchester, near Oxford, whence he removed to the see of Winchester. He was a great benefactor of Malmesbury and king Ina's chief adviser. He ruled the diocese for about forty years.

HEDWIG (Bl) Queen   PC. Feb 28
1371–1399. She succeeded her father Louis on the throne of Poland at the age of thirteen. She was married to Jagiello of Lithuania, but she made it a a condition that he should become a Christian, which he did. Afterwards she was instrumental in bringing to the Faith many Lithuanians. She is venerated throughout Poland with a popular cult.

**HEDWIG (HADWIGIS) (Bl) Abs.
OSB.   AC. Sept 13**
d. *c*.887. A niece of Bl Warinus of Corvey. She became a Benedictine nun and abbess of Herford (*Herivordien*) in Westphalia.

**HEDWIG (JADWIGA) (St) W. OSB.
Cist.   RM. Oct 16**
c.1174–1243. Born at Andechs in Bavaria, but of Moravian descent, she was the daughter of the duke of Croatia and Dalmatia, and the aunt of St Elisabeth of Hungary. She was educated by the Benedictine nuns of Hitzingen in Franconia, and at the age of twelve was married to the duke of Silesia, head of the Polish royal family. She bore him seven children, who were in after-life the cause of great anxiety to their parents. The king and the queen were at one in fostering the religious life in their kingdom. Among other houses, they founded the Cistercian nunnery of Trebnitz, whither Hedwig retired in her widowhood. She was canonized in 1266.

HEGESIPPUS (St) C.   RM. Apr 7
d. *c*.180. A Jew and a native of Jerusalem who spent twenty years of his life in Rome. He is considered the father of ecclesiastical history and the first to trace the succession of popes from St Peter to his own day. Only a few chapters of his work remain. It was warmly commended by Eusebius and by St Jerome, who knew it well and made use of it.

**HEIMRAD (St) Mk. OSB.
                    PC. June 28**
d. 1019. A priest of Baden, who, after many pilgrimages, lived as a monk at Hersfeld, and then as a hermit at Hasungen in Westphalia. In his wanderings throughout Europe he was often taken for a lunatic rather than a pilgrim. His cult has never been officially confirmed.

**HELDRAD (ELDRAD) (St) Ab.
OSB.   AC. March 13**
d. 842. A native of Provence who spent his large fortune in good works, and then set out on a pilgrimage to Rome. He heard from other pilgrims of the Benedictine abbey of Novalese, at the foot of the Alps, and joined that community. After a time he was made abbot and ruled the house for thirty years. The library was his special care. He was moreover a great builder, and had an hospice erected at the highest point of Mt Cenis pass. Cult approved in 1904.

HELANUS (St) H.   RM. Oct 7
6th cent. An Irishman who crossed over to France, it is said, with six brothers and three sisters, and settled near Reims. He was ordained priest and ministered to the people of the neighbourhood.

**HELEN of POLAND (Bl) W. Poor
Clare   AC. March 6**
d. 1298. Daughter of Bela IV of Hungary. In 1256 she married Boleslas V of Poland, after whose death (1279) she lived as a Poor Clare at Gnesen. Cult approved in 1827.

HELEN VALENTINI (Bl) W.
AC. Apr 23
d. 1458. A lady of Udine noted by her contemporaries both for her devotion to the duties of married life for twenty-five years and for her charity and austerities as an Augustinian tertiary after her husband's death. Cult confirmed in 1848.

HELEN (St) V.   RM. May 22
d. *p*.418. A maiden mentioned in the Acts of St Amator of Auxerre as assisting him on his deathbed.

HELEN (HELENA) (St) VM.
AC. June 24
Otherwise Alena, q.v.

HELEN of SKÖFDE (St) WM.
AC. July 31
d. *c*.1160. A noble Swedish lady, who, left a widow, spent her fortune in the service of the poor and the church. She was barbarously put to death in a family feud. Canonized in 1164.

HELEN (St) M.   RM. Aug 13
See Centolla and Helen.

HELEN (St) Empress   RM. Aug 18
c.250-330. An Asiatic by birth, probably a native of Bithynia (certainly not of Britain), who became the wife of Constantius Chlorus, to whom she bore a child who became Constantine the Great. Helen became a Christian after the Edict of Milan (313), and spent the rest of her life in the East and in Rome. She helped in the building of several Roman basilicas and many churches in the Holy Land. Her name is chiefly associated with the discovery of the True Cross in a rock-cistern near Mt Calvary.

HELEN DUGLIOLI (Bl) W.
AC. Sept 23
1472-1520. A native of Bologna, who, to please her mother, married against her own inclinations, and lived a happy married life for thirty years. After her husband's death she devoted herself completely to works of charity. Already revered as a saint during her life, she was venerated as such after her death. Cult confirmed in 1828.

HELEN ENSELMINI (Bl) V. Poor Clare   AC. Nov 4
d. 1242. A native of Padua, who at the age of twelve received the veil of the Poor Clares from St Francis himself at Arcella, near her native city. It is narrated of her that her only food for months was the Blessed Eucharist. Before her death she became blind and dumb. Cult approved in 1695.

HELEN (ILONA) of HUNGARY (Bl) V. OP.   PC. Nov 9
d. *c*.1270. A Dominican nun in Veszprem, and novice mistress of St Margaret of Hungary. She is reputed to have been marked with the stigmata. Venerated as Blessed in Hungary and in the Dominican order.

HELEN GUERRA (Bl) V. Foundress
AC. Dec 23
1835-1914. The foundress of the Sisters of St Zita, also called the Handmaids of the Holy Ghost, was born at Lucca (Tuscany), and her life was characterized by zealous devotion to the Holy Ghost and to the propagation of the faith. Her Congregation is prominent in mission territories. St Gemma Galgani was a pupil in her schools. Beatified 1959.

HELIA (HELIADA) (St) Abs. OSB.
AC. June 20
d. *c*.750. A Benedictine abbess of the nunnery of Öhren (*Horreum*) at Trèves.

HELICONIS (HELCONIDES) (St) M.   RM. May 28
d. ? 250. A woman of Thessalonica, who was arrested at Corinth and beheaded, during the persecution of Decius.

HELIER (HELEROUS) (St) M.
AC. July 16
6th cent. A native of Tongres (Limburg), who lived as a hermit in the island of Jersey and was murdered by heathen whom he was endeavouring to convert.

HELIMENAS (St) M.   RM. Apr 22
See Parmenius, and Comp.

HELINAND (ELINANDUS) (Bl or St) C. OSB. Cist.   AC. Feb 3
d. 1237. A native of Pronleroy (Oise) in the diocese of Beauvais, who from being a court singer, was converted and became a Cistercian at Froidmont. The Cistercians venerate him as a saint.

HELIODORUS, DESAN and MARJAB (SS) MM.   PC. Apr 9
c.355. Heliodorus was a bishop in Mesopotamia who with two priests, and many faithful were put to death in the persecution of Shapur II.

HELIODORUS, VENUSTUS and Comp. (SS) MM.   RM. May 6
3rd cent. A group of seventy-seven martyrs who suffered under Diocletian. Heliodorus and seven others seems to have been martyred in Africa; St Ambrose claims the greater part of the rest for Milan.

HELIODORUS (St) Bp. RM. July 3
c.332–390. A Dalmatian who, early in life, became an intimate friend of St Jerome, whom he followed to Palestine and helped financially and otherwise, in the preparation of the Vulgate. Later he settled in Aquileia and was made bishop of Altinum, a small town, since destroyed near Venice. He was a great bishop, and a brave opponent of Arianism.

HELIODORUS, DAUSA, MARIAHLE, ABDISO and Comp. (SS) MM.   PC. Aug 20
d. 362. A group of 9,000 Christians were deported by the Persians, of these 300 were set aside by Shapur and invited to renounce their faith. Two hundred and seventy-five refused and were martyred. To this number belongs Abdicius (q.v.), RM. Apr 22.

HELIODORUS (St) M. RM. Sept 28
See Mark, Alphius, etc.

HELIODORUS and Comp. (SS) MM.   RM. Nov 21
d. c.270. A group of martyrs, who suffered under Aurelian in Pamphylia.

HELLADIUS (St) M.   RM. Jan 8
See Theophilus and Helladius.

HELLADIUS of TOLEDO (St) Bp.
RM. Feb 18
d. 632. A native of Toledo, and a minister of the court of the Visigothic kings. He loved to pay frequent visits to the abbey of Agali (Agallia) near Toledo on the banks of the Tagus, until one day he joined the community and eventually was made its abbot (605). In 615 he was promoted archbishop of Toledo.

HELLADIUS of AUXERRE (St) Bp.
RM. May 8
d. 387. Bishop of Auxerre in France for thirty years. He converted his own successor St Amator to a devout life.

HELLADIUS (St) M.   RM. May 28
See Crescens, Dioscorides, etc.

HELPERS, FOURTEEN HOLY
See under Fourteen Holy Helpers.

HELWISA (Bl) H. OSB. AC. Feb 11
d. p.1066. A recluse under the obedience of the Benedictine abbey of Coulombs in Normandy.

HEMITERIUS and CHELEDONIUS (SS) MM.   RM. March 3
? 4th cent. Two Spanish martyrs, believed to have been soldiers, who

suffered at Calahorra in Old Castile. Their Acts have been lost; but both Prudentius and St Gregory of Tours have handed down to us the few details we have of them.

HEMMA (*several*)
Otherwise Gemma, q.v.

HENEDINA (St) M.   RM. May 14
See Justa, Justina and Henedina.

HENRY
Note. A Teuton name latinized into Henricus. The most common variants in other languages are—German, Heinrich; French, Henri; Danish, Eric; Spanish and Portuguese, Enrique; Hungarian, Emeric; Italian, Enrico (Arrigo, Amerigo—whence America) etc.

HENRY (St) H.   AC. Jan 16
d. 1127. A Dane by birth, he renounced his own country and lived as a recluse on Cocket Island, off the coast of Northumberland, under the obedience of the monks of Tynemouth to whom the island belonged. Tynemouth itself was a daughter-house of St Alban's. He was buried at Tynemouth.

HENRY of UPSALA (St) Bp. M.
                          AC. Jan 19
d. *c.*1156. An Englishman who accompanied Nicholas Breakspear (later Pope Adrian IV) to Sweden and Norway. Made Bishop of Upsala in Sweden (1152) he was helped in his apostolate by King St Eric IX. He then went to Finland as a member of an expedition led by the same king. He was murdered by a Finn whom he had excommunicated. He was canonized in 1158 and is venerated as a martyr and as the patron saint of Finland.

HENRY MORSE (Bl) M. SJ.
                          AC. Feb 1
d. 1645. A native of Norfolk (or Suf-

folk?) and a convert, who after being a member of the Inns Court, studied for the priesthood at Douai in Rome. He entered the Society of Jesus in 1625 and worked in London. He was martyred for his priesthood at Tyburn. Beatified in 1929.

HENRY SUSO (Bl) C. OP.
                          AC. March 2
*c.*1295-1365. A native of Bihlmeyer, near Constance, who joined the Friars Preachers at an early age, was prior in several houses of the order, and excelled as a director of souls. He is one of the greatest Dominican mystics and his *Book of the Eternal Wisdom* is still one of the most widely read of Christian classics. Cult approved in 1381.

HENRY of GHEEST (Bl) C. OSB. Cist.   AC. Apr 4
d. *c.*1190. A Cistercian monk at Villers, in the diocese of Namur. His relics were solemnly raised in 1599.

HENRY WALPOLE (Bl) M. SJ.
                          AC. Apr 7
d. 1595. A native of Docking, Norfolk, who was educated at Norwich, Cambridge (Peterhouse) and Gray's Inn. He was reconciled to the Church, and studied for the priesthood at the English College, Rome, there entering the Society of Jesus (1584). Ordained in 1588, he worked at York. Here also he was martyred for his priesthood. Beatified in 1929.

HENRY the SHOEMAKER (Bl) C.
                          ? PC. June 9
d. 1666. Henry Michael Buche—"der gute Heinrich"—was a native of Luxemburg, and a shoemaker by trade. In 1645 he settled at Paris and, with the help of Baron de Renti, founded the confraternity of SS Crispinus and Crispinianus (Frères Cordonniers), for

his fellow-craftsmen. He is usually called "saint" or "blessed" but there is no evidence of cult.

HENRY of TREVISO (Bl) C.
AC. June 10
d. 1315. Usually called in Italy, San Rigo (a diminutive form of Arrigo). He was born at Bolzano in the Tyrol, but lived at Treviso, earning his daily bread as a hired labourer (*facchino*). In his old age he lived on alms. Cult approved by Benedict XIV.

HENRY (HERIC) (Bl) C. OSB.
AC. June 24
d. *c*.880. A native of Hery (Yonne), who became a Benedictine, and the headmaster of the monastic school, at Saint-Germain d'Auxerre. He was also a hagiographer.

HENRY ZDIK (Bl) Bp. O. Praem.
PC. June 25
d. 1150. A son of King Wratislas I of Bohemia who was elected bishop of Olmütz in 1126. In 1137 he went to Palestine and donned the Premonstratensian habit at Jerusalem. On his return to his diocese he introduced the Premonstratensians in many places and founded for them the abbey of Strahov.

HENRY of ALBANO (Bl) Bp. Card. OSB. Cist.
AC. July 4
d. 1188. Usually surnamed "Henricus Gallus". He was a French Cistercian who became cardinal bishop of Albano in 1179, and died at Arras.

HENRY ABBOT (Bl) M. AC. July 4
d. 1597. A native of Howden, in Yorkshire. He was a layman and a convert, and was, for this reason, hanged at York. Beatified in 1929.

HENRY II (St) Emperor RM. July 15
972–1024. Henry the Good was born in Bavaria and was educated by St Wolfgang of Ratisbon. From being duke of Bavaria he was raised to the imperial throne in 1002. He, with his wife St Cunegundis, were providentially raised up to protect the Church in that troublous period. Henry, though very much a political and temporal ruler, had always at heart the welfare of religion, and readily co-operated with the Benedictine abbeys of that time—Cluny, Montecassino, Camaldoli, Einsiedeln, St Emmeran, Verdun, Gorsch—in the restoration of ecclesiastical and social discipline. He himself tried to become a Benedictine, and was for this reason officially declared by Pius X the patron saint of the Benedictine Oblates. Canonized in 1146.

HENRY of COLOGNE (Bl) C. OP.
PC. Oct 23
d. 1225. One of the first Dominicans recruited from among the students of the university of Paris, who became the first prior of the friary at Cologne. He was a friend of Bl Jordan.

HENRY of ZWIEFALTEN (Bl) C. OSB.
PC. Nov 4
d. *p*.1250. A Benedictine monk of the abbey of Zwiefalten, who became prior of Ochsenhausen. Both monasteries were in Swabia.

HERACLAS (St) Bp.   RM. July 14
d. 247. An Egyptian, brother of St Plutarch the martyr. He was at first a pupil and afterwards the successor of Origen as head of the catechetical school of Alexandria. He was raised to the patriarchal see in 231.

HERACLEAS (St) M.   RM. Sept 29
See Eutychius, Plautus and Heracleas.

HERACLIDES (St) M. RM. June 28
See Plutarch, Serenus, etc.

HERACLIUS (St) M. RM. March 2
See Paul, Heraclius, etc.

**HERACLIUS and ZOSIMUS (SS)
MM.   RM. March 11**
d. c.263. African martyrs who suffered at Carthage under Valerian and Gallienus.

HERACLIUS (St) M.   RM. May 26
See Felicissimus, Heraclius and Paulinus.

**HERACLIUS of SENS (St) Bp.
                          RM. June 8**
d. c.515. The fourteenth bishop of Sens. He was present in the cathedral of Reims at the baptism of Clovis (Dec 25, 496). He built the abbey of St John the Evangelist at Sens, where he was buried.

HERACLIUS (St) M.   RM. Sept 1
See Priscus, Castrensis, etc.

HERACLIUS (St) M.   RM. Oct 22
See Alexander, Heraclius and Comp.

**HERADIUS, PAUL, AQUILINUS
and Comp. (SS) MM.   RM. May 17**
d. 303. Five martyrs put to death at Nyon (*Noviodunum*) on the lake of Geneva, under Diocletian.

HERAIS (St) VM.   RM. Sept 22
Otherwise Irais, q.v.

HERBERT (St) H.   AC. March 20
d. 687. A priest, friend of St Cuthbert, who lived as a solitary on the island named after him on Lake Derwentwater. The two saints were granted their prayer to die on the same day.

**HERBERT HOSCAM (St) Bp.
                          AC. Aug 20**
d. 1180. An Englishman by birth, who became archbishop of Conza, in the Basilicata, Italy. He is venerated as the principal patron saint of Conza.

**HERBERT (HABERNE, HER-
BERN) (St) Bp. OSB.   AC. Oct 30**
? Abbot of Marmoutier, and afterwards archbishop of Tours.

**HERCULANUS of PIEGARE (Bl) C.
OFM.   AC. June 1**
d. 1541. A native of Piegare, near Perugia, he joined the Franciscans, and became one of their foremost preachers. Beatified in 1860.

**HERCULANUS of BRESCIA (St)
Bp.   RM. Aug 12**
d. c.550. A bishop of Brescia in Lombardy.

HERCULANUS (St) M. RM. Sept 5
d. ? c.180. A martyr who suffered at Porto, near Rome, probably under Marcus Aurelius.

HERCULANUS (St) M. RM. Sept 25
2nd cent. A Roman soldier, mentioned in the untrustworthy Acts of St Alexander I as having been converted by the pontiff and martyred shortly afterwards.

**HERCULANUS (St) Bp.
                 RM. Nov 7 and March 1**
d. 549. A bishop of Perugia, beheaded by the soldiers of Totila, the marauding leader of the Ostro-Goths.

**HEREBALD (HERBAND) (St) C.
                          AC. June 11**
8th cent. A native of Britain who embraced the solitary life in Brittany, where a church is dedicated to him.

HERENA (St) M.   RM. Feb 25
See Donatus, Justus, etc.

HERENIA (St) M.   RM. March 8
See Cyril, Rogatus, etc.

**HERESWITHA (St) W. OSB.
                          AC. Sept 3**
d. c.690. A Northumbrian princess,

sister of St Hilda and mother of SS Sexburga, Withburga and Ethelburga. She spent the closing years of her life as a nun at Chelles in France.

HERIBALDUS (St) Bp. OSB.
AC. Apr 25
d. *c*.857. A Benedictine monk and abbot of the monastery of St Germanus, at Auxerre, who was promoted bishop of the same city.

HERIBERT (St) Bp. RM. March 16
d. 1022. Born at Worms, and educated by the Benedictines of Gorze, he became chancellor to the emperor Otto III and (998) archbishop of Cologne. He was an outstanding churchman, learned, zealous and enterprising. He built the Benedictine abbey of Deutz on the Rhine where he was buried.

HERLINDIS and RELINDIS (SS) Abs. OSB.
AC. Oct 12
d. *c*.745 and 750. Daughters of Count Adelard, who built for them the nunnery of Maaseyk, on the Meuse, of which they became respectively first and second abbesses. They were friends of SS Willibrord and Boniface. See Relindis.

HERLUIN (Bl) Ab. OSB.
PC. Aug 26
d. 1078. A native of Normandy who was bred to the profession of arms and served as a knight at the court of the count of Brionne. He left it to found a monastery on his own estate at Bonneville, of which he became abbot. In 1040 the community moved to a new site on the banks of the little river Bec. One of the first novices was Bl Lanfranc; shortly afterwards came St Anselm. Under these three great men Bec became the foremost school of Christendom. Herluin has always been given the title of *Beatus*.

HERMAGORAS and FORTUNATUS (SS) MM.
RM. July 12
d. *c*.66. According to tradition, St Hermagoras was a disciple of St Mark, by whom he was appointed first bishop of Aquileia. After a fruitful apostolate he and his deacon Fortunatus were beheaded under Nero.

HERMAN of ZÄHRINGEN (Bl) Mk. OSB.
AC. March 25
d. 1074. Margrave of Zähringen, who became a monk at Cluny.

HERMAN JOSEPH (Bl) C.
O. Praem.
AC. Apr 7
c.1150–1241. A native of Cologne, who, at an early age, began to have mystical experiences which made him famous throughout the Germanies. He joined the Premonstratensians at Steinfeld and has left some remarkable mystical writings. He had a special devotion to St Ursula.

HERMAN of HEIDELBERG (Bl) H. OSB.
PC. Sept 3
d. *c*.1326. A Benedictine monk professed at Niederaltaich in Bavaria in 1320, who lived as a hermit. An altar is dedicated to him in the parish church of Rinchnach.

HERMAN the CRIPPLE (*CONTRACTUS*) (Bl) Mk. OSB.
PC. Sept 25
d. 1054. His nickname "the Cripple" describes his physical condition. He was offered as a child of seven to the abbey of Reichenau on the Rhine, and became the most famous religious poet of his age. He has always been given the title of *Beatus*.

HERMAN (Bl) Ab. O. Praem.
AC. Dec 23
d. *c*.1200. A Jew, born in Cologne, who became a Christian and joined the

Premonstratensians. He was elected first abbot of Scheda in the archdiocese of Cologne.

HERMAS (St) Bp.   RM. May 9
1st cent. A Roman, whom St Paul mentions in his Epistle to the Romans (XVI, 14). A Greek tradition makes him bishop of Philippi and a martyr.

HERMAS, SERAPION and POLYAENUS (SS) MM.   RM. Aug 18
? Roman martyrs who were dragged by their feet over rough ground till they expired; they were the victims of the infuriated mob. It seems that their biographer has united their stories quite arbitrarily into one. Hermas may be Hermes (Aug 28).

HERMAS (St) M.   RM. Nov 4
See Nicander and Hermas.

HERMELLUS (St) M.   RM. Aug 3
The same as Hermylus (q.v.).

HERMENEGILD (St) M.
                                RM. Apr 13
d. 585. Son of the Visigothic king of Spain Leovigild, and brought up an Arian at the court of Seville. He became a Catholic on his marriage to the daughter of Sigebert of Austrasia. His father disinherited him on account of his change of religion, whereupon he rose in arms, was defeated and captured and, on refusing to give up the Catholic faith, was put to death at the instigation of his stepmother.

HERMENEGILD (St) Mk. OSB.
                                AC. Nov 5
d. 953. A Spanish Benedictine of Salcedo in the diocese of Tuy, in Spanish Galicia—one of those who helped in the spreading of Benedictinism throughout N.W. Spain under St Rudesind.

HERMENGAUDIUS (ARMENGOL) (St) Bp.   RM. Nov 3
d. 1035. Bishop of Urgell, in the Spanish Pyrenees, from 1010 till 1035. He built the cathedral and gave its canons a rule of life based on that of St Augustine.

HERMENLAND (HERMELAND, HERBLAND, ERBLON)
                                RM. March 25
d. c.720. A native of the diocese of Noyon, he served in his youth as royal cup-bearer. Then he withdrew to Fontenelle and became a monk under St Lambert. He was ordained priest and sent, with a band of twelve monks, to establish a new abbey on the island of Aindre, in the estuary of the Loire.

HERMES, AGGAEUS and CAIUS (SS) MM.   RM. Jan 4
d. c.300. There is some uncertainty as to where these martyrs suffered. The RM. says at Bologna, under Maximian; this could be Bologna, a town of Mesia in Asia Minor. The feast day in their honour at Bologna, Italy, was abolished in 1914. Bononia on the Danube is another possibility.

HERMES and ADRIAN (SS) MM.
                                RM. March 1
d. c.290. Martyrs who suffered under Maximian Herculeus. The RM. says "at Marseilles" but most writers now identify this group of martyrs—Hermes and Adrian are only the first in a list of twenty-six—with "the Massylitan martyrs on whose birthday St Augustine delivered a discourse" (see RM. Apr 9). The original reading of the martyrology was *Massylis* (Marula) in Numidia, the spelling of which is very similar to the Latin *Massilia* (Marseilles).

HERMES and Comp. (SS) MM.
                                RM. Aug 28
d. c.120. Roman martyrs who perished

under the judge Aurelian, and are mentioned in the Acts of Pope St Alexander. Although their Acts are not trustworthy, the cult of St Hermes was both ancient and widespread.

HERMES (St) M.   RM. Oct 22
See Philip, Severus, etc.

HERMES (St) M.   RM. Nov 2
See Publius, Victor, etc.

HERMES (St) M.   RM. Dec 31
d. *c.270*. A cleric, of the rank of exorcist, who is believed to have suffered under Aurelian. He may be the same as the martyr commemorated on Jan. 4.

HERMIAS (St) M.   RM. May 31
d. 170. A veteran soldier, martyred at Comana in Cappadocia—not in Pontus, as Baronius thought. He has a prominent place in the Greek liturgy.

HERMIONE (St) V.   AC. Sept 4
d. *c.117*. One of the daughters of Philip the Deacon, mentioned in the Acts of the Apostles (XXI, 9) as a prophetess. She is said to have died a martyr at Ephesus.

HERMIPPUS (St) M.   RM. July 27
See Hermolaus, Hermippus and Hermocrates.

HERMOCRATES (St) M.
                         RM. July 27
See Hermolaus, Hermippus and Hermocrates.

HERMOGENES (St) M. RM. Apr 17
See Peter and Hermogenes.

HERMOGENES, CAIUS, EXPEDITUS, ARISTONICUS, RUFUS and GALATA (SS) MM.   RM. Apr 19
4th cent. Armenian martyrs who are believed to have suffered at Melitene.

The cult of St Expeditus (whose name appears in some documents as Elpidius) in order to receive a speedy answer, dates from the 17th century, and is of German origin.

HERMOGENES (St) M. RM. Apr 25
See Evodius, Hermogenes and Callistus.

HERMOGENES (St) M. RM. Dec 10
See Mennas, Hermogenes and Eugraphus.

HERMOGENES, DONATUS and Comp. (SS) MM.   RM. Dec 12
? Twenty-four martyrs, said to have been driven into a marsh and there left to perish of cold and exhaustion.

HERMOGIUS (St) Bp. OSB.
                            AC. June 26
d. *c.942*. A native of Tuy and founder of the abbey of Labrugia (915) in Spanish Galicia. He was taken captive by the Moors and brought to Cordova, but was subsequently given his freedom; his nephew, the boy St Pelagius, being retained there as a hostage. St Hermogius resigned his see and retired to Ribas del Sil.

HERMOLAUS, HERMIPPUS and HERMOCRATES (SS) MM.
                            RM. July 27
d. *c.305*. St Hermolaus, an aged priest of Nicomedia, having succeeded in converting St Pantaleon, the imperial physician, was martyred with him and with the two brothers Hermippus and Hermogenes.

HERMYLUS and STRATONICUS (SS) MM.   RM. Jan 13
d. 315. Hermylus, a deacon of *Singidunum* (Belgrade) and Stratonicus his servant, were drowned in the Danube under Licinius. The value of the *Life* however has been questioned.

HERNAN (St) C. AC. Sept 15
6th cent. A native of Britain, who took refuge in Brittany at the time of the Anglo-Saxon conquest. He lived as a solitary at a place called after him Loc-Harn, and he is the patron saint of that village.

HERODION, ASYNCRITUS and PHLEGON (SS) MM. RM. Apr 8
1st cent. Herodion, whom St Paul styles his kinsman (Rom XVI, 11), with Asyncritus and Phlegon, likewise mentioned by the Apostle, are said to have become bishops, Herodion of Patras, Asyncritus of Marathon and Phlegon of Hyrcania, and to have been done to death at the instigation of the Jews.

HERON (St) M. RM. June 28
See Plutarch, Serenus, etc.

HERON (St) Bp. M. RM. Oct 17
d. *c.*136. The disciple, and successor of St Ignatius in the see of Antioch, which he governed for twenty years (*c.*116–136). He died a martyr.

HERON, ARSENIUS, ISIDORE and DIOSCORUS (SS) MM. RM. Dec 14
d. 250. The three first named were burnt to death at Alexandria in Egypt under Decius. Dioscorus, a boy, was whipped and then dismissed.

HEROS (St) M. RM. June 24
See Orentius, Heros, etc.

HERULPH (HARIOLFUS) (St) Bp. OSB. AC. Aug 13
d. 785. A son of the count of Ellwangen. He became a Benedictine at St Gall and afterwards founded the abbey of Ellwangen (764) in the diocese of Augsburg. He was later raised to the see of Langres.

HERUNDO (St) V. RM. July 23
See Romula, Redempta and Herundo.

HERVEUS (HERVÉ) of TOURS (St) C. AC. Apr 16
d. 1021. A native of Touraine, he became treasurer of the Abbey of St Martin of Tours, and lived for a time as a hermit, but died among the canons of St Martin.

HERVEUS (HERVÉ) (St) Ab. AC. June 17
d. *c.*575. A Welsh saint and singer, blind from his childhood. He was taken very young to Brittany, where he grew up to become a teacher and minstrel. Though blind he became abbot of Plouvien, whence he migrated with part of his community to Lanhouarneau. He is still a most popular saint in Brittany. In art he is represented as blind, and led about by a wolf.

HERVEUS (Bl) H. AC. July 18
d. 1130. A native of the British Isles, he led the life of an anchorite on the island of Chalonnes, in Anjou.

HESPERIUS (St) M. RM. May 2
Otherwise Exuperius, q.v.

HESSO (ESSO) (Bl) Ab. OSB. AC. Dec 27
d. 1133. Benedictine monk and procurator of Hirschau under St William. He was sent to Beinwil in Switzerland as its first abbot (1085).

HESYCHIUS (St) Bp. RM. May 15
See Torquatus, Ctesiphon, etc.

HESYCHIUS (St) M. RM. June 15
d. *c.*302. A Roman soldier martyred at Dorostorum (Silistria) in Maesia, together with the veteran St Julius.

HESYCHIUS (St) M. RM. July 7
See Peregrinus, Lucian, etc.

HESYCHIUS (St) M. RM. Sept 2
See Diomedes, Julian, etc.

HESYCHIUS (St) H.   RM. Oct 3
d. *c.*380. A disciple of St Hilarion, under whom he became a monk at Majuma, near Gaza, in Palestine. He followed his master from solitude to solitude, and when St Hilarion fled to Sicily, St Hesychius spent three years searching for him. At St Hilarion's death (371) he conveyed the remains back to Majuma, where he lived until his own death.

HESYCHIUS (St) M.   RM. Nov 7
See Hieron, Nicander, etc.

HESYCHIUS of ANTIOCH (St) M.
                              RM. Nov 18
d. *c.*303. A Roman soldier who cast away his military belt (the *cingulum militare*) proclaiming himself a Christian. As a punishment for this he was drowned in the river Orontes.

HESYCHIUS (St) Bp. M. RM. Nov 26
See Faustus, Didius, etc.

HEWALD (SS) MM.   RM. Oct 3
Otherwise Ewald, q.v.

HIA (IA, IVES) (St) V.   AC. Feb 3
Otherwise Ia, q.v.

HIDULPHUS (St) Mk. OSB.
                              AC. June 23
d. *c.*707. Count of Hainault and a courtier at the royal palace of Austrasia. He married St Aye, but by mutual consent they became religious, Hidulphus entering the abbey of Lobbes, which he had helped to found.

HIDULPHUS (St) Bp. OSB.
                              AC. July 11
d. 707. A native of Ratisbon who became a monk of the abbey of Maximinus, at Trèves. At a later date he was consecrated a regionary bishop; but about the year 676 he resigned, and founded the Benedictine abbey of Moyenmoutier. When he died he was

abbot both of Moyenmoutier and Bonmoutier (Galilaea, afterwards called Saint-Dié).

HIERLATH (St) Bp.   AC. Feb 1
Otherwise Jarlath, q.v.

HIERO (IERO) (St) M. AC. Aug 17
d. 885. An Irish missionary in Holland, where he died a martyr.

HIERON, NICANDER, HESYCHIUS and Comp. (SS) MM.
                              RM. Nov 7
d. *c.*300. A group of thirty-three Armenian martyrs, who suffered at Mitilene under Diocletian.

HIERONIDES, LEONTIUS, SERAPION, (SELESIUS) SELEUCUS, VALERIAN and STRATON (SS) MM.   RM. Sept 12
d. *c.*300. Martyrs, cast into the sea at Alexandria in Egypt under Diocletian. Hieronides was a deacon far advanced in years; Leontius and Serapion were brothers. The name Selesius should be Seleucus.

HIEROTHEUS (St) Bp. RM. Oct 4
? The alleged teacher and friend of St Dionysius the Areopagite. Modern writers either deny his existence or postdate him to the 4th or 5th century.

HIEU (St) V.   AC. Sept 2
d. *c.*657. A Northumbrian maiden who received the veil from St Aidan, by whom she was made abbess of Tadcaster in Yorkshire. By some St Hieu is thought to be one and the same with St Bega or Bee.

HILARIA, DIGNA, EUPREPIA, EUNOMIA, QUIRIACUS, LARGIO, CRESCENTIAN, NIMMIA, JULIANA and Comp. (SS) MM.   RM. Aug 12
d. *c.*304. Hilaria is the alleged mother of

St Afra of Augsburg (q.v.). She and her three maids were seized while visiting the tomb of St Afra and burnt alive. The others (Quiriacus, etc., twenty-five in all) were Roman martyrs buried on the Ostian Way.

HILARIA (St) M.   RM. Dec 3
See Claudius, Hilaria, etc.

HILARIA (St) M.   RM. Dec 31
See Donata, Paulina, etc.

HILARINUS (St)   RM. Aug 7
See Donatus and Hilarinus.

HILARINUS (St) M.   PC. Aug 23
See Altigianus and Hilarinus.

HILARION (St) M.   RM. July 12
See Proclus and Hilarion.

HILARION (St) Ab.   RM. Oct 21
c.291–371. A native of Gaza in Palestine, Hilarion became a Christian while studying at Alexandria, and took St Antony the Great as his model. On his return to Gaza, he introduced there the eremitical life. Disciples soon flocked around him and he founded several monasteries in Palestine. The latter part of his life is the story of his escapes from the crowds who followed him on account of his miracles. He lived on Mt Sinai, in Egypt, Sicily, Dalmatia, Paphos and Cyprus, where he died at the age of eighty.

**HILARY (HILARUS) (St) Pope
          RM. Feb 28**
d. 468. A Sardinian by birth, promoted to high office in the Roman curia by St Leo the Great, who sent him as his legate to the "Robber Synod of Ephesus" from which he escaped with difficulty (449). He was made pope in 461 and worked energetically against the Nestorians and Eutychians, as well as in consolidating the Church in Sandi, Africa and Gaul.

HILARY (St) Bp. and Dr.
**   RM. Jan 14**
d. 368. Born at Poitiers of pagan patrician parents, he studied rhetoric and philosophy and married early in life. Shortly after he became a Christian and in 353 was elected bishop of Poitiers. At once he began his masterly campaign against Arianism, and for this reason was exiled to Phrygia by the Arian emperor Constantius. But in Phrygia he was even more objectionable to the Arians, who clamoured for his recall. He returned to Poitiers in 360. Hilary is the Doctor of the Divinity of Christ. He was officially declared a Doctor of the Church in 1851.

HILARY, TATIAN, FELIX, LARGUS and DENIS (SS) MM.
**   RM. March 16**
d. *c*.284. Hilary was a bishop of Aquileia, Tatian his deacon, and the rest laymen. All were beheaded under Numerian.

HILARY (St) M.   RM. Apr 9
See Demetrius, Concessus, etc.

HILARY (St) Bp.   RM. May 5
c.400–449. Born in Lorraine, while still a pagan he gained high office in the local administration. His relative and friend, St Honoratus, invited him to the monastery recently founded at Lérins, and Hilary received baptism there, and joined the community. When St Honoratus became bishop of Arles he took Hilary as his secretary. St Hilary succeeded to the see and showed himself a zealous prelate, though not always prudent. In fact, he was twice reproved by the Holy See. His sanctity, however, won for him popular veneration in life and after death.

HILARY (St) Ab.   AC. May 15
d. 558. A hermit near the river Ronco in Italy. Joined by others he built the monastery called Galeata, afterwards known as Sant'Ilaro, which at a later period was handed over to the Camaldolese.

HILARY (St) Bp.   AC. May 16
d. 376. Bishop of Pavia. One of the prelates of N. Italy who fought Arianism.

HILARY (St) Bp.   AC. May 20
4th cent. Bishop of Toulouse.

HILARY (St) Bp.   AC. June 3
? 4th cent. Bishop of Carcassonne.

HILARY (St) M.   RM. Sept 27
See Florentinus and Hilary.

HILARY of MENDE (St) Bp.
                              RM. Oct 25
d. 535. Born at Mende, the ancient *Gavallus*, in S. France, he received baptism on coming to man's estate, became a hermit on the banks of the Tarn, monk of Lérins, and finally bishop of Mende.

HILARY of VITERBO (St) M.
                              RM. Nov 3
See Valentine and Hilary.

HILARY (St) Ab. OSB. PC. Nov 21
d. *c.*1045. A native of Matera in S. Italy, he became abbot of San Vincenzo at Volturno (1011–1045). He revived the ancient glory of his monastery.

HILDA (St) Abs. OSB. AC. Nov 17
617–680. A native of Northumbria and a kinswoman of King St Edwin. She was baptized when a child by St Paulinus (631) and at the age of thirty-three joined the nuns of Hartlepool, by the river Wear in Northumberland, of whom soon after she became the abbess. Later on, she migrated also as abbess to the double monastery of Whitby at Streaneshalch. Her influence was certainly one of the decisive factors in securing unity in the English Church. Although she and her double community had professed and favoured the Celtic rule and observances, they gave them up after the council of Whitby convened by St Hilda herself in 664, when the Roman observances, including the Roman monastic Rule of St Benedict, were definitely adopted throughout England. Five of her monks, including St Wilfrid of York and St John of Beverley, became bishops. Hilda is one of the greatest Englishwomen of all time.

HILDEBERT (St) Ab. M. OSB.
                              AC. Apr 4
d. 752. Abbot of the Benedictine monastery of St Peter at Ghent. He was killed by some fanatics for his defence of holy images, and was venerated as a martyr.

HILDEBRAND (Bl) M. PC. Apr 11
See Stephen and Hildebrand.

HILDEBRAND (St) Pope OSB.
                              RM. May 25
Otherwise Gregory VII, q.v.

HILDEGARD (Bl) Empress
                              AC. Apr 30
d. 783. A daughter of the duke of Swabia. In 771 she was married to Charlemagne. Hildegard bore him eight children during the twelve years of their married life. She befriended monks and nuns, among whom she had a special predilection for St Lioba. She is considered as the foundress of Kempten Abbey, where she was buried.

HILDEGARD (St) Abs. OSB.
                              RM. Sept 17
1098–1179. Surnamed "the Sibyl of the Rhine". Born at Bockelheim, she joined the Benedictines at Diessenberg when she was only eight years old, and in

early womanhood was chosen abbess of the place. She removed the community to Mt St Rupert, near Bingen (*c*.1147), and founded another daughter-house in the neighbourhood. Her claim to fame, however, rests on her amazing writings. "Hildegard was the first of the great German mystics, a poetess and a prophetess, a physician and a political moralist, who rebuked popes and princes, bishops and lay-folk, with complete fearlessness and unerring justice" (Attwater). Accused by her numerous enemies, she was defended by St Bernard and by his pope-disciple Bl Eugene III. "Hildegard's mystical writings have provoked comparison with Dante and William Blake . . . she was alike one of the greatest figures of the 12th century, of the followers of St Benedict, and of the women of all time" (Attwater).

HILDEGRIN (St) Bp. AC. June 19
d. *c*.827. Younger brother of St Ludger, q.v., and his fellow-worker in the evangelization of the Saxons. At a later period (802?) he was promoted bishop of Châlons-sur-Marne. It is usually stated that towards the end of his life he became a monk, and abbot of the Benedictine monastery of Werden.

**HILDEGUND (St) W. O. Praem.
AC. Feb 6**
d. 1183. Wife of Count Lothair. In her widowhood she turned her castle of Meer, near Cologne, into a Premonstratensian nunnery and entered there with her daughter, in the teeth of fierce family opposition. Hildegund became the prioress of the new foundation.

**HILDEGUND, or Joseph (Bl) N.
OSB. Cist.   PC. Apr 20**
d. 1188. The Cistercian menology states: "Hildegund, died a novice at the abbey of Schönau, disguised in male apparel and calling herself Brother Joseph. She died most holily and is famous for her miracles." Hers is a romantic story. She was born in the Rhineland and, dressed as a boy, she accompanied her father to the Holy Land; on her return she joined the Cistercian monks at Schönau; her sex was discovered after death. Of the several women of whom similar stories are related, Hildegund is almost the only one in whose story there seems to be a measure of truth. Her cult is, however, only a popular one.

HILDELID (HILDILID, HILDELTHA) (St) Abs. OSB. AC. March 24
d. *c*.717. A young Anglo-Saxon princess who took the veil either at Chelles or at Faremoutier, in France. She was recalled to England by St Erconwald to train her sister Ethelburga of Barking. When the latter became abbess Hildelid stayed on as one of her nuns, and eventually succeeded her as abbess. She won the admiration of SS Aldhelm, Bede and Boniface.

**HILDEMAR (Bl) M. OSA.
AC. Jan 13**
d. 1097(8). German by origin, he was a court chaplain to William the Conqueror in England. Then he became a hermit at Arrouaise in Artois. He was joined by many disciples for whom he founded the monastery of Arrouaise under the Augustinian rule of canons regular. He was killed by an assassin who posed as a novice.

**HILDEMAR (St) Bp. OSB.
AC. Dec 10**
d. *p*.844. A monk of Corbie who was appointed bishop of Beauvais in 821.

**HILDEMARCA (St) Abs. OSB.
AC. Oct 25**
d. *c*.670. A nun of St Eulalia at Bor-

deaux, who was invited by St Wandrille to govern his new monastery at Fécamp.

HILDUARD (HILWARD, GARIBALD) (St) Bp. OSB.   AC. Sept 7
d. *c*.750. A missionary bishop in Flanders, founder of St Peter's abbey at Dickelvenne, between Ghent and Audenarde, in the Schelde.

HILLONIUS (St) C.   AC. Jan 7
Otherwise Tillo, q.v.

HILSINDIS (Bl) Abs. OSB. AC. May 4
d. 1028. Of the family of the dukes of Lorraine. In her widowhood she was the abbess-foundress of the nunnery of Thorn, on the Marne.

HILTRUDE (St) V. OSB. RM. Sept 27
d. *c*.790. A recluse in a cell near the abbey of Liessies, under the obedience of its abbot, who was her own brother, Gundrad.

HILTUTUS (St) Ab.   AC. July 7
Otherwise Illtyd, q.v.

HIMELIN (St) C.   AC. March 10
d. *c*.750. An Irish, or Scottish, priest, who died at Vissenaeken, near Tirlemont, in Belgium, on his return from a Roman pilgrimage. He is still venerated at Vissenaeken.

HIMERIUS (St) Bp.   RM. June 17
d. *c*.560. A native of Calabria, who from being a monk, was raised to the see of Amelia (*Ameria*) in Umbria. He is described as a very austere man, first with himself and then with others. In 995 his relics were translated to Cremona, where he is venerated as one of its principal patron saints.

HIMERIUS (IMIER) (St) Ab.
                            AC. Nov 12
d. *c*.610. A monk-hermit and a missionary in the district of the Swiss Jura, now

called after him Immertal, Val-Saint-Imier.

HIPPARCHUS (St) M.   AC. Dec 9
See Samosata Martyrs.

HIPPOLYTUS (St) M.   RM. Jan 30
? A martyr renowned at Antioch. The details given in the RM. are borrowed from the story of St Hippolytus of Rome.

HIPPOLYTUS (St) M.   RM. Feb 3
See Felix, Symphronius, etc.

HIPPOLYTUS GALANTINI (Bl) C.
                            AC. March 20
1565–1619. A native of Florence, and a silk-weaver by trade. From his twelfth year he assisted the priests in teaching Christian doctrine to the children. This practice was imitated by others, whom Bl Hippolytus formed into the congregation of Italian Doctrinarians. It soon spread throughout Italy. Beatified in 1825.

HIPPOLYTUS, CONCORDIA and Comp. (SS) MM.
                RM. Aug 13 and Nov 19
d. *c*.236. A native of Rome who became a member of the Roman clergy, among whom he was known for his rigoristic leanings. He censured Pope St Callistus I, causing himself to be elected antipope. He was exiled to Sardinia and there reconciled to the church before his martyrdom. He is one of the most important ecclesiastical writers of his time. His story has been overlaid by legends. One connects him with the death of St Laurence; and St Concordia (a genuine martyr of whom however nothing is known) is worked into the story. The legend of Hippolytus of Porto has no basis beyond the fact that this Hippolytus was venerated with a basilica at Porto. See also Pontian (Nov 19).

HIPPOLYTUS of PORTO (St) Bp. M. RM. Aug 22

? d. *c*.236. This saint is really St Hippolytus of Rome commemorated on Aug 13. The confusion arose through this saint having a basilica dedicated to him at Rome. The RM. makes him a bishop of Porto, martyred by drowning under Alexander.

HIPPOLYTUS (St) Bp. OSB. AC. Nov 28

d. *c*.775. Abbot-bishop of Saint-Claude, in France.

HIPPOLYTUS (St) M.   RM. Dec 2

See Eusebius, Marcellus, etc.

HIRENARCHUS, ACACIUS and Comp. (SS) MM.   RM. Nov 27

d. *c*.305. Martyrs of Sebaste in Armenia. They include Acacius, a priest, seven women, and Hirenarchus, converted on witnessing the courage of the other martyrs.

HOMOBONUS (St) C. RM. Nov 13

d. 1197. A merchant of Cremona, who throughout his life practised the most scrupulous honesty and was conspicuous for his charity to the poor. One day, during the celebration of Mass, at which he assisted every day, he fell prostrate on the ground and was picked up dead. Two years after his death his fellow-citizens petitioned the Holy See for his canonization and their petition was granted at once (1199).

HONESTUS (St) M.   AC. Feb 16

d. 270. A native of Nîmes, who was ordained priest and sent into Spain by St Saturninus to preach the gospel, which he did with much fruit. He appears to have been martyred at Pampeluna in Spanish Navarre.

HONORATA (St) V.   RM. Jan 11

d. *c*.500. The sister of St Epiphanius, bishop of Pavia. She was a nun at Pavia, when Odoacer, the king of the Heruli, dragged her into captivity. She was ransomed by her brother and returned to Pavia.

HONORATUS of ARLES (St) Bp. RM. Jan 16

d. 429. Born probably in Lorraine of a Roman consular family, he renounced paganism in his youth and went to the East to study monasticism. Returning to France, he founded on the Mediterranean islet of Lérins, the abbey of that name. In 426 he was forced to accept the archbishopric of Arles; but died only three years later.

HONORATUS of FONDI (St) Ab. ?OSB.   RM. Jan 16

6th cent. The abbot-founder of the monastery of Fondi on the confines of Latium and Campania. St Gregory the Great gives (Dialogues Bk I) a pleasing, though all too short, account of his life.

HONORATUS of MILAN (St) Bp. RM. Feb 8

d. 570. Appointed bishop of Milan in 567, at a time when much trouble was being caused by the Arian disputes and by the Lombard invasion. He was driven from his see by barbarians, and died in exile.

HONORATUS of AMIENS (St) Bp. RM. May 16

d. *c*.600. A native of Ponthieu who became bishop of Amiens. The church and thoroughfare of Saint-Honoré, in Paris, take their name from him.

HONORATUS, FORTUNATUS, ARONTIUS (ORONTIUS), SABINIAN (SAVINIAN) (SS) MM. RM. Aug 27 and Sept 1

d. 303. Martyrs beheaded at Potenza under Maximian. They are one of the groups commemorated under the title of "The Twelve Holy Brothers", q.v.

HONORATUS of VERCELLI (St) Bp.   RM. Oct 28
c.330-415. A native of Vercelli who was trained in the monastic and the ecclesiastical life by St Eusebius. He accompanied his master into his exile at Scythopolis (355), and in his wanderings through Cappadocia, Egypt and Illyricum. In 396 he was elected bishop on the recommendation of St Ambrose, to whom he administered holy viaticum.

HONORATUS of TOULOUSE (St) Bp.   AC. Dec 21
d. 3rd cent. Born in Spanish Navarre, he succeeded St Saturninus in the see of Toulouse. He consecrated St Firminus II bishop of Amiens.

HONORATUS (St) M.   RM. Dec 22
See Demetrius, Honoratus and Florus.

HONORATUS (St) M. RM. Dec 29
See Dominic, Victor, etc.

HONORÉ (St) Bp.   RM. May 16
Otherwise Honoratus of Amiens, q.v.

HONORINA (St) VM.   AC. Feb 27
? One of the early martyrs of Gaul. Her Acts have been lost. Her cult is most ancient in Normandy.

HONORIUS of BUZANCAIS (St or Bl) M.   AC. Jan 9
d. 1250 (?) Born at Buzancais in Berry, France, Honorius was a rich and charitable cattle merchant. On his return from a journey, he found out that he had been robbed by his servants and remonstrated with them. He was killed for this reason, at Parthenay in Poitou and venerated as a martyr. Canonized in 1444.

HONORIUS of BRESCIA (St) Bp.   RM. Apr 24
d. c.586. A hermit near Brescia, who was chosen bishop of that city (c.577).

HONORIUS of CANTERBURY (St) Bp. OSB.   RM. Sept 30
d. 653. A Roman by birth and a Benedictine by profession, he succeeded St Justus as archbishop of Canterbury (627). He was consecrated at Lincoln by St Paulinus, and himself consecrated bishops St Felix for the East Angles and St Ithamar, the first English born bishop, for Rochester.

HONORIUS (St) M.   RM. Nov 21
See Demetrius and Honorius.

HONORIUS, EUTYCHIUS and STEPHEN (SS) MM.   RM. Nov 21
d. c.300. Spanish martyrs, who suffered at Asta, in Andalusia, under Diocletian.

HONORIUS (St) M.   RM. Dec 30
See Mansuetus, Severus, etc.

HOPE (St) VM.   RM. Aug 1
See Faith, Hope, and Charity.

HORMISDAS (St) Pope RM. Aug 6
d. 523. Born at Frosinone in Latium, he succeeded St Symmachus in 514. He is best remembered for the confession of faith called the Formula of Hormisdas, which was accepted in the East (519) and thus ended the Monophysite schism of Acacius. His son, St Silverius, became pope in 536.

HORMISDAS (St) M.   RM. Aug 8
d. 420. A noble Persian youth, who refused to apostatize, and was degraded by King Varannes to the rank of an army camel-driver and subsequently executed.

HORRES (St) M.   RM. March 13
See Theusetas, Horres, etc.

HORTULANUS (St) Bp. M.
RM. Nov 28
See Valerian, Urban, etc.

HOSANNA of CATTARO (Bl) V. Tert. OP.   AC. Apr 27
d. 1565. Her baptismal name was Catherine Cosie, and she was the daughter of dissident orthodox parents in Montenegro. She abjured the schism at Cattaro, and became a Dominican tertiary, taking the new name of Hosanna. Cult confirmed in 1928.

HOSANNA of MANTUA (Bl) V. Tert. OP.   AC. June 18
1449–1505. A native of Mantua, daughter of the patrician, Andreasio. She spent her large fortune in the service of the poor as a Dominican tertiary. Cult confirmed by Leo X and Innocent XII.

HOSPITIUS (St) H.   RM. May 21
d. c.580. A hermit at the place now called after him Cap-Saint-Hospice, between Villefrance and Banlieu. His relics were translated to Lérins on May 21, the day on which his feast is now celebrated.

HROZNATA (Bl) M. O. Praem.
AC. July 19
1160–1217. A member of a noble family of Bohemia, who married and lost by sudden death his wife and only child. He then founded the Premonstratensian abbey of Tepl in Bavaria, and was himself professed therein. He died of starvation in a dungeon, into which he had been thrown by robbers. Cult approved in 1897.

HUBERT (St) Bp.   RM. Nov 3
d. 727. A courtier of Pepin of Heristal who, having lost his wife, entered the ecclesiastical state. According to a late legend his conversion happened while he was hunting, in circumstances similar to those narrated of St Eustace and others. He is also said by some writers to have joined the community of Stavelot. Eventually he succeeded St Lambert as bishop of Maestricht (c.706) whence he transferred the see to Liège. He is venerated as the patron saint of hunters.

HUBERT (HUGBERT) of BRETIGNY (St) C. OSB.   AC. May 30
d. c.714. At the age of twelve he entered, in spite of much opposition from his family, the abbey of Brétigny, near Noyon. There his life was an uninterrupted series of portentous happenings.

HUGH of FOSSE (Bl) O. Praem.
AC. Feb 10
1164. Born at Fosse near Namur in Belgium, he was ordained priest and in 1119 joined St Norbert the founder of the premonstratensians, whose companion and assistant he became, and whom he succeeded as abbot of Prémontré and superior general of the order. Cult confirmed in 1927.

HUGH dei LIPPI-UGUCCIONI (St) C. OSM.   RM. Feb 12 and May 3
d. 1282. A Florentine by birth. One of the Seven Founders of the Servite Order. He accompanied St Philip Benizi to France and Germany and was vicar-general of the order in Germany for eight years. He died on Mt Senario.

HUGH of VAUCELLES (Bl) OSB. Cist.   AC. March 29
d. 1239. From being dean of the church at Cambrai he became a monk at the Cistercian abbey of Vaucelles.

HUGH of GRENOBLE (St) Bp. OSB.   RM. Apr 1
1053–1132. A native of Dauphiné, who, although a layman, was at the age of

twenty-five already a canon of Valence. He was appointed bishop of Grenoble in 1080. Convinced of his own inefficiency, he retired to the austere abbey of Chaise-Dieu and received the Benedictine habit. Pope Gregory VII, however, ordered him back to Grenoble. He gave to St Bruno the land of La Grande Chartreuse. He was canonized in 1134, two years after his death.

HUGH of BONNEVAUX (Bl or St) Ab. OSB. Cist.   AC. Apr 1
d. 1194. A nephew of St Hugh of Grenoble who became a Cistercian at Mezières. In 1163 he was made abbot of Léoncel, and in 1169 promoted to Bonnevaux. He was possessed of singular powers of divination and exorcism, but he is chiefly remembered as the mediator between Alexander III and Barbarossa (1177).

HUGH of ROUEN (St) Bp. OSB.
RM. Apr 9
d. 730. At a very early age he became a monk, either at Fontenelle or Jumièges. Then he was called to be *primicerius* of Metz and shortly after was made bishop of Rouen (722) as well as of Paris, being at the same time abbot of Fontenelle and Jumièges. He made use of all these offices to foster piety and learning. Before his death, however, he resigned them all and died at Jumièges as a simple monk.

HUGH of ANZY-LE DUC (St) C. OSB.   AC. Apr 20
d. *c.*930. A native of Poitiers, he was trained from infancy at the Benedictine abbey of Saint-Savin, Poitou, where he became a monk. Later he was sent to several houses to revive monastic observance, including the newly founded abbey of Cluny where he helped Bl Berno. He died as prior of Anzy-le-Duc. His relics were elevated in 1001.

HUGH the GREAT of CLUNY (St) Ab. OSB.   RM. Apr 29
1024–1109. Born at Samur, he made his profession at Cluny (1039), was ordained priest at twenty, and elected abbot at twenty-five. He was abbot from 1049 till 1109, and during this period he was the adviser of nine popes, consulted and revered by all the sovereigns of Europe, and the ruler of over 200 monasteries. He and his Cluniac monk St Gregory VII were instrumental in promoting the powerful revival of spiritual life throughout W. Europe which characterizes the 11th century. He founded a hospital at Marcigny in which he loved to wait upon the lepers with his own hands. Few men have been so universally esteemed. Canonized in 1120.

HUGH of MARCHIENNES (Bl) Ab. OSB.   PC. June 11
d. 1158. Born at Tournai and educated at Reims, he became a Benedictine at St Martin, Tournai, and abbot of Marchiennes in 1148.

HUGH of MONTAIGU (Bl) Bp. OSB.   AC. Aug 10
d. 1136. A nephew of St Hugh of Cluny, under whom he was educated and professed a Benedictine at Cluny. In 1096 he was made bishop of Auxerre.

HUGH (LITTLE) (St) M. AC. Aug 18
d. 1255. A boy of Lincoln, aged nine, who was put to death by Jews. King Henry III conducted the judicial investigations which resulted in eighteen Jews being hanged for their crime.

HUGH GREEN (Bl) M. AC. Aug 19
d. 1642. A Londoner, educated at Peterhouse, Cambridge. After his conversion he studied for the priesthood at Douai, and was ordained there in 1612. He worked in Dorset, and was hanged for his priesthood at Dorchester.

HUGH MORE (Bl) M.
AC. Aug 28

d. 1588. Born at Grantham in Lincoln-shire, he was educated at Oxford (Broadgates Hall) and Gray's Inn. He became a convert at Reims and was hanged for this at Lincoln's Inn Fields. Beatified in 1929.

HUGH of SASSOFERRATO (Bl) C. OSB. Silv.
AC. Sept 19

d. c.1290. Born at Serra San Quirico in the diocese of Camerino, he studied at Bologna. He received the monastic habit from St Silvester, of whom he was a devoted disciple. He died at Sasso-ferrato. Cult approved in 1747.

HUGH CANEFRO (St or Bl) C.
AC. Oct 8

1168–1230. Priest and chaplain of the knights of St John of Jerusalem at Genoa.

HUGH of MÂCON (Bl) Bp. OSB. Cist.
PC. Oct 10

d. 1151. A Cistercian under St Stephen, and then abbot of Pontigny (1114). In 1137 he was elected bishop of Auxerre, the first Cistercian to be raised to the episcopate.

HUGH of AMBRONAY (St) Ab. OSB.
AC. Oct 21

9th–10th cent. Third abbot of the Bene-dictine monastery of Ambronay in the diocese of Belley.

HUGH FARINGDON (Bl) Ab. M. OSB.
AC. Nov 15

d. 1539. Hugh Faringdon (*vere* Cook) became abbot of Reading in 1520. He was an intimate friend of Henry VIII, but at the dissolution he refused to sur-render his abbey. He was martyred at Reading with two prebendaries of the abbey (doubtless monks).

HUGH of NOARA (St) Ab. OSB. Cist.
AC. Nov 17

d. p.1172. First abbot of the Cistercian abbey of Noara in Sicily, founded in 1172 by the community of Sambucina.

HUGH of LINCOLN (St) Bp. O. Cart.
RM. Nov 17

1140–1200. A native of Burgundy and a canon regular, who at the age of twenty joined the Carthusians. In 1175 he was invited by King Henry II to found the first English Charterhouse at Witham in Somerset, which he did in the face of obstacles of all kinds. In 1181 he was raised to the see of Lincoln, and gov-erned it zealously and wisely; the present cathedral of Lincoln was begun during his episcopate. He died, aged sixty, deeply lamented by all, especially by the Jews, whom he had always defended and befriended. At his magnificent funeral the kings of England and Scot-land helped to carry the bier. Canonized in 1220.

HUGOLINUS of GUALDO (Bl) C. OSA.
AC. Jan 1

d. 1260. A hermit of St Augustine who ruled as prior a monastery of that order at Gualdo, in Umbria. Cult approved in 1919.

HUGOLINUS ZEFFERINI (Bl) C. OSA.
AC. March 22

d. c.1470(?). An Augustinian hermit friar who lived at Cortona (or perhaps Mantua). Cult confirmed in 1804.

HUGOLINUS (St) M. OFM.
RM. Oct 10

See Daniel, Samuel, etc.

HUGOLINUS MAGALOTTI (Bl) C. Tert. OFM.
AC. Dec 11

d. 1373. A native of Camerino who lived as a hermit after having joined the third order of the Friars Minor. Cult con-firmed in 1856.

HUMBELINE (St) Abs. OSB.
AC. Feb 12
1092–1135. A younger sister of St Bernard of Clairvaux. She married a rich man and was leading a worldly life when a visit to her brother in Clairvaux resulted in her spiritual conversion. She asked and obtained her husband's consent to become a nun, and entered the Black Benedictine nunnery of Jully-les-Nonnais, near Troyes, of which she became abbess. She founded Tart nunnery for the Cistercians, but she herself remained a Black Benedictine at Jully, where she died in St Bernard's arms. Cult approved in 1763.

HUMBERT of SAVOY (Bl) C.
AC. March 4
1136–1188. Humbert III was king of Savoy, and was three, perhaps four times married. Coming to the throne at the age of thirteen, he learnt holiness and the art of government from Bl Amedius of Lausanne. Ever just and pious, in his old age he retired to the Cistercian abbey of Haute Combe, where he died in the Cistercian habit. Cult confirmed in 1838.

HUMBERT (St) Ab. OSB.
AC. March 25
d. c.680. A disciple of St Amandus who became the joint founder and first abbot of the abbey of Marolles in Flanders.

HUMBERT of ROMANS (Bl) C. OP.
PC. July 14
d. 1277. The fifth master general of the Dominicans. He was particularly successful in the development of the foreign missions, and in the definitive planning of the studies among the Friars Preachers. Cult not yet confirmed.

HUMBERT (Bl) C. OSB. AC. Oct 26
d. 7th or 8th cent. Monk of Fritzlar in Hesse and prior of Buraburg.

HUMBERT (Bl) Ab. OSB. Cist.
PC. Dec 7
d. 1148. A monk of Chaise-Dieu who went over to Clairvaux in 1117. St Bernard made him prior and then sent him as abbot to Igny (1127). Humbert sought to return to Clairvaux, but St Bernard ordered him back to Igny under pain of monastic excommunication. On Humbert's death St Bernard delivered a most touching homily to his brethren at Clairvaux.

HUMILIANA de'CERCHI (Bl) Tert. OFM.
AC. May 19
1220–1246. Daughter of a Florentine family, she married at the age of sixteen. After the early death of her husband she became the first cloistered Franciscan tertiary at Florence. Cult approved by Innocent XII.

HUMILIS of BISIGNANO (Bl) C. OFM.
AC. Nov 27
1582–1637. A native of Bisignano in Calabria, and a Franciscan lay-brother. He became so widely known for his sanctity that he was called to Rome, where both Gregory XV and Urban VIII consulted him. Beatified in 1882.

HUMILITAS (or ROSANNA) (St) Abs. OSB. Vall.
AC. May 22
1226–1310. Born at Faenza, in the Romagna, at fifteen years of age she was compelled to marry a frivolous young man named Ugoletto. After nine years of married life he became seriously ill, and on his recovery consented to become a religious and allowed Humilitas to receive the veil. She first lived as a recluse near the Vallumbrosan church of St Apollinaris where her husband was a monk, and later, persuaded by the general of the Vallumbrosans, founded and ruled two houses for Vallumbrosan nuns.

HUMPHREY (St) H.   RM. June 12
Otherwise Onuphrius, q.v.

HUMPHREY (HUNFRID) (St) Bp.
OSB.   AC. March 8
d. 871. A monk of the Benedictine
abbey of Prüm, in the Ardennes, at the
time of its greatest splendour. He became bishop of Therouanne and ruled
at the same time the abbey of St Bertin.
He was a source of strength and comfort
to the people during the Norman invasion. He had the feast of the Assumption of Our Lady kept with especial
splendour in his diocese.

HUMPHREY MIDDLEMORE (Bl)
M. O. Cart.   AC. June 19
d. 1535. A Carthusian monk, belonging
to the London Charterhouse, who was
hanged at Tyburn with two others of his
brethren. Beatified in 1886.

HUNA (St) C. OSB.   AC. Feb 13
d. c.690. A monk-priest at Ely under St
Etheldreda, whom he assisted in her
last moments, afterwards retiring to a
hermitage in the Fens where he died.

HUNEGUND (St) N. OSB.
                          AC. Aug 25
d. c.690. According to her biographer,
she was compelled to marry against her
wish, and prevailed on her bridegroom
to accompany her to Rome, where she
received the veil at the hands of Pope
St Vitalian. They returned to their
country and Hunegund entered the
nunnery of Homblières, while her former betrothed served there as chaplain.

HUNGER (St) Bp.   AC. Dec 22
d. 866. Bishop of Utrecht from 856.
During the Norman invasion he fled to
Prüm, where he died.

HUNNA (St) W.   AC. Apr 15
d. 679. The wife of an Alsatian nobleman. Her neighbours called her "the
holy washerwoman", because she was
wont to help them all in that capacity.
Canonized in 1520.

HYACINTH (St) M.   RM. Feb 10
See Zoticus, Irenaeus, etc.

HYACINTH (St) M.   RM. July 3
d. c.120. A chamberlain of the emperor
Trajan at Caesarea in Cappadocia. He
was imprisoned and offered as susten-
ance only meat consecrated to idols.
This he constantly refused and died in
consequence of starvation.

HYACINTH (St) M.   RM. July 17
? A martyr of Amastris in Paphlagonia,
put to death for having cut down a tree
consecrated to an idol.

HYACINTH (St) M.   RM. July 26
d. ? c.110. A martyr under Trajan. His
existence is certain, but his Acts are
thoroughly untrustworthy.

HYACINTH (St) C. OP. RM. Aug 17
1185-1257. Surnamed "the Apostle of
Poland". Silesian by birth, and a canon
of Cracow, he received the Dominican
habit from St Dominic himself. In
three apostolic journeys he is said to
have travelled through Poland, Pome-
ania, Denmark, Sweden, Norway, Russia, and as far as Tibet and China.
However, the details of his life are very
uncertain. He died at Cracow and was
canonized in 1594.

HYACINTH, ALEXANDER and
TIBURTIUS (SS) MM. RM. Sept 9
? Martyrs who are said to have suffered
at some place in the Sabine country,
about thirty miles from Rome.

HYACINTH ORFANEL (Bl) M.
OP.   AC. Sept 10
1578-1622. A native of Llana, Valencia,
Spain. He joined the Dominicans at
Barcelona and was sent to the missions
of Japan. He was burnt alive at Nagasaki, after many years of apostolic
labours. Beatified in 1867.

HYACINTH (St) M.   RM. Sept 11
See Protus and Hyacinth.

**HYACINTH, QUINTUS, FELI-
CIAN and LUCIUS (SS) MM.**
RM. Oct 29
? Martyrs of Lucania in S. Italy.

**HYACINTH CASTAÑEDA (Bl) M.
OP.   AC. Nov 7**
d. 1773. Born at Sétavo in the diocese
of Valencia, Spain. After his profession
as a Friar Preacher and his ordination
to the priesthood, he was sent to the
mission, first to China, then to Tonkin,
where he was beheaded. Beatified in
1906.

**HYACINTH of MARISCOTTI (St)
Tert. V. OFM.   RM. Jan 30**
1585–1640. A lady of Viterbo, who, at
the age of twenty, was passed over by the
Marquis Cassizucchi in favour of her
younger sister, whom he married. Hyacinth became so very troublesome that
her family almost forced her into the
convent of Franciscan tertiaries at
Viterbo. Here, she began by scandal-
ously ignoring or transgressing the Rule,
was then converted to better ways, but
relapsed, and finally, during twenty-
four years, gave herself up to a life of
heroic humility, prayer, patience and
penance. Canonized in 1807.

HYDROC (St) C.   AC. May 5
5th cent. The patron saint of Lanhydroc
in Cornwall.

**HYGBALD (HUGBALD, HIG-
BALD, HYBALD) (St) H. OSB.**
AC. Sept 18
d. c.690. An abbot in Lincolnshire to
whom several churches are dedicated.

HYGINUS (St) Pope M. RM. Jan 11
d. c.142. The probable dates of his
pontificate are 138 to 142; but even this
much is not certain. It is also doubtful
whether he died a martyr. His pontificate was occupied with the struggle
against Gnosticism.

HYPATIUS (St) M.   RM. June 3
See Lucillian, Claudius, etc.

HYPATIUS (St) C.   RM. June 17
d. c.450. Born in Phrygia, at the age of
nineteen he embraced the solitary life,
first in Thrace, and then at Chalcedon
in Bithynia, where he became abbot of
a flourishing *laura*. He was a determined opponent of Nestorianism.

HYPATIUS (St) M.   RM. June 18
See Leontius, Hypatius and Theodulus.

**HYPATIUS and ANDREW (SS)
MM.   RM. Aug 29**
d. 735. Natives of Lydia. Hypatius was
a bishop, and Andrew a priest. They
were martyred at Constantinople under
Leo the Isaurian for their defence of the
veneration of sacred images.

HYPATIUS (St) Bp. M. RM. Nov 14
d. c.325. A bishop of Gangra in Paphlagonia, who attended the council of
Nicaea and was a prominent defender
of the divinity of Christ. While on his
return from Nicaea, he was attacked by
a band of heretics and stoned to death.

HYPERECHIOS (St) C. PC. Aug 7
? An Egyptian desert father; a collection of 160 sayings attributed to him
were published by Rosweyde's *Vitae
Patrum*.

HYWYN (St) C.   AC. Jan 6
d. p.516. Probably a companion of St
Cadfan on his return journey (516) from
Brittany to Cornwall and Wales. He is
said to have been the founder of Aber-
daron in Carnarvonshire. Several
churches in W. England known as St
Owen's or St Ewen's possibly have him
for their titular saint.

I

IA (HIA, IVES) (St) VM.
AC. Feb 3

d. 450. An Irish maiden, sister of St Ercus, who crossed into Cornwall, with SS Fingar, Piala, and other missionaries, and there suffered martyrdom at the mouth of the Hayle river. She has left her name to St Ives in Cornwall.

IA and Comp. (SS) MM.
RM. Aug 4

d. 360. A Greek slave, who suffered martyrdom in Persia with many other Christian captives (the figure usually given is nine thousand) during the persecution of King Shapur II. The name signifies "violet", and the circumstances attending his martyrdom are not known.

IAGO (St) Apostle
RM. July 25

Note. An antiquated Spanish form of the name of St James. Iago is now always used with the prefixed hagiological title of Sant (Saint) in this way: Santiago.

IBAR (IBERIUS, IVOR) (St) C.
AC. Apr 23

5th cent. One of the missionaries—SS Kiaran, Ailbe, Declan, etc.—who evangelized Ireland at the time of, or as some writers hold, shortly before, St Patrick. St Ibar preached chiefly in Leinster and in Meath.

IDA of ARGENSOLLES (Bl) Abs. OSB. Cist.
AC. Jan 13

d. 1226. A Black Benedictine nun of St Leonard's, Liège, who was elected abbess of the Cistercian nunnery of Argensolles, in the diocese of Soissons.

IDA of HOHENFELS (Bl) N. OSB.
AC. Feb 24

d. *c.*1195. Wife of Eberhard, count of Spanheim, and, after his death, a Benedictine nun at Bingen.

IDA of BOULOGNE (Bl) W.
AC. Apr 13

1040–1113. A daughter of Godfrey IV, duke of Lorraine, descended from Charlemagne. She was the mother of Godfrey and Baldwin de Bouillon. After the death of her husband she endowed several monasteries in Picardy, herself living as a Benedictine oblate under the obedience of the abbot of St Vaast.

IDA of LOUVAIN (Bl) N. OSB. Cist.
PC. Apr 13

d. *c.*1300. A native of Louvain. She joined the Cistercians at the nunnery of Rossendael, near Malines, where she was favoured by God with a life-long series of amazing supernatural charismata.

IDA of NIVELLES (Bl) N. OSB.
AC. May 8

d. 652. She is also named Itta or Iduberga. She was the wife of Pepin of Landen, after whose death (640) she became a Benedictine at Nivelles under her own daughter St Gertrude.

IDA of HERZFELD (St) W.
AC. Sept 4

d. *c.*813. Great-granddaughter of Charles Martel. She married and was very happy in her married life; but lost her husband very young. She then founded the nunnery of Herzfeld in Westphalia, devoted herself to good works, and died at the convent.

IDA of TOGGENBURG (Bl) N. OSB. AC. Nov 3

1156–1226. She married a Count Henry of Toggenburg, to whom she bore no child, and from whom she suffered much persecution. She escaped, and at last succeeded in obtaining her husband's consent to her becoming a nun in the Benedictine convent of Fieshingen.

IDABERGA (several)

Otherwise Edburga, q.v.

IDESBALD (Bl) Ab. OSB. Cist. AC. Apr 18

1100–1167. Born in Flanders, he spent his youth at the court of the count of Flanders. In 1135 he was made canon of Furnes, but resigned his office to become a Cistercian at the abbey of our Lady of the Dunes on the sand-hills between Dunkirk and Nieuport. He became the third abbot and ruled for twelve years. Cult confirmed in 1894.

IDUS (St) Bp. AC. July 14

5th cent. A disciple of St Patrick by whom he was baptized and appointed bishop of Alt-Fadha in Leinster.

IGNATIUS of ANTIOCH (St) Bp. M. RM. Feb 1

d. c.107. Surnamed Theophorus (the God-bearer). Bishop of Antioch in Syria for forty years. Under Trajan he was carried to Rome, where he was thrown to the wild beasts in the amphitheatre during the public games. On his way to Rome he wrote seven epistles, which are still extant, and which show the whole system of Christianity—doctrinal, sacramental and hierarchical —as perfect then as it is today. His relics are kept at St Peter's, Rome, and his

name is mentioned in the canon of the Roman Mass.

IGNATIUS of AFRICA (St) M. RM. Feb 3

See Laurentinus, Ignatius and Celerina.

IGNATIUS de LACONI (St) C. OFM. Cap. AC. May 11

1701–1781. Vincent de Laconi was born in Sardinia of parents of modest means. His childish devotion was so remarkable he would be at the church doors before dawn waiting in prayer for them to be opened. Received with some difficulty into the Franciscan Order, he made profession as Br Ignatius in 1722. He passed his life in menial tasks and in begging for his convent at Cagliari. Illiterate, he loved to listen to the Gospels, especially the Passion of Christ being read, and was favoured with the gifts of prophecy and miracles. He would pass whole hours in prayer before the tabernacle. Canonized 1951.

IGNATIUS DELGADO (Bl) Bp. M. OP. AC. July 11

1761–1838. A Spaniard by birth, Ignatius Delgado y Cebrián professed the Dominican rule and was sent to the missions in Tonkin. He laboured for nearly fifty years and was appointed vicar apostolic of E. Tonkin and consecrated bishop. He died in his cage at Annam from hunger and exposure. Beatified in 1900.

IGNATIUS de AZEVEDO and Comp. (BB) MM. SJ. AC. July 15

d. 1570. A band of forty Portuguese and Spanish Jesuit missionaries, who were put to death by the Huguenot skipper, Jacques Sourie, near the Canary Islands, while on their way to the West Indies. Ignatius was the superior and leader of the band. He was born at Coimbra, where he joined the Society of Jesus in

1548. He was a religious of outstanding ability, highly revered by his superiors. Cult officially confirmed in 1854.

IGNATIUS of LOYOLA (St)
Founder   RM. July 31
1491–1556. Iñigo de Recalde de Loyola was born on the estate of his family at Loyola in the Basque province of Guipuzcoa (Spain) and, after some time as a page at court, joined the army and was grievously wounded at the siege of Pampeluna in 1521. On his recovery he turned his mind to the service of the militant church. He prepared himself by a retreat at Montserrat and Manresa, where he wrote his epoch-making classic, *The Book of Spiritual Exercises*. At Paris he gathered nine companions and together they took their first vows at the church of Montmartre. Ignatius's aim was simply this: to work for the greater glory of God under the obedience of the pope. In 1537 he called his little band the Society of Jesus and in April 1541, all took their final vows in the Benedictine basilica of St Paul-outside-the-Walls, Rome. Ignatius was naturally elected the first general and ruled the Society until his death. Before this time the original band had already become a veritable army scattered throughout the world—from Japan in the Far East to the furthermost West Indies. Ignatius was canonized in 1622.

IGNATIUS JORJES (Bl) M.
**   AC. Sept 10**
d. 1622. The four-year-old son of Dominic Jorjes and Isabel Fernandez. He was beheaded with his mother at Nagasaki (see Charles Spinola).

IGNATIUS of CONSTANTINOPLE
(St) Bp.   RM. Oct 23
c.799–877. Son of the Byzantine emperor Michael, he was successively monk, priest, abbot, and patriarch (842)

of his native Constantinople. He stood firm against intrigue and corruption, even in high places, and openly refused holy communion to Bardas Caesar on account of his public incest. Ignatius was driven from the see, and Photius intruded. After nine years Ignatius was recalled and governed the see till his death.

ILDEPHONSUS (St) Bp. RM. Jan 23
607–667. Nephew of St Eugene of Toledo. He was born also at Toledo, studied at Seville under St Isidore, became monk and abbot of Agli (Agalia), on the Tagus near Toledo, and was made archbishop of that city in 657. He was responsible for the unification of the Spanish liturgy and excelled as a writer, chiefly on Mariology.

ILLADAN (ILLATHAN, IOLLA-
DHAN) (St) Bp.   AC. June 10
6th cent. Bishop of Rathliphthen (now Rathlihen) in Offaly, Ireland.

ILLIDIUS (ALLYRE) (St) Bp.
**   RM. July 7**
d. 385. The fourth bishop of Clermont, France. St Gregory of Tours had a great veneration for him.

ILLOG (St) C.   AC. Aug 8
Otherwise Ellidius, q.v.

ILLTYD (ILLTUT) (St) Ab.
**   AC. Nov 6**
d. c.505. One of the most celebrated of the Welsh saints, but unfortunately the details of his life have not reached us in trustworthy form. From being a courtier and minister, he embraced the monastic life under St Cadoc, and later founded the great abbey of Llan-Illtut, or Llantwit, whence issued most of the Welsh saints of that period. According to some the original foundation was on Caldey Island. He is said to have died in Brittany.

ILLUMINATA (St) V.   RM. Nov 29
d. *c*.320. A maiden of Todi, in Italy, where she is still held in great veneration.

ILLUMINATUS (St) Mk. OSB.
RM. May 11
d. *c*.1000. A Benedictine monk of the abbey of San Mariano, in his native township of Sanseverino in the Marches of Ancona.

ILLUMINATUS (St) C. OFM.
AC. May 11
d. *c*.1230. Said to have been a disciple of St Francis of Assisi. He is often confused with his homonym of Sanseverino.

IMANA of LOSS (IMAINA, HIM-
MANNA, IMAINE) (Bl) Abs. OSB.
PC. Oct 21
d. 1270. Cistercian abbess of Salzinnes, near Namur, and afterwards of Flines, in the diocese of Cambrai.

IMELDA LAMBERTINI (Bl) V.
OP.   AC. May 12
d. 1333. Daughter of Count Egano Lambertini of Bologna, she was a pupil at the Dominican convent of that city, and "is stated to have received her first holy communion miraculously at the age of eleven, and to have died immediately after". (Attwater.) Cult confirmed in 1826.

IMELIN (St) Ab.   AC. March 10
Otherwise Emilian, q.v.

IMMA (IMMINA) (St) Abs. OSB.
AC. Nov 25
c.700–752. A native of Würzburg and abbess of a nunnery at Karlburg in Franconia.

INA and ETHELBURGA (SS)
PC. Sept 8
d. 727. Ina was king of Wessex from 688 till 726. As such he is best remembered

as the restorer of Glastonbury. About the year 726 he resigned and, with his wife Ethelburga, journeyed to Rome, where he ended his days in practices of piety and penance. They have never been formally recognized as saints.

INAN (St) H.   AC. Aug 18
Otherwise Evan, q.v.

INDALETIUS (St) Bp. RM. May 15
See Torquatus, Ctesiphon, etc.

INDES, DOMNA, AGAPES and
THEOPHILA (SS) MM. RM. Dec 28
d. 303. A group of martyrs, who suffered at Nicomedia under Diocletian.

INDRACT (St) M.   AC. Feb 5
d. *c*.710. An old legend makes him an Irish chieftain, who, on his return from a Roman pilgrimage, was put to death, with his sister St Dominica (Drusa) and others, by heathen Saxons, near Glastonbury, where their relics were enshrined. A still later legend has made them contemporaries of St Patrick.

INÉS de BENIGANIM (Bl) V.
OSA. Erem.   AC. Jan 21
1625–1696. Born near Valencia, in Spain, she entered the nunnery of Augustinian hermitesses at Beniganim with the new name of Josepha Maria. In Spain she is usually called by her baptismal name as above. Beatified in 1888.

INÉS, INEZ (*several*)
Note. The Spanish and Portuguese forms respectively of the name Agnes, q.v.

INGEN (St) M.   RM. Dec 20
See Ammon, Zeno, etc.

INGENUINUS (St) Bp. RM. Feb 5
Otherwise Genuinus, q.v.

IÑIGO (St) Ab. OSB.   RM. June 1
Otherwise Eneco, q.v.

INISCHOLUS   RM. Apr 29
See Corfu, Martyrs of.

INJURIOSUS and SCHOLASTICA (SS)   AC. May 25
d. *c*.550. A married couple of Auvergne, who lived the whole of their married life as brother and sister, *"Les Deux Amants"*.

**INNOCENT of TORTONA (St) Bp.
    RM. Apr 17**
d. *c*.350. He was a confessor under Diocletian, being scourged and just escaping death. After Constantine's peace, he was ordained a priest and consecrated bishop of Tortona in Italy (*c*.326).

INNOCENT (St) M.   RM. June 17
See Isaurus, Innocent, etc.

INNOCENT (St) Bp.   AC. June 19
d. 559. Bishop of Le Mans, in France, for over forty years.

**INNOCENT V. (Bl) Pope OP.
    RM. June 22**
1245–1277. Born at Tarentaise in Burgundy, he entered the Dominican order and acquired great fame as a theologian and as a preacher. In 1272 he was made archbishop of Lyons, and during his episcopate the general council was held in that city, in which he took a prominent part. Created cardinal of Ostia, he was made pope in 1276, but died only a few months later. Beatified 1898.

**INNOCENT, SEBASTIA (SABBATIA) and Comp. (SS) MM.
    RM. July 4**
? A group of thirty-two martyrs who suffered at Sirmium, now Mitrovica, in the Balkans.

INNOCENT I (St) Pope RM. July 28
d. 417. A native of Albano, near Rome, St Innocent was pope from 402 till 417. The outstanding event in his pontificate was the sack of Rome by the Goth Alaric in 410. He firmly maintained the supremacy of the Roman see, both in the West, in the case of the African synods against Pelagianism, and in the East, witness the appeal of St John Chrysostom.

INNOCENT XI (Bl) Pope AC. Aug 12
1611–1689. Born at Como, he was elected Pope in 1676. He was outstanding for charity, evangelical simplicity and poverty. He withstood the autocracy of Louis XIV of France, strove to check nepotism, to stir up exemplary life among the clergy and to encourage catechetical instruction. He condemned Jansenism, Quietism and the errors of Molinos. Beatified 1956.

INNOCENT (St) M.   RM. Sept 22
See Theban Legion.

**INNOCENTS, The Holy (SS) MM.
    RM. Dec 28**
1st cent. From a very early date "the men children that were in Bethlehem and in all the borders thereof" (Matt. II, 16), murdered by Herod, have been liturgically venerated as martyrs. Prudentius most fittingly styles them *Flores Martyrum*. Their number is not known, and this has led to the multiplication of their relics in many churches.

IPHIGENIA (St) V.   RM. Sept 21
1st cent. An alleged maiden of Ethiopia converted by St Matthew the apostle and evangelist.

**IRAIS (HERAIS, RHAIS) (St) VM.
    RM. Sept 22**
d. *c*.300. An Egyptian maiden of Alexandria, or of Antinoë, beheaded under Diocletian.

IRCHARD (St) Bp.   AC. Aug 24
7th cent. An apostle of the Picts and
disciple of St Ternan, born in Kincardineshire, and said to have been consecrated bishop in Rome by St Gregory
the Great.

IRENAEUS (St) M.   RM. Feb 10
See Zoticus, Irenaeus, etc.

**IRENAEUS of SIRMIUM (St) Bp.
M.   RM. March 25**
d. 304. A bishop in Pannonia (Hungary),
who suffered martyrdom under Diocletian at Sirmium (Mitrovica). His
Acts are authentic and most touching.

IRENAEUS (St) M.   RM. March 26
See Theodore, Irenaeus, etc.

IRENAEUS (St) M.   RM. Apr 1
See Quintian and Irenaeus.

**IRENAEUS, PEREGRINUS and
IRENE (SS) MM.   RM. May 5**
d. c.300. Martyrs of Thessalonica, burnt
at the stake under Diocletian.

**IRENAEUS of LYONS (St) Bp. M.
RM. June 28**
c.125–202. A native of Asia Minor and
a disciple of St Polycarp, who was a
pupil of St John the Apostle. He
migrated to Gaul, and became bishop
of Lyons (c.177). Tradition adds that
he was a martyr, but of this we have no
proof. St Irenaeus is the first great
ecclesiastical writer of the West. His
work against Gnosticism is a witness to
the apostolic tradition, derived from St
John: in it we find already a testimony
to the primacy of the Roman see.

**IRENAEUS and MUSTIOLA (SS)
MM.   RM. July 3**
d. 273. Irenaeus, a deacon, and Mustiola,
a noble lady, were martyred at Chiusi in
Tuscany under Aurelian for having

ministered to other martyrs and buried
their bodies.

**IRENAEUS and ABUNDIUS (SS)
MM.   RM. Aug 26**
d. c.258. They were Roman martyrs.
According to their *Passio* they were
drowned in the public sewers during the
persecution of Valerian.

**IRENAEUS, ANTONY, THEO-
DORE, SATURNINUS, VICTOR
and Comp. (SS) MM.   RM. Dec 15**
d. c.258. A group of twenty-two martyrs, who suffered under Valerian.

IRENE (St) VM.   RM. Apr 5
d. 304. The sister of SS Agape and
Chionia, q.v.

IRENE (St) M.   RM. May 5
See Irenaeus, Peregrinus, etc.

IRENE (St) M.   RM. Sept 18
See Sophia and Irene.

IRENE (St) VM.   RM. Oct 20
d. c.653. A Portuguese nun who suffered
death in defence of her chastity. Her
shrine is at Santarem (*Sancta Irenes*)
the ancient Scalabris. The legend as
handed down to us is full of fiction, but
the essential facts are certain.

IRENION (St) Bp.   RM. Dec 16
d. 389. A bishop of Gaza in Palestine in
the time of Theodosius the Great.

**IRMENGARD (Bl) Abs. OSB.
AC. July 16**
d. 866. Daughter of King Louis the
German, grandson of Charlemagne. By
her father she was appointed abbess,
first of Buchau and then of Chiemsee.
Cult confirmed in 1928.

IRMINA (St) Abs. OSB. RM. Dec 24
d. 708. Daughter of Dagobert II. At

the age of fifteen she was given in marriage but on the day of her wedding her betrothed died. She then persuaded her father to build for her the nunnery of Oehren (*Horreum*) near Trèves, under the Benedictine Rule. She was a generous benefactress of both Celtic and Saxon monks; and built Echternach for St Willibrord (698). She died at the monastery of Weissenburg, another foundation of her father's.

ISAAC JOGUES (St) M. SJ.
    AC. March 16
d. 1646 (Oct 18). A Jesuit missionary who arrived in Canada in 1636, and after several heroic adventures, was tomahawked by the Mohawks in an Iroquois village. Canonized in 1930.

ISAAC (St) H. **RM. Apr 11**
d. *c*.550. A Syrian monk, who fled from the Monophysite persecution and founded a *laura* at Monteluco, near Spoleto, in Umbria. He was one of the restorers of eremitical life in 6th-century Italy.

ISAAC (ISACIUS) (St) M.
    RM. Apr 21
See Apollo, Isacius and Crotates.

ISAAC (St) Ab. **AC. May 30**
d. *c*.410. A brave defender of the Catholic faith against the Arian emperor Valens, whom he publicly denounced. He narrowly escaped death, and became a monk, and eventually abbot, of a large monastery at Constantinople.

ISAAC (St) M. **RM. June 3**
d. 852. Born at Cordova, in Spain, he became very proficient in Arabic and was made a notary under the Moorish government. He resigned this office to embrace the monastic life at Tabanos, about seven miles from Cordova. In a

public debate at Cordova he denounced Mohammed and was put to death at the age of twenty-seven.

ISAAC the GREAT (St) Bp.
    AC. Sept 9
d. *c*.440. Son of the Armenian patriarch (or katholikos) St Nerses the Great, to whose office he succeeded. He is the real founder of the Armenian church. He translated a large part of the Bible, founded monasteries, and was practically the only ruler—ecclesiastical and civil—of the Armenians. He died a centenarian.

ISAAC (ISACIUS) (St) Bp. M.
    RM. Sept 21
? An Eastern martyr, honoured chiefly in Cyprus, of which he was Bishop.

ISAAC (St) M. OSB. **RM. Nov 12**
See Benedict, John, etc.

ISABEL FERNANDEZ (Bl) M.
    AC. Sept 10
d. 1622. A Spanish lady, widow of Dominic Jorjes, beheaded with her son Ignatius at Nagasaki, for having given shelter to Bl Charles Spinola, q.v. Beatified in 1867.

ISABELLA (St) Queen RM. July 8
Otherwise Elisabeth, q.v.

ISABELLE of FRANCE (Bl) V.
Poor Clare **AC. Feb 26**
d. 1270. The only sister of St Louis of France. She declined marriage with the emperor of Germany, and after the death of her mother, Blanche of Castile, founded the convent of Poor Clares at Longchamps, near Paris, where she lived as a nun, without, however, taking vows. Beatified in 1520.

ISACIUS (ISAAC) **RM. Apr 21**
See Apollo, Isacius and Crotates.

ISAIAS, SABAS and Comp. (SS)
MM.   RM. Jan 14
d. 309. Thirty-eight monks on Mt
Sinai, massacred by pagan Arabs. This
massacre was followed by several others
in the neighbourhood of the Red Sea.

ISAIAS BONER (Bl) C. OSA.
                          AC. Feb 8
d. 1471. Born at Cracow, where also he
studied theology. He joined the Augustinians and was employed chiefly in
teaching Scripture, which he did with
extraordinary zeal and success.

ISAIAS (St) M.   RM. Feb 16
See Elias, Jeremias, etc.

ISAIAS (ISAIAH) (St) Prophet
                          RM. July 6
d. c.681. One of the four greater prophets of the OT. Tradition tells us that
he was sawn in two by order of King
Manasses of Juda, and buried under an
oak tree. His tomb was still venerated
in the 5th century of our era.

ISARNUS (YSARN) of TOULOUSE
(St) Ab. OSB.   AC. Sept 24
d. 1048. Born at Marseilles, he was
educated, and became a monk and
abbot, at St Victor's, Marseilles. He was
famous for his charity, chiefly towards
criminals.

ISAURUS, INNOCENT, FELIX,
JEREMIAS and PEREGRINUS (SS)
MM.   RM. June 17
? Athenians who during one of the
persecutions concealed themselves in a
cave at Apollonia in Macedonia. On
being discovered they were beheaded.

ISBERGA (ITISBERGA) (St) V.
OSB.   AC. May 21
d. c.800. A supposed sister of Charlemagne. She was a nun at Aire (Aria) in
the Artois. She is venerated as the
patroness of Artois.

ISCHYRION and Comp. (SS) MM.
                 RM. June 1 and Dec 22
d. 250. Ischyrion was an Egyptian official who was impaled for the Faith under
Decius. The Ischyrion commemorated
in the RM. on June 1 is identical with
the one mentioned on Dec 22.

ISIDORA (St) V.   AC. May 1
c.365. A nun in an Egyptian monastery
who, to escape being honoured in the
cloister, fled to a desert hermitage where
she died.

ISIDORE of ANTIOCH (St) Bp. M.
                          RM. Jan 2
Baronius introduced this saint into the
RM. on the strength of a notice in the
Hieronymen martyrology which read:
In Antiochia Siridoni episcopi eiusdem
loci. No such bishop is known.

ISIDORE of NITRIA (St) Bp.
                          RM. Jan 2
4th cent. Mentioned by St Jerome as
"a holy venerable bishop" who had
welcomed him to Egypt. Some think
that he is identical with St Isidore of
Pelusium (Feb 4).

ISIDORE the EGYPTIAN (St) C.
                          RM. Jan 15
d. 404. An Egyptian priest, who was in
charge of the hospice for pilgrims at
Alexandria. He defended St Athanasius
and had much to suffer at the hands of
the Arians. Accused of Origenism by St
Jerome, Isidore went to Constantinople
where he was befriended by St John
Chrysostom.

ISIDORE of PELUSIUM (St) C.
                          RM. Feb 4
d. c.450. An Egyptian abbot of a monastery at Pelusium. He was much esteemed
by St Cyril of Alexandria. A great
number of his letters are still extant.

ISIDORE (St) M.   RM. Feb 5
The RM. places him at Alexandria, but he is probably a duplicate of Isidore of Chios (May 15) q.v.

ISIDORE of SEVILLE (St) Bp. and Dr.   RM. Apr 4
*c.*560–636. A native of Cartagena, in Spain, and brother to SS Leander, Fulgentius and Florentina. He was educated by St Leander whom he succeeded in the see of Seville in 600. He presided over several synods, reorganized the Spanish church, encouraged monastic life, completed the Mozarabic liturgical rite, was responsible for the decree of the council of Toledo in 633, and was himself an encyclopaedical writer on theology, scripture, biography, history, geography, astronomy and grammar. Declared Doctor of the Church by Benedict XIV.

ISIDORE (St) M.   RM. Apr 17
See Elias, Paul and Isidore.

**ISIDORE the FARMER (St) C.
                          RM. May 10**
d. 1170. A native of Madrid, he spent his whole life working in the fields on an estate just outside the city. He was married to St Mary de la Cabeza. Canonized in 1622 and venerated as the patron saint of Madrid.

**ISIDORE of CHIOS (St) M.
                          RM. May 15**
d. ? 251. A martyr of Chios under Decius.

ISIDORE (St) M.   AC. Aug 4
See Epiphanes and Isidore.

ISIDORE (St) M.   RM. Dec 14
See Heron, Arsenius, etc.

ISMAEL (St) Bp.   AC. June 16
6th cent. A disciple of St Teilo, and by him consecrated bishop. Several Welsh churches are dedicated to him.

ISMAEL (St) M.   RM. June 17
See Manuel, Sabel and Ismael.

**ISNARD de CHIAMPO (Bl) C. OP.
                          AC. March 22**
d. 1244. A native of Chiampo, diocese of Vicenza, he received the Dominican habit at the hands of St Dominic himself (1219) and was the founder and first prior of the friary at Pavia. It is narrated of him that, in spite of his mortified life, "he was excessively fat and people used to ridicule him about it when he was preaching". (Attwater h. l.) Cult confirmed in 1919.

ISSELL (ISSEY) (St) Bp. AC. Feb 9
Otherwise Teilo, q.v.

ISSERNINUS (St) Bp.   AC. Dec 6
See Auxilius, Isserninus and Secundinus.

ISSEY (St) Ab.   AC. Feb 9
Otherwise Teilo, q.v. Perhaps also a Cornish variant of Ita.

**ITA (YTHA, MEDA) (St) V.
                          AC. Jan 15**
d. *c.*570. In popular veneration among the Irish she is second only to St Bridget. She was a native of Drum in Co. Waterford. She founded the nunnery of Hy Conaill, in Co. Limerick and soon attracted thither large numbers of maidens. Her life is full of incredible anecdotes.

ITHAMAR (St) Bp.   AC. June 10
d. *c.*656. A native of Kent, and the first Anglo-Saxon to be appointed bishop, being promoted to the see of Rochester after St Paulinus.

**ITTA (IDUBERGA) (Bl) N. OSB.
                          AC. May 8**
Otherwise Ida of Nivelles, q.v.

IVAN (St) H.   AC. June 24
9th cent. A hermit in Bohemia, who had renounced a brilliant position at court. He was buried by St Ludmilla, duchess of Bohemia.

IVE (IVES) (St) VM.   AC. Feb 3
Otherwise Ia, q.v.

IVES (St) Bp.   AC. Apr 24
Otherwise Ivo, q.v.

IVETTA (JUTTA) (Bl) W.
AC. Jan 13
1158–1228. A Dutch mystic who was left a widow and the mother of two children at the age of eighteen. Consecrating her widowhood to God, she undertook the care of lepers, till she took to the solitary life at Huy, near Leyden. She spent more than forty years as a solitary, and was famous for discernment of spirits and gifts of counsel.

IVO (St) Bp.   AC. Apr 24
? According to the medieval legend he was a Persian bishop, who became a hermit in Huntingdonshire. The town of St Ives in Huntingdonshire takes its name from him (but not that in Cornwall).

IVO (YVO) HÉLORY (St) C.
RM. May 19
1253–1303. A native of Brittany, born near Tréguier. He studied at Paris and Orleans and he practised law in his native city, both in the ecclesiastical and in the civil courts. He defended the poor and unprotected as well as the rich and was called "the Advocate of the Poor". Canonized in 1347, and venerated by lawyers as their patron saint.

IVO of CHARTRES (St) Bp. OSA.
AC. May 23
d. 1115. The provost of the Augustinian canons regular of Saint-Quentin, who in 1091 was made bishop of Chartres. He was renowned for his knowledge of canon law, and was consulted by King Philip of France on difficult canonical questions. Upright and just, Ivo opposed the rapacity of ecclesiastical dignitaries. He wrote much on canon law.

IVOR (St) Bp.   AC. Apr 23
Otherwise Ibar, q.v.

J

JACOBINUS de' CANEPACI (Bl) C. OC. AC. March 3
1438–1508. A native of the diocese of Vercelli, in Piedmont, and a Carmelite lay-brother there. Cult approved in 1845.

JACOPONE da TODI (Bl) C. OFM. PC. Dec 25
d. 1306. Jacopone Benedetti was a native of Todi, who read law at Bologna, married, and lived in easy circumstances. In 1268 he lost his wife and his sorrow knew no bounds. He became a "fool for Christ's sake" and eventually joined the Friars Minor. Unfortunately his tempestuous temperament led him to join the party of the Franciscan Spirituals; he wrote against the pope and was put in prison. He is the alleged author of the *Stabat Mater*, etc. Cult never confirmed.

JACUT and GUETHENOC (SS) CC. AC. Feb 8
5th cent. Sons of SS Fragan and Gwen, and brothers of the more celebrated St Gwenaloe or Winwaloë. They became disciples of St Budoc, and like him were driven from Britain by the invading Saxons.

JADER (St) Bp. M. RM. Sept 10
See Nemesian, Felix, etc.

JADWIGA (*several*)
Otherwise Hedwig, q.v.

JAMBERT (St) Bp. OSB. AC. Aug 12
d. 790. Abbot of St Augustine's, Canterbury, chosen to succeed St Bregwin as archbishop in that see (766).

JAMES (*several*)
Note. James is the English form of the Hebrew Jacob, latinized into Jacobus. Hence the modern variants in different languages: in Italian, Giacomo; in French, Jacques; in Spanish, Santiago, Iago, Jaime, Diego; in Portuguese, Iago, Diogo; in Catalan, Jaume.

JAMES of TARENTAISE (St) Bp. AC. Jan 16
d. ? 429. A Syrian by origin he became a monk and a disciple of St Honoratus at Lérins and venerated at Chambéry as an apostle of Savoy and the first bishop of Tarentaise.

JAMES the HERMIT (St) C. RM. Jan 28
6th cent. The RM. says: "In Palestine the memory of St James the Hermit, who, after a lapse from the faith, lay hid long in a tomb for penance, and, renowned for miracles, passed to the Lord." A later legend changes the "lapse from the faith" into one of homicide, committed under most romantic circumstances.

JAMES the ALMSGIVER (Bl) C. or M. AC. Jan 28
d. 1304. Born near Chiusi in Lombardy, Bl James studied law, but on attaining manhood became a priest and restored a ruined hospital, where he tended the sick and gave legal advice gratuitously. Having discovered that the former revenues of this hospital had been unjustly appropriated, he found it necessary to sue the bishop of Chiusi in the courts and won his case. The bishop

retaliated by hiring assassins who murdered the saint.

JAMES KISAI (St) M. SJ.
RM. Feb 5

d. 1597. A native of Japan, temporal coadjutor of the Society of Jesus, and catechist at Ozaka. He was crucified at Nagasaki at the age of sixty-four. Canonized in 1862.

JAMES SALÈS and WILLIAM SAULTEMOUCHE (BB) MM. SJ.
AC. Feb 7

d. 1593. James Salès born in 1556, joined the Society of Jesus. In 1592, in company with William Saultemouche, a temporal coadjutor, he was sent to preach at Aubenas in the Cévennes. His sermons, in which he attacked the teaching of the Protestants, were a great success. Early in February, 1593, a band of Huguenot raiders dragged the Jesuits before an improvised court of Calvinist ministers. After a heated theological discussion Salès was shot, while Saultemouche was stabbed to death. Both were beatified in 1926.

JAMES FENN (Bl) M.   AC. Feb 12
d. 1584. A native of Montacute, near Yeovil, Somerset, he was educated at Oxford (Corpus Christi College and Gloucester Hall), became a schoolmaster and married. On his wife's death he studied at Reims and was ordained priest (1580). Four years later he was martyred at Tyburn. Beatified in 1929.

JAMES of VITERBO (Bl) C. OSA. Erem.
AC. Feb 13

d. 1308. He became an Augustinian Hermit in his native city and taught theology with considerable renown, being known as *Doctor Speculativus*. He became bishop of Benevento, and was transferred to Naples in 1303. Cult confirmed by Pius X.

JAMES CARVALHO and Comp. (BB) MM. SJ.
AC. Feb 25

d. 1624. A Portuguese Jesuit who laboured as a missionary in the Far East. Together with sixty other Christians he was slowly martyred by exposure to cold at Sendai in Japan. They were beatified 1867.

JAMES CAPOCCI (Bl) Bp. OSA.
AC. March 14

d. 1308. Born at Viterbo. From being an Augustinian friar he was promoted (1302) to the see of Benevento and in 1303 transferred to Naples. Cult approved in 1911.

JAMES BIRD (Bl) M.
AC. March 25

d. 1593. A native of Winchester who, at the age of nineteen, was hanged in that city for being reconciled to the Church. Beatified in 1929.

JAMES of PADUA (Bl) M. OFM.
AC. Apr 9

See Bl Thomas of Tolentino and Comp.

JAMES of CERTALDO (Bl) C. OSB. Cam.
AC. Apr 13

d. 1292. James Guidi was born at Certaldo, the son of a knight of Volterra. He joined the Camaldolese Benedictines at the abbey of SS Clement and Justus at Volterra. He spent there sixty years, during forty of which he acted as parish priest of the abbey church. His father and his brother joined the abbey as lay-brothers. Twice he refused the abbacy.

JAMES of CERQUETO (Bl) C. OSA.
AC. Apr 17

d. 1367. A native of Cerqueto, near Perugia. He joined the Augustinian friars in the latter city. Cult approved in 1895.

JAMES D'OLDO (Bl) C. Tert.
OFM.   AC. Apr 19
d. 1404. A native of Lodi who married and for a time gave himself up to pleasure and good living. He was converted to higher things during a time of pestilence, became, with his wife, a Franciscan tertiary, turned his house into a church, and eventually was ordained priest.

JAMES DUCKETT (Bl) M.
AC. Apr 19
d. 1602. A native of Gilfortrigs, Skelsmergh, Westmorland, who became a convert and settled as a bookseller in London. After several terms of imprisonment, amounting to altogether nine years, for printing and selling Catholic books, he was hanged at Tyburn for the same reason. Beatified in 1929.

JAMES BELL (Bl) M.   AC. Apr 20
d. 1584. A native of Warrington, Lancs, and educated at Oxford. He was ordained priest under Queen Mary, conformed to the state Church under Elizabeth, repented and was reconciled to the true Church. On this account he was hanged at Lancaster in his sixty-fourth year. Beatified in 1929.

JAMES of PERSIA (St) M.
RM. Apr 22
4th cent. A priest martyr under Shapur II.

JAMES of BITETTO (Bl) C. OFM.
AC. Apr 27
d. c.1485. Surnamed also "of Sclavonia", or "of Illyricum", or "of Zara", or "of Dalmatia". He was a native of Sebenico in Dalmatia, and donned the Franciscan habit as a lay-brother at Zara; but spent most of his life at the friary of Bitetto, near Bari, in S. Italy. Cult approved by Innocent XII.

JAMES of NUMIDIA (St) M.
RM. Apr 30
See Marianus, James, etc.

JAMES the LESS (St) Apostle
RM. May 1
d. c.62. James the Less (*Jacobus Minor*) or "the Younger", surnamed also "the Just", was a cousin of our Lord, and one of the twelve. After the Resurrection he became the first bishop of Jerusalem. He is the author of one of the canonical epistles. He was martyred at Jerusalem by being thrown from a pinnacle of the temple and then stoned to death.

JAMES WALWORTH (Bl) M.
O. Cart.   AC. May 11
d. 1537. A monk of the London Charterhouse, hanged in chains at York under Henry VIII. Beatified in 1886.

JAMES of NOCERA (Bl) C. OSB.
AC. May 27
d. 1300. A native of Nocera in Umbria, and a monk of Santa Croce di'Fontavellana.

JAMES BERTONI (Bl) C. OSM.
AC. May 30
c.1444–1483. A native of Faenza. At the age of nine he joined the Servites, whom he served as procurator of the friary from the time of his ordination till his death. Cult confirmed in 1766.

JAMES SALOMONE (Bl) C. OP.
AC. May 31
1231–1314. A native of Venice who joined the Dominicans at Santa Maria Celeste, in that city, and held office in several houses of the Order until he died of cancer at Forlí. Cult approved in 1526.

JAMES of STREPAR (Bl) Bp. OFM.
AC. June 1
c.1350–1411. Of Polish birth, he joined

the Franciscans and worked very successfully as vicar-general of the Franciscan missions among the schismatics and pagans of W. Russia. In 1392 he was appointed archbishop of Halicz in Gallicia. Cult approved in 1791.

JAMES BUZABALIAO (St) M.
RM. June 3
d. 1886. Son of the royal bark-cloth maker and a soldier of King Mwanga of Uganda. He was baptized in 1885 and burnt alive at Namuyongo in the following year. See Uganda (Martyrs of).

JAMES of TOUL (St) Bp.
AC. June 23
d. 769. Born probably at Bertigny in Haute Marne. It is commonly asserted that he was a monk of Hornbach in the diocese of Metz, before he was raised to the see of Toul (756). He was a great benefactor of the Benedictines. He died at Dijon, praying before the tomb of St Benignus, while on his return from a pilgrimage to Rome.

JAMES LACOP (St) M. O. Praem.
RM. July 9
d. 1572. A native of Oudenarden, Flanders. He was a Norbertine at Middelburg, and in 1566 he apostatized, wrote and preached against the Church; then he repented, returned to his abbey and was martyred by the Calvinists with the group of Gorkum martyrs, q.v. Canonized in 1867.

JAMES of VORAGINE (Bl) Bp. OP.
AC. July 13
c.1230–1298. A native of Varezze (Voragine), in the diocese of Savona, he took the Dominican habit (1244), was provincial of Lombardy (1267–1286), and finally was consecrated archbishop of Genoa at Rome (1292). His highest title to fame is the compilation of the *Legenda*

Aurea Sanctorum, a classic now known everywhere as *The Golden Legend*. Beatified in 1816.

JAMES of NISIBIS (St) Bp.
RM. July 15
d. c.340. A Syrian who became a monk and eventually was promoted bishop of Nisibis in Mesopotamia. We have very few authentic facts concerning him, but he will always be remembered as an ecclesiastical writer; indeed, among the Syrian Fathers, second only to St Ephrem.

JAMES ANDRADE (Bl) M. SJ.
AC. July 15
d. 1570. Born at Pedrogao in the diocese of Coimbra, Portugal. He was a Jesuit priest and a companion of Bl Ignatius de Azevedo, whose martyrdom he shared. Beatified in 1854.

JAMES the GREATER (St) Apostle
RM. July 25
d. 43 The son of Zebedee and Salome and brother of St John the Evangelist, called with him to the apostolate by our Lord. He was the first of the Twelve to be martyred (Acts XII, 2) under King Herod Agrippa. A 9th-century legend makes him apostle of Spain and points to Compostella as the place where his body is enshrined; the legend grew, under Cluniac influence, and spread throughout W. Europe, so that Compostella became, after Jerusalem and Rome, the most famous place of pilgrimage in Christendom. St James is the patron saint of Spain.

JAMES GERIUS (Bl) C. OSB. Cam.
AC. Aug 5
d. 1345. A Camaldolese monk of Florence who died aged thirty-three. His great devotion was the "Sacred Will of God".

369

JAMES the SYRIAN (St) C.
RM. Aug 6
d. *p*.500. A Syrian by birth, who led a solitary life in the environs of Amida (Diarbekir) in Mesopotamia.

JAMES NAM (Bl) M.   AC. Aug 12
d. 1838. A native Tonkin priest, attached to the Society of Foreign Missions of Paris. Beheaded with BB Antony Dich, his host, and Bl Michael Mi. Beatified in 1900.

JAMES the DEACON (St) C. OSB.
AC. Aug 17
7th cent. An Italian monk and deacon, companion of St Paulinus in his mission to Northumbria, where he remained in spite of the pagan reaction which set in after the death of St Edwin.

JAMES GUENGORO (Bl) M.
AC. Aug 18
d. 1620. A native Japanese child, aged two, son of BB Thomas and Mary Guengoro, with whom he was crucified at Cocura. Beatified in 1867.

JAMES DENXI (Bl) M. AC. Aug 19
d. 1622. A Japanese sailor on board the ship of Bl Joachim Firaiama, q.v. He was beheaded at Nagasaki. Beatified in 1867.

JAMES of MEVANIA (Bl) C. OP.
AC. Aug 23
d. 1301. James Bianconi was a native of Mevania—now Bevagna—in the diocese of Spoleto, and the founder and first prior of the Dominican friary in his native city. Cult approved in 1400 and again in 1674.

JAMES CLAXTON (Bl) M.
AC. Aug 28
d. 1588. Born in Yorkshire and educated at Reims, where he was ordained in 1582. He was hanged for his priesthood at Isleworth. Beatified in 1929.

JAMES FAYAXIDA (Bl) M. Tert.
OP.   AC. Sept 8
d. 1628. A Japanese who became a Dominican tertiary and was beheaded at Nagasaki. Beatified in 1867.

JAMES CHASTAN (Bl) Mk.
AC. Sept 22
See Lawrence Imbert, etc.

JAMES GRIESINGER (Bl) C. OP.
AC. Oct 11
1407–1491. Born at Ulm in Swabia, he joined the army, but abandoned this profession to take the Dominican habit as a lay-brother at Bologna (1441). For the rest of his life he was employed in painting on glass, in which art he excelled. Beatified in 1825.

JAMES the PERSIAN (St) M.
RM. Nov 1
See John and James.

JAMES of SASSEAU (St) C. OSB.
AC. Nov 19
d. *c*.865. A native of Constantinople and an army officer, after many travels he came to Gaul, was ordained priest at Clermont and joined the Benedictines near Bourges, whence at a later date he retired to the solitude of Sasseau (*Saxiacum*).

JAMES BENFATTI (Bl) Bp. OP.
AC. Nov 26
d. 1338. A native of Mantua and a Friar Preacher. He was a master in theology and in 1303 was chosen bishop of Mantua, in which office he merited the title of "Father of the Poor". Cult confirmed in 1859.

JAMES INTERCISUS (St) M.
RM. Nov 27
d. 421. A Persian officer of high rank who apostatized to keep the favour of King Yezdegird; but repented, and,

under King Varanes V, was martyred by being cut into twenty-eight parts. Hence his surname of *Intercisus* (cut into pieces). The RM. adds that many other Christians suffered with him.

JAMES della MARCA (St) C. OFM.
RM. Nov 28

1391–1475. James Gangala was born in the March of Ancona (the ancient Picenum). He studied law, but abandoned that career to join the Friars Minor. He became a fellow-missionary of St John Capistran, and for forty years he never let a day pass without preaching the Word of God.

JAMES THOMPSON (alias HUDSON) (Bl) M.
AC. Nov 28

d. 1582. Born at York and educated for the priesthood at Reims, he was ordained in 1581, and hanged the following year at York for his priesthood. Beatified in 1895.

JAMES (St) M.
AC. Dec 9

See Samosata Martyrs.

JANE (*several*)

The English feminine form of John. The variants in other modern languages are numerous. In hagiology, however, the principal are: In Italian, Giovanna; in French, Jeanne; in Spanish, Juana; in Portuguese and Catalan, Joana. Another English form is Joan.

JANE OF BAGNO (Bl) V. OSB.
Cam.   AC. Jan 16

d. 1105. Born at Fontechiuso in Tuscany, she became a Camaldolese lay-sister at Santa Lucia, near Bagno, in Tuscany. Cult approved in 1823.

JANE de LESTONNAC (St)
Foundress   AC. Feb 2

1556–1640. She was born at Bordeaux, the daughter of a Calvinist mother, and a niece of Montaigne. After the death of her husband, in her forty-seventh year, she entered the Cistercian novitiate which she had to leave on account of ill-health. She now felt called to found a new religious institute for the education of girls with the object of stemming the tide of Calvinism. Her scheme was approved by Paul V in 1607 and the first house was opened at Bordeaux. The Order spread rapidly, some thirty houses being established, and she ruled them all as superioress general. But as the result of a calumny and intrigue on the part of one of the sisters she was deposed, and spent some years in seclusion. Her character was completely vindicated before she died. Canonized 1949.

JANE of VALOIS (St) Foundress
AC. Feb 4

1461–1504. The daughter of Louis XI of France, who married her to the duke of Orleans, afterwards King Louis XII. Her husband obtained a decree of nullity of marriage, and she retired to Bourges, where, together with the Franciscan Bl Gabriel Mary, she founded the order of nuns of the Annunciation—known as *Les Annonciades*. Canonized 1949.

JANE MARY BONOMO (Bl) V.
OSB.   AC. March 1

1606–1670. Born at Asiago, diocese of Vicenza, in N. Italy and educated by the Poor Clares at Trent. She became a Benedictine at Bassano in 1622 and fell into ecstasy for the first time at the ceremony of profession. She held the offices of novice mistress, abbess (three times) and prioress. She was bitterly persecuted by some members of her own community. Beatified in 1783.

JANE MARY de MAILLÉ (Bl) V.
Tert. OFM.   AC. March 29

1331–1414. The daughter of the Baron

de Maillé, she married the Baron de Silly, with whom she lived in virginity for sixteen years. After his death (1362) she joined the Franciscan tertiaries and retired to Tours, where she spent the rest of her life in much poverty and privation due to the persecution of her husband's relatives. Cult confirmed in 1871.

JANE of TOULOUSE (Bl) V. Tert. OC.   AC. March 31

d. 1286. A native of Toulouse, she was affiliated to the Carmelite Order, as a tertiary, by St Simon Stock, and is for this reason venerated as the foundress of the Carmelite third order. She spent her time and substance in training young boy-candidates for the Carmelite Friars. Cult confirmed in 1895.

JANE of PORTUGAL (Bl) V. OP.   AC. May 12

1452–1490. Born at Lisbon, a daughter of King Alphonsus V of Portugal. In 1473 she entered the Dominican convent at Aveiro, but her family would not allow her to take her vows until 1485, when the Portuguese succession was secured. She had to suffer much annoyance on this account. Cult confirmed in 1693.

JANE of ARC (St) V.   RM. May 30

Otherwise Joan of Arc, q.v.

JANE GERARD (Bl) M. AC. June 26

d. 1794. One of the Sisters of Charity of Arras in France, who were arrested in 1792, and guillotined at Cambrai. Beatified in 1920.

JANE SCOPELLI (Bl) V. OC.   AC. July 9

c.1428–1491. A native of Reggio d'Emilia, Italy. She was the foundress and first prioress of the Carmelite nunnery at Reggio, for which she refused all endowments except those

freely given to the nuns as alms. Cult confirmed in 1771.

JANE of ORVIETO (Bl) Tert. OP.   AC. July 23

d. 1306. Usually called Vanna, an Italian derivative of Giovanna (Jane). She was born at Carnajola, near Orvieto, where also she took the Dominican habit of the third order. Cult approved in 1754.

JANE of AZA (Bl) W. OP. AC. Aug 8

d. c.1190. Born at the family castle of Aza, near Aranda, in Old Castile, she married Felix de Guzman, to whom she bore two sons and a daughter and finally —in answer to prayer before the shrine of St Dominic of Silos—the Dominic who became the founder of the friars preachers. Cult approved in 1828.

JANE DELANOUE (Bl) V.
Foundress   AC. Aug 16

1666–1732. Jane Delanoue was the twelfth child of a man who ran a small business in the village of Fenet, near Saumur, in the diocese of Angers. After a pious childhood, her father being dead, she continued to run the business and became somewhat remiss in her piety. Recalled to grace and granted an extraordinary vision, she began to serve the poor women and sick persons. For their care she founded the Institute of the Sisters of St Anne, taking herself the name of Jane of the Cross. After practising heroic virtue, and founding several houses of the Institute, she died at Fenet. Beatified 1947.

JANE FRANCES FRÉMIOT de CHANTAL (St) W. Foundress
                          RM. Aug 21

1572–1641 (Dec 13). Jane Frances Frémiot was born at Dijon, in Burgundy, and in 1592 married the Baron de Chantal. They spent together eight years of happy married life and had four children; then the Baron died as the result of a hunting accident. St Jane now found her spiritual father and friend in St Francis de Sales, under whose guidance, she founded the new Order of the Visitation, chiefly for widows and ladies who could not stand the austerities of the older orders. Sixty-six convents were established during her lifetime. Her last years were a period of intense suffering in body and mind. St Francis described her as "the perfect woman". She died at Moulins, but her remains rest at Anneçy in Savoy.

JANE ANTIDE THOURET (St) V. Foundress   RM. Aug 24
1765–1828. Born near Besançon, the daughter of a tanner. In 1787 she joined the Sisters of Charity of St Vincent de Paul, but on the outbreak of the Revolution she was forced to return home. She now (1798) started at Besançon, a school of her own for poor girls. Soon her helpers in this and in other works of charity were so numerous as to lead her to found a new Institute of Daughters of Charity which was approved by the Holy See before the Foundress's death. Canonized by Pius XI.

JANE-ELIZABETH BICHIER des AGES (St) V. Foundress RM. Aug 26
1773–1832. Of noble rank, she was born in the diocese of Bourges. After the French Revolution she entrusted herself to the guidance of St Andrew Fournet (q.v.), and in spite of grave difficulties at the outset founded the Congregation of the Daughters of the Cross for teaching and service in Hospitals. She died at Le Pay, Poitiers. Canonized 1947.

JANE SODERINI (Bl) V. Tert. OSM.   AC. Sept 1
1301–1367. Born at Florence and educated by St Juliana Falconieri, under

whom she became a Servite tertiary. Beatified in 1827.

JANE-LOUISE BARRÉ and JANE-REINÉ PRIN (BB) MM. AC. Oct 17
d. 1794. Two Ursuline nuns, called in religion, respectively, Sister Cordula and Sister Laurentina, guillotined at Valenciennes. They formed part of a group of martyrs, listed in this book under the title Ursuline Nuns, MM., q.v.

JANE of SEGNA (Bl) V. AC. Nov 17
d. 1307. Born at Segna, near Florence, she tended sheep. Both the Vallumbrosans and the Franciscans claim her as one of their tertiaries. Cult approved in 1798.

JANE of CÁCERES (Bl) Abs. OSB. Cist.   PC. Dec 8
d. 1383. Cistercian abbess of the nunnery of St Benedict, at Castro, near Cáceres, in W. Spain. She was killed by marauding soldiers.

JANUARIA (St) M.   RM. March 2
See Paul, Heraclius, etc.

JANUARIA (St) M.   RM. July 17
See Scillitan Martyrs.

JANUARIUS (St) M.   RM. Jan 7
See Felix and Januarius.

JANUARIUS (St) M.   RM. Jan 19
See Paul, Gerontius, etc.

JANUARIUS, MAXIMA and MACARIA (SS) MM.   RM. Apr 8
? African martyrs of whom nothing further is known. The names are sometimes given as SS Januarius, Maximus and Maccarius.

JANUARIUS (St) M.   RM. Apr 29
See Corfu, Martyrs of.

JANUARIUS (St) M. RM. July 10
See Seven Brothers.

JANUARIUS, MARINUS, NABOR and FELIX (SS) MM. RM. July 10
? African martyrs, of whom nothing further is known.

JANUARIUS and PELAGIA (SS) MM. RM. July 11
d. 320. Martyrs beheaded at Nicopolis in Lesser Armenia under Licinius.

JANUARIUS (St) M. RM. July 15
See Catulinus, Januarius, etc.

JANUARIUS (St) M. RM. Aug 6
See Sixtus II and Comp.

JANUARIUS and Comp. (SS) MM. RM. Sept 19
d. 304. Januarius, bishop of Benevento, Festus, his deacon, Desiderius, lector or reader, Sosius, deacon of the church of Misenum, Proculus, deacon of Pozzuoli, and two other Christians, Eutyches and Acutius, were beheaded at Pozzuoli, under Diocletian. The body of St Januarius (Gennaro) was eventually enshrined at Naples, of which city he has become the patron saint. The yearly liquefaction of some of his blood preserved in a phial is a well-known phenomenon, of which there are records for the past four hundred years. No natural explanation has been found, although many have been advanced.

JANUARIUS (St) M. RM. Oct 13
See Faustus, Januarius and Martial.

JANUARIUS (St) M. RM. Oct 24
See Felix (Africanus), Audactus, etc.

JANUARIUS (St) M. RM. Oct 25
See Protus and Januarius.

JANUARIUS (St) M. RM. Dec 2
See Severus, Securus, etc.

JANUARIUS (St) M. RM. Dec 15
See Faustinus, Lucius, etc.

JAPAN (Martyrs of) (SS and BB) MM. RM. Feb 5 (and AC. several dates)
d. 1597 and 1614 and the following years. There are two main groups of Japanese martyrs: the first comprises six Franciscans, three Jesuits and seventeen lay people. The friars were Spanish or Portuguese with one Mexican; the rest were Japanese. All were crucified near Nagasaki in 1597. They were canonized by Pius IX in 1862. The second group is formed of thirty-six Jesuits, twenty-six Franciscans, twenty-one Dominicans, and five Augustinians, and one hundred and seven lay victims. They were martyred between 1614 and 1644, and were beatified by Pius IX and Leo XIII at different dates. Most of the religious were Spanish; most of the lay people native Japanese. Each is given a special notice in this book.

JARLATH (HIERLATH) (St) Bp. AC. Feb 1
d. c.480. One of St Patrick's disciples, who succeeded St Benignus in the see of Armagh.

JARLATH (St) Bp. AC. June 6
d. c.550. The founder and first abbot-bishop of Tuam, in Connaught, Ireland, where he established a monastic school which became famous. St Brendan of Clonard and St Colman of Cloyne were pupils there.

JARMAN (St) Bp. AC. July 3
Otherwise Germanus, q.v.

JASON (St) RM. July 12
1st cent. The Acts of the Apostles (XVII, 5) say that St Paul stayed at Jason's house in Thessalonica. St Paul

mentions him in his Epistle to the Romans (XVI, 21). In the Greek legend he is described as a bishop of Tarsus in Cilicia, going to Corfu, evangelizing that island, and dying there. The RM. wrongly identifies him with the Mnason mentioned in the Acts (XXI, 16) "a Cyprian, an old disciple", with whom St Paul was staying in Jerusalem and whom tradition makes bishop of Tamasus in Cyprus.

JASON (St) M.   **RM. Dec 3**
See Claudius, Hilaria, etc.

JEHUDIEL   **AC. Apr 20**
See Seven Angels who stand before the throne of God.

JEREMIAS (St) M.   **RM. Feb 16**
See Elias, Jeremias, etc.

JEREMIAS (St) Prophet RM. May 1
c.590 B.C. The second of the greater prophets. The tradition concerning him is that at the age of fifty-five he was stoned to death in Egypt by the Jews who shared his captivity. His feast is observed chiefly at Venice, where some of his alleged relics are enshrined.

JEREMIAS (St) M.   **RM. June 7**
See Peter, Wallabonsus, etc.

JEREMIAS (St) M.   **RM. June 17**
See Isaurus, Innocent, etc.

JEREMIAS (St) M.   **RM. Sept 15**
See Emilas and Jeremias.

JERMYN (GERMAN) GARDINER (Bl) M.   **AC. March 7**
d. 1544. Educated at Cambridge, he became secretary to Stephen Gardiner, bishop of Winchester, and was executed at Tyburn with BB John Larke and John Ireland, for denying the royal supremacy. Beatified in 1886.

JEROME LU (Bl) M.   AC. Jan 28
c.1810–1858. Born at Mao-Cheu in China. He worked as a native catechist and was beheaded in his native town. Beatified in 1909.

JEROME of VALLUMBROSA (Bl) C. OSB. Vall.   AC. June 18
d. 1135. A Vallumbrosan monk who retired to the hermitage of the abbey, called *Masso delle celle*, where he spent thirty-five years, living all the time, it is said, only on bread and water.

JEROME of WERDEN (St) M. OFM.   RM. July 9
1522–1572. A native of Werden in Holland, who spent several years in Palestine as a Franciscan missionary. He was a powerful preacher against Calvinism. At the time of his martyrdom he was the vicar of the friary at Gorkum under St Nicholas Pieck (see Gorkum, Martyrs of).

JEROME of PAVIA (St) Bp.
                    AC. July 19
d. 787. Bishop of Pavia, 778–787.

JEROME EMILIANI (St) C.
                    RM. July 20
1481–1537. A Venetian who in his youth served in the army of the Republic. Being taken prisoner he was miraculously set free after praying to our Lady. He took holy orders and devoted himself to charitable works. In 1532 he founded a congregation of clerks regular vowed to the care of orphans. They were called *Somaschi*, from the little town in Lombardy — Somasca — where they started. Jerome died of a contagious malady caught while tending the sick. Canonized in 1767, and in 1928 declared the patron saint of orphans and abandoned children.

JEROME of the CROSS de TORRES M. Tert. OFM.   AC. Sept 3

d. 1632. A Japanese secular priest, educated in the seminary of Arima and ordained at Manila. He returned to Japan (1628), was arrested (1631) and burnt alive at Nagasaki. Beatified in 1867.

JEROME (St) C. Dr.   RM. Sept 30

c.342–420. Eusebius Hieronymus Sophronius was born at Stridonium in Dalmatia. He studied in Rome, particularly the classics for which he developed a life-long passion. He then travelled extensively in Italy and Gaul, lived as a hermit in Palestine, returned to Rome, where, after his ordination to the priesthood, he joined the Roman clergy and acted as secretary to the pope, and finally, having come to be on bad terms with those who surrounded him, went back to Palestine and settled at Bethlehem. He spent the rest of his life translating, and commenting, the Bible, and became the most learned biblical scholar of his day. He himself was the first to appreciate this fact and was apt to resent any opposition to his way of thinking. However, he acknowledged his own shortcomings, particularly his shortness of temper, with a rather tempestuous but virile humility. His place as an exponent of Catholic dogma is still the highest ever allotted to a biblical scholar. He died at Bethlehem and is officially venerated as a Doctor of the Church.

JEROME HERMOSILLA (Bl) M. OP.   AC. Nov 1

d. 1861. A native of La Calzada, in Old Castile, who after his profession in the Dominican Order, was sent to Manila, where he was ordained priest and in 1828 appointed to the mission of E. Tonkin. He succeeded Bl Ignatius Delgado as vicar-apostolic and was consecrated bishop. Arrested in 1861 he was tortured and beheaded. Beatified 1906.

JEROME de ANGELIS (Bl) M. SJ.   AC. Dec 4

d. 1623. A native of Castrogiovanni in Sicily, who became a Jesuit at Messina and was sent to the missions of the Far East. He worked for twenty-two years in various parts of Japan and finally, betrayed to the persecutors, was martyred by burning at Yeddo, together with BB Simon Yempo and Francis Gálvez. Beatified in 1867.

JEROME RANUZZI (Bl) C. OSM.   AC. Dec 12

d. 1455. Born at Sant' Angelo in Vado (Urbino), he took his religious vows as a Servite and eventually became the personal adviser of Duke Frederick of Montefeltro, of Urbino. On this account he was surnamed "the Angel of Good Counsel". Cult approved in 1775.

JOACHIM SACCACHIBARA (St) M. Tert. OFM.   RM. Feb 5

d. 1597. A native of Japan, doctor of the Franciscan Fathers. He was crucified at Nagasaki with twenty-four companions. Beatified in 1627. Canonized in 1862.

JOACHIM of FIORE (de FLORIS) (Bl) Ab. OSB. Cist.   PC. March 30

c.1130–1202. Born at Celico in Calabria, after a pilgrimage to Palestine, he joined the Cistercians at Sambucina and in 1176 was made abbot of Corazzo; about the year 1190 he inaugurated at Fiore a new Cistercian Congregation. He was a prolific ascetical and biblical writer, and his commentary on the Apocalypse gave him the title of "the Prophet" by which he is described by Dante: "the Calabrian abbot Joachim, endowed with prophetic spirit" (Paradiso, XII). Unfortunately, after his death the Franciscan Spirituals made use of his books to uphold their heretical tendencies. The holy abbot, however, has always been given the title of *Beatus*.

JOACHIM PICCOLOMINI (Bl) C. OSM.   RM. Apr 16
d. 1305. A member of the illustrious Piccolomini family of Siena, he joined the Servites as a lay-brother under St Philip Benizi. Beatified by Paul V.

JOACHIM (St) Patriarch
                            RM. Aug 16
1st cent. B.C. Joachim is now the usual name given to the father of our Lady. Other names attributed to him are: Heli, Cleopas, Eliacim, Jonachir, Sadoc. Nothing is known about him. Liturgically, he has been honoured in the East from time immemorial; in the West only since the 16th century. The traditions concerning him rest only on the apocryphal Gospel of James.

JOACHIM FIRAIAMA-DIAZ (Bl) M.   AC. Aug 19
d. 1622. A Japanese captain of a ship at Manila. When bringing Bl Peter Zuñiga and Louis Flores to Japan his ship was captured by Dutch Protestant pirates, and brought to Firando. He and his crew, all members of the Confraternity of the Holy Rosary, were beheaded at Nagasaki. Beatified in 1867.

JOACHIM ROYO (Bl) M. OP.
                            AC. Oct 28
d. 1748. A Spanish missionary of the Dominican Order, who was sent to China to work under Bl Peter Sanz, and was ordained there. He was strangled in prison at Fu-tsheu. Beatified in 1893.

JOACHIM HO (Bl) M.   AC. Nov 24
d. 1839. A Chinese, martyred at Kouei-Tcheou. Beatified in 1900.

JOAN of ARC (St) V.   RM May 30
1412–1431. Called "the Maid of Orleans"—*La Pucelle*. She was born at Domrémy in Lorraine, the daughter of a peasant. When she was seventeen, while minding her father's sheep, she heard supernatural voices commanding her to take up arms and lead the French army against the English invaders of France. Accordingly, Charles VII entrusted her with an armed force, and Joan's rapid successes enabled him to be crowned at Reims. However, as Joan herself had predicted, she was captured by the Burgundians and handed over to the English. She was tried by an ecclesiastical court presided over by the bishop of Beauvais, a tool of the English, and condemned to be burnt alive at the stake as a heretic. The sentence was executed at Rouen, May 31, 1431. In 1456 the case was re-tried and Joan was declared innocent. After centuries of popular veneration she was beatified in 1909 and canonized in 1920. In 1922 she was declared the patroness of France.

JOANNA (St) W.   RM. May 24
1st cent. The wife of Chuza, steward of Herod Antipas, tetrarch of Galilee. She is mentioned by St Luke (viii, 3) in his gospel as one of the holy women who ministered to our Lord.

JOANNICIUS (St) H.   RM. Nov 4
750–846. A native of Bithynia who, after serving as a soldier, retired at the age of forty to lead a solitary life near Mt Olympus. Popular veneration, however, drove him from solitude to solitude. He was a strenuous opponent of Iconoclasm. His memory is held in high honour among the Greeks.

JOANNINUS de SAN JUAN (Bl) M.
                            AC. July 15
d. 1570. A nephew of the captain of the

ship which carried Bl Ignatius de Azevedo (q.v.) and his companions. He voluntarily joined the martyrs and was thrown into the sea by the French Calvinist pirates.

JOAQUINA VEDRUNA de MAS (St) W. Foundress   AC. May 19
1783–1854. A Spanish lady, wife of Theodore de Mas, of the Spanish nobility, who died in the Napoleonic wars. Joaquina then retired to Vich, where she founded the Institute of the Carmelite Sisters of Charity, now spread throughout Spain and S. America. She died at Barcelona during a cholera epidemic. Canonized 1959.

JOAVAN (St) Bp.   AC. March 2
d. c.576. A Romano-Briton who passed over to Brittany to live under his uncle St Paul of León, from whom he received episcopal consecration as coadjutor.

JOB (St) Patriarch   RM. May 10
? 1500 B.C. The man "simple and upright and fearing God and avoiding evil", whose patience forms the subject matter of a canonical book of Scripture. (See also James V, 11.) His liturgical cult obtains chiefly in the East.

JODOC (JUDOCUS, JOSSE, JOST) (St) C.   RM. Dec 13
See Judocus.

JOEL (Bl or St) Ab. OSB.   AC. Jan 25
d. 1185. A disciple of St John of Matera, founder of the Benedictine Congregation of Pulsano. St Joel was its third general.

JOEL (St) Prophet   RM. July 13
8th cent. B.C. One of the twelve minor prophets. His body is said to be enshrined under the high altar of the cathedral of Zara in Dalmatia.

JOHN
Note. This is the most popular proper name in Christendom. The original Hebrew form has been Hellenized and Latinized into Joannes, whence the numerous variants in all languages. For hagiological purposes we mention only the following: Italian, Giovanni; French, Jean; Spanish, Juan; Portuguese, Xuan; Catalan, Jean; Dutch, Jan; German, Johann; Russian, Iwan, Ivan. There are also numerous diminutive forms, e.g., Italian, Giovannino, Nanino; Spanish, Juanito; French, Jeannin; Old English, Johnikin, etc. Moreover, especially in the Latin countries, the name is very often used in combination with others, as follows: Gianpier, Gianluigi, Jean-Benoît, Jean-François, Juan-José, Juan-Maria, etc. No less than seventy-three of the post-Reformation English martyrs— one canonized, forty-eight *Beati*, nineteen *Venerabiles*, five *dilati*—were called John.

JOHN NEPOMUCENE NEUMANN (Bl) Bp. C.SS.R. Founder   AC. Jan 5
1811–1860. From Bohemia, his native soil, missionary zeal led him to America in 1836, where he laboured in the district of Niagra until 1840 when he became a Redemptorist. As superior, and even more fully with his consecration as Bishop of Philadelphia, he devoted himself to the ministry of the word, the education of youth, the building of churches, the decorum of divine worship and, above all, to the care of orphans and the needy. He also founded the Sisters of the Third Order of St Francis. Beatified 1963.

JOHN de RIBERA (St) Bp.   AC. Jan 6
1532–1611. A native of Seville, and the son of the duke of Alcalá, viceroy of Naples. He was educated at the university of Salamanca and ordained priest

378

in 1557. He remained at Salamanca as professor of theology, gifts became widely known and gained him the esteem of Pope Pius V, and of Philip II of Spain. He was appointed bishop of Badajoz, but transferred shortly after to the archbishopric of Valencia, with the added dignity of viceroy of that province. While all may not regard him as an enlightened statesman, one cannot but admire his conscientious devotion to duty and his heroic patience in bearing the responsibilities of his office. Canonized 1959.

JOHN CAMILLUS the GOOD (St) Bp. RM. Jan 10

d. *c.* 660. Bishop of Milan. The Lombard invasion forced the bishops of Milan to live away from that city eighty years. With John Camillus the line of resident bishops recommenced. He worked successfully against Arianism and the Monothelitism.

JOHN of RAVENNA (St) Bp. RM. Jan 12

d. 494. Bishop of Ravenna from 452 to 494. He is said to have saved his flock from the fury of Attila the Hun, and mitigated its sad lot when the city was taken by Theodoric, king of the Ostro-Goths.

JOHN GASPARD CRATZ (Bl) M. SJ. AC. Jan 12

d. 1737. A German Jesuit, born at Duren near Cologne. He entered the Order at Macao in 1730. Sent to China with three Portuguese companions, he was arrested at Tonkin in 1736, and martyred in the following year.

JOHN CALABYTES (St) H. RM. Jan 15

d. *c.*450. Born at Constantinople, he disappeared from home and became at the age of twelve a monk at Gomon on

the Bosphorus. After some years he returned home so changed in appearance that his parents did not recognize him. He lived on their charity in a small hut—Calybe in Greek, whence *Kalabytes*—near their home until his death, so runs the legend, which is remarkably reminiscent of that of St Alexis of Rome and other saints.

JOHN of ROME (St) C. OSB. RM. Jan 17

See Antony, Merulus and John.

JOHN the ALMONER (St) Abp. RM. Jan 23

d. ? 616. A Cypriot, who became patriarch of Alexandria (*c.*608). He set himself to redress social evils by means of almsgiving. He compiled a list of the 7,500 poor of the diocese, and one of his first episcopal acts was the distribution of 80,000 pieces of gold to hospitals and monasteries. He followed this policy systematically till his death.

JOHN GROVE (Bl) M AC. Jan 24

d. 1697. A layman, servant of Bl William Ireland, SJ., with whom he was martyred at Tyburn for alleged complicity in the Oates Plot. Beatified in 1929.

JOHN CHRYSOSTOM (St) Bp. Dr. RM. Jan 27

*c.*344–407 (Sept 14). Surnamed *Chrysostom* ("Golden Mouthed") on account of his great eloquence, and also "the Doctor of the Eucharist". He was born at Antioch, tried the monastic life in his youth and ruined his health, and was then ordained priest. It was as a priest at Antioch that he delivered that series of sermons which made him famous throughout the East. In 398, much against his own will, he was raised to the see of Constantinople, where his ardent zeal, which knew no compromise, brought down upon him the imperial wrath. In 403, at a gathering of bishops known as the Synod of the Oak, he was deposed and banished, but public opinion was so strongly in his favour that the court was unable to prevent his triumphant return. Two months later, however, on account of another of his outspoken denunciations of vice, he was exiled again to Armenia, in defiance of the pope who strenuously espoused the saint's cause. John died in exile on Sept 14. Besides being the most prolific of the Greek Doctors, St John was famous for his revision of the Greek Liturgy.

JOHN of WARNETON (Bl) Bp.
AC. Jan 27

d. 1130. Born at Warneton, in French Flanders, a disciple of St Ivo of Chartres, he became a canon regular at Mont-Saint-Eloi, near Arras, and was eventually raised to the see of Thérouanne, which he accepted only under a papal order. He was a great founder of monasteries. Though he had a reputation for strictness, he showed himself extremely gentle when dealing with certain individuals who had conspired against his life.

JOHN MARY MZEC (Bl) M.
AC. Jan 27

d. 1887. A negro of Uganda who baptized many in the hour of death. Beheaded in January, 1887. Beatified in 1912.

JOHN of REOMAY (RÉOMÉ) (St) Ab.
RM. Jan 28

425–539. Born at Dijon, he was first a solitary at Reomay. When disciples gathered round him he escaped in secret and became a monk of Lérins. Here he learnt the traditions of St Macarius, and when summoned back to Reomay, he regulated his monastery

according to them. He was one of the pioneers on monastic life in the West.

JOHN (St) M.
RM. Jan 31

See Cyrus and John.

JOHN ANGELUS (Bl) C. OSB.
AC. Jan 31

d. c.1050. A native of Venice and a Benedictine at Pomposa in the diocese of Ferrara, under St Guy, q.v.

JOHN BOSCO (St) Founder
RM. Jan 31

1815–1888. Born at Becchi, Castelnuovo d'Asti, in Piedmont, son of a peasant. After his ordination to the priesthood in 1841 he began at Turin his life-long work of educating boys. From the first he had a clear programme of education in his mind—viz., to educate through love, to compel the boys to love their teachers, their studies, and all the conditions which surround their education. A group of willing helpers offered themselves to Don Bosco and in 1860 the new Institute was approved by the Holy See. St John placed it under the protection of our Lady Help of Christians and of St Francis of Sales—*Salesians*. It grew rapidly and spread throughout Europe and the foreign missions. He also formed on the same lines a new sisterhood, the Daughters of Mary Auxiliatrix, for the education of girls. Canonized in 1934.

JOHN of the GRATING (St) Bp. OSB. Cist.
AC. Feb 1

1098–1163. Surnamed *de Craticula* "of the Grating", from the metal railings that surrounded his shrine. He was a Breton who entered Clairvaux and was professed under St Bernard. He returned to Brittany as abbot-founder of Buzay and Bégard and finally was promoted to the bishopric of Aleth, which see he transferred to Saint-Malo. He introduced Canons Regular into the diocese, and some sources treat him as a Canon, and a friend of St Bernard, but not a monk under him.

JOHN NELSON (Bl) M. SJ.
AC. Feb 3
d. 1578. A native of Skelton, near York. He began his studies for the priesthood at Douai at the age of forty and was ordained in 1575. He was sent to London, but was soon arrested and subsequently executed at Tyburn. He became a Jesuit shortly before his death.

JOHN SPEED (Bl) M. AC. Feb 4
d. 1594. *Alias* Spence. A layman, born at Durham, and martyred also at Durham for befriending priests. Beatified in 1929.

JOHN ZAKOLY (Bl) Bp. PC. Feb 3
d. 1494. Bishop of Csanad in Hungary, he entered the Pauline Order and died Prior of the monastery of Diosgyör.

JOHN de BRITTO (St) M. SJ.
RM. Feb 4
1647–1693. A native of Lisbon, he joined the Society of Jesus in 1662 and was soon after sent to the missions of the Far East. He worked in Malabar, Tanjore, Marava and Madura, first as a simple religious and afterwards as superior. He joined the Brahmin caste in an endeavour to reach the nobility, and his methods were in many other respects unconventional and enlightened. He was captured and tortured and ordered to leave the country; but he refused and was martyred at Oreiour in India. Canonized 1947.

JOHN MOROSINI (Bl) Ab. OSB.
PC. Feb 5
d. 1012. A native of Venice who became a Benedictine at Cuxá in the Catalonian

Pyrenees. At a later period he returned to Venice where he founded and was the first abbot of San Giorgio Maggiore (c.982). Most writers call him *beatus*, although there is no evidence of cult.

JOHN SOAN de GOTO (St) M. SJ.
RM. Feb 5
d. 1597. A Japanese temporal-coadjutor of the Society of Jesus, and catechist at Ozaka. Crucified at Nagasaki in his nineteenth year, with many companions. Canonized in 1862.

JOHN KISAKA (or KIMOIA) (St) M. Tert. OFM. RM. Feb 5
d. 1597. A Japanese silk-weaver, born at Meaco. He was baptized and received into the third order of St Francis shortly before his crucifixion at Nagasaki with twenty-five companions.

JOHN of MATHA (St) Founder
RM. Feb 8
1160–1213 (Dec 17). A native of Faucon in Provence, who studied at Paris and later founded the order of Trinitarians for the redemption of captives, which was approved by Pope Innocent III. It is said that John himself ransomed many captives at Tunis, but of this and many other episodes of his life there are no trustworthy records. He died at Rome.

JOHN CHARLES CORNY (Bl) M.
AC. Feb 8
1809–1837. Born at Loudun, in the diocese of Poitiers, France. He belonged to the Paris Society of Foreign Missions and worked in Annam. He was seized at Ban-no, Tonkin, kept in a cage for three months being put often in irons and brutally beaten. He was finally beheaded (Sept 20). Beatified in 1900.

JOHN BUONAGIUNTA (St)
RM. Feb 12
See Seven Holy Founders.

JOHN NUTTER and JOHN MUNDEN (BB) MM.   AC. Feb 12

d. 1584. John Nutter was born near Burnley, Lancs, and was a fellow of St John's College, Cambridge. He studied for the priesthood at Reims, and was ordained in 1581. Bl John Munden, a native of Coitley, S. Maperton, Dorset, studied at New College, Oxford, became a schoolmaster, went to Reims and to Rome for his ecclesiastical training and was ordained in 1582. They were martyred at Tyburn with three other priests. Beatified in 1929.

JOHN LANTRUA of TRIORA (Bl) M. OFM.   AC. Feb 13

1760–1816. A native of Triora in Liguria, who at the age of seventeen joined the Friars Minor. After having been guardian of Velletri, near Rome, he volunteered for the Chinese missions, where at that time a fierce persecution was raging. He arrived there in 1799 and worked with great success in spite of many obstacles. At length he was seized and martyred by strangulation at Ch'angsha Fu. Beatified in 1900.

JOHN BAPTIST of the CONCEPTION (Bl) C.   AC. Feb 14

1561–1613. A native of Almodovar, Toledo, Spain. He entered the Trinitarian Order at Toledo and seventeen years later joined the party of reform in that Order. As superior, he inaugurated such a revival at Valdepeñas in 1597. The reform, called the Discalced Trinitarians, was approved by Rome and John had to endure on this account the bitter opposition of the "unreformed". At the time of his death thirty-four houses had adopted the reform. Beatified in 1819.

JOHN PIBUSH (Bl) M.   AC. Feb 18

d. 1601. Born at Thirsk, Yorks, and educated at Reims. Ordained in 1587, he was sent to the English Mission, where he spent his time mostly in prison and was finally executed at Southwark, solely for his priesthood. Beatified in 1929.

JOHN PETER (NÉEL) (Bl)   AC. Feb 18

1832–1862. A French missionary priest working in Kuy-tsheu, China, who was arrested, tied to a horse's tail by his hair, and beheaded at Kuy-tsheu. Beatified in 1909.

JOHN the SAXON (Bl) M.   AC. Feb 22

d. 895. Apparently a native of Old Saxony and a monk in some French abbey who was invited by King Alfred to restore religion and learning in the English abbeys after the devastation of the Danes. The king appointed him abbot of Athelingay. John worked zealously in furthering the king's wishes. Two French monks of his own community murdered him one night in church.

JOHN of HUNGARY (Bl) OFM.   PC. Feb 23

d. 1287. Of French origin, he was the first Franciscan to work in Hungary. In the chronicle of his Order he is styled "Saint".

JOHN THERISTUS (St) Mk. OSB.   RM. Feb 24

d. 1129. Of Calabrian parentage, he was born in Sicily, whither his mother had been carried as a slave by the Saracens. He contrived to escape to Calabria while still a child, and there he became a Benedictine. Theristus means Harvester, a reference to a miraculous harvesting supposed to have been performed by the Saint.

JOHN of GORZE (St) Ab. OSB.
AC. Feb 27
d. *c*.975. Born at Vandières, near Metz. After some years spent in administering his large estates, he made a pilgrimage to Rome, and on his return restored, and entered, the abbey of Gorze (933). The emperor Otto I sent him as his ambassador to the khalif Abd-er-Rahman of Cordova, where he stayed for two years. In 960 he was made abbot of Gorze, and the wise reforms which he introduced spread even to distant Benedictine abbeys. The saint is said to have been gifted with a prodigious memory.

JOHN-JOSEPH of the CROSS (St)
C. OFM.   RM. March 5
1654–1734. Carlo Gaetano was born on the island of Ischia, off the coast of Naples. In 1670 he joined the Franciscan-Alcantarines and was given the new name of Gianguiseppe (John-Joseph). He held various offices in the Order and finally that of superior of the new Italian branch of the Alcantarines. Canonized in 1839.

JOHN LARKE and JOHN IRELAND (BB) MM. AC. March 7
d. 1544. Both were secular priests. John Larke was rector of St Ethelburga's Bishopsgate, then of Woodford, Essex, and finally of Chelsea, to which he was nominated by St Thomas More. John Ireland, after being chaplain to the same saint, was made rector of Eltham, Kent. Both were martyred at Tyburn, with Bl Jermyn Gardiner. John Larke was beatified in 1886 and John Ireland in 1929.

JOHN of GOD (St) Founder
RM. March 8
1495–1550. Born at Montemoro Novo, diocese of Evora, in Portugal, John followed various vocations for the first forty years of his life—shepherd, soldier, peddler, superintendent of slaves in Morocco, vendor of religious books in the district near Gibraltar, etc. He was led to a more perfect life by a sermon of Bl John of Avila, but the fervour of his conversion produced in him such extravagant behaviour that he was taken for a madman. Finally, in 1540, he settled at Granada and founded a hospital where he tended the sick. This was the beginning of the new Order of Brothers Hospitallers (Brothers of St John of God). St John was canonized in 1690 and declared patron of the sick and of hospitals in 1886.

JOHN of VALLUMBROSA (Bl) C.
OSB. Vall.   AC. March 10
d. *c*.1380. A Florentine monk of the Holy Trinity in his native city. As a result of poring over forbidden books night and day, he took secretly to the practice of the Black Art and became a necromancer, and a slave to vice and depravity. On being found out, he was summoned before the abbot-general of Vallumbrosa and, after first denying ultimately confessed his guilt and was imprisoned in a pestilential gaol. This proved his salvation: he became truly penitent and by voluntary fasting reduced himself to a skeleton, so that his fellow monks implored him to return to community life. He, however, preferred to remain in prison till his death, living as a hermit to a very old age and attaining to great sanctity. He was an elegant writer, and a great friend of St Catherine of Siena, who often appeared to him.

JOHN OGILVIE (Bl) M. SJ.
AC. March 10
d. 1615. Born at Drum-na-Keith, Banffshire, and brought up a Calvinist, he was received into the Church at Louvain (1596), at the age of seventeen. He joined the Society of Jesus (1599)

and worked in Austria and in France till 1613. He then returned to his native Scotland where he was beginning to make converts when he was betrayed and imprisoned. For eight days and nights on end he was forcibly kept from sleep so that he should reveal the names of other Catholics. The attempt was unsuccessful. He was hanged at Glasgow. Beatified in 1929.

JOHN RIGHI of FABRIANO (Bl) C. OFM.   AC. March 11

1469–1539. John Baptist Righi was a native of Fabriano, province of Ancona, who professed the Franciscan rule and lived a hermit's life at Massaccio. Cult approved in 1903.

JOHN SORDI, OR CACCIAFRONTE (Bl) Bp. M. OSB.   AC. March 16

d. 1183. A native of Cremona who joined the abbey of St Lawrence in his native city, and became abbot in 1155. He is described as most loyal to, and gentle with his monks. He sided with the pope against the emperor Barbarossa, by whom he was banished from his abbey. He lived as a hermit near Mantua, and, in 1174, the bishop of this city being deposed by the pope, Bl John was raised to the see. But, some three years afterwards, the former bishop repented and Bl John asked permission to resign in his favour, being himself transferred to Vicenza (1177). Here he was killed by a man whom he had rebuked for embezzling episcopal revenues.

JOHN AMIAS (or ANNE) (Bl) M.   AC. March 16

d. 1589. Born near Wakefield, he began life as a clothier and married, but on his wife's death, studied for the priesthood at Reims and was ordained in 1581. He was executed for his priesthood at

York, together with Bl Robert Dalby. Beatified in 1929.

JOHN BRÉBEUF and JOHN de la LANDE (SS) MM. SJ.   RM. March 16 and Oct 18

d. 1649 and 1646. Two Jesuit martyrs, belonging to the group of the North American Martyrs (q.v.). John Brébeuf, born at Condé in 1596, was a priest who landed at Quebec in 1615 and worked chiefly among the Hurons for thirty-four years. He was martyred by the Iroquois in 1649. John de la Lande, a native of Dieppe was a lay brother, and was martyred in 1646. Both were canonized, with four companions, in 1930.

JOHN SARKANDER (Bl) M.   AC. March 17

1576–1620. Born in Austrian Silesia, he became a parish priest of Holleschau in Moravia. He converted many Hussites and Bohemian Brethren, but as a result, he was unjustly accused by the heretics of conspiring to bring Polish troops into the country, and was ordered to reveal what he heard in confession from his penitent the baron of Moravia. On refusing he was cruelly racked and left to die in prison. Beatified in 1859.

JOHN the SYRIAN of PINNA (St) H.   RM. March 19

6th cent. According to the RM. he was a Syrian monk who settled at Pinna, near Spoleto, where for forty-four years he was abbot of a large monastic colony. It is probable that he was a refugee from Monophysite persecution.

JOHN BAPTIST SPAGNUOLO (Bl) C. OC.   AC. March 20

1448–1516. Usually called *Baptista Mantuanus*. His family name *Spagnuolo* denotes his Spanish origin. He was, however, born at Mantua, studied at

Padua, joined the Carmelites (1464) and in 1513 became their prior-general. He is famous as a Latin poet—he wrote over 50,000 lines of Latin verse—and he is considered one of the most eminent representatives of Christian Humanism in Italy. Beatified in 1885.

JOHN of PARMA (Bl) C. OFM.
AC. March 20

1209–1289. A native of Parma, who after his profession in the Franciscan Order and his ordination, taught theology at Bologna and Naples. In 1247 he was elected seventh minister general of the Franciscans and held the office until 1257. He visited the Franciscan provinces of different countries, including England. He was sent to Constantinople as papal legate. His final years he lived in retirement at Greccio. Cult approved in 1777.

JOHN, SERGIUS and Comp. (SS) MM.
AC. March 20

d. 796. A group of twenty monks of the *laura* of St Sabas, near Jerusalem, who were killed in one of the anti-Christian Arab raids. Many more were wounded, and a few escaped. One of the last category, Stephen the poet, has left a detailed account of the event.

JOHN del BASTONE (Bl) C. OSB. Silv.
AC. March 24

d. 1290. One of the first disciples of St Silvester at Monte Fano.

JOHN of LYCOPOLIS (St) H.
RM. March 27

c.305–394. Surnamed "The Egyptian" or "the Prophet of the Thebaid". He was born near Assiut, in Egypt, and was a carpenter by trade. At the age of twenty-five he journeyed to a mountain near Lycopolis and lived there for forty years as a recluse. He was consulted by the emperor Theodosius and greatly admired by his contemporaries SS

Jerome, Augustine, Cassian, Palladius, etc. He was remarkable for his gift of prophecy.

JOHN DAMASCENE (St) C. Dr.
RM. March 27

c.676–749. A native of Damascus, where his father was the caliph's vizier. He was educated by Cosmos, a Greek monk who had been brought into Syria as a slave. After succeeding his father as vizier, he retired to the *laura* of St Sabas at Jerusalem and embraced there the monastic life. He boldly resisted the Iconoclast emperor, Leo the Isaurian, but he is best remembered as a theologian. He was the author of the first real *Summa Theologica*, as well as of numerous liturgical hymns. He was the last of the Greek fathers and the first of the Christian Aristotelians. Leo XIII proclaimed him Doctor of the Church in 1890.

JOHN of CAPISTRANO (St) C. OFM.
RM. March 28

1386–1456 (Oct 23). A native of Capistrano in the Abruzzi, he began life as a lawyer, and was made governor of Perugia in the Papal States. When he was thirty he was left a widower and became a Franciscan and a life-long friend of St Bernardinus of Siena. His whole religious life was spent as papal legate to various states, Palestine, Milan, France, Sicily, Austria, Bavaria, Poland, Bohemia, and Silesia. The most important was that to Bohemia, where his conduct in connexion with the Hussite movement has been adversely criticized. St John played a large part in inspiring the heroic resistance of the Hungarians to the Turks. Canonized in 1724.

JOHN CLIMACUS (St) Ab.
RM. March 30

c.525–605. Called *"Climacus"* from the title of his book *The Climax*, or *Ladder of Perfection*, which is a classic in ascetical literature. He was born in Palestine and, at the age of sixteen, became a monk on Mt Sinai and afterwards a solitary in different places in the Arabian Desert. He was already seventy-five when he was made abbot of Sinai, but four years later he resigned and died as a hermit. By some his life is given later dates, and his death placed after 650.

JOHN PAYNE (Bl) M.   AC. Apr 20 d. 1582. Born in the diocese of Peterborough, he was educated for the priesthood at Douai, where he was ordained in 1576. He worked on the English mission at Ingatestone in Essex until his martyrdom at Chelmsford. Beatified in 1886.

JOHN of PENNA (Bl) C. OFM. **AC. Apr 3** d. 1271. A native of Penna San Giovanni in the diocese of Fermo who, after being ordained priest, joined the Franciscans at Recanati and founded several houses in Provence, where he lived for twenty-five years. (See his life in ch. 45 of the *Little Flowers of St Francis*.) Cult approved by Pius VII.

JOHN of VESPIGNANO (Bl) C. **AC. Apr 9** d. 1331. Born at Vespignano in the diocese of Florence. During the civil wars he devoted himself to works of charity among the refugees who flocked to Florence. Cult approved by Pius VII.

JOHN of CUPRAMONTANA (Bl) C. OSB. Cam.   AC. Apr 11 d. 1303. A Camaldolese monk-hermit who lived many years in the cave of Cupramontana, on Mt Massaccio.

JOHN LOCKWOOD (Bl) M. **AC. Apr 13** d. 1642. John Lockwood, *alias* Lascelles,

was born at Sowerby, Yorks, and studied for the priesthood at Rome. Ordained in 1597, he was sent to the English mission, where he worked from 1598 till 1642. At the age of eighty-one he was hanged, drawn and quartered for his priesthood at York. Beatified in 1929.

JOHN of VILNA (St) M. AC. Apr 14 See SS Antony, John and Eustace.

JOHN of GRACE-DIEU (Bl) Ab. OSB. Cist.   PC. Apr 20 d. 1280. A Benedictine monk of St Denis, who passed over to the Cistercians and became successively abbot of Igny, of Clairvaux (1257) and of Grace-Dieu (*c.*1262).

JOHN FINCH (Bl) M.   AC. Apr 20 d. 1584. A yeoman farmer of Eccleston in Lancashire, who suffered at Lancaster for being reconciled to the Church and for harbouring priests. Beatified in 1929.

JOHN of VALENCE (Bl) Bp. OSB. Cist.   AC. Apr 26 d. 1146. A native of Lyons, he was a canon of that city, and after a pilgrimage to Compostella, entered Clairvaux under St Bernard. In 1117 he was sent to found Bonneval (*Bona Vallis*) on the Loire, and proved to be an excellent abbot. In 1141 he was raised to the see of Valence, but had to be carried by main force to the altar to be consecrated. Cult approved in 1901.

JOHN of CONSTANTINOPLE (St) Ab.   RM. Apr 27 d. 813. Abbot of the monastery called *Cathares* at Constantinople, a staunch opponent of the Iconoclast emperor Leo the Armenian by whom he was imprisoned and exiled.

JOHN BAPTIST THAUH (Bl) M. **AC. Apr 28** d. 1840. A native catechist in Tonkin, attached to the Society of Foreign Missions. He was beheaded with Bl Peter Hieu, q.v.

JOHN-LOUIS BONNARD (Bl) M.
AC. May 1

1824–1852. A missionary priest, a native of France, who belonged to the Paris Society of Foreign Missions and was beheaded in Annam. Beatified in 1900.

JOHN HOUGHTON (Bl) M. O.
Cart.   AC. May 4

d. 1535. A native of Essex and prior of the London Charterhouse. As such, he was the first to oppose Henry VIII's Acts of Succession and Supremacy, giving to his monks and the whole of England a magnificent example of fidelity to the Catholic faith, for which he was martyred at Tyburn, with four companions. He is the proto-martyr of the post-reformation English martyrs. Beatified in 1886.

JOHN HAILE (Bl) M.   AC. May 5

d. 1535. A secular priest, vicar of Isleworth, Middlesex. He was martyred at Tyburn with Bl John Houghton, q.v.

JOHN of BEVERLEY (St) Bp. OSB.
RM. May 7

d. 721. He was born at Harpham in Yorkshire and studied at Canterbury under SS Adrian and Theodore; then he became a monk at Whitby. Eventually he was consecrated bishop of Hexham, whence he was transferred to York as metropolitan. As such he ordained St Bede to the priesthood. He was the founder of Beverley Abbey, to which he retired in his old age.

JOHN of CHÂLON (St) Bp.
AC. May 9

d. c.475. The third bishop of Châlonsur-Saone. He was consecrated by St Patiens of Lyons.

JOHN of AVILA (Bl) C. AC. May 10

d. 1569. Born at Almodovar, in New Castile, he studied law at Salamanca and theology at Alcalá (*Complutum*). After his ordination he was preparing to sail for the missions of the West Indies and Mexico, but was detained by the archbishop of Seville. He spent the forty years of his priestly career evangelizing Andalusia—preaching, writing, directing souls (among others those of SS Teresa, Francis Borgia, John of God, Louis of Granada) and converting sinners. His ascetical writings, chiefly his letters, rank high among the Spanish classics. He is usually called "the Apostle of Andalusia". Beatified in 1894.

JOHN ROCHESTER (Bl) M. O.
Cart.   AC. May 11

d. 1537. He was born at Terling, Essex, and a professed Carthusian of the London Charterhouse. He was martyred at York, with Bl James Walworth. Beatified in 1886.

JOHN STONE (Bl) M. OSA.
AC. May 12

d. 1538. An Augustinian friar at Canterbury, martyred in that place for denying the royal supremacy.

JOHN the SILENT (St) Bp.
RM. May 13

454–558. Born at Nicopolis in Armenia, before his twentieth year he had already founded a monastery and become a monk in his native city. At the age of twenty-eight he was chosen bishop of Colonia (Taxara). He resigned after nine or ten years, and hiding his episcopal dignity, entered the *laura* of St Sabas near Jerusalem. Here he spent the rest of his life, part of it as a "walledup" recluse.

JOHN BAPTIST de la SALLE (St)
Founder   RM. May 15

1654–1719. A native of Reims and a

canon of the cathedral chapter (1667), before he was ordained a priest (1678). His life-work was the foundation, on new, original and revolutionary educational principles, of the congregation of the Brothers of the Christian Schools. In the teeth of extreme opposition, he succeeded in establishing his system and his new Institute on solid foundations. He died in retirement at Saint-Yon. Canonized in 1900.

JOHN NEPOMUCEN (St) M.
RM. May 16

c.1345–1393. A native of Nepomuk, in Bohemia, he became canon of Prague and eventually court chaplain and confessor to Queen Sophie, second wife of the dissolute Wenceslaus IV. He was of a retiring disposition, and repeatedly refused bishoprics which were offered to him. In 1393, or according to another tradition 1383, he was, by order of Wenceslaus, thrown into the river Moldau and drowned. A tradition, still widely credited in Central Europe, attributes his martyrdom to his refusal to reveal to the king what he had heard from the queen in sacramental confession. Canonized in 1729.

JOHN of PARMA (St) Ab. OSB.
AC. May 22

d. c.982. He was born at Parma and early in life was made canon of the cathedral in that city. He is said to have made six pilgrimages to Jerusalem and to have taken the Benedictine habit there. He was abbot of St John's, at Parma (973–c.982) then under the Cluniac observance. He is a minor patron of Parma.

JOHN of CETINA (Bl) M. OFM.
AC. May 22

d. 1397. A Spanish Franciscan, who with Bl Peter de Dueñas (q.v.) was commissioned to evangelize the Moors at Granada and was martyred in the attempt.

JOHN FOREST (Bl) M. OFM.
AC. May 22

d. 1538. Born in all probability at Oxford, where, after his profession as a Friar Minor, he was also educated in the Franciscan college. He was stationed at Greenwich when he became confessor to Queen Catherine of Aragon. He opposed the queen's divorce and the king's supremacy in matters spiritual, and was for this cause burnt to death at Smithfield under conditions of most revolting cruelty. Beatified in 1886.

JOHN BAPTIST MACHADO (Bl) M. SJ.
AC. May 22

1580–1617. Born at Terceira, in the Azores, he became a Jesuit at Coimbra, and in 1609 was dispatched to the Japanese missions. He was beheaded at Nagasaki with two companions. Beatified in 1867.

JOHN BAPTIST de ROSSI (St) C.
RM. May 23

1698–1764. Born at Voltaggio, diocese of Genoa, he studied at the Roman College and, after his ordination in 1721, remained in Rome as a member of the Roman clergy. In 1737 he was made canon of Santa Maria in Cosmedin at the foot of the Aventine. His main work as missioner and catechist was among the teamsters, farmers and herdsmen of the Campagna, and among the sick and prisoners. Canonized in 1881.

JOHN of MONTFORT (Bl) Knight
AC. May 24

d. 1177(8). A Knight Templar of Jerusalem. Wounded in a battle against the Saracens he was taken to Cyprus, where he died at Nikosia. His feast was for a long time celebrated at Cyprus on May 25.

JOHN del PRADO (St) M. OFM.
RM. May 24

d. 1636. Born at Morgobresio, León, Spain. While following his theological course of Salamanca he joined the bare-footed Franciscans of the Strict Observance. Eventually he was sent to Morocco with special ecclesiastical powers, and was martyred there with two other Spanish friars.

JOHN HOAN (Bl) M.   AC. May 26

c.1789–1861. Born at Kim-long, in Cochin-China, he was ordained priest, and worked zealously until his martyrdom by beheading under King Yu-Duc near Dougl Hoi. Beatified in 1909.

JOHN I (St) Pope M.   RM. May 27

d. 526. A Tuscan, who was ordained for the Roman clergy, became archdeacon and finally pope (523). In 526 he went to Constantinople on an embassy from Theodoric the Arian king of the Ostrogoths. On his return Theodoric cast the pope into prison on suspicion of having conspired with the emperor Justin. The pope died there of want and hardship. Some modern writers contest his claim to martyrdom.

JOHN SHERT (Bl) M.   AC. May 28

d. 1582. Born at Shert Hall, near Macclesfield, Cheshire and educated at Brasenose College, Oxford. After his conversion he studied at Douai and Rome and was ordained in 1576. In 1579 he began his work on the English mission. He suffered at Tyburn with BB Thomas Ford and Robert Johnstone. Beatified in 1886.

JOHN de ATARÉS (St) H.
AC. May 29

d. c.750. A hermit in the diocese of Jaca, in the Aragonese Pyrenees, whose cell was situated under a huge rock, where at a later time the Benedictine abbey of St John de la Peña (of the Rock) was built. The saint and the place are famous in Spanish history, since the abbey of La Peña became the cradle of the Christian kingdoms of Navarre and Aragon.

JOHN PELINGOTTO (Bl) C. Tert. OFM.   AC. June 1

1240–1304. A native of Urbino, the son of a merchant. He was received into the Franciscan third order, and devoted his whole life to prayer and works of charity. Cult approved in 1918.

JOHN STOREY (Bl) M.   AC. June 1

d. 1571. He was born in N. England and educated at Oxford, where he received the degree of Doctor of Law and subsequently was appointed president of Broadgate Hall and first Regius Professor of civil law. He married (after 1547), became a member of parliament, and opposed several laws against the Catholic faith, enacted under Edward VI and Elizabeth. He was imprisoned and managed to escape abroad, but was followed by Elizabeth's secret agents, kidnapped, brought back to England and martyred at Tyburn for alleged treason.

JOHN de ORTEGA (St) H.
AC. June 2

d. c.1150. A priest of the diocese of Burgos, in Spain, who after sundry pilgrimages to Palestine, Rome, and Compostella, became a hermit in a small village near Burgos, and helped St Dominic de la Calzada (q.v.) in the work of building bridges and hospices, opening roads, etc. His feast is liturgically observed in the diocese of Burgos.

JOHN GRANDE (Bl) C. AC. June 3

1546–1600. Born at Carmona in Andalusia, Spain, he worked in the linen trade but abandoned that occupation to become a hermit at Marcena. From this time up to his death, punning on his Spanish surname—*Grande* i.e. Great —he always called himself *Juan Grande Pecador*—John the Great Sinner. He left his cell to work in the prisons and hospitals at Xeres, where a recently opened hospital was entrusted to his care. This he handed over to St John of God, taking the habit of the latter's new order at Granada. He died at Xeres while still caring for the prisoners and the sick. Beatified in 1853.

JOHN MARIA MUZEYI (St) M.
                                RM. June 3
d. 1886. He practised the corporal works of mercy until his martyrdom by order of King Mwanga of Uganda. See Uganda (Martyrs of).

JOHN of VERONA (St) Bp.
                                RM. June 6
7th cent. The successor of St Maurus in the see of Verona, in N. Italy.

JOHN DAVY (Bl) M. O. Cart.
                                AC. June 6
d. 1537. A Carthusian monk, professed at the London Charterhouse, starved to death at Newgate, where he was imprisoned for resisting Henry VIII's spiritual supremacy. He suffered with a group of six other Carthusians. Beatified in 1886.

JOHN RAINUZZI (Bl) C. OSB.
                                AC. June 8
d. ? 1330. A Benedictine monk of St Margaret's monastery, at Todi. His charity earned for him the title of "John the Almsgiver", by which he is often called.

JOHN DOMINIC (Bl) Bp. OP.
                                AC. June 10
1356–1418. Born at Florence, he entered the Dominican Order, in which he dis-

tinguished himself as one of the leaders in the restoration of discipline. In 1408 he was named archbishop of Ragusa and created cardinal. He was one of those who worked most successfully for the healing of the Great Schism of the West, and, as papal legate for Hungary and Bohemia, converted many Hussites. Cult confirmed in 1832.

JOHN of SAHAGUN (of ST FACUNDO) (St) C. OSA.
                                RM. June 12
1419–1479. Born at Sahagun, province of León, in Spain, and educated by the Benedictines at the great abbey of his native town, and then at Salamanca and Burgos. While still quite young he held several benefices in the diocese of Burgos, but eventually he surrendered all but one. In 1463 this too he gave up to become an Augustinian at Salamanca, where he held the offices of novice-master and prior. By his fearless preaching he effected a great change in the social life of Salamanca. Canonized in 1690.

JOHN of PULSANO (of MATERA) (St) Ab. OSB.   AC. June 20
d. 1139. A native of Matera in the Basilicata, who early in life entered a Benedictine monastery, where his austerity was not looked upon with much favour. He next joined the monks of Montevergine under St William the founder, but left him to become a popular preacher at Bari. Finally he settled at Pulsano, near Monte Gargano, where he established an abbey, the first of a series of foundations which coalesced into a new Benedictine congregation. He died at Pulsano. He is often called, from his birthplace, St John of Matera.

JOHN BAPTIST ZOLA (Bl) M. SJ.
                                AC. June 20
1576–1626. Born at Brescia in Italy, he

became a Jesuit (1595) and was sent to India (1602) and thence to Japan (1606). He settled at Tacacu; but in 1614 was banished to China. On his return to Japan he was captured and burnt alive at Nagasaki. Beatified in 1867.

JOHN KINSACO (Bl) M. SJ.
AC. June 20

d. 1626. A native of Ocinozu in Japan, who became a Jesuit novice, and was arrested and burnt alive at Nagasaki. Beatified in 1867.

JOHN FENWICK and JOHN GAVAN (BB) MM. SJ. AC. June 20

d. 1679. John Fenwick was born at Durham and educated at Saint-Omer. He became a Jesuit in 1656. John Gavan, a Londoner by birth, was also educated at Saint-Omer and received into the Society of Jesus in 1660. Both were martyred at Tyburn, with three other Jesuits, for alleged complicity in the Oates Plot. Beatified in 1929.

JOHN RIGBY (Bl) M. AC June 21

d. 1600. A layman, born at Harrock Hall, near Wigan, Lancs, who was condemned for being reconciled to the Catholic Church and executed at Southwark. Beatified in 1929.

JOHN I of NAPLES (St) Bp.
RM. June 22

5th cent. The bishop of Naples who translated the body of St Januarius from Puteoli to Naples, "whom blessed Paulinus bishop of Nola, called to the heavenly kingdoms" (RM.).

JOHN IV of Naples (St) Bp.
AC. June 22

d. 835. Locally known as *San Giovanni d'Acquarola*, or "the Peacemaker". Bishop of Naples, where he is now venerated as one of the patron saints of the city.

JOHN (St) M.
RM. June 23

d. 362. A Roman priest beheaded under Julian the Apostate. The relic venerated as the head of John the Baptist at San Silvestro in Capite, the English church in Rome, is supposed to be in reality the head of this martyred priest. According to the RM. he was buried by the priest Concordius.

JOHN the BAPTIST (St) Prophet M.
RM. June 24

1st cent. "The man sent from God", the voice crying in the wilderness: "Prepare ye the way of the Lord", of whom Christ said "among those that are born of women there is not a greater prophet". His career as a forerunner of the Messiah is fully described in the four Gospels. Patristic tradition maintains that St John was freed from original sin and sanctified in his mother's womb: hence from the earliest time the Church has liturgically celebrated the nativity of St John. His martyrdom under Herod is also commemorated (August 29). St John has always been, and still is, one of the most popular of saints. Liturgically, he even ranks above St Joseph, the foster-father of our Lord.

JOHN of TUY (St) H.
AC. June 24

9th cent. A native of Spanish Galicia, who lived as a hermit near Tuy. His body is now enshrined in the Dominican church at Tuy.

JOHN the SPANIARD (Bl) C. O. Cart.
AC. June 25

1123-1160. A native of Almanza in Spain, who, when still a boy, travelled to France and studied at Arles. He became a Carthusian at Montrieu, was transferred to the Grande Chartreuse under St Anthelmus and finally sent as founder and first prior of the charterhouse of Reposoir, near lake Geneva.

He was the first to draw up constitutions for the Carthusian nuns. Cult approved in 1864.

JOHN and PAUL (SS) MM.
RM. June 26

? Roman martyrs who suffered at Rome, but not as traditionally asserted under Julian the Apostate. Their names occur in the canon of the Mass, and there is a stately basilica erected in their name on the Coelian Hill. Their Acts, however, are held by most scholars to be merely a pious fiction.

JOHN of the GOTHS (St) Bp.
AC. June 26

d. c.800. A bishop of the Goths in S. Russia, noted for his defence of the veneration of images. He was driven from his see by the invading Khazars, and died in exile.

JOHN of CHINON (St) H.
RM. June 27

6th cent. A native of Brittany who became a hermit at Chinon in Touraine, where he was the spiritual adviser of Queen St Radegund.

JOHN SOUTHWORTH (Bl) M.
AC. June 28

d. 1654. A Lancashire man who became a student at Douai. He was ordained in 1619 and sent to the English mission, where his ministrations during the plague of 1636 were specially noteworthy. He was arrested and imprisoned as early as 1627, but was subsequently released. He was executed at Tyburn for his priesthood under the commonwealth. Beatified in 1929.

JOHN CORNELIUS SJ. and JOHN CAREY (BB) MM.
AC. July 4

d. 1594. Bl John Cornelius was born at Bodmin of Irish parents. He became a fellow of Exeter College, Oxford, and a student at Reims and then at Rome, where he was ordained priest in 1583. He worked for ten years on the English mission at Lanherne and became a Jesuit only in 1594. He was condemned for the priesthood. Bl John Carey was a layman, an Irish servant of Bl Thomas Bosgrave and a fellow-servant of Bl Patrick Salmon. The four were martyred at Dorchester. Beatified in 1929.

JOHN FISHER (St) Card. Bp. M.
RM. June 13, AC. July 9

1469–1535 (June 22). Born at Beverley in Yorkshire, the son of a draper. He was educated at Cambridge and ever afterwards was connected with the life of the university, of which he eventually became chancellor. As such he did much to further the growth and progress of his Alma Mater, of which he may justly be considered the second founder. In 1504 he was appointed bishop of Rochester and proved to be the most faithful of the English bishops of that period: he upheld the cause of the queen against her adulterous husband, Henry VIII, and refused to take the oath of supremacy. He was for this reason beheaded on Tower Hill. Shortly before his death he had been created cardinal by the pope. He died with the words *Te Deum* on his lips. Canonized in 1935.

JOHN of COLOGNE (St) M. OP.
RM. July 9

d. 1572. A native of Cologne who became a Dominican and parish priest of Horner, Holland. He was hanged with the other Gorkum martyrs, q.v. They were canonized in 1867.

JOHN of OSTERWICK (St) M. OSA.
RM. July 9

d. 1572. A native of Holland who joined the Augustinians at Briel and was director and confessor of a community of Augustinian nuns at Gorkum when the town was taken by the Calvinists. He suffered with the group of the Gorkum Martyrs, q.v.

JOHN of BERGAMO (St) Bp.
RM. July 11

d. *c*.690. A bishop of Bergamo (*c*.656 to *c*.690) renowned for his learning and great success in combating Arianism. The letters BM. appended to his name, instead of being read *Bonae Memoriae* —"of good memory", were wrongly taken for *Beati Martyris*—"of the Blessed Martyr"—and he was in consequence formerly considered to have been a martyr.

JOHN the GEORGIAN (St) Ab.
AC. July 12

d. *c*.1002. This John is usually surnamed "the Iberian", i.e., the Georgian, and also "the Hagiorite". With his wife's consent, he and his son St Euthymius became monks on Mt Olympus in Bithynia. Thence they migrated to Mt Athos in Macedonia, where they founded the monastery of Iviron (Iweron—the Iberian), which otill exists.

JOHN GUALBERT (St) Ab. OSB. Vall.
RM. July 12

d. 1073. A Florentine by birth, of the noble family of the Visdomini. As a young man he spent his time in worldly amusements, until one Good Friday, having pardoned his brother's murderer, he saw the image of the crucifix miraculously bow its head in acknowledgement of Gualbert's good action. Thereupon John became a Benedictine at San Miniato del Monte, at Florence. When it seemed likely that he would be appointed abbot he left the abbey for a more secluded spot and founded the monastery of Vallumbrosa—*Vallis Umbrosa*—near Fiesole, under St Benedict's Rule. His foundation soon grew into a

powerful Congregation spread chiefly through Tuscany and Lombardy. St John died at Passignano, one of his own foundations, and was canonized in 1193.

JOHN JONES (Bl) M. OFM.
AC. July 12

d. 1598. John Jones, alias Buckley, was born at Clynog Fawr, Carnarvon. He became a Franciscan Observant at Rome and worked on the London mission from 1592 till 1597. He was martyred for his priesthood at Southwark. Beatified in 1929.

JOHN NAISEN (Bl) M. AC. July 12
d. 1626. A wealthy Japanese layman from Arima. When the persecutors threatened him with the prostitution of his wife, his constancy gave way for a time, but he repented and was burnt alive at Nagasaki. Beatified in 1867.

JOHN TANACA (Bl) M. AC. July 12
d. 1626. A Japanese layman who gave shelter to Bl Balthasar de Torres. After a long imprisonment at Omura he was burnt alive at Nagasaki. Beatified in 1867.

JOHN FERNANDEZ, born at Lisbon.

JOHN of SAN MARTIN, born at Toledo.

JOHN de BAEZA, a Spaniard by birth.

JOHN de ZAFRA, born at Toledo.

JOHN de MAVORGA, born in Aragon.

JOHN FERNANDEZ (BB) MM. SJ.
AC. July 15

d. 1570. Born at Braga, Portugal.

All belonged to the Society of Jesus; the first two were clerics and the rest temporal-coadjutors. All suffered martyrdom with Bl Ignatius de Azevedo and comp., q.v.

JOHN PLESINGTON (Bl) M.
AC. July 19

d. 1697. Born at Dimples, near Garstang, Lancs, and educated at Valladolid, he worked on the mission in Cheshire, and was hanged for his priesthood at Chester. Beatified in 1929.

JOHN of EDESSA (St) H.
RM. July 21

6th cent. A Syrian monk of Edessa and an associate of St Simeon Salus.

JOHN and BENIGNUS (SS) OSB.
AC. July 21

d. 707. Said to have been twin brothers and monks of Moyenmoutier under St Hidulphus.

JOHN LLOYD (Bl) M. AC. July 22

d. 1679. A native of Brecknockshire who received his priestly education at Valladolid and then served the Welsh mission. He was executed for his priesthood at Cardiff with Bl Philip Evans, SJ. Beatified in 1929.

JOHN CASSIAN (St) Ab.
AC. July 23

c.360–433. An Eastern monk who received his monastic training in Egypt, and afterwards established himself at Marseilles, where he founded the abbey of St Victor and a nunnery, and ruled both from Lérins. His *Conferences* and his *Institutes* were commended by St Benedict as authoritative treatises on the training of monks, and in consequence have exerted a lasting influence in the Christian world.

JOHN of TOSSIGNANO (Bl) Bp.
AC. July 24

d. 1446. John Tavalli was born at Tossignano, near Imola, and, after his studies at the university of Bologna, joined the order of the Gesuati. In 1431 he was raised to the see of Ferrara. He is best remembered as the translator of the Bible into Italian. Cult confirmed by Benedict XIV.

JOHN BOSTE (Bl) M. AC. July 24

d. 1594. Born at Dufton in Westmorland and educated at Queen's College, Oxford, and after his conversion, at Reims. He was ordained in 1581 and laboured in the northern counties for twelve years until his martyrdom for the priesthood at Durham. Beatified in 1929.

JOHN INGRAM (Bl) M.
AC. July 26

d. 1594. Born at Stoke Edith, Herefordshire. He became a convert, studied at New College, Oxford, and afterwards at Reims and Rome. After his ordination in 1589, he worked in Scotland. He was condemned for his priesthood, and suffered at Gateshead.

JOHN BAPTIST LO (Bl) M.
AC. July 29

1825–1861. A Chinese servant beheaded at Tsin-gai. Beatified in 1909.

JOHN SORETH (Bl) C. OC.
AC. July 30

c.1420–1471. A native of Caen in Normandy. He joined the Carmelites and was their prior general from 1451 to 1471. He was a forerunner of St Teresa in his efforts to return to the primitive observance and to admit nunneries into the order. Cult approved in 1865.

JOHN COLOMBINI (Bl) Founder
RM. July 31

c.1300–1367. A Native of Siena, who became a prominent citizen, held the office of *Gonfalionere* (first magistrate), and is described as an ambitious, avaricious and bad-tempered man. While reading the story of the conversion of St Mary of Egypt, he was suddenly converted and eventually formed a small society of lay persons devoted to penance and deeds of charity. They were called *Gesuati* and were approved in 1367. Bl John was beatified by Gregory XIII.

JOHN FELTON (Bl) M.
AC. Aug 8

d. 1570. Born at Bermondsey, of a Norfolk family. He was living at Southwark when the bull of Pope St Pius V excommunicating Queen Elizabeth reached London, and he bravely affixed a copy to the door of the Bishop of London's house. For this he was martyred in St Paul's churchyard. Beatified in 1886.

JOHN of SALERNO (Bl) C. OP.
AC. Aug 9

c.1190–1242. A native of Salerno, who received the religious habit from St Dominic and became the founder of the Dominican friary of Santa Maria Novella at Florence (1221). Cult approved in 1783.

JOHN of ALVERNIA (Bl) C. OFM.
AC. Aug 9

1259–1322. Born at Fermo, he joined the Friars Minor in 1272, and thereafter lived a semi-eremitical life on Mt Alvernia, whence he evangelized the surrounding district. He was famous for his gift of infused knowledge. Cult approved in 1880.

JOHN of RIETI (Bl) C. OSA. Erem.
AC. Aug 9

d. c.1350. John Bufalari was a native of Castel Porziano, near Rome, and an Augustinian friar-hermit at Rieti. Cult approved in 1832.

JOHN BAPTIST VIANNEY (St) C.
RM. Aug 4 and 9

1786–1859. More often called "the Curé d'Ars". Born at Dardilly, near Lyons,

he was a farm-hand and already nineteen when he began his studies for the priesthood, which he completed only with considerable difficulty. He was, however, ordained in 1815 and three years after was appointed parish priest of Ars, a small village near Lyons, where he worked for the rest of his life, and for which he won world-wide fame. His chief work was the direction of souls: his confessional was thronged with all classes of persons, who flocked to him from far and wide, and during the last ten years of his life he spent in it sixteen to eighteen hours a day. He was gifted with discernment of spirits, prophecy and hidden knowledge, and was often tormented by evil spirits. Canonized in 1925 and declared patron saint of parishpriests.

JOHN and PETER BECCHETTI (BB) CC. OSA. Erem.
AC. Aug 11

13th cent. Descendants of the family of St Thomas Becket (Becchetti) from a branch that settled at Fabriano, in Italy. Both belonged to the Augustinian hermits, and Bl John is said to have taught at Oxford. Cult approved in 1835.

JOHN BAPTIST PETRUCCI (Bl) M. OSM.
AC. Aug 11

See Laurence Nerucci, etc.

JOHN BERCHMANS (St) C. SJ.
RM. Aug 13

1599–1621. Born at Diest in Brabant, the son of a master-shoemaker. He studied at Malines and there also he entered the Society of Jesus at the age of seventeen and was sent to Rome for his novitiate. His short life of twenty-two years was remarkable for the heroic fidelity with which he kept the minutest points of regular observance. He was canonized in 1888, and is venerated as patron of young mass-servers.

JOHN of SAINT MARTHA (Bl) M. OFM.   AC. Aug 16

1578–1618. Born at Prados, near Tarragona, in Spain, after his ordination (1606) he was sent to Japan, where he is said to have gained a perfect mastery of the language. Arrested at Meaco in 1615, he was beheaded after a three years' imprisonment. Beatified in 1867.

JOHN of MONTE MARANO (St) Bp. OSB.   AC. Aug 17

d. 1094. A Benedictine monk, probably of Montecassino. He was nominated bishop of Monte Marano by Gregory VII (1074) while that pope was in exile at Salerno. His cult was approved in 1906, and he is venerated as the principal patron saint of Monte Marano.

JOHN and CRISPUS (SS) MM.   RM. Aug 18

According to the Roman Martyrology, they were Roman priests who devoted themselves to recovering and burying the bodies of the martyrs, for which they themselves suffered martyrdom. Their names are taken from the untrustworthy Acts of SS Simplicius, Faustinus and Beatrix.

JOHN NANGATA, JOHN YANO and JOHN FOIAMON (BB) MM.   AC. Aug 19

d. 1662. The two first named were sailors in the ship on which Bl Peter Zuñiga (q.v.) was a traveller, and the last named was a scribe on the same ship. They were beheaded at Nagasaki. Beatified in 1867.

JOHN EUDES (St) Founder RM. Aug 19   RM. Aug 19

1601–1680. A native of Ri, France, who after his ordination (1625) entered the French Oratory and devoted himself wholeheartedly to the "home-mission", twice risking his life in attending victims of the plague. In 1641 he founded the Sisterhood of our Lady of Charity of the Refuge to care of women of ill repute and in 1643 the Society of Jesus and Mary—*Eudists*—for the education of priests. He was moreover the originator of the liturgical cult of the Sacred Heart. He died at Caen, and was canonized in 1925.

JOHN KEMBLE (Bl) M.   AC. Aug 22

1599–1679. A native of Herefordshire. After his studies and ordination at Douai, he served the missions of Monmouthshire and Herefordshire for fifty-three years (1625–1679). In his eighty-first year he was hanged, drawn and quartered at Hereford for being a priest. Beatified in 1929.

JOHN WALL (Bl) M. OFM.   AC. Aug 22

d. 1679. Born near Preston, in Lancs, he was educated at Douai and in Rome. Here he joined the Friars Minor with the new name of Fr Joachim of St Anne (1651). In 1656 he joined the Worcester mission which he served until the year of his martyrdom for his priesthood at Worcester. Beatified in 1929.

JOHN of CARAMOLA (Bl) C. OSB. Cist.   PC. Aug 26

d. 1339. A native of Toulouse who became a hermit on Mt Caramola in the Basilicata, Italy, and afterwards a Cistercian lay-brother at the abbey of Sagittario, near Chiaramonte, Naples.

JOHN BASSAND (Bl) C. OSB. Cel.   AC. Aug 26

1360–1445. A native of Besançon, where he joined the Canons Regular of St

Paul. Shortly after, however, he passed over to the Celestine Benedictines at Paris. He held important offices in the congregation, and was spiritual director of St Colette. He made great efforts to establish his congregation in England and Aragon.

JOHN (St) M.   RM. Aug 27
See Marcellinus, Mannea, etc.

JOHN (St) Bp.   RM. Aug 27
d. 813. Bishop of Pavia, in Lombardy, 801–813.

JOHN ROCHE (Bl) M. AC. Aug 30
d. 1588. John Roche (*alias* Neale) was an Irish waterman who was condemned to death for rescuing a priest. He suffered at Tyburn with five companions: BB Richard Leigh, etc. Beatified in 1929.

JOHN du LAU (Bl) Bp. M.
AC. Sept 2
d. 1792. Archbishop of Arles. During the French Revolution he was imprisoned in the Carmelite church in the rue de Rennes at Paris, and later martyred, by the mob, with the approval of the Legislative Assembly, for refusing the oath and constitution of the clergy which had been condemned by the Holy See. He forms part of the group September (Martyrs of) q.v.

JOHN of PERUGIA and PETER of SASSOFERRATO (BB) MM. OFM.
AC. Sept 3
d. 1231. These two Franciscan friars, priest and lay-brother respectively, were sent by St Francis of Assisi in 1216 to preach to the Mohammedans in Spain. They worked in the district between Teruel and Valencia. Having been seized in a mosque at Valencia and refusing to apostatize they were beheaded. Cult approved in 1783.

JOHN of NICOMEDIA (St) M.
RM. Sept 7
d. 303. A Christian of rank, who, when the edict of persecution against the Christians was first published at Nicomedia, removed it and tore it to pieces. He was burnt alive.

JOHN of LODI (St) Bp. OSB.
AC. Sept 7
d. 1106. A native of Lodi Vecchio in Lombardy, who, after being a hermit for some years, entered the abbey of Fontavellana, where he professed the Benedictine Rule under St Peter Damian. In 1072 he was chosen prior of the abbey and in 1105 bishop of Gubbio. He wrote the life of St Peter Damian.

JOHN MAKI (Bl) M.   AC. Sept 7
d. 1627. An adopted son of Bl Louis Maki. He was burnt alive at Nagasaki. Beatified in 1867.

JOHN DUCKETT (Bl) M. AC. Sept 7
d. 1644. A kinsman of Bl James Duckett, the bookseller (q.v.). He was born at Underwinder, near Sedbergh, Yorks, educated for the priesthood at Douai and ordained in 1639. He ministered to the Catholics at Durham. Martyred for his priesthood at Tyburn with Bl Ralph Corby. Beatified in 1929.

JOHN TOMAKI and JOHN INAMURA (BB) MM. Tert. OP.
AC. Sept 8
d. 1628. Japanese laymen and Dominican tertiaries, beheaded at Nagasaki for helping the missionaries. Bl John Tomaki was a very active Christian and the proud father of four martyr sons. Beatified in 1867.

JOHN KINGOCU (Bl) M. SJ.
AC. Sept 10
d. 1622. Born at Amanguchi in Japan, he was a catechist of Bl Charles Spinola,

by whom he was received into the Society of Jesus in the prison at Omura. He was beheaded at Nagasaki. Beatified in 1867.

JOHN of COREA (Bl) M. AC. Sept 10
d. 1622. A boy of twelve, son of Bl Antony of Corea and his wife Mary, beheaded at Nagasaki. Beatified in 1867.

JOHN-GABRIEL PERBOYRE (Bl) M.   AC. Sept 11
See Gabriel Perboyre.

JOHN the DWARF (St) H.
AC. Sept 15
5th cent. John, nicknamed *Kolobos*, "the Dwarf", was a native of Basta in Lower Egypt. He became a disciple of St Poemen in the desert of Skete, and is described as short-tempered and conceited by nature, but gentle and humble by grace. He was also famous for his absentmindedness. In obedience to orders he watered a walking stick, and when it sprouted, it was called "the tree of obedience".

JOHN (St) M.   RM. Sept 16
See Abundius, Abundantius, etc.

JOHN de MASSIAS (Bl) C. OP.
AC. Sept 18
1585–1645. A native of Ribera, in Estremadura, Spain, who crossed over to S. America and worked on a cattle ranch before becoming a Dominican lay-brother at Lima. He was employed as the doorkeeper of the friary to the end of his life. Beatified in 1837.

JOHN EUSTACE (Bl) Ab. OSB. Cist.   PC. Sept 20
d. 1481. A canon regular at Mons who became a Cistercian and eventually was made first abbot of Jardinet, in the diocese of Namur. He was deputed to restore discipline in several other houses.

JOHN (St) M.   RM. Sept 23
See Andrew, John, etc.

JOHN of MEDA (St) Ab. OSB.
AC. Sept 26
d. 1159 (?). A native of Meda, and a member of the clergy of Milan, who about the year 1134 joined the *Humiliati* and advised them to adopt St Benedict's Rule, which they did, although they continued to call themselves canons. Canonized by Alexander III.

JOHN MARK (St) Bp.
RM. Sept 27
1st cent. The RM. makes this John Mark (see Acts XII, 25) a bishop of Byblos in Phoenicia. Nowadays most biblical scholars identify him with St Mark the evangelist, first bishop of Alexandria.

JOHN of CORDOVA (St) M.
RM. Sept 27
See Adolphus and John.

JOHN COCHUMBUCO (Bl) M.
AC. Sept 28
d. 1630. A tertiary of St Augustine and a native catechist to Bl Bartholomew Gutierrez. Beheaded at Nagasaki, and beatified in 1867.

JOHN de MONTMIRAIL (Bl) C. OSB. Cist.   AC. Sept 29
1165–1217. Besides other titles of nobility he was Seigneur de Montmirail on the Marne. He was bred to arms and married and had several children, but as soon as he could win his wife's consent, he became a Cistercian at Longpoint, where he died. He is venerated liturgically by the Cistercians and in several French dioceses.

JOHN of GHENT (Bl) C. OSB.
PC. Sept 29
d. 1439. A Benedictine of the abbey of

Sainte-Claude on the Jura Mountains. A collaborator with St Joan of Arc, known as "the Hermit of St Claude".

JOHN of DUKLA (Bl) C. OFM. AC. Oct 1
d. 1484. A native of Dukla in Polish Galicia, who became a Franciscan Conventual at Lemberg, and at the instigation of St John of Capistrano passed over to the Observants, and worked successfully among the Ruthenian schismatics. Cult approved in 1739.

JOHN ROBINSON (Bl) M. AC. Oct 1
d. 1588. Born at Ferrensby, Yorks. Having become a widower he went to Reims to study for the priesthood and was ordained there in 1585. He was executed for his priesthood at Ipswich. Beatified in 1929.

JOHN HEWITT (Bl) M. AC. Oct 5
d. 1588. *Alias* Weldon and Savell. A native of Yorkshire, he was educated at Caius College, Cambridge and studied for the priesthood at Reims. He was ordained in 1586 and hanged for his priesthood at Mile End Green. Beatified in 1929.

JOHN LEONARDI (St) Founder RM. Oct 9
c.1550–1609. A native of Diecimo in the diocese of Lucca. While serving as an apprentice to a pharmacist at Lucca he studied for the priesthood and was ordained in 1571. He worked with great zeal among the prisoners and in hospitals and, with the help of two laymen and some priests, founded the Institute of Clerks Regular of the Mother of God, approved in 1593. He is reckoned one of the founders also of the College of Propaganda Fide in Rome, and was appointed visitor of the Vallombrosans and Monteverginians.

JOHN of BRIDLINGTON (St) C. OSA. AC. Oct 11
d. 1379. John Thwing, a student at the university of Oxford, joined the community of Augustinian canons at Bridlington and in due course ruled it as prior for seventeen years. Canonized in 1403. Nothing else is known about him.

JOHN CANTIUS (St) C. RM. Oct 20
c.1395–1473 (Dec 24). Born at Kenty in Silesia, he graduated at the university of Cracow, and was appointed there to the chair of Sacred Scripture. For some time he took charge of a parish but, fearing the responsibility of the care of souls, returned to his biblical teaching, which he carried on until his death. He made a practice of sharing his earnings with the poor. Canonized in 1767.

JOHN of SYRACUSE (St) Bp. OSB. AC. Oct 23
d. c.609. Bishop of Syracuse from 595 till c.609.

JOHN BUONI (Bl) C. OSA. Erem. RM. Oct 23
d. 1249. A native of Mantua who in early life was a licentious jester at various Italian courts. In 1208, after a severe illness, he changed his life completely and retired to do penance as a hermit near Cesena, whither a number of disciples followed him. They were given the Augustinian rule (*Boniti*) by Innocent IV, and soon they coalesced with similar hermits to form the order of Augustinian hermit friars. Cult approved in 1483.

JOHN ANGELO PORRO (Bl) C. OSB. AC. Oct 24
d. 1504. A native of Milan who joined the Servites, and after a time spent at Monte Senario, returned to Milan where he worked to the end of his life. Cult approved in 1737.

JOHN DAT (Bl) M.   AC. Oct 28
1764-1798. A native of W. Tonkin, ordained to the priesthood in 1798. After three months' captivity he was beheaded in the same year. Beatified in 1900.

JOHN of AUTUN (St) Bp.
                                 RM. Oct 29
? A bishop-saint venerated at Autun, of whom no particulars are extant.

JOHN SLADE (Bl) M.   AC. Oct 30
d. 1583. A native of Manston, Dorset (?) and a student at New College, Oxford. He became a schoolmaster, and was martyred at Winchester for denying the royal supremacy in spiritual matters. Beatified in 1929.

JOHN and JAMES (SS) MM.
                                    RM. Nov 1
d. c.344. Persian martyrs who suffered under King Shapur II. John is described as a bishop.

JOHN BODEY (Bl) M.   AC. Nov 2
d. 1583. Born at Wells, Somerset, and a fellow of New College, Oxford. He became a convert and studied law at Douai. He returned to England and became a schoolmaster. He was condemned for repudiating the royal supremacy in spiritual matters and was hanged at Andover. Beatified in 1929.

JOHN ZEDAZNELI (St) Ab.
                                     AC. Nov 4
6th cent. The leader of the group of Syrian monks, who evangelized Georgia (Iberia) and introduced the monastic life there.

JOHN BAPTIST CON. (Bl) M.
                                     AC. Nov 7
1805-1840. A native of Tonkin, a layman and married, who was beheaded for the faith. Beatified in 1900.

JOHN of RATZEBURG (St) Bp. M.
                                    AC. Nov 10
d. 1066. A native of Scotland, who became a missionary in Germany. He was appointed bishop of Ratzeburg and evangelized the Baltic coastal region, where he was martyred.

JOHN of POLAND (St) M. OSB.
                                    RM. Nov 12
See Benedict, John and Comp.

JOHN CINI "della PACE" (Bl) C. Tert. OFM.   AC. Nov 12
d. 1433. Surnamed "the Soldier", or "Stipendario", or from his domicile, *"de Porta pacis"*, *"della pace"*. He was a native of Pisa, bred to arms, who in 1396, became a Franciscan tertiary and founded several charitable organizations and a confraternity of flagellants. Cult approved in 1856.

JOHN LICCI (Bl) C. OP.
                                    AC. Nov 14
1400-1511. Born at Caccamo in the diocese of Palermo, in Sicily. He joined the Dominican Order and died at the age of 111. Cult confirmed in 1753.

JOHN THORNE (Bl) M. OSB.
                                    AC. Nov 15
d. 1539. A Benedictine at Glastonbury and treasurer of the abbey at the time of the dissolution. He was executed at Glastonbury with his abbot, Bl Richard Whiting and a brother-monk, Bl Roger James. The charge against John Thorne was that of *sacrilege*, the sacrilege consisting in his having hidden various treasures of the abbey church to save them from the rapacious hands of the king. Beatified in 1895.

JOHN EYNON and JOHN RUGG (BB) MM. OSB.   AC. Nov 15
d. 1539. John Eynon was priest in

charge of St Giles, at Reading, and John Rugg a prebendary of Chichester living at Reading Abbey. Both were executed at Reading with the abbot Bl Hugh Faringdon. They are generally considered to have been monks of the abbey. Beatified in 1895.

JOHN XOUN (Bl) M.   AC. Nov 18

d. 1619. A Japanese layman, born at Meaco and baptized by the Jesuits at Nagasaki. He was a member of the confraternity of the Holy Rosary. Burnt alive at Nagasaki. Beatified in 1867.

JOHN of the CROSS (St) Dr. OC.
RM. Nov 24

1542–1591. Juan de Yepes was born at Fontiberos in Old Castile, the son of a weaver. He joined the Carmelites at Medina (1562) and from 1564 to 1567 was a student of theology at Salamanca. He now fell under the influence of St Teresa and was her first "half-friar" of the first house of the reform, founded for men, at Duruelo. From 1572 to 1577 he was the confessor of St Teresa at Avila. There followed a most trying period of ill-treatment, calumny and imprisonment at Toledo, until, in 1578 the Discalced were definitely separated from the Calced Carmelites. St John was now made prior successively of several houses, and in 1585 visitor of Andalusia. The last years of his life were again a period of intense humiliation, misunderstanding and physical suffering. He died in obscurity at Ubeda. St John's highest title to fame are his mystical writings (*The Ascent of Mount Carmel, The Dark Night of the Soul, The Spiritual Canticle, etc*) which, besides being superb masterpieces of Spanish literature, contain a thorough exposition of Catholic mysticism. St John was canonized in 1726 and declared a Doctor of the Church in 1926.

JOHN ANGELOPTES (St) Bp.
AC. Nov 27

d. 433. Bishop of Ravenna, 430–433. He was appointed by the pope metropolitan of Aemilia and Flaminia. The nickname *Angeloptes* means "the man who saw an angel": it was given him because, according to the legend, an angel visible to him alone once came and assisted him in the celebration of mass.

JOHN IVANANGO and JOHN MONTAJANA (BB) MM.
AC. Nov 27

d. 1619. Japanese laymen, both belonging to the royal family of Firando. They were beheaded at Nagasaki with eight companions. Beatified in 1867.

JOHN of VERCELLI (Bl) C. OP.
AC. Dec 1

d. 1283. Born at Mosso Santa Maria, near Vercelli, he studied at Paris and taught law at Paris and Vercelli. He then joined the Friars Preachers, among whom he held several offices ending with that of master-general (1264–1283). He was commissioned by the pope to draw up the *Schema* for the second ecumenical council of Lyons. Cult approved in 1903.

JOHN BECHE (Bl) Ab. M. OSB.
AC. Dec 1

d. 1539. As a young Benedictine Beche took his D.D. at Oxford (1515) and eventually became abbot of St Werburgh at Chester, whence in 1533 he was promoted to the abbacy of Colchester. He was a great friend of SS John Fisher and Thomas More, and opposed Henry VIII's ecclesiastical policy. He took the oath of supremacy, but when in 1538 his abbey was dissolved, he openly denied the king's right to do this. Within the year he was charged with treason and executed at Colchester. Beatified in 1895.

JOHN RUYSBROECK (Bl) C. OSA.
AC. Dec 2

1293–1381. A native of Ruysbroeck, near Brussels, who after his ordination was appointed to a canonry at Sainte-Gudule. In 1343 he founded, and ruled as first prior, the monastery of Groenendael, for Augustinian canons. It was here that he composed his numerous spiritual works, which have entitled him to a prominent place among medieval mystical writers. Cult confirmed in 1908.

JOHN ARMERO (Bl) C. OP.
PC. Dec 2

d. 1566. A Dominican lay-brother at Baeza, Spain, who was directed by his superiors to take Holy Orders. His two great interests in life were study and prayer before the Blessed Sacrament. He is the object of a popular cultus.

JOHN (St) M.   RM. Dec 3
See Claudius, Crispin, etc.

John the WONDER-WORKER (St) Bp.   RM. Dec 5
d. p.750. Bishop of Polybotum in Phrygia, one of the most strenuous champions of orthodoxy against the emperor Leo, the Image-Breaker. Such was his fame as a wonder-worker that the emperor did not dare to interfere with him.

JOHN GRADENIGO (Bl) H. OSB.
AC. Dec 5

d. 1025. A Venetian nobleman, who was professed as a Benedictine at Cuxa, in the Catalonian Pyrenees, together with his friend St Peter Urseolo. After a life of manifold vicissitudes, he died as a hermit near Montecassino.

JOHN ALMOND (Bl) M.
AC. Dec 5

d. 1612. A native of Allerton, near Liverpool, and educated at Much Woolton, Reims, and Rome. Ordained in 1598 he worked on the English mission from 1602 till 1612. He was put to death for his priesthood at Tyburn. Beatified in 1929.

JOHN MASON (Bl) M.
AC. Dec 10

d. 1591. A native of Kendal, Westmorland. He was a layman and was hanged at Tyburn for relieving priests. He suffered with four companions. Beatified in 1929.

JOHN ROBERTS (Bl) M. OSB.
AC. Dec 10

1577–1610. Born at Trawfynydd in Merionethshire, he was brought up nominally a Protestant, but was always a Catholic at heart. At the age of nineteen he went up to St John's College, Oxford, and in 1598 was entered at the Inns of Court as a student of law. This same year travelling on the Continent on holiday, he was received into the Church at Notre Dame, Paris, and went to Valladolid in October for his ecclesiastical course. While there he joined the Benedictines at San Benito el Real (1599), and was professed the following year at Compostella. In December, 1602, after his ordination, he set out for the English mission. His resourcefulness and courage made him an outstanding figure even among the priests of the English mission. Six or seven times he was imprisoned and released; during the plague of 1603 his services to the sick in London made his name known throughout the land. Meanwhile, he was the chief assistant of Dom Augustine Bradshaw in the founding of St Gregory's, at Douai (now Downside Abbey). He was captured in his priestly vestments while saying Mass and executed for his priesthood at Tyburn. Beatified in 1929.

JOHN MARINONI (Bl) C.
AC. Dec 13

1490–1562. A Venetian, canon of St Mark's cathedral, who gave up his canonry to join (1530) St Cajetan, the founder of the Theatines. He was a ubiquitous preacher, the exclusive theme of his sermons being Christ crucified. He refused the archbishopric of Naples, the city in which he died. Cult approved in 1762.

JOHN BREAD-and-WATER (Bl) C. OSB. Cist.
AC. Dec 14

d. *p.*1150. A Cistercian lay-brother of the abbey of Sagramenia (*Sacra Moenia*) in Spain, founded in 1142. On account of Bl John's life-long fasting on bread and water the people nicknamed him Brother John Bread-and-Water. (*Pan y Agua*).

JOHN and FESTUS (SS) MM.
RM. Dec 21

? Martyrs honoured in Tuscany.

JOHN VINCENT (St) Bp. OSB.
RM. Dec 21

d. 1012. A native of Ravenna, who became a Benedictine at St Michael of Chiusa, and then a hermit on Monte Caprario; finally he was made bishop of a diocese in the neighbourhood.

JOHN CIRITA (Bl) H. OSB.
PC. Dec 23

d. *c.*1164. A Spanish Benedictine who was first a hermit in Galicia and then a monk at Toronca in Portugal. He was instrumental in handing over the abbey to the Cistercians, and is said to have written the rule of the Knights of Avis.

JOHN (St) Apostle and Evang.
RM. Dec. 27

d. *c.*100. Often surnamed in English the Divine i.e. the theologian. A Galilean, the son of Zebedee and brother of St James the Greater, John was a fisher-man by profession until called by Christ to be an apostle. He became in fact "the Disciple whom Jesus loved," whom our Lord, dying on the Cross, made the guardian of his mother. He wrote the fourth Gospel, chiefly to prove Christ's Divinity, three canonical epistles and the Apocalypse (Revelation). After the resurrection he spent most of his time at Ephesus. A very ancient tradition holds that he was cast into a cauldron of boiling oil at Rome under Domitan, but was preserved unhurt and banished to Patmos. This tradition used to be liturgically commemorated in the Western Church on May 6—St John before the Latin Gate, *ante Portam Latinam*. St John died at Ephesus at a great age.

JOHN ALCOBER (Bl) M. OP.
AC. Dec 30

1694–1748. Born at Gerona, in Spain, after his profession in the Dominican order, he was sent to China (1728) and for sixteen years he worked in the province of Fo-kien. Arrested in 1746, he was strangled in the prison at Futsheu. Beatified in 1893.

JOHN-FRANCIS REGIS (St) C. SJ.
RM. Dec. 31

1597–1640. Born at Font-Couverte in the diocese of Narbonne, in Languedoc. At the age of eighteen he entered the Society of Jesus at Béziers, was ordained in 1631, and from that moment knew no rest, spending himself in preaching the gospel to unlettered farming folk of Languedoc and Auvergne, providing for prisoners and fallen women, establishing confraternities of the Bl Sacrament, and effecting everywhere numerous conversions among the Huguenots. He died while preaching a mission (Dec. 30) and was canonized in 1737.

Note. There are some two hundred or

more other saints, named John—e.g. John Thauler, John Gelibert, John Wagner, John Duns Scotus, John of Jesus-Mary, John of Lerida, etc.—who are usually called *Beati* in their respective orders or nations, but there is no evidence of their being the object of any cult, whether official or popular.

**JOLENTA of HUNGARY (Bl) W.
Poor Clare   AC. March 6**
Otherwise Helen of Poland, q.v.

JONAS (St) H.   RM. Feb 11
4th cent. A monk of Demeskenyanos in Egypt under St Pachomius. He was the gardener of the community for eighty-five years, working in his capacity during the day, and at night plaiting ropes and singing psalms.

**JONAS, BARACHISIUS and Comp.
(SS) MM.   RM. March 29**
d. 327. Jonas and Barachisius were brothers, born at Beth-Asa in Persia. They suffered martyrdom under Shapur II. We have an eye-witness's account of their passion: the brutal inventiveness of the persecutors in devising new tortures was only surpassed by the quiet heroism of the martyrs. Some nine companions suffered at the same time.

**JONAS (JONAH) (St) Prophet.
RM. Sept 21**
? 8th cent. B.C. One of the twelve minor Prophets and the subject of a canonical book of the Bible. Modern writers regard the book as a much later composition. In the time of St Jerome his supposed tomb was shown at Diospolis.

JONAS (YON) (St) M.   RM. Sept 22
3rd cent. A companion or disciple of St Dionysius of Paris, who preached in the neighbourhood of that city, and was martyred.

**JONATUS (St) Ab. OSB.
AC. Aug 1**
d. c.690. A monk of Elnone under St Amandus. He was abbot first of Marchiennes (c.643–652), and then of Elnone (c.652–659).

**JORANDUS (St) H. OSB.
AC. Nov 2**
d. 1340. A monk-hermit at Kergrist and later Saint-Juhec in Pédernec.

**JORDAN of SAXONY (Bl) C. OP.
AC. Feb 15**
d. 1237. Jordan joined the Dominican order under St Dominic himself in 1220, and while yet a novice, attended the first general chapter of the order at Bologna. He was later elected second master-general and under him the new order advanced apace, spread throughout Germany and reached Denmark. He was a powerful preacher and one of his sermons won St Albert the Great for the order. He was shipwrecked and drowned when on a voyage to the Holy Land. Cult confirmed in 1828.

**JORDAN of PISA (Bl) C. OP.
AC. March 6**
d. 1311. Bl Jordan received the Dominican habit at Pisa in 1280. After having studied at Paris he returned to Italy and he became a preacher of very great renown at Florence. It was he who began to make use of the Italian vernacular, instead of Latin, in his sermons, and he is reckoned as one of the creators of the Italian language. Cult approved in 1833.

**JORDAN FORZATEI (Bl) Ab. OSB.
AC. Aug 7**
1158–1248. A native of Padua, where he became a monk and then abbot of the Benedictine abbey of St Justina. He was entrusted with the government of the city by Frederick II. The tyrant Count

Ezzelino cast him into prison where he remained for three years. He died at Venice. His feast is observed at Padua, Treviso, Praglia, etc.

JORDAN of PULSANO (Bl) Ab. OSB.   AC. Sept 5
d. 1152. A monk of Pulsano under the founder St John of Pulsano, whom he succeeded as abbot general of the congregation (1139–1152).

JOSAPHAT (St) Bp. M.
RM. Nov 12
1584–1623. A native of Vladimir in Poland, who, at the age of twenty, became a monk of the Byzantine rite and abbot of Vilna. He devoted himself unsparingly to the work of reuniting schismatics with the Holy See. In his thirty-ninth year he was consecrated archbishop of Polotsk in Lithuania, where he continued his labours, refusing to be dragged into politics. He was martyred by a mob of schismatics. He was the first of the Orientals to be formally canonized in Rome (1867).

JOSAPHAT (St) M.   RM. Nov 27
See Barlaam and Josaphat.

JOSCIUS (JOSBERT, VALBEBERTUS) (Bl) C. OSB.   AC. Nov 30
d. 1186. A Benedictine monk of Saint-Bertin (Saint-Omer) in the diocese of Arras, renowned for his devotion to the *Ave Maria*. The legend adds, that after his death, a rose tree grew out of his mouth and that the name of Mary was written on the leaves of one of the roses!

JOSEPH (*several*)
Note. The spelling is the same in most modern languages, excepting the Italian: Giuseppe, and the Spanish: José. In both Italy and Spain the name is frequently joined to that of our Lady, viz. Giuseppe Maria, José Maria. The feminine form takes the following variants: Italian: Giuseppa, Giuseppina; Spanish: Josefa, Josefina, French: Josephine.

JOSEPH MARY TOMMASI (Bl) Card.   AC. Jan 1
1649–1713. A son of the duke of Palermo. He joined the Theatines and was stationed in Rome, where he devoted his great natural gifts to the methodical study of the Liturgy and produced several very valuable works on this subject. He was the confessor of Cardinal Albani, who, on being elected pope (Clement XI), was ordered by Bl Joseph to accept the papacy under pain of mortal sin. The pope retaliated by appointing Bl Joseph cardinal. He was wont to teach the catechism to the children in his titular church. Beatified in 1803.

JOSEPH of FREISING (Bl) Bp. OSB.   AC. Jan 17
d. 764. A Benedictine of Freising, who in 764 became third bishop of that Bavarian see. In 752 he founded the monastery of St Zeno at Isen. His relics are at Isen.

JOSEPH of LEONISSA (St) C. OFM. Cap.   RM. Feb 4
1556–1612. A native of Leonissa, in the States of the Church, who became a Capuchin (1574). He was sent as a missionary to Turkey, chiefly to care for the Christian galley-slaves. During his stay at Constantinople he suffered both imprisonment and torture. He returned to Italy and died after an operation for cancer. Canonized in 1745.

JOSEPH (JOSIPPUS) of ANTIOCH (St) M.   RM. Feb 15
? A deacon who, with seven others, is stated to have suffered martyrdom at Antioch.

JOSEPH TSHANG-TA-PONG (Bl) M.   AC. March 12
c.1754–1815. A Chinese catechist martyr. Beatified in 1909.

JOSEPH of ARIMATHAEA (St) C.
RM. March 17
1st cent. "The noble counsellor" (Mark, XV, 43), mentioned in the gospels in connexion with our Lord's burial. Later legends concerning him are numerous: in the sacristy of San Lorenzo, Genoa, is the *Sacro Catino*, in which Joseph is said to have caught the blood of Christ at the crucifixion; in England there is the well-known story which connects St Joseph with Glastonbury. None of these legends have any evidence to support them.

JOSEPH (St) Patriarch
RM. March 19
1st cent. Spouse of our Lady and foster-father of our Lord. All that we know of him is to be found in Matt. I–II and Luke I–II. He is described with the all-embracing phrase "a just man". (Matt. I, 9.) From the circumstance of his not being mentioned in the history of the Passion, it is believed that he was then already dead. Devotion to him as a saint, widespread in the East from early ages, has, since the 14th century, grown in the West to such an extent that Pope Pius IX formally constituted him the patron of the universal Church. Besides the feast of his *Transitus* on March 19, he has now a second feast St Joseph the Workman on May 1.

JOSEPH ORIOL (St) C.
RM. March 23
1650–1702. The son of humble parents, citizens of Barcelona, Joseph Oriol succeeded in his ambition to become a priest, took the degree of doctor of theology, and was appointed canon of Santa Maria del Pino in his native city.

He lived on bread and water for twenty-six years, carrying on at the same time a very active apostolate, being particularly successful with soldiers and children. Canonized in 1909.

JOSEPH of PERSIA (St) M.
RM. Apr 22
d. 376. A priest martyr under Shapur II: he suffered with St Acepsimas.

JOSEPH BENEDICT COTTOLENGO (St) C.   RM. Apr 30
1786–1842. Born at Bra, near Turin, where he became canon of the church of *Corpus Domini*. In 1827 he opened a small house near his church for the sick and derelict which in 1832 was transferred to Valdocco, and called the Little House of Divine Providence. The *Piccola Casa* soon grew into a veritable township, comprising asylums, orphanages, hospitals, schools, workshops, almshouses of all descriptions, and catering for all needs. To meet the large daily expenditure required to keep up all these institutions the saint continued to depend almost entirely on alms: he kept no books of accounts and made no investments and his trust in Divine Providence never once failed him. From his time to this the *Piccola Casa* has cared for a daily average of from 8,000 to 9,000 inmates. Throughout his life he was first and foremost a man of prayer. Canonized in 1934.

JOSEPH LUU (Bl) M.   AC. May 2
c.1790–1854. A native catechist, born at Cai-nhum, Cochin-China, who died in prison at Vinh-long. Beatified in 1909.

JOSEPH MUKASA (St) M.
RM. June 3
d. 1886. Majordomo to King Mwanga of Uganda who ordered him to be put to death. See Uganda (Martyrs of).

JOSEPH the HYMNOGRAPHER (St) Bp.   AC. June 14

d. *c*.845. Bishop of Salonica, brother of St Theodore Studites. He bravely opposed the Iconoclast emperor, Theophilus. He is one of the great liturgical poets of the Byzantine Church.

JOSEPH CAFASSO (St) C.
                                RM. June 22
1811–1860. Born at Castelnuovo d' Asti, he was ordained priest in 1833, and three years later was appointed professor of moral theology at the ecclesiastical college at Turin. Ten years later he was appointed superior of the college, and remained in that position till his death. He led a very penitential life and was renowned for his devotion to the Bl Sacrament and as a confessor. Canonized 1947.

JOSEPH YUEN (or UEN) (Bl) M.
                                AC. June 24
1765–1815. A native priest of Tonkin, he suffered a year's imprisonment and was finally strangled. Beatified in 1900.

JOSEPH HEIU (HIEN) (Bl) M. OP.
                                AC. June 27
d. 1840. A native Dominican priest of Annam, who was beheaded at Nam-Dinh. Beatified in 1900.

JOSEPH PETER VYEN (Bl) M. Tert. OP.   AC. July 3

1778–1838. A native catechist, born in E. Tonkin, who died in prison. Beatified in 1900.

JOSEPH BARSABAS (St) Disciple
                                RM. July 20
1st cent. Surnamed "the Just" (Acts I, 23). He was the competitor of St Matthias for the twelfth place among the apostles left vacant by Judas Iscariot.

JOSEPH of PALESTINE (St) C.
                                RM. July 22
d. *c*.356. A Jew belonging to the biblical school of Tiberias. After prolonged interior resistance he became a Christian and was much favoured by the emperor Constantine, who bestowed on him the title of *Comes* (count). He devoted himself to building churches and spreading the Gospel in the Holy Land. He was the host of St Eusebius of Vercelli, St Epiphanius and others.

JOSEPH FERNANDEZ (Bl) M. OP.
                                AC. July 24
1775–1838. A Spaniard and a professed friar of the Dominican order. He was sent to Tonkin in 1805, and having been ordained priest, was appointed provincial vicar in Tonkin, where later he was beheaded. Beatified in 1900.

JOSEPH TSHANG (Bl) M.
                                AC. July 29
c.1832–1861. A young native seminarian, born in the province of Su-tchuen China. He was beheaded at Tsin-gai with three companions. Beatified in 1909.

JOSEPH NIEN (VIEN) (Bl) M.
                                AC. Aug 21
1786–1838. A priest in Tonkin, beheaded at Hung-An. Beatified in 1900.

JOSEPH CALASANCTIUS (St) Founder   RM. Aug 27

1556–1648. Joseph Calasanz was born at Peralta, near Barbastro, in Aragon. Ordained priest in 1583, he was engaged in pastoral work until in a vision he learned that he was to go to Rome. He did so in 1592 and at once joined the Confraternity of Christian Doctrine for the free schooling of neglected children. He gradually organized it into a religious order, called *Le Scuole Pie* (Religious Schools), whose members were, and are still, known as *Scolopi*, or

Piarists. The new congregation had to pass through a period of violent persecution, mainly from other religious engaged in similar work. In his old age Joseph was unjustly accused, brought before the Holy Office and removed from control of the Congregation. Later, however, he was restored. Canonized in 1767.

JOSEPH CANH (Bl) M. Tert. OP.
AC. Sept 5
1765–1838. A native physician of Tonkin, and a Dominican tertiary, beheaded in 1838. Beatified in 1900.

JOSEPH of ST HYACINTH (Bl) M. OP.   AC. Sept 10
d. 1622. A native of Villareal in the Spanish Mancha. He was provincial vicar of the Dominican missions in Japan and spoke Japanese perfectly. He was burnt alive at Nagasaki. Beatified in 1867.

JOSEPH ABIBOS (St) Ab.
AC. Sept 15
d. c.590. Abbot of Alaverdi in Georgia; one of the thirteen Syriac disciples of St John Zedazneli.

JOSEPH of CUPERTINO (St) C. OFM.   RM. Sept 18
1602–1663. Joseph Desa was born at Cupertino, near Brindisi. He tried his vocation in several places, but was summarily dismissed on account of his "poor intelligence". Finally he was received by the Conventual Franciscans of Grotella as a stable-hand and a lay tertiary. On account, however, of the rare spiritual gifts which now began to be manifest in him, he was professed as a friar and duly ordained priest. From this time on his life is an amazing, and perfectly authenticated, succession of preternatural phenomena. The most remarkable of these was his power of

levitation: he would fly straight from the church door to the altar over the heads of the worshippers; once he flew to an olive tree and remained kneeling on a branch for half an hour. Happenings like these were almost every day occurrences, witnessed by hundreds of persons. Withal he was a simple, gentle, humble follower of St Francis. His brethren, however, resented so much publicity, and on this account the saint had much to suffer from them. Canonized in 1767.

JOSEPH THI (Bl) M.   AC. Oct 24
d. 1860. A native captain in the army of King Tu-duc of Cochin-China. He was garroted at An-hoa. Beatified in 1909.

JOSEPH NGHI (Bl) M. AC. Nov 8
d. 1840. A native priest of Tonkin, attached to the Society of Foreign missions of Paris. He was beheaded. Beatified in 1900.

JOSEPH PIGNATELLI (St) C. SJ.
AC. Nov 11
1737–1811. A native of Saragossa and a scion of one of the noblest Aragonese families, who at the age of fifteen joined the Jesuits at Tarragona. After his profession he taught at Manresa, Bilbao and Saragossa. After the banishment of the Jesuits from Spain he went to Corsica, and thence to Ferrara, in charge of the young Jesuits. Finally, after the suppression of the Society in 1773, he resided at Bologna for twenty years, contributing to the temporal support of his religious brethren, and strengthening their courage with brotherly advice. At the same time he worked hard for the restoration of his beloved Institute. In 1799 he was allowed to open a quasi-novitiate, and in 1804 he became the first Italian provincial of the restored Order—"the link between the old and the new Society". Pius XI described

him as a priest of "manly and vigorous holiness". Canonized in 1954.

JOSEPH MKASA (St) M. AC. Nov 16
d. 1885. A Negro, prefect of the royal pages of Uganda, baptized in 1881 and beheaded in 1885. Canonized in 1964.

JOSEPH MARCHAND (Bl) M.
                                    AC. Nov 30
1803–1835. Born at Passavant in the diocese of Besançon, in France. He joined the Missionary Seminary of Paris, and was sent to Annam, where he died while the flesh was being torn from his body with red-hot tongs. Beatified in 1900.

JOSEPH KHANG (Bl) M. Tert. OP.
                                    AC. Dec 6
1832–1861. Born at Tra-vi, province of Nam-Dinh, Tonkin, he was a servant of Bl Jerome Hermosilla, whom he tried to deliver from prison. Caught in the attempt, he was punished with one hundred and twenty lashes and after other most cruel tortures, was beheaded. Beatified in 1906.

JOSEPHA-MARIA of St AGNES
(Bl) V. OSA.   AC. Jan 21
Otherwise Bl Inés de Beniganim, q.v.

JOSEPHINE (ANN-JOSEPH)
LEROUX (Bl) VM.   AC. Oct 23
1747–1794. Born at Cambrai, she became an Ursuline nun at Valenciennes under the name of Josephine. When the convents were closed by the French Revolution she retired to Mons in Hainault, but returned to Valenciennes in 1793. The following year she was captured and guillotined with ten other Ursulines. Beatified in 1920.

JOSHUA (JOSUE) (St) Patriarch
                                    RM. Sept 1
15th cent. B.C. The leader of the Israel-ites into the land of Canaan. All that we know of him is to be found in the Pentateuch and in the canonical book which bears his name. He figures, with Gideon, in both the Eastern and Western martyrologies.

JOSSE (JOST, JODER) (St)
                                    RM. Dec 13
Otherwise Judocus, q.v.

JOVINIAN (St) M.   RM. May 5
d. c.300. A fellow missioner with St Peregrinus of Auxerre, whom he served as reader (*lector*). He is believed to have survived his bishop, and to have died a martyr.

JOVINUS and BASILEUS (SS) MM.
                                    RM. March 2
d. c.258. Two martyrs, who suffered in Rome under Gallienus and Valerian, and were buried on the Latin Way.

JOVINUS (St) M.   RM. March 26
See Peter, Marcian, etc.

JOVITA (St) M.   RM. Feb 15
See Faustinus and Jovita.

JUCUNDA (St) M.   RM. July 27
See Felix, Julia and Jucunda.

JUCUNDA (St) V.   RM. Nov 25
d. 466. A virgin of Reggio in Aemilia, Italy, a spiritual daughter of St Prosper, bishop of that city.

JUCUNDIAN (St) M.   RM. July 4
? An African, who was martyred by being cast into the sea.

JUCUNDINUS (St) M. RM. July 21
See Claudius, Justus, etc.

JUCUNDUS (St) M.   RM. Jan 9
See Epictetus, Jucundus, etc.

JUCUNDUS of BOLOGNA (St) Bp.
RM. Nov 14
d. 485. A bishop of Bologna who flourished in the 5th or 6th century.

JUDE THADDAEUS (St) Apostle
RM. Oct 28
1st cent. One of the Twelve, brother of St James the Less and therefore related by blood to our Lord. He is the writer of one of the canonical epistles. The tradition is that he preached in Mesopotamia, and afterwards, together with St Simon, in Persia, where he was martyred.

JUDGOENOC (JUDGANOC, JOUVEN) (St) RM. Dec 13
Otherwise Judocus, q.v.

JUDICAËL (St) King AC. Dec 17
d. 658. King of Brittany, much beloved by his people. After a victorious reign he abdicated and spent the last twenty years of his life in the monastery of Gaël, near Vannes.

JUDITH (St) OSB. AC. June 29
See Salome and Judith.

JUDOCUS (JUDGANOC, JOSSE, etc.) (St) H. RM. Dec 13
d. 668. A priest, brother of King Judicaël of Brittany, and on the abdication of the latter for some months occupant of the throne. After a pilgrimage to Rome, he left Brittany and retired to Villiers-Saint-Josse, near Saint-Josse-sur-Mer, where he ended his life as a solitary.

JULIA of CERTALDO (Bl) V. OSA.
AC. Feb 15
d. 1367. Julia began life as a domestic servant, but in her nineteenth year she joined the third order of St Augustine at Florence. Returning to her native city of Certaldo, she lived as an an-choress beside the church of SS Michael and James. She died aged forty-eight, on Jan 9. Cult confirmed in 1819.

JULIA BILLIART (Bl) V. Foundress AC. Apr 8
1751–1816. Marie Rose Julia Billiart was born at Cuvilly in Picardy, the daughter of a peasant farmer. At the age of fourteen she took a vow of chastity, and gave herself up to the service and instruction of the poor. Soon her health completely broke down, and she remained a helpless cripple until miraculously cured in 1804. During the French Revolution (1794–1804) pious friends gathered round her couch seeking to give a permanent shape to their works of charity. Thus developed the Institute of Notre Dame, for the Christian education of girls, which was definitely established at Amiens in 1804. Beatified in 1906.

JULIA of SARAGOSSA (St) M.
RM. Apr 16
See Saragossa (Martyrs of).

JULIA (St) VM. RM. May 22
5th cent. A noble maiden of Carthage sold into slavery by the Vandal conquerors. The ship on which she was being taken to Gaul touched at Corsica. A heathen festival was just being observed by the islanders, and when Julia refused to join in it, she was forthwith nailed to a cross.

JULIA (St) M. RM. July 15
See Catulinus, Januarius, etc.

JULIA LOUISE of JESUS (Bl) M. OC. AC. July 17
Otherwise Rose Chrétien, q.v.

JULIA of TROYES (St) VM.
RM. July 21
d. p.272. A maiden of Troyes, France,

seized by the soldiers of the emperor Aurelian after his victory over the usurper Tetricus. Committed to the charge of Claudius, an officer of the army, she succeeded in converting him to Christ, and both were beheaded at Troyes under the same Aurelian.

JULIA of NICOMEDIA (St) M.
RM. July 27
See Felix, Julia and Jucunda.

JULIA of LISBON (St) M.
RM. Oct 1
See Verissimus, Maxima and Julia.

JULIA (St) VM. RM. Oct 7
d. c.300. A martyr, either in Egypt or in Syria, under Diocletian.

JULIA of MÉRIDA (St) VM.
RM. Dec 10
d. c.304. A fellow-sufferer with St Eulalia at Mérida in Spain, under Diocletian.

JULIA (Bl) V. OSB. Cam, AC. Dec 15
? A Camaldolese nun in St Benedict's convent, at Arezzo, Italy.

JULIAN of CAGLIARI (St) M.
RM. Jan 7
? A martyr honoured at Cagliari in Sardinia, whose relics were discovered and enshrined in 1615. Locally he is often styled *Comes* (Count), but nothing is now known of his history.

JULIAN (St) M. RM. Jan 8
See Lucian, Maximian and Julian.

JULIAN, BASILISSA, ANTONY, ANASTASIUS, CELSUS, MARCIONILLA and Comp. (SS) MM.
RM. Jan 9
d. c.304. Julian and Basilissa, a married couple, took vows of continence and turned their house into a hospital for the poor and indigent. Antony was a priest; Anastasius a new convert; Marcionilla a married woman and Celsus her little son. All except Basilissa, were put to death at Antioch—which Antioch it is not known—under Diocletian. The very existence, however, of Julian and Basilissa is questioned.

JULIAN SABAS the ELDER (St) C.
RM. Jan 17 and Oct 18
d. 377. A Mesopotamian solitary who did much to encourage the Christians when persecuted by Julian the Apostate. He was called on to go to Antioch to visit the triumphant Arian party. St John Chrysostom and Theodoret have left us an account of his life.

JULIAN (St) M. RM. Jan 27
See Datius, Reatrus, etc.

JULIAN of SORA (St) M.
RM. Jan 27
d. c.150. A Dalmatian, arrested, put to the torture and beheaded at Sora in Campania, under Antoninus Pius (138–161).

JULIAN of LE MANS (St) Bp.
RM. Jan 27
? 3rd cent. Honoured as the first bishop of Le Mans in France. Various English churches and places dating from Norman and Plantagenet times have this Julian for their titular.

JULIAN of CUENCA (St) Bp.
RM. Jan 28
1127–1208. A native of Burgos in Spain who, on the recapture of Cuenca in New Castile from the Moors by King Alphonsus IX, was appointed bishop of that city. In his longing to help the poor he is said to have spent all his spare time earning money for them by the work of his hands. He is the principal patron saint of the diocese of Cuenca.

JULIAN MAUNOIR (Bl) C. SJ.
AC. Jan 28

1606–1683. Born at Saint-Georges-de-Reitembault in France, he was piously brought up by his parents, and entered the Society of Jesus and took vows in 1625. Being ordained in 1637 he desired to go on the Canadian mission but was destined to become an apostle in Brittany. He mastered the language, and preached so effectively that he is said to have recalled 30,000 to God within two years. He laboured thus for forty years, being joined by a number of secular priests, and finally died worn out with his labours in the town of Plévin. Beatified in 1951.

JULIAN (St) M.   RM. Feb 12
See Modestus and Julian.

JULIAN the HOSPITALLER (St) C.
AC. Feb 12

? Also surnamed "the Poor". The legend, very popular in the Middle Ages, runs as follows: Julian in error slew his own parents; in penance he and his wife went to Rome to obtain absolution and, on their return home, built a hospice by the side of a river, where they tended the poor and the sick and rowed travellers across the river. Julian is for this reason venerated as patron saint of boatmen, innkeepers and travellers. Probably the whole story is fictitious. It may be a variant of that of St Julian of Jan 9 (q.v.).

JULIAN of LYONS (St) M.
RM. Feb 13

? A martyr registered in the RM. as having suffered at Lyons in France, though many maintain that he was martyred at Nicomedia.

JULIAN of EGYPT and Comp.
RM. Feb 16

? It is said that this saint Julian was the leader of 5,000 martyrs who suffered in Egypt. Nothing, however, is known of him and his fellow-sufferers. One text substitutes *militibus* for *millibus* i.e. five soldiers not five thousand persons.

JULIAN of CAESAREA (St) M.
RM. Feb 17

d. 308. According to Eusebius, this St Julian was a native of Cappadocia who happened to be present at Caesarea in Palestine at the martyrdom of St Pamphilus and ten companions. He instantly offered himself to the executioners to make up the number of twelve and was roasted to death at a slow fire.

JULIAN (St) M.   RM. Feb 19
See Publius, Julian, etc.

JULIAN (St) M.   RM. Feb 24
See Montanus, Lucius, etc.

JULIAN, CRONION (surnamed EUNUS) and BESAS (SS) MM.
RM. Feb 27 and Oct 30

d. 250. Martyrs at Alexandria in Egypt under Decius. Julian, too infirm to walk, was carried to the court by his two slaves, both Christians. One apostatized through fear, the other, Eunus, bravely shared his master's lot. They were carried on camels through Alexandria, scourged, and finally, burnt to death. Besas, a sympathetic soldier, was killed by the mob for having sought to shield them. We have these particulars from St Dionysius of Alexandria.

JULIAN of TOLEDO (St) Bp.
RM. March 8

d. 690. Monk of Agali under St Eugene, whom he succeeded first as abbot in the same monastery and then (680) as archbishop of Toledo. He was the first bishop to exercise the primacy over the whole Iberian Peninsula. Besides presiding over several national councils and revising and developing the Mozarabic liturgy, he was a voluminous writer. He was an outstanding churchman in the Spain of his day.

JULIAN of ANAZARBUS (St) M.
RM. March 16
d. *c.*302. A Christian of senatorial rank of Anazarbus in Cilicia who suffered under Diocletian. After being tortured he was taken to the coast, sewn up in a sack half-filled with scorpions and vipers and cast into the sea. His body was recovered and enshrined at Antioch, where St John Chrysostom delivered a sermon in his praise.

JULIAN (St) M.   RM. March 23
? The RM. styles him a confessor but it appears certain that he was also a martyr. Nothing more is known about him.

JULIAN of ST AUGUSTINE (Bl) C.
OFM.   AC. Apr 8
d. 1606. Born at Medinaceli in the diocese of Segovia, in Castile. After being twice rejected he was finally admitted to the Franciscan Order as a lay-brother at Santorcaz. He accompanied the Franciscan preachers on their missions and it was his custom to ring the bell through the streets to summon people to the sermon. Beatified in 1825.

JULIAN CESARELLO de VALLE
(Bl) C. OFM.   AC. May 11
? Born and died at Valle in Istria where his tomb is venerated. Cult approved in 1910.

JULIAN (St) M.   RM. May 23
See Quintian, Lucius, etc.

JULIAN of PERUGIA (St) M.
RM. June 5
See Florentius, Julian, etc.

JULIAN (St) C.   RM. June 9
d. *c.*370. A captive from the West who was sold into slavery in Syria. On regaining his freedom he entered a monastery in Mesopotamia under St Ephrem.

JULIAN (St) M.   RM. July 18
One of the alleged sons of St Symphorosa, q.v.

JULIAN (St) M.   RM. July 20
See Sabinus, Julian, etc.

JULIAN (St) M.   RM. Aug 7
See Peter, Julian, etc.

JULIAN, MARCIAN and Comp.
(SS) MM.   RM. Aug 9
d. 730. A group of about ten citizens of Constantinople (among them a patrician lady, named Mary) who opposed by force the attempts of the Iconoclasts to deface the picture of our Lord set up over the Brazen Gate of the city. They were put to death by order of Leo the Isaurian.

JULIAN (St) M.   RM. Aug 12
See Macarius and Julian.

JULIAN (St) M.   RM. Aug 25
? Baronius describes him as a Syrian priest, but nothing certain is known about him.

JULIAN of AUVERGNE (St) M.
RM. Aug 28
3rd cent. A native of Vienne in France, an officer in the imperial army, and secretly a Christian. On the outbreak of persecution, probably under Decius, he fled but gave himself to his pursuers and was martyred near Brionde. His feast day was fixed by St Germanus of Auxerre.

JULIAN (St) M.   RM. Sept 2
See Diomedes, Julian, etc.

JULIAN (RENATUS) MASSEY (Bl) M. OSB.   AC. Sept 2

d. 1792. Julian (his baptismal name was René) Massey was a Benedictine monk of St Melania of Rennes, of the Congregation of St Maur. He was martyred at Paris with the September martyrs, q.v. Beatified in 1926.

JULIAN (St) M.   RM. Sept 4

See Theodore, Oceanus, etc.

JULIAN (St) M.   RM. Sept 13

See Macrobius and Julian.

JULIAN MAJALI (Bl) Ab. OSB.   AC. Oct 4

d. 1470. A Benedictine of San Martino delle Scale in Sicily. He was held in high esteem by popes and kings. Six years before his death he became a recluse.

JULIAN, EUNUS, MACARIUS and Comp. (SS) MM.   RM. Oct 30

d. c.250. Martyrs of Alexandria in Egypt. St Julian and St Eunus are identical with the martyrs of that name commemorated on Feb 27; St Macarius is again mentioned on Dec 8. The duplication has been caused by the inserting in the RM. of another group of sixteen martyrs, which includes the above-mentioned. This larger group is commemorated in the Greek calendar on this day.

JULIAN (St) M.   RM. Nov 1

See Caesarius and Julian.

JULIAN of APAMEA (St) Bp.   RM. Dec 9

3rd cent. Bishop of Apamea in Syria. He distinguished himself in the controversies with the Montanist and Kata-Phrygian heretics.

JULIANA of BOLOGNA (St) W.   RM. Feb 7

d. 435. A matron of Bologna in Italy whose piety and charity are extolled by St Ambrose of Milan. Her husband, having with her consent left her to become a priest, she devoted herself to bringing up her four children and to the service of the church and the poor.

JULIANA (St) VM.   RM. Feb 16

d. 305. The RM. describes this virgin martyr as having suffered at Nicomedia in Asia Minor, but it is more probable that she was martyred in the neighbourhood at Naples, perhaps at Cumae, where her relics are supposed to be enshrined.

JULIANA (St) VM.   RM. March 20

See Alexandra, Claudia, etc.

JULIANA of CORNILLON (Bl) V. OSA.   AC. Apr 6

1192–1258. Born at Retinnes near Liége she became an Augustinian nun and prioress at Mt Cornillon. As such she promoted the institution of the feast of Corpus Christi. On this account she was reviled as a visionary and driven from Cornillon. Recalled by the bishop of Liége she was expelled definitely from her convent in 1248. She took refuge at the Cistercian nunnery of Salzinnes, and when this place was burnt down, she retired to Fosses, where she lived as a recluse. Her great achievement was the institution of the feast of Corpus Christi. Cult confirmed in 1869.

JULIANA of NORWICH (Bl) H. OSB.   May 13

d. c.1423. Dame Juliana of Norwich is one of the most celebrated of English mystics. She was a recluse at Norwich and was under the spiritual direction of the Benedictines of that city. "The book in which she narrates her visions, *Revelations of Divine Love*, is the tenderest and most beautiful exposition in the English language of God's loving dealings with men." (Attwater, h.l.) She has never been beatified.

JULIANA FALCONIERI (St) V. Tert. OSM.   **RM. June 19**
1270–1340. A lady of Florence who, at the age of sixteen embraced the Rule of the Servite Friars, of whom her uncle St Alexis Falconieri, was a co-founder. In 1304 the community of Servite Tertiaries, known as the "Mantellate" of which she was the first superior was formally established and admitted into the Order by St Philip Benizi. She received Holy Viaticum miraculously on her death-bed. Canonized in 1737.

JULIANA (St) M.   **RM. Aug 12**
See Hilaria, Digna, etc.

JULIANA PURICELLI (Bl) V. OSA.   **AC. Aug 14**
1427–1501. A native of Busto-Arizio in upper Italy, who, as an Augustinian nun, was the first companion of Bl Catherine da Pallanza at the Sacro Monte sopra Varese, where she died. Cult approved in 1769.

JULIANA (St) VM.   **RM. Aug 17**
See Paul and Juliana.

JULIANA (St) M.   **RM. Aug 18**
See Leo and Juliana.

JULIANA of COLLALTO (Bl) V. OSB.   **AC. Sept 1**
d. 1262. Born near Treviso of the noble Collalto family. At the age of ten she became a Benedictine at Salarola, whence, in 1222, she migrated with Bl Beatrix of Este, to Gemmola. In 1226 she became the abbess-foundress of SS Biagio and Cataldo at Venice. Cult approved by Gregory XVI.

JULIANA of PAVILLY (St) Abs. OSB.   **AC. Oct 11**
d. c.750. A servant girl, who became a nun at Pavilly in Normandy under St Benedicta, and finally abbess of the same nunnery. She is called "the Little Sister of Jesus".

JULIANA (St) M.   **RM. Nov 1**
See Cyrenia and Juliana.

JULIE BILLIART (Bl) V. AC. Apr 8
French form for Julia Billiart, q.v.

JULIETTE VEROLOT (Bl) M. OC.   **AC. July 17**
d. 1794. Called in religion Sister St Francis Xavier. She was born in the diocese of Troyes and became a Carmelite nun at Compiègne, the last Carmelite to be professed there (Jan 12, 1789) before the outbreak of the French Revolution. She was guillotined with her community at Compiègne. Beatified in 1906.

JULIOT (St) M.   **RM. June 16**
See Quiricus and Julitta. (The Cornish form of the name.)

JULITTA (St) VM.   **RM. May 18**
See Theodotus, Thecusa, etc.

JULITTA (St) M.   **RM. June 16**
See Quiricus and Julitta.

JULITTA (St) M.   **RM. July 30**
d. 303. A rich lady of Caesarea in Cappadocia, who, after losing her property, was condemned to be burnt at the stake.

JULIUS (St) M.   **RM. Jan 19**
See Paul, Gerontius, etc.

JULIUS of NOVARA (St) C.   **RM. Jan 31**
d. p.390. Julius was a priest and his brother Julian a deacon. They were authorized by the emperor Thedosius, to devote themselves to converting the heathen temples into Christian churches.

JULIUS I (St) Pope.   RM. Apr 12
d. 352. A Roman; he ruled the church
from 337 to 352. He received the appeal
of St Athanasius, whom he defended
against his Arian accusers. The letter he
wrote to the East on this occasion is one
of the most momentous pronounce-
ments of the Roman see. He built
several churches in Rome, and ranks as
one of the most distinguished occupants
of the Holy See.

JULIUS of DOROSTORUM (St) M.
RM. May 27
d. *c.*302. A veteran soldier of the Roman
army put to death at Dorostorum on the
Danube (now Silistria in Rumania)
under Diocletian. Other soldiers of his
legion were martyred about the same
time.

**JULIUS and AARON with others
(SS) MM.**   RM. July 1
d. *c.*305. According to tradition these
martyrs met their death at Caerleon-
upon-Usk under Diocletian.

JULIUS (St) M.   RM. Aug 19
d. *c.*190. A Roman senator mentioned
in the unreliable *Passio* of SS Eusebius,
Pontian etc. There is no archeological
evidence of his existence.

JULIUS (St) M.   RM. Dec 3
See Ambicus, Victor and Julius.

**JULIUS, POTAMIA, CRISPIN,
FELIX, GRATUS and Comp. (SS)
MM.**   RM. Dec 5
d. 302. Twelve African martyrs, who
suffered at Thagura in Numidia under
Diocletian.

JULIUS (St) M.   RM. Dec 20
? A martyr registered in the martyrolo-
gies as having suffered at Gelduba
(Gildoba) in Thrace.

JUNIAN (St) Ab.   AC. Aug 13
d. 587. Founder and first abbot of
Mairé (*Mariacum*) in Poitou, France,
and then a recluse at Chaulnay.

JUNIAN (St) H.   AC. Oct 16
5th cent. A hermit at Commodoliacus—
now Saint-Junien (Haute Vienne), in
the diocese of Limoges, France.

JUNIAS   AC. May 17
See Andronicus and Junias.

JURMIN (St) C.   AC. Feb 23
7th cent. An E. Anglian prince, son, or
more probably, nephew of King Anna.
His relics were eventually enshrined at
Bury St Edmunds.

JUST (St)
The titular saint of a parish in Cornwall.
He may be identical with Justus (or
Justin), a boy-martyr commemorated
on Oct 18, or with the Justus com-
memorated on Aug 12.

**JUSTA, JUSTINA and HENEDINA
(SS) MM.**   RM. May 14
d. *c.*130. Saints, said to have been venerated in Sardinia, where they were
martyred under Hadrian (117–138),
either at Cagliari or at Sassari.

JUSTA (St) M.   RM. July 15
See Catulinus, Januarius, etc.

JUSTA and RUFINA (SS) VV, MM.
RM. July 19
d. 287. Two sisters of Seville, in Spain,
potters by trade, who suffered under
Diocletian. They are greatly honoured
in the Mozarabic liturgy and are now
venerated as principal patron saints of
Seville. It is to be noted that in the early
MSS Justa is given as Justus.

JUSTIN of CHIETI (St) C.
RM. Jan 1
d. *c.*?540. This saint has been from time

immemorial venerated at Chieti. Some writers describe him as a bishop of that city.

JUSTIN the PHILOSOPHER or JUSTIN MARTYR (St) M.
RM. Apr 13 and 14

c.100–165. Born at Nablus in Palestine of pagan parents. He was converted to Christ when about thirty years of age by reading the Scriptures and witnessing the heroism of the martyrs. His two *Apologies for the Christian Religion* and his *Dialogue with the Jew Tryphon* are among the most instructive second-century writings which we possess. He was beheaded in Rome with other Christians.

JUSTIN (St) M.   RM. July 18
One of the alleged sons of St Symphorosa, q.v.

JUSTIN de JACOBIS (Bl) Bp. C.
AC. July 31

1800–1860. He was a great Apostle of Africa and the true founder of the Abyssinian mission. Born at San Fele in Lucania, he was noted for his youthful piety. He became a Vincentian and was chosen by the Congregation de Propaganda Fide as Prefect Apostolic for Abyssinia. In 1838 he left for his mission field with a few companions. There he adapted his whole way of life to that of the country, and amid persecution, prison and hardship laboured with indefatigable zeal; he founded missions and named a native clergy; his converts are reckoned at 12,000, among them Bl Ghebre Michael. In 1849 he was constrained to accept the title of Vicar Apostolic and episcopal consecration. Beatified in 1939.

JUSTIN (St) M.   RM. Aug 1
d. *c*.290. A child said to have been martyred at Louvre, near Paris. He may be identical with Justus, the boy-martyr of

Beauvais, commemorated on Oct 18. At any rate his story appears to have been taken from the same source.

JUSTIN (St) M.   RM. Sept 17
d. 259. A priest who devoted himself to burying the bodies of martyrs, and was eventually martyred himself. His relics were transferred to Frisingen in Germany.

JUSTIN (St) M.   RM. Dec 12
See Maxentius, Constantius, etc.

JUSTINA BEZZOLI (Bl) N. OSB.
AC. March 12

d. 1319. Francuccia (in religion Justina) Bezzoli, was born at Arezzo, and at the age of thirteen entered the Benedictine convent of St Mark in her native city, whence she migrated to that of All Saints, also Benedictine, at Arezzo. Later she lived as a recluse at Civitella, and finally returned to community life at All Saints. Cult confirmed in 1890.

JUSTINA (St) M.   RM. May 14
See Justa, Justina and Henedina.

JUSTINA (St) M.   RM. June 16
See Aureus, Justina, etc.

JUSTINA (St) VM.   RM. Sept 26
See Cyprian and Justina.

JUSTINA (St) VM.   RM. Oct 7
d. *c*.300. A virgin-martyr of Padua under Diocletian. A medieval forgery associates her with St Prosdocimus "a disciple of blessed Peter". Her cult spread throughout Italy on account of the Benedictine abbey dedicated in her name at Padua, which became the cradle of the Cassinese Congregation of St Justina.

JUSTINA (St) VM.   RM. Nov 30
? A maiden martyred at Constantinople.

JUSTINIAN (STINAN) (St) M.
AC. Dec 5
6th cent. A hermit, a native of Brittany, who became a recluse on the Isle of Ramsey off the coast of S. Wales, where he was murdered by evildoers and was thenceforward venerated as a martyr.

JUSTUS (St) M. RM. Feb 25
See Donatus, Justus, etc.

JUSTUS (St) M. RM. Feb 28
See Macarius, Rufinus, etc.

JUSTUS of URGELL (St) Bp.
RM. May 28
d. *p.*527. The first recorded bishop of Urgell in Spanish Catalonia. He is numbered by St Isidore among the "viri illustres", of whom he wrote the lives. St Justus has left us a very interesting commentary on the *Song of Songs*.

JUSTUS (St) M. RM. July 2
See Ariston, Crescentian, etc.

JUSTUS of POLAND (St) H. OSB. Cam. AC. July 9
d. 1008. One of the four Polish Brethren —viz. SS Benedict, Andrew, Barnabas and Justus. All were Camaldolese monks.

JUSTUS (St) M. RM. July 14
? A Roman soldier in the imperial army martyred at Rome (or perhaps at New Rome, i.e. Constantinople).

JUSTUS (St) M. RM. July 21
See Claudius, Justus, etc.

JUSTUS and PASTOR (SS) MM.
RM. Aug 6
d. *c.*304. Two brothers, aged respectively thirteen and nine years, who were scourged and beheaded at Alcalá under Diocletian. Prudentius numbers them among the most glorious martyrs of Spain.

JUSTUS (St) AC. Aug 12
Otherwise Ust, q.v.

JUSTUS of LYONS (St) Bp.
RM. Sept 2 and Oct 14
d. 390. A deacon of Vienne who was bishop of Lyons in 350. In 381 he attended the council of Aquileia and then instead of returning to his see, repaired to Egypt, where, in spite of remonstrances, he lived as a hermit till his death.

JUSTUS of BEAUVAIS (St) M.
RM. Oct 18
d. 287. A child-martyr, aged nine, who is alleged to have suffered at Beauvais. He is probably identical with some other saint of this name, and certainly his Acts, as we now possess them, are pure fiction.

JUSTUS of TRIESTE (St) M.
RM. Nov 2
d. 303. A citizen of Trieste martyred under Diocletian by being cast into the sea. He is still much honoured at Trieste.

JUSTUS of CANTERBURY (St) Bp. OSB. RM. Nov 10
d. 627. A Roman Benedictine, one of those sent by St Gregory the Great in 601 to reinforce the mission to the Anglo-Saxons. In 604 St Augustine of Canterbury consecrated him bishop of Rochester, and in 624 he succeeded St Mellitus at Canterbury itself. Pope Boniface V, in sending Justus the *Pallium*, writes to him in words of high appreciation.

JUSTUS and ABUNDIUS (SS) MM.
RM. Dec 14
d. 283. Spanish martyrs who suffered under Numerian. After a futile attempt to burn them at the stake, they were beheaded. The Mozarabic liturgy has a solemn office in their honour.

JUTHWARE (St) V.   AC. July 1
7th cent. Sister of St Sidwell. They were
probably of British lineage and appear
to have lived in Devonshire before the
Anglo-Saxons of Wessex penetrated into
that county.

JUTTA (Bl) W.   AC. Jan 13
Otherwise Bl Ivetta, q.v.

JUTTA (St) W.   AC. May 5
d. 1250. A Thuringian of noble family
whose husband lost his life crusading
in the Holy Land, and who, after providing for her children, became a recluse
near Kulmsee in Prussia. She is venerated as patroness of Prussia.

JUTTA (JULITTA) (Bl) Abs. OSB.
Cist.   AC. Nov 29
d. c.1250. Foundress and first abbess
(1234–c.1250) of the Cistercian nunnery
of Heiligenthal.

JUTTA (JUDITH) (Bl) Abs. OSB.
                        AC. Dec 22
d. 1136. Sister of the count Palatine of
Spanheim, she became a recluse in a cell
near the monastery-church of Disenberg
(Disibodi Mons). Here she was entrusted
with the education of St Hildegarde.
Other disciples gathered round her and
she formed them into a Benedictine
community, which she ruled for twenty
years.

JUVENAL of NARNI (St) Bp.
                        RM. May 3
d. 369. First bishop of Narni, in central
Italy, ordained, it is said by Pope St
Damasus. His biographers have confused him with other saints of the same
name, with the result that we have no
certainty as to the details of his career.

JUVENAL of BENEVENTO (St) Bp.
                        RM. May 7

d. c.132. A saint of Narni. His reputed
shrine is at Benevento.

JUVENAL ANCINA (Bl) Bp.
                        AC. Sept 12
1545–1604. Born at Fossano in Piedmont, he became professor of medicine
at the university of Turin and as such
he accompanied the ambassador of
Savoy to Rome as his private physician
(1575). At Rome he came under the
influence of St Philip Neri and joined
the Oratory in 1575. He was duly ordained and sent to Naples to open a
new oratory there. He was noted especially for his work for the poor. Finally
in 1602 he was made bishop of Saluzzo
and at once set out on his first episcopal
visitation. On his return he was poisoned
by a friar whose evil life he had rebuked.
Beatified in 1869.

JUVENTINUS and MAXIMUS (SS)
MM.   RM. Jan 25
d. 363. Officers in the army of Julian the
Apostate. For criticizing the laws against
Christians and refusing to sacrifice to
idols, they were degraded, imprisoned,
scourged and finally beheaded at Antioch in Syria.

JUVENTIUS of PAVIA (St) Bp.
                RM. Feb 8 and Sept 12
1st cent. (?). The tradition is that St
Hermagoras, bishop of Aquileia, the disciple of St Mark, despatched SS Syrus
and Juventius to evangelize Pavia
(Ticinum), of which city the latter became the first bishop. The RM. commemorates him a second time with St
Syrus on Sept 12.

JUVENTIUS (St) M.   RM. June 1
? A Roman martyr, whose relics were
translated in the 16th century to the
Benedictine abbey of Chaise-Dieu,
Evreux, France.

K

Note. For Katherine and similar names sometimes written with an initial K, see also C and CH.

KANTEN (CANNEN) (St) C. AC. Nov 5
8th cent. A Welsh saint. Founder of Llanganten Abbey (Brecknock).

KARANTOC (St) Jan 16
Probably identical with St Carantac of May 16, q.v.

KEA (KAY, KENAN) (St) Bp. AC. Nov 5
6th cent. A British saint who has left his name to Landkey in Devon. He passed some of his life in Brittany, where he is venerated as St Quay. The details of his life are very uncertain.

KEBIUS (St) Bp. AC. Nov 8
Otherwise Cuby (Cyby), q.v.

KELLACH (St) Bp. AC. May 1
Otherwise Ceallach, q.v.

KENAN (CIANAN) (St) Bp. AC. Nov 24
d. c.500. An Irish bishop. He was with St Patrick a disciple of St Martin of Tours. He was the first bishop in Ireland to build his cathedral (Damleag or Duleek, in Meath) of stone.

KENELM (St) King M. AC. July 17
d. 821. Said to have been a Mercian prince, who at the age of seven succeeded to the throne of his father, King Kenulph. He was murdered in the forest of Clent by order of his sister Cynefrith. In medieval England he was universally venerated as a saint and martyr.

KENNERA (St) VM. AC. Oct 29
4th cent. A recluse at Kirk-Kinner, Galloway, Scotland. She had been educated with St Ursula and also with St Regulus of Patras.

KENNETH (KINED) (St) H. AC. Aug 1
6th cent. A Welsh hermit, the son of a chieftain. He made his cell among the rocks in the peninsula of Gower.

KENNETH (St) Ab. RM. Oct 11
Otherwise Canice (or Canicus), q.v.

KENNOCHA (KYLE, ENOCH) (St) V. AC. March 25
d. 1007. A Scottish nun belonging to a convent in Fife. Formerly she was held in great veneration in Scotland, especially in the district round Glasgow.

KENNY (St) Ab. RM. Oct 11
Otherwise Canice, q.v.

KENTIGERN MUNGO (St) Bp. AC. Jan 14
d. 603. The surname *Mungo* means "darling". He began his missionary labours at Cathures, on the Clyde, on the site of the present city of Glasgow, and was consecrated first bishop of the Strathclyde Britons. Driven into exile, he preached around Carlisle and then went to Wales, and he is said to have stayed with St David at Menevia. Tradition credits him with having founded the monastery of Llanelwy (St Asaph), but it is now thought that he

was not the founder, but merely the abbot of that monastery for a time. Returning to Scotland, he continued his missionary labours, making Glasgow his centre. He died while taking a bath. He is venerated as the apostle of N.W. England and S.W. Scotland.

KENTIGERNA (St) W. AC. Jan 7
d. 734. Daughter of Kelly, prince of Leinster and mother of St Coellan. After her husband's death she left Ireland and became a recluse on the island of Inchebroida, in Loch Lomond, where a church is dedicated in her name.

KERIC (St) Ab.   AC. Feb 17
Otherwise Guevrock, q.v.

KERRIER (St)
              AC. March 5, RM. Sept 9
A variant of the name Kieran, q.v., Piran, Queranus.

KESSOG (MACKESSOG) (St) Bp.
              AC. March 10
d. c.560. Born at Cashel, Ulster. Even as a child he is said to have worked miracles. He became a missionary and laboured in Scotland, where he was consecrated bishop. It is not certain where he died: according to one tradition he was martyred at Bandry. He is the patron of Lennox.

KESTER (St) M.   RM. July 25
Otherwise Christopher, q.v.

KEVERNE (St)   Nov 18
6th cent. A Cornish saint, friend of St Kieran or Piran, with whom indeed some identify him.

KEVIN (COEMGEN, CAOIMH-GHIN) (St) Ab.   AC. June 3
d. c.618. The name has been Latinized as Coemgenus. A native of Leinster, he was educated by St Petroc of Cornwall who was then in Ireland. He is best

remembered as the abbot-founder of Glendalough, one of the most famous names in Irish history. His extant biographies abound in romantic but untrustworthy legends, which, however, may be based on actual facts. He is one of the patron saints of Dublin.

KEVOCA (KENNOTHA, QUIVOCA) (St)   AC. March 13
7th cent. She is honoured at Kyle in Scotland. Possibly she should be identified with St Mochoemoc.

KEWE (KWYA, CIWA) (St)
                          AC. Feb 8
Otherwise Kigwe, q.v.

KEYNA (KEYNE, KEAN) (St) V.
              AC. Oct 8
5th cent. A Welsh saint, an alleged daughter of Brychan of Brecknock. She lived as a recluse in Somersetshire—at Keynsham, so called after her—but she returned to Wales to die. Many churches were dedicated in her honour.

KIARA (CHIER) (St) V.
              AC. Jan 5 (Oct 16)
d. c.680. An Irish maiden, directed in the religious life by St Fintan Munnu. She lived near Nenagh, Co. Tipperary, at a place now called after her Kilkeary.

KIERAN (KIERNAN, KYRAN, CIARAN) (St) Bp.   AC. March 5
d. c.530. Styled "the first-born of the saints of Ireland". A native of Ossory, he was probably consecrated bishop by St Patrick. He has certainly been venerated from time immemorial as the first bishop of Ossory and as founder of the Monastery of Saighir. He is wrongly identified with St Piran of Cornwall.

KIERAN (KYRAN, Latin: QUERANUS) (St) Ab. RM. Sept 9
d. c.556 (?). Surnamed "The Younger". He was born in Connacht, and was

trained in the monastic life by St Finian of Clonard, where he was one of the "Twelve Apostles of Ireland". At a later date he became the abbot-founder of Clonmacnois in West Meath, on the Shannon, and gave his monks an extremely austere monastic rule, known as "the Law of Kieran".

KIGWE (KEWE) (St) V. AC. Feb 8
? She is probably the same as St Ciwa, a 6th- or 7th-century saint venerated in Monmouthshire. The name is also spelt: Ciwg, Cwick, Kigwoe, etc.

KILDA (St)
An unidentified saint whose name has been given to an Island off the Scottish coast, in which there is a well-known St Kilder's or St Kilda's Well.

KILIAN (CHILIANUS), COLMAN and TOTNAN (SS) MM.
RM. July 8
d. c.689. Irish missionary monks who were commissioned by Pope John V to evangelize Franconia and East Thuringia, where they were martyred after a successful apostolate.

KILIAN (St) Ab.   AC. July 29
7th cent. An Irish abbot of a monastery in the island of Inishcaltra, and author of a life of St Brigid.

KILIAN (St) C.   AC. Nov 13
Otherwise Chillien, q.v.

KINGA (St) V. Tert. OFM.
AC. July 24
d. 1292. A niece of St Elizabeth of Hungary and great-niece of St Hedwig. She shared with her husband, Prince Boleslaus of Poland, the sufferings to which the Tartar invasion subjected that land. She died a Franciscan tertiary in the nunnery she had founded at Sandez. Her name is also given as Cunegunde, Kioga, Zinga, etc.

KINGSMARK (CYNFARCH) (St) C.
AC. Sept 8
5th cent. Said to have been a Scottish chieftain who lived in Wales, where some churches are dedicated to him.

KINNIA (St) V.   AC. Feb 1
5th cent. An Irish maiden, baptized by St Patrick, and by him also consecrated to God. She is greatly venerated in Co. Louth.

KITT (St) M.   RM. July 25
Otherwise Christopher, q.v.

KIZITO (St) M.   RM. June 3
d. 1886. At fourteen, he was the youngest of the martyrs put to death by King Mwanga of Uganda. See Uganda (Martyrs of).

"KLAUS" (St)   RM. Dec 6
A corrupt form of the name Nicholas (Niklaus), q.v.

KYBI (St) Bp.   AC. Nov 8
Otherwise Cuby, q.v.

KYNEBURGA, KYNESWIDE and TIBBA (SS) OSB.   AC. March 6
d. c.680. Kyneburga and Kyneswide, were daughters of Penda of Mercia famous for his fierce opposition to Christianity. The former became the abbess-foundress of Dormancaster, now Castor, in Northamptonshire, and was succeeded by her sister as abbess. Tibba was their kinswoman, who joined them at the convent. Their relics were enshrined at Peterborough Abbey.

KYNESWIDE (St) V. OSB.
AC. March 6
See SS Kyneburga, Kyneswide and Tibba.

KYRAN (St) Ab.   RM. Sept 9
Otherwise Kieran, q.v.

KYRIN (KYRSTIN) (St) Bp.
AC. March 14
Otherwise Boniface, q.v.

L

LACTAN (LACTINUS) Ab.
AC. March 19
d. 672. Born near Cork, in Ireland, he was educated at Bangor under SS Comgall and Molua. St Comgall sent him to be abbot-founder of Achadh-Ur, now Freshford in Kilkenny.

LADISLAS (Bl) M. OFM. PC. Feb 12
See Antony of Saxony, etc.

LADISLAS BATHORY (Bl)
PC. Feb 27
d. c.1484. A Pauline hermit on the mountains of Buda. He translated the bible into Hungarian. Not officially beatified.

LADISLAS (LANCELOT) (St) King
RM. June 27
1040–1095. Son of Bela, king of Hungary, to which kingdom, after his accession in 1077, he added Dalmatia and Croatia. His enlightened government, with regard both to church and state affairs, makes him one of the great national heroes of Hungary. He fought just and successful wars against the Poles, Russians and Tartars. He died while preparing to take part, as commander-in-chief, in the first crusade. Canonized in 1192. The Hungarians call him Laszlo.

LADISLAS of GIELNIOW (Bl) C.
OFM. **AC. Sept 25**
1440–1505 (May 4). A Pole by birth, he joined the Observant Franciscans at Warsaw and eventually became their minister provincial. As such he sent Franciscan missionaries to Lithuania.

He himself was an untiring preacher and travelled the whole length and breadth of Poland evangelizing the country. Beatified in 1586.

LAETANTIUS (St) M. RM. July 17
See Scillitan Martyrs.

LAETUS (St) M. **RM. Sept 1**
See Vincent and Laetus.

LAETUS (St) Bp. M. **RM. Sept 6**
See Donatian, Praesidius, etc.

LAETUS (St) Priest **RM. Nov 5**
d. 533. Honoured in the diocese of Orleans, his relics being enshrined in the village of St Lié in that diocese. He is said to have embraced the monastic state at the age of twelve years.

LAICIN (St) Ab. **AC. Jan 20**
Otherwise Molagga, q.v.

LAMALISSE (St) H. AC. March 3
7th cent. A Scottish hermit who has left his name to an islet (Lamlash) off the coast of the isle of Arran.

LAMBERT of LYONS (St) Bp.
OSB. **RM. Apr 14**
d. 688. Born in N. France and reared at the court of Clotaire III, he became a monk at Fontenelle under St Wandrille whom he succeeded as abbot in 666. In 678 he was raised to the see of Lyons.

LAMBERT of SARAGOSSA (St) M.
RM. Apr 16
d. c.900. A servant, killed near Saragossa in Spain, by his Saracen master

during the Moorish occupation. His cult was promoted by Pope Hadrian VI.

LAMBERT PÉLOGUIN (St) Bp. OSB.　　　　　　AC. May 26

c.1080–1154. He was born in the diocese of Riez, France, and became a Benedictine at Lérins. In 1114 he was made bishop of Vence in Provence, and ruled his diocese for forty years. His relics are still enshrined at Vence.

LAMBERT (Bl) Ab. OSB.　　　　　　AC. June 22

d. 1125. From childhood he was trained in the monastic life at the Benedictine abbey of Saint-Bertin, of which he eventually became the fortieth abbot. He finished the abbey church and introduced the Cluniac observances.

LAMBERT (Bl) Ab. OSB. Cist.　　　　　　AC. July 12

d. 1163. He became a Cistercian monk at Morimond and afterwards ruled successively as abbot Clairfontaine, Morimond and Cîteaux (1155–1161). The last two years of his life he spent in retirement at Morimond, where he died.

LAMBERT (Bl) Ab. OSB. Cist.　　　　　　AC. Aug 22

d. 1151. A brother of St Peter of Tarentaise, and, like him, a Cistercian monk at Bonnevaux. In 1140 he was sent to preside as abbot-founder over the new Abbey of Chézery, in the diocese of Belley, France.

LAMBERT (St) Bp. OSB.　　　　　　RM. Sept 17

d. 709. Born at Maestricht, he became bishop of that city in 668, but in 674 he was driven from his see by the tyrant Ebroin. He now lived for seven years at the Benedictine abbey of Stavelot as a simple monk. He was recalled to his see by Pepin of Heristal, and did much to foster the apostolate of St Willibrord. He was murdered in the then village of Liège, and has ever since been venerated as a martyr.

LAMBERT and VALERIUS (BELLÈRE, BERLHER) (SS) CC. OSB.　　　　　　AC. Oct 9

d. c.680. Disciples of St Gislenus, and his fellow-workers in preaching the Gospel.

LANDELINUS (St) Ab. OSB.　　　　　　RM. June 15

c.625–686. Born near Bapaume, in N. France, Landelinus, though carefully brought up by St Aubert of Cambrai, was for a time led astray and turned robber, but repented and became a monk. Afterwards he was ordained priest and founded the abbeys of Lobbes (*Lanbacum*) in 654, Aulne (656), Walers (657) and Crespin (Crepy, *Crespiacum*) in 670, which he governed till his death.

LANDERICUS (LANDRY) (St) Bp. OSB.　　　　　　AC. Apr 17

7th cent. The eldest son of SS Madelgarus and Waldetrudis. From 641 to 650 he was bishop of Meaux, but on the death of his father, the abbot of Soignies, Landericus resigned his see in order to undertake the government of that abbey.

LANDERICUS (St) Bp. AC. June 10

d. c.661. Bishop of Paris from 650 to his death. He is best remembered as the founder of the first hospital—*Hôtel-Dieu*—in Paris.

LANDERICUS (St) M. OSB.　　　　　　AC. June 10

d. 1050 (?). A Benedictine monk of Novalese in Savoy, drowned in the R. Arc by some malefactors whom he had reprimanded.

LANDOALD and AMANTIUS (SS) CC.   **RM. March 19**
d. *c*.668. Said to have been a Roman priest and his deacon, sent by the Pope to evangelize what is now Belgium and N.E. France. They founded the church at Wintershoven.

LANDRADA (St) V. OSB.
                                             AC. July 8
d. *c*.690. Foundress and first abbess of the nunnery of Münsterbilsen, in Belgic Luxemburg.

LANDULF VARIGLIA (St) Bp. OSB.   **AC. June 7**
1070–1134. Born at Asti in Piedmont, he took the Benedictine habit at San Michele in Ciel d'Oro at Pavia and became bishop of Asti in 1103.

LANFRANC of CANTERBURY (Bl) Bp. OSB.   **PC. May 28**
c.1005–1089. Born of a family of senatorial rank at Pavia, he studied at Bologna, taught civil law at Pavia, and in 1042 became a Benedictine at Bec in Normandy, where he founded the school which was to become famous throughout Christendom. He left Bec to be the first abbot of St Stephen's at Caen and in 1070 was raised to the see of Canterbury. Both as a zealous churchman and as a theological writer he left his mark on the ecclesiastical as well as on the civil history of his time. He has always been given the title of *Beatus*, although he does not seem to have been honoured with a public cult.

LANFRANC BECCARIA (Bl) Bp. OSB. Vall.   **AC. June 23**
d. 1194. He was born near Pavia, and in 1178 was made bishop of that city. During his episcopate he was troubled much by heretics and rapacious civil magistrates. He left the city and joined the monks of S. Sepolcro, but was recalled. At the time of his death he had definitely determined to become a Vallumbrosan.

LANTFRID, WALTRAM and ELILANTUS BB or (SS) OSB.
                                             AC. July 10
d. *p*.770. Three brothers who became founders of Benediktbeuren in Bavaria and succeeded one another as abbots of the monastery. St Lantfrid, the first to be abbot, was still alive in 770.

LANUINUS (Bl) C. O. Cart.
                                             AC. Apr 14
d. 1120. A disciple of St Bruno, who accompanied the saint to Calabria, where he succeeded him as prior of the charterhouse which he founded at Torre in the diocese of Squillace. He was also appointed visitor apostolic of all the monastic houses in Calabria. Cult confirmed in 1893.

LANZO (Bl) Mk. OSB.   PC Apr 1
d. *c*.1100. Described by William of Malmesbury as "the most perfect religious of his century", Lanzo was a monk of Cluny who became Prior of St Pancras in London.

LARGIO (St) M.   RM. Aug 12
See Hilaria, Digna, etc.

LARGUS of AQUILEIA (St) M.
                                             RM. March 16
See Hilary, Tatian, etc.

LARGUS of ROME (St) M.
                                             RM. Aug 8
See Cyriacus, Largus, etc.

LASAR (LASSAR, LASSERA) (St) V.   **AC. March 29**
6th cent. An Irish nun, niece of St Forchera. She was in early life placed under the care of SS Finan and Kiernan at Clonard. Her name means "Flame".

LASERIAN (St) Bp.   AC. Apr 18

d. 639. Otherwise Molaisse, and (probably) Lamliss. He was an Irishman by birth and the founder of the monastery and bishopric of Leighlin. He was appointed by Pope Honorius I apostolic legate to Ireland, where he strenuously upheld the Roman observance. He was prominent at the synod of Whitefield (635).

LASSA (St) M.   AC. Feb 9

See Ammon, Emilian, etc.

LASZLO (St) King   RM. June 27

Magyar form of Ladislas, q.v.

LATINUS of BRESCIA (St) Bp.
RM. March 24

d. 115. Flavius Latinus is said to have been a successor of St Viator (q.v.) and third Bishop of Brescia (84–115). He is said to have suffered imprisonment and torture with other Christians.

LAUDO (St) Bp.   RM. Sept 22

Otherwise Lauto, q.v.

LAURA (St) Abs. M.   AC. Oct 19

d. 864. A native of Cordova in Spain. In her widowhood she became a nun at Cuteclara. Condemned as a Christian by the Moorish conquerors she was thrown into a cauldron of molten lead.

LAURENCE GIUSTINIANI (St) Bp.
RM. Jan 8

1381–1455. A scion of the noble Venetian family of the Giustiniani, who at the age of nineteen joined the canons regular of San Giorgio in Alga, of whom in due time he became the general. In 1433 he was forced to accept the see of Castello, and in 1451 was translated to that of Grado which (with its patriarchal title) was transferred at the same time from Grado to Venice. His writings on mystical contemplation are sublime in their simplicity. Canonized in 1690.

LAURENCE WANG (Bl) M.
AC. Jan 28

1811–1858. A Chinese catechist, born at Kuy-yang and beheaded at Mao-Ken. Beatified in 1909.

LAURENCE of CANTERBURY (St)
Bp. OSB.   RM. Feb 2

d. 619. One of the Benedictines sent by Pope St Gregory the Great to convert England. St Augustine sent him back to Rome to report to St Gregory on the progress of the English mission and to bring back reinforcements for the work. Succeeding to the archbishopric of Canterbury in 604, he had much to suffer during the pagan reaction in Kent under Eadbald and thought of escaping to France, but was forcibly rebuked by St Peter in a dream, and in the end succeeded in converting Eadbald. The Irish Stowe Missal commemorates him by name in the canon of the Mass.

LAURENCE the ILLUMINATOR
(St) Bp.   AC. Feb 3

d. 576. A Syrian Catholic, driven by the Monophysite persecution to Italy, where he was ordained and founded a monastery near Spoleto. Chosen bishop of that city, he held the see for twenty years: he then resigned and founded the famous abbey of Farfa in the Sabine hills near Rome. St Laurence was renowned as a peacemaker, and his title, it is said, derives from his gift of healing blindness, both spiritual and physical.

LAURENCE of SIPONTO (St) Bp.
AC. Feb 7

d. c.546. Surnamed Majoranus. Bishop of Siponto from 492 to his death. He is said to have built the sanctuary of St Michael on Mt Gargano.

LAURENCE HUNG (Bl) M.
AC. Apr 27

c.1802–1856. A native priest of Tonkin,

beheaded near Ninh-biuh, in W. Tonkin. Beatified in 1909.

LAURENCE of NOVARA and Comp. (SS) MM.   RM. Apr 30

d. *c*.397. Said to have come from the West (Spain or France?) and to have assisted St Gaudentius, bishop of Novara in Piedmont. He was put to death with a group of children whom he was instructing.

LAURENCE RICHARDSON (*vere* JOHNSON) (Bl) M.   AC. May 30

d. 1582. A native of Great Crosby in Lancashire, he was educated at Brasenose College, Oxford, and after his conversion, studied for the priesthood at Douai. He was ordained in 1577 and was sent to the English mission, where he worked in Lancashire. He was martyred at Tyburn. Beatified in 1886.

LAURENCE of VILLAMAGNA (Bl) C. OFM.   AC. June 6

1476–1535. Born at Villamagna, in the Abruzzi, of the noble family del Mascoli, he joined the Franciscan order and he became a most powerful and successful preacher. Cult approved in 1923.

LAURENCE HUMPHREY (Bl) M.   AC. July 7

1571–1591. A native of Hampshire and a convert, he was only twenty years of age when he was hanged, drawn and quartered at Winchester for his conversion to the Catholic faith. Beatified in 1929.

LAURENCE of BRINDISI (St) C. OFM. Cap.   RM. July 22

1559–1619. A native of Brindisi who joined the Capuchins and was sent to Germany as one of the pioneers of the Capuchin Order in that country. He preached throughout Central Europe,

and was appointed chaplain to the forces of the Archduke Matthias fighting against the Turks. He contributed to the success of the Christian army by his prayers and shrewd military advice. He died at Lisbon during one of his diplomatic missions. Canonized in 1881.

LAURENCE of ROME (St) M.   RM. Aug 10

d. 258. The *Passio* of St Laurence was written at least a century after his death, and although accepted by the Fathers of the Church leaves room for doubt in the details. According to this account St Laurence, one of the Deacons of Pope Sixtus II, was put to death three days after the martyrdom of that Pope, by being roasted alive on a gridiron. See Sixtus II (Aug 7). Whatever may be said of the historical value of his Acts the fact remains that Laurence has always been venerated, both in the West and in the East, as the most celebrated of the numerous Roman martyrs—witness the writings of SS Ambrose, Leo the Great, Augustine and Prudentius. His martyrdom must have deeply impressed the Roman Christians. His death, says Prudentius, was the death of idolatry in Rome, which from that time began to decline. He was buried on the Via Tiburtina, at the *Campus Veranus*, where his basilica now stands, and his name is mentioned in the canon of the Mass.

LAURENCE NERUCCI, AUGUSTINE CENNINI, BARTHOLOMEW DONATI, and JOHN BAPTIST PETRUCCI (BB) MM. OSM.   AC. Aug 11

d. 1420. Four Servite friars sent from Siena to Bohemia by Pope Martin V to combat the Hussite heresy. With sixty other Servites they were burnt in a church at Prague while singing the *Te Deum*. Cult approved in 1918.

LAURENCE LORICATUS (Bl) H. OSB.   AC. Aug 16

d. 1243. Born at Fanello, near Siponto, he was bred to arms and, having accidentally killed a man, undertook a pilgrimage to Compostella. On his return in 1209 he joined the Benedictines at Subiaco and obtained leave to live as a recluse in the ruins of one of the twelve monasteries founded there by St Benedict. His name Loricatus was given to him on account of a coat of mail which he wore next his skin. His relics are enshrined at the Sagro Speco, Subiaco. Cult approved in 1778.

LAURENCE ROCOUYEMON (Bl) M.   AC. Aug 19

d. 1622. A Japanese merchant on the ship of Bl Joachim Firaiama. He was beheaded at Nagasaki. Beatified in 1867.

LAURENCE JAMADA (Bl) M.   AC. Sept 8

d. 1628. Son of Bl Michael Jamada, and a Dominican tertiary. He was beheaded at Nagasaki. Beatified in 1867.

LAURENCE IMBERT, Bp. PETER MAUBANT, JAMES CHASTAN and Comp. (BB) MM.   AC. Sept 22

d. 1839–1846. These martyrs perished in the persecution of the Christians which raged in Corea from 1839 till 1846. Imbert, a native of Aix-en-Provence, was a member of the Paris Society of Missions. He worked first as a missionary priest in China and then as a bishop in Corea. With Maubant and Chastan, missionary priests of the same society, he was exiled and cruelly tortured to death in 1839. With them were beatified in 1925 seventy-six native converts (including Bl Andrew Kim, q.v.) who suffered death in the next few years with heroic constancy.

LAURENCE of AFRICA (St) M.   RM. Sept 28

See Martial, Laurence, and Comp.

LAURENCE of RIPPAFRATTA (Bl) C. OP.   AC. Sept 28

d. 1457. Born at Rippafratta in Tuscany, he joined the Friars Preachers at Pisa under Bl John Dominic, and was made novice-master at Cortona. St Antoninus and BB Benedict of Mugello and Fra Angelico were his novices. Cult approved in 1851.

LAURENCE XIZO (Bl) M.   AC. Sept 28

d. 1630. A native of Japan and a tertiary of St Augustine. He was condemned to death for having sheltered the Augustinian fathers and was beheaded at Nagasaki. Beatified in 1867.

LAURENCE O'TOOLE (St) Bp. OSA.   RM. Nov 14

1128–1180. Lorcan O'Tuathail was born in Leinster, and at the age of twelve became an Augustinian canon at Glendalough of which he was made abbot at the age of twenty-five. Eight years later he was promoted to the archbishopric of Dublin. In 1179 he attended the Lateran Council at Rome and was made papal legate in Ireland. He carried out many reforms in his diocese and was much engaged in negotiating on behalf of the Irish with King Henry II of England. It was while on an embassy to the latter that he died at the Augustinian abbey of Eu in Normandy. Canonized in 1226.

LAURENCE PE-MAN (Bl) M.   AC. Nov 24

d. 1856. A Chinese labourer and convert of Bl Augustine Chapdelaine. He was beheaded after torture at Su-Lik-Hien (Prov. of Kwang-Si). Beatified in 1900.

LAURENTIA (St) M.   RM. Oct 8

See Palatias and Laurentia.

LAURENTINUS, IGNATIUS and CELERINA (SS) MM.   RM. Feb 3
3rd cent. African martyrs, of whom St Cyprian writes movingly in his 34th Epistle. SS Laurentinus and Ignatius were uncles, and St Celerina, an aunt, of the deacon St Celerinus (q.v.), who is commemorated on the same day.

**LAURENTINUS SOSSIUS (Bl) M.
                                    AC. Apr 15**
d. 485. A boy aged five, said to have been killed by the Jews on Good Friday at Valrovina in the diocese of Vicenza, in Italy. Cult approved in 1867.

LAURENTINUS (St) M. RM. June 3
See Pergentinus and Laurentinus.

LAURIANUS (St) M.   RM. July 4
d. ? c.544. Said to have been a Hungarian by birth, ordained deacon in Milan, and later appointed archbishop of Seville. The place of his supposed martyrdom is given as Bourges in France. All these details are open to grave doubt.

LAURUS (St) M.   RM. Aug 18
See Florus, Laurus, etc.

**LAURUS (LÉRY) (St) Ab.
                                    AC. Sept 30**
7th cent. A native of Wales, who crossed over to Brittany and became the abbot-founder of the monastery afterwards called after him Saint-Léry, on the R. Doneff.

LAUTO (LAUDO, LAUDUS, LÔ) (St) Bp.   RM. Sept 22
d. 568. Bishop of Coutances in Normandy for forty years (528–568). He appears to have been one of the most energetic prelates of that period. His family estate has become the village of Saint-Lô.

LAWDOG (St)   AC. Jan 21
6th cent. Titular of four churches in the diocese of St David's, Wales, and perhaps identical with St Lleuddad (Laudatus), abbot of Bardsey.

**LAZARUS of MILAN (St) Bp.
                                    RM. Feb 11**
d. c.450 (March 14). An archbishop of Milan who was the support of his flock during the invasion of the Ostrogoths. His feast was translated to Feb 11, in deference to the Milanese custom of not keeping saints' days in Lent.

LAZARUS (St) C.   RM. Feb 23
d. c.867. Surnamed Zographos (the Painter). He was a monk of Constantinople, and a skilled painter, who in the time of Theophilus (829–842), one of the iconoclast emperors, busied himself in restoring the sacred pictures, defaced by the heretics. For this he was cruelly tormented by the Emperor. Later he was restored to honour and sent as ambassador to Rome.

LAZARUS (St) M.   RM. March 27
See Zanitas, Lazarus, etc.

LAZARUS (St)   AC. June 21
The poor man in our Lord's parable (Luke XVI). The military Order of St Lazarus, founded during the crusades, one of whose duties was to take care of lepers, was named after him. Hence also the words *Lazaretto*, for a hospital, *Lazarone*, for a poor man of the street, etc. The Abyssinians keep his feast on June 21.

LAZARUS (St) Bp.   RM. Dec 17
1st cent. The disciple and friend of our Lord raised by Him from the dead. (John XI). The Greek tradition states that he died bishop of Kition in Cyprus. The French legend which connects him with Marseilles is first heard of in the

11th century, and has no historical foundation whatever: it is probably due to confusion with an early bishop of Aix, called Lazarus.

LEA (St) W.   RM. March 22
d. 384. A Roman lady who, after the death of her husband, joined the community of St Marcella, where she spent her life serving the nuns.

LEAFWINE (St) C. OSB. AC. Nov 12
Otherwise Lebuin, q.v.

LEANDER (St) Bp.   RM. Feb. 27
d. 596. The elder brother of SS Fulgentius, Isidore and Florentina. He entered a monastery in his early youth and was later sent to Constantinople on a diplomatic mission. There he met St Gregory the Great, whose close friend he became and whose *Moralia* was published at his request. On his return to Spain Leander was appointed archbishop of Seville. He proved himself a great prelate: revised and unified the Spanish liturgy, converted St Hermenegild, was instrumental in winning the Visigoths from Arianism and was responsible for the holding of two national synods at Toledo (589 and 590). He founded the episcopal school of Seville. In Spain he is liturgically honoured as a Doctor.

**LEBUIN (LEAFWINE) (St) C. OSB.
                                        AC. Nov 12**
d. c.773. A Benedictine of Ripon who crossed over to Holland and took part in the missionary work inaugurated by St Boniface. He worked with St Marcellinus (July 14) under St Gregory of Utrecht and founded the church at Deventer. From there he went forth to preach to the Saxons and Frisians.

LEBUINUS (St) Bp. M. RM. Nov 12
Otherwise Livinus, q.v.

LEGER (St) Bp. M.   RM. Oct 2
Otherwise Leodegarius, q.v.

LELIA (St) V.   AC. Aug 11
? An Irish maiden, who seems to have lived at a very early period and to have been connected with the dioceses of Limerick and Kerry. Several placenames in Ireland perpetuate her memory.

**LEO CARASUMA (St) M.
                                        RM. Feb 5**
d. 1597. A native of Corea, who after being a pagan priest was converted to the Faith and was the first to be received into the third order of St Francis in Japan. As a catechist of the Franciscans, he was crucified at Nagasaki. Beatified in 1627 and canonized in 1862.

**LEO and PAREGORIUS (SS) MM.
                                        AC. Feb 18**
d. c.260. Martyrs of Patara in Lycia, greatly venerated in the East. Their alleged Acts may be merely a pious romance.

**LEO of CATANIA (St) Bp.
                                        RM. Feb 20**
703-787. Known in Sicily as St Leo *"il Maraviglioso"*, the wonder-worker. He was a priest of Ravenna who became bishop of Catania in Sicily. He was highly esteemed for his learning. The story of his life has been embellished with many delightful, though unreliable, *"Fioretti"*.

**LEO of SAINT-BERTIN (Bl) Ab.
OSB.   AC. Feb 26**
d. 1163. Of noble Flemish birth, Leo was appointed abbot of Lobbes where he succeeded in making good the ravages of war. In 1138 he was given charge of the great abbey of Saint-Bertin, which he ruled for twenty-five years. In 1146 he joined the second

crusade and reached Jerusalem and on his return brought with him the alleged relic of our Lord's Blood which ever since has been worshipped at Bruges. The abbey of St Bertin was destroyed by fire in 1152, but Bl Leo was energetic in its rebuilding.

LEO, DONATUS, ABUNDANTIUS, NICEPHORUS and Comp. (SS) MM.   RM. March 1
? A group of thirteen martyrs, believed to have laid down their lives for Christ in Africa.

LEO of ROUEN (St) Bp. M.
AC. March 1
c.856–900. Born at Carentan in Normandy, he is said to have been bishop of Rouen, and afterwards to have resigned in order to preach the gospel in Navarre and the Basque provinces—both French and Spanish—devastated by the Saracen invasion. Pirates beheaded him near Bayonne, of which city he is now the patron saint. The whole story is untrustworthy.

LEO LUKE (St) Ab. C.
PC. March 1
d. c.900. He became abbot of a Basilian monastery of Cooleoni in Sicily, and is honoured also in Calabria. He died a centenarian after eighty years of monastic life.

LEO (St) Bp. M.   RM. March 14
? The RM. has the following entry: "At Rome, in the Agro Verano, St Leo, bishop and martyr." This is all that is known about him. He may have been a victim of the Arians.

LEO the GREAT (St) Pope and Dr.
RM. Apr 11
d. 461. Born probably in Tuscany and joining the Roman clergy, he became archdeacon under Celestine I and Sixtus III, and was raised to the papal throne in 440. Ever conscious of his supreme jurisdiction and responsibility as the successor of St Peter, he combated Pelagians, Manicheans, Priscillianists, and, especially, the Eutychians and Nestorians. His celebrated *Tomos*, or Dogmatic Letter, addressed to Flavian, patriarch of Constantinople, in which he defined the exact Catholic belief on the twofold nature and one person in Christ, marks an epoch in Catholic theology. It was acclaimed as the teaching of the Church at the council of Chalcedon (451). The most famous action of his pontificate was his meeting with Attila outside the gates of Rome, which resulted in the salvation of Rome (452), but he was unable to stop Genseric the Vandal from pillaging it in 455.

LEO IX (St) Pope   RM. Apr 19
1002–1054. A cousin of the emperor Conrad the Salic, born in Alsace, and in baptism named Bruno. He was made bishop of Toul in 1026 and constrained to accept the papal office in 1048. He took with him to Rome, as his spiritual adviser, Hildebrand, the future Gregory VII, and the reform of the Roman curia now began in earnest. Leo combated simony, condemned Berengarius, and strove to prevent the schism between the Eastern and the Western churches then being engineered by the emperor Michael Coerularius. While at Benevento, a city belonging to the Holy See, he was taken prisoner by the Normans. He was released, but shortly after died before the high altar in St Peter's.

LEO of SENS (St) Bp.
RM. Apr 22
d. 541. Bishop of Sens for twenty-three years. He defended the rights of his own see against the pretensions of King Childebert.

LEO of TROYES (St) Ab.
RM. May 25
d. *c*.550. A monk who succeeded St Romanus in the government of the monastery of Mantenay, near Troyes.

LEO TANACA (Bl) M.   AC. June 1
d. 1617. A Japanese catechist to the Jesuit Fathers. Beheaded at Nagasaki, and beatified in 1867.

LEO III (St) Pope   RM. June 12
d. 816. A Roman by birth, who became pope in 795. While attempting to suppress the unruly factions of Rome he was himself seized and put to the torture. He then called to his help Charlemagne, who re-established order in Rome, and who was by Pope Leo crowned emperor of the West in St Peter's (800). Leo refused to add the "filioque" to the Nicene creed.

LEO (St) M.   RM. June 30
See Caius and Leo.

LEO II (St) Pope   RM. July 3
d. 683. A Sicilian who became pope in 681. He governed the church only two years and the oustanding event of his pontificate was the condemnation of Pope Honorius I for having been remiss in formally denouncing the Monothelites.

LEO of LUCCA (St) Ab. OSB.
AC. July 12
d. 1079. Born at Lucca in Tuscany, he entered the Benedictine abbey of La Cava, near Naples, under its founder St Alferius, whom he succeeded as abbot in 1050. He stood in great favour with Duke Gisulf II of Salerno. Cult approved—as a saint in 1579 and again in 1893.

LEO IV (St) Pope OSB. RM. July 17
d. 855. A Roman and a monk of the Benedictine abbey of San Martino, he was chosen pope in 847. He enclosed the whole Vatican city with a wall (the Leonine city), and through his prayers and exhortations to the soldiers the Saracens from Calabria were utterly routed at Ostia. His benefactions to churches take up twenty-eight pages in the *Liber Pontificalis*. The English king Alfred visited Rome during his pontificate (853) and Leo stood godfather for him at his confirmation.

LEO and JULIANA (SS) MM.
RM. Aug 18
? Leo was martyred at Myra, in Lycia, and Juliana at Strobylum. Juliana may be identified with the martyr of Ptolemais. (See Paul and Juliana.)

LEO SUCHEIEMON (Bl) M.
AC. Aug 19
d. 1622. A native Japanese, pilot of the ship of Bl Joachim Firaiama. Beheaded at Nagasaki. Beatified in 1867.

LEO II of CAVA (Bl) Ab. OSB.
AC. Aug 19
1239–1295. The fifteenth abbot of the Benedictine abbey of La Cava, near Naples. He ruled from 1268 to 1295. Cult approved in 1928.

LEO COMBIOGE (Bl) M.
AC. Sept 8
d. 1628. A Japanese catechist, member of the third order of St Dominic. Beheaded at Nagasaki. Beatified in 1867.

LEO SATZUMA (Bl) M. AC. Sept 10
d. 1622. A Japanese catechist, and a Franciscan tertiary. He was burnt alive at Nagasaki with Bl Charles Spinola (q.v.), on the day of the great martyrdom.

LEO (St) M. OFM.   RM. Oct 10
See Daniel and Comp.

LEO of MELUN (St) C. RM. Nov 10
? A saint held in veneration from time immemorial at Melun, near Paris. He is now identified by scholars with St Leo the Great, who died on Nov 10.

LEO of NONANTULA (St) Ab. OSB.   AC. Nov 20
d. 1000. Monk and abbot of the Benedictine monastery of Nonantula, near Modena.

LEO NACANIXI (Bl) M. AC. Nov 27
d. 1619. A Japanese layman, born at Amangucchi, of the royal family of Firando. He was beheaded with ten companions at Nagasaki. Beatified in 1867.

LEOBALD (LEODEBOD) (St) Ab. OSB.   AC. Aug 8
d. 650. Abbot-founder of Fleury, afterwards called Saint-Benoît-sur-Loire, in the diocese of Orleans. He had been a monk at Saint-Aignan, in the same diocese.

LEOBARD (LIBERD) (St) C,
RM. Jan 18
d. 593. A recluse at Tours who shut himself up in a cell near the abbey of Marmoutier and lived there for twenty-two years under the direction of St Gregory of Tours.

LEOBINUS (LUBIN) (St) Bp.
RM. Sept 15
d. c.556. Born near Poitiers, the son of a peasant family. Early in life he became a hermit, then a priest, abbot of Brou, and finally bishop of Chartres—one of the most distinguished occupants of that important see.

LEOCADIA (St) VM.   RM. Dec 9
d. c.303. According to the RM. she was a maiden of Toledo, who died in prison, after having been condemned to death, under Diocletian. Her cult at Toledo

dates from the 5th century, at the latest. In Flanders she is known as St Locaie.

LEOCRITIA (LUCRETIA) (St) VM.
RM. March 15
d. 859. A maiden of Cordova, Spain, born of Moorish parents, but early converted to Christianity and in consequence driven from her home. She was sheltered by St Eulogius, and both were flogged and beheaded.

LEODEGARIUS (St) Bp. M. OSB.
RM. Oct 2
c.616–678. Nephew of the bishop of Poitiers by whom he was educated. In 653 he was made abbot of the monastery of St Maxentius, where he introduced the Benedictine rule. On the death of King Clovis II he assisted St Bathildis, the queen regent during the minority of her son, Clotaire III. In 659 he became bishop of Autun, in which capacity he reformed church discipline and imposed on all the monasteries the observance of the Rule of St Benedict. His connexion with the court brought upon him the full fury of the tyrant Ebroin, mayor of the palace, who had the saint degraded, imprisoned, blinded and finally murdered. He is widely venerated in France as St Leger.

LEOMENES (St) M.   RM. Dec 23
See Theodulus, Saturninus, etc.

LEONARD of AVRANCHES (Bl)
Bp. C.   PC. March 4
d. c.614. In his early years he was a torment to the countryside, but being converted, largely by the prayers of his mother, he was elected Bishop of Avranches, and venerated by the people as a saint.

LEONARD MURIALDO (Bl) C.
Founder   AC. March 30
1828–1890. As a native of Turin he

belongs to the times and the distinguished quadrumvirate of saintly priests, John Bosco, Joseph Cafasso, Joseph Cottolengo with himself the fourth as the guide of Christian Social Work. In fact, "conservative Catholics" dubbed him "a socialist" for advocating an eight-hour day for workers in 1885. His Congregation of St Joseph continues to care for young apprentices. Beatified in 1963.

LEONARD (Bl) H. OSB. Cam.
AC. May 15
d. c.1250. Monk-hermit at Camaldoli.

LEONARD WEGEL (WICHEL, VECHEL) (St) M.   RM. July 9
d. 1572. Born at Bois-le-duc, in Holland, he studied for the priesthood at Louvain, and was appointed parish priest of Gorkum, where he was noted for his opposition to Calvinism. He was one of the group of the Gorkum martyrs, q.v. Canonized in 1867.

LEONARD of CAVA (Bl) Ab. OSB.
AC. Aug 18
d. 1255. Eleventh abbot of La Cava, in S. Italy, from 1232 till his death. Cult confirmed in 1928.

LEONARD of VANDOEUVRE (St) Ab.   AC. Oct 15
d. c.570. A hermit, who became the abbot-founder of Vandoeuvre, now Saint-Leonard-aux-Bois, near Le Mans.

LEONARD of NOBLAC (St) Ab.
RM. Nov 6
d. c.559. A French courtier converted by St Remigius of Reims. On the advice of that saint, St Leonard retired to the abbey of Micy near Orleans, and later became a hermit in a neighbouring forest, now called Noblac. His cult was widespread in the west during the Middle Ages.

LEONARD of RERESBY (St) C.
PC. Nov 6
13th cent. A native of Thryberg in Yorkshire. According to local tradition, he was a crusader, who, taken prisoner by the Saracens, was miraculously set free and returned safely home.

LEONARD KIMURA and Comp. (BB) MM.   AC. Nov 18
d. 1619. A Japanese nobleman, who, after his conversion, became a temporal coadjutor in the Society of Jesus, and with others of his countrymen was burnt to death at Nagasaki.

LEONARD of PORT MAURICE (St) C. OFM.   RM. Nov 26
1676–1751. Born at Porto Maurizio, on the Italian Riviera, he studied in the Roman College and became a Franciscan of the Strictest Observance in the convent of St Bonaventure on the Palatine. Soon after his ordination he began his career as a missionary, spreading everywhere devotion to the Blessed Sacrament, to the Sacred Heart, to the Immaculate Conception and to the Stations of the Cross: he is said to have established the Way of the Cross in five hundred and seventy-two places including the Colosseum in Rome. He was a prolific ascetical writer, his works filling thirteen volumes. In 1744 he was sent to restore discipline in Corsica. In 1751 he was called to Rome by Benedict XIV but died on the night after his arrival at his old friary of St Bonaventure. Canonized in 1867.

LEONIANUS (St) C.   AC. Nov 6
d. c.570. A Pannonian by birth, he was taken as a captive to Gaul, and, on regaining his freedom, lived as a recluse near Autun. Later he embraced the monastic life at the abbey of St Symphorianus, also at Autun. Cult approved in 1907.

LEONIDAS and Comp. (SS) MM.
RM. Jan 28
d. 304. Egyptian martyrs, associated with SS Philemon and Apollonius (q.v.). All suffered under Diocletian.

LEONIDAS (St) M.   RM. Apr 22
d. 202. The father of Origen, and himself a distinguished philosopher. He was martyred at Alexandria, his native city, under Septimius Severus.

LEONIDES (St) M.   RM. Aug 8
See Eleutherius and Leonides.

LEONIDES (St) M.   RM. Sept 2
See Diomedes, Julian, etc.

LEONILLA (St) M.   RM. Jan 17
See Speusippus, Eleusippus, etc.

LEONIS (St) VM.   RM. June 15
See Lybe, Leonis and Eutropia.

LEONORIUS (LUNAIRE) (St) Ab. Bp.   AC. July 1
d. c.570. A son of Hoel, king of Brittany, but born in Wales, educated by St Illtyd, and consecrated bishop by St Dubricius. Crossing to Brittany, then ruled by his brother Hoel II, he founded the monastery of Pontual, near Saint Malo.

LEONTIA (St) M.   RM. Dec 6
See Dionysia, Dativa, etc.

LEONTIUS of CAESAREA (St) Bp.
RM. Jan 13
d. 337. Bishop of Caesarea in Cappadocia and one of the fathers of the council of Nicaea (325). He is specially praised by St Athanasius and described as "an angel of peace" by the Greeks.

LEONTIUS (St) Bp. M.
RM. March 19
See Apollonius and Leontius.

LEONTIUS (St) Bp. AC. March 19
d. 640. Bishop of Saintes. A friend of St Malo, whom he received into his diocese when he was exiled from Brittany.

LEONTIUS (St) M.   RM. Apr 24
See Eusebius, Neon, etc.

LEONTIUS, HYPATIUS and THEODULUS (SS) MM.
RM. June 18
d. ? 135. Greeks martyred at Tripoli in Phoenicia at an early date.

LEONTIUS, MAURICE, DANIEL and Comp. (SS) MM.   RM. July 10
d. c.320. A band of forty-five martyrs who suffered together at Nicopolis in Armenia under the emperor Licinius and were among the last martyrs of the great persecution.

LEONTIUS the YOUNGER (St) Bp.
AC. July 11
c.510–565. A soldier who served against the Visigoths. He married and went to reside at Bordeaux; he was forced to accept the see and government of that city, his wife taking the veil.

LEONTIUS, ATTIUS, ALEXANDER and Comp.   RM. Aug 1
d. c.300. Three Christians of Perge in Pamphylia, who, together with six farm labourers, were martyred under Diocletian for having destroyed the altar of Artemis.

LEONTIUS the ELDER (St) Bp.
AC. Aug 21
d. c.541. Bishop of Bordeaux, the immediate predecessor of St Leontius the Younger (v. July 11).

LEONTIUS (St) M.   RM. Sept 12
See Hieronides, Leontius, etc.

LEONTIUS (St) M.   RM. Sept 27
Mentioned in the RM. as a companion in martyrdom of SS Cosmas and Damian, q.v.

LEONTIUS (St) Bp.   AC. Dee 1
d. c.432. Bishop of Fréjus in France from c.419 to c.432. He was a great friend of Cassian, who dedicated to him his first ten conferences.

LEOPARDINUS (St) Ab. M.
**   AC. Nov 24**
d. 7th cent. Monk and abbot of the monastery of St Symphorian of Vivaris in the province of Berry, France. He perished at the hands of assassins and was forthwith venerated as a martyr.

LEOPARDUS (St) M. RM. Sept 30
d. 362. A servant, or slave, in the household of Julian the Apostate. His execution probably took place in Rome.

LEOPOLD of GAICHE (Bl) C.
OFM.   AC. Apr 2
1732–1815 (Apr 15). A native of Gaiche, in the diocese of Perugia, he joined the Franciscans, and after his ordination was professor of philosophy and theology, and apostolic missionary for the Papal States. During the Napoleonic invasion he was compelled to put off his habit and became parish priest, although then seventy-seven years of age. Beatified in 1893.

LEOPOLD the GOOD (St) C.
**   RM. Nov 15**
1073–1136. Born at Melk in Austria, a grandson of the emperor Henry III. In 1096 he succeeded his father as fourth margrave of Austria. He married Agnes, daughter of Henry IV, by whom he had eighteen children. He ruled firmly and successfully for forty years, and was especially interested in the spread of religious institutions. He was the foun-

der of Mariazell (Benedictine), Heiligenkreuz (Cistercian) and Klosterneuburg (Augustinian). He was buried in the last mentioned monastery.

LEOTHADIUS (LÉOTHADE) (St)
Ab. OSB.   AC. Oct 23
d. 718. Of noble Frankish family, Léothade became a monk and shortly after abbot of Moissac, in S. France. Later he was raised to the see of Auch.

LEOVIGILD and CHRISTOPHER
(SS) MM.   RM. Aug 20
d. 852. Leovigild was a monk of SS Justus and Pastor of Cordova, and Christopher of the monastery of St Martin de La Rojana, near Cordova. They were martyred at Cordova under Abderrahman II.

LESBOS (Martyrs of)   RM. Apr 5
? Five maidens venerated by the Greeks as having suffered martyrdom in the island of Lesbos.

LESMES (St) Ab. OSB.   AC. Jan 30
The Spanish form of Adelelmus, q.v.

LETARD (St) Bp.   AC. Feb 24
Otherwise Liudhard, q.v.

LEU (St) Bp.   RM. Sept 1
French form for Lupus of Sens, q.v.

LEUCHTELDIS (LIUTHILD) (St)
V.   AC. Jan 23
Otherwise Lufthild, q.v.

LEUCIUS (St) M.   RM. Jan 11
See SS Peter, Severus and Leucius.

LEUCIUS of BRINDISI (St) Bp.
**   RM. Jan 11**
d. c.180. Venerated as the first bishop of Brindisi whither he is said to have come as a missionary from Alexandria. Another saint of the same name, likewise

bishop of Brindisi, who flourished at the beginning of the 5th century, is mentioned by St Gregory the Great.

LEUCIUS (St) M.   RM. Jan 28
See Thyrsus, Leucius and Callinicus.

LEUDOMER (LOMER) (St) Bp.
**   AC. Oct 2**
d. *c*.585. A French bishop of Chartres.

LEUS (LEO) (St)   AC. Aug 1
A priest of the 4th cent. whose relics were transported to Viguenza in the diocese of Ferrara.

LEUTFRID (LEUFROI) Ab. OSB.
**   RM. June 21**
d. 738. Abbot-founder of the monastery La - Croix - Saint - Ouen (afterwards Saint-Leufroy), near Evreux, which he governed for nearly fifty years. In art he is represented surrounded by a group of the poor children it was his delight to befriend.

LEVAN (St) C.   AC. June 8
6th cent. An Irish saint who came over to Cornwall and who has given his name (spelt also Levin—possibly an abbreviated form of Silvanus) to a parish in that county.

LEWINA (St) VM.   AC. July 24
5th cent. The first surviving record of this saint dates from 1058, when her relics were translated from Seaford in Sussex, where she is said to have been venerated, to Berg in Flanders. She is supposed to have been a British maiden martyred by the Saxon invaders.

LEZIN (St) Bp.   AC. Feb 13
Otherwise Lucinius, q.v.

LIAFDAG (St) Bp. M.   PC. Feb 3
c.980. He was made Bishop in Jutland

to meet the needs of the growing number of Christians, but was soon put to death by the pagans.

LIBENTIUS (LIÄWIZO) (St or Bl) Bp. OSB.   AC. Jan 4
938–1013. Born in S. Swabia, he became bishop of Hamburg in 988, professing at the same time the Benedictine Rule at the cathedral abbey of Hamburg. He is venerated as one of the apostles of the Slavs.

LIBERALIS (St) C.   AC. Apr 27
d. *c*.400. A priest of the district round Ancona, who worked zealously for the conversion of the Arians and suffered much at their hands. His relics are enshrined at Treviso.

LIBERATA (St) V.   AC. Jan 16
5th cent. Sister of St Epiphanius of Pavia and St Honorata, she was a virgin, living however in her parents' house.

LIBERATA (St) V.   RM. Jan 18
d. 580. A maiden of Como, at which city she, with her sister St Faustina, founded the nunnery of Santa Margarita. Both died in 580. Their relics are in Como Cathedral.

LIBERATA (St) V.   RM. July 20
Otherwise Wilgefortis, q.v.

LIBERATUS, BONIFACE, SERVUS, RUSTICUS, ROGATUS, SEPTIMUS and MAXIMUS (SS) MM.   RM. Aug 17
d. 483. Liberatus was abbot of a monastery in Africa, the rest were his monks: Boniface, a deacon; Servus and Rusticus, sub-deacons; Rogatus and Septimus, simple monks; Maximus, a child educated in the monastery. All were martyred by the Arian king Hunneric.

LIBERATUS da LORO (Bl) C. OFM.   AC. Sept 6
d. 1258. Born at San Liberato, in Piceno, of the Brumforti family, he joined the Franciscans, among whom at a later date he introduced the initial austerity of the Order, aided by BB Humilis and Pacificus. His cult was forbidden in 1730, but restored in 1731 and again approved in 1868.

LIBERATUS and BAJULUS (SS) MM.   RM. Dec 20
? Martyrs venerated at Rome, of whom nothing certain is known.

LIBERIUS (St) Bp.   RM. Dec 30
d. c.200. A bishop of Ravenna, venerated as one of the founders of that see.

LIBERT (LIEBERT) (St) Bp.
                                AC. June 23
d. 1076. Bishop of Cambrai from 1051 till his death. He went on a pilgrimage to Palestine, but failing to reach the Holy Places, he built instead, on his return to his diocese, the abbey of the Holy Sepulchre. He excommunicated the lord of Cambrai and was on that account brutally persecuted.

LIBERT (St) M. OSB.   AC. July 14
d. 783. Born at Malines, baptized and educated by St Rumoldus, from whom he received the Benedictine habit. Afterwards he migrated to the abbey of Saint-Trond, where he was put to death by invading barbarians.

LIBORIUS (St) Bp.   RM. July 23
d. 390. Bishop of Le Mans from 348 to 390. He is the patron saint of Paderborn, whither his relics were translated in 836.

LICERIUS (LIZIER) (St) Bp.
                                RM. Aug 27
d. c.548. Born in Spain, probably at Lérida (Ilerda). He went to France and in 506 was chosen bishop of Couserans (now in the diocese of Pamiers). The RM. wrongly makes him bishop of Lérida.

LICINIUS (St) M.   RM. Aug 7
See Carpophorus, Exanthus, etc.

LICINIUS (LESIN) (St) Bp.
                                RM. Nov 1
d. c.616. Count of Anjou under King Chilperic. He became a monk and afterwards was chosen bishop of Angers (586), and consecrated by St Gregory of Tours. He wished to resign, but his people would on no account allow him to do so.

LIDANUS (St) Ab. OSB. AC. July 2
1026–1118. A native of Antina in the Abruzzi who became the abbot-founder of the Benedictine abbey of Sezze in the Papal States. He deserves well of humanity for his work in draining the Pontine Marshes. In his old age he retired to Montecassino. He is the patron saint of Sezze.

LIDWINA (St) V.   AC. Apr 14
Otherwise Lydwina of Schiedam, q.v.

LIÉ (*several*)
French form of Laetus and Leo, q.v.

LIEPHARD (St) Bp. M.   AC. Feb 4
d. 640. An Englishman by birth and perhaps a bishop, said to have been the companion of King Cadwalla on the latter's pilgrimage to Rome. While on his way back to England, Liephard was done to death near Cambrai.

LIGORIUS (St) M.   RM. Sept 13
? An eastern saint who met his death at the hands of a pagan mob. His relics are enshrined at Venice.

LILIOSA (St) M.   RM. July 27
See George, Aurelius, etc.

LIMBANIA (St) V. OSB. AC. Aug 15
d. 1294. A Cyprian by birth who became a Benedictine nun at Genoa, and then lived as a recluse in a cave below the church of St Thomas in that city. Cult approved by Paul V. (*Note.* In 1509 the church of St Thomas was handed over to the Augustinians and this is the reason why Limbania is often described as an Augustinian.)

LIMNAEUS (St) H.   AC. Feb 22
See Thalassius and Limnaeus.

LINUS (St) Pope M.   RM. Sept 23
d. c.79. The immediate successor of St Peter in the see of Rome, which he ruled for twelve years (67–79). He is traditionally venerated as a martyr, but there is no evidence for his martyrdom. His name is mentioned in the Canon of the Mass.

LIOBA (St) Abs. OSB. RM. Sept 28
d. c.779. An Anglo-Saxon by birth and a kinswoman of St Boniface, St Lioba professed the Benedictine Rule at Wimborne. In 748, at the request of St Boniface, she, with a band of missionary nuns, left England for the German mission and was at once appointed abbess of Bischoffsheim and was given the general supervision of all the daughter-houses founded from that nunnery. "Lioba ruled her home in the very spirit of St Benedict's moderation and gentleness, and insisted equally on manual work and studies for all her nuns" (Attwater). She was greatly loved by her nuns and a close friend of the empress St Hildegard, Charlemagne's wife, while the tender affection which subsisted between herself and St Boniface forms one of the most charming episodes in church history. St Lioba's convents were one of the most powerful factors in the conversion of Germany by the Benedictines.

LIPHARDUS (LIFARD) (St) Ab.
                                  RM. June 3
d. c.550. A prominent lawyer of Orleans who at the age of fifty embraced the solitary life and eventually became the abbot-founder of the monastery of Meung-sur-Loire.

LITTEUS (St) M.   RM. Sept 10
See Nemesian, Felix, etc.

LIUDHARD (St) Bp.   AC. Feb 24
d. c.600. Frankish chaplain to Queen Bertha of Kent. He is said to have been a bishop and to have played an important part in the conversion of King Ethelbert, q.v. He was buried in the abbey of SS Peter and Paul, at Canterbury.

LIUTWIN (St) Bp. OSB.
                                  AC. Sept 29
d. c.713. Founder and monk of Mettlach, and then bishop of Trèves.

LIVINUS (LEBWIN) (St) Bp. M.
                                  RM. Nov 12
d. c.650. An Irishman by birth, he was ordained priest by St Augustine of Canterbury, and crossed over to Flanders, where for some years he preached the gospel with great success. At some time during this period he is said to have been consecrated bishop in Ireland. He was martyred near Alost in Brabant. He is perhaps to be identified with St Lebuinus.

LIZIER (St) Bp.   RM. Aug 27
Otherwise Licerius, q.v.

LLEUDADD (LAUDATUS) (St) Ab.
                                  AC. Jan 15
6th cent. A Welsh saint, abbot of Bardsey (Carnarvon), who accompanied St Cadfan to Brittany. By some scholars he is thought to be no other than St Lô of Coutances.

LLEWELLYN (LLYWELYN) and GWRNERTH (SS) CC. AC. Apr 7
6th cent. Welsh monks at Welshpool and afterwards at Bardsey.

LLIBIO (St) C.   AC. Feb 28
6th cent. The patron saint of Llanllibio in the isle of Anglesey.

LÔ (St) Bp.   RM. Sept 22
Otherwise Lauto, q.v.

LOARN (St) C.   AC. Aug 30
5th cent. A native of W. Ireland and a disciple of St Patrick. Some writers describe him as a regionary bishop of Downpatrick.

LOCAIE (St) VM.   RM. Dec 9
Otherwise Leocadia, q.v.

LOLANUS (St) C.   AC. Sept 2
d. c. ? 1034. A Scottish bishop. The legend which makes him a native of Galilee who preached the gospel in Scotland during the 5th century deserves no credence.

LOLLIAN (St)   AC. Dec 9
See Samosata Martyrs.

LOMAN (LUMAN) (St) Bp.
**   AC. Feb 17**
d. c.450. Said to have been a nephew of St Patrick and the first bishop of Trim in Meath.

LOMBARDS (Martyrs under the) (SS)   RM. March 2
d. c.579. A group of eighty martyrs slain by the Lombards in Campania for refusing "to adore the head of a goat" (RM.). They are also mentioned by St Gregory the Great.

LOMER (LAUDOMARUS) (St) Ab.
**   AC. Jan 19**
d. 593. A shepherd boy near Chartres,

then priest, he became a hermit. Disciples came and so he founded the monastery of Corbion near Chartres. He lived to be over a hundred.

LONDON (Martyrs of)
Three main groups of post-Reformation martyrs may be listed under the above heading, namely: (I) those of 1582, executed for being concerned in a spurious plot called the conspiracy of Reims and Rome; (II) those of 1588, following on the defeat of the Armada; (III) those of 1591, following on a stricter enforcement of the laws against Catholics. Each martyr receives in this book a special notice.

LONGINUS (St) M. RM. March 15
1st cent. This is the name given by tradition to the soldier who pierced the side of our Lord hanging on the Cross (John XIX, 34). The centurion who acknowledged Christ to be the son of God, after the crucifixion, is also called Longinus. (Matt. XXVII, 54.) He is said to have died a martyr in Cappadocia, his alleged native country.

LONGINUS (St) M.   RM. Apr 24
See Eusebius, Neon, etc.

LONGINUS (St) Bp. M.
**   RM. May 2**
See Vindemnialis, Eugene and Longinus.

LONGINUS (St) M.   RM. June 24
See Orentius, Heros, etc.

LONGINUS (St) M.   RM. July 21
See Victor, Alexander, etc.

LONOCHILUS (LONGIS, LENOGISIL) and AGNOFLEDA (SS)
**   AC. Apr 2**
d. 653 and 638. The first was a priest who founded a monastery in Maine,

France. Agnofleda vowed her virginity to God and cast herself on his protection. Both were calumniated as a result, but their innocence was proved miraculously.

LORGIUS (St) M.   RM. March 2
See Lucius, Absalom and Lorgius.

LOTHARIUS (St) Bp. OSB.
AC. June 14
c.756. Founder of a monastery in the forest of Argentan, which was later called after him Saint-Loyer-des-Champs. Afterwards he was raised to the see of Séez, which he ruled for thirty-two years.

LOUIS
See also under Aloysius.

LOUIS IBARCHI (St) M.
RM. Feb 5
1585–1597. A Japanese boy of twelve who served Mass for the Franciscan missionaries in Japan. He was crucified at Nagasaki with twenty-five companions. Canonized in 1867.

LOUIS MARY GRIGNON de MONTFORT (St) C.   RM. Apr 28
1673–1716. Born in Brittany of poor parents. Some charitable persons having defrayed the cost of his education, he was ordained priest in 1700. He became chaplain to a hospital at Nantes, where he founded the institute of Sisters of the Divine Wisdom. He now began his missionary activities throughout France, and in order to train helpers in his forceful methods of preaching, he formed, shortly before his death, Missionaries of the Company of Mary. His writings, especially his little treatise on "True Devotion to our Lady" are of great doctrinal value. He was a Dominican tertiary, but never a professed member of that order.

LOUIS of CORDOVA (St) M.
RM. Apr 30
See Amator, Peter and Louis.

LOUIS (LUDWIG) von BRUCK (St) M.   AC. Apr 30
d. 1429. A boy born of Swiss parents at Ravensburg in Swabia, who was murdered by the Jews at Easter.

LOUIS BONNARD (Bl) M.
AC. May 1
See John-Louis Bonnard.

LOUIS MARY PALAZZOLO (Bl) C.
Founder   AC. June 15
1827–1886. A native of Bergamo, he was ordained priest in 1880. A spirit akin to John Bosco, he also applied all his energy to the Christian education of young people and adults, the preservation of girls, especially children of the working class, and the care of the sick and the poor. Heirs to these tasks are the Congregations he established—the Poor Little Sisters, and the Brothers of the Holy Family. Beatified in 1963.

LOUIS NAISEN (Bl) M.   AC. July 12
1619–1626. A Japanese boy of seven years, son of BB John and Monica Naisen. He was beheaded at Nagasaki. Beatified in 1867.

LOUIS CORREA (Bl) M. SJ.
AC. July 15
d. 1570. A Jesuit cleric, born at Evora in Portugal. A companion of Bl Ignatius de Azevedo, q.v.

LOUIS BERTRÁN (Bl) M. OP.
AC. July 29
d. 1629. Born at Barcelona a kinsman of St Louis Bertrán, the apostle of Colombia. After his profession in the Dominican Order, he was sent to the Philippine Islands in 1618 and then to Japan, where he worked until his martyrdom.

He was burnt alive with two companions at Omura. Beatified in 1867.

LOUIS SOMEYON (? MATZUO) (Bl) M.   AC. Aug 17

d. 1627. A Japanese layman, of the third order of St Francis, beheaded at Nagasaki. Beatified in 1867.

LOUIS of TOULOUSE (St) Bp. OFM.   RM. Aug 19

1274–1297. Son of Charles II of Anjou, king of Naples, great-nephew of St Louis of France and of St Elisabeth of Hungary. He was born probably at Nocera and grew up in Provence. He spent seven years as a hostage for his father at Barcelona and in Tarragona. At the age of twenty-three he was ordained and joined the Friars Minor. Reluctantly he accepted the see of Toulouse, but died only six months later. Canonized in 1317.

LOUIS FLORES (Bl) M. OP.
                               AC. Aug 19

1570–1622. Born at Antwerp, he went with his parents to Mexico, where he joined the Dominicans. After serving as novice-master, he was sent in 1602 to the Philippine Islands. In 1620, while on a journey, he was captured by the Dutch, handed over to the Japanese, tortured, and imprisoned for two years, and finally burnt alive at Nagasaki. Beatified in 1867.

LOUIS IX (St) King   RM. Aug 25

1214–1270. Born at Poissy, near Paris, he succeeded to the throne under the regency of his mother Blanche of Castile in 1226. He reigned for forty-four years. In his private life he was more austere and more prayerful than a religious, as a ruler he was energetic but considerate to his people, especially to the poor, and he was a brave warrior who knew how to lead his armies to victory, as when he

defeated King Henry III of England at Taillebourg in 1242. He was the father of eleven children and a devoted husband. He led the two crusades: in the first he was made prisoner in Egypt, and during the second he died of dysentery before Tunis. He was canonized, with the universal approbation of Western Christendom, in 1297.

LOUIS SOTELO (Bl) M. OFM.
                               AC. Aug 25

d. 1624. Born of a noble family at Seville, in Spain, he became a Franciscan at Salamanca. After his ordination he was sent to Manila (1601) and then to Japan (1603). He was arrested and shipped back to Spain (1613), but after a visit to Rome, he returned to Japan (1622). Again arrested at Nagasaki, he was burnt alive at Ximabara. Beatified in 1867.

LOUIS SASANDA (Bl) M. OFM.
                               AC. Aug 25

d. 1624. Son of Bl Michael Sasanda, a martyr at Yeddo, Japan. In 1613, he accompanied Bl Louis Sotelo to Mexico, where he became a Franciscan. In 1622 he was ordained at Manila. Two years later he was burnt alive at Ximabara, with Bl Louis Sotelo and comp. Beatified in 1867.

LOUIS BABA (Bl) M. Tert. OFM.
                               AC. Aug 25

d. 1624. A Japanese catechist. He accompanied Bl Louis Sotelo to Europe. On his return to Japan he was arrested, received the Franciscan habit in prison at Omura, and was burnt alive at Ximabara. Beatified in 1867.

LOUIS BARREAU de la TOUCHE (Bl) M. OSB.   AC. Sept 2

d. 1792. A French Benedictine of the congregation of St Maur, monk of Saint-Florent-de-Saumur, and nephew of Bl

Augustine Chevreux, with whom he was massacred at Paris (see September, Martyrs of).

LOUIS MAKI (Bl) M.   AC. Sept 7
d. 1627. A Japanese layman, burnt alive at Nagasaki for having allowed Bl Thomas Tzughi to say Mass in his house. Beatified in 1867.

LOUIS NIFAKI (Bl) M. Tert. OP.
AC. Sept 8
d. 1628. A Japanese Dominican tertiary, beheaded at Nagasaki with his two sons, Francis and Dominic, for having sheltered the missionaries. Beatified in 1867.

LOUIS CAVARA (Bl) M. SJ.
AC. Sept 10
d. 1622. A page at the court of Arima, Japan, who was later exiled by the apostate prince, Michael. Received into the Society of Jesus by Bl Charles Spinola, he was burnt alive at Nagasaki. Beatified in 1867.

LOUIS (LUDWIG) (Bl) C.
PC. Sept 11
1200–1227 Landgrave of Thuringia and husband of St Elisabeth of Hungary. An able ruler and brave warrior, he died at Otranto while following the emperor Frederick II to the crusade. His cult has never been confirmed, but is certainly well deserved.

LOUIS the GREAT (Bl) C.
PC. Sept 11
d. 1382. One of the greatest of the Kings of Hungary; later of Poland too. Fought for the expansion of the Church in the Balkans. Never officially beatified, his cult is chiefly in Poland.

LOUIS ALLEMAND (Bl) Bp. Card.
AC. Sept 16
d. 1450. Appointed archbishop of Arles in 1423 and cardinal shortly after, Louis was one of the leaders of the "Council

party" during the troubled period of the Western Schism. He was one of those who elected and remained faithful to the antipope Felix V. On this account he was deprived of the cardinalate and excommunicated by Eugenius IV. Pope Nicholas V restored him, and from this time till his death Louis attended exclusively to the government of his diocese. In his private life, he was always a model of virtue.

LOUIS CHAKICHI (Bl) M. AC. Oct 2
d. 1622. A Japanese layman who released Bl Louis Flores from prison at Firando. He was burnt alive at Nagasaki. His wife and children were beheaded. Beatified in 1867.

LOUIS BERTRÁN (St) C. OP.
RM. Oct 9
1526–1581. A native of Valencia, in Spain, and a blood relation of St Vincent Ferrer; like him he was a Dominican. After filling very successfully the office of novice-master, he was in 1562 sent to evangelize S. America, and for seven years worked in what are now Colombia, Panama and some of the West Indian islands. Under obedience he returned to Spain, and served as prior in several houses. Canonized in 1671.

LOUIS MORBIOLI (Bl) C.
AC. Nov 16
1439–1495. A native of Bologna, who as a young man was notorious for his loose living, even after he had contracted marriage. He was converted by sickness, became a Carmelite tertiary, and went about teaching Christian doctrine to the young, and begging alms which he gave to the poor. Cult confirmed in 1842.

LOUISE degli ALBERTONI (Bl) W.
RM. Jan 31
1474–1533. A Roman born, she married James de Citara to whom she bore three

children. After his death she put on the habit of the third order of St Francis and spent her life in works of charity. Cult approved in 1671.

LOUISE de MARILLAC (St) Foundress   RM. March 15
1591–1660. Born in Paris. She wished to become a nun, but on the advice of her confessor, married Antony Le Gras. After his death (1625), Louise spent the remainder of her life in co-operating with St Vincent de Paul in the establishment of the Sisters of Charity. The sisters took their vows for the first time in 1638, and Louise remained their superioress till her death. Beatified in 1920, canonized in 1934.

LOUISE of SAVOY (Bl) W. Poor Clare   AC. July 24
1462–1503. Daughter of Bl Amadeus IX, duke of Savoy, and cousin of Bl Joan of Valois. In 1479 she was married to Hugh of Châlons, who left her a widow when she was only twenty-seven. She now joined the Poor Clares at Orbe and was employed in collecting food for the community, which she did most graciously and cheerfully. Cult approved in 1839.

LOUISE of OMURA (Bl) M.
**   AC. Sept 8**
d. 1628. A Japanese woman martyred at Omura.

LOUP (St) Bp.   RM. July 29
Otherwise Lupus of Troyes, q.v.

LOUTHIERN (St) Bp.   AC. Oct 17
6th cent. An Irish saint, patron of St Ludgran in Cornwall, possibly identical with St Luchtighern, abbot of Ennistymon, associated with St Ita.

LUANUS (LUGID, MOLUA) (St) Ab.   AC. Aug 4
554–609? Originally from Limerick he became a disciple of St Comgall and founder of many monasteries (the number is given as 120). His rule was most austere, but he was of great tenderness to man and beast.

LUBIN (St) Bp.   RM. Sept 15
Otherwise Leobinus, q.v.

LUCANUS (St) M.   RM. Oct 30
5th cent. A martyr who is believed to have suffered at Lagny, near Paris, where his relics were enshrined.

LUCERIUS (St) Ab. OSB.
**   AC. Dec 10**
d. 739. While still a child he joined the Benedictines of Farfa near Rome under its restorer, St Thomas of Maurienne, whom he eventually succeeded as abbot.

LUCHESIUS (Bl) C.   AC. Apr 28
d. 1260. Born near Poggibonsi, in Umbria, he married Bl Bonadonna and was in business as a grocer, money changer and corn merchant. About the year 1221 he and his wife gave themselves to a life of alms-deeds and penance as Franciscan tertiaries. They are venerated as the first to have become tertiaries, but this is not quite established.

LUCHTIGHERN (St) Ab.
**   AC. Apr 28**
See under Louthiern.

LUCIAN of ANTIOCH (St) M.
**   RM. Jan 7**
d. 312. A native of Edessa, where he distinguished himself as a scriptural scholar. He travelled to Antioch where he opened a school of exegesis, and then to Nicomedia, where he was martyred after nine years in prison. The Arians endeavoured to claim the authority of his name for their errors. He is highly praised by SS John Chrysostom and Jerome.

LUCIAN, MAXIMIAN and JULIAN (SS) MM. RM. Jan 8
d. *c*.290. Alleged to have been missionaries from Rome martyred at Beauvais.

LUCIAN (St) M. RM. May 28
See Emilius, Felix, etc.

LUCIAN (St) M. RM. June 13
See Fortunatus and Lucian.

LUCIAN (St) M. RM. July 7
See Peregrinus, Lucian, etc.

LUCIAN, FLORIUS and Comp. (SS) MM. RM. Oct 26
d. *c*.250. A group of martyrs who suffered at Nicomedia under Decius. Their Acts were fancifully embellished at a later date.

LUCIAN, METROBIUS, PAUL, ZENOBIUS, THEOTIMUS and DRUSUS (SS) MM. RM. Dec 24
? African martyrs who suffered at Tripoli.

LUCIDIUS (St) Bp. RM. Apr 26
? A bishop of Verona, famous for his life of prayer and study.

LUCIDUS (St) H. OSB. AC. July 28
d. ? 938. Benedictine monk of St Peter's, near Aquara in S. Italy. He died as a recluse in the cell of Santa Maria del Piano.

LUCILLA, FLORA VV., EUGENE, ANTONINUS, THEODORE and Comp. (SS) MM. RM. July 29
d. *c*.260. A band of twenty-three martyrs who suffered under Gallienus. It seems that this group should be identified with the three groups commemorated on the following days: June 24 (SS Faustus, etc.), June 25 (SS Lucy and Comp.), July 6 (SS Lucy, Antoninus, etc.).

LUCILLA (St) VM. RM. Aug 25
See Nemesius and Lucilla.

LUCILLIAN, CLAUDIUS, HYPATIUS, PAUL and DIONYSIUS (SS) MM. RM. June 3
d. 273. Lucillian is said to have become a Christian in his old age. He was crucified at Byzantium, and on the same occasion the four youths, mentioned above, were beheaded. Another version of the story states that Lucillian was the father, the four youths his sons, and makes Paula (q.v.), a lady commemorated on the same day, their respective wife and mother.

LUCINA (three of the same name) (St) RM. June 30
Some modern writers affirm that there were three Roman saints of this name. (I) St Lucina of apostolic times, mentioned in the (spurious) Acts of SS Processus and Martinianus. (II) St Lucina who ministered to the martyrs under Decius (250). (III) St Lucina, connected with St Sebastian and other martyrs under Diocletian. The first is commemorated on June 30.

LUCINUS (LEZIN) (St) Bp. AC. Feb 13
d. *c*.618. A courtier who eventually became bishop of Angers, which see he ruled for many years.

LUCIOLUS (St) M. RM. March 3
See Felix, Luciolus, etc.

LUCIUS (St) M. RM. Feb 8
See Paul, Lucius and Cyriacus.

LUCIUS and Comp. (SS) MM. RM. Feb 11
d. 350. Lucius, bishop of Adrianople, played a leading part in the council of Sardica (347). Under the protection of Pope St Julius I, he returned to Adrianople, but refused to be in communion

with the Arian bishops condemned at Sardica. On this account he was martyred with a group of his faithful Catholics by order of the emperor Constantius.

LUCIUS (St) M.   RM. Feb 15
See Saturninus, Castulus, etc.

LUCIUS, SILVANUS, RUTULUS, CLASSICUS, SECUNDINUS, FRUCTULUS and MAXIMUS (SS) MM.   RM. Feb 18
? African martyrs, whose names Baronius inserted in the RM. on the authority, he states, of reliable MSS.

LUCIUS (St) M.   RM. Feb 24
See Montanus, Lucius, etc.

LUCIUS, ABSOLON and LORGIUS MM.   RM. March 2
The names are first met in the martyrology of Usuard. The RM. says they were martyred at Caesarea in Cappadocia.

**LUCIUS I (St) Pope M.
          RM. March 4**
d. 254. He succeeded St Cornelius as Pope in 253, and was at once sent into exile. On the death of the emperor Gallus he returned triumphantly to his flock, but his pontificate lasted only eight months. Although referred to as a martyr by St Cyprian, there is no evidence or probability of his having been put to death; he was a Confessor of the faith.

LUCIUS (St) M.   RM. Apr 22
See Apelles, Lucius and Clement.

**LUCIUS of CYRENE (St) Bp.
          RM. May 6**
1st cent. One of the "prophets and doctors" mentioned as being in the church at Antioch when Paul and Barnabas were set apart for their apostolate (Acts XIII, 1). He is stated to have been "of Cyrene", whence the tradition that he was the first bishop of that city in the Ptolemais (Africa).

LUCIUS (St) M.   RM. May 23
See Quintian, Lucius, etc.

**LUCIUS and Comp. (SS) MM.
          RM. Aug 20**
? The story of Lucius is wrapped in obscurity. According to the RM. he came from Cyrene to Cyprus, and this may imply a confusion with Lucius of Cyrene (May 6).

LUCIUS (St) Bp. M.   RM. Sept 10
See Nemesian, Felix, etc.

LUCIUS (St) M.   RM. Oct 4
See Caius, Faustus, etc.

LUCIUS (St) M.   RM. Oct 19
See Ptolemy, Lucius, etc.

LUCIUS (St) M.   RM. Oct 25
See Theodosius, Lucius, etc.

LUCIUS (St) M.   RM. Oct 29
See Hyacinth, Quintus, etc.

**LUCIUS, ROGATUS, CASSIAN and CANDIDA (SS) MM.
          RM. Dec 1**
? Roman martyrs.

LUCIUS (St) King.   RM. Dec 3
d. c.200. King of Britain. According to a tradition, first heard of in the sixth century, he asked Pope St Eleutherius (d. c.189) to send missionaries into Britain, where he founded the dioceses of London and Llandaff and whence he eventually set out as a missionary to the Grisons in Switzerland. Present-day scholars incline to regard the whole story as fictitious.

LUCIUS (St) M.   RM. Dec 15
See Faustinus, Lucius, etc.

LUCRETIA (St) VM. RM. March 15
Otherwise Leocritia, q.v.

LUCRETIA (St) VM.   RM. Nov 23
d. 306. A Spanish maiden, martyred at
Mérida (Emerita) in W. Spain.

LUCY (Bl) VM.   AC. Feb 19
1813–1862. A Chinese school-teacher
beheaded at Kuy-tszheu. Beatified in
1909.

**LUCY (LUCIA) FILIPPINI (St) V.
                        RM. March 25**
1672–1732. Born in Tuscany, she
joined Rosa Venerini at Montefiascone
and helped her in the work of training
school-mistresses. This was the origin
of the flourishing Italian institute of the
Maestre Pie, or Filippine, of which St
Lucy is venerated as the co-foundress.
Canonized in 1930.

**LUCY (LUCIA, LUCEIA) and 20
Comp. (SS) MM.   RM. June 25**
See the notice of SS Lucilla, etc., of
July 29.

**LUCY, ANTONINUS, SEVERI-
NUS, DIODORUS, DION and
Comp. (SS) MM.   RM. July 6**
See the notice of SS. Lucilla, etc., of
July 29.

**LUCY BUFALARI (Bl) V. OSA.
                        AC. July 27**
d. 1350. Born at Castel Porziano, near
Rome, a sister of Bl John of Rieti, she
took the veil in the Augustinian convent
of Amelia where she became prioress.
She is venerated as patroness against
diabolical possession. Cult confirmed in
1832.

**LUCY de FREITAS (Bl) M.
                        AC. Sept 10**
d. 1622. Of Japanese birth, but married

to a Portuguese, Philip de Freitas. For
having given shelter to the missionaries
she was burnt alive at Nagasaki on the
day of the great martyrdom. Beatified
in 1867.

**LUCY and GEMINIAN (SS) MM.
                        RM. Sept 16**
d. c.300. A Roman widow (said to have
been 75 years old) and a neophyte, who
were martyred together under Diocletian. Their Acts are untrustworthy.

**LUCY of CALTAGIRONE (Bl) V.
OFM.   AC. Sept 26**
d. ? 1304. Born at Caltagirone in Sicily,
she became a Poor Clare at Salerno.
Cult approved in 1514.

LUCY CHAKICHI (Bl) M. AC. Oct 2
d. 1622. The wife of Bl Louis Chakichi,
q.v. She was beheaded with her two
boys, Andrew and Francis (q.v.), at
Nagasaki. Beatified in 1867.

**LUCY of SETTEFONTI (Bl) V.
OSB, Cam.   AC. Nov 7**
d. 12th cent. Born at Bologna, she took
the Camaldolese habit in the convent of
St Christina, at Settefonti, diocese of
Bologna. The Camaldolese venerate her
as the foundress of their sisterhoods.

**LUCY BROCOLELLI (Bl) V. Tert.
OP.   AC. Nov 15**
1476–1544. Born at Narni in Umbria,
after three years of virginal wedlock she
was allowed by her husband to become
a Dominican regular tertiary at Viterbo,
where she received the *Stigmata*. In
1499 she was sent as the first prioress of
the convent of Ferrara, but she proved
a very incapable superior, and was deposed, treated with un-Christian cruelty
by her successor, and forgotten by all.
Thus she lived thirty-nine years without
ever complaining. Cult confirmed in
1710.

LUCY of SYRACUSE (St) VM.
RM. Dec 13
d. 304. A Sicilian maiden who suffered at Syracuse under Diocletian. She is one of the most famous of the Western virgin-martyrs, and is still daily commemorated in the canon of the Mass. Her *Acta*, however, though written before the 6th century, are unfortunately not trustworthy.

LUDAN (LUDEN, LOUDAIN) (St) C.   AC. Feb 12
d. *c*.1202. The saint of this name honoured at Scherkirchen in Alsace is said to have been a Scottish or Irish pilgrim who died in that country on his way back from Jerusalem.

LUDGER (St) Bp. OSB.
RM. March 26
d. 809. A Frisian by birth, educated under St Gregory in the abbey school of Utrecht and under Bl Alcuin in England. Returning to his fatherland as a missionary, he worked chiefly in Westphalia, of which he is the apostle. His gentleness did more to attract the Saxons to Christ than all the armies of Charlemagne. He lived for a time at Montecassino, learning the Benedictine observance. He was the founder and the first bishop of Münster.

LUDMILLA (St) M.   AC. Sept 16
d. 921. Duchess of Bohemia entrusted with the education of the young prince St Wenceslaus. She fell a victim to the jealousy of her daughter-in-law, by whose orders she was strangled by hired assassins at Tetin.

LUDOLPH (St) Bp. O. Praem.
AC. March 29
d. 1250. A Premonstratensian canon who became bishop of Ratzeburg and had to endure much persecution at the hands of the Duke Albert of Sachsen-Lauenberg.

LUDOLPH (St) Ab. OSB.
AC. Aug 13
d. 983. Abbot of New Corvey in Westphalia from 971 to 983. During his abbacy there was a marked revival of the monastic school and studies.

LUDOLPH (Bl) OSB.   PC.
11th cent.? Abbot founder of Fontoavellana. It is not certain what rule they followed; apparently there were elements from St Benedict, and others from St Columban, or they may have been Camaldolese, following a visit from St Romuald.

LUDOVICUS PAVONI (Bl) C.
Founder   AC. Apr 1
1784-1849. From the cradle to the grave his life was lived in his native Brescia. Ordained in 1807 he did not spare himself in the fulfilment of priestly tasks, particularly in the care of the young. This ideal urged him to create the religious institute known as the Sons of Mary Immaculate. Beatified in 1947.

LUDWIN (LEODWIN, etc.) (St) Bp. OSB.   AC. Sept 29
d. 713. Born in Austrasia and educated under St Basinus, he married early in life. Left a widower, he founded the abbey of Mettlach (*Mediolacus*) and became a monk there. Later he was raised to the see of Trèves.

LUFTHILD (St) V.   AC. Jan 23
d. ? 850. A saint honoured in the neighbourhood of Cologne. She is said to have lived as an anchoress in that locality.

LUKE (St) M.   RM. Feb 6
See Silvanus, Luke, etc.

LUKE the YOUNGER   AC. Feb 7
d. *c*.946. A Greek farm labourer who was admitted as a novice to a monastery at Athens, and became a solitary on

Mt Joannitza, near Corinth. He worked so many miracles in this place that it was known as *Soterion* (place of healing) and he himself as the Thaumaturgus (the wonder-worker).

LUKE BELLUDI (Bl) C. OFM.
                                    AC. Feb 17
1200–1285. He received the Franciscan habit from St Francis himself at Padua and became the intimate associate of St Antony of Padua, at whose death he assisted. On his own death he was laid in the empty tomb from which the body of St Antony had been taken. Cult confirmed in 1927.

LUKE (St) M.   RM. Apr 22
See Parmenius and Comp.

LUKE KIRBY (Bl) M.   AC. May 30
d. 1582. Born in N. England and educated, probably, at Cambridge. After his conversion he studied for the priesthood at Rome and Douai. On his return to England as a priest (1580) he was arrested and subjected in the Tower to the terrible torture known as the "scavenger's daughter". He was finally martyred at Tyburn.

LUKE BANABAKIUTU (St) M.
                                    RM. June 3
d. 1886. A Negro, baptized in 1881 and burnt alive at Namuyongo in Uganda. See Uganda (Martyrs of).

LUKE LOAN (Bl) M.   AC. June 4
1756–1840. An old priest, native of Tonkin, beheaded for his priesthood.

LUKE KIEMON (Bl) M. AC. Aug 17
d. 1627. A native of Japan, and a Franciscan tertiary, beheaded at Nagasaki. Beatified in 1867.

LUKE MELLINI (Bl) Ab. OSB. Cel.
                                    AC. Aug 24
d. *c*.1460. A Benedictine monk of the Celestine congregation. Pope Nicholas V appointed him general of the Celestines.

LUKE BANFY (Bl) Bp. M.
                                    PC. Aug 28
d. *c*.1178. Primate of Hungary and Archbishop of Esztergom, he defended the Church against royal despotism. His canonization, started by Gregory IX, was interrupted by the Tartar invasion of Hungary.

LUKE (St) M.   RM. Sept 10
See Apelles, Lucius and Clement.

LUKE (St) Evangelist   RM. Oct 18
1st cent. A Greek of Antioch, and a physician by profession, who became the fellow worker of St Paul and remained with him till the great apostle's martyrdom. He wrote the third gospel —"St Paul's Gospel"—and the Acts of the Apostles. The later tradition that he was a painter seems to be based on the picturesque style of his narrative. There is no evidence that he died a martyr.

LUKE de NOSTRA (Bl) H.
                                    PC. Dec 5
14th cent. A Hungarian Pauline hermit, friend and confessor of King Louis the Great (1342–1382).

LULLUS (St) Bp. OSB.
                                    RM. Oct 16
d. 787. An Anglo-Saxon monk of Malmesbury, and a kinsman of St Boniface, whom he joined in Germany, becoming his archdeacon and chief assistant. In 751 he was sent to Rome, and on his return Boniface consecrated him regionary bishop and his coadjutor in the see of Mainz, which he ruled after his master's martyrdom.

LUNAIRE (St) Bp.   AC. July 1
Otherwise Leonorius, q.v.

LUPERCULUS (LUPERCUS) (St) Bp. M.   AC. March 1

300. A French, or Spanish, martyr under Diocletian. He is venerated chiefly at Tarbes, near Lourdes.

LUPERCUS (St) M.   RM. Apr 16

See Saragossa (Martyrs of).

LUPERCUS (St) M.   RM. Oct 30

See Claudius, Lupercus and Victorius.

LUPERIUS (St) Bp.   RM. Nov 15

6th (or 8th) cent. A bishop of Verona, of whom nothing further is known.

LUPICINUS and FELIX (SS) Bps.   RM. Feb 3

5th cent. Described in the Martyrologies as bishops of Lyons. To St Lupicinus is usually assigned the date 486. Nothing else is known of either saint.

LUPICINUS (St) Ab. RM. March 21

d. c.480. Brother of St Romanus of Condat (Feb 28), with whom he founded the abbeys of St Claud (Condat) in the Jura and Lauconne.

LUPICINUS (St) Bp.   RM. May 31

5th cent. Bishop of Verona, described as "the most holy, the best of bishops".

LUPUS (St) M.   RM. Aug 23

? A slave who gave his life for Christ.

LUPUS of CHÂLONS (St) Bp.   AC. Jan 27

d. c.610. Bishop of Châlons-sur-Saône, famous for his charity to the afflicted. We have a letter of St Gregory the Great addressed to him 601.

LUPUS of TROYES (St) Bp.   RM. July 29

384–478. A native of Toul who married the sister of St Hilary. After seven years husband and wife separated by mutual consent, Lupus becoming a monk at Lérins. In 426 he was made bishop of Troyes. In the course of his episcopate he accompanied St Germanus of Auxerre to Britain to rid the country of Pelagianism, and in 453 he succeeded in saving Troyes from being sacked by Attila. He died at the age of ninety-four.

LUPUS of SENS (St) Bp. RM. Sept 1

d. 623. A monk of Lérins who became bishop of Sens in 609. He was slandered and banished from his see under Clotaire, but was recalled by his own people and his cause fully vindicated.

LUPUS of LYONS (St) Bp.   RM. Sept 25

d. 542. A monk of a monastery near Lyons who became archbishop of that see. He had much to suffer in the political troubles which followed the death of St Sigismund, king of Burgundy.

LUPUS (St) M.   RM. Oct 14

See Saturninus and Lupus.

LUPUS of SOISSONS (St) Bp.   AC. Oct 19

d. c.540. A nephew of St Remigius of Reims who became bishop of Soissons.

LUPUS of BAYEUX (St) Bp.   AC. Oct 25

5th cent. A bishop of Bayeux, said to have ruled that diocese about the year 465.

LUPUS of VERONA (St) Bp.   RM. Dec 2

? A bishop of Verona of whom nothing is known save the bare name.

LUTGARD (St) V. OSB. Cist.   RM. June 16

1182–1246. Born at Tongres in Brabant, she became a Black Benedictine nun at the age of twenty, and after some years, in order to escape being made abbess she migrated to the Cistercian nunnery of Aywières. Here she lived for thirty years a wonderful life full of mystical experiences: she is an outstanding figure among the women mystics of the Middle Ages. She was blind for eleven years before her death.

LUXORIUS, CISELLUS and CAMERINUS (SS) MM. RM. Aug 21

d. *c*.303. Sardinian martyrs, beheaded under Diocletian. According to his *Passio* Luxorius had been a soldier in the imperial army; the other two were boys whom he encouraged to brave martyrdom.

LYBE, LEONIS and EUTROPIA (SS) VV. MM.   RM. June 15

d. 303. Martyrs under Diocletian, at Palmyra in Syria. Lybe was beheaded; Leonis, her sister, died at the stake; and Eutropia, a girl of twelve, was, by order of the judge, used as a target for the soldiers to shoot at.

LYBOSUS (St) M.   RM. Dec 29

See Dominic, Victor, etc.

LYCARION (St) M.   RM. June 7

? A martyr who suffered in Egypt.

LYDIA (St) M.   RM. March 27

See Philetus, Lydia, etc.

LYDIA PURPURARIA (St) Matron   RM. Aug 3

1st cent. A native of Thyatira (now Ak-Hissar), a city in Asia Minor famous for its dye-works, whence Lydia's trade—*purpuraria*, purple seller. She was at Philippi in Macedonia when she became St Paul's first convert in Europe and afterwards his hostess (Acts XVI, 14–15).

LYDWINA of SCHIEDAM (Bl) V.   AC. Apr 14

1380–1433. In the words of her proper office she was "a prodigy of human suffering and heroic patience". The daughter of a labourer, at the age of sixteen she met with an accident and became completely bedridden. The disease increased in virulence up to the moment of her death. Through it all she was favoured by God with mystical experiences. She suffered greatly.

LYÉ (*several*)

Note. Both St Leo of Troyes (May 25) and St Leo of Melun (Nov 10) are frequently called Lié or Lyé, which is also a French form of Laetus.

LYONS and VIENNE (Martyrs of)   RM. June 2

See Photinus (Pothinus), Sanctius, etc.

LYTHAN (LLYTHAOTHAW) (St)   AC. Sept 1

? Titular saint of two Welsh churches in the Llandaff diocese.

LYUTIUS (St) H. OSB.   ? AC. July 28

d. *c*.1038. A monk of Montecassino, who died as a hermit at La Cava. Some writers identify him with St Lucidus, q.v.

M

MABYN (St)   **AC. Sept 21**
6th cent. Welsh and Cornish saints, Mabyn, Mabon, Mabenna, are associated with St Teilo, and have originated some place-names, but nothing definite can be stated in regard to them. One of the daughters of the chieftain Brychan of Brecknock is venerated as St Mabenna; and the place-name Ruabon (Denbighshire) perpetuates the name of another saint of similar name.

MACAILLE (St) Bp.   **AC. Apr 25**
d. c.489. A disciple of Mel who became bishop of Croghan, Offaly. He assisted St Mel in receiving Brigid's vows. He seems to be other than his contemporary, St Maccai, also a disciple of St Patrick, venerated in the isle of Bute.

MACANISIUS (St) Bp. AC. Sept 3
d. 514. Or *Aengus Mc Nisse*. He is said to have been baptized as an infant by St Patrick, by whom he is also alleged to have been consecrated bishop. He became the abbot-founder of a monastery, probably at Kells, which grew into the diocese of Connor.

MACARIA (MACARIUS) (St) M.
     RM. Apr 8
See Januarius, Maxima, etc.

MACARIUS the YOUNGER (St) H.
     RM. Jan 2
d. c.408. Surnamed also "of Alexandria". He is said to have abandoned the trade of a fruiterer to become a monk in the Thebaid in Upper Egypt, c.335. Thence passing into Lower Egypt, he took up his abode in the desert of Nitria. Lucius, the intruded Arian patriarch of Alexandria, banished him on account of his unflinching orthodoxy.

MACARIUS the ELDER (St) H.
     RM. Jan 15
c.300–390. Known also as "Macarius of Egypt" or "the Great". Born in Upper Egypt, in his youth he retired to a solitary hut, where he combined assiduous prayer with the tending of sheep and the plaiting of baskets. To escape notice he migrated to the desert of Skete, where he was promoted to the priesthood and passed the remaining 60 years of his life. His chief duty was to say daily Mass for the several thousand members of the monastic colony. He was banished for a time for having upheld the Catholic faith against the Arians.

MACARIUS, RUFINUS, JUSTUS and THEOPHILUS (SS) MM.
     RM. Feb 28
d. c.250. Martyrs under Decius. The RM. claims them for Rome; other martyrologies for Alexandria. They are said to have been potters by trade.

MACARIUS of JERUSALEM (St) Bp.   **RM. March 10**
d. c.335. Bishop of Jerusalem from 314 till his death. It is said that during his episcopate St Helen found the True Cross and that it was he who identified it. He planned Constantine's basilica of the Holy Sepulchre and of the Resurrection, which was completed before his death.

452

MACARIUS the WONDER-WORKER (St) Ab. RM. Apr 1

d. 830. Abbot of Pelecete, near Constantinople. He was singled out as the special object of their persecution by the iconoclast emperors Leo the Armenian and Michael the Stammerer. After several years in prison he died in exile.

MACARIUS of ANTIOCH (St) Bp. RM. Apr 10

d. 1012. Said to have been a native of Antioch in Pisidia and a bishop, who travelled westward as a pilgrim and was received by the Benedictines of St Bavo, Ghent, in whose hospice he died of the plague, then raging in Belgium.

MACARIUS (St) Bp. RM. June 20

d. c.350. A bishop of Petra in Palestine. He took part in the council of Sardica against the Arians, who succeeded in securing his banishment to Africa, where he died. His name was originally Arius, but he has been renamed Macarius to distinguish him from the founder of Arianism, whom Macarius opposed throughout his life.

MACARIUS and JULIAN (SS) MM. RM. Aug 12

? Described by the RM. as martyrs of Syria. The earlier martyrologies treat them as confessors; possibly they were monks.

MACARIUS (St) M. RM. Sept 5

See Eudoxius, Zeno, etc.

MACARIUS (St) M. RM. Sept 6

See Faustus, Macarius and Comp.

MACARIUS and Comp. (SS) MM. RM. Oct 30

d. c.250. The RM. places them at Alexandria but they seem to be identical with the group noticed under Feb 28.

MACARIUS (St) M. RM. Dec 8

This Macarius, who suffered at Alexandria, also seems to be identical with those noticed under Feb 28 and Oct 30.

MACARIUS the SCOT (Bl) Ab. OSB. AC. Dec 19

d. 1153. A Benedictine monk who crossed over to Würzburg from Scotland (or Ireland) and was elected first abbot of St James's monastery, founded by Bishop Embricho (1125–1146).

MACARIUS (St) M. RM. Dec 20

See Eugene and Macarius.

MACARTIN (MACARTAN, MACCARTHEN) (St) Bp. AC. March 24

d. c.505. An early disciple and companion of St Patrick, by whom he is said to have been consecrated bishop of Clogher. His name in Irish is Aedh mac Carthin.

MACCABEAN MARTYRS (SS) RM. Aug 1

See Machabees.

MACCALDUS (St) Bp. AC. Dec 28

Otherwise Maughold, q.v.

MACCALLIN (MALCALLAN) Ab. OSB. AC. Jan 21

d. 978. An Irishman who made a pilgrimage to St Fursey's shrine at Péronne, and entered the Benedictine abbey of Gorze. Later he became a hermit and later still abbot of St Michael's monastery at Thiérache and Waulsort (*Valciodorum*), near Dinant, on the R. Meuse.

MACCALLIN (MACALLAN, MACCULIN DUS) (St) Bp. AC. Sept 6

d. c.497. An Irish bishop of Lusk, who is venerated also in Scotland, which country he is known to have visited.

MACDARA (St)
The saint who has given its name to St Macdaras Island off the coast of Galway.

MACEDO (St) M.   RM. March 27
See Philetus, Lydia, etc.

MACEDONIUS (St) H. AC. Jan 24
d. c.430. A Syrian hermit who wandered for forty years in Syria, Phoenicia and Cilicia, living all the time on barley; hence his surname of *Kritophagos* "the barley-eater".

MACEDONIUS, PATRICIA and MODESTA (SS) MM.
RM. March 13
d. c.304. A group of three martyrs, husband, wife and daughter, whom the RM. assigns to Nicomedia. Earlier martyrologies extend the group to twenty-two names.

MACEDONIUS (St) Bp.
AC. Apr 25
d. 516. A patriarch of Constantinople who suffered deportation for his zeal in defence of the Council of Chalcedon. He died in exile.

MACEDONIUS, THEODULUS and TATIAN (SS) MM.   RM. Sept 12
d. 362. Martyrs of Phrygia, roasted alive on gridirons at Mevos for having broken into the temple and destroyed the idols during the restoration of paganism under Julian the Apostate.

MACERATUS (St) M.
See Peregrinus, Maceratus, etc.

MACHABEES (SS) MM. RM. Aug 1
d. 166 B.C. These are the only saints of the Old Testament liturgically venerated in the Western Church. Prominent among them were a scribe by name Eleazar, ninety years of age, and a mother with her seven sons (2 Mac. VI, VII), all Jews and probably natives of Antioch, martyred under Antiochus IV Epiphanes for refusing to eat the flesh of swine forbidden by the Jewish Torah. Their relics are said to be enshrined in the church of St Peter *ad vincula* in Rome.

MACHABEO (GILDA-MARCHAI-BEO) (St) Ab.   AC. March 31
1104–1174. An Irishman, abbot of the monastery of SS Peter and Paul at Armagh from 1134 till his death.

MACHAI (St) Ab.   AC. Apr 11
5th cent. A disciple of St Patrick, who founded a monastery in the isle of Bute.

MACHAN (St) Bp.   AC. Sept 28
? A Scottish saint trained in Ireland and consecrated bishop in Rome.

MACHAR (MACHARIUS, MOCHUMNA) (St) Bp. AC. Nov 12
6th cent. An Irishman by birth, he was baptized by St Colman and became a disciple of St Columba at Iona. Afterwards he was sent with twelve disciples to convert the Picts, and fixed his episcopal residence at Old Aberdeen.

MACHUDD (MACHELL) (St) Ab.
AC. Nov 15
7th cent. Abbot-founder of Llanfechell (Anglesey).

MACHUTUS (MACLOVIUS) (St) Bp.   RM. Nov 15
Otherwise Malo, q.v.

MACKESSOG (KEGSAG) (St)
AC. March 10
Otherwise Kessog, q.v.

MACRA (St) VM.   RM. Jan 6
d. 287. A maiden of Reims, martyred at Fismes in Champagne under the prefect Rictiovarus, before the outbreak of the

persecution under Diocletian. In art she is usually represented with a pair of pincers in her hand, in memory of one of the fiendish tortures to which she was subjected.

MACRINA the ELDER (St) W.
RM. Jan 14
d. *c*.340. The paternal grandmother of SS Basil and Gregory of Nyssa. In her youth she had been directed by St Gregory Thaumaturgus, and during the persecution of Diocletian she and her husband were forced to remain concealed for seven years or more in a hiding place on the shores of the Black Sea. They had much to suffer later under Licinius. Nevertheless they succeeded in rearing one of the most saintly families in Cappadocia.

MACRINA the YOUNGER (St) V.
RM. July 19
d. *c*.380. Granddaughter of St Macrina the Elder (v. Jan 14) and eldest daughter of SS Basil and Emmelia. She was one of ten children among whom were SS Basil the Great and Gregory of Nyssa. She helped her parents in the training of her younger brothers and sisters and afterwards became a nun and abbess.

MACRINA (St) VM.   RM. July 20
Otherwise Margaret, q.v.

MACRINUS (St) M.   RM. Sept 17
See Valerian, Macrinus and Gordian.

MACROBIUS (St) M.   RM. July 20
See Sabinus, Julian, etc.

MACROBIUS and JULIAN (SS)
MM.   RM. Sept 13
d. *c*.321. Martyrs who seem to have suffered under Licinius—Macrobius, a Cappadocian, at Tomis on the Black Sea, and Julian, a priest, in Galatia. It appears, however, that these two mar-

tyrs have been confused with those of Sept 17, Valerian, Macrinus (Macrobius) and Gordian (Julian).

MACULL (St) Bp.   AC. Apr 25
Otherwise Maughold, q.v.

MADALBERTA (St) V. OSB.
AC. Sept 7
d. 706. Daughter of SS Vincent Madelgarus and Waldetrudis. She was educated by her aunt, St Aldegund, the foundress of Maubeuge, where she took the veil. About the year 697 she succeeded her sister, St Aldetrudis, as abbess.

MADELEINE (*several*)
French form of Magdalen. See under Mary Magdalen.

MADELGISILUS (French:
MAUGUILLE) (St) H. OSB.
AC. May 30
d. *c*.655. An Irish monk, disciple and trusted confidant of St Fursey. After some years of monastic life at St Riquier, he, together with St Pulgan, retired to a solitude, near Monstrelet, where he died.

MADEN (MADERN, MADRON)
(St) C.   AC. May 17
d. *c*.545. A Breton hermit of Cornish descent, to whom many churches are dedicated, the most noted being that at St Madern's Well in Cornwall, the reputed site of his hermitage.

MADIR (St) M.   RM. March 3
Otherwise Hermiterius, q.v.

MADOES (MADIANUS) (St) C.
AC. ? Jan 31
? A saint who has left his name to a place in the Carse of Gowrie. Some identify him with St Modoc or Aidan of Ferns. Another tradition makes of him a fellow missionary to Scotland with St

Boniface Quiritinus or Curitan, who appears to have been sent from Rome to preach in N. Britain. It seems impossible to disentangle the facts from the legendary accretions.

**MADRUN (MATERIANA) (St) W.
                                        AC. Apr 9**
5th cent. A Welsh or Cornish saint to whom some Welsh churches are dedicated.

**MAEDHOG (AEDHAN,
MOGUE) (St) Ab.   AC. Apr 11**
6th cent. An Irish abbot, whose chief monastery was at Clonmore. He was closely associated with SS Onchu and Finan.

**MAEDOC (MODOC, AEDAN,
EDAN, AIDUS) (St) Bp. AC. Jan 31**
Otherwise Aidan, q.v.

MAEL (MAHEL) (St) C. AC. May 13
6th cent. A disciple of St Cadfan with whom he came from Brittany into Wales. He became one of the solitaries of the isle of Bardsey.

**MAELMUIRE (MARIANUS) (St) C.
                                        AC. July 3**
d. p.1167. Maelmuire O'Gorman was an abbot of Knock (Louth), and is best known as a composer in Irish verse of an Irish menology.

MAELRHYS (St) C.   AC. Jan 1
6th cent. A saint of the isle of Bardsey, probably a Breton by birth, venerated in N. Wales.

**MAELRUBIUS (MAOLRUBHA)
(St) C.   AC. Apr 21**
d. 724. A member of St Comgall's community at Bangor, who migrated to Iona. He afterwards founded a church at Applecross on the N.W. coast of Scotland. Cult approved in 1898.

MAETHLU (St) C.   AC. Dec 22
Otherwise Amaethlu, q.v.

**MAFALDA (St) N. OSB. Cist.
                                        AC. May 2**
1203-1252. Daughter of King Sancho II of Portugal. At the age of twelve she was married to King Henry I of Castile, but her marriage was declared null by the Holy See on account of consanguinity. She at once entered the Cistercian nunnery of Arouca in Portugal and there professed the Benedictine Rule. Cult, as a saint, approved in 1793.

MAGDALEN (*several*)
See under Mary Magdalen.

**MAGDALVEUS (MADALVEUS,
MAUVÉ) (St) Bp. OSB. AC. Oct 5**
d. c.776. Born at Verdun, he became a monk of St Vannes, and afterwards (c.736) bishop of his native city.

MAGENULPUS (St) C.   AC. Oct 5
Otherwise Meinuph, q.v.

**MAGI (Three Holy Kings):
BALTHASAR, CASPAR (GASPAR)
and MELCHIOR (SS)   AC. Jan 6**
1st cent. According to a very ancient, though not altogether constant tradition the Wise Men from the East were three in number (Matt. II). The idea, traced back to the 6th century, that they were kings was almost certainly suggested by the passage in the psalm: "The kings of Tharsis and the islands shall offer presents; the kings of the Arabians and of Saba shall bring gifts." Names were attributed to them as early as the 8th century. A magnificent medieval shrine in Cologne cathedral contains their reputed bones.

MAGINA (St) M.   RM. Dec 3
See Claudius, Crispinus, etc.

MAGINUS (Catalan: MAGÍ) (St) M. RM. Aug 25

d. *c*.304. Born at Tarragona, in Spain, he evangelized the people of the *Montes Brufagani* near his native city, and was finally beheaded under Diocletian.

MAGLORIUS (St) Bp. RM. Oct 24

d. *c*.586. Maglorius, or Maelor, was born in S. Wales and educated under St Illtyd. He was a kinsman of St Samson, with whom he crossed over to Brittany, where they became abbots of two monasteries, St Samson of Dol and St Maglorius of Lammeur. St Samson became moreover bishop of Dol, and on his death he is said to have been succeeded by St Maglorius, who finally retired to the Channel Islands and built an abbey on Sark, where he died.

MAGNERICUS (St) Bp. RM. July 25

d. 596. Of Frankish descent, he was the first of his race to be raised to the see of Trèves (*c*.566). He was an intimate friend of St Gregory of Tours, and one of the most illustrious of the prelates of his time.

MAGNOALDUS (St) Ab. AC. Sept 6

Otherwise Magnus, q.v.

MAGNOBODUS (MAINBOEUF) (St) Bp. AC. Oct 16

d. *c*.670. A Frank of noble birth, appointed at the demand of the people bishop of Angers.

MAGNUS (St) M. RM. Jan 1

A martyr mentioned in the RM., of whom nothing is known.

MAGNUS (MANNUS) (St) M. RM. Feb 4

See Aquilinus, Geminus, etc.

MAGNUS (St) M. RM. Feb 15

See Saturninus, Castulus, etc.

MAGNUS (St) M. AC. Apr 16

d. 1116. A native of the Orkneys, over which he was set as governor by the king of Norway, the then overlord of the islands. When his life was threatened by conspirators, he escaped to the court of Scotland, where he gave himself up to a life of penance. In the end he was murdered by his cousin Hakon for political reasons, but has nevertheless been always venerated as a martyr.

MAGNUS (St) M. RM. Aug 6

See Sixtus II and Comp.

MAGNUS of ANAGNI (St) Bp. M. RM. Aug 19

d. *c*.250. In the RM. he is described as a bishop martyred under Decius. Actually he seems to be a duplicate of St Andrew the Tribune, q.v. (Aug 19), surnamed by the Greeks "the Megalomartyr" and listed in the martyrologies as *Andreas Tribunus Magnus Martyr*. Apparently a scribe put a comma after *Tribunus*, and thus made one martyr into two.

MAGNUS (St) Bp. OSB. AC. Aug 19

d. 660. Born at Avignon, he was appointed governor of the city. After his wife's death he joined the monks of Lérins, whither his son St Agricola had preceded him. In 656 he was raised to the see of Avignon. His existence is doubtful, as he is first mentioned in a document of 1458, and his cult cannot be traced. There was, however, a bishop named Magnus at the Council of Châlons-sur-Saône (630).

MAGNUS, CASTUS and MAXIMUS (SS) MM. RM. Sept 4

? They probably belong to the group of seventeen martyrs (SS Rufinus, Silvanus, etc.) put to death at Ancyra in Galatia. Their names seem to have been separated from the remainder of the group, whose entry occurs on the same day.

MAGNUS (MAGNOALDUS, MAGINOLD, MANG, etc.) (St) Ab. OSB.   AC. Sept 6
d. *c.*666. A fellow-missionary with the Irish saints Columbanus and Gall. He became the abbot-founder of Füssen in Bavaria.

MAGNUS (St) Bp.   RM. Oct 6
d. *c.*660. A Venetian born, who became bishop of Oderzo in the province of Treviso, on the Adriatic. In 638, owing to the incursions of the Lombards, he transferred his see to Citta Nuova, then called Heraclea in honour of the emperor Heraclius.

MAGNUS (St) Bp.   RM. Nov 5
d. 525. Archbishop of Milan from *c.*520 to 525. Little further is known about him.

MAGUIL (St)   AC. May 30
Otherwise Madelgisilus, q.v.

MAHARSAPOR (St) M. AC. Oct 10
d. 421. A Persian who was martyred under Varanes V. After a three years' imprisonment he was thrown into a pit and left to die of starvation.

MAIDOC (MADOC) (St) Bp.
AC. Feb 28
There are several Welsh and Irish saints of this name. Hardy gives the following variants: Aidnus, Aidan, Edan, Aldus, Edus, Eda, Maidoc, Maedoc, Modoc, Modog, Moedoc, Moeg, Mogue, Madog. The best known saints of this name are St Aidan of Ferns (Jan 31) and St Aidan of Lindisfarne (Aug 31). The St Maidoc assigned to Feb 28 may be the 6th century abbot-bishop after whom Llanmadog in Glamorganshire is called.

MAIDOC (MO-MHAEDOG) (St) Ab.   AC. March 23
5th cent. An Irish abbot of Fiddown in Kilkenny.

MAILDULF (St) Ab.   AC. May 17
d. 673. An Irishman by birth who came to England and founded the great abbey of Malmesbury, where he had St Aldhelm among his disciples, and where he ended his days.

MAIMBOD (St) M.   AC. Jan 23
d. *c.*880. An Irish missionary who was put to death by pagans while evangelizing the country people near Kaltenbrunn in Alsace, diocese of Besançon.

MAINARD (Bl) Ab. OSB.
AC. Dec 10
d. 1096. Abbot and founder of the monastery and Congregation of the Holy Cross at Sassovivo in the diocese of Foligno.

MAINE (MEVENUS, MEWAN, MEEN) (St) C.   AC. June 21
d. 617. A Welsh or Cornish disciple of St Samson, whom he accompanied to Brittany. He founded there the monastery since known as Saint-Méon. He died at a great age.

MAJOLUS (French: MAIEUL) (St) Ab. OSB.   RM. May 11
*c.*906–994. Born at Avignon, he studied at Lyons and while still very young he was chosen archdeacon of Mâcon. He was offered the see of Besançon, but he fled instead to Cluny and became a monk there, and shortly after, in 954, was made abbot-coadjutor to St Aymard. In 965 he succeeded as the head of the Cluniac congregation, which under him grew and spread throughout W. Europe. He was the friend of emperors and popes and several times refused the tiara. He died at Souvigny.

MAJORICUS (St) M.   RM. Dec 6
d. *c*.490. According to the RM. he was the son of St Dionysia, who encouraged him to suffer martyrdom and buried him in her own house. For the account given by Victor of Utica see Dionysia, Dativa, etc. The martyrdom took place in Africa under the Arian Hunneric the Vandal.

MALACHY (St) Prophet RM. Jan 14
5th cent. B.C. The last of the twelve Minor Prophets. The tradition is that he was a native of Sapha. The Jews erroneously identify him with Esdras (Ezra).

MALACHY O'MORE (St) Bp.
RM. Nov 3
1095–1148. Maolmhaodhog ua Morgair was born at Armagh and ordained priest by St Celsus. He was successively vicar general to St Celsus, abbot of Bangor, bishop of Connor and archbishop of Armagh (1132). He worked zealously to restore ecclesiastical discipline and succeeded in replacing once and for all the Celtic liturgy by the Roman. In 1138 he resigned the primatial see and made a pilgrimage to Rome, staying for a while at Clairvaux, then at the acme of its fame under St Bernard. He wished to remain a monk there, but this was not allowed by the pope. Instead he left at Clairvaux several young Irishmen who four years later were the pioneer monks of Mellifont abbey in Ireland. He made a second pilgrimage to Rome and on his way back died at Clairvaux in St Bernard's arms. He was formally canonized in 1190. The "prophecies of the popes" attributed to him were first found in Rome in 1590—that is, over four centuries after his death.

MALARD (St) Bp.   AC. Jan 15
d. *p*.650. A bishop of Chartres who took part in the council of Châlon-sur-Saône (650).

MALCHUS (St) M.   RM. March 28
See Priscus, Malchus and Alexander.

MALCHUS (St) Bp. OSB.
AC. Apr 10
d. 12th cent. An Irishman who became a monk of Winchester in England and was consecrated by St Anselm first bishop of Waterford. He was one of the preceptors of St Malachy O'More. His life has been confused with those of several among his contemporaries.

MALCHUS (St) H.   RM. Oct 21
d. *c*.390. A Syrian monk at Chalcis near Antioch. After about twenty years of monastic life he was kidnapped by the Bedouins, who sold him for a slave. He was given an already married woman to wife, but they lived as brother and sister. After some seven years of bondage they succeeded in escaping together and Malchus returned to his monastery. St Jerome knew him there and wrote his life.

MALCOLDIA (Bl) H. OSB.
AC. March 15
d. *c*.1090. Benedictine nun and then a recluse near the abbey church of St Anastasia, at Asti.

MALO (MACHUTIS, MACLOU)
(St) Bp.   RM. Nov 15
d. 621. A Welshman who became a monk at Llancarfan and eventually migrated to Brittany with a band of Welsh missionaries. He settled at a place called Alethnow St Malo—of which he is recognized as the first bishop. For a time he was banished and resided at Saintes.

MALRUBIUS (St) M.   AC. Aug 27
d. *c*.1040. An anchorite in Merns (Kincardineshire) Scotland. He was martyred by Norwegian invaders.

MAMAS (MAMMAS, MAMANS) (St) M.   RM. Aug 17

d. *c.*275. A shepherd of Caesarea in Cappadocia, martyred under Aurelian. He is greatly venerated throughout the East. His *Acta* are not reliable.

MAMELTA (St) M.   RM. Oct 17

d. *c.*344. Said to have been a heathen priestess at Bethfarme in Persia, who, on being converted to Christ, was stoned and finally drowned in a lake.

MAMERTINUS (St) Bp.
AC. March 30

d. *c.*462. A convert of St Germanus, he became a monk, and then abbot, of SS Cosmas and Damian at Auxerre in France.

MAMERTUS (MAMMERTUS) (St) Bp.   RM. May 11

d. 475. Archbishop of Vienne, 461–475. He is best remembered as the originator of the Rogation Days before the Ascension, which he established in his diocese in consequence of the many calamities which afflicted his people.

MAMILIAN (MAXIMILIAN) (St) M.   RM. March 12

? A Roman martyr, of whom nothing definite is known.

MAMILIAN (St) Bp.   AC. Sept 15

d. 460. A bishop of Palermo in Sicily, said to have been exiled to Tuscany by the Arian king Genseric. His relics were eventually taken back to Palermo.

MAMILLUS (St) M.   RM. March 8

See Cyril, Rogatus, etc.

MAMMEA (St) M.   RM. Aug 27

Otherwise Mannea. See Marcellinus, Mannea, etc.

MANAHEN (St) Prophet
RM. May 24

1st cent. Mentioned in the Acts of the Apostles (XIII, 1) as the foster-brother of King Herod Antipas and as a prophet. He is supposed to have died at Antioch in Syria.

MANAKUS (MANACCUS) (St) Ab.
AC. Oct 14

6th cent. A Welshman, abbot of Holyhead, connected with St Cuby. He appears to have died in Cornwall. Manaccan (Minster), near Falmouth, is said to owe its name to him.

MANCIUS (St)   RM. March 15

5th (or 6th?) cent. Of Roman origin, he appears to have been bought as a slave by Jewish traders and taken to Evora in Portugal, where he was martyred by his masters.

MANCIUS ARAKI (Bl) M.
AC. July 8

d. 1626. A Japanese layman, brother of Bl Matthew Araki. For giving shelter to the missionaries he was imprisoned at Omura, where he died of consumption. His body was burnt at Nagasaki (July 12). Beatified in 1867.

MANCIUS of the HOLY CROSS (Bl) M. OP.   AC. July 29

d. 1629. An aged catechist, burnt alive at Omura with Bl Louis Bertrán. Beatified in 1867.

MANCIUS of ST THOMAS (Bl) M. OP.   AC. Sept 12

d. 1622. A Japanese catechist imprisoned and burnt alive with Bl Thomas Zumárraga and companions at Omura. Beatified in 1867.

MANCIUS XIZIZOIEMON (Bl) M.
AC. Sept 25

d. 1630. A native of Japan, and a tertiary of St Augustine, beheaded at Nagasaki. Beatified in 1867.

MANCUS (St)   AC. May 31

See Winnow, Mancus and Myrbad.

MANDAL (St) M.   RM. June 10
See Basilides, Tripos, etc.

MANEHILDIS (MÉNÉHOULD) (St) V.   AC. Oct 14
d. *c.*490. Born at Perthois, she was the youngest of seven sisters, all of whom are honoured as saints in different parts of Champagne. She is the patroness of Sainte-Ménéhould on the R. Aisne.

MANETTUS (MANETIUS, MANETTO) (St) C. OSM.
                     RM. Aug 20 and Feb 12
d. 1268. Benedict dell' Antella was a Florentine merchant who became one of the Seven Founders of the Servite Order, q.v. From provincial of Tuscany he became general of the Order. In 1246 he attended the council of Lyons, and at the request of St Louis introduced the Order into France. He resigned his generalate to St Philip Benizi and retired to Monte Senario, where he died in the following year.

MANEZ (MANNES, MANES) (Bl) C. OP,   AC. July 30
d. 1230. Manez de Guzmán, an elder brother of St Dominic, was born at Calaruega. He joined the original sixteen members of the Order of Preachers in 1216 and later was prior of St James's in Paris, and the founder of a convent for nuns at Madrid. Cult approved in 1834.

MANIRUS (St) Bp.   AC. Dec 19
? One of the apostles of N. Scotland. His work seems chiefly to have been the promoting of good feeling and union among the newly converted Highlanders.

MANNEA (St) M.   RM. Aug 27
See Marcellinus, Mannea, etc.

MANNONIUS (St) M.   RM. Apr 29
See Corfu, Martyrs of.

MANNUS (St) M.   RM. Feb 4
Otherwise Magnus, q.v.

MANSUETUS (St) Bp. RM. Feb 19
d. *c.*690. A Roman by birth, he was appointed to the see of Milan (*c.*672) and ruled it with vigour and wisdom. He wrote a treatise against the Monothelites.

MANSUETUS (MANSUY) (St) Bp.
                     RM. Sept 3
d. *c.*350. Bishop of Toul in France (*c.*338–350). His biography as it has come down to us is full of fictitious matter.

MANSUETUS (St) M.   RM. Sept 6
See Donatian, Praesidius, etc.

MANSUETUS (St) Bp. M.
                     RM. Nov 28
See Papinianus and Mansuetus.

MANSUETUS, SEVERUS, APPIAN, DONATUS, HONORIUS and Comp. (SS) MM.   RM. Dec 30
d. *c.*483. A group of ten martyrs, who suffered at Alexandria in connexion with the troubles raised by the Monophysites.

MANUEL (*several*)
The Spanish, Portuguese and Catalan form of Emmanuel, q.v.

MANUEL, SABEL and ISMAEL (SS) MM.   RM. June 17
d. 362. Persian magnates sent to negotiate for peace with Julian the Apostate at Chalcedon. The tradition is that Julian, finding that they were Christians, had them beheaded. Theodosius the Great dedicated a church in their honour near Byzantium.

MAOLRUAIN (St) Ab.   AC. July 7
d. 792. Abbot-founder of the monastery

461

of Tallaght in Ireland and compiler of the martyrology named after that place.

MAPPALICUS and Comp. (SS) MM.   RM. Apr 17

d. 250. African martyrs who suffered at Carthage under Decius. They are highly praised by St Cyprian.

MAPRILIS (St) M. RM. Aug 22

See Martial, Saturninus, etc.

MARANA and CYRA (SS) MM.
         RM. Aug 3

5th cent. Two maidens who embraced the eremitical life near Beroea in Syria. It is recorded of them that they observed continuous silence throughout the year except on Whit Sunday.

MARCELLA (St) W. RM. Jan 31

d. 410. She belonged to the nobility of Rome, and after the early death of her husband turned her house into a sort of "retreat" for ladies of the aristocracy. St Jerome was her guest for three years and under his direction she devoted herself to the study of the Bible, to prayer and to alms-deeds. When Alaric sacked Rome, Marcella was cruelly scourged for concealing, as the Goths thought, her wealth, which she had already distributed to the poor. She died from the effects of this treatment shortly after.

MARCELLA (St) M. RM. June 28

See Plutarch, Serenus, etc.

MARCELLIAN (St) M. RM. June 18

See Mark and Marcellian.

MARCELLIAN (St) M. RM. Aug 9

See Secundian, Marcellian and Verian.

MARCELLINA (St) V. RM. July 17

d. c.398. Born in Rome, the elder sister of St Ambrose of Milan and of St Satyrus. She received the veil of a consecrated virgin from the hands of Pope Liberius on Christmas Day, 353. She outlived both her brothers. Her remains are enshrined at Milan.

MARCELLINUS (St) M. RM. Jan 2

See Argeus, Narcissus and Marcellinus.

MARCELLINUS of ANCONA (St)
         RM. Jan 9

d. c.566. A native of Ancona, who was promoted to that see c.550. He is mentioned by St Gregory the Great.

MARCELLINUS (St) M. RM. Apr 6

d. 413. Marcellinus was the imperial representative in Africa at the time of the Donatist disturbances. He and his brother the judge Agrarius endeavoured to enforce the decisions of a conference at Carthage against those heretics, but the Donatists resorted to false accusation, and the two brothers were put to death without even the formality of a trial. St Augustine was an intimate friend of Marcellinus, to whom the holy Doctor dedicated his masterpiece "De civitate Dei".

MARCELLINUS, VINCENT and DOMNINUS (SS) RM. Apr 20

d. c.374. African missionaries who crossed over to Gaul and preached in Dauphiné. St Marcellinus was consecrated first bishop of Embrun by St Eusebius of Vercelli. The relics of the three saints are venerated at Digne, in the Alps of Savoy.

MARCELLINUS (St) Pope M.
    RM. Apr 26 (and Oct 25)

d. 304. A native of Rome, he was pope from 296 to his death, during the persecution under Diocletian. It seems to be the fact that Marcellinus was guilty of some personal weakness during the persecution, though the story of his lapse as told in the Roman Breviary up to the year 1883 is now discredited. He certainly died a good death, in all probability as a martyr. St Marcellinus is mentioned a second time in the RM. on Oct 25.

MARCELLINUS and PETER (SS) MM.   RM. June 2

d. 304. Marcellinus was a priest and Peter probably an exorcist, both belonging to the Roman clergy. Although their extant Acts are unreliable, these two martyrs were certainly greatly venerated by the Romans, since their names occur in the canon of the Latin Mass and Constantine built a basilica over their tombs.

MARCELLINUS (St) M. RM. June 5

See Florentius, Julian, etc.

MARCELLINUS (or MARCELLIANUS) (St) M.   RM. June 18

See Mark and Marcellian.

MARCELLINUS (MARCHELM, MARCULF) (St) C.   RM. July 14

d. c.762. An Anglo Saxon who followed St Willibrord to Holland. Together with St Lebuin he preached the gospel to the people of Over-Yssel. In 738 he accompanied St Boniface to Rome. He died at Oldensee (Oldenzeel), but his remains were transferred to Deventer.

MARCELLINUS (or MARCELLUS), MANNEA, JOHN, SERAPION, PETER and Comp. (SS) MM.   RM. Aug 27

d. c.303. According to their authentic *Acta*, Marcellinus, a tribune, with his wife Mannea, his three sons, John, Serapion and Peter, a bishop, three clerics, eight laymen and another woman, that is the entire Christian congregation of a small place, now said to be Oxyrinchus, in Egypt, were taken to Thmuis and beheaded. Marcellinus is often known as Marcellus.

MARCELLINUS of RAVENNA (St) Bp.   RM. Oct 5

3rd cent. The second or third bishop of Ravenna, said to have occupied that see in the second half of the third century.

MARCELLINUS, CLAUDIUS, CYRINUS (QUIRINUS) and ANTONINUS (SS) MM. RM. Oct 25

d. 304. Claudius, Cyrinus and Antoninus are named on this day as having been beheaded together with Pope St Marcellinus. See April 26.

MARCELLUS (St) Pope M.   RM. Jan 16

d. 309. St Marcellus was pope for one year only (308–309). He seems to have been exiled by Maxentius, but not to have died a martyr. The story of his having been forced to work as a slave in the stables seems to be legendary.

MARCELLUS (St) M.   RM. Feb 19

See Publius, Julian, etc.

MARCELLUS (St) Bp.   RM. Apr 9

d. 474. A native of Avignon, he was educated by his own brother St Petronius, bishop of Die (not of Saint-Dié), whom he succeeded in the see, being consecrated by St Mamertus, bishop of Vienne. He suffered much from the Arians, and died after a long episcopate.

MARCELLUS and ANASTASIUS (SS) MM.   RM. June 29

d. 274. Roman missionaries sent into Gaul to preach the gospel. They were put to death in the neighbourhood of Bourges. Marcellus was beheaded and Anastasius scourged to death.

MARCELLUS (St) Bp. M.   RM. Aug 14

d. 389. A native of Cyprus, who from being a conscientious civil magistrate was elected to the see of Apamea in Syria. While supervising the destruction of a pagan shrine, at Aulona, in accordance with the edict of Theodosius the Great, he was attacked and murdered by the mob.

MARCELLUS (St) M.   RM. Aug 27
Otherwise Marcellinus, q.v.

MARCELLUS (St) M.   RM. Sept 4
d. *c*.178. A priest of Lyons who escaped from prison and, being again arrested, was buried up to the waist on the banks of the Saône and left to die. It is said that he survived three days.

MARCELLUS (St) Bp. M.
RM. Sept 4
? A bishop of Trèves (or of Tongres) listed in the RM. His name seems to have been invented in the 10th century.

MARCELLUS (St) Mk. OSB.
PC. Sept 27
d. *c*.869 (?). An Irishman (or Scot) by birth, he became a monk at St Gall in Switzerland and is best known as the tutor of Bl Notker Balbulus.

MARCELLUS, CASTUS, EMILIUS and SATURNINUS (SS) MM.
RM. Oct 6
? Martyrs of Capua, of whom no particulars are extant.

MARCELLUS and APULEIUS (SS) MM.   RM. Oct 7
? Apocryphal saints perhaps to be identified with Niceta and Aquilina, q.v.

MARCELLUS (St) M.   RM. Oct 30
d. 298. A centurion of the Roman army stationed at Tangier. During a festival in honour of the birthday of the emperor he refused to join in the celebrations, threw away his arms and insignia and declared himself a Christian. The

notary, who refused to write the official report of the case and who was in consequence martyred, was St Cassian (v. Dec 3). The *Acta* of St Marcellus are quite reliable.

MARCELLUS (St) Bp.   RM. Nov 1
d. *c*.430. A bishop of Paris, who was buried in the old Christian cemetery outside the walls of the city, where now is the suburb of Saint-Marceau.

MARCELLUS (St) M.   RM. Nov 16
See Elpidius, Marcellus, etc.

MARCELLUS (St) M.   RM. Nov 26
d. 349. A priest of Nicomedia, in Asia Minor, who during the reign of the emperor Constantius was seized by the Arians and killed by being hurled from a high rock.

MARCELLUS (St) M.   RM. Dec 2
See Eusebius, Marcellus, etc.

MARCELLUS (St) Ab. RM. Dec 29
d. *c*.485. Surnamed "Akimetes" the "non-rester". A native of Apamea in Syria, who joined the monks called *Akimetes*, because they recited the divine office in relays throughout the day and night. He became the third abbot of their chief abbey at Constantinople, and under his rule the *Akimetes* grew in number and influence. He was present at the council of Chalcedon.

MARCELLUS (St) M.   RM. Dec 30
See Sabinus, Exuperantius, etc.

MARCHELM (St)   RM. July 14
Otherwise Marcellinus, q.v.

MARCIA (St) M.   RM. March 3
See Felix, Luciolus, etc.

MARCIA (St) M.   RM. June 5
See Zenais, Cyria, etc.

MARCIA (St) M.   RM. July 2
See Ariston, Crescentian, etc.

MARCIAN (St) M.   RM. Jan 4
See Aquilinus, Geminus, etc.

MARCIAN (St) C.   RM. Jan 10
d. c.471. A native of Constantinople, though connected with a Roman family. He was ordained priest and appointed treasurer of the church of St Sophia. In this capacity he superintended the building of several churches, notably of that of the Anastasis. He was wrongly suspected of Novatianism and had to suffer much on this account.

MARCIAN (St) Bp.   RM. March 6
d. 120. Said to have been a disciple of St Barnabas and first bishop of Tortona in Piedmont, where he is alleged to have been martyred under Hadrian, after an episcopate of forty-five years. The theory has been advanced that St Marcian of Tortosa is to be identified with St Marcian of Ravenna.

MARCIAN (St) M.   RM. March 26
See Peter, Marcian, etc.

MARCIAN (St) M.   RM. Apr 17
See Fortunatus and Marcian.

MARCIAN of AUXERRE (St) Mk.
RM. Apr 20
d. c.470. A native of Bourges, of humble birth, who was admitted as a lay-brother into the abbey of SS Cosmas and Damian at Auxerre. There he discharged menial duties and had charge of the cattle of the abbey.

MARCIAN of RAVENNA (St) Bp.
RM. May 22
d. c.127. The fourth bishop of Ravenna, where he is known as San Mariano. He ruled the diocese from c.112 to c.127.

MARCIAN, NICANOR, APOLLO-NIUS and Comp. (SS) MM.
RM. June 5
d. c.304. According to the RM. they were a group of Egyptian martyrs who suffered under Diocletian. Their Acts are, however, quite unreliable. It is more probable that Marcian and Nicander (not Nicanor) were soldiers in the Roman army, who suffered either in Bulgaria or Rumania.

MARCIAN of SYRACUSE (St) Bp. M.   RM. June 14
d. c.255. Said to have been "the first bishop of the West", having been, according to the Sicilian legend, sent to Syracuse by St Peter himself. It is more likely that Marcian was sent to Sicily by a pope of the 3rd century. He is said to have been thrown from a tower by the Jews.

MARCIAN (St) M.   RM. June 17
See Nicander and Marcian.

MARCIAN (St) Bp.   AC. June 30
d. c.757. Bishop of Pampeluna, in Spanish Navarre. He signed the decrees of the sixth council of Toledo in 737.

MARCIAN (St) M.   RM. July 11
d. 243. A youth martyred at Iconium in Lycaonia. He is specially notable for his courage in confessing Christ.

MARCIAN (St) M.   RM. Aug 9
See Julian, Marcian, and Comp.

MARCIAN of SAIGNON (St) Ab.
AC. Aug 25
d. 485. Born at Saignon (Vaucluse) he became the abbot-founder of St Eusebius at Apt, diocese of Avignon.

MARCIAN (St) M.   RM. Sept 16
See Abundius, Abundantius, etc.

MARCIAN (St) M.   RM. Oct 4
See Mark, Marcian, and Comp.

MARCIAN (St) M.   RM. Oct 25
See Martyrius and Marcian.

MARCIAN (St) H.   RM. Nov 2
d. 387. He left the emperor's court and
gave up a brilliant military career in
order to lead the solitary life in the
desert of Chalcis. He had several illustrious disciples.

MARCIANA (St) VM.   RM. Jan 9
d. *c*.303. A maiden of Mauritania,
accused of having shattered a statue of
the goddess Diana and thrown to the
wild beasts in the amphitheatre, where
she was gored to death by a bull. The
Mozarabic office has a special hymn in
her honour.

MARCIANA (St) M.   RM. May 24
See Susanna, Marciana, etc.

MARCIANA (St) VM.   RM. July 12
d. *c*.303. The RM. assigns this virgin-
martyr to Toledo in Spain, but she is
almost certainly identical with St
Marciana of Mauretania (v. Jan 9).

MARCIONILLA (St) M. RM. Jan 9
See Julian, Basilissa, etc.

**MARCIUS (MARK, MARTIN) H.
OSB.   RM. Oct 24**
d. *c*.679. An Italian hermit at Montecassino, mentioned by St Gregory the
Great in the life of St Benedict. The
Cassinese tradition adds that Marcius
(or Martin) became a monk at the abbey
and then retired into a cave on Mount
Massicus (Mondragone) where he died.

**MARCOLINO of FORLÌ (Bl) C.
OP.   AC. Jan 24**
1317–1397 (Jan 2). Marcolino Amanni
was born at Forlì and became a Domini-

can in his early years. He was a model
religious, but it was only after his death
that his brethren realized his heroic
sanctity. Cult confirmed in 1750.

MARCULFUS (St) Ab.   AC. May 1
d. 558. The abbot-founder of a monastery of hermit-monks, on the Egyptian
model, at Nanteuil. His relics were in
898 enshrined at Corbigny, diocese of
Laon, and thither the kings of France
resorted after their coronation. After
touching the relics of the saint they
healed those afflicted with "the king's
evil" (scrofula).

MARD (St) Bp.   RM. June 8
Otherwise Medard, q.v.

MARDARIUS (St) M.   RM. Dec 13
See Eustratius, Auxentius, etc.

**MARDONIUS, MUSONIUS,
EUGENE and METELLUS (SS)
MM.   RM. Jan 24**
d. ?. Four martyrs burnt at the stake
somewhere in Asia Minor.

MARDONIUS (St) M.   RM. Dec 23
See Migdonius and Mardonius.

MAREAS (St) Bp. M.   RM. Apr 22
d. 342. A Persian bishop martyred under King Shapur II. Together with him
there suffered twenty-one other bishops,
nearly two hundred and fifty clerics,
many monks and nuns, and a great
number of lay people. The church of
Persia was brought to the verge of
extinction.

MARGARET (*several*)
Note. The Latin, Spanish, Portuguese
and Catalan form of this name is Margarita; the Italian Margherita and the
French Marguerite. There are numerous diminutives of the same name in all
languages.

MARGARET of RAVENNA (Bl) V.
PC. Jan 23
d. 1505. Born at Russi, near Ravenna, Margaret was from her youth almost blind and suffered much from want of sympathy on the part of those around her; nevertheless in course of time she gained many friends by her patience and humility. With the help of a priest she formed a religious association of persons living in the world, but this did not survive her. Her cult has never been officially confirmed.

MARGARET of HUNGARY (St) V.
OP.   RM. Jan 18
1252–1270. Daughter of Bela IV, king of Hungary. She founded a convent for Dominican nuns on an island in the Danube near Budapest and herself joined the community. Her life was most penitential. Canonized in 1943.

MARGARET of ENGLAND (St) M.
OSB. Cist.   AC. Feb 3
d. 1192. Born in Hungary, probably of an English mother and related to St Thomas of Canterbury. She lost her mother in the Holy Land, made a pilgrimage to our Lady of Montserrat in Spanish Catalonia and joined the Cistercian nuns at Sauve-Benite, in the diocese of Puy-en-Velay. She was greatly venerated in that district.

MARGARET of CORTONA (St)
Tert. OFM.   RM. Feb 22
1247–1297. Born at Laviano in Tuscany, a farmer's daughter, she was the mistress of a young nobleman for nine years. In his sudden death she saw a judgment from heaven, and publicly confessing her sins in the church of Cortona, she placed herself under the direction of the Franciscan friars. She became a tertiary herself and the foundress of a convent and a hospital where she and her nuns tended the sick. She

suffered from calumny and obloquy, but God favoured her with supernatural charismata. Canonized in 1728.

MARGARET CLITHEROW (Bl) M.
AC. March 25
1556–1586. Margaret Middleton was born at York, married John Clitherow and shortly after became a Catholic. For this she was imprisoned for two years, and on her release she began to shelter priests in her house. She was again arrested, and, refusing to plead, was condemned to the horrible penalty of being pressed to death. The sentence was carried out at York. Beatified in 1929.

MARGARET of CITTÀ-DI-CAS-
TELLO (Bl) V. Tert. OP. AC. Apr 13
d. 1320. Born at Meldola, in the diocese of S. Angelo in Vado, Italy, she was left a foundling at Città-di-Castello and was brought up by several families in the city, being usually occupied in looking after children. She died at the age of thirty-three, after passing her life in poverty, in blindness and in complete innocence of soul. Cult approved in 1609.

MARGARET of AMELIA (Bl) V.
OSB.   PC. Apr 20
d. 1666. A Benedictine abbess of the nunnery of St Catherine at Amelia, possessed of mystical gifts.

MARGARET POLE (Bl) M.
AC. May 28
d. 1541. Margaret Plantagenet was a niece of Edward IV and Richard III. She married Sir Reginald Pole, to whom she bore five children. Left a widow she was created countess of Salisbury in her own right and appointed governess to Princess Mary, daughter of Henry VIII. When her son Cardinal Pole opposed the royal supremacy and refused to return to England, Henry revenged

himself on the cardinal's mother, and lodged her in the Tower of London for two years. Finally she was condemned for high treason by Bill of Attainder and beheaded on Tower Hill at the age of seventy. Beatified in 1886.

MARGARET of VAU-LE-DUC (Bl)
V. OSB. Cist.   **PC. June 4**
d. 1277. Daughter of Duke Henry II of Brabant, she became a Cistercian nun, and second abbess, of the convent of Vau-le-Duc in Brabant, which had been founded by her father. She has always been venerated as a *beata* by the Cistercians.

MARGARET of SCOTLAND (St)
W.   **RM. June 10 and Nov 16**
c.1050–1093 (Nov 16). Granddaughter of King Edmund Ironside of England and granddaughter of St Stephen of Hungary. In 1070 she married King Malcolm III Canmore of Scotland. She used her influence as queen for the good of religion and for the promotion of justice, ever having a special thought for the poor. She had six sons and two daughters, one of whom was "Good Queen Maud", wife of Henry I. Among the foundations she made was the Benedictine abbey of Dunfermline, where she was buried. Canonized in 1251.

MARGARET or MARINA (St) VM.
    RM. July 20
d. c.304. Said to have been a maiden of Antioch in Pisidia martyred under Diocletian. This much is probably true; everything else related in her *Acta* is pure legend, including, of course, the story of the fierce dragon which swallowed her before she was beheaded. Nevertheless, she is one of the most popular of maiden-martyr saints and her cult is very ancient. In the East she is known as Marina.

MARGARET of FAENZA (Bl or St)
Abs. OSB. Vall.   **AC. Aug 26**
d. 1330. A native of Faenza, she became a Vallombrosan nun under St Humilitas at the convent of St John the Evangelist, near Florence, and eventually its second abbess.

MARGARET the BAREFOOTED
(St) W.   **RM. Aug 27**
d. 1395. A poor girl of Sanseverino, near Ancona, in Italy, who in her fifteenth year was married to a man who ill-treated her. She bore it all with patience for many years.

MARGARET WARD (Bl) M.
    AC. Aug 30
d. 1588. A gentlewoman of Congleton, Cheshire, hanged at Tyburn for rescuing a priest. Beatified in 1929.

MARGARET of LOUVAIN (Bl) V.
    AC. Sept 2
1207–1225. Surnamed in Belgium "Marguerite la Fière". Born at Louvain, she worked as a maid-servant at an inn in the same city. She was murdered by robbers whom she had seen kill and rob her employers. The Cistercian Caesarius of Heisterbach states that she was about to become a Cistercian nun. Cult approved in 1905.

MARGARET MARY ALACOQUE
(St) V.   **RM. Oct 17**
1647–1690. Born at L'Hautecourt in Burgundy. In 1671 she joined the Order of the Visitation at Paray-le-Monial. From a revelation made to her by our Lord in 1675 she was led to enter upon her great work, the spreading of public and liturgical devotion to the Sacred Heart. After violent opposition, met with chiefly in Jansenistic milieus, the devotion triumphed and became extremely popular in the Church. St Margaret was canonized in 1920.

MARGARET LEROUX (Bl) V.
AC. Oct 23

d. 1794. An Ursuline nun of Valenciennes, who formed part of the group of martyrs guillotined on Oct 23. She was born at Cambrai in 1747 and was professed in 1769. Her name in religion was Ann-Joseph, or Mother Josephine. See Ursuline Nuns.

MARGARET of LORRAINE (Bl) W.
Poor Clare   AC. Nov 6

1463-1521. A daughter of Duke Frederick of Lorraine, she married in 1488 René, duke of Alençon, who died in 1492 leaving her a widow with three children. She devoted herself exclusively to their upbringing and to works of charity. When they were of age, she founded a convent of Poor Clares at Argentan, and entered there in 1519. Cult confirmed in 1921.

MARGARET of SAVOY (Bl) W.
Tert. OP.   AC. Nov 23

d. 1464. Born at Pinerolo, daughter of Duke Amadeo II of Savoy. In 1403 she married Theodore Paleologus, marquis of Montferrat, after whose death (1418), influenced by St Vincent Ferrer, she joined the Dominican tertiaries. In 1426 she founded a house at Alba in Liguria, of which she became the first Dominican prioress. Cult confirmed in 1669.

MARGARET of HOHENFELS (Bl)
V. OSB.   AC. Dec 26

d. p.1150. She belonged to the family of the Hohenfels and became a Benedictine nun at Bingen under St Hildegard, by whom she was appointed prioress.

MARGARET COLONNA (Bl) V.
Poor Clare   AC. Dec 30

d. 1284. Daughter of Prince Odo Colonna of Palestrina. She turned her family castle on the mountain side above Palestrina into a convent of Poor Clares, for whom her brother, Cardinal James Colonna, adapted a mitigated version of the Franciscan Rule. Cult confirmed in 1847.

MARGUERITE BOURJEOYS (Bl)
V. Foundress   AC. Jan 19

1620-1700. Born at Troyes, she went to Canada as tutor to the children of the French garrison of Montreal. In 1688 she founded the Congregation of the Sisters of Notre Dame de Montreal, dedicated to the apostolate of Canada. She obtained from Louis XIV the royal patent to teach throughout Canada. Her Congregation subsequently spread to the United States, receiving Papal approval in 1889. Beatified in 1950.

MARI (St) Bp.
AC. Aug 5

See Addai and Mari.

MARIANA of JESUS (Bl) V. O.
Merc.   AC. Apr 27

1565-1624. Surnamed "the Lily of Madrid". Mariana Navarra de Guevara was born in Madrid and joined the community of Discalced Mercedarians in the same city, where she distinguished herself by her life of penance. Beatified by Pius VI.

MARIANA de PAREDES (St) V.
AC. May 26

1618-1645. Known as the "Lily of Quito". Her family name was Mariana de Paredes y Flores, but she chose to call herself Mariana of Jesus. She was born at Quito, in Ecuador, and was of Spanish descent. She tried her vocation as a religious, but failed. After this, she lived as a solitary in the house of her brother-in-law. During the earthquakes at Quito in 1645 she offered herself as a victim for the city and died shortly after. Canonized in 1950.

MARIANUS SCOTUS (Bl) Ab. OSB.   AC. Feb 9

d. 1088. His Irish name Muirdach Mac-Robartaigh was latinized as Marianus. He was born in Donegal. In 1067, setting out with some companions on a pilgrimage to Rome, he was, while on his way thither, induced to become a Benedictine at Michelsberg, near Bamberg, whence he migrated to Upper Minster at Ratisbon. In 1078 he founded and became the abbot of the abbey of St Peter, also at Ratisbon, thus originating the congregation of Scottish monasteries in S. Germany. Throughout his life Bl Marianus occupied his free time in copying manuscripts.

MARIANUS (St) Mk.   RM. Apr 20

Otherwise Marcian of Auxerre, q.v.

MARIANUS, JAMES and Comp. (SS) MM.   RM. Apr 30

d. 259. Martyrs of Lambesa, an ancient town in Numidia (Algeria). Marianus was a reader and James a deacon. Their *Acta* are touching and authentic. The true day of their martyrdom was May 6.

MARIANUS (St) H.   RM. Aug 19

d. c.515. A solitary in the forest of Entreaigues, near Evaux, in Berry, France. His life was written by St Gregory of Tours.

MARIANUS (St) M.   RM. Oct 17

See Victor, Alexander and Marianus.

MARIANUS (St) M.   RM. Dec 1

See Diodorus, Marianus, and Comp.

MARIANUS SCOTUS (Bl) H. OSB.   AC. Dec 22

d. 1086. Born in Ireland, his real name was Moelbrigte, i.e., servant of Brigid.

After becoming a monk, he migrated to Cologne (1056), then to Fulda, where for a time he lived as a recluse, and finally (1069) to Mainz. He wrote a "Chronicle of the World".

MARINA (*several*)

Note. Marina is the Latin form of the Greek name Pelagia, a fact which has caused a few duplicates in our martyrologies.

MARINA (St) VM.

RM. June 18 (and July 17)
? In the ancient martyrologies this saint is variously named Maria, Marina, or even Marinus. Moreover, she is simply called *virgin*, not martyr. Some identify her with St Margaret (July 20); others with the Marina who lived in a monastery of men dressed as a boy, i.e., a duplicate of the Greek St Pelagia (Oct 8). Her life served as a model for the legends of SS Euphrosyne, Maria, Theodora, etc. The RM. makes her a martyr at Alexandria.

MARINA of SPOLETO (Bl) V. OSA.   AC. June 18

d. c.1300. Marina Vallarina was an Augustinian nun of Spoleto in Umbria. Her cult at Spoleto seems to have died out.

MARINA (St) VM.   RM. July 18

? The RM. states that she was a martyr of Orense in Spanish Galicia. All records concerning her are lost. The name was introduced into the Roman Martyrology by Baronius (second revision).

MARINUS (AMARINUS) (St) M. OSB.   RM. Jan 25

See Amarinus.

MARINUS (St) M.   RM. Jan 29

Otherwise Maurus. See Papias and Maurus.

MARINUS and ASTERIUS (SS) MM. RM. March 3
d. 262. Marinus was a Roman soldier stationed at Caesarea in Palestine, who, when on the point of being promoted to the rank of centurion, was denounced as a Christian by a jealous rival and forthwith martyred. Asterius, or Astyrius, a senator, buried the body, and it seems, although it is not certain, that he too died a martyr.

MARINUS, VIMIUS and ZIMIUS (SS) CC. OSB. AC. June 12
d. *p.*1100. Surnamed the "*Tres Sancti Exules*", the "Three Holy Exiles". They were Benedictine monks of the Scots abbey of St James at Ratisbon, who, *c.*1100, became hermits at Griesstetten.

MARINUS, THEODOTUS and SEDOPHA (SS) MM. RM. July 5
? Martyrs who suffered at Tomi on the Black Sea.

MARINUS (St) M. RM. July 10
See Januarius, Marinus, etc.

MARINUS (St) M. RM. Aug 8
d. *c.*305. An aged man, martyred at Anazarbus in Cilicia under Diocletian.

MARINUS (St) Ab.-Bp. OSB. AC. Aug 19
*c.*800. A Benedictine abbot-bishop of the monastery of St Peter at Besalú in Spanish Catalonia.

MARINUS (St) H. RM. Sept 4
4th cent. He is said to have been born on an island off the coast of Dalmatia, and to have been by profession a stonemason, to have been ordained a deacon by Gaudentius, bishop of Rimini, and finally to have died a hermit where now stands the tiny Republic of San Marino, which is called after him.

MARINUS (St) M. OSB. AC. Nov 24
d. 731. Born in Italy, he became a Benedictine at Maurienne in Savoy, and afterwards a hermit near the monastery of Chandor, where he was put to death by the Saracens.

MARINUS (Bl) Ab. OSB. AC. Dec 15
d. 1170. A Benedictine monk of La Cava in S. Italy, where he held the office of treasurer before he was elected abbot in 1146. He received the abbatial blessing at Rome from Pope Eugene III. He was a close friend both of the supreme pontiffs and of the kings of Sicily, and he acted as mediator between the two powers in 1156. Cult confirmed in 1928.

MARINUS (St) M. RM. Dec 26
d. 283. He is described as a Roman, the son of a senator, who was beheaded under Numerian, after having been miraculously delivered from torture chambers, wild beasts, fire, water, etc. His *Acta* are probably a pious romance.

MARIUS (MARIS), MARTHA, AUDIFAX and ABACHUM (SS) MM. RM. Jan 19
d. *c.*270. A Persian nobleman, who with his wife Martha and their two sons Audifax and Abachum journeyed to Rome to venerate the tombs of the Apostles. While in the holy city they busied themselves in burying the bodies of those who were then being martyred in the persecution of Claudius II. They too were arrested, the three men beheaded and St Martha drowned.

MARIUS (St) RM. Jan 27
Otherwise Maurus, q.v.

MARK dei MARCONI (Bl) C. AC. Feb 24
1480–1510. Born of a poor family at Milliarino, near Mantua, he joined the

Hieronymites of Bl Peter of Pisa in the monastery of St Matthew of Mantua, where he spent his life. Cult approved in 1906.

MARK BARKWORTH (Bl) M. OSB.
AC. Feb 27
d. 1601. Bl Mark Barkworth (*alias* Lambert) was born in Lincolnshire and educated at Oxford. After his conversion he studied for the priesthood at Rome and Valladolid and was received into the Benedictine Order at the abbey of our Lady of Hirache, near Estella, in Spanish Navarre. He was the first to die at Tyburn in the Benedictine habit after the suppression of the monasteries.

MARK (St) M.   RM. March 13
See Horres, etc.

MARK (St) M.   RM. March 19
See Quintus, Quintilla, etc.

MARK of MONTEGALLO (Bl) C. OFM.   AC. March 20
1426–1497. Born at Montegallo, diocese of Ascoli Piceno, he became a physician and married. Later, by mutual consent, both he and his wife joined the Franciscans. Bl Mark was ordained priest and travelled the length and breadth of Italy preaching and establishing charitable pawnshops for the poor, known in Italy as *Monti di Pietà*.

MARK and TIMOTHY (SS) MM.
RM. March 24
d. c.150. Two Roman martyrs of post-apostolic times, mentioned by Pope St Pius I in a letter to the bishop of Vienne in Gaul.

MARK of ARETHUSA (St) M. Bp.
AC. March 29
d. c.362. Bishop of Arethusa on Mt Lebanon. In 351 he was present at the synod of Sirmium where he produced a creed for which he was unjustly accused

of Arianism by Baronius, who excluded his name from the RM. He has since been vindicated by the Bollandists. St Mark died a martyr under Julian the Apostate.

MARK FANTUCCI (Bl) C. OFM.
AC. Apr 10
1405–1479. Born at Bologna, he first studied law and in 1430 became a Friar Minor. He held several offices in the order and preached throughout Italy, Istria and Dalmatia, visiting also the friars in Austria, Poland, Russia and the Levant. He died at Piacenza. Cult approved in 1868.

MARK (St) Evangelist   RM. Apr 25
d. 75. He is generally thought to have been the young man who ran away when our Lord was arrested (Mark XIV, 51–52) and the "John who is surnamed Mark" of Acts XII, 25. He accompanied SS Paul and Barnabas on their first missionary journey. Afterwards he followed St Peter to Rome, where, in the words of the RM., he was "the disciple and interpreter of St Peter", whose preaching he set down in writing in the gospel which bears his name. St Peter calls him "my son Mark" (1 Pet V, 13). According to tradition he afterwards went to Alexandria where he established the church and died a martyr. His body was in the 9th century translated to Venice.

MARK of GALILEE (St) Bp. M.
RM. Apr 28
d. 92. Said to have been a Galilean by descent and the first missionary bishop and martyr in the province of the Marsi (Abruzzi) in Italy.

MARK of LUCERA (St) Bp.
AC. June 14
d. c.328. A bishop in local veneration in S. Italy.

MARK and MARCELLIAN (SS) MM. RM. June 18 (and July 29) d. *c*.287. Roman martyrs, twin brothers and deacons, who suffered at Rome under Maximian Herculeus. Their basilica in the catacombs of St Balbina was rediscovered in 1902.

MARK, MUCIAN, an unnamed boy, and PAUL (SS) MM. RM. July 3 ? The entry in the RM. reads as follows: "The holy martyrs Mark and Mucian who were slain with the sword for Christ's sake. When a little boy called upon them with a loud voice that they should not sacrifice to idols, he was ordered to be whipped, and as he then confessed Christ more loudly, he was slain too, together with one Paul who was exhorting the martyrs."

MARK CALDEIRA (Bl) M. SJ. AC. July 15 d. 1570. A native of Feira, diocese of Oporto, Portugal, and a Jesuit novice. He was martyred with Bl Ignatius de Azevedo, q.v.

MARK XINEIEMON (Bl) M. AC. Aug 19 d. 1622. A Japanese merchant on the ship of Bl Joachim Firaima (q.v.). He was beheaded at Nagasaki. Beatified in 1867.

MARK (St) M. RM. Aug 31 See Robustian and Mark.

MARK (St) M. RM. Sept 1 See Priscus, Castrensis, etc.

MARK, STEPHEN, SJ. and MELCHIOR, SJ. (BB) MM. AC. Sept 7 d. 1619. Bl Mark Crisin (Körösy) was a Croat and a canon, Bl Stephen Pongracz a Hungarian Jesuit and Bl Melchior Grondech a Czech Jesuit. The three were most brutally massacred by the Calvinist soldiers at Körösi in Hungary. Beatified in 1905.

MARK of MODENA (Bl) C. OP. AC. Sept 23 d. 1498. Born at Modena he joined the Friars Preachers and was a very successful preacher in N. and Central Italy. Cult approved in 1857.

MARK CRIADO (Bl) M. OS. Trin. AC. Sept 25 1522–1569. Born at Andujar, in Andalusia, in 1536 he joined the Trinitarians. He was tortured and slain at Almeria by the Moors. Cult approved by Leo XIII.

MARK (St) Bp. RM. Sept 27 Otherwise John Mark, q.v.

MARK, ALPHIUS, ALEXANDER and Comp. (SS) MM. RM. Sept 28 d. *c*.303. The RM. says: "At Antioch in Pisidia, the martyrs Mark, a shepherd, Alphius, Alexander and Zosimus, his brothers, Nicon, Neon, Heliodorus, and thirty soldiers, who through the miracles of blessed Mark believed in Christ, and were crowned with martyrdom in divers manners and places."

MARK, MARCIAN and Comp. MM. RM. Oct 4 d. 304. Egyptian martyrs under Diocletian. Mark and Marcian were brothers. The rest are described as "victims of all ages and both sexes" and their number as "innumerable". They seem, however, to be duplicates of other groups.

MARK (St) Pope RM. Oct 7 d. 336. A Roman by birth, who was chosen pope in 336 and died within the year.

MARK (St) Bp. M. RM. Oct 22 d. *c*.156. The first bishop of Jerusalem not of Jewish extraction. He is said to have ruled that see for twenty years and to have died a martyr: both statements are mere conjectures.

MARK (St)   RM. Oct 24
Otherwise Marcius, q.v.

MARK (St) M.   RM. Oct 25
See Theodosius, Lucius, etc.

MARK (Bl) Ab. OSB.   AC. Nov 13
d. c.1280. A Benedictine abbot of Sant' Angelo di Scala, of the Congregation of Montevergine.

MARK (St) M.   RM. Nov 16
See Rufinus, Mark, etc.

MARK and STEPHEN (SS) MM.
                            RM. Nov 22
d. c.305. Mark, with another martyr by name Stephen, suffered at Antioch in Pisidia under Galerius.

MARK (St) M.   RM. Dec 15
See Faustinus, Lucius, etc.

MARNOCK (MARNANUS, MAR-NAN, MARNOC) (St) Bp.
                            AC. March 1
d. c.625. An Irish monk under St Columba at Iona, and afterwards a missionary bishop, who died at Annandale, and was much venerated in the neighbourhood of the Scottish border. He has given his name to Kilmarnock in Scotland. His feast is celebrated again on Oct 25.

MARO (St) Ab.   AC. Feb 14
d. c.435. A Syrian hermit, who lived on the bank of the R. Orontes between Homs and Apamea. He was greatly revered by St John Chrysostom and by Theodoret. The monastery of Beit-Marun, built around his shrine, gave its name to the body of Syrian Catholics called Maronites.

MARO, EUTYCHES and VIC-TORINUS (SS) MM.   RM. Apr 15
d. c.99. According to the *Gesta Nerei et Achillei* they belonged to the entourage of St Flavia Domitilla, whom they accompanied in her exile to the island of Ponza. Eventually they returned to Rome and suffered martyrdom under Trajan. The RM. mentions Victorinus again on Sept 5 as a bishop, but little credence can be given to the legend of these martyrs.

MAROLUS (St) Bp.   RM. Apr 23
d. 423. A Syrian by origin, he was raised to the see of Milan in 408. The Christian poet Ennodius wrote a poem in his honour.

MAROTAS (St) M.   RM. March 27
See Zanitas, Lazarus, etc.

MAROVEUS (St) Ab. OSB.
                            AC. Oct 22
d. c.650. Monk of Bobbio. Abbot-founder of the monastery of Precipiano, near Tortona.

MARQUARD (St) Bp. M. OSB.
                            AC. Feb 2
d. 880. A monk at New-Corbey in Saxony, he ruled the see of Hildesheim from 874 to 880 and fell in battle against the Norsemen at Ebsdorf. (See Bruno and Comp. MM. Feb 2.)

MARTANA (St) M.   RM. Dec 2
See Eusebius, Marcellus, etc.

MARTHA (St) M.   RM. Jan 19
See Marius, Martha, etc.

MARTHA (St) VM.   RM. Feb 23
d. 251. A Spanish maiden, beheaded at Astorga under Decius. Her relics are enshrined in the old Benedictine abbey of Ribas de Sil and at Ters, diocese of Astorga.

MARTHA (St) V.   RM. July 29

d. *c*.80. Sister of St Lazarus and of St Mary of Bethany (identified in the West with St Mary Magdalen). She was the hostess of our Lord in their house at Bethany (Luke X, 38, John XI, 2) who was "careful and troubled about many things". For this reason she has become the type of the active life. The story of her subsequent journey to S. Gaul merits no credence.

MARTHA WANG (Bl) M.
AC. July 29

d. 1861. A native woman of Tonkin who carried letters from the imprisoned seminarians BB Joseph Tshang and Paul Tcheng to their bishop. She was arrested and beheaded with them at Tsingai. Beatified in 1909.

MARTHA, SAULA and Comp. (SS) VV. MM.   RM. Oct 20

? The entry in the RM. reads: "At Cologne the passion of the holy virgins Martha and Saula with many others." They are now usually assigned to the mythical cycle of St Ursula and her 11,000 virgins (Oct 21), and it is thought that these martyrs of Oct 20 formed the first nucleus of the Ursuline legend. Indeed, it seems that the name Ursula derives from Sa-ula.

MARTIA (St) M.   RM. June 21

See Rufinus and Martia.

MARTIAL (St) M.   RM. Apr 16

See Saragossa, Martyrs of.

MARTIAL of LIMOGES, Bp. ALPINIAN and AUSTRICLINIAN (SS)   RM. June 30

d. *c*.250. First bishop of Limoges, the reputed apostle of the Limousin, and, according to St Gregory of Tours, one of the seven missionary bishops sent from Rome to preach the gospel in Gaul.

His memory is still held in great veneration in the Limousin. Other legends connected with the saint are medieval forgeries. Alpinian and Austriclinian were priests who collaborated with him.

MARTIAL (St) M.   RM. July 10

See Seven Brothers.

MARTIAL, SATURNINUS, EPICTETUS, MAPRILIS, FELIX and Comp. (SS) MM.   RM. Aug 22

d. *c*.300. ? The names occur in the *Passio of St Aurea* (q.v.); otherwise unidentifiable.

MARTIAL, LAURENCE and Comp. (SS) MM.   RM. Sept 28

? A group of twenty-two African martyrs, who suffered in the province now called Algeria.

MARTIAL (St) M.   RM. Oct 13

See Faustus, Januarius and Martial.

MARTIN of LEÓN (St) C. OSA.
AC. Jan 12

d. 1203. Born at León, in Old Castile, he joined the Augustinian canons regular, first at San Marcelo and then at St Isidore in his native city. He was a prolific ascetical writer.

MARTIN MANUEL (St) M.
AC. Jan 31

d. 1156. Born at Auranca, near Coimbra, in Portugal. As archpriest of Soure he was captured by the Saracens and died in prison at Cordova of ill-treatment at their hands.

MARTIN LOYNAZ of the ASCENSION (St) M. OFM.   RM. Feb 5

d. 1597. Born at Vergara, near Pampeluna, in Spanish Navarre, he studied at Alcalá, and became a Franciscan in 1586. He did missionary work in Mexico, Manila, and finally Japan. He was crucified at Nagasaki. Canonized in 1862.

MARTIN (Bl) M.   **AC. Feb 18**
1815–1862. A native Chinese catechist and host of Bl John Peter Néel. He was beheaded at Kuy-tsheu. Beatified in 1909.

MARTIN of BRAGA (St) Bp.
     AC. March 20
d. 580. Born in Pannonia, he became a monk in Palestine, and later travelled in Spanish Galicia where he preached to the pagan Suevi. He was bishop first of Mondoñedo (*Dumium*) and then of Braga, and introduced monasticism throughout N.W. Spain. Several of his highly interesting writings are still extant.

MARTIN of TONGRES (St) Bp.
     RM. June 21
d. *c*.350. He is said to have been the seventh bishop of Tongres and is venerated as the apostle of the Hesbaye district in Brabant.

MARTIN of VIENNE (St) Bp.
     RM. July 1
d. *p*.132. Alleged third bishop of Vienne, sent thither by Pope St Alexander.

MARTIN of TRÈVES (St) Bp. M.
     RM. July 19
d. *c*.210. Listed in the episcopal records of Trèves as the tenth bishop of that see. There is no conclusive evidence for his martyrdom.

MARTIN GÓMEZ (Bl) M. Tert. OFM.   **AC. Aug 17**
d. 1627. A native Japanese, of Portuguese descent, beheaded at Nagasaki. Beatified in 1867.

MARTIN de HINOJOSA (St) Bp. OSB. Cist.   **AC. Sept 3**
d. 1213. A member of the illustrious Castilian family of the Hinojosas. He became a Cistercian and eventually founded the abbey of Huerta, by the R. Jalón, near Soria (1164), of which he was the first abbot. In 1185 he became bishop of Sigüenza, but resigned in 1192 to live again as a monk.

MARTIN III (Bl) OSB. Cam.
     AC. Sept 13
d. 1259. Abbot and prior general of Camaldoli (1248–1259). He is best known as the compiler of the new constitutions of the order.

MARTIN (St) Ab. OSB. AC. Sept 28
See Willigod and Martin.

MARTIN CID (St) Ab. OSB. Cist.
     AC. Oct 8
d. 1152. Born at Zamora, in Spain, he became the abbot-founder of the Cistercian abbey of Val-Paraiso, for which St Bernard himself supplied the pioneer community. He is still greatly venerated in the diocese of Zamora and by the Cistercians.

MARTIN (St) C.   **RM. Oct 24**
Otherwise Marcius, q.v.

MARTIN of VERTOU (St) Ab.
     RM. Oct 24
d. 601. Abbot-founder of Vertou Abbey, near Nantes, of Saint-Jouin-de-Marnes and of other monastic establishments. The particulars of his life, as they have come down to us, are rather confused. He is venerated in the province of Poitou.

MARTIN PORRES (St) C. OP.
     AC. Nov 5
1569–1639. Born at Lima, in Peru, son of a Spanish knight of Alcantara and of a negro or Indian mother from Panama, Martin became a barber and studied surgery, and entered as a lay-brother at the Dominican friary of Lima. Here he

nursed the sick and "became a friend to all the poor in the city, especially the African slaves, and including stray cats and dogs". (Attwater, h.l.) When he was dying the Spanish Viceroy, the Count of Chinchón, came to kneel by his bed and ask for his blessing. Canonized in 1962.

MARTIN TINH and MARTIN THO (BB) MM.   AC. Nov 8
d. 1840. Martin Tinh was a native of Tonkin and a priest, martyred at the age of eighty with his companion, a taxgatherer, Martin Tho, also a native of Tonkin.

MARTIN of TOURS (St) Bp.
RM. Nov 11 (and July 4)
c.316–397. Born in Upper Pannonia (now Hungary), the son of a Roman officer. He was educated at Pavia and at the age of fifteen enrolled in the imperial cavalry. The episode of his sharing his cloak with a poor beggar and the subsequent heavenly vision which led to his baptism has become famous. He left the army and placed himself in the hands of St Hilary, bishop of Poitiers, living for ten years as a recluse and founding a community of monk-hermits at Ligugé. In 371 he was promoted to the see of Tours, but he accepted the office with great reluctance, and, establishing another great monastic centre at Marmoutier, he continued to live there privately as a monk, while publicly he devoted himself with burning zeal to the discharge of his episcopal duties. He opposed Arianism and Priscillianism, but befriended the Priscillianists when they were persecuted and condemned the practice of invoking the civil power to punish heretics. He was the greatest of the pioneers of Western monachism before St Benedict, who had a particular veneration for St Martin. His shrine at Tours was a great resort of pilgrims.

MARTIN I (St) Pope. M.
RM. Nov 12 (and Sept 16)
d. 655. Born in Tuscany, he was raised to the papacy in 649. At once he convened a council and condemned the Monothelites, of whom the reigning emperor Constans II was one. The imperial wrath now fell upon the pontiff, who in 653 was deported by force to Naxos, in the Aegean Sea, the following year condemned to death at a mock trial at Constantinople, and finally taken as prisoner to the Chersonese where he died of starvation.

MARTIN of ARADES (St) C. OSB.
AC. Nov 26
d. 726. A monk of Corbie, in France, chaplain and confessor to Charles Martel.

MARTIN of SAUJON (St) Ab.
RM. Dec 7
d. c.400. A disciple of St Martin of Tours, who, in his turn, became the abbot-founder of the monastery of Saujon, near Saintes.

MARTINA (St) VM.
RM. Jan 1 and 30
d. 228. A Roman martyr under Alexander Severus. She has a basilica dedicated in her honour at the Roman Forum, and there the sarcophagus containing her remains was found in 1634. Her "Passion" is entirely apocryphal and is borrowed from those of St Prisca and St Tatiana.

MARTINIAN (MATERNIAN) (St) Bp.   RM. Jan 2
d. c.435. Bishop of Milan (423–c.435). He took part in the council of Ephesus and wrote against Nestorianism.

MARTINIAN (St) H.   AC. Feb 13
d. c.400. A hermit who lived near Caesarea in Palestine. Zoe, a woman

of evil repute, tempted him to become her paramour; instead she was converted and persuaded to become a nun at Bethlehem. The story is questionable.

MARTINIAN (St) M.   RM. July 2
See Processus and Martinian.

MARTINIAN, SATURIAN and Comp. (SS) MM.   RM. Oct 16
d. 458. Four Afro-Roman brothers, reduced to slavery in the house of an Arian Vandal in Mauretania. They were encouraged to suffer for Christ by their fellow-slave, Maxima by name. The four brothers were martyred under Genseric by being dragged to death by horses. Maxima died in peace, in a convent.

MARTIUS (St) C.   AC. Apr 13
d. c.530. A native of Auvergne, he lived an austere and primitive life on the mountainside, but later built a monastery for his disciples.

MARTYRIUS (MARTORY) (St) M.   RM. Jan 23
6th cent. A solitary in the Abruzzi (Valeria), whom St Gregory the Great extols in his Dialogues (*Dial.* I, II).

MARTYRIUS (St) M. RM. May 29
See Sisinius, Martyrius and Alexander.

MARTYRIUS and MARCIAN (SS) MM.   RM. Oct 25
d. 351. Martyrius, a subdeacon, and Marcian, a chorister, were martyred at Constantinople under the Arian patriarch Macedonius on a trumped-up charge of sedition.

MARUTHAS (St) Bp.   RM. Dec 4
d. c.415. One of the most prominent personalities of the Syrian church. He was bishop of Maiferkat in Mesopotamia and devoted all his energy to the reorganization of the church in Persia and E. Syria, as well as to the preservation of the memory of the numerous Syrian and Persian martyrs under Shapur. He collected their *Passiones*, and wrote liturgical hymns in their honour. St John Chrysostom highly valued his friendship.

MARY CHRISTINA (Bl) AC. Jan 31
1812–1836. Born at Cagliari in Sardinia, daughter of Victor Emmanuel, king of Savoy and of Mary Teresa, niece of the emperor Joseph II. In 1832 she married Ferdinand II, king of the two Sicilies, to whom she bore a son before her death at the age of twenty-three. Beatified in 1872.

MARY of PROVIDENCE (Bl) V. Foundress   AC. Feb 7
1825–1871. Born at Lille, she founded the Congregation of the Helpers of the Holy Souls, aided by the advice of the Curé d'Ars, to make atonement on behalf of the souls in Purgatory by works of charity. Her Congregation is now spread throughout the world and particularly in mission territories. Her boundless patience under various trials, especially her sufferings in the crucible of incurable cancer, demonstrated more clearly the great soul she was. Beatified in 1957.

MARY (MILEDA, MLADA) (Bl) Abs. OSB.   PC. Feb 8
d. 994. Daughter of Boleslas I, duke of Bohemia. She became the abbess-foundress of the nunnery of St George, at Prague (967). She has always been venerated as a *beata*.

MARY (St) VM.   RM. Feb 11
See Saturninus, Dativus and Comp.

MARY MAMALA (Bl) W. Poor Clare   AC. March 31
d. 1453. A member of the Spanish

family of the dukes of Medina-Sidonia. She married Henry de Guzmán, and in her widowhood joined the Poor Clares at Seville.

MARY of EGYPT (St) H.
RM. Apr 2

5th cent. An Egyptian by birth, who became an actress and then lived as a courtesan at Alexandria. After her conversion, which took place, it is said, at the Holy Sepulchre at Jerusalem, she fled into the desert beyond the Jordan, where she spent the remainder of her life doing penance, and where she was found dead by two disciples of St Cyriacus. The story is doubtful, and its elaborate additions may be ignored. See also St Zosimus, H.

MARY of CLEOPHAS (St)
RM. Apr 9

1st cent. The wife of Cleophas or Alpheus (John XIX, 25) and the mother of the apostle St James the Less. She was one of the "three Marys" who followed our Lord from Galilee and who stood at the foot of the cross on Calvary. The legends which have grown up around her name deserve no credence.

MARY MARGARET DUFROST de LAJEMMERAIS D'YOUVILLE (Bl)
W. Foundress   AC. Apr 11

1701–1771. Born at Varennes, Canada, she experienced the joys and hardships of a poor backwoods home, the early loss of her father, eleven years of married life and the untimely death of her husband and four of her six children. These trials did not break her spirit but rather helped to develop a life of union with God and of service of her neighbour, especially those visited by suffering. She founded the Sisters of Charity to serve the sick and the needy. Beatified in 1959.

MARY BERNARD SOUBIROUS (St) V.
RM. Apr 16

Otherwise Bernadette Soubirous, q.v.

MARY of the INCARNATION (Bl) W. OC.
AC. Apr 18

d. 1618. Barbara Avrillot, who in her young days was styled "the beautiful Acarie", was married to Peter Acarie, a French government official. After his death in 1613, Barbara joined the Carmelites as a lay-sister and took the new name of Mary-of-the-Incarnation. She introduced into France the Discalced Carmelites of St Teresa. Beatified in 1791.

MARY SAINTE-EUPHRASIE PELLETIER (St) V.
RM. Apr 24

Otherwise Euphrasia Pelletier, q.v.

MARY-ANN of JESUS
Apr 27

Otherwise Mariana of Jesus, q.v.

MARY DOMINIC MAZZARELLO (St) V. Co-Foundress
AC. May 14

1837–1881. She was born at Mornese in the diocese of Acqui, N. Italy, of humble parents. After a devout childhood in which she worked in the fields, she joined the Pious Union of Mary Immaculate. First one and then other companions joined her in a life of regular piety, and so insensibly her Institute, the Daughters of Mary Auxiliatrix came into being. Under the direction of St John Bosco it received full canonical formation and status, and undertook for girls what the Salesians were doing for boys. St Mary Dominic was obliged to become first Superior General in 1874. She died in 1881 after a long illness, and was canonized in 1951.

MARY-MAGDALEN of CANOSSA (Bl) V. Foundress
AC. May 14

1774–1835. She was a daughter of the Marquis of Canossa. Her father died while she was a child, and her mother married again, abandoning her children. She managed her late father's household till she was thirty-three. Then, after a brief period of serving hospitals in Venice in 1808, she founded the first house of her Institute, the Daughters of Charity, at Verona, its scope being the education of poor girls, the service of hospitals and the teaching of the cate- chism in parishes. When the foundress died in 1835 she left several houses in N. Italy; since then well over 400 houses have been established in all parts of the world. Beatified in 1941.

MARY-MAGDALEN ALBRIZZI (Bl) V. OSA.   AC. May 15
d. 1465. Born at Como, she entered a nunnery at Brunate, near her native city, of which she became prioress. While prioress she affiliated the convent to the Augustinian friars. She was remarkable for her promotion of frequent com- munion among her nuns. Cult approved in 1907.

MARY-MAGDALEN SOPHIE BARAT (St) V. Foundress
RM. May 25
1779–1865. Madeleine Sophie Barat was a native of Joigny, in Burgundy, and opened the first convent of her new congregation of nuns, called the Society of the Sacred Heart of Jesus, at Amiens in 1801. She was a lady of great charm and enterprise, and before her death she had established houses throughout Europe, America and Africa—one hundred and five foundations in all, during her life-time. Canonized in 1925.

MARY-ANN de PAREDES (St) V.
AC. May 26
Otherwise Mariana de Paredes, q.v.

MARY-BARTHOLOMEW BAG- NESI (Bl)   AC. May 27
Otherwise Bartholomaea Bagnesi, q.v.

MARY-MAGDALEN de'PAZZI (St) V. OC.   RM. May 29
1566–1607 (May 25). A native of Florence, where she became a Discalced Carmelite at the age of sixteen. Throughout her life she was subject to remarkable mystical experiences and was tried with many kinds of suffering —spiritual and physical. She filled various conventual offices with remark- able ability. Canonized in 1669.

MARY (St) M. OSB. Cist.
AC. June 1
See Bernard, Mary, etc.

MARY-MAGDALEN of CARPI (Bl) V. OSM.   AC. June 10
d. 1546. A Servite lay-sister at Carpi, collector of alms for her community.

MARY of OIGNIES (Bl) W.
AC. June 23
d. 1213. Born at Nivelles in Belgium, she married early in life, but persuaded her husband not to consummate the marriage. They then turned their house into a leper hospital, and tended the sick there. Finally Mary became a recluse in a cell near the church of Oignies, where she was favoured with supernatural charismata.

MARY-MAGDALEN FONTAINE (Bl) M.   AC. June 26
1723–1794. Born at Etrépagny (Eure), she entered the noviciate of the sisters of Charity of St Vincent de Paul in 1748, and from 1767 was the superior of the house of that Institute at Arras. She was guillotined at Cambrai during the French Revolution together with three religious of her community. Beatified in 1920.

MARY (St) W.   RM. June 29
1st cent. Mentioned in the Acts of the Apostles (XII, 12), as the mother of John, surnamed Mark (q.v.). From the

text it appears that Mary's house was a place of assembly for the apostles and the faithful generally. Subsequent traditions about her are conflicting.

MARY GORETTI (St) VM.
AC. July 5

1890–1902. Born at Corinaldo, near Ancona, Italy, she showed marked signs of youthful holiness. She was pursued by a youth inflamed with lustful desires for her. Finally, when all were working in the fields, he came upon her alone, but she died in defence of her chastity under the repeated blows of his knife rather than give way to him. Her canonization in 1950 was attended by her mother, family and an enormous crowd. Some thirty to forty miracles worked by her are on record.

MARY ROSE (Bl) M. OSB.
AC. July 6

1741–1794. Her baptismal name was Susanne-Agatha de Loye. She was born at Sérignan, near Orange, and in 1762 became a Benedictine in the nunnery of Caderousse. At the outbreak of the French Revolution she was expelled from the convent, and in May 1794 she was arrested and guillotined, the first of a band of thirty-one martyrs put to death at Orange. Beatified in 1925.

MARY-MAGDALEN POSTEL (St)
V. Foundress   RM. July 16

1756–1846. Born at Barfleur. Early in life she opened a school for girls, but soon the French Revolution stopped her work. During that trying period she obtained permission to administer the Bl Sacrament to the dying. In 1805 she reopened her school at Cherbourg, and this proved to be the origin of the Sisterhood of Christian Schools, which, after severe trials, spread and flourished throughout the world. Canonized in 1925.

MARY ST-HENRY (MARGUERITE-ELÉONORE de JUSTAMOND) and MARY-MAGDALEN du ST-SACREMENT (MAGDALEN-FRANÇOISE de JUSTAMOND) (BB) MM. OSB. Cist.
AC. July 16

d. 1794. Sisters by blood and Cistercian nuns at the convent of St Catherine at Avignon. They were guillotined at Orange during the French Revolution. Beatified in 1925.

MARY MAGDALEN LIDOIN (In religion: Mère Thérèse de St Augustine, Prioress) MARY ANN PIEDCOURT (Soeur de Jésus Crucifié), MARY HANISSET (Soeur Thérèse du Coeur de Marie), MARY TRÉSEL (Soeur Thérèse de St Ignace), MARY DUFOUR (Soeur Sainte Marthe) (BB) MM. OC.
AC. July 17

d. 1794. They belong to the community of Carmelite Nuns of Compiègne, q.v., guillotined at Paris during the French Revolution. The first four were solemnly professed choir sisters, Bl Mary Dufour a lay-sister.

MARY MAGDALEN (St)
RM. July 22

1st cent. Mary Magdalen is mentioned in the four gospels as one of the most devoted followers of our Lord. Chiefly under the influence of St Gregory the Great's writings, the Western liturgies have identified her with the unnamed sinner (Luke VII, 37, cf. Luke VIII, 2) and Mary the sister of Martha and Lazarus (John XI). This identification is challenged by Eastern tradition and by the writings of the Eastern Fathers. The story connecting St Mary Magdalen with France is pure legend.

MARY-MAGDALEN MARTIN-ENGO (Bl) V. OFM. Cap.
AC. July 27

1687–1737. A native of Brescia, where she entered the convent of Capuchin nuns. She filled the post of novice-mistress and prioress with marked success. Beatified in 1900.

MARY the CONSOLER (St)
AC. Aug 1

8th cent. Said to have been the sister of St Anno bishop of Verona.

MARY the BLESSED VIRGIN, Mother of God (St)
RM. Aug 15 and as below

d. ? 45. The Virgin Mother of God is venerated with a special cult, called *hyperdoulia*, by the Catholic Church, as the highest of God's creatures. The invocation of Mary pervades all Catholic devotion, public and private, and among Catholics her name is more commonly bestowed at baptism than any other. The principal events of the life of our Lady are the object of special liturgical feasts celebrated by the universal Church and listed in the RM. as follows: (1) Dec 8: her Immaculate Conception, viz., the singular privilege by which God preserved her from all stain of original sin at the first moment of her conception. (2) Sept 8: her birthday as a Jewish child and a lineal descendant of the royal family of David. (3) Sept 12: her most holy name of Mary. (4) Nov 21: her Presentation, i.e., the offering of her to God for the first time by her parents in the temple at Jerusalem. (5) March 25: the Annunciation, when Gabriel the Archangel was sent by God to declare unto her that she was chosen to be the Mother of God. (6) July 2: the Visitation, viz. Mary's visit to her cousin St Elizabeth, the mother of St John the Baptist. (7) Oct 11: her divine Motherhood, in virtue of which she is truly entitled to the name of *Theotokos—Deipara—* Mother of God. (8) Feb 2: the Purification, when Mary took her Child to present Him for the first time in the temple at Jerusalem. (9) On the Friday after Passion Sunday and on Sept 15: the Seven Sorrows of our Lady. (10) Aug 15: Mary's Assumption soul and body into heaven. Other feasts refer to special events connected with our Lady's patronage over the Church; these are (11) Aug 5: feast of the dedication of her principal Roman basilica "of the Snow". (12) July 16: feast of our Lady of Mt Carmel. (13) Sept 24: the apparition of our Lady of Ransom. (14) Oct 7: feast of the Most Holy Rosary. (15) Feb 11: feast of our Lady's miraculous apparitions to St Bernadette Soubirous at Lourdes. Moreover, each nation and almost every diocese of the Catholic Church venerates our Lady under some special title, thus literally fulfilling her prophecy: *All generations shall call me blessed* (Luke I, 48).

MARY-MAGDALEN KIOTA (Bl) M.
AC. Aug 16

d. 1620. Wife of Bl Simon Kiota. She was crucified with her husband at Cocura, Japan. Beatified in 1867. (*She is not to be identified with Bl Mary Magdalen Kiota of Nagasaki, q.v.*)

MARY-MAGDALEN KIOTA (Bl) M. Tert. OP.
AC. Aug 17

d. 1627. A Japanese princess, kinswoman to the king of Bungo, and a Dominican tertiary. She was burnt at Nagasaki for having sheltered the missionaries. Beatified in 1867.

MARY VAZ (Bl) M.
AC. Aug 17

d. 1627. A Japanese woman, wife of Bl Caspar Vaz. She was a Franciscan tertiary. Beheaded at Nagasaki. Beatified in 1867.

MARY GUENGORO (Bl) M.
AC. Aug 18
d. 1620. A Japanese, wife of Bl Thomas Guengoro. She was crucified at Cocura with her husband and her son James. Beatified in 1867.

MARY de MATTHIAS (Bl) V.
Foundress   AC. Aug 20
1805–1866. She was born at Vallecorsa, S. Italy. Bl. Gaspar Buffalo chose her at the age of seventeen to found a Congregation for women corresponding to that which he was founding for teaching boys. In 1834 she opened her first school at Acuto, and this became the cradle of the new Congregation, the Adorers of the Most Precious Blood. By the time of her death, her sisters were conducting about seventy schools. Beatified in 1950.

MARY-MICHAELA (St) Foundress
RM. Aug 24
1809–1865. Michaela Dermaisières, viscountess of Sorbalán, was born at Madrid. She was educated by the Ursulines and afterwards lived with her family at Guadalajara, where she began her active life of charity. In 1848 she founded the Institute of Handmaids of the Blessed Sacrament and of Charity which was approved in 1859. She died at Valencia from the cholera, which she contracted in ministering to its victims. In Spain she is surnamed *La Loca del S.mo Sacramento*—the mad-woman of the Bl Sacrament. Canonized in 1934.

MARY de la CABEZA (Bl)
AC. Sept 9
d. c.1175. Born at Torrejon, she married St Isidore the Farmer, q.v., after whose death she retired to Caraquiz. Cult approved in 1697.

MARY TANAURA, MARY TANACA, and MARY MAGDALEN SANGA (BB) MM.   AC. Sept 10
d. 1622. Japanese women beheaded at Nagasaki, the last two with their respective husbands, BB Paul Tanaca and Antony Sanga. Beatified in 1867.

MARY TOCUAN and MARY XOUN (BB) MM.   AC. Sept 10
d. 1619. Japanese women martyred with their husbands.

MARY VICTORIA FORNARI-STRATA (Bl) Foundress AC. Sept 12
1562–1617. Mary Victoria Fornari was born at Genoa and married Angelo Strata, by whom she had six children. In 1589 he died. After Mary Victoria had educated and provided for her children, she founded the congregation of nuns called the Blue Annonciades, of whom she was the first superior. Beatified in 1828.

MARY de CEREVELLON (St) V.
O. Merc.   RM. Sept 19
d. 1290. Also called, in her native Catalan, Maria de Socós, "Mary of help", She was born at Barcelona and became one of the first nuns of the Mercedarian Order (our Lady of Ransom) and the superioress of the convent at Barcelona. Cult confirmed in 1690.

MARY-TERESA COUDERC (Bl) V.
Foundress   AC. Sept 26
1805–1885. At the age of twenty under the guidance of Father Terma she founded the Society of Our Lady of the Cenacle at La Louvesc, France. The intention was to attract pilgrims to the tomb of St John Francis Regis there, and induce them to spend time there in recollection. The Institute developed as one of Retreat Houses for women and rapidly spread throughout Europe and to America. Although obliged in 1835 to resign the administration of her Institute through ill-health, she lived to the age of eighty. Beatified in 1951.

MARY FRANCES (St) V. RM. Oct 6
1715–1791. Anna Maria Gallo was born at Naples of a middle-class family. Her father was brutal and avaricious and was especially harsh towards her when she refused to marry the man he had chosen for her. In 1731 she became a Franciscan tertiary with the new name of Mary Frances of the Sacred Wounds. She continued to live at home until she got a position as housekeeper to a priest, a post which she filled for thirty-eight years. God favoured her with extraordinary graces, including the mystical marriage.

MARY-DESOLATA TORRES ACOSTA (Bl) V. Foundress Oct 11
1826–1887. This truly great woman was born in a poor quarter of Madrid. She tried unsuccessfully to become a Dominican nun. In 1848 she responded to the call of a priest to found an institute for the care of the sick in their own homes. A subsequent priest-director of the young Institute (Handmaids of Mary) removed her and appointed another Superior in her place, with the result that the Institute nearly perished. But after an examination by the Bishop she was re-appointed and lived to found forty-six houses. She died in Madrid in 1887. Beatified in 1950.

MARY-MAGDALEN dei PANATTIERI (Bl) V. OP.   AC. Oct 13
1443–1503. Born at Trino, in the diocese of Vercelli, in Piedmont, she modelled herself on St Catherine of Siena, and like her became a Dominican tertiary in her own home, devoted to charitable works among her neighbours. Cult approved by Leo XIII.

MARY MAGDALEN DEJARDIN (in religion Soeur Marie-Augustine) and MARY LOUISE VANOT (Soeur Natalie) (BB) MM.   AC. Oct 17

d. 1794. Two Ursuline sisters, belonging to the community of Valenciennes, guillotined in that town during the French Revolution together with nine others of the same community. Beatified in 1920. See also Ursuline Nuns, MM.

MARY-TERESA de SOUBIRAN (Bl) V. Foundress   AC. Oct 20
1834–1889. Born of noble parents in Castelnaudary, Carcassonne, she wished to become a Carmelite nun, but under the guidance of her uncle, a canon, she founded a Béguinage in 1855, and took the name of Mary-Teresa. In order to attain her apostolic ends more fully she transformed the Béguinage into the Institute of Mary Auxiliatrix, with the approval of the Bishop. But through the machinations of one of her subjects she was driven from her own Congregation, overwhelmed with calumnies and deprived of her property. Thus in 1868 she sought refuge in the Institute of Our Lady of Charity in which she was allowed to take vows and in which she persevered till her death. Only then did the truth come out. She enjoyed mystical gifts of a high order. Beatified in 1946.

MARY SALOME (St)   RM. Oct 22
1st cent. One of the "three Marys". She was the wife of Zebedee, the mother of St James the Great and St John the Evangelist, and one of the pious women who ministered to our Lord during His public life. She also witnessed His death on the cross, burial and resurrection.

MARY the SLAVE (St) M. RM. Nov 1
d. c.300. A slave-girl in the household of a Roman patrician who was venerated as a martyr on account of her sufferings during the persecution of Diocletian.

MARY (St) VM.   RM. Nov 24
See Flora and Mary.

MARY (St) M.   **RM. Dec 2**
See Eusebius, Marcellus, etc.

MARY of ST MARTIN (Bl) N. OSB. Cam.   **AC. Dec 4**
d. 1240. A Camaldolese nun of the convent of Pugnano, near Pisa.

MARY-JOSEPH ROSSELLO (St) V. Foundress   **AC. Dec 7**
1811–1888. Born at Albisola in the diocese of Savona of poor parents, Benedicta Rossello showed early signs of unusual virtue. Unable to enter a religious order for want of a dowry or sufficient health, she became a Franciscan tertiary. In 1837 she laid the foundations of her new Institute, the Daughters of Our Lady of Mercy, which spread rapidly through Italy and South America. Known in religion as Sister Mary-Joseph, she suffered from constant sickness, but ruled her Institute with heroic courage amid many difficulties until her death in 1888. Canonized in 1949.

MARY CRUCIFIXA di ROSA (St) V. Foundress   **AC. Dec 15**
1813–1885. She was born of a well-to-do business family. From her childhood she showed a lively piety and sympathy with the poor. When cholera broke out in 1836 she gave herself wholeheartedly to tending its victims, and in the course of this work gathered the first companions of her Institute, the Servants of Charity. The Society formed in 1839 was approved by Pius IX in 1851. Her love for Christ crucified showed itself in the addition of the name Crucifixa, and in her great austerities. Her Order today has three hundred houses and three thousand religious. Canonized in 1954.

MARY of the ANGELS (Bl) V. OC.   **AC. Dec 16**
1661–1717. Mary Ann Fontanella was born at Baldinero, near Turin, the daughter of Count Fontanella. In 1676 she entered the Carmel of St Christina at Turin and soon her life was a replica of that of SS Teresa and Magdalen de' Pazzi. She founded the Carmel of Moncaglieri, which still exists. Beatified in 1865.

MARY of PISA (Bl) W. Tert. OP.   **AC. Dec 22**
d. 1431. A member of the Mancini family of Pisa. She received extraordinary mystical favours such as the apparition of her Guardian Angel from childhood. She married at the early age of twelve and was left a widow and the mother of two children at sixteen. She married again, but lost her second husband eight years later. Mary then became a Dominican tertiary and later took charge of a new foundation of that order, noted for its strict observance. Cult confirmed by Pius IX.

MASCULAS (St) M. RM. March 29
See Armogastes and Comp.

MASSA CANDIDA (SS) MM.   **RM. Aug 24**
d. c.260. The name *Massa Candida* (the white mass) denotes a group of martyrs who suffered at Utica in N. Africa under Gallienus and Valerian. The RM. gives their number as three hundred, but modern writers limit it to one hundred and fifty. According to the RM. they were called the white mass because they were thrown into a lime pit, and their remains became conglomerated into one great white mass, but it now appears that *Massa Candida* was a locality near Utica.

MASSALIUS (St) M.   **RM. Apr 29**
See Corfu, Martyrs of.

MATERNIAN (St) Bp.   **RM. Jan 2**
Otherwise Martinian, q.v.

MATERNUS (St) Bp.   RM. July 18
d. *c.*307. Bishop of Milan, raised to the
see by popular acclamation in 295. He
had much to suffer during the persecution of Diocletian, but survived it and
died in peace.

MATERNUS (St) Bp.   RM. Sept 14
d. *c.*325. The first bishop of Cologne
about whom we have positive evidence.
His name is in fact mentioned in connexion with the Donatist controversy.
A medieval legend, which was still
defended by St Peter Canisius, identifies this Maternus with the son of the
widow of Naim and makes him a
disciple of St Peter.

MATHIAS MULUMBA (St) M.
RM. June 3
d. 1886. A Chief of several villages, who
was martyred by King Mwanga of
Uganda. See Uganda (Martyrs of).

MATHILDIS (St) Queen
RM. March 14
Otherwise Matilda, q.v.

MATHURIN (MATURINUS) (St)
C.   RM. Nov 1
d. 388. Born in the district of Sens, he
was converted and ordained priest by
Polycarp, bishop of that city. In his
turn he converted his own parents and
evangelized his native district with signal success.

MATILDA of SPANHEIM (Bl) V.
OSB.   PC. Feb 26
d. 1154. A German recluse, first at
Mainz, under the obedience of her
brother, the abbot of St Albans's,
Mainz; and then near Spanheim when
he became abbot of a new abbey there.

MATILDA (MATHILDIS, MAUD)
(St) W.   RM. March 14
d. 968. Wife of the German king Henry

the Fowler. She was of a very generous
disposition and founded, among others,
the Benedictine abbeys of Nordhausen,
Pöhlde, Engern and Quedlinburg. She
was a widow for thirty years and had to
suffer much at the hands of her sons,
Otto and Henry, by whom she was
despoiled of most of her possessions.
She died at Quedlinburg and the Benedictines venerate her as one of their
oblates.

MATRONA (St) VM. RM. March 15
d. *c.*?350. The serving-maid of a rich
Jewess of Thessalonica, scourged to
death at the orders of her mistress when
she discovered that she was a Christian.
The Acts are not very clear.

MATRONA (St) M.   RM. March 20
See Alexandra, Claudia, etc.

MATRONA (St) H.   RM. May 18
See Theodotus, Thecusa, etc.

MATRONIAN (St) H.   RM. Dec 14
? A native of Milan, who became a
hermit, and whose relics are said to
have been enshrined by St Ambrose in
the church of S. Nazario.

MATTHEW ALONSO LEZINIANA
(Bl) M. OP.   AC. Jan 22
d. 1745. Born at Navas del Rey in the
diocese of Valladolid, Spain. After his
profession in the Dominican Order and
his ordination he was sent to the
Philippine Islands and thence to Tonkin, where he was eventually beheaded.
Beatified in 1906.

MATTHEW of GIRGENTI (Bl) Bp.
OFM.   AC. Feb 3
d. 1450. Matthew Gimarra was born at
Girgenti in Sicily and became a Conventual Franciscan. He afterwards
migrated to the Observants and worked
zealously under St Bernardinus of

Siena. Pope Eugene IV forced him to accept the bishopric of Girgenti, but as a result of much opposition he had to resign the see. He died in a Franciscan friary at Palermo. Cult confirmed in 1767.

MATTHEW of BEAUVAIS (St) M.
AC. March 27
d. c.1098. A native of Beauvais who took the cross under bishop Roger of Beauvais and joined the First Crusade. He was taken prisoner by the Saracens and beheaded on refusing to renounce Christ.

MATTHEW PHUNG (Bl) M.
AC. May 26
c.1801–1861. Born at Ke-lay in Cochin-China, he became a catechist, for which he was beheaded near Dong-hoi in N. Cochin-China. Beatified in 1909.

MATTHEW GAM (Bl) M.
AC. May 27
1812–1847. A native Tonkin Christian who brought the missionaries of the Paris Foreign Missions from Singapore to Annam in his boat. He was imprisoned in 1846, tortured and beheaded. Beatified in 1900.

MATTHEW ALVAREZ (Bl) M. Tert. OP.
AC. Sept 8
d. 1628. A Japanese catechist and Dominican tertiary who was beheaded at Nagasaki. Beatified in 1867.

MATTHEW (Bl) H. OSB. Cam.
AC. Sept 11
d. 1303. A Camaldolese hermit, disciple of Bl John of Massaccio, whose cave on Mt Massaccio he inherited.

MATTHEW (St) Apostle
RM. Sept 21
1st cent. Matthew, or Levi, before he was called by our Lord to be an apostle, was a tax-gatherer at Capharnaum. We have a legendary account of his career after the coming down of the Holy Ghost, but the gospel narrative provides the only trustworthy data concerning him. He is the author of the first gospel, which he addressed to his fellow-Jews. It is not known where he preached or whether he died a martyr.

MATTHEW CARRERI (Bl) C. OP.
AC. Oct 7
d. 1471. Born at Mantua, he joined the Dominicans and spent his life in preaching throughout Italy. Cult approved in 1483.

MATTHEW de ESKANDELY (Bl) M.
AC. Oct 8
d. c.1309. Born in Buda, Hungary, he went as a missionary to the East, being apparently the first Catholic missionary in China, where he was martyred.

MATTHEW (St) M. OSB.
RM. Nov 12
See Benedict, John, etc.

MATTHEW (Bl) Card. OSB.
PC. Dec 25
d. 1134. A canon of Reims who became a Cluniac monk at Saint-Martin-des-Champs (1108) and prior there in 1117. In 1125 he was created cardinal bishop of Albano and in 1128 papal legate in France and Germany. He was a staunch upholder of the Cluniac ideal and a great friend of St Peter the Venerable.

MATTHEW of CITTÀ DELLA PIEVE (Bl) C. OSM.
PC.?
d. 1348. The ninth superior general of the Servites (1344–1348). His cult has not yet been confirmed.

MATTHIA dei NAZAREI (Bl) Abs. OSB.
AC. Dec 30
d. 1213. Born at Metalica in the March

of Ancona, she received the Benedictine veil at the nunnery of Santa Maddalena, at Metalica, of which she became abbess, a position which she held for forty years. At a later date the convent adopted the rule of the Poor Clares, and for this reason Bl Matthia is often called a Poor Clare. Cult confirmed in 1756.

MATTHIAS (St) Bp.   RM. Jan 30
d. *c.*120. A bishop of Jerusalem of Jewish descent. He governed the see at a time when his flock was in great part dispersed.

MATTHIAS of MEACO (St) M.
                                RM. Feb 5
d. 1597. Born at Meaco, he became a Franciscan tertiary and was crucified at Nagasaki with St Peter Baptist and twenty-five companions. Canonized in 1862.

MATTHIAS (St) Apostle
                                RM. Feb 24
1st cent. He was chosen by lot by the Eleven to take the place of Judas Iscariot among the apostles (Acts I, 21–22). The traditions concerning his later life are not consistent. It seems, however, that he was martyred in Colchis.

MATTHIAS of ARIMA (Bl) M.
                                AC. May 22
d. 1622. A native Japanese catechist of the Jesuit Fathers and servant of the provincial. Because he would not betray his master he was subjected to a most revolting martyrdom. Beatified in 1867.

MATTHIAS MURUMBA (St) M.
                                RM. June 3
d. 1886. A negro judge in Uganda. He was first a Mohammedan, then a Protestant, and in 1881 became a convert to the Catholic Faith. He was martyred on Kumpala hill. See Uganda (Martyrs of).

MATTHIAS ARAKI (Bl) M.
                                AC. July 12
d. 1626. A Japanese layman, brother of Bl Mancius Araki, q.v. He was burnt alive at Nagasaki for having sheltered the European missionaries. Beatified in 1867.

MATTHIAS COSACA and MATTHIAS NAKANO (BB) MM.
                                AC. Nov 27
d. 1619. Japanese laymen belonging to the royal family of Firando. They were imprisoned at Omura, their native place, and beheaded at Nagasaki. Beatified in 1867.

MATURINUS (St) C.   RM. Nov 1
Otherwise Mathurin, q.v.

MATURUS (St) M.   RM. June 2
See Photinus (Pothinus), Sanctus, etc.

MAUD and MAUDE
Note. Saints of this name should be sought under other forms of the word, which is either a variant of Mechtilde, Matilda, or a diminutive of Magdalen (Maudlin).

MAUGHAN (MAWGAN, MORGAN) (St)   AC. Sept 26
Otherwise Meugant, q.v.

MAUGHOLD (MACCALDUS) (St) Bp.   AC. Dec 28
d. *c.*488. An Irishman said to have been a brigand, converted by St Patrick and by him sent to the Isle of Man, where his episcopate was very successful.

MAURA (St) M.   RM. Feb 13
See Fusca and Maura.

MAURA (St) M.   RM. May 3
See Timothy and Maura.

MAURA and BRITTA (SS) VV.
AC. Jan 15
? 4th cent. Two virgins whose life is not known, but whose relics were, according to St Gregory of Tours, found during the episcopate of his predecessor, St Euphronius.

MAURA (St) V.   AC. Sept 21
d. 850. A maiden of Troyes in Champagne, who died at the age of twenty-three after a life of prayer and good works.

MAURA (St) V.   AC. Nov 2
See Baya and Maura.

MAURA (St) VM.   RM. Nov 30
? A maiden martyred at Constantinople. One of the Ionian islands is named after her.

MAURICE CSAKY (Bl) C. OP.
PC. March 20
1281–1336. Maurice Csaky belonged to the royal house of Hungary. Some years after their marriage both he and his wife by mutual consent became religious, Maurice joining the Friars Preachers. Although never officially canonized or beatified, he is still venerated in Hungary.

MAURICE (St) M.   RM. July 10
See Leontius, Maurice, etc.

MAURICE and Comp. (SS) MM.
RM. Sept 22
See Theban Legion.

MAURICE of CARNOET (St) Ab. OSB. Cist.   AC. Oct 13
c.1114–1191. Born in the district of Loudéac, in Brittany, and educated at Paris, he joined the Cistercians at Langonel, in his native country (1144). In 1147 he was made abbot, and in 1177 he became the abbot-founder of Carnoet.

As abbot both of Langonel and of Carnoet he was a great friend and adviser of the dukes of Brittany. Cult confirmed by Clement XI.

MAURILIUS (St) Bp. OSB.
AC. Aug 9
d. 1067. A native of Reims, he became successively headmaster of the cathedral school at Halberstadt, a Benedictine monk at Fécamp in Normandy, abbot of St Mary's at Florence and archbishop of Rouen (1055). He was one of the leading churchmen of his day; he wrote against Berengarius.

MAURILIUS (St) Bp.   AC. Sept 3
d. 580. Bishop of Cahors. It is recorded that he knew the whole Bible by heart.

MAURILIUS (St) Bp.   RM. Sept 13
d. c.430. A native of Milan who migrated to France where he became a disciple of St Martin of Tours. About the year 407 he was raised to the see of Angers.

MAURINUS (St) Ab. M.
RM. June 10
? Abbot of a monastery—probably that of St Pantaleon—at Cologne. Venerated also as a martyr. All other data are lacking.

MAURITIUS (*several*)
Otherwise Maurice, q.v.

MAURONTUS (MAURONTIUS, MAURUNTIUS) (St) Ab. OSB.
AC. Jan 9
d. c.700. Abbot-founder of Saint-Florent-le-Vieil, in Anjou.

MAURONTUS (MAURONT) (St) Ab. OSB.   AC. May 5
d. 701. Eldest son of SS Adalbald and Rictrudis, he was reared at the court and succeeded his father as lord of Douai. He was just on the point of marrying

when he joined the Benedictines at Marchiennes. Eventually he became abbot-founder of Breuil-sur-lys, near Douai, of which town he is now the patron saint.

MAURONTUS (St) Bp. OSB.
AC. Oct 21

d. *c*.804. Abbot of St Victor at Marseilles, who was promoted to the see of the same city (*c*.767).

MAURUS (St) Ab. OSB.
RM. Jan 15

d. *c*.580. Eutychius, a noble Roman, was among the first to place his son, Maurus, under the care of St Benedict, the patriarch of Western monks, then at Subiaco. The youth grew up a faithful disciple of St Benedict and a pattern of obedience to his fellow monks. When Benedict migrated to Montecassino (*c*.525) he left Maurus in charge of the monasteries at Subiaco. The legend which makes St Maurus abbot-founder of Glanfeuil in France is now completely discredited.

MAURUS (St) Bp. OSB.
RM. Jan 20

d. 946. A Roman, nephew of Pope John IX, who ordained him priest. Next he became monk and abbot of Classe at Ravenna (926), and finally bishop of Cesena (934). He built for himself a cell on a hill near the city, where he would spend part of his time in prayer. After his death the cell grew into the Benedictine abbey of Santa Maria del Monte.

MAURUS (MARIUS, MAY) (St) Ab.
RM. Jan 27

d. *c*.555. Abbot-founder of Bodon in the diocese of Sisteron, France.

MAURUS (St) M.
RM. Jan 29

See Papias and Maurus.

MAURUS de CHAK (Bl) OP.
PC. March 20

d. 1336. Son of the Count Chak, he left the wealth and dignity of his family to enter the Dominican order. He died in Gyor, where his tomb was, till destroyed by the Turks. His miracles were collected for the Council of Ferrara but the Turkish invasion stopped the process.

MAURUS (WILLIAM) SCOTT (Bl) M. OSB.
AC. May 30

d. 1612. William (in religion, Maurus) Scott was born at Chigwell, in Essex, and became a student of law at Trinity Hall, Cambridge. By reading Catholic literature he was led to embrace Catholicism and was received into the Church by Bl John Roberts, OSB., who sent him to the Benedictine abbey at Satagún, in Spain. He became a monk of this abbey (1604) and after his ordination was sent back to England as a missionary. Shortly after his arrival he witnessed the martyrdom of Bl John Roberts and not long afterwards he himself was captured and martyred for his priesthood at Tyburn. Beatified in 1929.

MAURUS (St) M.
AC. June 16

See Felix and Maurus.

MAURUS, PANTALEEMON and SERGIUS (SS) MM.
RM. July 27

d. *c*.?117. Three martyrs venerated at Bisceglia on the Adriatic. Maurus is said to have been a native of Bethlehem, sent by St Peter to be the first bishop of Bisceglia. They are stated to have been martyred under Trajan, but their Acts are quite untrustworthy.

MAURUS (St) M.
RM. Aug 1

See Bonus, Faustus and Maurus.

MAURUS and Comp. (SS) MM.
RM. Aug 22
? A group of fifty martyrs, whose leader, Maurus, was a priest. All other data are uncertain. The RM. assigns them to Reims, and they seem to have suffered either under Valerian (*c*.260) or under Diocletian (*c*.300).

MAURUS (Bl) Bp. OSB.
PC. Oct 25
d. *c*.1070. A Benedictine abbot who in 1036 became Bishop of Pécs in Hungary. He wrote the lives of St Benedict Zorard and St Andrew Szkalka (q.v.).

MAURUS (St) Bp.   RM. Nov 8
d. 383. Second bishop of Verdun (353–383). His relics were enshrined in the 9th century, when many miracles are said to have taken place at his tomb.

MAURUS (St) Bp.   RM. Nov 21
d. *c*.600. Twelfth bishop of Verona, in N. Italy. Towards the end of his life he resigned and became a hermit.

MAURUS (St) M.   RM. Nov 22
d. *c*.284. Born of Christian parents in Proconsular Africa, he travelled to Rome, where he was martyred under Numerian. About ten different cities in Italy and in France claim to possess his relics.

MAURUS (St) M.   RM. Dec 3
See Claudius, Hilaria, etc.

MAURUS (Bl) Bp. OSB.
AC. Dec 4
d. *c*.1070. One of the Benedictine monks whom St Stephen of Hungary invited to his kingdom. He was a member of the community of Pannonhalma until 1036, when he was made bishop of Pécs (*Quinque Ecclesiae*). He is notable too as a hagiographer. Cult approved in 1848.

MAVILUS (MAJULUS) (St) M.
RM. Jan 4
d. 212. A martyr of Adrumetum in Africa, flung to the wild beasts in the arena, under Caracalla.

MAWES (MAUDETUS, MAUDEZ) (St) Ab.   AC. Nov 18
6th cent. An Irishman, who lived first as a solitary near Falmouth in Cornwall, and then passed over to Brittany where he is known as St Maudez.

MAWGAN (St)   AC. Sept 26
Otherwise Meugant, q.v.

MAXELLENDIS (St) VM.
AC. Nov 13
d. *c*.670. She was stabbed to death at Caudry, near Cambrai, by Hardouin of Solesmes, in a fit of rage because she wished to be a nun and refused to marry him.

MAXENTIA (St) VM.   AC. Nov 20
? An Irish or Scottish maiden who settled as a recluse near Senlis in France, where she was put to death at the place now called Pont-Sainte-Maxence. She is venerated at Beauvais.

MAXENTIOLUS (MEZENCEUL) (St) Ab.   AC. Dec 17
5th cent. A disciple of St Martin of Tours, who became the abbot-founder of our Lady of Cunault.

MAXENTIUS (MAIXENT) (St) Ab.
RM. June 26
c.448–515. Born at Agde in S. France, he was educated by St Severus and afterwards became a monk in a monastery of Poitou, now called after him Saint-Maixent, of which he eventually became abbot. He was highly esteemed by Clovis I and by the surrounding population whom he protected from the invading barbarians.

MAXENTIUS, CONSTANTIUS, CRESCENTIUS, JUSTIN and Comp. (SS) MM.   RM. Dec 12

d. *c*.287. Martyrs at Trèves, at the beginning of the reign of Diocletian.

MAXIMA (St) M.   RM. March 26

See Montanus and Maxima.

MAXIMA (St) M.   RM. Apr 8

See Januarius, Maxima and Macaria.

MAXIMA (St) V.   RM. May 16

? She is widely venerated in the diocese of Fréjus, in France, where several villages are called after her. Nothing, however, is known about her.

MAXIMA, DONATILLA and SECUNDA (SS) VV. MM.
RM. July 30

d. 304. Three maidens (Secunda was aged twelve), martyred at Tebourba in Proconsular Africa under Diocletian.

MAXIMA (St) M.   RM. Sept 2

d. 304. A Roman slave, who expired under the lash, during the persecution of Diocletian. She was condemned to death together with St Ansanus.

MAXIMA (St) M.   RM. Oct 1

See Verissimus, Maxima, etc.

MAXIMA (St)   RM. Oct 16

See Martinian, Saturian, and Comp.

MAXIMIAN of BEAUVAIS (St) M.
RM. Jan 8

See Lucian, Maximian, and Julian.

MAXIMIAN of RAVENNA (St) Bp.
RM. Feb 22

d. *c*.556. Consecrated bishop of Ravenna by Pope Vigilius in 546. He built the splendid basilica of St Vitalis, which was dedicated with much pomp in the presence of the emperor Justinian and his wife Theodora.

MAXIMIAN of CONSTANTI-NOPLE (St)   AC. Apr 21

d. 434. A Roman by birth, he became a priest and finally patriarch at Constantinople. He was highly esteemed by Pope Celestine I.

MAXIMIAN of SYRACUSE (St) Bp. OSB.   RM. June 9

d. 594. A Sicilian by birth and a monk of St Andrew's abbey on the Coelian Hill in Rome under St Gregory the Great. He served both Pope Pelagius and Gregory the Great as *Apocrisarius* in Constantinople. Recalled to Rome, he acted as minister to St Gregory, who finally appointed him bishop of Syracuse and apostolic legate in Sicily (591), where he died in the third year of his episcopate.

MAXIMIAN (St) M.   RM. Aug 21

See Bonosus and Maximian.

MAXIMIAN (St) Bp.   RM. Oct 3

d. 404. An African, a convert from Donatism, who was made bishop of Bagae (Bagaia) in Numidia. Finding his nomination displeasing to the people, he persuaded the Fathers of the council of Milevis to accept his resignation. Having deprived the Donatists of the basilica of Calvianum, he was grievously wounded and thrown from a tower by the heretics. Nursed back to life, he crossed over to Italy and obtained a decree of justification from the emperor Honorius.

MAXIMILIAN (St) M.
RM. March 12

d. 295. Otherwise Mamilian. The RM. appears to be wrong in placing his martyrdom at Rome. His Acts are genuine, and describe him as a young martyr who as a Christian refused to do military service and was therefore executed at Thebeste in Nimidia.

MAXIMILIAN (St) Bp. M.
RM. Oct 12
d. 284. A native of Novicum (the territory between the Inn and the Danube). He founded the church of Lorch (*Laurencum*), near Passau, and was martyred at Cilli in Styria, under Numerian. St Rupert of Salzburg erected churches in his name.

MAXIMILIAN (St) Bp. M.
RM. Oct 29
d. 284. A duplicate of St Maximilian of Lorch, coupled in the RM. with St Valentine, of whom nothing is known.

MAXIMINUS (St) M.　　RM. Jan 25
See Juventinus and Maximus.

MAXIMINUS of TRÈVES (St) Bp.
RM. May 29
d. *c*.349. Born at Silly near Poitiers and a brother of St Maxentius of Poitiers. In 333 he succeeded his teacher St Agrecius in the see of Trèves and became the valiant defender and host of St Athanasius of Alexandria and St Paul of Constantinople, exiled from their sees by the Arian emperor. He was a prominent opponent of Arianism in the councils of Milan, Sardica and Cologne. St Jerome describes him as "one of the most courageous bishops of his time".

MAXIMINUS of AIX (St) Bp.
RM. June 8
1st cent. (?). Venerated as the first bishop of Aix in Provence, and connected by legend with the mythical journey of St Mary Magdalen to Marseilles. Indeed, he is identified with the man born blind of John IX.

MAXIMINUS (MESMIN) (St) Ab.
RM. Dec 15
d. *c*.520. First abbot of the monastery of Micy, founded near Orleans by King Clovis.

MAXIMUS (St) Bp.　　RM. Jan 8
d. 511. There were two Bishops of Pavia of this name, both reputed as Saints. The one honoured today is the second. He assisted at Councils held at Rome under Pope Symmachus.

MAXIMUS of NOLA (St) Bp.
RM. Jan 15
d. *p*.250. Bishop of Nola. He ordained St Felix. During the persecution of Decius (250) he fled to the mountains, where he nearly died of exposure and hunger. He died at Nola worn out with the hardships he had endured for the Faith.

MAXIMUS (St) M.　　RM. Jan 25
Otherwise Maximinus. See Juventinus and Maximus.

MAXIMUS (St) M.　　RM. Feb 18
See Lucius, Silvanus, etc.

MAXIMUS, CLAUDIUS, PRAE-PEDIGNA, ALEXANDER and CUTIAS (SS) MM.　　RM. Feb 18
d. 295. These martyrs are supposed to have suffered under Diocletian, but their legend seems to be no more than a pious fiction.

MAXIMUS, QUINTILIAN and DADAS (SS) MM.　　RM. Apr 13
d. 303. Three brothers of Dorostorum, now Silistria on the Danube, in Bulgaria, beheaded at Ozobia under Diocletian. Maximus was a lector.

MAXIMUS (St) M.　　RM. Apr 14
See Tiburtius, Valerian and Maximus.

MAXIMUS and OLYMPIADES (SS) MM.　　RM. Apr 15
d. 251. Persian noblemen, martyred by being beaten to death with crowbars, under Decius.

MAXIMUS (St) M.   RM. Apr 30
d. *c*.251. A citizen of Ephesus, a merchant by profession, who on the publication of the edict of Decius against the Christians in 250, presented himself to the judge as a Christian and was accordingly martyred. His proconsular *Acta* are still extant.

MAXIMUS of JERUSALEM (St) Bp.
RM. May 5
d. *c*.350. A confessor of the faith under Diocletian. He survived the persecution, although a cripple for life, and eventually succeeded St Macarius in the see of Jerusalem. The Arians taking advantage of his simplicity used him as a tool against St Athanasius, but he afterwards made ample amends. The Greeks, however, do not venerate him.

MAXIMUS, BASSUS and FABIUS
(SS) MM.   RM. May 11
d. 304. Roman martyrs under Diocletian.

MAXIMUS (St) M.   RM. May 15
See Cassius, Victorinus, etc.

MAXIMUS and VICTORINUS (SS)
MM.   AC. May 25
d. *c*.384. Said to have been two brothers sent from Rome by Pope Damasus to preach in Gaul, and martyred by barbarians near Evreux.

MAXIMUS (St) Bp.   RM. May 29
? 6th cent. A bishop of Verona.

MAXIMUS (St) Bp. M. RM. June 10
4th cent. Tenth bishop of Naples (359). He died in exile and is honoured as a martyr.

MAXIMUS of TURIN (St) Bp.
RM. June 25
d. *c*.470. Bishop of Turin in the troublous times of the barbarian inroads into N. Italy. He is now best remem-

bered for his homilies and other ascetical writings, which are still extant.

MAXIMUS (St) M.   RM. July 20
See Sabinus, Julian, etc.

MAXIMUS of PADUA (St) Bp.
RM. Aug 2
2nd cent. Successor of St Prosdocimus as bishop of Padua. His alleged relics were found in 1053 and enshrined by Pope St Leo IX.

MAXIMUS HOMOLOGETES Ab.
and Comp. (SS) CC.   RM. Aug 13
580–662. A Greek of noble birth and a courtier at Byzantium, who became a monk, and later abbot, of Chrysopolis (Scutari). As such he firmly opposed the Monothelite heretics and upheld the authority of the Roman see. After assisting at the council of the Lateran held at Rome in 649 he stayed for some years in the Eternal City. In 655 he was seized by order of the Monothelite emperor, taken to Constantinople, maimed and exiled. He died near Batum in Transcaucasia. He was a prolific theological and ascetical writer. Several of his disciples, two of whom were named Anastasius, shared his exile and are honoured with him.

MAXIMUS (St)   RM. Aug 17
See Liberatus, Boniface, etc.

MAXIMUS (St) M.   RM. Aug 18
See Florus, Laurus, etc.

MAXIMUS (St) Ab.   RM. Aug 20
d. *c*.470. Abbot founder of Chinon in the diocese of Tours. A disciple of St Martin.

MAXIMUS (St) M.   RM. Aug 23
See Quiriacus, Maximus, etc.

MAXIMUS (St) M.   RM. Aug 25
Otherwise Maginus, q.v.

MAXIMUS (St) M.   RM. Sept 4
See Magnus, Castus, and Maximus.

MAXIMUS, THEODORE and
ASCLEPIODOTUS (SS) MM.
RM. Sept 15
d. c.310. Three martyrs, natives of Marcianopolis, an ancient town in what is
now Bulgaria, who suffered at Adrianopolis.

MAXIMUS (St) M.   RM. Sept 25
See Paul, Tatta, etc.

MAXIMUS (St) M.   RM. Sept 28
According to the best authorities, identical with the St Maximus, M., entered
under April 30 in the RM.

MAXIMUS of AQUILA (St) M.
RM. Oct 20
d. c.250. A deacon of Aquila in S. Italy,
conspicuous for his zeal, who was martyred by being cast down from an overhanging cliff near his native city, during
the persecution of Decius. He is now
venerated as the patron saint of Aquila.

MAXIMUS (St) M.   RM. Oct 30
d. 304. According to the RM. he was
martyred at Apamea in Phrygia, under
Diocletian. More likely, the place of his
martyrdom was Cuma (the ancient
Cumae) in Campania.

MAXIMUS of MAINZ (St) Bp.
RM. Nov 18
d. 378. The 19th bishop of Mainz, which
see he governed from c.354 to 378. He
suffered much at the hands of the Arians,
and was distinguished as a scholar and
writer.

MAXIMUS (St) M.   RM. Nov 19
d. c.255. A martyr who suffered in
Rome under Valerian.

MAXIMUS of RIEZ (St) Bp.
RM. Nov 27
d. 460. Appointed abbot of Lérins in
426 and promoted to the see of Riez,
much against his will, in 434, receiving
the episcopal consecration from St
Hilary. He was one of the most prominent prelates of the church of Gaul in
his time.

MAXIMUS (St) M.   RM. Dec 2
See Eusebius, Marcellus, etc.

MAXIMUS of ALEXANDRIA (St)
Bp.   RM. Dec 27
d. 282. A priest of Alexandria, who administered the patriarchate while St
Dionysius was in exile (251–264) and
finally succeeded him in the see (265–
282). He drove Paul of Samosata from
Egypt.

MAZOTA (St) V.   AC. Dec 23
? 8th cent. One of a band of nineteen
maidens who came over from Ireland to
Scotland and founded a community at
Abernethy on the Tay. Mazota seems
to have been their leader.

MBAGA TUZINDE (St) M.
RM. June 3
d. 1886. A page to King Mwanga of
Uganda and adopted son of the chief
executioner, he had to resist the pleas
of his family up to the very moment of
execution. He was burnt alive at Namuyongo. See Uganda (Martyrs of).

MECHTILD of SPANHEIM (Bl)
H. OSB.   PC. Feb 26
Otherwise Matilda of Spanheim, q.v.

MECHTILD (Bl) V.   AC. Apr 11
d. 1200. A virgin of Scottish origin who
passed with her brother into France and
spent her life as a recluse in the village
of Lappion, diocese of Laon.

MECHTILD of DIESSEN (St) Abs. OSB.   AC. May 31

1125–1160. Born at Andechs in Bavaria, daughter of Count Berthold of Andechs. At the age of five she was placed in a convent at Diessen, where in due time she professed the Benedictine Rule and became abbess. In 1153 she was entrusted by the bishop of Augsburg with the reform of the nunnery of Edelstetten, which she carried through in the teeth of fierce opposition, some of the nuns having in fact to be expelled. She was greatly revered by her contemporaries who credited her with the gift of miracles.

MECHTILD of MAGDEBURG (Bl) V. OSB.   AC. Oct 8

d. 1282. After living as a béguine for forty years, she became, towards the end of her life, a Benedictine at Helfta, where she was professed under Abbess Gertrude of Hackeborn and was a fellow-religious of St Mechtild of Hackeborn and St Gertrude the Great. Mechtild of Magdeburg was the first of the Helfta nuns known to have been favoured with mystical experiences.

MECHTILD of HACKEBORN (St) V. OSB.   AC. Nov 19

d. 1298. A Benedictine nun of Helfta, sister of the Abbess Gertrude of Hackeborn. She was the teacher and novicemistress of St Gertrude the Great. She too had mystical experiences, which were written down by St Gertrude in the *Book of Special Grace*.

MEDA (St) V.   AC. Jan 15

Otherwise Ita, q.v.

MEDAN (St)   AC. June 4

See Croidan, Medan, etc.

MEDANA (St) V.   AC. Nov 19

8th cent. An Irish maiden who passed over into Scotland and lived in Galloway. She is possibly identical with St Midnat venerated in West Mcath on Nov 18.

MEDARD (St) Bp.   RM. June 8

c.470–558. Born in Picardy, he was ordained when thirty-three years of age, and in 530 was raised to the see of Vermand, which he transferred to Noyon. At a later date he was entrusted also with the diocese of Tournai, which remained united with Noyon till 1146. See also St Gildard.

MEDERICUS (MERRY) (St) Ab. OSB.   RM. Aug 29

d. c.700. Born at Autun, he was offered to God at the age of thirteen in the abbey of St Martin of Autun, of which he eventually became abbot. Later he resigned and lived as a hermit in a cell near Paris, where now stands the church of Saint-Merry.

MEDRALD (MÉRALD, MÉRAUT) (St) Ab. OSB.   AC. Feb 23

d. c.850. A monk of Saint-Evroult (Ebrulfus) of Ouche: he became abbot of Vendôme.

MEDRAN and ODRAN (SS) CC.   AC. July 7

6th cent. Two brothers, disciples of St Kieran of Saghir, one of whom remained to the end with that holy man, while the other became the abbot-founder of a monastery at Muskerry.

MEEN (St) Ab.   AC. June 21

Otherwise Maine, q.v.

MEGINGAUD (MENGOLD, MEGINGOZ) (St) Bp. OSB.   AC. March 16

d. 794. Born of a Frankish family, he became a monk at Fritzlar (738), and after some years as teacher in the abbey school, was elected abbot. Later he succeeded St Burchard as bishop of Würzburg (c.754). In 787 he resigned and retired to the abbey of Neustadt where he died.

MEGINHARD (MEGINHER, MEGINARD) (Bl) Ab. OSB.
AC. Sept 26
d. 1059. A monk of Hersfeld in Germany who was chosen abbot in 1035. In 1037 he undertook the rebuilding of the monastery after it had been destroyed by fire. He was one of the best biblical scholars of the Middle Ages.

MEGINRATUS (St) M. RM. Jan 21
Otherwise Meinrad, q.v.

MEINGOLD (St)   AC. Feb 8
10th cent. There was a holy man, Meingold of Huy on the Meuse, who was venerated in Belgium after his death in the tenth century. Long afterwards he seems to have been confused with a certain Count Meingaud who was assassinated in 892.

MEINGOSUS (MEINGOS) (Bl) Ab. OSB.   AC. Apr 2
c.1200. Abbot of the great Benedictine abbey of Weingarten in Swabia from c.1188 to 1200.

MEINHARD (Bl) Bp. OSA.
AC. Apr 12
d. 1196. An Augustinian canon regular who went to preach in Latvia. In 1184 he was consecrated bishop and fixed his residence at Yxkill on the Düna. (The see was transferred to Riga in 1201.)

MEINRAD (St) M. OSB.
RM. Jan 21
d. 861. Born at Solgen in Swabia, of the noble family of Hohenzollern, and educated, professed and ordained a priest at the Benedictine abbey of Reichenau on the Rhine. Later he became a hermit in Switzerland, at the place where afterwards arose the abbey of Einsiedeln (i.e., Hermitage). He was a hermit twenty-five years and was murdered by robbers who thought to find hidden treasures in his cell. He has always been venerated as a martyr.

MEINULPH (St) C.   AC. Oct 5
d. c.859. A godson of Charlemagne. He founded the abbey of Bödeken in Westphalia, where he died.

MEINWERK (Bl) Bp.   AC. June 5
d. 1036. A relative of the emperor St Henry II by whom he was promoted to the see of Paderborn in 1009. On account of his building activities, which occupied him throughout his episcopal career, he has been called "the bishop-builder" and "the second founder of Paderborn". His cathedral school was famous all over N. Germany.

MEL (MELCHNO) (St) Bp.
AC. Feb 6
d. c 490. Said to have been one of the four nephews of St Patrick (viz., Mel, Melchu, Munis and Rioch), sons of Conis and Darerca, St Patrick's sister. They are further stated to have accompanied St Patrick to Ireland as missionaries, St Mel becoming the first abbot-bishop of Ardagh. The evidence, however, concerning him and his brothers is hopelessly entangled and conflicting.

MELAN (St) Bp.   AC. June 15
d. p.549. Bishop of Viviers from 519 till some time after 549, in which year he sent his representatives to the council held at Orleans.

MELANGELL (MONACELLA) (St) V.   AC. Jan 31
d. c.590. A virgin commemorated in certain Welsh calendars. She seems to

have been a recluse in Montgomery-shire.

MELANIA the ELDER (St) W.
AC. June 8
d. c.400. A patrician lady of Rome, of the family of the Valerii. She was interested in the Holy Land, which she was one of the first Roman matrons to visit.

MELANIA the YOUNGER and PINIAN (SS)   RM. Dec 31
5th cent. This Melania was the grand-daughter of St Melania the Elder. A Roman by birth, she belonged to the patrician family of the Valerii. She married her cousin St Pinian and they had two children who died young. About the year 410 husband and wife travelled to the East, the former entering a monastery and the latter a nunnery at Jerusalem. Melania outlived her husband, dying in 439.

MELANIUS (St) Bp.   RM. Jan 6
d. c.530. A Breton by birth, he was bishop of Rennes at the critical period when the Franks were overrunning Gaul. He is said to have almost completely succeeded in extirpating idolatry from his diocese. He was highly revered by King Clovis.

MELANIUS (St) Bp.   RM. Oct 22
Otherwise Mellonius, q.v.

MELANTIUS (St) Bp.   RM. Jan 16
Otherwise Melas, q.v.

MELAS (MELANTIUS) (St) Bp.
RM. Jan 16
d. c.385. A humble ascetic who was made Bishop of Rhinocolura, a little town on the Mediterranean near the boundary between Egypt and Palestine. During the Arian troubles he underwent imprisonment and banishment for the Catholic cause.

MELASIPPUS (St) Bp. RM. Jan 17
Otherwise Meleusippus, q.v.

MELASIPPUS, ANTONY and CARINA (SS) MM.   RM. Nov 7
d. 360. Antony, or Antoninus, was the child of Melasippus and Carina. All three were martyred at Ancyra, under Julian the Apostate. The parents died under torture, and their child was beheaded.

MELCHIADES (St) Pope M.
RM. Dec 10
Otherwise Miltiades, q.v.

MELCHIOR (St)   AC. Jan 6
One of the Magi, q.v.

MELCHIOR (Bl) M. SJ. AC. Sept 7
See Mark, Stephen and Melchior.

MELDON (MEDON) (St) Bp.
AC. Feb 7
6th cent. An Irishman who became an anchorite in France and died at Péronne, where he is the titular saint of several churches.

MELETIUS (St) Bp.   RM. Feb 12
d. 381. Born at Melitene in Armenia he became bishop of Sebaste (358) and then patriarch of Antioch (360) then in the throes of the Arian controversy. Within a month he was exiled by the Arian emperor. Recalled for a brief space, he was again banished and not fully reinstated till 378. In 381 he presided over the second general council of Constantinople, dying while the council was still sitting.

MELETIUS (St) M.   RM. May 24
? The *laus* in the RM. reads "The passion of the holy martyrs Meletius, a general of the army, and his 252 companions, who suffered martyrdom in various ways." Nothing more, that is

really trustworthy, can be stated about them.

MELETIUS (St) Bp. RM. Sept 21
? The Menology of Basil associates the name of this St Meletius with that of St Isacius, who is styled a martyr. They are both described as bishops in Cyprus.

MELETIUS (St) Bp. RM. Dec 4
d. *c*.295. A bishop in Pontus, he suffered much during the persecution of Diocletian. Eusebius, who knew him personally, tells us that Meletius derived his name from *Mel Atticum:* ("Attic honey") a phrase used to describe his eloquence. If so, we do not know his real name.

MELEUSIPPUS (St) M. RM. Jan 17
See Speusippus, Eleusippus, etc.

MELIOR (MIGLIORE, MILLORY) (Bl) H. OSB. Vall. AC. March 26
d. 1198. A priest and monk of Vallumbrosa, who after many years of cenobitical life, asked to become a recluse in the hermitage called *Massa delle Celle*, above Vallumbrosa. His relics are enshrined at Vallumbrosa in the "altar of the Ten Beati".

MELITINA (St) M. RM. Sept 15
Mid. 2nd cent. A maiden martyred at Marcianopolis in Thrace under Antoninus Pius. Her relics were translated to the isle of Lemnos.

MELITO of SARDIS (St) Bp.
         AC. Apr 1
d. *c*.180. A bishop of Sardis in Lydia and an ecclesiastical writer of the period of the Apologists. He had a great reputation, but very little of his work is extant.

MELLA (St) W. AC. Apr 25
d. *c*.780. Born in Connaught, Mella became the mother of two saints, Cannech

and Tigernach. After the death of her husband she embraced the religious life and died abbess of Doire-Melle, Leitrim.

MELLANIUS (St) Bp. RM. Oct 22
Otherwise Melanius, Mellonius, Mellon, Mellonus, Mello, Mullion, etc. In this dictionary we have adopted the form Mellonius, q.v.

MELLITUS (St) Bp. RM. Apr 24
d. 624. A Roman abbot, presumably from the monastery of St Andrew on the Coelian Hill, whom St Gregory the Great sent to England in the wake of St Augustine in 601 at the head of a second band of missionary monks. He spent three years in Kent, and then was stationed in London as its first bishop. He was banished to France for refusing holy communion to the apostate sons of King Sigebert. In 619 he was recalled to Kent to succeed St Laurence as archbishop of Canterbury.

MELLONIUS (St) Bp. RM. Oct 22
d. 314. Said to have been a Briton, born near Cardiff, in the district called St Mellon's, and to have been the first bishop of Rouen.

MELORIUS (St) M. AC. Oct 1
8th cent. Son of a king of Armorican Cornwall, done to death when a child. He was at one time venerated at Amesbury in Wiltshire, and his cult still survives at Quimper in Brittany.

MEMMIUS (MENGE, MEINGE) (St) Bp. RM. Aug 5
d. *c*.300. Founder and first bishop of the see of Châlons-sur-Marne, and the apostle of that district. He preached during the second half of the 3rd century, the legend which makes him a disciple of St Peter being now discredited.

MEMNON (St) M.   RM. Aug 20
See Severus, Memnon and Comp.

MEMORIUS and Comp. (SS) MM.
                                    RM. Sept 7
d. 451. Memorius, registered in the RM.
as Nemorius and popularly known as
St Mesmin, was a deacon of Troyes,
under St Lupus, by whom he was sent
with five companions to the camp of
Attila, to implore the mercy of the
barbarian leader. Attila had them all
beheaded. The story is not trustworthy.
The relics of the martyrs are still the
object of great veneration.

MENALIPPUS (St) M.   RM. Sept 2
See Diomedes, Julian, etc.

MENANDER (St) M.   RM. Apr 28
See Patrick, Acacius, etc.

MENANDER (St) M.   RM. Aug 1
See Cyril, Aquila, etc.

MENEDEMUS (St) M.   RM. Sept 5
One of the group Urban, Theodore,
and Comp. q.v.

MENEFRIDA (St) V.   AC. July 24
5th cent. Of the family of Brychan of
Brecknock. She is the patron saint of
Menver, in Cornwall.

MENEHOULD (St) V.   AC. Oct 14
5th cent. Patron saint of the French
town in the Argonne called after her.
With her five sisters, likewise honoured
as saints, she brought fame by her
sanctity to the diocese of Châlons-sur-
Marne.

**MENELEUS (French: MENELE,
MAUVIER) (St) Ab. OSB.**
                                    RM. July 22
d. c.720. Born in Anjou, he became a
monk of Carméry in Auvergne. Seven
years afterwards he left the abbey and

became the abbot-restorer of the monastery of Ménat near Clermont.

**MENEUS (or HYMENAEUS) and
CAPITO (SS) MM.   RM. July 24**
? Martyrs commemorated in both the
Greek and the Latin menologies, of
whom, however, nothing is known.

MENIGNUS (St) M. RM. March 15
d. 251. A martyr who suffered at Parium
on the Hellespont under Decius. He was
a dyer by trade. He tore down the
imperial edict against the Christians. In
punishment for this his fingers were
cut off. Later he was beheaded for the
faith.

MENNA (MANNA) V.   AC. Oct 3
d. c.395. A maiden of Lorraine said to
have been related by blood to SS Eucherius and Elaptius (MM.) and other
saints. The particulars of her life as they
have reached us are very unreliable.

MENNAS (MENAS) (St) Bp.
                                    RM. Aug 25
d. 552. A native of Alexandria who became superior of the hospice of St
Samson at Constantinople and later was
promoted patriarch of the latter city in
536. He condemned Origenism, but
subscribed to the decrees of the emperor
Justinian on "the Three Chapters" and
was for this reason excommunicated by
Pope Vigilius in 551. He submitted at
once, and died shortly after.

MENNAS (St) M.   RM. Nov 11
d. c.295. An Egyptian, martyred at
Karm Aba-Mina, near Alexandria. At a
later period he was said to have been an
officer in the imperial army and was
venerated as one of the great warrior
saints, whose cult was so much in vogue
during the Middle Ages. The legends
woven around his name are as numerous as they are untrustworthy.

MENNAS (St) H.   RM. Nov 11
d. 6th cent. A Greek from Asia Minor,
who became a hermit in the Abruzzi,
probably at Santomena (*Sanctus Menna*)
in the diocese of Conza. St Gregory the
Great (Dial., III, 26) enlarges upon his
virtues and miracles.

MENNAS, HERMOGENES, and
EUGRAPHUS (SS) MM. RM. Dec 10
d. *c*.312. Three martyrs who were beheaded at Alexandria under Diocletian.
Their *Passio* is worthless; it has been
falsely ascribed to St Athanasius.

MENODORA, METRODORA and
NYMPHODORA (SS) VV. MM.
                          RM. Sept 10
d. 306. Three sisters who were martyred
under Maximian Galerius near the
Pythian baths or hot springs in Bithynia.
These bare facts are certain; but not so
the later *Acta* based upon them.

MENULPHUS (MENOU) (St) Bp.
                          AC. July 12
7th cent. Said to have been an Irish pilgrim who became bishop of Quimper in
Brittany and died in the neighbourhood
of Bourges while on his return journey
from Rome.

MERCOLINO of FORLÌ (Bl) C. OP.
                          AC. Jan 24
Otherwise Marcolino of Forlì, q.v.

MERCURIA (St) M.   RM. Dec 12
See Ammonaria, Mercuria, etc.

MERCURIALIS (St) Bp.
                          RM. May 23
d. *c*.406. First bishop of Forlì in central
Italy. He was a zealous opponent of
paganism and Arianism. His life became
the subject of many extravagant legends.

MERCURIUS (St) M.   RM. Nov 25
d. *c*.250. An alleged Scythian officer in
the imperial army, martyred at Caesarea
in Cappadocia under Decius. He forms
one of the group of "Warrior Saints".

MERCURIUS and Comp. (SS) MM.
                          RM. Dec 10
d. *c*.300. (?) A group of soldiers told off
to escort Christian prisoners to their
place of execution at Lentini (*Leontium*)
in Sicily. The soldiers were so impressed
with the behaviour of the prisoners that
they too declared themselves believers
in Christ, and soldiers and prisoners
were beheaded together.

MEREWENNA (MERWENNA,
MERWINNA) (St) Abs. OSB.
                          AC. May 13
d. *c*.970. Abbess of Rumsey, a nunnery
in Hampshire, restored under King
Edgar the Peaceful.

MEREWENNA (St) V.   AC. Aug 12
? Titular saint of Marhamchurch, near
Bude in Cornwall. She is said to have
been one of the daughters of Brychan of
Brecknock.

MERIADEC (St) Bp.   AC. June 7
d. *c*.886 (?). Probably a Welshman by
birth. He became a hermit-priest and
later bishop of Vannes in Brittany,
where he is greatly venerated. The details of his life are of small historical
value.

MERIADEC (St) Bp.   AC. June 7
d. 1302. Born in Brittany, he was ordained priest and retired to a solitude to
live as a hermit, but was forced to
abandon it on being elected by the
clergy bishop of Vannes. He was known
far and wide for his charity to the poor.

MERINUS (St) H.   AC. Jan 6
6th cent. A disciple of Dunawd of Bangor and titular saint of churches in
Wales and Brittany.

MERINUS (MERRYN, MEADH-RAN) (St) Bp.   AC. Sept 15
d. c.620. A disciple of St Comgall at Bangor, venerated both in Scotland and in Ireland.

MERILILAUN (MEROLILAUN) (St) M.   AC. May 18
8th cent. A British pilgrim who met his death by violence near Reims while on his way to Rome and has since been popularly venerated as a martyr.

MERRI or MERRY (St) Ab.
          RM. Aug 29
Otherwise Medericus, q.v.

MERRYN (MEADHRAN) (St)
          AC. Sept 15
Otherwise Merinus, q.v.

MERULUS (St) Mk. OSB.
          RM. Jan 17
See Antony, Merulus and John.

MERWENNA (St) Abs. OSB.
          AC. May 13
Otherwise Merewenna, q.v.

MESME (St)   Aug 20
See Maximus.

MESMIN (St) M.   RM. Sept 7
Otherwise Memorius, q.v.

MESMIN (St)   RM. Dec 15
Otherwise Maximinus, q.v.

MESOPOTAMIA (Martyrs of)
          RM. May 23
d. c.307. A group of martyrs who suffered in Mesopotamia under Maximian Galerius.

MESROB (St) C.   AC. Nov 25
d. 441. Surnamed "the Teacher". A native of the province of Taron in Armenia, he became a disciple of St Nerses the Great and a monk. Later he became a missionary under St Isaac the Great. The Armenians attribute to him the invention of their alphabet and the translation of the New Testament into Armenian. He certainly organized schools and studies throughout the country. Indeed, he was one of the most remarkable oriental churchmen of his time.

MESSALINA (St) VM.   AC. Jan 19
d. 251. A maiden of Foligno, who received the veil from St Felician, bishop of that city. She is said to have visited him in prison and to have been thereupon delated as a Christian and clubbed to death.

MESSIANUS (St) M.   RM. Jan 8
Otherwise Maximian. See Lucian, Maximian and Julian.

METELLUS (St) M.   RM. Jan 24
See Mardonius, Musonius, etc.

METHODIUS (St) Bp.
          RM. Apr 6 and July 7
See Cyril and Methodius.

METHODIUS the CONFESSOR (St) Bp.   RM. June 14
d. 847. A Sicilian who founded a monastery on the island of Chios. He was sent to Rome to report on the iconoclastic persecution of the Holy See. On his return to Constantinople he was detained in prison for seven years. Finally in 842, the empress Theodora induced him to become patriarch of Constantinople. In this position he did excellent work in restoring the faith after thirty years of iconoclastic rule.

METHODIUS (St) Bp. M.
          RM. Sept 18
d. 311. Bishop of Olympus in Lycia, and then of Tyre in Phoenicia. He is generally supposed to have died a martyr at Chalcis. He is now better known

as an ecclesiastical writer of distinction, especially for his *Banquet of the Ten Virgins*, an imitation of Plato's *Symposion*, and for his treatise on the Resurrection.

METRANUS (METRAS) (St) M.
                                  RM. Jan 31
d. *c*.250. An Egyptian of Alexandria, martyred under Decius. St Dionysius of Alexandria, his bishop and contemporary, has left a vivid account of the martyrdom.

METROBIUS (St) M.   RM. Dec 24
See Lucian, Metrobius, etc.

METRODORA (St) VM.
                                  RM. Sept 10
See Menodora, Metrodora and Nymphodora.

METROPHANES (St) Bp.
                                  RM. June 4
d. 325. Bishop of Byzantium from 313 to 325, and supposed to have been the first occupant of that see. Very little, however, is known about him.

MEUGANT (MAWGHAN, MORGAN) (St)   AC. Sept 26
6th cent. He appears to have been a disciple of St Illtyd, to have lived as a hermit in several places in W. Britain, and to have died on the isle of Bardsey. Several churches in Wales and Cornwall are dedicated to him.

MEURIS and THEA (SS) MM.
                                  RM. Dec 19
d. *c*.307. Two maidens martyred at Gaza in Palestine. They are probably identical with the St Valentina and her anonymous fellow-martyr commemorated on July 25.

MAVENUS (MAVENNA) (St) Ab.
                                  AC. June 21
Otherwise Maine, q.v.

MEWAN (St) Ab.   AC. June 21
The Cornish form of the name Maine, q.v.

MEWROG (St) C.   AC. Sept 25
? A Denbighshire saint, concerning whom no particulars are extant.

MICAH (MICHAEAS) (St) Prophet
                                  RM. Jan 15
8th cent. B.C. One of the twelve minor prophets. His book contains the prophecy of Christ's birth in Bethlehem. His presence in the RM. is due to an alleged finding of his remains.

MICHAEL PINI (Bl) H. OSB. Cam.
                                  PC. Jan 27
c.1445–1522. Born at Florence, he was in high favour at the court of Lorenzo de' Medici before becoming a Camaldolese hermit (1502). After ordination to the priesthood he was walled up in his hermitage, where he remained till his death.

MICHAEL COZAKI (St) M.
                                  RM. Feb 5
d. 1597. A Japanese catechist and hospital nurse to the Franciscan missionaries. He was crucified at Nagasaki with St Peter Baptist and other companions including his own son, St Thomas Cozaki. Beatified in 1627, and canonized in 1862.

MICHAEL of the SAINTS (St) C. O. Trin.   RM. Apr 10
1591–1625. Born at Vich, in Spanish Catalonia, he joined the calced Trinitarians at Barcelona in 1603, and took his vows at Saragossa in 1607. This same year he passed over to the discalced Trinitarians and renewed his vows at Alcalá. After his ordination he was twice superior at Valladolid, where he died. He was one of the greatest apostles of the Holy Eucharist in 17th century Spain. Canonized in 1862.

MICHAEL ULUMBIJSKI (St) C.
AC. May 7
6th cent. One of the twelve companions of St John Zedazneli (Nov 7) in Georgia, q.v.

MICHAEL the ARCHANGEL (St)
RM. May 8 and Sept 29
One of the three angels (Michael, Gabriel, Raphael) liturgically venerated by the Church, and also described as one of the Seven Angels who stand before the throne of God (q.v.). Holy Scripture describes Michael as "one of the chief princes" (Dan. X, 13); and as the leader of the heavenly armies in their battle against the forces of hell (Apoc. XII, 7). He is mentioned also in the epistle of St Jude as "rebuking the devil". IIc has always been especially invoked by the Catholic Church both in the East and in the West. His feast on Sept 29 is probably the anniversary of the dedication of a church of St Michael and All Angels on the Salarian Way at Rome in the 6th century; that of May 8 commemorates his apparition on Mt Gargano in S. Italy (also 6th century). Another apparition in France (8th century) led to the foundation of Mont Saint-Michel "in peril of the sea" (*in periculo maris*), in Brittany.

MICHAEL GARICOITS (St)
Founder   **RM. May 14**
1797–1863. Born near Bayonne, the son of a Pyrenean peasant, he acted as servant to his parish priest, and later to the bishop of Bayonne, in return for his education. He was ordained priest in 1823, and after holding a curacy for a short time was appointed professor of philosophy, and eventually rector of the diocesan seminary. As such he founded in 1838 at Bétharram the congregation of Auxiliary Priests of the Sacred Heart, known as the Bétharram Fathers, for mission work among the people. After

encountering many initial difficulties the Congregation grew and spread beyond France and across the Atlantic. Canonized in 1947.

MICHAEL GEDROYE (Bl) OSA.
AC. May 4
d. 1485. Born near Vilna in Lithuania of noble parentage. He was a cripple and a dwarf. He took up his abode in a cell adjoining the church of the Augustinian canons regular at Cracow, and there he lived all his life, famous for his gifts of prophecy and miracles.

MICHAEL HO-DINH-HY (Bl) M.
AC. May 22
c.1808–1857. Born at Nhu-lam in Cochin-China of Christian parents, he became a Great Mandarin and superintendent of the royal silk mills. For a long time he did not practise his religion, but eventually became leader and protector of his fellow-Christians. He was for this reason beheaded at An-Hoa, near Hué, in N. Cochin-China. Beatified in 1909.

MICHAEL of SYNNADA (St) Bp.
RM. May 23
d. c.820. A disciple of St Tarasius of Constantinople, by whom he was consecrated bishop of Synnada in Phrygia. Tarasius also chose Michael as the bearer of his synodal letter to the pope St Leo III in Rome. Michael was a fearless opponent of the iconoclasts. He was for this reason banished to Galatia by the emperor Leo the Armenian.

MICHAEL TOZO (Bl) M.
AC. June 20
d. 1626. A native of Japan, catechist to Bl Balthassar Torres. He was burnt alive at Nagasaki. Beatified in 1867.

MICHAEL MI (Bl) M.   AC. Aug 12
d. 1838. Born in Tonkin. He was mayor

of Ke-Vinh, and a married man. He was martyred with BB Antony Dich his son-in-law and James Nam. Beatified in 1900.

MICHAEL KIRAIEMON (Bl) M. Tert. OFM.   AC. Aug 17

d. 1627. A native of Japan and tertiary of St Francis. Beheaded at Nagasaki. Beatified in 1867.

MICHAEL DIAZ (Bl) M.
AC. Aug 19

d. 1622. A Spanish merchant on the Japanese ship of Bl Joachim Firaiama (q.v.). He was beheaded at Nagasaki. Beatified in 1867.

MICHAEL CARVALHO (Bl) M. SJ.
AC. Aug 25

1577–1624. Born at Braga in Portugal, he entered the Society of Jesus in 1597 and was sent to Goa, where he was ordained priest and taught theology for fifteen years. He was next dispatched to Japan, which he reached after many adventures. In July 1623 he was arrested and finally roasted to death at Ximabura with BB Peter Vasquez, OP., Louis Sotelo, OFM. and two other Friars Minor. Beatified in 1867.

MICHAEL GHEBRE (Bl) M. CM.
AC. Sept 1

1791–1855. Born in Abyssinia of dissident parents, he became an orthodox monk in that country and was known for his zeal and scholarship. Contact with missionary fathers of St Vincent of Paul brought to him at the age of fifty the grace of conversion. In 1844 he was reconciled to the Catholic Church and in 1851 was ordained priest, having already joined the Vincentian Fathers. In 1855 a persecution was launched against the Ethiopian Catholics by their new *negus*, Theodore II. Michael was arrested and died from the ill-usage he received at the hands of his gaolers. Beatified in 1926.

MICHAEL JAMADA (Bl) M. Tert. OP.   AC. Sept 8

d. 1628. A Japanese and a Dominican tertiary, beheaded at Nagasaki. Beatified in 1867.

MICHAEL TOMAKI (Bl) M.
AC. Sept 8

1613–1626. A Japanese boy of thirteen beheaded at Nagasaki with his father, Bl John Tomaki, and his three brothers. Beatified in 1867.

MICHAEL XUMPO (Bl) M. SJ.
AC. Sept 10

1589–1622. A Japanese, who attached himself to the Jesuit missionaries when only eight years old. He was received into the Society of Jesus by Bl Charles Spinola in the prison at Omura and later burnt alive at Nagasaki. Beatified in 1867.

MICHAEL YAMIKI (Bl) M.
AC. Sept 10

1617–1622. The five-year-old son of Bl Damian Yamiki, beheaded at Nagasaki with his father on the day of the great martyrdom. Beatified in 1867.

MICHAEL FIMONAYA (Bl) M. Tert. OP.   AC. Sept 16

d. 1628. A Japanese catechist and Dominican tertiary, beheaded at Nagasaki. Beatified in 1867.

MICHAEL KINOXI (Bl) M. Tert. OSA.   AC. Sept 28

d. 1630. A native of Japan, beheaded at Nagasaki for having given shelter to the missionaries. He was an Augustinian tertiary. Beatified in 1867.

MICHAEL TAKEXITA (Bl) M.
AC. Nov 27

d. 1619. A Japanese layman, of the royal

family of Firando. He is described as a man of most amiable character. He was beheaded, at the age of twenty-five, at Nagasaki, with ten companions. Beatified in 1867.

MICHAEL NAKAXIMA (Bl) M. SJ.
AC. Dec 25

d. 1628. Born at Maciai in Japan. He concealed the missionary priests in his house and was admitted to the Society of Jesus. From the year 1627 to September 1628 he was kept a prisoner in his own house. He was then taken to Ximabara and after many tortures brought to the hot springs of Mt Ungen, where scalding water was poured upon him until he died. Beatified in 1867.

MICHAELA of the MOST HOLY SACRAMENT (St)   AC. Aug 26
Otherwise Mary-Michaela, q.v.

MICHELINA of PESARO (Bl) W. Tert. OFM.   AC. June 20

1300–1356. Michelina Metelli was born at Pesaro, in the duchy of Urbino, of the family of the counts of Pardi. At the age of twelve she married Duke Malatesta and was left a widow when she was only twenty. On the death of her only child she determined to change her life, but met with opposition from her parents who shut her up as a lunatic. When set free she gave up her fortune, became a Franciscan tertiary, and lived as such till her death. Cult confirmed in 1737.

MIDA (St) V.   AC. Jan 15
Otherwise Ita, q.v.

MIDAN (NIDAN) (St)
AC. Sept 30

d. c.610. A saint of Anglesey who flourished early in the 7th century.

MIDNAT (St) V.   AC. Nov 18
Otherwise Medana, q.v.

MIGDONIUS and MARDONIUS (SS) MM.   RM. Dec 23

d. 303. High officials at the imperial court of Rome. When the persecution broke out under Diocletian in 303, they refused to renounce their Christian faith. Migdonius was for this reason burnt at the stake and Mardonius drowned in a well.

MILBURGA (St) Abs. OSB.
RM. Feb 23

d. 722. The elder sister of St Mildred of Thanet, and abbess-foundress of Wenlock in Salop. Archbishop St Theodore consecrated her abbess and the nunnery is said to have greatly flourished under her rule. She had the gift of miracles and a mysterious power over birds.

MILDGYTHA (St) N. OSB.
AC. Jan 17

d. c.676. The youngest of the three holy virgins of Thanet—Milburga, Mildred and Mildgytha. She received the veil at Minster in Thanet, where her own mother, St Ermenburga, or Domneva, was abbess. Later she migrated to a convent in Northumbria, where she died.

MILDRED of THANET (St) Abs. OSB.   AC. July 13

d. c.700 (or 725?). One of the three daughters of St Ermenburga of Thanet. She was sent by her mother to be educated in the French nunnery of Chelles, and on her return, received the Benedictine habit from St Theodore of Canterbury at Minster in Thanet, where she eventually succeeded her mother as abbess. Her relics were first enshrined at Canterbury and afterwards removed to Holland, whence a part of them have been in recent times brought back to Minster. Mildred was one of the most popular saints in medieval England. In her life she is described as "ever merciful, of easy temper and tranquil".

MILES GERARD (Bl) M.
AC. Apr 30

d. 1590. *Alias* William Richardson. He was born near Wigan and became a schoolmaster. Afterwards he studied for the priesthood at Reims and was ordained in 1583. He was martyred for his priesthood at Rochester. Beatified in 1929.

MILLES (St) M.   RM. Apr 22
d. 380. A Persian bishop martyred under King Shapur II.

MILO (Bl) Bp.   PC. Feb 23
d. 1076. Born in Auvergne, he was made canon of Paris and dean of the chapter, and finally (1074) archbishop of Benevento in Italy. He died two years later.

MILO (Bl) Bp. O. Praem.
PC. July 16

d. 1159. Milo of Selincourt was a disciple of St Norbert. He became abbot of Donmartin in 1123 and bishop of Thérouanne in 1131. He was one of the ablest opponents of Gilbert de la Porrée.

MILO (Bl) H. OSB.   PC. Aug 18
d. *c*.740. His parents who were noble Franks both entered the cloister; Milo entered with his father at Fontenelle and later became a recluse.

MILTIADES (St) Pope RM. Dec 10
d. 314. Wrongly spelt in the RM. and elsewhere Melchiades. An African by birth, he was pope from 311 to 314, during which period the emperor Constantine granted toleration to the Church. St Miltiades is venerated as a martyr on account of his many sufferings during the persecution of Maximian.

MINERVINUS (St) M. RM. Dec 31
See Stephen, Pontian, etc.

MINERVIUS, ELEAZAR and Comp. (SS) MM.   RM. Aug 23
3rd cent. The details of the passion of these martyrs are wanting, and those given in the chronicles are untrustworthy. It seems fairly clear that they suffered at Lyons. Eight children are said to have been included in their number, and these are alleged to have been the children either of Minervius or of Eleazar. Eleazar is believed by some to have been a woman, perhaps the wife of Minervius.

MINIAS (Italian: MINIATO) (St) M.
RM. Oct 25

d. *c*.250. A soldier, stationed at Florence, where he spread the faith among his comrades, and where he was martyred under Decius.

MINNBORINUS (St) Ab. OSB.
AC. July 18

d. 986. An Irishman, who became abbot of St Martin at Cologne (974–986).

MIRO (Bl) C. OSA.   AC. Sept 12
d. 1161. An Augustinian canon regular at St John de las Abadesas, near Vich, in Spanish Catalonia.

MIROCLES (St) Bp.   RM. Dec 3
d. 318. Archbishop of Milan, one of the originators of the Ambrosian liturgy and chant.

MISAEL (MISHAEL, MISACH) (St)   RM. Dec 16
7th cent. B.C. One of the three Hebrew youths cast into the fiery furnace at Babylon and miraculously delivered unscathed therefrom (Dan. III).

MITRIUS (French: MITRE, METRE, MERRE) (St) M.
RM. Nov 13

d. 314. A Greek slave belonging to a tyrannical master at Aix in Provence.

He was savagely ill-used by his master
and by his fellow-slaves, and finally beheaded.

MNASON (St)   RM. July 12
Otherwise Jason, q.v.

MO
Note. The syllable mo (my) often prefixed to the names of Irish saints has an
honorific significance.

MOBEOC (MOBHEOC) (St) Ab.
                              AC. Jan 1
Otherwise Beoc, q.v.

**MOCHOEMOC (MOCHAEMHOG,
PULCHERIUS, VULCANIUS) (St)
Ab.**   AC. March 13
d. *c.*656. He was born in Munster and
brought up by his aunt, St Ita. He became a monk of Bangor in Co. Down
under St Comgall, and later the abbot-
founder of Liath-Mochoemoc. All
other information we have about him is
pure legend.

**MOCHELLOC (CELLOG, MOT-
TELOG, MOTALOGUS) (St)**
                              AC. March 26
d. *c.*639. Patron saint of Kilmallock in
Limerick. Authentic particulars of his
life are lacking.

MOCHTA (MOCHTEUS) (St) Bp.
                              AC. Aug 19
6th cent. A Briton by birth, he founded
the monastery of Louth in the East of
Ireland. His life is a tissue of miraculous fables.

MOCHUA (St) Ab.   AC. Jan 1
Otherwise Cuan, q.v. Several Irish
saints are honoured under the name of
Mochua on various days.

MOCHUDA (St) Bp.   AC. May 14
Otherwise Carthage the Younger, q.v.

MODAN (St) Ab.   AC. Feb 4
? 6th cent. The son of an Irish chieftain,
who preached at Stirling, Falkirk, and
along the Forth, retiring in his old age
to a solitude near Dumbarton.

MODANIC (St) Bp.   AC. Nov 14
? A Scottish bishop, whose feast was
kept at Aberdeen, but of whom we have
no reliable particulars.

**MODERAN (MODERAMNUS,
MORAN) (St) Bp. OSB.** AC. Oct 22
d. *c.*730. A native of Rennes who became bishop of that city in 703. About
the year 720 he made a pilgrimage to
Rome, resigned his see and ended his
days as a monk-hermit in the abbey of
Berceto, in the diocese of Parma.

MODESTA (St) M.   RM. March 13
See Macedonius, Patricia and Modesta.

MODESTA (St) Ab. OSB.
                              RM. Nov 4
d. *c.*680. Niece of St Mocoald, and first
abbess of the nunnery of Oehren (*Horreum*) at Trèves, to which office she was
appointed by its founder St Modoald.

MODESTUS (St) M.   RM. Jan 12
See Zoticus, Rogatus, etc.

MODESTUS (St) Bp. OSB.
                              AC. Feb 5
d. *c.*722. A monk under St Virgilius,
abbot-bishop of Salzburg. He was
appointed regionary bishop of Carinthia
and was largely responsible for the
evangelization of that country.

MODESTUS and JULIAN (SS) MM.
                              RM. Feb 12
? Modestus was martyred at Carthage,
Julian at Alexandria (in 160). The
former is venerated as the patron saint
of Cartagena in Spain. Their association
in the RM. is arbitrary.

MODESTUS and AMMONIUS (SS)
MM.   RM. Feb 12
? Martyrs at Alexandria in Egypt. They
are said to have been the children of St
Damien, martyr (Feb 12). Nothing is
known about them.

MODESTUS (St) M.   RM. Feb 12
d. c.304. A deacon, said to have been a
native of Sardinia, martyred under Diocletian. His relics were brought to
Benevento c.785.

MODESTUS (St) Bp.   RM. Feb 24
d. 489. Bishop of Trèves from 486 to
489, that is, during the difficult period
when the city came under Frankish
rule. His relics are venerated in the
church of St Matthias at Trèves.

MODESTUS (St) M.   RM. June 15
See Vitus, Modestus and Crescentia.

MODESTUS (St) M.   RM. Nov 10
See Tiberius, Modestus and Florentia.

MODOALD (St) Bp.   RM. May 12
d. 640. A native of Gascony, related by
blood and united in friendship with
most of the saints of the Merovingian
period. From being the adviser of King
Dagobert I, he was raised in 622 to the
see of Trèves, which he governed most
successfully till his death.

MODOC (St) Bp.   AC. Jan 31
Otherwise Aidan of Ferns, q.v.

MODOMNOCK (DOMNOC,
DOMINIC) (St) Bp.   AC. Feb 13
d. c.550. An alleged descendant of the
Irish royal line of O'Neil. He was a
disciple of St David in Wales, and
afterwards a hermit at Tibraghny in
Kilkenny, and, some writers add, a
bishop.

MODWENNA (St) V.   AC. July 5
Also called Edana, Medana, Monyna,

Merryn, and in French Modivene. Four
or five saints of this name are listed in
different menologies, but their lives are
hopelessly confused. Two seem to have
been more important than the rest: (1)
St Modwenna who succeeded St Hilda
as abbess of Whitby (d. c.695); and (2)
St Modwenna, abbess of Polesworth in
Warwickshire (d. c.900).

MOELIAI (MOELRAY) (St) Ab.
                             AC. June 23
d. c.493. A native of Ireland, baptized
by St Patrick, and by him set over the
newly founded monastery of Nendrum,
where he had SS Finian and Colman
among his disciples.

MOGUE (St) Bp.   AC. Jan 31
Otherwise Aidan, q.v.

MOLAGGA (LAICIN) (St) Ab.
                             AC. Jan 20
d. c.655. An Irishman, brought up in
Wales under St David. He founded a
monastery at Fulachmhin (Fermoy)
He is much venerated in S. Ireland.

MOLAISRE (St) Bp.   AC. Apr 18
Otherwise Laserian, q.v.

MOLLING (MOLING, MYLLIN,
MOLIGNUS, or DAIRCHILLA) (St)
Bp.   AC. June 17
d. 697. Born in Wexford, he is said to
have been a monk at Glendalough and
afterwards abbot at Aghacainid (Tegh-
molin, St Mullins). Later, he succeeded
St Aidan in the see of Ferns, having the
whole of Leinster under his jurisdiction.
He resigned some years before his death.

MOLOC (MOLLUOG, MURLACH,
LUGAIDH) (St) Bp.   AC. June 25
d. c.572. A Scot, who was educated in
Ireland and then returned to his native
land as a missionary. His main work as
a bishop was the evangelization of the

Hebrides. He died at Rossmarkie, but his shrine was at Mortlach.

MOLONACHUS (St) Bp.
AC. June 25

7th cent. A disciple of St Brendan who became bishop of Lismore in Argyle.

MOLUA (St) Ab.   AC. Aug 4
Otherwise Luanus, q.v.

MOMMOLINUS (St) Ab. OSB.
AC. Oct 16

Otherwise Mummolinus, q.v.

MOMMOLUS (St)
Otherwise Mummolus (q.v.)

MONACELLA (St) V.   AC. Jan 31
Otherwise Melangell, q.v.

MONALDUS of ANCONA, AN-TONY of MILAN and FRANCIS of FERMO (BB) MM. OFM.
PC. March 15

d. 1286. Three Franciscan friars who were sent to Armenia to preach the Gospel and were martyred there.

MONAN (St) M.   AC. March 1
d. 874. A saint trained under St Adrian of St Andrew's, and a missionary in the country about the Firth of Forth. He was slain by the Danes, together with a great number of fellow-Christians.

MONAS (St) Bp.   RM. Oct 12
d. 249. Bishop of Milan from 193 till his death, i.e., for fifty-six years. He lived through several persecutions.

MONEGUNDIS (St)   RM. July 2
d. 570. A woman of Chartres who, on the death of her two daughters, obtained the consent of her husband to become a hermit. She spent the better part of her life in a cell at Tours, where she died. Round her deathbed were gathered several nuns who had followed her example and who later united in forming the original community of Saint-Pierre-le-Puellier.

MONESSA (St) V.   AC. Sept 4
d. 456. Daughter of an Irish chieftain converted by St Patrick. The tradition is that she died on coming out of the baptismal font.

MONICA (St) W.   RM. May 4
332–387. Born at Carthage of Christian parentage, but married to a pagan husband, she was the mother of three children. Her husband's example led to the lapse from the Faith of her elder son, St Augustine, the future Doctor of the Church. Through her patience and gentleness she converted her husband, and after his death her prayers and tears were rewarded by the return of Augustine to the practice of the Catholic Faith. Monica followed him to Rome, where the longed-for conversion took place. She died the same year at Ostia, near Rome, on the way back to Africa with Augustine.

MONICA (Bl) M.   AC. July 12
d. 1626. A native Japanese woman, wife of Bl John Naisen, with whom she was beheaded at Nagasaki for having given shelter to Bl John Baptist Zola. Beatified in 1867.

MONINNE (or DARERCA) (St) V.
AC. July 6

d. 518. An Irish hermit at Sliabh Cuillin, where she died.

MONITOR (St) Bp.   RM. Nov 10
d. c.490. Twelfth bishop of Orleans.

MONON (St) M.   AC. Oct 18
c.645. A Scottish pilgrim who crossed over to the Continent and lived as a hermit in the Ardennes. He was murdered

at Nassogne, in Belgian Luxemburg, by some evil-doers whom he had reproved.

MONTANUS, LUCIUS, JULIAN, VICTORICUS, FLAVIAN and Comp. (SS) MM.   RM. Feb 24

d. 259. A group of ten African martyrs, disciples of St Cyprian of Carthage, who suffered in that city under Valerian. Their *Acta* are thoroughly authentic: the story of their imprisonment is told by themselves, and that of their martyrdom by eye-witnesses.

MONTANUS and MAXIMA (SS) MM.   RM. March 26

d. 304. Montanus, a priest, and Maxima, said to have been his wife, were drowned as Christians in the R. Save at Sirmium, in Dalmatia, or Singidunum, Pannonia.

MONTANUS (St) M.   RM. June 17

d. *c*.300. A soldier, who was taken to the island of Ponza, off the Italian coast, and martyred there by being thrown into the sea with a heavy stone tied round his neck. The Christians recovered his body and enshrined it at Gaeta.

MORANDUS (St) Mk. OSB.
AC. June 3

d. *c*.1115. Born of noble parentage near Worms, he was educated at the cathedral school of Worms, and after a pilgrimage at Compostella, received the Benedictine habit at Cluny from St Hugh the Great. Eventually he was sent to the new Cluniac foundation of St Christopher's at Altkirk, in Alsace, of which he was the first superior. He was greatly esteemed for his work as a missioner throughout the neighbouring countryside.

MORE, THOMAS (St) M. RM. July 9
See Thomas More.

MORICUS (Bl) C.   AC. March 30

d. 1236. A religious of the Order of the *Cruciferi*, whose story is told by St Bonaventure in his life of St Francis of Assisi. The Franciscans claim him as the fifth recruit to join the Friars Minor. He is honoured chiefly at Orvieto and among the Franciscans.

MOROC (St) Bp.   AC. Nov 8

9th cent. Abbot of Dunkeld and afterwards bishop of Dunblane. He appears to have left his name to several churches, and was venerated with a solemn office in the old Scottish rite.

MORWENNA (St) V.   AC. July 8

5th cent. A Cornish saint, to whom we owe several place-names. She is often confused either with the other saints of this name or with the Irish saints of the name of Moninne.

MOSES (St) Bp.   RM. Feb 7

d. *c*.372. An Arab who retired into the desert around Mt Sinai, and there worked as bishop of a roaming Arab flock.

MOSES (St) M.   RM. Feb 14
See Cyrion, Bassian, etc.

MOSES the BLACK (St) M.
RM. Aug 28

d. *c*.395. An Abyssinian Negro, born in slavery and of such vicious propensities that his master drove him from his household. He now became the chief of a gang of robbers. It was as a fugitive from justice that he took refuge among the hermits of Scete in Lower Egypt, by whom he was converted. He remained with them, was ordained priest, and became famous for his supernatural gifts. In his old age he was murdered by Bedouins against whom he refused to defend himself.

MOSES (St) Prophet   RM. Sept 4
15th cent. B.C. The Hebrew leader and lawgiver. What we know of him we learn from the Bible, chiefly from the Book of Exodus. He died at the age of one hundred and twenty, on the borders of the promised land. Where he was buried no man knows.

MOSES (St) M.   RM. Nov 25
d. 251. A Roman priest, noted for his zeal in preaching the gospel and for his firm stand against Novatianism. He was one of the victims under Decius.

MOSES (MOYSETES) (St) M.
                        RM. Dec 18
d. c.? 250. An African martyr, who probably suffered under Decius.

MOSEUS and AMMONIUS (SS) MM.   RM. Jan 18
d. 250. Two soldier-martyrs sentenced to forced labour for life in the mines and later burnt alive at Astas (Asracus) in Bithynia.

MOUNT ARARAT (Martyrs of)
                        RM. June 22
See Acacius.

MOUNT SINAI (Martyrs of)
                        RM. Jan 14
d. c.380. A group of monks on Mt Sinai, massacred by the marauding Bedouins. Another and larger group of solitaries done to death also by the Bedouins in the neighbouring desert of Raithu is commemorated on the same day in the RM.

MOVEAN (BITEUS) (St) Ab.
                        AC. July 22
? A disciple of St Patrick and abbot of Inis-Coosery, Co. Down. He seems also to have worked in Perthshire, where he is thought to have died as a hermit.

MUCIAN (St) M.   RM. July 3
See Mark, Mucian, etc.

MUCIUS (St) M.   RM. Feb 6
See Silvanus, Luke, etc.

MUCIUS (St) M.   RM. Apr 22
See Parmenius and Comp.

MUCIUS (St) M.   RM. May 13
d. 304. A Roman by origin, but born at Byzantium, Mucius became a priest and was martyred under Diocletian for having, it is said, overturned a pagan altar.

MUGAGGA (St) M.   RM. June 3
d. 1886. He was brought up and taught by the royal clothmaker. He was martyred by order of King Mwanga of Uganda. See Uganda (Martyrs of).

MUIRCHU (MACCUTINUS) (St) C.   AC. June 8
7th cent. An Irishman, who wrote a life of St Brigid and a life of St Patrick.

MUKASA KIRIWAWANVU (St) M.
                        RM. June 3
d. 1886. He served at the royal table of King Mwanga of Uganda by whose orders he was put to death. See Uganda (Martyrs of).

MULLION (St) Bp.   RM. Jan 6
Otherwise Melanius, q.v.

MUMMOLINUS (MOMMOLEN-US, etc.) (St) Bp. OSB. AC. Oct 16
d. c.686. A native of Constance in Switzerland, he became a monk at Luxeuil, and eventually was sent to St Omer and appointed superior of the Old Monastery (now Saint-Mommolin). Thence he migrated to the New Monastery, viz. Sithin, which had been founded by his great friend and fellow-monk St Ber-

tinus. Finally in 660 he was raised to the see of Noyon-Tournai.

MUMMOLUS (MOMMOLUS, MOMMOLENUS) (St) Ab. OSB.
AC. Aug 8

d. *c.*678. Second abbot of Fleury. He caused the relics of SS Benedict and Scholastica to be translated from Montecassino to France, and for this reason Fleury began to be known as Saint-Benoît-sur-Loire.

MUMMOLUS (MUMBOLUS, MOMLEOLUS, MOMBLE) (St) Ab. OSB.
AC. Nov 18

d. *c.*690. An Irishman, companion of St Fursey, whom he succeeded as abbot of Lagny, in the diocese of Meaux.

MUN (St) Bp.
AC. Feb 6

5th cent. Described as a nephew of St Patrick, who consecrated him bishop of what is now Co. Longford. He ended his days as a solitary in an island in Lough Ree.

MUNCHIN (St) Bp. (?)
AC. Jan 2

? Patron of the city and diocese of Limerick, St Munchin may have been first bishop of that see. He is said to have lived in the 7th century or earlier, but even this is uncertain.

MUNDUS (MUNDE, MUND, MOND) (St) Ab.
AC. Apr 15

d. *c.*962. A Scottish abbot who governed a large abbey and made several monastic foundations in Argyle. The details of his career are obscure.

MUNGO (St) Bp.
AC. Jan 13

Otherwise Kentigern, q.v.

MUNNU (MUNDUS, etc.) (St)
AC. Oct 21

Otherwise Fintan, q.v.

MURA McFEREDACH (MURAN, MURAMES) (St) Ab.
AC. March 12

d. *c.*645. Born in Donegal, he was appointed abbot of Fahan by St Columba. He is the special patron saint of the O'Neill clan and of Fahan in Co. Derry.

MUREDACH (MURTAGH) (St) Bp.
AC. Aug 13

d. *c.*455. A disciple of St Patrick, by whom he was consecrated first bishop of Killala. He ended his life as a hermit in the island of Innismurray.

MUREDHAE (Bl) Ab. OSB.
AC. Feb 9

Otherwise Marianus Scotus, q.v.

MURITTA (St) M.
RM. July 13

See Eugene, Salutaris, etc.

MUSA (St) V.
AC. Apr 2

d. 6th cent. A child living in Rome who was favoured with visions and mystical experiences. She is spoken of by St Gregory the Great, her contemporary.

MUSONIUS (St) M.
RM. Jan 24

See Mardonius, Musonius, etc.

MUSTIOLA (St) M.
RM. July 3

See Irenaeus and Mustiola.

MYDWYN (St)
AC. Jan 1

See Elvan and Mydwyn.

MYLLIN (St) Bp.
AC. June 17

The Welsh form of the name Molling, q.v.

MYLOR (St) C.
AC. Oct 1

Otherwise Melorius, q.v.

MYRBAD (St) C.
AC. May 31

See Winnow, Mancus and Myrbad.

MYRON (St) Bp.   RM. Aug 8
c.250–350. Surnamed "the Wonder-worker". A bishop in Crete, who died a centenarian.

MYRON (St) M.   RM. Aug 17
d. *c*.250. A priest who boldly faced the persecutors when they came to destroy his church, and was martyred at Cyzicus on the sea of Marmora.

MYROPE (St) M.   RM. July 13
d. *c*.251. A native of Chios in the Grecian archipelago, whence she used to make pilgrimages to the shrines of the martyrs. Accused of having hidden the body of the martyr St Isidore, she admitted having done so. She was scourged and died in prison from the effects of the punishment.

N

NAAL (St) Ab.　　　　　AC. Jan 27
Otherwise Natalis, q.v.

NABOR (St) M.　　　　RM. June 12
See Basilides, Cyrinus, etc.

NABOR (St) M.　　　　RM. July 10
See Januarius, Marinus, etc.

NABOR and FELIX (SS) MM.
　　　　　　　　　　RM. July 12
d. c.304. Martyrs at Milan under Diocletian. They owe their celebrity to
their solemn translation and enshrine-
ment by St Ambrose, nearly a century
later.

NAGRAN (Martyrs of) (SS)
　　　　　　　　　　RM. Oct 24
d. 523. A large group of martyrs (the
RM. gives their number as 340) massacred at Nagran (Nedjran) in S.W.
Arabia by Jews and heathen Arabs
under the Jew Dhu Nowas (Dunaan).
The leader of the martyrs was the chief
of the Beni Harith, Abdullah ibn Kaab
(the "Aretas" of the RM.). "After
these," adds the RM., "a Christian
woman was delivered to the flames, and
her son of five years old in his lisping
voice confessed Christ, and could not be
moved from his purpose by promises or
threats, but threw himself headlong into
the fire where his mother was burning."
The massacre of the Nagran martyrs
made such a deep impression that they
are even mentioned by Mohammed in
the Koran.

NAHUM (St) C.　　　　AC. July 17
See Seven Apostles of Bulgaria.

NAHUM (St) Prophet　　RM. Dec 1
c.660. B.C. One of the minor prophets,
supposed to have been a native of N.
Palestine. His short prophecy of three
chapters is directed against Niniveh.
He lived to see the destruction of
Niniveh which he had foretold.

NAMADIA (St) N. OSB. AC. Aug 19
d. c.700. Wife of St Calminius, and in
her widowhood a Benedictine nun at
Marsat.

**NAMASIUS (NAAMAT, NAMAT,
NAMATIUS) (St) Bp.**　　AC. Nov 17
d. c.559. Twenty-second bishop of
Vienne in France. Cult confirmed in
1903.

NAMATIUS (NAMACE) (St) Bp.
　　　　　　　　　　AC. Oct 27
d. p.462. Ninth bishop of Clermont in
France. He built the cathedral.

**NAMPHANION and Comp. (SS)
MM.**　　　　　　　　RM. July 4
d. c. ? 180. Namphanion, of Carthaginian descent, was martyred with several
companions, his compatriots, at Ma-
daura in Numidia. He is usually styled
by the African writers "the Arch-
martyr".

**NAMPHASIUS (NAMPHISIUS,
NAMPHOSIUS, NAUPHARY,
NAMPHRASE) (St) H. OSB.**
　　　　　　　　　　AC. Nov 12
d. c.800. A friend of Charlemagne, and
one of those who fought against the
Saracens in S. France. He afterwards
became a monk-recluse near Marcillac
(Lot).

NANTERIUS (NANTIER, NAN-TÈRE) (Bl) Ab. OSB.   AC. Oct 30
d. *c*.1044. A Benedictine abbot of the monastery of Saint-Mihiel (*S. Michaelis ad Mosam*) in Lorraine, diocese of Verdun.

NAPOLEON (NEOPOLUS) (St) M.
AC. Aug 15
d. *c*.300. An Egyptian martyr who suffered at Alexandria under Diocletian. He was put to the torture and so horribly maimed thereby that he expired while being carried back to his dungeon.

NARCISSUS (St) M.   RM. Jan 2
See Argeus, Narcissus, and Marcellinus.

NARCISSUS and FELIX (SS) MM.
RM. March 18
d. *c*.307. A bishop and his deacon honoured as martyrs at Gerona in Spanish Catalonia. This is all that is certain about these martyrs; their alleged escape to, and their apostolate in, Germany and Switzerland, with the subsequent conversion of St Afra, is legendary.

NARCISSUS and CRESCENTIO (SS) MM.   RM. Sept 17
d. *c*.260. They are mentioned in the Acts of St Lawrence the Martyr, which are only substantially authentic. St Lawrence used to distribute alms to the poor in the house of Narcissus, and there he cured Crescentio of his blindness. On the Salarian Way a cemetery bore the name of St Crescentio.

NARCISSUS (St) Bp.   RM. Oct 29
d. *c*.222. A Greek who was appointed bishop of Jerusalem when he was already a very old man. He was summoned to a council at Jerusalem at which he favoured the Roman custom of celebrating Easter. He was for this reason calumniated and for a time re-

tired from his see, but returned to it at the request of his people.

NARCISSUS (St) M.   RM. Oct 31
See Ampliatus, Urban and Narcissus.

NARNUS (St) Bp.   RM. Aug 27
? The alleged first bishop of Bergamo, said to have been consecrated by St Barnabas.

NARSES (St) Bp.   PC. Jan 3
340? Narses, Bishop of Subogord in Persia was arrested with his disciple Joseph and martyred. The date is uncertain.

NARSES (St) M.   RM. March 27
See Zanitas, Lazarus, etc.

NARSEUS (St) M.   RM. July 15
See Philip, Zeno, etc.

NARZALES (St) M.   RM. July 17
See Scillitan Martyrs.

NATALIA (St) M.   RM. July 27
See George, Aurelius, etc.

NATALIA (St) MW.   RM. Sept 8
See Adrian and Natalia.

NATALIA (St)   RM. Dec 1
d. *c*.311. A woman of Nicomedia, who bravely ministered to the martyrs imprisoned during the persecution of Diocletian. She is especially mentioned in the Acts of the martyr St Adrian (Sept 8). She survived the persecution and died in peace at Constantinople.

NATALIS (St) Ab.   AC. Jan 27
6th cent. The founder of monasticism in the northern parts of Ireland, and a fellow-worker with St Columba. He ruled the abbeys of Cill, Naile and Daunhinis. His holy well is still venerated.

NATALIS (NOEL) PINOT (Bl) M.
AC. Feb 21

1747–1794. Born at Angers, he was ordained priest in 1771 and worked in that diocese as parish priest of Louroux-Béconnais till the outbreak of the French Revolution. On his refusal to take the oath recognizing the civil constitution of the clergy he was extruded from his parish, but continued to minister to his flock at first in secret and afterwards openly. In 1794 he was captured when vested for Mass and guillotined still wearing his priestly vestments. Beatified in 1926.

NATALIS (St) Bp.   AC. May 13
d. 751. Bishop of Milan (740–751).

NATALIS (St) C.   AC. Sept 3
6th cent. A native of Benevento who became a priest and worked at Casale in Piedmont.

NATHALAN (St) Bp.   AC. Jan 19
d. 678. A Scot by birth and a rich man. He became an anchorite, and is especially praised for having earned his living by the cultivation of the soil, "which approaches nearest to divine contemplation". He was made bishop and resided at Tullicht. Cult confirmed in 1898.

NATHANAEL (St) Apostle
RM. Aug 24
Otherwise probably Bartholomew, q.v.

NATHY (DAVID) (St) Bp. AC. Aug 9
d. c.610. Disciple of St Finian of Clonard. He became the founder and abbotbishop of a monastery at Achonry, Sligo, where he is now venerated as the patron saint. Cult confirmed in 1903.

NAVALIS (St) M.   RM. Dec 16
See Valentine, Concordius, etc.

NAZARIUS (St) M.   RM. June 12
See Basilides, Cyrinus, etc.

NAZARIUS and CELSUS (SS) MM.
RM. July 28 and May 10

d. c.?68. Martyrs said to have been beheaded at Milan under Nero. Their Acts are certainly unreliable, and even the above mentioned data are open to doubt. The only certain fact is that St Ambrose searched for and discovered their alleged relics at Milan in 395.

NAZARIUS (St) Ab.   AC. Nov 18
d. c.450. Monk and abbot of Lérins.

NEACHTAIN (St) C.   AC. May 2
5th cent. A near kinsman of St Patrick, at whose death, according to tradition, he was present.

NEBRIDIUS (St) Bp.   AC. Feb 9
d. p.527. Bishop of Egara, a city since destroyed, near Barcelona in Spain.

NECTAN (St) M.   AC. June 17
6th cent. The patron saint of Hartland in Devonshire. He has always been venerated as a martyr, but nothing is known about him.

NECTARIUS (St) Bp.   AC. Sept 13
d. c.550. Bishop of Autun. A great friend of St Germanus of Paris.

NECTARIUS (St) Bp.   AC. May 5
d. c.445. Bishop of Vienne in Dauphiné.

NECTARIUS (St) Bp.   AC. Oct 11
d. 397. Successor of St Gregory Nazianzen and predecessor of St John Chrysostom in the see of Constantinople (381–397).

NEMESIAN, FELIX, LUCIUS, another FELIX, LITTEUS, POLYANUS, VICTOR, JADER, DATIVUS and Comp. (SS) Bps. MM.   RM. Sept 10
d. 257. Nine bishops of Numidia who, with numerous lower clergy and layfolk, were condemned to servitude in

the marble quarries of Sigum, where they ended their lives. We have still a letter of St Cyprian addressed to them.

NEMESIUS (St) M.   RM. Feb 20
See Potamius and Nemesius.

NEMESIUS (St) M.   RM. July 18
See Symphorosa and her children.

NEMESIUS (St)   RM. Aug 1
? A saint venerated near Lisieux, but of whose life we have no reliable account.

NEMESIUS and LUCILLA (SS) MM.   RM. Aug 25 (Oct 31, Dec 8)
d. c.260. Nemesius, a Roman deacon, and Lucilla, his daughter, were martyred at Rome under Valerian. Their Acts are not trustworthy.

NEMESIUS (St) M.   RM. Dec 19
d. 250. An Egyptian martyred at Alexandria under Decius. He was burnt at the stake between two thieves.

NEMORIUS (St) M.   RM. Sept 7
Otherwise Memorius, q.v.

NENNIUS (St) Ab.   AC. Jan 17
6th cent. An Irishman, disciple of St Finian of Clonard, reckoned as one of the "Twelve Apostles of Ireland". The particulars of his life are lost.

NENNOC (NENNOCHA, NINNOC) (St) V.   AC. June 4
d. c.467. A British maiden, one of the children of Brychan of Brecknock, said to have followed St Germanus of Auxerre to France and to have become abbess of one or more monasteries in Armorica.

NENNUS (NENUS, NEHEMIAS) (St) Ab.   AC. June 14
7th cent. An Irish abbot, successor of St Enda in the government of the monasteries of the isles of Arran and Bute.

NEOMISIA (St) V.   RM. Sept 25
See Aurelia and Neomisia.

NEON (St) M.   RM. Apr 24
See Eusebius, Neon, etc.

NEON (St) M.   RM. Aug 23
See Claudius, Asterius, etc.

NEON (St) M.   RM. Sept 28
See Mark, Alphius, etc.

NEON (St) M.   RM. Dec 2
See Eusebius, Marcellus, etc.

NEOPHYTUS (St) M. RM. Jan 20
d. 310. A youth, not yet fifteen years of age, martyred at Nicaea under Galerius.

NEOPHYTUS (St) M. RM. Aug 22
See Athanasius, Anthusa, etc.

NEOPOLUS (St) M.   RM. May 2
See Saturninus, Neopolus, etc.

NEOT (St) H. OSB.   AC. July 31
c.880. According to tradition he was a monk of Glastonbury and a priest, who became a hermit in Cornwall at the place now called Saint Neot. His relics were subsequently taken to St Neots in Huntingdonshire.

NEOTERIUS (St) M.   RM. Sept 8
See Ammon, Theophilus, etc.

NEPOTIAN (St) C.   AC. (?) May 4
d. 395. Nephew of St Heliodorus, bishop of Altino, by whom he was ordained priest after having abandoned his high position of an officer in the imperial bodyguard. He was much esteemed by St Jerome, who dedicated to him a treatise on the sacerdotal life. It seems, however, that he has never been the object of a public cultus.

NEPOTIAN (St) Bp.   AC. Oct 22
d. *c*.388. Bishop of Clermont (386–*c*.388).

NEREUS and ACHILLEUS (St) MM.   RM. May 12
d. *c*.100. Pretorian soldiers, baptized, it is said, by St Peter, exiled with St Flavia Domitilla to the isle of Pontia and later to Terracina, where they were beheaded. Their extant Acts are far from reliable.

NEREUS (St) M.   RM. Oct 16
See Saturninus, Nereus, etc.

NERONIAN MARTYRS (SS)   RM. June 24
d. 64. The *laus* of the RM. reads as follows: "At Rome, the birthday of very many holy martyrs who, under the emperor Nero, were falsely charged with the burning of the city, and by him were ordered to be slain by divers kinds of cruel deaths; some of them were covered with the skins of wild beasts, and cast to the dogs to be torn; others were crucified; others were delivered to the fire, and when daylight failed were used for lights in the night. All these were disciples of the Apostles and the first fruits of the martyrs whom the holy Roman Church, that fruitful field of martyrs, sent to their Lord before the Apostles' death." All the above facts are historically accurate; it is not certain, however, that Nero himself set fire to the city.

NERSES LAMBRONAZI (St) Bp.   AC. July 17
1153–1198. An Armenian by birth, nephew of St Nerses Glaiëtsi (see Aug 13), he became the Armenian archbishop of Tarsus, and was instrumental in bringing about the reunion of Little Armenia with the Holy See in 1198. He translated many Western works into

Armenian, including the Rule of St Benedict and St Gregory's Dialogues.

NERSES GLAIËTSI (St) Bp.   AC. Aug 13
1102–1173. He was called "Chnorhali" meaning "the Gracious" on account of his goodness and his agreeable literary style. As Catholicos he worked diligently at the union of the Greek and Armenian churches, but died before achieving it. He became bishop of the Armenians in 1166 and throughout his life he succeeded in maintaining perfect union and full communion with the Holy See. He excelled as a poet.

NERSES the GREAT (St) Bp. M.   AC. Nov 19
d. 373. Born in Armenia, educated in Cappadocia and married to a princess of the Mamikonian family by whom he became the father of St Isaac the Great (q.v.). In 353 he was consecrated patriarch by force. As such he worked zealously for certain reforms which proved unpalatable to King Arshak. Nerses was exiled, but recalled by the dissolute King Pap, who contrived to poison him.

NERSES and Comp. (SS) MM.   RM. Nov 20
d. 343. A group of at least twelve Persian martyrs, of whom the most illustrious were Nerses, bishop of Sahgerd, and his disciple Joseph. They suffered under Shapur II for refusing to worship the sun.

NESTABUS (St) M.   RM. Sept 8
See Eusebius, Nestabus, and Zeno.

NESTOR (St) Bp. M.   RM. Feb 26
d. 251. Bishop of Magydos in Pamphylia, crucified at Perge under Decius.

NESTOR (St) Bp. M. RM. March 4
See Basil, Eugene, etc.

NESTOR (St) M.   RM. Sept 8
d. 362. A youth of Gaza in Palestine, martyred under Julian the Apostate. After the horrors of the torture-chamber, he was, with others, being dragged half-dead to execution when the crowd intervened and insisted, out of pity, on his being left to die by the wayside. He was taken to a Christian home, where he expired.

NESTOR (St) M.   RM. Oct 8
d. c.304. A martyr of Thessalonica under Diocletian. His story, as handed down to us in his Acts, is certainly fabulous.

NEVOLO (Bl) H. OSB. Cam.
AC. July 27
d. 1280. A shoemaker by trade and married, he led a frivolous life until at the age of twenty-four he turned completely to God. He became first a Franciscan tertiary and later a Camaldolese lay-brother in the monastery of San Maglorio at Faenza. Cult approved in 1817.

NICAEAS (NICETAS) (St) Bp.
RM. June 22
d. c.414. Most modern writers identify him with St Nicetas of Remesiana (Jan 7), q.v.

NICAEAS and PAUL (SS) MM.
RM. Aug 29
? Catalogued as Syrian martyrs who suffered at Antioch.

NICANDER (St) M. RM. March 15
d. c.304. An Egyptian martyr beheaded under Diocletian. He was a physician and was condemned for ministering to the Christians in prison, and burying the dead.

NICANDER and MARCIAN (SS)
MM.   RM. June 17
d. 173 (or 304?). Two officers in the imperial army, martyred probably in the region now covered by Rumania and Bulgaria. Probably duplicates of SS Marcian and Nicanor (June 5), q.v.

NICANDER and HERMAS (SS)
MM.   RM. Nov 4
? St Nicander was a bishop and St Hermas a priest. They were martyred at Myra in Lycia (Asia Minor).

NICANDER (St) M.   RM. Nov 7
See Hieron, Nicander, etc.

NICANOR (St) M.   RM. Jan 10
d. c.76. A Jew by birth, one of the seven deacons chosen by the Apostles (Acts, VI, 5). The tradition is that he eventually came to Cyprus, where, years afterwards, he was martyred under Vespasian. It is more likely that he died in peace.

NICANOR (St) M.   RM. June 5
See Marcian, Nicanor, etc.

NICARETE (NICERAS) (St) V.
RM. Dec 27
d. c.405. A woman born at Nicomedia but resident at Constantinople, where she became the loyal friend and supporter of St John Chrysostom, whose exile and suffering she shared.

NICASIUS JONSON (St) M. OFM.
RM. July 9
c.1522–1572. Born in the castle of Hez, Brabant, he became a licentiate of theology and was the author of several controversial treatises against Protestantism. He was hanged at Briel, Holland, with eighteen companions. Canonized in 1867. (See Gorkum, Martyrs of.)

NICASIUS, QUIRINUS, SCUBICULUS and PIENTIA, V. (SS) MM.
RM. Oct 11
d. c.285. Nicasius was a regionary bishop

who, on a journey from Paris to Rouen, was slain for the faith along with his priest Quirinus, his deacon Scubiculus (Egobille) and other companions. The legend that Nicasius was one of the missionaries sent from Rome during the first century is now rejected; some even say that he is a duplicate of St Nicasius of Reims (see Dec 14).

NICASIUS, EUTROPIA, V. and Comp. (SS) MM.   RM. Dec 14
d. c.407 (or 451). Bishop of Reims, who, with his sister Eutropia and a number of his clergy and faithful, was martyred either by the Vandals in 407 or by the Huns in 451.

NICEPHORUS (St) M.   RM. Feb 9
d. 260. A martyr of Antioch under Valerian. It is reasonably contended that his story is a pious invention, written to inculcate the forgiveness of injuries.

NICEPHORUS (St) M.
                              RM. Feb 25
See Victorinus, Victor, etc.

NICEPHORUS (St) Bp. M.
                    RM. March 13 and June 2
758–828 (June 2). He began his career as imperial secretary at the court of Constantinople. In 806, though a layman, he was chosen patriarch of the city. His antecedents roused the hostility of the powerful monks of Studion and their abbot St Theodore, while the revival of iconoclasm by the emperor Leo the Armenian soon brought him into disagreement with the court. He was exiled to a monastery which he had founded on the Bosporus and there he spent the last fifteen years of his life.

NICETA and AQUILINA (SS) MM.
                              RM. July 24
? The names were originally Nicetas and Aquila and were applied to two alleged soldier-martyrs. In the apocryphal Acts of St Christopher the names are given a feminine form and are said to be those of two harlots.

NICETAS of REMESIANA (St) Bp.
                    RM. Jan 7 and June 22
d. c.414. A zealous missionary bishop in Dacia, i.e., modern Rumania and Yugoslavia. Many recent scholars assign to him the authorship or redaction of the thanksgiving hymn Te Deum.

NICETAS (St) Bp.   RM. March 20
d. c.735. Bishop of Apollonias in Bithynia, persecuted by the iconoclastic emperor Leo III. He died in exile in Anatolia.

NICETAS (St) Ab.   RM. Apr 3
d. 824. Abbot of Medikion at the foot of Mt Olympus in Bithynia. He suffered much in defence of the veneration of images against Leo the Armenian. He was imprisoned for six years in the isle of Glyceria, but after the emperor's death was set free and died in a hermitage near Constantinople.

NICETAS the GOTH (St) M.
                              RM. Sept 15
d. c.378. Surnamed in the East "the Great". He was an Ostrogoth, converted with many of his people by the Arian Ulphilas. He was a priest, and perhaps also, in good faith, an Arian. He was put to death by King Athanaric, who did his utmost to root out Christianity from his people.

NICETAS (St) C.   AC. Oct 6
d. c.838. A young patrician of Paphlagonia, who became prefect of Cilicia and then a monk at Constantinople. He opposed the blind fury of the iconoclasts and was exiled to Catisia, where he died.

## NICETIUS (NIZIER) of BESAN-ÇON (St) Bp.					AC. Feb 8

d. 611. Bishop of Besançon and a friend of St Columbanus of Luxeuil. He restored to Besançon the episcopal see, which after the invasion of the Huns had been transferred to Nyon, on the Lake of Geneva.

## NICETIUS (NIZIER) (St) Bp.					RM. Apr 2

d. 573. Became bishop of Lyons in 553 and governed the see for twenty years.

## NICETIUS (St) Bp.					RM. Dec 5

d. 566. The last of the Gallo-Roman bishops of Trèves, to which see he was raised in 532. He had been a monk and abbot in his native province of Auvergne. As a bishop he withstood the cruelty of the Frankish barbarians and excommunicated Kings Theudebert I and Clotaire, by whom he was exiled for a time. He restored discipline among the clergy, founded a school of clerical studies, rebuilt the cathedral and combated heresy.

## NICETUS (St) Bp.					RM. May 5

d. p.449. The fifteenth bishop of Vienne in Gaul.

## NICHOLAS STUDITES (St) Ab.					AC. Feb 4

d. 863. A native of Crete, who at an early age entered the monastery of the Studion at Constantinople. During the iconoclastic persecution he followed his abbot into banishment, and on his return, when peace was temporarily restored, succeeded as abbot. He went again into exile under the emperor Michael, refusing to recognize the usurping patriarch Photius. When the emperor Basil restored St Ignatius, the lawful patriarch, Nicholas considered himself too old to resume charge and died as a simple monk.

## NICHOLAS of HUNGARY (Bl) M. OFM.					PC. Feb 12

See Antony of Saxony, etc.

## NICHOLAS SAGGIO (Bl) C. O. Minim.					AC. Feb 12

d. 1709. Born of poor parents at Longobardi in Calabria, he became a laybrother in the Order of Minims of St Francis of Paola. Beatified by Pius VI.

## NICHOLAS PALEA (Bl) C. OP.					AC. Feb 14

1197–1255. Born at Giovinazzo, near Bari. As a young man he heard St Dominic preach at Bologna and joined the Friars Preachers. He established houses of the order at Perugia (1233) and at Trani (1254) and became provincial of the Roman province in 1230 and again in 1255. He died at Perugia. Cult confirmed in 1828.

## NICHOLAS of VANGADIZZA (Bl) C. OSB. Cam.					AC. Feb 21

d. c.1210. A Camaldolese monk and priest at the abbey of Vangadizza. A great helper of the holy souls.

## NICHOLAS of PRUSSIA (Bl) C. OSB.					PC. Feb 23

c.1379–1456. A native of Prussia who became one of the original members of the reformed abbey of St Justina at Padua under the Ven. Ludovico Barbo, the founder of the Benedictine Cassinese congregation. Nicholas lived successively at Padua, Venice, Padolirone, and finally at the abbey of San Niccolò del Boschetto, near Genoa, where he was novice-master and prior. Cult not yet officially approved.

## NICHOLAS OWEN (Bl) M. SJ.					AC. March 12

d. 1606. A Jesuit lay-brother who, both before and after entering the Society of Jesus, was employed in making hiding-places for hunted priests. He was twice imprisoned and tortured, and when he was arrested a third time and refused to give any information concerning the Gunpowder Plot, he was tortured so mercilessly that he died therefrom, being literally torn to pieces. Beatified in 1929.

NICHOLAS von FLÜE (St) H.
RM. March 21
1417–1487. Born near Sachseln, Canton Obwalden, Switzerland, the son of a peasant, he married and had ten children. Besides fighting bravely in the army of his canton, he was appointed judge and councillor for Obwalden. At the age of fifty he left his family with their consent and for nineteen years lived as a hermit at Ranft without any food besides Holy Communion. His advice was much sought after, especially by civil magistrates. He is still greatly venerated in Switzerland as "Bruder Klaus". Canonized in 1950.

NICHOLAS (Bl) C. OSB. Cist.
AC. Apr 1
d. c.1220. A Cistercian monk at Santa Maria dell' Arcu, near Neti, in Sicily.

NICHOLAS ALBERGATI (Bl) Bp.
O. Cart.   RM. May 9
1375–1443. A native of Bologna who in 1394 joined the Carthusians and in 1418, much against his will, was made archbishop of his native city. In 1426 he was created cardinal. He was called in as mediator between the emperor and the pope and the latter and the French king, and was prominent at the councils of Basle and Ferrara-Florence. He was a generous patron of learned men. Cult confirmed in 1744.

NICHOLAS the MYSTIC (St) Bp.
AC. May 15
d. 925. Patriarch of Constantinople. He was deposed and banished from his see by the emperor Leo the Wise, because he would not permit that monarch to marry a fourth time, this being forbidden in the Eastern Church. He is surnamed "the mystic" because he was the oldest member of the mystic, or secret, council of the Byzantine court.

NICHOLAS (Bl) Ab. OSB. Cist.
AC. May 31
d. c.1163. He and his father gave up splendid worldly prospects in order to receive the Cistercian habit from St Bernard. Nicholas became abbot of Vaucelles. He is venerated by the Cistercians.

NICHOLAS PEREGRINUS (St) C.
RM. June 2
1075–1094. A Greek who journeyed to S. Italy and wandered through Apulia, carrying a cross and crying out "*Kyrie eleison*". Crowds of people, especially children, followed him repeating the same cry. He was taken for a lunatic and treated as such, but after his death at Trani, at the age of nineteen years, so many miracles were alleged to have taken place at his tomb that he was canonized in 1098.

NICHOLAS PIECK and NICHOLAS POPPEL (SS) MM. RM. July 9
d. 1572. Two members of the group of the martyrs of Gorkum (q.v.). Nicholas Pieck was the Franciscan guardian of the friary at Gorkum. He was a native of Holland and a student of Louvain, and had made the conversion of Calvinists his life's work. Nicholas Poppel, also a Dutchman, was curate to Leonard van Wechel, another Gorkum martyr. Canonized in 1867.

NICHOLAS THE (Bl) M.
AC. June 13
d. 1839. A Tonkinese soldier who was

hacked asunder for the faith. He was a companion of Bl Augustine Huy, q.v.

NICHOLAS DINNIS (Bl) M. SJ.
AC. July 15
d. 1570. A native of Braganza in Portugal and a Jesuit novice. Companion of Bl Ignatius de Azevedo, q.v.

NICHOLAS HERMANSSÖN (Bl) Bp.   AC. July 24
1331–1391. Born at Skeninge in Sweden, and educated at Paris and Orleans, he was ordained priest and appointed tutor to the sons of St Brigid of Sweden. Eventually he became bishop of Linköping. He is greatly honoured in Sweden as a liturgist and poet. It is said, but cannot be proved, that he was canonized in 1414 (or 1416).

NICHOLAS APPLEINE (Bl) C.
AC. (?) Aug 11
d. 1466. A canon of St-Marcel-de-Prémery, diocese of Nevers. Cult approved by the bishop of Nevers in 1731.

NICHOLAS POLITI (Bl) H.
AC. Aug 17
1117–1167. Born at Adernò, in Sicily. He lived for thirty years as a hermit in a cave on Mt Etna. Cult approved by Julius II.

NICHOLAS of TOLENTINO (St) C. OSA. Erem.   RM. Sept 10
1245–1305. A native of Sant'Angelo, diocese of Fermo. In 1623 he joined the hermits of St Augustine. After his ordination to the priesthood he made a resolution to preach daily to the people, and this he did, first at Cingoli, and then for thirty years at Tolentino. He was also known for his work among the poor. Canonized in 1446.

NICHOLAS of FORCA-PALENA (Bl) C.   AC. Oct 1
1349–1449. A native of Palena, near Sulmona, and founder of the Hermits of St Jerome (*Romitani di San Girolamo*), for whom he established houses at Naples, Rome (Sant'Onofrio) and Florence. Afterwards he amalgamated his institute with the Hieronymites, founded by Bl Peter of Pisa. Cult approved in 1771.

NICHOLAS (St) M. OFM.
RM. Oct 10
See Daniel, Samuel, etc.

NICHOLAS I (St) Pope RM. Nov 13
d. 867. Surnamed "the Great", a Roman by birth and a member of the Roman clergy, he was elected pope in 858. He was remarkable for his energy and courage. Among those who were excommunicated by him were John, the recalcitrant archbishop of Ravenna, king Lothair of Lorraine for matrimonial irregularity, and Photius, the intruded patriarch of Constantinople. He also forced Archbishop Hincmar of Reims, after a struggle, to acknowledge the papal appellate jurisdiction. Nicholas was described by his contemporaries as the champion of the people. He confirmed St Anschar as papal legate in Scandinavia, and, through his missionaries, effected the conversion of Bulgaria.

NICHOLAS GIUSTINIANI (Bl) C. OSB.   AC. Nov 21
d. *p*.1180. A Venetian belonging to the noble family of the Giustiniani. He became a Benedictine in the monastery of San Niccolò del Lido. After all his brothers had been killed in battle at Constantinople the Doge obtained from the pope a dispensation for Nicholas to marry and beget heirs for the family. He accordingly married and had six sons and three daughters. In his old age Nicholas returned to the abbey. He has always been venerated at Venice.

NICHOLAS TAVIGLI (Bl) M. OFM.   AC. Dec 5

d. 1391. Born in the diocese of Sebenico in Dalmatia, he joined the Friars Minor, and was sent to the Bosnian mission, where he worked for twenty years among the Paterine schismatics. Thence he travelled to Palestine to preach to the Mohammedans and was by them cut to pieces at Jerusalem. Cult confirmed by Leo XIII.

NICHOLAS (St) Bp.   RM. Dec 6

d. c.350. One of the most popular saints in Christendom. His cult is based mainly on legend, since almost nothing is known of his life, excepting the bare facts that he was a bishop of Myra in Lycia, and that his alleged relics were stolen by Italian merchants in 1087 and now are enshrined at Bari. Legend, however, has abundantly supplied the lack of known data, as witness the life of the saint written by Simon Metaphrastes in the 10th century. To this day he is venerated as the patron saint of sailors, of captives, and especially of children. The last mentioned veneration derives from the story that he raised to life three children who had been pickled in a brine-tub. Numerous medieval observances were connected with this saint, for example, that of Santa Klaus (Sint Klaes, Sanctus Nicolaus), and the ceremony of the boy-bishop which still survives at Montserrat in Catalonia. St Nicholas is a patron saint of Russia.

NICHOLAS CHRYSOBERGES (St) Bp.   AC. Dec 16

d. 996. Patriarch of Constantinople (983–996). He was, and always remained, a staunch Catholic.

NICHOLAS FACTOR (St) C. OFM.   AC. Dec 23

1520–1582. Born at Valencia in Spain. He became a Franciscan in 1537 and spent his life as an itinerant preacher, pitilessly scourging himself before every sermon. He was beatified in 1786, St Paschal Baylon and Bl Louis Bertrand being used as witnesses in the process of beatification.

NICODEMUS (St) M.   RM. Aug 3

1st cent. The faithful, though timid, disciple of Christ mentioned in the gospel of St John (ch III), styled by our Lord "a master in Israel". He shared with St Joseph of Arimathaea the privilege of laying Christ in the tomb. One of the apocryphal gospels was circulated under his name. On Aug 3 is kept the feast of the finding of his body with that of St Stephen and others. He has always been venerated as a martyr.

NICOLINO MAGALOTTI (Bl) H.   AC. Nov 29

d. 1370. A Franciscan tertiary who lived as a hermit near Camerino for thirty years. Cult approved in 1856.

NICOMEDES (St) M.   RM. Sept 15

d. c.90. A Roman priest martyred in Rome at a very early period, some say under Domitian. In later legends he is associated with SS Nereus, Achilleus and Petronilla.

NICOMEDIA, Martyrs of (SS)

The RM. lists four anonymous groups of martyrs who suffered at Nicomedia on the Hellespont, for a time the principal residence of the Roman emperors in the East.

RM. March 18

d. c.300. A band of 10,000 massacred, it is said, following a fire in the imperial palace at Nicomedia.

RM. June 23

d. c.303. Numerous martyrs (some suggest 20,000) who hid in the mountains and caves, and were hunted down by the persecutors.

RM. Dec 23
d. *c*.304. A group of twenty martyrs.

RM. Dec 25
d. 303. Many thousands (the Greeks say 20,000) burnt alive by order of Diocletian in the great basilica of Nicomedia where they had assembled to celebrate Christmas.

Probably the above figures are exaggerated. There are other difficulties in accepting the stories as they stand, e.g., Christmas was not celebrated in the East until a later period.

NICON and Comp. (SS) MM.
RM. March 23
d. *c*.250. Nicon was a Roman soldier of distinction, who, while travelling in the East, became a Christian and a monk. His master, Theodosius of Cyzicus, left him in charge of two hundred disciples, and when persecution threatened Palestine they fled to Sicily where they were martyred under Decius. The RM. wrongly assigns them to Caesarea in Palestine.

NICON (St) M.   RM. Sept 28
See Mark, Alphius, etc.

NICON (St) C.   RM. Nov 26
d. 998. Surnamed *Metanoite*, because penance (in Greek *metanoia*) was always the theme of his preaching. He was an Armenian monk first at Khrysopetro and then in his native country, where he carried on missionary work. This he continued later in Crete and in Greece.

NICOSTRATUS, ANTIOCHUS
and Comp. (SS) MM.   RM. May 21
d. 303. A cohort of Roman soldiers said to have been put to death at Caesarea Philippi, in Palestine, under Diocletian. Nicostratus was their tribune. Their story occurs in the apocryphal *Acta* of St Procopius, M.

NICOSTRATUS (St) M.
RM. July 7 and Nov 8
See Four Crowned Martyrs.

NIDAN (St) C.   AC. Sept 30
Otherwise Midan, q.v.

NIDGER (NIDGAR, NITGAR) (Bl)
Bp. OSB.   AC. Apr 15
d. *c*.829. Said to have been abbot of the Benedictine monastery of Ottobeuren in Bavaria. He became bishop of Augsburg in 822.

NIGHTON (St) M.   AC. June 17
Otherwise Nectan, q.v.

NILAMMON (St) H.   RM. June 6
5th cent. An Egyptian monk and recluse. To avoid consecration as a bishop, he barricaded his cell and died in prayer, while the consecrating prelates were waiting outside.

NILUS (St) M.   RM. Feb 20
See Tyrannio, Sylvanus, etc.

NILUS (St) M.   RM. Sept 19
See Peleus, Nilus, etc.

NILUS the YOUNGER (St) Ab.
RM. Sept 26
d. 1004. A Greek of S. Italy, who, after a careless youth, joined the Basilian monks of the abbey of St Adrian in Calabria, of which he soon after became abbot. In 981 the invading Saracens drove the community to Vellelucio in the *Terra di Lavoro*, where they lived on land given them by Montecassino. While sick at Frascati shortly before his death Nilus designated that city as the place where his community were to be definitely established and there in fact the still flourishing abbey of Grottaferrata was founded by his disciple St Bartholomew. The monks of Grottaferrata profess the Basilian rule

and use the Greek rite, and they regard St Nilus as their founder and first abbot.

NILUS the ELDER (St) Ab.
RM. Nov 12

d. *c*.430. Surnamed "the Wise". An imperial official at Constantinople, who when already advanced in years embraced the solitary life with one of his sons on Mt Sinai. He was a staunch friend and defender of St John Chrysostom. He is now best remembered as an ascetical, theological and biblical writer of some distinction.

NIMMIA (St) M.   RM. Aug 12
See Hilaria, Digna, etc.

NINIAN (St) Bp.   RM. Sept 16
d. ? 432. A Briton who was educated in Rome, and thence sent to evangelize his native country. He established his episcopal see at Whithorn (*Candida Casa*, the White House) in Wigtownshire, so called because the cathedral was built of white stone. There was a monastery attached to it, and it was from this centre that Ninian and his monks evangelized the northern Britons and the Picts.

NINO (or CHRISTIANA) (St) V.
RM. Dec 15

d. *c*.320. A native of Colastri in Cappadocia. The RM. not knowing her local name, calls her "Christiana". As a slave or captive she was brought into Georgia (Iberia) and was the means of spreading Christianity in that country. She is venerated as the apostle of Georgia. Substantially her story is true, but many myths and contradictory legends have been added to it.

NISSEN (St) Ab.   AC. July 25
5th cent. An Irish convert of St Patrick, by whom he was set over a monastery at Montgarth (Mountgarret) in Wexford.

NITHARD (St) M. OSB. AC. Feb 4
d. 845. Monk of Corbie in Saxony and companion of St Anschar, whom he followed to Sweden as a missionary. He was martyred there by the pagan Swedes.

NIVARD (Bl) Mk. OSB. Cist.
PC. Feb 7

c.1100–*p*.1150. The youngest brother of St Bernard. He followed his brother to Clairvaux and eventually was appointed novice-master at Vaucelles. Our information as to his later career is rather confused. Cult not yet officially confirmed.

NIVARD (St) Bp.   AC. Sept 1
d. *c*.670. Archbishop of Reims. Brother-in-law of King Childeric II of Austrasia. He restored the abbey of Hautvilliers, where he was buried.

NIZIER (St) Bp.   RM. Apr 2
Otherwise Nicetius, q.v.

NOE MAWAGGALI (St) M.
RM. June 3

d. 1886. A potter by trade, he was put to death by King Mwanga of Uganda. See Uganda (Martyrs of).

NOEL (*several*)
The French form of Natalis, q.v.

NOMINANDA (St) M. RM. Dec 31
See Donata, Paulina, etc.

NONIUS ALVAREZ (Bl) OC.
AC. Nov 6

1360–1431. Nuñez Alvarez de Pereira was born at Bomjardin in Portugal and was bred to arms. He served his king in the wars for the independence of Portugal, and, after the death of his wife, became a Carmelite lay-brother at Lisbon. Cult confirmed in 1918.

NONNA (St) W.   RM. Aug 5
d. 374. Wife of St Gregory Nazianzen

the Elder, whom she converted to the Faith. Their three children, Gregory, Caesar and Gorgonius, are also venerated as saints.

NONNITA (NONNA, NON) (St) W. AC. March 3
5th–6th cent. The mother of St David of Wales. She ended her days as a nun, according to some writers in a nunnery in Brittany.

NONNOSUS (St) Mk. OSB.
RM. Sept 2
d. *c*.575. A Benedictine monk, *praepositus* in the abbey of Mt Soracte, near Rome. His wonderful deeds of faith are recorded by St Gregory the Great.

NONNUS (St) Bp.　　　RM. Dec 2
d. *c*.458. A monk of Tabennisi in Egypt, promoted in 448 to the see of Edessa. He laboured with great success among the Arabians around Heliopolis (Baalbeck). He is connected with the conversion of St Pelagia, the Penitent.

NORBERT (St) Bp. Founder
RM. June 6
c.1080–1134. Born of a princely family at Xanten, he led a worldly life at the German court and even received holy orders as a means to worldly advancement. In 1115 a narrow escape from death brought about his conversion. After endeavouring to reform the chapter of canons at Xanten, he became an itinerant preacher. In 1120 he was given the territory of Prémontré near Laon, and here he founded a community of canons regular under the Rule of St Augustine, since known as Norbertines or Premonstratensians. The new Order soon spread over Western Europe. Norbert himself was compelled to accept the see of Magdeburg, where he set about the reformation of his clergy, even resorting to force when it was

necessary. He was a zealous exponent of the doctrine of the Real Presence and fostered the cult of the Blessed Sacrament. Canonized in 1582.

NORTH AMERICA (Martyrs of) (SS) SJ.　RM. March 16 and Oct 18
1642–1649. A group of six Jesuit priests and two lay-brothers martyred in N. America at various dates between 1642 and 1649 while evangelizing the Red Indians. Their names are: John de Brébeuf, Isaac Jogues, Antony Daniel, Gabriel Lalemant, Charles Garnier and Noel Chabanel, priests; and John Lalande and René Goupil, lay-brothers. They were working among the Hurons when they met their death at the hands of the Iroquois, the mortal enemies of the Hurons. The Iroquois were animated by bitter hatred of the missionaries, whom they subjected to indescribable tortures before putting them to death. Canonized in 1930.

NOSTRIANUS (St) Bp. RM. Feb 14
d. *c*.450. Bishop of Naples, a valiant opponent of Arianism and Pelagianism.

NOTBURGA (St) V.　　AC. Sept 14
d. 1313. A Tyrolese serving-maid. She joyfully fulfilled her humble duties first in a noble household, then in that of a peasant. She made it one of her duties to help those poorer than herself. Her shrine is at Eben in the Tyrolese mountains. Cult confirmed in 1862.

NOTBURGA (NOITBURGIS) (St) N. OSB.　　　　　AC. Oct 31
d. *c*.714. A Benedictine nun in the convent of St Mary in the Capitol, at Cologne.

NOTHELM (St) Bp.　　AC. Oct 17
d. *c*.740. Archbishop of Canterbury, friend and collaborator of St Bede and correspondent of St Boniface.

NOTKER BALBULUS (Bl) Mk.
OSB.   **AC. Apr 6**
d. 912. Nicknamed *Balbulus*, i.e., the
Stammerer. He was born at Heiligau
(now Elgg) in the canton of Zurich and
when still a child entered the Benedictine abbey of St Gall, where he spent
his whole life, holding the offices of
librarian, guest-master and precentor.
He excelled as a musician and was the
originator of liturgical sequences, he
himself composing both the words and
the music of many of them. Cult confirmed in 1512.

NOVATUS (St)   **RM. June 20**
d. *c*.151. Alleged son of Pudens, the
senator, and brother of SS Praxedes and
Pudentiana.

NOVELLONE (Bl) H. OSB.
                                              AC. July 27
Otherwise Nevolo, q.v.

NOYALA (St) VM.   **AC. July 6**
? A British maiden, beheaded at
Beignan in Brittany. According to the
legend she walked to Pontivy holding
her head in her hands. She is greatly
venerated in Brittany.

NUMERIAN (MEMORIAN) (St) Bp.
OSB.   **RM. July 5**
d. *c*.666. Son of a rich senator of Trèves,
he first became a monk at Remiremont
under St Arnulph, and then went to
reside in the abbey of Luxeuil under
St Waldebert. Ultimately he was appointed bishop of his native city.

NUMIDICUS and Comp. (SS) MM.
                                               RM. Aug 9
d. 251. A group of African martyrs
burnt at the stake at Carthage under
Decius (not Valerian). Numidicus is
said to have been dragged still breathing
out of the ashes of the funeral pyre and
to have lived to be ordained priest by
St Cyprian. St Cyprian mentions a
priest named Numidicus but this group
of martyrs is unknown to the ancient
martyrologies.

NUNCTUS (NOINT) (St) Ab. M.
                                               AC. Oct 22
d. 668. Abbot of a monastery near
Mérida, in W. Spain. He was killed by
robbers and venerated thenceforward
as a martyr.

NUNILO and ALODIA (SS) VV.
MM.   **RM. Oct 22**
d. 851. Two sisters born at Adahuesca,
in the province of Huesca, Spain. After
their birth their Christian mother
married a Mohammedan, who brutally
persecuted them, had them imprisoned
at Alquézar, near Barastoro, and finally
beheaded at Huesca during the persecution of Abderrahman II. They are still
greatly venerated in Aragon.

NUNTIUS SULPRIZIO (Bl) C.
                                               AC. May 5
1817 1836. Born in the Abruzzi, he
accomplished the full mission of his
Christian life in the short span of
nineteen years in the ranks of simple
working men as an apprentice blacksmith. His patience under the handicaps
of health and fortune, his chastity and
the social evils of the 19th century set
him as a challenge to youth and workmen. Beatified in 1963.

NYMPHA (St) VM.   **RM. Nov 10**
See Tryphon, Respicius and Nympha.

NYMPHODORA (St) M.
                                              RM. March 13
See Theusetas, Horres, etc.

NYMPHODORA (St) VM.
                                              RM. Sept 10
See Menodora, Metrodora and Nym-
phodora.

O

OBDULIA (St) V. RM. Sept 5
? A virgin venerated at Toledo, where her relics are enshrined. Nothing is known about her beyond her name and cult.

OBITIUS (St) Mk. OSB. AC. Feb 4
d. *c.*1204. A knight of Brescia, who narrowly escaped drowning and, terrified by a vision of hell, gave himself to a life of austere penance as a Benedictine lay-brother in the service of the Benedictine nuns of St Julia at Brescia. Cult approved in 1900.

OCEANUS (St) M. RM. Sept 4
See Theodore, Oceanus, etc.

OCTAVIAN and Comp. MM.
  RM. March 22
d. 484. Octavian, archdeacon of the church at Carthage, and several thousand companions suffered martyrdom at that city under the Arian Vandal king Hunneric.

OCTAVIAN (Bl) Bp. OSB.
  AC. Aug 6
*c.*1060–1132. Born at Quingey in the diocese of Besançon and a brother of Pope Callixtus II. Educated by the Benedictines, he became a Benedictine himself at the abbey of St Peter in *Ciel d'Oro*, at Pavia. In 1129 he was promoted to the see of Savona. Cult confirmed in 1793.

OCTAVIUS, SOLUTOR and ADVENTOR (SS) MM. RM. Nov 20
d. 297. Patron saints of Turin, where they suffered martyrdom. At a later date their story became connected with the legend of the Theban Legion.

ODA (Bl) V. O. Praem. PC. Apr 20
d. 1158. Daughter of a noble family in Brabant, she avoided marriage with a young nobleman by disfiguring her face. She was then allowed to follow her religious vocation in the Premonstratensian nunnery of Rivroelles, of which she became prioress. Her cult has never been officially confirmed.

ODA (St) W. AC. Oct 23
d. *c.*723. A French princess married to the duke of Aquitaine. In her widowhood she devoted herself to the care of the poor and suffering. Her shrine is at Amay, near Liége.

ODDINO BARROTTI (Bl) C.
  AC. July 21
1324–1400. A native of Fossano in Piedmont who became parish priest at the church of St John the Baptist at Fossano and a Franciscan tertiary. Later he resigned his cure of souls and turned his house into a hospital. He is still greatly venerated at Fossano. Cult approved in 1808.

ODERISIUS (Bl) Card. OSB.
  AC. Dec 2
d. 1105. A son of the noble family of de' Marsi, in the diocese of Marsi, he was educated at Montecassino, where he became a Benedictine. In 1059 he was created cardinal deacon of St Agatha and shortly after cardinal priest of St Cyriacus in Termis. Finally, in 1087 he succeeded Bl Victor III as abbot of

Montecassino. He was a poet and patron of scholars and the mediator between the crusaders and the Greek emperor Alexius.

ODHRAN (ORAN) (St) Ab.
AC. Oct 27
Otherwise Otteran, q.v.

ODILIA (St) V. OSB. RM. Dec 13
Otherwise Ottilia, q.v.

ODILO (St) Ab. OSB. RM. Jan 1
c.962–1049. A scion of the noble family of Mercoeur in Auvergne. About the year 990 he joined the community of Cluny, became abbot coadjutor in 992 and abbot in 994. Gentle and kind, he was known throughout Christendom for his liberality to the needy. A friend of popes and princes, he was the promoter of the Truce of God and instituted the annual commemoration of the faithful departed (1031). Under his government the Cluniac houses increased from 37 to 65. He was surnamed by his contemporaries "the Archangel of Monks"— *Archangelus Monachorum.*

ODILO (Bl) Ab. OSB. AC. Oct 15
d. *p.*954. A Benedictine of Gorze in Lorraine, who in 945 was elected abbot of Stavelot-Malmédy. He raised the standard of studies and discipline in the abbey.

ODO of NOVARA (Bl) C. O. Cart.
AC. Jan 14
c.1105–1200. A native of Novara who became a Carthusian and was made prior of Geyrach in Slavonia. However, owing to difficulties with the bishop he resigned and became chaplain to a convent at Tagliacozzo in Italy, where he died at a very advanced age. Cult confirmed in 1859.

ODO of BEAUVAIS (St) Bp. OSB.
AC. Jan 28
801–880. Born near Beauvais, he gave up his profession of arms to become a Benedictine at Corbie, where he was tutor to the sons of Charles Martel. In 851 he succeeded St Paschasius Radbert as abbot. In 861 he was raised to the see of Beauvais, where his reforms greatly influenced the whole church of N. France. He was the mediator between Pope Nicholas I and Hincmar of Reims. Cult approved by Pius IX.

ODO of MASSAY (Bl) Ab. OSB.
AC. June 7
d. 967. A Benedictine abbot of Massay (935–967), a house belonging to the Cluniac observance.

ODO of CAMBRAI (Bl) Bp. OSB.
AC. June 19
1050–1113. A native of Orleans who became the headmaster (*scholasticus*) of the cathedral school at Tournai. In c.1090 he was converted to a higher life by reading St Augustine on free will, and founded a community of Benedictines in the disused abbey of St Martin at Tournai. In 1105 he was made bishop of Cambrai, but, on refusing to receive secular investiture, was exiled to the abbey of Anchin where he died. He was one of the most learned French scholars of the 11th century.

ODO the GOOD (St) Bp. OSB.
AC. July 4
d. 959. Born in East Anglia of Danish parents, he became a bishop in Wessex and was present at the battle of Brunanburh. In 942 he was appointed to Canterbury. He tried to escape consecration by declaring that, unlike previous archbishops, he was not a monk, and he consented to accept the dignity only after he had received the Benedictine habit from the hands of the abbot of Fleury. As archbishop he took a prominent part in the legislation of Kings Edmund and Edgar and paved the way

for the monastic restoration under SS Dunstan, Oswald (Odo's nephew) and Ethelwold.

ODO of URGELL (St) Bp.
RM. July 7
d. 1122. A scion of the house of the counts of Barcelona who, after following the profession of arms, entered the service of the Church. He was appointed archdeacon of Urgell in the Pyrenees and in 1095 was consecrated by Pope Urban II bishop of the same town. His outstanding characteristic was love of the poor.

ODO of CLUNY (St) Ab. OSB.
RM. Nov 18
c.879–942. Born in Maine, he was educated at the cathedral school of St Martin at Tours. In 909 he became a Benedictine at Baume under Bl Berno, the abbot-founder of Cluny, to the government of which latter abbey he succeeded in 927. Under his prudent and paternal rule Cluny began to exert its influence throughout France and in Italy, including Rome, where the saint was asked to restore the observance at St Paul-outside-the-Walls. He died at Tours, by the tomb of St Martin. He was one of the great abbots who enhanced the prestige of the Benedictine Order.

ODORIC of PORDENONE (Bl) C. OFM.
AC. Feb 3
1285–1331. Odoric Mattiuzzi was born at Villanova near Pordenone in Friuli, became a Franciscan, and spent some years as a recluse. Then he set out on his apostolic missions, journeying through the Near and the Far East and entering China and even Tibet. After sixteen years of such labours he returned to Europe to report to the pope at Avignon, but died at Udine. Cult confirmed in 1775.

ODRAN (St) M.
AC. Feb 19
d. c.452. The chariot-driver of St Patrick. He gave his life for his master by changing places with him in the chariot, when he knew that an ambush awaited him.

ODRAN (St) Ab.
AC. July 7
See Medran and Odran.

ODRIAN (St) Bp.
AC. May 8
? One of the early bishops of Waterford.

ODULPHUS (St) C. OSA.
AC. June 12
d. c.855. A native of Brabant, appointed canon of Utrecht by St Frederick, whom he greatly helped in the evangelization of Frisia. He founded a monastery of Augustinian canons at Stavoren. His relics are said to have been stolen in 1034 and taken to London and from there to Evesham abbey.

ODUVALD (St) Ab.
AC. May 26
d. 698. A Scottish nobleman who became a monk and later abbot of Melrose. He was a contemporary of St Cuthbert.

OFFA (St) Abs. OSB.
AC. Dec 31
d. c.1070. A Benedictine abbess of St Peter's at Benevento.

OGERIUS (OGLER) (Bl) Ab. OSB. Cist.
AC. Sept 10
d. 1214. A Cistercian abbot of Locedio, in the diocese of Vercelli. He wrote a series of sermons in defence of the doctrine of the Immaculate Conception. Cult confirmed in 1875.

OGMUND (St) Bp.
AC. March 8
d. 1121. Bishop of Holar in Iceland. He is venerated as one of the apostles of that island. Canonized in 1201.

OLALLA (St) VM.
RM. Dec 10
Otherwise Eulalia of Mérida, q.v.

OLAV of NORWAY (OLAVUS, OLAF, OLAUS, TOOLEY) (St) King M.   RM. July 29

995–1030. Son of King Harald of Norway. His early youth was spent, after the manner of his countrymen in those days, as a pirate. In 1010 he received baptism at Rouen and in 1013 helped Ethelred of England against the Danes. In 1015 he succeeded to the throne of Norway and at once summoned missionaries, chiefly from England, to complete the Christianization of the country. He succeeded to some extent, but his measures were harsh and he was driven from his kingdom. In an attempt to recover it he fell in battle at Stiklestadt. He is now regarded in Norway as the champion of national independence.

OLAV of SWEDEN (St) King M.   AC. July 30

d. c.950. A king of Sweden, murdered by his rebellious heathen subjects for refusing to sacrifice to idols at the spot where Stockholm now stands.

OLCAN (St) Bp.   AC. Feb 20

Otherwise Bolcan, q.v.

OLGA (St) W.   AC. July 11

c.879–969. Wife of Igor I, duke of Kiev, whom she married in 903. After his assassination in 945 she ruled the country for the rest of her life. In 958 she became a Christian and made great, though unsuccessful, efforts to introduce Christianity into Russia, a task which was achieved by her grandson St Vladimir.

OLIVA (St) VM.   AC. March 5

d. 138. Said to have been a martyr under the Emperor Adrian. Her body is venerated in the church of St Afra at Brescia.

OLIVA (St) V.   RM. June 3

? A nun of Anagni, near Rome, of whose life we have no authentic particulars.

OLIVA (OLIVIA, OLIVE) (St) VM.   AC. June 10

? A virgin martyr venerated both at Palermo and at Carthage. She is, however, a fictitious person, the heroine of a romance the scene of which is laid among the Mohammedans of Tunis, by whom also she is held in high veneration.

OLIVER (OLIVERIUS, LIBERIUS) (St) C. OSB.   AC. Feb 3

d. c.1050. A Benedictine monk of Santa Maria di Portonuovo at Ancona.

OLIVER PLUNKET (Bl) Bp. M.   AC. July 11

1629–1681. Born at Loughcrew in Co. Meath, he studied for the priesthood in Rome, where he was ordained in 1654. He remained there as professor of theology in the college de Propaganda Fide till 1669. In that year he was consecrated archbishop of Armagh and at once threw himself courageously into the task of restoring the Irish church, laid waste by continuous persecution. He was arrested on a charge of complicity in one of the sham plots of the time and, the Irish judges refusing to convict him of treason, he was brought for trial to London. Here, too, his first trial collapsed for lack of evidence, but on a second trial he was found guilty of treason "for propagating the Catholic religion". While in prison Bl Oliver made his Benedictine oblation in the hands of his fellow prisoner, Dom Maurus Corker, the president of the English Benedictines, to whom also he bequeathed his body, which is now enshrined at Downside Abbey. He was the last Catholic to be martyred at Tyburn. He was beatified in 1920 and his canonization is expected to take place before very long.

OLLEGARIUS (OLDEGAR, OLEGARI) (St) Bp. OSA.
RM. March 6
1060–1137. Born at Barcelona, he joined the Augustinian canons regular and was prior in several houses in France before being raised to the see of Barcelona in 1115. The following year he was transferred to the archbishopric of Tarragona. That diocese he successfully raised from the condition of neglect and decay into which it had fallen during the Moorish domination.

OLYMPIADES (St) M.
RM. Apr 15
See Maximus and Olympiades.

OLYMPIADES (St) M.   RM. Dec 1
d. 303. Said to have been a Roman of consular rank tortured to death at Almeria (now Amelia) in central Italy, under Diocletian.

OLYMPIAS (St) W.   RM. Dec 17
d. 408. A lady of noble birth at Constantinople who married Nebridius, prefect of the city. On her husband's death soon after their marriage she devoted herself to the service of the church, becoming a deaconess and establishing a "domestic community" of virgins in her own home. She loyally supported the cause of St John Chrysostom, and on this account was herself persecuted and exiled, her house being sold and her community disbanded. She died in exile at Nicomedia.

OLYMPIUS (St) Bp.   RM. June 12
d. p.343. A bishop of Aenos (now Enos) in Rumelia, a contemporary of St Athanasius. He was a staunch opponent of Arianism and was driven from his see by the Arian emperor Constantius.

OLYMPIUS (St) M.   RM. July 26
See Symphronius, Olympius, etc.

OMER (AUDOMARUS) (St) Bp. OSB.   RM. Sept 9
c.595–670. Born in the territory of Constance, he became a monk at Luxeuil, and after some twenty years was raised to the see of Thérouanne (which at that time embraced what is now called Pas-de-Calais and Flanders, in Belgic Gaul). The diocese sadly needed evangelization, and for this purpose St Omer secured the services of a numerous band of fellow-monks, who literally covered that district with abbeys. The saint himself was the co-founder of Sithin, over which he placed St Bertinus. Round this abbey grew up the town now known as Saint-Omer.

ONCHO (ONCHUO) (St) C.
AC. Feb 8
d. c.600. An Irish pilgrim, who was also a poet, a guardian of the Celtic traditions and a collector of holy relics. While pursuing his search for memorials of the Irish saints he died at Clonmore monastery, then governed by St Maidoc, and his body was there enshrined together with the relics he had gathered.

ONESIMUS (St) M.   RM. Feb 16
d. c.90. The slave who ran away from his master Philemon, was converted by St Paul in Rome, and was the occasion of the apostle's letter to Philemon. The RM. has confused him with another Onesimus, who was bishop of Ephesus after St Timothy.

ONESIMUS (St) Bp.   AC. May 13
d. c.361. Fifth bishop of Soissons.

ONESIPHORUS and PORPHYRIUS (SS) MM.   RM. Sept 6
d. c.81. Onesiphorus is mentioned by St Paul in the second epistle to Timothy (IV, 19). Tradition adds that he followed St Paul to Spain and then back to

the East, where he was martyred under Domitian somewhere on the Hellespont by being tied to wild horses and so torn to pieces. Porphyrius is described as a member of his household, who shared in the work and the martyrdom of his master.

ONUPHRIUS (HUMPHREY) (St) H.   RM. June 12
d. *c.*400. An Egyptian who lived as a hermit for seventy years in the desert of the Thebais, in Upper Egypt. He was a very popular saint in the Middle Ages, both in the East and in the West. He is the patron saint of weavers, probably because "he was dressed only in his own abundant hair and a loin-cloth of leaves".

**OPPORTUNA (St) Abs. OSB.
                                AC. Apr 22**
d. *c.*770. Born near Ayesmes in Normandy, sister of St Chrodegang, bishop of Séez. At an early age she entered the Benedictine abbey of Montreuil, of which she became abbess. She is described as "a true mother to all her nuns". Her cult has always been very flourishing in France.

OPTATIAN (St) Bp.   RM. July 14
d. *c.*505. Bishop of Brescia *c.*451–505.

OPTATUS (St) M.   RM. Apr 16
See Saragossa (Martyrs of).

**OPTATUS of MILEVIS (St) Bp.
                                RM. June 4**
d. *c.*387. Bishop of Milevis in Numidia. He was an excellent controversialist against the Donatists—resourceful and vigorous but conciliatory. He wrote six treatises against them which are praised by his contemporaries, chiefly by SS Augustine and Fulgentius of Ruspe. He is often quoted in modern controversial works against heresy and schism.

OPTATUS (St) Bp.   RM. Aug 31
d. *c.*530. A bishop of Auxerre who died in the second year of his episcopate.

ORAN (St) Ab.   AC. Oct 27
Otherwise Otteran, q.v.

**ORANGE (Martyrs of) (BB)
                                AC. July 6**
d. 1794. A group of thirty-two nuns—one Benedictine, two Cistercians, thirteen religious of the Institute of Perpetual Adoration and sixteen Ursulines—imprisoned during the French Revolution in the public gaol at Orange for several months and ultimately guillotined there. They were martyred on different days during the month of July. Beatified in 1925. Each receives a special notice in this book.

ORDONIUS (ORDOÑO) (St) Bp. OSB.   AC. Feb 23
d. 1066. Monk of the Benedictine abbey (Cluniac observance) of Sahagún, in the province of León, Spain, and afterwards bishop of Astorga (1062–1066).

ORENTIUS and PATIENTIA (SS) MM.   RM. May 1
d. *c.*240. Husband and wife, who lived at Loret, near Huesca, in N. Aragon. An ancient Spanish tradition makes them the parents of St Laurence the martyr.

ORENTIUS (or ORIENTIUS) of AUCH (St) Bp.   RM. May 1
d. *c.*439. A hermit in the Lavendan valley near Tarbes, whom the people of Auch insisted on having for their bishop. He governed that see for over forty years.

ORENTIUS, HEROS, PHARNACIUS, FIRMINUS, FIRMUS, CYRIACUS and LONGINUS (SS) MM.   RM. June 24
d. *c.*304. Described in the RM. as seven brothers who, on account of their faith,

were deprived of their military belt by Maximian, taken away to various places and put to death.

ORESTES (St) M.   **RM. Nov 9**
d. 304. A martyr of Cappadocia, tortured to death under Diocletian.

ORESTES (St) M.   **RM. Dec 13**
See Eustratius, Auxentius, etc.

ORGONNE (St) V.   **RM. Jan 30**
Otherwise Aldegund, q.v.

ORIA (St) V. OSB.   **AC. March 11**
Otherwise Aurea, q.v.

ORICULUS and Comp. (SS) MM.
                         RM. Nov 18
d. c.430. A group of martyrs, put to death by the Arian Vandals in the province of Carthage.

ORINGA (or CHRISTIANA) of the CROSS (Bl) V. OSA.   **AC. Jan 4**
d. 1310. Her life, which seems somewhat legendary, relates that she fled from home to escape marriage, and became a serving-maid at Lucca. Then she returned to her birthplace, Castello di Santa Croce, in Tuscany, and founded a convent under the Augustinian Rule.

ORLANDO (Bl) H. OSB. Vall.
                         AC. May 20
d. 1212. A Vallombrosan lay-brother who was celebrated as an exorcist.

ORMOND (ARMAND) (St) Mk.
                         AC. Jan 23
6th cent. Monk of the abbey of Saint Mairé, he became abbot in 587, in which task he was eminently successful.

ORONTIUS (St) M.   **RM. Jan 22**
See Vincent, Orontius and Victor.

ORORA (St)   **AC. Oct 20**
See Bradan and Orora.

ORSISIUS (St) H.   **AC. June 15**
d. c.380. A favourite disciple of St Pachomius, and his assistant in drawing up the rules for the cenobites. He succeeded Pachomius as abbot. Some twelve years before his death he was forced to resign by his monks. He is the author of an ascetical treatise which St Jerome translated into Latin.

OSANNA (*several***)**
Otherwise Hosanna, q.v.

OSBURGA (or OSBERGA) (St) Abs. OSB.   **AC. March 28**
d. c.1016. First abbess of the nunnery founded by King Canute at Coventry. Her cult was confirmed in the 15th century, and her feast is still kept in the diocese of Birmingham. The above data are commonly accepted, but she may be a saint of much earlier date.

OSEE (HOSEA) (St) Prophet
                         RM. July 4
8th cent. B.C. A prophet among the ten tribes of Israel. He seems to have been a contemporary of Isaiah. His prophecy was directed to his compatriots of Samaria, of which kingdom he foretells the destruction.

OSITH (St) M. OSB.   **AC. Oct 7**
Otherwise Osyth, q.v.

OSMANNA (OSANNA) (St) N. OSB.   **AC. June 18**
d. c.700. A nun of the Benedictine convent of Jouarre in France.

OSMANNA (or ARGARIARGA) (St) V.   **AC. Sept 9**
d. c.650. An Irish maiden who crossed over to Brittany and became a solitary in a hermitage near Brieuc.

OSMUND (St) Bp.   RM. Dec 4
d. 1099. A Norman noble attached to the court of William the Conqueror, with whom he came to England and by whom he was made chancellor. In 1077 he was appointed to the see of Salisbury (Old Sarum), where he finished the cathedral and instituted a chapter of secular canons. He is especially remembered as the compiler of the liturgical services for his diocese, now known as the "Sarum use". His hobby was bookbinding. Canonized in 1457.

OSTIANUS (St) C.   RM. June 30
? A saint venerated at Viviers. He is said to have been a priest, but nothing is now known about him.

OSWALD (St) Bp. OSB.
                        AC. Feb 28
d. 992. Born in England of a noble Danish family, he was educated under his uncle St Odo of Canterbury and was appointed dean of Winchester. Shortly after he crossed over to France and professed the Benedictine Rule at Fleury. At the suggestion of St Dunstan he was raised to the see of Worcester (960), and heartily identified himself with St Dunstan and with St Ethelwold in their efforts to revive monastic life and ecclesiastical discipline in England. St Oswald founded the abbey of Ramsey and the monastery at Worcester which later became the cathedral priory. In 972 he was promoted to the archbishopric of York, without relinquishing the government of the diocese of Worcester. He died while still on his knees after having performed his daily practice of washing the feet of twelve poor persons.

OSWALD (St) King M.
                        RM. Aug 5
604–642. The successor of King Edwin on the throne of Northumbria in the time of the Heptarchy. He was baptized at Iona during a period of exile among the Scots. In 635 he defeated the Welsh King Cadwalla near Hexham and with that victory his actual reign began. One of his chief aims was the complete evangelization of his country. In 642 he fell in battle at Maserfield fighting against the champion ¡of paganism, Penda of Mercia. He has always been venerated as a martyr.

OSWIN (St) King M.   AC. Aug 20
d. 651. A prince of Deira, part of the kingdom of Northumbria, he was educated by St Aidan. In 642 he succeeded St Oswald as ruler of Deira, but reigned only nine years, being killed at Gilling in Yorkshire by order of his cousin Oswy. He has ever since been venerated as a martyr.

OSYTH (OSITH) (St) M. OSB.
                        AC. Oct 7
d. c.675. She was brought up in a Benedictine nunnery the name of which is no longer known. Later she founded a nunnery herself at a place called Chich, now St Osyth, on a creek of the Colne in Essex. She was murdered there by Danish pirates.

OTGER (St) M. OSB.   AC. Sept 10
See Wiro, Phechelm, etc.

OTHMAR (OTMAR, AUDEMAR) (St) Ab. OSB.   RM. Nov 16
d. 759. Of Teutonic origin and already a priest, in 720 he was appointed abbot of the then dilapidated monastery of St Gall. He introduced at once the Benedictine Rule and a new period of prosperity began for the abbey, which soon became the most important in Switzerland. He was persecuted by two neighbouring counts, unjustly calumniated and condemned by an ecclesiastical tribunal. He bore his sufferings with great patience, and died in prison.

OTILLIA (ODILIA, OTHILIA, ADILIA) (St) Abs. OSB. RM. Dec 13

d. *c*.720. According to tradition St Ottilia was born blind and cast out for this reason by her family. She was adopted by a convent, where she miraculously recovered her sight. Eventually she became abbess foundress of Hohenburg (now Odilienberg) and of Niedermünster, both under the Benedictine Rule. Her life as it comes down to us abounds in extraordinary legends.

OTTERAN (ODHRAN) (St) Ab. AC. Oct 27

c.563. An Irish abbot of Meath who crossed over to Scotland with St Columba, and was the first to die at Iona. His feast is kept throughout Ireland. He has given its name to Oronsay.

OTTO (St) M. OFM. RM. Jan 16

See Berardus, Peter, etc.

OTTO of BAMBERG (St) Bp. RM. July 2

d. 1139. Born in S. Germany, he was chosen bishop of Bamberg under the emperor Henry IV, whom he endeavoured to reconcile with the Holy See. He was more successful in his missionary activities among the Pomeranians, and is honoured as their apostle. Canonized in 1189.

OTTO of HEIDELBERG (Bl) H. OSB. AC. Dec 28

d. 1344. A brother of Bl Herman of Heidelberg and, like him, a monk and priest at the Benedictine abbey of Niederaltaich in Bavaria. After his brother's death in 1326, Otto exercised his priestly office at the cell where Bl Herman had died.

OUDACEUS (In Welsh: Eddogwy) (St) Ab. (?) AC. July 2

d. *c*.600. Son of Budic, prince of Brittany, but brought up in Wales by his uncle St Teilo, whom perhaps he succeeded in the abbacy of Llandeilo Fawr. He is wrongly described as bishop of Llandaff.

OUEN (AUDOËNUS, ALDWIN, OWEN, DADO) (St) Bp. RM. Aug 24

610–684. Son of St Authaire (q.v.). He founded the abbey of Rebais, was consecrated bishop of Rouen in 641, attended the Synod of Châlons in 644, and died near Paris in 684.

OWEN (OWIN, OUINI) (St) H. OSB. AC. March 3

d. 680. After having been steward in the household of St Etheldreda, he became a monk at Lastingham under St Chad, and when the latter was appointed bishop of Mercia he settled St Owen with other monks in a house near Lichfield.

OYAND (St) Ab. RM. Jan 1

Otherwise Eugendus, q.v.

OYE (St) M. RM. Dec 11

Otherwise Eutychius, q.v.

OYS (St) C. AC. Apr 22

Otherwise Authaire, q.v.

P

PABIALI (St) C.   **AC. Nov 1**
5th (or 6th) cent. Son of the British prince Brychan by his Spanish wife Proistri: he is said to have gone to Spain. He is patron of a chapel called Party-pallai in Wales.

PABO (St) C.   **AC. Nov 9**
d. c.510. Surnamed "Post-Prydain", i.e., the prop of N. Britain. He was the son of a chieftain on the Scottish border and at first a soldier. Later he came to Wales and founded the monastery called after him Llanbabon, in Anglesey.

PACHOMIUS (St) Ab.   RM. May 9
d. 292–346. Born in the Upper Thebaid, he followed at first the profession of arms which he abandoned to receive baptism (314) and three years later became a hermit. In 318 he built his first monastery at Tabenna (Tabennisi), north of Thebes on the east bank of the Nile, and subsequently he established several others. He governed them all much as a present day superior general and wrote for them the first known cenobitical rule, thus departing from the then common type of eremitical monachism. At the time of his death he had seven thousand monks under his rule. He is one of the most outstanding figures in the history of monachism.

PACHOMIUS (St) Bp. M.
            RM. Nov 26
See Faustus, Didius, etc.

PACIANUS (St) Bp.   RM. March 9
d. c.390. Bishop of Barcelona from 365. He wrote much on matters of ecclesias-tical discipline, but most of it is lost. His treatise on penance is considered a classic. In his first letter against Nova-tian occurs the famous saying: "My name is Christian, my surname is Catholic".

PACIFICUS of CERANO (Bl) C. OFM.   **AC. June 8**
1424–1482. Pacificus Ramota was born at Cerano, diocese of Novara, and be-came a Friar Minor in 1445. He excelled both as a popular preacher and as a writer of moral theology, his *Summa Pacifica* being much used by his con-temporaries. Cult approved in 1745.

PACIFICUS of SAN SEVERINO (St) C. OFM.   **RM. Sept 24**
1653–1721. A native of San Severino, near Ancona, he joined the Franciscans of the Observance and was ordained priest in 1677. In his early years as a priest his preaching bore much fruit, but in 1688 he became deaf and blind and almost a cripple. From this time his life was one of intense suffering, blessed by God with supernatural charismata. Canonized in 1839.

PADARN (St) Bp.   RM. Apr 16
Otherwise Paternus, q.v.

PADUINUS (PAVIN) (St) Ab. OSB.
            AC. Nov 15
d. c.703. Monk and prior of St Vincent's abbey, at Le Mans, and later first abbot of St Mary's near the same city.

PAGANUS (Bl) Mk. OSB. AC. Feb 10
d. 1423. An Italian who became a pro-fessed monk of the Sicilian abbey of

San Niccolò d' Arena. He lived as a hermit near the monastery, but returned to it before his death.

PAGANUS of LECCO (Bl) M. OP. AC. Dec 26

d. 1274. He was admitted into the Dominican Order by St Dominic himself and lived in it for fifty years. He succeeded St Peter of Verna as inquisitor general and, like him, was murdered by heretics.

PALAEMON (St) Ab.   RM. Jan 11

d. 325. One of the earliest of the Egyptian hermits. He took refuge in Upper Egypt during the persecution under Diocletian. To him came St Pachomius to be trained in the monastic life. He was closely associated with Pachomius in organizing the hermits on cenobitical lines, and he eventually followed Pachomius to Tabennisi and died there.

PALATIAS and LAURENTIA (SS) MM.   RM. Oct 8

d. 302. Palatias was a lady of Ancona converted to Christ by her slave Laurentia. Both were martyred at Fermo, near Ancona, under Diocletian.

PALATINUS (St) M.   RM. May 30

See Sycus and Palatinus.

PALDO, TASO and TATO (SS) Abbots OSB.   AC. Jan 11

8th cent. Three brothers, natives of Benevento, who became monks at the abbey of Farfa, in Sabina, and eventually founded the monastery of San Vincenzo at the headwaters of the Volturno. Of this latter foundation they became successively abbots, Paldo dying c. 720, Taso c.729, and Tato c.739.

PALESTINE, Martyrs of (SS)

There are five groups of anonymous Palestinian martyrs listed in the RM.

RM. Feb 19

d. c.509. Saracen tribes under Persian rule invaded Palestine about this time and martyred the solitaries they found there, out of hatred for Rome and Christianity.

RM. May 16

d. c.614. Forty-four monks of the *laura* of St Sabbas, massacred during the war between Heraclius and Chosroas. (They are included among those listed under June 22, q.v.)

RM. May 28

d. c.410. A number of monks martyred by Arabs and other pagans who invaded Palestine early in the reign of Theodosius the Younger.

RM. June 22

d. c.614. A great number of martyrs (the RM. speaks of 1480) massacred at Samaria or in its neighbourhood during the war between Heraclius and Chosroas.

RM. Aug 16

? A group of thirty-three martyrs of whom no details are known.

PALLADIA (St) M.   RM. May 24

See Susanna, Marciana and Palladia.

PALLADIUS (St) H.   AC. Jan 28

d. c.390. A hermit near Antioch in Syria, a friend of St Simeon "the Ancient".

PALLADIUS (St) Bp.   AC. Apr 10

d. 661. An abbot of the abbey of St Germanus at Auxerre, who in 622 was appointed bishop of that city. He founded several monasteries.

PALLADIUS (St) Bp.   AC. July 7

d. 432. A deacon of the Roman church, consecrated bishop and sent (c.430) by Pope Celestine I to evangelize Ireland. He landed near Wicklow and after founding a few churches left for Scotland, where he died shortly after.

PALLADIUS (St) Bp.   AC. Oct 7
d. *c*.590. Bishop of Saintes (570–*c*.590). He is liturgically honoured in several dioceses of France, but his claim to the title of saint is disputed, not without reason.

PALMATIUS (St)   RM. May 10
See Calepodius, Palmatius, etc.

**PALMATIUS and Comp. (SS) MM.
RM. Oct 5**
d. *c*.287. Apocryphal martyrs of Trèves alleged (only since the 11th century) to have been put to death under Maximian Herculeus.

PALUMBUS (Bl) H. OSB. AC. Jan 4
d. *c*.1070. A monk-priest of the abbey of Subiaco, who lived for some years as a hermit near the monastery.

PAMBO (St) Ab.   AC. July 18
d. *c*.390. A disciple of the great St Antony and one of the pioneers of the eremitical life in the Nitrian desert. In his old age he was a venerable figure, visited by a great number of persons from East and West. Among these were St Athanasius, St Melania the Elder and Rufinus.

PAMMACHIUS (St) C. RM. Aug 30
d. 410. A Roman senator, married to one of the daughters of St Paula. On the death of his wife in 395 Pammachius donned the monastic habit and received priest's orders, spending the rest of his life and his immense wealth in the personal service of the sick and the poor. His great friends, SS Jerome and Paulinus of Nola, admired and encouraged him. His house became the present church of SS John and Paul (*Titulus Pammachii*).

PAMPHILUS (St) Bp. RM. Apr 28
d. *c*.700. Bishop of Sulmona (a see later joined to that of Valva) and Corfinium in the Abruzzi. He was accused to Pope Sergius of Arian practices, chiefly, it seems, on account of his singing Mass before daybreak on Sundays—but he completely vindicated himself.

**PAMPHILUS and Comp. (SS) MM.
RM. June 1**
d. 309. A native of Beirut (*Berytus*) in Phoenicia. He studied at Alexandria under Pierius, and then settled at Caesarea in Palestine, where he was ordained priest. Himself the greatest biblical scholar of his day, he fostered learning and protected all students. His household became famous for its practice of fraternal love, slaves and domestics being treated as sons and brothers. The historian Eusebius assumed the surname "Pamphili" in gratitude for favours received from St Pamphilus. After years of imprisonment and repeated tortures, he was martyred under Galerius. With him suffered his deacon and ten companions.

PAMPHILUS (St) Bp.   RM. Sept 7
d. *c*.400. A Greek by birth, consecrated bishop of Capua by Pope Siricius. His relics were enshrined at Benevento.

PAMPHILUS (St) M.   RM. Sept 21
? A Roman martyr, about whom nothing is known.

PANACEA (PANEXIA, PANASSIA) (St) V.   AC. May 1
1378–1383. Born at Quarona, diocese of Novara. When she was only five years old her stepmother killed her with a spindle while she was at prayer. Cult confirmed in 1867.

**PANCHARIUS (St) M.
RM. March 19**
d. 303. A Roman senator, a favourite officer of the emperor Maximian. At

the outbreak of the persecution he denied, or at any rate concealed, his religion, but on receiving a letter from his mother and sister, he nobly confessed Christ and was beheaded at Nicomedia.

PANCHARIUS (St) M.
AC. July 22

d. *c*.356. Bishop of Besançon. He suffered much at the hands of the officials of the Arian emperor Constantius.

PANCRAS (Latin: PANCRATIUS) (St) Bp. M.
RM. Apr 3

1st cent. According to the Sicilian tradition, this St Pancras was an Antiochene by birth, whom St Peter consecrated bishop and sent to Taormina (*Tauromenium*) in Sicily, where he was stoned to death.

PANCRAS (St) M.
RM. May 12

d. *c*.304 (?). A martyr of this name was certainly buried in the cemetery of Calepodius in Rome. Other particulars are lacking. His story as given in Cardinal Wiseman's *Fabiola* is of course a literary creation of the novelist's imagination. In the 7th century Pope St Vitalian sent relics of the saint to one of the Anglo-Saxon kings, and St Pancras thenceforward became very popular in England.

PANDONIA (St) V.
AC. Aug 26

Otherwise Pandwyna, q.v.

PANDWYNA (St) N. OSB.
AC. Aug 26

d. *c*.904. Born in Scotland or Ireland. She became a nun at Ettisley in Cambridgeshire.

PANNONIA (Martyrs of) (SS)
RM. Apr 9

? The RM. has this entry: "At Sirmium in Pannonia the passion of seven holy virgins and martyrs." Modern research has found no further particulars about them.

PANTAENUS (St) C.
RM. July 7

d. *c*.216. A Sicilian and a convert from Stoicism, Pantaenus became the head of the catechetical school of Alexandria, which under him began to be considered the intellectual centre of the Christian East. He is said to have ended his life as a missionary in India (more probably in Ethiopia).

PANTAGAPES (St) M.
RM. Sept 2

See Diomedes, Julian, etc.

PANTAGATHUS (St) Bp.
RM. Apr 17

475–540. A courtier in the service of King Clovis, he eventually left the court and received holy orders. He was afterwards raised to the see of Vienne.

PANTALEEMON (St) M.
RM. July 27

See Maurus, Pantaleemon and Sergius.

PANTALEON (St) M.
RM. July 27

d. *c*.305. His Greek name is *Panteleemon* which means "the All-compassionate". The name may have given rise to the legend of his life, which, as we have it now, is not to be trusted. The main facts are probably true: viz., that he was a physician by profession, who practised his art without taking any fees, and who was martyred under Diocletian, perhaps at Nicomedia.

PANTALUS (St) Bp. M.
AC. Oct 12

? A legendary bishop of Basle connected with the story of St Ursula.

PAPAS (St) M.
RM. March 16

d. *c*.300. A martyr of Lycaonia in Asia Minor under Diocletian.

PAPHNUTIUS (St) M. RM. Apr 19
? A priest put to death at Jerusalem.

PAPHNUTIUS the GREAT (St) Bp.
RM. Sept 11
d. *c*.356. An Egyptian who suffered for
the Faith under Maximinus Thrax by
having one eye plucked out and one leg
hamstrung. In 311 he joined St Antony
as monk, but shortly after was consecrated bishop of a see in the Upper
Thebaid. As such he assisted at the
council of Nicaea, where he is said to
have advocated the marriage of priests
before ordination. Throughout his life
he was a strenuous opponent of Arianism. He was in great favour with the
emperor Constantine.

PAPHNUTIUS and Comp. (SS)
MM. RM. Sept 24
d. *c*.303. Martyrs in Egypt under Diocletian.

PAPHNUTIUS (St) Ab. AC. Sept 25
d. *c*.480. The alleged father of the girl-
monk St Euphrosyne, q.v. He became a
monk and abbot in Egypt and is held in
great veneration in the East.

PAPIAS and MAURUS (SS) MM.
RM. Jan 29
d. *c*.303. Roman soldiers martyred at
Rome under Maximian.

PAPIAS (St) Bp. RM. Feb 22
d. *c*.120. Bishop of Hierapolis in the
valley of the Lycus in Phrygia, a contemporary and friend of St Polycarp of
Smyrna. He wrote much, but only a few
fragments of his works are extant.

PAPIAS (St) M. RM. Feb 25
See Victorinus, Victor, etc.

PAPIAS, DIODORUS, CONON and
CLAUDIAN (SS) MM. RM. Feb 26
d. *c*.250. Poor shepherds, natives of

Pamphylia (Asia Minor), tortured and
put to death under Decius.

PAPIAS (PAPIUS) (St) M.
RM. June 28
d. *c*.303. A martyr, possibly in Sicily,
under Diocletian.

PAPIAS (PAPIUS) (St) M.
RM. July 7
See Peregrinus, Lucian, etc.

PAPIAS (St) M. RM. Nov 2
See Publius, Victor, etc.

PAPINIANUS and MANSUETUS
(SS) MM. RM. Nov 28
5th cent. African bishops, martyred
under the Arian Vandal King Genseric,
who had overrun that Roman province.

PAPOLENUS (St) Ab.
AC. June 26
Otherwise Babolenus, q.v.

PAPPUS (PAPIUS) (*several*)
Otherwise Papias, q.v.

PAPULUS (PAPOUL) (St) M.
AC. Nov 3
d. *c*.300. A priest who worked as a missionary under St Saturninus in S.
France, and who like him was martyred
under Diocletian. His shrine is at
Toulouse.

PAPYLUS (St) M. RM. Apr 13
See Carpus, Papylus, etc.

PARAGRUS (St) AC. Dec 9
See Samosata Martyrs.

PARAGUAY (Martyrs of) (BB) SJ.
AC. Nov 17
d. 1628. Three Spanish Jesuits—Roch
(Roque) Gonzalez, Alphonsus Rodriguez and John de Castillo—founders of
the "reduction" of the Assumption on

the Jiuhi river in Paraguay. In 1628 they established the new mission of All Saints, and it was here that they were murdered by order of the local chief.

PARAMON and Comp. (SS) MM.
RM. Nov 29

d. 250. A group of three hundred and seventy-five martyrs, venerated especially by the Greeks. They are said to have suffered on the same day during the Decian persecution.

PARASCEVE (St) M.
RM. March 20

See Photina, Joseph, etc.

PARDULPHUS (PARDOUX) (St) Ab. OSB.
AC. Oct 6

c.658–738. Born at Sardent, near Guéret, diocese of Limoges, he first became a hermit, but afterwards joined the Benedictine community of Guéret, of which he became abbot. At the time of the Saracen invasion he remained alone in the abbey, which he saved by prayer.

PAREGORIUS (St) M. AC. Feb 18

See Leo and Paregorius.

PARIS (St) Bp.
RM. Aug 5

d. 346. According to the local tradition, Bishop of Teano, near Naples. His life is embellished with the usual legendary additions.

PARISIUS (St) C. OSB. Cam.
RM. June 11

1152–1267. Born probably at Treviso. At the age of twelve he received the Camaldolese habit, and was ordained priest in 1190. In that same year he was appointed chaplain and spiritual director of the Camaldolese nuns of St Christina outside the walls of Treviso, and he filled that office for seventy-seven years. His body is enshrined in the cathedral of Treviso.

PARMENAS (St) M.   RM. Jan 23

d. c.98. One of the seven deacons ordained by the Apostles (Acts VI, 5). Tradition says that after many years spent in preaching the gospel in Asia Minor, he was martyred at Philippi in Macedonia under Trajan.

PARMENIUS and Comp. (SS) MM.
RM. Apr 22

d. c.250. The priests Parmenius, Helimenas and Chrysotelus, and the deacons Luke and Mucius were beheaded near Babylon when the emperor Decius invaded Mesopotamia.

PARTHENIUS (St) M. RM. May 19

See Calocerus and Parthenius.

PASCHAL I (St) Pope OSB.
RM. Feb 11

d. 824. A Roman, and abbot of the Roman Benedictine monastery of St Stephen near the Vatican, he was raised to the papal throne in 817. He defended the Greek Catholics against the barbarous persecution of the iconoclast emperors. He is perhaps best remembered for his zeal in the recovery and enshrining of the bodies of St Caecilia and other martyrs.

PASCHAL BAYLON (St) C. OFM.
RM. May 17

1540–1592. Born of peasant stock at Torrehermosa in Aragon, he started life as a shepherd. Later he became a Franciscan lay-brother of the Alcantarine reform (1564). He spent his life mainly as doorkeeper in different friaries of Spain. All his life he was animated with an intense love for the Holy Eucharist, the true doctrine of which he triumphantly defended against a Calvinist preacher in France. Beatified in 1618, canonized in 1690. In 1897 he was declared patron of all Eucharistic confraternities and congresses.

PASCHARIUS (PASQUIER) (St) Bp.   **AC. July 10**
d. c.680. Bishop of Nantes. He founded the abbey of Aindre, where he placed St Hermenland of Fontenelle as first abbot.

PASCHASIA (St) VM.   AC. Jan 9
d. c.178 (?). A virgin martyr venerated at Dijon. Her cult is already described as ancient by St Gregory of Tours. Later legends connect her with St Benignus of Dijon.

PASCHASIUS (St) Bp. RM. Feb 22
d. c.312. The eleventh bishop of Vienne in Gaul.

PASCHASIUS RADBERT (St) Ab. OSB.   AC. Apr 26
d. c.851. Born in the Soissonnais, he became a monk of Corbie under St Adalard and was ordained deacon. For many years he held the offices of novice-master and headmaster, both at Old Corbie and at New Corvey, whither he accompanied his abbot in 822. In 844 he was made abbot of Corbie, an office which he found most uncongenial, and which he resigned about the year 850. He was prolific on biblical subjects and his most famous book is his treatise on the Holy Eucharist.

PASCHASIUS (St) C. RM. May 31
d. c.512. A Roman deacon who, in good faith, sided with the antipope Laurence against Pope Symmachus. He is mentioned by St Gregory the Great (Dial. IV, 40). He wrote some theological works which have been lost.

PASCHASIUS (St) M. RM. Nov 13
See Arcadius, Paschasius, etc.

PASICRATES, VALENTIO and Comp. (SS) MM.   RM. May 25
d. c.302. Four soldiers, martyred at Silistria, in Moesia (Bulgaria). They belong to the group of St Julius of Dorostorum, q.v.

PASTOR, VICTORINUS and Comp. (SS) MM.   RM. March 29
d. c.311. Seven martyrs who suffered at Nicomedia under Galesius.

PASTOR (St) Bp. RM. March 30
6th cent. (?). Bishop of Orleans. His name, however, does not appear in the ancient lists.

PASTOR (St) C.   RM. July 26
d. c.160. A Roman priest, said to have been brother to Pope St Pius I. He has left his name to the title (i.e. parish) of St Pudentiana in Rome—*Titulus Pastoris*.

PASTOR (St) M.   RM. Aug 6
See Justus and Pastor.

PATAPIUS (St) H.   RM. Dec 8
7th cent. An Egyptian monk, who migrated to Constantinople and passed his life as a hermit in the suburbs of the city. He is much venerated in the East.

PATERIUS (St) Bp.   RM. Feb 21
d. 606. A Roman monk, disciple and friend of St Gregory the Great. From being notary of the Roman Church, he was raised to the see of Brescia in Lombardy. He was a prolific writer on biblical subjects.

PATERMUTHIUS, COPRES and ALEXANDER (SS) MM. RM. July 9
d. c.363. Patermuthius was a notorious robber converted by an Egyptian hermit, St Copres. Patermuthius then became a hermit also. The RM. makes them martyrs together with Alexander, a converted soldier under Julian the Apostate; but the Acts of these alleged martyrs cannot be admitted as history.

PATERNIAN (St) Bp. RM. July 12
d. *c*.470. Bishop of Bologna *c*.450–470.
Probably identical with the following.

PATERNIAN (St) Bp. AC. Nov 23
d. *c*.343. A Christian who, towards the
end of the persecution of Diocletian
escaped to the mountains. Later he was
made bishop of Fano.

PATERNUS (Bl or St) H. OSB.
AC. Apr 10
d. 1058. A Scot by birth, he was one of
the first monks to enter the Benedictine
abbey of Abdinghof in Paderborn,
founded by St Meinwerk. Afterwards
he became a hermit and died in his cell,
refusing to leave it when the monastery
was destroyed by fire. Bl Marianus
Scotus visited the place a fortnight after
the fire. St Paternus was greatly revered
by St Peter Damian.

PATERNUS (or PERN) (St) Bp.
AC. Apr 15
d. *c*.500. Bishop of Vannes in Brittany,
consecrated *c*.465.

PATERNUS (or PADARN) (St) C.
AC. Apr 16
5th cent. A monk from Brittany, who,
with other monks from the same country, founded Llanbadarn Fawr (i.e., the
great monastery of Padarn) near Aber-
ystwyth in Wales. He preached the
gospel in the country round about.

PATERNUS (French: PAIR) (St)
Bp. RM. Apr 16 and Sept 23
d. *c*.574 (or 563). Born at Poitiers, he
became a monk at Ansion, and later a
hermit near Coutances. Eventually he
was raised to the see of Avranches in
Normandy. He is often confused with
St Paternus of Llanbadarn (see Apr 16).

PATERNUS (St) M. RM. Aug 21
d. *c*.255. The RM., based on doubtful
Acta, says that he came from Alexandria

to Rome, was arrested at Fondi and expired in the dungeon there.

PATERNUS (St) Bp. AC. Sept 28
2nd cent. Born at Bilbao in Spain. He
was one of the earliest bishops—some
say the first—of Eauze (now Auch) in
France.

PATERNUS (St) M. OSB.
RM. Nov 12
d. *c*.726. Born in Brittany, he was a
monk first at Cessier, in the diocese of
Avranches, and then at Saint-Pierre-le-
Vif, diocese of Sens. He was murdered
by malefactors whom he had admon-
ished to reform their lives.

PATIENS (St) Bp. RM. Jan 8
2nd cent. Venerated as the fourth
bishop and the patron saint of Metz.

PATIENS (St) Bp. RM. Sept 11
d. *c*.491. Archbishop of Lyons, highly
praised by his contemporary St Sidonius Apollinaris. He devoted all his
revenues to the relief of the poor.

PATIENTIA (St) M. RM. May 1
See Orentius and Patientia.

PATRICIA (PATRITIA) (St) M.
RM. March 13
See Macedonius, Patricia and Modesta.

PATRICIA (St) V. RM. Aug 25
d. *c*.665. According to the legend, she
was a maiden of Constantinople, related
to the imperial family. In order to
escape marriage she went on a pilgrimage to Jerusalem and then to Rome,
where she received the veil. She died at
Naples, of which city she is one of the
patrons.

PATRICIAN (St) Bp. AC. Oct 10
5th cent. A Scottish bishop driven from
his see by heathen invaders. He spent
the remainder of his life in the Isle of
Man.

PATRICK (St) Bp.   RM. March 16
? Registered in the RM. as bishop of
Auvergne, but his name is not to be
found in the lists of the sees of Auvergne. Quite probably the copyists
wrote *Arvernia* for *Hibernia*, i.e., Ireland,
and thus duplicated the apostle of that
country (see the following). At Malaga,
in Spain, is kept on March 16 the feast
of St Patrick, a native and bishop of that
city, who, according to the local tradition, fled to Auvergne, and died there
c.307.

PATRICK (St) Bp.   RM. March 17
c.389–461. A Romano-Briton by origin,
at the age of sixteen he was taken captive to Ireland (*c*.405). He escaped after
six years. He now pursued his education
in continental monasteries. About the
year 432, after having been consecrated
bishop by St Germanus at Auxerre, he
returned to Ireland as a missionary.
Whatever may be said of the extant data
supplied by his biographers, which in
some instances are obviously conflicting
or legendary, the fact remains that St
Patrick established the Catholic Church
throughout Ireland on lasting foundations: he travelled throughout the
country preaching, teaching, building
churches, opening schools and monasteries, converting chiefs and bards,
and everywhere supporting his preaching with miracles. His writings show
what solid doctrine he must have taught
his hearers. He was, moreover, the first
organizer of the Irish church, with the
primatial see at Armagh (established
c.444). He fully deserves his title of
"Apostle of Ireland".

**PATRICK, ACACIUS, MENAN-
DER and POLYAENUS (SS) MM.**
RM. Apr 28
? A group of martyrs of Prusa (Broussa)
in Bithynia. The Acts of Patrick are
considered authentic. The names of the

others have been added in the early
calendars.

PATRICK (St) Bp.   AC. May 24
d. *c*.469. The fourth bishop of Bayeux.
Liturgically venerated at Bayeux on
May 24.

PATRICK SALMON (Bl) M.
AC. July 4
d. 1594. A servant of Bl Thomas Bosgrave and martyred with him at Dorchester for sheltering a priest.

PATRICK de' PATRIZI (Bl) Mk.
OSB. Oliv.   PC. Aug 21
See Ambrose Piccolomini, etc.

PATRICK (St) Ab.   AC. Aug 24
d. *c*.450. Surnamed "Sen-Patrick"
(Patrick the Elder). Several traditions
mention him as a kinsman and contemporary of St Patrick of Ireland.
There is also St Patrick, abbot of
Nevers, France, likewise commemorated on Aug 24. It is impossible to
disentangle the conflicting data concerning these and other saints of the same
name.

PATROBAS (St)   RM. Nov 4
See Philologus and Patrobas.

PATROCLUS (St) M.   RM. Jan 21
d. *c*.275 (or 259). A very wealthy and
exceedingly charitable Christian of
Troyes, martyred in that city. His relics
were (960) translated to Soest in
Westphalia.

PATTO (Latin: PACIFICUS) (St)
Bp. OSB.   AC. March 30
d. *c*.788. A native of Britain who
crossed over to Saxony, became abbot
of a monastery there, and finally was
appointed bishop of Werden.

PAUL
Note. A very widely used name in all

Christian lands. The Latin form is Paulus, and its modern derivatives are: in Italian and Portuguese, Paolo; in English and French, Paul; in Spanish, Pablo; in Catalan, Pau.

PAUL the HERMIT (St) C.
RM. Jan 10 and 15

c.230–342. The life of this saint, written by St Jerome, tells us that he was an Egyptian of good birth and well educated. At the age of twenty-two he fled into the desert of Thebes to escape the persecution under Decius. He stayed there even after the ending of the persecutions until his death, that is, for ninety years. He was comforted in the end by a visit from St Antony. On a second visit St Antony found him dead and buried him.

PAUL, GERONTIUS, JANUARIUS, SATURNINUS, SUCCESSUS, JULIUS, CATUS, PIA and GER-MANA (SS) MM.   RM. Jan 19

2nd cent. (?). African martyrs, of the province of Numidia, about whom no particulars are given.

PAUL of TROIS-CHATEAUX (St) Bp.   RM. Feb 1

d. c.405. A native of Reims, who, escaping from the barbarian invasions, became a hermit near Arles, and eventually was chosen bishop of Trois-Châteaux (Augusta Tricastrinorum—a diocese now extinct) in Dauphiné.

PAUL MIKI (St) M. SJ. RM. Feb 5

1562–1597. Born at Tounucumada in Japan, son of a Japanese military chief, he was educated at the Jesuit college of Anziquiama, and in 1580 entered the Society of Jesus. He was famed as an orator and controversialist. His last sermon was delivered from the Cross on which he was martyred at Nagasaki. Canonized in 1862.

PAUL YUANKI or IBARKI and PAUL SUSUKI (SS) MM. RM. Feb 5

d. 1597. Japanese laymen, tertiaries of St Francis, interpreters and catechists to the Franciscan missionaries. Both were crucified at Nagasaki. Canonized in 1862.

PAUL, LUCIUS and CYRIACUS (SS) MM.   RM. Feb 8

? Martyrs at Rome.

PAUL of VERDUN (St) Bp. OSB.
RM. Feb 8

d. c.649. A courtier who retired first to Mt Voge (now Paulberg), near Trèves, as a hermit and afterwards entered the monastery of Tholey, where he was appointed headmaster of the monastic school. After some years (c.630) King Dagobert appointed him bishop of Verdun.

PAUL and NINETY COM-PANIONS (BB) MM. OP. PC. Feb 10

d. 1240. Paul was a lawyer of Hungarian origin at the University of Bologna. Induced by St Dominic to join the Friars Preachers, he brought the new order into Hungary. With ninety companions he was sent to Wallachia, where they were martyred by the Cumanians.

PAUL LIEOU (Bl) M.   AC. Feb 13

d. 1818. A Chinese layman who was martyred by strangulation. Beatified in 1900.

PAUL LOC (Bl) M.   AC. Feb 13

1831–1859. A native of An-nhon in Cochin-China, who, shortly after his ordination to the priesthood, was beheaded at Saigon. Beatified in 1909.

PAUL, HERACLIUS, SECUNDIL-LA and JANUARIA (SS) MM.
RM. March 2

d. c.305. Martyrs who suffered under

Diocletian at Porto Romano, at the mouth of the Tiber.

PAUL of PRUSA (St) Bp.
RM. March 7

d. 840. Bishop of Prusa (Plusias) in Bithynia. For his courageous resistance to the iconoclasts he was banished to Egypt where he died.

PAUL the SIMPLE (St) H.
RM. March 7

d. c.339. An Egyptian farmer who, at the age of sixty, discovered the adultery of his wife and forthwith left for the desert, where he placed himself under St Antony. His prompt obedience and childlike disposition were "the pride of the desert" and merited for him the surname of "the Simple". He is mentioned by Rufinus and Palladius.

PAUL (St) M.
RM. March 10

See Codratus, Dionysius, etc.

PAUL AURELIAN (St) Bp.
AC. March 12

d. c.575. A Romano-Briton by origin, he was born in Wales, and educated at Llantwit Major under St Illtyd, together with SS David, Samson, Gildas, etc. He dwelt for a time on Caldey Island, whence he crossed over into Brittany with twelve companions. He established a monastery at Porz-Pol on the isle of Ouessant and finally fixed his residence at Ouismor (now Saint-Pol-de-Léon), where he was consecrated bishop.

PAUL of CYPRUS (St) M.
RM. March 17

d. 775. A monk of Cyprus, who, in the reign of the iconoclast emperor Constantine Copronymus, refused to trample on a crucifix and was hung head downwards over a slow fire till he died.

PAUL, CYRIL, EUGENE and Comp. (SS) MM.
RM. March 20

? A group of seven martyrs, who suffered in Syria.

PAUL of NARBONNE (St) Bp.
RM. March 22

d. p.250. St Gregory of Tours (*Hist. Franc. I. 30*) writes that St Paul was consecrated at Rome towards the middle of the 3rd century and sent to Gaul to preach the gospel, which he did with great success at Narbonne. A much later legend identifies him with the Roman proconsul Sergius Paulus, converted by St Paul the Apostle (Acts XIII).

PAUL TINH (Bl) M.
AC. Apr 6

d. 1857. Born at Trinh-ha, Tonkin, he became a priest, and was beheaded at Son-tay, in W. Tonkin. Beatified in 1909.

PAUL of CORDOVA (St) M.
RM. Apr 17

See Elias, Paul and Isidore.

PAUL of the CROSS (St) C. Founder
RM. Apr 28

1694–1775 (Oct 18). Paolo Francesco Danei was born at Ovada in Piedmont. Inspired by a series of visions he with some companions went to live the religious life on Mt Argentaro, near Orbitello. In 1720 they received the habit of "Barefooted Clerks of the Cross and the Passion" (Passionists) from the bishop of Alessandria. In 1727 Paul was ordained priest in the Vatican basilica, and in 1747 the first general chapter of the new Congregation was held. St Paul lived to see its expansion throughout Italy. Canonized in 1867.

PAUL KHOAN (Bl) M. AC. Apr 28

d. 1840. A native of Tonkin, and a priest attached to the Paris Foreign

Missions for forty years. He was in prison for two years before he was beheaded. Beatified in 1900.

PAUL (St) M.   RM. May 15
See Peter, Andrew, etc.

PAUL (St) M.   RM. May 17
See Heradius, Paul, etc.

PAUL (St) M.   RM. May 28
See Crescens, Dioscorides, etc.

PAUL HANH (Bl) M.   AC. May 28
d. 1859. A native layman of Cochin-China. He abandoned his Faith and joined a band of outlaws. When arrested, he professed his religion, and, after frightful tortures, was beheaded near Saigon. Beatified in 1909.

PAUL (St) M.   RM. June 1
See Reverianus, Paul, and Comp.

PAUL (St) M.   RM. June 1
See Valens, Paul, and Comp.

PAUL (St) M.   RM. June 3
See Lucillian, Claudius, etc.

PAUL of CONSTANTINOPLE (St) Bp. M.   RM. June 7
d. c.350. A patriarch of Constantinople, whose episcopate was largely spent in exile for the Catholic faith. Elected in 336, he was exiled to Pontus in 337, whence he returned in 338, but was exiled again by an Arian synod, this time to Trèves. He returned to his see c.340, but in 342 was sent in chains to Mesopotamia by the emperor Constantius. Recalled in 344, he was banished for the last time to Kukusus in Armenia, where he was left without food for six days and then strangled.

PAUL BURALI d' AREZZO (Bl) Bp. Card.   AC. June 17
1511–1578. Born at Itri, diocese of Gaeta, he became a lawyer and practised his profession for ten years at Naples. In 1549 he was appointed royal counsellor, but in 1558 he joined the Theatine order and eventually was made superior at the houses of Naples and Rome. St Pius V appointed him bishop of Piacenza and created him cardinal. Finally he was promoted to the see of Naples. Beatified in 1772.

PAUL and CYRIACUS (SS) MM.
                                         RM. June 20
? Martyrs who suffered at Tomi on the Black Sea, in Lower Moesia.

PAUL XINSUKI (Bl) M. SJ.
                                         AC. June 20
d. 1626. A Japanese Jesuit, catechist to Bl Paul Navarro. He was burnt alive at Nagasaki. Beatified in 1867.

PAUL (St) M.   RM. June 26
See John and Paul

PAUL I (St) Pope   RM. June 28
d. 767. A Roman, educated with his brother, the future Pope Stephen III, at the Lateran school. He succeeded his brother in the papal chair in 757. His pontificate was uneventful except for the iconoclast excesses of the Byzantine emperor Constantine Copronymus, whom the pope valiantly opposed. As some compensation for the destruction in the East, St Paul restored and beautified several Roman churches and enshrined the relics of many saints.

PAUL GIUSTINIANI (Bl) OSB. Cam.   AC. June 28
1476–1528. A member of the Venetian house of Giustiniani. He joined the Camaldolese Benedictines, and eventually established the new Congregation of Monte Corona. He ranks among the Camaldolese as their most prolific writer. His feast is kept by the Camaldolese.

PAUL the APOSTLE (St) M.
RM. June 29 (30)

c.3–67. Born at Tarsus in Cilicia, a Jew of the tribe of Benjamin, a Pharisee, a Roman citizen, a tentmaker by trade, he was educated in the Sacred Law of the Jews at the feet of Gamaliel in Jerusalem. After taking an active part in the stoning of the first Christian martyr St Stephen, he placed himself whole-heartedly at the service of the Jewish authorities in their attempt to stamp out Christianity, but was miraculously converted on the road to Damascus, and received directly from Christ his mission to evangelize the Gentiles. He did so in at least four apostolic journeys, ex-tending from Cappadocia and Galatia perhaps as far as Spain, establishing churches everywhere, and ever sur-rounded by dangers of all sorts—he was shipwrecked, imprisoned, flogged, stoned, banished from several cities, persecuted by the hatred of his own people. Nevertheless he was always burning for more sufferings and con-quests for Christ, who recompensed him, even in this life, with the highest degree of mystical experience. His fourteen epistles, addressed mostly to the churches which he had founded, belong to the deposit of divine revela-tion. He was beheaded in Rome near the Ostian Way where the Church of Tre Fontane now stands. Liturgically he is honoured with St Peter, on June 29, as the co-founder of the Roman church; while the feast of his conversion is celebrated on Jan 25.

PAUL (St) M.
RM. July 3

See Mark, Mucianus and Paul.

PAUL of ST ZOILUS (St) M.
RM. July 20

d. 851. A Spanish deacon of Cordova who belonged to the community of St Zoilus in the same city and was most zealous in ministering to his fellow-Christians imprisoned by the Moham-medans. He was beheaded for the Faith, and his fellow Christians succeeded in securing his remains, which they en-shrined in the church of St Zoilus.

PAUL of GAZA (St) M. RM. July 25

d. 308. A martyr of Gaza in Palestine, beheaded under Maximian Galerius.

PAUL TCHENG (Bl) M. AC. July 29

d. 1861. A seminarian. Beheaded at Tsin-gai. Beatified in 1909.

PAUL and JULIANA (SS) MM.
RM. Aug 17

d. *c*.270. Brother and sister, beheaded at Ptolemais in Palestine under Aurelian.

PAUL SANCHIKI (Bl) M.
AC. Aug 19

d. 1622. A Japanese sailor on board the ship of Bl Joachim Firaiama. Beheaded at Nagasaki. Beatified in 1867.

PAUL (St) M.
RM. Aug 29

See Nicaeas and Paul.

PAUL TOMAKI and PAUL AY BARA Tert. OP. (BB) MM.
AC. Sept 8

d. 1628. Paul Tomaki was a boy of seven, beheaded with his father, Bl John Tomaki, q.v., and his three brothers at Nagasaki. Paul Aybara was a Japanese catechist and Dominican tertiary, likewise beheaded at Nagasaki. Beatified in 1867.

PAUL TANACA and PAUL NAN-GAXI (BB) MM.
AC. Sept 10

d. 1622. Japanese companions in martyrdom of Bl Charles Spinola, q.v.

PAUL FIMONAYA (Bl) M. Tert. OP.
AC. Sept 16

d. 1628. Son of Bl Michael Fimonaya

(q.v.) and a Dominican tertiary. Beheaded at Nagasaki. Beatified in 1867.

PAUL, TATTA, SABINIAN, MAXIMUS, RUFUS, and EUGENE (SS) MM. RM. Sept 25
? Paul and Tatta were husband and wife, the others were their sons. All died under torture in their native city of Damascus.

PAUL (St) M. RM. Oct 3
See Dionysius, Faustus, etc.

PAUL DOI BUONG (Bl) M.
AC. Oct 22
d. 1833. A native of Cochin-China and captain of the bodyguard of King Minh-Menh. As a Christian he became attached to the Society of Foreign Missions of Paris. He was arrested in 1832, degraded and beheaded. Beatified in 1900.

PAUL NAVARRO SJ. and Comp. (BB) MM. SJ. AC. Nov 1
d. 1622. Paul Navarro was born in 1560 at Laino, diocese of Cassano, in Italy. He became a Jesuit in 1587 and while still a scholastic was sent to India where he was ordained, and thence to Japan. He worked with great success as superior of Amanguchi. He was burnt alive at Ximabara. With him suffered two junior members of the Society and a servant.

PAUL NGAN (Bl) M. AC. Nov 8
d. 1840. A Tonkinese priest, beheaded with four other martyrs at Nam-Dinh. Beatified in 1900.

PAUL of LATROS (St) H.
AC. Dec 15
d. 956. Born near Pergamos. After the death of his parents he became a hermit first on Mt Olympus, then in a cave on Mt Latros in Bithynia, and finally on the isle of Samos. He died on Mt Latros.

PAUL MI (Bl) M. AC. Dec 18
d. 1838. A native of Tonkin, attached to the Society of Foreign Missions of Paris. Martyred by strangulation. Beatified in 1900.

PAUL (St) M. RM. Dec 19
See Darius, Zozimus, etc.

PAUL (St) M. RM. Dec 24
See Lucian, Metrobius, etc.

PAULA (St) V. OSB. Cam. AC. Jan 5
1318–1368. Born in Tuscany, she was entrusted in childhood to the Camaldolese nuns and remained with them all her life. She was instrumental in bringing the feuds between Pisa and Florence to a peaceful settlement.

PAULA (St) W. RM. Jan 26
347–404. A Roman lady of noble birth, she married a patrician, to whom she bore five children, among them St Eustochium and St Blaesilla. Left a widow when she was thirty-four Paula embraced the religious life, and for twenty years presided over the sisterhood founded by her near St Jerome's monastery at Bethlehem, where she also established a hospital. St Jerome became her spiritual director, and after her death her biographer.

PAULA GAMBARA-COSTA (Bl) Matron AC. Jan 31
1473–1515. Born at Brescia, she married at the age of twelve a young nobleman. She had much to suffer from her husband, who not only objected to her charities, admittedly lavish, but was also shamefully unfaithful to her. By her heroic patience she won him over to better things and passed the remainder of an austere life in peaceful wedlock. She died worn out with self-imposed penances. Cult confirmed by Gregory XVI.

PAULA (St) VM.   RM. June 3
d. *c*.273. A maiden of Nicomedia who ministered to the martyr St Lucillian (q.v.) and to four youths in prison, and was for this reason arrested and tortured, and finally sent to Byzantium, where she was beheaded.

PAULA FRASINETTI (Bl) Foundress   AC. June 11
1809–1882. Born at Genoa, she lived with her brother who was parish-priest at Quinto, one of the suburbs of the city, and there she began to teach poor children. This was the beginning of the Congregation of St Dorothy, which she lived to see flourishing throughout Italy and the New World. Beatified in 1930.

PAULA (St) VM.   RM. June 18
See Cyriacus and Paula.

PAULA (St) M.   RM. July 20
See Sabinus, Julian, etc.

PAULA (St) VM.   RM. Aug 10
See Bassa, Paula and Agathonica.

PAULA of MONTALDO (Bl) W. Poor Clare   AC. Oct 29
1443–1514. Born at Montaldo, near Mantua, at the age of fifteen she joined the Poor Clares at Santa Lucia in Mantua, where she was later elected abbess three times. She was favoured with mystical experiences. Cult approved in 1906.

PAULA-ELIZABETH CERIOLI (Bl) W. Foundress   AC. Dec 24
1818–1865. Constance Honorata Cerioli was born at Soncini, Cremona, and educated by the Visitation nuns. In spite of an inclination to the religious life, she accepted the will of her parents and married Cajetan Buzecchi-Tassis, by whom she had three children. All, however, died, as did her husband in 1854. Then she began to receive and care for orphan girls in her house at Como, whom she educated and taught to till the fields. Under her pious leadership there thus arose the Institute of the Sisters of the Holy Family, of which she, under the name of Paula-Elizabeth, was made Superior. Later she founded a similar orphanage for boys in 1863. She died of heart disease at forty-seven, leaving the memory of a saint. Beatified in 1950.

PAULILLUS (St) M.   RM. Nov 13
See Arcadius, Paschasius, etc.

PAULILLUS (St) M.   RM. Dec 19
See Cyriacus, Paulillus, etc.

PAULINA (Bl) W. OSB.   AC. March 14
d. 1107. A German princess, who, after the death of her husband, founded, with her son Werner, the double monastery at Zell (Paulinzelle). She died at Münsterschwarzach.

PAULINA (St) M.   RM. June 6
See Artemius, Candida and Paulina.

PAULINA (St) M.   RM. Dec 2
See Eusebius, Marcellus, etc.

PAULINA (St) M.   RM. Dec 31
See Donata, Paulina, etc.

PAULINUS of AQUILEIA (St) Bp.   AC. Jan 28
c.726–804. Born near Cividale in N. Italy he received a good education, and after the destruction of the Lombard kingdom in 774, was summoned to court by his great admirer Charlemagne, who in 784 sent him back to Italy as patriarch of Aquileia. Paulinus wrote much and competently against Adoptionism and was a firm supporter of the *Filioque*. He also carried on missionary work among the Avars.

PAULINUS of BRESCIA (St) Bp.
RM. Apr 29

d. *c*.545. Bishop of Brescia (*c*.524–545). His relics are enshrined in the church of San Pietro in Oliveto.

PAULINUS (St) M.　　RM. May 4

? A martyr whose relics are enshrined at Cologne, but of whom otherwise nothing is known.

PAULINUS of SINIGAGLIA (St) Bp.　　　　　　　　AC. May 4

d. 826. Bishop, and now patron saint, of Sinigaglia, in Italy. Nothing is known of his life.

PAULINUS (St) M.　　RM. May 26

See Felicissimus, Heraclius and Paulinus.

PAULINUS of NOLA (St) Bp.
RM. June 22

c.354–431. Pontius Meropius Anicius Paulinus was born at Bordeaux, the son of a Roman patrician who at that time held the office of praetorian prefect in Gaul. Paulinus was taught by the poet Ausonius. He was appointed prefect of Rome, but after the death of his only child (390) he retired from the world and went to Spain, where the people of Barcelona compelled him to accept the priesthood. Finally he settled as a hermit near Nola in Campania and here the people (410) chose him for their bishop. He proved to be one of the best prelates of his time, and was in friendly intercourse with most of his great contemporaries: Ambrose, Jerome, Augustine, Martin of Tours, Victricius of Rouen, etc. He had much to suffer during the invasion of Campania by the Goths under Alaric. Most of his poems and a number of his letters are still extant, and they show him to have been a Christian poet of distinction as well as a fluent writer of prose.

PAULINUS of ANTIOCH and Comp. (SS) MM.　　RM. July 12

? This St Paulinus is venerated as the first bishop and patron saint of Lucca in Tuscany. The legend adds that he was a native of Antioch sent to Lucca by St Peter, and that he was martyred (*c*.67) with a priest, a deacon and a soldier. The whole story is most untrustworthy and it is probable that this saint is to be identified with the bishop Paulinus who governed the see *c*.355–365.

PAULINUS of TRÈVES (St) Bp.
RM. Aug 31

d. 358. A native of Gascony who accompanied St Maximinus to Trèves and succeeded him as bishop in 349. He was a brave supporter of St Athanasius and was for this reason banished to Phrygia by the Arian emperor Constantius in 355. He died in exile, but his relics were brought back to Trèves.

PAULINUS of YORK (St) Bp. OSB.
RM. Oct 10

d. 644. A Roman monk sent to England with SS Mellitus and Justus (601) by Pope Gregory the Great to aid St Augustine in his labours. He spent twenty-four years in Kent, and in 625 was consecrated bishop of York and sent to evangelize Northumbria, which he did very successfully, baptizing King St Edwin at York on Easter Sunday, 627. After the king's death he was driven from his see and returned to Kent, where he administered the see of Rochester till his death.

PAULINUS of CAPUA (St) Bp.
RM. Oct 10

d. 843. Said to have been a native of England, who, while on a pilgrimage to Jerusalem, made a stay at Capua and was constrained by the inhabitants to become their bishop. After an episcopate of eight years he died at Sicopolis, whither he had fled during the invasion of the Saracens.

PAULINUS (St) Mk. OSB. AC. Nov 5
See Augustine and Paulinus.

PAULINUS (POLIN, PEWLIN, PAULHEN) (St) C.   AC. Nov 23
d. *c*.505 (?). A Welsh abbot, pupil of St Illtyd, founder (?) of the monastery of Whitland (Caermarthen), where he had among his disciples St David and St Teilo.

PAUSIDES (PAUSIS) (St) M.
RM. March 24
See Timolaus, and Comp.

PAUSILIPPUS (St) M.   RM. Apr 15
See Theodore and Pausilippus.

PEBLIG (PUBLICUS) C. AC. July 3
Otherwise Byblig, q.v.

PEGA (St) V.   AC. Jan 8
d. *c*.719. A sister of St Guthlac of Croyland. She too lived as a recluse, but seems to have died while on a pilgrimage to Rome. The village of Peakirk in Northamptonshire preserves her name.

PEGASIUS (St) M.   RM. Nov 2
See Acindynus, Pegasius, etc.

PELAGIA (St) M.   RM. March 23
See Domitius, Pelagia, etc.

PELAGIA (St) VM.   RM. May 4
d. *c*.300. A maiden of Tarsus in Cilicia, said to have been roasted to death for refusing to marry one of the sons of the emperor Diocletian. The story is regarded as apocryphal.

PELAGIA of ANTIOCH (St) VM.
RM. June 9
d. *c*.311. A girl of fifteen who was a

disciple of St Lucian at Antioch. When soldiers were sent to arrest her, she threw herself from the top of her house to avoid the loss of her virginity and was killed. St John Chrysostom, who greatly praised her courage, attributes her action to divine inspiration.

PELAGIA (St) M.   RM. July 11
See Januarius and Pelagia.

PELAGIA the PENITENT (St)
RM. Oct 8
Otherwise Marina (June 18) q.v.

PELAGIA (St) VM.   RM. Oct 19
See Beronicus, Pelagia, etc.

PELAGIUS of LAODICEA (St) Bp.
RM. March 25
d. *p*.381. A bishop of Laodicea. He championed the Catholic cause against Arianism and on that account was banished by the Arian emperor Valens. Recalled by Gratian, he was present at the council of Constantinople (381). The date of his death is not known.

PELAGIUS (St) M.   AC. Apr 7
? A priest martyred at Alexandria in Egypt. Mentioned in the Martyrology of St Jerome.

PELAGIUS (Spanish: PELAYO) (St) M.   RM. June 26
c.912–925. A young boy of Asturias left as a hostage with the Moors at Cordova. He was offered freedom and other rewards if he would turn Mohammedan and commit other shameful sins. These inducements were repeatedly put before him during the three years that he was kept in prison, and on his stubborn refusal he was put to the torture, which he endured for six hours, finally dying while under it. His relics were transferred to León in 967 and to Oviedo in

985. The Benedictine poetess Rhoswitha of Gandersheim (d. 973) wrote a long poem in his honour. He is still greatly honoured in Spain.

PELAGIUS (St) M.   RM. Aug 28
d. *c*.283. A boy martyred in Istria under Numerian. His relics were transferred to Città Nuova in Istria and part of them (*c*.915) to Constance on the Swiss lake of that name. He is venerated as the patron saint of Constance.

**PELAGIUS, ARSENIUS and SYL-
VANUS (SS) MM.   AC. Aug 30**
d. *c*.950. Hermits near Burgos in Old Castile, who, according to an old tradition, were done to death by the Saracens. Their cell was the origin of the Benedictine Abbey of Artanza. The three martyrs are still greatly venerated in the province of Burgos.

PELEUS (St) Bp. M.
RM. Feb 20 and Sept 19
See Tyrannio, Sylvanus, etc., and Peleus, Nilus, etc.

**PELEUS, NILUS, ELIAS and
Comp. (SS) MM.   RM. Sept 19**
d. *c*.310. Three Egyptian bishops (or priests) together with many priests and laymen (some say, with only one layman), were sentenced to labour in the quarries and finally burnt alive, probably at Phunon, near Petra, for celebrating the liturgy in the place of detention. Some identify this group with that listed in the RM. on Feb 20 under St Tyrannio, q.v.

PELEUSIUS (St) M.   RM. Apr 7
? According to the RM., a priest of Alexandria. Nothing is known of him.

PELINUS (St) Bp. M.   RM. Dec 5
d. 361. A martyr of Confinium, a town in Samnium now destroyed, who suffered under Julian the Apostate.

PEPIN of LANDEN (Bl) C.
AC. Feb 21
d. *c*.646. Pepin, duke of Brabant, mayor of the palace under Kings Clotaire II, Dagobert and Sigebert, and ancestor of the Carolingian dynasty of French kings, was the husband of Bl Ida and the father of St Gertrude of Nivelles and of St Begga. He is described as "a lover of peace and the constant defender of truth and justice". His feast was kept at Nivelles.

PEREGRINUS (Bl) C. OSA.
AC. March 20
See Evangelist and Peregrinus.

**PEREGRINUS LAZIOSI (St) C.
OSM.   RM. May 1**
1260–1345. A native of Forli who spent a very worldly youth, in the course of which during a popular revolt he struck St Philip Benizi across the face. Philip turned the other cheek and Peregrinus was converted on the spot and forthwith joined the Servites at Siena. He was afterwards sent back to Forli where he spent the rest of his long life. He was instantaneously cured of a cancer of the foot as a result of a vision, and is for that reason invoked against cancer. Canonized in 1726.

PEREGRINUS (St) M.
RM. May 5
See Irenaeus, Peregrinus and Irene.

PEREGRINUS (St) Bp. AC. May 16
d. *c*.138 (?). Bishop of Terni in Umbria and founder of its cathedral.

PEREGRINUS (St) Bp. M.
RM. May 16
d. *c*.304. A Roman by birth, venerated as the first bishop of Auxerre, to which see he is said to have been appointed by Pope Sixtus II. He was martyred under Diocletian.

PEREGRINUS I and PEREGRINUS II (BB) CC. OSB. Cam. AC. June 3
d. *c*.1291. Peregrinus I was a Camal-dolese abbot of Santa Maria dell' Isola. In 1290 he returned to Camaldoli as sacrist and prior. Peregrinus II was a simple monk who lived at Camaldoli and died about the same time as Peregrinus I.

PEREGRINUS (properly CETHE-US) (St) Bp. M.   RM. June 13
d. *c*.600. Bishop of Amiternum (now Aquila) in S. Italy. He was drowned in the river Aterno by the Arian Lombards for asking mercy for a condemned prisoner.

PEREGRINUS (St) M. RM. June 17
See Isaurus, Innocent, etc.

PEREGRINUS, LUCIAN, POM-PEIUS, HESYCHIUS, PAPIUS, SATURNINUS, GERMANUS, and ASTIUS (SS) MM.   RM. July 7
d. *c*.117. Astius was bishop of Dyrrachium (Durazzo) in Macedonia and was there crucified under Trajan. The others were Italians who had fled to Macedonia in order to escape the persecution in their own country and were seized on account of the sympathy they showed for Astius. They were loaded with chains, taken out to the sea and thrown overboard.

PEREGRINUS (St) H. RM. July 28
2nd cent. (?). He seems to have been a priest of the diocese of Lyons in the time of St Irenaeus, and during the persecution under Severus to have lived as a hermit in an island in the R. Saône.

PEREGRINUS (St) H.   AC. Aug 1
d. 643. An Irish, or Scottish, pilgrim, who, returning from a pilgrimage to the Holy Land, settled in a solitude near Modena where he passed the rest of his days.

PEREGRINUS, MACERATUS and VIVENTIUS (SS) MM.   AC. Aug 4
6th cent. A doubtful legend makes them Spaniards and brothers who perished in France, seeking to rescue their enslaved sister. The cult is entirely local.

PEREGRINUS (St) M. RM. Aug 25
See Eusebius, Pontian, etc.

PEREGRINUS of FALERONE (Bl) C. OFM.   AC. Sept 6
d. 1240. Born at Falerone in the diocese of Fermo, he became a follower of St Francis of Assisi, and after a pilgrimage to Palestine, lived as a lay-brother at San Severino.

PERFECTUS (St) M.   RM. Apr 18
d. 851. A Spanish priest of Cordova, martyred by the Mohammedans on Easter Sunday.

PERGENTINUS and LAURENTI-NUS (SS) MM.   RM. June 3
d. 251. Two brothers martyred at Arezzo under Decius. It is not certain whether they ever existed.

PERIS (St) C.   AC. Dec 11
? The patron saint of Llanberis in N. Wales. No record of him exists.

PERPETUA, FELICITAS, SATU-RUS (SATYRUS), SATURNINUS, REVOCATUS and SECUNDULUS (SS) MM.   RM. March 6 and 7
d. 203. Vivia Perpetua was a young married woman of good social position and Saturus was her brother. Felicitas, also married, was a slave. The others were catechumens. All were imprisoned together at Carthage. Secundulus died in prison: the others were thrown to the wild beasts in the amphitheatre on March 7. The feast of SS Perpetua and Felicitas is kept on the preceding day. Their Acts, which are of the highest

value and interest, both theologically and historically, are undoubtedly authentic. They were written by Saturus, one of the martyrs, and completed by an eye-witness, perhaps Tertullian. SS Perpetua and Felicitas are mentioned in the canon of the Roman Mass.

PERPETUA (St)   **RM. Aug 4**
d. *c*.80. A Roman matron said to have been baptized by St Peter and to have converted her husband and her son St Nazarius. (See Nazarius and Celsus.) Her relics are at Milan and Cremona.

PERPETUUS (St) Bp.   **RM. Apr 8**
d. *c*.490. Bishop of Tours (*c*.460–490). His alleged will is admittedly a forgery of the 17th century.

PERREUX (St) Ab.   **AC. June 4**
The Breton form of Petroc, q.v.

PERSEVERANDA (PECINNA, PEZAINE) (St) V.   **RM. June 26**
d. *c*.726. Said to have been a Spanish maiden, who with her sisters Macrina and Columba, travelled to Poitiers, where they founded a nunnery. While fleeing from the pirate Oliver, Perseveranda died of exhaustion in the place now called after her Sainte-Pezaine in Poitou.

PERSIA, Martyrs of (SS)
The RM. catalogues five anonymous groups of martyrs who suffered in Persia, as follows:
                                          RM. Feb 8
? 6th cent. Martyrs slain under Cabas.

                                        RM. March 10
? A group of forty-two martyrs of whom all details are lost.
                                          RM. Apr 6
? 345. Another group of one hundred and twenty martyrs, believed to have suffered under Shapur II (309–380).

                                          RM. Apr 22
d. 376. A vast number of martyrs put to death under the same king Shapur II on Good Friday. Among them were some twenty-five bishops, two hundred and fifty priests and deacons and very many monks and nuns.

                                          RM. May 9
? A group of three hundred and ten martyrs of whom, again, no details are known.

Eastern menologies give other dates and other figures, but a fair estimate of the Persian martyrs put to death during the first six centuries would bring the number up to ten thousand.

PETER (*several*)
Note. The name Petrus is the latinized form of the Greek Petros, which means Rock. Modern variants of Petrus are as follows: Italian, Pietro (antiquated form Piero); Spanish and Portuguese, Pedro; French, Pierre; Catalan, Pere; English, Peter.

PETER APSELAMUS and PETER ABSALON (SS) MM.   **RM. Jan 3**
311. Peter surnamed Apselamus, or Balsamus, was crucified at Aulona, near Hebron. Eusebius mentions a Peter Abselame (or Absalon) who was burnt at Caesarea. It is disputed whether these two are the same person.

PETER of CANTERBURY (St) Ab. OSB.   **AC. Jan 6**
d. *c*.608. A Benedictine monk of St Andrew's Rome, who was a member of the first band of missionaries sent to England by St Gregory the Great. He became first abbot of the monastery of SS Peter and Paul (afterwards St Augustine's), founded at Canterbury. While on a mission in France he was drowned at Ambleteuse, near Boulogne. Cult confirmed in 1915.

PETER of SEBASTE (St) Bp.
RM. Jan 9

d. *c*.391. A native of Cappadocia, and younger brother of St Basil and of St Gregory of Nyssa. He succeeded St Basil as abbot and in 380 was appointed bishop of Sebaste in Armenia. He took part in the general council of Constantinople (381). (Another Peter of Sebaste, Bishop, is also honoured as a Saint. He died about 320.)

PETER URSEOLUS (St) H. OSB.
RM. Jan 10

928–987. Born in Venice, Peter became, at the age of twenty, admiral of the Venetian fleet. In 976 he became Doge of Venice and succeeded in guiding the Republic safely through a time of dangerous political crisis. After two years, unknown to all—even to his family, he disappeared from Venice, to emerge as a monk in the Benedictine abbey of Cuxa, in the Spanish Pyrenees. He acted as sacristan of the abbey until some years later he retired to live as a hermit.

PETER, SEVERUS and LEUCIUS (SS) MM.
RM. Jan 11

? Peter and Leucius are mentioned in the Hieronymen martyrology as Confessors. To them the RM. adds Severus and describes all three as martyrs at Alexandria.

PETER of CASTELNAU (Bl) M. OSB. Cist.
AC. Jan 15

d. 1208. Born near Montpellier, he became archdeacon of Maguelonne (1199) and shortly after (*c*.1202) a Cistercian at Fontfroide. The following year Pope Innocent III appointed him apostolic legate and inquisitor for the Albigensians—in fact the leader of the famous expedition, of which St Dominic was a member, for the conversion of those heretics. While engaged in that work he was assassinated, his last words being: "May God forgive thee, brother, as fully as I forgive thee."

PETER (St) M. OFM.
RM. Jan 16

See Berardus, Peter, etc.

PETER THOMAS (St) Bp. OC.
AC. Jan 25

1305–1366 (Jan 6). A native of Breil in Gascony, Peter Thomas joined the Carmelites and in 1342 was sent to Avignon as procurator of his Order. There he entered the service of the papal court and was sent on diplomatic missions to Italy, Serbia, Hungary and the Near East, being appointed successively bishop of Patti and Lipari (1354), bishop of Coron in Morea (1359), archbishop of Candia (1363) and Latin patriarch of Constantinople (1364). On behalf of Pope Urban V and with the support of King Peter I of Cyprus he led a crusade against the Turks. In an unsuccessful attack on Alexandria he was severely wounded and died three months later at Cyprus. Throughout his active life he remained true to the spirit of his contemplative profession. Cult approved in 1608.

PETER NOLASCO (St) Founder
RM. Jan 31

c.1182–1258 (Dec 25). A native of Languedoc, who, after seeing service against the Albigenses, settled at Barcelona, where he became intimate with St Raymund of Peñafort. About the year 1218 both saints, with the help of James I of Aragon, reorganized a lay confraternity for ransoming captives from the Moors, which was gradually transformed into the Order of the Mercedarians (*B. V. Mariae de Mercede Redemptionis Captivorum*), of which St Peter Nolasco is revered as the chief founder. He personally ransomed several hundred captives. Canonized in 1628.

PETER of ZALANKEMEN (Bl) C.
PC. Jan 31
15th cent. He was an exemplary General of the Pauline Hermit Order (1488–1492).

PETER CAMBIAN (Bl) M. OP.
AC. Feb 2
d. 1365. Peter Cambian de Ruffi, a Dominican of distinction, was sent in 1351 as inquisitor general to Piedmont and Lombardy. He had chiefly to deal with the Waldenses, who ultimately trapped and killed him. Cult approved in 1856.

PETER BAPTIST (St) M. OFM.
RM. Feb 5
1545–1597. Born near Avila, in Spain, He joined the Friars Minor in 1567. He was sent as a missionary first to Mexico, then to the Philippine Islands (1583) and lastly (1593) to Japan. Political intrigues led to the arrest of Peter and twenty-six missionaries (six Franciscans, three Jesuits and seventeen native Franciscan tertiaries), who had never given a thought to politics. They were all crucified at Nagasaki. St Peter Baptist, who had the gift of working miracles, is considered as their leader. All were canonized in 1862.

PETER XUKEXICO (St) M.
RM. Feb 5
d. 1597. A Japanese layman. He was a Franciscan tertiary, a catechist, and house-servant and sacristan to the Franciscan missionaries in Japan. He belongs to the group of St Peter Baptist, q.v.

PETER IGNEUS (St) Card. Bp.
OSB. Vall.   RM. Feb 8
d. c.1089. He is said to have belonged to the Aldobrandini family of Florence. He took his vows at Vallumbrosa under St John Gualbert. Shortly after, in order to convict the bishop of Florence of simony, Peter miraculously passed through the flames unharmed, whence his surname of *Igneus*, "of the fire". At a later period he was created cardinal-bishop of Albano and sent to foreign countries as legate of the Holy See.

PETER of TREJA (Bl) C. OFM.
AC. Feb 20
d. 1304. One of the early Franciscans associated with Bl Conrad of Offida in his apostolate. They preached with great success throughout Italy. Bl Peter died at Sirolo in Piceno. Cult approved in 1793.

PETER the SCRIBE (St) M.
RM. Feb 21
d. 743. Surnamed also *Mavimenus*, from the town of Majuma in Palestine where he worked as a scribe (*chartularius*). He was put to death by the Arab sheik of Damascus.

PETER DAMIAN (St) Bp. Card.
Dr. OSB.   RM. Feb 23
1007–1072. Born at Ravenna, the youngest of many children, he was left an orphan in charge of a married brother, who ill-treated him and set him to herd swine. Another brother, Damian, archpriest of Ravenna, took pity on the child and paid for his schooling at Faenza and Parma. Peter soon joined the Benedictine community of Fontavellana, founded by Bl Rudolph twenty years before. Earnest in all his undertakings, Peter became a model monk and was chosen abbot. In 1057 he was summoned to Rome and created cardinal-bishop of Ostia. He served successive popes in various missions: as legate to Germany, to France, to Lombardy, as president, or papal representative, at sundry councils and synods; as visitor to bishoprics and abbeys. Meanwhile

he wrote unceasingly, mostly theological or ascetical works, but also poetry, his Latin verse being among the very best of the Middle Ages. He died at Faenza worn out by his labours. Declared doctor of the Church in 1828.

PETER ROQUE (Bl) M. CM.
AC. March 1
1758–1796. A native of Vannes in Brittany and a priest of the Congregation of the Mission (Vincentians) at Paris. He refused to take the constitutional oath during the French Revolution and was guillotined. Beatified in 1934.

PETER PAPPACARBONE (St) Bp.
OSB.   AC. March 4
d. 1123. He was born at Salerno, and became a monk of Cava under the second abbot St Leo I. About the year 1062 he was sent to Cluny, where he stayed some six years. In 1079 he was made bishop of Policastro, but resigned and returned to Cava, where Leo I appointed him coadjutor abbot. He succeeded to the abbacy in the same year (1079), but showed himself too strict, and in view of the remonstrances of the community he withdrew to another house. He was soon recalled and under his new, more paternal, régime, the abbey prospered exceedingly: he is said to have given the habit to over three thousand monks. When he died Cava numbered twenty-nine subject abbeys, ninety priories and over three hundred and forty cells.

PETER de GEREMIA (Bl) C. OP.
AC. March 10
1381–1452. A native of Palermo, who was a student of law at Bologna when he decided to join the Friars Preachers. He became one of the best known preachers and missionaries of his age. Cult approved in 1784.

PETER the SPANIARD (St) C.
RM. March 11
? A Spanish pilgrim to Rome who settled as a hermit at Babuco, near Veroli. He wore a coat of mail next to his skin.

PETER of NICOMEDIA (St) M.
RM. March 12
d. 303. A chamberlain (*cubicularius*) in the palace of Diocletian at Nicomedia. He was one of the first victims of the last great persecution. His flesh was torn from his bones, salt and vinegar were poured into his wounds, and finally he was roasted to death over a slow fire.

PETER the DEACON (St) C.
AC. March 12
d. *p*.605. The disciple, secretary and companion of St Gregory the Great, to whom the great pope dictated the four books of his Dialogues. He is venerated as the patron saint of Salassola, diocese of Biella, in Upper Italy. He is usually described as a Benedictine.

PETER II of CAVA (Bl) Ab. OSB.
AC. March 13
d. 1208. The ninth abbot of Cava, near Salerno, from 1195 to 1208. He is described as "an enemy of all litigation", which, for that time, is no small praise. Cult confirmed in 1928.

PETER and APHRODISIUS (SS)
MM.   RM. March 14
5th cent. Martyrs under the Arian Vandals in N.W. Africa. Nothing else is known about them.

PETER LIEOU (Bl) M.
AC. March 17
d. 1834. A Chinese layman. Converted when young, he was exiled for his faith to Tartary (1814). In 1827 he was allowed to return. During a fresh persecution, he gained entry into the prison

to comfort and strengthen his sons and was strangled. Beatified in 1900.

PETER of GUBBIO (Bl) C. OSA. Erem.   AC. March 23

d. *c.*1350 (?). Born at Gubbio in Umbria, of the family of the Ghisleni. He became a hermit of St Augustine, and was provincial of his congregation. His shrine is at Gubbio. Cult confirmed by Pius IX.

PETER, MARCIAN, JOVINUS, THECLA, CASSIAN, and Comp. (SS) MM.   RM. March 26

? Roman martyrs, of whom nothing certain is known. Some registers have *Theodula* instead of *Thecla*.

PETER MARGINET (Bl) C. OSB, Cist.   AC. March 26

d. 1435. A Cistercian monk of Poblet, near Tarragona, in Spain, and the cellarer of the abbey. From a life of high fervour he lapsed into one of crime, apostatized and became the leader of bandits. After some years he repented, went back to the abbey and spent the rest of his life doing penance.

PETER REGALADO (St) C. OFM. RM. March 30

1390–1456. A Spaniard of noble birth of Valladolid who entered the Franciscan order and effected a strict reform in several friaries, notably at Aguilar del Campo in New Castile.

PETER of POITIERS (St) Bp. AC. Apr 4

d. 1115. Bishop of Poitiers (1087–1115). A fearless prelate who publicly denounced the sacrilegious tyranny and licence of King Philip I and of William VI, count of Poitiers and duke of Aquitaine. He befriended and helped Bl Robert d'Arbrisselle in founding the abbey of Fontrevault.

PETER CERDAN (Bl) C. OP. AC. Apr 5

d. 1422. A Dominican friar, who accompanied St Vincent Ferrer in his travels and apostolate. He died at Grans, diocese of Barbastro, Aragon.

PETER of SIENA (Bl) M. OFM. AC. Apr 9

See Bl Thomas of Tolentino and Comp.

PETER of MONTEPIANO (Bl) C. OSB. Vall.   AC. Apr 12

d. 1098. A Vallumbrosan abbot of San Virgilio at Brescia, who ended his life as a hermit at Montepiano in Tuscany.

PETER GONZALEZ (or TELMO) (St) C. OP.   AC. Apr 14

1190–1246. Born at Astorga in Spain he became a canon of Palencia and subsequently joined the Dominicans. He was chosen by King St Ferdinand of Castile as his confessor and court-chaplain, and in that position did much to foster the crusade against the Moors and to obtain a kindly treatment for the Moorish captives when Cordova and Seville were taken. He also worked among the sailors and peasants of Galicia. Spanish sailors often call him Telmo, or Elmo thought to be a corruption of Erasmus—that saint being an earlier patron of mariners.

PETER and HERMOGENES (SS) MM.   RM. Apr 17

? Peter, a deacon, and Hermogenes, his servant, were martyred at an unknown date, probably at Antioch.

PETER of BRAGA (St) Bp. M. RM. Apr 26

? The alleged first bishop and martyr of Braga in Portugal. The local tradition connects him with the apostolate of St James the Great, q.v., in Spain. He is thought, however, to have lived in the 5th or 6th century.

PETER ARMENGOL (St) M.
O. Merc.   RM. Apr 27
1238–1304. He belonged to the house of the counts of Urgell, in the Spanish Eastern Pyrenees. He spent his youth in dissipation, but in 1258 joined the Mercedarians and devoted all his energies to the ransoming of captives. He offered himself as a hostage for eighteen Christian children, and was put to frightful tortures in his African captivity, being for this reason considered a martyr. He died near Tarragona.

PETER CANISIUS (St) C. Dr. SJ.
                              RM. Apr 27
1521–1597. A native of Nijmwegen in Holland. He was received into the Society of Jesus by Bl Peter Faber (1543). He was the leader of the Catholic counter-Reformation in German lands, being constantly engaged in preaching, teaching, writing, instructing, advising, arbitrating, in Germany, Austria, Switzerland, Bohemia, Poland. His short catechism in Latin and German had passed through two hundred editions before his death and was translated into twelve European languages. He also wrote theological, ascetical and historical treatises. He has been rightly called "the Second Apostle of Germany". Canonized and declared Doctor of the Church in 1925.

PETER CHANEL (St) M.
                              AC. Apr 28
1803–1840. Peter Louis Mary Chanel was born at Cluet, diocese of Belley, in France, of a family of peasants. He was ordained priest in 1827 and appointed parish priest of Crozet. In 1831 he entered the Society of Mary (Marist Fathers) and was sent to Oceania as superior of the first missionary band. He was martyred on Fortuna Island by the native king. He is the first martyr of Oceania. Canonized in 1954.

PETER HIEU (Bl) M.   AC. Apr 28
d. 1840. A native catechist of Tonkin, attached to the Society of Foreign Missions of Paris. He was beheaded with two companions. Beatified in 1900.

PETER MARTYR (St) OP.
                    RM. Apr 29 (and Apr 6)
1206–1252. Born at Verona of heretical (Catharist) parents, he joined the Dominicans and was appointed inquisitor of Lombardy, then swarming with Catharists. He preached very successfully throughout northern and central Italy, until at length the Catharists succeeded in waylaying him on the road between Como and Milan. He was canonized in the following year (1253).

PETER (St) M.   RM. Apr 30
See Amator, Peter and Louis.

PETER of PAVIA (St) Bp.
                              RM. May 7
d. c.735. A bishop of Pavia during the reign of his kinsman Luitprand, king of the Lombards. His episcopate was brief.

PETER of TARANTAISE (St) Bp.
OSB. Cist.   RM. May 8
1102–1175. Born near Vienne in Dauphiné, at the age of twelve he joined the Cistercians at Bonnevaux and before he was thirty he was sent as first abbot to the foundation of Tamié. In 1142 he was chosen archbishop of Tarantaise, but after holding this position thirteen years he disappeared and was eventually found serving his novitiate as a lay-brother in a remote Cistercian abbey in Switzerland. He was compelled to return to his diocese, where he made a name for himself as an upholder of papal rights. Canonized in 1191.

PETER, ANDREW, PAUL and
DIONYSIA (SS) MM.   RM. May 15
d. 251. Peter was a young man of

Lampsacus on the Hellespont, martyred at Troas with SS Paul, Andrew and Dionysia, under Decius.

PETER CELESTINE (St) Pope, Founder, OSB.   RM. May 19

1210–1296. Born at Isernia in the Abruzzi, he became a hermit and a priest. In 1246 he received the Benedictine habit from the abbot of Faizola, but he returned to the solitary life at Morone, near Sulmona (1251) where he gathered numerous disciples and founded the new Benedictine congregation named after him. In 1294 he was elected pope and was compelled by the cardinals to accept, but he proved an utter failure and resigned the same year. His successor Boniface VIII kept him in custody till his death. Canonized in 1313.

PETER de DUEÑAS (Bl) M. OFM.   AC. May 19

1378–1397. Born at Palencia, Spain, he became a Franciscan and in 1396 accompanied Bl John de Cetina to Granada to preach the gospel to the Moors. Both were beheaded in the following year.

PETER WRIGHT (Bl) M. SJ.   AC. May 19

d. 1651. Born at Slipton in Northamptonshire, he became a convert to the Catholic faith and studied for the priesthood at Ghent and in Rome. In 1629 he joined the Jesuits and was a chaplain to the royalist army during the Civil War. He was condemned to death for his priesthood and executed at Tyburn.

PETER PARENZI (St) M.   AC. May 22

d. 1199. A Roman by birth, he was sent to Orvieto (1199) as papal governor to repress the excesses of the Catharist heretics. He adopted severe measures,

with the result that the heretics seized him and put him to a cruel death.

PETER of the ASSUMPTION (Bl) M. OFM.   AC. May 22

d. 1617. Born at Cuerva, archdiocese of Toledo. He went to Japan with a band of fifty Franciscan missionaries (1601) and was appointed guardian of the friary at Nagasaki. He was beheaded at Nagasaki with Bl John Machado (q.v.). He is the first martyr of the second great Japanese persecution. Beatified in 1867.

PETER VAN (Bl) M.   AC. May 25

c.1780–1857. A native catechist beheaded at Son-tay, in W. Tonkin. Beatified in 1909.

PETER SANZ (Bl) Bp. M. OP.   AC. May 26

d. 1747. Born at Asco in Catalonia he joined the Dominicans (1697) and was sent to the Philippine Islands (1712) whence (1713) he proceeded to China. In 1730 he was nominated vicar apostolic of Fo-Kien and titular bishop of Mauricastro. In 1746 he was imprisoned and finally beheaded at Futsheu. Beatified in 1893.

PETER ARNAUD (Bl) M.   AC. May 28

d. 1242. A layman, notary of the inquisition at Toulouse, put to death by the Albigenses at Avignonet with eleven inquisitors. Cult approved in 1866.

PETER PETRONI (Bl) C. O. Cart.   AC. May 29

1311–1361. A Sienese by birth, he became (1328) a Carthusian at Maggiano near Siena. His thoughtful charity was instrumental in the conversion of Boccaccio.

PETER (St) M.   RM. June 2

See Marcellinus and Peter.

PETER, WALLABONSUS, SABINIAN, WISTREMUNDUS, HABENTIUS and JEREMIAS (SS) MM. RM. June 7

d. 851. Spaniards living at Cordova under the Moorish rule. Peter was a priest; Wallabonsus, a deacon; Sabinian and Wistremundus monks of St Zoilus at Cordova; Habentius a monk of St Christopher's; Jeremias, a very old man, had founded the monastery of Tábanos, near Cordova. For publicly reprobating Mohammed they were martyred under Abderrahman II. Jeremias was scourged to death, the others were beheaded.

PETER TU (Bl) M. OP. AC. June 10

d. 1838. A native Dominican priest of Tonkin, beheaded at Ninh-Tai.

PETER RODRIGUEZ and Comp. (BB) MM. (?) PC. June 11

d. 1242. A group of seven Portuguese knights of Santiago, whose leader was Bl Peter Rodriguez. All were murdered during an armistice by the Moors at Tavira in Algabes, Portugal. Cult not yet approved.

PETER GAMBACORTA (Bl) Founder AC. June 17

1355-1435. Born at Pisa or Lucca. After a misspent youth, he repented and retired to the solitude of Montebello, diocese of Urbino, where, it is said, he converted twelve robbers, with whom he founded the institute of the Poor Brothers of St Jerome. When his father and two brothers were murdered, Peter refused to leave his cell, and, like his sister, Bl Clare Gambacorta, fully forgave the assassins.

PETER RINXEI (Bl) M. SJ. AC. June 20

1589-1626. A Japanese who was educated at the Jesuit seminary of Arima. He became the catechist of Bl Francis Pacheco, by whom he was received into the Society while in prison. Burnt alive at Nagasaki. Beatified in 1867.

PETER of TARANTAISE (Bl) Pope RM. June 22

Otherwise Innocent V, q.v.

PETER of JUILLY (Bl or St) OSB. Cist. AC. June 23

d. 1136. An Englishman and a companion and friend of St Stephen Harding at Molesme. He was appointed chaplain and confessor to the Benedictine nuns of Juilly-les-Nonnais, subject to Molesme, where St Bernard's sister, St Humbeline, was abbess. Peter is described as a great preacher and wonder-worker. He died at Juilly.

PETER JAMES of PESARO (Bl) C. OSA. AC. June 23

d. c.1496. An Augustinian friar in the monastery of St Nicholas at Pesaro. Cult approved by Pius IX.

PETER the APOSTLE (St) M. RM. June 29 (Jan 18, Feb 22, Aug 1, Nov 18)

d. c.67. Simon, son of Jona, was a Galilean fisherman, a married man living at Bethsaida. He was a disciple of St John the baptist before he was called, with his elder brother Andrew to be a disciple of Christ, by whom he was at once named "Rock" (Kephas, Petros, Petra, Peter). The culminating episode narrated of him in the gospel, is that of his confession of Christ as the Son of God (Matt. XVI, 15-19), to which Christ answered with the solemn promise: "Thou art Peter and upon this rock I will build my church . . . and I will give thee the keys of the kingdom of heaven." This promise was ratified by Christ after his resurrection with the threefold injunction to feed His flock. As one of the most ancient catalogues of the popes puts it, St Peter "succeeded our Lord as bishop of Rome and of the universal church". After Christ's ascension he presided at Jerusalem, preached in Samaria, was perhaps for a time bishop of Antioch and finally fixed his permanent see in Rome, where he was martyred, head downwards according to tradition, in the circus of Nero on the Vatican Hill. Liturgically he is commemorated several times in the year, but his chief feast is that of June 29 on which day he has been honoured with St Paul at least since the beginning of the 4th century.

PETER of LUXEMBURG (Bl) Bp., Card.   AC. July 4

1369–1387. Born at Ligny in Lorraine, of the family of the counts of Lützelburg. As a boy he showed an inclination to the clerical state, and, according to the abuse of the time, was forthwith given sundry canonries at Paris, Chartres and Cambrai and was made archdeacon of Dreux. At the age of fourteen he was appointed bishop of Metz. At sixteen he was created cardinal of San Giorgio in Velabro. He died at the age of eighteen. He was a youth of great promise and holiness of life. Beatified in 1527.

PETER the HERMIT (Bl) C.   PC. July 8

d. 1115. A soldier of European birth who became a hermit for a time in Palestine. Then he returned to Europe and preached the first Crusade throughout Italy, France and part of the Germanies. He accompanied the first expedition to the East and followed once more the profession of arms. He fought at the siege of Antioch and the capture of Jerusalem. Subsequently he founded the monastery of Neumoutier at Huy in Flanders, where he died. He was never officially beatified.

PETER van ASCHE (St) M. OFM.   RM. July 9

d. 1572. Born at Asche near Brussels. He was a Franciscan lay-brother at Gorkum in Holland, and was hanged by the Calvinists at Briel.

PETER of PERUGIA (St) Ab. OSB.   AC. July 10

d. 1007. Peter Vincioli was born near Perugia and belonged to the family of the counts of Agello. He was the abbot-founder of the monastery of St Peter at Perugia, where he has an altar dedicated to him in the abbey church.

PETER TU (Bl) M.   AC. July 10

d. 1840. A native catechist of Tonkin, beheaded at Anam. Beatified in 1900.

PETER ARAKI-COBIOJE (Bl) M.   AC. July 12

d. 1626. A Japanese layman burnt alive at Nagasaki for sheltering Christians. Beatified in 1867.

PETER KHANH (Bl) M.   AC. July 12

c.1780–1842. A native priest of Tonkin, beheaded at Con-co in W. Tonkin. Beatified in 1909.

PETER NUÑEZ and PETER FONTURA (BB) MM. SJ.   AC. July 15

d. 1570. Two Portuguese Jesuits, fellow-martyrs of Bl Ignatius de Azevedo. The former was a cleric, a native of Fronteria; the latter a lay-brother, born at Braga.

PETER BERNA (Bl) M. SJ.   AC. July 15

d. 1583. Born at Ascona, on the lake of Locarno, Ticino, Switzerland, he studied at the German College in Rome and joined the Jesuits. He went to India with Bl Rudolph Acquaviva and was ordained at Goa. After some years of missionary work he was put to death with Bl Rudolph, q.v.

PETER TUAN (Bl) M. AC. July 15
1766–1838. A native priest of Tonkin, who died in prison of wounds received for the Faith while awaiting the decree of decapitation. Beatified in 1900.

PETER of the HOLY MOTHER of GOD (Bl) M. OP.   AC. July 29
d. 1629. A Japanese catechist and a Dominican. He was burnt alive at Omura with Bl Louis Bertrán. Beatified in 1867.

PETER of MOGLIANO (Bl) C. OFM.   AC. July 30
d. 1490. Born at Mogliano, diocese of Fermo, he studied law at Perugia and joined the Observant Franciscans there. Later on he went about preaching with St James della Marca, q.v. "It is said of him that he would die laughing." (Attwater, h.i.) Cult approved in 1760.

PETER QUI (Bl) M.   AC. July 31
d. 1859. Born at Bung in Cochin-China he was ordained priest and beheaded for that reason near Chau-doc, in W. Cochin-China. Beatified in 1909.

PETER (St) M.   RM. Aug 1
See Cyril, Aquila, etc.

PETER of OSMA (St) Bp. OSB.
AC. Aug 2
d. 1109. A French monk of Cluny, one of the numerous Cluniac monks who settled in Spain from c.1050 to c.1130. He first became archdeacon of Toledo under the Cluniac archbishop Bernard de la Sauvetat, who in 1101 nominated him bishop of Osma in Old Castile. St Peter is venerated as the principal patron saint of the cathedral and diocese of Osma.

PETER of ANAGNI (St) Bp. OSB.
RM. Aug 3
d. 1105. Born at Salerno, he became a Benedictine monk in his native city. In 1062 Pope St Gregory VII appointed him to the see of Anagni. He built a new cathedral there, took part in the first crusade and was sent as papal legate to Constantinople. Canonized four years after his death.

PETER JULIAN EYMARD (St)
Founder   AC. Aug 3
1811–1868. A native of La Mure ('Isère). He was ordained in 1834 and worked for some time as a parish priest, but subsequently joined the congregation of the Marist Fathers, as a member of which he became renowned as a preacher and confessor. In 1856 he was dispensed from his vows in that Institute, and in the following year founded another of his own, the Congregation of priests of the Blessed Sacrament, with the special object of fostering devotion to the Holy Eucharist. Shortly after he established a congregation of women with similar aims. In both enterprises he was encouraged by St John Vianney. Canonized in 1963.

PETER, JULIAN, and Comp. (SS) MM.   RM. Aug 7
d. c.260. A band of twenty or more Roman martyrs under Valerian and Gallienus. Julian should probably be Juliana.

PETER BECKET (BECCHETTI) (Bl)   AC. Aug 11
See John and Peter Becchetti.

PETER FABER (Bl) C. SJ.
AC. Aug 11
1506–1546. Peter Lefèvre was born at Villaret in Savoy and was already a priest and a student at Paris when he attached himself to St Ignatius of Loyola. After the official approbation of

the Society of Jesus (1540) he worked at Worms, Spires, Mainz, and especially at Cologne. He was a man of very winning manners, of great ability and of untiring energy. He died in Rome, when about to leave for the Council of Trent.

PETER ZUÑIGA (Bl) M. OSA.
AC. Aug 19

1585–1622. A native of Seville, he spent his youth in Mexico, where his father was the sixth viceroy. On his return to Spain he joined the Augustinians at Seville, and after being ordained priest asked to be sent to Japan. He arrived at Manila in 1610 and in Japan in 1620, and two years later was burnt alive at Nagasaki with Bl Louis Flores, Bl Joachim Firayama and the captain of the vessel which had brought him. The crew of twelve who were Christians were beheaded. All were beatified in 1867.

PETER VASQUEZ (Bl) M. OP.
AC. Aug 25

d. 1624. Born at Berin, in Galicia, he joined the Dominicans in Madrid and ultimately was appointed to the missions in Japan. He was burnt alive at Ximabura with Bl Louis Sotelo and Comp. Beatified in 1867.

PETER (St) M.   RM. Aug 27
See Marcellinus, Mannea, etc.

PETER of TREVI (St) C.
RM. Aug 30

d. c.1050. Born at Carsoli in the diocese of Marsi, Italy. He was ordained to the priesthood and preached with signal success to the peasants of the districts of Tivoli, Anagni and Subiaco. He died while still young at Trevi, near Subiaco. Canonized in 1215.

PETER of SASSOFERRATO (Bl) M. OFM.   AC. Sept 3
See under John of Perugia.

PETER CLAVER (St) C. SJ.
RM. Sept 8

1581–1654. Born at Verdú, near Barcelona, in Spain, the son of a farmer, he became a Jesuit in 1609 and was stationed at Majorca, where he was inspired by St Alphonsus Rodriguez with the desire to work for souls in America. In 1610 he was sent there, and received priest's orders at Cartagena in Central America. During the following forty years he worked chiefly at Cartagena, at that time the central slave-mart of the West Indies, dedicating his life by a special vow to the service of the outcast Negroes. He is said to have baptized, and cared for over 300,000 of them. During the last four years of his life he was a sick man and was often neglected by his brethren. He was canonized in 1888 and declared patron of all the Catholic missions among the Negroes in 1896.

PETER MARTINEZ (St) Bp. OSB.
RM. Sept 10

d. c.1000. Surnamed also St Peter of Mozonzo. He was a native of Spanish Galicia, and about the year 950 became a Benedictine at the abbey of St Mary of Mozonzo. Later he was appointed abbot of St Martin de Antealtares, at Compostella and finally (c.986) archbishop of that city. He is one of the heroes of the Spanish Reconquest, as also one of the supposed authors of the Salve Regina.

PETER de AVILA (Bl) M. OFM.
AC. Sept 10

1562–1622. Born at Palomares in Castile, he was sent to Manila with Bl Louis Sotelo (1617) then to Japan. He was burnt alive at Nagasaki on the day of the Great Martyrdom. Beatified in 1867.

PETER SAMPO (Bl) M. SJ.
AC. Sept 10

d. 1622. Born in the province of Ochu,

in Japan. He was received into the Society of Jesus by Bl Charles Spinola in the prison of Omura. Burnt alive at Nagasaki on the day of the Great Martyrdom. Beatified in 1867.

PETER NANGAXI, PETER SANGA, and PETER IKIEMON (BB) MM.   AC. Sept 10 and 11

d. 1622. Three Japanese children martyred with their parents at Nagasaki. Peter Nangaxi, a boy of seven years, was the son of BB Paul and Thecla; Peter Sanga, a boy of three years, was the second son of BB Antony and Mary Magdalen Sanga, of Corea; Peter Ikiemon, a boy of seven years, was the son of Bl Bartholomew. The three were beheaded: the first two on the 10th, the third on the 11th of September. Beatified in 1867.

PETER of CHAVANON (St) C. OSA.   AC. Sept 11

1003–1080. A native of Langeac, in Haute Loire, he became a secular priest and then founded an abbey of Augustinian canons regular at Pébrac in Auvergne and ruled it as its first provost.

PETER-PAUL of ST CLAIRE (Bl) M. OFM.   AC. Sept 12

d. 1622. Born at Saigo in Arima, Japan, he became a catechist under Bl Apollinaris Franco. He was burnt alive at Omura. Beatified in 1867.

PETER ARBUES (St) M. OSA.
RM. Sept. 17

1442–1485. Born at Epila in Aragon he studied philosophy at Huesca, and theology and canon law at Bologna. In 1478 he became an Augustinian canon regular at Saragossa, and in 1484 was made inquisitor of Aragon. What has been written about his cruelty is un-

historical and uncritical: not a single sentence of death or of torture can be traced to him; but his integrity was feared by the Crypto-Jews (the *Marranos*) who murdered him in his cathedral. Canonized in 1867.

PETER MAUBANT (Bl) M.
AC. Sept 22

See Laurence Imbert.

PETER (St) M.   RM. Sept 23

See Andrew, John, etc.

PETER ACOTANTO (Bl) C. OSB.
AC. Sept 23

d. c.1180. Born of a noble Venetian family, he spent his life tending the sick. Some years before his death he retired to live as a recluse in a cell near the Benedictine abbey of San Giorgio Maggiore in Venice, under the obedience of the abbot. Cult approved by Clement VIII.

PETER CUFIOJE (Bl) M.
AC. Sept 28

d. 1630. A Japanese Augustinian tertiary, beheaded at Nagasaki for sheltering the Augustinian missionaries. Beatified in 1867.

PETER (St) M.   RM. Oct 3

See Dionysius, Faustus, etc.

PETER of DAMASCUS (St) Bp. M.
RM. Oct 4

d. c.750. A bishop of Damascus who was maimed, blinded, exiled and ultimately bound to a cross and beheaded by the Arab rulers of the city for preaching against their prophet.

PETER of SEVILLE (St) M.
RM. Oct 8

? A martyr venerated at Seville, of whom only the name is known. Later legends are admitted to be fables.

PETER TUY (Bl) M.   AC. Oct 11
d. 1833. A native Tonkinese priest beheaded at the age of seventy under King
Minh-Menh. Beatified in 1900.

PETER of ALCÁNTARA (St) C.
OFM.   RM. Oct 19
1499–1562. Born at Alcántara in Estremadura, at the age of fifteen he became a
Franciscan Observant and after his
ordination (1524) initiated at Pedrosa a
still more severe Franciscan reform
which was known as *Alcantarine* and
received papal approval. St Peter is also
remembered as one of the group of
great Spanish mystics and his treatise
on prayer was much valued, and used
by St Francis of Sales. He encouraged
and defended St Teresa, whose confessor and admirer he was. St Teresa
held him in great esteem and speaks
with awe of his austerities and penances
as "incomprehensible to the human
mind"; they had reduced him, she tells
us, to a condition in which he looked as
if "he had been made of the roots of
trees". Canonized in 1669.

PETER CAPUCCI (Bl) C. OP.
                                AC. Oct 21
1390–1445. Born at Città di Castello
(the ancient *Tifernum*), he joined the
Dominicans and was raised to the
priesthood at Cortona. He became
known as "the preacher of death", because he used to preach with a skull in
his hands. Cult confirmed by Pius VII.

PETER (St) M.   RM. Oct 25
See Theodosius, Lucius, etc.

PETER ONIZUKO (Bl) M. SJ.
                                AC. Nov 1
d. 1622. A Japanese born at Faciram,
Arima. He became a Jesuit postulant
and attached himself to Bl Paul Navarro,
with whom he was burnt alive at
Ximabara. Beatified in 1867.

PETER ALMATÓ (Bl) M. OP.
                                AC. Nov 1
d. 1861. Born at Sasserra, diocese of
Vich, Spain, he became a Dominican
and was sent to the Philippine Islands,
and thence to Ximabara under Bl
Jerome Hermosilla, with whom he was
beheaded. Beatified in 1906.

PETER-FRANCIS NÉRON (Bl) M.
                                AC. Nov 3
1818–1860. Born in Bornay, in Jura, he
was admitted into the seminary of
Foreign Missions of Paris (1846), ordained priest (1848) and sent to Hong-
Kong. He worked in W. Tonkin as
director of the central seminary until
his martyrdom by beheading. Beatified
in 1919.

PETER OU (Bl) M.   AC. Nov 7
d. 1814. Originally an innkeeper, on his
conversion he became a catechist and
instructed about six hundred persons.
He was strangled at Tsen-y-Fou, of the
Su-Tchuen Province. Beatified in 1900.

PETER DUMOULIN-BORIE,
PETER CHOA and VINCENT
DIEM (BB) MM.   AC. Nov 24
d. 1838. Bl Peter Dumoulin was born at
Cors, diocese of Tulle, France, in 1808,
and entered the seminary for Foreign
Missions at Paris in 1829, being sent to
Tonkin after his ordination in 1832. In
1836 he was arrested and received when
in prison his appointment as titular
bishop and vicar apostolic of W.
Tonkin. BB Peter Choa and Vincent
Diem were natives of Tonkin and
priests. The bishop was beheaded, the
two priests strangled at Dong-Hoi.
Beatified in 1900.

PETER of ALEXANDRIA (St) Bp.
M.   RM. Nov 26
d. 311. An Alexandrian who, as a young
man, was a "confessor" during the

Decian persecution. Then he became the head of the catechetical school and as such combated extreme Origenism. In 300 he was raised to the patriarchal see and in that position he figured as one of the opponents of the Meletian schism, being also one of the first to detect the dangerous teaching of Arius. He was martyred under Galerius Maximus, "the seal and complement of martyrs" as the Copts term him, because he was the last to be put to death as a Christian by public authority at Alexandria.

PETER (St) M.   RM. Nov 28
See Stephen, Basil, etc.

PETER CHRYSOLOGUS (St) Bp. Dr.   RM. Dec 2 and 4
406–c.450. Born at Imola, he became deacon there, and then successive archdeacon and archbishop of Ravenna (c.433). He is chiefly famed for his assiduity and eloquence in preaching, whence the name given him of *Chrysologus*, "Golden Speech". A great number of his sermons are still extant. He was declared a Doctor of the Church in 1729.

PETER PASCUAL (St) Bp. M.
                     RM. Dec 6
1227–1300. Peter Pascual, or Pascualez (latinized as *Paschasius*), was born at Valencia in Spain. About the year 1250 he was ordained priest and was for some time tutor to the son of the king of Aragon. Later he was raised to the see of Jaén, which at that time was still under Moorish government. His heroic exertions in ransoming captives, and his preaching and writing against Islam were rewarded with martyrdom at Granada. Cult confirmed in 1673.

PETER, SUCCESSUS, BASSIAN, PRIMITIVUS and Comp. (SS) MM.
                     RM. Dec 9

? Martyrs in Africa, of whom nothing is known.

PETER FOURIER (St) OSA.
Founder   RM. Dec 9
1565–1640. Born at Mirecourt in Lorraine, he joined the Augustinian canons regular, and some time after his ordination (1585) was put in charge of the neglected parish of Mattaincourt. Here he founded the Congregation of Notre Dame for the education of girls. He failed, however, in similar efforts to establish a new congregation for teaching boys. Canonized in 1897.

PETER TECELANO (Bl) C. OFM.
                     AC. Dec 10
d. 1287. Born at Campi in Tuscany, he started life as a comb-maker at Siena. On the death of his wife he joined the Franciscans as a lay-brother and carried on his trade in the friary for the remainder of his long life. He attained a high degree of mystical prayer. Cult confirmed in 1802.

PETER DUONG and PETER TRUAT (BB) MM.   AC. Dec 18
d. 1838. Native catechists in Tonkin, martyred in Annam. Beatified in 1900.

PETER de la CADIRETA (Bl) M. OP.   PC. Dec 20
d. 1277. Born at Moya in Spain, he became a Dominican friar. He was stoned to death by heretics while preaching at Urgell. His body is venerated in the church of St Dominic at Urgell.

PETER MASSALENUS (Bl) C. OSB. Cam.   AC. Dec 20
1375–1453. Peter de Massalenis was born at Othoca in Sardinia. After repeated pilgrimages to the Holy Land he joined the Camaldolese Benedictines at San Michele di Murano, Venice (1410). He was famed for his gift of mystical contemplation.

PETER THI (Bl) M.   AC. Dec 20
1763–1839. A native of Tonkin and a priest. At the age of sixty he was beheaded at Ha-Noi. Beatified in 1900.

PETER the VENERABLE (Bl) Ab. OSB.   AC. Dec 25
c.1092–1156. Peter de Montboissier was born in Auvergne, and became a monk at Cluny in 1109. At twenty he was prior of Vézelay and in 1122 succeeded to the abbacy of Cluny. He was one of the most eminent churchmen of his age, and during the thirty-four years of his reign Cluny retained its position as the greatest and most influential abbey in Christendom. Calm and serene in his charity, he was the counterpart of his tempestuous contemporary, friend, admirer, and, on some points, rival, St Bernard of Clairvaux. At Cluny he regulated the finances, raised the standard of studies (he was himself a poet and a theological writer of distinction) and received the vanquished Abelard under his roof. He died, according to his wish, on Christmas Day, after having preached about the feast to his monks. His name was inserted in French martyrologies, and his feast is observed in the diocese of Arras on Dec 29.

PETER of SUBIACO (Bl) M. OSB.   PC. Dec 31
d. 1003. The twenty-second abbot of Subiaco. For defending the rights of his abbey he was blinded by the baron of Monticello and died in prison.

PETROC (PETROCK, PEDROG, PERREUX) (St) Ab.   AC. June 4
d. c.594. Said to have been the son of a Welsh chieftain, and to have studied in Ireland and settled in Cornwall, where he undoubtedly exercised a very active apostolate. There he founded a monastery at a place called after him, Petroc-

ston (Padstow) and another at Bodmin where he died. In Brittany he is venerated under the name of Perreux.

PETRONAX (St) Ab. OSB.
**   AC. May 6**
d. c.747. A native of Brescia who was induced by Pope St Gregory II in 717 to visit Montecassino, destroyed in 580 by the Lombards, with a view to restoring the cenobitical life there. He found a few hermits who elected him their abbot and Benedictine life began afresh. St Willibald, bishop of Eichstätt and St Sturmius of Fulda, were monks under him. He is surnamed "the second founder of Montecassino".

PETRONILLA of MONCEL (Bl)
Abs. Poor Clare   AC. May 14
d. 1355. Of the family of the counts of Troyes. She was the first abbess of the convent of Poor Clares at Moncel in Burgundy, founded by King Philip le Bel.

PETRONILLA (St) V.   RM. May 31
1st cent. (?). A Roman virgin venerated from the earliest times. Later legends connect her with St Peter, to whom she is said to have ministered. The RM. goes further and describes her as the daughter of the Apostle, which she certainly was not.

PETRONIUS (St) Bp.   AC. Jan 10
d. c.463. The son of a senator of Avignon. He became a monk of Lérins and bishop of Die from c.456 to 463.

PETRONIUS (St) Bp.   RM. Sept 6
d. c.450. A bishop of Verona.

PETRONIUS (St) Bp.   RM. Oct 4
d. c.445. Born in Byzantium, he was sent by the emperor Theodosius the Younger to report to the pope on the case of

Nestorius. While in Italy he was raised to the see of Bologna. He is said to have built the monastery of St Stephen in that city, reproducing the general lines of the buildings of the Holy Places at Jerusalem, which he had visited.

PHAEBADIUS (FIARI) (St) Bp.
AC. Apr 25
d. c.392. A bishop of Agen in S. Gaul, who, together with his friend St Hilary of Poitiers, succeeded in stamping out Arian heresy in Gaul. He was one of the best known prelates of his time and presided at several councils. St Jerome mentions him among "the illustrious men" of the Church.

PHAGANUS (St)
AC. Jan 3 (RM. May 26)
Otherwise Fugatius, q.v.

PHAINA (St) VM.   RM. May 18
See Theodotus, Thecusa, etc.

PHAL (PHELE) (St)   RM. May 16
Otherwise Fidolus, q.v.

PHARA (St) Abs.   RM. Dec 7
Otherwise Burgundofara (Apr 3) q.v.

PHARAÏLDIS (VAREIDE, VERYLDE, VEERLE) (St) V.
AC. Jan 4
d. c.740. She seems to have been born in Ghent and was married against her will, having dedicated her virginity to God. She was maltreated by her husband, either because she insisted on living as a virgin or because he objected to her nocturnal visits to the churches. She is one of the patron saints of Ghent.

PHARNACIUS (St) M. RM. June 24
See Orentius, Heros, etc.

PHARO (St) Bp.   RM. Oct 28
Otherwise Faro, q.v.

PHELIM (FIDLEMINUS) (St) Bp.
AC. Aug 9
6th cent. Said to have been a disciple of St Columba. The city of Kilmore sprang up round the place where his cell stood. Principal patron of Kilmore.

PHILADELPHIUS (St) M.
RM. May 10
See Alphius, Philadelphus and Cyrinus.

PHILADELPHUS (St) M.
RM. Sept 2
See Diomedes, Julian, etc.

PHILAPPIAN (St) M.   RM. Jan 30
See Felician, Philappian, etc.

PHILASTRIUS (St) Bp. RM. July 18
d. c.387. A Spaniard who was appointed bishop of Brescia at the time of the Arian troubles. He wrote a book against the Arians, which is still extant. St Gaudentius, his successor, praises him for his "modesty, quietness and gentleness towards all men", and because he helped the poor.

PHILEAS and Comp. (SS) MM.
RM. Feb 4 and Nov 26
d. c.304–311. Martyrs whose passion is related by their contemporary, the historian Eusebius. Phileas, bishop of Thmuis, an ancient city in Lower Egypt, was beheaded. From his prison at Alexandria he wrote a letter to his flock describing the sufferings of his fellow Christian prisoners. With him suffered a Roman tribune named Philoromus and a great number of people from Thmuis and its neighbourhood. See also Faustus, Didius, etc.

PHILEMON and APOLLONIUS (SS) MM.   RM. March 8
d. c.305. Philemon was an actor and musician at Antinoe, who was converted by the deacon Apollonius of the

same city. They were brought to Alexandria, bound hand and foot, and cast into the sea. They suffered under Diocletian.

PHILEMON and DOMNINUS (SS) MM.   RM. March 21
? Romans by birth, who preached the gospel in various parts of Italy and were finally put to death, where is not certain.

PHILEMON and APPHIA (APPIA) (SS) MM.   RM. Nov 22
d. c.70. Philemon is the Christian of Colossae, master of the runaway slave Onesimus, to whom St Paul's shortest epistle is addressed, Apphia is supposed to have been Philemon's wife. Both are said to have been stoned to death at their home at Colossae.

PHILETUS, LYDIA, MACEDO, THEOPREPIUS (THEOPRE-PIDES), AMPHILOCHIUS and CRONIDAS (SS) MM.
RM. March 27
d. c.121. Martyrs of Illyria under Hadrian. The RM. describes Philetus as a senator, Lydia as his wife, Macedo and Theoprepius as their sons, Amphilochius as a captain, and Cronidas as a notary. Their *Acts* are not reliable.

PHILIBERT (St) Ab. OSB.
RM. Aug 20
c.608–684. Born in Gascony and educated at the court of King Dogobert I. At the age of twenty he became a monk at Rébais and shortly afterwards its abbot. However he left this abbey and, after visiting several famous Columbanian houses (which were at that time adopting the Rule of St Benedict), founded and ruled the abbey of Jumièges, not far from Fontenelle. He opposed Ebroin, the tyrannical mayor of the palace, and was imprisoned and ex-

iled. Before his death he had established the Abbey of Noirmoutier, restored Quinçay and aided several others.

PHILIBERT (St) M.   RM. Aug 22
See Fabrician and Philibert.

PHILIP (*several*)
Note. Philip is the English form of the Latin Philippus; the French is: Philippe; the Italian, Filippo; the Spanish, Felipe.

PHILIP BERRUYER (Bl) Bp.
AC. Jan 9
d. 1260. A nephew of St William of Bourges, and, like his uncle, archbishop of that diocese.

PHILIP of VIENNE (St) Bp.
AC. Feb 3
d. c.578. Bishop of Vienne in Gaul (c.560–578).

PHILIP of JESUS (St) M. OFM.
RM. Feb 5
d. 1597. Born in Mexico City of Spanish parents, Philip became a Franciscan at Puebla, but left the Order in 1589 and travelled to the Philippines as a merchant. He repented and rejoined the Franciscans at Manila (1590). On his way home to be ordained in Mexico, his ship was driven by a storm to Japan (1596) where he was arrested with St Peter Baptist and crucified at Nagasaki. Canonized in 1862.

PHILIP of GORTYNA (St) Bp.
RM. Apr 11
d. c.180. A bishop of Gortyna in Crete, author of a work, now lost, against the Marcionite Gnostics.

PHILIP the APOSTLE (St)
RM. May 11
d. c.80. One of the Twelve, a native of Bethsaida, he always takes the fifth place in the catalogue of the Apostles,

and is mentioned three times as a confidant of our Lord in St John's gospel. After the ascension he is believed to have preached in Asia Minor and to have been martyred at Hierapolis in Phrygia. His relics are venerated in Rome.

PHILIP of ZELL (St) H. OSB.
AC. May 3

d. *c.*770. An Anglo-Saxon pilgrim who settled as a hermit near Worms and became a great friend of King Pepin. Being joined by several disciples, he founded the monastery of Zell—thus called from his own original *cell*—which in subsequent times grew into the town of Zell.

PHILIP of AGIRONE (St)
RM. May 12

? A saint venerated in the little hill town of Agirone in Sicily as the first missionary sent to that country by the Holy See. The story abounds in contradictory, as well as improbable, statements.

PHILIP SUZANNI (Bl) C. OSA.
AC. May 24

d. 1306. A native of Piacenza who joined the Augustinian Order in that city. He was famed for his spirit of prayer and compunction. Cult approved in 1756.

PHILIP NERI (St) C. Founder
RM. May 26

1515–1595. A native of Florence, he worked first as an assistant to a merchant at San Germano, at the foot of Montecassino (1534–1541). Then he settled in Rome as tutor in the house of a Florentine nobleman. Meanwhile he devoted all his leisure time to the study of theology and to the silent unobtrusive service of his neighbour. He thought of going to the foreign missions, but a Benedictine of St Paul's told him that his apostolate was in Rome. In 1548 he gathered fourteen companions into a congregation which ultimately received a definite shape as the Congregation of the Oratory. It was not until 1551 that he was ordained priest. During the thirty-three years that followed Philip and his Oratory constituted the centre of religious life in Rome. In 1583 his institute was officially approved with its motherhouse at the church of La Valicella, which St Philip rebuilt on a magnificent scale. He fully deserves the title given him of "Second Apostle of Rome". Canonized in 1622.

PHILIP THE DEACON (St)
RM. June 6

1st cent. One of the seven deacons ordained by the Apostles (Acts VI, 5). He worked in Samaria, baptized the eunuch of Queen Candace of Ethiopia (ib. VI, 8), and was the host of St Paul at Caesarea (ib. XXI, 8). His four daughters (ib. XXI, 9) are honoured as saints with him.

PHILIP POWEL (Bl) M. OSB.
AC. June 30

d. 1646. A native of Tralon in Brecknockshire, he was educated at Abergavenny grammar school, and joined the Benedictines at St Gregory's, Douai (now Downside) in 1614, being ordained priest in 1621. In the following year he was sent to the English mission and worked chiefly in Devon but also in Somerset and Cornwall for twenty years. Martyred at Tyburn. Beatified in 1929.

PHILIP MINH (Bl) M.   AC. July 3

1815–1853. Born at Caimong in W. Cochin-China, he joined the Society for Foreign Missions and was ordained priest of Mac-Bat in E. Cochin-China. He was beheaded at Vinh-hong. Beatified in 1900.

PHILIP (St) M.   RM. July 10
One of the Seven Brothers, q.v.

**PHILIP, ZENO, NARSEUS and
Comp. (SS) MM.   RM. July 15**
? Martyrs of Alexandria. The "companions" consisted of ten little children.

**PHILIP EVANS (Bl) M. SJ.
                                       AC. July 22**
1645–1679. Born in Monmouthshire and educated at Saint-Omer, he joined the Jesuits (1665) and served on the Welsh mission. Martyred for his priesthood at Cardiff in consequence of the "Oates plot". Beatified in 1929.

PHILIP (St) M.   RM. Aug 17
See Straton, Philip and Eutychian.

**PHILIP BENIZI (St) C. OSM.
                                       RM. Aug 23**
1233–1285. Born at Florence (Aug 15), where, after his studies at Paris and Padua, he practised medicine. In 1253 he joined the Servite Order as a lay-brother, until 1259, when he was directed by his superiors to receive holy orders. Soon he was known as one of the most zealous preachers in Italy, was made superior of several friaries, and, in 1267, the fifth general of the Order. In the following year the cardinals were for putting him forward as a candidate for the papacy, but he fled by night and hid in a cave until another was elected. He established new foundations of his institute throughout Italy and the German lands, and was untiring in visiting them. Moreover he intervened as peacemaker in the feud between Guelphs and Ghibellines. Canonized in 1671.

PHILIP (St) M.   RM. Sept 2
See Diomedes, Julian, etc.

PHILIP (St) M.   RM. Sept 13
3rd cent. The alleged father of St

Eugenia, in whose household SS Protus and Hyacinth are said to have been employed. Since St Eugenia's story is thought now to be only a pious romance, the very existence of St Philip is problematical.

**PHILIP ODERISI (Bl) Bp. OSB.
                                       AC. Sept 18**
d. 1285. From being a monk of Fontavellana he was raised to the see of Nocera in Umbria, which he occupied from 1254 to 1285. He was a great friend and defender of the early Friars Minor.

**PHILIP HOWARD (Bl) M.
                                       AC. Oct 19**
d. 1595. Earl of Arundel and Surrey. He was converted from a life of indifference and neglect of his religion and became a fervent and conscientious Catholic. In 1585 he was committed to the Tower of London and in 1589 sentenced to death. The sentence was never carried out but he remained a prisoner until his death at the age of thirty-eight. Beatified in 1929.

PHILIP (St) Bp. M.   RM. Oct 22
d. c.270. A bishop martyr of Fermo in Italy, whose relics are enshrined in his cathedral.

**PHILIP, SEVERUS, EUSEBIUS and
HERMES (SS) MM.   RM. Oct 22**
d. 304. Philip was bishop of Heraclea near Constantinople; Severus was his deacon; Eusebius and Hermes, two of the inferior clergy. During the persecution under Diocletian they were all arrested and brought to trial. It was insistently demanded of them that they should deliver up the sacred books of the church to be burnt. On their refusal they were taken to Adrianopolis and burnt at the stake. We have a copy of the legal process instituted against them, a document of undeniable authenticity.

By mistake the recent editions of the RM. register these martyrs as having suffered under Julian.

PHILIPPA MARERI (Bl) V. Poor Clare   AC. Feb 16
d. 1236. Born at Cicoli in the Abruzzi. After having met St Francis of Assisi in her parents' home she decided to become a hermit, and did so on a mountain above Mareri. Eventually she founded and ruled as first abbess, a Franciscan nunnery at Rieti under the direction of Bl Roger of Todi.

**PHILIPPA de GHELDRE (Bl) W.
                                    PC. Feb 26**
1462–1547. Of noble birth, she married the Duke of Lorraine. Her life however was marked by tribulation. An orphan from the cradle, she was early a widow and was deprived of most of her fortune. She entered a convent of Poor Clares at Port à Mousson in 1519, and lived a life of great austerity. Cult never officially confirmed.

PHILIPPA GUIDONI (Bl) Abs. OSB.   AC. Aug 29
d. 1335. A disciple of Bl Santuccia of Gubbio. Foundress and first abbess of the Benedictine convent of Santa Maria di Valverde at Arezzo.

PHILIPPA (St) M.   RM. Sept 20
See Theodore, Philippa, etc.

**PHILIPPINE DUCHESNE (Bl) V.
                                    AC. Nov 18**
Otherwise Rose-Philippine Duchesne, q.v.

PHILO and AGATHOPODES (AGATHOPUS) (SS)   RM. Apr 25
d. c.150. The two deacons of Antioch who (c.107) attended St Ignatius, their bishop, to his martyrdom in Rome. They took back to Antioch such relics

of the saint as they were able to recover and are believed to have written the "Acts" of his trial and death.

**PHILOGONIUS (St) Bp.
                                    RM. Dec 20**
d. 324. A lawyer at Antioch and a confessor under Licinius. After the death of his wife he became bishop of Antioch and was one of the first to denounce Arianism. St John Chrysostom preached a panegyric, still extant, in honour of St Philogonius.

PHILOLOGUS and PATROBAS (SS)   RM. Nov 4
1st cent. Roman Christians saluted by St Paul in his epistle to the Romans (XVI, 14–18).

PHILOMENA (St) V.   RM. July 5
d. a.500. A saint venerated at San Severino (*Septempeda*) near Ancona. Nothing is now known of her.

PHILOMENA (PHILUMENA)
In 1802 the remains of a young woman were discovered in the catacomb of St Priscilla on the Via Salaria. The tomb was closed by three stones bearing the description LUMENA PAX TE CUM FI. The conclusion was drawn that here was buried a martyr called St Philomena, and a shrine was set up at Mugnano, in the diocese of Nola. The cult spread throughout the world. Further archaeological investigation proved however that the disarrangement of the stones was a regular habit of the sextons in the 4th century when they re-used materials already engraved, and intended to indicate that it was NOT the same person. The shrine was dismantled and cultus forbidden by decree of Rome, 1961.

PHILOMENUS (St) M. RM. Nov 14
See Clementinus, Theodotus and Philomenus.

PHILOMENUS (St) M. RM. Nov 29
d. 275. A martyr of Ancyra in Galatia
under Aurelian.

PHILONILLA (St)   RM. Oct 11
See Zenais and Philonilla.

PHILOROMUS (St) M.   RM. Feb 4
See Phileas, and Comp.

PHILOTERUS (St) M.
                            RM. May 19
d. 303. A nobleman of Nicomedia, martyred there under Diocletian. His supposed Acts are quite untrustworthy.

PHILOTHEUS (St) M.   RM. Nov 5
See Domninus, Theotimus, etc.

PHILOTHEUS (St) M.   AC. Dec 9
See Samosata, the Seven Martyrs of.

PHLEGON (St) M.   RM. Apr 8
See Herodion, Asyncritus and Phlegon.

PHOCAS (St) M.   RM. March 5
d. c.320. A martyr of Antioch, suffocated in a bath. His Acts are not reliable.
Often confused with St Phocas the
Gardener (see July 23).

PHOCAS (St) Bp. M.   RM. July 14
d. 117. Bishop of Sinope on the Black
Sea, martyred under Trajan.

PHOCAS the GARDENER (St) M.
                            AC. July 23
d. c.303. A gardener near Sinope on the
Black Sea martyred under Diocletian.
His existence, martyrdom and ancient
cult are established facts. He is still
greatly venerated in the East.

PHOEBE (St)   RM. Sept 3
1st cent. A matron who worked as a
deaconess at Cenchreae near Corinth,
highly commended by St Paul and the
bearer to Rome of his epistle to that
church (Rom. XVI, 1–3). It has been
suggested, without the slightest foundation, that she was St Paul's wife.

**PHOTINA, JOSEPH, VICTOR,
SEBASTIAN, ANATOLIUS, PHO-
TIUS, PHOTIS (PHOTIDES),
PARASCEVE and CYRIACA (SS)
MM.   RM. March 20**
? This group of martyrs constitutes a
historical puzzle. The Greek tradition
identifies Photina with the Samaritan
woman of St John's gospel (chap. IV)
and makes Joseph and Victor her sons.
They are alleged to have been martyred
with other Christians at Rome under
Nero. Baronius may have put them in
the RM. because he believed that the
head of St Photina was preserved at St
Paul's outside-the-walls.

**PHOTINUS (or POTHINUS),
SANCTIUS (SANCTUS), VETIUS,
EPAGATHUS, MATURUS, PONTI-
CUS, BIBLIS (BIBLIDES), ATTA-
LUS, ALEXANDER, BLANDINA
and Comp. (SS) MM.   RM. June 2**
d. 177. Martyrs of Lyons, the details of
whose martyrdom are given in an authentic letter written by the churches of
Vienne and Lyons to those of Asia. The
writer may have been St Irenaeus. The
martyrs were at first set upon by the
pagan mob, but afterwards they were
tried and condemned on account of their
religion, by the regular tribunals. Photinus, their leader, bishop of the city,
an old man of ninety years, expired in
his dungeon from the ill-usage he received. The others were thrown to the
wild beasts in the amphitheatre at the
public games. The slave-girl, Blandina,
enmeshed in a net and tossed by a wild
bull, and the boy, Ponticus, who was
one of the last to suffer, have ever
excited special admiration. The whole
description is most graphic. They suffered under Marcus Aurelius.

PHOTINUS (St) M.   RM. Aug 12
See Anicetus, Photinus, etc.

PHOTIS (St) M.   RM. March 20
See Photina, Joseph, etc.

PHOTIUS (St) M.   RM. March 4
See Archelaus, Cyril and Photius.

PHOTIUS (St) M.   RM. March 20
See Photina, Joseph, etc.

PIA (St) M.   RM. Jan 19
See Paul, Gerontius, etc.

PIALA (St) M.   AC. Dec 14
See Fingar, Phiala, and Comp.

**PIATON (PIATO, PIAT) (St) M.
                          RM. Oct 1**
d. *c*.286. Said to have been a native of
Benevento in Italy, sent by the pope to
evangelize the districts of Tournai and
Chartres. He is thought to have died a
martyr at Tournai under Maximian.

PIENTIA (St) VM.   RM. Oct 11
See Nicasius, Quirinus, etc.

PIERIUS (St) C.   RM. Nov 4
d. *c*.310. A priest of Alexandria, writer
of several philosophical and theological
treatises.

PIGMENIUS (St) M. RM. March 24
d. 362. A Roman priest thrown into the
Tiber under Julian the Apostate.

PINIAN (St) M.   RM. Dec 31
See Melania and Pinian.

PINNOCK (St)   Nov 6
A church in Cornwall is called St Pin-
nocks, but it is probable that Pinnock is
a corruption of Winnock.

PINYTUS (St) Bp.   RM. Oct 10
d. *p*.180. A Greek bishop in Crete numbered among distinguished ecclesiastical
writers by Eusebius.

**PIONIUS and Comp. (SS) MM.
                          RM. Feb 1**
d. 251. A priest of Smyrna who, with
fifteen companions, suffered under
Decius. They were arrested while liturgically commemorating the anniversary
of the martyrdom of St Polycarp. They
were burnt at the stake after a long
cross-examination and after having been
put to severe torture. We have an eye-
witness's account of their death.

PIOR (St) H.   AC. Jan 17
d. *c*.395. An Egyptian solitary, a disciple of St Antony.

PIPERION (St) M.   RM. March 11
See Candidus, Piperion and Comp.

PIRAN (PYRAN) (St) C. AC. March 5
5th or 6th cent. A hermit near Padstow
in Cornwall, titular of the church of the
canons regular at Truro. Many writers
identify him with St Kieran, q.v. He is
venerated as the patron saint of miners.

PIRMIN (St) Bp. OSB. RM. Nov 3
d. 753. According to the latest researches, Pirmin was born in S. Aragon
and became a monk there. The name of
his monastery is not known. When the
Saracens invaded Spain, he fled, and
travelled as far as the Rhineland where
he established several abbeys—Reichenau, Murbach, Amorbach—and restored others, notably Dissentis, introducing into them all the Benedictine
Rule. He was ordained by the pope a
chorepiscopus, or regionary bishop; he
was never bishop of Meaux. He is one
of the great Benedictine apostles in
German lands.

PISTIS (FAITH) (St) VM. RM. Aug 1
See Faith, Hope and Charity.

PIUS V (St) Pope OP.   RM. May 5
1504–1572. Michael Ghislieri was born in Piedmont, joined the Dominicans in 1518, was ordained priest in 1540, taught philosophy and theology for sixteen years and in 1556 was nominated bishop of Sutri and inquisitor for Lombardy. In 1557 he was created cardinal and in 1559 was transferred to the see of Mondovi, finally being elected pope in 1565. Of an austere and severe disposition he was well fitted for the task of combating the loose discipline of that time in many ecclesiastical quarters, including the Roman curia. He insisted on the exact observance of the decrees of the Council of Trent, organized an expedition against the Turks which won the victory of Lepanto (1570), promoted ecclesiastical learning, reformed liturgical worship, excommunicated Queen Elizabeth of England and fought Protestantism everywhere. Canonized in 1712.

PIUS I (St) Pope M.   RM. July 11
d. c.154. Pope from c.142 to c.154. He may have been a brother of Hermas, the writer of the work called The Shepherd; if so, Pius, like his brother, was born a slave. His pontificate was one of active opposition to the Gnostics, notably the Gnostic Marcion. It is not proved that he died a martyr.

PIUS X (St) Pope   RM. Sept 3
1835–1914. Joseph Sarto was born in 1835 in Riese, diocese of Treviso near Venice, then part of the Austrian Empire. His parents were very poor; his father owned a cow and a strip of land, and worked part-time as caretaker of the village hall, and postman. Joseph used to walk four miles barefoot to school to save shoe-leather. From 1850 he studied at the minor seminary at Treviso, and went on to Padua. He served nine years as curate to the parish

priest of Tombolo, and the latter formed a high opinion of his virtues. Promotion followed: in 1867 he was parish priest of Salzano; in 1884 Bishop of Mantua, and 1893 Patriarch of Venice and Cardinal. Very unexpectedly to himself was elected Pope at the Conclave of 1903, and as Pope he continued the simple personal life he had always observed. The keynote of his pontificate was *Omnia Instaurare in Christo*. It was distinguished by his decrees on early and frequent Communion, on liturgical reform, on the teaching of the Catechism. Other notable activities were his condemnation of Modernism, his reorganization of the Roman Curia and initiation of the codification of Canon Law. Greatly saddened by the outbreak of the World War in August 1914, he died on the 20th of that month. His will ran: I was born poor; I lived poor; I wish to die poor. Canonized in 1954.

PLACID (PLACIDUS, PLAIT) (St) Ab. OSB.   AC. May 7
d. c.675. Abbot in the basilica of St Symphorian at Autun.

PLACID (St) M.   AC. July 11
See Sigisbert and Placid.

PLACID (Bl) Ab. OSB. Cist.   AC. June 12
d. 1248. Born at Rodi, near Amiterno in Italy, of working class parents. He became a Cistercian monk at St Nicholas in Corno, then a hermit at Ocre in the Abruzzi, and ultimately the abbot-founder of the monastery of Santo Spirito, near Val d'Ocre. It is narrated of him that he took his sleep in a standing posture for thirty-seven years.

PLACID, EUTYCHIUS, VICTORINUS, FLAVIA, DONATUS, FIRMATUS, FAUSTUS, and Comp. (SS) MM.   RM. Oct 5

? A heterogeneous group of martyrs, some of whom, notably Placid, have been venerated as Sicilian martyrs since the 4th century, their names being included in the martyrology compiled by St Jerome. In the 12th century this Sicilian Placid was identified with Placid the disciple of St Benedict at Subiaco (d. *c.*550) who was also thought to have died a martyr. This latter Placid is the Placid now liturgically honoured in the RM. Of him we know only what St Gregory tells us in Book II of the Dialogues, viz. that he was the son of the Roman patrician Tertullus, that he, when a mere child was offered to God at Subiaco and placed under the care of St Benedict, and that he was saved from drowning by the miraculous intervention of St Benedict and St Maurus. The death of St Placid, St Benedict's disciple, is usually said to have taken place *c.*550.

PLACID (St) M.   RM. Oct 11
See Anastasius, Placid, etc.

PLACIDE VIEL (Bl) V. AC. March 4
1815–1877. Born on a farm in Normandy she was introduced by her aunt to St Marie-Madeleine Postel, the first Mother General of the Sisters of the Christian Schools. She entered the Order in 1833 and became Assistant-General at the age of twenty-six. This was the cause of some resentment against her, but on the death of Mother Postel in 1846 she succeeded her, and in 1859 obtained Papal approval of the Institute. Her organizing work during the Franco-Prussian War was heroic and probably hastened her end. Beatified in 1951.

PLACIDIA (St) V.   RM. Oct 11
d. *c.*460. A virgin venerated at Verona. She has been often erroneously identified with Placidia the daughter of the emperor Valentinian III.

PLATO (St) Ab.   RM. Apr 4
d. 813. A Greek monk, and abbot, first of Symboleon on Mt Olympus in Bithynia, and then Sakkudion near Constantinople. He opposed the divorce and subsequent attempted marriage of the emperor Constantine Porphyrogenitus, who retaliated by persecuting and imprisoning him.

PLATO (St) M.   RM. July 22
d. *c.*306. A rich youth martyred at Ancyra in Galatia. He was a brother of St Antiochus (q.v.). He is held in great veneration in the East.

**PLATONIDES and Comp. (SS)
MM.**   RM. Apr 6
d. *c.*308. A deaconess and foundress of a nunnery at Nisibis in Mesopotamia. The RM. wrongly calls her a martyr and ascribes her to Ascalon. Nothing is known about her companions.

PLAUTILLA (St) W.   RM. May 20
d. *c.*67. The alleged mother of St Flavia Domitilla. She is said to have been baptized by St Peter and to have been present at the martyrdom of St Paul.

PLAUTUS (St) M.   RM. Sept 29
See Eutychius, Plautus and Heracleas.

PLECHELM (St) M. OSB.
                              AC. July 15
See Wiro, Plechelm and Otger.

PLEGMUND (St) Bp. OSB.
                              PC. Aug 2
d. 914. The tutor of King Alfred. At that monarch's request, consecrated archbishop of Canterbury by Pope Formosus.

**PLUTARCH, SERENUS, HERA-
CLIDES, HERON, a second SERE-
NUS, RHAIS, POTAMIOENA and
MARCELLA (SS) MM. RM. June 28**
d. 202. Martyrs of Alexandria under

Septimius Severus. They were pupils of Origen at the catechetical school of Alexandria. The virgin Potamioena was lowered slowly into a cauldron of boiling pitch. Her mother St Marcella suffered at the same time.

PODIUS (St) Bp. OSA. RM. May 28
d. 1002. A son of the margrave of Tuscany who became a canon regular and eventually ruled the see of Florence from 990 to 1002.

POEMON (POEMEN) (St) H.
RM. Aug 27
d. c.450. His name is often written in its Latin form "Pastor." One of the most famous of the fathers of the Egyptian desert. He dwelt at Skete, where he became abbot of the numerous groups of hermits, who lived in the abandoned ruins of a pagan temple at Terenuth.

POL de LÉON (St) Bp. AC. March 12
Otherwise Paul Aurelian, q.v.

POLIUS (St) M.   RM. May 21
See Timothy, Polius and Eutychius.

POLLIO (St) M.   RM. Apr 28
d. c.304. A lector of the church of Cybalae in Pannonia, burnt alive under Diocletian.

POLYAENUS (St) M.   RM. Apr 28
See Patrick, Acacius, etc.

POLYAENUS (St) M.   RM. Aug 18
See Hermas, Serapion and Polyaenus.

POLYANUS (St) M. Bp. RM. Sept 10
See Nemesian, Felix, etc.

POLYCARP of SMYRNA and Comp. (SS) MM.
RM. Jan 26 and Feb 23
d. 156 (or 166). Converted to the Faith by St John the Evangelist c.80, Polycarp

became bishop of Smyrna c.96. He with his friend St Ignatius of Antioch were the link between the Apostles and subsequent generations of Christians in Asia Minor, and, through their disciple St Irenaeus of Lyons, in Gaul. We have an authentic record of St Polycarp's martyrdom in a letter written by eye-witnesses of the church of Smyrna. His profession of faith before the proconsul is a touching example of loyal devotion to Christ. He said that he had served Christ eighty-six years when he was burnt alive with twelve of his own flock, under Marcus Aurelius. Polycarp's letter to the Philippians, still extant, was during at least three centuries publicly read in the churches of Asia.

POLYCARP (St) C.   RM. Feb 23
d. c.300. A Roman priest of whom mention is made in the Acts of the martyrs for his zeal in ministering to those detained in prison for their faith.

POLYCARP of ALEXANDRIA (St) M.   AC. Apr 2
d. 303. A martyr beheaded at Alexandria after many torments.

POLYCARP and THEODORE (SS) MM.   RM. Dec 7
? Martyrs at Antioch in Syria.

POLYCHRONIUS (St) Bp. M.
RM. Feb 17
? Bishop and martyr at Babylon. The RM. says that he was put to death by Decius, but that emperor never made an expedition against the Persians. As St Polychronius of Dec 6 had also a feast on Feb 17, it is suggested that this feast masked the translation of his relics, and there was only one person.

POLYCHRONIUS (St) M.
RM. Dec 6
4th cent. A priest who, in the reign of

the emperor Constantius, was slain by Arians while he was celebrating Mass. He was present at the council of Nicaea (325).

POLYDORE PLASDEN (Bl) M.
                              AC. Dec 10
d. 1591. Born in London and educated for the priesthood at Reims and in Rome, he was ordained in 1588 and martyred at Tyburn for his priesthood. Beatified in 1929.

POLYEUCTUS (St) M. RM. Feb 13
d. c.259. A Roman officer martyred at Melitene in Armenia under Valerian. His Acts, as given by Metaphrastes, are as touching as any in early Christian literature. Corneille has used some elements of the martyr's story in his tragedy *Polyeucte*.

POLYEUCTUS, VICTORIUS and DONATUS (SS) MM. RM. May 21
? Martyrs of Caesarea in Cappadocia, of whom we know no more than the names (variously spelt) registered in the martyrologies.

POLYXENA (St) M. RM. Sept 23
See Xantippa and Polyxena.

POMPEIUS (St) M. RM. Apr 10
See Terence, Africanus, etc.

POMPEIUS (St) M. RM. July 7
See Peregrinus, Lucian, etc.

POMPEIUS (St) Bp. RM. Dec 14
d. c.290. Bishop of Pavia.

POMPILIUS MARIA PIROTTI (St) C. RM. July 15
1710–1756. Born at Montecalvo, diocese of Benevento, he joined the Piarist fathers (Scolopi) at Naples in 1727 and devoted his life to teaching in the schools of his Order. He died at Lecce in Apulia. Canonized in 1934.

POMPONIUS (St) Bp. RM. Apr 30
d. 536. Bishop of Naples (508–536). He was a strong opponent of Arianism, then under the patronage of the Gothic king Theodoric.

POMPOSA (St) VM. RM. Sept 19
d. 835. A nun of Peñamelaria near Cordova. She was beheaded by the Moors at Cordova.

PONS (St) M. RM. May 14
Otherwise Pontius, q.v.

PONTIAN (St) M. RM. Jan 19
d. 169. An Italian martyr who suffered at Spoleto under Marcus Aurelius. His Acts are only substantially accurate.

PONTIAN NGONDWE (St) M. RM. June 3
d. 1886. A member of the Royal Guard of King Mwanga of Uganda by whose orders he was put to death. See Uganda (Martyrs of).

PONTIAN (St) M. RM. Aug 25
See Eusebius, Pontian, etc.

PONTIAN (St) Pope M. RM. Nov 19
d. c.236. He succeeded St Urban I in the chair of Peter about the year 230. He was exiled by the emperor Maximinus to Sardinia c.235, where he is said to have succumbed to ill-treatment. With him the RM. commemorates St Hippolytus as his fellow exile in Sardinia.

PONTIAN and Comp. (SS) MM. RM. Dec 2
d. c.259. A group of five Roman martyrs who suffered under Valerian.

PONTIAN (St) M. RM. Dec 11
See Trason, Pontian and Praetextatus.

PONTIAN (St) M. RM. Dec 31
See Stephen, Pontian, etc.

PONTICUS (St) M.   RM. June 2
See Photinus (Pothinus), Sanctius, etc.

PONTIUS (St) C.   RM. March 8
d. *c*.260. A deacon of the church of
Carthage. He was the attendant of St
Cyprian in his exile and at his trial and
execution. He has left us a graphic
account of the life and passion of St
Cyprian.

PONTIUS of CIMIEZ (St) M.
RM. May 14
d. 258 (?). A martyr of Cimella (Cimiez)
near Nice. His relics, translated into
Languedoc, have given its name to the
town of Saint-Pons.

PONTIUS of FAUCIGNY (Bl) Ab.
OSA.   AC. Nov 26
d. 1178. Born in Savoy, at the age of
twenty he joined the canons regular at
Abondance in the Chablais. He founded
and was abbot of the monastery of St
Sixtus, whence he was promoted to the
abbacy of Abondance. He was held in
high veneration by St Francis of Sales.
Cult confirmed in 1806.

PONTIUS of BALMEY (Bl) Bp.
O. Cart.   PC. Dec 13
d. 1140. Born at Balmey, he became a
canon of Lyons. Later he founded on
his paternal estate the charterhouse of
Meyriat and joined the Carthusians. He
was appointed bishop of Belley in 1121,
but resigned before his death and returned to Meyriat.

POPPO (St) Ab. OSB. RM. Jan 25
978–1048. Born in Flanders, he first
followed a military career and led an
unbridled life. He then made a penitential pilgrimage to Jerusalem and Rome
and on his return became a Benedictine
at St Thierry, Reims (1006). Two years
later he migrated to Saint-Vannes and
helped Bl Richard in the revival of

monastic discipline. Shortly after he was
appointed provost of St Vaast, Arras,
and soon became known to the emperor
St Henry, who chose him as one of his
most trusted advisers. In 1021 the
emperor made Poppo abbot of Stavelot-Malmédy and soon the revival
spread to several of the most ancient
abbeys of Lotharingia and neighbouring
territories: Hautmont, Marchiennes,
St Maximinus of Trèves, St Vaast at
Arras, etc. Poppo ruled all these houses
as a sort of superior general. He is one
of the greatest monastic figures of the
11th century.

PORCARIUS and Comp. (SS) MM.
OSB.   RM. Aug 12
d. *c*.732. Porcarius was the second of
this name to be abbot of Lérins, an
island off the coast of Provence. The
whole community of five hundred
monks—except the youngest members
whom the abbot had sent away to safety,
were massacred by the Saracens.

PORPHYRIUS and SELEUCUS
(SS) MM.   RM. Feb 16
d. 309. Palestinian martyrs put to death
at Caesarea. We owe the account of their
martyrdom to the historian Eusebius.

PORPHYRIUS (St) Bp. RM. Feb 26
d. 420. A wealthy Greek who became a
hermit first in the desert of Skete in
Egypt and then in Palestine on the
banks of the Jordan. Much against his
will he was raised to the see of Gaza,
which he ruled with extraordinary
energy, ability and success. He almost
completely uprooted the remnants of
paganism in his diocese. His biography
written by his deacon Mark is one of the
most valuable historical sources of the
5th century.

PORPHYRIUS (St) M. RM. May 4
d. 250. A priest who is said to have

preached in Umbria, chiefly at Camerino, and to have been beheaded under Decius. He belongs to the apocryphal legend of St Venantius (May 18), q.v.

PORPHYRIUS (St) M. RM. Aug 20
? Connected with the apocryphal legend of St Agapitus of Palestrina (Aug 18), whose story was transferred to the equally unhistorical legend of St Venantius.

PORPHYRIUS (St) M. RM. Sept 6
See Onesiphorus and Porphyrius.

PORPHYRIUS (St) M. RM. Sept 15
d. 362. Said to have been a horse-dealer and an actor, who, while playing before Julian the Apostate and burlesquing the baptism of Christians, suddenly declared himself a believer and was at once slain.

PORPHYRIUS (St) M. RM. Nov 4
d. 271. A martyr at Ephesus under Aurelian.

PORTIANUS (St) Ab. RM. Nov 24
d. 533. A slave who became a monk and, in course of time, abbot of Miranda in Auvergne. He fearlessly faced the Merovingian king Thierry of Austrasia and obtained from him the release of his Auvergnate prisoners.

POSSESSOR (St) Bp. AC. May 11
d. c.485. A city magistrate of Verdun, who became bishop of that city in 470. He and his flock were reduced to great distress by the invasions of the barbarians—Franks, Vandals, Goths, etc.

POSSIDIUS (St) Bp. RM. May 16
d. 450. A favourite disciple, and the biographer, of St Augustine of Hippo. He became bishop of Calama in Numidia, whence he was driven by the Arian Vandals, and ended his days in Apulia.

He was one of the ablest controversialists of his time.

POTAMIA (St) M. RM. Dec 5
See Julius, Potamia, etc.

POTAMIOENA the YOUNGER (St) VM. AC. June 7
d. c.304. A young girl put to death at Alexandria under Diocletian.

POTAMIOENA the ELDER (St) VM. RM. June 28
See Plutarch, Serenus, etc.

POTAMIUS and NEMESIUS (SS) MM. RM. Feb 20
? Martyrs in Cyprus. Nothing is known of them. Eusebius attaches them to the Church of Alexandria.

POTAMON (St) Bp. M. RM. May 18
d. c.340. Bishop of Heraclea in Upper Egypt. During the persecution of Maximinus Daza (310) he was sentenced to the mines, lamed in one leg and deprived of one eye. Released after Constantine's decree of toleration, he was present at the council of Nicaea. He supported his metropolitan St Athanasius and was as a result fiercely persecuted by the Arians, who ultimately compassed his death.

POTENTIAN (St) M. RM. Dec 31
See Sabinian and Potentian.

POTENTIANA (St) M. RM. May 19
Otherwise Pudentiana, q.v.

POTHMIUS and NEMESIUS (SS) MM. RM. Feb 20
Otherwise Potamius and Nemesius, q.v.

POTHINUS (St) Bp. M. RM. June 2
Otherwise Photinus, q.v.

POTITUS (St) M.   RM. Jan 13
? Honoured as a boy-martyr in the diocese of Naples. His extant Acts are legendary.

PRAEJECTUS (PRIEST, PREST, PREILS, PRIX) (St) Bp. M.
RM. Jan 25
d. 676. He became Bishop of Clermont in Auvergne with the approval of Childeric II in 666. A great administrator, and fosterer of monasticism, he was slain by evil-doers at Volvic in the Vosges.

PRAEPEDIGNA (St) M.
RM. Feb 18
See Maximus, Claudius, etc.

PRAESIDIUS (St) M.   RM. Sept 6
See Donatian, Praesidius, etc.

PRAETEXTATUS (PRIX) (St) Bp. M.   RM. Feb 24
d. 586 (Apr 14). Bishop of Rouen (550–586). For his courage in denouncing the crimes of the wicked queen Fredegonda he was cruelly persecuted and exiled. Recalled after seven years he was put to death by her order on Easter Sunday in his own church.

PRAETEXTATUS (St) M.
RM. Dec 11
See Trason, Pontian and Praetextatus.

PRAGMATIUS (St) Bp.
RM. Nov 22
d. c.520. Bishop of Autun. His diocese suffered much during the war between the sons of Clovis.

PRAXEDES (St) V.   RM. July 21
2nd cent. Said to have been the daughter of the Roman senator Pudens and sister of St Pudentiana. One of the most ancient churches in Rome perpetuates her memory.

PRIAM (St) M.   RM. May 28
See Emilius, Felix, etc.

PRILIDIAN (St) M.   RM. Jan 24
See Babilas, Urban, etc.

PRIMAEL (St) H.   AC. May 16
d. c.450. A native of Britain who crossed over to Brittany and became a hermit in the diocese of Quimper, where churches are dedicated to him.

PRIMIAN (St) M.   RM. Dec 29
See Dominic, Victor, etc.

PRIMITIVA (St) M.   RM. Feb 24
? An early martyr, probably of Rome. Some old martyrologies have "Primitivus".

PRIMITIVA (St) VM.   RM. July 23
? An early martyr, probably of Rome. Very probably identical with the Primitiva of Feb 24. Several ancient lists write her name "Primitia"; others, "Privata".

PRIMITIVUS (St) M.   RM. Apr 16
See Saragossa Martyrs.

PRIMITIVUS (St) M.   RM. June 10
See Getulius, Caerealis, etc.

PRIMITIVUS (St) M.   RM. July 18
See Symphorosa and her sons.

PRIMITIVUS (St) M.   RM. Nov 27
See Facundus and Primitivus.

PRIMITIVUS (St) M.   RM. Dec 9
See Peter, Successus, etc.

PRIMUS (St) M.   RM. Jan 3
See Cyrinus, Primus and Theogenes.

PRIMUS and DONATUS (SS) MM.
RM. Feb 9
d. 362. Two African deacons slain by

the Donatist schismatics when the latter were trying to get possession of the Catholic church at Lavallum in N.W. Africa.

PRIMUS and FELICIAN (SS) MM.
RM. June 9

d. c.297. Two aged brothers, Roman citizens, beheaded under Diocletian on the Via Nomentana. Their Acts are not altogether trustworthy.

PRIMUS, CYRIL and SECUNDARIUS (SS) MM.
RM. Oct 2

? Martyrs at Antioch in Syria in one of the early persecutions.

PRINCIPIA (St) V.
AC. May 11

d. c.420. A Roman virgin, a disciple of St Marcella.

PRINCIPIUS (St) Bp.
RM. Sept 25

d. c.505. The elder brother of St Remigius of Reims. He became bishop of Soissons.

PRIOR (St) H.
AC. June 17

c.295–395. An Egyptian hermit, one of the first disciples of St Antony.

PRISCA (St) VM.
RM. Jan 18

3rd cent. (?). A virgin martyr venerated from ancient times in Rome, where a church is dedicated in her honour on the Aventine, but of whom nothing authentic is known.

PRISCIAN (St) M.
RM. Oct 12

See Evagrius, Priscian, etc.

PRISCIAN (St) M.
RM. Oct 14

See Carponius, Evaristus and Priscian.

PRISCILLA (St) W.
RM. Jan 16

1st cent. The wife of Manius Acilius Glabrio and mother of the senator Pudens. The tradition is that she was the hostess in Rome of St Peter the Apostle, whose headquarters were at her villa, near the Roman catacombs which to this day bear her name.

PRISCILLA (St)
RM. July 8

See Aquila and Priscilla.

PRISCILLIAN (St) M.
RM. Jan 4

See next below.

PRISCUS, PRISCILLIAN and BENEDICTA (SS) MM.
RM. Jan 4

? The names are taken from the untrustworthy Acts of St Bibiana, in which it is stated that they were Christians buried by her father, Flavian. The martyrologist Ado treated them as martyrs.

PRISCUS, MALCHUS and ALEXANDER (SS) MM.
RM. March 28

d. 260. Martyrs thrown to the wild beasts during the public games at Caesarea in Palestine under Valerian.

PRISCUS and Comp. (SS) MM.
RM. May 26

d. c.272. Priscus, a Roman military officer, several soldiers under his command, and a number of citizens of Besançon were martyred near Auxerre at a place where they had concealed themselves.

PRISCUS (St) M.
RM. Sept 1

d. c.66. The alleged first bishop of Capua, whither he is supposed to have been sent by St Peter. He is said to have been a disciple of our Lord and to have died a martyr under Nero.

PRISCUS, CASTRENSIS, TAMMARUS, ROSIUS, HERACLIUS, SECUNDINUS, ADJUTOR, MARK, AUGUSTUS, ELPIDIUS, CANION and VINDONIUS (SS) CC.
RM. Sept 1 and Feb 11

5th cent. Priscus, an African bishop,

with his priests, were cast adrift in a rudderless boat by the Arian Vandals. They reached S. Italy, where eventually Priscus became bishop of Capua and several of the others were in time promoted to different sees. The Acts, however, are untrustworthy and it seems that the companions of St Priscus are Campanian saints unconnected with the story of the Roman Martyrology. One opinion interprets Priscus Castrensis as meaning "Priscus formerly Bishop of Castra in N. Africa".

PRISCUS (St) M.   RM. Sept 20
? A native of Phrygia, martyred by being first stabbed with poniards and then beheaded.

PRISCUS, CRESCENS and EVA-GRIUS (SS) MM.   RM. Oct 1
? Martyrs at Tomi on the Black Sea.

PRIVATUS (St) Bp. M. RM. Aug 21
d. 260. A bishop of Gévaudan (now Mende) in Gaul. He was seized by invading barbarians, but was offered his life on condition of his revealing the hiding place of his flock; on his refusal he was beaten to death.

PRIVATUS (St) M.   RM. Sept 20
See Dionysius and Privatus.

PRIVATUS (St) M.   RM. Sept 28
d. 223. A Roman citizen, scourged to death under Alexander Severus.

PRIX (St) M.   RM. Jan 25
Otherwise Praejectus, q.v., or Praetextatus (Feb 24).

PROBUS (St) Bp.   RM. Jan 12
d. *p.*591. A bishop of Verona, about whom no particulars are extant.

PROBUS (St) Bp.   RM. March 15
d. *c.*571. Bishop of Rieti in central Italy.

St Gregory the Great describes the death-bed scene of St Probus, when St Juvenal and St Eleutherius appeared to him in a vision.

PROBUS and GRACE (SS)
                                        AC. July 5
? Cornish saints, by tradition husband and wife. The church of Tressilian, or Probus, is dedicated in their honour.

PROBUS (St) M.   RM. Oct 11
See Tharacus (Tarachus), Probus and Andronicus.

PROBUS (St) Bp.   RM. Nov 10
d. *c.*175. A Roman who became sixth bishop of Ravenna. His relics are still venerated in the cathedral of Ravenna.

PROBUS (St) M.   RM. Nov 13
See Arcadius, Paschasius, etc.

PROCESSUS and MARTINIAN (SS) MM.   RM. July 2
? Roman martyrs greatly venerated in Rome: their tomb and basilica were on the Aurelian Way. Their connexion with the apostles Peter and Paul in the Mamertine jail is mere legend.

PROCHORUS (St) Bp. M.
                                        RM. Apr 9
1st cent. One of the seven deacons ordained by the apostles. The tradition is that he afterwards became bishop of Nicomedia and was martyred at Antioch.

PROCLUS and HILARION (SS) MM.   RM. July 12
d. 115. Martyrs of Ancyra in Galatia in the reign of Trajan.

PROCLUS (St) Bp.   RM. Oct 24
d. 447. A disciple of St John Chrysostom. He became patriarch of Constantinople in 434. His treatment of heretics,

chiefly Nestorians, was characterized by great gentleness. According to tradition he instituted the singing of the Trisagion in the liturgy in miraculous circumstances.

PROCOPIUS (St) C.   RM. Feb 27
See Basil and Procopius.

PROCOPIUS (St) Ab. OS. Bas.
AC. July 4
c.980–1053 (March 25). Born in Bohemia, he studied at Prague, where he was ordained and became a canon. Later he became a hermit, and finally abbot-founder of Sazaba abbey in Prague. Canonized in 1804.

PROCOPIUS (St) M.   RM. July 8
d. 303. The first victim of the Diocletian persecution in Palestine. He was a reader in the church of Scythopolis and was beheaded at Caesarea Maritima. The account of his martyrdom is given by his contemporary Eusebius the historian. It has been much distorted by later legend.

PROCULUS, EPHEBUS and APOLLONIUS (SS) MM.
RM. Feb 14
d. 273. Mentioned as martyrs at Terni in the untrustworthy Acts of St Valentine of Terni. The Bollandists identify this Proculus with the bishop of Terni venerated on April 14.

PROCULUS (St) Bp. M. RM. Apr 14
? A martyr of Terni, in Italy, who suffered martyrdom under Maxentius. The RM. says he was Bishop, but there is no authority for this.

PROCULUS (St) M.   RM. June 1
d. c.304 (?). Said to have been a Roman officer, martyred at Bologna under Diocletian. He has been held in great veneration at Bologna from very ancient times.

PROCULUS (St) Bp. M.
AC. July 12
d. 542. Bishop of Bologna (540–542). He was martyred by the Goths.

PROCULUS (St) M.   RM. Aug 18
See Florus, Laurus, etc.

PROCULUS (St) M.   RM. Sept 19
See Januarius, and Comp.

PROCULUS (St) Bp. M. RM. Nov 4
d. p.717. Bishop of Autun, said to have been put to death by the invading Huns.

PROCULUS (St) Bp. M. RM. Dec 1
d. c.542. Bishop of Narni (others say of Terni), put to death by order of Totila, king of the Goths.

PROCULUS (St) Bp.   RM. Dec 9
d. c.320. Bishop of Verona. He was a confessor during the persecution of Diocletian, but ultimately died in peace in his episcopal city.

PROJECTUS (St) M.   RM. Jan 24
See Thyrsus and Projectus.

PROJECTUS (St) Bp. M.
RM. Jan 25
Otherwise Praejectus, q.v.

PROSDOCE (St) M.   AC. Oct 4
See Domina, Berenice.

PROSDOCIMUS (St) Bp.
RM. Nov 7
d. c.100. First bishop of Padua, greatly venerated in N.E. Italy. That he was sent from Antioch by St Peter is now generally denied by historians.

PROSPER of REGGIO (St) Bp.
RM. June 25
d. c.466. A bishop of Reggio in Emilia, venerated as principal patron of the city and diocese of Reggio.

PROSPER of AQUITAINE (St) C.
RM. June 25

c.390–463. A native of Aquitaine, a layman and, probably, a married man, Prosper devoted his fine intellect to the study of theological questions and became an enthusiastic admirer of St Augustine, whose doctrine on grace he defended against the Semi-Pelagians. He worked for a time in the Roman curia. He was a prolific writer and a powerful controversialist.

PROSPER of ORLEANS (St) Bp.
RM. July 29

d. c.453. A bishop of Orleans, who has often been confused with St Prosper of Aquitaine and St Prosper of Reggio.

PROTASIUS (PROTASE) (St)
RM. June 19

See Gervase and Protase.

PROTASIUS (St) M.   RM. Aug 4

? A martyr honoured at Cologne. Probably identical with the fellow-sufferer of St Gervase (June 19).

PROTASIUS (St) Bp.   RM. Nov 24

d. 352. Bishop of Milan 331–352. He espoused the cause of St Athanasius against the Arians, doing so with special effect at the synod of Sardica (343).

PROTERIUS (St) Bp. M.
AC. Feb 28

d. 458. Patriarch of Alexandria. He replaced Dioscorus, who had been deposed by the council of Chalcedon, and did his utmost to counter the plots of the Eutychians, who were leading his flock astray. They, however, succeeded in compassing his death on Good Friday.

PROTHADIUS (PROTAGIUS) (St) Bp.
AC. Feb 10

d. 624. The successor of St Nicetius in the see of Besançon, he was consulted on all important matters by Clotaire II.

PROTOGENES (St) Bp.
RM. May 6

4th cent. A bishop of Carrhae in Syria, who, while still a priest, had been banished by the Arian emperor Valens. He was recalled under Theodosius and consecrated bishop.

PROTOLICUS (St) M. RM. Feb 14

See Bassus, Antony and Protolicus.

PROTUS (St)   RM. May 31

See Cantius, Cantian, etc.

PROTUS and HYACINTH (SS) MM.
RM. Sept 11

d. c.257. According to tradition they were Romans by birth, brothers, and servants in the house of St Philip; and they are said to have been martyred in Rome. The relics of St Hyacinth were beyond any doubt discovered in the cemetery of St Basilla at Rome in 1845. The Acts, however, of these martyrs, as handed down to us, are largely legendary.

PROTUS and JANUARIUS (SS) MM.
RM. Oct 25

d. 303. Protus, a priest, and Januarius, a deacon, were sent by the pope to work in Sardinia, where they were beheaded at Porto Torres, not far from Sassari, in the persecution of Diocletian.

PROVINUS (St) Bp.   AC. March 8

d. c.420. A native of Gaul who became a disciple of St Ambrose at Milan. Later he was coadjutor to St Felix, bishop of Como, whom he succeeded in the see (391).

PRUDENTIA (Bl) V. OSA. Erem.
PC. May 6

d. 1492. Prudentia Castori joined the

hermits of St Augustine at Milan and later became the abbess-foundress of a new convent at Como, where she died.

PRUDENTIUS GALINDO (St) Bp.
AC. Apr 6

d. 861. A Spaniard who in his youth fled from the Saracens to the court of France, where he changed his baptismal name Galindo to Prudentius. He became bishop of Troyes and played a prominent part in the controversy on predestination against Gottschalk and Scotus Erigena. His feast is still kept at Troyes.

PRUDENTIUS (St) Bp. RM. Apr 28

d. *p*.700. A native of Armentia, in the province of Alava, Spain. After having been a hermit for some years he was ordained priest and became bishop of Tarazona (not Tarragona) in Aragon. He is the patron saint of the diocese of Tarazona.

PSALMODIUS (French: PSAL-MET) (St) H.   AC. June 14

7th cent. Of Irish or Scottish descent, and a disciple of St Brendan. He crossed into France and lived as a hermit near Limoges. He is identical with St Sauman (or Saumay).

PTOLEMY (St) Bp. M.
RM. Aug 24

1st cent. Said to have been a disciple of St Peter and bishop of Nepi in Tuscany and there to have suffered martyrdom.

PTOLEMY and LUCIUS (SS) MM.
RM. Oct 19

d. *c*.165. Roman martyrs under Antoninus Pius. Ptolemy was put to death for instructing a woman in the Christian religion. One Lucius and an unnamed man protested against the injustice of the sentence and were also martyred.

We owe the account of their passion to St Justin Martyr, their contemporary.

PTOLEMY (St) M.   RM. Dec 20
See Ammon, Zeno, etc.

PUBLIA (St) W.   RM. Oct 9

d. 362. A Syrian matron, head of a community of women at Antioch, illtreated by order of Julian the Apostate. While the emperor was passing through Antioch, he overheard the community singing the verse: "The idols of the Gentiles are silver and gold, let them that fashion them be made like unto them," and interpreted the words as an insult to himself.

PUBLICUS (St)   AC. July 3
Otherwise Byblig, q.v.

PUBLIUS (St) Bp. M.   RM. Jan 21

d. *c*.112. Tradition identifies this saint with the Publius, "chief man of the island of Malta", who befriended St Paul after his shipwreck (Acts XXVIII, 7). He is said to have become bishop of Athens and to have died a martyr under Trajan. Other sources describe him simply as the first bishop of Malta.

PUBLIUS (St) Ab.   AC. Jan 25

d. *c*.380. An abbot of Zeugma in Syria, who housed his large community in two separate buildings, one for the Greeks and the other for the Syrians.

PUBLIUS, JULIAN, MARCELLUS and Comp. (SS) MM.   RM. Feb 19
? Martyrs in Proconsular Africa.

PUBLIUS (St) M.   RM. Apr 16
See Saragossa Martyrs.

PUBLIUS, VICTOR, HERMES and PAPIAS (SS) MM.   RM. Nov 2
? Martyrs in N.W. Africa.

PUBLIUS (St) Bp. M. RM. Nov 12
See Aurelius and Publius.

PUDENS (St) M. RM. May 19
2nd cent. A Roman senator baptized by
the apostles, the father of St Pudentiana.
He is by many identified with the
Pudens mentioned by St Paul (2 Tim.
IV, 21).

**PUDENTIANA (or POTENTIANA)
(St) V. RM. May 19**
2nd cent. A Roman maiden, daughter of
the senator St Pudens. She is said to
have died at the age of sixteen. We know
very little that is really certain about her.

**PULCHERIA AUGUSTA (St) V.
RM. Sept 10**
d. 453. Daughter of the Eastern emperor Arcadius, she was regent during
the minority of her brother Theodosius
II, and empress after his death. She was
a devoted adherent of the see of Rome
and a firm opponent of Monophysitism.

PUPULUS (St) M. RM. Feb 28
See Caerealis, Pupulus, etc.

PUSICIUS (St) M. RM. Apr 21
See Simeon, Abdechalas, etc.

PUSINNA (St) V. PC. Apr 23
5th–6th cent. A holy virgin of Champagne who had six sisters all honoured
widely as saints. They lived mostly at
home.

PYRAN (St) AC. March 5
Otherwise Piran, q.v.

Q

QUADRAGESIMUS (St) C.
                    RM. Oct 26
d. c.590. A shepherd and subdeacon at
Policastro, who, according to the testimony of St Gregory the Great, raised
a dead man to life.

**QUADRATUS (CODRATUS),
THEODOSIUS, EMMANUEL and
Comp. (SS) MM.   RM. March 26**
d. c.304. A group of forty-three martyrs,
under the leadership of St Quadratus,
bishop in Anatolia, put to death under
Diocletian.

QUADRATUS (St) M.   RM. May 7
d. 257. A martyr said to have been kept
in prison for years at Nicomedia, Nicaea
and Apamea, previous to his martyrdom
at Herbipolis under Valerian.

QUADRATUS (St) M. RM. May 26
? A martyr in Proconsular Africa in
whose honour St Augustine preached a
panegyric.

QUADRATUS (St) Bp. RM. May 26
d. c.130. Bishop of Athens and the first
to write an Apology for the Christian
religion, which he addressed to the
emperor Hadrian.

QUADRATUS (St) Bp. RM. Aug 21
3rd cent. Bishop of Utica highly praised
by St Augustine: "He taught his whole
people, clergy and laity, to confess
Christ." They were all martyred. His
cult was widespread in Africa.

**QUARTUS and QUINTUS (SS)
MM.   RM. May 10**
? Two citizens of Capua, condemned
and executed in Rome, whose remains
were taken back to Capua and there
enshrined.

QUARTUS (St) ? Bp.   RM. Nov 3
1st cent. The disciple of the apostles
whom St Paul (Rom. XVI, 23) mentions as "greeting the Christians of
Rome". Some traditions describe Quartus as one of the seventy-two disciples
(Luke X), others add that he was a
bishop.

QUENTIN (St) M.   RM. Oct 31
Otherwise Quintinus, q.v.

QUERANUS (St)
Otherwise Piran, Kieran, q.v., "Qui-
rinus" may be taken as one of the
Latinized forms of the names of both St
Kieran of Ossory and St Kieran of
Saghir. Another would be Queranus, as
above.

QUINCT—
Note. For names in Quinct— see
Quint—

QUINIDIUS (St) Bp.   RM. Feb 15
d. c.579. From being a hermit at Aix in
Provence he was raised to the see of
Vaison, also in Provence.

QUINTA (St) M.   RM. Feb 8
Otherwise Cointha, q.v.

**QUINTIAN and IRENAEUS (SS)
MM.   RM. Apr. 1**
? Armenian martyrs, of whom nothing
is known.

QUINTIAN, LUCIUS, JULIAN and Comp. (SS) MM.   RM. May 23
d. *c.*430. Three of a group of African martyrs under the Arian Vandal King Hunneric. The group seems to have numbered nineteen and to have included several women.

QUINTIAN (St) Bp.   RM. June 14
? Bishop of an unidentified see in France. The RM. mistakenly ascribes him to Rodez.

QUINTIAN (St) Bp.   RM. Nov 13
d. *c.*527. An African by birth, he fled to Gaul to escape the Arian-Vandal persecution. Eventually he became bishop of Rodez, but was driven thence, this time by the Arian Visigoths, and went to Auvergne, where St Euphrasius made him his successor in the see of Clermont.

QUINTIAN (St) M.   RM. Dec 31
See Stephen, Pontian, etc.

QUINTILIAN (St) M.   RM. Apr 13
See Maximus, Dadas and Quintilian.

QUINTILIAN (St) M.   RM. Apr 16
See Saragossa, Martyrs of.

**QUINTILIS (St) Bp. M.
                RM. March 8**
? A martyr of Nicomedia. Most ancient records mention St Capitolinus as a fellow-martyr.

**QUINTINUS (QUENTIN) (St) M.
                RM. Oct 31**
d. 287. According to the traditional story, often recast and much embellished, Quentin was a Roman by birth who went as a missionary to Gaul. He evangelized the district round Amiens and was martyred at the town on the Somme now called Saint-Quentin. He is beyond doubt a historical person.

QUINTIUS, ARCONTIUS and DONATUS (SS) MM.   RM. Sept 5
? Martyrs venerated at Capua and elsewhere in S. Italy.

**QUINTIUS (QUENTIN) (St) M.
                AC. Oct 4**
d. *c.*570. A citizen of Tours and an official at the court of the Frankish king. The reigning queen, having tried in vain to seduce him, had him assassinated at L'Indrois, near Montresor.

QUINTUS (St) M.   RM. Jan 4
See Aquilinus, Geminus, etc.

QUINTUS, QUINTILLA, QUARTILLA, MARK and Comp. (SS) MM.   RM. March 19
? Martyrs venerated at Sorrento, near Naples. The three first-named were probably a brother and two sisters.

QUINTUS, SIMPLICIUS and Comp. (SS) MM.   RM. Dec 18
d. *c.*255. Martyrs in Proconsular Africa under the emperors Decius and Valerian.

**QUIRIACUS (St) Bp. M.
                RM. May 4**
Otherwise Cyriacus, q.v.

QUIRIACUS (St) M.   RM. Aug 12
See Hilaria, Digna, etc.

**QUIRIACUS, MAXIMUS, ARCHELAUS and Comp. (SS) MM.
                RM. Aug 23**
d. *c.*235 (or 250?). Stated to have been bishop, priest and deacon of Ostia respectively, and to have been martyred with a number of Christian soldiers under Alexander Severus. Some modern writers place the martyrdom twenty or more years later.

QUIRIACUS (St) H.   RM. Sept 29
d. *c.*550. A Greek who lived as a hermit

in various lauras of Palestine. He is said to have died when long past his hundredth year.

QUIRICUS (French: CYR) and JULITTA (SS) MM.   RM. June 16

d. 304. Julitta was a widow of noble birth from Iconium, and was martyred at Tarsus. Previous to her own martyrdom her three-year-old son Quiricus had been brained before her eyes because he had scratched the face of the infuriated magistrate. Modern writers regard the story as fictitious.

QUIRINUS (St) M.   RM. March 25

d. c.269. A Roman martyr who suffered under Claudius II. He was one of those befriended and buried by SS Marius, Martha and Comp. (q.v.).

QUIRINUS (St) M.   RM. March 30

d. c.117. The jailer of Pope St Alexander I, by whom he was converted with his daughter St Balbina. He was martyred shortly after under Hadrian. The story forms part of what modern writers describe as "the Romance called the Passion of St Alexander", q.v. (May 3).

QUIRINUS (St) Bp. M.   RM. June 4

d. 308. Bishop of Siscia (Sisak, or Seseg) in Croatia. He fled from his city to escape the persecution of Galerius, was captured and brought back and ordered to sacrifice to the gods. He refused, was barbarously beaten and handed over to the governor of Pannonia Prima at Sabaria (now Szombathely in Hungary). There, on his continued refusal to apostatize, he was drowned in the river Raab.

QUIRINUS (St) M.   RM. June 4

? A martyr at Tivoli, near Rome.

QUIRINUS (St) M.   RM. Oct 11

See Nicasius, Quirinus, etc.

QUITERIA (St) VM.   RM. May 22

? A Spanish saint greatly venerated on the borders of France and Spain, especially in Spanish and French Navarre. Her traditional story is wholly untrustworthy.

QUIVOX (EVOX) (St)   AC. March 13

Otherwise Kevoca, q.v.

QUODVULTDEUS (St) Bp.   RM. Feb 19

d. c.450. A bishop of Carthage exiled by the Arian Genseric, king of the Vandals, after the capture of the city in 439. He ended his days at Naples.

R

RABANUS MAURUS (Bl) Bp. OSB. AC. Feb 4

*c.*776–856. Born at Mainz, he was offered as a child to the abbey Fulda, and there he spent practically his whole life. After receiving his early education at the abbey, he completed it at Tours, where he studied for two years under Alcuin. Already a monk of Fulda, he was appointed headmaster of the abbey school in 799, ordained deacon (801) and priest (814), and elected abbot in 822. In 847 he resigned this office, but in the same year was appointed archbishop of Mainz. He governed his diocese with remarkable ability and was noted for his charity to the poor, three hundred of whom were entertained daily at his house. Rabanus was the outstanding scholar of his century and one of the most prolific writers of any age. His biblical commentaries, homilies, martyrology and poetical works (he composed the *Veni Creator Spiritus*) have by no means lost their value or interest.

RACHILDIS (St) H. OSB. PC. Nov 23

d. *c.*946. A female recluse who lived walled up in a cell near that of St Wiborada, under the obedience of the abbot of St Gall in Switzerland.

RACHO (RAGNOBERT) (St) Bp. AC. Jan 25

d. *c.*660. The first Frankish bishop of Autun.

RADBOD (St) Bp. OSB. AC. Nov 29

d. 918. The great-grandson of the last pagan king of Friesland, Radbod became bishop of Utrecht in 900. He at once put on the Benedictine habit, all his predecessors having been monks, and ruled the monastic cathedral and the diocese as an exemplary abbot-bishop. At the end of his life he retired to Deventer, where he died.

RADEGUND (St) Queen. RM. Aug 13

518–587. Daughter of the pagan king of Thuringia, whose assassination was avenged by the Frankish king Clotaire I. The latter had the child, then twelve years old, baptized and educated, and eventually married her; but much ill-usage, crowned by the king's murder of her brother, compelled Radegund to leave him. She received the veil from St Medard and founded the great nunnery of the Holy Cross at Poitiers, where she spent the last thirty years of her life.

RADEGUND (St) V. PC. Aug 13

d. *c.*1300. A serving maid at the castle of Wellenburg, near Augsburg, who occupied herself much in works of charity. While on an errand of mercy to a neighbouring hospital she was set upon and torn to pieces by wolves. She at once became the object of a popular cult.

RADINGUS (St) Ab. AC. Sept 17

Otherwise Rodingus, q.v.

RADULPHUS (RADULF) (*several*)

Otherwise Ralph, q.v.

RAINGARDIS (Bl) W. OSB.
PC. June 24
d. 1135. Mother of St Peter the Venerable, abbot of Cluny. In her widowhood she became a Benedictine nun at Marcigny. She was venerated as a saint by the Cluniac Benedictines.

RAITHU (Martyrs of) (SS)
RM. Jan 14
d. c.510. Forty-three anchorites living in the desert of Raithu, near the Red Sea, who were massacred by savages from Ethiopia or by Saracens.

RALPH (several)
Note. Ralph is the English form of Radulphus, which is more common in its French form of Raoul. There are many other variants: Radult, Raul, Radolph, Randulph, Rodolfo, Rudolf, Rodolphe, Rollon, Ruph, etc.

RALPH ASHLEY (Bl) M. SJ.
AC. Apr 7
d. 1606. A Jesuit lay-brother martyred at Worcester for being found in attendance upon Bl Edward Oldcorne. Beatified in 1929.

RALPH (Bl) Bp. OSB. Cist.
AC. Apr 14
d. 1241. Cistercian monk and abbot (1209) of Thoronet Abbey. Later, bishop of Sisteron, France (1216–1241).

RALPH (St) Bp. OSB. AC. June 21
d. 866. In his boyhood he was entrusted to the care of the abbot of Solignac and, according to Benedictine historians, became a monk there. He later held several abbacies, including that of St Medard, Soissons. In 840 he was made bishop of Bourges, and as such he fostered learning, founded monasteries and in general promoted the public welfare.

RALPH MILNER (Bl) M. AC. July 7
d. 1591. A husbandman, born at Stackstead, Hants, martyred at Winchester for relieving Bl Roger Dickenson. Beatified in 1929.

RALPH de la FUTAYE (de FLAGEIO) (Bl) Ab. OSB. AC. Aug 16
d. 1129. A Benedictine of Saint-Jouin-de-Marne, who helped Bl Robert of Arbrissel to establish a new Benedictine congregation, and then became the abbot-founder (1092) of the double monastery of Saint-Sulpice, diocese of Rennes.

RALPH CORBY (*vere* CORBINGTON) (Bl) M. SJ. AC. Sept 7
d. 1644. Born in Dublin, he was educated at St Omer and then studied for the priesthood at Seville and Valladolid. In 1631 he was admitted to the Society of Jesus and ordained priest. He was sent to the English mission and ministered in Co Durham. He was martyred at Tyburn for his priesthood. Beatified in 1929.

RALPH CROCKETT (Bl) M.
AC. Oct 1
d. 1588. Born at Barton-on-the-Hill in Cheshire, he was educated at Christ's College, Cambridge, and at Gloucester Hall, Oxford. He became a schoolmaster in Norfolk and Suffolk. Later he studied for the priesthood at Reims, where he was ordained in 1586. He was arrested while engaged in priestly work in England and martyred at Chichester. Beatified in 1929.

RALPH SHERWIN (Bl) M.
AC. Dec 1
d. 1581. Born at Rodsley in Derbyshire, he gained a fellowship at Oxford, where he was known as a classical scholar of distinction. After his conversion he studied for the priesthood at Douai and Rome, and was ordained in 1580. Within a few months he was in England and in

prison. Queen Elizabeth offered him preferment if he would turn Protestant: on his indignant refusal he was martyred at Tyburn. He is the protomartyr of the Venerable English College, Rome. Beatified in 1886.

RALPH of VAUCELLES (Bl) Ab. OSB.   AC. Dec 30

d. 1152. An Englishman he became St Bernard's disciple at Clairvaux, by whom he was later sent to be the abbotfounder of Vaucelles, diocese of Cambrai. He has a cult among the Cistercians.

RAMBERT (RAGNEBERT, RAGNOBERT) (St) M. AC. June 13

d. c.680. A courtier of high standing and much influence at the court of Thierry III of Austrasia. Ebroin, mayor of the palace, had him exiled and then ambushed and murdered in the Jura mountains. He has always been considered a martyr.

RAMBOLD (RAMNOLD) (St) Ab. OSB.   AC. June 17

d. 1001. Monk of St Maximinus at Trèves, called to Ratisbon by St Wolfgang to be abbot of St Emmeram. He died at the age of one hundred.

RAMIRUS and Comp. (SS) MM. AC. March 13

d. c.554 (or 630). Prior of the Monastery of St Claudius at Leon, Spain. Two days after the martyrdom of his abbot, St Vincent, he, with all the monks of the community, was massacred by the Arian Visigoths while chanting the Nicene creed in the choir of the abbey church.

RAMÓN (several)

The Spanish form of Raymund, q.v.

RANDCALD (St) M. OSB. AC. Feb 21

See Germanus and Randcald.

RANULPHUS (RAGNULF) (St) M. RM. May 27

d. c.700. A martyr of Thélus, near Arras. He was the father of St Hadulph, bishop of Arras-Cambrai.

RAPHAEL the ARCHANGEL (St) RM. Oct 24

One of the three angels whom the Church venerates liturgically by name, and also described as one of the Seven Angels who stand before the throne of God (q.v.). His name means "the Healer of God", and his ministrations in favour of men are described in the book of Tobias. He is commonly identified with the angel of the sheep-pool (John V, 1–4). His feast was added to the calendar of the universal church in 1922.

RASSO (or RATHO) (Bl) Mk. OSB. AC. May 17

d. 953. Count of Andechs in Bavaria, remarkable for his great stature. He was a brave warrior, leader of the Bavarians against the invading Hungarians. In middle age he made a pilgrimage to Palestine and Rome, and on his return founded the abbey of Wörth in Bavaria (now called after him Grafrath), in which he took the Benedictine habit.

RASYPHUS (St) M.   RM. July 23

? A martyr venerated in Rome from early times. He may be identical with a St Rasius whose relics are enshrined in the Pantheon.

RASYPHUS and RAVENNUS (SS) MM.   AC. July 23

5th cent. Said to have been natives of Britain who took refuge in N. France from the Anglo-Saxon invaders. There they became hermits and were ultimately slain for the Faith at Macé, diocese of Séez. Their relics are enshrined in Bayeux cathedral.

RATHARD (Bl) C.   AC. Aug 8
d. 815. A member of the family of the counts of Andechs in Bavaria, he became a priest and founded the Augustinian monastery of Diessen.

RAVENNUS (St) M.   AC. July 23
See Rasyphus and Ravennus.

RAVERRANUS (RAVERIANUS) (St) Bp. OSB.   AC. Nov 7
d. 682. Bishop of Séez. He resigned his see and became a Benedictine monk at Fontenelle.

RAYMUND of PEÑAFORT (St) C. OP.   RM. Jan 23
1175–1275. A kinsman of the kings of Aragon, he was born at Villafranca in Catalonia and studied and taught at Barcelona, where he became a priest and a dignitary of the cathedral. In 1222 he joined the Dominican Order and began to preach to the Moors and the Albigenses. Called to Rome by Gregory IX, he was appointed penitentiary and confessor to the pope and was entrusted with the task of systematizing and codifying the canon law. This he did in his five books of the decretals, finished in 1234, which remained the most authoritative codification of ecclesiastical legislation till 1917. In 1238 he was chosen master-general of his Order and in that capacity encouraged St Thomas Aquinas to write the *Contra Gentiles*. In his later years Raymund resided in Majorca. The part he took, if any, in the foundation of the Mercedarians is still open to controversy. Canonized in 1601.

RAYMUND of FITERO (St) Ab. OSB. Cist.   AC. March 15
d. 1163. A native of Aragon who became a canon of the cathedral of Tarazona and then a Cistercian at the abbey of Scala Dei in France. From there he was sent to found and govern the abbey of Fitero in Spanish Navarre. In 1158, the city of Calatrava in New Castile being abandoned by the Templars and threatened by the Moors, he founded for its defence the military Order of Calatrava under the Benedictine Rule and the Cistercian Customary. Under him this Order won for itself a glorious name in Spanish history. Raymund's cult, as a saint, was approved in 1719.

RAYMUND of BARBASTRO (St) Bp. OSA.   AC. June 21
d. 1126. Born at Durban, near Coserans, in France, he became an Augustinian canon regular at Pamiers and in 1104 second bishop of the recently recaptured city of Barbastro in Aragon. He is the principal patron of the city and diocese of Barbastro.

RAYMUND LULL (Bl) M.   AC. July 3
c.1232–1315. Born at Palma, Majorca, he married young and led a gay life as seneschal at the court of Aragon. At the age of about thirty he was converted by a series of apparitions, became a Franciscan tertiary and devoted his whole life to the conversion of the Moors. He was unsuccessful in his attempts to interest the Holy See and the courts of Western Europe in this enterprise. He himself learned Arabic and three times went to preach the gospel to the Moors of Tunis. Twice he was banished, and on the third occasion he was stoned to death. In the interests of his life's work he travelled extensively in Italy, France, England and Germany, wrote copiously in Latin, Arabic and Catalan, and encouraged the study of oriental religion and culture. For a time he taught Arabic metaphysics at the university of Paris. He was a theologian (*Doctor Illuminatus*), a philosopher, a poet, an

alchemist and a chemist. His feast is kept by the Friars Minor.

RAYMUND of TOULOUSE (St) C. AC. July 8

d. 1118. A chanter in the church of St Sernin at Toulouse who, after the death of his wife, received a canonry in the same church and was noted for his generosity to the poor and for his personal austerity.

RAYMUND NONNATUS (St) Card. O. Merc.   RM. Aug 31

d. 1240. A member of the Mercedarian Order, which was instituted in Spain for the ransoming of Christian captives from the Moors of the Barbary Coast. He succeeded St Peter Nolasco as its second master general. He spent his whole substance in purchasing the freedom of Christian slaves and surrendered himself as a hostage to secure the liberation of one of their number until his Order succeeded in ransoming him in his turn. He was created cardinal by Gregory IX.

RAYMUND of CAPUA (Bl) C. OP. AC. Oct 5

d. 1399. Raymund delle Vigne was born at Capua, joined the Dominicans and held various offices in different friaries of the Order. He became the spiritual director of St Catherine of Siena when living in that city, and with her his name will be always linked. Later he became master general of the Dominicans and restored discipline with such success that he has been called the second founder of the Order. He wrote lives of St Catherine and of St Agnes of Montepulciano. Beatified in 1899.

RAYNALD of NOCERA (St) Bp. OSB.   AC. Feb 9

d. 1225. Born of German parents near Nocera in Umbria, he took the Benedictine habit at Fontavellana and in 1222 was raised to the see of Nocera, of which city he is now venerated as the principal patron.

RAYNALD of RAVENNA (Bl) Bp. AC. Aug 18

d. 1321. Raynald Concorrezzo was born at Milan, became a canon of Lodi and was then raised to the see of Vicenza (1296). After holding various offices in the papal states he became archbishop of Ravenna (1303). He was a friend and defender of the Knights Templars. Cult approved in 1852.

RAYNALD de BAR (Bl) Ab. OSB. Cist.   PC. Dec 16

d. 1151. A monk of Clairvaux who was appointed abbot of Cîteaux in 1133. He is remembered chiefly as the compiler of the first collection of Cistercian statutes. He was also instrumental in bringing about the union of the Benedictine congregations of Obazine and Savigny with Cîteaux.

RAYNERIUS (RAYNIER) (St) Mk. OSB.   AC. Feb 22

d. c.967. Benedictine monk at Beaulieu in the neighbourhood of Limoges.

RAYNERIUS INCLUSUS (Bl) H. AC. Apr 11

d. 1237. A hermit who lived in a cell near the cathedral of Osnabrück. He spent twenty-two years in his cell (*inclusus* means "shut up").

RAYNERIUS (RANIERO, RAINERIUS) (St) H.   RM. June 17

d. 1160. Raniero Scacceri was a native of Pisa. After a sinful youth he undertook several penitential pilgrimages to Jerusalem and afterwards lived as a conventual oblate in the Benedictine abbey of St Andrew at Pisa and then in that of San Vito in the same city, where he died.

RAYNERIUS of SPALATRO (St) M. OSB.   AC. Aug 4
d. 1180. A Camaldolese monk of Fontavellana, raised to the see of Cagli in 1156 and to the archbishopric of Spalatro in 1175. He was murdered by members of his flock for his defence of ecclesiastical immunity.

RAYNERIUS of AREZZO (Bl) C. OFM.   AC. Nov 3
d. 1304. Raniero Mariani was a native of Arezzo. He became a Franciscan laybrother and died at Borgo Sansepolcro. Cult confirmed in 1802.

RAYNERIUS of TODI (Bl) C. OFM. Cap.   AC. Nov 5
d. c.1586. Born at Sansepolcro, he married to please his parents, but on the death of his wife became a Capuchin friar. He died at Todi. Cult confirmed by Pius VII.

RAYNERIUS (St) Bp.   RM. Dec 30
d. 1077. Bishop of Aquila (*Forconium*) in the Abruzzi.

REATRUS (RESTIUS) (St) M.
                                RM. Jan 27
See Datius, Reatrus, etc.

REDEMPTA (St) V.   RM. July 23
See Romula, Redempta and Herundo.

REDEMPTUS (St) Bp.   RM. Apr 8
d. 586. Bishop of Ferentini (*in Hernicis*), a town to the south of Rome. He was a friend of St Gregory the Great, who bears witness to his sanctity.

REDEMPTUS of the CROSS (Bl) M. OCD.   AC. Nov 29
See Dionysius and Redemptus.

REGIMBALD (REGINBALD, REGIMBAUT, REGINOBALDUS) Bp. OSB.   AC. Oct 13
d. 1039. A Benedictine monk of the abbey of SS Ulric and Afra at Augsburg. In 1015 he migrated to the abbey of Ebersberg. In 1022 he became abbot of Lorsch and later founded therefrom the daughter-abbey of Heiligenberg. In 1032 he was appointed bishop of Speyer.

REGINA (REGNIA, REINE) (St) VM.   RM. Sept 7
d. c.?286. A virgin martyr venerated at Autun from an early date. We have no particulars of her life.

REGINALD of SAINT-GILLES (Bl) C. OP.   AC. Feb 1
1183–1220. Born at Saint-Gilles in Languedoc. After having taught canon law at the university of Paris from 1206 to 1211 he was appointed dean of Saint-Agnan, Orleans. He met St Dominic in Rome and became one of his ablest disciples. He helped to establish the Dominicans at Bologna and Paris. Cult confirmed in 1885.

REGINALD MONTEMARTI (Bl) C. OP.   AC. Apr 9
1292–1348. He was born near Orvieto and became a Dominican. He died at Piperno. Cult approved in 1877.

REGINALD (Bl) H. OSB. AC. July 2
d. c.1095. A Benedictine monk of Baume who lived as a hermit in the cell occupied by St Adegrin more than a century before.

REGINTRUDIS (Bl) Abs. OSB.
                                AC. May 26
d. c.750. Fourth abbess of Nonnberg near Salzburg.

REGULA (St) VM.   AC. Sept 11
See Felix and Regula.

REGULUS (French: RIEUL) (St)
Bp.   RM. March 30
d. *c*.260. Said to have been a Greek by
origin. He is honoured as the first bishop
of Senlis. An old tradition connects him
with Arles.

REGULUS (RULE) (St) Ab.
                          AC. March 30
? 4th cent. The legendary abbot who
brought the relics of St Andrew from
Greece to Scotland. His cult is very
ancient, but we have no Life earlier
than the 9th century.

REGULUS (St) M.   RM. Sept 1
d. *c*.545. An African driven into exile by
the Arian Vandals. He landed in Tuscany and appears to have been martyred
under Totila.

REGULUS (French: REOL) (St) Bp.
OSB.   AC. Sept 3
d. 698. A monk of Rebais under St
Philibert. He succeeded St Nivard
(*c*.670) as archbishop of Reims. He was
the founder of the great abbey of Orbais
(680).

REINE (St) VM.   RM. Sept 7
Otherwise Regina, q.v.

REINELDIS (RAINELDIS, REIN-
ALDES) V. and Comp. (SS) MM.
                          RM. July 16
d. *c*.680. Daughter of St Amelberga and
sister of St Gudula. She was a nun of
Saintes in Hainault and was put to
death, together with two clerics, by the
Huns who were then ravaging the
country.

REINHARD (Bl) Ab. OSB.
                          AC. March 7
d. *p*.1170. Monk and headmaster of the
abbey school of Stavelot-Malmédy.
About 1130 he was appointed first
abbot of Reinhausen in Saxony.

REINOLD (RAINALD, REYNOLD)
(St) M. OSB.   AC. Jan 7
d. 960. Said to have belonged to the
family of Charlemagne. He was a
Benedictine monk of the abbey of St
Pantaleon at Cologne. He was in charge
of the building operations there and was
killed by the stonemasons with their
hammers and his body flung into a pool
near the Rhine. It is said to have been
found later by divine revelation.

RELINDIS (RENILDIS, RENULA,
RENULE) (St) Abs. OSB.
                          AC. Feb 6
d. *c*.750. Educated with her sister Herlindis in the Benedictine nunnery of
Valenciennes. She became an expert in
embroidery and painting. On the death
of her sister, St Boniface appointed her
abbess of the convent of Maaseyk,
founded by her parents. See Herlindis
and Relindis.

REMACLUS (St) Bp. OSB.
                          AC. Sept 3
d. *c*.663. A native of Aquitaine and a
courtier. He became a monk and after
his ordination to the priesthood was
appointed first abbot of Solignac near
Limoges, and then of Cougnon in
Luxemburg. About the year 648 he
founded the twin abbeys of Stavelot and
Malmédy in the Ardennes, and in 652
he became bishop of Maestricht. After
eleven years as a bishop he resigned and
returned to Stavelot, where he died.

REMBERT (St) Bp. OSB.
                          RM. Feb 4
d. 888. Born in Flanders and a monk of
Turholt. He shared with St Anschar the
apostolate to Scandinavia and succeeded
him in the see of Hamburg-Bremen
(865). He died on June 11, but the RM.
commemorates him also on the day of
his episcopal consecration. He wrote an
excellent biography of St Anschar.

REMEDIUS (St) Bp.   RM. Feb 3
? A bishop of Gap in the French Alps.

REMI (REMY) *(several)*
The French form of Remigius, q.v.

REMIGIUS (St) Bp.   AC. Jan 19
d. *c*.772. A natural son of Charles Martel. He was bishop of Rouen from 755 till his death. He worked successfully for the introduction of the Roman rite and chant into Gaul.

REMIGIUS (Bl or St) Bp. OSB.
AC. March 20
d. 783. A son of Duke Hugh of Alsace and a nephew of St Ottilien. He was educated at, and became abbot of, Münster near Colmar, and in 776 was raised to the see of Strasburg. Pope Leo IX authorized his feast for the abbey of Münster.

REMIGIUS (St) Bp.   RM. Oct 1
d. *c*.533 (Jan 13). A Gallo-Roman by birth, he was elected in 459, while still a layman, to the see of Reims. During the seventy-four years of his episcopate he was the most influential prelate of Gaul, the culminating event in his life being the conversion and baptism of Clovis, king of the Franks, on Easter eve 496. The sources for his biography are not very trustworthy.

REMIGIUS (St) Bp.   PC. Oct 28
d. 875. Royal arch-chaplain and in 852 archbishop of Lyons. He combated Gottschalk's doctrine on predestination but defended the latter's person against his metropolitan Hincmar of Reims.

REMO (St) Bp.   RM. Oct 13
Remo is a corrupt form of Romulus, q.v.

RENATUS (French: RENÉ)
GOUPIL (St) M.   AC. March 16
d. 1642. He was a laybrother and a

surgeon and acted as assistant to the missionaries to the Red Indians. He was the first to be martyred (Sept 29) being tomahawked for making the sign of the cross on the brow of some children. See N. America (Martyrs of).

RENATUS (French: RENÉ) MASSEY (Bl) M. OSB.   AC. Sept 2
A Maurist monk and Prior of Saint Florent de Saumur, one of the September Martyrs of 1792 (q.v.).

RENATUS (French: RENÉ) (St) Bp.
AC. Nov 12
d. *c*.422. Said to have been bishop first at Angers and then at Sorrento in S. Italy. Probably this is a mistaken identification of two different persons.

RENOVATUS (St) Bp. AC. March 31
d. *c*.633. A converted Arian, he became monk and then Abbot of Cauliana in Lusitania. Finally he became Bishop of Merida, and governed the see for twenty-two years.

REOL (REOLUS) (St) Bp. AC. Sept 3
Otherwise Regulus, q.v.

REPARATA (St) VM.   RM. Oct 8
d. *c*.250. A virgin martyr of Caesarea in Palestine, martyred at the age of twelve under Decius. Her Acts are spurious.

REPOSITUS (St) M.
RM. Aug 29 and Sept 1
See Vitalis, Sator and Repositus.

RESPICIUS (St) M.   RM. Nov 10
See Tryphon, Respicius and Nympha.

RESTITUTA (St) VM. RM. May 17
d. 255 (or 304). An African maiden martyred at Carthage either under Valerian or Diocletian. Her relics are said to be enshrined in the cathedral of Naples.

RESTITUTA and Comp. (SS) MM. RM. May 27

d. 272. Said to have been a Roman maiden of patrician parentage who fled to Sora in Campania to escape the persecution under Aurelian and who was martyred there with several companions.

RESTITUTUS (St) M. RM. May 29

d. *c.*299. A Roman martyr under Diocletian. His Acts are not trustworthy.

RESTITUTUS (St) M. RM. June 10

See Crispulus and Restitutus.

RESTITUTUS, DONATUS, VALERIAN, FRUCTUOSA and Comp. (SS) MM. RM. Aug 23

d. *c.*?305. A group of sixteen Syrian martyrs put to death at Antioch. Some may have been African. The grouping was made by Florus of Lyons (*c.*850).

RESTITUTUS (St) Bp. M. RM. Dec 9

? Bishop of Carthage, in whose honour St Augustine preached a sermon which is now lost.

REVERIANUS, PAUL and Comp. (SS) MM. RM. June 1

d. 272. Reverianus, a bishop, and Paul, a priest, Italians by birth, appear to have been sent as missionaries to Gaul by the Holy See. They evangelized Autun and the surrounding district and were martyred with several companions under Aurelian.

REVOCATA (St) M. RM. Feb 6

See Saturninus, Theophilus and Revocata.

REVOCATUS (St) M. RM. Jan 9

See Vitalis, Revocatus and Fortunatus.

REVOCATUS (St) M. RM. March 7

See Perpetua, Felicitas, etc.

REYNE (St) VM. RM. Sept 7

Otherwise Regina, q.v.

RHAIS (St) M. RM. June 28

See Plutarch, Serenus, etc.

RHAIS (St) VM. RM. Sept 22

Otherwise Irais, q.v.

RHEDIUS (RHEDIW) (St) AC. Nov 11

? A Welsh saint whose name is perpetuated by the dedication of a church in his honour at Llanllyfni in Carnarvonshire.

RHETICUS (RHETICIUS, RHETICE) (St) Bp. AC. July 20

d. 334. A Gallo-Roman raised to the see of Autun *c.*310. In 313 he was present at the Lateran synod which condemned the Donatists.

RHIAN (RANUS, RIAN) (St) Ab. AC. Mar 8

? The saint who has left his name to Llanrhian in Pembrokeshire. He is described as an abbot, but we have no authentic details of his life.

RHIPSIME (RIPSIMIS), GAIANA and Comp. (SS) VV. MM. RM. Sept 29

d. *c.*290. A band of virgin martyrs venerated from early times as the first to suffer for Christ in the Armenian Church. Their existence is certainly established, but their Acts arc in no way trustworthy.

RHODOPIANUS (St) M. RM. May 3

See Diodorus and Rhodopianus.

RHUDDLAD (St) V. AC. Sept 4

? 7th cent. Patron of Llanrhyddlad, at the foot of Moel Rhyddlad in Anglesey.

RIBERT (St) Ab. OSB. AC. Sept 15

7th cent. Monk and abbot of Saint-

Valèry-sur-Somme. He may have been also a regionary bishop in Normandy and Picardy. He is the patron of numerous parishes in the diocese of Rouen.

RIBERT (RIBARIUS) (St) Ab. OSB.
AC. Dec 19
d. *c*.790. Seventeenth abbot of Saint-Oyend. He is much venerated in Franche-Comté.

RICHARD the SACRIST (Bl) Mk.
OSB. Cist.   AC. Jan 28
d. *p*.1142. An Englishman who became a Cistercian monk and sacristan of the abbey of Dundrennan in Kirkcud-brightshire.

RICHARD of VAUCELLES (St) Ab.
Ab. OSB. Cist.   AC. Jan 28
d. 1169. An Englishman who became a Cistercian and was made by St Bernard second Abbot of Vaucelles, near Cambrai.

RICHARD the KING (St) C.
RM. Feb 7
d. 722. According to the earlier Italian legend this saint was a prince in Wessex and father of SS Willibald, Winebald and Walburga: he died at Lucca on a pilgrimage to Rome. A later legend makes him duke of Swabia. Both legends have been proved to be quite untrustworthy.

RICHARD (St) M.   AC. March 25
d. 1179. He was a child crucified by fanatical Jews at Pontoise. The body was transferred to Paris.

RICHARD of CHICHESTER (St)
Bp.   RM. Apr 3
1197–1253. Richard de Wych was born at Droitwich in Worcestershire and pursued his studies at Oxford, Paris and Bologna. Returning to England (1235), he was chosen chancellor of Oxford university. He then became the legal

adviser of the archbishops of Canterbury, St Edmund Rich and St Boniface of Savoy. Having been ordained priest in France, he was raised to the see of Chichester, and in the early years of his episcopate he had to defend himself against the rapacity of Henry III. He died at Dover while engaged in preaching the crusade. Canonized in 1262.

RICHARD REYNOLDS (Bl) M.
Bridg.   AC. May 4
c.1490–1535. Born at Devon, he studied at Christ's College, Cambridge, was elected a fellow of Corpus Christi College in 1510, took the degree of B.D. in 1513 and was appointed university preacher. In the same year he was professed a Bridgettine monk at Syon Abbey, Isleworth. He was one of the first band of martyrs executed at Tyburn for their opposition to the royal supremacy. Beatified in 1886.

RICHARD THIRKELD (THIR-
KILD) (Bl) M.   AC. May 29
d. 1583. Born in Co. Durham, he was educated at Queen's College, Oxford, and when already advanced in years completed his studies for the priesthood at Douai and Reims, being ordained in 1579. He ministered to the Catholics of Yorkshire and was condemned and executed for his priesthood at York. Beatified in 1886.

RICHARD NEWPORT (*alias:*
SMITH) (Bl) M.   AC. May 30
d. 1612. Born at Harringworth in Northamptonshire, he was educated for the priesthood at Rome and ordained in 1597. On his return to England he worked in the London district and was executed at Tyburn for his priesthood.

RICHARD of ANDRIA (St) Bp.
RM. June 9
d. *p*.1196. An Englishman who became

bishop of Andria in Italy. By a confusion of dates at a much later period he has been ascribed, quite erroneously, to the fifth century (453).

RICHARD of ST VANNES (Bl) Ab. OSB. AC. June 14

d. 1046. Nicknamed "Gratia Dei", from a phrase frequently on his lips. From being dean of the cathedral of Reims, he became a Benedictine at St Vannes, Verdun. He was a personal friend of St Odilo of Cluny and of the emperor St Henry, who is said to have asked Richard to confer the monastic habit on him.

RICHARD LANGHORNE (Bl) M. AC. July 14

d. 1679. Born in Bedfordshire, he read law at the Inner Temple and was called to the bar in 1654. He was executed at Tyburn for alleged complicity in the "Popish Plot". Beatified in 1929.

RICHARD FEATHERSTONE (Bl) M. AC. July 30

d. 1540. Educated at Cambridge, he became tutor to the princess Mary and archdeacon of Brecknock. As one of the chaplains to Queen Catherine of Aragon he defended her in convocation and was forthwith attainted for treason and executed at Tyburn. Beatified in 1886.

RICHARD KIRKMAN (Bl) M. AC. Aug 22

d. 1582. Born at Addingham, near Skipton in Yorkshire, he was educated at Douai and ordained in 1579. He was appointed tutor in the family of Dymoke of Scrivelsby. He was martyred at York for denying the queen's supremacy in spiritual matters. Beatified in 1886.

RICHARD HERST (Bl) M. AC. Aug 29

d. 1628. Richard Herst (also Hurst or Hayhurst) was born near Preston in Lancashire and worked there as a farmer. He was condemned ostensibly for murder but in fact because he was a Catholic recusant. He was hanged at Lancaster. Beatified in 1929.

RICHARD LEIGH and RICHARD MARTIN (BB) MM. AC. Aug 30

d. 1588. Richard Leigh (*alias* Garth or Earth) was born in London, educated at Reims and Rome and ordained in 1586. Richard Martin was a Shropshire gentleman who was educated at Broadgates Hall, Oxford. They were martyred together at Tyburn with Bl Edward Shelley, Bl John Roche, Bl Margaret Ward, and Ven Richard Lloyd (*alias* Flower) of Anglesey. Leigh for being a priest and Martin for sheltering priests. Beatified in 1929.

RICHARD BERE (Bl) M. AC. Aug 31 (?)

d. 1537. Born at Glastonbury, he was educated at Oxford and the Inns of Court. He became a Carthusian at the London Charterhouse and was starved to death in Newgate, with others of his community, for opposing the divorce plans of Henry VIII.

RICHARD of ST ANN (Bl) M. OFM. AC. Sept 10

1585–1622. Born of Spanish parents in Flanders, he was a tailor at Brussels when he joined the Friars Minor as a lay-brother. He was sent as a missionary to Mexico and thence (1611) to the Philippines, where he was raised to the priesthood at Cebu. In 1613 he went to Japan, where he was martyred at Nagasaki on the day of the great martyrdom. Beatified in 1867.

RICHARD ROLLE (Bl) C. PC. Sept 29

c.1300–1349. Born at Thornton in Yorkshire, he lived as a hermit at Hampole and elsewhere in that county. He is best known as one of the foremost mystical writers of his time. At one time he had a very considerable popular cult.

RICHARD GWYN (*alias* WHITE) (Bl) M.   AC. Oct 17
1537–1584. Born at Llanidloes, in Montgomeryshire, he was educated at St John's College, Cambridge. He renounced Protestantism, married and became a schoolmaster in Flintshire and Denbighshire. He was imprisoned for four years before he was martyred for his Catholic faith at Wrexham. In jail he wrote numerous religious poems in Welsh. He is the proto-martyr of Wales.

RICHARD WHITING (Bl) M. Ab. OSB.   AC. Nov 15
d. 1539. Born at Wrington in Somerset, he became a Benedictine monk at Glastonbury and was sent to Cambridge for his higher education. In 1525 he became abbot of Glastonbury. At the dissolution he refused to surrender his abbey to the Crown and was condemned to death for treason. He was hanged with the usual brutalities on the summit of Tor Hill overlooking Glastonbury. Beatified in 1895.

RICHARD LANGLEY (Bl) M.
AC. Dec 1
d. 1586. A Yorkshire gentleman of Ousethorpe near Pocklington, hanged at York for sheltering priests in his house. Beatified in 1929.

RICHARDIS (St) Empress
AC. Sept 18
d. c.895. She was married at twenty-two to the emperor Charles the Fat, and after nineteen years of married life was accused of unfaithfulness. Her innocence was established, but she ceased to cohabit with her husband and retired to the nunnery of Andlau, which she herself had founded, and lived there as a nun till her death. She is venerated as a Benedictine oblate. Her relics were elevated by order of Pope Leo IX.

RICHARIUS (RIQUIER) Ab.
RM. Apr 26
d. c.645. Born at Centula (Celles) near Amiens, he became a priest and founded an abbey in his native place, afterwards called after him Saint-Riquier. He was the first to devote himself to the work of ransoming captives. After some years as abbot he resigned and spent the rest of his life as a hermit.

RICHALM (Bl) Ab. OSB. Cist.
AC. Dec 2
d. 1219. Cistercian abbot of Schönthal (*Speciosa Vallis*) in Würtemberg.

RICHILDIS (Bl) N. OSB.
AC. Aug 23
d. c.1100. A Benedictine nun at Hohenwart in Upper Bavaria, diocese of Augsburg. After several years of community life she became an anchoress.

RICHIMIRUS (St) Ab. OSB.
AC. Jan 17
d. c.715. An abbot who, under the patronage of the bishop of Le Mans, founded a monastery in that diocese (afterwards called after him Saint-Rigomer-des-Bois) and gave it the Rule of St Benedict.

RICTRUDIS (St) W. OSB.
AC. May 12
d. 688. Born in Gascony, she married St Adalbald, by whom she had four children—all saints, viz. Maurontius, Eusebia, Clotsindis and Adalsindis. After her husband's death she received the veil from St Amandus and became the abbess-foundress of Marchiennes, ruling that house for forty years.

RIEUL (St) Bp.   RM. March 30
Otherwise Regulus, q.v.

RIGOBERT (St) Bp. OSB.
RM. Jan 4
d. *c*.745. Monk and abbot of Orbais.
In 721 he was made archbishop of
Reims, but some years later was
banished by Charles Martel. He returned to Orbais and resumed monastic
life. On being recalled to Reims he
came to terms with the intruded prelate
and himself became a hermit.

RINGAN, RINGEN
Variant forms of Ninian and Ninnian
respectively.

RIOCH (St) Ab.   AC. Aug 1
d. *c*.480. Described as a nephew of St
Patrick and abbot of Innisboffin, Longford, Ireland.

RIQUIER (St) Ab.   RM. Apr 26
Otherwise Richarius, q.v.

**RITA (MARGARITA) of CASCIA
(St) W. OSA.   RM. May 22**
d. 1457. Born near Spoleto, she married
a rude ill-tempered husband who died
a violent death. Her two sons, who had
sworn vengeance against their father's
murderers, died shortly afterwards filled
with the spirit of forgiveness. Rita now
entered a convent of Augustinians at
Cascia, where she sanctified herself
under the strain of a chronic and very
painful malady. She was canonized in
1900. In Spanish-speaking countries she
is surnamed *La Abogada de Imposibles*,
the saint of desperate cases.

RITBERT (St) Ab. OSB.
AC. Sept 15
d. *c*.690. Monk and abbot of a small
monastery at Varennes. He had previously been a disciple of St Ouen.

**RIXIUS VARUS (RICTIOVARUS)
(St) M.   RM. July 6**
The RM. reads: "On the same day the
holy martyr Lucy, a native of Campania,
who, being tried and sharply tortured
under the vicar Rixius Varus, converted
him to Christ. . . . They suffered and
were crowned together." Rixius Varus
is notorious in the Martyrology as a
persecuting prefect under whom hundreds of martyrs died. Modern scholars,
however, not only reject the legend of
his conversion, but even query his
existence.

**RIZZERIO (RICHERIUS) (Bl) C.
OFM.   AC. Feb 7**
d. 1236. Referred to in the *Fioretti* as
Rinieri. Born at Muccia in the Italian
Marches. While studying at Bologna he
heard St Francis preaching and at once
attached himself to him. He was much
beloved by Francis and was present at
his death. He later became provincial of
the Marches. Cult approved in 1836.

RO
Corruption of Maelrubius, q.v.

ROBERT of REIMS (St) Bp. OSB.
RM. Jan 4
Otherwise Rigobert, q.v.

ROBERT SOUTHWELL (Bl) M. SJ.
AC. Feb 21
1561–1595. Born at Horsham St Faith's
in Norfolk, at the age of 17 he joined
the Jesuits in Rome and worked as a
priest in London from 1584 to 1592.
He was betrayed and kept three years in
jail, being tortured thirteen times. He
was martyred at Tyburn. He holds a
place in English literature as a religious
poet. Beatified in 1929.

**ROBERT of ARBRISSEL (Bl) Ab.
OSB.   PC. Feb 24**
d. 1117. A native of Arbrissel in Brit-

tany who became chancellor of the university of Paris and then vicar general of Rennes (1085). At Rennes his activities as preacher and reformer caused such a reaction that he had to quit Brittany. In 1099 he founded the Order of Fontevrault on the borders of Poitou and Anjou. This Order consisted of both men and women. Its members lived under the Benedictine Rule, the abbess being in supreme command over both nuns and monks, the position of the latter being really that of chaplains to the nuns. After a stormy career Robert retired to Fontevrault and lived out the remainder of his life as a simple monk.

ROBERT DALBY (Bl) M.
AC. March 16
d. 1589. Born at Hemingborough in Yorkshire. He was a convert from the Protestant ministry and was ordained priest at Reims in 1588. He was hanged for his priesthood at York.

ROBERT of BURY ST EDMUNDS (St) M.   AC. March 25
d. 1181. A child said to have been put to death by Jews on Good Friday at Bury St Edmunds, where his relics were enshrined in the abbey church.

ROBERT of CHAISE-DIEU (St) Ab. OSB.   RM. Apr 17
d. 1067. Robert de Turlande, a native of Auvergne, was a priest and canon noted for his love of the poor, for whom he founded a hospice. After spending many years at Cluny under St Odilo and having made a pilgrimage to Rome, he retired to a solitude near Brioude in Auvergne, where he was joined by many disciples. Buildings soon arose which developed into the great abbey of *Casa Dei* or Chaise-Dieu, housing some 300 monks. To these Robert gave the Benedictine Rule, and the foundation

became the mother-house of an important Black Benedictine congregation.

ROBERT WATKINSON (Bl) M.
AC. Apr 20
d. 1602. Born at Hemingborough in Yorkshire, he studied for the priesthood at Douai and Rome and was ordained in 1602 at the age of twenty-three. The same year he suffered at Tyburn for his priesthood.

ROBERT of SYRACUSE (St) Ab. OSB.   AC. Apr 25
d. *a.* 1000. Benedictine abbot of a monastery at Syracuse in Sicily.

ROBERT ANDERTON (Bl) M.
AC. Apr 25
d. 1586. Born at Chorley, Lancs, he was educated at Brasenose College, Oxford. After his conversion he studied for the priesthood at Reims and was ordained in 1585. The following year he was martyred in the Isle of Wight. Beatified in 1929.

ROBERT of MOLESMES (St) Ab. OSB. Cist.   RM. Apr 29
1018–1110 (March 21). Born near Troyes in Champagne, he became a Benedictine monk at Moutier-la-Celle. He was made prior soon after his novitiate and then abbot of St Michael of Tonnerre. He left this monastery to become superior of some hermits in the forest of Collan. In 1075 he migrated with this little community to Molesmes. As the community grew Robert felt less satisfied with the life and withdrew to a hermitage at Or. He was recalled to Molesmes but again left it, this time in the company of SS Stephen Harding and Alberic. In 1098 they founded at Cîteaux a new monastery more in consonance with their monastic ideals. However, the monks of Molesmes appealed to Rome and obtained Robert's recall

(1099), and he ruled that abbey thenceforward until his death.

ROBERT of BRUGES (Bl) Ab. OSB. Cist.   AC. Apr 29

d. 1157. Robert Gruthuysen was a native of Bruges. In 1131 he followed St Bernard to Clairvaux, and in 1139 was sent back to Belgium as abbot of Dunes. In 1153 he succeeded St Bernard as abbot of Clairvaux.

ROBERT LAWRENCE (Bl) M. O. Cart.   AC. May 4

d. 1535. The prior of the charterhouse at Beauvale, Notts. He was one of the first group of Carthusians to be martyred at Tyburn under Henry VIII. Beatified in 1886.

ROBERT BELLARMINE (St) Bp. Card. Dr, SJ.

RM. May 13 and Sept 17

1542–1621. (Sept 17). Born at Montepulciano, he was educated by the Jesuits and joined that Society in 1560. As a young man he held professorships of Greek, Hebrew and theology. It was at Louvain that he first made his reputation as a controversialist, and from that time onward his pen and voice were busy in defence of Catholic doctrine against its Protestant opponents. He was created cardinal in 1598 and archbishop of Capua in 1602. Recalled to Rome in 1605, he became head of the Vatican library and theological adviser to the popes. He was canonized in 1930 and declared a Doctor of the Church the following year.

ROBERT JOHNSON (Bl) M.

AC. May 28

d. 1582. Born in Shropshire and educated at Rome and Douai, he was ordained in 1576. He began to minister to the Catholics in London in 1580. Two years later he was hanged at Tyburn. Beatified in 1886.

ROBERT SALT (Bl) M. O. Cart.

AC. June 6 (?)

d. 1537. A lay-brother of the London Charterhouse, starved to death, with six of his brethren, at Newgate under Henry VIII. Beatified in 1886.

ROBERT of NEWMINSTER (St) Ab. OSB. Cist.   RM. June 7

d. 1159. A Yorkshire priest who took the Benedictine habit at Whitby and obtained permission to join some monks of York who were attempting to live according to a new interpretation of the Benedictine Rule at Fountains Abbey (1132). Fountains soon became Cistercian and one of the centres of the White Monks in N. England. Newminster Abbey was founded from it in 1137, and Robert became its first abbot. He is described as "gentle in companionship, merciful in judgment."

ROBERT of FRASSINORO (St) Ab. OSB.   AC. June 8

d. *p*.1070. Abbot of the Benedictine monastery of Frassinoro near Modena.

ROBERT of SALENTINO (Bl) Ab. OSB. Cel.   AC. July 18

1272–1341. A Benedictine monk, disciple of St Peter Celestine at Murrone and founder of fourteen monasteries of the Celestine congregation.

ROBERT MORTON (Bl) M.

AC. Aug 28

d. 1588. Born at Bawtry in Yorkshire, he studied for the priesthood at Reims and Rome and was ordained in 1587. He suffered for his priesthood the following year at Lincoln's Inn Fields, London. Beatified in 1929.

ROBERT FLOWER (Bl) H.

PC. Sept 24

d. 1218 (or 1235?). Born at York, he became a postulant at Newminster, but left that abbey to become a hermit, living in a cave by the river Nidd near Knaresborough. His cult has never been officially confirmed.

ROBERT WILCOX and ROBERT WIDMERPOOL (BB) MM.
AC. Oct 1
d. 1588. Robert Wilcox was born at Chester and educated at Reims, where he was ordained in 1585. Robert Widmerpool was a gentleman of Nottinghamshire who was educated at Oxford and followed the profession of a schoolmaster. They were martyred together at Canterbury, the former for his priesthood. Beatified in 1929.

ROBERT SUTTON (Bl) M.
AC. Oct 5
d. 1588. Born at Kegwell in Leicestershire, he was a schoolmaster in London and was hanged at Clerkenwell for having been reconciled to the Catholic Church. Beatified in 1929.

ROBUSTIAN (St) M.
RM. May 24
? An early Milanese martyr, possibly one and the same with the following.

ROBUSTIAN and MARK (SS) MM.
RM. Aug 31
? Martyrs venerated at Milan from early times, of whom nothing further is known.

ROCH (St) C.   RM. Aug 16
1350–1379. A citizen of Montpellier in France who devoted his life to the service of the plague-stricken. He was a pilgrim and laboured for the sick especially in Italy. He is invoked as a protector against pestilence. The Latin form of his name is Rochus, the Italian Rocco, the Spanish Roque. Scottish corruptions of the name are Rollock, Rollox and Seemirookie.

ROCH (ROQUE) GONZALEZ (Bl) M. SJ.   AC. Nov 17
See Paraguay, Martyrs of.

RODERICK (St) M. RM. March 13
Otherwise Rudericus, q.v.

RODINGUS (ROUIN) (St) Ab. OSB.
AC. Sept 17
d. c.690. An Irish monk and priest who preached in Germany and entered the abbey of Tholey near Trèves. Distracted by the visits of his converts, he migrated to the forest of Argonne, where he became the abbot-founder of Wasloi, afterwards called Beaulieu. His cult is very ancient.

RODOLPH or RODULPH (*several*)
Otherwise Rudolph, q.v.

RODRIGO (St) M. RM. March 13
The Spanish form of Roderick or Rudericus, q.v.

ROGATIAN (St) M. RM. Feb 11
See under Saturninus, Dativus, etc.

ROGATIAN (St) M. RM. May 24
See Donatian and Rogatian.

ROGATIAN and FELICISSIMUS (SS) MM.   RM. Oct 26
d. 256. Rogatian, a priest, and Felicissimus, a layman, belonged to the church of Carthage. They are mentioned by St Cyprian as having "witnessed a good confession for Christ." These words are usually taken as referring to their martyrdom.

ROGATIAN (St) M. RM. Dec 28
See Castor, Victor and Rogatian.

ROGATUS (St) M. RM. Jan 12
See Zoticus, Rogatus, etc.

ROGATUS and ROGATUS (SS) MM.   RM. March 8
See Cyril, Rogatus, etc.

ROGATUS, SUCCESSUS and Comp. (SS) MM.   RM. March 28
? A band of eighteen martyrs put to death in proconsular Africa.

ROGATUS (St) M.   RM. June 10
See Aresius, Rogatus, etc.

ROGATUS (St) M.   RM. Aug 17
See Liberatus, Boniface, etc.

ROGATUS (St) M.   RM. Dec 1
See Lucius, Rogatus, etc.

ROGELLUS and SERVUS-DEI (SS) MM.   RM. Sept 16
d. 852. A monk and his young disciple martyred at Cordova for publicly denouncing Mohammedanism.

ROGER of ELLANT (Bl) Ab. OSB. Cist.   AC. Jan 4
d. 1160. An Englishman who joined the Cistercian Order at Lorroyen-Berry, France, and in 1156 was chosen abbot of the new monastery of Ellant in the diocese of Reims.

ROGER of TODI (Bl) C. OFM.
AC. Jan 28
d. 1237. Ruggiero da Todi was one of the early Franciscans, having been admitted to the Order by St Francis himself, who appointed him spiritual director of the convent of Poor Clares at Rieti. He died at Todi. Cult confirmed by Benedict XIV.

ROGER LEFORT (Bl) Bp.
AC. March 1
d. 1367. Son of the lord of Ternes in the Limousin. He became a jurist and while still only a subdeacon was raised to the see of Orleans (1321). In 1328 he was translated to Limoges and in 1343 to Bourges. He instituted a feast in honour of our Lady's conception. In his will he left all his property for the education of poor boys.

ROGER DICKENSON (Bl) M.
AC. July 7
d. 1591. Born at Lincoln and educated at Reims, where he was ordained in 1583. He was hanged at Winchester for his priesthood together with Bl Ralph Milner, a layman, who had sheltered him. Beatified in 1929.

ROGER JAMES (Bl) M. OSB.
AC. Nov 15
d. 1539. At the time of his death he was the youngest monk of the Glastonbury community, where he held the office of sacristan. He was executed with his abbot, Bl Richard Whiting, and a fellow monk, Bl John Thorne, on Tor Hill near Glastonbury under Henry VIII. Beatified in 1895.

ROLAND de' MEDICI (Bl) H.
AC. Sept 15
d. 1386. A scion of the illustrious Florentine family of that name. For twenty-six years he lived without any shelter in the forests of Parma. He died at Borgone. Cult confirmed in 1852.

ROLLOCK, ROLLOX, SEEMI-ROOKIE (St) C.   RM. Aug 16
Scottish variants of Roch (in the case of the third, of Saint-Roch), q.v.

ROMANA (St) V.   RM. Feb 23
d. 324. A Roman maiden who died at the age of eighteen while living as a solitary in a cave on the banks of the Tiber. She figures in the spurious life of Pope St Sylvester.

ROMANUS of CONDAT (St) Ab.
RM. Feb 28
d. c.460. A Gallo-Roman who, at the age of thirty-five, went to live as a hermit in the Jura mountains, whither he was followed by his brother, St Lupicinus. Many disciples soon gathered round the two brothers, who thereupon

founded the abbeys of Condat (later known as Saint-Oyend) and Leuconne, over which they ruled jointly, and the nunnery of La Beaume (afterwards St-Romain-de-la-Roche) presided over by their sister.

ROMANUS of SUBIACO (St) Ab. OSB.   RM. May 22
d. c.560. The monk, living in a community near Subiaco, who discovered the hermitage of the youthful St Benedict, when the latter first fled from the world, and bestowed on him the monastic habit and his daily food. There is no historical evidence of his having been an abbot.

ROMANUS (BORIS) and DAVID (GLEB) (SS) MM.   AC. July 24
d. 1010. Sons of St Vladimir, the first Catholic duke of Muscovy. Their zeal for the propagation of the Christian faith led to their martyrdom at the hands of their heathen fellow-countrymen. Benedict XIII approved their feast for the Russian Catholics. Romanus, called by the Russians Boris, is the patron saint of Moscow.

ROMANUS OSTIARIUS (St) M. RM. Aug 9
d. 258. The accounts we have of him are untrustworthy. His martyrdom was connected with that of St Laurence and he died about the same time. He may have been a doorkeeper; the RM. makes him a soldier.

ROMANUS of NEPI (St) Bp. M. RM. Aug 24
1st cent. A bishop-martyr of Nepi in Tuscany, said to have been a disciple of St Ptolemy (q.v.).

ROMANUS AYBARA (Bl) M. Tert. OP.   AC. Sept 8
d. 1628. A Japanese layman, father of Bl Paul Aybara, beheaded at Nagasaki. He was a Dominican tertiary. Beatified in 1867.

ROMANUS the MELODIST (St) C. AC. Oct 1
d. c.540. A Syrian Jew by origin, he became a deacon at Berytos and a priest at Constantinople. He is the greatest of the Greek hymnographers, about 1000 hymns being attributed to him. Some eighty of these have come down to us: they are marked by poetic inspiration, depth of feeling and purity of style.

ROMANUS of AUXERRE (St) Bp. M.   RM. Oct 6
d. ? 564. An alleged bishop of Auxerre. His existence is doubtful.

ROMANUS of ROUEN (St) Bp. RM. Oct 23
d. 639. A courtier of Clothaire II who became bishop of Rouen c.629. He devoted himself to the care of prisoners, particularly those condemned to death.

ROMANUS and BARULAS (SS) MM.   RM. Nov 18
d. 304. Romanus was a young deacon martyred at Antioch in Syria under Diocletian. His companion Barulas is described in the RM. as a young boy, but we know nothing authentic about him.

ROMANUS of LE MANS (St) C. RM. Nov 24
d. 385. A Gallo-Roman priest who converted the pagans at the mouth of the Gironde and died at Blaye. He seems to have exercised a special influence over sailors.

ROMANUS MATEVOCA (Bl) M. AC. Nov 27
d. 1619. A Japanese layman, born at Omura of the royal family of Firando. He was beheaded at Nagasaki with ten companions. Beatified in 1867.

ROMANUS (St) M.   AC. Dec 9
See Samosata Martyrs.

ROMARICUS (St) Ab. OSB.
RM. Dec 8
d. 653. A Merovingian nobleman converted by St Amatus. He was professed a monk at Luxeuil and founded on his estate the abbey of Habendum (afterwards called Remiremont, i.e. *Romarici Mons*), of which Amatus became the first abbot and he himself the second. The *laus perennis* was performed there by relays of seven choirs.

ROME (Martyrs of) (SS)
The RM. catalogues the following groups of martyrs who suffered at Rome:
RM. Jan 1
d. *c*.304. Thirty soldiers martyred under Diocletian.
RM. Jan 2
d. *c*.303. Many martyrs who suffered under Diocletian for refusing to give up the holy books.
RM. Jan 13
d. 262. Forty soldiers who suffered on the Via Lavicana under Gallienus.

RM. Feb 10
? 250. Ten soldiers martyred on the Via Lavicana.
RM. March 1
d. 269. Two hundred and sixty martyrs condemned to dig sand on the Salarian Way and subsequently shot to death with arrows in the amphitheatre under Claudius II.
RM. March 2
d. 219. A large number of martyrs put to death under Alexander Severus and the prefect Ulpian.
RM. March 4
d. 260 (?). A group of nine hundred martyrs buried in the catacombs of Callistus on the Appian Way, of whom no particulars are extant.

RM. March 14
d. *c*.67. Forty-seven martyrs baptized by St Peter, according to an account which is not very trustworthy; they are said to have suffered under Nero on the same day. The details of the RM. are from the Acts of SS Processus and Martinian.
RM. March 25
? A group of two hundred and sixty-two martyrs who seem to be identical with those of March 1.
RM. Apr 10
d. *c*.115. A number of malefactors detained in the public jail and baptized by Pope St Alexander during his imprisonment there: they were taken to Ostia and put on board an old boat which was then sent out to sea and scuttled.

RM. June 17
? A group of two hundred and sixty-two martyrs stated to have suffered under Diocletian and buried on the old Via Salaria; they seem to be identical with those of March 1 and March 25.
RM. June 24
This group has already been catalogued in this book under the heading "Neronian Martyrs," q.v.
RM. July 2
c.68. Three soldiers who, according to the legend, were converted at the passion of St Paul and martyred.
RM. Aug 5
d. 303. Twenty-three martyrs who suffered on the Salarian Way under Diocletian.
RM. Aug 10
d. 274. One hundred and sixty-five martyrs put to death under Aurelian.
RM. Oct 25
d. 269. Forty-six soldiers and one hundred and twenty-one civilians martyred under Claudius II.

RM. Dec 22
d. *c.*303. A group of thirty martyrs who suffered under Diocletian and were buried on the Via Lavicana "between the two laurels."

Quite possibly there were many other similar groups. It is also likely that not all the data given in the RM. are trustworthy. Nevertheless the RM.'s description (June 24) of Rome as "a fruitful field of martyrs" is historically very exact.

ROMEO (ROMAEUS) (Bl) C. OC.
AC. March 4
d. 1380. An Italian Carmelite laybrother, the companion of St Avertanus. Having set out together from Limoges on a pilgrimage to the Holy Land, both died, apparently from plague, at Lucca.

ROMUALD (St) Ab. OSB. Founder
RM. Feb 7 and June 19
*c.*951–1027. A native of Ravenna, of the ducal family of the Onesti. In his youth he saw his father commit a murder and resolved to atone for that crime by becoming a monk at the Benedictine abbey of Classe near Ravenna. In 996 he was elected abbot of the monastery, but he resigned in 999 and from that time forward led a wandering life in central and northern Italy and the country of the Pyrenees establishing hermitages and monasteries. The best known of these latter, which remains to this day, is that of Camaldoli near Arezzo (1009). The Camaldolese Benedictines combine the eremitical life of the Eastern type with the cenobitical monachism of the West. Romuald made repeated attempts to embark upon missionary work among the Slavs. He died on June 19. Feb 7 is the anniversary of the translation of his relics from Val di Castro, near Camaldoli, where he died, to Fabriano.

ROMULA, REDEMPTA and HERUNDO (SS) VV,
RM. July 23
d. *c.*580. Three Roman maidens who lived an austere life of retirement and prayer near the church of St Mary Major. St Gregory the Great held them in high esteem.

ROMULUS (St) M.
RM. Feb 17
See Donatus, Secundian, etc.

ROMULUS (St) M.
RM. March 24
See Timolaus and Comp.

ROMULUS and SECUNDUS (SS) MM.
RM. March 24
? Two brothers who suffered in proconsular Africa. In some MSS the name of Secundus appears as Secundulus.

ROMULUS (St) Ab. OSB.
AC. March 27
d. *c.*730. Abbot of St Baudilius near Nîmes. About 720 he and his community fled before the invading Saracens and settled in a ruined monastery at Saissy-les-Bois in the Nivernais.

ROMULUS and Comp. (SS) MM.
RM. July 6
d. *c.*90. Said to have been appointed by St Peter first bishop of Fiesole and to have been martyred with several companions under Domitian.

ROMULUS (St) M.
RM. Sept 5
d. *c.*112. An official of the court of Trajan who, for remonstrating with the emperor on his cruelty to the Christians, was made to share their fate.

ROMULUS (St) Bp.
AC. Oct 13
d. *p.*641. A bishop of Genoa concerning whom we have no trustworthy documents. He died at Matuziano, a coast town on the Riviera, since called after him, San Remo.

ROMULUS and CONINDRUS (SS) Bps.   AC. Dec 28

d. *c*.450. Two of the first preachers of Christianity in the Isle of Man, contemporaries of St Patrick.

RONALD (St) M.   AC. Aug 20

d. 1158. A chieftain of Orkney who, in discharge of a vow, built the cathedral of St Magnus at Kirkwall. He was murdered by rebels and is venerated as a martyr.

RONAN (St) Bp.

Otherwise Ruadan, q.v.

There are several saints of this or a similar name venerated especially in Ireland.

ROQUE (St) C.   RM. Aug 16

The Spanish form of Roch, q.v.

ROSALIA (St) V.

RM. Sept 4 and July 15

d. ? 1160. According to the Sicilian tradition she was a girl of good family who became an anchoress in a cave on Mt Coschina, near Bivona, and later in a grotto on Mt Pellegrino, three miles from Palermo. Her alleged relics were found in 1624 and she was acclaimed the patron saint of Palermo.

ROSE de LOYE (Bl) M. OSB.

AC. July 6

See Mary Rose.

ROSE CHRÉTIEN (Bl) M. OC.

AC. July 17

1741–1794. A native of Evreux who married very young and, on being left a widow, entered the Carmel of Compiègne, taking the name of Soeur Julie-Louise. She was guillotined at Paris with her community. See Carmelite Nuns of Compiègne.

ROSE of LIMA (St) V. Tert. OP.

RM. Aug 30

1586–1617. Born of Spanish parents at Lima in Peru. From childhood her life was an exact replica of that of St Catherine of Siena. She lived in her own home as a Dominican tertiary and, like her model, was favoured with extraordinary mystical gifts. She is the first American born to have been canonized (1671) and is venerated as the patron saint of S. America.

ROSE of VITERBO (St) V.

RM. Sept 4

1234–1252. Born at Viterbo of poor parents. She had the highest spiritual gifts from earliest years and used to preach in the streets against the Ghibellines and in favour of the pope. She sought admittance to the convent of Poor Clares and was repeatedly refused. After her death, however, her body was, by order of Pope Alexander IV (1258), laid to rest in that convent. Canonized in 1457.

ROSE-PHILIPPINE DUCHESNE (Bl) V.   AC. Nov 18

1769–1852. Born at Grenoble, she joined the Visitation nuns. When these were scattered during the Reign of Terror she stayed with her family at Grenoble and, in spite of the difficult times, gathered together a community there. In 1804, at the suggestion of St Magdalen Sophie Barat, she incorporated her community into the Society of the Sacred Heart. Her life's desire was to work in the missions, and in 1818 she landed at New Orleans and set up a missionary centre at St Charles, Missouri. In the teeth of many difficulties she founded six more mission stations and went herself to work among the Pottowatomies at Sugar Creek. Later she worked in the Rocky Mountain mission area. In her old age she returned to St Charles to die. Beatified in 1940.

ROSE ELISABETH (St) Abs. OSB.
AC. Dec 13
See Elizabeth Rose.

ROSELINE de VILLENEUVE (Bl)
V. O. Cart. AC. Jan 17
d. 1329. A Carthusian nun of noble
family who became prioress of Celle
Roubaud in Provence. She was favoured
with frequent visions and other mystical
phenomena. Cult confirmed in 1851.

ROSENDO (St) Bp. OSB.
AC. March 1
The Spanish form of Rudesind, q.v.

ROSIUS (St) RM. Sept 1
See Priscus, Castrensis, etc.

ROSULA (St) M. RM. Sept 14
See Crescentian, Victor, etc.

ROSWINDA (St) N. OSB. AC. Dec 13
See Einhildis and Roswinda.

ROTRUDIS (St) V. AC. June 22
d. c.869. A saint whose relics were enshrined at the Benedictine abbey of
Saint-Bertin at Saint-Omer. According
to popular belief she was a daughter, or
sister of Charlemagne.

ROUIN (St) Ab. AC. Sept 17
Otherwise Rodingus, q.v.

RUADAN (RUADHAN, RODAN)
(St) Ab. AC. Apr 15
d. 584. One of the leading disciples of
St Finian of Clonard and abbot-founder
of the monastery of Lothra.

RUADAN (RUADHAN, RUAN,
RUMON, RONAN) (St) AC. June 1
6th cent. A bishop sometimes confused
with the Irish saint Ruadan or Ronan.
He was patron of the abbey of Tavistock
in Devonshire, and of several places in
Cornwall and Brittany.

RUDERICUS (RODERICK) and
SALOMON (SOLOMON) (SS) MM.
RM. March 13
d. 857. Roderick was a priest at Cabra,
near Cordova, who was betrayed by his
Mohammedan brother and imprisoned
at Cordova. In prison he met his fellow-
martyr, Salomon, a layman. They were
both martyred at Cordova.

RUDESIND (ROSENDO) (St) Bp.
OSB. AC. March 1
907–977. Born of a noble family in
Spanish Galicia, he became bishop of
Mondoñedo (the ancient *Dumium*) at
the age of eighteen. Shortly after he
replaced an unworthy prelate, as administrator of the see of Compostella.
In this capacity he opposed with equal
success the depredations of the Normans and the Saracens. Driven from
Compostella by the ex-bishop, he
founded the abbey of Celanova and
became a monk there. He built further
monasteries, imposing on these, as well
as on others already founded, the strict
observance of the Rule of St Benedict.
He was elected second abbot of Celanova, where he died. Canonized in 1195.

RUDOLPH ACQUAVIVA and
Comp. (BB) MM. SJ. AC. July 27
d. 1583 (July 25). Rudolph was born at
Atri in 1550 and was a nephew of
Claudio Acquaviva, fifth general of the
Jesuits. He too became a Jesuit and was
sent to the Jesuit missions in the East
Indies. He was martyred on the penin-
sula of Salsette, near Goa, with four
companions. Beatified in 1893.

RUDOLPH (Bl) Ab. OSB. Vall.
AC. Aug 1
d. 1076. Guest Master under St John
Gualbert, he succeeded him as abbot
general on his death. Cult recognized
in 1602.

RUDOLPH of GUBBIO (St) Bp. OSB. AC. Oct 17
d. *c*.1066. A monk of Fontavellana under St Peter Damian. In 1061, while still very young, he was appointed bishop of Gubbio. He is described as "a miracle of unselfishness."

RUELLINUS (RUELLIN) (St) Bp. AC. Feb 28
6th cent. Successor of St Tudwal in the see of Tréguier in Brittany.

RUFFINUS (St) M. AC. July 24
See Wulfhade and Ruffinus.

RUFILLUS (RUFFILIUS) (St) Bp. RM. July 18
d. 382. The alleged first bishop of Forlimpopoli (*Forum Pompilii*) in Emilia.

RUFINA, MODERATA, ROMANA, SECUNDUS and Seven Companions (SS) MM. AC. Apr 6
? 4th cent. Martyrs at Sirmium, Pannonia.

RUFINA and SECUNDA (SS) VV. MM. RM. July 10
d. 257. Two Roman maidens martyred under Valerian and buried at Santa Rufina on the Aurelian Way. Their later Acts are apocryphal.

RUFINA (St) VM. RM. July 19
See Justa and Rufina.

RUFINA (St) M. RM. Aug 31
See Theodotus, Rufina and Ammia.

RUFINIAN (St) M. RM. Sept 9
See Rufinus and Rufinian.

RUFINUS (St) M. RM. Feb 28
See Macarius, Rufinus, etc.

RUFINUS (St) M. RM. Apr 7
See Epiphanius, Donatus, etc.

RUFINUS (St) M. RM. June 14
See Valerius and Rufinus.

RUFINUS and MARTIA (SS) MM. RM. June 21
? Martyrs in one of the early persecutions at Syracuse.

RUFINUS (St) M. RM. July 30
? A martyr in one of the early persecutions at Assisi.

RUFINUS and Comp. (SS) MM. RM. Aug 11
? Rufinus is described in the RM. as "bishop of the Marsi." Probably he is identical with St Rufinus of Assisi (July 30). Of his companions nothing is known.

RUFINUS (St) RM. Aug 19
? A saint, probably a priest, venerated at Mantua from early times.

RUFINUS (St) Bp. RM. Aug 26
5th cent. A bishop of Capua, whose relics are enshrined in the cathedral of that city.

RUFINUS, SILVANUS and VICTALICUS (SS) MM. RM. Sept 4
? Three children who formed part of a large group of martyrs put to death at Ancyra in Galatia.

RUFINUS and RUFINIAN (SS) MM. RM. Sept 9
? Two brothers martyred at a time and place unknown.

RUFINUS, MARK, VALERIUS and Comp. (SS) MM. RM. Nov 16
? African martyrs.

RUFUS of MELITENE (St) M. RM. Apr 19
See Hermogenes, Caius, etc.

RUFUS (St) H.   **AC. Apr 2**
? A hermit at Glendalough, where he was buried. Some writers call him a bishop.

RUFUS (St) M.   **RM. Aug 1**
See Cyril, Aquila, etc.

RUFUS of CAPUA (St) Bp. M.
                   RM. Aug 27
? The RM. makes him Bishop of Capua and disciple of St Apollinaris of Ravenna. He is however to be identified with the St Rufus commemorated with St Carpophorus (see below).

RUFUS and CARPOPHORUS (SS) MM.   **RM. Aug 27**
d. 295. Martyrs of Capua under Diocletian. According to the untrustworthy Acts Rufus was a deacon. Of Carpophorus (the MSS has Carpone) nothing is known.

RUFUS (St) M.   **RM. Sept 25**
See Paul, Tatta, etc.

RUFUS of METZ (St) Bp.
                   RM. Nov 7
d. c.400. An early bishop of Metz. He was bishop for about twenty-nine years. He is perhaps identical with the Rufus of Metz mentioned c.386 in connection within the Priscillianist controversy.

RUFUS of AVIGNON (St) Bp.
                   RM. Nov 12
d. c.200. Venerated as the first bishop of Avignon. He certainly existed, but the biographies we have of him are quite unhistorical.

RUFUS of ROME (St) Bp. (?)
                   RM. Nov 21
d. c.90. The disciple whom St Paul greets in Rom. XVI, 13. Some identify him with the son of Simon of Cyrene mentioned in Mark XV 21. A later tradition makes him a bishop in the East.

RUFUS and Comp. (SS) MM.
                   RM. Nov 28
d. 304. A Roman citizen who was martyred with his entire household under Diocletian.

RUFUS and ZOSIMUS (SS) MM.
                   RM. Dec 18
d. c.107. Citizens of Philippi brought to Rome with St Ignatius of Antioch and thrown to the beasts in the Roman amphitheatre two days before the latter's martyrdom.

RULE (St) Ab.   **AC. March 30**
Otherwise Regulus, q.v.

RUMOLDUS (RUMBOLD, ROMBAULD) (St) Bp. M. OSB.
                   RM. June 24
d. c.775. A monk, probably of an Anglo-Saxon abbey, who became a regionary bishop and worked under St Willibrord in Holland and Brabant. He was murdered near Malines. He is now the titular of Malines cathedral. The RM. and later legends say that he was of Irish descent and bishop of Dublin.

RUMON (St) Bp.   **AC. June 1**
Otherwise Ruadan, q.v.

RUMWOLD (St) C.   **AC. Aug 28**
d. c.650. Said to have been a three-days' old infant, prince of Northumbria, who, immediately after baptism, pronounced aloud the profession of faith and then died. He was at one time honoured with a cult, chiefly in Northants and Bucks.

RUPERT (HRODBERT, ROBERT) (St) Bp. OSB.   **RM. March 27**
d. c.717. He seems to have been of French, not Irish, descent. Having been

appointed bishop of Worms, he set himself to spread Christianity in S. Germany. He started operations at Ratisbon and pushed his way along the Danube. The duke of Bavaria gave him the old ruined town of Iuvavum, which Rupert rebuilt and called Salzburg. Here he founded the abbey of St Peter, with school and church attached, and also the nunnery of Nonnberg, over which he placed his sister Erentrudis. He is venerated as the first archbishop-abbot of Salzburg and as the apostle of Bavaria and Austria.

RUPERT and BERTHA (SS)
AC. May 15

9th cent. A hermit who lived with his mother Bertha on a hill near Bingen. The hill has been since called after him Rupertsberg. During the 12th century St Hildegard greatly fostered the cult of both saints.

RUPERT (Bl) Ab. OSB.
PC. Aug 15

d. 1145. He was prior of St George's abbey in the Black Forest when (1102) he was asked to become abbot of Ottobeuren in Bavaria. He accepted, and during the forty-three years of his abbacy Ottobeuren attained great prosperity and influence. He introduced there the Cluny-Hirschau customary.

RUSTICA (St) M.   RM. Dec 31
See Donata, Paulina, etc.

RUSTICUS (Bl) Ab. OSB.
AC. March 12

d. 1092. A monk of Vallumbrosa who was chosen third abbot general of the Congregation in 1076. His relics were elevated in 1200.

RUSTICUS (St) M.   AC. Aug 9
? 4th cent. Martyr of Sirmium, Pannonia.

RUSTICUS of VERONA (St) M.
RM. Aug 9

See Firmus and Rusticus.

RUSTICUS (St) M.   RM. Aug 17
See Liberatus, Boniface, etc.

RUSTICUS (St) Bp.   RM. Sept 24
d. 446. Bishop of Clermont in Auvergne 426–446.

RUSTICUS (St) M.   RM. Oct 9
See Dionysius, Rusticus and Eleutherius.

RUSTICUS (St) Bp.   RM. Oct 14
d. 574. Bishop of Trèves. Accused of sexual impurity by St Goar, he resigned and retired to the hermitage of the same St Goar.

RUSTICUS (St) Bp.   RM. Oct 26
d. c.462. A monk of Lérins who was raised to the see of Narbonne. He was present at the council of Ephesus in 431.

RUTILIUS (St) M.   RM. Aug 2
d. 250. A native of Proconsular Africa. During the persecution of Decius he fled from place to place and even paid money to obtain exemption from sacrifice, but he was at last arrested and bravely confessed Christ. The story is given by Tertullian (De fuga in persecutione).

RUTILUS and Comp. (SS) MM.
RM. June 4

? Martyrs at Sabaria in Pannonia (Sabar in modern Hungary).

RUTULUS (St)   RM. Feb 18
See Lucius, Silvanus, etc.

S

SABAS (St) M.   RM. Jan 14
See Isaias, Sabas, etc.

SABAS (SAVA) (St) Bp. AC. Jan 14
1174-1237. Rastho, youngest son of
Stephen Nemanya, king of Serbia,
became a monk at Mt Athos, where he
received the name of Sabas (in Slavonic
Sava) and followed the observance till
nearly sixty years of age. He was then
appointed archbishop of Serbia and
managed the ecclesiastical affairs of that
kingdom with tact and skill. He was
instrumental in securing the papal
recognition of his brother Stephen II as
king of Serbia. He is venerated as one
of the principal patron saints of Yugoslavia.

**SABAS (SABBAS) and Comp. (SS)
MM.**   RM. Apr 12
d. 372. A Goth who held the office of
lector in a local church of what is now
Rumania. He was captured by heathen
Gothic soldiers, and on refusing to eat
food which had been sacrificed to idols,
was tortured to death and thrown into
the river Mussovo at a spot near Tirgo-
vist. Several others suffered with him.
He is greatly venerated in the East.

SABAS and Comp. (SS) MM.
     RM. Apr 24
d. 272. A Christian officer of Gothic
descent martyred with seventy companions at Rome under Aurelian. Some
writers identify him with his namesake
of Apr 12.

SABAS (St) C.   AC. July 17
See Seven Apostles of Bulgaria.

SABBAS (St) Ab.   RM. Dec 5
439-532. A Cappadocian who, at a very
early age, fled to Palestine, where for
many years he lived a hermit's life in
various places. He eventually founded a
laura (Mar Saba, which still flourishes)
in the mountainous desert of Judaea
between Jerusalem and the Dead Sea.
He was appointed archimandrite over
all the Palestinian houses and in that
capacity played a prominent part in the
campaign against the Eutychian heresy.
He is regarded as one of the founders of
Eastern monachism.

SABBATIUS (St) M.   RM. Sept 19
See Trophimus, Sabbatius, and Dorymedon.

SABEL (St) M.   RM. June 17
See Manuel, Sabel and Ismael.

SABINA (St) M.   RM. Aug 29
? The famous basilica on the Aventine
is dedicated to her. Was she a wealthy
lady who founded it in the 3rd or 4th
century, or, as her Passion asserts, a
Roman martyr? The former seems
more probable, but we do not know.

SABINA (St) V.   RM. Aug 29
d. ? 275. The alleged sister of St Sabinian of Troyes, where she is venerated
together with the latter. The martyrologist Usuard placed her on this date.

SABINA (St) M.   RM. Oct 27
See Vincent, Sabina and Christeta.

**SABINIAN (French: SAVINIEN)
(St) M.**   RM. Jan 29
d. ? 275. A martyr honoured at Troyes

in France as having suffered there in one of the early persecutions (under Aurelian?). The French tradition claims that he was a native of Samos, whence with his sister St Sabina he fled to Gaul.

SABINIAN (St) M.   RM. June 7
See Peter, Wallabonsus, etc.

SABINIAN (St) M.
                    RM. Aug 27 and Sept 1
See Honoratus, Fortunatus, etc.

SABINIAN (St) M.   RM. Sept 25
See Paul, Tatta, etc.

SABINIAN (St) Ab. OSB.
                              AC. Nov 22
d. c.720 (or c.770?). Third abbot of Moutier-Saint-Chaffre (Ménat).

SABINIAN and POTENTIAN (SS) MM.   RM. Dec 31
d. c.300. Sabinian is honoured as the first bishop of Sens. Potentian was perhaps his successor. Both were martyred and are now venerated as the patron saints of the diocese of Sens. The legend that they were immediate disciples of St Peter is now discarded.

SABINUS (St) M.   RM. Jan 25
See Donatus, Sabinus and Agape.

SABINUS (St) Bp.   RM. Feb 9
d. c.566. Bishop of Canosa (the ancient Canusium, now destroyed) in Apulia and a friend of St Benedict. Pope St Agapitus I entrusted him with an embassy (535-536) to the emperor Justinian. He is the patron saint of Bari, where his relics are now enshrined.

SABINUS (St) M.   RM. March 13
d. 287. An Egyptian of noble birth,

martyred by drowning in the Nile under Diocletian.

SABINUS (St)   RM. July 11
d. 5th cent. A saint venerated in the neighbourhood of Poitiers. He is said to have been a disciple of St Germanus of Auxerre. The local tradition considers him a martyr.

SABINUS (SAVINUS) and CYPRIAN (SS) MM.   RM. July 11
? Two martyrs, brothers, venerated at Brescia in Italy, but probably the Brixia of the RM. refers to La Bresse in Poitou, where these two saints are also venerated.

SABINUS, JULIAN, MAXIMUS, MACROBIUS, CASSIA, PAULA and ten Comp. (SS) MM.
                              RM. July 20
? A group of Syrians put to death for the faith at Damascus.

SABINUS (French: SAVIN) (St) H.
                              AC. Oct 9
d. c. ? 820. Venerated as one of the apostles of the Lavedan, a district of the Pyrenees which includes Lourdes. He is said to have been born at Barcelona, educated at Poitiers, professed as a Benedictine at Ligugé, and finally to have become a hermit. All these statements are very doubtful.

SABINUS (St) Bp.   AC. Oct 15
d. c.760. Bishop of Catania in Sicily. After a few years as bishop he resigned and became a hermit.

SABINUS (St) Bp.   RM. Dec 11
d. 420. Bishop of Piacenza and a close friend of St Ambrose, who used to send him his writings for revision and approval. While still a deacon he was sent by

Pope St Damasus to settle the Meletian schism at Antioch.

SABINUS, EXUPERANTIUS, MARCELLUS, VENUSTIAN and Comp. (SS) MM.   RM. Dec 30

d. 303. Sabinus is described as a bishop who was martyred near Spoleto. His see is unknown, but Faenza, Assisi, Spoleto and Chiusi each claim him. Venustian and his family were converts of Sabinus, while Exuperantius and Marcellus are said to have been his deacons.

SACER (MO-SACRA) (St) Ab.
                        AC. March 3
7th cent. An Irish saint, abbot-founder of the monastery of Saggard, Dublin.

SACERDOS (SARDOT, SADROC, SARDOU, SERDON, SERDOT) (St) Bp. OSB.   RM. May 4

670–c720. Born in the neighbourhood of Sarlat in Périgord, he became a monk and eventually the abbot-founder of Calabre (*Calabrum*, Calviat) He was appointed bishop of Limoges, resigning his see shortly before his death.

SACERDOS (St) Bp.   RM. May 5
d. c.560. A Spanish saint venerated at Murviedro (the ancient Saguntum), and said to have been bishop of that city.

SACERDOS (St) Bp.   RM. Sept 12
d. 551. Bishop of Lyons 544–551 and adviser of King Childebert. He presided at the council of Orleans in 549.

SADOC and Comp. (BB) MM. OP.
                        AC. June 2 or May 5
d. 1260. Sadoc was received into the Dominican Order by St Dominic himself and sent to Hungary. Later he passed on to Poland, where he founded a house at Sandomir and became its prior. When the town was pillaged by

the Tartars, Sadoc and his forty-nine friars were butchered while singing the Salve Regina.

SADOTH (SADOSH, SCHADOST) and Comp. (SS) MM.   RM. Feb 20

d. 345 (or 342). Sadoth was the metropolitan of Seleucia-Ctesiphon in Persia. He, with one hundred and twenty-eight other Christians, was arrested in the persecution of Shapur II. Most of these were martyred at once, but Sadoth, with eight companions, was detained for five months in a filthy prison at Bei-Lapat before being executed.

SADWEN (SADWRN) (St) C.
                        AC. Nov 29
6th cent. Brother of St Illtyd and disciple of St Cadfan. Some Welsh churches are dedicated to him. He has been confused with St Saturninus (RM. Nov 29).

SAGAR (St) Bp. M.   RM. Oct 6
d. c.175. Bishop of Laodicea in Phrygia, put to death under Marcus Aurelius. It seems impossible to accept the tradition that he was a disciple of St Paul.

SAIR (St) Bp.   AC. July 1
Otherwise Servan, q.v.

SALABERGA (St) Abs. RM. Sept 22
d. c.665. As a child she was cured of blindness by St Eustace of Lisieux. She married very young, and her husband died after two months. Her second husband was St Blandinus, to whom she bore five children, two of whom are venerated as saints. In later years husband and wife decided to become religious. Salaberga entered the nunnery of Poulangey and was subsequently the foundress of St John the Baptist at Laon, where she died.

SALAUN (SALOMON) (St) C.
                        AC. Nov 1
d. 1358. A poor man of Leseven in

Brittany. Content to be despised and considered "a fool for Christ's sake," he reached a high degree of contemplation. He is venerated at N.D. de Folgoet in Brittany.

SALLUSTIA (St) M.   RM. Sept 14
See Caerealis and Sallustia.

SALLUSTIAN (St)   RM. June 8
? A saint honoured in Sardinia from time immemorial. In some martyrologies he is described as a martyr, in others as a hermit.

SALOME and JUDITH (SS) OSB.
AC. June 29
9th cent. Salome is said to have been an Anglo-Saxon princess, exiled from her native country. She was befriended by a pious Bavarian widow named Judith. Both became anchoresses under the obedience of the Benedictine abbey of Oberaltaich.

SALOME (St)   RM. Oct 22
See Mary Salome.

SALOMEA (Bl) W. Poor Clare.
AC. Nov 17
c. 1219–1268. Daughter of Prince Lesko of Poland. At the age of three she was betrothed to Prince Coloman of Hungary and was left a widow before her 23rd year in 1241. She founded the convent of Poor Clares at Zawichost, later removed to Skala, where she became a nun and ended her days. Beatified in 1673.

SALOMON (St) M.   RM. March 13
See Rudericus and Salomon.

SALONIUS (St) Bp.   RM. Sept 28
Otherwise Solomon, q.v.

SALUTARIS (St) M.   RM. July 13
See Eugene, Salutaris, etc.

SALVATOR of HORTA (St) C.
OFM.   RM. March 18
1520–1567. Born at Santa Columba, diocese of Gerona, Spain, he was a shoemaker by trade before he joined the Franciscans as a lay-brother at Barcelona. He spent most of his life as cook of the friary of Horta, near Tortosa. He died at the friary of Cagliari in Sardinia. Canonized in 1940.

SALVINUS (St) Bp.   AC. Sept 4
d. c.420. Third bishop of Verdun (c. 383–420).

SALVINUS (St) Bp.   RM. Oct 12
d. 562. Bishop of Verona. His relics are enshrined in the church of St Stephen in that city.

SALVIUS (SALVE, SAUVE) (St) Bp.
RM. Jan 11
d. c.625. Bishop of Amiens. There is no reason to suppose that he was a martyr as stated in the RM. He has been confused with other saints of the same name.

SALVIUS (St) M.   RM. Jan 11
? A martyr in Proconsular Africa.

SALVIUS (Bl) Ab. OSB. PC. Feb 10
d. 962. Benedictine abbot of Albelda in N. Spain. He was a prudent adviser at the courts of Navarre and Castile at the time of the Reconquest.

SALVIUS and SUPERIUS (SS) MM.
d. c.768. Salvius was a regionary bishop in the district of Angoulême, who went to Valenciennes to evangelize the Flemish. The cupidity of a baron led to his death, and with a companion he was hastily interred. When the bodies were discovered the companion was found first (*Superius*).

SALVIUS (St) Bp.   RM. Sept 10
d. 584. A lawyer who became a monk

and abbot, then a hermit, and finally bishop of Albi (574–584). He died while tending the sick during an epidemic which was ravaging his diocese.

SALVIUS (French: SAIRE) (St) H.
AC. Oct 28
6th cent. A hermit at the place now called after him Saint-Saire in Normandy. Some writers identify him with Salvius of Albi.

SAMONAS (St) M.   RM. Nov 15
See Gurias and Samonas.

SAMOSATA, The SEVEN MAR-TYRS of (SS)   AC. Dec 9
d. c.311. Their names were: Hipparchus and Philotheus, magistrates, and their converts James, Paragrus, Abibus, Romanus and Lollian. They were crucified at Samosata on the Euphrates for refusing to join in the public rejoicing, including pagan rites, after Maximinus's victory over the Persians.

SAMSON (SAMPSON) (St) C.
RM. June 27
d. c.530. Surnamed "the Hospitable" (Xenodochius). He was a distinguished citizen of Constantinople who studied medicine and was ordained priest in order to devote his life to the spiritual and physical care of the sick and destitute. He founded and equipped a magnificent hospital near St Sophia.

SAMSON (SAMPSON) (St) Bp.
RM. July 28
d. c.565. Born in Glamorgan, Wales, he became a disciple of St Illtyd at Llanwit Major, and then for a time monk and abbot of the monastery on Caldey Island. He left Caldey and visited Ireland: then, on his return to England, he sojourned in Cornwall and was consecrated bishop by St Dubricius. Finally he crossed over to Brittany and spent the rest of his life evangelizing that country, fixing his central residence at Dol (c.525). His name is still held in benediction throughout Brittany and Wales. He is indeed one of the greatest missionaries Britain has ever produced.

SAMTHANA (St) V.   AC. Dec 19
6th cent. An Irish saint, abbess-foundress of Cluain-Bronach in Meath.

SAMUEL (St) M.   RM. Feb 16
See Elias, Jeremias, etc.

SAMUEL of EDESSA (St) PC. Aug 9
d. p.496. He is mentioned by Gennadius in his work on Ecclesiastical Authors. Samuel wrote in Syriac against the Nestorians, Eutychians and Timotheans.

SAMUEL (St) Prophet RM. Aug 20
11th cent. B.C. The 1st book of Kings, often for this reason called the 1st book of Samuel, contains the history of the prophet, the wonders of his birth and childhood (i, ii); his judgeship of Israel (iv–vii); his anointing of Saul as king (viii–x); his replacing of Saul by David (xvi); and his death (xxv).

SAMUEL (St) M.   RM. Oct 10
See Daniel, Samuel, etc.

SANCHA (SANCTIA) (Bl) V. OSB.
AC. March 13
c.1180–1229. Daughter of King Sancho I of Portugal, sister of BB Teresa and Mafalda. She helped the first Franciscan and Dominican foundations in Portugal and afterwards (1223) joined the Cistercians at Cellas. Cult approved in 1705.

SANCHO (SANCTIUS, SANCIUS) (St) M.   RM. June 5
d. 851. Born at Albi in France, he was brought to Cordova as a prisoner of

war, educated at the Moorish court there, and enrolled in the guards of the Emir. He was martyred by impalement on refusing to embrace Mohammedanism.

SANCTAN (St) Bp.   AC. May 9
6th cent. Bishop of the Irish sees of Kill-da-Les and Kill-na-Sanctan (Dublin). He was probably of British birth.

SANCTES BRANCASINO (Bl) C. OFM.   AC. Aug 14
d. 1390. Born at Monte Fabri, diocese of Urbino, he became a Franciscan laybrother at Scotameto, where he spent most of his life. Cult approved by Clement XIV.

**SANCTES of CORI (Bl) C. OSA.
AC. Oct 5**
d. 1392. A native of Cori, diocese of Velletri, who joined the Augustinians and became famous as a zealous missioner. Cult approved by Leo XIII.

SANCTIAN (St) M.   AC. Sept 6
See Augustine, Sanctian and Beata.

SANCTINUS (St) Bp.   RM. Sept 22
d. c.300. Alleged to have been the first bishop of Meux and a disciple of St Dionysius of Paris. He is probably to be identified with a St Sanctinus claimed by the diocese of Verdun.

**SANCTUS (SANCTIUS) (St) M.
RM. June 2**
See Photinus (Pothinus), Sanctus, etc.

SANDILA (SANDALUS, SANDO-LUS, SANDULF) (St) M. RM. Sept 3
d. c.855. A Spanish martyr of Cordova under the Moorish domination.

SANDRATUS (SANDRADUS) Ab. OSB.   AC. Aug 24
d. 986. Monk of the abbey of St Maxi-

minus at Trèves. In 972 he was sent by the emperor Otto I to restore monastic observance at St Gall. Shortly after he was made abbot of Gladbach, and in 981 also abbot of Weissenburg. He died at Gladbach.

SANTUCCIA TERREBOTTI (Bl) W. OSB.   AC. March 21
d. 1305. Born at Gubbio in Umbria, she married and bore a daughter who died young. Santuccia and her husband then decided to enter religion. She became a Benedictine at Gubbio and rose to be abbess. Under her the community migrated to Santa Maria in Via Lata, on the Julian Way, Rome, where they continued to live the Benedictine life, though usually called the Servants of Mary. The people nicknamed them Le Santuccie.

SAPIENTIA (St) W.   RM. Sept 30
Otherwise Sophia, q.v.

SAPOR (SHAPUR), ISAAC and Comp. (SS) MM.   AC. Nov 30
d. 339. A band of Persian martyrs under Shapur II. Sapor and Isaac were bishops: the former died in prison, the latter was stoned to death. SS Mahanes, Abraham and Simeon suffered at the same time.

**SARAGOSSA, The EIGHTEEN MARTYRS of, viz. OPTATUS, LUPERCUS, SUCCESSUS, MARTIAL, URBAN, JULIA, QUINTILIAN, PUBLIUS, FRONTO, FELIX, CAECILIAN, EVENTIUS, PRIMITIVUS, APODEMIUS, and four named SATURNINUS (SS)
RM. Apr 16**
d. c.304. Martyrs of Saragossa in Spain under the emperor Diocletian and the prefect Dacian. Prudentius, who lived at Saragossa a lifetime later, describes their martyrdom.

SARAGOSSA, The INNUMERABLE MARTYRS of (SS)
RM. Nov 3

d. *c*.304. An exceedingly large number of martyrs put to death at Saragossa under Diocletian by the savage prefect Dacian, who had been sent to Spain to enforce the decrees. He published an edict banishing all Christians from the city, and while they were leaving he ordered the soldiers to fall upon and massacre them. Eighteen of them are mentioned by Prudentius and received a special notice in the RM. on April 16.

SARBELIUS (SHARBEL) and BARBEA (BEBAIA) (SS) MM.
RM. Jan 29

d. 101. Brother and sister martyred at Edessa under Trajan. Previous to their martyrdom they were tortured with red-hot irons. Before his conversion Thatueles Sarbelius had been the pagan high priest of the city.

SARDON (St) Bp.   RM. May 4
Otherwise Sacerdos, q.v.

SARMATA (St) M.   RM. Oct 11
d. 357. An Egyptian disciple of St Antony, murdered in his monastery by a band of marauding Bedouins and venerated as a martyr.

SATOR (St) M.
RM. Aug 29 and Sept 1
See Vitalis, Sator and Repositus.

SATURIAN (St) M.   RM. Oct 16
See Martinian, Saturian, etc.

SATURNINA (St) VM. RM. June 4
? A maiden said to have come from Germany into the neighbourhood of Arras and there to have met her death in defending herself against an assault on her virginity. The story is now held to be a romance.

SATURNINUS (St) M. RM. Jan 19
See Paul, Gerontius, etc.

SATURNINUS, THYRSUS and VICTOR (SS) MM.   RM. Jan 31
d. *c*. ? 250. Egyptians martyred at Alexandria.

SATURNINUS, THEOPHILUS and REVOCATA (SS) MM. RM. Feb 6
? A group of martyrs concerning whom neither place nor date of martyrdom is known.

SATURNINUS, DATIVUS, FELIX, AMPELIUS and Comp. (SS) MM.
RM. Feb 11

d. 304. A group of forty-six martyrs of Albitina in Africa. They were arrested at Mass and sent to Carthage for examination. Saturninus was a priest, and with him suffered his four children, viz., Saturninus and Felix, lectors, Mary, a virgin, and Hilarion, a young child. Dativus and another Felix were senators. Other names from this group which have come down to us are: Thelica, Ampelius, Emeritus, Rogatian and Victoria, a maiden of undaunted courage. The child Hilarion, when threatened by the magistrates, while his companions were being tortured, replied: "Yes, torture me too; anyhow, I am a Christian". They all appear to have died in prison. Their Acts bear the stamp of authenticity.

SATURNINUS, CASTULUS, MAGNUS and LUCIUS (SS) MM.
RM. Feb 15
d. 273. These martyrs belonged to the flock of St Valentine, bishop of Terni in Italy. They were buried at Passae (Rocca San Zenone).

SATURNINUS (St) M.
RM. March 7
See Perpetua, Felicitas, etc.

SATURNINUS and Comp. (SS)
MM.   RM. March 22
? A group of ten martyrs of N.W. Africa.

SATURNINUS (St) Bp.
RM. Apr 7
4th cent. Bishop of Verona. No details
of his career are extant.

SATURNINUS (SS) MM.
RM. Apr 16
Four of the same name among the group
of Saragossa Martyrs, q.v.

SATURNINUS (St) M. RM. Apr 29
See Corfu, Martyrs of.

SATURNINUS, NEOPOLUS,
GERMANUS and CELESTINE
(SS) MM.   RM. May 2
d. 304. Saturninus was martyred at
Alexandria under Diocletian, not at
Rome as stated in the RM. Of the
others nothing is known.

SATURNINUS (St) M. RM. July 7
See Peregrinus, Lucian, etc.

SATURNINUS (St) M. RM. Aug 22
See Martial, Saturninus, etc.

SATURNINUS (St) M. RM. Oct 6
See Marcellus, Castus, etc.

SATURNINUS and LUPUS (SS)
MM.   RM. Oct 14
? Martyrs at Caesarea in Cappadocia.

SATURNINUS, NEREUS and
Comp. (SS) MM.   RM. Oct 16
d. c.450. A band of some three hundred
and sixty-five martyrs who suffered in
Proconsular Africa under the Vandal
king Genseric. Some authorities maintain that this is merely a second listing
of the band of martyrs led by SS Martinian and Saturian, q.v.

SATURNINUS (St) M.
RM. Oct 30
d. 303. A martyr of Cagliari, in Sardinia,
under Diocletian. According to his
untrustworthy Acts he was beheaded
during a pagan festival of Jupiter.

SATURNINUS (St) M. RM. Nov 27
See Basileus, Auxilius and Saturninus.

SATURNINUS and SISINIUS (SS)
MM.   RM. Nov 29
d. ? 309. Saturninus was a Roman
priest, though by birth, it is said, a
Carthaginian. He and his deacon
Sisinius were sentenced to hard labour
and subsequently martyred. They were
buried in the cemetery of St Thraso on
the Salarian Way. They have no connexion with SS Cyriacus, Largus and
Smaragdus, as has been alleged.

SATURNINUS (French: SERNIN)
(St) Bp. M.   RM. Nov 29
d. c.257. A missionary from Rome who
evangelized the district round Pampeluna in Spanish Navarre, and then the
territory and city of Toulouse. He is
venerated as the first bishop of Toulouse.
He is said to have been martyred in the
persecution of Valerian by being fastened behind a wild bull which dragged
him about until he was dashed to pieces.

SATURNINUS (St) C. AC. Nov 29
Otherwise Sadwen, q.v.

SATURNINUS (St) M. RM. Dec 15
See Irenaeus, Antony, etc.

SATURNINUS (St) M. RM. Dec 23
See Theodulus, Saturninus, etc.

SATURNINUS (St) M. RM. Dec 29
See Dominic, Victor, etc.

SATURUS (St) M.   RM. March 7
See Perpetua, Felicitas, etc.

SATURUS (St) M.   RM. March 29
See Armogastes and Comp.

SATURUS (several)
Otherwise Satyrus, q.v.

SATYRUS (St) M.   RM. Jan 12
d. ? An Arab by birth, who was martyred in Achaia (or at Antioch) for insulting an idol. Another version says that the idol fell to the ground when Satyrus made the sign of the cross over it. There is complete confusion in the sources.

SATYRUS (St) C.   RM. Sept 17
d. c.392. The elder brother of St Ambrose of Milan. As a lawyer he undertook the administration of the temporal affairs of the diocese of Milan. His high sense of justice, his integrity and his generosity are eulogized by Ambrose in the funeral sermon "On the death of a brother".

SAULA (St) VM.   RM. Oct 20
See Martha, Saula and Comp.

SAUMAN (SAUMAY) (St) H.
AC. June 14
Otherwise Psalmodius, q.v.

SAUVE (St) Bp.   RM. Sept 10
Otherwise Salvius, q.v.

SAVINA (St) Matron   RM. Jan 30
d. 311. A woman of Milan who, during the persecution of Diocletian, busied herself in ministering to the martyrs in prison and in interring their bodies after execution. She died while praying at the tomb of SS Nabor and Felix.

SAVINIAN (SAVINIEN) (several)
Otherwise Sabinian, q.v.

SAVINUS (several)
Otherwise Sabinus, q.v.

SAVINUS (Bl) H. OSB. Cam.
AC. May 19
See Bellatanus, Savinus.

SAWL (St) C.   AC. Jan 15
6th cent. A Welsh chieftain, father of St Asaph. The traditions concerning him are very obscure.

SAZAN (St) M.   AC. Oct 1
See Aizan and Sazan.

SCANNAL (St) C.   AC. May 3
d. p.563. Scannal of Cell-Coleraine was a disciple of St Columba and a celebrated missionary.

SCARTHIN (St) C.   AC. Jan 6
Otherwise Schotin, q.v.

SCHADOST (St) M.   RM. Feb 20
Otherwise Sadoth, q.v.

SCHENUTE (SINUTIUS) (St) Ab.
AC. July 1
d. c.460. An Egyptian who became a monk at Deir-al-Abiad in 371. He is said to have become in the course of time superior of a very large number of monks and nuns, the number being given as over four thousand. It seems to have been under him that the custom arose of religious binding themselves by public vows.

SCHOLASTICA (St) V. OSB.
RM. Feb 10
d. c.550. Sister of St Benedict. She became a nun and lived near Montecassino under the direction of her brother. She is regarded as the first nun of the Benedictine Order. St Gregory narrates that, at her last meeting with her brother, she obtained by prayer a sudden heavy rainstorm, which prevented Benedict from returning to his monastery and thus prolonged their interview through the night: three days later Benedict saw

her soul ascend to heaven in the semblance of a dove. The tradition that St Scholastica was a nun dates from the 11th century. Before then she was considered a devout and holy woman living in the vicinity of the Abbey of Montecassino.

SCHOLASTICA (St)   AC. May 25
See Injuriosus and Scholastica.

SCHOTIN (SCARTHIN) (St) C.
**   AC. Jan 6**
6th cent. While still a youth Schotin left Ireland to become a disciple of St David in Wales. On his return to his native country he for many years led the life of an anchorite at Mt Mairge, Leix. He is said to have established a school for boys at Kilkenny.

SCILLITAN MARTYRS (SS)
**   RM. July 17**
d. 180. Twelve martyrs, seven men and five women, who suffered at Scillium in Proconsular Africa under Septimius Severus. Their names are: Speratus, Narzales, Cythinus, Veturius, Felix, Acyllinus, Laetantius, Januaria, Generosa, Vestina, Donata and Secunda. The official Acts of these martyrs are still extant.

SCUBICULUS (St) M. RM. Oct 11
See Nicasius, Quirinus, etc.

SEACHNALL (SECHNALL,
SECUNDINUS) (St) Bp. AC. Nov 27
d. 457. A nephew and disciple of St Patrick. In 433 he was appointed first bishop of Dunsauglin, Meath, and later served as assistant bishop of Armagh. He wrote the earliest Latin poem of the Irish church—an alphabetical hymn in honour of St Patrick.

SEBALD (St) H. OSB. RM. Aug 19
d. c.770. First a hermit near Vicenza,

then a co-worker with St Willibald in the Reichswald. He was probably an Anglo-Saxon missionary.

SEBASTE, MARTYRS of
**   RM. March 10**
See Forty Armenian Martyrs.

SEBASTIA (St) M.   RM. July 4
See Innocent, Sebastia, and Comp.

SEBASTIAN (St) M.   RM. Jan 20
d. ? 288. One of the most renowned of the Roman martyrs. According to his Acts, which however are not trustworthy, he was an officer in the imperial army and a favourite of Diocletian. Nevertheless when it was discovered that he was a Christian no mercy was shown to him. Tied to a tree, his body was made a target for the Roman archers, and he was finally dispatched with clubs. His cult, both at Rome and at Milan, dates from the 4th century. In 367 Pope St Damasus built a basilica over his tomb on the Appian Way, and this is now one of the seven principal churches of Rome.

SEBASTIAN VALFRÉ (Bl) Orat.
**   AC. Jan 30**
1629–1710. Born at Verduno, diocese of Alba, N. Italy, he joined the Oratorians at Turin after his ordination to the priesthood, and there he spent the remainder of his life. He became prefect of the Oratory and was much in request as a spiritual director. He acquired in full measure the spirit of St Philip Neri. Beatified in 1834.

SEBASTIAN (St) M.   RM. Feb 8
See Dionysius, Emilian and Sebastian.

SEBASTIAN APARICIO (Bl) C.
OFM.   AC. Feb 25
d. 1600. Born in Spanish Galicia, he

became a farm labourer and then valet to a gentleman of Salamanca. He emigrated to Mexico, where he was engaged by the government in building roads and in conducting the postal service between Mexico and Zacateca. After the death of his second wife, when he was seventy years old, he became a Franciscan lay-brother at Puebla de los Angeles. He lived for another twenty-six years, his chief occupation being to beg alms for the community. Beatified in 1787.

SEBASTIAN (St) M. RM. March 20
See Photina, Joseph, etc.

SEBASTIAN NEWDIGATE (Bl) M. O. Cart. AC. June 19
d. 1535. Born at Harefield, Middlesex, and educated at Cambridge, he professed the Carthusian Rule in the London Charterhouse. He was executed at Tyburn for denying the royal supremacy. BB Humphrey Middlemore and William Exmew suffered with him. Beatified in 1886.

SEBASTIAN KIMURA (Bl) M. SJ. AC. Sept 10
d. 1622. A grandson of the first Japanese baptized by St Francis Xavier. At the age of eighteen he joined the Jesuits and worked as a catechist at Meaco. He was the first Japanese to be ordained priest. After two years imprisonment at Omura he was burnt alive with Bl Charles Spinola. Beatified in 1867.

SEBASTIAN MONTAÑOL (Bl) M. OP. PC. Dec 10
d. 1616. A Spanish Dominican and a missionary in Zacateca, Mexico, where he was put to death by the Indians whom he had rebuked for having profaned the Sacred Host. Though he has never been officially declared a martyr, he has always been the object of a popular cult.

SEBASTIAN MAGGI (Bl) C. OP. AC. Dec 16
d. 1494. A native of Brescia, he became a Friar Preacher and was noted for his zeal in enforcing religious observance. He was twice vicar of the Lombard province and was for a time confessor of Savonarola. He died in Genoa. Cult confirmed in 1760.

SEBASTIAN (Bl) Bp. OSB. AC. Dec 30
d. c.1036. A Benedictine monk who became Archbishop of Esztergom (1002) and Primate of Hungary in the time of St Stephen.

SEBASTIANA (St) M. RM. Sept 16
1st cent. A woman converted by St Paul. Beheaded at Heraclea in Thrace under Domitian.

SEBBE (SEBBA, SEBBI) (St) C. OSB. RM. Aug 29
d. c.694. King of the East Saxons at the time of the Heptarchy. After a peaceful reign of thirty years he received the monastic habit in London and died shortly after.

SECUNDA (St) VM. RM. July 10
See Rufina and Seconda.

SECUNDA (St) M. RM. July 17
One of the Scillitan Martyrs, q.v.

SECUNDA (St) VM. RM. July 30
See Maxima, Donatilla and Secunda.

SECUNDARIUS (St) M. RM. Oct 2
See Primus, Cyril and Secundarius.

SECUNDEL (St) H. AC. Aug 1
6th cent. He lived with St Friard, q.v.

SECUNDIAN (St) M. RM. Feb 17
See Donatus, Secundian, etc.

SECUNDIAN, MARCELLIAN and VERIAN (SS) MM.   RM. Aug 9
d. 250. Tuscan martyrs who suffered near Civitavecchia under Decius. Secundian seems to have been a prominent government official; the others are described as "scholastics". Nothing certain can be stated about this group.

SECUNDILLA (St) M.
                         RM. March 2
See Paul, Heraclius, etc.

SECUNDINA (St) VM. RM. Jan 15
d. c.250. A Roman maiden, scourged to death in the neighbourhood of Rome in the persecution of Decius.

SECUNDINUS (St) M. RM. Feb 18
See Lucius, Silvanus, etc.

SECUNDINUS (St) Bp. M.
                         RM. Apr 29
See Agapius and Comp.

SECUNDINUS (St) M. RM. May 21
d. c.306. A Spanish martyr at Cordova under Diocletian.

SECUNDINUS (St) Bp. M.
                         RM. July 1
See Castus and Secundinus.

SECUNDINUS, AGRIPPINUS, MAXIMUS, FORTUNATUS and MARTIALIS (SS) MM. AC. July 15
? 4th cent. Martyrs in Pannonia.

SECUNDINUS (St) M. RM. Sept 1
See Priscus, Castrensis, etc.

SECUNDINUS (St) Bp. AC. Dec 6
See Auxilius, Isserninus and Secundinus.

SECUNDULUS (St) M.
                         RM. March 7
See Perpetua, Felicitas, etc.

SECUNDUS (St) M.   RM. Jan 9
See Epictetus, Jucundus, etc.

SECUNDUS (St) M. RM. March 24
See Romulus and Secundus.

SECUNDUS (St) M. RM. March 29
d. 119. A patrician of Asti in Piedmont and a subaltern officer in the imperial army. He was beheaded at Asti under Hadrian.

SECUNDUS (St) Bp.   RM. May 15
See Torquatus, Ctesiphon, etc.

SECUNDUS and Comp. (SS) MM.
                         RM. May 21
d. 357. Secundus, a priest of the church of Alexandria, was martyred with a great multitude of clergy and laity, including many women, by the intruded Arian patriarch George. The latter was supported in his occupation of the see of Alexandria by the emperor Constantius, the rightful patriarch, St Athanasius, having been driven into exile.

SECUNDUS (St) M.   RM. June 1
d. 304. An alleged martyr at Amelia, drowned in the Tiber under Diocletian. He is the patron saint of several places in central Italy, but his historical existence cannot be proved.

SECUNDUS (St) M.   RM. July 31
See Democritus, Secundus and Dionysius.

SECUNDUS (St) M.   RM. Aug 7
See Carpophorus, Exanthus, etc.

SECUNDUS (St) M.   RM. Aug 26
3rd cent. A legendary soldier, said to have belonged to the Theban legion and to have been martyred near Ventimiglia.

SECUNDUS, FIDENTIAN and VARICUS (SS) MM.   RM. Nov 15
? Martyrs of Proconsular Africa, of whom nothing is known.

SECUNDUS (St) M.   **RM. Dec 19**
See Darius, Zosimus, etc.

SECUNDUS (St) M.   **RM. Dec 19**
See Cyriacus, Paulillus, etc.

SECUNDUS (St) M.   **RM. Dec 29**
See Dominic, Victor, etc.

SECURUS (St) M.   **RM. Dec 2**
See Severus, Securus, etc.

SEDNA (St) Bp.   **AC. March 10**
d. *c*.570. Bishop of Ossory and friend
of St Luanus.

SEDOPHA (St) M.   **RM. July 5**
See Marinus, Theodotus and Sedopha.

SEDUINUS (St) Bp.
                  ? RM. July 15
Possibly identical with St Swithin of
Winchester, q.v.

SEEMIE-ROOKIE (St) C.
                  RM. Aug 16
See Roch.

SEINE (St) Ab.   **RM. Sept 19**
Otherwise Sequanus, q.v.

SEIRIOL (St) C.   **AC. Jan 2**
6th cent. A Welsh saint whose memory
is perpetuated by the name of the island
of Ynys-Seiriol.

SELESIUS (SELEUCUS) (St) M.
                  RM. Sept 12
See Hieronides, Leontius, etc.

SELEUCUS (St) M.   **RM. Feb 16**
See Porphyrius and Seleucus.

SELEUCUS (St)   **RM. March 24**
? A Syrian saint honoured in the East
and often described as a martyr. Our
only record of him is in the Eastern
Calendars.

SELYF (St) M.   **AC. June 25**
Otherwise Solomon, q.v.

SENACH (SNACH) Bp.
                  AC. Aug 3
6th cent. A disciple of St Finian and his
successor at Clonard.

SENAN (SENAMES) (St) Bp.
                  AC. March 8
d. *c*.560. An Irish monk of Kilmanagh
in Ossory. Having established a monastery, probably at Enniscorthy, he is said
to have then visited Rome and on his
way home to have stayed with St David
in Wales. On his return to Ireland he
founded more churches and monasteries,
notably one at Inishcarra near Cork.
Finally he settled on Scattery Island in
the Shannon estuary, where he was
buried. There are indications that he
spent some time in Cornwall.

SENAN (St) H.   **AC. Apr 29**
7th cent. Said to have been a hermit in
N. Wales. There is much confusion in
the records of saints of this and similar
names, and consequently it is impossible
to give any precise account of them.

SENATOR (St) Bp.   **RM. May 28**
d. 480. A Milanese priest who, as a
young man, attended the council of
Chalcedon as a legate of Pope St Leo
the Great. Afterwards he became archbishop of Milan.

SENATOR (St) Bp.   **AC. May 28**
d. 480. Bishop of Pavia.

SENATOR (St)   **RM. Sept 26**
? A saint of Albanum, of whom nothing
is known. Albanum may be Albano near
Rome or Apt, the ancient Alba Helve-
tiorum, in S. France.

SENNEN (St) M.   **RM. July 30**
See Abdon and Sennen.

SENORINA (St) V. OSB.
AC. Apr 22
d. 982. She was related to St Rudesind of Mondoñedo. Entrusted to the care of her aunt, the abbess Godina, at the convent of St John of Venaria (Vieyra), she joined the community and later became its abbess. As such she removed the community to Basto in the diocese of Braga.

SEPTEMBER (Martyrs of) (BB)
AC. Sept 2–3
d. 1792. A group of one hundred and ninety-one martyrs who met their death during the French Revolution. They were imprisoned by the Legislative Assembly for refusing the oath to support the civil constitution of the clergy which had been condemned by the Holy See. They were massacred by the mob, with the connivance of the Assembly, on Sept 2 and 3, 1792. The most prominent members of the group were: John Mary du Lau, archbishop of Arles, Francis de la Rochefoucauld, bishop of Beauvais, his brother Louis, bishop of Saintes, Augustine Ambrose Chevreux, OSB., last superior general of the Maurists, and Charles de la Calmette, count of Valfons. One hundred and twenty were massacred at the Carmelite church (Les Carmes) in the rue de Rennes, Paris. Beatified in 1926.

SEPTIMINUS, JANUARIUS and FELIX (SS) MM.
RM. Aug 28 and Sept 1
A group among the Twelve Holy Brothers, q.v.

SEPTIMUS (St) M.   RM. Aug 17
See Liberatus, Boniface, etc.

SEPTIMUS (St) M.   RM. Oct 24
See Felix (Africanus) Audactus (Adauctus), etc.

SEQUANUS (SEINE, SIGO) Ab.
RM. Sept 19
d. c.580. Monk of Réomay and abbot-founder of a monastery at Segreste, diocese of Langres, which was later called after him Saint-Seine.

SERAPHIA (St) VM.   RM. July 29
Otherwise Serapia, q.v.

SERAPHINA (or FINA) (St) V.
AC. March 12
d. 1253. Born at San Geminiano in Tuscany, she led a life of constant suffering, being the victim of repulsive diseases and continuous neglect. She was never a nun, but seems to have lived at home under the obedience of the Benedictines. She is greatly venerated at San Geminiano as Santa Fina.

SERAPHINA SFORZA (Bl) V. Poor Clare   AC. Sept 9
1434–1478. Born at Urbino, the daughter of Guido, count of Urbino and lord of Gubbio, she married in 1448 Alexander Sforza, duke of Pesaro, who treated her with great ignominy and expelled her from her home. She took refuge in the convent of Poor Clares and eventually professed their rule and became abbess. Beatified in 1754.

SERAPHINA (St)   RM. July 29
d. ? c.426. The RM. ascribes this saint to a *Civitas Mamiensis*, which some writers place in Armenia, others in Spain, others in Italy.

SERAPHINUS (St) C. OFM. Cap.
RM. Oct 12
1540–1604. Born at Montegranaro, he took the Capuchin habit as a lay-brother in 1556 and spent the whole of his uneventful life at the friary of Ascoli-Piceno. He is said to have been the spiritual adviser of high ecclesiastical and civil dignitaries. Canonized in 1767.

SERAPIA (St) VM.   RM. July 29
d. 119. A slave of Syrian extraction in the household of St Sabina, whom she converted to the Faith. She was beheaded under Hadrian.

SERAPION (St) M.   RM. Feb 25
See Victorinus, Victor, etc.

SERAPION (St) M.   RM. Feb 28
See Caerealis, Pupulus, etc.

SERAPION (St) Bp.   RM. March 21
d. *c*.370. An Egyptian monk who was consecrated bishop of Thmuis in Lower Egypt and distinguished himself by his firm opposition to Arianism. He was a great friend of St Athanasius and of St Antony. He was the author of several works; his Euchologium, a valuable liturgical source was discovered in 1899.

SERAPION of ARSINOE (St) C.
**   AC. ? March 21**
d. 4th cent? One of the most famous of the desert fathers, he ruled over 10,000 monks scattered through the desert.

SERAPION (St) M. RM. March 26
See Theodore, Irenaeus, etc.

SERAPION the SINDONITE (St) C.
**   AC. May 21**
d. *c*.356. Born in Egypt, he became a monk and pushed self-denial to extreme limits. He made a pilgrimage to Rome.

SERAPION (St) M.   RM. July 13
d. *c*.195. An oriental martyr who suffered under Septimus Severus, probably in Macedonia.

SERAPION (St) M.   RM. Aug 27
See Marcellians, Mannavea, etc.

SERAPION (St) Bp.   RM. Oct 30
d. 199. A bishop of Antioch praised by

Eusebius and St Jerome for his theological writings, which however are no longer extant.

SERAPION (St) M.   RM. Nov 14
d. 252. A martyr of Alexandria who perished in a riot raised against the Christians. The mob cast him down from the roof of his own house, a high building.

SERAPION (St) M. O. Merc.
**   RM. Nov 14**
d. 1240. Said to have been born in England and to have fought against the Moors in Spain under the banner of Castile. In Spain he joined the Mercedarian Order and surrendered himself as a hostage at Algiers, where he was crucified for preaching the gospel while awaiting his ransom. Cult confirmed, as a saint, in 1728.

SERDOT (St) Bp.   RM. May 4
Otherwise Sacerdos, q.v.

SERENA (St)   RM. Aug 16
d. *c*.290. Described in the RM. as "sometime wife of the emperor Diocletian", but his information is derived from the spurious Acts of St Cyriacus.

SERENICUS Ab. and SERENUS
H. (SS) OSB.   AC. May 7
d. *c*.669. Two brothers belonging to a patrician family of Spoleto. They received the Benedictine habit at the tomb of the apostles, which was then in Benedictine custody. Later they settled in France as hermits near the river Sarthe. Serenus remained a hermit till the end of his life, but Serenicus became the head of a community of some one hundred and forty disciples who gathered round him. On these he imposed the Benedictine Rule and other Roman practices.

SERENUS (CERNEUF, SIRENUS) (St) M.   **RM. Feb 23**
d. *c*.303. A Greek monk who lived as a hermit at Sirmium, now Mitrovica, in the Balkans. He was martyred under Diocletian.

SERENUS (St) H. OSB. AC. May 7
See Serenicus and Serenus.

SERENUS (St) M.   RM. June 28
See Plutarch, Serenus, etc.

SERENUS (St) Bp.   AC. Aug 9
d. 606. Bishop of Marseilles. St Gregory wrote him several letters, in which he recommended to him the Roman missionaries travelling to England and twice reprimanded him for his iconoclastic tendencies.

SERF (St) Bp.   AC. July 1
Otherwise Servan, q.v.

SERGIUS (St) M.   RM. Feb 24
d. 304. A monk, perhaps a priest, in Cappadocia, martyred under Diocletian. His relics are said to have been translated to Ubeda, near Tarragona, in Spain.

SERGIUS (St) M.   AC. March 20
See John, Sergius, and Comp.

SERGIUS (St) M.   RM. July 27
See Maurus, Pantaleemon and Sergius.

SERGIUS (St) Pope   RM. Sept 8
d. 701. Of Syrian parentage, but born at Palermo in Sicily and admitted to membership of the Roman clergy, Sergius governed the Church as Pope from 687 to 701. He opposed the interference of the Byzantine emperors in ecclesiastical affairs and refused to sign the decrees of the synod known as Trullanum. He blessed and fostered the missionary enterprise of the English monks in Friesland and Germany and defended St Wilfrid.

SERGIUS and BACCHUS (SS) MM.   **RM. Oct 7**
d. 303. High officers of the Roman army in Syria. For refusing to join in pagan sacrifices they were dressed in women's clothes and led through the streets of Arabissus. Then Bacchus was beaten to death, and Sergius was beheaded a week later.

SERLO (Bl) Ab. OSB.   PC. March 3
d. 1104. A Norman by birth, he became a canon of Avranches and later a Benedictine monk at Mont Saint-Michel. Four years later (1074), on the recommendation of St Osmund, he was appointed abbot of Gloucester, receiving the abbatial blessing from St Wulstan. When he arrived at Gloucester the community consisted of two adult monks and eight boys: when he died he left a community of over one hundred professed monks. He was noted for his building activities and his fearless defence of ecclesiastical rights and the moral law.

SERLO (Bl) Ab. OSB. Cist.   **AC. Sept 10**
d. 1158. A Benedictine of Chérisy who became abbot of Savigny in 1140. He united the whole congregation of Savigny to the Cistercians in 1147 and was thenceforward a devoted member of the latter order.

SERNIN (St) Bp. M.   RM. Nov 29
Otherwise Saturninus, q.v.

SEROTINA (St) M.   RM. Dec 31
See Donata, Paulina, etc.

SERVAN (SERF, SAIR) (St) Bp.   **AC. July 1**
? Apostle of the Orkney Islands. The traditions concerning him are very contradictory and extravagant. He died and was buried at Culross.

SERVANDUS and GERMANUS (SS) MM.   RM. Oct 23

d. *c*.305. Said to have been sons of St Marcellus of León (Oct 30). They were put to death at Cadiz while on their way under arrest to Tangiers. They are held in great veneration throughout S. Spain.

SERVATUS (French: SERVAIS) (St) Bp.   RM. May 13

d. 384. Bishop of Tangres in the Low Countries. He was the host of St Athanasius when the latter was an exile in the West.

SERVILIAN (St) M.   RM. Apr 20

See Sulpicius and Servilian.

SERVILIUS (St) M.   RM. May 24

See Zoëllus, Servilius, etc.

SERVITE MARTYRS (BB)
                                          AC. Aug 31

d. 1420. Sixty-four Servite friars burnt to death in their church at Prague by the Hussites. The group included four friars from Tuscany who had been sent to Bohemia to preach against the Hussite heresy. Cult confirmed in 1918.

SERVULUS (St) C.   RM. Dec 23

d. *c*.590. A cripple who begged for alms at the door of the church of St Clement in Rome, sharing what he received with other beggars. St Gregory the Great describes the beautiful scene of Servulus's death.

SERVUS (St) M.   RM. Aug 17

See Liberatus, Boniface, etc.

SERVUS (St) M.   RM. Dec 7

d. 483. A layman of noble birth in Proconsular Africa. He was seized and tortured to death under the Arian Vandal king Hunneric.

SERVUS-DEI (St) M.   RM. Jan 13

See Gumesindus and Servus-Dei.

SERVUS-DEI (St) M.   RM. Sept 16

See Rogellus and Servus-Dei.

SETHRIDA (SAETHRYTH) (St) Abs. OSB.   AC. Jan 10

d. *c*.660. Stepdaughter of Anna, king of the East Angles (635–644). She became a nun at Faremoutier-en-Brie under St Fara, whom she succeeded as abbess. She was half-sister to SS Ethelreda and Ethelburga.

SETON (Mother) ELIZABETH ANNE BAYLEY (Bl)

See Elizabeth Anne Bayley Seton.

SEVEN ANGELS who stand before the throne of God   AC. Apr 20

See Tob. XII 15; Apoc. VIII, 2–5. The names usually given to them are Michael, Gabriel, Raphael (these three names occur in the Bible), Uriel, Shealtiel, Jehudiel and Berachiel. A church at Palermo is dedicated to the Seven Angels, their feast being observed there on Apr 20.

SEVEN APOSTLES of BULGARIA (SS) CC.   AC. July 17

The Bulgarians venerate liturgically their first seven apostles; they are, besides the well-known Cyril and Methodius, q.v., Gorazd, Nahum, Sabas, Angelarius and Clement of Okharida. The last-named, who is the most important after Cyril and Methodius, died on July 17, 916.

SEVEN BROTHERS (SS) MM.
                                          RM. July 10

d. *c*.150. The seven alleged sons of the Roman martyr Felicitas, q.v. Their names are: Januarius, Felix and Philip, scourged to death; Sylvanus, thrown over a precipice; Alexander, Vitalis and Martial, beheaded. They seem to have suffered at Rome under Antoninus Pius. Modern scholars deny that they were brothers: the fact that they were commemorated on the same day led to the legend of their being related by blood and the sons of Felicitas.

SEVEN HOLY FOUNDERS (SS)
RM. Feb 12

Their names are: Bonfilio Monaldo, Alexius Falconieri, (Benedict) Manettus dell'Antello, (Bartholomew) Amedeo de Amideis, (Ricovero) Uguccio Uguccione, (Gherordino) Sostenes Sostegni, (John) Buonagiunta Monetti. They were young Florentine members of the Confraternity of Our Lady who, on Aug 15, 1233, in obedience to a vision of the Mother of God, withdrew to Mt Senario and laid the foundation of the Order of the Servants of Mary, known as Servites. The chief devotion of this Order is to the Seven Sorrows of Our Lady. Bonfilio was the first superior General, Buonagiunta the second, Manettus the fourth. Amedeo was first prior of Carfaggio. Uguccio and Sosteneo established the order in France and Germany respectively. Alexis remained a lay-brother and was the last to die (1310). They were canonized conjointly by Leo XIII in 1887, when their common feast was added to the Roman Missal for the universal Church.

SEVEN SAINTLY ROBBERS
(SS) MM.   RM. Apr 29

See Corfu (Martyrs of).

SEVEN SLEEPERS (SS) MM.
RM. July 27

250–362. The legend of the Seven Sleepers states that seven youths of Ephesus were walled up in a cave under Decius in the year 250 and were found alive there in the time of Theodosius II (362), having spent the intervening period in sleep. There are three or four sets of different names and a large number of variants of the legend. One of the most ingenuous of these was written by St James of Sarug in Syriac (c.500). The origin of the legend is probably to be traced to the discovery of some forgotten relics. Baronius, although he left the *memoria* of the Seven Sleepers in the RM., doubted the authenticity of their story.

SEVERA (St) V. Abs.   RM. July 20
d. c.680. Sister of St Modoald, bishop of Trèves. First abbess of St Gemma (later Sainte-Sevère) at Villeneuve, diocese of Bourges.

SEVERA (St) Abs. OSB. AC. July 20
d. c.750. Benedictine abbess of the great nunnery of Oehren at Trèves.

SEVERIAN and AQUILA (SS) MM.
RM. Jan 23

? A husband and wife martyred at Julia Caesarea in Mauritania.

SEVERIAN (St) Bp. M. RM. Feb 21
d. c.452. A bishop of Scythopolis (Bethsan) in Galilee who, on his return from the council of Chalcedon, was murdered by the Eutychian heretics with the connivance of the empress Eudoxia.

SEVERIAN (St) M.   RM. Apr 20
See Victor, Zoticus, etc.

SEVERIAN (St) M.   RM. Sept 9
d. 320. An Armenian senator who, having witnessed the martyrdom of the forty martyrs of Sebaste, openly professed his Christianity and was torn with iron rakes until he died. He suffered at Sebaste under Licinius.

SEVERIAN (St) M.   RM. Nov 8
One of the Four Crowned Martyrs, q.v.

SEVERINUS (St) Ab.   RM. Jan 8
d. 476. An Eastern hermit who undertook the evangelization of Noricum

(corresponding to modern Austria), where he established several monastic foundations, notably one on the Danube near Vienna, where he died. Six years after his death the monks were driven from the country and carried his relics to Naples, where the great Benedictine monastery of San Severino was built to enshrine them.

SEVERINUS (St) Bp.   RM. Jan 8
Under this date the RM. commemorates a St Severinus, bishop at Naples, brother of St Victorinus M. The entry in the RM. is the result of a confusion between the saint noticed above and St Severinus of Septempeda (June 8), brother of St Victorinus of Camerino.

SEVERINUS (St) Ab.   RM. Feb 11
d. ? 507. A Burgundian said to have been the abbot of Agaunum in Switzerland. He is also alleged to have restored to health Clovis, first Christian king of the Franks. The historical evidence for these assertions is not good.

SEVERINUS (St) Bp.   RM. June 8
d. 550. Bishop of Septempeda, now called after him Sanseverino, in the Marches of Ancona. He and his brother Victorinus distributed their great wealth among the poor and became hermits at Montenero. They were forced by Pope Vigilius (540) to become bishops, the former of Septempeda, the latter of Camerino. Severinus died shortly before Septempeda was destroyed by Totila the Ostrogoth.

SEVERINUS (St) M.   RM. July 6
See Lucy, Antoninus, etc.

SEVERINUS (St) M.   RM. Aug 7
See Carpophorus, Exanthus, etc.

SEVERINUS (St) Bp.   RM. Oct 23
d. c.403. Said to have been born at Bordeaux. He was bishop of Cologne and a prominent opponent of Arianism.

SEVERINUS (French: SEURIN) (St) Bp.   RM. Oct 23
d. c.420. Said to have been an oriental by birth. He was bishop of Bordeaux c.405–420.

**SEVERINUS BOËTHIUS (St) M.
                                   AC. Oct 23**
d. 523. Anicius Manlius Torquatus Severinus Boëthius is known to history as a Roman statesman in the service of Theodoric the Ostrogoth and as an eminent philosopher, author of *De consolatione philosophiae*. About the year 534 he fell into disfavour with the barbarian king and was beheaded at Pavia after a long imprisonment. His relics are enshrined at the cathedral of Pavia, where his feast is observed. His feast is also kept at the church of Santa Maria in Portico, Rome. Cult confirmed in 1883.

**SEVERINUS (St) H. OSB.
                                      RM. Nov 1**
d. c.699. A Benedictine monk who lived as a hermit at Tivoli. His relics are in the church of St Laurence at Tivoli.

SEVERINUS, EXUPERIUS and FELICIAN (SS) MM.   RM. Nov 19
d. 170. Martyrs of Vienne in Gaul under Marcus Aurelius.

SEVERINUS (St) H.   RM. Nov 27
d. c.540. A hermit who lived first at Paris and then in a cell at Novientum near Paris.

SEVERINUS (St) Bp.   RM. Dec 21
d. c.300. Bishop of Trèves.

SEVERUS (St) M.   RM. Jan 11
See Peter, Severus and Leucius.

SEVERUS (St) Bp.   RM. Feb 1
d. *c*.348. A native of Ravenna who became bishop of that city in 283. He accompanied the papal legate to the synod of Sardica (344).

SEVERUS (St) Bp.   AC. Feb 1
d. *c*.690. Born of poor parents in the Cotentin, he became successively priest, abbot and bishop of Avranches. Before his death he resigned his see and returned to monastic life.

SEVERUS (St) C.   RM. Feb 15
d. *c*.530. A parish priest of Interocrea (Androcca) in the Abruzzi. St Gregory the Great relates that he brought a dead man back to life that he might receive the Last Sacraments. The relics of Severus were translated to Münster-Maifeld, diocese of Trèves, in the 10th century.

SEVERUS and SIXTY-TWO COMPS. (SS) MM.   AC. Feb 21
3rd–4th cent. Martyrs at Syrmium, Pannonia.

SEVERUS (St) Bp.   RM. Apr 29
d. 409. Bishop of Naples and a famous wonder-worker. He raised a dead man to life in order that he should bear witness in favour of his persecuted widow.

SEVERUS (St) C.   AC. Aug 1
d. *c*.500. A priest of noble family and famous for his charity, he has been honoured from time immemorial in the village that bears his name, St Sever de Rustan in Bigorre (Hautes-Pyrenées).

SEVERUS (St) C.   RM. Aug 8
d. *p*.445. A priest who came from afar (some accounts say from India) and evangelized the district round Vienne in Gaul.

SEVERUS, MEMNON and Comp. (SS) MM.   RM. Aug 20
d. *c*.300. Severus was a priest and Memnon a centurion at Bizya in Thrace, where they were beheaded for the faith. Thirty-seven Christian soldiers from Philippopolis were at the same time thrown into a furnace.

SEVERUS (St) C.   RM. Oct 1
This saint seems to be identical with Severus, Feb 15, q.v.

SEVERUS (St) Bp.   RM. Oct 15
d. *c*.455. Born in Gaul, he was a disciple of St Germanus of Auxerre and of St Lupus of Troyes. He accompanied Germanus to Britain to oppose the Pelagian heresy. He preached the gospel to the Germans on the lower Moselle and became bishop of Trèves (446–*c*.455).

SEVERUS (St) M.   RM. Oct 22
See Philip, Severus, etc.

SEVERUS (St) Bp. M.   RM. Nov 6
d. 633. Bishop of Barcelona, martyred under the Arian Visigoths, who put him to death by driving nails into his temples. He is a minor patron of Barcelona.

SEVERUS (St) M.   RM. Nov 8
One of the Four Crowned Martyrs, q.v.

SEVERUS, SECURUS, JANUARIUS and VICTORINUS (SS) MM.   RM. Dec 2
d. *c*.450. African martyrs who suffered under the Vandals.

SEVERUS (Bl) Bp. OSB.   PC. Dec 9
d. 1067. A Benedictine of Brevnov who became bishop of Prague (1031–1067) and was noted for his activities as a builder of churches. He is always styled either saint or blessed by Czech hagiographers.

SEVERUS (St) M.   RM. Dec 30
See Mansuetus, Severus, etc.

SEXBURGA (St) W. Abs. OSB.
AC. July 6
d. *c*.699. Daughter of Anna, king of the
East Angles, sister of SS Etheldreda,
Ethelburga and Withburga, and half-
sister of St Sethrida. She married
Erconbert, king of Kent, by whom she
became the mother of SS Ermengilda
and Ermengota. As queen she founded
the nunnery of Minster in Sheppey.
Left a widow after twenty-four years of
happy married life, she became a nun
at Milton in Kent, whence she migrated
to Ely, where she became abbess.

SEXTUS (St) M.   RM. Dec 31
See Stephen, Pontian, etc.

SEZIN (St) Bp.   AC. March 6
d. *c*.529. A native of Britain who
laboured in Ireland at the time of St
Patrick and then crossed over to Guic-
Sezni in Brittany, where he is said to
have founded a monastery and where his
relics are now venerated.

SHEALTIEL   AC. Apr 20
See Seven Angels who stand before the
throne of God.

SIAGRIUS (St) (*several*)
Otherwise Syagrius, q.v.

SIARDUS (SIARD) (St) O. Praem.
PC. Nov 13
d. 1230. Premonstratensian abbot of
Mariengaarden in Frisia (1196–1230).

SIBYLLINA BISCOSSI (Bl) V. Tert.
OP.   AC. March 23
1287–1367. Born at Pavia and left an
orphan, at the age of twelve she became
blind and was adopted by a community
of Dominican tertiaries. In 1302 she
retired to a cell near the Dominican
friary at Pavia, and there she lived as a

recluse till the age of eighty, doing
penance and working miracles. Cult
approved in 1853.

SIDNEY HODGSON (Bl) M.
AC. Dec 10
d. 1591. A layman and a convert
hanged at Tyburn for relieving priests.
Beatified in 1929.

SIDONIUS APOLLINARIS (St) Bp.
RM. Aug 23
c.430–486. Caius Sollius Apollinaris
Sidonius was born at Lyons and ranks
as one of the last of the great Gallo-
Romans. He was first a soldier and
married the daughter of Avitus, emperor of the West. In 468 he served the
state as chief senator and prefect of
Rome. After his term of office he retired
to his country estate in Gaul, and while
there, although a married man, he was
promoted to the see of Clermont. As a
bishop he saved his people from the
fury of the Gothic invaders under
Alaric, for which purpose he not only
employed skilful diplomacy but also
introduced into his diocese and reorganized days of public prayers called
"Rogation Days". Sidonius was a man
of letters. He wrote Latin verse with
facility, but his letters are now much
more important than the twenty-four
poems of his which are still extant.

SIDONIUS (French: SAËNS) (St)
Ab. OSB.   AC. Nov 14
d. *c*.690. An Irishman who became a
monk at Jumièges under St Philibert
(644). Later he was appointed by St
Ouen first abbot of a small monastery
which that bishop had founded near
Rouen: this monastery was in after ages
called Saint-Saëns.

SIDRONIUS (St) M.   RM. July 11
d. *c*.270. A Roman martyr under Aurelian. In the Middle Ages his relics were

translated to Flanders. Another St Sidronius is venerated at Sens in France. The history of the two saints has been confused, and the traditions concerning them are untrustworthy.

SIDWELL (SATIVOLA) (St) VM.
AC. Aug 1
? Probably of British (not Anglo-Saxon) lineage. She is said to have lived in the West of England, and there are churches dedicated to her in Devonshire, chiefly in the neighbourhood of Exeter. Particulars of her life, and as to how she came to be venerated as a martyr, are lacking.

SIFFRED (SIFFREIN, SYFFROY, SUFFREDUS) (St) Bp.   AC. Nov 27
d. 540 (or 660 ?). A native of Albano, near Rome, who became a monk at Lérins and later bishop of Carpentras in Provence, where he is now venerated as the principal patron saint of the diocese.

SIGEBERT (St) King   AC. Feb 1
631–656. Sigebert III, son of Dagobert I, was king of Austrasia, i.e., Eastern France. Under the influence of Bl Pepin of Landen, of St Cunibert of Cologne and of other saintly persons, the young king grew up to be a clean-living and pious man. He died at the age of twenty-five. Though not a very successful monarch, he was revered as the founder of numerous hospitals, churches and monasteries. The abbeys of Stavelot and Malmédy were founded by him.

SIGEBERT (St) King M. OSB.
AC. Sept 27
d. 635. The first Christian king of East Anglia. He was baptized in France and, assisted by SS Felix and Fursey, he introduced Christianity into his realm. He took the monastic habit (at Dun-

wich ?), but was forcibly removed from the cloister by his warrior subjects and fell while leading them in battle against Penda of Mercia. His opponents being pagans, he was venerated as a martyr.

SIGFRID (St) Bp. OSB. AC. Feb 15
d. c.1045. An English priest and monk, probably of Glastonbury. At the invitation of King Olaf of Norway he went to that country as a missionary and fixed his residence at Wexiow. Great success attended his efforts, one of his converts being Olaf, king of Sweden. He is said to have been canonized by Pope Adrian IV.

SIGFRID (St) Ab. OSB. AC. Aug 22
d. 690. Monk and disciple of St Benet Biscop, by whom he was appointed abbot of Wearmouth in 686. They both died in the same year.

SIGFRID (Bl) Mk OSB. AC. Dec 15
d. 1215. A Benedictine monk of Reinhardsbrunn in Thuringia. From the year 1212 he lived as a hermit at Georgenberg.

SIGHARDUS (Bl) Ab. OSB. Cist.
AC. Apr 5
d. 1162. Cistercian monk of Jouy. In 1141 he founded and became the first abbot of Bonlieu, or Carbon-Blanc, near Bordeaux.

SIGIBALD (St) Bp.   AC. Oct 26
d. c.740. Bishop of Metz 716–c.740. He was promoter of learning, a builder of schools and abbeys (notably Neuweiter and Saint-Avold) and an able administrator.

SIGIRANUS (CYRAN, SIRAN, SIGRAM) (St) Ab. OSB. AC. Dec 5
d. c.655 (or 690?). Born of a noble Frankish family, he was first cup-bearer at the court of Clotaire II and later

archdeacon of Tours, of which city his father was bishop. Ultimately he became a monk and abbot-founder of Meobecq and of Lonrey (*Longoretum*). The latter was afterwards called after him Saint-Cyran.

SIGISBERT, Ab. and PLACID, M. (SS) AC. July 11
d. c.650 (or c.750 ?). Sigisbert was the abbot-founder of the great Benedictine abbey of Dissentis in Switzerland. He built it on land given him by St Placid, a wealthy landowner who joined the new community as a monk and was later murdered for defending the ecclesiastical rights of the abbey. Sigisbert survived him several years. Cult approved in 1905.

SIGISMUND (St) King, M. RM. May 1
d. 523. A Vandal by extraction and disposition, he was king of the Burgundians for one year. During that period he ordered one of his sons to be strangled for rebuking his step-mother. He atoned for this sin by giving generously to the Church and the poor. Being defeated in battle he disguised himself in a monk's habit and hid in a cell near the abbey of Agaunum, which he had built. There he was found by his enemies and put to death. He is honoured as a martyr.

SIGOLENA (SEGOULÈME) (St) Abs. OSB. AC. July 24
d. c.769. Daughter of a nobleman of Aquitaine and a widow early in life, she became a nun in the convent of Troclar on the Tarn, S. France, where she was later chosen abbess. She is co-patroness of the diocese of Albi.

SIGOLINUS (SIGHELM) (St) Ab. OSB. AC. Oct 29
d. c.670. Abbot of Stavelot and Malmédy, in Belgium.

SIGRADA (St) N. OSB. AC. Aug 8
d. c.678. Mother of SS Leodegarius and Warinus. In her widowhood she became a nun in the convent at Soissons. She died shortly after the martyrdom of her two sons, victims of the cruelty of Ebroin, mayor of the palace.

SILAS (or SILVANUS) (St) C. RM. July 13
1st cent. Silas, disciple and companion of St Paul, is mentioned both as Silas (Acts XV, 22; XVIII, 5) and as Silvanus (2 Cor. I, 19; 1 Thess. I, 1; 2 Thess. I, 1; 1 Pet. V, 12). Legend makes him the first bishop of Corinth. The Greeks distinguish Silas from Silvanus and commemorate both on July 20.

SILAUS (SILAVE, SILANUS) (St) Bp. AC. May 17
d. 1100. Said to have been an Irish bishop who died at Lucca on his way back from a pilgrimage to Rome. He is the subject of many extravagant legends.

SILIN (SULIAN) (St) C. AC. Sept 1
6th cent. A prince of N. Wales who became a hermit on an island off the coast of Anglesey. Later he became a missionary in Brittany.

SILLAN (SILVANUS) (St) Ab. AC. Feb 28
d. c.610. A disciple of St Comgall at Bangor, Co. Down, and his second successor as abbot of that monastery.

SILVANUS, LUKE and MUCIUS (SS) MM. RM. Feb 6
d. 312. Silvanus was bishop of Emesa in Phoenicia, Luke his deacon, and Mucius his lector. After long imprisonment the three were martyred under Maximian. The RM. identifies this Silvanus with the companion of St Tyrannio, q.v. (Feb 20).

SILVANUS (St) Bp.   RM. Feb 10
? Bishop of Terracina. He is described as a "Confessor", which would mean that he had suffered for the Faith, by imprisonment, or torture, or even death.

SILVANUS (St) M.   RM. Feb 18
See Lucius, Silvanus, etc.

SILVANUS (St) Bp. M. RM. Feb 20
See Tyrannio, Silvanus, etc.

SILVANUS (St) M.   RM. March 8
See Cyril, Rogatus, etc.

**SILVANUS and Comp. (SS) MM.
RM. May 4**
d. c.311. A group of forty-one martyrs from Egypt and Palestine, of whose martyrdom an account is given by Eusebius. Silvanus was bishop of Gaza and was sentenced to the mines in Palestine, but being too old for heavy work, he was beheaded instead, together with forty others similarly incapacitated.

SILVANUS (St) M.   RM. May 5
? A Roman martyr.

SILVANUS (St) H.   AC. May 15
4th cent. An actor who left the world and became a monk at Tabennisi under St Pachomius. After twenty years of monastic life he became lax and was excommunicated by Pachomius. This led to a second conversion and to the beginning of a new life of sanctification. He is honoured by the Greeks.

SILVANUS (St) M.   RM. May 24
See Zöellus, Servilius, etc.

SILVANUS (St) M.   RM. July 10
One of the Seven Brothers, MM., q.v.

SILVANUS (St) M.   RM. July 10
See Bianor and Silvanus.

SILVANUS (St) M.   RM. Sept 4
See Rufinus, Silvanus and Vitalicus.

SILVANUS (St)   RM. Sept 22
? A saint venerated from ancient times at Levroux, diocese of Bourges. Legend identifies him with the Zacchaeus of the gospel.

SILVANUS (St) M.   RM. Nov 5
See Domninus, Theotimus, etc.

SILVANUS (St) Bp.   RM. Dec 2
d. c.450. A monk at Constantinople. Later bishop of Troas in Phrygia.

**SILVERIUS (St) Pope, M.
RM. June 20**
d. c.537. A native of Frosinone in Campania and son of Pope St Hormisdas. He was only a sub-deacon when promoted to the Roman see. For refusing to countenance the restoration of the monophysite bishop Anthimos to the see of Constantinople he incurred the violent hatred of the empress Theodora. He was summarily condemned on a charge of high treason, deported to the East and finally banished to an islet off Naples, where he was left to die of privation, or perhaps actually murdered.

**SILVESTER (St) Bp.
AC. March 10**
c.420. A companion of St Palladius in the evangelization of Ireland.

SILVESTER (St) Ab.   AC. Apr 15
d. c.625. Second abbot of Moutier-Saint-Jean (Réome), diocese of Dijon.

**SILVESTER VENTURA (Bl) Mk.
OSB. Cam.   AC. June 9**
d. 1348. A native of Florence and a carder and bleacher of wool by trade. At the age of forty he joined the Camaldolese at S. Maria degli Angeli at Florence as a lay-brother, and served the com-

munity as cook. He was favoured with ecstasies and heavenly visions, and the angels were wont to come and cook for him. His spiritual advice was much sought after.

SILVESTER (St) Bp.   RM. Nov 20
d. *c*.525. Bishop of Châlons-sur-Saône from *c*.484 to *c*.525. St Gregory of Tours describes him as "the glory of confessors".

SILVESTER GOZZOLINI (St) Ab. OSB.   RM. Nov 26
1177–1267. Born at Osimo, he read law at Padua and Bologna, then became a secular priest and canon at Osimo. Later he retired to live as a hermit at Montefano, near Fabriano. In 1231, directed by St Benedict in a vision, he instituted a new congregation of Benedictines known from the colour of their habit as the Blue Benedictines. The congregation spread rapidly, and Silvester governed it "with unbounded wisdom and gentleness" for thirty-six years. It was approved by Innocent IV in 1247. St Silvester represents the new efflorescence of Benedictinism in Italy which synchronized with the foundation of the new orders of friars. He was equivalently canonized in 1598.

SILVESTER (St) Pope RM. Dec 31
d. 335. Silvester was a Roman, and governed the Church as Pope from 314 to 335. In 313 Constantine had, by the Edict of Milan, granted toleration to Christianity, and Silvester was therefore enabled to govern the Church free from persecution. Very little that is historically certain is known about his life, though there are various legends which connect his name with that of Constantine. During his pontificate the first general council was held at Nicaea to deal with the Arian heresy, and he was represented at the council by bishop Hosius of Cordova. The major part of his remains are enshrined at San Silvestro in Capite, Rome.

SILVINUS (St) Bp. OSB.
**   RM. Feb 17**
d. *c*.720. A courtier who gave up his worldly life and became a pilgrim. At Rome he was consecrated a regionary bishop and evangelized the district round Thérouanne. After some forty years of unceasing apostolate, a feature of which was the ransoming of numerous slaves, he retired to the Benedictine abbey of Auchy-les-Moines, where he lived the few remaining years of his life as a monk.

SILVINUS (St) Bp.   RM. Sept 12
d. *c*.550. Bishop of Verona. Nothing further is known about him.

SILVINUS (St) Bp.   RM. Sept 28
d. 444. Bishop of Brescia. He was raised to the episcopate in extreme old age.

SILVIUS (St) M.   RM. Apr 21
See Arator, Fortunatus, etc.

SIMBERT (SIMPERT, SINTBERT) (St) Bp. OSB.   AC. Oct 13
d. *c*.809. Pupil, monk and abbot at the abbey of Murbach, near Colmar in Alsace. In 778 he was made bishop of Augsburg, but retained the government of Murbach. He was a remarkable prelate in every respect, but especially as a restorer of ecclesiastical discipline and studies. Canonized by Nicholas V.

SIMEON STYLITES the ELDER (St) H.   RM. Jan 5
390–459. Born at Sis in Cilicia, the son of a shepherd and a shepherd himself in his youth. He joined a community of Syrian monks but was dismissed on account of his excessive austerities. He then became a hermit attaching himself

by chains to a rock, but so many people came to see him that, in order to gain greater solitude, he took to living on a platform mounted on a pillar. He gradually raised the height of the pillar till it reached sixty-six feet, and it was on the flat summit of this, about three feet in width, that he spent the remaining thirty-seven years of his life: hence the name Stylites, which means "raised on a pillar". For forty years he passed the whole of Lent without taking any food. His pillar stood on a hill on the borders of Syria and Cilicia, and the wild tribes of the desert flocked to him for baptism and spiritual advice. The above facts are quite authentic, being based on the testimony of eye-witnesses.

SIMEON the ANCIENT (St) C.
AC. Jan 28
d. c.390. He lived from early youth in a cave in Syria, and later founded two monasteries on Mt Sinai. He often visited his friend Palladius.

SIMEON (St) Bp. M.   RM. Feb 18
d. c.107. The son of Cleophas and a kinsman of our Lord (Mat. XIII, 55; Mk. VI, 3; John XIX, 25). He succeeded St James the Less in the see of Jerusalem and was crucified in extreme old age under Trajan.

SIMEON, ABDECHALAS, ANANIAS, USTHAZANES, PUSICIUS and Comp.   RM. Apr 21
d. 341. Persian martyrs under Shapur II. Simeon was bishop of Seleucia-Ctesiphon, Abdechalas and Ananias his priests, Usthazanes the king's tutor (a repentant apostate), and Pusicius the overseer of the king's workmen. They suffered with a band of over one hundred other Christians—bishops, priests and clerics of various ranks. Pusicius's virgin daughter was also martyred with them. The Acts are authentic.

SIMEON of TRÈVES (St) H. OSB.
RM. June 1
d. 1035. A native of Syracuse who, after being educated at Constantinople, lived as a hermit by the Jordan. He then joined a community at Bethlehem, but migrated later to Mt Sinai and again became a hermit, first in a small cave near the Red Sea and then on the summit of Sinai. Thence he was sent by the abbot of Mt Sinai on a mission to the duke of Normandy. After a series of adventures he settled at Trèves, where he was walled up by the archbishop and lived under the obedience of the abbot of the great Benedictine monastery of St Martin. It was the abbot of this monastery who assisted Simeon at his death and wrote his life. St Simeon was the second saint to be formally canonized (1042).

SIMEON SALUS (St) H.
RM. July 1
d. p.588. An Egyptian who lived as a hermit for close on thirty years in the desert of Sinai, by the Red Sea, and afterwards at Emesa in Phoenicia. He received the nickname *Salus* meaning fool on account of his eccentric behaviour.

SIMEON of PADOLIRONE (St) Mk.
OSB.   RM. July 26
d. 1016. An Armenian who, after spending some time as a hermit, went on pilgrimage to Jerusalem, Rome, Compostella and St Martin of Tours. He was renowned for the miracles he worked on these journeys. Finally he settled at the Cluniac abbey of Padolirone near Padua, where he passed the rest of his life. Canonized by Benedict VIII.

SIMEON STYLITES the YOUNGER (St) H.   RM. Sept 3
521–597. A native of Antioch who as a child joined the community of St John

Stylites. As a boy he began to live on a pillar, and he continued to live thus uninterruptedly for sixty-nine years, until his death. In his earlier years he did not always remain on the same pillar, but he remained on his last pillar (on the Wonderful Mountain, near Antioch) for forty-five years. He was ordained priest and celebrated Mass at a small altar on the pillar itself. He was consulted by prelates and princes, as well as the common people.

SIMEON SENEX (St)   RM. Oct 8
1st cent. The "just and devout man who awaited the consolation of Israel" (Luke II, 25), who took the Infant Saviour in his arms when he was brought to the Temple and who on that occasion sang the *Nunc dimittis* (ib.).

SIMEON of CAVA (Bl) Ab. OSB.
AC. Nov 16
d. 1141. Abbot of the great Benedictine abbey of La Cava, in S. Italy, from 1124 to 1141. He was highly esteemed by Pope Innocent II and by Roger II of Sicily. It was during his abbacy that Cava reached the peak of its splendour. Cult confirmed in 1928.

SIMILIAN (French: SAMBIN) (St)
Bp.   RM. June 16
d. 310. Third bishop of Nantes. St Gregory of Tours testifies to his sanctity.

SIMITRIUS and Comp. (SS) MM.
RM. May 26
d. *c.*159. A band of twenty-three Roman martyrs, arrested while assembled for prayer in the *titulus* or church of St Praxedes and beheaded without trial.

SIMON FIDATI of CASCIA (Bl) C.
OSA. Erem.   AC. Feb 3
d. 1348. Born at Cascia in Umbria, he joined the friar-hermits of St Augustine

and was a prominent figure as a writer, preacher and adviser in the life of most of the cities of central Italy. In recent times scholars have claimed to find in his book *De Gestis Domini Salvatoris* the source of several of Luther's heretical doctrines.

SIMON of ST BERTIN (Bl) Ab.
OSB.   AC. Feb 4
d. 1148. Successively monk of Saint-Bertin, abbot of Auchy, and abbot of Saint-Bertin (1131). His election as abbot of Saint-Bertin was contested, and he was unable to take up his office until 1138.

SIMON of TRENT (St) M.
RM. March 24
d. 1474. A child living at Trent in N. Italy who is said to have been murdered by Jews at Eastertide out of hatred of Christ. The confession of the Jews was obtained under torture. The trial was reviewed at Rome by Sixtus IV in 1478 but he did not authorize the cult of St Simon. This however was done by Sixtus V in 1588, largely on account of the miracles. In 1965 the Sacred Congregation of Rites forbade all future veneration. The cause of the child's death is considered quite uncertain.

SIMON RINALDUCCI (Bl) S. OSA.
AC. Apr 20
d. 1322. A native of Todi, he became an Austin friar, a famous preacher, and for a time provincial of Umbria. He kept silence under an unjust accusation rather than cause scandal among his brethren. Cult confirmed in 1833.

SIMON STOCK (St) C. OC.
AC. May 16
d. 1265. Born at Aylesford in Kent, he joined the Carmelites and eventually (1247) became the sixth general of the order. As such he was instrumental in

establishing houses at the principal university cities of Europe: Cambridge (1248), Oxford (1253), Paris (1260), Bologna (id.), and in modifying the rule so that the Carmelites became an order of mendicant friars rather than of hermits. According to a Carmelite tradition our Lady gave Simon the brown scapular with all the privileges attached to it. Though never formally canonized, Simon is venerated throughout the Church as a canonized saint. He died at Bordeaux.

SIMON ACOSTA and SIMON LOPEZ (BB) MM. SJ.   AC. July 15
d. 1570. The former was born at Oporto in Portugal and became a Jesuit lay-brother; the latter was a native of Ourem, also in Portugal, and was a Jesuit cleric. Both formed part of the missionary expedition of Bl Ignatius Azevedo, q.v.

SIMON of LIPNICZA (Bl) C. OFM.
AC. July 30
d. 1482. A native of Lipnicza in Poland who, as a result of hearing a sermon by St John Capistran, joined the Friars Minor and became a powerful preacher himself. He died while tending the sick during a plague at Cracow. Beatified in 1685.

SIMON KIOTA and Comp. (BB) MM.   AC. Aug 16
d. 1625. A Japanese, member of one of the old Christian families of Bungo and an officer in the royal army. He served as a catechist and at the age of sixty was crucified with his wife and three companions (Bl Thomas Ghengoro, his wife and their child James) at Cocura. Beatified in 1867.

SIMON of CRESPY (St) Mk. OSB.
AC. Sept 18
d. c.1080. Count of Crespy in Valois and a descendant of Charlemagne. He was brought up at the court of William the Conqueror. The sight of his father's decomposing body led him to desire the monastic life, and with William's leave, though the latter wished him to marry, he set out for Rome. On the way thither he stopped at the Benedictine abbey of Condat in the Jura and there took the habit. After his profession he was employed by St Gregory VII and others in bringing about reconciliations between princes and potentates. It was while he was at Rome engaged in a mission of this kind that he died, being attended at his deathbed by Pope Gregory.

SIMON of GENOA (Bl) A. OSB. Cam.   AC. Sept 18
d. 1292. A Genoese who became a hermit at Camaldoli.

SIMON de ROJAS (Bl) C. O. Trin.
AC. Sept 28
1522–1624. A native of Valladolid who became a Trinitarian, in which order he became a superior and a famous missionary. In later life he was appointed confessor at the court of Philip III and tutor to the royal family. Beatified in 1766.

SIMON (St) Apostle   RM. Oct 28
1st cent. In the gospels he is surnamed "the Cananean", i.e., "the Zealot". His name occurs only in the lists of the apostles. The tradition of the West places the scene of his labours in Egypt and Mesopotamia, but there are several other different traditions among the Christians of the East, and nothing positive can be stated about his life and activities.

SIMON BALLACHI (Bl) C. OP.
AC. Nov 3
d. 1319. Born at Sant' Arcangelo near Rimini, the son of Count Ballachi and

nephew of two archbishops of Rimini. At the age of twenty-seven he became a Dominican lay-brother in his native city and was remarkable for his extraordinary austerities. Cult confirmed in 1821.

SIMON of AULNE (Bl) C. OSB. Cist.   AC. Nov 6

d. 1215. A Cistercian lay-brother at Aulne renowned for his gift of mystical prayer, his visions and his ecstasies. On this account he was invited to Rome by Innocent III.

SIMON YEMPO (Bl) M. AC. Dec 4

d. 1623. A native of Japan who became a Buddhist monk. Having been converted to Christianity and become a lay catechist, he was burnt alive at Yeddo. Beatified in 1867.

SIMON HOA (Bl) M.   AC. Dec 12

d. 1840. A native of Cochin-China, a physician and mayor of his village. He was attached to the Foreign Missions of Paris. After most cruel tortures he was beheaded for the Faith. Beatified in 1900.

SIMPLICIAN (St) Bp. RM. Aug 16

d. 400. A friend and adviser of St Ambrose, whom he succeeded in the see of Milan. He was already an old man and governed the see only three years. He played a leading part in the conversion of St Augustine, by whom he was always remembered with deep gratitude.

SIMPLICIAN (St) M.   RM. Dec 31

See Stephen, Pontian, etc.

SIMPLICIUS (St) Pope
                         RM. March 10

d. 483. A native of Tivoli who was pope from 468 to 483. He upheld the decrees of the council of Chalcedon and supported the Eastern Catholics against the Monophysite heretics, who were backed by three successive Byzantine emperors.

SIMPLICIUS and Comp. (SS) MM.
                         RM. May 10

See Calepodius, Palmatius, etc.

SIMPLICIUS (St) M.   RM. May 15

d. 304. A martyr of Sardinia, buried alive under Diocletian.

SIMPLICIUS of BOURGES (St) Bp.
                         AC. June 16

d. 477 (March 1). He was already married and the father of a large family when the bishops of the province raised him to the see of Bourges. He defended the Church against the Arian Visigoths and the ambitions of lay magnates.

SIMPLICIUS of AUTUN (St) Bp.
                         RM. June 24

d. c.360. A married man who lived a virginal life with his wife and was raised to the see of Autun. As a bishop he worked zealously and successfully to uproot paganism.

SIMPLICIUS, FAUSTINUS and BEATRIX (SS) MM.   RM. July 29

d. 303. Said to have been two brothers and their sister martyred in Rome under Diocletian. Their Acts are not trustworthy.

SIMPLICIUS, CONSTANTIUS and VICTORIAN (SS) MM.
                         RM. Aug 26

? According to the RM., Simplicius and his two sons were martyred under Aurelian, but it seems that three separate martyrs have been artificially grouped by a hagiographer, Simplicius of Rome, Victorianus of Amiternum and Constantius of Perugia (q.v. Jan 29).

SIMPLICIUS (St) Ab. OSB.
                         AC. Oct 22

d. c.570. A disciple of St Benedict and third abbot of Montecassino. His relics were elevated in 1071.

SIMPLICIUS (St) M.   RM. Nov 8
See Four Crowned Martyrs.

SIMPLICIUS of VERONA (St) Bp.
RM. Nov 20
d. c.535. Bishop of Verona.

SIMPLICIUS (St) M.   RM. Dec 18
See Quintus, Simplicius, and Comp.

SINAI (Martyrs of)(SS) RM. Jan 14
See Isaias, Sabas and Comp.

SINCHEALL (St) Ab. AC. March 26
5th cent. A disciple of St Patrick. Abbot-founder of the monastery and school at Killeigh, Offaly, Ireland, where he had one hundred and fifty monks under his direction.

SINDIMIUS (St) M.   RM. Dec 19
See Cyriacus, Paulillus, etc.

SINDULPHUS of REIMS (St) H.
RM. Oct 20
d. 660. A native of Gascony who lived as a hermit at Aussonce, near Reims.

SINDULPHUS of VIENNE (St) Bp.
RM. Dec 10
d. c.669. The thirty-first bishop of Vienne in Gaul.

SIRAN (St) Ab. OSB.   AC. Dec 5
Otherwise Sigiranus, q.v.

SIRICIUS (St) Pope   RM. Nov 26
d. 399. A native of Rome who ruled the Church from 384 to 399. His episcopate is very important for the development of the Roman primacy. His letter—called the first papal decretal—to Archbishop Himerius of Tarragona marks an epoch in the history of the papal authority.

SIRIDION (St) Bp.   RM. Jan 2
? Probably a scribe's error for Isidore. See Isidore of Antioch.

SIRMIUM (Martyrs of) (SS)
RM. Feb 23 and Apr 9
d. c.303. Two anonymous groups of martyrs are catalogued in the RM. as having suffered under Diocletian at Sirmium, now Mitrovica in the Balkans: (i) a band of seventy-two, on Feb 23, put to death probably in 303; and (ii) a group of seven maidens commemorated on Apr 9 and probably martyred in the same year.

SISEBUTUS (St) Ab. OSB.
AC. March 15
d. 1082. Abbot of the Benedictine monastery of Cardena in the diocese of Burgos, Spain. Under him the abbey became a powerful focus of ecclesiastical and civil life. He gave shelter to the Cid (Rodrigo Diaz de Vivar), the celebrated hero of the Christian Spanish Reconquest.

SISENANDUS (St) M.
RM. July 16
d. 851. Born at Badajoz in Estremadura, he became a deacon in the church of St Acisclus at Cordova. He was beheaded under Abderrahman II.

SISINIUS, DIOCLETIUS and FLORENTIUS (SS) MM.
RM. May 11
d. 303. Martyrs at Osimo, near Ancona, under Diocletian. They were stoned to death at the same time as the better known Roman priest, St Anthimus.

SISINIUS, MARTYRIUS and ALEXANDER (SS) MM.
RM. May 29
d. 397. Said to have been Cappadocians, received by St Vigilius of Trent on the recommendation of St Ambrose and sent to evangelize the Tyrol. They were martyred by a pagan mob who were celebrating the festival of the Ambarvalia.

SISINIUS (St) Bp.   **RM. Nov 23**
d. *p*.325. Bishop of Cyzicus and a confessor of the Faith under Diocletian. He was dragged by wild horses, but survived and was present at the council of Nicaea.

SISINIUS (St) M.   **RM. Nov 29**
See Saturninus and Sisinius.

SISOES (St) H.   **AC. July 4**
d. *c*.429. He lived as a hermit in Egypt for sixty-two years. To some extent he resembled St Antony in the influence he exercised.

SITHIAN (St) Bp.   **AC. July 15**
Otherwise Seduinus, possibly identical with Swithun, q.v.

SIVIARD (St) Ab. OSB.
    RM. March 1
d. *c*.729. Benedictine monk at Saint-Calais, on the R. Anisole. He succeeded his own father as abbot of the monastery. To him we owe an interesting life of St Calais, founder of the abbey.

SIXTUS I (XYSTUS) Pope, M.
    RM. Apr 3
d. 127. A Roman. Pope from 117 to 127. The martyrologies refer to him as a martyr but there are no *Acta*.

SIXTUS II (XYSTUS) Pope, and Comp. MM.   **RM. Aug 6**
d. 258. He reigned for one year: 257–258. While preaching in the catacomb of Praetextatus during the celebration of the liturgy he was seized with his deacons Felicissimus and Agapitus and martyred. His name is mentioned in the canon of the Roman Mass. The RM. commemorates with them Januarius, Magnus, Vincent and Stephen, subdeacons, and Quartus, all as martyrs. Quartus owes his existence to a bad manuscript in which "diaconus Quar-

tus" was written for "diacones quattuor". It is probable that St Sixtus suffered with all his seven deacons, the six mentioned today, and, later, St Laurence.

SIXTUS III (XYSTUS) Pope
    RM. Aug 19
d. 440. Pope from 432 to 440. A Roman by birth. As pope he is best remembered for having opposed Nestorianism and Pelagianism and for having restored several Roman basilicas, among them S. Maria Maggiore.

SIXTUS (XYSTUS) of REIMS (St) Bp.   **RM. Sept 1**
d. *c*.300. First bishop of Reims, *c*.290–300. He was sent from Rome and established his see at Soissons before moving it to Reims.

SLEBHENE (SLEBHINE) (St) Ab.
    AC. March 2
d. 767. An Irish monk who was abbot of Iona from 752 to 767.

SMARAGDUS (St) M.   **RM. Aug 8**
See Cyriacus, Largus, etc.

SOBEL (St) M.   **RM. Aug 5**
See Cantidius, Cantidian and Sobel.

SOCRATES and DIONYSIUS (SS) MM.   **RM. Apr 19**
d. 275. Martyrs of Pamphylia, stabbed to death under Aurelian.

SOCRATES and STEPHEN (SS) MM.   **RM. Sept 17**
d. *c*.304. Alleged British martyrs under Diocletian. The RM. assigns them to Britain, but it seems certain that Socrates was martyred in Abretania, a province of Mysia in Asia Minor, and that a scribe changed the name to Britannia. Bithynia has also been suggested as the place of martyrdom.

SOLA (SOL, SOLUS, SUOLO) (St)
H. OSB.   **AC. Dec 3**
d. 794. An Anglo-Saxon monk and
priest who followed St Boniface to
Germany and lived as a hermit first near
Fulda under the obedience of that
abbey and later near Eichstätt. Finally
he settled on a piece of land bestowed
on him by Charlemagne, on which he
founded the abbey of Solnhofen as a
dependency of Fulda.

SOLANGIA (SOLANGE) (St) VM.
                                      AC. May 10
d. c.880. A poor shepherdess of the
neighbourhood of Bourges, who, for
resisting the attempts of the local lord
on her chastity, was brutally murdered
by him.

SOLEMNIS (SOLEINE) (St) Bp.
                                      RM. Sept 25
d. c.511. Bishop of Chartres c.490–511.
He was present at the baptism of Clovis.

SOLINA (St) VM.   **AC. Oct 17**
d. c.290. A Gascon maiden who escaped
to Chartres to avoid marriage to a pagan.
She was beheaded at Chartres.

SOLOCHON and Comp. (SS) MM.
                                      RM. May 17
d. 305. Three Egyptian soldiers in the
imperial army, stationed at Chalcedon.
They were clubbed to death for the
Faith under Maximian.

SOLOMON (St) M. RM. March 13
See Rudericus and Salomon.

SOLOMON I (St) M.   AC. June 25
d. 434. Born in Cornwall, husband of
St Gwen and father of St Cuby (Cybi).
He reigned as a kinglet in Brittany and
was assassinated by heathen malcontents among his subjects.

SOLOMON III (Breton: SELYF)
(St) M.   **AC. June 25**

d. 874. King of Brittany and a brave,
though at times brutal, warrior against
Franks, Northmen and his own rebellious subjects. The Bretons count him
among their many national heroes. He
did penance for the crimes of his youth,
and when he was assassinated the
people at once acclaimed him a martyr.

SOLOMON (SALOMON, SALONI-
US) (St) Bp.   **RM. Sept 28**
d. p.269. First bishop of Genoa. His
true name was Salonius: it was changed
into Salomon by a scribe's error.

SOLUTOR (St) M.   RM. Nov 13
See Valentine, Solutor and Victor.

SOLUTOR (St) M.   RM. Nov 20
See Octavius, Solutor and Adventor.

SOPATRA (St) V.   RM. Nov 9
See Eustolia and Sopatra.

SOPHIA (St) VM.   RM. Apr 30
d. c.250. A maiden of Fermo in central
Italy, martyred under Decius.

SOPHIA and IRENE (SS) MM.
                                      RM. Sept 18
d. c.?200. Martyrs beheaded in Egypt.

SOPHIA (St) W.   RM. Sept 30
d c.138. The mother of the virgin martyrs Faith, Hope and Charity, who,
according to a Roman tradition, suffered
at Rome under Hadrian. Three days
later Sophia, while praying at their
tomb, herself passed peacefully away.
The story seems to have come from the
East and is thought by some to be an
allegorical explanation of the cult of the
Divine Wisdom, from whom proceed
Faith, Hope and Charity.

SOPHONIAS (ZEPHANIAH) (St)
Prophet   **RM. Dec 3**
7th cent. B.C. Said to have been of the

tribe of Simeon. He prophesied in Judaea in the days of King Josiah: his most remarkable prophecy regards the ultimate conversion of the Jews. There are no trustworthy traditions concerning him.

SOPHRONIUS (St) Bp.
RM. March 11
d. *c.*639. A Syrian from Damascus who became patriarch of Jerusalem in 633. He is an ecclesiastical writer of distinction. His life's work, however, was the condemnation of Monothelism. He was engaged in this campaign when the Saracens occupied Jerusalem and drove him from his see (638). He is said to have died of grief shortly after.

SOPHRONIUS (St) Bp.   RM. Dec 8
6th cent. An alleged bishop of Cyprus.

SOSIPATER (St)   RM. June 25
2nd cent. A kinsman and disciple of St Paul (Rom. XVI, 21). He accompanied the apostle on some of his journeys, and tradition connects his later life with the island of Corfu.

SOSIUS (St) M.   RM. Sept 19
See Januarius and Comp.

SOSTENEO (St) C.   RM. May 3
One of the Seven Founders of the Servite Order, q.v.

SOSTHENES and VICTOR (SS) MM.   RM. Sept 10
d. 307. Martyrs at Chalcedon under Maximian. They were among the executioners appointed to torture St Euphemia and were converted through her prayers and the example of her fortitude.

SOSTHENES (St)   RM. Nov 28
1st cent. The ruler of the synagogue at Corinth mentioned in Acts XVIII, 17.

He became a disciple of St Paul and is probably the "brother" mentioned in 1 Cor. I, 1. Greek tradition makes him the first bishop of Colophon in Asia Minor.

SOSTRATUS, SPIRUS, ERACLIUS, EPERENTIUS and CECILIA (SS) MM.   AC. July 8
? 4th cent. Martyrs of Syrmium, Pannonia.

SOTER (St) Pope, M.   RM. Apr 22
d. 174. A native of Fondi, near Gaeta. He was pope from 166 to 174 and was an active opponent of Montanism. He is supposed to have died a martyr.

SOTERIS (St) VM.   RM. Feb 10
d. 304. A Roman maiden martyred under Diocletian. She seems to have been a sister of the great-great-grandmother of St Ambrose, by whom she is often mentioned.

SOZON (St) M.   RM. Sept 7
d. *c.*304. A shepherd in his native Cilicia. At a pagan celebration he pulled off the golden hand of an idol, broke it up and distributed the pieces among the poor. He was forthwith burnt at the stake.

SPECIOSUS (St) Mk. OSB.
RM. March 15
d. *c.*555. A wealthy landowner of Campania who, with his brother Gregory, received the habit from St Benedict at Montecassino. He was attached to the new foundation at Terracina, but died at Capua while on an errand undertaken for the benefit of his monastery.

SPERANDEA (SPERANDIA) (St) Abs. OSB.   AC. Sept 11
d. 1276. A relative of St Ubald of Gubbio. She became a Benedictine at Cingoli, in the Marches of Ancona, and

eventually abbess of her nunnery. She is venerated as the patron saint of Cingoli.

SPERATUS (St) M.   RM. July 17
See Scillitan Martyrs.

SPES (St) Ab.   RM. March 28
d. *c.*513. An abbot of Campi in central Italy. He was totally blind for forty years, but fifteen days before his death his eyesight was restored.

SPES (HOPE, ELPIS) (St) VM.
RM. Aug 1
See Faith, Hope and Charity.

SPEUSIPPUS, ELEUSIPPUS, MELEUSIPPUS and LEONILLA (SS) MM.   RM. Jan 17
d. 175. According to the legend, which probably has no basis in fact, these saints were three brothers born at one birth, natives of Cappadocia, martyred with their grandmother Leonilla under Marcus Aurelius. Their alleged relics were brought to Langres, where their church bears the name of St Geome (Holy Twins).

SPINULUS (SPINULA, SPIN) (St) Ab. OSB.   AC. Nov 5
d. 707 (or 720). A Benedictine monk of Moyenmoutier under St Hidulphus. Later he became the abbot-founder of the small abbey of Bégon-Celle (now Saint-Blaisien).

SPIRIDION (St) Bp.   RM. Dec 14
d. *c.*348. He began life as a shepherd and rose to be bishop of Tremithus in his native island of Cyprus. Under Diocletian he was condemned to lose an eye and forced to labour in the mines. He survived the persecution and was one of the venerable "confessors of the Faith" present at the council of Nicaea, where he was a strong opponent of Arianism.

STACHYS (St) Bp.   RM. Oct 31
1st cent. The Christian saluted by St Paul (Rom. XVI, 9) as "my beloved". The tradition is that St Andrew consecrated him bishop of Byzantium.

STACTEUS (St) M.   RM. July 18
One of the alleged sons of St Symphorosa, q.v.

STACTEUS (St) M.   RM. Sept 28
? A Roman martyr of whom no particulars are available.

STANISLAUS (St) Bp. M.
RM. May 7
1030–1079. Stanislaus Szczepanovsky was born near Cracow and educated at Gnesen and Paris. In 1072 he was raised to the see of Cracow. He excommunicated King Boleslaus the Cruel for his evil life, and that monarch in consequence slew the saint with his own hand while he was celebrating Mass. Pope St Gregory VII laid Poland under an interdict and Boleslaus fled the country and died a fugitive in Hungary. Stanislaus was canonized in 1253. Some Polish historians contend that the saint was plotting to dethrone Boleslaus.

STANISLAUS KOSTKA (St) C. SJ.
RM. Aug 15
1550–1568. Born at Rostkovo in Poland, the son of a senator, he was sent in 1563 to Vienna to study at the Jesuit college recently established in that city. Despite fierce opposition from his family he resolved to become a Jesuit himself. St Peter Canisius sent him to Rome, where he was received into the Jesuit novice-ship by St Francis Borgia in Oct 1567. He died within a year, but during that brief period he had gained a reputation for angelic innocence. Canonized in 1726.

STEPHANA de QUINZANI (Bl) V. OP.   AC. Jan 2

1457–1530. She was born near Brescia and at the age of fifteen joined the Dominican tertiaries. After living at home for many years she founded a convent called San Paolo, near Soncino, of which she became first abbess. She was noted for her ecstasies and for the marks of the sacred stigmata, which were attested by many eye-witnesses. Cult confirmed by Benedict XIV.

STEPHEN

Note. Stephen is the English variant of the Graeco-Latin Stephanus (crowned). Other modern variants of the same name are: Italian, Stefano; French, Etienne; Spanish, Esteban; German, Stephan; Hungarian, Istvan.

STEPHEN du BOURG (St) O. Cart.   PC. Jan 4

d. 1118. A canon of St Rufus at Valence who became one of the first companions of St Bruno at the foundation of the Grande-Chartreuse. He was sent (1116) to found the charterhouse at Meyria, and there he died.

STEPHEN of LIÈGE (Bl) Ab. OSB.   AC. Jan 13

d. 1059. A canon of St Denis, Liège, who became a Benedictine monk at St Vannes, Verdun. Later he returned to Liège as abbot-founder of St Laurence.

STEPHEN BELLESINI (Bl) C. OSA. Erem.   AC. Feb 3

1774–1840. A native of Trent who joined the Augustinian hermits at Bologna and studied there and at Rome. Owing to the disturbances following the French Revolution he retired to his home in the Trentino, where he held the post of government inspector of schools. At the earliest opportunity, however, he returned to the religious life and was appointed novice master in Rome and later parish priest at the shrine of our Lady at Genazzano. Here he died as a result of his devoted ministrations to the victims of the cholera epidemic. Beatified in 1904.

STEPHEN of GRANDMONT (St) Ab.   RM. Feb 8

1046–1124. Born at Thiers in Auvergne, the son of the lord of the district, he accompanied his father at the age of twelve to the tomb of St Nicholas of Bari. He fell ill at Benevento and remained there, being educated by Archbishop Milo. On his return to France he founded at Murat a congregation of Benedictine monk-hermits on the model of those he had seen in Calabria. He ruled them for forty-six years but does not seem ever to have become a monk himself. After his death the large community migrated to Grandmont, whence the name of Grandmontines given to this new branch of the Benedictine order. Stephen was canonized in 1189 at the request of Henry II of England.

STEPHEN CUÉNOT (Bl) Bp. M.   AC. Feb 8

1802–1861. Born at Beaulieu, France, he joined the society of Foreign Missions at Paris and was sent to Annam. In 1833 he was appointed vicar apostolic of E. Cochin-China, receiving episcopal consecration at Singapore. After fifteen years more of fruitful labour he was one of the first to be arrested on the outbreak of the persecution of 1861. He died in prison (perhaps from poison) on Nov 4, shortly before the date fixed for his execution. Beatified in 1909.

STEPHEN of LYONS (St) Bp.   RM. Feb 13

d. 512. Bishop of Lyons. He was active in converting the Arian Burgundians to the Catholic faith.

STEPHEN of RIETI (St) Ab.
RM. Feb 13
d. *c*.590. An abbot at Rieti whom St Gregory the Great describes as "rude of speech but of cultured life".

STEPHEN of OBAZINE (St) Ab.
OSB. Cist.   AC. March 8
d. 1154. Stephen and another priest withdrew into the forest of Obazine near Tulle, France, to lead a solitary life. When disciples wished to join them they obtained leave of the bishop of Limoges to build a monastery. The new abbey had no written rule, and St Stephen arranged for its affiliation to the Cistercian order, and was himself blessed as its first abbot.

STEPHEN of PALESTRINA (Bl)
Card. Bp. OSB. Cist. PC. March 17
d. 1144. A monk of Clairvaux who was promoted to the cardinalate and to the see of Palestrina (1141). By Cistercian writers he is always called either saint or blessed.

STEPHEN IX or X (Bl) Pope, OSB.
PC. March 29
d. 1058. A distinguished ecclesiastic he became a monk of Montecassino. In 1057 he first became abbot of Montecassino and then Pope. His pontificate though brief was vigorous and worthy.

STEPHEN (St) M.   RM. Apr 1
See Victor and Stephen.

STEPHEN and HILDEBRAND (BB)
MM. OSB. Cist.   PC. Apr 11
d. 1209. Two Cistercians, the former an abbot, the latter a monk, slain by the Albigenses at Saint-Gilles in Languedoc. They are venerated at Saint-Gilles, though their cult has not been officially confirmed.

STEPHEN HARDING (St) Ab. OSB.
Cist.   RM. Apr 17
d. 1137. An English monk of Sherborne who, after a pilgrimage to Rome, joined St Robert at Molesmes and with him migrated to Cîteaux. Here he became successively sub-prior under St Robert, prior under St Alberic, and third abbot (1109). As such he was responsible for the original constitutions of the Cistercians, as also for the Charter of Charity which he presented to the general chapter of Cîteaux in 1119. To him therefore, much more than to St Robert, the Cistercians owe their definite status as a new branch of the Benedictines. It was Stephen who received St Bernard and his thirty companions at Cîteaux and two years later sent him to become the abbot-founder of Clairvaux and the principal exponent of the Cistercian ideal. St Stephen was canonized in 1623.

STEPHEN de PÉTERVÁRAD (Bl)
M. OFM.   AC. Apr 22
d. 1334. A Hungarian Franciscan in the Balkans. Being tortured by the Mohammedan Tartars, he denied his faith, but recovering his courage, solemnly professed it before the Khan, and was cruelly put to death.

STEPHEN of ANTIOCH (St) Bp. M.
RM. Apr 25
d. 481. A patriarch of Antioch who was a special target for the fury of the Monophysite heretics. In the end they attacked him at the altar, struck him down and flung his body into the River Orontes.

STEPHEN (St) M.   RM. Apr 27
See Castor and Stephen.

STEPHEN of NARBONNE and
Comp. (BB) MM.   AC. May 28
d. 1242. Stephen was a member of the Inquisition of Toulouse: he was a Franciscan. Together with eleven com-

panions — Benedictines, Franciscans, Dominicans, and one secular priest— he was murdered at Avignonet by the Albigensian heretics. Cult approved in 1866.

STEPHEN of CORVEY (St) Bp. M. OSB. AC. June 2
d. ? 1075. A monk of Corvey in Saxony who was appointed regionary bishop in Sweden, where he worked as a missionary with signal success. He was the first to plant the faith on the shores of the Sound. He was martyred, probably at Nora.

STEPHEN BANDELLI (Bl) C. OP. AC. June 12
d. 1450. Born at Castelnuovo, diocese of Piacenza, where he became a Dominican. He was an eminent preacher and reformer. Cult approved in 1856.

STEPHEN of REGGIO (St) Bp. M. AC. July 5
1st cent. Said to have been ordained first bishop of Reggio by St Paul and to have been martyred under Nero. It is only since the 17th century that this story has gained currency and that he has been venerated as the principal patron of Reggio.

STEPHEN de ZUDAIRA (Bl) M. SJ. AC. July 15
d. 1570. Born at Viscaya in Spain, he became a Jesuit lay-brother and formed one of the martyr-band headed by Bl Ignatius de Azevedo, q.v.

STEPHEN del LUPO (St) Ab. OSB. AC. July 19
d. 1191. Benedictine monk of San Liberatore di Majella, and afterwards abbot-founder of St Peter's at Vallebona, near Manopello, in Italy. He is said to have been befriended by a wolf: hence his nickname of "del lupo".

STEPHEN I (St) Pope, M. RM. Aug 2
d. 257. A Roman of the *gens Julia*. He became pope in 254, and during his short pontificate he was occupied with the question of the re-baptizing of heretics. He invoked the apostolic tradition in favour of the Roman practice and met with stout opposition from St Cyprian. Tradition says that he was beheaded while seated in his chair during the celebration of his Mass in the catacombs, but the earliest liturgical documents present him as a bishop and confessor.

STEPHEN (St) M. RM. Aug 6
See Sixtus II and Comp.

STEPHEN of CARDEÑA and Comp. (SS) MM. OSB. RM. Aug 6
d. 872. Abbot of the great Castilian monastery of Cardeña, near Burgos, in which were housed over two hundred monks. The abbot and community were slain by Saracens from S. Spain. The cult was approved in 1603 and Card. Baronius composed the proper lessons for their office. As these martyrs are first heard of in an inscription of the 13th century, there is considerable doubt as to their existence; the name Stephen for the abbot is an even later addition.

STEPHEN of HUNGARY (St) King RM. Sept 2
d. 1038. On the death of his father Geza (997) Stephen succeeded as sovereign of the Magyars of Hungary. He married Gisela, a sister of the emperor St Henry II, and they set their hands to the common task of christianizing their people. With the help of the Holy See and as a result of numerous victories over external and internal foes, Stephen gradually welded the Magyars into a national unity. He organized dioceses and founded abbeys (among them the

great Benedictine abbey of Pannon-halma, which still stands), and secured the services of prominent foreign monks, notably of St Gerard Sagredo, abbot of San Giorgio Maggiore at Venice, who became the tutor of the king's son, the young St Emeric. The latter died in the prime of life, and the declining years of St Stephen were darkened by many misfortunes and difficulties. His relics were enshrined in 1083 by order of St Gregory VII. To this day the Magyars consider him their greatest national saint and hero.

STEPHEN of CHATILLON (St) Bp. O. Cart.   **AC. Sept 7**
d. 1208. Born at Lyons of the noble family of the Chatillons, he entered the charterhouse of Portes, where he became prior in 1196. In 1203 he was raised to the see of Dié. Cult approved in 1907.

STEPHEN PONGRACZ (Bl) M. SJ.   **AC. Sept 7**
See Mark, Stephen and Melchior.

STEPHEN of PERUGIA (St) Ab. OSB.   **AC. Sept 16**
d. 1026. Third abbot of the Benedictine monastery of St Peter at Perugia, where an altar is dedicated to him.

STEPHEN (St) M.   RM. Sept 17
See Socrates and Stephen.

STEPHEN of CAJAZZO (St) Bp. OSB.   **AC. Oct 29**
935–1023. Born at Macerata and educated at Capua, he was appointed abbot of San Salvatore Maggiore and later, in 979, bishop of Cajazzo. He is now venerated as the principal patron of the city and diocese.

STEPHEN of APT (St) Bp.
                                                            PC. Nov 6
975–1046. Born at Agde, he was elected bishop of Apt, S. France, in 1010. He rebuilt the cathedral.

STEPHEN (St) M.   RM. Nov 21
See Honorius, Eutychius and Stephen.

STEPHEN (St) M.   RM. Nov 22
See Mark and Stephen.

STEPHEN, BASIL, PETER, ANDREW and Comp. (SS) MM.
                                                            RM. Nov 28
d. 764. St Stephen, surnamed "the Younger", was born at Constantinople in 714 and became a monk and abbot of Mt St Auxentius. He firmly opposed the fanatical iconoclasm of the emperor Constantine Copronymus. When all attempts to win him over to heresy had failed, the emperor had him put to death, along with SS Basil, Peter, Andrew and a band of over three hundred monks.

STEPHEN (St) M.   RM. Dec 3
See Claudius, Crispin, etc.

STEPHEN VINH (Bl) M.
                                                            AC. Dec 19
d. 1839. A peasant of Tonkin and a Dominican tertiary. Strangled at Ninh-Tai with four companions. Beatified in 1900.

STEPHEN the DEACON (St) Protomartyr   RM. Dec 26 (Aug 3)
d. 33. The disciple chosen by the apostles, "full of faith and the Holy Ghost" as the first of the seven deacons (Acts VI, 1–5). He was stoned to death by the Jews at the instigation of the Sanhedrin, thus becoming the Christian protomartyr. His dying prayer obtained the conversion of St Paul, who was actively engaged in his martyrdom. The RM. commemorates on Aug 3 the finding of the reputed relics of St Stephen at Kafr Gamala in 415, and on May 7 their translation to Rome.

STEPHEN of LORÁNDHÁZA (Bl) Mk.   **AC. Nov 6**
d. 1519. General of the Hungarian Pauline Order, and biographer of St Paul the Hermit. He died in the monastery of St Peter in Sümeg.

STEPHEN (Bl) Mk.   **AC. Dec 8**
d. 1300. Third General of the Pauline Order.

STEPHEN, PONTIAN, ATTALUS, FABIAN, CORNELIUS, SEXTUS, FLOS, QUINTIAN, MINERVINUS and SIMPLICIAN (SS) MM.
                                  RM. Dec 31
? Catalogued as martyrs of Catania in Sicily.

STERCATIUS (St) M.   RM. July 24
See Victor, Stercatius and Antinogenes.

STILLA (Bl) V.   **AC. July 19**
d. c.1141. Daughter of Count Wolfgang II of Abenberg and a sister of Archbishop Conrad I of Salzburg. She founded the church of St Peter at Abenberg, near Nuremburg, where she was buried and venerated as a saint. Cult confirmed in 1927.

STRATON, PHILIP and EUTYCHIAN (SS) MM.   **RM. Aug 17**
d. c.301? Citizens of Nicomedia, they were burnt at the stake. In most MSS a fourth martyr is added, by name Cyprian. Their Acts have no value.

STRATON (St) M.   **RM. Sept 9**
? A martyr who was bound to two trees bent towards each other and torn asunder by their recoil. Place and era unknown.

STRATON (St) M.   **RM. Sept 12**
See Hieronides, Leontius, etc.

STRATONICUS (St) M. RM. Jan 13
See Hermylus and Stratonicus.

STURMIUS (STURMI) (St) OSB.
                                  RM. Dec 17
d. 779. The first German to become a Benedictine. As a child he was entrusted to St Boniface and educated by St Wigbert in the abbey of Fritzlar. He was ordained and sent to evangelize the Saxons. Under orders from Boniface, whose favourite disciple he was, he led an expedition to discover a suitable site for a central abbey for Germany. He chose Fulda, and the abbey of that name was founded there in 744. Sturmius was then dispatched to Montecassino to learn the true Benedictine observance, and on his return he was appointed abbot of Fulda. One of his lasting achievements was the establishment of the celebrated school at Fulda. Dearly loved by his monks, Sturmius was considered as second only to Boniface as the apostle of the Germanies. Canonized in 1139.

STYLIANUS (St) H.   RM. Nov 26
d. 390. A hermit in the vicinity of Adrianople in Paphlagonia. His life has come down to us in a naively legendary form.

STYRIACUS (St)   **RM. Nov 2**
See Carterius, Styriacus, etc.

SUAIRLECH (St) Bp. AC. March 27
d. c.750. First bishop of Fore, Westmeath, Ireland, from c.735 to c.750.

SUCCESSUS (St) M.   RM. Jan 19
See Paul, Gerontius, etc.

SUCCESSUS (St) M. RM. March 28
See Rogatus, Successus and Comp.

SUCCESSUS (St) M.   RM. Apr 16
See Saragossa (Martyrs of).

SUCCESSUS (St) M.   RM. Dec 9
See Peter, Successus, etc.

SULINUS (St) Ab.   AC. Sept 1
Otherwise Silin, q.v.

SULPICIUS (II) PIUS (St) Bp.
                          RM. Jan 17
d. 647. Bishop of Bourges from 624 to
647. He devoted himself to the care and
defence of the poor and persecuted,
particularly those who were victims of a
certain official of King Dagobert. He is
the titular saint of the church and seminary of Saint-Sulpice at Paris.

SULPICIUS (I) (St) Bp. RM. Jan 29
d. 591. Bishop of Bourges from 584 to
591. Though often called Sulpicius
Severus, he is not to be confused with
the celebrated man of letters of that
name, whose name was likewise for
some centuries included in the RM.

SULPICIUS and SERVILIAN (SS)
MM.   RM. Apr 20
d. c.117. Roman martyrs whose conversion is traditionally ascribed to the
prayers of St Flavia Domitilla. They
were beheaded under Trajan.

SULPICIUS of BAYEUX (St) Bp.
M.   AC. Sept 4
d. 843. Bishop of Bayeux from c.838 to
843. He was slain by the Normans at
Livry, diocese of Versailles.

SUNAMAN (St) M. OSB.
                          AC. Feb 15
See Winaman, Unaman and Sunaman.

SUNNIVA (SUNNIFA) (St) V.
                          AC. July 8
10th cent. According to the legend,
Sunniva was an Irish princess who fled
from her country with her brother
Alban and a number of other maidens.
They were shipwrecked off the coast of
Norway and succeeded in landing at
Selje Island. Here they were slain by
people from the mainland. Their

alleged relics were enshrined at Bergen.
The whole story seems to be a somewhat
modified version of the legend of St
Ursula.

SUPERIUS (St) M.   RM. June 26
See Salvius and Superius.

SURANUS (St) Ab.   RM. Jan 24
d. c.580. Abbot of a monastery at Sora,
near Caserta, who distributed all the
goods of the monastery among the
refugees from the Lombards. When the
latter arrived and found that nothing
remained in the abbey to plunder, they
slew Suranus on the spot. We owe the
story to St Gregory the Great (Dial.
IV, 22).

SUSANNA (St) VM.   AC. Jan 18
See Archelais, Thecla, etc.

SUSANNA, MARCIANA, PALLA-
DIA and Comp. (SS) MM.
                          RM. May 24
2nd cent. Wives of certain soldiers belonging to the military unit commanded
by St Meletius. They were put to death
together with their children and other
martyrs in Galatia. Their Acts are
legendary.

SUSANNA COBIOJE (Bl) M.
                          AC. July 12
d. 1628. Wife of Bl Peter Araki Cobioje.
Six months before her death she was
hung naked by her hair from a tree for
eight hours. She was beheaded at
Nagasaki. Beatified in 1867.

SUSANNA (St) VM.   RM. Aug 11
d. 295. The Acts of this saint are wholly
untrustworthy, but there certainly was a
famous Roman martyr of this name, and
to her is dedicated the Roman church of
St Susanna. She had no connexion with
St Tiburtius commemorated on the
same day.

SUSANNA (St) VM.   RM. Sept 19
d. 362. According to the RM. she was the daughter of a pagan priest and a Jewess. Being converted to Christ after their death, she was made a deaconess at Eleutheropolis, where she was martyred under Julian the Apostate.

SUSO, HENRY (Bl) C.   AC. Oct 25
See Henry Suso.

SWITHBERT (St) Bp. OSB.
                              RM. March 1
647–715. A Northumbrian Benedictine, he formed one of the group of twelve missionary monks who in 690 crossed over to Friesland under the leadership of St Willibrord. He preached the gospel with great success, mainly in Hither Friesland. In 693 he was consecrated regionary bishop by St Wilfrid at Ripon and returned to preach along the right bank of the Rhine. His work here was undone by the Saxon invaders, and he retired to the small island of Kaiserswerth in the Rhine, near Düsseldorf. Here he founded a Benedictine monastery (710) and here he died.

SWITHBERT the YOUNGER (St) Bp.   **AC. Apr 30**
d. 807. An Englishman, perhaps a Benedictine monk, who joined the missionaries in Germany and was made bishop of Werden in Westphalia.

SWITHUN (SWITHIN) (St) Bp.
           AC. July 15. RM. July 2
d. 862. He was born in Wessex and spent his youth at the Old Abbey at Winchester, but it is not certain that he ever became a monk. After being ordained priest he was made chaplain to Egbert, king of the W. Saxons and tutor to the young prince Ethelwolf. In 852 he was appointed bishop of Winchester. The origin of the popular saying: "If it rains on St Swithun's day" etc., is not known.

SWITHUN WELLS (Bl) M.
                              AC. Dec 10
d. 1591. A gentleman of Bambridge, Hants, executed at Gray's Inn Fields for sheltering a priest named Edmund Genings, q.v., who suffered with him. Beatified in 1929.

SY
Note. Names beginning with Sy are quite as often written Si. Sometimes too the initial letters Sy stand for the Greek Su.

SYAGRIUS (SIACRE) (St) Bp. OSB.
                              AC. May 23
d. *c.*787. A kinsman of Charlemagne. He became a monk of Lérins and later abbot-founder of the monastery of St Pons at Cimiez in Provence, whence he was promoted to the see of Nice (777).

SYAGRIUS (SIACRE) (St) Bp.
                              RM. Aug 27
d. 600. Bishop of Autun *c.*560–600. He played a prominent part in the ecclesiastical and political life of his time. He entertained St Augustine and his fellow monks on their way to England.

SYCUS and PALATINUS (SS) MM.
                              RM. May 30
? Martyrs of Antioch in Syria. Probably the original entry was: Hesychius Palatinus (March 2), q.v.

SYLVESTER, SYLVANUS (*several*)
Otherwise Silvester, Silvanus, q.v.

SYLVIA (St) W.   RM. Nov 3
d. *c.*572. The mother of St Gregory the Great. Over her former house on the Coelian Hill at Rome a chapel was built in her honour.

SYMMACHUS (St) Pope
                              RM. July 19
d. 514. A Sardinian by birth, he became pope in 498. His pontificate was a

troubled one owing to the activities of his enemies, who set up an antipope. He was a holy and able pope and well deserved the title "father of the poor" which was bestowed upon him.

SYMPHORIAN (St) M. RM. July 7
See Claudius, Nicostratus, etc.

SYMPHORIAN (St) M. RM. Aug 22
d. *c*.180. A member of a senatorial family at Autun, put to death under Marcus Aurelius for refusing to sacrifice to the goddess Cybele. He is one of the most celebrated martyrs of France.

SYMPHORIAN (St) M. RM. Nov 8
One of the Four Crowned Martyrs, q.v.

SYMPHOROSA (St) M. RM. July 2
See Ariston, Crescentian, etc.

SYMPHOROSA and Comp. (SS) MM. RM. July 18
d. *c*.135. A martyr of Tivoli under Hadrian, widow of the martyr St Getulius. The RM. describes her as the mother of seven other martyrs, viz., Crescens, Julian, Nemesius, Primitivus, Justin, Stacteus and Eugene. Her Acts, however, are very untrustworthy, being a Christian adaptation of the story of the Maccabees. She was not the mother of seven martyrs, and these seven martyrs were not brothers, nor were they martyred together.

SYMPHRONIUS (St) M. RM. Feb 3
See Felix, Symphronius, etc.

SYMPHRONIUS, OLYMPIUS, THEODULUS and EXUPERIA (SS) MM. RM. July 26
d. 257. Symphronius was a Roman slave who brought about the conversion of the tribune Olympius, the latter's wife Exuperia and their son Theodulus. They were all burnt to death under Valerian.

SYNCLETICA (St) V. RM. Jan 5
d. *c*.400. A wealthy lady of Alexandria who abandoned the world and lived as a recluse in a disused tomb till her eighty-fourth year. For a long time she suffered from temptations and spiritual desolation, and in her later years from cancer and consumption.

SYNCROTAS, ANTIGONUS, RUTILUS, LIBIUS, SENEROTAS and ROGATIANUS (SS) MM. AC. Feb 23
4th cent. Martyrs of Syrmium, Pannonia.

SYNESIUS and THEOPOMPUS (SS) MM. RM. May 21
Identical with Theopemptus and Theonas of Jan 3, q.v., Theonas being also known as Synesius.

SYNESIUS (St) M. RM. Dec 12
d. 275. A lector of the Roman church martyred under Aurelian.

SYNTYCHE (St) RM. July 22
d. 1st cent. A female member of the church of Philippi, described by St Paul as his fellow labourer in the gospel and as one whose name is in the book of life. (Philip. IV, 2–3).

SYRA (SYRIA) (St) V. AC. June 8
7th cent. An alleged sister of St Fiacre (Flaker) who followed her brother from Ireland to France and there lived as a recluse.

SYRA (St) V. OSB. AC. Oct 23
d. *c*.660. Nun of Faremoutier, whence she was summoned by Bishop Ragneboldus to be abbess of a convent at Châlons-sur-Marne.

SYRIAN MARTYRS (SS) RM. July 31
d. 517. A group of three hundred and

fifty monks slain by the Monophysites for defending the decrees of the council of Chalcedon.

SYRIAN MARTYRS (SS)
RM. Nov 14

d. 773. A large number of women cruelly put to death at Emesa in Phoenicia by the Mohammedan conquerors of the country.

SYRUS of GENOA (St) Bp.
RM. June 29

d. c.380. Bishop of Genoa from c.324 to c.380. He had been parish priest of St Romulus (now San Remo). He is the titular of the cathedral of Genoa and principal patron of the city and diocese. His feast is kept on July 7.

SYRUS (St) Bp. M.
RM. Dec 9

1st cent. (?). Alleged first bishop of Pavia. He probably belongs to the 3rd or 4th century. He is the principal patron of Pavia. See also Juventius (Feb 8).

SYTHA (St) V.
AC. May 19

Otherwise Osyth, q.v.

T

TABITHA (or DORCAS) (St) W.
                                    AC. Oct 25
1st cent. A widow of Joppe who believed in Christ. She was raised from the dead by St Peter (Acts IX, 36–43).

TALARICAN (St) Bp.   AC. Oct 30
? 6th cent. A bishop, probably Pictish, in whose honour various Scottish churches were dedicated. Mentioned in the Aberdeen Breviary.

TALIDA (St) V.   AC. Jan 5
4th cent. Palladius relates that she was abbess of one of the twelve nunneries at Antinoë in Egypt, and that she had been eighty years at her convent when he visited her.

TALMACH (St) C.   AC. March 14
7th cent. A disciple of St Barr at Lough Erc, and founder of a monastery which he placed under the same saint.

TAMMARUS (St) C.   RM. Sept 1
See Priscus, Castrensis, etc.

TANCA (St) VM.   AC. Oct 10
d. c.637. A young girl of the neighbourhood of Troyes in France, who lost her life in defence of her virginity and is locally venerated as a virgin martyr.

TANCO (TANCHO, TATTA) (St) Bp. M. OSB.   AC. Feb 6
d. 808. An Irish monk who became abbot of the Benedictine monastery of Amalbarich in Saxony, and who was eventually promoted to the see of Werden. He died at the hands of a pagan mob whose savage customs he had denounced.

TARACUS (St) M.   RM. Oct 11
Otherwise Tharacus, q.v.

TARAGHTA (St) V.   AC. Aug 11
Otherwise Attracta, q.v.

TARASIUS (THARASIUS) (St) Bp.
                                    RM. Feb 25
d. 806. A patrician of Constantinople. Though a layman he was chosen patriarch, and he accepted on condition that a general council should be convened to end the iconoclastic persecution. He was accordingly consecrated (Christmas 784) and the second council of Nicaea held, the decrees of which were approved by the pope. Shortly after, however, on his refusing to countenance the emperor's bigamous marriage, he was cruelly persecuted by the empress Irene. On the other hand St Theodore and his monks of Studium accused the patriarch of being too lenient. Tarasius is highly venerated in the Orthodox Church.

TARBULA (TARBO, TARBA) (St) VM.   RM. Apr 22
d. 345 (May 5). Sister of St Simeon, the great bishop-martyr of Persia, and a virgin consecrated to God. After her brother's death Tarbula was accused by Jews of having caused by witchcraft the sickness of King Shapur's wife, and she was put to death by being sawn in two.

TARKIN (St) Bp.   AC. Oct 30
Otherwise Talarican, q.v.

TARSICIA (TARSITIA) (St) V.
                                    AC. Jan 15
d. c.600. Said to have been a grand-

daughter of Clotaire II and sister of St Ferreolus of Uzès. She lived as a recluse near Rodez, where she is now venerated.

TARSICIUS, ZOTICUS, CYRIA-CUS and Comp. (SS) MM.
RM. Jan 31
? Martyrs at Alexandria.

TARSICIUS (St) M.   RM. Aug 15
d. ? 255. The inscription upon his tomb, written by Pope St Damasus, informs us that Tarsicius, while carrying the Blessed Sacrament to some Christians in prison, was seized by a heathen mob and preferred to die rather than expose to profanation the Sacred Mysteries. The story was embellished by Cardinal Wiseman in his *Fabiola*.

TARSILLA (St) V.   RM. Dec 24
d. *c*.581. An aunt of St Gregory the Great, sister of St Emiliana and niece of Pope St Felix. In her paternal home she led a life of seclusion and mortification.

TARSUS (Martyrs of) (SS)
RM. June 6
d. *c*.290. A group of twenty martyrs at Tarsus in Cilicia under Diocletian.

TASSACH (St) Bp.   AC. Apr 14
d. *c*.495. One of St Patrick's earliest disciples and first bishop of Raholp (Co. Down). He was a skilful artisan and made crosses, croziers and shrines for St Patrick. It was he who administered the last sacraments to St Patrick.

TASSILO (Bl) Mk. OSB.
AC. Dec 13
d. *p*.794. Duke of Bavaria and one of the greatest benefactors of the Benedictine monks. After founding many abbeys and churches he himself became a monk at Jumièges, whence he migrated to Lorsch, where he died.

TASSO (TASO) (St) Ab. OSB.
AC. Jan 11
See Paldo, Taso and Tato.

TATE (St) W.   AC. Apr 5
Otherwise Ethelburga, q.v.

TATHAI (TATHAN, TATHAEUS, ATHAEUS) (St) H.   AC. Dec 26
Early 6th cent. A nephew of St Samson of Dol who settled in Glamorganshire, where he founded a church.

TATIAN (St) M.   RM. March 16
See Hilary, Tatian, etc.

TATIAN DULAS (St) M.
RM. June 15
Otherwise Dulas, q.v.

TATIAN (St) M.   RM. Sept 12
See Macedonius, Theodulus and Tatian.

TATIANA (St) M.   RM. Jan 12
d. *c*.230. According to the RM., a woman put to death in Rome under Alexander Severus. On this day the Greeks also honour a St Tatiana together with two others, Euthasia and Mertios, MM.

TATION (St) M.   RM. Aug 24
d. *c*.304. A martyr beheaded at Claudipolis in Bithynia under Diocletian.

TATO (St) Ab. OSB.   AC. Jan 11
See Paldo, Taso and Tato.

TATTA (St) M.   RM. Sept 25
See Paul, Tatta, etc.

TATWIN (St) Bp. OSB. AC. July 30
d. 734. Monk of Bredon, or Brenton, in Worcestershire. He succeeded St Brithwald in the see of Canterbury in 731 and received the pallium in 733.

TAURINUS (St) Bp.   RM. Aug 11
d. *c*.412. Bishop of Evreux in Normandy. The legend connecting him with St Denis of Paris is now rejected by all scholars.

TAURION (St) M.   RM. Nov 7
See Auctus, Taurion and Thessalonica.

TEATH (TEATHA, EATHA) (St)
Otherwise Ita, q.v.   **AC. Jan 15**
The title-saint of the church of St Teath in Cornwall is perhaps another of that name, for there is believed to have been a St Teath from Wales, one of the daughters of Brychan of Brecknock.

TEGLA (THECLA) (St) V.
                              AC. June 1
? The patron saint of the church and holy well at Llandegla in Denbighshire.

TEILO (TEILIO, TEILUS, THELIAN, TEILAN, TEILOU, TELIOU, DILLO, DILLON, etc.) (St) Bp.   AC. Feb 9
d. *c*.580. Born at Penally, near Tenby, in S. Wales, and educated by St Dubricius. He was a companion and friend of SS David and Samson. He became the founder and abbot-bishop of Llandaff monastery (Llandeilo Fawr) in Carmarthenshire.

TELEMACHUS (St) M.   RM. Jan 1
Otherwise Almachius, q.v.

TELESPHORUS (St) Pope M.
                              RM. Jan 5
d. 136. A Calabrian Greek, he was pope for ten years, and according to the Roman tradition suffered martyrdom under Hadrian.

TENENAN (St) Bp.   AC. July 16
d. *c*.635. A Briton by birth who became a hermit in Brittany and was eventually raised to the see of Léon.

TERENCE, AFRICANUS, POMPEIUS and Comp. (SS) MM.
                              RM. Apr 10
d. 250. A band of fifty martyrs, imprisoned with a number of snakes and scorpions, and finally beheaded at Carthage under Decius.

TERENCE (St) Bp. M. RM. June 21
1st cent. Bishop of Iconium in apostolic times. Some hagiographers conjecture that he is identical with the Tertius mentioned as his amanuensis by St Paul in his epistle to the Romans (XVI, 22).

TERENCE of TODI (St) M.
                              RM. Sept 27
See Fidentius and Terence.

TERENCE of METZ (St) Bp.
                              AC. Oct 29
d. 520. Sixteenth bishop of Metz.

TERENTIAN (St) Bp. M. RM. Sept 1
d. 118. Bishop of Todi in Umbria. He was racked, had his tongue cut out, and was finally beheaded under Hadrian.

TERESA EUSTOCHIUM VERZERI (Bl) V. Foundress   AC. March 3
1801–1852. Born at Bergamo of noble parents she attempted three times to become a Benedictine nun. Failing in this she gave herself to the instruction of young girls. Thus she came to found the Daughters of the Sacred Heart in 1831. Both the numbers and the scope of the Institute grew, so as to include a wide range of charitable works. The Bishop of Bergamo, at first favourable, turned against her, but approval was given by Rome in 1841. Worn out with labour she died comparatively young at Brescia. Beatified in 1946.

TERESA MARGARET REDI (St) V. OCD.   RM. March 7
1747–1770. Anna Maria, in religion

Teresa Margaret, Redi became a Discalced Carmelite nun at the convent of St Teresa at Florence in 1765. She died at the age of twenty-three, her short life in religion being remarkable for penance and prayer. Canonized in 1934.

TERESA (TARASIA) (St) N. OSB. Cist. AC. June 17
d. 1250. Daughter of King Sancho I of Portugal. She married her cousin Alphonsus IX, king of León, but the marriage was declared null by the Holy See on the grounds of consanguinity. She returned to Portugal and entered the Cistercian convent at Lorvao, near Coimbra, where she died. Cult confirmed, with the title of saint, by Clement XI in 1705.

TERESA FANTOU (Bl) VM.
AC. June 26
d. 1794. A Sister of Charity of Arras. With three other Sisters she was arrested by the French revolutionaries in 1794, brought to Cambrai and there guillotined. Beatified 1920.

TERESA SOIRON (Bl) VM.
AC. July 17
d. 1794. A sister of Bl Catherine Soiron. She was a maid in the service of the Princess Lamballe. During the French Revolution she attached herself to the Carmelite Nuns of Compiègne, q.v., with whom she was executed.

TERESA of JESUS IBARS (Bl) V. Foundress AC. Aug 26
1843–1897. Born at Aytona in Catalonia, she experienced the hardships of life on a farm in her youth before qualifying as a teacher at Lérida. Of deep interior life, she tried to become a religious but without success. Finally, with the advice of her spiritual director, she started an Institute of her own at Barbastro on Jan 27, 1872, under the title of "Little Sisters of the Poor". Her deep spiritual insight, firmness of spirit, unflagging industry and endurance were responsible for the foundation of no less than fifty-eight houses of her congregation during her lifetime. Beatified in 1958.

TERESA of LISIEUX (St) V. OCD.
RM. Oct 3
1873–1897. Marie Françoise Thérèse Martin (her religious name was Teresa of the Infant Jesus) was born at Alençon, entered the Carmelite Order at Lisieux at the age of fifteen, and such was her progress in the spiritual life that she was appointed novice-mistress at the age of twenty-two. Two years later she died, her short life having been remarkable for its humility, simplicity and silently heroic endurance of suffering. Since her death she has worked innumerable miracles, and her cult has spread throughout the world. Pius XI declared her, together with St Francis Xavier, patron saint of foreign missions. Canonized 1925. In English-speaking countries she is often known as the Little Flower of Jesus.

TERESA (St) V. OCD. RM. Oct 15
1515–1582. Teresa Cepeda de Ahumada was born at Avila in Old Castile and at the age of eighteen entered the Carmelite convent in her native town. In 1562 she founded her first reformed convent of St Joseph at Avila, and from that year till her death she was always on the move, opening new houses (fifteen directly and seventeen through others), smoothing away difficulties for her nuns, placating those in authority (both clerical and lay), who often fiercely opposed her and called her the "roving nun". All this time she was being favoured with remarkable mystical experiences, which she described, under obedience, in treatises which may be

regarded as veritable text-books of mystical prayer and rank as classics of Spanish literature. She is the saint of sound common sense, of sane good humour, of generous ideals, "one of the greatest, most attractive and widely appreciated women the world has ever known". (Attwater, h.l.) She died at Alba de Tormes. Canonized 1622.

TERNAN (St) Bp.   AC. June 12
? 5th cent. An early missionary bishop among the Picts in Scotland. He is said to have resided at Abernethy and to have been consecrated by St Palladius. He is the reputed founder of the abbey of Culross in Fifeshire.

TERNATIUS (TERNISCUS) (St) Bp.   AC. Aug 8
d. c.680. Eleventh bishop of Besançon.

TERTIUS (St) M.   RM. Dec 6
See Dionysia, Dativa, etc.

TERTULLA (St) VM.   RM. Apr 29
See Agapius and Comp.

TERTULLIAN (St) Bp. RM. Apr 27
d. c.490. Eighth bishop of Bologna.

TERTULLINUS (St) M. RM. Aug 4
d. 257. A Roman priest, martyred under Valerian two days after his ordination.

TETRICUS (St) Bp. AC. March 20
d. 572. Son of St Gregory, bishop of Langres, and uncle of St Gregory of Tours. He succeeded his father in the see of Langres about the year 540.

TETRICUS (St) Bp. M. OSB.
**   AC. Apr 12**
d. 707. Abbot of the Benedictine monastery of St Germanus at Auxerre. He was raised to the see of Auxerre by popular acclamation. The saint met his death at the hand of his archdeacon

Raginfred, who slew him with a sword as he lay asleep on a bench.

TETTA (St) Abs. OSB. AC. Sept 28
d. c.772. Abbess of Wimborne in Dorsetshire. She helped St Boniface by sending him band after band of missionary nuns from her community, among whom were SS Lioba, Thecla, etc. She is said to have ruled over some five hundred nuns.

TEUZZO (Bl) C. OSB.   AC. Aug 9
d. c.1072. Monk of St Mary's Abbey (La Badia) at Florence. During some fifty years he lived as a recluse near his monastery. He supported St John Gualbert in his campaign against simony.

THADDEUS (TADHG) (Bl) Bp.
**   AC. Oct 25**
d. 1497. Thaddeus McCarthy (Machar) was made bishop of Ross in 1482 but driven from his see in 1488. The Holy See next nominated him bishop of Cork and Cloyne, but he was not allowed into the diocese. Then the perplexed bishop went to Rome to plead his cause personally, but died on his way home at Ivrea in Piedmont. Cult approved 1910.

THADDEUS (St) Apostle
**   RM. Oct 28**
Otherwise Jude, q.v.

THADDEUS LIEU (Bl) M.
**   AC. Nov 24**
d. 1823 (Nov 30). A Chinese priest in the province of Zyu-Thuan. He was imprisoned for two years and then strangled. Beatified 1900.

THAIS (St) Penitent   AC. Oct 8
d. c.348. A wealthy and beautiful courtesan of Alexandria converted by St Paphnutius (other accounts say St Bessarion or St Serapion) and walled up, for three years in a cell. Only to-

wards the end of her life was she admitted to full conventual life with the other nuns. Some modern writers consider the story a moral tale with no foundation of fact.

THALASSIUS and LIMNAEUS (SS) HH.   AC. Feb 22
5th cent. Two Syrian hermits who lived in a cave near Cyrrhus. Our knowledge of them is due to the historian Theodoret, who knew them personally.

THALELAEUS (St) H. AC. Feb 27
d. *c*.450. Surnamed Epiclautos, i.e., weeping much. A hermit who dwelt at Gabala in Syria, next to the shrine of an idol, where he converted many of the pagan pilgrims. For many years he lived in an open barrel.

THALELAEUS, ASTERIUS, ALEXANDER and Comp.
                                  RM. May 20
d. ? 284. Thalelaeus practised medicine and attended his patients gratis at Anazarbus in Cilicia. He suffered martyrdom at Aegae, a town on the coast of that province, and not at Edessa as has been sometimes stated. The RM. adds Asterius and Alexander, two of his executioners, and others of the spectators, who were converted by the constancy of the martyr.

THALUS (St) M.   RM. March 11
See Trophimus and Thalus.

THAMEL and Comp. (SS) MM.
                                  RM. Sept 4
d. *c*.125. A converted pagan priest, martyred with four or five others (one of them his own sister) somewhere in the East, under Hadrian.

THARACUS (TARACHUS), PROBUS and ANDRONICUS (SS) MM.   RM. Oct 11
d. 304. Tarachus, aged sixty-five, was a retired officer of the Roman army, Probus a Roman citizen from Pamphilia, and Andronicus a young man of good birth from Ephesus. They were beheaded near Tarsus in Cilicia under Diocletian. The authenticity of their Acts is disputed.

THARASIUS (St) Bp.   RM. Feb 25
Otherwise Tarasius, q.v.

THAW (St)   AC. Sept 1
Otherwise Lythan, q.v.

THEA (St) M.   RM. Dec 19
See Meuris and Thea.

THÉAU (St)   AC. Jan 7
Otherwise Tillo, q.v.

THEBAN LEGION, The (SS) MM.
                                  RM. Sept 22
d. *c*.287. The story of the Theban Legion is as follows. In the army of Maximinian Herculeus there was a legion (6,600 men) consisting of Christians recruited in Upper Egypt. When the emperor marched his army across the Alps to suppress a revolt in Gaul he camped near Agaunum, in Switzerland, and prepared for the battle with public sacrifices. The Christian legion refused to attend (another version says that they refused to attack innocent people) and were in consequence twice decimated. When they still persevered in their refusal they were massacred *en masse*. Among those who suffered were Maurice, the *primicerius*, Exuperius, Candidus, Vitalis, two Victors, Alexander (at Bergamo) and Gereon (at Cologne). At Agaunum, now St-Maurice-en-Valais, a basilica was built (*c*.369–391) to enshrine the relics of the martyrs. The story can therefore be accepted as substantially true, but it is almost unbelievable that the whole legion was Christian and that the whole

of it was put to death. Probably a very large number of soldiers were put to death and that gave rise to the story as now told.

THECLA (St) VM.   AC Jan 18
See Archelais, Thecla, etc.

THECLA (St) M.   RM. March 26
See Peter, Marcian, etc.

THECLA (St) M.   RM. Aug 19
See Timothy, Thecla and Agapius.

THECLA (St) M.   RM. Aug 30
See Boniface and Thecla.

THECLA (St) VM.   RM. Sept 3
See Euphemia, Dorothea, etc.

THECLA NANGAXI (Bl) M.
**   AC. Sept 10**
d. 1622. A Japanese woman, wife of Bl Paul Nangaxi, beheaded at Nagasaki (see Charles Spinola).

THECLA (St) VM.   RM. Sept 23
1st cent. According to the 2nd century novel called the *Acts of Paul and Thecla*, which abounds in extravagant stories and is not quite orthodox in doctrine, Thecla was a maiden of Iconium who heard St Paul preaching while she sat at her chamber window, became a Christian and followed the apostle dressed in boy's clothes. Several times she underwent most cruel tortures for the Faith—in the prayer for the dying the Roman Ritual refers especially to "three most cruel torments"—and finally died a solitary in Seleucia. The story seems to have a foundation of fact, but it is not possible to disentangle truth from fiction.

THECLA (St) Abs. OSB. RM. Oct 15
d. c.790. A Benedictine nun of Wimborne under St Tetta. She was one of the party which set out for the German mission under St Lioba. She was named by St Boniface first abbess of Ochsenfürt, and then of Kitzingen on the Main, over which she ruled for many years.

THECUSA (St) VM.   RM. May 18
See Theodotus, Thecusa, etc.

THELIAU (St) Bp.   AC. Feb 9
Otherwise Teilo, q.v.

THELICA (St) M.   RM. Feb 11
See under Saturninus, Dativus, etc.

THEMISTOCLES and DIO-
SCORUS (SS) MM.   RM. Dec 21
d. 253. Themistocles was a shepherd of Myra in Lycia who was beheaded for refusing to reveal the hiding-place of St Dioscorus.

THENEVA (THENEW, THENOVA, DWYNWEN) (St) W.   AC. July 18
7th cent. The mother of St Kentigern and together with him the patron saint of Glasgow.

THEOBALD (THIBAUD) of VIENNE (St) Bp.   AC. May 21
d. 1001. Archbishop of Vienne 970–1001. Cult confirmed 1903.

THEOBALD ROGGERI (Bl) C.
**   AC. June 1**
d. 1150. Born at Vico in Liguria of a good family, he left home and chose to work as a cobbler at Alba in Piedmont. After a pilgrimage to Compostella he earned his living as a carrier, sharing his wages with the poor and suffering.

THEOBALD (THIBAUT) (St) H. OSB. Cam.   RM. June 30
1017–1066. Born in Brie, the son of Count Arnoul of Champagne, he was bred to arms, but at the age of eighteen, filled with a desire for greater perfection

as a result of reading the lives of the saints, he became a pilgrim and then a hermit. Finally he settled at Salanigo, near Vicenza, received the Camaldolese habit and was ordained priest. Canonized by Alexander II in 1073.

THEOBALD of MARLY (St) Ab. OSB. Cist.   AC. July 27
d. 1247. Born in the castle of Marly, the son of Buchard of Montmorency, he was a distinguished knight at the court of Philip Augustus of France. He abandoned his worldly prospects and entered the Cistercian abbey of Vaux-de-Cernay (1220), becoming prior in 1230 and abbot in 1235. He was highly esteemed by St Louis of France.

THEOCTISTE (St) V.   RM. Nov 10
10th cent. A nun of Lesbos who became a solitary in the isle of Paros. The story of her last Holy Communion seems to be an adaptation from the life of St Mary of Egypt.

THEODARD (St) Bp. OSB.
**   AC. May 1**
d. 893. Educated at the Benedictine abbey of St Martin at Montauriol, he became archbishop of Narbonne. He died at St Martin's Abbey, having been clothed with the Benedictine habit. Later the abbey was named after him, St Audard.

THEODARD (St) Bp. M. OSB.
**   RM. Sept 10**
d. c.670. A disciple of St Remaclus at Malmédy-Stavelot and his successor as abbot (653) and as bishop of Maestricht (663). On a journey undertaken in defence of his church he was murdered by robbers in the forest of Bienwald, near Speyer.

THEODEMIR (St) M.   RM. July 25
d. 851. A monk martyred at Cordova under Abderrahman II.

THEODICHILDIS (TELCHILDIS) (St) Abs. OSB.   AC. June 28
d. p.660. A nun of Faremoutier, she became the first abbess of Jouarre, diocese of Meaux.

THEODORA (St) Empress
**   AC. Feb 11**
d. 867. Wife of the iconoclast emperor Theophilus. During the regency of her son, Michael the Drunkard, she did her utmost to restore the veneration of images. She ended her life in a convent. Her claim to sanctity is questionable.

THEODORA (St) M. RM. March 13
See Theusetas, Horres, etc.

THEODORA (St) M.   RM. Apr 1
d. c.120. According to the *Acta* of Pope Alexander I, she was sister of St Hermes (Aug 28) whom she assisted in prison and under torture. She was herself martyred some months later. Brother and sister were buried side by side.

THEODORA V. and DIDYMUS (SS) MM.   RM. Apr 28
d. 304. A maiden of Alexandria, sentenced to prostitution, but delivered from the brothel by St Didymus, who was still a pagan. This led to his conversion, and the two saints were martyred together. The Acts are considered trustworthy.

THEODORA (St) VM.   RM. May 7
See Flavia Domitilla, Euphrosyne and Theodora.

THEODORA (St) Penitent
**   RM. Sept 11**
d. 491. The current story of this saint is similar to that of St Pelagia of Antioch (Oct 8) q.v. The RM., however, simply says: "At Alexandria, St Theodora, who fell through lack of care, but repenting of her deed, persevered in the

religious habit, unknown, with won-
drous abstinence and patience, until her
death."

THEODORA (St) Matron
                                    RM. Sept 17
d. c.305. A Roman lady of noble birth
and great wealth, who, during the persecution of Diocletian, generously devoted
herself and her riches to the service of
the martyrs. She seems to have died
while the persecution was still raging.

THEODORE of EGYPT (St) H.
                                    RM. Jan 7
4th cent. A monk of Egypt, disciple of
St Ammonius.

THEODORE STRATELATES (St)
M.   RM. Feb 7
d. 319. He is said to have been a general
(stratelates) in the army of Licinius, by
whose order he was tortured and crucified at Heraclea in Thrace. He is probably identical with St Theodore Tyro
of Amasea (Nov 9).

THEODORE (St) M. RM. March 17
See Alexander and Theodore.

THEODORE, IRENAEUS, SERA-
PION and AMMONIUS (SS) MM.
                                    RM. March 26
d. 310. Theodore, bishop of Pentapolis
in Libya, Irenaeus, his deacon, and
Serapion and Ammonius, his two lectors, suffered under Gallienus by having
their tongues cut out. However, they
survived and died in peace, being nevertheless venerated as martyrs.

THEODORE and Comp. (SS) MM.
OSB.   AC. Apr 9
d. 870. Theodore was abbot of Croyland, and he and his large community
were put to death by the Danes. Besides
the abbot, several others are mentioned
by name: Askega, prior; Swethin, sub-

prior; Elfgete, deacon; Savinus, subdeacon; Egdred and Ulrick, acolytes;
Grimkeld and Agamund (Argamund),
both centenarians.

THEODORE and PAUSILIPPUS
(SS) MM.   RM. Apr 5
d. c.130. Martyrs near Byzantium under
Hadrian.

THEODORE TRICHINAS (St) H.
                                    RM. Apr 20
d. p.330. A hermit near his native city
of Constantinople. He is surnamed
Trichinas, "the hairy", because his only
garment was a rough hair-shirt.

THEODORE of SIKION (St) Bp.
                                    RM. Apr 22
d. 613. Born at Sikion in Galatia, the
son of an imperial messenger, he became
a monk at Jerusalem and in after life
the abbot-founder of several monasteries. About 590 he was made bishop of
Anastasiopolis in Galatia. He was a
great fosterer of the cult of St George.

THEODORE of TABENNA (St) Ab.
                                    RM. Apr 27
d. c.368. Usually called "Theodore the
Holy" by the Greeks. He was trained in
the monastic life by St Pachomius,
whom he succeeded as abbot of Tabenna. His feast is kept in the East on
May 16, but the actual date of his death
was Apr 27.

THEODORE of BOLOGNA (St) Bp.
                                    RM. May 5
d. c.550. A bishop of Bologna c.530–
c.550.

THEODORE of PAVIA (St) Bp.
                                    RM. May 20
d. 778. Bishop of Pavia 743–778. He
had much to endure, including repeated
banishment, at the hands of the Arian
Lombard kings.

THEODORE of CYRENE (St) Bp.
M.   RM. July 4
d. c.310. Bishop of Cyrene in Libya.
He had great skill in copying books, and
was brutally martyred under Diocletian
for refusing to deliver up his manuscripts of the Holy Scriptures.

THEODORE (St) M.   RM. July 29
See Lucilla, Flora, etc.

THEODORE (St) M.   RM. Sept 2
See Zeno, Concordius and Theodore.

THEODORE, OCEANUS, AMMI-
ANUS and JULIAN (SS) MM.
                        RM. Sept 4
d. c.310. Oriental martyrs, burnt at the
stake, probably under Maximian Herculeus.

THEODORE (St) M.   RM. Sept 5
See Urban, Theodore, etc.

THEODORE (St) M.   RM. Sept 15
See Maximus, Theodore and Asclepiodotus.

THEODORE of CANTERBURY
(St) Bp.   RM. Sept 19
c.602–690. Born at Tarsus in Cilicia, he
spent some time at Athens and became a
monk at Rome. He was sixty-six years
old when St Vitalian appointed him
to the see of Canterbury at the suggestion of the African St Adrian. These two
travelled to England together, Adrian
becoming abbot of the monastery of SS
Peter and Paul of Canterbury and acting
as adviser to the new archbishop. Theodore is rightly called the second
founder of the see of Canterbury and
the first primate of the English Church.
He visited all parts of the country,
consolidated or re-established dioceses,
promoted learning and opened schools,
and held the first national council at
Hertford in 673. His activities involved
him in disputes on questions of juris-

diction with St Chad and St Wilfrid,
but these controversies were conducted
with dignity and settled in a spirit of
charity. St Theodore has a claim to be
considered one of the greatest figures in
English history.

THEODORE, PHILIPPA and
Comp. (SS) MM.   RM. Sept 20
d. 220. A group of four Christians crucified at Perge in Pamphilia under Helio-
gabalus. They were: Theodore and
Socrates, soldiers; Dionysius, a former
pagan priest; and Philippa, Theodore's
mother. They expired after three days
on the cross.

THEODORE (THEODORET) of
ANTIOCH (St) M.   RM. Oct 23
d. 362. A priest, treasurer of the Church
of Antioch, martyred under Julian the
Apostate for continuing to minister to
the faithful in spite of the imperial
decrees to the contrary.

THEODORE (THEUDAR, CHEF)
(St) Ab.   RM. Oct 29
d. c.575. A priest, disciple of St Caesarius of Arles and abbot of one of the
monasteries of Vienne in Gaul. He made
several ecclesiastical and monastic foundations and died as a recluse in the
church of St Laurence in Vienne.

THEODORE GUÉNOT (Bl) Bp. M.
                        AC. Nov 4
1802–1861. A native of Bessieux, diocese
of Besançon. He joined the Society of
Foreign Missions and after his ordination was sent to Cochin-China. Later
he was appointed vicar apostolic of that
region and titular bishop of Metello-
polis. He was arrested and sentenced
to death, but died in prison as a result
of ill-treatment.

THEODORE TYRO (St) M.
                        RM. Nov 9
d. c.306. Said to have been a recruit

(hence his nickname of Tyro) in the Roman army, who set fire to the temple of Cybele at Euchaïta, near Amasea in Pontus, for which he paid the penalty by being burnt alive at the same place. Beyond the fact of his martyrdom nothing certain is known about him. He is greatly venerated in the East as one of the "three soldier saints", viz., SS George, Demetrius and Theodore. He is almost certainly identical with St Theodore Stratelates.

THEODORE STUDITES (St) Ab.
RM. Nov 11

759–826. A native of Constantinople who became a monk at the monastery of the Studium (more correctly *Studios*) in that city. In 799 he became abbot, and under his rule the monastery developed into a centre from which a monastic revival spread throughout the East, its influence reaching to Mt Athos and later to Russia, Rumania and Bulgaria. Studium stood for all that is lasting in monastic observance: liturgical prayer, community life, enclosure, poverty, studies and manual work (the monks excelled in calligraphy). The community, with St Theodore at their head, uncompromisingly defended the supreme authority of the see of Rome, the veneration of images (against a series of iconoclastic emperors), and opposed Caesaropapism in every form. Theodore suffered banishment for seven years on this account. He is one of the great figures of monastic history.

THEODORE (St) Bp. M.
RM. Nov 26
See Faustus, Didius, etc.

THEODORE (St) M.   RM. Dec 7
See Polycarp and Theodore.

THEODORE (St) M.   RM. Dec 14
See Drusus, Zosimus and Theodore.

THEODORE (St) M.   RM. Dec 15
See Irenaeus, Antony, etc.

THEODORE the SACRISTAN (St)
C.   RM. Dec 26

d. 6th cent. A contemporary of St Gregory the Great, from whom we derive all our information concerning his life. Theodore was a sacristan (*mansionarius*) in the basilica of St Peter, Rome, where, while busy about his duties in the church, he engaged in visible intercourse with the angels.

THEODORE, M. and THEOPHANES Bp. (SS)   RM. Dec 27

c.841 and c.845. Two brothers, monks of the *laura* of St Sabbas in Jerusalem, who were prominent in defence of the veneration of images. They were cruelly persecuted by the Byzantine emperors. Verses were cut in the flesh of their faces (for this reason they are called *Graphi*, "the Written-on"), and they were otherwise ill-treated. Theodore died in prison in consequence of his sufferings. Theophanes survived him a few years and according to the RM. became bishop of Nicaea.

THEODORET (St) M.
RM. Oct 23
Called Theodorus in the RM. (see above, Oct 23).

THEODORIC II of ORLEANS (St)
Bp. OSB.   AC. Jan 27

d. 1022. Monk of Saint-Pierre-le-Vif at Sens. He was summoned to court as counsellor and afterwards nominated bishop of Orleans. He died at Tonnerre on his way to Rome.

THEODORIC (St) Bp. M.
AC. Feb 2
d. 880. Third Bishop of Ninden. He fell in battle against the Norsemen at Ebsdorf, Saxony. See Bruno and Comp.

THEODORIC (THIERRY, THEODERICUS) (St) Ab. RM. July 1
d. *c*.533. Educated by St Remigius of Reims, by whom he was appointed abbot of Mont d'Or, near Reims.

THEODORIC of EMDEN (St) M. OFM. RM. Oct 9
d. 1572. A Dutch Friar Minor, confessor to the Franciscan nuns at Gorkum. He was hanged at Briel with the group of Gorkum martyrs, q.v.

THEODORIC (St) Bp. AC. Aug 5
d. 863. Bishop of Cambrai-Arras, *c*.830–863.

THEODORIC of ST-HUBERT (THIERRY) (Bl) Ab. OSB.
AC. Oct 25
d. 1087. Educated at Maubeuge, he became a Benedictine at Lobbes, and in 1055 abbot of St Hubert in the Ardennes. Here and at the neighbouring abbeys of Stavelot-Malmédy he introduced with great success the Cluniac observance.

THEODOSIA (St) M. RM. March 20
See Alexandra, Claudia, etc.

THEODOSIA (St) M. RM. March 23
See Domitius, Pelagia, etc.

THEODOSIA (St) VM. RM. Apr 2
d. 308. A maiden of Tyre, eighteen years old, who, on a visit to Caesarea in Palestine, seeing some martyrs on their way to execution, asked them to pray for her. Whereupon she was seized, tortured, and finally cast into the sea.

THEODOSIA and Comp. (SS) MM.
RM. May 29
d. *c*.303. Theodosia, the alleged mother of St Procopius, is said to have been martyred at Caesarea Philippi in Palestine under Diocletian. She is said to have been put to death with twelve

other women. The whole story seems to be a fabrication.

THEODOSIA (St) VM.
AC. May 29
d. 745. A nun of Constantinople who led a group of other nuns in an attempt to resist by force the soldiers who were sent to destroy the image of Christ over the main door of their monastery. She was tortured and put to death.

THEODOSIUS the CENOBIARCH (St) Ab. RM. Jan 11
423–529. A Cappadocian who was put in charge of the church of Our Lady situated on the road between Jerusalem and Bethlehem. He next founded a monastery in the desert of Juda by the Dead Sea, where several hundred monks were soon living under his rule. He divided them according to nationality—Greeks, Armenians and Arabs—and built a church for each group. The patriarch of Jerusalem appointed him visitor to all the cenobitical communities in Palestine—as distinct from eremitical—whence the title cenobiarch given to the saint. The Byzantine emperor tried unsuccessfully to bribe Theodosius to support Monophysitism. The saint died at the age of one hundred and five.

THEODOSIUS of ANTIOCH (St) Mk. AC. Jan 11
d. *c*.412. A native of Antioch, of good family, he left the world to found a monastery near Rhosus in Cilicia. He died and was buried at Antioch.

THEODOSIUS (St) Bp. AC. Feb 14
d. 554. Bishop of Vaison in France and predecessor of St Quinidius.

THEODOSIUS (St) M.
RM. March 26
See Quadratus, Theodosius, etc.

THEODOSIUS (St) Bp.
RM. July 17
d. 516. Bishop of Auxerre c.507–516.

THEODOSIUS, LUCIUS, MARK and PETER (SS) MM. RM. Oct 25
d. 269. They belong to a group of fifty soldiers martyred at Rome under Claudius II.

THEODOTA (St) M. RM. July 17
d. c.735. A lady of Constantinople martyred under the iconoclastic emperor Leo the Isaurian for hiding three holy icons from the imperial officers.

THEODOTA and her three Sons (SS) MM. RM. Aug 2
d. 304. Martyrs of Nicaea. Theodota with Evodius (q.v.) and her other two sons were cast into a furnace and perished in the flames. Their Acts are not trustworthy.

THEODOTA (St) Penitent.
? AC. Sept 29
d. c.318. Described as a penitent harlot, martyred at Philippopolis in Thrace. According to her untrustworthy Acts her executioners exhausted their ingenuity in devising fresh tortures for her.

THEODOTUS (St) M. RM. Jan 4
See Aquilinus, Geminus, etc.

THEODOTUS (St) Bp. RM. May 6
d. c.325. Bishop of Cyrenia in Cyprus. He suffered a long term of imprisonment under Licinius.

THEODOTUS, THECUSA, ALEXANDRA, CLAUDIA, FAINA (PHAINA), EUPHRASIA, MATRONA and JULITTA (SS) MM.
RM. May 18
d. 304. According to their Acts, Theodotus was an innkeeper of Ancyra who

was martyred there under Diocletian for giving Christian burial to the bodies of the seven virgins mentioned above, also martyrs of Ancyra. The Bollandist Father Delehaye contends that the Acts are merely a moral tale.

THEODOTUS (St) M. RM. July 5
See Marinus, Theodotus and Sedopha.

THEODOTUS, RUFINA and AMMIA (SS) MM. RM. Aug 31
d. c.270. Theodotus and Rufina were the parents, and Ammia the fostermother, of St Mamas (v. Aug 17). They also are said to have suffered in Cappadocia under Aurelian. The untrustworthy Acta of St Mamas is the sole source of our knowledge.

THEODOTUS (St) Bp. RM. Nov 2
d. 334. A bishop of Laodicea at the time of the Arian troubles and a great friend of the Arianizing Eusebius the historian, who is loud in his praise. Theodotus subscribed to the Nicene formula, but seems to have sided with the Arians and the semi-Arians up to his death.

THEODOTUS (St) M. RM. Nov 14
See Clementinus, Theodotus and Philomenus.

THEODULA (St) VM.
RM. March 25
Otherwise Dula, q.v.

THEODULPHUS (THIOU) (St) Bp. OSB. RM. June 24
d. 776. The third abbot-bishop of the great Benedictine abbey of Lobbes, near Liége.

THEODULUS (St) M. RM. Feb 17
d. 309. An aged man in the household of Firmilian, governor of Palestine, by whom he was ordered to be crucified at Caesarea in Palestine.

THEODULUS (St) C.
RM. March 23
? A priest of Antioch in Syria, of whom nothing else is known. His name is also given as Theodore and Theodoricus.

THEODULUS, ANESIUS, FELIX, CORNELIA and Comp. (SS) MM.
RM. March 31
? Martyrs in Proconsular Africa.

THEODULUS (St) M.   RM. Apr 4
See Agathopodes and Theodulus.

THEODULUS (St) M.   RM. May 2
See Exuperius, Zoe, etc.

THEODULUS (St) M.   RM. May 3
See Alexander, Eventius and Theodulus.

THEODULUS (St) M. RM. June 18
See Leontius, Hypatius and Theodulus.

THEODULUS (St) M.   RM. July 26
See Symphronius, Olympius, etc.

THEODULUS (THEODORE) of GRAMMONT (St) Bp.   AC. Aug 17
4th cent. An early bishop of Valais whose cult was widespread in that region, Switzerland and Savoy. A later life placing him in the 9th century, has led to much confusion about his identity.

THEODULUS (St) M. RM. Sept 12
See Macedonius, Theodulus and Tatian.

THEODULUS, SATURNINUS, EUPORUS, GELASIUS, EUNICIAN, ZETICUS, CLEOMENES (LEOMENES), AGATHOPUS, BASILIDES and EVARISTUS (SS) MM.   RM. Dec 23
d. 250. Martyrs of Crete who suffered under Decius.

THEOFRID (THEOFROY) (St) Bp. OSB.   AC. Jan 26
d. c.690. A monk of Luxeuil who became abbot of Corbie (622) and a regionary bishop.

THEOFRID (THEOFROY, CHAFFRE) (St) Ab. OSB.   AC. Oct 19
d. 728. A native of Orange who became monk and abbot of Carmery-en-Velay (Monastier-Saint-Chaffre). He died as a consequence of ill-treatment received at the hands of the invading Saracens and has been ever since venerated as a martyr.

THEOGENES (St) M.   RM. Jan 3
See Cyrinus, Primus and Theogenes.

THEOGENES and Comp. (SS) MM.
d. 258. According to the RM. Theogenes was bishop of Hippona (Hippo Regius) in Africa, where he suffered with thirty-six of his flock under Valerian. A modern opinion places these martyrs at Laodicea in Phrygia.

THEOGER (THEOGAR, DIETHGER) (Bl) Bp. OSB.   PC. Apr 29
d. 1120. A native probably of Alsace who became successively canon · of Mainz, monk of Hirschau, prior of Raichenbach on the Murg, abbot of St Georgen in the Black Forest (1090) and bishop of Metz (1118). However, after his consecration at Corbie he retired to the abbey of Cluny, where he died.

THEOGONIUS (St) M. RM. Aug 21
See Bassa, Theogonius, etc.

THEONAS (St) M.   RM. Jan 3
See Theopemptus and Theonas.

THEONAS of EGYPT (St) Mk.
AC. Apr 4
d. c.395. A famous solitary who lived near Oxyrinchus in the Thebaid.

THEONAS (St) M.   RM. Apr 20
See Victor, Zoticus, etc.

THEONAS (St) Bp.   RM. Aug 23
d. 300. Bishop of Alexandria 281–300.
He fostered sacred studies, chiefly by his
care of the catechetical school of his
episcopal city. He was also known as a
determined opponent of Sabellianism.

THEONESTUS (St) Bp. M.
                                RM. Oct 30
d. 425. Said to have been bishop of
Philippi in Macedonia, to have been
driven from his see by the Arians, and
to have been sent by the pope with
several companions (among whom was
St Alban of Mainz) to evangelize Germany. Arrived at Mainz, they were
obliged to flee from the invading Vandals, and on their way home Theonestus
was martyred at Altino in the Veneto.
Probably Theonestus is a local martyr
of Altino having no connexion with the
others.

THEONILLA (St) M.   RM. Aug 23
See Claudius, Asterius, etc.

THEOPEMPTUS and THEONAS
(SS) MM.   RM. Jan 3
d. 284. Theopemptus was bishop of
Nicomedia. Theonas was a magician
converted by the example of Theopemptus and after him martyred. Their
Acts are wholly untrustworthy, though
the martyrs themselves seem to be
historical personages.

THEOPHANES VÉNARD (Bl) M.
                                AC. Feb 2
1829–1861. A native of the diocese of
Poitiers who joined the Society of
Foreign Missions at Paris, was ordained
in 1852 and arrived in Tonkin in 1854.
After teaching in an Annamite semi-
nary he took up work in W. Tonkin.
He was barbarously put to death in a
persecution which soon after broke out.
Beatified 1909.

THEOPHANES (St) Ab.
                                RM. March 12
d. 818. A native of Constantinople and
educated at the imperial court, he
married early in life, but two years later
allowed his wife to become a nun and
himself joined the monks of Polychro-
nion. Some time later he founded two
monasteries and governed one of them
as abbot, viz., that of Mt Sigriana, near
Cyzicus. For his steadfast opposition to
iconoclasm he was banished by Leo the
Armenian to Samothrace, where he died
from the ill-treatment he had received.

THEOPHANES and Comp. (SS)
MM.   RM. Dec 4
d. c.815. Four officers of the court of
Leo the Armenian, imprisoned and
tortured for their opposition to iconoclasm. Theophanes died under torture;
the rest survived and eventually became monks.

THEOPHANES (St) Bp. C.
                                RM. Dec 27
See Theodore and Theophanes.

THEOPHILA (St) VM. RM. Dec 28
See Indes, Domna, etc.

THEOPHILUS and HELLADIUS
(SS) MM.   RM. Jan 8
? Africans martyred in Libya, where
they had preached the gospel. Theophilus was a deacon, Helladius a layman. They were tortured and thrown
into a furnace.

THEOPHILUS the PENITENT (St)
                                Feb 4
c.538. Metaphrastes is responsible for
the spread of the legend connected with
this saint. He is said to have been archdeacon of Adana in Cilicia and, having

been deposed from his office through a calumny, to have made a pact with the devil. He repented, and our Lady appeared to him and returned the pact, which was then torn up and publicly burnt. Goethe made use of this legend in his *Faust*.

THEOPHILUS the LAWYER (St) M, RM. Feb 6
d. *c*.300. Said to have been beheaded at Caesarea in Cappadocia. He figures in the legend of St Dorothy, where he is surnamed *Scholasticus*, i.e., the lawyer.

THEOPHILUS (St) M. RM. Feb 6
See Saturninus, Theophilus and Revocata.

THEOPHILUS (St) M. RM. Feb 28
See Macarius, Rufinus, etc.

THEOPHILUS (St) Bp. RM. March 5
d. *c*.195. A bishop of Caesarea in Palestine and a prominent opponent of the Quartodecimans, a sect which insisted on keeping Easter on the Jewish Passover day, whether it fell on a Sunday or not.

THEOPHILUS (St) Bp. RM. March 7
His real name is Theophylact, q.v.

THEOPHILUS (St) Bp. RM. Apr 27
d. *p*.427. Bishop of Brescia and successor to St Gaudentius.

THEOPHILUS of CORTE (St) C. OFM. RM. May 19
1676–1740. Biagio Arrighi was born at Corte in Corsica and joined the Friars Minor, taking the name of Theophilus (1693). He was ordained priest at Naples and taught theology at Civitella in the Roman Campagna. Later he became a famous missioner in Italy and Corsica and a zealous worker for the revival of Franciscan observance. Canonized in 1930.

THEOPHILUS (St) M. RM. July 22
d. 789. An officer of the imperial forces stationed in Cyprus when the Saracens invaded the island. As admiral of the Christian fleet he refused to flee when the battle went against him. He was taken prisoner and after one year's incarceration was martyred for refusing to deny Christ.

THEOPHILUS (St) M. RM. July 23
See Trophimus and Theophilus.

THEOPHILUS (St) M. RM. Sept 8
See Ammon, Theophilus, etc.

THEOPHILUS (St) Mk. OSB. RM. Oct 2
d. *c*.750. A native of Bulgaria, who became a monk of a monastery in Asia Minor, in which the community followed the Western Rule of St Benedict. For opposing iconoclasm he was fiercely persecuted, maltreated and finally exiled by the emperor Leo the Isaurian.

THEOPHILUS (St) Bp. RM. Oct 13
d. 181. An Eastern philosopher who became a Christian as a result of reading the Scriptures with a view to attacking them. He became bishop of Antioch. He is now best known as one of the Apologists of the second century.

THEOPHILUS (St) M. RM. Nov 3
See Germanus, Theophilus, etc.

THEOPHILUS (St) M. RM. Dec 20
See Ammon, Zeno, etc.

THEOPHYLACT (St) Bp. RM. March 7
d. 845. Wrongly called Theophilus in the RM. An Asiatic monk who became bishop of Nicomedia. He opposed

the iconoclastic fury of Leo the Armenian, by whom he was banished to Caria, where he died thirty years later.

THEOPISTES and THEOPISTUS (SS) MM.   RM. Sept 20
See Eustace, Theopistes, etc.

THEOPOMPUS (St) M.
                                              RM. May 21
See Synesius and Theopompus.

THEOPREPIUS (St) M.
                                            RM. March 27
See Philetus, Lydia, etc.

THEOROGITHA (THORDGITH, THORCTGYD) (St) N.   AC. Jan 25
See Thordgith.

THEOTICUS (St) M. RM. March 8
See Arianus, Theoticus, etc.

THEOTIMUS (St) Bp. RM. Apr 20
d. 407. Bishop of Tomi on the Black Sea. He defended Origen against St Epiphanius of Salamis. He evangelized the barbarian tribes of the Lower Danube, who were then pressing into imperial territory.

THEOTIMUS (St) M.   RM. Nov 5
See Domninus, Theotimus, etc.

THEOTIMUS and BASILIAN (SS) MM.   RM. Dec 18
? Martyrs of Laodicea in Syria.

THEOTIMUS (St) M.   RM. Dec 24
See Lucian, Metrobius, etc.

THEOTONIUS (St) C. OSA.
                                             AC. Feb 18
1086–1166. Born in Spain, he was educated at Coimbra in Portugal and became archpriest of Viseu. He resigned that office to go on pilgrimage to the Holy Land, and on his return joined

the Augustinian canons regular at Coimbra. Highly esteemed by King Alphonsus of Portugal, he was fearless in rebuking vice and exact in the performance of the divine service. Cult approved by Benedict XIV.

THERESA (*several*).
Otherwise Teresa, q.v.

THESPESIUS (St) M.   RM. June 1
d. *c*.230. A Cappadocian martyred under Alexander Severus.

THESPESIUS (St) M. RM. Nov 20
See Eustace, Thespesius and Anatolius.

THESSALONICA (St) M.
                                              RM. Nov 7
See Auctus, Taurion, and Thessalonica.

THETHMAR (THEODEMAR) (St) C.   AC. May 17
d. 1152. A native of Bremen who became a missionary among the Wends under St Vicelinus. He was probably a Premonstratensian. He died at Neumünster.

THEUDERIUS (St) Ab.
                                              RM. Oct 29
See Theodore (Theudar).

THEUSETAS, HORRES, THEODORA, NYMPHODORA, MARK and ARABIA (SS) MM.
                                            RM. March 13
? Theusetas was the parent of the young boy Horres. The whole group was put to death at Nicaea in Bithynia. Earlier martyrologies have a much longer list of martyrs in this group.

THIEMO (THEODMARUS) (St) Bp. M. OSB.   AC. Sept 28
d. 1102. Of the family of the counts of Meglin in Bavaria. He became a Benedictine at Niederaltaich, where he

gained great celebrity as an artist in metal, a painter and a sculptor. In 1077 he was chosen abbot of St Peter's, Salzburg, and in 1090 archbishop of the same city. He was persecuted, imprisoned and exiled for his loyalty to the principles of Gregory VII. As an exile he joined the crusaders, was captured and imprisoned at Ascalon, and after long and cruel tortures was martyred at Corozain for refusing to apostatize to Islam.

THIENTO and Comp. (BB) MM.
OSB.   **AC. Aug 10**
d. 955. An abbot of Wessobrunn in Bavaria who was martyred with six of his monks by the invading Hungarians.

THIERRY (St) C.   **RM. July 1**
Otherwise Theodoric, q.v.

THILLO (St) Ab. OSB.   **AC. Jan 7**
Otherwise Tillo, q.v.

THIOU (St) Bp.   **RM. June 24**
Otherwise Theodulphus, q.v.

THOMAIS (St) M.   **RM. Apr 14**
d. 476. An Alexandrian woman, wife of a fisherman. Tempted to an act of impurity by her father-in-law, she refused and was murdered by him.

THOMAS PLUMTREE (Bl) M.
AC. Jan 4
d. 1570. A native of Lincolnshire, educated at Corpus Christi College, Oxford, and rector of Stubton. He was chaplain to the insurgents of the North. Before being martyred in the market-place at Durham he was offered his life if he would turn Protestant. Beatified 1886.

THOMAS of CORI (Bl) C. M.
AC. Jan 19
1655–1729. A native of Cori, diocese of Velletri, who, after being a shepherd in the Roman Campagna, became an Observant Franciscan (1675), and, after his ordination to the priesthood, was stationed at Civitella. He spent the remainder of his life in preaching and ministering to the inhabitants of the mountain district around Subiaco. Beatified 1785.

THOMAS REYNOLDS (Bl) M.
AC. Jan 21
d. 1642. Thomas Reynolds, whose true name was Green, was born at Oxford and educated for the priesthood at Reims, Valladolid and Seville. After his ordination in 1592 he returned to England and worked on the English mission for nearly fifty years. He must have been about eighty years of age when he was hanged for his priesthood at Tyburn, together with Bl Bartholomew Roe, OSB. Beatified 1929.

THOMAS XICO or DAUKI (St) M.
RM. Feb 5
d. 1597. A Japanese layman, Franciscan tertiary, catechist, and interpreter to the Franciscan missionaries in Japan. Crucified at Nagasaki with twenty-five companions. Canonized 1862.

THOMAS COZAKI (St) M.
RM. Feb 5
d. 1597. A Japanese boy of fifteen, son of St Michael Cozaki. He served Mass for the Franciscan missionaries and was crucified at Nagasaki with twenty-five companions, including his own father. Canonized 1862.

THOMAS SHERWOOD (Bl) M.
AC. Feb 7
1551–1578. A Londoner, who was preparing to go to Douai to study for the priesthood when he was betrayed, imprisoned and racked in the Tower in order to force him to disclose the place where he had heard Mass. He was finally executed at Tyburn on the charge

of denying the queen's ecclesiastical supremacy. Beatified 1886.

THOMAS of FOLIGNO (Bl) M. OFM.   PC. Feb 12

See Antony of Saxony.

THOMAS HEMERFORD (Bl) M.
AC. Feb 12

d. 1584. A Dorsetshire man who was educated at St John's College and Hart Hall, Oxford. He studied for the priest-hood at the English College, Rome, where he was ordained in 1583. The following year, with four priest-com-panions, he was hanged at Tyburn for his priesthood. Beatified 1929.

THOMAS of SZOMBATHELY (Bl) Mk.   AC. March 7

15th cent. General of the Hungarian Pauline Order 1476-1480 and 1484-1488, he was renowned for his austerities and gifts of prophecy, and also as a theo-logical writer.

THOMAS AQUINAS (St) Dr OP.
RM. March 7

c.1226–1274. Surnamed the "Angelic Doctor." Born at Roccasecca, near Aquino, Naples, and educated as an oblate by the Benedictines at Monte-cassino, he joined the then recently founded Dominicans, studied and re-ceived the doctorate of theology at the university of Paris, and thenceforward taught that subject at Paris (1252–1260), Orvieto (1261–1264), Rome (1265–1267), Viterbo (1268), Paris (1269–1271) and Naples (1272–1274). He died at Fossanova, near Rome, on his way to the council of Lyons. Canonized in 1323 and declared Doctor of the Church in 1567 and patron saint of Catholic universities and centres of study in 1880, St Thomas is the acknowledged prince of Catholic theologians, and his *Summa Theologica* is unrivalled as an authority in that branch of sacred learning.

THOMAS (or THOMASIUS) of COSTACCIARO (Bl) H. OSB. Cam.
AC. March 25

d. 1337. Born at Costacciaro in Umbria, the son of poor peasants. He joined the Camaldolese at Sitria, then retired to Monte Cupo as a hermit, where he lived for many years. At the time of his death his existence had been almost forgotten.

THOMAS of TOLENTINO and Comp. (BB) MM. OFM. AC. Apr 9

d. 1322. A native of Tolentino in Italy, who became a Franciscan and went to preach the gospel in Armenia and Persia. He was on his way to Ceylon, with a view to proceeding to China, when he was seized at Thama in Hin-dustan and beheaded by the Moham-medans. Three companions, BB James of Padua, Peter of Siena, Franciscans, and Demetrius of Tiflis, layman, suffered with him. Cult approved 1894.

THOMAS PICKERING (Bl) M. OSB.   AC. May 9

d. 1679. A native of Westmoreland who joined the Benedictines as a lay-brother at St Gregory's, Douai (now at Down-side) and took his vows in 1660. He was sent to England and attached to the small community of Benedictine chap-lains who served the royal chapel. He was a victim of the "Popish Plot," being falsely accused and hanged at Tyburn. Beatified 1929.

THOMAS FORD (Bl) M. AC. May 28

d. 1582. A native of Devon who was educated at Trinity College, Oxford, where he was converted to the Catholic Faith. He studied for the priesthood at Douai, was ordained there in 1573, and sent on the English mission in 1576. He worked in Oxfordshire and Berkshire until his arrest and martyrdom at Tyburn with BB John Shert and Robert Johnson. Beatified 1886.

THOMAS COTTAM (Bl) M. SJ.
AC. May 30

1549–1582. Born at Dilworth in Lancashire of Protestant parents, he graduated at Brasenose College, Oxford, and was converted to the Catholic Faith. He crossed over to Douai and then went to Rome to study for the priesthood. At Rome he was received into the Society of Jesus. He returned to England in 1580, but was arrested on landing at Dover and imprisoned in the Tower. Two years later he was hanged at Tyburn with three priest-companions. Beatified 1886.

THOMAS DU (Bl) M. Tert. OP.
AC. May 31

1774–1839. A native of Tonkin who was ordained priest, became a Dominican tertiary and worked in the province of Nam-Dingh. He was tortured and beheaded. Beatified 1900.

THOMAS GREEN, THOMAS SCRYVEN and THOMAS REDING (BB) MM. O. Cart.   AC. June 15

d. 1537. Thomas Green (or Greenwood) was a fellow of St John's College, Cambridge, who took monastic vows and was ordained priest at the London Charterhouse. The other two were lay-brothers of the same charterhouse. These three, with four companions, were starved to death at Newgate. Beatified 1886.

THOMAS WOODHOUSE (Bl) M. SJ.   AC. June 19

d. 1573. A secular priest who resided in Lincolnshire and acted also as a private tutor in Wales. In 1561 he was committed to the Fleet prison, where he was kept in custody till his death. During his imprisonment he was admitted by letter to the Society of Jesus. He was hanged at Tyburn. Beatified 1886.

THOMAS WHITBREAD (Bl) M. SJ.
AC. June 20

d. 1679. Thomas Whitbread, *alias* Harcourt, was a native of Essex. He was educated at St Omer and joined the Jesuits in 1635. He was provincial of the English mission and at the time of the Popish Plot was convicted with four other priests of his Order on a bogus charge of conspiring to murder Charles II. He was hanged at Tyburn. Beatified 1929.

THOMAS CORSINI (Bl) C. OSM.
AC. June 23

d. 1343. A native of Orvieto who became a Servite lay-brother and spent his life collecting alms for his friary. He is credited with many visions. Beatified 1768.

THOMAS GARNET (Bl) M. SJ.
AC. June 23

d. 1608. Born in Southwark, a nephew of Fr Henry Garnet, SJ. Educated for the priesthood at St Omer and Valladolid. He worked first as a secular priest but in 1604 was admitted to the Society of Jesus. Hanged at Tyburn for his priesthood. Beatified 1929.

THOMAS TOAN (Bl) Tert. OP.
AC. June 27

1767–1840. A native catechist of Tonkin who, having shown signs of apostatizing, repented and was in consequence cruelly scourged and exposed to the sun and insects without food or drink for twelve days until his death. Beatified 1900.

THOMAS MAXFIELD (Bl) M.
AC. July 1

d. 1616. A native of Enville, Staffs., he was educated for the priesthood at Douai and ordained in 1615. The following year he was hanged for his priesthood at Tyburn. Beatified 1929.

THOMAS BOSGRAVE (Bl) M.
AC. July 4
d. 1594. A gentleman, nephew of Sir J. Arundel, hanged at Dorchester with two of his servants for sheltering priests. Beatified 1929.

THOMAS WARCOP (Bl) M.
AC. July 4
d. 1597. A gentleman of Yorkshire, hanged with three companions at York for sheltering priests. Beatified 1929.

THOMAS ALFIELD (Bl) M.
AC. July 6
d. 1585. Born at Gloucester and educated at Eton and King's College, Cambridge. He was reconciled to the Catholic Church and went abroad to study for the priesthood at Douai and Reims. After his ordination in 1581 he returned to England and was arrested while engaged in distributing copies of Dr Allen's *True and Modest Defence*. For this he was hanged at Tyburn. Beatified 1929.

THOMAS MORE (St) M. RM. July 6
1478–1535. A native of London, More studied at Canterbury Hall, Oxford, and read Law at the Inns of Court, being called to the bar in 1501. He married twice and was the ideal husband, devoted to wife and children, devout, cheerful and charitable. In 1516 he published his *Utopia*, which gained for him a European reputation as a scholar and humanist. From this time he was more and more in favour with Henry VIII and Cardinal Wolsey, whom in 1529 he succeeded as Lord Chancellor. Soon, however, he found himself unable to support the king on the question of the royal divorce. He resigned the chancellorship and on refusing to take the oath of supremacy, declaring the king supreme head of the Church in England, was imprisoned in the Tower. After fifteen months' incarceration he was beheaded on Tower Hill. In the decree of his canonization in 1935 Pius XI described him as the "Martyr of the Papacy."

THOMAS TUNSTAL (Bl) M. OSB.
AC. July 13
d. 1616. Thomas Tunstal, *alias* Helmes, was born at Whinfell, near Kendal, Westmorland. He was educated for the priesthood at Douai, ordained there in 1609, sent to the English mission in 1610 and imprisoned almost at once. He spent the rest of his life in prison, and while there was received into the Benedictine Order. He was hanged for his priesthood at Norwich. Beatified 1929.

THOMAS ABEL (Bl) M. AC. July 30
d. 1540. A doctor of Oxford university, chaplain to Queen Catharine of Aragon and a loyal defender of the validity of her marriage. He was kept a prisoner in the Tower of London for six years and finally executed at Smithfield for refusing to acknowledge the king's spiritual supremacy. Beatified 1886.

THOMAS WELBOURNE (Bl) M.
AC. Aug 1
d. 1605. A native of Hutton Bushel in Yorkshire and a schoolmaster by profession who was hanged at York for persuading people to turn Catholic. Beatified 1929.

THOMAS of DOVER (St) M. OSB.
AC. Aug 5
d. 1295. Thomas Hales was a Benedictine monk of St Martin's Priory, Dover, a cell of Christ Church, Canterbury. On Aug 5, 1295 the French raided Dover and all the monks went into hiding except Thomas, who was too old and infirm to get away. The raiders found him in bed and ordered him to

disclose the whereabouts of the church plate: he refused and was murdered. Miracles occurred at his tomb and he was forthwith venerated as a martyr. There was an altar dedicated to him in Dover Priory church in 1500, and his image figured among those of the English saints at the English College, Rome.

THOMAS WO YINYEMON (Bl) M.
AC. Aug 17
d. 1627. A Japanese layman beheaded at Nagasaki for sheltering the missionary priests. Beatified in 1867.

THOMAS GUENGORO (Bl) M.
AC. Aug 18
d. 1620. A Japanese layman. With his wife and his little son he was crucified at Cocura for sheltering Bl Simon Kiota. Beatified 1867.

THOMAS COYANANGHI (Bl) M.
AC. Aug 19
d. 1622. A Japanese passenger on the ship of Bl Joachim, beheaded at Nagasaki. Beatified 1867.

THOMAS of HEREFORD (St) Bp.
RM. Aug 25
c.1218–1282. Born at Hambledon, near Great Marlow, the son of the Norman Baron William of Cantalupe. He was a brilliant student at Oxford and Paris, became chaplain to Pope Innocent IV, and in 1262 chancellor of Oxford University. In 1265 he was appointed chancellor of England, but on being deprived of this office by Henry III, he returned at once to his beloved Oxford. He was raised to the bishopric of Hereford in 1275. The seven years of his episcopate were taken up with a continuous struggle in defence of the rights of his diocese and in untiring pastoral activities. He died at Montefiascone in Italy, whither he had gone to plead the cause of his see before the pope. Canonized 1320.

THOMAS PERCY (Bl) M.
AC. Aug 26
1528–1572. Earl of Northumberland, condemned to death and executed at York for his part in the rising of the North against Elizabeth. During the period of nearly three years' imprisonment which preceded his martyrdom he was repeatedly offered his freedom on condition of his apostasy to Protestantism. Beatified 1896.

THOMAS HOLFORD (Bl) M.
AC. Aug 28
d. 1588. Thomas Holford, *alias* Acton or Bude, was born at Aston in Cheshire of Protestant parents and became a schoolmaster in Herefordshire, where he embraced the Catholic faith. After his studies and ordination at Reims (1583) he worked in Cheshire. He was hanged for his priesthood at Clerkenwell. Beatified 1929.

THOMAS FELTON (Bl) M. O.
Minim.   AC. Aug 28
1568–1588. Born at Bermondsey, son of Bl John Felton. He was educated at Reims and became a friar minim. He was hanged at Isleworth in his twentieth year. Beatified 1929.

THOMAS TZUGHI (Bl) M. SJ.
AC. Sept 6
d. 1627. A Japanese, educated by the Jesuit fathers at Arima, whom he joined in 1589. He was noted for his gift of oratory. Exiled to Macao, he returned in disguise. He separated himself from the Society of Jesus, but only for one day; he then repented of his act and engaged himself again in missionary work with renewed zeal. He was burnt alive with several companions at Nagasaki. Beatified 1867.

THOMAS of ST HYACINTH (Bl) M. OP. AC. Sept 8

d. 1628. A Japanese catechist attached to the Dominican missionaries, burnt alive with Bl Dominic Castellet and companions. Beatified 1867.

THOMAS TOMAKI (Bl) M. AC. Sept 8

d. 1628. A Japanese boy, ten years old, beheaded with his father, Bl John Tomaki, and his three brothers. Beatified 1867.

THOMAS XIQUIRO (Bl) M. AC. Sept 10

d. 1622. A Japanese layman, seventy years old, highly respected by his fellow-citizens, beheaded at Nagasaki with Bl Charles Spinola. Beatified 1867.

THOMAS of the HOLY ROSARY (Bl) M. OP. AC. Sept 10

d. 1622. A Japanese catechist, attached to the Dominican missionaries, with several of whom he was beheaded at Nagasaki. Beatified 1867.

THOMAS ZUMARRAGA (Bl) M. OP. AC. Sept 12

1575–1622. A native of Vitoria in Spain who joined the Dominicans and was sent to their missions in Japan. He was imprisoned for three years at Suzuta (Omura) and ultimately burnt alive at Omura with several companions. Beatified 1867.

THOMAS ACAFOXI (Bl) M. AC. Sept 19

d. 1622. A Japanese nobleman from Fingo who acted as catechist to Bl Leonard Kimura. Burnt alive at Nagasaki. Beatified 1867.

THOMAS JOHNSON (Bl) O. Cart. AC. Sept 20

d. 1537. A priest of the London charterhouse imprisoned with others of his community at Newgate for opposition to Henry VIII's ecclesiastical policy. He died in prison from starvation. Beatified 1886.

THOMAS DIEN (THIEN) (Bl) M. AC. Sept 21

d. 1838. A native seminarist in Cochin-China, attached to the Foreign Missions of Paris. He was cruelly scourged and finally strangled, being eighteen years old at the time of his death. Beatified 1900.

THOMAS of VILLANUEVA (St) Bp. OSA. RM. Sept 22

1488–1555 (Sept 8). Born at Fuellana, near Villanueva, Spain, the son of a miller. He studied at Alcalá and joined the Augustinians at Salamanca. After his ordination in 1520 he was appointed prior successively of the Augustinian friaries of Salamanca (where he taught moral theology in the university), Burgos and Valladolid. Later he became in turn provincial of Andalusia and Castile, court chaplain and (1544) archbishop of Valencia. As archbishop his outstanding characteristic was self-sacrifice: he was known as the grand almoner of the poor. He left a number of theological writings. Canonized 1658.

THOMAS CUFIOJE (Bl) M. AC. Sept 28

d. 1630. A Japanese layman, Augustinian tertiary, beheaded at Nagasaki. Beatified 1867.

THOMAS HÉLYE (Bl) C. AC. Oct 19

1187–1257. Born at Biville in Normandy, he led an ascetic life in the house of his parents and devoted part of his time to teaching the catechism to the poor. He was ordained priest at the request of his bishop and became an itinerant preacher throughout Normandy. Later he was appointed almoner to the king. He died at the castle of Vauville, Manche. Cult confirmed 1859.

THOMAS THWING (THWENG) (Bl) M.   AC. Oct 23

d. 1680. Born at Heworth in Yorkshire and educated at Douai, he was ordained in 1665 and returned to England where he worked for fifteen years on the Yorkshire mission. He was martyred at York for his alleged part in the Oates plot. Beatified 1929.

THOMAS BELLACCI (Bl) C. OFM. AC. Oct 31

1370–1447. A native of Florence who joined the Franciscan friary at Fiesole, where, though only a lay-brother, he was made novice-master. Later he worked successfully to introduce the Franciscan Observance into Corsica and S. Italy and combated the Fraticelli in Tuscany. When over seventy he went to preach in Syria and Abyssinia where, to his sorrow, he narrowly escaped martyrdom by the Mohammedans. Cult approved 1771.

THOMAS of WALDEN (Bl) C. OC. PC. Nov 2

c.1375–1430. Thomas Netter was born at Saffron Walden and joined the Carmelites. He was an active opponent of Lollardism and a prominent member of the council of Constance. King Henry V chose him as his confessor and died in his arms. He died at Rouen.

THOMAS of ANTIOCH (St) H. RM. Nov 18

d. 782. A Syrian monk who dwelt in the vicinity of Antioch. He is venerated as a protector against pestilence.

THOMAS COTENDA and Comp. (BB) MM.   AC. Nov 27

d. 1619. A scion of the Japanese royal family of Firando. He was educated by the Jesuits and lived in exile at Naga-saki, where he was ultimately beheaded with ten companions. Beatified 1867.

THOMAS SOMERS (Bl) M. AC. Dec 10

d. 1610. Thomas Somers (*alias* Wilson) was born at Skelsmergh, Westmorland, and started life as a schoolmaster. Later he went to Douai and became a priest. On returning to England he worked on the London mission. Together with Bl John Roberts, OSB., he was hanged at Tyburn for his priesthood. Beatified 1929.

THOMAS HOLLAND (Bl) M. SJ. AC. Dec 12

d. 1642. Thomas Holland (*alias* Sanderson, *alias* Hammond), born at Sutton, near Prescot, Lancs., was educated at St Omer and Valladolid and became a Jesuit in 1624. He was hanged for his priesthood at Tyburn. Beatified 1929.

THOMAS DE and Comp (BB) MM. Tert. OP.   AC. Dec 19

d. 1839. A native of Tonkin, a tailor by trade and a Dominican tertiary, who was strangled with four companions for giving shelter to the missionaries. Beatified 1900.

THOMAS of FARFA (St) Ab. OSB. AC. Dec 10

d. c.720. A native of Maurienne in Savoy. After becoming a Benedictine he went on pilgrimage to the Holy Land and on his return settled as a hermit near Farfa in Italy. With the help of his friend, the duke of Spoleto, he restored the abbey of Farfa to its former splendour.

THOMAS the APOSTLE (St) RM. Dec 21

1st cent. Surnamed "Didymus," i.e, the twin. All we know for certain about him is derived from the gospel narrative, where the chief episode related of him concerns his unbelief and subsequent profession of faith in Christ's resurrection (John XX, 24 sqq.). According to a very ancient tradition he is said to have preached in S. India and there to have suffered martyrdom, but there is no decisive proof of this.

THOMAS BECKET (St) Bp. M.
RM. Dec 29

1118–1170. Born in London of Norman parents, he was sent to Paris to study and entered the service of Archbishop Theobald of Canterbury, who sent him to Bologna and Auxerre to follow a course of civil and canon law and in 1154 made him his archdeacon. He soon became a bosom friend of Henry II, who in 1155 appointed him chancellor of the kingdom and in 1162 archbishop of Canterbury. Up to this time Thomas had led a rather worldly life, but he now gave himself up completely to the faithful discharge of his pastoral duties. Being forced to oppose the king's wanton interference in ecclesiastical matters, he was brutally done to death in his cathedral by royal retainers. The whole kingdom at once proclaimed him a martyr, and the Church confirmed the title by canonizing him in 1173. His shrine became one of the most famous in Christendom.

THOMASIUS (THOMASSO) (Bl) H. OSB. Cam.   AC. March 25
Otherwise Thomas of Costacciaro, q.v.

THOMIAN (TOIMEN) Bp.
AC. Jan 10

d. c.660. Archbishop of Armagh 623–c.660. He wrote a letter to the Holy See on the paschal controversy.

THORDGITH (THORCTGYD, THEORIGITHA) N. OSB.
AC. Jan 26

d. c.700. Novice-mistress at the abbey of Barking under St Ethelburga. She is described as a miracle of patience under suffering.

THORLAC THORHALLI (St) C. OSA.   PC. Dec 23

1133–1193. Born in Iceland, he was ordained deacon before he was fifteen and priest at the age of eighteen. He was then sent to study at Paris and Lincoln. In 1177 he became bishop of Skalholt in his native island. By vigorous measures he succeeded in stamping out simony and incontinency. He was "canonized" in 1198 by the Althing, but his cult has never been officially confirmed.

THRACE (Martyrs of) (SS)
RM. Aug 20

? A group of thirty-seven martyrs put to death somewhere in Thrace. They were cast into a furnace after their hands and feet had been cut off.

THRASEAS (St) Bp. M.   RM. Oct 5

d. c.170. Bishop of Eumenia in Phrygia, an opponent of the Montanists, martyred at Smyrna.

THRASILLA (St) V.   RM. Dec 24
Otherwise Tarsilla, q.v.

THYRSUS and PROJECTUS (SS) MM.   RM. Jan 24
? Martyrs of whom we know only the names.

THYRSUS, LEUCIUS and CALLINICUS (SS) MM.   RM. Jan 28

d. 251. Martyrs of Apollonia in Phrygia. Their alleged relics were brought to Constantinople and thence to Spain and France: for this reason St Thyrsus had a full office in the Mozarabic liturgy, and he is also patron of the ancient cathedral of Sisteron in the Basses Alpes, France.

THYRSUS (St) M.   RM. Jan 31
See Saturninus, Thyrsus and Victor.

THYRSUS (St) M.   RM. Sept 24
See Andochius, Thyrus and Felix.

TIBBA (St) N. OSB.   AC. March 6
See Kyneburga, Kyneswide and Tibba.

**TIBERIUS, MODESTUS and FLO-
RENTIA (SS) MM.   RM. Nov 10**
d. 303. Martyrs who met their death
under Diocletian at Agde, diocese of
Montpellier.

**TIBURTIUS, VALERIAN and
MAXIMUS (SS) MM.   RM. Apr 14**
d. ?. Three names which occur in the
Acta of St Caecilia—Valerian as her
husband, Tiburtius as his brother and
Maximus as an official. Their tombs in
the Cemetery of Pretextatus were visited
by pilgrims in the Middle Ages. Though
the *Acta* of St Caecilia are regarded as a
romance, these saints might be authentic martyrs, to whom the author of St
Caecilia's life had assigned imaginary
rôles.

TIBURTIUS (St) M.   RM. Aug 11
d. *c*.288. A martyr at Rome. He was
later connected with the soldier-martyr
St Sebastian. His cult is ancient but
there are no trustworthy biographical
details.

TIBURTIUS (St) M.   RM. Sept 9
See Hyacinth, Alexander and Tiburtius.

**TIGERNACH (TIGERNAKE,
TIERNEY, TIERRY) (St) Bp.
                            AC. Apr 4**
d. 549. Said to have been abbot of the
monastery of Clones and to have succeeded St Macartin as bishop at Clogher. His life, in its present form, cannot
be taken as a historical document.

**TIGIDES and REMEDIUS (SS) Bps.
                            RM. Feb 3**
6th cent. ? Two bishops who succeeded
one another in the see of Gap (French
Alps).

**TIGRIDIA (or TRIGIDIA) (St) Abs.
OSB.   AC. Nov 22**
d. *c*.925. A daughter of Count Sancho
García, of Old Castile, who founded for
her the Benedictine nunnery of Oña,
near Burgos (later it became a monastery
of monks). St Tigridia is greatly venerated in the province of Burgos.

**TIGRIUS and EUTROPIUS (SS)
MM.   RM. Jan 12**
d. 404–405. Tigrius was a priest and
Eutropius a reader in the church of
Constantinople; both were loyal ad-
herents of their bishop St John Chrysostom. When the latter was banished
they were falsely accused of setting fire
to the cathedral and senate-house of
Constantinople and were put to the
torture. Eutropius died under it;
Tigrius seems to have survived and to
have been deported into Asia.

**TILBERT (GILBERT) (St) Bp.
OSB.   AC. Sept 7**
d. 789. Bishop of Hexham, 781–789.
No details are known of his life.

**TILLO (THILLO, THIELMAN,
THÉAU, TILLOINE, TILLON,
TILMAN, HILLONIUS, etc.) (St)
OSB.   AC. Jan 7**
d. *c*.702. Born in Saxony, he was kidnapped by robbers and carried as a
slave to the Low Countries, where he
was ransomed by St Eligius of Noyon.
He became a monk at Solignac, and
after his ordination to the priesthood,
evangelized the district round Tournai
and Courtrai. He returned to Solignac,
where he passed the last years of his
life.

TIMOLAUS and Comp. (SS) MM.
RM. March 24
d. 303. A group of eight martyrs, beheaded at Caesarea in Palestine under Diocletian. Eusebius gives the names of the rest: Dionysius (two), Romulus, Pausis, Alexander (two), and Agapius.

TIMON (St) M.   RM. Apr 19
1st cent. One of the first seven deacons, chosen by the Apostles (Acts VI, 5). There are only conflicting traditions as to the rest of his life.

TIMOTHY (St) Bp. M. RM. Jan 24
d. 97. "The beloved son in faith" of St Paul, whom he accompanied on his missionary journeys and by whom he was ordained bishop of Ephesus, while yet young. The Apostle wrote to him two epistles which are among the canonical books. According to a very ancient tradition, St Timothy was stoned to death for denouncing the worship of Diana.

TIMOTHY (St) M.   RM. March 24
See Mark and Timothy.

TIMOTHY and DIOGENES (SS) MM.   RM. Apr 6
d. ? 345. Martyrs at Philippi in Macedonia, victims probably of the Arians.

TIMOTHY and MAURA (SS) MM.
RM. May 3
d. 298. Husband and wife, martyred at Antinoë in Egypt, by being nailed to a wall, where they lingered for nine days, consoling each other. They had been married only three weeks. Timothy, who was a reader, had been condemned for refusing to deliver the Sacred Books.

TIMOTHY, POLIUS and EUTY-CHIUS (SS) MM.   RM. May 21
? Three deacons in the African province of Mauretania Caesariensis, martyred under Diocletian.

TIMOTHY (St) M.   RM. May 22
See Faustinus, Timothy and Venustus.

TIMOTHY (St) Bp. M.
RM. June 10
d. 362. Bishop of Prusa in Bithynia, martyred under Julian the Apostate.

TIMOTHY, THECLA and AGAPI-US (SS) MM.   RM. Aug 19
d. 304–306. Timothy, bishop of Gaza in Palestine, was burnt alive in his episcopal city (304). Thecla was condemned to be thrown to the wild beasts. Agapius was cast into the sea at Caesarea in Palestine (306).

TIMOTHY (St) M.   RM. Aug 22
d. c.306. A Roman martyr of the time of Diocletian. His remains were enshrined in a chapel near St Paul-outside-the-Walls and venerated there during the Middle Ages.

TIMOTHY (St) M.   RM. Aug 23
See Apollinaris and Timothy.

TIMOTHY of MONTECCHIO (Bl)
C. OFM.   AC. Aug 26
1414–1504. A native of Montecchio, near Aquila, in Italy, he became a Franciscan Observant and was celebrated for his supernatural gift of infused knowledge. Cult confirmed in 1870.

TIMOTHY and FAUSTUS (SS)
MM.   RM. Sept 8
? Martyrs at Antioch in Syria.

TIMOTHY (St) M.   RM. Dec 19
d. c.250. A deacon, burnt alive in Africa under Decius.

TITIAN (St) Bp.   RM. Jan 16
d. 650. For thirty years a bishop in the neighbourhood of Venice. The seat of his bishopric (Opitergium or Oderzo) has since been destroyed.

TITIAN (St) Bp.   RM. March 3
d. *c*.536. Said to have been a German by
birth, who became bishop of Brescia.

TITUS (St) Bp. RM. Jan 4 and Feb 6
d. ?. *c*.96. One of the favourite disciples
of St Paul, by whom he was consecrated
first bishop of Crete. St Paul addressed
to him one of the pastoral epistles. He
died in Crete (at Gortyna?).

TITUS (St) M.   RM. Aug 16
d. 410 (or 426?). A Roman deacon, put
to death by a soldier during the sack of
Rome by the Goths, while he was distributing alms to the half-starved
population.

TOBIAS (St) M.   RM. Nov 2
See Carterius, Styriacus, etc.

TOCHUMRA (St) V.   AC. June 11
? A virgin venerated in the diocese of
Kilmore. She is invoked by women in
labour.

TOIMAN (St) Bp.   AC. Jan 10
Otherwise Thomian, q.v.

TOLA (St) Bp.   AC. March 30
d. *c*.733. An Irish abbot-bishop of
Disert Tola (Meath).

TOOLEY (St) King M. RM. July 29
A corrupt form of the name of St Olaus
or Olav, q.v.

TORANNAN (St) Bp.   AC. June 12
Otherwise Ternan, q.v.

TORELLO (Bl) H. OSB. Vall.
                              AC. March 16
1201–1281. Born at Poppi in Tuscany,
he was led astray by evil companions,
but repented and received the habit of
a recluse from the Vallumbrosan abbot
of San Fedele. He lived as a recluse,
walled up in his cell, for sixty years.

Vallumbrosans and Franciscans claim
him. It seems certain that he was, at any
rate, a Vallumbrosan oblate. Cult confirmed by Benedict XIV.

TORPES (St) M.   RM. Apr 29
d. ? *c*.65. A martyr at Pisa, said to have
suffered under Nero. The legends we
have about him are altogether unreliable.

**TORQUATUS, CTESIPHON,
SECUNDUS, INDALETIUS, CAE-
CILIUS, HESYCHIUS, and EU-
PHRASIUS (SS) MM. RM. May 15**
1st cent. According to a tradition,
which, however, is not very ancient,
they were disciples of the Apostles, by
whom they were sent to evangelize
Spain. They worked chiefly in the
South, as follows: Torquatus at Guadix,
near Granada; Ctesiphon at Verga
(Vierzo?); Secundus at Avila; Indaletius at Urci, near Almeria; Caecilius
at Granada; Hesychius at Gibraltar;
Euphrasius at Andujar. Most of them
suffered martyrdom. The Mozarabic
liturgy had a common feast for all seven.

TORTHRED (St) M.   AC. Apr 9
Perhaps a variant of Theodore, q.v.

TOTNAN (St) M.   RM. July 8
See Kilian, Colman and Totnan.

TOULOUSE (Martyrs of) (BB)
                              AC. May 29
d. 1228. A group of twelve martyrs—
four of the secular clergy, three Dominicans, two Benedictines, two Franciscans, one layman—put to death by the
Albigensians near Toulouse on the eve
of the Ascension. They died singing the
Te Deum. Cult confirmed in 1866.

TOUREDEC (St) M.   AC. Apr 9
Otherwise Torthred, perhaps a variant
of Theodore, q.v.

TRANQUILLINUS (St) M.
                            RM. July 6
d. ? 288. A Roman martyr connected
with the legend of St Sebastian, q.v.

**TRASON, PONTIAN and PRAE-
TEXTATUS (SS) MM.** RM. Dec 11
d. c.302. Roman martyrs under Diocletian, put to death for ministering to
the Christian prisoners awaiting martyrdom.

TREA (St) V.   AC. Aug 3
5th cent. Converted to Christianity by
St Patrick. She passed the rest of her
life as a recluse at Ardtree, Derry.

TREMORUS (St) M.   AC. Nov 7
6th cent. Infant son of St Triphina. He
was murdered at Carhaix in Brittany by
his stepfather, Count Conmore. He is
patron saint of Carhaix.

**TRESSAN (French: TRÉSAIN) (St)
C.**   AC. Feb 7
d. 550. An Irish missionary, ordained
priest by St Remigius, who worked at
Mareuil on the Marne.

TRÈVES (Martyrs of) (SS)
                              RM. Oct 6
d. 287. The entry in the RM. is as
follows: "At Trèves, the commemoration of the almost innumerable martyrs
who were slain in divers ways in the
persecution of Diocletian, under the
governor Rictiovarus, for the faith of
Christ."

**TRIDUNA (TREDWALL, TRAL-
LEN) (St) V.**   AC. Oct 8
8th or 4th cent? A maiden connected
with the legend of St Regulus's mission
to Scotland.

TRIEN (TRIENAN) (St) Ab.
                              AC. March 22
5th cent. One of St Patrick's disciples,
abbot of Killelga.

TRILLO (DRILLO, DREL) (St) C.
                              AC. June 15
6th cent. The son of a Breton chieftain,
who crossed over into Wales with St
Cadfan. He is the patron saint of Llandrillo (Denbigh) and of Llandrillo
(Monmouth).

TRIPHINA (St) W.   RM. July 5
6th cent. The mother of St Tremorus
the infant-martyr. She passed the latter
years of her life in a convent in Brittany.

TRIPHINA (St) M.   RM. July 5
See Agatho and Triphina.

TRIPHYLLIUS (St) Bp.
                              RM. June 13
d. c.370. A lawyer converted to Christianity who was made bishop of Nikosia
Cyprus. He was a companion of St
Spiridion and a loyal supporter of St
Athanasius against the Arians, who
bitterly persecuted him.

TRIPOS (St) M.   RM. June 10
See Basilides, Tripos, etc.

TRIVERIUS (St) H.   AC. Jan 16
d. c.550. Born in Neustria, he showed
from childhood a strong leaning to the
contemplative life. He lived as a hermit
near the monastery of Thérouanne,
until he moved to Dombes. The village
of Saint Trivier commemorates his
name. He is honoured at Lyons and in
the diocese of Belley.

TROADIUS (St) M.   RM. Dec 28
d. 250. A martyr of Neo-Caesarea in
Pontus, in the persecution under
Decius.

**TROJAN (French: TROYEN) (St)
Bp.**   RM. Nov 30
d. 533. Said to have been born of a Jewish father and a Saracen mother. He
became a priest at Saintes under St
Vivian, whom he succeeded in the see.

TRON or TROND (St) Ab. OSB.
RM. Nov 23
Otherwise Trudo, q.v.

TROPHIMUS and THALUS (SS)
MM.   RM. March 11
d. *c*.300. Martyrs at Laodicea in Syria, crucified under Diocletian.

TROPHIMUS and EUCARPIUS
(SS) MM.   RM. March 18
d. *c*.304. Two pagan soldiers told off to hunt up Christians; they were converted and burnt alive at Nicomedia under Diocletian.

TROPHIMUS and THEOPHILUS
(SS) MM.   RM. July 23
d. *c*.302. Martyrs, beheaded at Rome under Diocletian.

TROPHIMUS, SABBATIUS and
DORYMEDON (SS) MM.
RM. Sept 19
d. *c*.277. Asiatic martyrs under the emperor Probus. They suffered probably at Antioch in Syria.

TROPHIMUS (St) Bp. RM. Dec 29
d. *c*.280. First bishop of Arles, sent to Gaul from Rome *c*.240–260. Since 452 (Synod of Arles) the church of Provence has identified him with St Trophimus, the disciples of St Paul (Acts XX, 4; XXI, 29; II Tim. IV, 20).

TRUDO (TRUDON, TRON,
TROND, TRUYEN, TRUDJEN)
(St) Ab. OSB.   RM. Nov 23
d. *c*.695 A Benedictine under St Remaclus, he was ordained priest by St Clodulphus of Metz, and eventually founded and governed an abbey on his paternal estate (*c*.660), which was afterwards called after him St Trond. It is situated between Louvain and Tongres.

TRUDPERT (St) H.   AC. Apr 26
d. *c*. ? 644. A solitary in Münstethal.

The Benedictine abbey of St Trudpert arose on that site. According to his life he was of Irish origin, and was murdered by servants, and so venerated as a martyr. This life is however considered a legend.

TRUMWIN (St) Bp. OSB.
AC. Dec 2
d. *c*.700. He was appointed (681) by St Theodore and King Egfrid bishop over the Southern Picts, and set up his see at the monastery of Abercorn on the Firth of Forth. In 685 King Egfrid was killed by the Picts and St Trumwin and all his monks had to flee South. He retired to Whitby and there he lived an exemplary monastic life.

TRYPHAENA (TRIPHENES) (St)
M.   RM. Jan 31
? A matron of Cyzicus on the Hellespont who, after having been tortured in divers manners, was thrown to a savage bull and gored to death.

TRYPHENNA and TRYPHOSA
(SS)   RM. Nov 10
1st cent. Two converts of St Paul from Iconium in Lycaonia, mentioned by the apostle in his Epistle to the Romans (XVI, 12). Tradition represents them as protectresses of St Thecla.

TRYPHON (St) M.   RM. Jan 4
See Aquilinus, Geminus, etc.

TRYPHON and Comp. (SS) MM.
RM. July 3
? A group of thirteen martyrs, who suffered at Alexandria in Egypt.

TRYPHON, RESPICIUS and
NYMPHA (SS) MM.   RM. Nov 10
d. 251. Tryphon was a gooseherd at Campsada near Apamea in Syria and was martyred in Nicaea under Decius. The names of Respicius and Nympha

have been joined to that of Tryphon only since the 11th century; we know nothing about either saint.

TRYPHONIA (St) W.   RM. Oct 18
3rd cent. A Roman widow martyred in the Holy City. In legend she has been made wife either of the emperor Decius, or of Decius's son, Messius Decius. Her *Acta* are worthless.

TRYPHOSA (St)   RM. Nov 10
See Tryphenna and Tryphosa.

TUDA (St) Bp.   PC. (?) Oct 21
d. 664. An Irish monk who succeeded St Colman in the see of Lindisfarne, a staunch adherent of the Roman practices. He died of the pestilence within the first year of his appointment. He does not seem to have enjoyed a public cult.

TUDE (St) Bp. M.   RM. June 17
Otherwise Antidius, q.v.

TUDINUS (St) Ab.   AC. May 9
Otherwise Tudy, q.v.

TUDNO (St) C.   AC. June 5
6th cent. The saint after whom Llandudno in Carnarvon is named. Several Welsh legends refer to him.

TUDWAL (TUGDUAL, TUGDUALUS) (St) Bp.   AC. Nov 30
d. c.564. A Welsh monk who crossed over into Brittany and became bishop of Tréguier. Three places in the Lleyn Peninsular in Carnarvonshire perpetuate his memory.

TUDY (TUDCLYD, TYBIE) (St) V.
AC. Jan 30
5th cent. Daughter of Brychan of Brecknock. She has left her name to Llandybie in Carmarthenshire.

TUDY (TUDINUS, TEGWIN, THETGO) (St) Ab.   AC. May 9
5th cent. A Breton saint, disciple of St Maudez (Mawes) and fellow-worker with St Corentinus. He was first a hermit and then an abbot near Landevennec in Brittany; like St Mawes, he spent some time in Cornwall, where a church and parish still bear his name.

TUGDUAL (St) Bp.   AC. Nov 30
Otherwise Tudwal, q.v.

TURIAF (TURIAV, TURIAVUS) (St) Bp.   RM. July 13
d. c.750. A Breton who succeeded St Samson as bishop of Dol.

TURIBIUS de MOGROBEJO (St) Bp.   RM. March 23
1538–1606. Torbibio Alfonso de Mogrobejo was born at Mayorga, prov. of León, Spain. He was professor of law at Salamanca, and, though a layman, was made president of the court of the Inquisition at Granada. Philip II appointed him to the see of Lima in Peru (1580) and the saint, fearing God but no man, with boundless zeal and untiring energy renewed the face of the Church in Peru. Canonized in 1726.

TURIBIUS of ASTORGA (St) Bp.
RM. Apr 16
d. c.460. Bishop of Astorga in Spain, champion of Catholic doctrine against the Priscillianists.

TURIBIUS of PALENCIA (St) Ab.
AC. Apr 16 (?)
d. c.528. Probably a bishop. The abbotfounder of the great abbey of Liébana in Asturias, which eventually became a Benedictine centre.

TURKETIL (St) Ab. OSB.
AC. July 11
887–975. A nephew of King Edred of

England and his chancellor. In 948 he became a monk and shortly after abbot of Croyland, which he restored, attaching a cloistral school to the monastery.

TURNINUS (St) C.   AC. July 17
8th cent. An Irish priest who worked as a missionary with St Foillan in the Netherlands, and more particularly in the vicinity of Antwerp.

TUTILO (St) Mk. OSB.
AC. March 28
d. c.915. Monk of St Gall in Switzerland. Handsome, eloquent, quickwitted, a giant in strength and stature, poet, orator, architect, painter, sculptor, metal worker, mechanic, musician who played and taught several instruments at the abbey school, he was characterized by his obedience and recollection.

TUTO (TOTTO) (Bl) Bp. OSB.
AC. May 14
d. 930. Monk and abbot of St Emmeram at Ratisbon. He became bishop of the same city and secretary to the emperor Arnold.

TUTO (TOTTO) (Bl) Ab. OSB.
AC. Nov 19
d. 815. Abbot-founder (764) of the great Benedictine abbey of Ottobeuren in Bavaria.

TWELVE HOLY BROTHERS, The (SS) MM.   RM. Sept 1
d. c.303 ? The relics of several groups of martyrs, who had suffered in S. Italy, were brought together and enshrined at Benevento in 760. A legend grew up according to which all these martyrs were the sons of SS Boniface and Thecla, q.v.; they were said to have been arrested in Africa and brought to Italy where they were put to death. This legend is now considered to have no historical foundation. The several groups comprised in the so-called "twelve brothers," or Martyrs of the South, are (1) Aug 27. At Potenza in the Basilicata, Arontius or Orontius, Honoratus, Fortunatus and Sabinian. (2) Aug 28. At Venosa in Apulia, Septiminus, Januarius and Felix. (3) Aug 29. At Velleianum in Apulia, Vitalis, Sator (or Satyrus) and Repositus. (4) Sept 1. At Sentianum in Apulia, Donatus and another Felix.

TWYNNELL (St)
This occurs as a place-name in Pembrokeshire. It is possibly a corrupt form of the name of St Winneur, or Winoc, or Winwaloë.

TYCHICUS (St) Bp.   RM. Apr 29
1st cent. A disciple of St Paul the Apostle (Acts 20: 4; 21: 29) and his fellow-worker (Col. 4: 7; Eph. 6: 21 sq.). He is said to have ended his days as bishop of Paphos in Cyprus.

TYCHON (St) Bp.   RM. June 16
d. c.450. Bishop of Amathus in Cyprus. He energetically fought against the last remnants of paganism in the island, especially the cult of Aphrodite.

TYDECHO (St)   AC. Dec 17
6th cent. A Welshman, brother of St Cadfan. He and his sister dwelt in Merionethshire. Several churches are dedicated in his honour.

TYDFIL (St) M.   AC. Aug 23
d. c.480. Of the clan of Brychan. She is venerated at Merthyr-Tydfil, Glamorgan, where she was slain by the marauding Picts or Saxons.

TYRANNIO, SILVANUS, PELEUS, NILUS and ZENOBIUS (SS) MM.
RM. Feb 20
d. c.304. The RM. entry commemorates

an unknown number of Martyrs of Tyr. According to the Bollandists, Tyrannio and Zenobius, whose names are included, suffered at Antioch in 310, Silvanus at Emesa; Peleus and Nilus were, according to Eusebius, Egyptian bishops, among the martyrs of Palestine.

TYRE (Martyrs of)   RM. Feb 20
d. 302–310. The RM. has this entry: "At Tyre in Phoenicia, the commemoration of blessed martyrs whose number the wisdom of God alone can tell . . ." The group of the preceding entry were among this number.

TYSILIO (TYSSEL, TYSSILO, SULIAU) (St) Ab.   AC. Nov 8
d. *c*.640. A Welsh prince, who became abbot of Meifod in Montgomeryshire and founded several churches in the other parts of Wales; finally (*c*.617) he migrated to Brittany and died at Saint-Suliac.

U

UBALD BALDASSINI (St) Bp.
                              RM. May 16
*c.*1100–1160. Born at Gubbio near Ancona, he was made dean of the cathedral and introduced community life among the canons. In 1128 he became bishop of his native city. His character was remarkable for its combination of gentleness with courage, and it was by these qualities that he succeeded in disarming the tyrannical Frederick Barbarossa. Canonized 1192.

UBALD ADIMARI (Bl) C. OSM.
                              AC. Apr 9
1246–1315. He belonged to the nobility of Florence, and as a leader in the Ghibelline party he was notorious for his wild and dissolute life. In 1276 he was converted by St Philip Benizi who admitted him to the Servite institute. Ubald spent the remainder of his life on Mt Senario, a model to penitent souls. Cult confirmed 1821.

UBRIC (St) Bp.   RM. July 4
Otherwise Ulric, q.v.

UDA (St) V.   AC. Jan 30
Otherwise Tudy, q.v.

UGANDA (Martyrs of) (SS)
                              AC. June 3
1885–1887. Twenty-two negroes of Uganda, boys and young men from thirteen to thirty years of age, for the most part pages of King Mwanga. They were converts of the White Fathers and were martyred with horrible cruelty. Their heroic courage rivalled that of the early martyrs. Canonized in 1964. Each has a separate entry in this book.

UGUCCIO (St) C.
                    RM. May 3 and Feb 12
One of the Seven Founders of the Servite Order, q.v.

UGUZO (LUCIUS) M.
                              AC. Aug 16
? A poor shepherd in the mountains of Carvagna (Italian Alps) who gave his savings to the poor and the churches. He was killed through envy by one of his former masters. His cult has flourished at Milan since 1280 and has been rcpeatedly approved by Rome.

ULCHED (ULCHAD, YLCHED) (St)   AC. Apr 6
? The holy man who has given his name to the church of Llechulched in Anglesey.

ULFRID (WOLFRED, WILFRID) (St) M.   AC. Jan 18
d. 1029. A native of England who became a missionary in Germany and Sweden. He was martyred for destroying the idol of Thor.

ULMAR (St) Ab. OSB. AC. July 20
Otherwise Wulmar, q.v.

ULPHIA (WULFIA, OLFE, WULFE) (St) H.   AC. Jan 31
8th cent. Said to have lived as a solitary near Amiens under the direction of the aged hermit St Domitius. At a later period the convent of the Paraclete was built over her tomb.

ULPIAN (St) M.   RM. Apr 3
Otherwise Vulpian, q.v.

ULRIC (St) H.   **AC. Feb 20**
Otherwise Wulfric, q.v.

ULRIC of EINSIEDELN (Bl) C.
OSB.   **AC. May 29**
d. *p*.978. Son of St Gerold. He became
a monk at the Swiss abbey of Einsiedeln
and was appointed treasurer. After his
father's death he retired to live as a
hermit in the latter's cell. His feast is
observed at Einsiedeln.

ULRIC (ULDARICUS, UDAL-
RIC) (St) Bp.   **RM. July 4**
d. 973. A native of Augsburg, at the age
of seven he was sent to be educated at
the Swiss Benedictine abbey of St Gall.
In 923 he was nominated bishop of
Augsburg and became the protector of
his people against the invading Magyars. In his old age he retired to St Gall
and took one of his nephews as his
coadjutor: this led to an unjust charge
of nepotism. Canonized 993.

ULRIC of CLUNY (St) Mk. OSB.
                        AC. July 14
c.1018–1093. Born at Ratisbon, he became archdeacon of Freising and then
went on a pilgrimage to Rome and
Jerusalem. On his return he joined the
Benedictines at Cluny under St Hugh
(1061). He held the following offices in
rapid succession: novice master (as such
he wrote the famous Cluniac Customary), prior and confessor of the
Cluniac nunnery of Marcigny, prior of
Peterlingen, prior of Rüggersburg, and
finally prior-founder of Zell in the Black
Forest. Throughout life he suffered from
violent headaches.

ULTAN (St) Ab. OSB.   **AC. May 2**
d. *c*.686. An Irishman, brother of SS
Fursey and Foillan and a monk with
them at Burghcastle near Yarmouth.
Thence he crossed over to Belgium,
where he was warmly welcomed by St

Gertrude of Nivelles. He was chaplain
to her nunnery and taught chant to the
nuns until he succeeded his brother St
Foillan in the abbacies of Fosses and
Peronne.

ULTAN (St) H. OSB.   **AC. Aug 8**
8th cent. An Irishman and monk-priest
of St Peter's monastery at Craik. He
excelled in the art of illumination.

ULTAN (St) Bp.   **AC. Sept 4**
7th cent. There are a score or so of Irish
saints named Ultan. Besides the two
listed above the most important seems
to have been a bishop of Ardbraccan,
noted for his fondness for children and
said to have collected the writings of
St Brigid.

ULTIUS (St) Bp.   **AC. Jan 8**
Otherwise Wulsin, q.v.

UNAMAN (St) M. OSB. AC. Feb 15
See Winaman, Unaman and Sunaman.

UNI (UNNI, UNNO, HUNO) (St)
Bp. OSB.   **AC. Sept 17**
d. 936. A Benedictine of New Corvey in
Saxony, who in 917 was appointed
bishop of Bremen-Hamburg. He evangelized Sweden and Denmark with
signal success and died at Birka in
Sweden.

URBAN (St) M.   **RM. Jan 24**
See Babilas, Urban, etc.

URBAN (St) M.   **RM. March 8**
See Cyril, Rogatus, etc.

URBAN of LANGRES (St) Bp.
                        RM. Apr 2
d. *c*.390. Sixth bishop of Langres,
nominated to that see in 374. In some
parts of Burgundy and neighbouring
provinces he is honoured as the patron
saint of vine dressers.

URBAN (St) Ab. OSB.   AC. Apr 6
d. *c*.940. Abbot of the Benedictine
monastery of Peñalba in the diocese of
Astorga, Spain. He helped St Gennadius to bring about a Benedictine revival.

URBAN (St) M.   RM. Apr 16
See Saragossa (Martyrs of).

URBAN I (St) Pope M.   RM. May 25
d. 230. A Roman, successor of Callistus
in the papal chair (222–230). During his
pontificate the Church seems to have
enjoyed comparative peace. He does not
appear to have died a martyr.

URBAN (St) M.   RM. July 2
See Ariston, Crescentian, etc.

URBAN II (Bl) Pope OSB.
RM. July 29
1042–1099. Odo of Lagery was born at
Chatillon-sur Marne and belonged to
the family of the counts of Semur. He
studied at Reims under St Bruno and
became archdeacon of that church. In
1070 he joined the Benedictines of
Cluny and was soon appointed grand
prior under St Hugh. In 1078 he was
created cardinal bishop of Ostia and in
1088 was elected pope. As prior, as
cardinal and as pope he followed and
fostered the Gregorian policy of ecclesiastical reform. As pope he had as
adviser St Bruno, the founder of the
Carthusians. Urban is perhaps best
remembered as the promoter of the
first crusade at the council of Clermont,
in consequence of an appeal from the
Byzantine emperor Alexius I. Beatified
1881.

URBAN, THEODORE and Comp.
(SS) MM.   RM. Sept 5
d. 370. a group of eighty priests and
clerics who, in the time of the Arian
emperor Valens, were deliberately left
to perish in a burning ship for having

appealed to the emperor against the
persecution of the Catholics.

URBAN (St) M.   RM. Oct 31
See Ampliatus, Urban and Narcissus.

URBAN (St) Bp.   RM. Nov 28
See Valerian, Urban, etc.

URBAN (St) Bp.   RM. Dec 7
d. *c*.356. Bishop of Teano in Campania.

URBAN V (Bl) Pope OSB.
RM. Dec 19
1310–1370. William of Grimoard was
born in Languedoc and educated at the
universities of Montpellier and Toulouse. He became a Benedictine at the
priory of Chiriac and was sent to take
his doctorate at Paris and Avignon. He
affiliated himself to the Cluniacs and
was made abbot of St Germanus at
Auxerre, and then of St Victor at
Marseilles. In 1361 he was sent as papal
legate to Italy (the papacy then being
at Avignon) and in the following year,
although not yet a cardinal, was elected
pope. He succeeded in transferring the
papacy back to Rome, but in 1370 he
was forced to retire to France, dying the
same year. Cult confirmed 1870.

URBITIUS (St) Bp.   AC. March 20
d. *c*.420. Bishop of Metz. He built a
church in honour of St Felix of Nola
which became the abbey church of the
monastery of St Clement.

URBITIUS (Spanish: ÚRBEZ) (St)
H. OSB.   AC. Dec 15
d. *c*.805. Said to have been born at
Bordeaux, to have become a monk in
France, and to have been taken prisoner
by Saracens and brought to Spain. He
managed to escape and settled as a
hermit in the valley of Nocito, Aragonese
Pyrenees, near Huesca. There is no
trustworthy biography of the saint, but

his cult is still very flourishing in that district.

URCISCENUS (St) Bp. RM. June 21
d. *c*.216. Reckoned as the seventh bishop of Pavia, *c*.183–216.

URPASIAN (St) M. AC. March 13
d. 295. A Christian of the household of Diocletian who was burnt alive at Nicomedia.

URSACIUS (St) RM. Aug 16
Otherwise Arsacius, q.v.

URSICINUS (St) M. RM. June 19
d. *c*.67. Said to have been a physician at Ravenna who, on being sentenced to death for being a Christian, wavered, but was encouraged by the soldier St Vitalis and accepted martyrdom. His Acts are not trustworthy.

URSICINUS (St) Bp. RM. July 24
d. *c*.380. Registered as the fourth bishop of Sens. An opponent of Arianism.

URSICINUS (St) Bp. OSB. AC. Oct 2
d. 760. Abbot of Disentis in Switzerland, who became bishop of Chur in 754. In 758 he resigned and became a hermit.

URSICINUS (St) Bp. RM. Dec 1
d. *p*.347. A bishop of Brescia in Lombardy who took part in the council of Sardica (347). His shrine at Brescia still exists.

URSICINUS (St) Bp. AC. Dec 20
d. *c*.585. Bishop of Cahors, often mentioned by the historian St Gregory of Tours.

URSICINUS (St) Ab. AC. Dec 20
d. *c*.625. An Irish missionary monk, companion of St Columbanus. He became the abbot-founder of the monas-

tery of St Ursanne, from which the Swiss town so called takes its name.

URSICIUS (St) M. RM. Aug 14
d. 304. An Illyrian tribune in the imperial army beheaded at Nicomedia under Diocletian.

URSINUS (St) Bp. RM. Nov 9
3rd cent. Though alleged to have been one of several disciples of Christ sent by the apostles to be bishops in Gaul, it is certain that he flourished in the 3rd century and that he was the first bishop of Bourges.

URSMAR (St) Bp. OSB. RM. Apr 19
d. 713. Abbot-bishop of the great Benedictine abbey of Lobbes on the Sambre and founder of Aulne and Wallers, also in present-day Belgium. His work as regionary bishop in Flanders was of great importance.

URSULA and Comp. (SS) VV. MM. RM. Oct 21
4th cent. A group of maidens martyred at Cologne, probably under Diocletian. In the fourth century a church was built at Cologne in their honour. Medieval legends greatly embellished the scanty historical facts. The number of, probably, eleven (XI MM VV, i.e., eleven martyr-virgins) was increased to eleven thousand (XIM VV, i.e., XI Millia Virginum—11,000 virgins) and a convenient legendary setting was found for the increased number. Pope Benedict XIV intended to delete the entry concerning them from the RM.

URSULINA (Bl) V. AC. Apr 7
1375–1410. A young woman of Parma who, alleging supernatural visions, visited Clement VII at Avignon and Boniface IX at Rome with a view to putting an end to the papal schism. After a pilgrimage to the Holy Land she was refused admittance to Parma

and had to retire to Bologna, where she died.

URSULINE NUNS (BB) MM.
AC. Oct 17

d. 1794. A group of eleven Ursuline nuns guillotined at Valenciennes for having reopened their school in spite of the prohibition of the French revolutionary authorities. Each has a special entry in this book. Beatified 1920.

URSUS (St) C.
PC Feb 1

6th cent. Of Irish origin, he preached against the Arians in the South of France and became archdeacon of Aosta.

URSUS (St) Bp.
RM. Apr 13

d. 396. Of a noble Sicilian family, he became a convert and fled from his father's wrath to Ravenna, where in 378 he became bishop.

URSUS (St) Bp.
RM. July 30

d. 508. A recluse at the church of St Amator of Auxerre, who was made bishop of that city when he was already seventy-five years of age.

URSUS (St) M.
RM. Sept 30

See Victor and Ursus.

UST (JUSTUS) (St)
AC. Aug 12

? He gives its title to the church of St Just a few miles from Penzance. He is described indiscriminately as a hermit, as a martyr, and as a bishop. Possibly there were several saints of this name, whose lives have been amalgamated.

USTHAZANES (St) M.
RM. Apr 21

See Simeon, Abdechalas, etc.

UTTO (Bl) Ab. OSB.
AC. Oct 3

c.750–820. Abbot-founder of the Benedictine monastery of Metten in Bavaria. Cult approved 1909.

UVAL (St) Bp.
AC. Nov 20

Otherwise Eval, q.v.

V

VAAST (St) Bp.   RM. Feb 6
Otherwise Vedast, q.v.

VACZ (Bl) H.   AC. Nov 26
11th cent. Hermit at Visegrád, in the mountains of Pilis, Hungary. Considered by the Pauline Order as the forerunner of their founder Bl Eusebius (1260).

VALENS and Comp. (SS) MM.
            RM. May 21
? Said to have been a bishop martyred at Auxerre with three boys.

VALENS, PAUL and Comp. (SS) MM.   RM. June 1
d. 309. Martyrs at Caesarea in Palestine, companions of St Pamphilus. Valens was an aged deacon of the church of Jerusalem. They suffered under Diocletian.

VALENS (St) Bp.   RM. July 26
d. 531. Bishop of Verona, 524–531.

VALENTINA and Comp. (SS) VV. MM.   RM. July 25
d. 308. Virgin martyrs in Palestine under Maximian Galerius. See Meuris and Thea.

VALENTINE (St) Bp.   AC. Jan 7
d. c.470. An abbot who became a missionary bishop in Rhaetia. He died at Mais in the Tyrol. Some years later his body was translated to Trent and finally to Passau.

VALENTINE (St) M.   RM. Feb 14
d. 269. A priest and physician in Rome martyred under Claudius the Goth and buried on the Flaminian Way. In 350 a church was built over his tomb. The custom of sending "Valentines" on Feb 14 is based on the medieval belief that birds began to pair on the 14th of February.

VALENTINE (St) Bp. M.
            RM. Feb 14
d. c.269. A bishop of Terni (*Interamna*) about sixty miles from Rome, martyred under Claudius the Goth. Some writers, we believe rightly, identify this saint with the St Valentine recorded above.

VALENTINE (St) Bp.   AC. May 2
d. c. Bishop of Genoa, c.295–307. His relics were discovered and enshrined in 985.

VALENTINE (St) Bp. M.
            RM. July 16
d. c.305. A bishop of Trèves (or more probably Tongres) martyred under Diocletian.

VALENTINE (St) Bp.   AC. Sept 2
4th cent. Fourth bishop of Strasburg.

VALENTINE (St) H.   AC. Oct 25
See Fructus, Valentine and Engratia.

VALENTINE (St) Bp.   RM. Oct 29
Coupled in the RM. with St Maximilian. Nothing is known of him.

VALENTINE BERRIO-OCHOA (Bl) Bp. M. OP.   AC. Nov 1
1827–1861. Born at Ellorio, diocese of Vitoria, Spain. After his profession in the Dominican Order he was sent to the

Philippine Islands and thence (1858) to Tonkin as a bishop titular and vicar apostolic. He was beheaded with Bl Jerome Hermosilla. Beatified in 1909.

VALENTINE and HILARY (SS) MM. RM. Nov 3
d. *c.*304. A priest and his deacon, beheaded at Viterbo, near Rome, under Diocletian.

VALENTINE, FELICIAN and VICTORINUS (SS) MM.
RM. Nov 11
d. *c.*305. Martyrs at Ravenna under Diocletian.

VALENTINE, SOLUTOR and VICTOR (SS) MM. RM. Nov 13
d. *c.*305. Martyrs at Ravenna under Diocletian. Probably a duplicate of Nov 11. To both groups some martyrologies add a number of other names.

VALENTINE, CONCORDIUS, NAVALIS and AGRICOLA (SS) MM. RM. Dec 16
d. *c.*305. In all probability a repetition of the two preceding entries. Since St Peter Chrysologus (d. *c.*450) writes that St Apollinaris was the only martyr of Ravenna, it may be that St Valentine and Comp. were merely venerated in that city, and only later said to have been martyred there.

VALENTINIAN (St) Bp.
AC. Nov 3
d. *c.*500. Bishop of Salerno in S. Italy.

VALENTIO (St) M. RM. May 25
See Pasicrates, Valentio, etc.

VALERIA (Martyrs of) (SS)
RM. March 14
8th cent. The RM. has this entry: "In the province of Valeria, the birthday of two holy monks, whom the Lombards

slew by hanging them on a tree: and there, although dead, they were heard even by their enemies singing psalms". The story is taken from St Gregory the Great (Dial. IV, 21).

VALERIA (St) M. RM. Apr 28
? 1st cent. The alleged mother of SS Gervase and Protase and wife of St Vitalis. She seems to be a fictitious personage. See Vitalis.

VALERIA (St) M. RM. June 5
See Zenais, Dyria, etc.

VALERIA (St) VM. RM. Dec 9
? This saint probably never existed. She is said to have been converted to the Faith by St Martial of Limoges, and to have been beheaded there. (Cf. Martial of Limoges).

VALERIAN (St) M. RM. Apr 14
See Tiburtius, Valerian and Maximus.

VALERIAN (St) Bp. AC. May 13
d. *c.*350. Third bishop of Auxerre. A champion of the Catholic Faith against Arianism.

VALERIAN (St) Bp. AC. July 23
d. *c.*460. A monk of Lérins who was promoted to the see of Cimiez (now united to that of Nice).

VALERIAN (St) M. RM. Aug 23
See Restitutus, Donatus, etc.

VALERIAN (St) M. RM. Sept 12
See Hieronides, Leontius, etc.

VALERIAN (St) M. RM. Sept 15
d. 178. A companion of St Photinus (Pothinus) of Lyons. He succeeded in escaping from prison and reappeared at Tournus, near Autun, where he again preached to the people. He was captured a second time and beheaded.

VALERIAN, MACRINUS and GORDIAN (SS) MM.   RM. Sept 17
? Martyrs ascribed by some to Noyon, by others to Nevers, by others to Nyon (near Berne, Switzerland), by others to a place called Noviodunum near the mouth of the Danube in Lower Moesia.

VALERIAN (St) Bp.   RM. Nov 27
d. 389. Bishop of Aquileia in N. Italy. He succeeded immediately after an Arian bishop and his pontificate, 369–389, was spent in combating that heresy.

VALERIAN, URBAN, CRESCENS, EUSTACE, CRESCONIUS, CRESCENTIAN, FELIX, HORTULANUS and FLORENTIAN (SS) Bps.   RM. Nov 28
5th cent. African bishops banished from their country by the Arian king Genseric. They died in exile and were afterwards honoured as confessors of the Faith.

VALERIAN (St) Bp. (M) RM. Dec 15
d. 457. Bishop of Abbenza in Africa, who, when over eighty years of age, was left to die of exposure for refusing to give up the sacred vessels. He died under the Arian Genseric, king of the Vandals.

VALERIUS (St) Bp.   AC. Jan 16
d. c.453. A hermit taken from his solitude by the people of Sorrento, who made him their bishop.

VALERIUS (St) Bp.   RM. Jan 28
d. 315. Bishop of Saragossa in Spain, under whom St Vincent served as deacon. He was arrested, and exiled under Diocletian; but survived and died in peace in his episcopal city.

VALERIUS (St) Bp.   RM. Jan 29
d. c.320. Legendary second bishop of Trèves and alleged disciple of St Peter.

More probably he was bishop of that city at the beginning of the fourth century.

VALERIUS (St) Bp.   AC. Feb 19
d. p.450. Bishop of Antibes in S. France.

VALERIUS (St) Bp.   AC. Feb 20
? Mentioned by St Gregory of Tours as the first bishop of Conserans in France.

VALERIUS (St) Ab.   AC. Feb 21
d. 695. A native of Astorga in Spain, who became a monk and abbot of San Pedro de Montes. He has left several ascetical writings: he is in fact the last representative of the Isidorian revival in Spain.

VALERIUS and RUFINUS (SS) MM.   RM. June 14
d. c.287. Roman missionaries in Gaul who were martyred at Soissons.

VALERIUS (St) C. OSB. AC. Oct 9
See Lambert and Valerius.

VALERIUS (St) M.   RM. Nov 16
See Rufinus, Mark, etc.

VALÉRY (St) Ab.   RM. Apr 1
Otherwise Walericus, q.v.

VAMNES (St) M.   AC.
d. ?423. A convert to Christianity, he was put to death by the Persian King Bahram V for having rescued a monk cruelly tormented.

VANDRILLE (St) Ab. RM. July 22
Otherwise Wandrille, q.v.

VANNE (VAUNE) (St) Bp. AC. Nov 9
Otherwise Vitonus, q.v.

VARELDE (VEERLE, VERYLDE) (St) V.   AC. Jan 4
Otherwise Pharaïldis, q.v.

VARICUS (St) M.   RM. Nov 15
See Secundus, Fidentian and Varicus.

VARUS (St) M.   RM. Oct 19
d. 307. A Roman soldier in Upper Egypt who, being on guard at a prison in which certain monks condemned to death were confined, on seeing one of them expire in his dungeon, insisted on taking his place and was forthwith hanged from a tree. The Acts are genuine.

VASIUS (French: VAISE, VAIZE) (St) M.   AC. Apr 16
d. *c*.500. A rich citizen of Saintes, in France, murdered by his relatives for distributing his property among the poor.

VEDAST (VAAST, VAAT, GASTON, FOSTER) (St) Bp. RM. Feb 6
d. 539. A fellow-worker with St Remigius in the conversion of the Franks. For close on forty years he ruled the united sees of Arras-Cambrai.

VEEP (VEEPUS, VEEPY, WIMP, WENNAPA) (St) V.   AC. July 1
6th cent. Patron saint of St Veep in Cornwall. St Veep (in Welsh, Gwenafwy) was a daughter of Caw, chief of North Britain and a sister of St Samson of York. Driven south by the Picts, she settled in Cornwall, where place-names still recall her memory.

VEHO (St) Bp.   AC. June 15
Otherwise Vouga, q.v.

VELLEICUS (WILLEIC) (St) Ab. OSB.   AC. Aug 29
8th cent. An Anglo-Saxon, who followed St Swithbert to the apostolate in Germany and became abbot of Kaiserswerth, on the Rhine.

VENANTIUS (St) Bp. M. RM. Apr 1
d. ?*c*.255. A bishop in Dalmatia, whose body was brought from Spalato to the Lateran by Pope John IV in 641.

VENANTIUS (St) M.   RM. May 18
d. *c*.250. Said to have been a boy of fifteen who died a martyr at Camerino, near Ancona, under Decius. Nothing certain is known about him: Pope Clement X, a former bishop of Camerino, raised the feast of St Venantius to the double rite and composed the proper hymns of his office.

VENANTIUS (St) H.   AC. May 30
d. *c*.400. Elder brother of St Honoratus, the founder of Lérins. After living as hermit on an island near Cannes, both travelled to the East to study the monastic life, and Venantius died at Modon in Morea.

VENANTIUS (St) Bp.   AC. Aug 5
d. 544. The most celebrated of the ancient Bishops of Viviers. His life, written in the 12th century, has no value.

VENANTIUS (St) Ab.   RM. Oct 13
5th cent. An abbot of the monastery of St Martin at Tours.

VENANTIUS FORTUNATUS (St) Bp.   AC. Dec 14
c.535–605. Born near Treviso in N. Italy, at the age of thirty he settled at Poitiers and was ordained priest. He became known to Queen St Radegunde who befriended him. He was a prolific writer and poet; the hymn *Vexilla Regis* was composed by him. Not all his other compositions, however, reach the same excellence. Shortly before his death he was made bishop of Poitiers. His feast is celebrated in several Italian and French dioceses.

VENERANDA (St) VM. RM. Nov 14
2nd cent. Described by the RM. as a

martyr and ascribed to Gaul. It seems that Veneranda is a later corruption of Venera (from *dies Veneris*—Friday) the Latin counterpart of *Parasceves*, and that she is identical with a Parasceves, at one time venerated by the Greeks.

VENERANDUS (St) M. RM. Nov 14
d. 275. An influential citizen of Troyes in France, martyred under Aurelian.

VENERANDUS (St) Bp. AC. Dec 24
d. 423. Born of a senatorial family of Clermont in Auvergne, he became bishop of the same city (385–423).

VENERIUS (St) Bp.   RM. May 4
d. 409. Ordained deacon by St Ambrose, eventually he was promoted to the see of Milan. He is best remembered as a loyal supporter of St John Chrysostom.

VENERIUS (St) Ab. OSB.
                        RM. Sept 13
7th (or 9th) cent. A hermit, and then abbot on the island of Tino in the Gulf of Genoa. His "Life" is very untrustworthy.

VENTURA SPELLUCCI (Bl) Ab. OSB.   AC. May 3
12th cent. Born at Spello near Assisi, he joined the Italian Cruciferi, under the Benedictine Rule, and eventually built an abbey-hospice on his family estate which he ruled as abbot till his death.

VENTURINUS of BERGAMO
                        PC. March 28
1304–1346. A celebrated Dominican preacher, he was entrusted with preaching the crusade against the Turks. He accompanied the expedition, preached successfully to schismatics and died at Smyrna.

VENUSTIAN (St) M.   RM. Dec 30
See Sabinus, Exuperantius, etc.

VENUSTUS (St) M.   RM. May 6
See Heliodorus, Venustus, etc.

VENUSTUS (St) M.   RM. May 22
See Faustinus, Timothy and Venustus.

VERANUS (St) Bp.   AC. Sept 10
d. *c*.480. Son of St Eucherius of Lyons, he became a monk at Lérins, and afterwards bishop of Vence (Alpes Maritimes) France.

VERANUS (St) Bp.   RM. Oct 19
d. 590. Native of Vaucluse, who became bishop of Cavaillon, in France.

VERANUS (St) Bp.   RM. Nov 11
5th cent. Ascribed by the RM. to Lyons. Probably he is identical with St Veranus of Vence (Sept 10).

VERDA (St) M.   AC. Feb 21
See Daniel and Verda.

VERECUNDUS (St) Bp.
                        RM. Oct 22
d. 522. Bishop of Verona.

VEREMUNDUS (St) Ab. OSB.
                        AC. March 8
d. 1092. A native of Navarre, he entered the Benedictine abbey of Our Lady of Hirache. He eventually became abbot, and during his abbacy the monastery was reckoned the most influential religious centre of Navarre. St Veremundus himself was the advisor of its kings. He was remarkable for his charity towards the poor and for his zeal for the accurate recitation of the Divine Office. In the controversy concerning the use of the Mozarabic rite, he won for it the approval even of the Roman see which was for suppressing it.

VERENA (St)   RM. Sept 1
3rd cent. Said to have been an Egyptian maiden, related to a soldier of the

Theban Legion, who travelled to Switzerland in search of him, and settled as a recluse near Zurich. Her cult is very ancient.

VERGILIUS (St) Bp.   RM. Nov 27
Otherwise Virgilius, q.v.

VERIAN (St) M.   RM. Aug 9
See Secundian, Marcellian, and Verian.

VERIDIANA (St) H. OSB. Vall.
**   RM. Feb 1**
d. 1242. A maiden of Castelfiorentino in Tuscany, who after a pilgrimage to Compostella, was walled up as a recluse in her native town, where she lived for thirty-four years under the obedience of a Vallumbrosan abbey. Cult approved in 1533.

VERISSIMUS, MAXIMA and
JULIA (SS) MM.   RM. Oct 1
d. c.302. Martyrs at Lisbon under Diocletian. Full office in the Mozarabic Breviary.

VERONICA of BINASCO (Bl) V.
OSA.   RM. Jan 13
d. 1497. Born at Binasco, near Milan, the daughter of poor peasants, with whom she worked in the fields. She joined the Augustinian nuns of Milan as a lay-sister and spent her life in collecting alms for the convent in the streets of the city. She experienced wonderful ecstasies and visions. Cult confirmed in 1517.

VERONICA GIULIANI (St) Abs.
OFM. Cap.   RM. July 9
1660–1727. Born at Mercatello, diocese of Urbino, in Italy, Veronica became a Capuchin nun at Città di Castello, in Umbria, where she spent the rest of her life, being novice-mistress for thirty-four years. Her mystical experiences (visions, revelations, stigmata, etc.)

were accurately authenticated by eye-witnesses. Though in a state of almost continuous supernatural vision, she was in no way visionary, but a most practical and level-headed religious. Canonized in 1839.

VERONICA (St)   AC. July 12
1st cent. According to tradition, when our Lord fell beneath His cross on the road to Calvary, a compassionate woman wiped His face with a towel, on which a picture of the same Holy Face remained imprinted. Numerous legends have grown up around her; the derivation of her name from the Graeco-Latin word *Veron Ikon*—true image—is only a hypothesis.

VERULUS, SECUNDINUS,
SIRICIUS, FELIX, SERVULUS,
SATURNINUS, FORTUNATUS
and Comp. (SS) MM.   RM. Feb. 21
d. c.434? Martyrs in N. Africa. Hadrumetum is given as the place, and the number was apparently twenty-six. The RM assigns them to the Vandal persecution, but there is a wide variety of opinion.

VERUS (St) Bp.   RM. Aug 1
d. p.314. Bishop of Vienne in France. He assisted at the synod of Arles in 314.

VERUS (St) Bp.   RM. Oct 23
4th cent. The third bishop of Salerno.

VESTINA (St) M.   RM. July 17
One of the Scillitan Martyrs, q.v.

VETIUS (St) M.   RM. June 2
See Photinus, Sanctius, etc.

VETURIUS (St) M.   RM. July 17
One of the Scillitan Martyrs, q.v.

VIAL (VIAU) (St)   AC. Oct 16
Otherwise Vitalis, q.v.

VIATOR (St) H.   RM. Oct 21
d. *c*.390. A disciple of St Justus, archbishop of Lyons, whom he accompanied into the solitude to live as a hermit.

VIATOR (St) Bp.   RM. Dec 14
d. *c*.378. Said by the local tradition to have been one of the first bishops of Brescia, and later of Bergamo, during the first century. Probably he was never bishop of Brescia, but only of Bergamo, from 344 to 378.

VIBIANA (St) VM.   AC. Sept 1
The Roman virgin martyr whose body is now venerated at Los Angeles, California, of which she is the principal patron. See Bibiana (RM. Dec 2).

VICELINUS (St) Bp.   AC. Dec 12
d. 1154. A disciple of St Norbert, who worked with considerable success among the Wagrian Wends in N.E. Germany and died a bishop at Lübeck.

VICTOR (St) M.   RM. Jan 22
See Vincent, Orontius and Victor.

VICTOR (St) M.   RM. Jan 31
See Saturninus, Thyrsus and Victor.

VICTOR (St) M.   RM. Feb 25
See Victorinus, Victor, etc.

VICTOR (Bl) Mk. OSB.
                          AC. Feb 25
d. 995. A Benedictine monk of St Gall in Switzerland who became a recluse in the Vosges, where he died.

VICTOR (St) H.   RM. Feb 26
7th cent. A hermit at Arcis-sur-Aube, in Champagne. His feast was celebrated by the Benedictines of Montiramey at whose request St Bernard wrote hymns in honour of the saint.

VICTOR, VICTORINUS, CLAUDIAN and BASSA (SS) MM.
                          RM. March 6
? A group of martyrs, natives of Bithynia, who perished in prison at Nicomedia. Bassa was the wife of Claudian.

VICTOR (St) M.   RM. March 10
? Perhaps he suffered in N. Africa under Decius. He is mentioned by St Augustine. (*In Psalm* CXV, 15).

VICTOR (St) M.   RM. March 20
See Photina, Joseph, etc.

VICTOR (St) M.   RM. March 30
See Domninus, Victor, and Comp.

VICTOR and STEPHEN (SS) MM.
                          RM. Apr 1
? Martyrs in Egypt.

VICTOR (St) Bp. M.   RM. Apr 2
d. 554. A Bishop of Capua in S. Italy and an ecclesiastical writer.

VICTOR (St) M.   RM. Apr 12
d. *c*.300. A catechumen, martyred at Braga in Portugal under Diocletian. He was thus baptized in his own blood.

VICTOR, ZOTICUS, ZENO, ACINDYNUS, CAESAREUS, SEVERIAN, CHRYSOPHORUS, THEONAS and ANTONINUS (SS) MM.   RM. Apr 20
d. *c*.303. Martyrs at Nicomedia. The apocryphal *Acta* of St George connect them with his martyrdom.

VICTOR the MOOR (St) M.
                          RM. May 8
d. 303. A soldier from Mauritania in Africa, martyred at Milan under Maximian. He is associated by St Ambrose with the martyrs SS Nabor and Felix.

VICTOR and CORONA (SS) MM.
RM. May 14
d. c.176. Husband and wife martyred, it seems, in Syria. Their *Acta* abound in details of an untrustworthy character.

VICTOR (St) M.   RM. May 17
See Adrio, Victor, and Basilla.

VICTOR ALEXANDER, FELICIAN and LONGINUS (SS) MM.
RM. July 21
d. 304. Victor, an army officer stationed at Marseilles, suffered martyrdom there with three prison-guards whom he had converted. In the 4th century St John Cassian built a monastery over their tomb, which afterwards became a Benedictine abbey.

VICTOR, STERCATIUS and ANTINOGENES (SS) MM.
RM. July 24
d. 304. Said to have been three brothers, martyred at Merida in Estremadura, Spain. Probably, however, only Victor belongs to Merida; the other two to the group who suffered with St Theozonus of Sebaste in Armenia.

VICTOR I (St) Pope M. RM. July 28
d. c.199. Perhaps an African by birth. He was pope for about ten years: c.189–c.199. The paschal controversy was then vexing the Church, and Victor threatened the Asiatics with excommunication in a synod held at Rome. He is said to have been the first to use Latin in the celebration of the liturgy. It is not certain that he died a martyr.

VICTOR of VITA (St) Bp.
RM. Aug 23
d. c.535. A native of Carthage, and Bishop either of that city or of Utica (as stated in the RM.). Baronius identified him (without proof) with Victor of Vita who wrote the history of the Hunneric persecution.

VICTOR (Spanish: VITORES) (St) M.   RM. Aug 26
d. c.950. According to the *Passio* composed in the 15th century, Victor was a Spanish priest martyred by the Moors in the 9th or 10th century. More ancient documents show him to have been an African martyr put to death at Caesarea in Mauretania in the early persecutions.

VICTOR (St) Bp. M.   RM. Sept 10
See Nemesian, Felix, etc.

VICTOR (St) M.   RM. Sept 10
See Sosthenes and Victor.

VICTOR (St) M.   RM. Sept 14
See Crescentian, Victor, etc.

VICTOR III (St) Pope OSB.
RM. Sept 16
c.1027–1087. A native of Benevento, the only son of the duke of that city. His secular name was Dauferius, which he changed into that of Desiderius on becoming a Benedictine at Montecassino (1047) and into that of Victor on his election to the papacy (1087). He became a monk in the teeth of family opposition: he was successively at La Cava, at St Sophia in Benevento, at a house on an island in the Adriatic, at Salerno as a student of medicine, in the Abruzzi as a hermit, back at Salerno and finally at Montecassino. He was chosen abbot in 1057 and under him the abbey attained its high level of prosperity and glory: the community rose to two hundred monks; basilica and monastery were rebuilt on a larger scale; arts, learning, sanctity flourished. In 1086 he was acclaimed pope by the cardinals at Montecassino itself. It was not a happy choice, and the abbot was persuaded to accept only after one year of delay—the year in which he died. Cult confirmed in 1727 and again (conferring the title of saint) by Leo XIII.

VICTOR (St) M.   RM. Sept 22
See Theban Legion.

VICTOR and URSUS (SS) MM.
                           RM. Sept 30
d. c.286. Two soldiers connected with
the Thebian Legion and venerated at
Soleure in Switzerland.

VICTOR and Comp. (SS) MM.
                           RM. Oct 10
d. c.286. A group of three hundred and
thirty soldiers, connected with the
Theban Legion who were martyred at
Xanten on the Lower Rhine.

**VICTOR, ALEXANDER and
MARIANUS (SS) MM.** RM. Oct 17
d. 303. A group of martyrs in the Diocletian persecution who suffered at
Nicomedia.

VICTOR (St) M.   RM. Nov 2
See Publius, Victor, etc.

VICTOR (St) M.   RM. Nov 13
See Valentine, Solutor and Victor.

VICTOR (St) M.   RM. Dec 3
See Ambicus, Victor and Julius.

VICTOR of PIACENZA (St) Bp.
                           AC. Dec 7
d. 375. First bishop of Piacenza, c.322–
375. He was a brave champion of the
Catholic faith against the Arians.

VICTOR (St) M.   RM. Dec 15
See Irenaeus, Antony, etc.

VICTOR (St) M.   RM. Dec 18
See Victurus, Victor, etc.

VICTOR (St) M.   RM. Dec 28
See Castor, Victor and Rogatian.

VICTOR (St) M.   RM. Dec 29
See Dominic, Victor, etc.

VICTORIA (St) VM.   RM. Feb 11
See Saturninus, Dativus, etc.

VICTORIA (St) M.   RM. Nov 17
See Acisclus and Victoria.

**VICTORIA (and ANATOLIA) (SS)
VV. MM.**   RM. Dec 23
d. 250. Two sisters, martyred at Rome,
for refusing to marry pagan husbands.
Their *Acta* are unfortunately worthless.
Anatolia is not mentioned in the RM.

VICTORIAN of ASAN (St) Ab.
                           AC. Jan 12
d. c.560. A native of Italy, who settled
in France for a time, and then became
the abbot-founder of Asan (now called
after him San Victorian) in the Aragonese Pyrenees, diocese of Barbastro. He
is highly praised by St Venantius
Fortunatus.

**VICTORIAN, FRUMENTIUS and
Comp. (SS) MM.**   RM. March 23
d. 484. Victorian, a former pro-consul
in Africa, and four wealthy merchants
were martyred at Adrumetum under
King Hunneric, for refusing to become
Arians.

VICTORIAN (St) M.   RM. May 16
See Aquilinus and Victorian.

VICTORIAN (St) M.   RM. Aug 26
See Simplicius, Constantius and Victorian.

VICTORICUS (St) M. RM. Feb 24
See Montanus, Lucius, etc.

**VICTORICUS, FUSCIAN and
GENTIAN (SS) MM.**   RM. Dec 11
d. c.287. Victoricus and Fuscian are
described as early missionaries in Gaul,
martyred near Amiens; and Gentian as
an old man killed while endeavouring to
protect them when they were arrested.

VICTORINUS, VICTOR, NICE-
PHORUS, CLAUDIAN, DIO-
SCORUS, SERAPION AND
PAPIAS (SS) MM.   RM. Feb 25
d. 284. Citizens of Corinth exiled to
Egypt in 249 and martyred in various
ways and with great brutality, under
Numerian, at Diospolis in the Thebaid.

VICTORINUS (St) M.
                          RM. March 6
See Victor, Victorinus, etc.

VICTORINUS (St) M.
                          RM. March 29
See Pastor, Victorinus, etc.

VICTORINUS (St) M. RM. Apr 15
See Maro, Eutyches and Victorinus.

VICTORINUS (St) M. RM. May 15
See Cassius, Victorinus, etc.

VICTORINUS (St) C. RM. June 8
d. 543. Brother of St Severino, bishop of
Septempeda (now San Severino), with
whom he led an eremitical life near
Ancona.

VICTORINUS (St) M. RM. July 7
See Four Crowned Martyrs.

VICTORINUS (St) Bp. AC. Sept 5
d. 644. Bishop of Como. A great opponent of Arianism.

VICTORINUS (St) Bp. M.
                          RM. Sept 5
See Maro, Eutyches and Victorinus.

VICTORINUS (St) M.   RM. Oct 5
See Placid, Eutychius, etc.

VICTORINUS of PETTAU (St) Bp.
M.   RM. Nov 2
d. c.303. A bishop of Pettau in Styria
(Upper Pannonia), and an exegete of
distinction.

VICTORINUS (St) M.   RM. Nov 8
One of the Four Crowned Martyrs, q.v.

VICTORINUS (St) M. RM. Nov 11
See Valentine, Felician and Victorinus.

VICTORINUS (St) M.   RM. Dec 2
See Severus, Securus, etc.

VICTORINUS (St) M. RM. Dec 18
See Victurus, Victor, etc.

VICTORIUS (St) M.   RM. May 21
See Polyeuctus, Victorius and Donatus.

VICTORIUS (St) Bp.   RM. Sept 1
d. c.490. A disciple of St Martin of
Tours who became bishop of Le Mans
c.453.

VICTORIUS (St) M.   RM. Oct 30
See Claudius, Lupercus and Victorius.

VICTRICIUS (St) Bp.   RM. Aug 7
d. 407. A Roman officer, who retired
from the army, because he thought the
military service incompatible with the
profession of Christianity. He was sentenced to death, but the sentence was
not carried out. He became a missionary
among the northern tribes of France
and later as bishop of Rouen (380) was
one of the leading prelates of Gaul.

VICTURUS, VICTOR, VICTORI-
NUS, ADJUTOR, QUARTUS and
Comp.   RM. Dec 18
? A group of thirty-five martyrs in
N.W. Africa.

VIGEAN (St) Ab.   AC. Jan 20
Otherwise Fechin, q.v.

VIGILIUS (St) Bp. M. AC. March 11
d. 685. Successor of St Palladius (661)
in the see of Auxerre. By order of the
mayor of the palace, Waraton, he was
killed in a forest near Compiègne.

VIGILIUS (St) Bp. M. RM. June 26
d. 405. A Roman patrician who studied at Athens, and with his family settled in the Trentino. He was made bishop of Trent and succeeded in practically up-rooting paganism from his diocese. He was stoned to death in the Val di Rendena for overturning a statue of Saturn.

VIGILIUS (St) Bp. RM. Sept 26
d. *p.*506. A bishop of Brescia in Lombardy.

VIGOR (St) Bp. RM. Nov 1
d. *c.*537. A disciple of St Vedast, who became bishop of Bayeux.

VILLANA de' BOTTI (Bl) Matron.
AC. Feb 28
d. *c.*1360. Daughter of a rich Florentine merchant. In her youth she wished to enter a convent but was opposed by her father. She married and abandoned herself completely to worldliness and vanity. One day, it is said, on looking into a mirror she saw, instead of her own reflection, the figure of a demon. She completely changed her life, became a Dominican tertiary, and, in spite of much obloquy, persevered in heroic works. Cult confirmed in 1824.

VILLANUS (St) Bp. OSB. AC. May 7
d. 1237. A native of Gubbio who became a monk at Fontavellana, and in 1206 was raised to the see of his native city.

VILLICUS (St) Bp. AC. Apr 17
d. 568. Bishop of Metz, 543–568. He was praised for his virtues by Venantius Fortunatus.

VIMIN (WYNNIN, GWYNNIN) (St) Bp. AC. Jan 21
6th cent. A Scottish bishop, whose his-tory is very confused. He is said to have been the founder of the monastery of Holywood.

VIMIUS (St) C. OSB. AC. June 12
See Marinus, Vimius, etc.

VINCENT STRAMBI (St) Bp. CP.
AC. Jan 1
1745–1824. Born at Civitavecchia, he was ordained priest in 1767 and shortly afterwards joined the Passionists. He filled almost all the offices of the Order, being at the same time an indefatigable missioner. He was created bishop of Macerata and Tolentino in 1801 and was exiled in 1808 for refusing to take the oath of allegiance to Napoleon. At the end of his life he was summoned by Leo XII to the Vatican as papal adviser. Canonized in 1950.

VINCENT da CUNHA (Bl) M. SJ.
AC. Jan 12
d. 1737. A Jesuit cleric sent to Tonkin in 1736 and martyred there with Bl John Gaspard Cratz and two companions.

VINCENT the DEACON (St) M.
RM. Jan 22
d. 304. A native of Huesca who became deacon to St Valerius at Saragossa and was martyred at Valencia under Diocletian. He has always been widely venerated at the Western Church. St Augustine, St Leo and Prudentius wrote in his honour. In some places he is honoured as the patron of vinedressers.

VINCENT of DIGNE (St) Bp.
AC. Jan 22
d. 380. An African by birth who succeeded St Domninus in the see of Digne. He is the principal patron saint of the city and diocese of Digne.

VINCENT, ORONTIUS and VICTOR (SS) MM. RM. Jan 22

d. 305. Vincent and Orontius were brothers, natives of Cimiez, near Nice. They preached the gospel to the people of the Spanish Pyrenees and were martyred, with St Victor, at Puigcerda, in the province of Gerona. Their bodies were subsequently brought to Embrun, France.

VINCENT PALLOTTI (St) C.
Founder   AC. Jan 23
1798–1850. He was born at Rome of a noble family and became a secular priest in 1820. After a short period of theological teaching he dedicated himself to pastoral work in Rome. His apostolic labours were matched only by his austerities, and in 1837 during the cholera plague he constantly endangered his life. His Society, the Pallottines, or the Society of Catholic Action, numbered only twelve during his life, but has since spread all over the world. In 1836 he started the special observance of the Octave of the Epiphany for the reunion of the Oriental Church with Rome. He was especially interested also in the English Mission. Canonized in 1963.

VINCENT (St) M.   RM. Jan 27
See Datius, Reatus, etc.

VINCENT of TROYES (St) Bp.
AC. Feb 4
d. c.546. Bishop of Troyes, c.536–546.

VINCENT of SIENA (Bl) C. OFM.
AC. Feb 14
d. 1442. A Friar Minor for twenty-two years, the companion of St Bernardinus of Siena in his travels through Italy.

VINCENT KADLUBEK (Bl or St)
Bp. OSB. Cist.   AC. March 8
d. 1223. Born in the Palatinate, he studied in France and Italy, and was

appointed provost at Sandomir in Poland. In 1208 he was consecrated bishop of Cracow, but resigned (1218) and became a Cistercian at Jedrzejo Abbey. He is one of the earliest Polish chroniclers. Cult approved in 1764.

VINCENT FERRER (St) C. OP.
RM. Apr 5
c.1350–1418. A native of Valencia in Spain, at an early age he entered the Dominican Order and soon became the adviser of the king of Aragon and of the Avignon pope, with whom he sided in good faith. To heal the schism of the papacy he travelled through Spain, France, Switzerland and Italy, preaching penance, working miracles and converting thousands, being endowed with the gift of tongues. When it became clear to him that the Avignon party were not in the right, he turned his efforts towards bringing them into obedience to the legitimate pope. His authority acquired as a preacher and sustained by numerous miracles was tremendous. He died at Vannes in Brittany.

VINCENT of COLLIOURE (St) M.
RM. Apr. 19
d. c.304. A martyr at Collioure, in Languedoc, under Diocletian. His *Acta* are worthless. Some have identified him with St Vincent of Gerona (Jan 22).

VINCENT (St)   RM. Apr 20
See under Marcellinus, Vincent and Domninus.

VINCENT (St) Ab. OSB.
AC. May 9
d. c.950. Abbot of St Peter de Montes, disciple and successor of St Gennadius.

VINCENT of LÉRINS (St) C.
RM. May 24
d. c.445. A member of a noble family of

Gaul who in early life followed a military career but later abandoned it to become a monk at Lérins, where he was ordained priest. He is best known as the writer of the *Commonitorium*, in which he deals with the doctrine of exterior development in dogma and formulates the principle that only such doctrines are to be considered true as have been held "always, everywhere and by all the faithful." (*Quod semper, quod ubique, quod ab omnibus*).

VINCENT of PORTO (St) M.
RM. May 24
? A martyr at Porto Romano, the former port of Rome which has long since disappeared.

VINCENT of BEVAGNA (St) Bp. M.
AC. June 6
d. 303. First bishop of Bevagna in Umbria, martyred under Diocletian.

VINCENT of AGEN (St) M.
RM. June 9
d. ? c.292. A deacon martyred at Agen in Gascony for having disturbed a feast of the Gallic druids.

VINCENT CAUN (Bl) M. SJ.
AC. June 20
d. 1626. A native of Seul in Corea who in 1591 was carried to Japan as a prisoner of war. He became a Christian and entered the Jesuit seminary at Arima, spending thirty years as a catechist in Japan and in China. He was burnt alive at Nagasaki with Bl Francis Pacheco and companions. Beatified in 1867.

VINCENT YEN (Bl) M. OP.
AC. June 30
c.1765–1838. A native of Tonkin, he became a Dominican in 1808, and laboured as a priest in the mission field. From the publication of the edict of persecution in 1832, he lived six years in hiding, but was finally betrayed and beheaded at Hai-Duong. Beatified in 1900.

VINCENT de PAUL (St) C.
RM. July 19
1576–1660. Born either at Pouy, near Dax, in France or at Tamarite, in Aragon, Spain, he studied with distinction at Saragossa and at Toulouse and was ordained priest at the age of twenty. He fell into the hands of corsairs and was taken captive to Tunis but contrived to escape and went to Paris. Here, under the guidance of Berulle, he embarked upon his life work of active charity. No one was excluded from his ministrations: he organized relief for all: abandoned orphans, sick children, fallen women, the poor, the destitute, the blind, the insane. He began to preach missions and retreats and enlisted for this work a number of priests whom he grouped into a new religious institute: the Lazarists, or Vincentians (Priests of the Mission, *Congregatio Missionis*). In 1633 he organized the congregation of the Sisters of Charity, who have been ever since a worldwide and glorious feature of Catholic life. He was canonized in 1737 and has been declared patron saint of all societies devoted to works of charity.

VINCENT (St) M. RM. July 24
? A Roman, martyred outside the walls of the city on the road to Tivoli.

VINCENT (St) M. RM. Aug 6
See Sixtus II and Comp.

VINCENT of AQUILA (Bl) C. OFM.
AC. Aug 7
d. 1504. A native of Aquila, who became a Franciscan lay-brother and was famed for his mystical gifts. Cult approved in 1785.

VINCENT (St) M.   RM. Aug 25
See Eusebius, Pontian, etc.

VINCENT and LAETUS (SS) MM.
RM. Sept 1
? 5th cent. The RM. ascribes these martyrs to Spain, and they are actually venerated at Toledo as natives of that diocese; but it seems that they should be identified with St Vincent of Xaintes, the first bishop and patron of Dax in Gascony and St Laetus, one of his deacons.

VINCENT CARVALHO (Bl) M.
OSA.   AC. Sept 3
d. 1632. A native of Alfama near Lisbon who joined the Augustinians at Santa Maria de la Gracia, Lisbon. In 1621 he was sent to Mexico, and thence in 1623 travelled to Japan. He was burnt alive at Nagasaki. Beatified in 1867.

VINCENT of ST JOSEPH (Bl) M.
OFM.   AC. Sept 10
1596–1622. Born at Ayamonte, diocese of Seville, he migrated to Mexico, where he became a Franciscan lay-brother (1615). In 1618 he accompanied Bl Louis Sotelo to Manila and in 1619 was sent to Japan. He was arrested in 1620 and after two years of inhuman incarceration, was burnt alive at Nagasaki. Beatified in 1867.

VINCENT of LEON (St) Ab. M.
RM. Sept 11
d. c.554 (or 630), March 11. Abbot of St Claudius, at Leon, in Spain. He was martyred at the hands of the Arian Visigoths. (See Ramirus.)

VINCENT MADELGARUS (St) Ab.
OSB.   AC. Sept 20
d. 677. Madelgarus was the husband of St Waldetrudis, who bore him four children, all saints: Landericus, Dentlin, Madalberta and Aldetrudis. About the year 653 his wife became a nun and Madelgarus took the Benedictine habit with the name of Vincent in the monastery of Haumont which he founded. Later he established another abbey at Soignies, which he ruled, and where he died.

VINCENT, SABINA and CHRISTETA (SS) MM.   RM. Oct 27
d. 303. Martyrs at Avila, in Spain. Their *Acta* are not trustworthy.

VINCENT LIEM (Bl) M. OP.
AC. Nov 7
d. 1773. A member of a noble family in Tonkin who became a Dominican and a priest and worked under Bl Hyacinth Castañeda, OP. He was beheaded. Beatified in 1906.

VINCENT DIEM (Bl) M. AC. Nov 24
d. 1838. A Tonkinese native priest, martyred in Tonkin by beheading. Beatified in 1900.

VINCENT ROMANO (Bl) C.
AC. Dec 20
1751–1836. Born not far from Naples at Tor' del Greco, he was a soul akin to the Curé d'Ars. Throughout his life he lived at Tor' del Greco as the father of the orphan, consoler of the afflicted and protector of the oppressed. He was persecuted first by the French invaders and then by certain Italian political societies. Beatified in 1963.

VINCENTIAN (French: VIANCE, VIANTS) (St) H.   AC. Jan 2
d. c.730. A disciple of St Menelaus, who became a hermit in the diocese of Tulle (Auvergne).

VINCENZA MARY LOPEZ VICUÑA (Bl) V. Foundress
AC. Jan 18
1847–1890. Born at Cascante in Spanish Navarre, she declined the marriage her

parents wanted her to contract, and overcoming their opposition dedicated herself at the age of nineteen to the service of God. Shocked at the dangers and difficulties of the lives of domestic servants she founded in 1876 the Daughters of Mary Immaculate in order to look after those in need. Papal approval was given in 1888. She died overwhelmed with her business affairs and sickness in 1890, and was beatified in 1950.

VINCENZA GEROSA (St) V.
AC. June 28

1784–1847. An Italian woman, who till her fortieth year led an undistinguished domestic life. She then came to know Bl Bartolomea Capitanio, the foundress of the Italian Sisters of Charity at Lovere. When the foundress died in 1833, Bl Vincenza succeeded her and under her guidance the institute expanded in a wonderful way. Canonized in 1950.

VINDEMIALIS, EUGENE and LONGINUS (SS) MM. RM. May 2

d. c.485. African bishops, put to death by the Arian Vandal King Hunneric who had beforehand inflicted on them most horrible tortures.

VINDICIAN (St) Bp. AC. March 12

d. 712. A disciple of St Eligius, who became bishop of Arras-Cambrai, and with great courage protested against the excesses of the Merovingian kings and the all-powerful mayors of the palace. In his last days he lived mostly in the Abbey of St Vaast.

VINDONIUS (St)   RM. Sept 1

See Priscus, Castrensis, etc.

VINTILA (St) H. OSB. AC. Dec 23

d. 890. A Benedictine monk who died as a recluse at Pugino, near Orense, in Spanish Galicia.

VIRGILIUS of ARLES (St) Bp.
AC. March 5

d. c.610. A monk of Lérins who was promoted to the metropolitan see of Arles. Probably it was he who consecrated St Augustine bishop of Canterbury at the request of Pope St Gregory the Great.

VIRGILIUS (FEARGAL) (St) Bp. OSB.   RM. Nov 27

d. 784. An Irish monk, who undertook a pilgrimage to Palestine but remained in Bavaria to help St Rupert the apostle of Austria. St Virgilius was eventually made abbot of the Benedictine abbey of St Peter at Salzburg and archbishop of that city (c.765). He is venerated as the apostle of Carinthia. Canonized in 1232 by Gregory IX.

VIRIDIANA (St) H. OSB. Vall.
AC. Feb 1

See Veridiana.

VIRILA (St) Ab. OSB.   AC. Oct 1

d. c.1000. A Benedictine abbot of the Navarrese abbey of St Saviour, Leyre. He is undoubtedly an historical personage, but his life has been overlaid with much legendary—though often very beautiful—accretion.

VISSIA (St) VM.   RM. Apr 12

d. c.250. An Italian maiden, martyred at Fermo, near Ancona, under Decius.

VITALIAN (St) Pope   RM. Jan 27

d. 672. Pope from 657 to 672. The whole of his pontificate was troubled by the Monothelite controversy in the East. He consecrated St Theodore of Tarsus, whom he sent to England as archbishop of Canterbury.

VITALIAN (St) Bp.   RM. July 16

? A bishop of Capua in S. Italy.

VITALIAN (St) Bp.   AC. July 16
d. 776. Bishop of Osimo in Italy.

VITALICUS (St) M.   RM. Sept 4
See Rufinus, Silvanus and Vitalicus.

VITALIS, REVOCATUS and FORTUNATUS (SS) MM.   RM. Jan 9
? Vitalis appears to have been a bishop and Revocatus and Fortunatus his two deacons. They were martyred at Smyrna.

VITALIS (St) M.   RM. Jan 9
See Epictetus, Jucundus, etc.

VITALIS of GAZA (St) H.
AC. Jan 11
d. c.625. An aged monk of Gaza who undertook the reclamation of fallen women, and caused great scandal by the methods he employed. He was vindicated after his death.

VITALIS, FELICULA and ZENO (SS) MM.   RM. Feb 14
? Probably Roman martyrs. Nothing is known about them.

VITALIS (St) M.   RM. Apr 21
See Arator, Fortunatus, etc.

VITALIS of MILAN (St) M.
? 1st cent. The alleged father of SS Gervase and Protase and husband of St Valeria. The Acts are spurious and cult has been discontinued.

VITALIS (St) H. OSB.
AC. May 31
d. ? 1370. Monk of Monte Subasio, near Assisi, and then for twenty years a hermit under the obedience of the abbot of Monte Subasio at Santa Maria delle Viole, also near Assisi.

VITALIS (St) M.   RM. July 2
See Ariston, Crescentian, etc.

VITALIS (St) M.   RM. July 10
One of the Seven Brothers, q.v.

VITALIS, SATOR and REPOSITUS (SS) MM.   RM. Aug 29 and Sept 1
? 3rd or 4th cent. Martyrs of Velleianum in Apulia. They belong to the group known as the Twelve Holy Brothers, q.v.

VITALIS of SAVIGNY (Bl) Ab.
OSB.   AC. Sept 16
c.1063–1122. In early life he acted as chaplain to Robert, count of Mortain, half-brother of William the Conqueror; then he spent seventeen years as a hermit; finally (1112) he founded the abbey of Savigny in Normandy which soon became the mother house of numerous monasteries throughout France and England. Bl Vitalis visited the British Isles in this connexion. He died while presiding in choir at the recitation of the office of Our Lady. The Bollandists give his feast on Jan 7.

VITALIS (St) M.   RM. Sept 22
One of the alleged martyrs of the Theban Legion, q.v.

VITALIS (VIAL) H. OSB. AC. Oct 16
d. c.740. An Anglo-Saxon who became a Benedictine at Noirmoutier, and afterwards a hermit on Mt Scobrit, near the Loire.

VITALIS (St) Bp. OSB. AC. Oct 20
d. 745. St Rupert's successor as abbot of St Peter's at Salzburg, and as archbishop of that city (717–745).

VITALIS (St) M.   RM. Nov 3
See Germanus, Theophilus, etc.

VITALIS and AGRICOLA (SS) MM.
RM. Nov 4
d. c.304. Martyrs at Bologna under Diocletian. St Vitalis was a slave of St

Agricola. The slave suffered martyrdom in the presence of his master with such courage that Agricola was inspired by his example to face a shameful death—probably crucifixion—for Christ's sake.

VITONUS (VANNE, VAUNE) (St) Bp.   **AC. Nov 9**
d. *c*.525. Bishop of Verdun, *c*.500–525. At a later period a great Benedictine abbey of Lorraine was dedicated to him, which in 1600 became the centre of the Congregation of St Vannes.

VITUS, MODESTUS and CRESCENTIA (SS) MM.   **RM. June 15**
? Martyrs from S. Italy, perhaps Sicilians, whose cult is certainly very ancient, but whose Acts have reached us in various embellished versions. St Vitus (Guy) is described as a child, St Crescentia being his nurse and St Modestus Crescentia's husband. St Vitus is patron against epilepsy and the nervous disorder called St Vitus's dance.

VITUS (St) Mk. OSB.   **AC. Sept 5**
d. *c*.1095. A Benedictine monk of Pontida, near Bergamo, under its founder St. Albert.

VIVALDUS (UBALDO, GUALDO) (Bl) C.   **AC. May 11**
d. 1300. Disciple and companion of Bl Bartholomew Buonpedoni. When the latter became a leper, Vivaldus nursed him for twenty years. He was a Franciscan tertiary. Cult approved in 1909.

VIVENTIOLUS (St) Bp. RM. July 12
d. 524. Monk of St Oyend (Condat) who became archbishop of Lyons. A great friend of St Avitus of Vienne.

VIVENTIUS (St) H.   **RM. Jan 13**
d. *c*.400. A Samaritan who after becoming a priest travelled to the West and

attached himself to St Hilary of Poitiers. He closed his life as a hermit. His *Life* written in the 10th century lacks credibility.

VIVENTIUS (St) M.   **AC. Aug 4**
See Peregrinus, Maceratus, etc.

VIVIAN (St) Bp.   **AC. Jan 21**
Otherwise Vimin, q.v.

VIVIAN (St) Bp.   **RM. Aug 28**
d. *c*.460. A bishop of Saintes in W. France, who protected his people during the invasion of the Visigoths.

VIVIAN (St) VM.   **RM. Dec 2**
Otherwise Bibiana, q.v.

VIVINA (St) V.   **RM. Dec 17**
Otherwise Wivina, q.v.

VLADIMIR (St) King   AC. July 15
956–1015. Great Prince of Kiev in Russia. He was baptized before his marriage to the sister of the Byzantine emperor, and invited the Greek clergy to evangelize Russia. His two sons Boris and Gleb (known in the Western Church as Romanus and David) are venerated as martyrs. St Vladimir is honoured by the Russian Catholics as their patron saint.

VODOALDUS (VOEL, VODALUS, VODALIS) (St) H.   **AC. Feb 5**
d. *c*.725. An Irish or Scottish monk who crossed over to Gaul as a missionary and died a recluse near Soissons.

VOLCUIN (Bl) Ab. OSB. Cist.
                                           AC. Sept 18
d. 1154. A Cistercian monk at the German abbey of Altenkamp, whence he was sent as prior to a new foundation at Walkenried (1129) and later as abbot to a third foundation at Sittichenbach, or Sichem (1141) in Westphalia.

VOLKER (Bl) M. OSB.
AC. March 7
d. 1132. A missionary monk of Siegburg put to death by the Obotrites, whom he was evangelizing.

VOLOC (St) Bp. AC. Jan 29
d. *c*.724. An Irish missionary bishop who worked in Scotland.

VOLUSIAN (St) Bp. M.
RM. Jan 18
d. 496. A senator of Tours and a married man who was afflicted with a bad-tempered wife. He was chosen bishop of Tours and shortly after driven from his see by the Arian Visigoths. He died in exile at Toulouse. His martyrdom is not established.

VOTUS, FELIX and JOHN (SS) HH. AC. May 29
d. *c*.750. Votus and Felix were brothers, natives of Saragossa, who went in search of a hermitage and found one in the fastnesses of the Aragonese Pyrenees, already inhabited by St John. The three lived together and died about the same time. The hermitage was situated beneath a huge rock (*Peña*) where shortly afterwards arose the great Benedictine abbey of St John de la Peña. See John of Atarés.

VOUGA (VOUGAR, VEHO, FEOCK, FIECH) (St) Bp.
AC. June 15
6th cent. An Irish bishop who settled in Brittany and there lived as a hermit in a cell near Lesneven.

VULCHERIUS (St) Ab.
AC. March 13
Otherwise Mochoemoc, q.v.

VULGANIUS (St) H. OSB.
AC. Nov 3
d. *c*.704. An Irishman or Welshman, who crossed over to France, evangelized the Atrebati, and finally lived as a hermit at Arras, under the obedience of the abbot of St Vaast.

VULGIS (St) Bp. OSB. AC. Feb 4
d. *c*.760. Regionary bishop (*chorepiscopus*) and abbot of the Benedictine monastery of Lobbes in Hainault.

VULMAR (St) Ab. OSB. RM. July 20
Otherwise Wulmar, q.v.

VULPHY (WULFLAGIUS) (St) H.
AC. June 7
d. *c*.643. A parish priest at Rue, near Abbeville, who retired to the desert and died a solitary. His memory was greatly venerated at Montreuil-sur-Mer.

VULPIAN (St) M. RM. Apr 3
d. *c*.304. A Syrian put to death at Tyre in Phoenicia under Diocletian. He is said to have been sewn up in a leathern sack, together with a dog and a serpent, and so cast into the sea.

VULSIN (St) Bp. AC. Jan 8
Otherwise Wulsin, q.v.

VYEVAIN (Bl) Bp. AC. Aug 26
d. 1285. An archbishop of York, who was honoured with a liturgical cult at Pontigny in France.

W

WACCAR, GUNDEKAR, ELLE-
HER, HATHAWULF (SS) MM.
OSB.   RM. June 5
d. 755. Mentioned by name and as
monks among the fifty-two companions
who shared St Boniface's martyrdom.
It is very probable that most of the
others, if not all, were Benedictines.

WALBERT (VAUBERT) (St)
                         AC. May 11
d. c.678. Duke of Lorraine and count of
Hainault, husband of St Bertilia and
father of SS Waldetrudis and Alde-
gundis.

WALBURGA (St) Abs. OSB.
                         RM. Feb 25
d. 779. Sister of SS Willibald and Winebald. She became a nun at Wimborne
in Dorset under St Tatta and followed
St Lioba to Germany at the invitation of
St Boniface. She died abbess of Heidenheim, whence her relics were translated
to Eichstätt. Remarkable cures are
ascribed to the use of a fluid which
exudes from the rock on which her
shrine is placed.

WALDALENUS (St) Ab.
                         AC. May 15
7th cent. Abbot-founder of Bèze, and
brother of St Adalsindis.

WALDEBERT (WALBERT, GAU-
BERT) (St) Ab. OSB.   RM. May 2
d. c.668. A Frankish noble who left the
army to become a monk at Luxeuil.
About the year 628 he was made abbot,
and shortly afterwards (c.630) he introduced the Rule of St Benedict. Under
him the monastery reached the peak of

its religious and cultural influence in
W. Europe. He helped St Salaberga to
establish her great nunnery at Laon.

WALDERIC (Bl) Ab. OSB.
                         AC. Nov 29
d. c.817. Abbot-founder of Murrhardt,
which he built with the help of the
emperor Louis the Pious.

WALDETRUDIS (VAUDRU) (St)
W. Abs. OSB.   RM. Apr 9
d. c.688. Daughter of SS Walbert and
Bertilia, wife of St Vincent Madelgarus,
and mother of SS Landericus, Dente-
linus, Madalberta and Aldetrudis.
When her husband became a monk she
founded a nunnery and took the veil
there. Around her nunnery there grew
up the town of Mons in Belgium, where
her memory has always been greatly
honoured.

WALDRADA (St) Abs.   AC. May 5
d. c.620. First abbess of the nunnery of
Saint-Pierre-aux-Nonnais at Metz.

WALEMBERT (GAREMBERT) (Bl)
C. OSA.   AC. Dec 31
1084-1141. A native of the district of
Furness in Belgium who became a hermit and then built an Augustinian abbey
on Mont-Saint-Martin in the diocese of
Cambrai, of which he became the first
superior.

WALERICUS (VALÉRY) (St) Ab.
                         RM. Apr 1
d. c.622. A monk under St Columbanus
at Luxeuil, then a missionary in N.
France, where he became the abbot-

founder of Leuconay at the mouth of the Somme. Two towns in that district are called Saint-Valéry after him.

WALFRID (GUALFREDO) della GHERARDESCA (St) Ab. OSB.
AC. Feb 15
d. *c.*765. A citizen of Pisa who married and had five sons and one daughter. In middle life he joined with two other married men in founding the abbey of Palazzuolo, between Volterra and Piombino, and a nunnery nearby for their wives and Walfrid's daughter. Walfrid ruled Palazzuolo as first abbot and was succeeded as second abbot by one of his sons. Cult confirmed in 1861.

WALHERE (St) M.   AC. June 23
? A priest in the Walloon district of Belgium. On remonstrating with an ecclesiastic for his unedifying life he was murdered by the latter, and has since been venerated as a martyr, chiefly at Dinant.

WALLABONSUS (St) M.
RM. June 7
See Peter, Wallabonsus, etc.

WALPURGIS (St) V.   RM. Feb 25
Otherwise Walburga, q.v.

WALSTAN (St) C.   AC. May 30
d. 1016. Born at Bawburgh in Norfolk, he spent his life as a farm labourer at Taverham and Costessey, being remarkable for his charity to all in need. His cult, although a local one, is undisputed.

WALTER (GUALTERIUS, GAUTIER) (Bl) C. OSB. Cist.
AC. Jan 22
d. 1222. A native of Brabant who was bred to arms. On becoming a knight he was a familiar figure at tournaments until he found his way to the Cistercian abbey of Himerode. There he was appointed guest master and attracted many to the monastic life by his affability and tact. He died at Villers.

WALTER of BRUGES (Bl) Bp. C.
AC. Jan 22
d. 1307. A native of Bruges he became a Franciscan and studied at Paris. Named Bishop of Poitiers, he felt it his duty to excommunicate his metropolitan, Bertrand de Got. The latter became Pope as Clement V and deposed Walter. He retired to the religious life, and was miraculously vindicated after his death.

WALTER of PONTOISE (St) Ab. OSB.   AC. Apr 8
d. 1099. A Picard who became a professor of philosophy and rhetoric but later joined the Benedictines of Rebais in order to escape worldly applause. Against his will he was made abbot of Pontoise. He fled from his abbey several times, once to Cluny and on the last occasion to Rome, where he placed his resignation in the hands of the pope, who however refused to accept it but gave him orders to return to Pontoise and never again to leave it. He died on Good Friday.

WALTER (St) Ab.   AC. Apr 9
Otherwise Gaucherius, q.v.

WALTER (Bl) Ab. OSB.   AC. Apr 21
d. 1158. Abbot of the Benedictine monastery of Mondsee in Upper Austria.

WALTER (St) Ab. OSA. AC. May 11
d. 1070. An Augustinian canon and abbot of L'Esterp in the Limousin.

WALTER (St) Ab. OSB.   AC. June 4
d. *c.*1250. A Roman who became first a hermit and afterwards the founder and first abbot of Serviliano in the Marches of Ancona.

WALTER (St) Ab. OSB.
AC. ? June 4

d. 1150. An Englishman who became abbot of Fontenelle in France. He is commended for his humility, piety and zeal by Pope Innocent II.

WALTER PIERSON (Bl) M.
O. Cart.   AC. June 6

d. 1537. A Carthusian lay-brother of the London Charterhouse left with six companions to starve to death in prison.

WALTER (Bl) C. OFM.
AC. Aug 2

d. c.1258. One of the first friars and companions of St Francis. He was sent by the founder to establish the order in Portugal, where he died at Guemarraens.

WALTER of AULNE (Bl) Mk. OSB.
Cist.   AC. Nov 26

d. c.1180. A canon of Liége who followed St Bernard to Clairvaux and then became the first prior of the abbey of Aulne in Brabant.

WALTHEOF (WALTHEN, WALÈNE) (St) Ab. OSB. Cist.
AC. Aug 3

d. 1160. Son of the earl of Huntingdon, he was educated at the court of the king of Scotland, where he became a great friend of St Aelred. He joined the Augustinian canons at Nostell, but later migrated to the Cistercians and eventually became abbot of Melrose, rebuilt for him by King David. His outstanding characteristics were cheerfulness and unbounded generosity to the poor.

WALTMANN (Bl) Ab. O. Praem.
AC. Apr 11

d. 1138. A disciple of St Norbert, whom he accompanied to Cambrai to preach against heresy and who left him there as abbot of St Michael's.

WALTO (BALTO) (Bl) Ab. OSB.
AC. Dec 27

d. 1156. Abbot of Wessobrünn in Bavaria. His sanctity attracted many friends and benefactors to the abbey.

WALTRAM (Bl or St) OSB.
AC. July 10

See Lantfrid, Waltram, etc.

WANDO (VANDO) (St) Ab. OSB.
AC. Apr 17

d. c.756. Monk and abbot of Fontenelle. As a result of a false accusation he was exiled to Troyes but reinstated after his innocence had been proved. He died at Fontenelle.

WANDRILLE (WANDREGISILUS, VANDRILLE) (St) Ab. OSB.
RM. July 22

d. 666. Born near Verdun, he served in the king's palace, where he had among his fellow-courtiers seven or eight future saints. In spite of his desire for the monastic life he was appointed count of the palace and married. After a pilgrimage to Rome he entered (637) the abbey of Roumain-Moutier, and some ten years afterwards founded the abbey of Fontenelle, which became the great missionary centre of that district as well as a school of arts and crafts. Soon it had a community of over three hundred monks.

WANINGUS (VANENG) (St) Ab. OSB.
AC. Jan 9

d. c.686. Born in the diocese of Rouen. From a courtier at the court of Clothair III he became a monk, and assisted his friend St Wandrille in the foundation of Fontenelle. Soon after he himself made another, no less celebrated and important, at Fécamp.

WARINUS (GUARINUS, WARREN) (St) M.
AC. Aug 25

7th cent. Son of St Sigrada, and put to

death by Ebroin, mayor of the palace, who was at war with his brother, the bishop, St Leodegarius.

WASTRADA (St) Matron
AC. July 21
d. *c.*760. Mother of St Gregory of Utrecht. Towards the end of her life she retired to a convent and probably became a nun, though contemporary evidence of this is lacking.

WENCESLAUS (St) M. RM. Sept 28
d. 935. Duke of Bohemia. He received a pious upbringing from his grandmother the martyr St Ludmilla. He took over the reins of government at the time of a pagan reaction. This he tried to stem with great patience and mildness, but in the end he met his death as a result of a political conspiracy. He was murdered by his own brother Boleslav at the door of the church of Alt-Bunzlau. He is the patron of Bohemia.

WENDOLINUS (WENDELINUS, WENDEL) (St) C.   AC. Oct 21
d. 607 (or 650 ?). A shepherd who became famous for his sanctity and is venerated at St Wendel on the Nahe in W. Germany. A later legend makes him an Irish hermit and abbot of Tholey in the diocese of Trèves.

WENN (St) W.   AC. Oct 18
Otherwise Gwen, q.v.

WENNAPA (St) V.   AC. July 1
Otherwise Veep, q.v.

WENOG (St)   AC. Jan 3
? A Welsh saint, mentioned in various calendars, but of whose life nothing is known.

WEONARD (St)   AC. Apr 7
Otherwise Gwrnerth, Guainerth. See Llewellyn and Gwrnerth.

WERBURG (St) V. OSB.   AC. Feb 3
d. *c.*699. Daughter of St Ermenilda and of King Wulfhere of Mercia. She became a nun of Ely under St Etheldreda and later founded the nunneries of Hanbury near Tutbury, Trentham in Staffordshire and Wedon in Northamptonshire. She died at Trentham, but her body was transferred to Chester, of which city she is the patron saint.

WERBURG (St) Matron AC. Feb 3
d. *c.*785. Wife of a Ceolred of Mercia. In her widowhood she retired to a convent (Bardney ?) of which she became abbess.

WERENFRID (St) C. OSB.
AC. Aug 14
d. *c.*760. An Englishman who worked with St Willibrord among the Frisians. He died at Arnheim.

WERNHER (WERNER) (St) M.
AC. Apr 19
d. 1275. A boy in the service of a Jewish family at Oberwesel, alleged to have been martyred by that family on Maundy Thursday after he had received Holy Communion.

WIBORADA (GUIBORAT, WEIBRATH) (St) M. OSB.   AC. May 2
d. 925. She belonged to the Swabian nobility. When her brother Hatto became a Benedictine monk at St Gall, she asked to be walled up in an anchorhold not far from the monastery, where she lived the rest of her life under the obedience of the abbey. She occupied her time in binding books and doing similar work for the abbey. She was martyred by the invading Hungarians. Canonized in 1047.

WICTERP (WIHO, WICHO) (St) Bp.   AC. Apr 18
d. 749. Abbot of Ellwangen. He took an active part in the foundation of the

abbeys of Füssen, Wessobrünn and Kempten, all of which became famous in mediaeval Germany. St Wicterp became the tenth bishop of Augsburg.

WIDRADUS (French: WARÉ) (St) Ab. OSB.   **AC. Oct 3**
d. 747. Restorer of the abbey of Flavigny, diocese of Dijon, and founder of Saulieu (*Sanctus Andochius*—Saint-Andoche) in the diocese of Autun.

WIDUKIND (Bl) C.   **AC. Jan 7**
Otherwise Wittikund, q.v.

WIFRED (Bl) Ab. OSB. AC. Dec 13
d. 1021. A Benedictine monk, prior and abbot of St Victor at Marseilles (1005–1021).

WIGBERT (St) C.   **AC. Apr 12**
d. 690. An Anglo-Saxon who became a disciple of St Egbert in Ireland. He spent two years as a missionary in Friesland, but returned to Ireland to die.

WIGBERT (St) Ab. OSB. RM. Aug 13
d. *c*.746. An English monk who was invited by St Boniface to cross over into Germany. He did so, and Boniface appointed him abbot of Fritzlar, near Cassel. A few years later he was appointed to Ohrdruf in Thuringia, but before his death Boniface allowed him to return to Fritzlar.

WILFETRUDIS (St) Abs. OSB.
                              AC. Nov 23
d. *p*.670. Second abbess of the Benedictine nunnery of Nivelles in Brabant, which had been founded by her aunt St Gertrude.

WILFRID the YOUNGER (St) Bp. OSB.   **AC. Apr 29**
d. 744. A monk and favourite disciple of St John of Beverley at Whitby. He was appointed abbot of the cathedral community at York, and shortly afterwards coadjutor of St John of Beverley, whom he succeeded in the see. Before his death he retired to a monastery, presumably Ripon.

WILFRID (WALFRIDUS) Bp. OSB.   **RM. Oct 12**
d. 709. A Northumbrian who became the champion of the Roman See in England. Born at Ripon, he became a monk at Lindisfarne under the Celtic régime, but he left to adopt the Roman observance elsewhere. After a short stay at Canterbury he went to Rome (653–657). On his return to Northumbria he founded the abbey of Ripon under the Roman observance. In 664 he was consecrated bishop at Compiègne and played a leading part in the council of Whitby when Roman usages were adopted for the whole of England. The remainder of Wilfrid's life was occupied with long journeys, with appeals to Rome (the first recorded in English history) to recover his see (see St Chad), and with missionary work among the Frisians and South Saxons.

WILFRIDA (WULFRITHA) (St) Abs. OSB.   **AC. Sept 9**
d. *c*.988. Mother of St Edith of Wilton by King Edgar. After Edith's birth Wilfrida retired to Wilton, where she took the veil at the hands of St Ethelwold. As a nun, and later as abbess, her edifying life made ample amends for the irregularity of her connexion with Edgar.

WILGEFORTIS (St) V. RM. July 20
? I.e. Virgo-Fortis. She was known in England as Uncumber, in the Low Countries as Ontkommena, in Germany as Kümmernis, in Gascony as Livrade, in Spain as Librada. Her story is a worthless romance abounding in absurdities, e.g., that she was one of

724

nine sisters all born at one birth, that she miraculously grew a beard in order to escape marriage, etc.

WILLA (Bl) H. OSB.   AC. Oct 15
d. *c*.1050. A Benedictine nun at Nonnberg, near Salzburg, who died a recluse.

WILLEHAD of DENMARK (St) M. OFM.   RM. July 9
1482–1572. A Danish Franciscan who, on the introduction of Lutheranism into his country, was sent into exile and repaired to the Franciscan friary of Gorkum in Holland. He was ninety years of age when he was hanged by the Protestants with eighteen companions at Briel.

WILLEHAD (St) Bp. OSB.
RM. Nov 8
d. *c*.790. A Northumbrian monk, probably of York or Ripon, who *c*.765 went to evangelize the Frisians. Later he crossed the Weser and preached to the Saxons, but he had to abandon this mission and retired to the Benedictine abbey of Echternach. Eventually he was consecrated bishop and fixed his see at Bremen.

WILLEIC (St) Mk. OSB.
PC. March 2
d. 726. A disciple of St Swithbert, who made him prior of the abbey at Kaiserwerth, a position he held till his death.

WILLIAM (*several*)
Note. The English form of the Teutonic WILLHELM, which has been Latinized into GULIELMUS or GUILIELMUS, whence the Italian GULIELMO, the French GUILLAUME, and the Spanish GUILLERMO.

WILLIAM of DIJON (St) Ab. OSB.
AC. Jan 1
962–1031. Son of the count of Volpiano,

William was born near Novara and educated in a monastery. He became a Benedictine at Locedio, near Vercelli, whence he migrated to Cluny under St Majolus (987). Sent to restore the abbey of St Benignus at Dijon, he made this a centre from which he extended the Cluniac observance throughout Burgundy, Normandy, Lorraine and N. Italy. Gentle with the poor, in his dealings with the great he showed remarkable firmness. Towards the end of his life he founded the abbey of Fruttuaria in Piedmont and rebuilt that of Fécamp, where he died.

WILLIAM of BOURGES (St) Bp. OSB. Cist.   RM. Jan 10
d. 1209. William de Donjeon was born at Nevers and shortly after his ordination was made canon of Soissons, and later of Paris. He joined the monks of Grandmont, whence he migrated to the Cistercians of Pontigny. He was appointed successively abbot of Fontaine-Jean, abbot of Châlis and bishop of Bourges (1200). He made a great many converts among the Albigenses. Canonized 1217.

WILLIAM PATENSON (Bl) M.
AC. Jan 22
d. 1592. A native of Durham, he studied for the priesthood at Reims and was ordained there in 1587. He was condemned for his priesthood and hanged, drawn and quartered at Tyburn. Beatified 1929.

WILLIAM IRELAND (Bl) M. SJ.
AC. Jan 24
d. 1679. His true name was Iremonger and he was a native of Lincolnshire. He was educated at St Omer and received into the Society of Jesus there in 1655. He was martyred at Tyburn for alleged complicity in the imaginary Popish Plot. Beatified 1929.

WILLIAM SAULTEMOUCHE (Bl) M. SJ. AC. Feb 7

See James Salès and William Saultemouche (Feb 7).

WILLIAM of MALEVAL (St) H. OSB. RM. Feb 10

d. 1157. A Frenchman by birth, after some years of care-free military life he went on a pilgrimage to the Holy Land and on his return was made superior of an abbey near Pisa. Failing to maintain discipline there, as well as in a foundation of his own on Monte Bruno, he embraced the eremitical life in the solitude of Maleval near Siena (1155). He was joined by some disciples. After William's death, Gregory IX gave them the Rule of St Benedict, but they were eventually absorbed by the Augustinian hermits.

WILLIAM RICHARDSON (Bl) M. AC. Feb 17

d. 1603. William Richardson, *alias* Anderson, was born at Wales near Sheffield and educated for the priesthood at Valladolid and Seville, where he was ordained in 1594. He was martyred for his priesthood at Tyburn. Beatified 1929.

WILLIAM HARRINGTON (Bl) M. AC. Feb 18

d. 1594. Born at Mt St John, Felixkirk, in Yorkshire, he studied and was ordained (1592) at Reims. He was only twenty-seven years of age when he was hanged, drawn and quartered for his priesthood at Tyburn. Beatified 1929.

WILLIAM HART (Bl) M. AC. March 15

d. 1583. A native of Wells, he was educated at Lincoln College, Oxford, and on being reconciled to the Catholic Church studied for the priesthood at Douai, Reims and Rome. After his ordination (1581) he returned to England and was betrayed by an apostate in the house of Bl Margaret Clitherow. Executed at York. Beatified 1886.

WILLIAM of PEÑACORADA (St) H. OSB. AC. March 20

d. *c.*1042. Monk of the Benedictine (Cluniac) monastery of Satagún, province of León, Spain. In 988 he fled with the other monks from the Saracens and settled in the solitude of Peñacorada, where he eventually built the monastery of Santa Maria de los Valles, later named after him San Guillermo de Peñacorada.

WILLIAM of NORWICH (St) M. AC. March 24

d. 1144. A boy of twelve, apprentice to a tanner at Norwich, who is alleged to have been murdered by two Jews out of hatred of Christianity. The case for the crime does not seem to be established.

WILLIAM TEMPIER (Bl) Bp. AC. March 27

d. 1197. From being a canon regular at Saint-Hilaire-de-la-Celle, Poitiers, he was promoted to the see of that city and proved a brave champion of ecclesiastical liberty.

WILLIAM of ESKILSOË (St) C. OSA. RM. Apr 6

d. 1203. A Frenchman, canon regular at the church of St Geneviève, Paris, who was sent to Denmark to reform a community of canons regular at Eskilsoë (Ise Fjord) and then founded the abbey of Ebelholt, Zeeland. He worked in Denmark for thirty years. Canonized 1224.

WILLIAM CUFITELLA (Bl) H. AC. Apr 7

d. 1411. A native of Noto in Sicily, who for seventy years lived as a hermit at Scicli. He was a Franciscan tertiary. Cult approved 1537.

WILLIAM GNOFFI (Bl) H.
AC. Apr 16
d. *c*.1317. A native of Polizzi, near Palermo, who atoned for a sin of the flesh by leading a very penitential life.

WILLIAM FIRMATUS (St) H.
AC. Apr 24
d. 1103. A canon and medical practitioner at Saint-Venance, who, in consequence of a divine warning against avarice, gave all to the poor and spent the rest of his life on pilgrimages and as a hermit at Savigny and Mantilly.

WILLIAM MARSDEN (Bl) M.
AC. Apr 25
d. 1586. Born in Lancashire and educated at St Mary Hall, Oxford. He studied for the priesthood and was ordained at Reims (1585). Shortly after, he was executed for his priesthood in the Isle of Wight. Beatified 1929.

WILLIAM of PONTOISE (St) C.
AC. May 10
d. 1192. An Englishman who lived as a hermit at Pontoise in France. Some writers say that he was a Benedictine of St Martin's abbey.

WILLIAM de NAUROSE (Bl) C. OSA. Erem.
AC. May 18
1297-1369. A native of Toulouse, who joined the Augustinian hermits and was famed as a very zealous missionary priest. Cult confirmed 1893.

WILLIAM of ROCHESTER (St) M.
AC. May 23
d. 1201. Said to have been a native of Perth in Scotland, who was murdered at Rochester while on a pilgrimage to Canterbury. As a result of miracles wrought after his death he was acclaimed a martyr by the people and his body was enshrined in the cathedral of Rochester.

WILLIAM of DONGELBERG (Bl) Mk. OSB. Cist.
AC. May 24
d. *c*.1250. A Cistercian monk at the abbey of Villers in Belgium.

WILLIAM of GELLONE (St) Mk. OSB.
AC. May 28
755-812. Duke of Aquitaine and a member of Charlemagne's entourage. He manifested the qualities of the ideal Christian knight when campaigning against the Saracens in S. France. Afterwards he built a monastery at Gellone, diocese of Lodève, not far from Aniane, which he peopled with monks from the latter abbey, himself joining the community as a lay-brother. Later the abbey was renamed after him Saint-Guilhem-du-Desert. Canonized 1066.

WILLIAM ARNAUD (Bl) M. OP.
AC. May 29
d. 1242. The inquisitor general in S. France against the Albigensians, by whom he was killed with eleven companions. See Toulouse (Martyrs of).

WILLIAM FILBY (Bl) M.
AC. May 30
d. 1582. Born in Oxfordshire, he was educated at Lincoln College, Oxford, and, after his conversion, at Reims, where he was ordained in 1581. He was martyred at Tyburn with three companions. Beatified 1886.

WILLIAM SCOTT (Bl) M. OSB.
AC. May 30
Otherwise Maurus Scott, q.v.

WILLIAM of YORK (St) Bp.
RM. June 8
d. 1154. William Fitzherbert, or "of Thwayt", was a nephew of King Stephen and was appointed archbishop of York in 1142. Powerful enemies, chiefly the newly arrived White Monks supported by St Bernard of Clairvaux,

contested the appointment on the ground of simony, but Pope Innocent II, St Bernard's great friend, decided in favour of William, who was consecrated and enthroned. His enemies, however, did not rest till they had him deposed from his see. William went into retirement and lived a very mortified life, giving to all an heroic example of patience and resignation, until the Holy See restored him to York, where he was received by his people with unbounded joy. Canonized 1226.

WILLIAM GREENWOOD (Bl) M. O. Cart.   AC. June 16

d. 1537. A lay-brother of the London Charterhouse, starved to death at Newgate with six companions. Beatified 1886.

WILLIAM EXMEW (Bl) M. O. Cart.
AC. June 19

d. 1535. Educated at Christ's College, Cambridge, and sub-prior of the London Charterhouse. He was martyred with BB Humphrey Middlemore and Sebastian Newdigate, q.v.

WILLIAM HARCOURT (Bl) M. SJ.
AC. June 20

d. 1679. A native of Lancashire who became a Jesuit at St Omer (1632) and worked on the English mission from 1645 to 1678, chiefly in London. He was martyred at Tyburn with five Jesuit companions for alleged complicity in the "Popish Plot". Beatified 1929.

WILLIAM of MONTEVERGINE (St) Ab. Founder   RM. June 25

1085–1142. A native of Vercelli who, after a pilgrimage to Compostella, settled as a hermit on the summit of Monte Virgiliano, now Monte Vergine, between Nola and Benevento. Here he was joined by a band of hermit-monks to whom he gave a rule based on that of St Benedict, which was definitively adopted by the community under William's successor. He died at the daughter house of Guglieto, near Nusco.

WILLIAM ANDLEBY (Bl) M.
AC. July 4

d. 1597. Born at Etton, near Beverley, and educated at St John's College, Cambridge. After his conversion he studied at Douai and was ordained priest in 1577. He laboured in Yorkshire for twenty years. He was condemned for his priesthood and martyred at York with three Catholic laymen. Beatified 1929.

WILLIAM of HIRSAU (Bl) Ab.
OSB.   AC. July 4

d. 1091. A monk of St Emmeram at Ratisbon, who after being named abbot of the recently restored abbey of Hirsau in Würtemberg, introduced there the observance of Cluny. He founded a monastic school, restored the *scriptorium*, attended to the instruction and well-being of the tenants and serfs of the abbey estates, supported Gregory VII against Henry IV, wrote learned treatises and founded seven new abbeys. These activities, coupled with great holiness of life, show him to have been typical of the great Benedictine abbots of his time.

WILLIAM of BRETEUIL (St) Ab.
OSB.   AC. July 14

d. 1130. Abbot-restorer of the monastery of Breteuil, in the diocese of Beauvais, which had been practically destroyed during the Norman invasions.

WILLIAM WARD (Bl) M.
AC. July 26

d. 1641. His true name was Webster and he was a native of Thornby in Westmorland. He was educated at Douai and ordained there in 1608. He spent thirty-three years on the English mission, of which twenty were passed in prison. He was martyred for his priesthood at Tyburn. Beatified 1929.

WILLIAM of SAINT-BRIEUC (St) Bp.   RM. July 29

d. 1234. William Pinchon was born in Brittany, and shortly after receiving holy orders, was appointed successively canon and bishop of Saint-Brieuc (1220). During the fourteen years of his episcopate he suffered banishment to Poitiers and other penalties for maintaining the rights of the Church. Canonized 1253.

WILLIAM HORNE (Bl) M. O. Cart.   AC. Aug 4

d. 1540. A lay-brother of the London Charterhouse, martyred at Tyburn with two companions. Beatified 1886.

WILLIAM FREEMAN (Bl) M.   AC. Aug 13

d. 1595. William Freeman, *alias* Mason, was a Yorkshire convert, who had been educated at Magdalen College, Oxford He was ordained at Reims in 1587 and sent on the English mission. He laboured in Worcestershire and Warwickshire and was executed for his priesthood at Warwick. Beatified 1929.

WILLIAM LACEY (Bl) M.   AC. Aug 22

d. 1582. Born at Horton, near Settle, in Yorkshire. He was a gentleman of means and a staunch Catholic. He was married twice, and during the fourteen years of his married life his house was a refuge for supporters of the Old Religion. After the death of his second wife he went to Reims to study for the priesthood and was ordained in Rome. He ministered to the Catholics round York, and was captured in York prison while acting as Deacon to the Sung Mass of Bl Thomas Bell. He was martyred at York with Bl Richard Kirkman. Beatified 1886.

WILLIAM DEAN (Bl) M.   AC. Aug 28

d. 1588. A native of Linton in Craven, Yorkshire, he was a convert minister, who was ordained at Reims in 1581. He was martyred for his priesthood at Mile End Green. Beatified 1929.

WILLIAM GUNTER (Bl) M.   AC. Aug 28

d. 1588. Born at Raglan in Monmouthshire, and educated and ordained at Reims (1587). Condemned for his priesthood and hanged at Shoreditch. Beatified 1929.

WILLIAM of ROESKILDE (St) Bp.   AC. Sept 2

d. 1067. An Anglo-Saxon, chaplain to King Canute. He crossed over to Denmark and was made by the same king bishop of Roeskilde. Besides being a very successful missionary, William steadfastly resisted the anti-Christian policy and crimes of King Sweyn Estridsen.

WILLIAM BROWNE (Bl) M.   AC. Sept 5

d. 1605. A layman, a native of Northamptonshire, condemned and executed for the Faith at Ripon. Beatified 1929.

WILLIAM WAY (Bl) M.   AC. Sept 23

d. 1588. A native of Devon who was educated and ordained (1586) at Reims. He was martyred for his priesthood at Kingston-on-Thames. Beatified 1929.

WILLIAM HARTLEY (Bl) M.   AC. Oct 5

d. 1588. A native of Wilne, near Derby, he was educated at St John's College, Oxford, and became an Anglican minister. After his conversion he studied at Reims, where he was ordained (1580). He was hanged for his priesthood at Shoreditch. Beatified 1929.

WILLIAM of SAVIGNY (Bl) Mk. OSB. AC. Oct 20
d. *c.*1122. A novice at Savigny under Bl Vitalis.

WILLIAM (St) Mk. OSB. PC. Nov 3
See Acheric and William.

WILLIAM de PAULO (Bl) Ab OSB. AC. Nov 30
d. 1423. Born at Catania, he professed the Benedictine Rule at San Niccolò dell' Arena, and at a later period was sent to restore monastic discipline at Maniaco.

WILLIAM of FENOLI (Bl) C. O. Cart. AC. Dec 19
d. *c.*1205. A Carthusian lay-brother at the charterhouse *Casularum* in Lombardy. Cult confirmed 1860.

WILLIAM HOWARD (Bl) M. AC. Dec 29
1616–1680. Grandson of Bl Philip Howard, and Viscount Stafford. He was accused of complicity in the "Popish Plot" and after two years' imprisonment was beheaded on Tower Hill. Beatified 1929.

WILLIBALD (WILLEBALD) (St) Bp. OSB. RM. July 7
*c.*700–786. Born in Wessex, he was a brother of SS Winebald and Walburga and a cousin of St Boniface. At the age of five he was offered as a monk at Waltham in Hampshire. In 721 he accompanied his father and brother on a pilgrimage to Rome and the Holy Land. He visited all the holy places and many Eastern monastic lauras and stayed for two years at Constantinople. On his return to Italy he lived at Montecassino for ten years and helped in the monastic restoration under St Petronax, filling the offices of sacristan, dean and porter. While on a visit to Rome he was sent by the pope to Germany to help St Boniface in his missionary labours, and was soon after consecrated by the latter bishop of Eichstätt. With his brother St Winebald he founded the double abbey of Heidenheim, over which they placed their sister Walburga as abbess. Canonized in 938 by Leo VII.

WILLIBRORD (St) Bp. OSB. RM. Nov 7
*c.*658–739. A Northumbrian by birth and a Benedictine of Ripon, he crossed over to Ireland to be trained in the missionary life. Thence he went to Friesland (*c.*690) accompanied by eleven other English monks. Six years later he was consecrated bishop and established his see at Utrecht. His labours among the Frisians bore much fruit, but he was less successful in Heligoland and Denmark. With the help of Pepin of Heristal he founded the monastery of Echternach in Luxemburg as the centre of his missionary expeditions, and thither he retired to die.

WILLIGIS (St) Bp. AC. Feb 23
d. 1011. The son of a wheelwright of Schöningen, he became a canon of Hildesheim and as such attracted the attention of the emperor Otto III, who made him his chaplain and (971) chancellor of the Empire. About two years later he was appointed archbishop of Mainz, and Boniface VII created him vicar apostolic for Germany. Perhaps the greatest statesman of his age, Willigis was first and foremost a churchman, and ever remained humble and charitable in his dealings with others. In 1002 he consecrated the emperor St Henry II. In art he is shown with a wheel, which he chose for his arms as symbolizing his father's trade.

WILLIGOD and MARTIN (SS) Abbots OSB. AC. Sept 28
d. ? *c.*690. Monks of Moyenmoutier who

became co-founders and successive abbots of the monastery of Romont.

WILTRUDIS (St) W. OSB.
                                    AC. Jan 6
d. *c*.986. The wife of Duke Berthold of Bavaria, who after her husband's death (*c*.947) founded (*c*.976) the nunnery of Bergen, near Neuburg on the Danube, under the Benedictine Rule, and herself became a nun and its first abbess. She was renowned for her skill in artistic handicrafts.

WINAMAN, UNAMAN and SUNAMAN (SS) MM. OSB.
                                    AC. Feb 15
d. *c*.1040. Missionary monks, nephews of the English missionary St Sigfrid of Wexiow, whom they followed to the Swedish mission. They were martyred by pagans at Wexiow.

WINEBALD (VINEBAUD) (St) Ab. OSB.   **AC. Apr 6**
d. *c*.650. At first a hermit, he afterwards took the monastic habit at Saint-Loup-de-Troyes, of which monastery he was chosen abbot.

WINEBALD (St) Ab. OSB.
                                    AC. Dec 18
d. 761. An Englishman, brother of SS Willibald and Walburga. When on pilgrimage to the Holy Land with his brother, Winebald was taken ill and remained at Rome, where he studied for seven years. Eventually he became a Benedictine in Rome and passed into Germany at the invitation of St Boniface. In time he became the abbot of Heidenheim, a double abbey built for him and his sister by their brother, then bishop of Eichstätt.

WINEWALD (St) Ab. OSB.
                                    AC. Apr 27
d. *c*.731. The successor of St Bercthun as abbot of Beverley.

WINEFRED (WINEFRIDE, WENEFRIDA, GWENFREWI, GUINEVRA, etc.) (St) VM.
                                    RM. Nov 3
d. *c*.650. A native of Wales, she is said to have been a niece of St Beuno and to have been murdered by Caradog of Hawarden for refusing his amorous advances, a spring of water gushing forth on the spot where her head fell. This was the origin of the Holy Well, which has been a centre of pilgrimages for over a thousand years. Another version of the legend adds that she was restored to life by St Beuno and that she became a nun and abbess of Gwytherin in Denbighshire. She is evidently an historical personage, but it is equally evident that her true story can no longer be reconstructed.

WININ (St) Bp.   **AC. Sept 10**
The Welsh form of the name of St Finian, q.v.

WINNOW, MANCUS and MYRBAD (SS) CC.   **AC. May 31**
Probably 6th cent. Three Irish saints who lived in Cornwall, where they have churches dedicated in their honour.

WINOC (St) Ab. OSB.   RM. Nov 6
d. ? 717. He was of royal blood and probably of British origin, though brought up in Brittany. He became a monk at Sithiu under St Bertinus, by whom eventually he was sent to establish a new foundation among the Morini at Wormhoult, of which he became abbot. From that centre he evangelized the whole neighbourhood.

WINWALOË (GUENGALOEUS, GWENNO, WONNOW, WYNWALLOW, VALOIS, etc.) (St) Ab.
                                    AC. March 3
d. *c*.532. Born in Brittany of parents exiled from England, he became a

731

disciple of St Budoc on Isle Verte and abbot-founder of Landevennec near Brest. Several Cornish churches are dedicated to St Winwaloë, which seems to indicate that the saint had some connexion with those parts.

WIOMAD (WEOMADUS, WIO-MAGUS) (St) Bp. OSB.   AC. Nov 8
d. *c.*790. Monk of St Maximinus at Trèves. He became abbot of Mettlach and finally bishop of Trèves (*c.*750–790).

WIRNTO (Bl) Ab. OSB.
                               AC. Oct 29
d. 1127. A Benedictine of Göttweig in Austria, who became abbot of Form-bach in Bavaria.

WIRO, PLECHELM and OTGER (SS) MM. OSB.   RM. May 8
d. *c.*739. British missionaries in Fries-land under St Willibrord (or perhaps under St Switbert). They were martyred while preaching the gospel in that country. The centre of Wiro's apostolic labours was Peterkloster, afterwards renamed Odilienberg. According to the RM. Wiro was a bishop *Scotiae*.

WISINTO (Bl) Mk. OSB.
                               AC. Dec 31
d. *a.* 1250. A monk and priest of the great Austrian abbey of Kremsmünster. He has always been venerated as a saint by the Austrian Benedictines.

WISTAN (St) M.   AC. June 1
d. 849. Of the royal house of Mercia. He is said to have been put to death by Bertulph, king of Mercia, when the latter was regent of the kingdom during Wistan's youth. The saint's shrine was in Evesham abbey.

WISTREMUNDUS (St) M.
                               RM. June 7
See Peter, Wallabonsus, etc.

WITHBURGA (St) V. OSB.
                               AC. July 8
d. *c.*743 (March 17). Youngest daughter of King Anna of East Anglia. After her father had fallen in battle she took the veil and lived mostly at Dereham, a nunnery which she had founded.

WITTA (St) Bp. OSB.   AC. Oct 26
Otherwise Albinus, q.v.

WITTIKUND (Bl) C.   AC. Jan 7
d. *c.*804. A duke of Westphalia who as a pagan resisted the arms of Charlemagne. It is related that he was converted by a miraculous vision, and baptized in 785. Thereafter he was most zealous in pro-pagating Christianity and restoring churches. He died in warfare with the Suevi.

WIVINA (VIVINA) (St) Abs. OSB.
                               RM. Dec 17
d. 1170. A Flemish lady of the house of Oisy. In her twenty-third year she secretly left her father's house and became an anchoress in a wood near Brussels, called Grand-Bigard. The count of Brabant offered her the land and she built a nunnery, placing it under the direction of the Benedictines of Afflighem, near Alost. She was the first abbess.

WOLFGANG (St) Bp. OSB.
                               RM. Oct 31
924–994. A native of Swabia, who was educated by the Benedictines at Reich-enau, and after being dean of the cathe-dral school at Trèves, became a Benedictine at Einsiedeln (964). He was made headmaster of the abbey school which became under him the most flourishing institution of its kind in those parts. In 971 he was raised to the priesthood and with a group of monks went as a missionary to the Magyars; but in the following year (972) he was

promoted to the see of Ratisbon. He was one of those monk-bishops who have left their mark on the history of their times. He was tutor to the emperor Henry II, restored abbeys (St Emmeram at Ratisbon being one of the most important of these), raised the standard of education, reformed ecclesiastical discipline and was a great benefactor of the poor, being known as their *Eleemosynarius Major* (Great Almoner). Canonized by Leo IX in 1052.

WOLFHELM (Bl) Ab. OSB.
AC. Apr 22

d. 1091. A Rhinelander, he joined the Benedictine abbey of St Maximinus at Trèves. From there he transferred to St Pantaleon's at Cologne, and then became abbot successively of Gladbach, Siegburg and Brauwcilcr, at which last-named he ended his days. He is described as a great student of Holy Writ and a great lover of the Holy Rule.

WOLFRID (Bl) Ab. OSB.
AC. June 21

d. *c.*990. Abbot-founder (*c.*973) of Hohentwiel.

WOOLLOS (St)   AC. Jan 19
Otherwise Gundleus, q.v.

WORONUS (St)   AC. Apr 7
Otherwise Goran, q.v.

WULFHADE and RUFFINUS (SS) MM.   AC. July 24
d. 675. Two princes of the royal family of Mercia, baptized by a hermit and thereupon put to death by the king their father, who was as yet unconverted.

WULFHILDA (St) Abs. OSB.
AC. Sept 9

d. 980. Abbess-foundress of Horton nunnery in Dorsetshire. She was later put in charge of Barking abbey on its restoration as a nunnery by King Edgar. When the king died, Queen Elfrida drove her out, but she was recalled by King Ethelred and died abbess of Barking.

WULFRAM (St) Bp. OSB.
RM. March 20

d. *c.*703. A courtier-priest who was given the see of Sens, which he occupied for only two and a half years. He then undertook the work of the evangelization of the Frisians, and after spending some time at Fontenelle, he set out with some of the monks. After spending many years among the Frisians he returned to Fontenelle, where he died.

WULFRIC (St) H.   AC. Feb 20
d. 1154. A priest who, after leading a worldly life, became a hermit at Haselbury-Plucknett, near Crewkerne, in Somerset. The Cistercians lay claim to him, but he was attached to no Order.

WULMAR (ULMAR, ULMER, VILMARUS, VOLMAR, VILMER, etc.) (St) Ab. OSB.   AC. July 20
d. 689. Born near Boulogne in Picardy, he married, but was separated by force from his wife and became a Benedictine lay-brother at Haumont in Hainault. Here he was employed in keeping cattle and hewing wood for the abbey, but after a time, being considered worthy of the priesthood, he was ordained and eventually became the founder and first abbot of the monastery of Samer (*Salviniacum*) afterwards called after him Saint-Vulmaire, near Boulogne.

WULSIN (St) Bp. OSB. AC. Jan 8
d. 1005. Described as "a loyal and trusty monk whom St Dunstan loved like a son with pure affection". When St Dunstan restored Westminster Abbey (958) he made Wulsin superior there and finally abbot (980). In 993

he was promoted to the see of Sherborne.

WULSTAN (WULFSTAN, ULF-
STAN, WOLSTAN) Bp. OSB.
RM. Jan 19

d. 1095. A native of Long Itchington in
Warwickshire, he studied at the abbeys
of Evesham and Peterborough. Then he
became a priest and joined the Benedictines at Worcester, where he filled the
offices of precentor and prior. Finally
he was raised to the see of Worcester
(1062), which he governed so wisely
that he was the only English bishop
who was allowed to retain his see after
the Conquest. During his episcopate,
which lasted thirty-two years, he rebuilt
his cathedral. He died while engaged in
his daily practice of washing the feet of
twelve poor men. Canonized 1203.

WYNNIN (St) Bp.   AC. Jan 21
Otherwise Vimin, q.v.

X

XANTIPPA and POLYXENA (SS)
VV.   RM. Sept 23
1st cent. Described in the RM. as "disciples of the Apostles", but we have no trustworthy information about them.

XYSTUS (*several*)
Otherwise Sixtus, q.v.

Y

YMAR (St) M. OSB. **AC. Nov 12**
d. *c*.830. A monk of Reculver in Kent, martyred by the Danes.

YOLANDA (IOLANTHA) (Bl) W.
AC. June 15
d. 1298. Daughter of Bela IV, King of Hungary, niece of St Elizabeth, she married Boleslaus, the devout prince of Pomerania. She was a tertiary of St Francis. Beatified in 1827.

YON (St) M. **AC. Sept 22**
Otherwise Jonas, q.v.

YRCHARD (YARCARD) (St) Bp.
AC. Aug 24
5th cent. A Scottish priest, consecrated bishop by St Ternan, and like him a missionary among the Picts.

YRIEIX (St) Ab. **AC. Aug 25**
See Aredius.

YSARN (St) Ab. OSB. **AC. Sept 24**
d. 1048. Born near Toulouse, he became a Benedictine monk, and then abbot of St Victor's at Marseilles. Under his government the abbey became the centre of a Benedictine congregation with houses in S. France and N.E. Spain.

YTHA (St) V. **AC. Jan 15**
Otherwise Ita, q.v. In Cornwall she is known as St Ide or St Syth.

YVO (St) C. **RM. May 19**
Otherwise Ivo, q.v.

YWI (YVIUS) (St) H. OSB.
AC. Oct 8
d. *c*.690. A monk of Lindisfarne ordained deacon by St Cuthbert. His relics were translated to Wilton, near Salisbury.

Z

ZACCHAEUS (St) Bp. RM. Aug 23
d. *c*.116. This Zacchaeus or Zacharias is reckoned by St Epiphanius and other Fathers to have been the fourth bishop of Jerusalem.

ZACCHAEUS (St) M. RM. Nov 17
See Alphaeus and Zacchaeus.

ZACHARY (St) Pope RM. March 22
d. 752. Born at San Severino in Calabria of a Greek family. Chosen pope in 741, he showed himself worthy of that office: he successfully negotiated peace between the Lombards and the Greek empire; sanctioned the assumption of the Frankish crown by Pepin; seconded the missionary work of St Boniface and confirmed him as archbishop of Mainz; planned and undertook the restoration of Montecassino under St Petronax, himself consecrating the abbey church in 748; gave the Benedictine habit to St Ratchis, king of the Lombards; and in many other ways furthered the reconstruction of Europe.

ZACHARY (St) Bp. M. RM. May 26
d. *c*.106. Said to have been the second bishop of Vienne in Gaul, and to have died a martyr under Trajan.

ZACHARY (St) M. RM. June 10
? Described by the RM. as a martyr at Nicomedia.

ZACHARY (ZECHARIAH) (St)
Prophet RM. Sept 6
6th cent. B.C. A fellow-prophet of Aggaeus (Haggai). Both prophesied under King Darius (*c*.520 B.C.) and exhorted the people to rebuild the Temple.

ZACHARY (ZACHARIAS) (St)
Prophet RM. Nov 5
1st cent. Father of St John the Baptist, known to us from Luke I. Nothing is known of the rest of his life.

ZAMA (St) Bp. RM. Jan 24
d. *c*.268. The first bishop of Bologna of whom there is any record. He is said to have been consecrated by Pope St Dionysius *c*.260.

ZAMBDAS (ZABDAS, BAZAS) (St)
Bp. RM. Feb 19
d. *c*.304. Said to have been the thirty-seventh bishop of Jerusalem. He has been connected with the legend of the Theban legion.

ZANITAS, LAZARUS, MAROTAS, NARSES and Comp. (SS) MM.
RM. March 27
d. 326. A group of Persian martyrs who suffered under Shapur II. The remaining five martyrs of this group were: Elias, Abibos, Sembeeth, Mares and Sabas.

ZEBINAS (St) M. RM. Nov 13
See Antoninus, Zebinas, etc.

ZEBINUS (St) H. AC. Feb 23
5th cent. A hermit in Syria who trained St Maro, St Polychronius and others in the monastic life.

ZDISLAVA BERKA (Bl) Matron, OP. AC. Jan 1
d. 1252. Born in Bohemia of noble

parents, she married a man of her own rank to whom she bore four children. Her generosity towards the poor caused difficulties with her husband, whom she conciliated by her heroic patience. She died as a Dominican tertiary in the priory of St Lawrence, which she had founded. Cult approved in 1907.

ZENAIS, CYRIA, VALERIA and MARCIA (SS) MM.   RM. June 5
? Zenais seems to have suffered at Constantinople. The other martyrs of this group are traditionally believed to have been contemporaries of our Lord and among the early martyrs of the Church.

ZENAIS and PHILONILLA (SS) MM.   RM. Oct 11
1st cent. Two holy women, perhaps sisters, related to St Paul the Apostle. They were natives of Tarsus.

ZENAS (St) M.   RM. June 23
See Zeno and Zenas.

ZENO (St) M.   RM. Feb 14
See Vitalis, Felicula and Zeno.

ZENO (St) M.   RM. Apr 5
? A martyr who was burnt alive. Date and place unknown.

ZENO (St) Bp.   RM. Apr 12
d. 371. Bishop of Verona, 362–371, at the time of Julian the Apostate. He is best remembered as an ecclesiastical writer of distinction, his main subject being the virgin-birth of our Lord.

ZENO (St) M.   RM. Apr 20
See Victor, Zoticus, etc.

ZENO and ZENAS (SS) MM.   RM. June 23
d. c.304. Zeno, a wealthy citizen of Philadelphia near the Dead Sea, freed all his slaves and gave his property to the poor. Zenas, a former slave, re-mained with him as a servant. Both were beheaded under Diocletian.

ZENO and Comp. (SS) MM.   RM. July 9
d. c.300. According to the RM. this group of martyrs numbered 10,204. The entry is in fact a record of the wholesale slaughter, ordered by Diocletian, of the Christians who had been condemned to work on the building of the baths named after him. Zeno seems to have been the chief spokesman of these martyrs.

ZENO (St) M.   RM. July 15
See Philip, Zeno, etc.

ZENO, CONCORDIUS and THEODORE (SS) MM.   RM. Sept 2
d. 302. Zeno and his two sons were martyred at Nicomedia under Diocletian.

ZENO and CHARITON (SS) MM.   RM. Sept 3
d. 303. Martyrs in the East under Diocletian.

ZENO (St) M.   RM. Sept 5
See Eudoxius, Zeno, etc.

ZENO (St) M.   RM. Sept 8
See Eusebius, Nestabus, and Zeno.

ZENO (St) M.   RM. Dec 20
See Ammon, Zeno, etc.

ZENO (St) M.   RM. Dec 22
d. 303. A soldier at Nicomedia. As a punishment for laughing when Diocletian was offering a sacrifice to Ceres his jaws were broken and he was beheaded.

ZENO (St) Bp.   RM. Dec 26
d. c.399. A cousin of the martyr-brothers Eusebius, Nestabus and Zeno, commemorated on Sept 8. He survived Julian's persecution and was made bishop of Gaza.

738

ZENOBIA (St) M.   RM. Oct 30
See Zenobius and Zenobia.

ZENOBIUS (St) M.
                    RM. Feb 20 and Oct 29
See Tyrannio, Silvanus, etc.

ZENOBIUS (St) Bp.   RM. May 25
d. *c*.?390. Bishop of Florence. A great
friend of St Ambrose and also of St
Damasus, by whom he was sent as
papal representative to Constantinople
in connexion with the Arian troubles.

ZENOBIUS (St) M.   RM. Oct 29
d. 310. A priest and physician at Sidon,
who was martyred at Antioch under
Diocletian by being torn with iron hooks.

ZENOBIUS and ZENOBIA (SS)
MM.   RM. Oct 30
d. 285–290. Bishop and physician at
Aegae (now Alexandretta) on the coast
of Asia Minor. He is probably identical
with St Zenobius of Antioch (Oct 29),
in which case his martyrdom took place
somewhat later, under Maximian. Zenobia is said to have been his sister.

ZENOBIUS (St) M.   RM. Dec 24
See Lucian, Metrobius, etc.

ZEPHYRINUS (St) Pope M.
                          RM. Aug 26
d. 217. Pope from 199 to 217. He does
not seem to have died a martyr.

ZETICUS (St) M.   RM. Dec 23
See Theodulus, Saturninus, etc.

ZIMIUS (St) C. OSB.   AC. June 12
See Marinus, Vimius, etc.

ZITA (St) V.   RM. Apr 27
1218–1278. A native of Monsagrati near
Lucca, at the age of twelve she entered
the service of a family at Lucca, with
whom she remained all her life. She

would give her food and clothing to the
poor—and sometimes her master's too.
For this she was at first misunderstood
and maltreated, but she ended by gain-
ing the confidence of the whole household. She was canonized in 1696 and is
greatly venerated, especially in Italy, as
the patron saint of domestic servants.

ZOË (St) M.   RM. May 2
See Exuperius, Zoë, etc.

ZOË (ZOA) (St) M.   RM. July 5
d. *c*.286. A Roman lady, said to have
been the wife of a high official of the
imperial court, put to death for the
Faith.

ZOËLLUS, SERVILIUS, FELIX,
SILVANUS and DIOCLES (SS)
MM.   RM. May 24
? Martyrs at Istria (or in Syria?).

ZOILUS and Comp. (SS) MM.
                          RM. June 27
d. *c*.301. A youth martyred with nineteen companions at Cordova under Diocletian. The Benedictine abbey of San
Zoil de Carrión, province of León, in
N. Spain, was founded to enshrine their
relics.

ZOSIMA (St) M.   RM. July 15
See Eutropius, Zosima and Bonosa.

ZOSIMUS and ATHANASIUS (SS)
MM.   RM. Jan 3
d. 303. Martyrs in Cilicia under Diocletian. Another account says that Zosimus was put to the torture and that
Athanasius, a spectator, was converted
and forthwith tortured also, but that
both survived and died in peace as
hermits.

ZOSIMUS (St) Bp.   RM. March 30
d. *c*.660. A Sicilian, placed at the age of
seven in the monastery of Santa Lucia

(Benedictine or Basilian) near Syracuse. After being a simple monk for thirty years, he was successively made abbot and bishop of the city. He died at the age of ninety.

ZOSIMUS (St) H.   RM. Apr 4
5th cent. A Palestinian anchorite who lived on the banks of the Jordan, the supposed confidant and biographer of St Mary of Egypt.

ZOSIMUS (St) M.   RM. June 19
d. 110. A martyr of Spoleto in Umbria under Trajan.

ZOSIMUS (St) M.   RM. Sept 28
See Mark, Alphius, etc.

ZOSIMUS (St) H.   RM. Nov 30
6th cent. A hermit in Palestine, surnamed the Wonder-Worker.

ZOSIMUS (St) M.   RM. Dec 14
See Drusus, Zosimus and Theodore.

ZOSIMUS (St) M.   RM. Dec 18
See Rufus and Zosimus.

ZOSIMUS (St) M.   RM. Dec 19
See Darius, Zosimus, etc.

ZOSIMUS (St) Pope   RM. Dec 26
d. 418. A Greek, whose short pontificate was marked by the condemnation of the Pelagian heresy.

ZOTICUS, ROGATUS, MODESTUS, CASTULUS and Comp. (SS) MM.   RM. Jan 12

? A group of between forty and fifty soldiers martyred in Africa.

ZOTICUS (St) M.   RM. Jan 12
Identical with St Getulius, the martyr of Tivoli (June 10), q.v.

ZOTICUS (St) M.   RM. Jan 31
See Tarsicius, Zoticus, etc.

ZOTICUS, IRENAEUS, HYACINTH, AMANTIUS and Comp. (SS) MM.   RM. Feb 10
d. 120. A group of ten soldiers martyred in Rome and buried in the Via Lavicana.

ZOTICUS (St) M.   RM. Apr 20
See Victor, Zoticus, etc.

ZOTICUS (St) M.   RM. July 21
d. 204. Bishop of Comana in Cappadocia, famous for his zeal against the Montanist heretics and for his martyrdom.

ZOTICUS (St) M.   RM. Aug 22
See Agathonicus, Zoticus, etc.

ZOTICUS (St) M.   RM. Oct 21
See Dasius, Zoticus, etc.

ZOTICUS (St)   RM. Dec 31
d. c.350. A Roman priest who migrated to Constantinople at the time when Constantine transferred thither the capital of the empire. Zoticus built in that city a hospital for the poor and for orphans. He was a confessor of the Faith under the Arian emperor Constantius.